ORGANIZATIONAL BEHAVIOR

AN EXPERIENTIAL APPROACH

EIGHTH EDITION

Joyce S. Osland

SAN JOSÉ STATE UNIVERSITY

David A. Kolb

CASE WESTERN RESERVE UNIVERSITY

Irwin M. Rubin

TEMENOS, INC.

Marlene E. Turner

SAN JOSÉ STATE UNIVERSITY

PEARSON

Prentice Hall

Upper Saddle River, New Jersey 07458

Library of Congress Cataloging-in-Publication Data
Organizational behavior: an experiential approach / Joyce S. Osland . . . [et. al.]. —8th ed.
    p.   cm.
    Rev. ed. of: Organizational behavior / Joyce S. Osland, David A. Kolb, Irwin M. Rubin. 7th ed. c2001.
    Includes bibliographical references and index.
    ISBN 0-13-144151-5.
    1. Psychology, Industrial.   2. Organizational behavior.   I. Osland, Joyce.
    II. Osland, Joyce. Organizational behavior.
HF5548.8.K552 2009
158.7—dc22   2006028549

Acquisitions Editor: Jon Axelrod
VP/Editorial Director: Jeff Shelstad
Product Development Manager: Ashley Santora
Assistant Editor: Keri Molinari
Editorial Assistant: Kristen Varina
Marketing Manager: Anne Howard
Marketing Assistant: Susan Osterlitz
Associate Director, Production Editorial: Judy Leale
Managing Editor: Renata Butera
Production Editor: Angela Pica
Permissions Coordinator: Charles Morris
Associate Director, Manufacturing: Vinnie Scelta
Manufacturing Buyer: Diane Peirano
Manager, Creative Services: Christy Mahon
Interior Design and Composition Liaison: Suzanne Duda
Designer: Steve Frim
Cover Design: Bruce Kenselaar
Cover Illustration: Getty Images
Composition: Preparé
Full-Service Project Management: Preparé
Printer/Binder: Bindright

Pearson Education LTD.
Pearson Education Singapore, Pte. Ltd
Pearson Education, Canada, Ltd
Pearson Education–Japan
Pearson Education Australia PTY, Limited
Pearson Education North Asia Ltd
Pearson Educación de Mexico, S.A. de C.V.
Pearson Education Malaysia, Pte. Ltd.

10 9 8 7 6 5 4 3 2 1
ISBN 0-13-144151-5

▲▲

To
Asbjorn, Jessica, Michael, Katrina,
Ellie, Joe, Zoe, and Anna
Alice and Jonathan
Beth, Steven, and Corey
Anthony and Tony

▲▲

Contents

Foreword

This book–or better, the body of experiences it proposes–seeks to communicate some knowledge of general psychological principles, and some skills in applying that knowledge to social and organizational situations. Science tries to illuminate concrete reality by disclosing the general laws and principles that make the reality what it is. The generalization gives meaning to the concrete instance, but the instance carries the generalization into the real world and makes it usable. Experiencing social situations and then analyzing that experience brings generalization and concrete reality into effective union.

In teaching undergraduate and graduate management courses, I have frequently encountered students who hold a magical belief in a real world, somehow entirely different from any world they had hitherto experienced, and different, too, from the world of their textbooks. In teaching experienced executives, I have as frequently encountered people who balked at the proposal to apply general psychological principles to the concrete experiences of their everyday world. If there are skeptics of either variety in a group that undertakes one of these exercises, they can conduct their own tests of the relevance of theory to experience and vice versa. That is what the exercises are about.

But are the exercises themselves "real"? Can you really simulate social or organizational phenomena in a laboratory? The answer hangs on what we know of people—of their readiness to take roles, or, more accurately, their inability not to take roles when they find themselves in appropriate social situations, but this in itself is a psychological generalization: people are role-takers. Like any generalization, it should be tested empirically; and the exercises do just that. Each participant can be his or her own witness to the reality—or lack of it—of what has gone on.

But the purpose of the exercises is not just to increase understanding of principles, or understanding of concrete situations in terms of principles. They can be useful also as a means of developing skills for group situations: skills of observing, skills of self-insight, skills of understanding the behaviors and motives of others, skills of adapting behavior to the requirements of a task and the needs of groups and persons.

There is no magic to it. Learning here, like all learning, derives from time and attention directed to relevant material. The exercises provide the material. The time, attention, and active participation must be supplied by those who take part in them.

Herbert A. Simon

Preface

The eighth edition of *Organizational Behavior: An Experiential Approach,* which we refer to as the "workbook," has been revised from cover to cover, line by painstaking line, to provide you with an up-to-date, easily understood textbook. This edition is the latest improvement on an experiment that began over 35 years ago. The first edition of this book, developed at MIT in the late 1960s, was the first application of the principles of experience-based learning to teaching in this field. Since then the field has changed, the practice of experience-based learning has grown in acceptance and sophistication, and we, the authors, have changed. We are delighted to announce the addition of a new coauthor, Marlene Turner, who is an example of that rare breed of well-rounded people who are good at everything. Dr. Turner wins awards for both her scholarship and teaching and is highly skilled at practicing what she teaches at the College of Business at San José State University.

In comparison with previous editions, this edition is focused on teaching students to think like organizational behavior experts. Exercises and debriefings have been modified to accelerate the development of expertise by emphasizing pattern recognition of cues and the action scripts they elicit. We have added three new chapters–Setting the Global Stage (the introductory unit), Decoding Human Behavior and Personality, Chapter 4, and Creativity, Chapter 12. Even more emphasis has been placed on cross-cultural issues. We made substantial revisions in every chapter, adding recent research findings, new information on companies, and, in some chapters, new vignettes and experiential exercises. As always, our objective was not to overwhelm students with a comprehensive array of theories and findings, but to provide them with the essential content and experiences they need to become effective, expert managers and good employees. In every edition, our goal is to reflect the state of the art in the practice of experiential learning and to bring these approaches to bear on the latest thinking and research in the field of organizational behavior.

This book is intended for students and managers who wish to explore the personal relevance and conceptual bases of the phenomena of organizational behavior and to develop their expertise in this field. There are two goals in the experiential learning process. One is to learn the specifics of a particular subject matter. The other is to learn about one's own strengths and weaknesses as a learner (i.e., learning how to learn from experience). Thus, the book is focused upon exercises, self-analysis techniques, and role plays to make the insights of behavioral science meaningful and relevant to practicing managers and students. Each chapter is designed as an educational intervention that facilitates each stage of the experience-based learning process. Exercises and simulations are designed to produce experiences that create the phenomena of organizational behavior. Observation schemes and methods are introduced to facilitate your understanding of these experiences. Theories and models are added to aid in forming generalizations and mental models. And finally, the intervention is structured in a way that encourages learners to experiment with and test what they have learned, either in class or other areas of their lives. Our purpose is to teach students *how* to learn so that they will become continuous learners, capable of responding to demands for change and new skills throughout their career. Learning is no longer a special activity reserved for the classroom, but an integral and explicit part of work itself.

In addition to teaching students to be lifelong learners, the exercises and the order of the chapters are designed to facilitate self-knowledge and teamwork. Students should leave this course with a much clearer understanding of themselves and the effect their behavior has on others. Students work in the same learning groups throughout the course. In these groups, members share their experiences and provide support, advice, feedback, and friendship to each other. A by-product of this group approach is the creation of a class environment that facilitates learning.

A companion edited volume, *The Organizational Behavior Reader*, Eighth Edition, is also published by Prentice Hall. Many footnotes in the workbook make reference to complementary articles that have been reprinted there. These are simply cited as *"Reader"* in the endnotes.

A preface is a place to publicly thank the many people who have helped us. Our feelings of pride in our product are tempered by the great indebtedness we feel to many others whose ideas and insights preceded ours. It is a tribute to the spirit of collaboration that pervades our field that the origin of many of the exercises recorded here is unknown. We have tried throughout the manuscript to trace the origins of those exercises we know about and in the process we may, in many areas, fall short of the original insight. For that we can only apologize. The major unnamed contributors are our students. In a very real sense, this book could never have been completed without their active participation in our explorations.

We wish to thank James McIntyre, our coauthor in the first four editions of this book, for his generous and creative contributions. While much has changed and will continue to change through successive editions of this book, Jim's presence will always be there.

By sharing their experiences, resources, insights, and criticisms on previous editions, many instructors have been invaluable guides in the revision process. In particular, Nancy Adler, Janet Bennett, Allan Bird, Bruce Drake, Howard Feldman, Martin Gannon, Anne Lawrence, Don McCormick, Stan Malos, Bob Mehler, Stephen Miller, Asbjorn Osland, Rolanda Pollard, Anthony Pratkanis, Preston Probasco, Sully Taylor, Meg Virick, Joel West, George Whaley, Judith White, Robert Wood, and Bill Zachary were very helpful in a variety of ways. The reviewers did an excellent, thorough job.

Our greatest debt of gratitude goes to Pam Wells, research and teaching assistant extraordinaire. We would also like to thank the wonderful students who have helped us at various stages of the process: Angela Bywaters, Anu Sairaj, Arundhati Chatterjee, Liana Mortazavi, and Namrata Patel. Melanie Visalli did a terrific editing job by catching errors and making the book more understandable. We're grateful to Nicole Campbell, Prabha Chandrasekar, Kathryn Hetzner, Toby Matoush, Jodi Sanders, Barbara Somers, and Tehmina Wajahat for their help with this project and everything else we do. We were fortunate to have good managers of our own as we balanced revising the workbook with our other tasks; Abdel El-Shaieb and William Jiang, chairs of the Department of Organization & Management, and Bruce Magid, Dean, at San José State University, were very supportive. It was a pleasure, as always, to work with the Prentice Hall crew—Keri Molinari, Charles Morris, Angela Pica, Ashley Santora, Jennifer Simon—and with Stefania Magaldi and Fran Daniele at Preparé Inc. Finally, we are extremely grateful to our spouses for their faith, patience, countless sacrifices, and good ideas. We owe you!

Joyce S. Osland
David A. Kolb
Irwin M. Rubin
Marlene E. Turner

Reviewers

Cathleen McGrath, *Loyola Marymount University*
Thomas Timmerman, *Tennessee Technological University*
T. Roger Manley, *Florida Institute of Technology*
Anne Harper, *Humber College*

Setting the Global Stage: Introduction to the Workbook

▲▲▲

I hear and I forget
I see and I remember
I do and I understand
          CONFUCIUS

Organizations—and the way we choose to design them—profoundly affect how we live, work, and go about our daily lives. We spend an astonishing amount of time interacting with organizations. The clothes you wear, the buildings in which you live, the school you attend, the books you read, the entertainment you enjoy, the food and water you consume—all are most likely products of people in organizations.

Organizations and the people who comprise them are the subject of the field of organizational behavior. One of the criticisms sometimes leveled at organizational behavior is that it is just "common sense." There are several reasons why this is not always the case. First, in fact, many commonsense truisms are actually paradoxical—for example, "Nothing ventured, nothing gained" as opposed to "Better safe than sorry"or "Two heads are better than one" versus "Too many cooks spoil the broth." Which of these sayings should you follow? Which is true? Thus, common sense is not always so "common" nor is it always accurate. And so it is with common sense in relation to organizational behavior. Ask yourself the following question: Are workers who are satisfied with their jobs more productive than workers who are not satisfied with their jobs? Like many people, you probably answered yes to that question. But a great deal of research shows that there is very little relationship between a person's degree of job satisfaction and that person's performance.[1] In this case, applying a commonsense answer to a common organizational problem would be not so sensible.

Second, if organizational behavior is nothing more than common sense, all organizations should be wonderfully effective and profitable. Yet, as we know, truly outstanding organizations that stand the test of time are the exception rather than the norm. Indeed, the interesting question is, "If so much of organizational behavior is common sense, why isn't it common practice?" Our answer, not surprisingly, is that effective management of organizational behavior requires an extensive knowledge base and a number of critical skills that must be carefully developed, honed and practiced before they become "common sense."

WHO CARES?

Perhaps a more fundamental question is: Who cares? Why should we worry about how organizations are designed or how people behave in them? The most simple answer is because it makes a difference in how companies and organizations perform. A great deal of research has demonstrated positive relationships between how organizations manage their employees and various measures of firm performance including productivity, stock market value, sales, quality, turnover, commitment, and satisfaction.[2] Moreover, such positive relationships have been observed in a number of different industries including the automotive, financial services, manufacturing, airline transportation, and food service.[3] One estimate shows that changing human resources practices just a tad results in a 10 to 20 percent increase in market value.[4] There is no lack of examples of exceptional companies that place a premium value on their employees.

Toyota Motor Corporation, one of the most admired companies in the world, believes that people are its core and that challenging and respecting employees is critical to its success.[5] Southwest Airlines, one of the few profitable airlines companies in the United States, has the following mission:

> *To Our Employees:*
> *We are committed to provide our Employees a stable work environment with equal opportunity for learning and personal growth. Creativity and innovation are encouraged for improving the effectiveness of Southwest Airlines. Above all, Employees will be provided the same concern, respect, and caring attitude within the organization that they are expected to share externally with every Southwest Customer.*[6]

Notice that the mission statement is directed not at shareholders, not at financiers, and not even at customers. Rather, it tangibly demonstrates Southwest's belief that its employees are its core competitive advantage and that organizational success and profits rest squarely on their shoulders.

Based on research and best practices, the field of organizational behavior has compiled a great deal of knowledge over the years about what makes for successful businesses, leaders, managers, and employees. And yet, implementing this knowledge remains a fundamental challenge.[7] The expertise and skills needed to successfully craft and guide organizations are complex, subtle, and intricate. Throughout this book, you'll find research and tips on developing expertise that will help you be more successful in understanding the nuances of organizational behavior and the challenges and opportunities that lie before you.

WHAT IS ORGANIZATIONAL BEHAVIOR?

Organizational behavior (OB) is defined as a field of study that endeavors to understand, explain, predict, and change human behavior that occurs in the organizational context.[8] The origin of the field dates back to the early 1940s and the group climate experiments of Kurt Lewin, known as the father of OB, and his associates in 1943. Early scholars in the field came from industrial and social psychology and later from sociology and organizational psychology. Today, however, faculty obtain their Ph.D.s in organizational behavior. People with a master's degree in this field generally work inside organizations in training, HR, and organizational development or as external consultants with a consulting firm or their own business. Ph.D.s in organizational behavior tend to teach in schools of business and executive education programs, publish research and books, and consult to organizations. Many famous management consultants and gurus have advanced degrees in organizational behavior. The field expanded from an industrial-business focus to a wider application of behavioral science knowledge in various professional fields, such as health care management, law, public administration, education, and so forth.

CHARACTERISTICS OF ORGANIZATIONAL BEHAVIOR

Organizational behavior is characterized by the following traits. It is a relatively young *multidisciplinary* field that pulls from the disciplines of psychology, sociology, anthropology, political science, and economics. It consists of *three levels of analysis: individual, group, and organizational.* One of the basic tenets of organizational behavior is that behavior (B) is a function of the person and the environment, $B = f(P)(E)$.[9] People act in different ways in different settings, different groups, and different organizations. *Environmental forces* have a major impact on behavior within organizations. External changes such as the global economy, industrial and economic conditions, labor market forces, and societal and political changes affect our expectations in the workplace and the psychological contract we have with employers.

Knowledge in the field is accumulated by using the *scientific method*, which means that theories and relationships are tested to see whether they can actually predict behavior. The field has a *performance orientation*, and much of the research looks at performance at all three levels of analysis. Researchers are constantly trying to determine what makes for success in organizations and determining the most effective way to do things. Therefore, organizational behavior is an *applied science*—its purpose is to develop knowledge that is useful to managers and employees. Because of the emphasis on performance and application, it comes as no surprise that OB is a *change-oriented* discipline. Strategies for improving performance or modifying behavior have always been important to the field, particularly the subfield of organizational development (OD).

Because of the variety and complexity of human behavior, there are few simple answers to questions about organizations. Organizational behavior scholars and consultants often respond to questions with "It depends," followed up by many questions about the particular situation and maybe even a request to observe what's going on. To managers and students looking for quick answers, such a response may seem evasive. However, the management literature abounds with examples of companies that made policy and management decisions based on a small fragment of the entire picture and lived to regret it. That is why this course is designed to broaden your appreciation of the complexity of organizational behavior.

WORKBOOK OBJECTIVES—WHAT'S IN IT FOR YOU?

After completing this workbook, we hope that you will have developed your abilities to*: (1) diagnose an organizational situation; (2) know what would be the most effective action to take; and (3) cultivate a behavioral repertoire of the skills you need to carry out the appropriate action.* Our hope is that you will master the basic organizational behavior theories and concepts *and* be able to apply them to understand human behavior in any organization (work, home, etc.). We study this field because it helps us function more effectively in organizations. Regardless of our position in the hierarchy, mastering OB allows us to understand what is occurring around us and know how to make improvements. It teaches us the necessary skills to be an effective employee, team member, manager, or leader. Many people reach a plateau in their careers because they have risen as far as their technical skills allow. Good "people skills" are usually a prerequisite for higher management jobs. As one professor stated in an attempt to sell his OB course to students, "The difference between understanding organizational behavior and not understanding it is the difference between a six-figure and a five-figure salary." We can't promise you a six-figure salary if you master everything in this course. But, if you do your part, you should finish the course with: greater self awareness, more analytical skills, increased interpersonal and team skills, and more organizational expertise. Plus, you will have a much greater chance of creating and running successful businesses and organizations.

Both employees and managers in today's business organizations work in an environment characterized by a more rapid rate of change and greater demands for adaptation, more interdependence in various types of partnerships and teams, more demand for intercultural skills as the workforce becomes more diverse and global, and higher performance demands in a more competitive global economy. Our responsibility as textbook authors is to keep an eye on the environment and predictions about the future to provide an up-to-date educational experience for students. The eighth edition of the Workbook has four overarching themes that set the stage for this course, which are described in the following sections.

EXPERIENTIAL LEARNING

We agree with Confucius in his quotation at the beginning of this Introduction—we think the best way to understand this field is by 'doing'. Organizational behavior is a complex, often intensely personal subject that does not always come alive sufficiently in traditional lectures. This book was the very first application of experiential learning in our field. We began developing and testing the feasibility of experiential learning methods for teaching organizational psychology and behavior almost four decades ago. Our initial attempts to substitute exercises, games, and role plays for more traditional educational approaches were met in many quarters by polite skepticism and resistance. Today, however, experiential learning approaches are an integral part of management school curricula and management training programs everywhere. In experiential learning theory, knowledge is created through the transformation of experience—learning from your own experience.

Each workbook chapter begins with learning objectives and a vignette to illustrate the topic in a real life application. The Class Preparation questions ground students in their own experience and begin to draw out what you already know and want to learn about the subject. Most chapters have an assessment instrument to provide you with feedback on yourself or your organization. The Knowledge Base summarizes key theories and issues, providing you with mental frameworks and facts. The core of each chapter is an action-oriented behavioral simulation that allows you to generate your own data and lessons about each topic. Debriefing formats are provided to facilitate your ability to observe and share the personal reactions you have experienced, along with guidelines for critiquing the skills you will practice. The summarized learning points help to integrate your learning. The action scripts for employees, managers, and organizational architects provide tips and practical advice. Finally, at the end of each chapter, there is a Personal Application Assignment to integrate your learning using one of your own experiences. This design takes students through the entire learning cycle in each chapter and facilitates two of the workbook's experiential learning goals: *(1) learning how to learn from all of your experiences and (2) practicing and receiving feedback on the skills required of effective employees and managers.*

TAKING A HOLISTIC APPROACH—THE ROLE OF EMOTION, COGNITION, AND CONTEXT

Experiential learning lends itself to a holistic approach that includes both rational thought and feelings. Our thoughts and our feelings about those thoughts run simultaneously. In part because of a greater understanding of how the brain works, the idea of emotional intelligence has received increased attention lately from both researchers and business practitioners. Some management scholars, however, have long understood the important role of emotions. To take just one example, Wills and Barham found that successful senior international managers displayed emotional self-awareness, emotional resilience, and cultural empathy about how people from other cultures both think and feel. They also demonstrated psychological maturity, which was based in part on a value system that guided their lives, and cognitive complexity, the ability to perceive and integrate many dimensions in a situation.[10] This argues for a holistic approach in management development—a focus on feelings and thoughts accompanied by a consideration of the role of values and character. Context also plays a crucial role because organizational, cultural, and situational conditions all affect how we behave. In this edition, we take a more holistic approach that focuses on rational thought and feelings in context.

The next section builds on the idea of cognitive complexity, which correlates with higher levels of managerial performance and organizational effectiveness.[11] The ability to perceive work situations in a more complex fashion and see multiple relationships and patterns among the various elements relates to expert cognition.

BECOMING AN OB EXPERT

The focus of the workbook has always been to teach critical thinking in the field of organizational behavior and help students perceive organizations through new lenses that capture greater complexity. In this edition, however, we go a step farther with our third theme and try to teach you how to think like OB experts (e.g., highly skilled managers, management consultants, and professors who have mastered this field) and to develop the intuition on which they rely. Experts perform at higher levels because they perceive the world differently and use more sophisticated processes of insightful thinking.[12] They differ from novices in the following ways.

1. When experts look at a problem, they differentiate more readily between relevant and irrelevant information.[13] For example, expert managers are good at decoding the values, attitudes, behaviors and expectations of those with whom they work. Therefore, they can determine whether or not individual characteristics have to be taken into consideration. Is an executive against a new strategic proposal because in reality it is a bad idea, because he's currently depressed, or because he wasn't the first to come up with the idea and doesn't want a rival to get ahead? Novices sometimes overlook the significance of important cues or assign too much importance to red herrings, irrelevant cues.

2. Experts combine relevant information—sets of cues—into meaningful patterns to allow for a more accurate diagnosis of the problem.[14] For instance, chess experts, known as grand masters, can recall approximately 50,000 significant patterns in the game.[15] Patterns help experts of all types to tap into the knowledge that guides their subsequent decisions. In this way, pattern recognition functions like an index[16] or a hyperlink to their knowledge base. Novices perceive fewer patterns when they look at situations.

3. Experts possess an encyclopedia of knowledge that is more extensive than that of novices, and they are better at determining the importance of different types of knowledge and the level of difficulty involved in specific problems.[17] Knowledge alone, however, is not sufficient to develop expertise,[18] which is one of the reasons this course goes beyond traditional lectures and tests to incorporate experiential learning and assignments that build expertise.

4. Experts are also better at perceiving the interaction among cues and understanding the meaning of invisible or absent cues.[19] For instance, expert managers can drop into a meeting at a foreign subsidiary and notice that employees are not contributing ideas or taking initiative to solve problems as they should be. They perceive what is missing by matching what is typical in their previous experiences against what they are seeing or, in this case, failing to see. A novice may not have learned that participation is usually crucial or they may mistakenly assume that passive behavior is normal in that particular culture.

5. Experts are also better at reacting to nonroutine situations[20] and making decisions under pressure. Expert chess players make quicker high-quality decisions under pressure than less skilled players.[21] Experts are also more likely to generate a high-quality solution in their first attempt without needing to compare alternative solutions.[22]

6. Because of the knowledge base and the experience they accrue, experts' perceptions of their work become more complex than that of novices. For example, an exploratory study of cognitive complexity in French and British CEOs in four industries found that CEOs of firms with an international geographic scope or foreign parents had more complex cognitive maps of their own industry than did CEOs in the same industry whose jobs were less international.[23]

7. Although there is no difference in the way novices and experts reason analytically,[24] experts complement their analytical skills with intuitive reasoning.[25] Intuition is "a cognitive conclusion based on a decision maker's previous experiences and emotional inputs."[26] Experts "chunk" information, grouping relevant patterns of information together, thereby allowing them to produce accurate observations and solutions speedily without appearing to engage in much rational analysis.[27] This evolves into intuition— "a sophisticated form of reasoning based on chunking that an expert hones over years of job-specific experience."[28]

The development of expert thinking and intuition can be accelerated with the right kind of training,[29] and we have modified the workbook to do just that. In each chapter, we've included the content information that we deem most useful to expert managers—the knowledge base you need to acquire. When possible, we tell you about differences in the way novices and experts tend to approach situations. The chapters contain information that experts use as cues to diagnose organizational behavior and action scripts they use to be effective. The group exercises provide you with an opportunity to test your own expertise. You will be able to practice and get feedback on picking up on cues, distinguishing between relevant and irrelevant cues, starting to see patterns and interpreting them accurately, putting your knowledge base to work, and considering alternative action scripts and their potential impact.

To visualize the kind of sense-making that can occur in any instance of organizational behavior, look at the simplified version of the Recognition-Primed Decision Model[30] shown below in Exhibit I.1. Gary Klein developed this model as a result of his work with expert decision makers.[31] In a given situation, cues are generated, which allow experts to recognize patterns. These patterns tell expert what to do and lead to specific action scripts that tell them how to do it. Rather than comparing numerous possible actions to select the best one, experts quickly perceive the action script or scripts that fit the pattern and then they "mentally game out an option to see if it will work."[32] In mental simulation, they try to foresee how events and consequences might unfold. If they like what they "see," they proceed with that action. For mental simulation to be effective, however, we need accurate mental models. Gary Klein points out their importance in the following quotation.

Mental models are our beliefs about how various processes work. They direct our explanations and expectations. Effective executives understand the importance of helping their subordinates build better mental models. One explained to me how he would never hire a chief financial officer who only had experience in accounting. Once people gain accounting experience, he believed they should switch to operations, as a plant controller or a group supervisor, or to production control, and then move up to corporate controller, followed by a stint managing a division. Only then can they understand the workings of the corporation well enough to become CFO.[33]

The more cues that are on your "radar screen," the better your understanding of organizations and people. The more patterns and action scripts you have available, the more expertise you will have. Organizations are like puzzles that need to be decoded. In such a complex field, there is seldom one right answer. Instead, we will focus on seeing different perspectives and ways of thinking about behavior. Careful observation of how you and your classmates behave during group exercises, plus mastering the theories in the workbook, will help you develop mental mod-

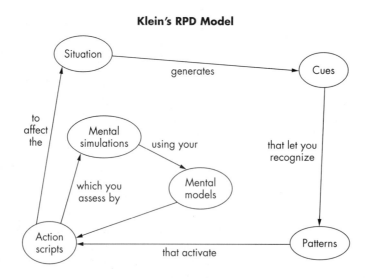

EXHIBIT I-1 Recognition-Primed Decision Model

Source: G. Klein, *The Power of Intuition* (New York: Doubleday, 2004): 26. Used with the author's permission.

els, pattern recognition, and action scripts. By the end of the book, we hope that you will be able to think and act more like an OB expert.

DEVELOPING A GLOBAL MIND-SET

Our final theme is to globalize the workbook's content even more than we have in the past to better prepare students for global business. Whether or not businesses proactively seek to compete beyond the borders of their country globalization brings global competitors, employees, and practices to their doorstep. In addition to understanding the pros and cons of globalization, we see a growing need to learn how to work with people from other cultures, to understand different business practices, and to develop a global mind-set. A global mind-set is *the ability to develop and interpret criteria for personal and business performance that are independent from the assumptions of a single country, culture, or context; and to implement those criteria appropriately in different countries, cultures, and contexts.*"[34] Experts believe that global mind-set leads to higher performance[35] in part because *complex environments demand a matching degree of complexity in humans, which is known as Ashby's law of requisite variety.*[36]

In recent years, increased outsourcing and the use of virtual, multicultural teams spurred a demand for greater intercultural knowledge and skills. Exhibit I.2 lists some of the basic tools of this knowledge base, the cultural value dimensions that are frequently used to compare and contrast cultures and to decode cultural behavior.[37] The following paragraphs provide a brief description of each dimension and an example of work behavior that they influence. We will refer to these dimensions in later chapters.

Several values describe how individuals view and relate to the people, objects, and issues in their sphere of influence. Regarding their relationship with the surrounding world, they may see themselves as either *mastering* their environment or seeking to live in *harmony* with it.[38] Mastery cultures tend to be more dynamic, competitive, and likely to use technology to manipulate the environment and achieve goals. Harmony cultures believe in understanding and integrating with the environment, rather than attempting to change it. This view extends to how people think they should control each other in the workplace.

A related dimension, *locus of control*, refers to beliefs about how much people either control their own destiny (internal locus of control or inner-oriented) or are at the mercy of uncontrollable forces, such as fate or luck (external locus of control or outer-oriented).[39] These values can influence how proactive people and organizations are in their strategy and planning efforts and how accountable employees are for their actions. The *trustworthy-untrustworthy* dimension influences how long it takes to establish trust.[40] If members of a culture assume that human nature is basically untrustworthy, they will approach new business relationships with more caution and employ more control mechanisms to guard against unethical behavior. Yet another dimension related to human nature concerns our beliefs about whether it is *mutable or immutable*—subject to change or set in stone. If a culture believes that humans cannot change, this determines who is hired (people who are fully developed versus those who simply show potential) and how much opportunity employees are given to learn more acceptable workplace behaviors.

Cultures have different beliefs about time, known as *synchronic versus sequential*[41] (also called polychronic versus monochronic).[42] A synchronic approach to time means that people do several things at the same time. They may easily work on a variety of projects at once while receiving different individuals or groups in their office whom they deal with simultaneously. The latter practice can be disconcerting to people from a sequential culture who are more likely to expect "first come-first served" norms. A sequential approach means that people tend to divide activities in a sequence, focusing more on one aspect at a time. Many jobs today involve multitasking, but we would expect to find more efforts to carve out blocks of uninterrupted time to dedicate to only one activity in sequential cultures. Another time-related belief concerns the dominant orientation to time as either *past, present or future*.[43] For example, with regard to decision making, a focus on the past implies that more attention is given to following precedents and tradition, whereas a present orientation may lead to more immediate, short-term considerations. A future orientation raises more consideration of the long-term consequences of decisions.

Environment
How individuals view and relate to the people, objects and issues in their sphere of influence

Mastery	Harmony
Internal locus of control	External local of control
Trustworthy human nature	Untrustworthy human nature
Mutable human nature	Immutable human nature

Time
How individuals perceive the nature of time and its use

Sequential (monochronic)		Synchronic (polychronic)
Past	Present	Future

Work Relationships
How people work together and define their identity and status

Individualistic	Collectivistic
Achievement	Ascription
Universalistic	Particularistic

Power
How individuals view differential power relationships

Hierarchy/high power distance	Equality/low power distance

Structure
How individuals approach change, risk, ambiguity and uncertainty

Order/high uncertainty avoidance	Flexibility/low uncertainty avoidance

Action
How individuals conceptualize actions and interactions

Being/feminine	Doing/masculine
Relationship	Task

Source of Truth
Where groups seek the "right" answers

Expert	Experience

Adapted from A. Bird and J. Osland, "Making Sense of Intercultural Collaboration," *International Studies of Management & Organization 35*(4) (2005/2006): 115–135; and M. E. Phillips and N. A. Boyacigiller, "Learning Culture: An Integrated Framework for Cultural Analysis," Symposium presentation at the Academy of Management Meeting, San Diego, California (1998).

EXHIBIT I-2 **Dimensions of Cultural Values**

The concept of *individualism versus collectivism* is the most extensively studied dimension.[44] Individualism is a cultural pattern found in most northern and western regions of Europe and in North America. It is defined as the extent to which people are responsible for taking care of themselves and giving priority to their own interests. Collectivism is characterized by individuals who subordinate their personal goals to the goals of some collective. Individuals give their loyalty to a group and, in return, the group takes responsibility for the individual. Collectivism is common in Asia, Africa, South America, and the Pacific. In individualistic cultures, people define themselves as an entity that is separate from the group. There is an emphasis on personal goals and less concern and emotional attachment to groups. Successes are individual successes whereas in collectivist cultures, successes are group successes. Competition is interpersonal in individualistic cultures; in collectivist cultures, it occurs between groups. People in collectivist cultures define themselves as part of a group. They are concerned for the integrity of the group and have an intense emotional attachment to the group. For example, the bond between a mother and son (Indo-European collectivist cultures) or father and son (East Asian collectivist cultures) will be stronger than the bond between a wife and a husband because the family group is the most important. Vertical relationships (parent-child, boss-subordinate) are more important in collectivist cultures, whereas horizontal relationships (spouse-spouse, friend-friend) are more important in individualistic cultures.

In-groups are also very important in collectivist cultures. In the previous family example, the extended family is the in-group; other examples include tribes, castes and villages. In-group members in collectivist cultures warrant very different treatment than out-group members who are often treated with hostility and distrust. In contrast, people in individualistic cultures tend to treat people more consistently because they see themselves as belonging to more and larger in-groups (for example, people like us in terms of social class, race, beliefs, attitudes, interests, or people from our region or state). However, the individualists' ties are not as strong with all these groups as the collectivists' ties are with their in-group.

There is an emphasis on harmony and face-saving in collectivist cultures. In contrast, people in individualistic cultures are more likely to value confrontation and "clearing the air." Individualistic cultures have more short-term relationships and use contracts in business dealings. Collectivistic cultures think in terms of long-term relationships, which make the use of contracts less important.

Not everyone in an individualistic culture is individualistic; the same is true for collectivist cultures. In both types of cultures, one can find allocentric people who value social support and idiocentric people who value achievement.[45] Individualistic cultures have higher gross national products, but they also have more social ills and higher heart attack rates. Collectivist cultures report lower degrees of loneliness, alienation, and social problems. However, they may have more government corruption if in-group loyalty dictates that those in power will try to enrich their in-group rather than concern themselves with the country as a whole.

Another source of identity concerns how cultural members gain status—via *achievement versus ascription.*[46] In achievement cultures, people are expected to accomplish things to earn status (e.g., working hard, becoming successful). Ascription cultures bestow (ascribe) status on their members based on their family, age, class, gender or education. In achievement cultures, the first question one generally asks a stranger is "What do you do?" In an ascription culture, the question is more likely to be "Where are you from? Are you related to the 'so-and-so's' from that region. Where did you go to school?" If you've begun to mumble that you can find both of these values, as well as the others in Exhibit I.2, in the same culture, you're correct. The context determines which cultural values are more figural in a specific circumstance.[47] But comparing cultures to others, we find marked tendencies to give greater importance to one end of these value dimensions than another. United States culture values achievement (the Horatio Alger myth of pulling oneself up by the bootstraps); nevertheless, some people benefit greatly from ascribed status. Despite low grades, their family name and wealth enables them to attend Ivy League schools where they make connections that advance their career. When asked about their success, however, they are likely to attribute it to their personal achievements, an explanation more in keeping with the dominant cultural belief.

The *universalistic-particularistic* dimension refers to cultural beliefs about the world and relationships.[48] Universalistic cultures believe that the rules apply equally to everyone, resulting in the same treatment. Particularistic cultures expect one's relationship to influence the treatment that one receives, and therefore, exceptions for friends or important people are normal. These values often determine whether personnel decisions and ethical practices are perceived as fair or unfair.

Cultures also vary in their acceptance of differential power relationships and ways to guarantee responsible behavior. In *hierarchical* cultures, the social fabric is maintained by a hierarchy of ascribed roles.[49] This is accompanied by an acceptance that power is distributed unequally, what culture expert Geert Hofstede calls high ital *power distance.*[50] Those at the top have a greater voice and more freedom to act as they wish. In contrast, equality cultures, similar to Hofstede's low power distance cultures, assume that people are equal and that power should be distributed more evenly. People are socialized to make commitments to bosses on a more voluntary basis, rather than responding to their role in the hierarchy. This value dimension influences how many layers we find in the organizational structure, who has a voice in decisions, and whether superiors are automatically respected or expected to earn that respect.

Another set of values concern structure as it relates to change, risk, and uncertainty. Cultures vary in their beliefs about *order versus flexibility*. Cultures that value order prefer predictability and clarity, while flexible cultures are more comfortable with ambiguity and change. Hofstede referred to these dimensions as low or high *uncertainty avoidance*. A cultural belief in order can be seen in greater career stability, more formal rules, and less openness to change.

Cultures tend to conceptualize their primary mode of activity in terms of *being or doing*.[51] In being cultures (what Hofstede calls *feminine* cultures), the emphasis is on enjoying life in the moment and nurturing others, whereas doing cultures (Hofstede's *masculine* cultures) emphasize achievement, assertiveness, and materialism. This dichotomy is often described as working to live (being) versus living to work (doing). These values influence how employees perceive work rewards; doing cultures are comfortable rewarding good performance while being cultures may express concern that merit pay or bonuses could have a negative impact on their co-workers or the work environment.

We'll introduce the next dimension, *relationship versus task*, with a story.

A second grade teacher asked her students to solve this problem: "There are four blackbirds sitting in a tree. You take a slingshot and shoot one of them. How many are left?"
"Three," answered the seven-year-old European with certainty. "One subtracted from four leaves three."
"Zero," answered the seven-year-old African with equal certainty. "If you shoot one bird, the others will fly away."[52]

The European perceived the question as a hypothetical situation that required a literal answer (task). In contrast, the African focused on the relationship among the birds and the predictable behavior that would result from a shot (relationship). In some cultures, such as the United States, task is the primary focus, and people quickly get down to business. In many other cultures, such as in Italy, Senegal, and Ecuador, people expect to establish a relationship first so they can trust one another enough to do business with them. Like the students' answers, one orientation is not better than the other; they are simply different and must be taken into consideration when working across cultures.

Finally, cultures vary in their views of what anthropologists call the source of truth. Some cultures believe that the right answers are obtained from *experts* while others trust their own *experience*. Do people believe that truth comes primarily from scientific research, legal precedent, the opinion of experts, tradition, personal experience, or trial-and-error experimentation?[53] For example, U.S. Americans value expert opinion, but they are more likely to question authority than many cultures and to rely, instead, on their own experience.

In addition to viewing culture as a constellation of values, anthropologists note that culture reflects the answers different groups have found to the basic problems that confront all humankind. Old age and dying represent an inescapable challenge for every society, but how they deal with the end of life derives primarily from particular cultural values and beliefs about medicine, the afterlife, the prestige and respect due the elderly, family obligations, and so forth. Culture provides us with ready-made solutions to basic human issues and a sense of identity. Each culture has an internal logic that makes perfect sense once it is understood. Novices, however, tend to see "strange" behavior through the lens of their own cultural norms and assumptions. Experts develop a global mind-set in part by learning these value dimensions and being able to recognize them in the workplace, without assuming different cultural beliefs and behaviors are "wrong" simply because they are different.

Through exposure to other cultures, we come to a deeper understanding of our own culture and its biases. Hofstede argued that management theories developed by U.S. scholars contain a cultural bias and therefore do not apply all over the world.[54] U.S. Americans, according to Hofstede, value equality (low power distance), are individualists (extremely high individualism) who willingly tolerate uncertainty (low uncertainty avoidance), value achievement and striving more than nurturance and support (above average masculinity) and have a short-term orientation. He contends that U.S. management techniques are largely based on these values. His argument inspired a great deal of research on comparative business practices. In response to his warning, we are careful to include theories that cross cultural borders and to note cultural limitations. As a result, this workbook is used successfully all over the world. Understanding the impact of culture on organizational behavior is an important skill for anyone who works in organizations. We encourage you to take advantage of the learning possibilities from the cultural diversity in your classroom or workplace and invite you to raise questions about the universality of both theories and behavior.

CLASS ACTIVITY: MAPPING THE MULTICULTURAL CLASSROOM

One of the ways firms develop a global mind-set is by hiring a diverse workforce and then leveraging the cultural diversity within their own organization. Following their example, the purpose of this exercise is to begin creating a productive multicultural learning community, in which we can benefit from learning about different cultural perspectives and scripts (Time allotted: 65 minutes).

STEP 1. Visual representation of student cultural influences. (10 minutes)
Visualize the classroom as the world, with the North Pole at the front of the room, the South Pole at the opposite end, with Africa and Europe along the wall to your far left and Latin America and North America along the wall to your far right. The Middle East, Asia, and Australia are toward the middle of the room. Go stand where you were raised on this world map and then check to see whether your position is correct relative to other students. You will have to ask them for their location to place yourself in the right spot. If you moved around while growing up, choose the location where your schooling had the most impact on you. Look around to see what areas are represented in your class.

STEP 2. Group discussion of classroom norms of behavior. (10 minutes)
Form a group with the people who were raised in geographical areas closest to you, introduce yourselves, and answer the questions below. (Your groups should be no larger than about six members. If you are the only person from a large region, join another person who is a sole representative like you or join the closest group.) The instructor will call upon someone in your group to report out your consolidated answers about classroom norms of behavior, so be prepared.
a. How were students expected to behave in the classroom where you were raised?
b. How were teachers expected to behave in the classroom where you were raised?

STEP 3. Reports to total group (15 minutes)
The instructor will have a spokesperson from each group briefly relay their answers, which will be written on the board.

STEP 4. Plenary Discussion (30 minutes)
1. Do you see any differences in norms that could affect what takes place in our classroom?
2. If there are different expectations about class participation in the room, how can we find a solution?
3. Have you ever studied in another country?
a. What was the most significant cultural difference you observed in the classroom when you were abroad?
b. What did you learn about your own culture as a result of your study abroad experience?

4. What cues do you think an expert in intercultural communication would pay attention to in a multicultural classroom? What action scripts would they have?

5. Given our cultural and/or regional differences, what behavioral norms should we adopt to create an effective multicultural classroom? The criteria that determine effectiveness are that students are comfortable, can talk openly about cultural differences, and maximize the opportunity to learn from people of different backgrounds.

THE PLAN OF THIS BOOK

The book is organized into four parts progressing from a focus on the individual to the group, organization, and the organization-environment interface. Part I examines many of the different mental maps that individuals possess. Chapters 1 and 7 consider the individual's relationship with the organization over time through the concepts of the psychological contract and career development. Chapter 2 reviews the principal theories of management and managerial functions. Chapter 3 focuses on the learning process for both individuals and organizations. Chapter 4 explains how to understand and decode personality and work with difficult people. Chapter 5 lays out the motivational determinants of human behavior in organizations, whereas Chapter 6 centers on individual values, ethical decision making, and the ways to create an ethical workplace.

While the primary focus of Part I is self-awareness and the appreciation of individual differences, in Part II there is more emphasis on the skill-building needed to develop effective work relationships and teams. It begins with a grounding in interpersonal communication in Chapter 8 and progresses to perception and attribution in Chapter 9. Chapter 10 focuses on team dynamics, while Chapters 11 and 12 deal, respectively, with problem management and creativity. Conflict and negotiation are addressed in Chapter 13. Managing diversity, both domestic and international, is the focus of Chapter 14.

Part III focuses on the knowledge and skills needed by managers and leaders to accomplish their goals and visions with the help of others. Leadership itself is the focus of Chapter 15, followed by the critical leadership functions in the managerial role in subsequent chapters—creating, maintaining, and changing organizational culture (Chapter 16), decision making (Chapter 17), exercising power and influence (Chapter 18), coaching and empowerment (Chapter 19), and performance management and appraisal (Chapter 20).

Part IV is concerned with the system-wide architecture required for effective organizations. Chapter 21 looks at the key issues pertaining to organization structure and design. Chapter 22 describes the process of planned change and organization development. There are four integrative cases at the end of the book that relate to topics from various chapters.

YOUR ROLE AS A LEARNER

You may find as you work with this book that a new role is being asked of you as a learner. Rather than assuming the role of a passive recipient, here you are given the opportunity to become an active creator of your own learning. This is an opportunity for you to develop new and different relationships with fellow students and faculty members responsible for this course. As you may already have sensed, the experiential learning approach provides numerous opportunities for shared leadership in the learning process.

 **LEARNING POINTS**

1. Organizational behavior is defined as a field of study that endeavors to understand, explain, predict, and change human behavior that occurs in the organizational context.

2. Kurt Lewin is viewed as the founder of this relatively young field.

3. Organizational behavior has the following characteristics:
   a. Multidisciplinary nature
   b. Three levels of analysis: individual, group, organizational
   c. Acknowledgment of environmental forces
   d. Grounded in the scientific method
   e. Performance orientation
   f. Applied orientation
   g. Change orientation
4. The course objectives are:
   a. Learn to diagnose organizational situations
   b. Know what would be the most effective action to take
   c. Have the repertoire of skills needed to implement that action.
5. The overarching themes of the book are 1) learning to learn from experience, 2) taking a holistic approach that includes cognition, emotion, and context, 3) developing a global mind-set, and 4) developing OB expertise.
6. In experiential learning theory, knowledge is created through the transformation of experience
7. In addition to possessing a larger knowledge base, experts differ from novices in their ability to distinguish between relevant and irrelevant information, to combine relevant information into meaningful patterns and perceive more patterns, to make decisions under pressure, and to complement their analytical skills with intuition.
8. Klein's circular model of Recognition Primed Decision Making starts with a situation that generates cues that let the expert recognize patterns that activate action scripts to affect the situation. Experts assess action scripts by mental simulation that uses mental models of how things work.
9. The more patterns and action scripts people have available, the more expertise they possess.
10. Global mind-set is the ability to develop and interpret criteria for personal and business performance that are independent from the assumptions of a single country, culture, or context; and to implement those criteria appropriately in different countries, cultures, and contexts.
11. Culture provides us with ready-made solutions for basic human problems and a sense of identity, but it can also limit our ability to see and appreciate alternative behaviors.
12. Cultural dimensions with regard to beliefs about the environment, time, work relationships, power, structure, action, and the source of truth help us compare and contrast cultures and decode cultural behavior.
13. Hofstede warned that U.S. management theories are culturally biased and do not apply everywhere.

ENDNOTES

[1] M. T. Iaffaldano and P. M. Muchinsky, "Job Satisfaction and Job Performance: A Meta-analysis," *Psychological Bulletin, 97*(2) (1985): 251–273; T. A. Judge, C. J. Thoresen, J. E. Bono, and G. Patten, "The Job-Satisfaction-Job Performance Relationship: A Qualitative and Quantitative Review," *Psychological Bulletin 127*(3) (2001): 376–407.

[2] P. M. Wright, T. M. Gardner, L.M. Moynihan, and M. R. Allen, "The Relationship between HR Practices and Firm Performance: Examining Causal Order." *Personnel Psychology 8* (2005): 409–446.

[3] Wright, Gardner, Moynihan, and Allen, "The Relationship between HR Practices and Firm Performance"; B. E. Becker and M. A. Huselid, "High Performance Work Systems and Firm Performance: A Synthesis of Research and Managerial Implications," in G. Ferris (ed.), *Research in Personnel and Human Resource Management 16* (1998): 53–101.

[4] Becker and Huselid. "High Performance Work Systems and Firm Performance."

[5] J. K. Liker, *The Toyota Way: 14 Management Principles from the World's Greatest Manufacturer* (New York: McGraw-Hill, 2004).

[6] "The Mission of Southwest Airlines," http://www.southwest.com /about_swa/mission.html. Accessed 8/3/06.

[7] J. Pfeffer and C. O'Reilly, *Hidden Value: How Great Companies Achieve Extraordinary Results with Ordinary People* (Cambridge, MA: Harvard Business School Press, 2000).

[8] J. A. Wagner and J. R. Hollenbeck. *Management of Organizational Behavior* (Englewood Cliffs, NJ: Prentice Hall, 1995).

[9] K. Lewin, *A Dynamic Theory of Personality* (New York: McGraw-Hill, 1935).

[10] S. Wills and K. Barham, "Being an International Manager," *European Management Journal 12*(1) (1994): 49–58.

[11] K. Weick, *The Social Psychology of Organizing* (Reading, MA: Addison-Wesley, 1979); I. M. Duhaime and C. R. Schwenk, "Conjectures on Cognitive Simplification in Acquisition and Divestment Decision Making," *Academy of Management Review 10* (1985): 287–295; E. Jacque, "The Development of Intellectual Capability: A Discussion of Stratified Systems Theory," *Journal of Applied Behavioral Science 22* (1986): 361–383.

[12] R. Sternberg and J. Davidson (Eds.), *The Nature of Insight* (Cambridge, MA: MIT Press, 1994).

[13] Sternberg and Davidson, *The Nature of Insight.*

[14] Sternberg and Davidson, *The Nature of Insight.*

[15] M. J. Prietula, and H. A. Simon, "The Experts in Your Midst," *Harvard Business Review 67*(1) (January–February, 1989): 120–124.

[16] Simon in A. M. Hayashi, "When to Trust Your Gut," *Harvard Business Review 79*(2) (February 2001): 59–65.

[17] G. A. Klein and R. R. Hoffman, "Seeing the Invisible: Perceptual-Cognitive Aspects of Expertise," in M. Rabinowits (ed.), *Cognitive Science Foundations of Instruction* (Hillsdale, NJ: Lawrence Erlbaum Associates, 1993): 203–226.

[18] Klein, and Hoffman, "Seeing the Invisible."

[19] Ibid.

[20] Ibid.

[21] N. Charness, "Search in Chess: Age and Skill Differences." *Journal of Experimental Psychology: Human Learning and Memory 7* (1981): 467–476; R. Calderwood, G.A. Klein, and B.W. Crandall, "Time Pressure, Skill, and Move Quality in Chess," *American Journal of Psychology 101* (1988): 481–493.

[22] G.A. Klein, *Sources of Power* (Cambridge, MA: MIT Press, 1988).

[23] R. Calori, G. Johnson and P. Sarnin, "CEO's Cognitive Maps and the Scope of the Organization," *Strategic Management Journal 15*(6) (1994): 15437–15457.

[24] M. T. H. Chi, P. J. Feltovich, and R. Glaser, "Categorization and Representation of Physics Problems by Experts and Novices," *Cognitive Science 5* (1981): 121–152; G. Klein, J.K. Phillips, E. Rall, and D. A. Peluso, "A Data/frame Theory of Sensemaking," in R. Hoffman (ed.), *Expertise Out of Context: Proceedings of the 6th International Conference on Naturalistic Decision Making (Mahweh, NJ: Lawrence Erlbaum, 2006)* (In press).

[25] Prietula and Simon, "The Experts in Your Midst."

[26] L. A. Burke and M. K. Miller, "Taking the Mystery Out of Intuitive Decision Making" *Academy of Management Executive 13*(4) (1999): 92–99.

[27] Prietula and Simon, "The Experts in Your Midst."

[28] Ibid.: 121–122.

[29] G. Klein, *The Power of Intuition* (NY: Doubleday, 2004).

[30] Ibid: 26.

[31] G. Klein, *Intuition at Work* (New York: Currency, 2003).

[32] G. Klein and K. Weick, "Decision: Making the Right Ones. Learning from the Wrong Ones," *Across the Board 37*(6) (2000): 18.

[33] Klein, *The Power of Intuition.*

[34] M. Maznevski and H. Lane, "Shaping the Global Mindset: Designing Educational Experiences for Effective Global Thinking and Action," in N. Boyacigiller, R. M. Goodman and M. Phillips (eds.), *Teaching and Experiencing Cross-*

Cultural Management: Lessons from Masters Teachers (London and New York: Routledge, 2004): 172.

[35] C. A. Bartlett and S. Ghoshal, "What is a Global Manager?" *Harvard Business Review 70*(5) (1992): 124–131; K. Ohmae, "Managing in a Borderless World," *Harvard Business Review 67*(3) (1989): 152–161.

[36] W. R. Ashby, *An Introduction to Cybernetics* (New York: Wiley, 1956).

[37] For a comprehensive treatise on culture, see M. Y. Brannen, C. Gomez, M. Peterson, L. Romani, L. Sagiv, and P. Wu, "People in Global Organizations: Culture, Personality, and Social Dynamics," in H. Lane, M. Maznevski, M. Mendenhall and J. McNett (eds.), *Handbook of Global Management* (Oxford: Blackwell, 2004): 26–54.

[38] F. Kluckhohn and F. Strodtbeck, *Variations in Value Orientations* (Evanston, IL: Row, Peterson, 1961).

[39] C. Hampden-Turner and F. Trompenaars, *Building Cross-Cultural Competence: How to Create Wealth from Conflicting Values* (Chichester: John Wiley, 2000); J. B. Rotter, "Generalized Expectancies for Internal vs. External Control of Reinforcement," *Psychological Monograph 80* (1966): 1–28.

[40] Kluckhohn and Strodtbeck, *Variations in Value Orientations,* were the first to write about this dimension; they termed human nature as either good or evil.

[41] E. T. Hall, *Beyond Culture* (New York: Anchor Press/Doubleday, 1976).

[42] E. T. Hall and M. Hall, *Hidden Differences: Doing Business with the Japanese* (New York: Prentice Hall, 1988).

[43] Kluckhohn, and F. Strodtbeck, *Variations in Value Orientation.*

[44] H. C. Triandis, R. Bontempo, M. J. Villareal, M. Asai, and N. Lucca, "Individualism and Collectivism: Cross-Cultural Perspectives on Self-Ingroup Relationships," *Journal of Personality and Social Psychology 54*(2) (1988): 323–338; and H. C. Triandis, R. Brislin, and C. H. Hui, "Cross-Cultural Training Across the Individualism-Collectivism Divide," *International Journal of Intercultural Relations 12* (1988): 269–89.

[45] H. C. Triandis, B. Bontempo, M. J. Villarreal, M. Asai, and N. Lucca, "Individualism and Collectivism: Cross-Cultural Perspectives on Self-Ingroup Relationships."

[46] T. Parsons, and E. Shils (eds.), *Toward a General Theory of Action* (Cambridge, MA: Harvard University Press, 1951); and C. Hampden-Turner and F. Trompenaars, *Riding the Waves of Culture: Understanding Cultural Diversity in Global Business,* 2nd ed. (New York: McGraw-Hill, 1998).

[47] J. S. Osland and A. Bird, "Beyond Sophisticated Stereotyping: Cultural Sensemaking in Context," *Academy of Management Executive 14* (2000): 65–77.

[48] T. Parsons and E. Shils (eds.), *Toward a General Theory of Action*; C. Hampden-Turner and Trompenaars, *Riding the Waves of Culture.*

[49] S. H. Schwartz, "Beyond Individualism/Collectivism: New Cultural Dimensions of Values," in U. Kim, H. C. Triandis, C. Kagitcibasi, S. Choi, and G. Yoon (eds.), *Individualism and Collectivism: Theory, Method, and Applications* (Thousand Oaks, CA: Sage, 1994): 85–119.

[50] References to Hofstede in the following paragraphs are taken from G. H. Hofstede, *Culture's Consequences: Competing Values, Behaviors, Institutions, and Organizations across Nations,* 2nd ed. (Thousand Oaks, CA: Sage, 2001). For a review of research based on Hofstede's work, see B. L. Kirkman, K. B. Lowe, and C. B. Gibson, "A Quarter Century of *Culture's Consequences*: A Review of Empirical Research Incorporating Hofstede's Cultural Values Framework," *Journal of International Business Studies 37* (2006): 285–320.

[51] F. Kluckhohn, and F. Strodtbeck, *Variations in Value Orientation.*

[52] "Cultural Diversity in Today's Corporation," *Working Woman* (January 1991): 45.

[53] M. E. Phillips and N. A. Boyacigiller, "Learning Culture: An Integrated Framework for Cultural Analysis," Symposium presentation at the Academy of Management Meeting, San Diego, California (1998).

[54] G. Hofstede, "Cultural Constraints in Management Theories," *Academy of Management Review 7*(1) (1993): 81–93.

Part 1

▲▲▲

UNDERSTANDING YOURSELF AND OTHER PEOPLE AT WORK

Mental Maps

The goal of the first section is to help you become aware of your mental maps or models, as well as those of fellow participants in the course. Although the concept has existed since ancient times, the term *mental models* was coined in the 1940s by Kenneth Craik, a Scottish psychologist. This term refers to "the images, assumptions, and stories that we carry in our minds of ourselves, other people, institutions, and every aspect of the world. Like a pane of glass framing and subtly distorting our vision, mental models determine what we see and then how we act." * One way to understand our behavior is to make these usually tacit maps visible. In this section, you will have an opportunity to examine mental maps about psychological contracts, theories of management, learning styles, personality, motivation, ethics, and values. We hope you'll finish the section with more self-knowledge and a greater appreciation for the differences you find in other people.

CHAPTER 1 The Psychological Contract and Commitment

CHAPTER 2 Theories of Managing People

CHAPTER 3 Individual and Organizational Learning

CHAPTER 4 Decoding Human Behavior and Personality

CHAPTER 5 Individual and Organizational Motivation

CHAPTER 6 Ethics and Values

CHAPTER 7 Personal Growth and Work Stress

* P. Senge, A. Kleiner, R. Ross, and B. Smith, *The Fifth Discipline Fieldbook: Strategies and Tools for Building a Learning Organization* (New York: Currency, 1993): 235.

Chapter 1

▲▲

THE PSYCHOLOGICAL CONTRACT AND COMMITMENT

OBJECTIVES   By the end of this chapter, you should be able to:

A. Define the psychological contract and discuss the obligations of the contract currently in place.

B. Explain the importance of the psychological contract and what happens when it is violated.

C. Explain the benefits of committed employees and what employers can do to foster commitment.

D. Describe external influences that affect workplace expectations.

E. Explain the self-fulfilling prophecy and how managers can apply this concept.

F. Explain the pinch model.

G. Make a psychological contract with your professor.

CREATING A GREAT PLACE TO WORK

Every year, *Fortune* magazine publishes a list of the 100 best companies to work for. It is one of the magazine's most popular issues of the year. People love to read about companies where the grass may be greener. And managers find they can pick up tips that they can apply to their organizations to make them better places to work.

WORK ENVIRONMENT AND ITS IMPACT

Everybody, whether a senior manager or frontline employee, would prefer to work in a good working environment. Since most people spend the majority of their waking hours at work, the quality of the work experience has a big impact on their lives. Everyone wants to look forward to going to work in the morning. And no one enjoys coming home from work feeling frustrated and discouraged from his or her experiences at work.

But there is more than quality of life involved with this issue. The quality of the workplace impacts directly on issues of customer service and productivity. The connection to customer service has been shown in numerous studies. A famous 1998 study published in the Harvard Business Review article "The Employee-Customer-Profit Chain at Sears" showed that an increase in employee satisfaction at a store resulted in an increase in customer satisfaction, which in turn resulted in higher profitability for the store. There have been similar studies in the hospital industry, showing that improvements in workplace environments result in better patient satisfaction.

The Great Place to Work Institute has seen extremely strong evidence of the same phenomenon from its work in surveying the best workplaces. A few months ago, Frank Russell Co., a firm that provides investment services for large pension funds among other clients, did two comparisons. The company took a hypothetical portfolio of stocks from the companies that were on the first Fortune 100 Best Companies to Work For list in 1997 and compared the overall financial results through 2003 with a portfolio of stocks from the Standard & Poor's 500 (an established stock market index similar to the Dow Jones industrial average). The results were astonishing. Money invested in the "100 Best" portfolio would have returned almost three times more than the same amount a portfolio in the S&P 500 during the past six years. The results were even more remarkable if, instead of holding onto the stocks of the 100 best companies, an investor had changed the portfolio to reflect the changes in the list annually. (Every year, a new list of the 100 Best is published based on our annual survey. Typically, about 20 companies are replaced.) If investors updated their portfolio with each year's 100 Best list, they would have seen the original investment outperform a comparable S&P 500 portfolio by more than a factor of five.

As shown, the best workplaces tend to have higher productivity and profitability as well as better customer satisfaction. Among the obvious reasons for this result is that the best workplaces typically have much lower staff turnover than their competitors. (In a study we conducted in 2001 that was published in *Fortune*, the 100 Best companies had an average staff turnover that was 50 percent lower than their competitors.) High staff turnover is very costly to any enterprise, whether a for-profit corporation, a nonprofit organization, or a governmental agency, because of the increased costs associated with recruiting and training new staff. Similarly, organizations with reputations as good employers also tend to attract high quality staff. The better the quality of the staff, the better able the staff will be in performing their duties.

A less tangible—though equally important—reason organizations with great workplaces deliver better service and products is employee morale. Better morale translates into environments where employees are more likely to provide better service.

CREATING A "GREAT PLACE TO WORK"

Before moving on to the subject of how a great workplace is created, the criteria should be defined. I define a great place to work as one where employees trust the people they work for, have pride in what they do and enjoy the people they work with. This definition is based on the hundreds of interviews I conducted in the 1980s for the first edition of my book, *The 100 Best Companies to Work for in America* (co-authored with Milton Moskowitz). From those interviews, I observed that employees insisted that the most important factor that distinguished their workplaces was a very high level of trust between the employees and the management.

What do employees at great workplaces mean by trust? There are three aspects of trust. The first is credibility—what employees think about the management's believability, competence, and integrity. It all begins with whether they can believe what someone tells them. If management's word cannot be taken to be true, trust is impossible. At great workplaces, management goes out of its way to be believable by doing the following:

Sharing information broadly. The Container Store, a Dallas-based retailer that was No. 1 on the Fortune 100 Best list in 2000 and 2001, makes it a point to share information about such matters as daily sales results from each store with all of the employees.

Accessibility to employees. The Great Place to Work Institute has found that even at large companies such as Continental Airlines or Procter and Gamble, the top executives go to great lengths to meet with ordinary employees whenever possible. In smaller companies, this is often done in more informal ways such as having lunch in the employee cafeteria. At East Alabama Medical Center, a county-run facility, the CEO makes it a point to visit every ward of the hospital every day. Frequently these companies have an open door policy. The point is that top managers make sure that people within the organization see them as fellow human beings rather than figures living in an ivory tower. To be able to trust, employees need to feel some sense of what kind of people are in management—whether they are trustworthy. That cannot be done unless employees have been able to size management up for themselves.

Willingness to answer hard questions. It is not enough to share information and be personally accessible. Leaders of the best workplaces also realize that they need to face difficult questions from their employees. Thus, the Great Place to Work Institute has seen a myriad of mechanisms to ensure that employees have regular opportunities to get straight answers to difficult questions. In the past few years, informal breakfasts of randomly selected employees with the CEO have become common. At J.M. Smucker, the jelly and jam maker that was No. 1 on the 2004 Fortune 100 Best list, the CEO and president conduct quarterly town hall meetings at each of their sites throughout the country where they answer any question that is asked of them. If they cannot provide an answer immediately, they make certain that each of the questions is answered through a company newsletter later. The key point is that management makes itself available for genuine dialogue with employees. Instead of concentrating on one-way, top-down communication, the emphasis on two-way communication is what distinguishes the best employers.

Delivering on promises. Closely related to the question of believability is that of integrity. People do not believe someone, no matter how good that person's communications skills are, unless he or she follows through on what has been said will be done. Several years ago, the Great Place to Work Institute was asked to do a workplace assessment of a large division of a major telecommunications company. A very charismatic leader who was an excellent communicator ran the division. He shared information with everyone, was accessible, and held regular question-and-answer conferences with staff. But the institute discovered that the staff did not trust him because he was too nice. When people would come into his office, he would invariably make commitments or implied promises. The employee would leave the office and feel good about the situation and about the executive, in the short run. But the problem was that sometimes he delivered on his promises and sometimes he did not. As a result, people did not know whether his word was any good. They liked him but did not trust him. The Great Place to Work Institute recommended that he follow a simple discipline: After every meeting, make a list of every promise that he had made. In a matter of weeks, his list became shorter and shorter and the level of trust within the division began to grow.

The second major aspect of trust relates to what employees think management thinks about them. While the first aspect of trust revolves around how employees perceive the management's credibility, it is equally important that employees feel that the management shows them respect. In other words, employees can feel that management has a high degree of credibility, is believable, and demonstrates competence and integrity. But they must also feel that management has their best interests at heart to genuinely extend their trust. This is done in two main ways:

Showing recognition and appreciation. The institute has found that the best employers make a special effort to say "thank you" in a variety of ways to employees. It becomes part of the fabric of daily existence in these companies. L.L. Bean, a mail-order catalogue retailer, has developed a particularly good method of singling out those who deserve special recognition. A committee of employees selects some five workers a year from dozens of employee nominations for an award called Bean's Best. The committee then organizes special celebrations complete with celebratory horns and champagne at the winners' own work sites.

Demonstrating personal concern. Respect is also a very personal matter. To select companies for the Great Place to Work Institute's lists, staff distribute to several hundred randomly selected employees at each firm an employee survey called the Great Place to Work Trust Index. Based on a correlation study of the results of the trust index, the institute found the following statement to be the most significant: "Management shows a sincere interest in me as a person, not just an employee." In particular, people are especially concerned with how they will be treated when faced with a personal event of significance—an illness, a death in the family, births, and so on. The best employers find ways to show genuine concern in those circumstances.

Becoming a great workplace may not be rocket science, but it does require paying attention to the basic issue of trust in the relationship between management and employees. Trust is a delicate commodity that must be earned daily. But when it is present, both management and employees benefit.

Source: Reprinted with permission from Robert Levering, "Creating a Great Place to Work: Why It Is Important and How It Is Done," (August 2004). San Francisco: Great Place to Work® Institute, Inc. www.greatplacetowork.com.

CLASS PREPARATION

A. Read "Creating a Great Place to Work."

B. Answer the following questions.

    1. Have you ever had a job experience that did not work out as you thought it would?

    2. What expectations of yours were not met?

    3. Were there any expectations on the part of your boss that were not met?

    4. What trends have you observed that are organizational changing the workplace?

C. Answer and score the organizational commitment questionnaire.

D. As you read the chapter, make a list of cues and patterns that will help you diagnose the psychological contracts in an organization and understand when they are being violated.

Organizational Commitment Questionnaire (OCQ)

Think about your organization as you respond to the following statements. If you are not working, choose the organization that is most relevant to you. Circle the number between 1 and 7 on the scale below that most accurately describes your opinion.

1-strongly disagree	2-moderately disagree	3-slightly disagree	4-neither disagree nor agree
5-slightly agree	6-moderately agree	7-strongly agree	

1	I am willing to put in a great deal of effort beyond that normally expected in order to help this organization be successful.	1 2 3 4 5 6 7
2	I talk up this organization to my friends as a great organization to work for.	1 2 3 4 5 6 7
3	I feel very little loyalty to this organization.	1 2 3 4 5 6 7
4	I would accept almost any type of job assignment in order to keep working for this organization.	1 2 3 4 5 6 7
5	I find that my values and the organization's values are very similar.	1 2 3 4 5 6 7
6	I am proud to tell others that I am part of this organization.	1 2 3 4 5 6 7
7	I could just as well be working for a different organization as long as the type of work was similar.	1 2 3 4 5 6 7
8	This organization really inspires the very best in me in the way of job performance.	1 2 3 4 5 6 7
9	It would take very little change in my present circumstances to cause me to leave this organization.	1 2 3 4 5 6 7
10	I am extremely glad that I chose this organization to work for over others I was considering at the time I joined.	1 2 3 4 5 6 7
11	There's not too much to be gained by sticking with this organization indefinitely.	1 2 3 4 5 6 7
12	Often, I find it difficult to agree with this organization's policies on important matters relating to this organization.	1 2 3 4 5 6 7
13	I really care about the fate of this organization.	1 2 3 4 5 6 7
14	For me this is the best of all possible organizations for which to work.	1 2 3 4 5 6 7
15	Deciding to work for this organization was a definite mistake on my part.	1 2 3 4 5 6 7

Scoring the survey:

A) Add up the scores you circled for items (#1, 2, 4, 5, 6, 8, 10, 13, & 14).

# 1 ___	# 2 ___	# 4 ___	
# 5 ___	# 6 ___	# 8 ___	
# 10 ___	# 13 ___	# 14 ___	Subtotal A = _____

B) For items #3, 7, 9, 11, 12, & 15 ONLY, subtract the number that you circled from 8, in order to obtain your score. For example: If you circled 5, your score would be 3 (8 − 5 = 3). Using your newly obtained scores, add up these six items.

8 − #3 _____ = _____	8 − #7 _____ = _____	
8 − #9 _____ = _____	8 − #11 _____ = _____	
8 − #12 _____ = _____	8 − #15 _____ = _____	Subtotal B = _____

C) Add Subtotal A (above) with Subtotal B (above) to obtain a composite score and divide by 15 to get your average score

A____ + B____ = Composite Score _____ ÷ 15 = Average Score.

Interpreting your score: The average scores on this instrument can range from 1 (very low commitent) to 7 (very high commitent). Compare your score to the averages shown below for different types of employees in a 2563-person validation study to discover how your commitment level relates.

TYPES OF EMPLOYEES	AVERAGE SCORE
Scientist and Engineers	4.4
Public Employees	4.5
Classified University Employees	4.6
Telephone Company Employees	4.7
Hospital Employees	5.1
Bank Employees	5.2
Auto Company Managers	5.3
Retail Management Trainees	6.1

Source: R. T. Mowday and R. M. Steers, "The Measurement of Organizational Commitment," *Journal of Vocational Behavior, 14* (1979): 224–247.

 **THE KNOWLEDGE BASE**

As we saw in the opening vignette, if you had invested in the 100 Best Companies to Work for in America, rather than their competitors not on this list, you would have had an equal or sometimes substantially higher return on your investment.[1] A positive relationship with employees is a competitive advantage. The issue of trust is a crucial factor in the employee–employer relationship. The credibility and integrity this requires relates to the psychological contract they develop. When individuals join an organization, they form an unwritten, implicit or (less frequently) explicit, psychological contract with the organization. *Psychological contracts are defined as an individual's beliefs, shaped by the organization, regarding the terms and conditions of a reciprocal exchange agreement between individuals and their organization.*[2] They refer to the mutual expectations employees and employers have of each other. Such contracts help predict both the type of outputs employers will get from employees as well as the rewards employees will receive for their efforts from the organization. The psychological contract is based on people's perception that they have been promised a future return for their contributions, creating an obligation to reciprocate. This concept is rooted in *social exchange theory, which argues that people enter into relationships in which not only economic but also social obligations play a role and that people are most comfortable when the exchange is balanced.*[3]

Psychological contracts differ from employment contracts because they focus on a dynamic relationship that defines the employees' psychological involvement with their employer. The actions of both parties mutually influence the psychological contract. For example, high company expectations about what employees should contribute to the company can produce increased individual performance; when individuals perform at a high level, they come to expect more than just a paycheck. They may also expect respectful treatment, challenging jobs, training that will help them develop and grow, and a share in the financial profits their increased performance levels have made possible. Psychological contracts also differ from employment contracts because they reflect each party's perception of the expectations involved, which means their interpretations may not be similar. In fact, employees are generally more likely than supervisors to perceive that employers have not lived up to their part of the psychological contract, particularly with regard to pay, advancement, and good employer–employee relationships.[4]

Even though such expectations may never formally be stated, they do exist, and they have a tangible impact on the relationship between employee and employer. For example, employees who perceived that both they and their employer had mutual high obligations to each other (rather than mutual low obligations or unbalanced obligations) reported more organizational commitment and support, more positive beliefs about the future of their career, and less intention to leave the firm.[5] However, if a new employee is given the impression that hard work will be rewarded with a promotion and raise in the near future and neither are forthcoming, the psychological contract is broken because the organization has failed to meet the employee's expectations about both advancement and credibility. On the other hand, if an organization agrees to pay the cost of an employee's MBA program, the boss may expect the employee to work harder or be more loyal because the company is contributing more to him or her than to other employees.

Broken psychological contracts occur when someone fails to fill an obligation, either by reneging on a promise or due to incongruence in how the employee and employer interpret the contract. Contract breaches change their relationship[6] and also affect employee attitudes and behavior. The trust and good faith of the employer–employee relationship is destroyed and cannot easily be rebuilt. Violations cause less damage to the relationship if employees believe that employers were *unable*, rather than simply *unwilling*, to keep a promise. When a psychological contract is broken, intense emotional reactions such as moral outrage, shock, indignation, betrayal, resentment, and anger result. The disillusionment over broken psychological contracts can lead to decreased employee job satisfaction, performance, commitment, attendance, discretionary effort, and desire to continue with the organization, and increased organizational cynicism.[7] A company staffed by employees who feel cheated or betrayed cannot expect to be a high-performance company.

More than half the employees in one study reported violations of their psychological contract in their first job upon graduating from college.[8] Such discrepancies between expectations and reality are, therefore, fairly common. Job seekers can try to avoid disillusionment by gaining a more realistic idea about what to expect from organizations through internships and by asking more questions during the job interview process. When employees received realistic job previews during the hiring process, their retention rate was higher, which represents thousands of dollars in savings for employers.[9] *Realistic job previews (RJPs) are a recruitment technique that gives accurate information about job duties, and especially about the major sources of job satisfaction and dissatisfaction prior to organizational entry.*[10] Therefore, they provide a more accurate view of the psychological contract. If you check out the student evaluations on record before registering for classes, this is a simple form of RJP. When Cisco recruits "passive" job seekers who aren't actively looking for a new job, they connect them with employees in similar jobs so they hear the inside scoop on what it's really like to work for Cisco in that job. This innovation partly explains Cisco's lower-than-average turnover rate.[11]

Certainly both prospective employees and employers would be better off if their expectations were made explicit from the beginning.[12] But often we are not aware of our expectations until they have been disappointed. That's why mechanisms or forums that allow for continued discussions and renegotiations of the contract are so crucial throughout the term of employment. Effective managers understand that the psychological contract is important because it links the individual to the organization, reflects the trust that is a fundamental feature of the employment relationship, and motivates individuals to fulfill their obligations if they believe the other party will do the same. They ensure that the mutual expectations that comprise the contract are both understood and fulfilled so the employer–employee relationship is carefully maintained.

THE CURRENT PSYCHOLOGICAL CONTRACT

The tremendous rate of change that businesses undergo as they adapt to global competition and changing markets, technology, and economic conditions has resulted in marked changes in workplace expectations and psychological contracts. Corporate mergers, downsizing, restructuring, reengineering, outsourcing and subcontracting, and relatively low union representation have changed the picture of employment over the last 30 years. More and more jobs in Europe, North America, and some Asian countries have been transformed from full-time, ongoing work (for core employees) to contingent, temporary employment (for peripheral employees). Originally, low-skilled manufacturing jobs were outsourced to countries that paid lower wages; at present, higher-skilled jobs such as engineering and research and development work are also outsourced. Silicon Valley venture capitalists won't even look at new business plans that don't include outsourcing arrangements. The reality that many businesses view the entire world as their potential labor pool is a major change for workers all over the globe and increases competition for jobs. Massive terminations further drive home the message that psychological contracts have changed.

After World War II, the terms of the prevailing psychological contract between Americans and their corporate employers were relatively simple. Employees were willing to work their way up the corporate ladder slowly in return for the promise of a sufficiently high promotion in their middle age to allow them to live comfortably during their retirement years. They had a fairly high degree of job security and internal career opportunities with little risk exposure.[13] This contract was always somewhat unbalanced because the company was expected to be loyal to employees, while the employees could resign whenever they wished. Lifelong job security is now viewed as an unaffordable luxury, even in Japanese business where it was previously common practice. The current employment contract has changed from long-term employment relationships and paternalism to employment based on business needs. Employees are rewarded for skills and performance (with higher pay in some cases), rather than tenure, and they are responsible for maintaining their own employability via personal reskilling and retraining. Since employers cannot offer long-term employment, they provide valuable employees with interesting and challenging work and training or risk losing them to their competitors. In return for high pay and stock options (which represent shared risk exposure), many employers expect long hours of hard work, flexibility, and commitment from highly skilled professionals, but they have less expectation of employee loyalty. For employees, there has been a simultaneous loss of job security accompanied by increasing demands for performance, flexibility, and innovation. This has led to greater job-related stress and the dawning realization that, whether they wanted to or not, many employees have become "free agents" who have to look out for their own interests.

How do employees react to the broken psychological contracts that accompany corporate restructuring? Some employees modify their expectations and make whatever sacrifices are necessary to retain their jobs, while others give more importance to family and nonwork interests. Still others place more emphasis on developing their reputational capital (i.e., building their resumes so they are more attractive to other companies) than on institution-building activities that would benefit their current employer. According to one study, only three Americans in ten are loyal to their employers.[14] The key question for managers and human resource professionals is "How do organizations promote commitment on the part of employees who no longer trust in job security?"

EMPLOYEE COMMITMENT

Scholarly definitions of commitment include these aspects: emotional attachment to the organization; identification with the organization; involvement in the organization; strong belief in, and acceptance of, the organization's goals and values; a willingness to exert considerable effort on behalf of the organization; and a strong desire to remain in the organization.[15] Committed employees yield several advantages for employers: higher performance and job satisfaction, greater ability to adapt to unforeseen circumstances, higher attendance, longer job tenure, and more organizational citizen behavior (OCB).[16] *Organizational citizenship behavior refers to "discretionary contributions that are organizationally related, but are neither explicitly required nor contractually rewarded by the organization, yet nevertheless contribute to its effective functioning."*[17] Commitment is more likely when employees are satisfied with their jobs;[18] when they perceive organizational justice in policies, procedures, and awards;[19] and when they are mentored.[20] Recommended ways to earn employee commitment are clarifying and communicating the organization's mission, guaranteeing organizational justice, creating a sense of community, and supporting employee development.[21] A study of knowledge workers in high technology and financial services found that the greatest influence on the level of employee commitment and intention to stay with the company was meritocracy (rewards and promotions based on performance and merit), followed by fair treatment.[22] Knowledge employees have tacit knowledge and skills that they may not be motivated to share fully with the company unless the expectations of their psychological contract are met. Stock option plans, which have been on the upswing in recent years, give employees an ownership stake in financial outcomes and may increase their identity with the firm. However, employee commitment has to do with more than money.

A comparison of different types of employment relationships found that employees perform better, are more committed, and demonstrate more citizenship behavior when they have long-term relationships with employers, when they work in teams, and when employers invest in employee careers.[23] Despite the current predilection for downsizing and using contingent workers, the research continues to find that lack of job security and lack of employer concern for employee development does not result in high performance.

Another factor that influences both commitment and turnover is workplace incivility. Incivility is defined *as low-intensity deviant behavior that violates workplace norms for mutual respect; it may or may not be intended to harm the target.*[24] Surveys indicate that incivility has been experienced by 20 to 75 percent of employees, which suggests that this is a serious problem that is on the rise.[25] Examples range from rudeness, sarcasm, public reprimands, to bluntly refusing demands for extra help from coworkers and supervisors. The cost of workplace incivility is not insignificant. It wastes the time of executives asked to deal with complaints and, for employees who are the targets of incivility, the results are decreased work effort, time spent at work, productivity, performance, motivation, creativity, and helping behaviors, and less OCB. One of eight subjects in one study quit his or her job due to incivility.[26] Confronting the instigators of incivility, who tend to be people in higher positions of power, is not always feasible; however, their targets may resort to indirect methods to get revenge—spreading rumors about them, withholding important information, and engaging in sabotage or even theft. If the organization fails to take action, its reputation may suffer when people tell family and friends stories of their poor treatment at work. Furthermore, when no action is taken to stop or punish incivility, employees report decreased job satisfaction and organizational loyalty and increased turnover.[27] When employees fail to receive civil, respectful treatment, which is a basic tenet of their psychological contract, their commitment to the organization may decrease.

Commitment is fostered by teamwork that builds important social relationships at work, challenging jobs that develop employees and allow them to utilize their talents, and pride in their organization. Other answers to developing committed employees come from research on "healthy companies." The seven values found in such organizations are (1) commitment to self-knowledge and development (continuous learning), (2) firm belief in decency (fair treatment, equity), (3) respect for individual differences (celebration of diversity), (4) spirit of partnership (strong belief in community, shared effort, teamwork, widespread participation), (5) high priority for health and well-being, (6) appreciation for flexibility and resilience (change is managed well), and (7) a passion for products and process (concern for both what is produced and how that happens, balancing stakeholder interests—family support, community responsibility, and environmental protection).[28] Not all organizations believe in these dimensions or put them into practice, but they reflect the growing belief that the contribution of the workforce is the ultimate key to the success of any company.

EXTERNAL INFLUENCES AND CHANGING EXPECTATIONS

In addition to the changing business conditions mentioned previously, other factors affect the psychological contract and commitment. Labor market conditions and the employment rate influence both employer and employee behavior. At the turn of the century, one of managers' top concerns was employee retention, which was manifested by "employee friendly" policies to help them compete in attracting and keeping good talent. Some companies moved beyond salary and traditional benefits (e.g., health insurance and pensions) to offer career-advancement and work–family programs. After the dot.com bust and 9/11, jobs became more scarce, creating a "buyers' market" for employers. In 2006, some firms argue that even traditional benefits like pensions and health care prevent them from competing effectively. Business ups and downs and the changes in the job market can influence how much money and attention firms spend on employees and, therefore, impact the psychological contract. In addition, when the demand for labor is weak, some employees are simply grateful to have a job, and they put up with treatment they would not accept if more alternatives were available. Therefore, turnover rates do not always tell the same tale about employee commitment. A Conference Board survey of 5,000 U.S. workers in 2004 found that 50 percent were satisfied with their jobs, compared with 59 percent in 1995; 14 percent were very satisfied, down from 18.4 percent in 1995. The biggest decline occurred among workers earning $25,000 to $35,000 and among workers aged 35 to 44. Dissatisfaction is attributed to rapid technological changes, employer pressure for greater productivity, and shifting worker expectations. While satisfied with their coworker relationships, only one in three was satisfied with his or her pay, and there were substantial complaints about bonus plans, promotion policies, health plans, and pension benefits.[29]

Another example of changing expectations concerns the way we do business and with whom we work. The ever-increasing demands for high performance, quality, customer service, and innovation resulted in different organizational forms—from telecommuting to virtual global teams who have never met in person to organizational alliances between historically fierce competitors. More pieces of firms are being moved around both globally and domestically to save costs. Learning to work in foreign countries where outsourcing takes place or where new markets have opened is always a challenging learning curve. Domestically the proliferation of small and midsized firms, spearheaded by pioneer-like entrepreneurs beginning in the 1990s continues to produce innovations and provide jobs in settings that bear little resemblance to traditional corporations.[30]

In many countries, the percentage of retired to active workers raises concerns about the availability of workers, social security, and immigration. By 2010, one-third of the U.S. workforce will be over 50 years of age. Some observers forecast a labor shortage and the continuing presence of elder workers. Firms like Home Depot and Borders have already started to hire older workers to preserve a trained workforce and mirror the demographics of their customers.[31] However, the U.S. case could be influenced by unforeseen factors, so it is too soon to predict the impact of the upcoming Baby Boomer retirement.

The nomadic nature and the changing complexion of the workforce will continue. According to one projection, the average high school or college graduate is expected to hold 13 different jobs in his or her career.[32] In a longitudinal study, the U.S. Bureau of Labor tracked people born between 1957 and 1964 for the first 20 years of their worklife. This group, which is categorized as young baby boomers, has held an average of 10.2 jobs from ages 18 to 38 and changed jobs more quickly in their late teens and early twenties.[33] Almost a third (31 percent) of workers ages 25 and older have worked 10 years or more with their current employer.[34] The composition of the U.S. workforce will consist of 47 percent women by the year 2012; white non-Hispanics will account for 65 percent, Hispanics 15 percent, African Americans 12 percent, and Asians 6 percent.[35]

Different generations hold unique expectations about work. The Baby Boomers (born between 1946 and 1964) are often called the "me" generation. Known for their concern with self-fulfillment at work, they were the first generation to fight against hierarchical authority and demand a voice in decision making at work. Work is an important part of their lives, and some observers say they may be the last generation to show significant loyalty to corporate employers. For Generation X (born between 1965 and 1976), work holds less importance than for Baby Boomers, and their identity is less tied to work. Family and nonwork activities hold more importance, and many do not want their children to come home to an empty house as "latchkey kids," as some of them did. Gen Xers do not expect the government or corporations to ensure their economic security, so they have fewer expectations of prosperity and greater expectations about being contingent workers and changing careers. "Success for many Xers is survival, having a good time, and making their own decisions and having enough money to enjoy the material goodies. Social status is not important in this picture".[36]

It is early to make definitive conclusions about Generation Y's expectations about work. The sheer size of this generation (born between 1976 and 2001), which is even larger than the Baby Boom generation, indicates that they will have a significant impact on the workplace. According to reports, they are highly computer and Internet literate and prefer a fun environment with teams that provide them with a sense of belonging and flexible work hours. Some are seeking work that has more meaning, and they are more likely to be involved in community service and to be more optimistic than Generation X. They are interested in determining the lifestyle that suits them and, secondly, work that supports their lifestyle. Their generation is the most diverse yet, and they tend to be tolerant of diversity; the traits they admire most are honesty and caring. [37]

Finally, the last example of shifting expectations relates to changing value trends—in addition to differences in the values held by various generations, changing societal norms also affect our psychological contracts at work and home. For example, 50.7 percent of U.S. married couples have dual careers, and only 20.5 percent of families consist of a working husband and a stay-at-home wife who cares for the children. Currently 5.2 percent of U.S. fathers are "stay-at-home dads." [38] The "traditional" family is no longer the norm, forcing us to rethink our expectations of what it means to be a good employee, spouse or partner, and parent and to adapt our psychological contracts accordingly.

CULTURAL DIFFERENCES

Working with people from other cultures forces the realization that psychological contracts have a cultural flavor to them. According to Rousseau and Salk, "Promising new recruits that a job with the firm will help them be employable elsewhere might be attractive in a highly mobile society but might signal an employer's unreliability in a less mobile one." [39] Even the principal party in the contract varies by culture. In individualistic cultures, like the United States, employees perceive their psychological contract to be with the employer, and contracts are more likely to be idiosyncratic arrangements rather than similar deals for everyone. In Australia, the employee contract is with one's coworkers, while in France, it is with the state itself. [40]

The boss's role in the relationship with employees involves different expectations, such as the Latin American expectation that bosses will attend the family celebrations—baptisms, first communions, marriages, and funerals—of their employees. In multicultural settings it quickly becomes apparent that cultures have different views of psychological contracts, due to their values and ways of processing information. Cultural differences can also influence how employees react to violations, since they have learned different scripts for handling conflict, [41] which are explained in Chapter 13. For example, people from cultures that find direct confrontation uncomfortable may be less likely to bring violations to the attention of their supervisor. People from cultures that value loyalty and identify strongly with their employer may be more likely to remain after a violation than individualistic people who calculate the pros and cons of staying with the organization and do what is best for themselves.

Rousseau and Schalk identified three primary ways that psychological contracts vary internationally. [42] First, promises mean different things in different cultures. In some cultures, intention to fulfill a promise may be just as good as actually doing what one promised. The role of uncertainty and fate is larger in some cultures, which can make promises less binding and less subject to one's control. In addition, some cultures have extensive networks of obligation, and their members may have to break promises to one party in order to fulfill a promise to another party. Second, the zone of negotiability refers to which employment conditions are under negotiation in different countries. This is determined by societal tolerance for unequal outcomes and societal regulation related to state intervention and centralized collective bargaining. For example, in some Latin American countries, the government decides all employees should receive an across-the-board bonus or raise—this makes individual negotiations between employers and employees less relevant. Third, group identity influences psychological contracts because the way that people define "we" and "they" has a critical influence on trust and promise making. People tend to trust their in-group members (we) more than out-group members (they), which can determine the types of promises that are made and fulfilled in the workplace. Trust itself takes different forms in different cultures. In some it is earned and based on experience, while in others trust is based on faith. Trust in authorities in an Islamic country is both a duty and a reflection of great respect for the people in those roles. In contrast, for the Dutch, blind faith in authority figures is the equivalent of abdicating responsible judgment. [43]

A study of commitment in over 7,000 employees in seven countries found that commitment was present in all countries, but the level of commitment, its content, and the factors that led to commitment varied by culture. For example, the U.S. employees had the highest level of affective commitment (emotional ties, identification, and sense of belonging with the organization), followed by the Slovenians and the Japanese, while the West German sample had the lowest score. Two factors predicted commitment across all cultures—job satisfaction and an intrinsic orientation toward work (valuing work for itself, rather than money or external outcomes). But high income and job autonomy were more important in the individualistic countries, the United Kingdom and the United States, whereas helping others at work or feeling that one's work benefits society was more likely to foster commitment in Japan and Hungary.[44]

THE SELF-FULFILLING PROPHECY

Another important concept that relates to expectations and new employees is the *self-fulfilling prophecy, the phenomenon that occurs when people perform in accordance with a rater's expectations of them.* A manager's expectations for an employee cause the manager to treat the employee differently; therefore, the employee responds in a way that confirms the manager's initial expectations. We have Rosenthal and his albino rats to thank for this particular contribution to organizational behavior.

In an experiment, he gave the same strain of rats to different groups of students at Harvard.[45] The students' task was to teach their rats to run a maze. However, one group of students was told their rats were bright; the other group was told their rats were dull. Although there were no inherent differences between the two groups of rats, the so-called "bright" rats learned to run mazes better than the "dull" rats. Further inquiry revealed that the students found the "bright" rats more likeable and, therefore, had treated them differently. Intrigued, Rosenthal and Jacobson tried the same experiment with school children.[46] They randomly chose one child out of every five and told teachers that these children were "academic spurters." At the year's end, the "academic spurters" had improved their IQ by an average of 22 points. The teachers' expectations about these students affected the way they treated the children. The children's response to that treatment was to become "academic spurters." The critical variable in these examples is the teacher's (or rat handler's) expectation: Higher expectations were associated with higher learning. The children (and the rats) became what the teachers thought they were, which is a perfect example of a self-fulfilling prophecy.

We find the same self-fulfilling prophecy at work with newly hired people. Studies indicate that new hires who are immediately given challenging jobs are more likely to show high performance later on in their careers.[47] Today, many large corporations formally label those employees for whom they have high expectations as "fast-trackers" or "high potentials." As part of their succession management programs, companies pay special attention to this group and provide them with the experiences and opportunities that will prepare them to take a top leadership role in the future. Such programs can be very effective, but one of their by-products may be resentment and complaints (both valid and invalid) by "non-fast-trackers" who feel that they, too, could shine if they received the special treatment that goes along with higher expectations of one's performance. What is the practical significance in the workplace of understanding the self-fulfilling prophecy?

- Employees who are expected to do well will likely perform better than those who are not, even though there may be no differences between them.
- Supervisors and managers who have high expectations of their employees will be more likely to have their expectations met.

A MODEL FOR MANAGING PSYCHOLOGICAL CONTRACTS—THE PINCH MODEL

Given the changing expectations within our society and the varying expectations of different generations, groups, and cultures in the workplace, we should proceed on the assumption that other people's expectations are not necessarily the same as our own. To avoid misunderstandings and disillusionment, it is crucial to identify and share mutual expectations in an ongoing process.

Sherwood and Glidewell have developed a simple but powerful model, the pinch model, that describes the dynamic quality of psychological contracts and suggests ways of minimizing the potentially dysfunctional consequences of shifting expectations (Exhibit 1-1).[48] It provides a framework for

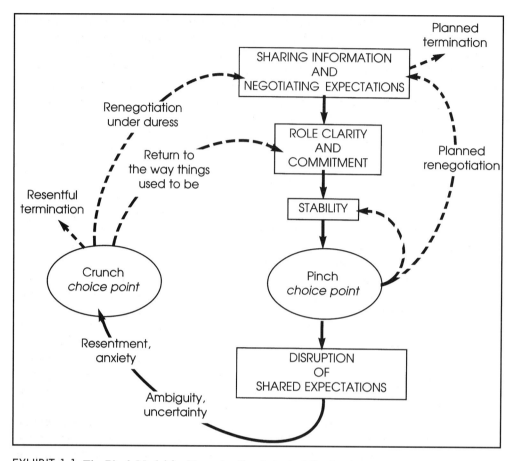

EXHIBIT 1-1 The Pinch Model for Managing Psychological Contracts
Source: J. J. Sherwood and J. C. Glidewell, "Planned Renegotiation: A Norm-Setting OD Intervention," in
Contemporary Organization Development: Orientations and Interventions, (ed.) W. W. Burke (Washington, D.C.: NTL
Institute, 1972): 35–46.

the continuous management of the psychological contract in the day-to-day work setting. The first
stage of any relationship between two individuals and/or an individual and an organization is characterized by a *sharing of information and a negotiating of expectations.* Suppose that a manager interviewing job candidates informs them that they will be expected to attend frequent company social
events after hours and on weekends. If this does not appear to be a reasonable expectation to some
candidates, they will deselect themselves, the equivalent of a *planned termination* in the model.

Assuming that both parties accept the other's expectations, they enter a stage of *role clarity
and joint commitment.* In other words, both the new employees and the manager understand and
accept the role the other party expects them to play and are motivated to meet those expectations.
The employee and employer both expect to move into a period of *stability* and productivity,
which allows them to focus their energies on work.

Even with the best intentions and full sharing of initial expectations, changes are likely to
occur over time. One or both of the parties begin to feel a "*pinch*" as Sherwood and Glidewell
call it. For example, an employee may have been more than willing to put in heavy overtime and
cover weekend shifts when he or she was single and new in town. But a marriage involving certain expectations about the time a couple should spend together might change the employee's
attitude toward demanding hours and the automatic assumption that this particular employee is
available to work them. Sherwood and Glidewell suggest that a pinch like this can be used as an
early warning sign to manage the psychological contract process before situations become disruptive. Discussing and renegotiating expectations at this point, a planned renegotation will lead
to either a return to stability or, if the differences cannot be resolved, a planned departure.
Employees sometimes respond to pinches by saying, "I don't have time to test this issue" or "If I

raise this issue with my bosses, they'll think I'm just complaining so I'll ignore it." But pinches have a habit of growing into larger problems if they are not handled in a planned manner rather than in the heat of emotion that accompanies the next stage, a *disruption of shared expectations*.

Since the "rules" that were accepted initially have been upset, one or both parties experience *heightened ambiguity and uncertainty*, which invariably result in *resentment and anxiety*. The situation may reach another choice point, or *crunch*. People often refer to crunches as the straw that broke the camel's back (e.g., the boss who unfairly accuses a dedicated employee of not working hard because the boss is misinformed, or a job promotion that goes to another employee who is clearly less qualified). Crunches force people to choose among three alternative actions. A common outcome is an effort to *return to the way things used to be*. The parties apologize for the misunderstanding, smooth over the conflict, and attempt to renew their commitment to one another under the terms of the old contract. Another possibility is that the two parties *renegotiate under duress* by again sharing information and negotiating their expectations. The final possibility is that little or no discussion occurs, and the result is some form of *resentful termination*. The termination may be either psychological ("I'll be darned if I'm going to do any more than I'm required to on this job" or "That's the last thing I ever do for that employee") or physical (absenteeism, tardiness, quitting, or firing).

In the classroom, the psychological contract is also very important. Generally only one of the parties makes its expectations explicit. Teachers begin a course by stating their requirements of students. Students are rarely asked to reciprocate, but woe to the teacher who fails to meet students' unstated expectations! One purpose of this unit is to introduce you to the concept of the psychological contract as it exists in the learning organization you are about to enter. In this way you will be able to move as quickly as possible to a period of stability and productivity (learning) and set in motion the processes of communication needed to deal with any subsequent pinches that may develop. We encourage participants to state their expectations in the upcoming class activity because it is the first step in taking responsibility for one's own learning in this course.

Although we do not often view the processes in the same terms, entering a classroom environment for the first time is very much like the first day on a new job. The typical orientation program in a company is usually very one sided. Most company communication flows from the organization to the individual: "These are our policies, procedures, expectations." One effect of this one-sided process is to cause new employees to feel that the organization is much more powerful than they are as individuals and may create a situation in which new employees, when asked their expectations, try to second-guess the company's expectations. Instead of trying to formulate and articulate their own expectations, the new employees (participants) often repeat what they think the organization (instructor) wants to hear.

Recall your last job interview. Remember how you tried to "look good" to the organization—to guess what it wanted. How much time did you spend talking about your own expectations and asking what the organization could contribute to your needs? Probably very little and then very cautiously.

Similarly, when organizations begin to socialize the incoming member to meet their norms and values and ways of doing things, they sometimes overdo this and oversocialize their members. For example, placing too much emphasis on the organization's expectations of newcomers may result in conformity and passivity. Managers can read passivity as a sign that new employees want and need more direction and control—they want to be told exactly what to do. This situation can create a feedback cycle (a vicious cycle in this case) that, in the long run, operates to the detriment of both the individual and the organization. Organizations need people who are innovative, creative, and independent thinkers to survive and remain productive in a rapidly changing environment. Individual growth and satisfaction also demand these same kinds of behavior. Occasionally, however, the new employee's first contact with the organization sets in motion a cycle that acts in direct opposition to these long-range goals and needs.

There is another way in which we can view the process of organizational socialization and the notion of the psychological contract. In approaching any new organization, an individual makes two classes of decisions: a decision to join and a decision to participate.[49] In some cases, such as being drafted into the military or taking required courses, individuals have no control over their own decision to join. The process by which we join an organization has implications for the second class of decisions—the decision to participate. This particular decision refers to whether or not a person chooses to play an active role in the organization or is content with merely being physically present. At work, employees who have made a decision to participate are involved and working hard to contribute. Those who have decided not to participate are simply marking time, putting in their hours. In the classroom, those who choose to participate take an active role in the course and become involved in their own learning process. In contrast, those who decide not to participate either sit passively or don't attend and work just enough to get by and fulfill the teacher's requirements for a grade. Their own expectations for learning, involvement, and stimulation go unsatisfied because they never made their expectations explicit when they joined.

Our purpose in encouraging students to participate in a joint expectation-setting exercise is to provide you with an opportunity to decide whether you want to join and participate in this course. Some educational systems and programs unwittingly encourage passivity in students when learners are not expected to take responsibility for their own learning. They are much more accustomed to instructors assuming full responsibility. Thus, when confronted with a genuine opportunity to participate in the learning process, they may become confused ("What kind of way is this to start a class?") or suspicious ("I wonder what the instructor is trying to do.").

When asked to articulate expectations, learners tend to be very vague and general, which is frustrating to everyone involved. Expectations are much more likely to be satisfied when a set of realistic, concrete goals can be developed. However, instructors must realize that learners who are not used to controlling their own education may struggle with accepting greater responsibility. The point is that both participants and instructors have a share of the responsibility for the learning process.

This point is an important one to reemphasize. Confusion sometimes develops as a result of this initial contracting session, along the lines of "Why all this talk about our expectations and stuff? You [the instructor] already have the course laid out, the syllabus typed, and the schedule planned!" As is true in any organization, the general thrust or goals are given. This is not a course in art or engineering. It is a course in organizational behavior, but there are many areas of flexibility: what specific goals you as a participating learner set within the general objectives, how you relate to peers and staff and who takes what responsibility for how goals are achieved, and what aspects of the course content receive greater emphasis. Differences might exist around these issues, and they need to be explored during the initial socialization process.

Clearly, within the context of the first class session of a few hours, all the possible conflicts that can arise will not be anticipated nor can all those identified be solved. More important than any concrete conclusions that may come out of this expectation-setting exercise is a series of norms for dealing with pinches. As a result of this contract exploration process, the legitimacy of raising issues and differences can be established, the right to question each other and particularly the instructor can be demonstrated, and a decision-making process of shared responsibility to resolve different points of view can be introduced.

CLASS ACTIVITY: INSTRUCTOR/PARTICIPANT INTERVIEWS

The purpose of the exercise is to model how an explicit psychological contract can be set in the classroom. In the first phase, the instructor learns about the participants' expectations for the course by interviewing group representatives. In the second phase, group representatives interview the instructor to discover his or her expectations of students. (Time allotted: 70 minutes)

STEP 1. The total group should divide into small discussion groups, four or five people who do not know each other per group, and introduce themselves. (5 minutes)

STEP 2. Unless your instructor provides different questions, discuss the general question areas in the accompanying Instructor's Interview Guide. Your instructor will want to hear all the different views expressed in your discussion, so there is no need to come to a group consensus on each question. Everyone should take notes in case he or she is chosen by the instructor as the group representative. Please finish on time. (15 minutes)

Instructor's Interview Guide

Few instructors ask students to articulate their expectations for a class. During the ensuing interview, the instructor will try to gain an understanding of your views in the following general areas:

1. What are your goals for this course? To increase self-awareness? To learn theories? To fulfill a requirement? To get a grade? To apply learning in your job? Something else?

2. How can the instructor best help you achieve your goals? By lectures, examinations, seminar discussions? (Think back to excellent professors/courses you've experienced and what made them great.)

3. What, if anything, have you heard about this textbook and/or this course from others?

4. What reservations, if any, do you have about this course?

5. What is the best thing that could happen in this course? What is the worst thing?

6. What are your resources for this course (prior work experience, courses in psychology, etc.)?

7. What norms of behavior or ground rules should we set to ensure that the course is successful (mutual respect, only one person talks at a time, punctuality, etc.)?

STEP 3.   Instructor's Interview. The instructor will choose a representative from each group, who will sit in the front of the room with the instructor like a panel. The instructor will ask them to give their names and then interview them (using the Instructor's Interview Guide) to understand their expectations for the course. The remainder of the class acts as observers. (15 minutes)

Participants' Interview of Instructor

STEP 4.   The class should reform into the same small discussion groups as in Step 1. Using the guide provided as a starting point (Participants' Interview Guide), groups should brainstorm a list of questions they want to ask the instructor. Please feel free to ask questions that do not appear in this guide. Take notes so that you have all the questions listed in case you are chosen as the spokesperson. (5 minutes)

Participants' Interview Guide

You will have the opportunity to ask the instructor any questions you feel are relevant to effective learning during this course and that will help you get to know the instructor. (Note: It is important that you ask questions that are of real concern to you at this point. Only in this way can potentially important problems or conflicts be identified and managed.) You probably have many ideas of your own, and the questions asked by the instructor during the first interview may suggest others to you. Be sure to ask specific questions.

Some areas you may want to discuss are the following:

1. The instructor's objectives for the course (What does he or she hope to accomplish?).

2. The instructor's theory of learning (i.e., How do people learn?).

3. The instructor's opinion on the question of evaluation.

4. The instructor's expectations of you.

5. The instructor's role in the class.

6. The instructor's background or anything else you think is important.

STEP 5.   Participants' Interview. The instructor will choose group representatives; they will interview the instructor to understand the instructor's expectations of them and the course. The remainder of the group acts as observers, paying particular attention to possible differences in expectations. (20 minutes)

STEP 6.   Plenary Discussion (10 minutes)
  a. Did you observe any potential pinches in our expectations?
  b. With respect to potential future pinches, whose responsibility is it to raise a pinch, and how should that be done (e.g., written comments, informal discussions at the end of meetings, mid-course evaluations)?
  c. What differences do you see when you compare this method of mutual interviews to the traditional way most courses begin?
  d. What is the impact of this exercise on you as a student?

LEARNING POINTS

1. The psychological contract is an individual's beliefs, shaped by the organization, regarding the terms and conditions of a reciprocal exchange agreement between individuals and their organization.

2. Social exchange theory states that people enter into relationships in which both economic and social obligations play a role and that they are most comfortable when exchanges are balanced.

3. Psychological contracts are important because they link individuals to organizations, reflect the trust that is a fundamental feature of the employment relationship, and motivate individuals to fulfill their obligations—if they believe the other party will do the same.

4. Psychological contracts differ from employment contracts because they are dynamic and perceptual; thus, the parties involved do not always share the same interpretation of the contract.

5. When psychological contracts are violated, people respond emotionally with moral outrage, shock, indignation, betrayal, resentment, and anger. Violated contracts also result in decreased employee satisfaction, performance, commitment, discretionary behavior to help the organization, and intentions to remain with the organization.

6. The use of realistic job previews (RJPs), a recruitment technique that gives accurate information about job duties, and especially about the major sources of job satisfaction and dissatisfaction prior to organizational entry, results in less turnover.

7. Commitment is defined as (a) emotional attachment to, identification with, and involvement in the organization; (b) strong belief in, and acceptance of, the organization's goals and values; (c) a willingness to exert considerable effort on behalf of the organization; and (d) a strong desire to remain in the organization.

8. Committed employees have higher performance, greater ability to adapt to unforeseen circumstances, higher attendance, longer job tenure, and more organizational citizenship behavior.

9. Employers can foster commitment by clarifying and communicating the organization's mission, guaranteeing organizational justice, creating a sense of community, and supporting employee development.

10. Organizational citizenship behavior (OCB) is defined as discretionary contributions that are organizationally related but are neither explicitly required nor contractually rewarded by the organization, yet nevertheless contribute to its effective functioning.

11. Workplace incivility is defined as low-intensity deviant behavior that violates workplace norms for mutual respect; it may or may not be intended to harm the target. It causes decreased work effort, time on the job, productivity, performance, motivation, creativity, and helping behaviors. If incivility is not curbed, decreased job satisfaction and organizational loyalty and increased turnover result.

12. External influences, such as adapting to a global economy, economic and employment conditions, demographics, and societal change, affect workplace expectations and psychological contracts.

13. The diverse nature of the U.S. workforce will increase according to predictions for the year 2012. Women will make up 47 percent of the workforce. White non-Hispanics will constitute 65 percent, Hispanics, 15 percent, African Americans, 12 percent, and Asians, 6 percent. Due to their higher birth rates, Hispanics will overtake African Americans as the second largest ethnic group around 2006.

14. The phenomenon of the self-fulfilling prophecy occurs when people perform in accordance with a rater's expectations of them. Managers with high expectations of employees are more likely to have their expectations met.

15. The pinch model illustrates how to manage the psychological contract and avoid major disruptions by heeding early warning signs that expectations have changed and need to be reconsidered.

16. In approaching any new organization, people make two classes of decisions: a decision to join and a decision to participate. Good managers and leaders are skilled at gaining participation.

DEVELOPING OB EXPERTISE

Because OB is a complex field, we can't tell you exactly what to do in every situation. Below, however, you will find many of the effective action scripts used by employees, team members, managers, leaders, and organizational architects who have OB expertise. Organizational architects are people who, regardless of their official title, design policies, procedures, and structure, generally on a system-wide basis. Our goal in this section is to help get the psychological contract on your radar screen so you will be alert to cues about how it is working and have a larger repertoire of actions you can take.

ACTION SCRIPTS

FOR EMPLOYEES

- Employees who are "expert" at managing psychological contracts understand that the contract is dynamic and continue to monitor changing expectations. A new boss, a major change effort, or a revolutionary shift in the environment or industry often result in new expectations and the need to be flexible.
- As newcomers, savvy employees are careful to choose the right mentors and to check with more than one person about what is expected of them. Organizational cynics of the bitter persuasion are often on the lookout for newcomers to inculcate with their negative view of what's going on—they want company and confirmation that their view is correct. While they can be very entertaining (and we'd be the last people to claim there is nothing to be cynical about in organizations), you are usually better off gathering a variety of perspectives on the psychological contract from people with a positive attitude and seeking out positive mentors.
- To some degree, workers influence the type of psychological contract they have with their employer. Employers generally have more loyalty and a less transactional approach to workers with a long-term commitment to the organization and to conscientious workers whose behavior they value.[50]
- Expert employees clarify expectations with their bosses and try to understand the constraints and pressures on administration.
- Like managers, employees should beware that their perceptions of how well each side is upholding the contract may be inaccurate. Sometimes we succumb to the human tendency to overvalue our contributions and downplay those of the other party (think about the last argument you had over household chores). We also tend to judge ourselves by our intentions, while judging others by their behavior, which is a higher standard.[51]
- Keep records of letters and emails that deal with expectations.
- Use effective negotiation and persuasion skills when necessary to create a new contract, rather than simply repeating demands.
- If the psychological contract has been broken, employees have alternative actions to choose from—exit (quit); voice (speak up and confront management on the discrepancy); loyalty or silence (accept the new reality); and neglect (work less or destructively harm the organization through sabotage or theft). (Neglect is seldom your best option.) Deciding on a strategy gives a greater sense of control over the situation. Some employees find it especially difficult to move beyond the injustice of broken psychological contracts and become embittered and cynical, which can lead to emotional exhaustion and burnout.
- The psychological contract among team members should be clarified and periodically evaluated to make sure there is consensus. To borrow Sherwood and Glidewell's terminology, when there appears to be a "pinch" or a "crunch," members take the initiative to address and resolve the problem.

- Team members who understand the importance of the contract talk about what trust means to each individual and commit themselves to behaving in ways that are reliable and trustworthy.

FOR MANAGERS

- Expert managers take action rather than ignoring pinches or crunches. For example, they may meet with individuals or groups to confront the issue by discussing their mutual perceptions of the contract in question, feelings about the violation, and why it occurred. Even if managers disagree with the employees' perception, they listen respectfully. When managers or leaders have made an error by reneging on a promise, they acknowledge their fault and work at regaining trust. When they are unable to meet the conditions of a contract, they negotiate a new one and think ahead about what the long-term consequences will be. If direct confrontation is not culturally appropriate, they use a mediator or communicate indirectly.
- They understand the repercussions of treating even one employee unfairly, because it sends the wrong message to all the others.
- They set aside time with new hires to discuss and establish explicit expectations early on and continue to do so on a frequent basis.
- They take the initiative to ensure that they and their employees perceive and interpret expectations in the same way, especially when cultural differences exist. Subordinates may not mention a pinch unless they are asked. Without shared perceptions of obligations, both sides can inaccurately assume a contract violation occurred.
- When managers are unsure about how an employee views the psychological contract, they can use the following sample questions to check out expectations:
  - What do you like/dislike about your job (or this relationship)?
  - Why do you continue with it?
  - Is there one thing that, if it were changed, would make you quit your job?
  - What are your expectations of me?
  - Do you think I am meeting them?
  - Is there any way I can help you do your job better?
  - What kind of supervision do you like best?
  - Does the organization or do I hinder you in completing your work?
  - Is there anything you would like to see changed?
- Some managers use the following matrix to judge whether mutual expectations are fairly balanced and reasonable. The contributions that individuals or organizations give should be balanced, more or less, by what they get. This matrix can be a good basis for discussion, but bear in mind that good human relationships are not based on a tit-for-tat mentality but on a flexible give-and-take approach.

	Expect to Get	Expect to Contribute
Individual (You)		
Organization or Group		

- Clear and immediate feedback is provided to employees who are not meeting the expectations set for them.
- Experts are on the lookout for other managers who feel they themselves have been poorly treated by the organization. Such managers are less likely to signal to others that the employer is trustworthy or to invest in subordinates.[52]

- When subordinates fail to give management the benefit of the doubt or excessively question decisions that have been made, this can signal lack of trust. Expert managers see these cues and follow up and see what can be done to restore trust.
- Effective managers earn employee trust by always doing what they say they will do.
- Along with trust, they foster good work group relationships, since both factors mitigate the strength of employee reactions to violated contracts.
- When they hear managers or supervisors talking callously or bragging about reneging on promises to employees, expert managers know this is a sign that the organization fails to understand the importance of trust, commitment and the psychological contract. Experts can sometimes educate others by pointing out the high costs of broken contracts in understandable terms, such as calculating turnover costs or pointing out the caliber of employees who quit due to broken contracts. They can also recommend and lead a system-wide effort to create a more trustworthy organization by adopting the actions in the next section.

FOR ORGANIZATIONAL ARCHITECTS

Prevention always takes less time than fixing a problem. This is especially true when dealing with humans who, as we have already seen in this chapter, often react badly to organizational errors. Organizational architects who know how to manage the psychological contract lay the groundwork for trust and commitment and minimize the risk of broken psychological contracts with these action scripts.

- The basis for healthy psychological contracts is an organizational commitment to developing a trusting relationship between management and employees and to fostering the communication and integrity that trust requires.[53]
- Psychological contracts are communicated through oral discussion, written documents, or organizational practices and procedures. Managers are trained to recognize that they are always setting precedents and shaping expectations when they communicate anything relating to employers and management obligations.
- Job announcements and publications are realistic.
- Interviewers are trained to be consistent in the information they give new hires and to foster consistency among everyone and everything that shapes contract expectations—top management, HR personnel, direct bosses, mentors, coworkers, HR policies, and PR publications.
- The intrinsic dimensions of the psychological contract (e.g., open and honest communication, managerial support, challenging and interesting work) are taken just as seriously as compensation by many employees, so these aspects of the contract should be discussed with potential hires and carefully managed with employees.
- Realistic job previews are provided during the hiring process so that new employees have accurate expectations. No one oversells the job or the organization just to reel in new hires who may later become disillusioned and leave when they discover the truth.
- Promises are documented to ensure clarity. It's easier to forget or confuse verbal promises. This problem is magnified when bosses change without leaving any record behind. New bosses should not have to deal with the debris of their predecessor's psychological contracts; it's difficult to establish new relationships when struggling to determine whether employees have a valid claim about what was promised to them or whether they are simply taking advantage of a new boss.
- Orientation programs are designed to clarify mutual expectations and obligations and help new hires be successful.
- Managers are trained to recognize cultural differences that can affect contracts, trust, and commitment.
- Testing for shared interpretations of the psychological contract can occur in personal interviews, focus groups, or employee opinion surveys.

- If circumstances beyond the organization's control cause a violation, these reasons are quickly and effectively communicated to employees.
- Prior to making an organizational change that will disrupt the current contract, the reasons for the change are explained beforehand, the resulting contract violation is acknowledged, and a new contract is established, which is as fair as possible.
- Organizational rewards are handled fairly and based on merit.
- Valuable employees are retained by providing them with interesting, challenging work and continued skill development.
- Given the symbolic message training sends about the value placed on investment in employees, the quality of training is very high.
- Performance review interviews are used as an opportunity for open and frank discussions about expectations, obligations, and rewards.[54]
- Sensitivity and responsiveness to the values and expectations of different generations in the workplace is promoted. These groups are helped to understand one another to prevent generational clashes.
- Zero-tolerance standards for incivility are set and consistently reinforced. Swift action is taken when employees are disrespectful, and they are held accountable for their actions. No excuses are made for employees, even if termination is necessary.[55]
- Job candidates are carefully screened by checking their work histories for instances of incivility.
- Three-hundred-sixty-degree feedback is employed so employees can anonymously identify the incivil behavior of more powerful employees.
- Post-departure interviews are used to determine whether incivility or broken psychological contracts play a role in turnover.

 PERSONAL APPLICATION ASSIGNMENT

The following assignment is modeled after Kolb's adult learning cycle, which appears in Chapter 3. Your instructor may want you to respond to the questions and submit them at next week's class or to use this guide as the basis for a longer paper. Each section of the assignment is worth 4 points that will be assigned according to the criteria that follow.[56]

The topic of this assignment is to think back on a significant incident when you experienced a pinch in a psychological contract. Pick an experience about which you are motivated to learn more; that is, there is something about it that you do not totally understand, that intrigues you, that makes you realize you lack certain skills, or that is problematic or very significant for you. It could have taken place at school, in a work relationship or a social one (with a club or group), or within a personal relationship.

A. Concrete Experience

   1. Objectively describe the experience (who, what, when, where, how). (2 points)

   2. Subjectively describe your feelings, perceptions, and thoughts that occurred during (not after) the experience. What did others seem to be feeling? (2 points)

B. Reflective Observation

    1. Looking back at the experience, what were the perspectives of the key actors (including you)? (2 points)

    2. Why did the people involved (including you) behave as they did? (2 points)

C. Abstract Conceptualization

    1. Relate concepts or theories from the assigned readings or the lecture to the experience. Explain thoroughly how they apply to your experience. Please apply at least two concepts or theories and cite them correctly. (4 points)

D. Active Experimentation

    1. What did you learn about psychological contracts from this experience? (1 point)

    2. What did you learn about yourself? (1 point)

    3. What action steps will you take to be more effective in the future? (2 points)

E. Integration, Synthesis, and Writing
   1. Did you integrate and synthesize the four sections? (1 point)
   2. Is your paper well written and easy to understand? (1 point)
   3. Is it free of spelling and grammar errors? (2 points)

ENDNOTES

[1] I. S. Fulmer, B. Gerhart, and K. S. Scott, "Are the 100 Best Better? An Empirical Investigation of the Relationship Between Being a 'Great Place to Work' and Firm Performance," *Personnel Psychology 56* (2003): 956–93.

[2] D. M. Rousseau, *Psychological Contract in Organizations: Understanding Written and Unwritten Agreements* (Newbury Park, CA: Sage, 1995).

[3] P. M. Blau, *Exchange and Power in Social Life* (New York: Wiley, 1964); A. W. Gouldner, "The Norm of Reciprocity: A Preliminary Statement," *American Sociological Review 25* (1960): 161–78; and S. J. Wayne, L. M. Short, and R. C. Liden. "Perceived Organizational Support and Leader-Member Exchange: A Social Exchange Perspective," *Academy of Management Journal 40* (1997): 82–111.

[4] S. W. Lester, J. M. Bloodgood, and M. C. Bolino, "Not Seeing Eye to Eye: Differences in Supervisor and Subordinate Perceptions of and Attributions for Psychological Contract Breach," *Journal of Organizational Behavior 24* (1) (2002): 39–57.

[5] L. M. Shore and K. Barksdale. "Examining a Degree of Balance and Level of Obligation in the Employment Relationship: A Social Exchange Approach," *Journal of Organizational Behavior 19* (1998): 731–44; T. Simons, "Behavioral Integrity: The Perceived Alignment between Managers' Words and Deeds as a Research Focus," *Organizational Science, 13* (1), (2002): 18–35.

[6] Simons, "Behavioral Integrity: The Perceived Alignment between Managers' Words and Deeds as a Research Focus."

[7] S. L. Robinson, and D. M. Rousseau, "Violating the Psychological Contract: Not the Exception but the Norm," *Journal of Organizational Behavior 15* (1994): 245–59; D. Blancero and S. A. Johnson, "Customer Service Employees and Discretionary Service Behavior: A Psychological Contract Model," Paper presented at the Academy of Management Conference, Boston, MA (1997); Lester, Bloodgood and Bolino,"Not Seeing Eye to Eye"; J. Coyle-Shapiro and I. Kessler, "Consequences of Psychological Contract for the Employment Relationship: A Large Scale Survey," *Journal of Management Studies 37* (2000): 903–930; R. A. Guzzo, K. A. Noonan, and E. Elron, "Expatriate Managers and the Psychological Contract," *Journal of Applied Psychology 79* (4) (1994): 617–26; W. H. Turnley and D. C. Feldman, "The Impact of Psychological Contract Violations on Exit, Voice, Loyalty and Neglect," *Human Relations 52* (1999): 895–922; J. L. Johnson, and A. M. O'Leary-Kelly, "The Effects of Psychological Contract Breach and Organizational Cynicism: Not all Social Exchange

Violations are Created Equal," *Journal of Organizational Behavior 24* (2003): 627–647; and R. Schalk, C. Freese, and J. Van den Bosch, "Het Psychologisch Contract Van Part-Timers en Full-Timers," *Gedrag en Organisatie 8*, (1995): 307–17.

[8] Robinson and Rousseau, "Violating the Psychological Contract: Not the Exception but the Norm."

[9] J. M. Phillips, "Effects of Realistic Job Previews on Multiple Organizational Outcomes: A Meta-Analysis," *Academy of Management Journal 41* (1998): 673–90.

[10] J. P. Wanous. "Realistic Job Previews," in *Encyclopedic Dictionary of Organizational Behavior*, ed. N. Nicholson (Cambridge, MA: Blackwell, 1995): 468–469.

[11] S. W. Lester, C. Eau, and J. Kickul. "Psychological Contracts in the 21st Century: What Employees Value Most and How Well Organizations are Responding to These Expectations, "*Human Resource Planning 24* (1) (2001): 10–21.

[12] D. M. Rousseau, and R. Schalk, *Psychological Contracts in Employment: Cross-National Perspectives.* (Thousand Oaks: Sage, 2000).

[13] Ibid.

[14] Walker Information, "The Walker Loyalty Report: Loyalty and Ethics in the Workplace," (Indianapolis, IN: Walker Information, 2003).

[15] These definitions were taken from J. P. Meyer and J. J. Allen, *Commitment in the Workplace: Theory, Research, and Application* (Thousand Oaks: Sage, 1997); and L. W. Porter, R. Steers, R. T. Mowday, and P.V. Boulian, "Unit Performance, Situational Factors, and Employee Attitudes in Spatially Separated Work Units," *Organizational Behavior and Human Performance 15* (1974): 87–98.

[16] Meyer and Allen, *Commitment in the Workplace: Theory, Research, and Application*; R. Mowday, L. W. Porter, and R. M. Steers, *Employee–Organization Linkages: The Psychology of Commitment, Absenteeism and Turnover* (New York: Academic Press, 1982); A. R. Elangovan, "Causal Ordering of Stress, Satisfaction and Commitment, and Intention to Quit: A Structural Equations Analysis," *Leadership and Organization Development Journal, 22*(4) (2001): 159–165. There is extensive research in this area; the research cited here is merely a sample.

[17] Meyer and Allan, *Commitment in the Workplace*: 34.

[18] I. E. Jernigan, J. M. Beggs, and G. F. Kohut, "Dimensions of Work Satisfaction as Predictors of Commitment Type," *Journal of Managerial Psychology 17*(7) (2002): 564–579.

[19] Meyer and Allen, *Commitment in the Workplace*; J. E. Mathieu and D. Zajac, "A Review and Meta-Analysis of the Antecedents, Correlates, and Consequences of Organizational Commitment," *Psychological Bulletin 108* (1990): 171–94.

[20] S. C. Payne, and A. H. Huffman, "A Longitudinal Examination of the Influence of Mentoring on Organizational Commitment and Turnover," *Academy of Management Journal 48*(1) (2005): 158–168.

[21] G. Dessler, "How to Earn Your Employees' Commitment," *Academy of Management Executive 13*(2) (1999): 58–67.

[22] P. C. Flood, T. Turner, N. Ramamoorthy, and J. Pearson, "Causes and Consequences of Psychological Contracts among Knowledge Workers in the High Technology and Financial Services Industries," *International Journal of Human Resource Management 12*(7) (2001): 1152–65.

[23] A. S. Tsui, J. L. Pearce, L. W. Porter, and A. M. Tripoli, "Alternative Approaches to the Employee-Organization Relationship: Does Investment in Employees Pay Off?" *Academy of Management Journal 40*(5) (1997): 1089–121.

[24] C. M. Pearson and C. L. Porath. "On the Nature, Consequences and Remedies of Workplace Incivility: No Time for 'Nice'? Think Again," *Academy of Management Executive 19*(1) (2005): 7.

[25] C. M. Pearson and C. L. Porath. "On the Nature, Consequences and Remedies of Workplace Incivility: No Time for 'Nice'? Think Again;" J. Graydon, W. Kasta, and P. Khan, "Verbal and Physical Abuse of Nurses," *Canadian Journal of Nursing Administration,* November–December (1994): 70–89; L. M. Cortina, V. J. Magley, J. H. Williams, and R. D. Langhout. "Incivility in the Workplace: Incidence and Impact," *Journal of Occupational Health Psychology, 6* (2001): 64–80; and H. J. Ehrlich and B. E. K. Larcom. "Ethnoviolence in the Workplace," Baltimore: Center for the Applied Study of Ethnoviolence, (1994).

[26] C.M. Pearson, C.L. Andersson, and L.M. Porath, "Assessing and Attacking Workplace Incivility," *Organizational Dynamics* Fall (2000): 123–137.

[27] Pearson and Porath, "On the Nature, Consequences and Remedies of Workplace Incivility: No Time for 'Nice'? Think Again."

[28] H. Rosen with L. Berger, *The Healthy Company: Eight Strategies to Develop People, Productivity, and Profits* (New York: Tarcher/Perigee, 1992).

[29] A. Geller, "Workers Less Satisfied With Jobs, Survey Says," (Associated Press) *San Jose Mercury News,* March 1, 2005, p. 2C.

[30] T. Petzinger, Jr., *The New Pioneers: The Men and Women Who Are Transforming the Workplace and Marketplace* (New York: Simon & Schuster, 1999).

[31] K. C. Hall. "More Job Opportunities Seen for Older Workers," (Associated Press) *San Jose Mercury News*, March 1, 2005, pp. 1C and 6C.

[32] L. Birch, "Thinking About Tomorrow," *Wall Street Journal*, May 24, 1999, R-30.

[33] "Number of Jobs Held, Labor Market Activity, and Earnings Growth Among Younger Baby Boomers: Recent Results From a Longitudinal Survey," *Bureau of Labor Statistics*. www.bls.gov/news.release/pdf/ nlsoy.pdf (accessed July 5, 2005).

[34] *Bureau of Labor Statistics*. www.bls.gov/news.release/pdf/ tenure.pdf (accessed June 23, 2005).

[35] "Labor Force," *Occupation Outlook Quarterly*, Winter (2003–2004): 42–48.

[36] G. Cole, R. Smith, and L. Lucas, "The Debut of Generation Y in the American Workforce," *Journal of Business Administration Online 1* (2) (2002): 3. Http://jbao.atu.edu/Fall2002/ cole_smith_lucas.pdf. Accessed 9/15/06.

[37] Ibid.

[38] U.S. Bureau of Labor Statistics, News-U.S. Department of Labor, released, June 9, 2005.

[39] Rousseau, and Schalk, *Psychological Contracts in Employment: Cross-National Perspective*, 8.

[40] Ibid.

[41] D. C. Thomas and K. Au, "Cultural Variation in the Psychological Contract," *Academy of Management Proceedings* (2000): 1–6; S. Ting-Toomey, *Communicating Across Cultures*. New York: Guilford (1999).

[42] Rousseau, and Schalk. *Psychological Contracts in Employment: Cross-National Perspective.*

[43] Ibid.

[44] D. M. Andolšek, and J. Štebe, "Multinational Perspectives on Work Values and Commitment," *International Journal of Cross Cultural Management 4*(2) (2004): 181–209.

[45] R. Rosenthal and K. L. Fode, "The Effect of Experimenter Bias on the Performance of the Albino Rat," *Behavioral Science 8* (1968): 183–89.

[46] R. Rosenthal and L. F. Jacobson, "Teacher Expectations for the Disadvantaged," *Scientific American 218* (1968): 19–23.

[47] D. W. Bray, R. J. Campbell, and D. L. Grant, *Formative Years in Business: A Long-Term AT&T Study of Managerial Lives* (New York: John Wiley, 1974) and D. E. Berlew and D.

T. Hall, "The Socialization of Managers: The Effects of Expectations on Performance," *Administrative Science Quarterly 11* (2) (September 1966): 207–33.

48 J. J. Sherwood and J. C. Glidewell, "Planned Renegotiation: A Norm Setting OD Intervention," *Contemporary Organization Development: Orientations and Interventions*, ed. W. W. Burke (Washington, DC: NTL Institute, 1972): 35–46.

49 See J. G. March and H. A. Simon, *Organization* (New York: John Wiley, 1963), especially Chapter 4, for a fuller discussion of this conceptual scheme.

50 Rousseau, "Psychological Contracts in the Workplace: Understanding the Ties that Motivate."

51 R. J. Paul, B. P. Niehoff, W. H. Turnley, "Empowerment, Expectations, and the Psychological Contract—Managing the Dilemmas and Gaining the Advantage," *The Journal of Socio-Economics* 29 (2000): 471–85.

52 Rousseau, "Psychological Contracts in the Workplace: Understanding the Ties that Motivate."

53 B. P. Nichoff and R. J. Paul, "The Just Workplace: Developing and Maintaining Effective Psychological Contracts," *Review of Business,* Spring (2001): 5–8.

54 R. S. Sims, "Human Resource Management's Role in Clarifying the New Psychological Contract," *Human Resource Management, 33*(3) (1994): 373–82.

55 The action scripts for dealing with incivility come from Pearson and Porath, "On the Nature, Consequences and Remedies of Workplace Incivility: No Time for 'Nice'? Think Again."

56 This guideline was originally developed by Don McCormick, Redlands University, Los Angeles.

Chapter 2

▲▲▲

THEORIES OF MANAGING PEOPLE

OBJECTIVES By the end of this chapter, you should be able to:

A. Describe seven theories of management and their "ideal" manager.

B. Explain the competing values framework and what constitutes a master manager.

C. Explain why it's important to identify your personal theories about management and organizational behavior.

D. Describe your personal theory of management.

E. Identify the managerial skills you need in today's global business environment.

THE JACK AND HERB SHOW

For a nationwide satellite broadcast, two of the most well-respected U.S. CEOs, former GE CEO Jack Welch and former Southwest Airlines CEO Herb Kelleher, met with *Fortune* editors John Huey and Geoffrey Colvin. The subject: how to create great companies and keep them that way.

Jack, let's start with a basic question. You've been in this job 17 years, and yet you're still bursting with energy. How come? What makes you so energized?

Jack Welch: There are a thousand things, I think. I have the greatest job in the world. We go from broadcasting, engines, plastics, the power system—anything you want, we've got a game going. So from an intellectual standpoint, you're learning every day. We get a great kick out of the fact that we have made this company think outside itself. We want people who get up every morning with a passion about finding a better way: finding from their associate in the office, finding from another company. We're constantly on the search. We brag about learning from Motorola, HP, Allied. Wal-Mart—we learned quick market intelligence from them. Toyota—asset management.

So we've designed a culture that gets people to look outside the company, and we've designed a reward system that's aligned with that. As Herb has said, the rewards of these jobs have to be in the soul and in the wallet. I get a sheet every week of stock optionees who've cashed options. This year we will see $1.6 billion in employee gains in stock options; $1.2 billion of that will be below any senior-management level. Some 40 percent of our optionees make $70,000 or less. If they got a thousand shares each of the past five years, they would today have a gain of $800,000. In five years they've gotten about 12 times their annual salary. That's a kick.

Sam Walton used to say that it takes a week to two weeks for employees to start treating customers the same way the employer is treating the employee. Everybody who's ever flown Southwest Airlines notices a big difference in the way you get treated at Southwest. What are you doing to these people to make them treat us so well?

Herb Kelleher: It's clearly the charisma of the chief executive officer.

But, seriously, your employees act as if they're empowered to make decisions and break rules. How do you encourage fun in a business where you've got people's lives in your hands every day?

Kelleher: There's something we call professional terminalism. People who emphasize too strongly the fact that they're professionals usually are not very good at what they do. What really adds up to professionalism is being very good at what you do in a very modest way. That's the way our people are: They're results oriented. Whether it's the best safety record in the world, the best customer service record in the world, the youngest jet fleet, or lower fares, our people are really focused.

GE also has an informality, which belies the image that most people would have of a huge, massive, financially driven global company. How does that work?

Welch: Informality gives you speed. It takes the crap out of the business equation, the pontificating. I can remember 20 years ago in this company when you went to a meeting, the lights went down, you read a script, you gave your pitch, and you got the hell out of the room. That was the game. Today you're in there having an open dialogue with self-confident people, real exchanges about real things.

Giving people self-confidence is by far the most important thing that I can do. Because then they will act. I tell people, if this place is stifling you, shake it, shake it, break it. Check the system, because it wants to be a bureaucracy. And if it doesn't work, get the hell out. If GE can't give you what you want, go get it somewhere else.

Jack, there's a story that at some point you quit, saying the GE bureaucracy had broken your spirit and you were leaving.

Welch: Right. It was after one year. But my boss's boss came up the night before the going-away party and convinced me that things would change. So I stayed. It was really about the absolute roteness of it all. I was in a group of seven in development engineering, and we all got our raise the same day, and we all got the same amount of money. And I thought I was a hell of a lot better than the other six. I didn't think it was a good deal.

Did your boss's boss make good?

Welch: Yes. He gave me a project where I was the only employee. I was able to call myself king, emperor, any title you wanted. And I hired one technician. And from that, we built a plastics business.

Well, that's self-confidence. You looked around, you decided you're worth more than everybody else, and quit. Let's turn to another subject. Herb, the figures I have are that 100,000 people applied for a job last year, and you hired 3,000. What's your advice to someone who wants a job at Southwest?

Kelleher: My first advice would be not to go for my job. Beyond that, I would say that if you're an altruistic, outgoing person who likes to serve others and enjoys working with a team, we want you. If you're the kind of person who enjoys a more secure, more regimented, more inflexible, more rule-governed type of environment, that doesn't mean that you're a bad person, but we're probably incompatible. We shouldn't even get engaged, much less get married.

Is it true that you should be prepared to tell a joke in the job interview?

Kelleher: No, that's not true. But it is true that we will say to someone, tell us how humor helped you get around one of the more difficult situations in your life.

People think it's kind of crazy, Jack, but we had a pilot-applicant class one day and we said, we don't interview you in suits; put on some Southwest Airlines shorts. Now, you may think that that seems kind of quirky and aberrational—irrational, even. But the ones who were delighted to do it because they thought it was a lark—those were the ones we hired.

You both run huge companies. How do you renew a big organization, renew your own spirit, and, most important, renew the sense of purpose of your employees?

Kelleher: The way that we accomplish that is that we constantly tell our employees—and Jack and I were discussing this earlier—think small and act small, and we'll get bigger. Think big, be complacent, be cocky, and we'll get smaller. One way we avoid complacency—and this may just be because I don't have a long attention span—is that we reject the idea of long-range planning. We say, do strategic planning, define what you are, and then get back together soon to define whether you need to change that. And have the alacrity of a puma. Because this plan about what we're going to do 10 years from now will almost certainly be invalidated in the next six months.

Welch: You need to believe that you are a learning institution and to constantly challenge everything you have. I was at Crotonville [the Connecticut site of GE's Leadership Development Center] on Monday night. I said, how many people can raise their hand and say they predicted the Asian crisis? Not one hand went up, including mine. I said, what does that tell you? All of this crap you planned for is meaningless, basically. What's important is that you're agile, in your thinking and in your action. We were getting steel casings for turbines in Mexico, which was making them for 40 percent less than they make them for here. Within 45 days our team had moved those casings out of Mexico to Korea, which was 40 percent below Mexico. That took just 45 days. You've also got to use the strength of a big company, and reduce its weaknesses. For example, a big company doesn't communicate as well as a small company. There's no chance. A big company moves more slowly. We think we're the fastest elephant at the dance, but we are an elephant.

So what does the big company do well? It can go to bat more often. I've made more mistakes in the 18 years I've been doing this job than probably any human being in America has made. Most of them, *Fortune* doesn't find out about, the *Wall Street Journal* doesn't find out about. (Of course. when I screw up Kidder Peabody, I get on the front page of everything.) But if I make small mistakes, no one sees them. We've made $10 billion to $15 billion of acquisitions every year for the past five years. Most don't even make the papers. A billion here, a billion there, two billion here. That's what a big company's balance sheet allows it to do: keep playing.

Jack, you're doing a total-quality thing 10 or 15 years after the rest of corporate America did it. Why are you doing it, and why now?

Welch: There was only one guy in the whole country who hated quality more than me. I always believed quality would come from just operating well and fast, and all these slogans were nonsense.

The guy who hated quality more was Larry Bossidy. He hated quality totally. Then he left GE and went to AlliedSignal. In order to resurrect AlliedSignal, Larry went out, saw Motorola, and did some stuff on Six Sigma. And he called me one day and he said, "Jack, this ain't b.s.—this is real stuff, this is really great stuff."

We poll 10,000 employees every year. In 1995 they came back and said, we desperately need a quality issue. So Six Sigma was something we adopted then. The results are fantastic. We're going to get $1.2 billion of gain this year. For years our operating margin was never over 10. It's been improving, and it's going to be 16.7 this year. Our working-capital turns were four for 35 years. It will be nine this year.

Herb, you're a company founder. Many people think there can't be a Southwest without Herb Kelleher. How do you follow your act?

Kelleher: The way I look at it is the United States was strong enough to live through Millard Fillmore and Warren G. Harding. And if we should make a mistake and get a successor who didn't subscribe to Southwest's value system, there will probably be an insurrection. So I think the culture is stronger than any individual who might try to fly in the face of it or defy it.

Finally, what keeps you guys awake at night?

Kelleher: What keeps me awake are the intangibles. It's the intangibles that are the hardest thing for a competitor to imitate. You can get airplanes, you can get ticket counter space, you can get tugs, you can get baggage conveyors. But the spirit of Southwest is the most difficult thing to emulate. So my biggest concern is that somehow, through maladroitness, through inattention, through misunderstanding, we lose the esprit de corps, the culture, the spirit. If we ever do lose that, we will have lost our most valuable competitive asset.

Welch: What do I worry about? I was in Hong Kong about a month ago when our stock crashed through 70 to 69 from a high of 96 [the stock was at 88 at the time of this interview]. People don't realize that 10 percent of our company is owned by our employees, including production workers, who own $2 billion worth. It is an incredible feeling of responsibility to take their savings and their life and have something go wrong with it.

Source: "The Jack and Herb Show," *Fortune 139*(1) (January 11, 1999): 163–66.

CLASS PREPARATION

A. Read "The Jack and Herb Show."

B. Fill out and score the Leadership Styles Questionnaire on the following page.

C. Answer the following questions.

  1. How would you describe the ideal manager?

  2. How did you arrive at this ideal— taking into consideration previous experiences, values, role models, education, training, reading, and so on?

  3. What values underlie your picture of the ideal manager?

  4. How would you score Jack Welch and Herb Kelleher on the questionnaire on the following page?

5. After reading the chapter, which theory(ies) of management seem(s) to be most prevalent in your workplace?

6. What struck you as the most significant idea in the chapter, one which might be useful in your current or former workplace?

Leadership Styles Questionnaire

This instrument is designed to help you better understand the assumptions you make about people and human nature. There are 10 pairs of statements. Assign a weight from 0 to 10 to each statement to show the relative strength of your belief in the statements in each pair. The points assigned for each pair must total 10 in each case. Be as honest with yourself as you can and resist the natural tendency to respond as you would like to think things are. This instrument is not a test. There are no right or wrong answers. It is designed to be a stimulus for personal reflection and discussion.

1. It's only human nature for people to do as little work as they can get away with. _____ (A)

    When people avoid work, it's usually because their work has been deprived of its meaning. _____ (B)
    10

2. If employees have access to any information they want, they tend to have better attitudes and behave more responsibly. _____ (C)

    If employees have access to more information than they need to do their immediate tasks, they will usually misuse it. _____ (D)
    10

3. One problem in asking for the ideas of employees is that their perspective is too limited for their suggestions to be of much practical value. _____ (E)

    Asking employees for their ideas broadens their perspective and results in the development of useful suggestions. _____ (F)
    10

4. If people don't use much imagination and ingenuity on the job, it's probably because relatively few people have much of either. _____ (G)

    Most people are imaginative and creative but may not show it because of limitations imposed by supervision and the job. _____ (H)
    10

5. People tend to raise their standards if they are accountable for their own behavior and for correcting their own mistakes. _____ (I)

    People tend to lower their standards if they are not punished for their misbehavior and mistakes. _____ (J)
    10

6. It's better to give people both good and bad news because most employees want the whole story, no matter how painful. _____ (K)

    It's better to withhold unfavorable news about business because most employees really want to hear only the good news. _____ (L)
    10

7. Because a supervisor is entitled to more respect than those below him or her in the organization, it weakens the supervisor's prestige to admit that a subordinate was right and he or she was wrong.

_____ (M)

Because people at all levels are entitled to equal respect, a supervisor's prestige is increased when he or she supports this principle by admitting that a subordinate was right and he or she was wrong.

_____ (N)
10

8. If you give people enough money, they are less likely to be concerned with such intangibles as responsibility and recognition.

_____ (O)

If you give people interesting and challenging work, they are less likely to complain about such things as pay and supplemental benefits.

_____ (P)
10

9. If people are allowed to set their own goals and standards of performance, they tend to set them higher than the boss would.

_____ (Q)

If people are allowed to set their own goals and standards of performance, they tend to set them lower than the boss would.

_____ (R)
10

10. The more knowledge and freedom people have regarding their jobs, the more controls are needed to keep them in line.

_____ (S)

The more knowledge and freedom people have regarding their jobs, the fewer controls are needed to ensure satisfactory job performance.

_____ (T)
10

Source: Adapted from M. Scott Myers, _Every Employee a Manager_ (New York: McGraw-Hill Book Company, 1970).

Scoring Instructions

Record the number you assigned to each of the following letters in the space provided, and then total each column.

Theory X		Theory Y	
A	_____	B	_____
D	_____	C	_____
E	_____	F	_____
G	_____	H	_____
J	_____	I	_____
L	_____	K	_____
M	_____	N	_____
O	_____	P	_____
R	_____	Q	_____
S	_____	T	_____
_____ (Total) Theory X Score		_____ (Total) Theory Y Score	

Theory X Assumptions (Traditional)	Theory Y Assumptions (Emerging)
1. People are naturally lazy; they prefer to do nothing.	1. People are naturally active; they set goals and enjoy striving.
2. People work mostly for money and status rewards.	2. People seek many satisfactions in work: pride in achievement, the work itself, sense of contribution, pleasure in association, stimulation of new challenges, etc.
3. The main force keeping people productive in their work is fear of being demoted or fired.	3. The main force keeping people productive in their work is desire to achieve their personal and social goals.
4. People remain children grown larger; they are naturally dependent on leaders.	4. People normally mature beyond childhood; they aspire to independence, self-fulfillment, and responsibility.
5. People expect and depend on direction from above; they do not want to think for themselves.	5. People close to the situation see and feel what is needed and are capable of self-direction.
6. People need to be told, shown, and trained in proper methods of work.	6. People who understand and care about what they are doing can devise and improve their own methods of doing work.
7. People need supervisors who will watch them closely enough to be able to praise good work and reprimand errors.	7. People need a sense that they are respected as capable of assuming responsibility and self-correction.
8. People have little concern beyond their immediate, material interests.	8. People seek to give meaning to their lives by identifying with nations, communities, churches, unions, companies, and causes.
9. People need specific instruction on what to do and how to do it; larger policy issues are none of their business.	9. People need ever-increasing understanding; they need to grasp the meaning of the activities in which they are engaged.
10. People appreciate being treated with courtesy.	10. People crave genuine respect from their fellow human beings.
11. People are naturally compartmentalized; work demands are entirely different from leisure activities.	11. People are naturally integrated; when work and play are too sharply separated, both deteriorate.
12. People naturally resist change; they prefer to stay in the old ruts.	12. People naturally tire of monotonous routine and enjoy new experiences; to some degree, everyone is creative.
13. Jobs are primary and must be done; people are selected, trained, and fitted to predefined jobs.	13 People are primary and seek self-realization; jobs must be designed, modified, and fitted to people.
14. People are formed by heredity, childhood, and youth; as adults they remain static; old dogs don't learn new tricks.	14. People constantly grow; it is never too late to learn; they enjoy learning and increasing their understanding and capability.
15. People need to be "inspired" (pep talk) or pushed or driven.	15. People need to be released, encouraged, and assisted.

Source: Douglas McGregor, *The Human Side of Enterprise* (New York: McGraw-Hill Book Company, 1960).

 **THE KNOWLEDGE BASE**

Just like Jack Welch and Herb Kelleher, two of the most effective CEOs in recent times, we all have our theories and mental maps about what makes successful managers and organizations. "Theory often gets a bum rap among managers because it's associated with the word "theoretical," which connotes "impractical."[1] Kurt Lewin, one of the earliest scholars to study organizational behavior, once said there is nothing so practical as a good theory. " A theory is a statement predicting which actions will lead to what results and why. Every action that managers take, and every plan they formulate, is based on some theory in the back of their minds that makes them expect the actions they contemplate will lead to the results they envision."[2] Everyone uses theories, but, unfortunately, not everyone uses theories that are valid and backed up by research. Good theories help us interpret the present and figure out what is going on and why. They allow us to make predictions about the consequences of managerial actions.[3] In this way, good theories take some of the uncertainty out of decision making and lead to better results.

Over the years, numerous theories have contributed to our general understanding of management. Some of the major schools of management thought are summarized in the following paragraphs to set the stage for the study of organizational behavior. Each reflected the theorist's model of excellent organizations and managers within their sociohistorical context.

Scientific Management   Frederick Taylor's scientific management,[4] the "one best way" of doing a job, which emerged in the late 1800s, emphasized the efficient division of labor into small, specialized, standardized jobs that were carefully matched with the capacities of workers. For the first time, Taylorism made it possible for engineers to research the most efficient way to do jobs. Taylor's goal was to develop workers to the best of their abilities and to convey the message that it was cooperation between capital and labor that resulted in success. By increasing profits, rather than arguing over their distribution, both labor and owners would prosper.

Taylor's name is often mistakenly associated with time-and-motion studies run amok and an inhumane emphasis on output. In fact, Taylor was concerned about both the proper design of the job and the worker. In Taylor's eyes, the ideal manager (perhaps with the aid of an engineer) scientifically determined the goals that needed to be accomplished, divided the work up in the most efficient way, trained workers to do the job, and rewarded them by wage incentives such as piecework. However, since foremen were cast as the "brains" who did planning rather than actual operations, workers came to be seen as little more than "a pair of hands." While that sounds pejorative, it was a perspective more easily understood when placed within the context of a country just beginning to industrialize. The labor force quite naturally consisted primarily of people from rural backgrounds without prior factory experience. In that era, workers were viewed as one more resource, much like machines.

Administrative Theory   The next phase in management history was termed administrative theory. At that time, beginning about the late 1920s, managers were grappling with the problems of organizing larger and larger organizations and defining the emerging role of the professional manager. Administrative theory came up with answers to both issues. Fayol defined the functions of a manager as planning, controlling, organizing, and commanding and advocated the study of management as a discipline.[5] Weber contributed greatly to our understanding of the "ideal" bureaucracy and the different types of authority that were appropriate for it.[6] In those days, bureaucracy did not have the negative connotations it does today. Indeed, bureaucracy was then viewed as a solution to the nepotism, favoritism, and unprofessional behavior found in organizations of the day. Proponents of administrative theory believed that if managers designed the organization correctly and followed the proven principles of management (e.g., having a limited number of people report to each supervisor, having only one boss for each worker, and engaging in merit-based selection of employees), the organization would succeed.

Human Relations School   The formula for organizational success was expanded by the famous Hawthorne studies[7] that took place in the late 1920s and 1930s. The Hawthorne studies contributed the idea that worker output was affected by numerous, heretofore ignored, variables: how workers were treated; how they felt about their work, coworkers, and boss; and what happened to them outside of work. When the researchers increased the lighting in the wire factory, productivity went up; but it also went up when the researchers dimmed the lighting till it approximated "moonlight"! The attention the workers received in the experiment from the researchers, rather than the varied work conditions being testing, caused them to work harder. This phenomenon has come to be known as the Hawthorne Effect.

The human relations school grew out of this research and acknowledged that workers had to be considered as more than "hands"; workers also had "hearts" (i.e., feelings and attitudes that affected productivity). And the norms or implicit rules of the work groups to which they belonged also affected productivity. Therefore, the effective manager was expected to pay attention to people's social needs and elicit their ideas about work issues. The human relations school of thought gained popularity at a time when the credibility of businesspeople was low due to the stock market crash and when feelings of exploitation fueled the union movement. Decreased immigration had made labor scarce, and, as a result, the needs of workers began to receive attention.

Theory X and Theory Y   Another example of mental maps that people have concerning management is McGregor's Theory X and Theory Y concept.[8] McGregor described two ends of a continuum of assumptions about people and human nature. These assumptions appear on page 34. The Leadership Style Questionnaire that you filled out as part of the class preparation is designed to help you assess the extent of your own Theory X versus Theory Y assumptions about people. Whether we incline more to the carrot (Theory Y) or the stick (Theory X) approach to motivation may be rooted in these assumptions. Understanding them is of crucial importance because of the potential that exists for self-fulfilling prophecies. For instance, if you believe people are lazy and incapable of thinking for themselves (Theory X assumptions), you will most likely manage them in a way that is consistent with these assumptions (e.g., watch over their shoulders all the time and call all the shots). This behavior can cause your subordinates to feel that they really have no responsibility in their job, which could lead them to work hard only when you are watching them closely. A self-fulfilling prophecy is thus set in motion, and your view of human nature is confirmed.

In some cultures, we find a stronger tendency toward a Theory X or Theory Y orientation. As we saw in Setting the Global Stage, one of the dimensions anthropologists use to differentiate cultures is their view of human nature. Is human nature good, evil, or neutral—in other words, trustworthy or untrustworthy? Cultures that tend to perceive humankind as innately untrustworthy tend toward a Theory X orientation (e.g., Latin American countries). Cultures that tend to perceive humankind as trustworthy are more likely to be characterized by a Theory Y orientation (e.g., Scandinavian countries). These generalizations do not mean that all managers in these cultures are similar but that we will find more aspects of either Theory X or Theory Y in their organizations and managerial style. There are other dimensions along which management theories of other cultures differ. Therefore, it's important to understand indigenous management theories when working overseas. European and U.S. theories are written about most frequently due in large part to the research emphasis of their universities, but this does not mean that other important theories are not alive and well around the world.

Decision-Making School   March and Simon,[9] writing in the late 1950s, were proponents of the decision-making school. They added yet another layer of complexity to our understanding of organizations with their description of organizations as social systems in which individual decisions are the basis of human behavior. One of their contributions was mentioned in the previous chapter: employees make the decision to join an organization, but once hired, they also have another decision to make—whether or not to participate and work as hard as they can. The outcome of this decision depends on the employee's rational analysis of the situation and the rewards involved. Now managers also had to take into account workers' "minds." The effective manager set the premises for employee decisions and relied on their rationality to make choices that would be best for both themselves and the organization. For example, if a CEO of a company in which marketing was seen as the springboard into top management decided that more emphasis needed to be placed on operations, he or she would promote more rapidly from operations positions. Employees would then realize that operations was the area receiving top-level attention, and ambitious workers would elect to work in that area. Understanding and manipulating the decision premises are unobtrusive methods of organizational control.

However, March and Simon also made the sobering observation that our decisions are limited by the number of variables our brains can handle, the time available, our reasoning powers, and so on; they called this *bounded rationality*. It means that we often "satisfice" (choose a solution that is merely good enough) rather than maximize or optimize (search and consider all the available information) when we make decisions. Furthermore, they noted that routine work drives out nonroutine work, which explains why it seems so much harder to launch important new projects than it is to maintain routine tasks. For theorists of this school, managerial effectiveness consisted of a thorough understanding of decision making.

Contingency Approach   By the middle of the 20th century, managers and scholars had identified many variables that were thought to be related to success, such as job specialization, managerial principles, worker attitudes and human relations, and rational decisions made by workers. In the 1960s, many scholars converged on the idea that there was no "one best way" to manage. Instead, they tried to identify which variables would be successful for particular situations.

This is still one of the dominant perspectives in the field of organizational behavior and is referred to as the *contingency approach;*[10] *the gist of this approach is that effectiveness varies according to the particular situation.* Good managers (and employees) analyze the situation and choose the most appropriate action. We know now that individuals, groups, cultural groups, occupational subgroups, industries, types of technology, managerial styles, organizations, and external environments can all vary enormously. As long as organizations fit their environment and as long as their various building blocks—their strategy, structure, systems, staff, style, skills, and superordinate overarching goals—fit together in a complementary fashion, very different types of organizations will still be effective. The particular building blocks in the previous sentence are known as the *7S model,*[11] which is discussed in greater detail in Chapter 21.

Procter & Gamble (P&G)[12] is an example of a company that has good "fit." The company regularly appears on *Fortune* magazine's lists of Most Admired Global Companies, Most Admired American Companies, 100 Best Companies to Work For, the Global *Fortune* 100, and the American *Fortune* 100.[13] Its management values about staffing are to (1) hire good people of high character, (2) treat them as individuals and develop their individual talents, and (3) provide a work environment that rewards individual achievement. The company is well known for its training programs and promotion from within. General managers are evaluated and rewarded for their success in terms of volume, profit, and people. P&G has developed systems (sometimes cumbersome) and skills (marketing, marketing research, and R&D) that reinforce its strategic goals. It has been very responsive to changing market conditions and demographics. Marketing strategies are customized for different ethnic groups, and it has made a major effort to integrate employees from diverse ethnic and cultural backgrounds. For example, the company has a reverse mentoring program that pairs junior female employees with a senior manager to help the mostly male higher-ups understand the issues women face.[14] P&G has also experimented with various structures to help it compete more effectively both domestically and globally. Its success is due, in large part, to its ability to keep the 7Ss in alignment and maintain the fit with its environment.

Open Systems Theory   According to open systems theory, which became popular due to the rapidly changing environment of the mid-1960s, an effective manager understood the interdependence among different parts of systems and recognized that organizations are embedded within the larger environment. *Open systems theory maintains that organizations and all the subdivisions within them take in resources and transform them into a service or product that is purchased or utilized by a larger system.*[15] Dealing with external entities is a crucial role for many managers. In this view, organizational effectiveness is governed by three major factors: the individuals who make up the organization, the organization itself, and the environment in which the organization exists. Effective management of the interfaces between these factors—between the individual and the organization and between the organization and its environment—is central to organizational success. The relationship between the individual and the organization is often mediated or linked by a work group.

Looking back on these theories of organization, one is reminded of the parable of the blind men who each touched a different part of the elephant and assumed that they understood the entire animal. How is it that previous theorists only touched on one part of organizing? One answer lies in the bounded rationality of their social context: most popular theories reflect ideas whose time has come, along with the personal predispositions and biases of the theorists themselves. Another answer is the increasing popularity of the concept of "paradox" regarding the process of organizing. Previous theories emphasized only one side of the equation (change versus stability, production versus social needs, Theory X versus Theory Y, etc.) rather than the balancing act that managers actually perform between them.

Competing Values Framework   According to Robert Quinn,[16] four of the previously explained theories help us understand the paradoxical nature of management. "Master managers" know how to balance the competing values of the rational goal model (similar to Taylor's scientific management with extra emphasis on profit) with those of the human relations model, and the competing values of the internal process model (comparable to administrative theory) with the open systems model. Exhibit 2–1 summarizes the differences among these models. Both organizational success and managerial effectiveness are linked to the ability to balance what at first blush appear to be the competing values of models that face one another diagonally in Exhibit 2–2, the rational goal model with the human relations model and the internal process model with the open systems model. Many of us (including theorists) have mental maps that cause us to see these models as mutually exclusive. Yet productivity and profit cannot be achieved without attention to the human resources responsible for productivity, and growth cannot be sustained if it is not also tempered by a certain degree of stability.

According to Quinn, none of these models is the one best way to organize or manage; in fact, too much emphasis on any one model will lead to failure. Too much of a good thing pushes the organization from what he calls the positive zone into the negative zone as shown in Exhibit 2–2. Overemphasis on productivity and lack of attention and sensitivity to human resources result in employee burnout and blind dogma—the oppressive sweatshop. In contrast, overemphasis on human resources and lack of attention to productivity result in extreme permissiveness, irrelevance, and inappropriate participation—the irresponsible country club. The other two poles are overemphasis on the external environment and change—the tumultuous anarchy—and excessive control and stability, which result in the frozen bureaucracy.[17]

	Rational Goal	Internal Process	Human Relations	Open Systems
Criteria of effectiveness	Productivity, profit	Stability, continuity	Commitment, cohesion, morale	Adaptability, external support
Means-ends theory	Clear direction leads to productive outcomes	Routinization leads to stability	Involvement results in commitment	Continual adaptation and innovation lead to acquiring and maintaining external resources
Emphasis	Goal clarification, rational analysis, and action taking	Defining responsibility, measurement, documentation	Participation, conflict resolution, and consensus building	Political adaptation, creative problem solving, innovation, change management
Climate	Rational economic: "the bottom line"	Hierarchical	Team oriented	Innovative, flexible
Role of manager	Director and producer	Monitor and coordinator	Mentor and facilitator	Innovator and broker

EXHIBIT 2-1 Characteristics of the Four Management Models in the Competing Values Framework
Adapted from R. E. Quinn, S. R. Faerman, M. P. Thompson, and M. R. McGrath, *Becoming a Master Manager: A Competency Framework* (New York: John Wiley & Sons, 1996), 10–11. Reprinted with permission of the publisher.

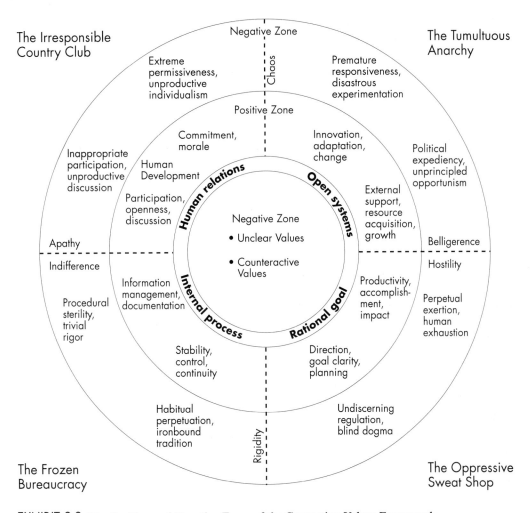

EXHIBIT 2-2 The Positive and Negative Zones of the Competing Values Framework
Adapted from Robert E. Quinn, *Beyond Rational Management* (San Francisco: Jossey-Bass, 1988), 7.

IBM is an example of a company that found itself in the negative zone and later regained its balance. When Louis Gerstner took over as chairman in 1993, he identified IBM's strengths as world-class technology, extraordinary people, and loyal customers. He identified IBM's weaknesses as excessive costs, a preoccupation with internal processes, and slowness;[18] the company had losses of $18 billion in the previous three years. Most critics agree that IBM banked too heavily and too long on its mainframe business and market position. Thus, IBM overemphasized its internal processes at the expense of the open systems values; it should have focused more on customers and the market.

Gerstner's lack of experience in the computer industry, except as a customer, turned out to be an advantage. Since he thought like a customer, he encouraged IBM to develop data-processing solutions built around customer needs, not IBM's hardware. His mantra became "The customer first, IBM second, and the business unit third." This strategy, made possible by the depth of IBM skills and talent and the breadth of its businesses, was also a good fit with the business environment. As one analyst stated, "The trends are with IBM for the first time in 15 years. It's service-led sales for them now, and that's appropriate because we are in a more solutions-oriented world." IBM was once again operating in the black (1998 pretax profits of $9.7 billion) and viewed as a leader in its industry[19]—IBM was back in the positive zone. Recently, IBM experienced some turbulent times, reporting disappointing revenue and profit growth.[20] However, its flexibility and adaptiveness are serving it well. The company is working to minimize or remove regional bureaucracies and give local sales and marketing teams more freedom to make decisions and move quickly. It sold its PC business to Lenovo, the Chinese firm. At the same time, it is centralizing its core functions such as customer service and research into centers located around the globe.[21] These actions got IBM back on track, reporting higher profit and renewed demand for its technology services.[22]

Theory and Practice

All of us have theories about management, which then guide our behavior. For example, if Manager A holds the belief that people are motivated primarily by money, he will see increased salary as a solution to low productivity. He may then see his role as little more than laying out the work that needs to be done and seeing that employees are well paid for doing it. In contrast, if Manager B believes that people's attitudes affect their productivity, she will try to improve morale and see her managerial role as including mentoring and coaching. These examples indicate more than the ubiquitous presence of theories or models of behavior. They also show that our theories determine what we actually see in situations. Manager A may never consider the possibility that morale issues may be involved, while Manager B may overlook the role of pay equity. Thus, our mental maps determine what we perceive when we look at situations, what role we are likely to take as a result of our theories of management, and what action scripts we will follow. Look, for example, at the bottom of Exhibit 2–1 to see the various roles that go along with each model in the competing values framework. The questions about your ideal manager in the class preparation section was assigned to help you clarify your personal theory about the role of effective managers.

The purpose of the class activity is to identify still more of your own theories about managing and organizing. This is the first step in being able to evaluate when your theories are adequate and when you need to learn or borrow other theories that may be more appropriate to specific situations. Quinn argues that master managers are capable of utilizing competing theories, either sequentially or simultaneously, to master the paradoxes found in organizations.[23] Streufert and Swezey claim that there is a correlation between reaching the executive suite and high "cognitive complexity."[24] *Cognitive complexity refers to the extent to which people are multidimensional in their thinking and to the number of different relationships they can make between different dimensions or concepts.* Managers with high cognitive complexity can perceive how various management theories apply to situations and can, therefore, choose those that make the most sense in a given situation. Such managers have a variety of maps in their cognitive bank. However, they must also have the behavioral flexibility to perform the various roles that follow from each theory of management.

Recent research findings highlight the importance of understanding the many facets of effective management. In their book reporting the results of interviews with over eighty thousand managers, Marcus Buckingham and Curt Coffman suggest that great managers: (a) select for talent and not just for experience, intelligence, and determination; (b) when setting expectations, they define outcomes, not the steps to get to the goals; (c) when motivating someone, they focus on enhancing strengths and not fixing weaknesses; and (d) when developing an employee, they find the right job that fits the individual, not just the next rung up the promotion ladder.[25] Another study of over 200 managers concluded that all engaged in the same activities: traditional management activities such as planning, budgeting, and decision-making; routine communication activities such as handling paperwork and passing on information; human resource development activities including motivating, reinforcing, training, and developing employees; and networking activities such as socializing, dealing with outsiders, and handling organizational politics.[26] But what about managers who were more effective than other managers? How did they spend their time? Interestingly, the researchers found different answers to these questions depending on how they measured manager effectiveness. Managers who were promoted more rapidly and more often tended to spend about 48 percent of their time networking, 28 percent of their time communicating, 13 percent on traditional management activities, and 11 percent on human resource development. But these generally were not the highest performers! Managers whose units had high quality and quantity of performance and whose employees were satisfied and committed to the organization spent about 45 percent of their time on communication, 27 percent on human resource development, 15 percent on traditional management, and 12 percent on networking. Managers who were effective on both measures (performance and promotions) comprised only about 10 percent of the research sample and had yet a different pattern of behavior. They tended to balance their time across all four activities.[27] In other words, managers who both obtained good performance results and were promoted tended to be good at all four activities. Thus, what constitutes an effective manager depends on the measure of effectiveness you use and the outcomes you want to achieve.

Clearly then, to be effective, today's managers must possess the capacity to analyze complex situations accurately and to choose appropriate responses. For example, do the individuals you supervise (or your managers) have a Theory X or a Theory Y orientation? Does this vary according to the tasks they are performing? What's the best way to manage them? Answering these questions successfully may mean introducing a different theory or going against one's natural way of doing things. Perhaps when life was less complex, it was sufficient for managers to espouse a "one best way" for managing and have a knee-jerk response to all situations. Today's environment, however, is too turbulent for routine responses, and today's global workforce is too diverse for just one theory of management.

What managers need now is a broad behavioral repertoire and the analytical skill to know what behaviors are most appropriate for each situation. Effectiveness also requires the self-control and self-discipline to do something other than "what comes naturally" when one's natural style would not work. The key then is learning—learning as many models or theories as possible, learning what's involved in different or changing situations, learning about different people and what makes them tick, and learning what works and what doesn't.

CLASS ACTIVITY: MANAGER OF THE YEAR ACCEPTANCE SPEECH

The purpose of this exercise is to focus on the link between the environment and managerial skills and to recognize espoused theories. (Time allotted: approximately 75 minutes)

STEP 1. Divide into groups of five to seven participants, preferably with students you do not know.

STEP 2. One of you (in each group) is about to receive the Manager of the Year Award. However, to maintain the suspense, you won't know who this lucky individual is until your instructor chooses a speaker at the end of the preparation period. Each of you should be prepared to give a five-minute acceptance speech that your entire group will help craft. The speech should come close to representing all your views, and you can also draw ideas from your class preparation assignment. The speech should include two subjects:
   a. A brief description of today's global business environment.
   b. The qualities and skills essential to a manager's success in today's global business world.
   (30 minutes)

STEP 3. The instructor designates the award winners from each group who then present their speeches to the entire class. Other Students should listen for common themes about managerial success in the speeches. Write down each quality and skill mentioned by the speakers in the appropriate category in the following chart, which contains the quadrants of the competing values framework in Exhibits 2–1 and 2–2. For example, interpersonal communication would fit in the human relations model, while setting clear goals would fall into the rational goal model. Keep track (using hatch marks) of how many times each quality or skill is mentioned. We'll refer to these as competencies, a term that encompasses both qualities and skills.
   (Time allotted: depends on the number of student groups; 5 minutes per group)

STEP 4.   Discuss as a class the following questions:
  a. What were the common themes you heard in the speeches?
  b. What competencies did you place in the human relations quadrant? Open systems? Rational goal? Internal process?
  c. Which quadrant(s) had the most competencies? The most frequently mentioned competencies? Were there any quadrants that were not mentioned at all? What implications can we draw from this?
  d. Was anything mentioned that did not fit into the four quadrants? What can we learn from this?

Analysis of the Speeches

Write the qualities and skills that you hear in the speeches in the appropriate category and mark how many times each competency is mentioned.	
Human Relations Model	Open Systems Model
Internal Process Model	Rational Goal Model
Items that cannot be categorized:	

LEARNING POINTS

1. Taylor's scientific management emphasized the efficient division of labor into small, standardized jobs that were matched to the capabilities of trained workers who received wage incentives.

2. Administrative theory focused on understanding the basic tasks of management—planning, controlling, organizing, and commanding—and developed guidelines or principles for managing large organizations and bureaucracies effectively.

3. The human relations school acknowledged the effect of the informal social system with its norms and individual attitudes and feelings on organizational functioning. This theory underlined the importance of employee morale and participation.

4. Theory X is based on the assumption that humans are inherently lazy, dislike responsibility, and prefer to be led. Theory Y is based on opposite perceptions of human nature—that humans are responsible, motivated to work hard and develop skills, and capable of self-direction.

5. The decision-making school described organizations as social systems based on individual decisions and contributed the idea of bounded rationality. Managers could control employee behavior by controlling the premises of decision making.

6. The contingency approach contends that there is no one best way to manage in every situation. Managers must find the appropriate method to match a given situation.

7. Successful organizations are characterized by good "fit" among strategy, structure, systems, staff, style, skills, and superordinate goals (the 7Ss). They must also fit their environment.

8. Open systems theory maintains that organizations and all the subdivisions within them take in resources and transform them into a service or product that is purchased or utilized by a larger system. All parts are interdependent, including the larger environment in which the organization is embedded.

9. In the competing values framework, master managers balance the paradoxes of four different models: rational goal model, internal process model, human relations model, and open systems model. Overemphasis on any one model will lead to failure.

10. The first step in managing the paradoxes of organizational effectiveness is understanding one's own theories of management.

11. Our theories or mental maps determine what we see when we look at situations and determine the roles we perform.

12. According to some researchers, great managers do the following:
    a. Select for talent and not just for experience, intelligence, and determination.
    b. When setting expectations, define outcomes, not the steps to get to the goals.
    c. When motivating someone, focus on strengths rather than fixing weaknesses.
    d. When developing an employee, find the right job that fits the individual, not just the next rung up the promotion ladder.

13. What constitutes an effective manager depends on the measure of effectiveness you use and the outcomes you want to achieve. Researchers found that all managers engage in four types of activities: (a) communication, (b) traditional management, (c) human resource development, and (d) networking. But, managers who were rapidly promoted spent a greater amount of time networking, whereas managers whose units had high quality and quantity of performance spent a greater amount of time communicating. Managers who were promoted and whose units had high performance balanced their time across all four activities.

14. Today's managers need to learn:
    a. How to analyze complex situations using a variety of models or theories.
    b. A broad repertoire of behaviors and knowledge about when to use them.
    c. How to adapt to rapidly changing environments.

ACTION SCRIPTS

FOR EMPLOYEES

- People often look down on those whose theories are dissimilar to their own. Employees who are more expert in management thinking, however, are more likely to look for pros and cons in different theories. One way to develop yourself is to seek out and work with people who have different beliefs. The payoff should be greater cognitive complexity and understanding of different mental maps.

- It is important to identify what *your* theory of management is. This will affect how you perceive and react to your manager.
- You also should identify your manager's theory of management. Understanding your manager's perspective on effectiveness will help you better understand his or her goals and interpret his or her actions more clearly.

FOR MANAGERS

- Expert managers are skilled at decoding situations and intuitively choosing the appropriate values and management theories to emphasize and to guide their actions.
- They gather as many perspectives as possible about situations. Just as there is no one best way of managing, there is not only one way to see a situation. Managers who can count on others to help them "see" what's going on and give their opinions on what could be done are fortunate. If, however, you give the impression that you don't like to hear a different perspective or receive advice, you won't—until it's too late to do much about it.
- Expert managers take the time to figure out whether employees seem to hold theory X or theory Y assumptions and manage them accordingly. In general, however, they try to create an environment that encourages employees to take initiative and responsibility and that allows them to keep learning at work. They understand that the environment also influences these orientations.
- The interdependence aspect of open systems theory means that changes in one part of the system will have repercussions elsewhere. Expert managers try to determine these consequences before making decisions and implementing changes.
- Interdependence within a system also means that problems are often rooted in other parts of the system. Experts take a systems approach when looking at problems. To develop this skill, you can ask yourself, "Have I thought about what's taking place on the individual, group, organizational, and environmental levels with regard to this particular situation?"
- Expert managers recognize that they operate within an organizational context and that different organizations value different managerial behavior. In general, however, try to balance your time across communication, traditional management, human resource development, and networking.
- They also understand that management thought evolves over time as conditions change, and they make a concerted effort to stay current by reading or attending seminars. Managing today's knowledge workers requires a theory Y approach. Defining outcomes for qualified employees and giving them the latitude to decide how they accomplish goals allows them to develop their skills and also frees managers from having to supervise their every step.
- Setting standards and measuring how well they are achieved provides clarity for the employee and generally leads to better performance.
- Strategies for developing yourself as a manager:
  - **Analyze yourself** To better understand yourself and your mental maps, fill out assessment instruments like the one at the beginning of the chapter. Ask other people to evaluate you, since this will provide another, perhaps more accurate, perspective. If you are surprised by their evaluations, discuss any differences in perception with an honest coworker or friend.
  - **Develop a change strategy** Select a specific area for improvement and set a goal that is possible to achieve in a particular time frame. You may want to keep a journal to record your questions, lessons, and progress. It is often helpful to work with a partner who provides the social support that makes it easier to change behavior.
  - **Learn about the skill you want to master** Educate yourself by reading books or attending workshops. Identify a good role model whom you can observe or who is willing to explain how to develop this skill. Ask someone to coach you on this skill.

- **Practice the skill and request feedback** Put yourself in situations that require the skill you want to develop so that you can get the practice you need. Ask others for feedback on what you are doing well and what still needs to be improved.

FOR ORGANIZATIONAL ARCHITECTS

- Organizational architects who are good at management usually make the effort to teach managers good theory *and* how to successfully apply theory—they value business education and ensure that employees have access to excellent training programs, and they disseminate knowledge. Rather than settling for quick fixes, they look for theories that fit their circumstances.
- Expert organizational architects carefully design their reward system. What management style does it reward? What management behaviors are reinforced? They analyze whether these are the appropriate ones for their organization at this point in time.
- They also consider how they allocate organizational resources and ensure that they are aligned with strategic goals. They make sure resources go to the best people and units and to those with the most potential.
- Finally, they pay close attention to how managers are developed. Many first-time managers are thrown into the role with little preparation or development. Instead, expert architects ensure that processes are in place to select managers for their *managerial* skills—not just because they excel at the jobs to be managed. As we all know, great sales representatives don't necessarily make great managers. Effective organizational designers ensure that managers have the opportunity to continue to develop and refine their skills.

PERSONAL APPLICATION ASSIGNMENT

A. What is your own theory of management? You can describe it in words or draw it as a model. (Keep a copy for yourself so that you can modify it as the course proceeds.)

B. Based on your theory of management and today's environment, answer the following questions:

1. What blind spots could your theory lead you to have?

2. What personal values seem to underlie your theory; that is, "People, managers, or organizations should/should not _____ (what?)."

3. What implicit assumptions, if any, are you making about human nature or human motivation?

4. What skills do you think are necessary to be a "master" manager?

5. Which of these do you already possess?

6. What skills would you like to work on during this course?

7. Write an action plan for learning these skills. How will you work on it? How will you know when your skills have improved?

ENDNOTES

[1] C. M. Christensen and M. E. Raynor, "Why Hard-Nosed Executives Should Care about Management Theory," *Harvard Business Review 81*(9) (2003): 67.

[2] Ibid.: 67.

[3] Ibid.: 66–74.

[4] F. A. Taylor, *The Principles of Scientific Management* (New York: W.W. Norton, 1911).

[5] H. Fayol, *General and Industrial Management*, trans. C. Storrs (London: Sir Isaac Pitman, 1949).

[6] M. Weber, *The Theory of Social and Economic Organization*, trans. T. Parsons (New York: Free Press, 1947).

[7] F. J. Roethlisberger and W. J. Dickson, *Management and the Worker* (Cambridge, MA: Harvard University Press, 1939).

[8] D. M. McGregor, *"The Human Side of Enterprise,"* (New York: McGraw-Hill, 1960). For a contemporary view, see "Survey: The X and Y Factors," *The Economist 378*(8461), January 21, 2006: 19.

[9] J. March and H. Simon, *Organizations* (New York: John Wiley, 1958).

[10] For a famous example of research on contingency theory, see P. R. Lawrence and J. W. Lorsch, *Organization and Environment: Managing Differentiation and Integration* (Homewood, IL: Richard D. Irwin, 1969).

[11] The 7S framework appears in R. Tanner Pascale and A.G. Athos, *The Art of Japanese Management* (New York: Simon & Schuster, 1981) and in R. H. Waterman Jr., T. J. Peters, and J. R. Phillips, "Structure Is Not Organization," *Business Horizons 23*(3) (1980): 14–26. For a critique of the framework, see R. M. Kanter, *Change Masters* (New York: Simon & Schuster, 1985).

[12] C. A. Bartlett and S. Ghoshal, *Transnational Management* (Homewood, IL: Irwin, 1992).

[13] http://money.cnn.com/lists/ index.html (Accessed June 25, 2006).

[14] R. Levering and M. Moskovitz, The 100 Best Companies to Work For. *Fortune 151* (January 24, 2005): 61–90.

[15] The original source of open systems theory came from the biologist von Bertalanffy. See L. von Bertalanffy. *General Systems Theory: Foundations, Development, Applications* (New York: Braziller, 1968). Subsequently, the theory was adapted for the field of management.

[16] R. E. Quinn, *Beyond Rational Management* (San Francisco: Jossey-Bass, 1988).

[17] Ibid.

[18] D. Kirkpatrick, "IBM from Big Blue Dinosaur to E-Business Animal" *Fortune 139* (April 26, 1999): 116–17; and "Blue Is the Colour," *The Economist 347*(8071) (June 6, 1998): 65–69.

[19] Ibid.

[20] S. Hamm, "Master Plan for A Big Blue World," *Business Week Online.* www.businessweek.com/technology/content/ may2005/tc20050523_4693_tc024.htm (accessed May 23, 2005).

[21] Ibid.

[22] C. Forelle, "IBM's Earning Hints at Recovery," *Wall Street Journal*, July 19, 2005, p. A3.

[23] Quinn, *Beyond Rational Management.*

[24] S. Streufert and R. W. Swezey, *Complexity, Managers, and Organizations* (Orlando, FL: Academic Press, 1986).

[25] M. Buckingham and C. Coffman, *First, Break All the Rules: What the World's Greatest Managers Do Differently* (New York: Simon and Schuster, 1999).

[26] F. Luthans, R. M. Hodgetts, and S. A. Rosenkrantz, *Real Managers* (Cambridge, MA: Ballinger Publishing Company, 1988).

[27] Ibid.

Chapter 3

▲▲▲

INDIVIDUAL AND ORGANIZATIONAL LEARNING

OBJECTIVES By the end of this chapter, you should be able to:

A. Describe the model of adult learning.

B. Identify individual learning styles and their characteristics.

C. Distinguish between adaptive and generative learning.

D. Describe the characteristics of a learning organization.

WHY DUMB THINGS HAPPEN TO SMART COMPANIES

Few people quarrel with the notion that companies must learn to invest in and manage knowledge if they hope to compete in an economy where, more than ever, knowledge is what we buy and sell. But how, they wonder, does one make the case for managing intellectual capital to CEOs and CFOs? And where do we start?

The two questions are cousins, since the best way to build support for any management effort is to start where you'll get early results. Mind you, the forgotten key to succeeding in management is not to stop there; quitting too soon condemns you to the hummingbird style of management, forever flitting and sipping from one blooming idea to another.

But you've got to start somewhere, and here's a way to figure out where: a list of nine symptoms of a "knowledge problem," something wrong with how your company manages its brainpower. The list comes from David H. Smith, head of knowledge development for Unilever, the giant (1996 sales: $52 billion) maker of ice cream, soaps and detergents, frozen foods, and personal products. Smith, a witty Englishman who works in the Netherlands, has a background in both information technology and business. Nine months ago he was given the task of "helping Unilever act more intelligently"—that is, learn faster and leverage what it knows. You can reconstruct the conversation, since you've had the same one: "The solution to our problem isn't to work harder. We've got to learn to work smarter ...." That, as Smith says, "is obviously true but also extremely trite." Besides, when your boss says, "Work smarter, Charlie," how, exactly, are you supposed to do that come Monday?

Like Lyme disease, knowledge problems have symptoms that sometimes mimic other problems, more benign or even more malign. But each of the following, says Smith, is a symptom that suggests that you don't manage knowledge well: People aren't finding it, moving it around, keeping it refreshed and up to date, sharing it, or using it.

The list is Smith's, the bells and whistles mine.

- **You repeat mistakes** "Your best teacher is your last mistake," Ralph Nader once told me. He, of course, has made a career out of publicizing companies that display this knowledge problem. It's rampant. Negligence lawyers don't wear Gucci loafers because companies make mistakes; they wear them because companies make the same mistake twice. The nature of icebergs being what it is, for every million-dollar lawsuit there must be tens of millions lost or wasted from repeated mistakes that are dumb but not tortious (actionable).

  Why does it happen? Fear, I'd guess, is the No. 1 reason: fear of being embarrassed, chewed out, or worse. Many people and companies are so busy trying to hide boners (from the boss, from stock analysts, from customers and competitors) that they tuck away the learning along with the evidence.

  You don't, obviously, want to encourage goofs just to learn from them. But the best way to avoid repeated errors is to study failure as assiduously as success. The history of medicine shows that you can learn as much from autopsies as you can from cures.

- **You duplicate work** "Reinventing the wheel" is the inevitable phrase, and most companies spend so much time doing it you would think they were suppliers to Schwinn. A classic example: You inspect the goods before you ship them, and your customer inspects them again after they arrive. Worse, you do the same thing in-house. Usually the underlying cause is a knowledge problem: Customer and supplier either don't know what each expects of the other, or they don't trust each other because they haven't shared processes or results.

  People fail to copy success for the same reasons that they succeed in copying mistakes: They're afraid or embarrassed to ask. Sometimes the problem is in systems and structures: They don't know where to look or looking takes too much time or they have no place to store corporate memory. Sometimes the problem is what one might call an overdeveloped engineer's mind: I know Eddie already did this, but I can do it better.

- **You have poor customer relations** If you're not selling schlock, why does a customer get peevish? Probably for one of three reasons, all knowledge problems. First, communication at the point of sale: Either he didn't understand what you were selling or you didn't understand what she was buying. Second, service: If I get the runaround when I have a problem, chances are the people who answer your 800 number are little more than switchboard operators who don't know what they should.

  The third reason is subtler and more interesting. Knowledge work tends to be custom work, or at least customized. That changes the nature of the transaction. You don't sell janitorial services the same way you sell mops. Too often salespeople are in a hurry to hear "yes" so they can write up the order. (Too often their incentives encourage that practice.) Result: You talked about the sale but not the deal.

- **Good ideas don't transfer between departments, units, or countries** This is the most common knowledge problem of all: How do we get people to share ideas rather than hoard them, to accept ideas rather than reject them? There's no easy answer. Says Hewlett-Packard's former CEO, Lewis Platt: "Knowledge transfer is a problem that yields to ten different initiatives, not one." Here's a starter kit:

  Set an example: Great bosses love teaching; great teachers produce great students. Once, interviewing Allied Signal former CEO Larry Bossidy, I confessed not knowing what working capital was. Bossidy positively lit up, grabbed a sheet of paper, scooted around the table, and taught me; his pleasure in teaching turned an interview into a sharing of minds.

  Nudge: Nothing will get the troops to use the new database faster than a leader who asks at a staff meeting, "I'd like to hear everyone's thoughts on Kay's posting about the situation in Germany. Bill, let's start with you: What do you think we should do?"

Create incentives: Says Robert Buckman, CEO of specialty-chemical maker Buckman Laboratories: "The most powerful incentives you have are salaries and promotions." Buckman makes sure—and makes it known—that he hands them out *based substantially on how well people share and borrow ideas.*

Benchmark: Be sure Phoenix knows it has twice as much bad debt as Dayton—and reward both if they close the gap.

Make it fun: When you return from a convention, which do you write up first, your expense account or your trip report? Which contains more creative thinking? Which is read more attentively? One group at Monsanto makes knowledge sharing fun by arming people with snazzy new Kodak digital cameras when they go on trips; when they get back, they show their pictures at the next staff meeting.

- **You're competing on price**   No company wants to find itself in a commodity business. What makes the difference? Why could an executive in General Electric's lighting business—light bulbs, for Pete's sake—tell me, in a mock-serious tone, "Cutting prices is not a core value of the General Electric Company," while some companies making computers—computers, for Pete's sake—are forced to do just that?

  The answer is almost always knowledge, or the lack of it. Whatever you sell, you can get out of the price game if you and your customer ride the learning curve together. Everything you learn about a customer—from how he likes pallets stacked to what his plans are—is an opportunity to make it harder for competitors to horn in. The result: margin.

- **You can't compete with market leaders**   Sometimes the big guys win because they've got something you ain't got, like prime-rate loans or Super Bowl-sized ad budgets. But don't blame your problems on scale until you have explored this question: What do they know that we don't know? Toyota, Wal-Mart, and Southwest Airlines are just three examples of formerly small companies that outwitted bigger competitors.

- **You're dependent on key individuals**   Remember the old Allan Sherman song?

  Oh, salesmen come and salesmen go
  And my best one is gone I know
  And if he don't come back to me
  I'll have to close the factory...

  Nothing's more dangerous than depending on a few key people. Usually this signals too little teamwork or an absence of ways to encourage star performers to reveal the secrets of their success. Note, though: The fault may not lie in your stars. Sometimes people have greatness thrust upon them because others are unwilling to achieve it themselves. HP's Lew Platt says, "You've got a knowledge problem when decisions are made too high in the organization." When things come to Platt's desk that shouldn't, he takes it as a sign that people lack knowledge that would let them think for themselves.

- **You're slow to launch new products or enter new markets**   It's obvious that being slow to market is a knowledge problem. But diagnosing its cause can be tricky; as with referred pain, the source may be far from the symptom. It could be a weak lab, a sludge-slowed commercialization process, a rigid budget bureaucracy, failure of competitor and market intelligence, or something else.

- **You don't know how to price for service**   Do you build the cost of service into your price? Sell a service contract? Bill by the hour, the day, the job? Let someone in the distribution channel handle it? Can you clearly explain why you do what you do, or are you just following industry practice?

  Of all the symptoms on Smith's list, this intrigues me most because the underlying knowledge problem is least self-evident. Here it is: If you don't know how to price for service or why to charge one way versus another, it's a sign that you don't fully understand what your customers do with whatever you sell them. Some customers just buy on price. More often, however, they are buying the solution to a problem. They don't want drills; they want holes. One adhesive company, Smith says, knew a way to help customers speed up assembly lines with the added benefit (for customers) of using less glue. But its sales force had no idea how to value and price this knowledge; worse, the reps were paid by the pound. If you know what customers are really paying for, you'd know better who should pay what.

Smith's list is diagnostic, not prescriptive. But each item on it is a knowledge problem with real business consequences that even a skeptical boss will want to fix. It's a start.

Source: Thomas A. Stewart, "Why Dumb Things Happen to Smart Companies." *Fortune 135*(12) (June 23, 1997), 159–60. Reprinted with permission of the publisher.

CLASS PREPARATION

A. Read "Why Dumb Things Happen to Smart Companies."

B. Answer the following questions concerning a real learning situation that you have recently faced or are currently facing (e.g., using a new computer program, playing an instrument, understanding the income tax laws, mastering a new management technique, giving a speech, playing a new sport).

1. Describe what you were (or are) trying to learn.

2. How did you go about learning to do it? What sequence of steps did you follow?

3. What was the outcome?

4. What was the best group learning experience you ever had? What was good about it?

5. What was your worst group learning experience? What made it that way?

6. In your opinion, what conditions promote adult learning?

C. Complete and score the Learning Style Inventory that follows.

D. After reading the chapter, what cues are you going to look for that will help you diagnose individual learning styles and organizational learning issues?

The Learning Style Inventory (LSI)*

The Learning Style Inventory describes the way you learn and how you deal with ideas and day-to-day situations in your life. Below are 12 sentences with a choice of endings. Rank the endings for each sentence according to how well you think each one fits with how you would go about learning something. Try to recall some recent situations where you had to learn something new, perhaps in your job or at school. Then, using the spaces provided, rank a "4" for the sentence ending that describes how you learn best, down to a "1" for the sentence ending that seems least like the way you learn. Be sure to rank all the endings for each sentence unit, using each number only once. Please do not allot the same number to two items.

Example of completed sentence set:

When I learn:

1 I am happy.   3 I am fast.   2 I am logical.   4 I am careful.

Remember:

4 = *most* like you   3 = *second most* like you   2 = *third most* like you   1 = *least* like you

	A		B		C		D	
1. When I learn:	I like to deal with my feelings.	___	I like to think about ideas.	___	I like to be doing things.	___	I like to watch and listen.	___
2. I learn best when:	I listen and watch carefully.	___	I rely on logical thinking.	___	I trust my hunches and feelings.	___	I work hard to get things done.	___
3. When I am learning:	I tend to reason things out.	___	I am responsible about things.	___	I am quiet and reserved.	___	I have strong feelings and reactions.	___
4. I learn by:	feeling.	___	doing.	___	watching.	___	thinking.	___
5. When I learn:	I am open to new experiences.	___	I look at all sides of issues.	___	I like to analyze things, break them down into their parts.	___	I like to try things out.	___
6. When I am learning:	I am an observing person.	___	I am an active person.	___	I am an intuitive person.	___	I am a logical person.	___
7. I learn best from:	observation.	___	personal relationships.	___	rational theories.	___	a chance to try out and practice.	___
8. When I learn:	I like to see results from my work.	___	I like ideas and theories.	___	I take my time before acting.	___	I feel personally involved in things.	___
9. I learn best when:	I rely on my observations.	___	I rely on my feelings.	___	I can try things out for myself.	___	I rely on my ideas.	___
10. When I am learning:	I am a reserved person.	___	I am an accepting person.	___	I am a responsible person.	___	I am a rational person.	___
11. When I learn:	I get involved.	___	I like to observe.	___	I evaluate things.	___	I like to be active.	___
12. I learn best when:	I analyze ideas.	___	I am receptive and open-minded.	___	I am careful.	___	I am practical.	___

Source: Reprinted from *The Kolb Learning Style Inventory, Version 3* (1999) by permission of the Hay Group, 116 Huntington Avenue, Boston, MA 02116. No part of the LSI instrument or information may be reproduced or transmitted in any form or by any means, without permission in writing from the Hay Group.

* *The Learning Style Inventory* is based on several tested theories of thinking and creativity. The ideas behind assimilation and accommodation originate in Jean Piaget's definition of intelligence as the balance between the process of adapting concepts to fit the external world (accommodation) and the process of fitting observations of the world into existing concepts (assimilation). Convergence and divergence are the two essential creative processes identified by J. P. Guilford's structure-of-intellect model.

Scoring the LSI: Enter your scores for each sentence completion in the correct space. For example, for item #1, if you ranked the first sentence completion option ("I like to deal with my feelings") as a 4, write a 4 in the first space above 1A. Next write the number you gave to 2C. Do that for the rest of your responses. Then add up the scores in each row to obtain your total for each dimension. Read The Knowledge Base for information on how to interpret your scores.

___ + ___ + ___ + ___ + ___ + ___ + ___ + ___ + ___ + ___ + ___ + ___   = ☐
1A   2C   3D   4A   5A   6C   7B   8D   9B   10B   11A   12B   CE Total

___ + ___ + ___ + ___ + ___ + ___ + ___ + ___ + ___ + ___ + ___ + ___   = ☐
1D   2A   3C   4C   5B   6A   7A   8C   9A   10A   11B   12C   RO Total

___ + ___ + ___ + ___ + ___ + ___ + ___ + ___ + ___ + ___ + ___ + ___   = ☐
1B   2B   3A   4D   5C   6D   7C   8B   9D   10D   11C   12A   AC Total

___ + ___ + ___ + ___ + ___ + ___ + ___ + ___ + ___ + ___ + ___ + ___   = ☐
1C   2D   3B   4B   5D   6B   7D   8A   9C   10C   11D   12D   AE Total

Plot your score for each learning mode on the graph below. Then connect these points to form a kite-like figure. To compare your score with others, look at the percentile rings. For example, if you had a score of 27 on Concrete Experience (CE), your score would be higher than 60% of those who scored at this level in the validation studies of this instrument.

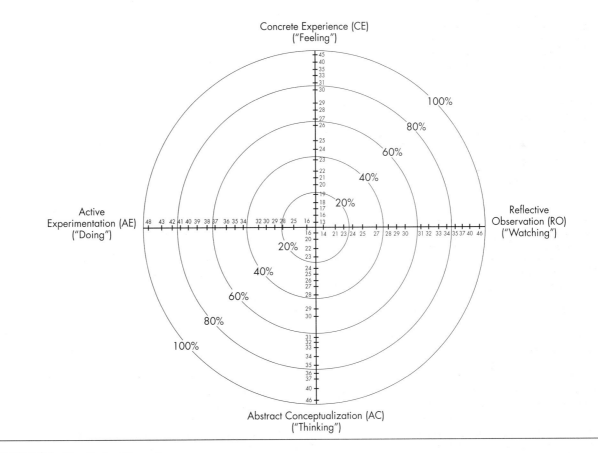

EXHIBIT 3-1 **The Cycle of Learning**

Source: Reprinted from *The Kolb Learning Style Inventory, Version 3* (1999) by permission of the Hay Group, 116 Huntington Avenue, Boston, MA 02116. No part of the LSI instrument or information may be reproduced or transmitted in any form or by any means, without permission in writing from the Hay Group.

While your kite shape explains your relative preferences for the four modes or phases of the learning cycle, your combined scores will explain which of the four dominant learning styles best describes you. Take your scores for the four learning modes, AC, CE, AE, and RO, listed on the previous page, and subtract as follows to get your two combination scores:

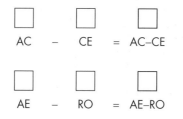

Next, plot these scores on the grid below to locate your data point. The closer your data point is to the center of the grid, the more balanced your learning style. If the data point falls near any of the far corners of the grid, you tend to rely heavily on that particular learning style. You can compare your score to those of other people using the percentile marks. Please read the descriptions of these styles and their strengths in the following pages.

Example: if your AC–CE score is –2 and your AE–RO score is +12, your style falls into the Accommodating quadrant, as shown below.

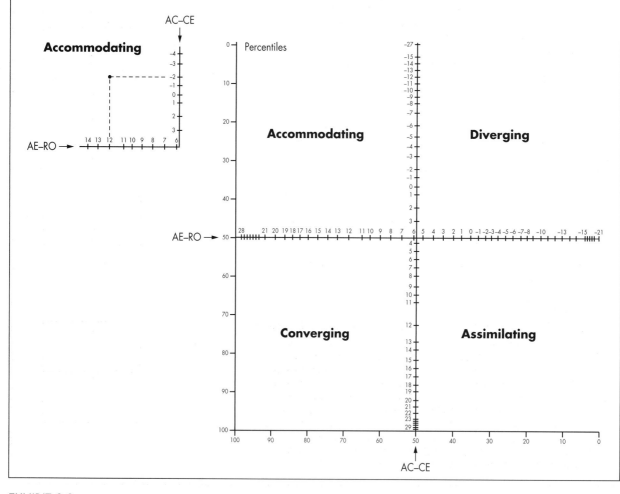

EXHIBIT 3-2 **Learning Style Type Grid**

Source: Reprinted from *The Kolb Learning Style Inventory, Version 3* (1999) by permission of the Hay Group, 116 Huntington Avenue, Boston, MA 02116. No part of the LSI instrument or information may be reproduced or transmitted in any form or by any means, without permission in writing from the Hay Group.

Diverging

Combines learning mode of Concrete Experience and Reflective Observation

People with this learning style are best at viewing concrete situations from many different points of view. Their approach to situations is to observe rather than take action. If this is your style, you may enjoy situations that call for generating a wide range of ideas, such as brainstorming sessions. You probably have broad cultural interests and like to gather information. This imaginative ability and sensitivity to feelings is needed for effectiveness in arts, entertainment, and service careers. In formal learning situations, you may prefer working in groups to gather information, listening with an open mind, and receiving personalized feedback.

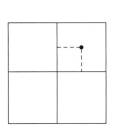

Assimilating

Combines learning mode of Reflective Observation and Abstract Conceptualization

People with this learning style are best at understanding a wide range of information and putting it into concise, logical form. If this is your learning style, you probably are less focused on people and more interested in abstract ideas and concepts. Generally, people with this learning style find it more important that a theory have logical soundness than practical value. This learning style is important for effectiveness in information and science careers. In formal learning situations, you may prefer lectures, readings, exploring analytical models, and having time to think things through.

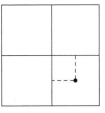

Converging

Combines learning mode of Abstract Conceptualization and Active Experimentation

People with this learning style are best at finding practical uses for ideas and theories. If this is your preferred learning style, you have the ability to solve problems and make decisions based on finding solutions to questions or problems. You would rather deal with technical tasks and problems than with social and interpersonal issues. These learning skills are important for effectiveness in specialist and technology careers. In formal learning situations, you may prefer to experiment with new ideas, simulations, laboratory assignments, and practical applications.

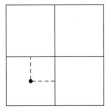

Accommodating

Combines learning mode of Active Experimentation and Concrete Experience

People with this learning style have the ability to learn primarily from "hands-on" experience. If this is your style, you probably enjoy carrying out plans and involving yourself in new and challenging experiences. Your tendency may be to act on "gut" feelings rather than on logical analysis. In solving problems, you may rely more heavily on people for information than on your own technical analysis. This learning style is important for effectiveness in action-oriented careers such as marketing or sales. In formal learning situations, you may prefer to work with others to get assignments done, to set goals, to do field work, and to test out different approaches to completing a project.

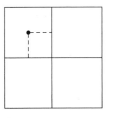

EXHIBIT 3-3 Learning Style Types

Source: Reprinted from *The Kolb Learning Style Inventory, Version 3* (1999) by permission of the Hay Group, 116 Huntington Avenue, Boston, MA 02116. No part of the LSI instrument or information may be reproduced or transmitted in any form or by any means, without permission in writing from the Hay Group.

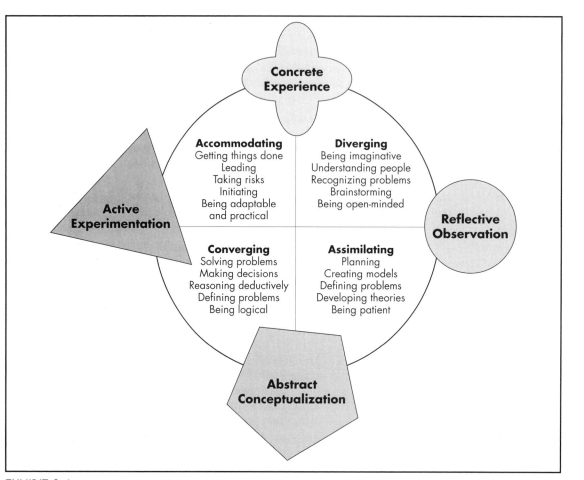

Concrete Experience

Accommodating
Getting things done
Leading
Taking risks
Initiating
Being adaptable
and practical

Diverging
Being imaginative
Understanding people
Recognizing problems
Brainstorming
Being open-minded

Active Experimentation

Reflective Observation

Converging
Solving problems
Making decisions
Reasoning deductively
Defining problems
Being logical

Assimilating
Planning
Creating models
Defining problems
Developing theories
Being patient

Abstract Conceptualization

EXHIBIT 3-4 **Basic Strengths of Each Learning Style**

Source: Reprinted from T*he Kolb Learning Style Inventory, Version 3* (1999) by permission of the Hay Group, 116 Huntington Avenue, Boston, MA 02116. No part of the LSI instrument or information may be reproduced or transmitted in any form or by any means, without permission in writing from the Hay Group.

 **THE KNOWLEDGE BASE**

Do not be puffed up because of your knowledge nor overconfident because you are a learned person. Take counsel with the ignorant as well as with the wise, for the limits of proficiency cannot be reached, and no person is ever fully skilled.

Egyptian Magistrate Ptah-Hotep to his son, c. 2400 B.C.

Learning became a business issue in the past two decades once companies realized its importance to survival. "We understand that the only competitive advantage the company of the future will have is its managers' ability to learn faster than their competitors. So the companies that succeed will be those that continually nudge their managers towards revising their views of the world."[1] This was one of the lessons Arie de Geus, senior planner, learned from Shell's efforts to analyze long-term corporate survival. Many companies, such as Asea Brown Boveri (ABB), 3M, Ford Motor, GE, FedEx, Motorola, and Johnsonville Foods, have worked hard to transform their companies into learning organizations. *A learning organization is an organization skilled at creating, acquiring, and transferring knowledge, and at modifying its behavior to reflect new knowledge and insights.*

Learning organizations succeed, in part, when individuals make explicit their knowledge and contribute it to the institutional collection of mental models and lessons. The structure and culture of the organization will then determine how quickly individual learning spreads, as seen in the following analogy from nature. Titmice travel in flocks and intermingle extensively; in contrast, robins have carefully defined boundaries and work hard and belligerently at keeping other robins out of their territory. When titmice learned to pierce the aluminum seals of the milk bottles delivered to U.K. doorsteps, that knowledge quickly spread throughout the species. Although individual robins may have learned this trick, their knowledge will never be disseminated to the species as a whole because they lack the capacity for institutional learning.[2] Much like territorial managers and departments, the robins' competitive relationships and their focus on turf result in hoarding, rather than sharing, knowledge.

Both companies and employees are being pressured to increase their learning capacity by the "white water" nature of today's business environment. According to Peter Vail, who coined this metaphor, managers in the past could paddle their canoes wherever they wanted on calm, still lakes. Now they are forced to learn to deal with a seemingly endless run of "white water," the rock-strewn, turbulent, fast-moving water in which canoeists struggle to stay afloat and unharmed. White water is exhilarating, but only if you possess the necessary skills. In a tumultuous environment in which people change jobs and even professions, no course or program of education can provide students with all the skills and knowledge they will need for the rest of their career. Our best response is to teach you *how* to learn so you can become a lifelong learner.

The Workbook is designed to create a learning environment that responds to the unique needs of adult learners. First, it is based on a *psychological contract of reciprocity*, a basic building block of human interaction. It is well documented that relationships that are based on a mutual and equal balance of giving and getting thrive and grow; those based on unequal exchange very quickly decay. Academic learning is often conceived as a process of getting rather than giving. Teachers give and students get. Yet in adult learning both giving and getting are critical. In getting, there is the opportunity to incorporate new ideas and perspectives. In giving, there is the opportunity to integrate and apply these new perspectives and to practice their use.

A second characteristic of an adult learning environment is that it is *experience based*. Ideally the motivation for learning comes not from the instructor's dispensation of rewards and grades but from problems and opportunities arising from the learner's own life experience. Their experience shows adults what they need to learn and also allows them to contribute to the learning of others.

Third, the adult learning environment emphasizes *personal application*. Since adults' learning needs arise from their own experience, the main goal of learning is to apply new knowledge, skills, and attitudes to the solution of the individual's practical problems.

Fourth, the learning environment is *individualized and self-directed*. In addition to unique experiences, each person also brings different learning goals and styles. This means that learning environments have to be flexible and attempt to meet the needs of different students. Learners, however, must also be willing to take responsibility for achieving their learning objectives and alert the group or instructor if problems arise.

A final characteristic of an adult learning environment is that it *integrates learning and living*. There are two goals in the learning process. One is to learn the specifics of a particular subject matter. The other is to learn about one's own strengths and weaknesses as a learner (i.e., learning how to learn from experience). This understanding helps in applying what has been learned and provides a framework for continued learning on the job.

A MODEL OF THE LEARNING PROCESS

Adults are often motivated to learn by a problem. A manager who has employees who habitually come late to work starts to chew on the problem. In addition to her individual reflections, she may consult management books or other managers who have solved this problem. Eventually, she will develop a mental model that explains her theory of tardiness: Employees come late to work because _____ (e.g., there are no negative consequences for doing so, employees rely on public transportation that is undependable, late employees are not committed to the organization, etc.). Based on this model, she will take action to solve the problem (e.g., negative sanctions, company transportation, beginning the disciplinary process for some employees). If her interventions are successful, she will have gained knowledge about workplace tardiness. *Knowledge is defined as the condition of knowing something through experience.* If, on the other hand, employees still come late, this becomes another concrete experience that sets the learning cycle in motion all over again.

By examining the learning process we can come closer to understanding how it is that people generate from their experience the concepts, rules, and principles that guide their behavior in new situations, and how they modify these concepts to improve their effectiveness. This process is both active and passive, both concrete and abstract. As shown in Exhibit 3–5, it can be conceived of as a four-stage cycle: (1) concrete experience is followed by (2) observation and reflection, which lead to (3) the formation of abstract concepts and generalizations, which lead to (4) hypotheses to be tested in future action, which in turn lead to new experiences.

There are several key observations about Kolb's model of the learning process.[3] First, this learning cycle is continuously recurring. We continuously test our concepts in experience and modify them as a result of our observation of the experience.

Second, the direction that learning takes is governed by one's felt needs and goals. We seek experiences that are related to our goals, interpret them in the light of our goals, and form concepts and test implications of these concepts that are relevant to these felt needs and goals. The implication of this fact is that the process of learning is erratic and inefficient when personal objectives are not clear.

Third, since the learning process is directed by individual needs and goals, learning styles become highly individual in both direction and process. For example, a mathematician may come to place great emphasis on abstract concepts, whereas a poet may value concrete experience more highly. A manager may be primarily concerned with active application of concepts, whereas a naturalist may develop exceptional observational skills. Each of us develops a learning style that has both weak and strong points. We may jump into experiences but fail to observe the lessons to be derived from these experiences; we may form concepts but fail to test their validity. In some areas, our objectives and needs may be clear guides to learning; in others, we wander aimlessly.

Several factors shape learning style: personality type, early education specialization, professional career, current job role and tasks.[4] Carl Jung's description of preferred ways of dealing with the world, partly measured by the Myers-Briggs Type Indicator (MBTI), explained in Chapter 4, seem to correlate with Kolb's learning styles. The way that students are taught or the areas in which they specialize creates a disposition to emphasize certain learning styles. Undergraduate majors in history, political science, English, psychology, and the arts tend to have a diverger learning style, while physical sciences and engineering majors tend to be convergers. Many undergraduates majoring in business and management tend to be accommodators, whereas those who specialize in economics, mathematics, sociology, and chemistry are more likely to be assimilators. The habits and approaches inculcated during career training and socialization also shape learning styles. People who work in the social services, the arts, and communications tend

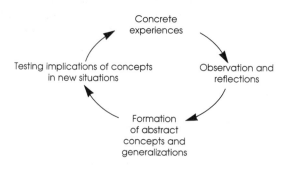

EXHIBIT 3-5 **The Learning Process**

to be divergers, while the science, information, and research professions have more members who are assimilators. Technology, economics, and environmental science professions tend to be peopled by convergers, and accommodators cluster in organizational careers (public finance, educational administration, management) and business. In the same vein, job demands and tasks also influence the development of learning styles.

INTERPRETING YOUR SCORES ON THE LEARNING STYLE INVENTORY

The Learning Style Inventory (LSI)[5] is a simple self-description test, based on Kolb's experiential learning theory, that is designed to measure your strengths and weaknesses as a learner in the four stages of the learning process. Effective learners rely on four different learning modes: concrete experience (CE), reflective observation (RO), abstract conceptualization (AC), and active experimentation (AE). That is, they must be able to involve themselves fully and openly, and without bias in new experiences (CE); they must be able to reflect on and observe these experiences from many perspectives (RO); they must be able to create concepts that integrate their observations into logically sound theories (AC); and they must be able to use these theories to make decisions and solve problems (AE).

The LSI measures your relative emphasis on the four learning modes by asking you to rank order a series of phrases that describe these different abilities. For example, one set of four words is feeling (CE), watching (RO), thinking (AC), and doing (AE). Combination scores indicate the extent to which you emphasize abstractness over concreteness (AC-CE) and the extent to which you emphasize active experimentation over reflection (AE-RO).

One way to better understand the meaning of your scores on the LSI is to compare them with the scores of others. The Cycle of Learning, Exhibit 3–1 on page 53, gives norms on the four basic scales (CE, RO, AC, AE) for 1,933 adults ranging from 18 to 60 years of age. About two-thirds of the group are men, and the group as a whole is highly educated (two-thirds have college degrees or higher). A wide range of occupations and educational backgrounds is represented, including teachers, counselors, engineers, salespersons, managers, doctors, and lawyers.

The raw scores for each of the four basic scales are listed on the crossed lines of the target. By circling your raw scores on the four scales and connecting them with straight lines you can create a graphic representation of your learning style profile. The concentric circles on the target represent percentile scores for the normative group. For example, if your raw score on abstract conceptualization was 31, you scored higher on this scale than 60 percent of the people in the normative group. If your CE score was −31, you scored higher than 80 percent of the normative group. Therefore, in comparison with the normative group, the shape of your profile indicates which of the four basic modes you tend to emphasize and which are less emphasized. No individual mode is better or worse than any other. Even a totally balanced profile is not necessarily best. The key to effective learning is being competent in each mode when it is appropriate. A high score on one mode may mean a tendency to overemphasize that aspect of the learning process at the expense of others. A low score on a mode may indicate a tendency to avoid that aspect of the learning process.

The LSI does not measure your learning style with 100 percent accuracy. Rather, it is simply an indication of how you see yourself as a learner. You will need data from other sources if you wish to pinpoint your learning style more exactly (e.g., how you make decisions on the job, how others see you learn, and what kinds of problems you solve best). Be aware of stereotyping yourself and others with your LSI scores. Your scores indicate which learning modes you emphasize in general. They may change from time to time and situation to situation. Think back to the learning experience you wrote about in the class preparation. Which of the following modes best describes your approach?

An orientation toward *concrete experience* focuses on being involved in experiences and dealing with immediate human situations in a personal way. It emphasizes the perception of feeling, focusing on the uniqueness and complexity of present reality as opposed to theories and generalizations—an intuitive, "artistic" approach as opposed to a systematic, scientific approach to problems. People with a concrete experience orientation enjoy and are good at relating to others. They are often skilled intuitive decision makers and function well in unstructured situations. People with this orientation value relating to people, being involved in real situations, and an open-minded approach to life.

An orientation toward *reflective observation* focuses on understanding the meaning of ideas and situations by carefully observing and impartially describing them. It emphasizes understanding as opposed to practical application, a concern with what is true or how things happen as opposed to what is practical—an emphasis on reflection as opposed to action. People with a reflective orientation enjoy thinking about the meaning of situations and ideas and are good at seeing their implications. They are good at looking at things from different perspectives and at appreciating different points of view. They like to rely on their own thoughts and feelings to form opinions. People with this orientation value patience, impartiality, and considered, thoughtful judgment.

An orientation toward *abstract conceptualization* focuses on using logic, ideas, and concepts. It emphasizes thinking as opposed to feeling, a concern with building general theories as opposed to understanding intuitively unique, specific areas—a scientific rather than an artistic approach to problems. A person with an abstract conceptual orientation enjoys and is good at systematic planning, manipulation of abstract symbols, and quantitative analysis. People with this orientation value precision, the rigor and discipline of analyzing ideas, and the aesthetic quality of a neat, conceptual system.

An orientation toward *active experimentation* focuses on actively influencing people and changing situations. It emphasizes practical applications as opposed to reflective understanding, a pragmatic concern with what works as opposed to what is absolute truth—an emphasis on doing as opposed to observing. People with an active experimentation orientation enjoy and are good at getting things accomplished. They are willing to take some risk to achieve their objectives. They also value having an impact and influence on the environment around them and like to see results.

IDENTIFYING YOUR LEARNING STYLE TYPE

It is unlikely that your learning style will be described accurately by just one of the four preceding paragraphs. This is because each person's learning style is a combination of the four basic learning modes. It is, therefore, useful to describe your learning style by a single data point that combines your scores on the four basic modes. This is accomplished by using the two combination scores, AC-CE and AE-RO. These scales indicate the degree to which you emphasize abstractness over concreteness and action over reflection, respectively. The Learning Style Type Grid, Exhibit 3–2 on page 54, shows the raw scores for these two scales on the crossed lines (AC-CE on the vertical and AE-RO on the horizontal) and percentile scores based on the normative group on the sides. By marking your raw scores on the two lines and plotting their point of intersection, you can find which of the four learning style quadrants you occupy. These four quadrants, labeled *accommodator*, *diverger*, *converger*, and *assimilator*, represent the four dominant learning styles. If your AC-CE score was −6 and your AE-RO score was 15, you would fall squarely into the accommodator quadrant. An AC-CE score of 5 and an AE-RO score of 8 would put you only slightly in the converger quadrant. The closer your data point is to the intersection where the lines cross, the more balanced is your learning style. If your data point is close to any of the four corners, this indicates that you rely heavily on one particular learning style.

The following is a description of the characteristics of the four basic learning styles based both on research and clinical observation (see also Exhibit 3-3). Exhibit 3-4 summarizes the strengths of each learning style.

The *divergent* learning style has the opposite strengths of the convergent style and emphasizes concrete experience and reflective observation. The greatest strength of this orientation lies in imaginative ability and awareness of meaning and values. The primary adaptive ability in this style is to view concrete situations from many perspectives and to organize many relationships into a meaningful gestalt. The emphasis in this orientation is on adaptation by observation rather than by action. This style is called "diverger" because a person of this type performs better in situations that call for generation of alternative ideas and implications, such as a brainstorming idea session. Divergers are interested in people and tend to be imaginative and feeling oriented. They generally have broad cultural interests and tend to specialize in the arts. This style is characteristic of individuals from humanities and liberal arts backgrounds. Counselors, organization development specialists, and personnel managers tend to be characterized by this learning style.

In *assimilation*, the dominant learning abilities are abstract conceptualization and reflective observation. The greatest strength of this orientation lies in inductive reasoning, in the ability to create theoretical models and in assimilating disparate observations into an integrated explanation. As in convergence, this orientation is less focused on people and more concerned with ideas and abstract concepts. Ideas, however, are judged less in this orientation by their practical value. For the assimilator, it is more important that the theory be logically sound and precise. This learning style is more characteristic of individuals in the basic sciences and mathematics rather than the applied sciences. In organizations, persons with this learning style are found most often in the research and planning departments.

The *convergent* learning style has the opposite strengths of the diverger style. It relies primarily on the dominant learning abilities of abstract conceptualization and active experimentation. The greatest strength of this approach lies in problem solving, decision making, and the practical application of ideas. Kolb called this learning style the "converger" because a person with this style seems to do best in such situations as conventional intelligence tests where there is a single correct answer or solution to a question or problem. In this learning style, knowledge is organized in such a way that, through hypothetical-deductive reasoning, it can be focused on specific problems. Research on individuals with this style of learning shows that convergent persons are controlled in their expression of emotion.[6] They prefer dealing with technical tasks and problems rather than with social and interpersonal issues. Convergers often specialize in the physical sciences. This learning style is characteristic of many engineers and technical specialists.

The *accommodative* learning style has the opposite strengths of assimilation, emphasizing concrete experience and active experimentation. The greatest strength of this orientation lies in doing things, in carrying out plans and tasks, and in getting involved in new experiences. The adaptive emphasis of this orientation is on opportunity seeking, risk taking, and action. This style is called "accommodation" because it is best suited for those situations in which one must adapt to changing immediate circumstances. In situations in which the theory or plans do not fit the facts, those with an accommodative style will most likely discard the plan or theory. (With the opposite learning style, assimilation, one would be more likely to disregard or reexamine the facts.) People with an accommodative orientation tend to solve problems in an intuitive trial-and-error manner, relying on other people for information rather than on their own analytical ability. Individuals with accommodative learning styles are at ease with people but are sometimes seen as impatient and "pushy." Their educational background is often in technical or practical fields such as business. In organizations, people with this learning style are found in action-oriented jobs, such as marketing, sales, or management.

As you can see, all styles have their unique strengths and weaknesses so, whenever possible, it is helpful to have groups with diverse learning styles. By doing so, we can avoid the problems that occur when there is an excess or a deficiency of a particular learning style in an organization or work unit, as illustrated in Exhibit 3-6 on page 67.

LEARNING STYLES AND MANAGEMENT EDUCATION

Differences in learning styles need to be addressed in management education. For example, managers who return to the university in midcareer experience something of a culture shock. Fresh from a world of time deadlines and concrete, specific problems that they must solve, they are suddenly immersed in a strange slow-paced world of generalities, where the elegant solution to problems is sought even when workable solutions are at hand. One gets rewarded here for reflection and analysis rather than concrete, goal-directed action. Managers who "act before they think—if they ever think" meet the scientists who "think before they act—if they ever act." Research on learning styles has shown that managers on the whole are distinguished by very strong, active experimentation skills and very weak reflective observation skills. Business school faculty members (and professors in general) usually have the reverse profile. To bridge this gap in learning styles, the management educator must somehow respond to pragmatic demands for relevance and the application of knowledge, while encouraging the reflective examination of experience that is necessary to refine old theories and to build new ones. In encouraging reflective observation, the teacher often is seen as an interrupter of action—as a passive "ivory tower" thinker. This is, however, a critical role in the learning process. Yet if the reflective observer role is not internalized by the learners themselves, the learning process can degenerate into a value conflict between teacher and student, each maintaining that theirs is the right perspective for learning.

Neither the faculty nor student perspective alone is valid. Managerial education will not be improved by eliminating theoretical analysis or relevant case problems. Improvement will come through the integration of the scholarly and practical learning styles. One approach to achieving this integration is to apply the experiential learning model directly in the classroom. This workbook provides simulations, role plays, and exercises (concrete experiences) that focus on central concepts in organizational behavior. They provide a common experiential starting point for participants and faculty to explore the relevance of behavioral concepts for their work. In traditional management education methods, the conflict between scholar and practitioner learning styles is exaggerated because the material to be taught is filtered through the learning style of faculty members in their lectures or presentation and analysis of cases. Students are "one down" in their own analysis because the data are secondhand and already biased. In the experiential learning approach, this filtering process does not take place because teacher and students alike are observers of immediate experiences that they both interpret according to their own learning style. In this approach to learning, the teachers' role is that of facilitators of a learning process that is basically self-directed. They help students to experience in a personal and immediate way the phenomena in their field of specialization. They provide observational schemes and perspectives from which to observe these experiences. They stand ready with alternative theories and concepts as students attempt to assimilate their observations into their own conception of reality. They assist in deducing the implications of the students' concepts and in designing new "experiments" to test these implications through practical, real-world experience.

LEARNING AND CULTURE

Another learning style difference that must be managed in the classroom relates to cultural diversity. Cultural differences have been found in LSI results for both managers and students[7]. Furthermore, in some cultures professors are perceived as experts with all the answers. They dispense their knowledge to students who are socialized not to interrupt or question but to act respectfully with teachers in or out of class. In many U.S. classrooms (but not all), students are encouraged, expected, or even forced to participate in class. Asking questions that may reflect badly on the professor's expertise, while not necessarily politic, is not taboo in the American milieu. Students in Asian classrooms are seldom expected to speak and would never say anything to embarrass a professor in public. Experiential learning may come as a shock to students who have been socialized to have more traditional expectations about learning and classroom roles. There is no question that some people will be more comfortable, at least in the beginning, than others in an experiential course. As a group, we should seek to understand and discuss the differences in our expectations and, when possible, make allowances for them. This lays the groundwork for an effective learning organization.

THE LEARNING ORGANIZATION

It was Woodrow Wilson who said, "I not only use all the brains that I have but all that I can borrow." Using all the available brainpower, knowledge, and wisdom is one of the basic premises of a learning organization. Some of the essential characteristics of learning organizations are:[8]

- *Systematic problem solving.* Employees are taught to solve problems using the scientific method, which focuses on data rather than assumptions and requires the use of simple statistical tools.
- *Experimentation.* Employees are encouraged to take risks and experiment with continuous improvements to ongoing programs or to test innovative ideas using pilot or demonstration projects. The results of these experiments are shared with the rest of the organization and guide decision making.
- *Learning from past experience.* Companies take time to reflect on and evaluate their successes and failures. They summarize and quickly disseminate the lessons learned.
- *Learning from others.* Companies look outward to find and adopt good ideas from other organizations. They visit and benchmark (study) excellent companies and learn from "best practices" and are not reluctant to implement ideas that were "not invented here" within their own company.
- *Transferring knowledge.* Learning organizations have mechanisms for quickly sharing knowledge among their members.

The popularity of learning organizations has given rise to numerous tools to help managers surface their assumptions and mental models, develop creative strategies for the future, resolve problems utilizing cross-functional teams (action-learning and total quality management groups), continuously improve work processes, and analyze possible scenarios for the future.[9] As with any organizational innovation, these tools do not succeed unless the other building blocks are in place, such as reward systems, management style, organizational systems, and a culture that fosters organizational learning. In the following passage, Jack Welch, former CEO of GE, describes the learning culture in his organization.[10]

GE is unique in that it is...a very large, multi-business company with a learning culture that has transformed the diversity of its businesses and its size—from what is sometimes perceived as a handicap—into a tremendous competitive advantage... At the heart of this culture is an understanding that an organization's ability to learn, and translate that learning into action rapidly, is the ultimate competitive business advantage. This appetite for ideas, this lust for learning, was born in the 1980s in a simple ritual called "Work-Out." Work-Out was nothing more complicated than bringing people of all ranks and functions—managers, secretaries, engineers, line workers, sometimes customers and suppliers—together into a room to focus on a problem or an opportunity, and then acting rapidly and decisively on the best ideas developed, regardless of their source. This simple process, and the growing reverence for the better idea that is spawned, is now in the cultural bloodstream of the company. It is reflected every day in the sharing and learning that goes on constantly among GE businesses and between our businesses and other companies. This boundaryless learning culture killed any view that assumed the "GE way" was the only way or even the best way.... GE is a bubbling cauldron of ideas and learning—with tens of thousands of people playing alternate roles of teacher and student.

One might assume that universities and their classrooms would be prime examples of learning organizations. Most universities, however, focus mainly on individual learning and incremental improvements in the programs they offer students. Distance learning is an exception, an innovation wherein students learn primarily from a professor and fellow students on the Web. It is an example of a new mental model about how students learn. The founders of distance learning questioned the basic assumption that students have to be physically present in a classroom; thus, distance learning is an example of generative learning, which is explained in the following section.

ADAPTIVE AND GENERATIVE LEARNING

For years Chris Argyris has studied the reasoning that underlies our actions and the relationship that exists with learning.[11] He concludes that we have two types of theories: espoused theories that we profess to believe ("Do as I say, not as I do") and theories in action that actually guide our behavior. We seldom examine the assumptions on which these theories are based. Indeed, we insulate them in defensive routines that prevent us from questioning their validity. An example of a defensive routine is smoothing over the conflict that arises on a team without ever looking carefully at the reasons for the conflict, thereby perpetuating the status quo.

This discovery led Argyris to describe two types of learning. Single-loop learning is like tracking the temperature on a gauge and responding to the feedback that it is too high or too low. It is now commonly referred to as *adaptive learning, which is defined as a coping approach that focuses on solving problems and making incremental improvements using the prevailing mental model.* A business example is the personal computer (PC) industry. Most companies followed the traditional practice of selling through the retail channel (computer stores such as CompUSA and retailers that sell computers) and have since focused on a coping approach—measuring what they were currently doing and improving it incrementally.

They did not, however, question their theories or mental models about the PC business. This is what distinguishes single- and double-loop learning. In double-loop learning, people question the assumptions that underlie their theories and ask themselves hard questions. Double-loop learning is currently known as generative learning. *Generative learning consists of continuous experimentation and feedback in an ongoing analysis of how organizations define and solve problems.*[12] As a result, it is a creative response rather than a coping response.

Michael Dell, founder and chairman of the Board of Directors of Dell Computer Corporation, did not have the option of using the retail channel when he started making and selling computers at age 19 in his college dorm room. Instead, he advertised in PC publications and sold custom-built computers through the mail. Customers saved money because Dell's prices did not include the middleman markup of 10 percent to 15 percent. Dell's direct-sales model is frequently cited as one of the most successful innovations in the PC industry. The company's mental model for doing business is based on maximum efficiency, a cash conversion cycle, meeting customers' needs, and providing excellent service. Most PC companies would agree that these goals are important, but not all of them turn this espoused theory into a theory in action as Dell did. For example, Dell makes each machine to order and maintains only four days of inventory while IBM has 20 days and HP has 28.[13] In 2005, one in 6 computers in the world were built by Dell.[14] Dell reports that it needs only four days to get parts and build and ship a computer to a customer.[15] Its direct link to customers provides the company with extensive firsthand information on customer needs. Dell was the first to sell computers on the Web, and its Web page was geared to a global market at a time when some of its competitors had nothing more than an 800 number on their Web pages. Dell's structure is segmented by customer sets, which are further subdivided when a unit grows too large so as not to lose focus. As Morton Topfer, Dell's vice chairman, noted, "Some people still measure themselves by how many people work for them or how many dollars they generate. At Dell success means growing so fast that we take half your business away. It's a different mind-set."[16] While the company has had its share of missteps, it has been quick to learn from them and get back on track. At present, Dell is focused on regaining its after-sales customer service reputation, damaged by managing costs (outsourcing call centers abroad and hiring temporary workers) rather than quality and service.[17] Time will tell if Dell's generative learning and mental models continue to produce performance measures that are higher than the industry averages.

Organizations must be careful not to rely on "old programming," obsolete mental maps, and adaptive learning. Companies that are unlikely to survive in a rapidly changing environment not only limit themselves to adaptive learning, they may even punish generative learning. There are numerous examples of employees who leave large, unresponsive corporations to form successful, competing companies where they can put their knowledge and ideas to work. Organizational cultures that stifle creativity and innovation are sometimes accused of playing the "whack the gopher game." [18] People who stick their necks out by asking questions that threaten defensive routines or by making radical suggestions get "whacked."

Some organizations employ *parallel learning structures, which are defined as part of the organization that operates alongside the normal bureaucracy with the purpose of increasing organizational learning by creating and/or implementing new thoughts and behaviors.* Parallel learning structures consist of "a steering committee and a number of small groups with norms and operating procedures that promote a climate conducive to innovation, learning, and group problem solving" that is not possible within the larger bureaucracy. [19] For example, one fast-growing semiconductor company created a parallel learning structure that focused on organizational adaptation to a competitive and stagnant market. The parallel structure came up with solutions that the larger organization then implemented.

MANAGING THE LEARNING PROCESS

To conclude, let us examine how managers and organizations can explicitly manage their learning process. We have seen that the experiential learning model is useful not only for examining the educational process but also for understanding managerial problem solving and organizational adaptation. But how can an awareness of the experiential learning model and our own individual learning style help improve individual and organizational learning? Two recommendations seem important.

First, learning should be an explicit objective that is pursued as consciously and deliberately as profit or productivity. Managers and organizational member should budget time to learn from their experiences. When important meetings are held or important decisions are made, time should be set aside to critique and learn from these events. All too few organizations have a climate that allows for free exploration of such questions as "What have we learned from this venture?" Usually, active experimentation norms dictate "We don't have time; let's move on."

This leads to the second recommendation. The nature of the learning process is such that opposing perspectives—action and reflection, concrete involvement, and analytical detachment—are all essential for optimal learning. When one perspective comes to dominate others, learning effectiveness is reduced. From this we can conclude that the most effective learning systems are those that can tolerate differences in perspective. This point can be illustrated by the case of an electronics firm that we have worked with over the years. The firm was started by a group of engineers with a unique product. For several years they had no competitors, and when some competition entered the market, they continued to dominate and do well because of their superior engineering quality. Today they are faced with stiff competition in their original product area, and, in addition, their very success has caused new problems. They are no longer a small intimate company but a large organization with plants around the world. The company has had great difficulty in responding to these changes because it still responds to problems primarily from an engineering point of view. Most of the top executives in the company are former engineers with no formal management training. Many of the specialists in marketing, finance, and personnel who have been brought in to help the organization solve its new problems feel like "second-class citizens." Their ideas just don't seem to carry much weight. What was once the organization's strength, its engineering expertise, has become to some extent its weakness. Because engineering has flourished at the expense of the development of other organizational functions such as marketing and the management of human resources, the firm is today struggling with, rather than mastering, its environment. As this example illustrates, effectively managing the learning process clearly has become a key competitive activity for managers who wish to ensure that their organization continues to flourish.

CLASS ACTIVITY: THE LEARNING STYLE INVENTORY

The objective of this exercise is to map and understand the individual learning styles in the classroom. (Time allotted: 1 hour)

STEP 1.   Individual self-assessment. (5 minutes) students should individually review their Learning Style Inventory (LSI) scores in the light of what they now know about learning styles and their own personal experiences in learning (e.g., their educational background, current job function, and positive and negative learning experiences).

   a. With this broader perspective, individuals should alter their position on the learning style type grid in Exhibit 3-2 on page 54 to reflect their current best judgment as to the learning style that best describes them. Do this by placing an X on the grid spot that best defines your learning style. You may agree with the position indicated by your LSI score. If so, place the X on top of the point of intersection you calculated earlier with the AC-CE and AE-RO scores. Or you may feel you are really farther away from or closer to the center or even in a different quadrant. If so, move the X accordingly.

STEP 2.   Visual representation of class learning styles. (10 minutes)

   a. Create a learning style grid large enough for the entire class to stand on. Using masking tape for the axes, create the grid on the floor of an open area.

   b. Individual group members should stand on this floor grid in the position corresponding to the X position they marked in Step 1.

   c. Look around and see how students are distributed on the grid.

STEP 3.   Group discussion on learning styles. (20 minutes)

   a. With their closest neighbors on the grid, students should form small groups of five to six people with homogeneous learning styles.

   b. Discuss the following questions, ensuring that all members have an opportunity to share their opinions. Please answer questions 2 and 3 based on your personal experience rather than the Workbook content. Take notes on the answers so a group representative can report your thoughts to the class as a whole.

   1. Do your learning profile scores seem valid to you? How do you characterize the way in which you learn? Does your learning style profile relate to the way you went about the recent learning situation you described in the pre-work assignment?

   2. What do you think is your greatest strength as a learner?

   3. What is your greatest weakness?

STEP 4.   Reports to the total group. (25 minutes) A representative of each small group should briefly report to the total group:

   a. Where each group stood on the grid.

   b. The main points of each group discussion—the content of the meeting.

   c. Observations about the process of the group meeting. How did it feel to be in a group of individuals who had learning styles similar to yours? Was the group's learning style reflected in the way the meeting ran? Do you prefer being in a group with similar or mixed learning styles?

   d. What connection can you make between this exercise and the readings for today's class?

Accommodating	Diverging
When there are too many accommodators:	When there are too many divergers:
• Trivial improvements	• Paralyzed by alternatives
• Meaningless activity	• Cannot make decisions
When there are too few accommodators:	When there are too few divergers:
• Work is not completed on time	• Lack of ideas
• Impractical plans	• Inability to recognize opportunities and problems
• Work is not goal-directed	
Converging	**Assimilating**
When there are too many convergers:	When there are too many assimilators:
• Solving the wrong problems	• Castles in the air
• Hasty decision making	• No practical applications
When there are too few convergers:	When there are too few assimilators:
• Lack of focus	• Unable to learn from mistakes
• No testing of ideas or theories	• No sound basis for work
• Scattered thoughts	• No systematic approach

EXHIBIT 3-6 **What Happens When There Are Too Many or Too Few People with Each Learning Style in an Organization**

CREATING A DIVERSE LEARNING COMMUNITY

The purpose of this activity is to form diverse learning groups in which you will work for the rest of the semester. (Time allotted: 45 minutes)

STEP 1.   Form learning groups of no more than six members. You probably already know how to work with people like you. Diversity should be the criterion for group composition because this will maximize your learning. Try to have at least one person from each of the four learning styles and people of different ages, genders, races, nationalities, occupations, and majors. Unless your instructor indicates otherwise, stand up and move around the room until you've created heterogenous groups that meet with everyone's approval. (10 minutes)

STEP 2.   In your learning group discuss your answers to the class preparation questions. (20 minutes)
   a.   What was your best group learning experience? What was good about it?
   b.   What was your worst group learning experience? What made it that way?
   c.   In your opinion, what conditions promote adult learning?
   d.   How could we turn this classroom into a highly effective learning organization?

STEP 3.   The group chooses one or more spokespersons who report the results of the group's discussion of questions c and d.

STEP 4.   The class and the instructor come to a consensus on how they will develop a learning organization in the classroom. (15 minutes)

 **LEARNING POINTS**

1. The rapid degree of change in today's business environment means that the ability of a company's managers to learn faster than their competitors is a key competitive advantage. Continuous learning is, therefore, a necessity for both individuals and organizations.

2. A learning organization is an organization skilled at creating, acquiring, and transferring knowledge, and at modifying its behavior to reflect new knowledge and insights.

3. Adult learning:
   a. Is based on reciprocity.
   b. Is based on experience.
   c. Has a problem-solving orientation.
   d. Is individualized and self-directed.
   e. Integrates learning and living.
   f. Needs to be applied.

4. The adult learning process is a cycle composed of the following modes: concrete experience, reflective observation, abstract conceptualization, and active experimentation. The process is both concrete and abstract, both reflective and active.

5. Individuals usually see themselves as having a predisposition or a learned facility for one of the four styles in Kolb's learning model: divergence, assimilation, convergence, and accommodation.

6. Learning communities and organizations profit from having members with different learning styles because each style has its own particular strengths.

7. Some of the essential characteristics of learning organizations are systematic problem solving, experimentation, learning from past experience, learning from others, and transferring knowledge.

8. Argyris claims we have two types of theories: espoused theories that we profess to believe and theories in action that actually guide our behavior.

9. People develop defensive routines that prevent them from questioning the validity of the assumptions underlying espoused theories and theories in action.

10. Adaptive learning (single-loop learning) has a coping orientation and focuses on solving problems or making incremental improvements in the current way of doing business. It involves refining the prevailing mental model.

11. Generative learning (double-loop learning) has a creative orientation and involves surfacing and reviewing the underlying assumptions about the prevailing mental model. Generative learning involves continuous experimentation and feedback in an ongoing analysis of how organizations define and solve problems.

12. Parallel learning structures are part of the organization that operate alongside the normal bureaucracy with the purpose of increasing organizational learning by creating and/or implementing new thoughts and behaviors.

ACTION SCRIPTS

FOR EMPLOYEES

- Many highly successful people report that they are continuous learners. Experts learn as much as they can about their job and industry.
- They can develop other learning styles by carefully observing people with different styles and through the following practices.[20]
- Develop diverger skills by:
  - Being sensitive to people's feelings
  - Being sensitive to values
  - Listening with an open mind
  - Gathering information
  - Imagining the implications of ambiguous situations
- Develop assimilator skills by:
  - Organizing information
  - Testing theories and ideas
  - Building conceptual models
  - Designing experiments
  - Analyzing quantitative data
  - Drawing models of speakers' message and situations
- Develop converger skills by:
  - Coming up with different ways of doing things
  - Experimenting with new ideas
  - Choosing the best solution
  - Setting goals
  - Making decisions
- Develop accommodator skills by:
  - Committing to goals and following through on them
  - Seeking out new opportunities
  - Practicing influence skills to get goals accomplished
  - Volunteering to lead teams
  - Getting personally involved with people
- Team leaders can help guide the group through all the phases in the learning cycle.
- When learning style differences are the cause of conflict among coworkers, an appreciation of these differences can alleviate the problem. People with OB expertise are more likely to perceive style differences, rather than personality, as the source of conflict.
- Experts consider whether they should adapt their communication style, based on their target audience's preferred learning style. For instance, accommodators may prefer models, bulleted action recommendations, whereas assimilators prefer models, detailed facts, and figures.

FOR MANAGERS

- Managers who are experts at learning are aware of their personal learning style so that they understand how they approach work issues and how they react to others who have different styles.
- When training others (even if it's only breaking in a replacement), they remember that people have a tendency to assume that everyone learns the same way they do. Since this is not true, they find out how the trainee learns best and adapt their instruction accordingly.
- They ensure that people with different learning styles are valued for their strengths. If they find themseves in a situation where this is not the case, they may want to give the work team or the

management group the Learning Style Inventory so that the differences can be understood in a positive manner. The LSI is often used as an opening exercise in team-building efforts.

- Most project teams benefit from an understanding of the learning cycle—divergence, assimilation, convergence, and accommodation—and a somewhat orderly progression through it. This prevents the frustration that occurs when teams jump ahead or loop back too often.
- In order to create a learning organization, managers should:[21]
    - Make time to reflect on work events and assume the stance, "What can we learn from this?" for both themselves and their employees.
    - Treat failure as a natural part of the learning process, which then leads to improvement. Employees should not be afraid to experiment and fail.
    - Avoid allowing an elite group or single point of view to dominate organizational decision making.
    - Create a climate of openness and supportiveness so that employees feel enough psychological safety to raise questions and generate new ideas.
    - Encourage the expression of conflicting ideas and train employees in conflict resolution.
    - Share with employees the data on performance, quality, consumer satisfaction, and competitiveness, so they can reflect on the company situation and make informed decisions.
    - Use cross-functional teams to benefit from different approaches and expertise.
    - Create norms that encourage people to question assumptions and challenge the status quo.
    - Focus on systems thinking by looking for interrelationships, examining entire work processes, and looking beyond symptoms for root causes.

FOR ORGANIZATIONAL ARCHITECTS

- Organizational architects who are expert at managing learning create a culture that values learning and different perspectives.
- They set up mechanisms that encourage reflection and learning from experiences, such as debriefings, postmortems, and lessons-learned web sites.
- They foster a strategic approach to learning so the link between learning and performance is clear to employees.
- Action learning teams, composed of diverse employees, emphasize the importance of learning and model how it can take place.

PERSONAL APPLICATION ASSIGNMENT

The topic of this assignment is to think back on a previous learning experience that was significant to you. Choose an experience about which you are motivated to learn more; that is, there was something about it that you do not totally understand, that intrigues you, that made you realize that you lack certain skills, or that was problematical or significant for you. It may have been an academic or a nonformal educational experience (e.g., tennis camp, a seminar, on-the-job training program).

A. Concrete Experience

    1. Objectively describe the experience (who, what, when, where, how). (2 points)

2. Subjectively describe your feelings, perceptions, and thoughts that occurred during (not after) the experience. What did others seem to be feeling? (2 points)

B. Reflective Observation
  1. Looking back at the experience, what were the perspectives of the key actors (including you)? (2 points)
  2. Why did the people involved (including you) behave as they did? (2 points)

C. Abstract Conceptualization
  1. Relate concepts or theories from the assigned readings or the lecture to the experience. Explain thoroughly how they apply to your experience. Please apply at least two concepts or theories and cite them correctly). (4 points)

D. Active Experimentation

    1. What did you learn from this experience? (1 point)

    2. What did you learn about yourself? (1 point)

    3. What action steps will you take to be more effective in the future? (2 points)

E. Integration, Synthesis, and Writing

    1. Did you integrate and synthesize the four sections? (1 point)

    2. Was the Personal Application Assignment well written and easy to understand? (1 point)

    3. Was it free of spelling and grammar errors? (2 points)

ENDNOTES

[1] A. de Geus, "Planning as Learning... At Shell, Planning Means Changing Minds, Not Making Plans," *Harvard Business Review 66*(2) (1988) 70–75.

[2] J. S. Wyles, J. G. Kunkel, and A. C. Wilson, "Birds, Behavior, and Anatomical Evolution," *Proceedings of the National Academy of Sciences*, USA, July 1983.

[3] D. Kolb, *Experiential Learning: Experience as the Source of Learning and Development* (Upper Saddle River, NJ: Prentice-Hall, 1984).

[4] D. A. Kolb, R. E. Boyatzis, and C. Mainemelis. "Experiential Learning Theory: Previous Research and New Directions." In R. J. Sternberg and L. F. Zhang (eds.), *Perspectives on Cognitive, Learning, and Thinking Styles*. (NJ: Lawrence Erlbaum, 2000):228–247.

[5] The Learning Style Inventory is copyrighted by David A. Kolb (1976) and distributed by McBer and Co., 137 Newbury St., Boston, MA 02116. Further information on theory, construction, reliability, and validity of the inventory is reported in The *Learning Style Inventory: Technical Manual,* available from McBer and Co. The theory and its implications are found in Kolb's book, *Experiential Learning: Experience as the Source of Learning and Development* (Upper Saddle River, NJ: Prentice-Hall, 1984). See D. C. Kayes, "Experiential Learning and its Critics: Preserving the Role of Experience in Management Learning and Education." *Academy of Management Learning and Education, 1*(2) (2002): 137–149 for a recent review of this theory.

[6] H. Liam, *Contrary Imaginations* (New York: Schocken Books, 1966).

[7] Y. Yamazaki, "Learning Styles and Typologies of Cultural Differences: A Theoretical and Empirical Comparison," *International Journal of Intercultural Relations 29* (5) (2005): 521–548.

[8] D. Garvin, "Building a Learning Organization," *Harvard Business Review 71* (4) (1993): 78–92. M. A. Gephart, V. J. Marsick, M. E. Van Buren, M. S. Spriro, and P. Senge. "Learning Organizations Come Alive," *Training & Development 50* (12) (December, 1996): 34–46.

[9] P. Senge, A. Kleiner, C. Roberts, R. Ross, and B. Smith. *The Fifth Discipline Fieldbook: Strategies and Tools for Building a Learning Organization* (New York: Currency, 1993); and R. M. Fulmer, P. Gibbs, and J. B. Keys. "The Second Generation Learning Organizations: New Tools for Sustaining Competitive Advantage," *Organizational Dynamics 27* (2) (Autumn 1998): 6–21.

[10] J. F. Welch, "A Learning Company and Its Quest for Six Sigma," an executive speech reprint, presented at the General Electric Company 1997 Annual Meeting, Charlotte, North Carolina (April 23, 1997): 2–3.

[11] C. Argyris, *Reasoning, Learning, and Action* (San Francisco: Jossey-Bass, 1982).

[12] M. E. McGill, J. W. Slocum, Jr., and D. Lei, "Management Practices in Learning Organizations," *Organizational Dynamics 22*(1) (Summer 1992): 5–17.

[13] A. Serwer, A. Lustgarten, and J. Mero. "The Education of Michael Dell," *Fortune 151* (5) (March 7, 2005): 72–82; R. V. Kasturi and M. Bell, "Case Study: Dell Online," *Journal of Interactive Marketing 12* (4) (1988): 63–83.

[14] Serwer, Lustgarten, and Mero. "The Education of Michael Dell.

[15] B. Breen, "Living in Dell Time," *Fast Company 88* (November 2004): 86–92.

[16] L. M. Fisher, "Inside Dell Computer Corporation: Managing Working Capital," *Strategy & Business* (First Quarter, 1998): 68–75.

[17] D. Kirkpatrick, "Dell in the Penalty Box" CNN.Money.Com. (September 5, 2006). http://money.cnn.com/ magazines/ fortune/fortune_archive/2006/09/18/8386121/index.htm. Accessed 9/17/06.

[18] This metaphor is attributed to Peter DeLisi of Digital Equipment Corporation in E. H. Schein's article, "How Can Organizations Learn Faster? The Challenge of Entering the Green Room," *Sloan Management Review 34* (2) (Winter 1993): 85–94.

[19] G. R. Bushe and A. B. Rami Shani, *Parallel Learning Structures: Increasing Innovation in Bureaucracies* (Reading, MA: Addison-Wesley, 1991): 9–10.

[20] Adapted from D. Kolb, "Strengthening and Developing Learning Style Skills." Hay Group, 116 Huntington Ave., Boston, MA 02116. Not to be used without permission in writing from the Hay Group.

[21] These suggestions are taken primarily from R. Tanner Pascale, *Managing on the Edge* (New York: Simon & Schuster, 1991): 236 -37 and the works cited in this chapter: Senge's *The Fifth Discipline*; McGill's et al., "Management Practices"; Schein's "Organizations Learn Faster"; and Garvin's "Building a Learning Organization."

Chapter 4

▲▲▲

DECODING HUMAN BEHAVIOR AND PERSONALITY

OBJECTIVES By the end of this chapter, you should be able to:

A. Describe the major influences on individual behavior in organizations.

B. Discuss the Big 5 Model of personality and summarize the research on the model.

C. Identify the four dimensions of the Myers–Briggs Type Indicator.

D. Discuss the interactionist approaches to personality and use them to discern the roots of individual behavior.

E. Diagnose the causes of a "difficult" employee's behavior and identify appropriate responses.

BUZZSAWS AND WHISTLEBLOWERS

"Oh, no. Not again! Doesn't she ever give up? I guess the 'Buzzsaw' is back at it," sighed Chris, a vice-president for finance at Northco, reading yet another memo from Peri, a manager in his department. Peri's first memo had appeared a few months earlier and lived up to her reputation of plain speaking. It was full of dire warnings that the company was about to "implode in a wave of accounting scandals." According to Peri, financial disaster was imminent, and the company was at risk of criminal prosecution.

Chris thought back to Peri's last performance appraisal. He recalled that she was often impatient with people and could be merciless with her criticisms. One supervisor had even noted, "When someone says something she thinks is nonsensical, Peri goes for the jugular; then later, when she realizes she has embarrassed the person or that he might have something to contribute, Peri tries to stop the bleeding, but it's too late. He's got blood gushing down his shirtfront."[1] But Chris also remembered that Peri could be a top performer, often qualifying for exceptional bonuses and getting the job done even under extremely difficult conditions and pressures.

This latest memo from the Buzzsaw was more of the same, warning of catastrophe and disaster—the accounting problems had continued and even worsened. Accounting practices, at least according to Peri, looked highly questionable; losses were claimed as gains. Peri wrote, "One of the overriding principles of accounting is that if you explain the 'accounting treatment' to a man on the street, would you influence his decisions? Would he sell or buy the stock based on a thorough understanding of the facts? If so, you best present it correctly and/or change the accounting."[2] (An accounting treatment refers to how accountants decide to deal with a specific accounting problem.) She was certain that the company would be sued, suggesting, "This is horrific. The plaintiff attorneys will be celebrating."[3] Even worse, she accused the company's external law and accounting firms of willingly turning a blind eye to the supposedly problematic activities. Peri was planning to go to the head of Human Resources to request a meeting with the CEO to go over her memo.[4]

Suppose you are Chris. Take a few minutes to think about what your response to Peri might be. Would you advise her to learn how to "get along"? Would you assume that being hypercritical is just part of her personality and advise her to calm down and focus on her "real job"? Would you suggest that she speak with the CEO? Would you prefer that she simply drop the subject all together? Or perhaps you think she might benefit from some training on conflict resolution and interpersonal skills?

If, like many people, you did not encourage her to continue her protests, you may have inadvertently contributed to condoning illegal activities. Peri's story, in reality, is modeled on that of Sherron Watkins, the Enron employee who *did* go to the CEO with her concerns about accounting practices that were later determined to be illegal. Sherron Watkins was in fact nicknamed the "Buzzsaw," and the quotes about her are from her actual supervisor. The statements directly attributed to Peri are taken from real memos that Ms. Watkins wrote while an employee at Enron. And indeed, Arthur Andersen, the auditor of the firm, did condone unacceptable practices, was fined heavily, and ultimately, like Enron, went bankrupt.

Why would some people write Peri off as a complainer or a troublemaker? One reason is that we have a tendency to assume that people cause their own behavior, and we attribute the causes of that behavior to individual characteristics, such as personality traits and motivation. In doing so, we often downplay the importance of situational factors as causes of behavior. Yet behavior, and particularly behavior in organizations, is a complex function of both individual characteristics and situational factors. Thus, in Peri's example, certainly some of her behavior could be attributed to her distinctive character—yet much of it was due to the unique nature of the situation in which she found herself as part of an organization that was clearly skirting the edges of the law. Unless managers learn to decode employee behavior, they can make the wrong call with disastrous results.

CLASS PREPARATION

A. Complete the following personality inventory and score the results.
B. Think about whether you believe your results accurately describe your personality. If so, when are you most likely to act in ways that are consistent with the results? Are there times when this does not describe you? If the results seem inaccurate, what parts do you disagree with? Why?

C. Think about an experience you had working with a difficult coworker or boss. Why was that person difficult to work with? How did you handle the situation? What was the outcome?

D. Read the Donor Services Department on page 673 and write up your answers to these questions.
   1. What do you want to accomplish in this situation with respect to Juana?
   2. What is causing Juana to act as she does?
   3. How do you think Joanna views Juana and the situation? Why?
   4. If you were Joanna, how would you handle the situation?
   5. What exactly would you say to Juana if you decide to confront her?

E. As you read the chapter, come up with a list of cues that you will look for when decoding behavior at work.

Five Factor Model Personality Inventory

Please use the rating scale to describe how accurately each of the statements below describes *you*. Describe yourself honestly as you generally are now, not as you wish you were or hope to be in the future. Compare yourself to people of your sex and age. Circle the number of the response that best describes you.

Response Options

1: Very Inaccurate   **2**: Moderately Inaccurate   **3**: Neither Inaccurate nor Accurate
4: Moderately Accurate   **5**: Very Accurate

1.	I am the life of the party.	1	2	3	4	5
2.	I feel little concern for others.	1	2	3	4	5
3.	I am always prepared.	1	2	3	4	5
4.	I get stressed out easily.	1	2	3	4	5
5.	I have a rich vocabulary.	1	2	3	4	5
6.	I don't talk a lot.	1	2	3	4	5
7.	I am interested in people.	1	2	3	4	5
8.	I leave my belongings around.	1	2	3	4	5
9.	I am relaxed most of the time.	1	2	3	4	5
10.	I have difficulty understanding abstract ideas.	1	2	3	4	5
11.	I feel comfortable around people.	1	2	3	4	5
12.	I insult people.	1	2	3	4	5
13.	I pay attention to details.	1	2	3	4	5
14.	I worry about things.	1	2	3	4	5
15.	I have a vivid imagination.	1	2	3	4	5
16.	I keep in the background.	1	2	3	4	5
17.	I sympathize with others' feelings.	1	2	3	4	5
18.	I make a mess of things.	1	2	3	4	5
19.	I seldom feel blue.	1	2	3	4	5
20.	I am not interested in abstract ideas.	1	2	3	4	5
21.	I start conversations.	1	2	3	4	5
22.	I am not interested in other people's problems.	1	2	3	4	5
23.	I get chores done right away.	1	2	3	4	5
24.	I am easily disturbed.	1	2	3	4	5
25.	I have excellent ideas.	1	2	3	4	5
26.	I have little to say.	1	2	3	4	5
27.	I have a soft heart.	1	2	3	4	5
28.	I often forget to put things back in their proper place.	1	2	3	4	5
29.	I get upset easily.	1	2	3	4	5
30.	I do not have a good imagination.	1	2	3	4	5
31.	I talk to a lot of different people at parties.	1	2	3	4	5
32.	I am not really interested in others.	1	2	3	4	5
33.	I like order.	1	2	3	4	5
34.	I change my mood a lot.	1	2	3	4	5

35. I am quick to understand things.	1	2	3	4	5
36. I don't like to draw attention to myself.	1	2	3	4	5
37. I take time out for others.	1	2	3	4	5
38. I shirk my duties.	1	2	3	4	5
39. I have frequent mood swings.	1	2	3	4	5
40. I use difficult words.	1	2	3	4	5
41. I don't mind being the center of attention.	1	2	3	4	5
42. I feel others' emotions.	1	2	3	4	5
43. I follow a schedule.	1	2	3	4	5
44. I get irritated easily.	1	2	3	4	5
45. I spend time reflecting on things.	1	2	3	4	5
46. I am quiet around strangers.	1	2	3	4	5
47. I make people feel at ease.	1	2	3	4	5
48. I am exacting in my work.	1	2	3	4	5
49. I often feel blue.	1	2	3	4	5
50. I am full of ideas.	1	2	3	4	5

Scoring the survey:

Add the numbers you circled for items #1, 11, 21, 31, and 41.

#1 _____   #11 _____   #21 _____   #31 _____   #41 _____ = **Subtotal A** _____

For items #6, 16, 26, 36, 46, subtract the number that you circled from 6. For example, if you circled 4, your score would be 2 (6 – 4 = 2). Using your newly obtained scores, add these five items.

6 – #6 _____ = _____
6 – #16 _____ = _____
6 – #26 _____ = _____
6 – #36 _____ = _____
6 – #46 _____ = _____

        Subtotal B = _____

Subtotal A _____ + **Subtotal B** _____ = **Total Extraversion** _____

Add the numbers you circled for items #7, 17, 27, 37, 42, and 47.

#7 _____   #17 _____   #27 _____   #37 _____   #42 _____   #47 _____ = **Subtotal A** _____

For items #2, 12, 22, 32, subtract the number that you circled from 6. For example, if you circled 4, your score would be 2 (6 – 4 = 2). Using your newly obtained scores, add these four items.

6 – #2 _____ = _____
6 – #12 _____ = _____
6 – #22 _____ = _____
6 – #32 _____ = _____

        Subtotal B = _____

Subtotal A _____ + **Subtotal B** _____ = **Total Agreeableness** _____

Add the numbers you circled for items #3, 13, 23, 33, 43, and 48.

3 ____   #13 ____   #23 ____   #33 ____   #43 ____   #48 ____ = **Subtotal A** ____

For items #8, 18, 28, and 38, subtract the number that you circled from 6. For example, if you circled 4, your score would be 2 (6 – 4 = 2). Using your newly obtained scores, add these four items.

6 – #8   ____ = ____
6 – #18 ____ = ____
6 – #28 ____ = ____
6 – #38 ____ = ____

     Subtotal B = ____

Subtotal A ____ + **Subtotal B** ____ = **Total Conscientiousness** ____

Add the numbers you circled for items #9 and 19.

#9 ____   #19 ____ = **Subtotal A** ____

For items #4, 14, 24, 29, 34, 39, 44, and 49, subtract the number that you circled from 6. For example, if you circled 4, your score would be 2 (6 – 4 = 2). Using your newly obtained scores, add these eight items.

6 – #4   ____ = ____
6 – #14 ____ = ____
6 – #24 ____ = ____
6 – #29 ____ = ____
6 – #34 ____ = ____
6 – #39 ____ = ____
6 – #44 ____ = ____
6 – #49 ____ = ____

     Subtotal B = ____

Subtotal A ____ + **Subtotal B** ____ = **Total Emotional Stability (neuroticism)** ____

Add the numbers you circled for items #5, 15, 25, 35, 40, 45, and 50.

#5 ___ #15 ___ #25 ___ #35 ___ #40 ___ #45 ___ #50 ___ = **Subtotal A** ____

For items #10, 20, 30, subtract the number that you circled from 6. For example, if you circled 4, your score would be 2 (6 – 4 = 2). Using your newly obtained scores, add up these three items.

6 – #10 ____ = ____
6 – #20 ____ = ____
6 – #30 ____ = ____

     Subtotal B = ____

Subtotal A ____ + **Subtotal B** ____ = **Total Openness to Experience** ____

Interpreting the Survey:

Each factor of the Big 5 Personality Inventory (Extraversion, Agreeableness, Conscientiousness, Emotional Stability [neuroticism], and Openness to Experience) has a range of possible scores from 5–50. The higher the score, the more you perceive this characteristic as descriptive of your personality.

 **THE KNOWLEDGE BASE**

A man can be a star of the first magnitude in gifts, will power and endurance, but so well balanced that he turns with the system to which he belongs without any friction or waste of energy. Another may have the same great gifts, or even finer ones, but the axis does not pass precisely through the center and he squanders half his strength in eccentric movements which weaken him and disturb his surroundings.

Herman Hesse, The Glass Bead Game

Managers have to decode and understand employee behavior so they know what action to take. This is not a simple task because there are many different factors that influence behavior. Think for a moment about how you behave in a classroom. What causes you to behave that way? Of course, your own personal characteristics influence what you do. But so also do the other people in the class, the instructor, the physical configuration of the room, the norms of the school, the discipline you are studying, and the culture of which you are a part. In just the same way, an employee's behavior is influenced by a number of different factors. As we see in Exhibit 4–1, behavior is influenced by the individual, the job, the work group, the organization, and the culture. A manager trying to understand an employee's behavior needs to consider all of these. For example, at the individual level, personal characteristics such as abilities, motivation, and personality may affect behavior. The job an employee performs affects how that person behaves. For example, regardless of their personalities, hospital nurses learn to be meticulous because errors are not tolerated in their job. Work-group characteristics such as norms, size, leadership, and structure also influence individual behavior. Reward systems, performance appraisal procedures, resources, and other organizational practices further impact how employees act. And all of these are impacted by the national, regional, and local culture to which they belong. Thus, managers need to take into account *both* the nature of the person and of the situation.

In this chapter, we will focus on one aspect of the individual, personality, to provide you with some tools to help you decode individual behavior. We will address the other components in Exhibit 4-1 elsewhere in the workbook.

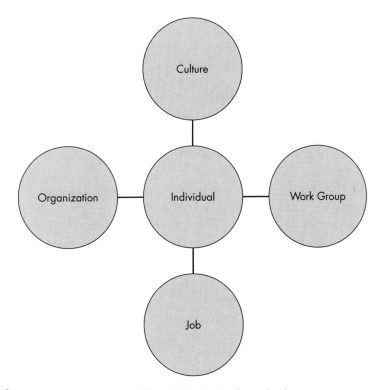

EXHIBIT 4-1 **Major Influences on Individual Behavior in Organizations**

Some managers view personality as the answer to all their dilemmas. Indeed, the personality testing business is a $400-million-a-year industry—suggesting that these managers are hardly alone in their views.[5] If it were possible to assess an individual's personality by asking a person to fill out a questionnaire and then predict that person's actions and thoughts with 100 percent certainty, it would truly be a gold mine for managers! It would be easy to assign people to jobs, form teams, match sales representatives with customers, and effectively handle all sorts of currently thorny organizational problems. Of course, in reality, personality has proven to be much more difficult to both identify with certainty and use in organizations. By the end of this chapter, we hope that you will have an informed view of personality and its components and understand how to apply this knowledge in organizations.

Personality can be defined as *an individual's relatively stable characteristic patterns of thought, emotion, and behavior, and the psychological mechanisms that support and drive those patterns.*[6] Current thinking on how personality develops emphasizes both genetic and environmental origins. Heredity does seem to play a role in personality development. Parents frequently comment that their children had unique personalities from a very early age, despite their parenting efforts. Although the family setting and life circumstances play a role in shaping personality, people are not passive recipients of environmental influences.[7] Even children are active creators of their own personalities because they can influence others' reactions and initiate their own social interactions. Adults likewise play a role in their own development by actively choosing the organizations they join, the jobs they take, the activities they participate in, and so forth. Thus, both nature (genetic) and nurture (environmental and situational aspects such as family, culture, and geographic location) factors play important roles in personality development.

Theories of personality vary in the emphasis they place on the importance of the nature of the individual and the importance of the situation or environment in determining personality and, ultimately, behavior. *Trait* theories, which emphasize the components of personality, tend to highlight the importance of individual characteristics in determining behavior and de-emphasize the role of the situation or environment. *Interactionist* theories emphasize the importance of the characteristics of the situation as well as the nature of the individual in understanding and predicting behavior.

TRAIT MODELS

Traits refer to broad, relatively regular dimensions of individual behavior.[8] When we describe someone as extroverted, aggressive, confident, or conscientious, we are using personality traits to characterize that person. *Trait models*, or theories, assume that personality is composed of a relatively stable set of traits or dimensions. According to these theories, although all individuals have these traits, people vary in the degree to which they exhibit specific dimensions. The theories differ, however, in the traits they consider to be the core components of personality. We will consider two popular trait theories, the Big Five Model and the Myers–Briggs Type Indicator (MBTI), as well as several other personality trait theories that have traditionally been of interest to managers.

The Big Five Model

Personality research has been compared to a search for the ultimate traits that define the human disposition. Trait research in the early part of the twentieth century was characterized by an ever-growing list of personality dimensions. This type of research typically involved asking people to complete questionnaires that measured various traits. The usefulness of this approach, however, was questioned when research failed to demonstrate strong linkages between traits and behavior such as job performance.[9] In the last few decades, additional research and more sophisticated analytical techniques have been used to support an emerging consensus among advocates that five factors or traits are the major structural units of personality. Called the Big Five Model, or the Five-Factor Model, this approach holds that personality is comprised of the "OCEAN" dimensions:[10]

- **Openness to experience:** This dimension refers to the extent that people actively seek out new and varied experiences and the extent to which they are aware of their thoughts, feelings, and impulses and are able to be attentive to many of them simultaneously.[11]

- **Conscientiousness:** People who are conscientious tend to be dependable and trustworthy and conform to social norms.[12]
- **Extroversion:** Extroversion refers to how outgoing, sociable, and assertive people are. Extroverts may also be very active and energetic, having many interests and hobbies.[13]
- **Agreeableness:** This dimension captures the extent to which people are likable, cooperative, and considerate.[14]
- **Neuroticism:** Neuroticism, also called emotional stability, in the Big Five approach refers to the tendency to experience chronic negative emotions such as worry, insecurity, self-pity, poor self-image, and mood swings.[15]

Of these five dimensions, conscientiousness appears to have the strongest relation to overall job performance across a wide variety of jobs.[16] People who score high on the conscientiousness dimension also may set higher goals for themselves, have higher performance expectations for other people, have greater motivation, be more satisfied in their jobs, and have higher occupational status than people who score low on this dimension.[17] There is some evidence that neuroticism or emotional stability is negatively related to performance.[18] Other personality dimensions appear to relate to performance in specific types of jobs. Extroversion may be related to performance in a sales job, where there is a high competitive and social component. Agreeableness may be related to performance in jobs where cooperation is necessary.[19] Openness to experience has not been a predictor of job performance,[20] although it may be a good selection criteria for international work. It is important to note that the effect of personality on these types of behavior is moderate rather than very strong.[21]

The Five-Factor Model has both its merits and its limitations. The questionnaire used to assess an individual is easy to administer and is of relatively low cost to be some stability in the dimensions for North Americans and Western Europeans. However, this model may not apply to all cultures. For example, studies of Italians show three rather than five dimensions. Research conducted in other cultures shows six, seven, and even nine dimensions.[22] Moreover, the same dimensions can have different meanings in different cultures.[23] The five-factor approach has also been criticized because it sometimes produces results that are not consistent across time or situations. In addition, the factors may exert only weak influences on behavior, which lessens the model's predictive ability.[24]

The Myers–Briggs Type Indicator

The *Myers–Briggs Type Indicator* (MBTI) is a personality profile partially based on psychologist Carl Jung's theory of personality. According to *Workforce Management*, the MBTI is administered over 2.5 million times a year.[25] The test is available in 19 different languages[26] and is used for a variety of organizational purposes including team building, management and leadership development, career counseling, hiring decisions, and performance effectiveness training.[27] For example, Dow Chemical's Polyolefin and Elastomers unit uses the MBTI to assign employees to tasks on various stages of the product development cycle.[28]

The MBTI suggests that there are four important components to personality:

- **Extroversion/Introversion (E/I)** This refers to how the individual interacts socially. Extroverts are outgoing and sociable, whereas introverts are shy and prefer to be alone.
- **Sensing/Intuiting (S/N)** This factor measures how people prefer to collect information. Those who score toward the sensing end of the dimension prefer to use their five senses to systematically obtain factual information. Intuitive individuals use instinct and subjective perception.
- **Thinking/Feeling (T/F)** This dimension captures how people evaluate information. Thinking types prefer to rely on logic and analysis, whereas feeling types rely more on their own and other people's reactions.
- **Judging/Perceiving (J/P)** This dimension refers to how people like to make decisions. Individuals who score on the judging end of the dimension are planners and like to control the decision-making process. Perceivers are more flexible, spontaneous, and adaptive in their decision style.

The MBTI is scored by combining all four pairs of traits into a matrix of 16 personality types. Individuals are categorized into one of the types based on how they respond on the test. The personality type represents the individual's preferences in the four separate categories, with each category composed of two opposite poles. According to the MBTI, each personality type has its preferred way of responding to the environment and its own set of strengths and weaknesses. For example, people whose personality type is ESTJ are focused on getting things done smoothly and efficiently. As an SJ, they have a core need for seeking the good of the community, a sense of belonging, and learning from the past. Conversely, an ENTJ focuses on implementing new ideas and challenges and is concerned primarily with competence and intellectual resourcefulness.[29]

Despite its popularity, there is little evidence supporting the MBTI as a valid personality measure. As such, managers are wise to be cautious in their use and interpretation of the MBTI.[30] Some researchers are attempting to construct more valid measures of the personality types by developing questionnaires that assess how people respond in different situations. For example, the Singer–Loomis Type Development Inventory asks people to indicate how they would respond in twenty different situations.[31]

Other Personality Traits

Self-esteem is the degree of regard people have for themselves.[32] Individuals high in self-esteem tend to be more satisfied in their jobs than those who are low in self-esteem. High self-esteem individuals also tend to be more resistant to influence.

Machiavellianism takes its name from Niccolo Machiavelli, author of a sixteenth-century treatise on power. People who are high in Machiavellianism believe that the ends justify the means and that manipulation is an acceptable way to influence other people. They also tend to be emotionally distant.[33]

Locus of control (see Setting the Global Stage) refers to the beliefs people have about why things happen to them. People with an internal locus of control tend to believe that they control their own fate and destiny. In contrast, people with an external locus of control tend to think that luck, chance, or other environmental factors control what happens to them.[34]

Summary of the Trait Approach

As we have seen, the trait approach is extremely popular in organizations. However, this perspective should be used with caution and with a clear understanding of just what the results can and cannot reliably tell managers. It is important to note that many of the relationships between personality traits and behavior are of moderate strength, at best. Moreover, most of the research studies have been correlational or observational in nature and are unable to determine whether personality causes behavior or vice versa. For example, we noted that neuroticism/emotional instability was associated with low performance. But we cannot tell if emotional instability caused low performance or if low performance caused the individual to report emotional instability. Managers should also carefully consider the legality of any personality tests that they may use. Some tests have been challenged on the basis of invasion of privacy and on discrimination of minorities. Another important point to remember is that labeling people according to their personality profile or type can result in yet another instance of the self-fulfilling prophecy discussed in Chapter 1. For example, one company actually required employees to wear badges revealing how they scored on a personality test.[35] We can easily see how a manager might perceive employees differently based on their badge type and that this, in turn, might result in employees responding in ways that confirm the manager's expectations. Simply knowing a person's score on a test can impact how others' perceive that individual and, in turn, how that person behaves. This highlights yet another critical issue: The nature of the situation can exert powerful influences on behavior. The interactionist models of personality discussed in the next section explicitly take this factor into account.

INTERACTIONIST MODELS

Like trait models, *interactionist models* hypothesize that personality is an important factor in determining an individual's behavior. They go a step further, however, and argue that situational factors can powerfully shape how that individual responds. We will consider two such models, the conditional reasoning approach and the cognitive–affective processing system.

The Conditional Reasoning Approach

The *conditional reasoning* approach suggests that individuals interpret what happens in their social environment based on their individual dispositions. These dispositions are a type of mental map. Individuals differ in their motives, in how they frame the world, and the assumptions that they make regarding events. In turn, these differences result in different types of behavior because people use different justification mechanisms to decide how best to adjust to their environment.[36]

Let's consider how two people with different dispositional motives might react. Ana is high in achievement motivation, which means she is motivated to succeed.[37] She very much believes that personal factors are important causes of performance and values hard work, learning, and experience. For Ana, a challenge is something to be met with confidence and even excitement. She is predisposed, according to the conditional reasoning approach, to believe that she is personally accountable for her success or failure and that she should take initiative to overcome the challenge. In contrast, Jay is high in fear of failure. Jay might also believe that his failure is due to external factors that are outside his control (e.g., a poor manager, irresponsible coworkers, etc.). For Jay, demanding tasks are a source of stress and anxiety. Instead of an opportunity to show what he can do, Jay believes a challenge will be a sure-fire way to demonstrate just how incompetent he really is. Thus, unlike Ana, Jay's primary reaction to a challenge would be avoidance. He might even reason that those who take a more relaxed approach are less likely to show signs of burnout or fatigue.

The conditional reasoning approach is a contingency model because it assumes that responses to situations depend on the personality of the individual faced with the situation. Individuals who are high in achievement motivation will react more positively to the idea of starting their own businesses than will individuals who are high in fear of failure. They will also more likely be drawn to some types of situations (e.g., situations where they can demonstrate exceptional performance) and to avoid other types of situations (e.g., ones where performance measurement is ambiguous). Indeed, according to the attraction–selection–attrition framework, different individuals will be attracted to different situations or organizations, will be selected by and become successful in different organizations, and will avoid or leave various types of organizations and situations depending on their preferences.[38]

As with all models, the conditional reasoning approach has both its strengths and its weaknesses. By taking into account how individuals make sense of their social environment, it underscores the importance of understanding individual motives and needs. However, it does not allow us to fully understand how the same individual might act differently in similar situations nor how dispositions change over time. Because little research has been conducted on this theory, it remains a promising direction for future development.

The Cognitive–Affective Processing System of Personality

The *cognitive-affective processing system* (CAPS) is depicted in Exhibit 4–2.[39] According to this model, the personality system is comprised of mental representations called cognitive–affective units (CAUs), which are defined as interpretations of people and situations, goals, expectancies, memories, and feelings. People differ in the content of these representations, in how accessible they are, and in how they are related to one another. These representations are affected by a rich array of factors, which include genetic, cultural, societal, and developmental components.

As an individual experiences various situations, different representations or CAUs become activated and are expressed in different behavioral responses. In other words, individuals act according to if–then types of relations, depending on the particular CAUs activated by the situation. Because individuals have different mental if–then relations, they also have differing patterns of behavior.[40]

According to the model, people will also interpret situations differently—even the same situation might be construed quite differently by people with different mental representations and different emotions. Thus, various people will pay attention to different features of the situation, interpret them both cognitively and affectively (emotionally) in different ways, and ultimately behave differently. This means that the relevant features of situations must be understood from the individual's point of view. Different cues will activate different patterns of behavior. Consider the example of Scott and how he reacts to criticism. In one instance, Scott reacts very aggressively—questioning the criticizer's motives and intelligence. In another case, Scott reacts quite passively—easily accepting the criticism and even offering suggestions for how to do things differently. What's going on here? In the first instance, Scott was criticized by peers and reacted quite defensively. Thus, the if–then relationship Scott used was, "If I am criticized by my peers, I have no reason to defer to them because they have no authority over me and have no right to criticize me." In the second instance, Scott was criticized by his manager. Here, his if–then profile might have been, "If I am criticized by my manager, I should accept what she says and try to improve." Clearly, other people might have different if–then rules for the same situations, prompting different behavioral reactions and judgments of that behavior by observers. This is one reason we often hear people commenting, "I never would have acted like that in his or her place."

How might this be used in organizations? The important point would be to identify features of the situations that are relevant to the employees in the organization and which trigger different

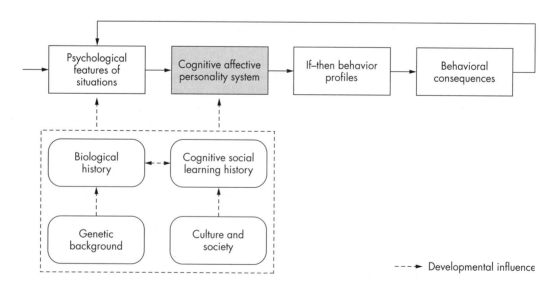

EXHIBIT 4-2 The Cognitive–Affective Personality System

Adapted from W. Mischel and Y. Shoda, "A Cognitive-Affective System Theory of Personality: Reconceptualizing Situations, Dispositions, Dynamics, and Invariance in Personality Structure," *Psychological Review 102* (2) (1995): 246–68.

patterns of if–then relations and behavior. Of course, this means that managers must understand how their employees view the particular situation and the organization—a process that can be quite labor intensive and time consuming.

Like other models of personality, this perspective has both its strengths and its weaknesses. The model is relatively comprehensive in its attempt to develop a model of personality that draws on individual, situational, and cultural influences. Although some research findings support the model,[41] much more work is needed to fully test it. Moreover, its application to organizational settings needs to be examined.

Summary of the Interactionist Approach

The interactionist models we discussed above explicitly look at how the nature of the individual's environment might interact with the individual's personality to influence behavior. These models emphasize the complex relationship between the individual and the setting. It is important to remember that they also emphasize that it is the individual's interpretation of key features of the situation that affects their behavior and that individual interpretations may have little or nothing in common. Indeed, individuals often interpret the same situation quite differently. These models suggest that managers must pay attention to how their employees interpret key features of their environments and understand what behaviors the employees feel are justified or appropriate in those situations.

Let's reconsider the opening vignette and our story of Peri. Taking the interactionist approach, Chris, her manager, might first look at Peri's interpretation of the situation as well as Peri's personality. Is Peri's prickly personality coming into play here? Is she simply overreacting to what she sees as less-than-perfect work? Or is the situation itself truly what is driving Peri's reactions? Are there problems that really need to be addressed? Clearly, a manager would need to do some detective work to discern the underlying causes of employee behavior. In reality, most behavior will be affected by multiple factors. Expert managers pay attention to the critical cues in each situation. Suppose you are Peri's manager. What cues would you pay attention to, and what action scripts would you employ?

This type of analysis helps managers develop an understanding of the rich complexity of human behavior, a skill that is especially critical in dealing with "difficult" people. One advice book gives examples of how to handle 30 different categories of difficult people in the workplace![42] Hopefully, we're only plagued with a few of them.

DEALING WITH "DIFFICULT" PEOPLE

When asked which work activities made them most uncomfortable, 73 percent of managers said that building relationships with people they dislike was their most worrying and troublesome chore.[43] Yet we have seen that effectively managing relationships with superiors, peers, and subordinates is one of the most critical tasks that managers face.

What can you do when you are confronted with a "difficult" person? Nigel Nicholson notes that managers are tempted to "sell" their viewpoint to that person or just give up.[44] Neither of these strategies is likely to be effective. Instead, he suggests trying the following steps:

1. **Create a rich picture of the problem person** Remember that we tend to think that people cause their own behavior, and we tend to downplay other causes. Think about the following when trying to analyze the causes of the behavior.
   - **The problem person** What motivates this person? What drives her? What obstacles are preventing him from achieving what he wants? What would happen if those obstacles were removed? In addition, you might consider how often this behavior has occurred. Has it occurred in similar situations?[45]
   - **Yourself** What might you be doing to encourage the problem behavior? Are you unknowingly rewarding some behaviors and punishing others? Is there something that you do that sets the person on the wrong track?

- **The situation** What might be causing both you and the problem person to behave poorly? Is there something happening in the organization that might have an impact? Has the company recently gone through layoffs? Is competition increasing? Have you gotten a new boss? Was there something that triggered this behavior?

2. **Reframe your goals** Try to think flexibly about what you want to happen. For example, consider a situation in which an employee is dealing with a large amount of email requests from a low-priority customer group. The employee is becoming more and more frustrated with the workload. He wants to stop answering these email messages and insists that he can't handle them any more. Instead of simply demanding that the employee complete the tasks, you might think about what you really want to accomplish. You might decide that you want the employee to have less work but also meet the needs of the customers. By framing your goals in this way, you can open up possibilities that you might have ignored. For example, perhaps there are routine questions that could be answered in a Web page with Frequently Asked Questions (FAQs).

3. **Stage the encounter** Schedule a face-to-face meeting to discuss the issues. Acknowledge the person's value and then describe the problem behavior as you see it in factual terms. Avoid saying things like, "You are so rude!" Instead, you might say, "I noticed in the last staff meeting that you interrupted other people five times in the first 15 minutes of the meeting." Clearly indicate that the problem behavior cannot continue and suggest that you would like to work together to find a solution that is acceptable to both of you. Then, begin to discuss possible solutions.

4. **Follow Up** Set aside time to monitor and reward progress or take corrective action.

CLASS ACTIVITY: THE DONOR SERVICES CASE: WHAT TO DO ABOUT JUANA?

The purpose of this exercise is to help you develop your skills in handling situations with difficult people (Time allotted: 55-70 minutes).

STEP 1.   Role-Play Preparation (20–25 minutes)

a. Form into groups of six members (preferably your learning groups).

b. Select one person to play the role of Juana and one person to play the role of Joanna in the Donor Services Department at the end of the book. The remainder of the group will act first as advisors during the preparation stage and then as observers during the role-play. Two people should volunteer to help Juana prepare for the role-play, and two others will help Joanna.

c. In your subgroup, discuss your answers to the case questions that you prepared before class. Discuss how Joanna or Juana should behave in the role-play. You can assume that Joanna has asked to meet with Juana privately in her office. Be sure to read the "Guidelines for Role-Plays" for tips on conducting the role-play and using the Observer Worksheet.

Guidelines for Role Plays

Participation Tips

- Read the case and pay careful attention to the character's actions, feelings, and thoughts. Why does this character act, think, and feel this way?
- During your preparation, imagine how the characters in the role-play might act in different circumstances. Try to plan how you would respond.
- During the role-play, let the assumptions that you made about the character guide your reactions. If you are confronted with an unexpected development, simply react as you think the character might react. Use your imagination!
- Avoid looking at the instructions during the role-play. Once you start, just let yourself take over the role.
- If you are assigned the manager role, use the role-play as an opportunity to practice your managerial skills. Assume that the situation is real and that the characters are really experiencing the situation.
- In this case, if you are the difficult person, don't "ham it up" and exaggerate your role so much that it is impossible to deal with you.
- Talk loudly enough so observers can hear.

Observation Tips:

- Pay attention to both **content** (what is being discussed) and **process** (how the participants behave and how the role-play progresses).
- Use the observer worksheet to help guide what you pay attention to in the role-play. Observe both **what** the participants do and **how often** the participants act that way.
- When the role-play is over, you may be asked to give the participants feedback. If so, try to use the following guidelines for giving constructive feedback:
  - Start by discussing what went well during the role-play.
  - Before giving your own ideas about how the role-play might have been better, ask the participants what they would do differently if they had the chance to "do it over."
  - Focus on actual behaviors and be specific rather than evaluative. For example, "You abruptly contradicted her three times" rather than "You were demeaning!"
  - If possible, give specific recommendations about how the role-play could have been improved.
  - Ask for feedback about how you gave feedback!

Facilitation Tips for the Instructor Leader:

- Do everything you can to make the role-play seem real and help the participants become involved. Introduce the participants by their characters' names. Describe the setting discussed in the instructions as vividly and faithfully as you can.
- Remind the participants that the instructions are the starting point; they should use those as a springboard for what happens in the role-play.
- Minimize distractions so that the participants and observers can focus on the role-play.

Adapted from D. Johnson and F. Johnson, *Joining Together*, (Boston: Allyn and Bacon, 2003).

Observer Worksheet

a. Use the scale below to evaluate Joanna and Juana's role play performance: answer the numbered questions by writing the number corresponding to your evaluation of each participant in the appropriate boxes. Write out answers to the lettered questions in the appropriate columns. Write other observations in the Comments column.

1	2	3	4	5
Needs work		Satisfactory		Excellent

To what extent did the participants:	Joanna	Juana	Comments
1. Create a rich picture of the other person?			
a. What motivates the person? What role does personality play? What if–then rules does the person use?			
b. What obstacles does the person face?			
c. What are the other person's real goals?			
2. Acknowledge how the participant's own character contributed to the problem?			
a. Did the character unknowingly reward some behaviors and punish others? Is there something that character did that set the person on the wrong track?			
b. Are there other ways that the character is contributing to the problem?			
3. Acknowledge the role of the situation?			
a. What might be causing both characters to behave poorly? Is there something happening in the organization that might have an impact?			
b. Was there something that triggered this behavior?			
4. Discuss the other person's behavior rather than focusing on personal traits or attributes?			

b. Answer the following questions.

What went well in this interaction?

What needed improvement?

Did you notice anything else that seems significant?

STEP 2.   Role-Play (15 minutes)

    a. In this step, Juana will go to Joanna's "office" and they will enact the meeting. All other group members should observe the role-play and critique it using the Observer Worksheet.

STEP 3.   Debriefing the Role-Play (20–30 minutes)

    a. What role did personality play in Joanna and Juana's analysis of each other's behavior? What about the role of the situation? What theories of personality did each person seem to be using to make sense of the situation?

    b. To what extent did Joanna and Juana try to follow the guidelines for dealing with difficult people? Did they:

       1. Create a rich picture of the other person?

       2. Understand what the other person's real goals were?

       3. Discuss the other person's behavior rather than focusing on personal traits or attributes?

    c. Did you observe anything that seemed to trigger a positive reaction by Juana or Joanna?

    d. Did you observe anything that seemed trigger a negative reaction by Juana or Joanna? How could that have been avoided?

    e. Was there anything else that could be improved? On Joanna's part? On Juana's part?

    f. Did Joanna and Juana arrive at an agreement? Do you think they solved the problem? Why or why not?

    g. What else did you learn from the role-play?

 **LEARNING POINTS**

1. An individual's behavior is influenced by characteristics of the individual, the job, the work group, the organization, and the culture. A manager trying to understand an employee's behavior needs to consider all of these.

2. Personality can be defined as an individual's relatively stable characteristic patterns of thought, emotion, and behavior, and the psychological mechanisms that support and drive those patterns.

3. Both nature (genetic) and nurture (environmental and situational aspects such as family, culture, and geographic location) factors likely play important roles in personality development.

4. Trait theories of personality emphasize the components of personality, highlight the importance of individual characteristics in determining behavior, and de-emphasize the role of the situation or environment.

5. Interactionist theories emphasize the importance of the characteristics of the situation as well as the nature of the individual in understanding and predicting behavior.

6. The Five-Factor Model holds that personality is comprised of the "OCEAN" dimensions:
   - *O*penness to experience actively seeking out new and varied experiences; awareness of one's thoughts, feelings, and impulses and able to be attentive to many of them simultaneously.
   - *C*onscientiousness dependable and trustworthy; conform to social norms.
   - *E*xtroversion outgoing, sociable, and assertive.[46]
   - *A*greeableness likable, cooperative, and considerate.
   - *N*euroticism (also called emotional stability) chronic negative emotions such as worry, insecurity, self-pity, poor self-image, and mood swings.

7. The Myers–Briggs Type Indicator (MBTI) is a personality profile partially based on psychologist Carl Jung's theory of personality. The MBTI suggests that there are four important components to personality that range along the following continua:

- Extroversion/Introversion (E/I) how the individual interacts socially.
- Sensing/Intuiting (S/N) how people prefer to collect information.
- Thinking/Feeling (T/F) how people evaluate information.
- Judging/Perceiving (J/P) how people like to make decisions.

8. The conditional reasoning approach suggests that individuals interpret what happens in their social environment differently based on their individual dispositions. These differences result in different types of behavior because people use different justification mechanisms to decide how best to adjust to their environment.

9. The cognitive–affective processing system (CAPS) holds that personality is comprised of mental representations called cognitive–affective units (CAUs), defined as interpretations of people and situations, goals, expectancies, memories, and feelings. People differ in the content of these representations, in how accessible they are, and in how they are related to one another. These representations are affected by genetic, cultural, societal, and developmental factors.

10. When dealing with a "difficult" person, avoid trying to "sell" your viewpoint. Instead, use the following guidelines to diagnose and manage the situation:
- Create a rich picture of the problem person, yourself, and the situation.
- Reframe your goals to focus on what you really want to accomplish.
- Schedule and carefully manage a face-to-face meeting to acknowledge the person's value, describe the problem behavior in factual terms, and discuss possible solutions.
- Follow up by setting aside time to monitor and reward progress or take corrective action.

 **ACTION SCRIPTS**

FOR EMPLOYEES

- Employees who are skilled at decoding behavior recognize that it is a complex phenomenon that is a function of both the person and the situation. They understand that this applies to their managers as well as their peers.
- When they try to understand why a person is acting in a particular way, they remember that we often overlook causes outside the individuals that influence their behavior. They always ask themself, "What other things could be causing this behavior?"
- They try to discern what if–then rules their peers and their managers are using to make sense of situations. They should be especially sensitive when people react differently in seemingly similar situations (e.g., criticism is accepted from managers but rejected from peers).
- They recognize the influences on their own behavior. They try to understand how their personality, situations, and the way they interpret situations affect how they behave.

FOR MANAGERS

- Expert managers create a rich picture of *all* their employees. They try to understand their personalities and the if–then rules they use to respond to situations.
- They systematically analyze the causes of employee behavior. They remember to pay attention to other characteristics of the individual, such as abilities and motivation. They check to be sure that the job, group, and organizational characteristics are exerting the intended consequences on behavior.
- They utilize their knowledge of cultural differences to understand behavior.

FOR ORGANIZATIONAL ARCHITECTS

- Organizational architects who understand personality design their employee selection system wisely.
    - They use personality tests cautiously when assessing employees.
    - They set up training programs in dealing with difficult employees for employees and managers.
    - They also provide training programs in cultural differences to help employees decode behavior.

PERSONAL APPLICATION ASSIGNMENT

The topic of this assignment is to think back on a personality-related experience that was significant for you. Choose an experience that intrigues you and that you want to learn more about.

A. Concrete Experience

    1. Objectively describe the experience (who, what, when, where, how) (2 points)

    2. Subjectively describe your feelings, perceptions, and thoughts that occurred during (not after) the experience. What did others seem to be feeling? (2 points)

B. Reflective Observation

    1. Looking back at the experience, what were the perspectives of the key actors (including you)? (2 points)

    2. Why did the people involved (including you) behave as they did? (2 points)

C. Abstract Conceptualization

    1. Relate concepts or theories from the assigned readings or the lecture to the experience. Explain thoroughly how they apply to your experience. Please apply at least two concepts or theories and cite them correctly. (4 points)

D. Active Experimentation

    1. What did you learn about motivation from this experience? (1 point)

    2. What did you learn about yourself? (1 point)

    3. What action steps will you take to be more effective in the future? (2 points)

E. Integration, Synthesis, and Writing

    1. Did you integrate and synthesize the four sections? (1 point)
    2. Was the Personal Application Assignment well written and easy to understand? (1 point)
    3. Was it free of spelling and grammar errors? (2 points)

ENDNOTES

[1] M. Swarz and S. Watkins, *Power Failure: The Inside Story of the Collapse of Enron* (New York: Currency Doubleday, 2003).

[2] Ibid.

[3] Ibid. and B. McLean and P. Elkind, *The Smartest Guys in the Room: The Amazing Rise and Scandalous Fall of Enron* (New York: Portfolio Penguin, 2003).

[4] Swarz and Watkins, *Power Failure: The Inside Story of the Collapse of Enron.*

[5] A. M. Paul, *The Cult of Personality* (New York: The Free Press, 2004).

[6] D. C. Funder, *The Personality Puzzle* (New York: Norton, 2001).

[7] G. Caprara and D. Cervone, *Personality: Determinants, Dynamics, and Potentials* (Cambridge: Cambridge University Press, 2000).

[8] L. A. Pervin, *Current Controversies and Issues in Personality*, 3rd ed. (New York: Wiley, 2002).

[9] R. M. Guion and R. F. Gottier, "Validity of personality measures in personnel selection," *Personnel Psychology 18* (1965): 135–64.

[10] O. John, "The Big Five Factor Taxonomy: Dimensions of Personality in the Natural Language and in Questionnaires,"

in L. A. Pervin, ed., *Handbook of Personality Theory and Research* (New York: Guilford, 1990): 66–100.

[11] R. R. McCrae and P. T. Costa, "Conceptions and Correlates of Openness to Experience," in R. Hogan, J. Johnson, and S. Briggs, (eds.), *Handbook of Personality Psychology* (San Diego: Academic Press, 1997): 826–848.

[12] J. Hogan and D. Ones, "Conscientiousness and Integrity at Work," in Hogan, Johnson, and Briggs, (eds.), *Handbook of Personality Psychology*: 849–872.

[13] D. Watson and L. Clark, "Extraversion and Its Positive Emotional Core," in R. Hogan, J. Johnson, and S. Briggs, (eds.), *Handbook of Personality Psychology* (San Diego: Academic Press, 1997): 767–794.

[14] W. Graziano and N. Eisenberg, "Agreeableness: A Dimension of Personality," in R. Hogan, J. Johnson, and S. Briggs, (eds.), *Handbook of Personality Psychology* (San Diego: Academic Press, 1997): 795–825.

[15] D. Wiebe and T. Smith, "Personality and Health: Progress and Problems in Psychosomatics," in R. Hogan, J. Johnson, and S. Briggs, (eds.), *Handbook of Personality Psychology* (San Diego: Academic Press,1997): 892–918; L. Morey, "Personality Diagnosis and Personality Disorders," in R. Hogan, J. Johnson, and S. Briggs, (eds.), *Handbook of Personality Psychology* (San Diego: Academic Press,1997): 919–947.

[16] M. R. Barrick, M. K. Mount, and T. A. Judge, "The FFM Personality Dimensions and Job Performance: Meta-analysis of Meta-analyses," *International Journal of Selection and Assessment 9* (2001): 9–30.

[17] M. R. Barrick and M. K. Mount, "The Big Five Personality Dimensions and Job Performance: A Meta-Analysis," *Personnel Psychology*, 44 (1991): 1–26; Barrick, Mount, and Judge, "The FFM Personality Dimensions and Job Performance: Meta-analysis of meta-analyses"; T. A. Judge, C. A. Higins, C. J. Thoresen, and M. R. Barrick, "The Big Five Personality Traits, General Mental Ability, and Career Success Across the Life Span," *Personnel Psychology 53* (1999): 621–652; L. A. Witt, L. A. Burke, M. R. Barrick, and M. K. Mount, "The Interactive Effects of Conscientiousness and Agreeableness on Job Performance," *Journal of Applied Psychology 87* (2002): 164–169; L. D. Goodstein and R. I. Lanyon, "Applications of Personality Assessment to the Workplace: A Review," *Journal of Business and Psychology 13* (1999): 291–322; G. M. Hurtz and J. J. Donovan, "Personality and Job Performance: The Big Five Revisited," *Journal of Applied Psychology 85*, (2000): 869–879; T.A. Judge and R. Iles, "Relationship of Personality to Performance Motivation: A Meta-Analytic Review," *Journal of Applied Psychology 87*, (2002): 797–807; M. R. Barrick, T. R. Mitchell, and G. L. Stewart, "Situational and Motivational Influences on Trait-Behavior Relationships," in M. R. Barrick and A. M. Ryan (eds.), *Personality and Work: Reconsidering the Role of Personality in Organizations* (San Francisco: Jossey-Bass, 2003): 60–82; J. W. Johnson, "Toward a Better Understanding of the Relationship Between Personality and Individual Job Performance," in Barrick and Ryan, (eds.), *Personality and Work: Reconsidering the Role of Personality in Organizations*: 83–120.

[18] Barrick, Mount, and Judge, "The FFM Personality Dimensions and Job Performance: Meta-analysis of meta-Analyses."

[19] Ibid.; M. R. Barrick, G. L. Stewart, and M. Piotrowski, "Personality and Job Performance: Test of the Mediating Effects of Motivation Among Sales Representatives," *Journal of Applied Psychology 87* (2002): 43–51; Barrick, Mitchell, and Stewart, "Situational and Motivational Influences on Trait-Behavior Relationships."

[20] Barrick, Mitchell, and Stewart, "Situational and Motivational Influences on Trait-Behavior Relationships."

[21] Pervin, *Current Controversies and Issues in Personality.*

[22] Caprara and Cervone, *Personality: Determinants, Dynamics, and Potentials.*

[23] Pervin, *Current Controversies and Issues in Personality.*

[24] Caprara and Cervone, *Personality: Determinants, Dynamics, and Potentials*; Pervin, *Current Controversies and Issues in Personality.*

[25] D. P. Shuitt, "At 60, Myers–Briggs Is Still Sorting Out and Identifying People's Types," *Workforce Management 82* (December, 2003): 82–85.

[26] C. Bell, "What Type Are You?: If You Feel That Your Job Isn't For You, Taking The Myers–Briggs Test May Hold Some Of The Answers," *The Guardian* (December 8, 2003): 5.

[27] J. Michael, "Using The Myers–Briggs Type Indicator As A Tool For Leadership Development? Apply With Caution," *Journal of Leadership and Organizational Studies 10* (2003): 68–81.

[28] A. Overholt, "A Nice Personality," *Fast Company 83* (April, 2004): 20.

[29] The Myers and Briggs Foundation, www.myersbriggs.org, (accessed July 31, 2005).

[30] Michael, "Using The Myers–Briggs Type Indicator As A Tool For Leadership Development? Apply With Caution."

[31] R. C. Arnau, D. H. Rosen, and B. Thompson. "Reliability and validity of scores from the Singer-Loomis Type Deployment Inventory," *Journal of Analytical Psychology 45* (3) (July 2000): 409-426. This test is available from Moving Boundaries, Inc., Gresham, OR.

[32] J. Brockner, *Self-Esteem at Work* (Lexington, MA: Lexington Books, 1998).

[33] R. Christie and F. L. Geis, *Studies in Machiavellianism* (New York: Academic Press, 1970).

[34] J. B. Rotter, "Generalized Expectancies for Internal Versus External Locus of Control," *Psychological Monographs 80* (609) (1966): whole issue.

[35] T. A. Stewart, "Escape from the Cult of Personality Tests," *Fortune 137* (March 16, 1998): 80.

[36] L. R. James and M. D. Mazerolle, *Personality in Work Organizations* (Thousand Oaks, CA: Sage, 2002).

[37] D. C. McClelland, *Human Motivation* (Glenview, IL: Scott, Foresman, 1985).

[38] James and Mazerolle, *Personality in Work Organizations.*

[39] W. R. Mischel, "Toward an Integrative Science of the Person," *Annual Review of Psychology 55* (2004): 1–22.

[40] W. R. Mischel and Y. Shoda, "A Cognitive–Affective System Theory of Personality: Reconceptualizing Situations, Dispositions, Dynamics, and Invariance in Personality Structure," *Psychological Review 102* (2) (1995): 246–268; W. R. Mischel and Y. Shoda, "Reconciling Processing Dynamics

and Personality Dispositions," *Annual Review of Psychology*, 49 (1998): 229–258; Y. Shoda, W. R. Mischel, and J. C. Wright, "Intuitive Interactionism in Person Perception: Effects of Situation-Behavior Relations on Dispositional Judgments," *Journal of Personality and Social Psychology*, *56* (1989): 41–43; Y. Shoda, W. R. Mischel, and J. C. Wright, "The Role of Situational Demands and Cognitive Competencies in Behavior Organization and Personality Coherence," *Journal of Personality and Social Psychology 65* (1993): 1023–1035.

[41] D. Cervone, "The Architecture of Personality," *Psychological Review 111* (2004): 183–204.

[42] M. Solomon. *Working with Difficult People* (Englewood Cliffs, NJ: Prentice Hall, 1990).

[43] I. Sager, "Up Front," *Business Week 3840* (July 7, 2003): 14.

[44] N. Nicholson, "How to Motivate Your Problem People," *Harvard Business Review 81* (2003): 56–65.

[45] R. M. Bramson, *Coping With Difficult People* (Garden City, NJ: Anchor Doubleday, 1981).

Chapter 5

▲▲▲

INDIVIDUAL AND ORGANIZATIONAL MOTIVATION

OBJECTIVES By the end of this chapter, you should be able to:

A. Explain and to apply the basic theories of motivation.

B. Explain how managers and organizations can foster and reward employee motivation.

C. Identify the characteristics of enriched, motivating jobs.

D. Describe five methods of job redesign.

E. Understand what demotivates employees.

A WINNING RECIPE

Sixteen years ago, Fernando Velez was a shy 18-year-old farm worker earning $4.25 an hour milking cows in central California. He didn't speak English, had no health insurance, no bank account—no real future. He was a citizen of the United States but felt like a foreigner. Then, in 1989, Velez was hired for an entry-level position at Ruiz Foods, the nation's largest manufacturer of frozen Mexican food products. He had no idea that he would soon learn how to become a more productive American.

Velez began taking educational courses offered at Ruiz Foods that taught him how to speak and read English and gave him other personal and professional tools that many people take for granted. Today, Velez is a packaging supervisor at Ruiz, overseeing 150 employees. He earns a respectable living. He's also earned something even more valuable—self-respect.

"I used to be intimidated because I couldn't speak English. When you don't speak English in this country, your opportunities are limited," says Velez, who also met his wife at Ruiz Foods. "The company provided me with one-on-one instruction for about four months. Those four months opened the door for me to learn what the United States truly had to offer me. Sometimes I think about it and I'm amazed at how far I've come."

Nurturing and educating employees is more than an after-hours benefit at Ruiz Foods. It's a practice that is at the very heart of the company—and has a very real impact on its success. In short, taking extraordinary steps to help employees makes good business sense, says Fred Ruiz, chair and co-founder of Ruiz Foods.

"Over the years, we've created a trust between the company and the people," says the 62-year-old Ruiz, whose 1,900-member workforce is nearly 90 percent Hispanic. They trust us—that we're going to take care of them, we're going to provide them with good benefits and a good environment. And we trust that they're going to make good products, that they're going to work very hard and protect our company.

"I learned a long time ago that in order to be successful, you have to rely on the power of people," he continues. "We solve all of our problems through our people. And we achieve all of our success through our people."

At Ruiz Foods, which recently celebrated its 40th year in business, employees are called "team members." Hundreds of them have been given the opportunity to improve their professional and personal lives by attending classes at the company's headquarters in Dinuba, California. The on-site education center functions in a typical classroom setting, with paid instructors. It is free to all employees and offered at various times throughout the day to accommodate staggered work shifts. The classes provide a twofold function:

- Helping employees function in the day-to-day world outside work, by teaching them English, how to count money, how to make change, how to open a checking account, etc. The company also hosts health fairs to educate employees on proper nutrition and on how to decrease the risk of diabetes and other diseases.
- Giving employees necessary professional tools to climb the company ladder, including classes on leadership, communication, and computer training to operate the numerous machines in the plant.

"The amount of pride and self-esteem that this creates for our team members is unbelievable," says Ruiz.

Making the most of every opportunity made the unlikely 40-year Ruiz family journey possible. It began when Fred and his father, Louis, used a tiny electric mixer, a cooking pot, a small chest freezer, and authentic Mexican recipes from Fred's mother, Rosie, and started selling frozen enchiladas and burritos to retail outlets through central California. Ruiz Foods has taken giant strides in recent years. The company's 350,000-square-foot plant in Dinuba has around-the-clock work shifts to produce 151 million chimichangas and 293 million taquitos per year. The company is building another facility in Texas and was the #2-ranked Hispanic-owned manufacturing firm in the United States and was selected for the Small Business Administration's Hall of Fame. Ruiz Foods sells more than 180 frozen-food products under the El Monterey brand throughout the United States and Canada. Incredibly, all of their products are still hand-rolled. A tour of the plant reveals not only a well-oiled machine at work but also a family-like atmosphere.

The Ruiz family insists on an honest day's work, but they also give a lot in return. Two years ago, the company created a housing program called *Una Casa Para Mi Familia* ("A House for My Family"), which helps employees and their families learn the process of buying a home. Two years ago, the company came up with the Birthday Club. Eight times per month—each and every month—company vice presidents can be found greeting employees and lending an attentive ear anytime from 4 A.M. to midnight, depending on which work shift is celebrating. They commemorate team member birthdays with gifts, cake, and, of course, food. During this time, employees are encouraged to give positive or negative feedback about their work experience.

"It allows us to shake hands with each and every team member throughout the year. We try to communicate the company values. But if people feel like we're not operating according to these values, we have an open-door policy." The company has more than 300 employees who have been with the team for more than 10 years—many have remained for more than 30 years. Nearly 10 percent of the workforce is made up of second-generation employees. "Every time that we have brought in a new piece of equipment that is going to eliminate jobs, we tell them that they should never be threatened by progress," Fred says. "We have to be more productive or else we'll lose our competitive edge. But at the same time, we've never fired anybody because of automation."

It's all part of the family environment that father and son spent years cultivating. "You've got all these people who work very hard for you," says Fred. "We've got everybody here, so why not take advantage of that by teaching them how to write a check, or how to borrow money, or reading or writing or English. It's a no-brainer. That's my job as the head of a company. How can I improve the lives of our team members?"

Even seasoned employees, such as production supervisor Rosa Alexander, continue to receive off-the-job training. "We continue to take leadership courses on improving our communication skills, how to deal with difficult people, team building, and how to communicate with coworkers," says Alexander, who began her career at Ruiz 24 years ago as an entry-level packer. She now oversees a 200-person crew. "If you really want to put forth the effort, the company is more than willing to go the extra mile for you. They show me the same respect today as they did years ago. You are never treated like just another number around here."

Source: This article was excerpted and adapted with permission from M. E. Stroder, "The Winning Recipe", *The Costco Connection*, (July 2005): 20–22.

HOW TO CHANGE YOUR BOSS

My boss has a couple of habits that drive me crazy. If s/he would just change them this would be a great place to work. Oh, that I could be the boss for one day and he be the subordinate. I know what I'd do in a flash. Don't get me wrong, I like working here. It's just a couple of those habits.

Do you ever wish that you could be the "boss for a day"? Do you long for the genie to come out of the bottle or for the good fairy to grant you three wishes? Your first wish would be to change your boss, your second to modify the way he behaves at times.

You have that wish. It's called behavior modification—the power to change (modify) the way your boss behaves. And the technique is simple if you will merely utilize the five, easy to follow, steps of positive reinforcement:

- Understand the purposes of positive reinforcement.
- State the undesired behavior.
- State the desired behavior.
- Create an opportunity for the desired behavior.
- Give verbal praise.

UNDERSTAND THE PURPOSES OF POSITIVE REINFORCEMENT

Just because you are the subordinate and he is the boss does not necessarily mean that you are forever under the whims and helpless control of your boss's every habit. It merely means that your "tool bag" is smaller than his and at times you have to be very skillful in using the few tools that you have available. Perhaps the most powerful tool in your bag is positive reinforcement.

One reason to utilize positive reinforcement is to change an undesirable behavior to a desirable behavior. Once the boss begins exhibiting the desired behavior, then positive reinforcement is utilized to maintain the behavior.

STATE THE UNDESIRED BEHAVIOR

At this step you want to clearly understand exactly what behavior to change. This is accomplished by specifically stating the undesired behavior that you want your boss to change. Two examples will help illustrate the process.

- *You*: (to yourself) Your boss comes to you several times each day and checks your work.
- *You*: Your boss frequently asks you to do things at the last minute, not giving you enough time to do the work properly.

Resist the temptation to dwell on this step. To linger will change the whole tone of this skill from "positive" to "negative." The key to successfully utilizing this procedure lies in accomplishing this step in the shortest amount of time. Merely state it and quickly move to the next step.

STATE THE DESIRED BEHAVIOR

Specifically state the desired behavior that you want your boss to show.

- *You*: (to yourself) You would like your boss to check your work once each day at the designated time.
- *You*: You want your boss to give you things enough ahead of time to do them right, or allow you to get others to help.

These become your goals. When your boss demonstrates this behavior, you'll know that you have succeeded. The good fairy actually can grant wishes, or perhaps you're the good fairy.

CREATE AN OPPORTUNITY FOR THE DESIRED BEHAVIOR

This can be accomplished in two ways. Either create an opportunity where your boss will show the desired behavior, or wait for it to occur naturally and then reinforce it.

In order to create the opportunity, your boss must first be aware of the particular behavior that is bothering you. This can only be achieved by you diplomatically explaining both the undesired behavior and the desired behavior.

In stating the undesirable behavior you must be careful to talk strictly about the behavior and refrain from discussing his personality. By talking about the observed behavior, you increase the likelihood that he can discuss it without becoming emotionally involved. If you choose to attack his personality, then you naturally will instigate a battle which can easily escalate to a war.

Second, you need to let the boss know how this makes you feel. Without the insight to your inner feelings, he is unable to share or understand the impact that this has on you.

Let's return to the two examples presented earlier:

- *You*: I wanted to chat with you about a minor thing that at times bothers me. Frequently during the day you check me and my work. Checking my work (notice we're talking about a behavior and not his personality - so important), and I know it's probably a silly FEELING of mine (giving him an "out" that you will cleverly take away from him in a minute), makes me FEEL as though I'm not capable of doing my job, to both our satisfactions, without some outside monitoring (behavior - not personality).
- *You*: I'm glad we have this chance to talk because there's something I need to share with you. Frequently, I'm asked to do things without enough lead time to do them properly. This makes me feel inadequate because when they don't get done or don't get done properly, I feel that this reflects on my ability, and in turn I feel incompetent.

Now we can return to creating an opportunity where your boss will show the desired behavior or waiting for the opportunity to occur naturally. Examples will clarify how this can be accomplished.

Example 1

- *You*: Perhaps you could try checking me once a day for a couple of days to see how that works.

  or

- You could wait for an opportunity when you know circumstances will allow your boss to be able to check you only at the end of the day. This could be when he is tied up on a project, in a day long meeting, or out of the office for most of the day.

Example 2

- *You*: It would help me greatly if you could give me more lead time.

  or

- When you anticipate a rush job, as is often the case, you can go to your boss and get the rush job early.

  or

- You can wait for a time when your boss just happens to give you enough time on a rush job.

  or, if that never happens

- You can select a time when he gives you a little more time than he normally gives you but it still is not enough time. (Here you are having to select a behavior, while not totally the desired behavior, that tends towards the desired behavior. This is the most difficult behavior to reinforce, but that's jumping ahead of ourselves.)

You've got the idea. Somehow, some way, you arrange for the desired behavior to occur. HURRAY! Your problems are forever solved. You knew the good fairy would cause you to live happily ever after … WRONG … We've left out the most important step, positive reinforcement—that super glue that will forever bind his new found behavior to the bag of tools that he readily uses.

GIVE VERBAL PRAISE

When the desired behavior is shown, give positive reinforcement—give it immediately after the desired behavior is shown—give it every time the desired behavior is shown in order to change the behavior and have it become second nature to him. Once he has internalized his newfound behavior (note that HE has done all this, and that's fine, you're big enough to let him think that he did it), you merely need to sporadically give positive reinforcement to him in order to maintain it. He'll probably take credit for it again.

To give positive reinforcement you do three things:

- State the desired behavior.
- Indicate why you like the desired behavior - that is, tell him how it makes you FEEL.
- Give ,verbal praise.

  The first two of these can be illustrated together.

- *You*: Today you checked my work just once. I think it's working great. I feel that you trust my ability to do the work and that in turn gives me greater confidence. A side benefit that I didn't realize is that I have more time because I don't spend as much time with you and I'm not wasting time wondering when you'll be coming by. This in turn allows me to accomplish still more. I'm sure that you also appreciate having some extra time.
- *You*: You've been consciously giving me some additional lead time. I'm better able to complete the work and have it ready for you when you need it. I appreciate that and it makes me feel good to know that you value my needs.

  Lastly, you merely give verbal praise. Again, with the three examples, all you need to say is

- *You*: Thanks a lot.

Giving positive reinforcement can do wonders when it comes to modifying your boss's behavior!

CLASS PREPARATION

A. Read "A Winning Recipe" and "How to Change Your Boss."

B. Fill out and score the Job Survey below.

C. Answer the questions at the end of the Donor Services Department on page 676.

D. Be prepared to take on the role of both Sam and Elena in the Motivation Counseling Session Role Play on page 114.

E. As you read the chapter, prepare a list of the motivation cues that relate to the Donor Services Department.

Job Survey

Here are some statements about your job. How much do you agree with each?

My Job	Strongly Disagree	Disagree	Slightly Disagree	Undecided	Slightly Agree	Agree	Strongly Agree
1. provides much variety permits me to be left on my own to do my own work	1	2	3	4	5	6	7
2. is arranged so that I often have the opportunity to see jobs or projects through to completion	1	2	3	4	5	6	7
3. provides feedback on how well I am doing as I am working	1	2	3	4	5	6	7
4. is relatively significant in our organization	1	2	3	4	5	6	7
5. gives me considerable opportunity for independence and freedom in how I do my work	1	2	3	4	5	6	7
6. gives me the opportunity to do a number of different things	1	2	3	4	5	6	7
7. provides me an opportunity to find out how well I am doing	1	2	3	4	5	6	7
8. is very significant or important in the broader scheme of things	1	2	3	4	5	6	7
9. provides an opportunity for independent thought and action	1	2	3	4	5	6	7
10. provides me with a great deal of variety at work	1	2	3	4	5	6	7

My Job	Strongly Disagree	Disagree	Slightly Disagree	Undecided	Slightly Agree	Agree	Strongly Agree
11. is arranged so that I have the opportunity to complete the work I start	1	2	3	4	5	6	7
12. provides me with the feeling that I know whether I am performing well or poorly	1	2	3	4	5	6	7
13. is arranged so that I have the chance to do a job from the beginning to end (i.e., a chance to do the whole job)	1	2	3	4	5	6	7
14. is one where a lot of other people can be affected by how well	1	2	3	4	5	6	7
15. the work gets done	1	2	3	4	5	6	7

Scoring:

_____	Skill variety	questions 1,7,11	_____	Autonomy	questions 2,6,10
_____	Task identity	questions 3,12,14	_____	Feedback about results	questions 4,8,13
_____	Task significance	questions 5,9,15			

 THE KNOWLEDGE BASE

Concern over productivity levels raises the question of how well companies can compete in both the domestic and global marketplace. One of the key factors that affects productivity is *motivation*, which is defined as *the psychological forces that determine the direction of people's behavior, their level of effort, and level of persistence.*[1] Motivation has always been an issue of concern for managers; it has long been recognized as one of the basic managerial functions. There persist, however, some commonsense notions about motivation that are misleading and just plain wrong. First among these notions is the idea that there are persons who are not motivated. This is incorrect. Every living human being is motivated. What managers really mean when they say that a worker is not motivated is that the worker is not motivated to do what the manager wants the worker to do. The same "lazy" employee who just goes through the motions at work may stay up all night laboring with great intensity on a sports car or devote many hours outside of the job to charity work. Although it is true that some people are more energetic than others, the most important factor to consider is how this energy is directed—toward what goals and objectives. The primary task for managing motivation, therefore, is channeling and directing human energy toward the activities, tasks, and objectives that further the organization's mission.

A second erroneous idea about motivation is that managers "motivate" workers and that motivation is something you do to someone else. Motivation is an internal state that directs individuals toward certain goals and objectives. Managers cannot directly influence this internal state; they can only create expectations on the part of employees that their motives will be satisfied by doing the organization's work and then provide the rewards that satisfy the employee's needs.

This distinction may appear subtle, but it is important because failure to understand it often leads managers to attempt to use motivation to manipulate employees. Manipulation is a very inefficient way of managing motivation because it requires that you as a manager maintain control of the carrot and stick. As a result, you must spend time scheming about how you will motivate those whom you supervise on a day-to-day basis. A more effective way of managing motivation is through understanding. If you understand the needs and objectives of your subordinates and even your peers, you can work with them to develop an equitable psychological contract that recognizes their particular desires and creates conditions where these motives can be satisfied in the work setting. The same is true of your own motivation. By becoming more aware of your own motives and desires, you can better organize your work and life activities to achieve satisfaction and productivity.

The sources of motivation are both intrinsic and extrinsic.[2] Intrinsic behavior is performed for its own sake. The work itself is pleasurable, and we see examples of this in people who love the work they do. It is common to hear people say, "I'm always surprised I get paid for doing something I enjoy so much!" This is a cue that they are intrinsically motivated. In contrast, extrinsic behavior is performed because of the consequences it brings—material or social rewards or even the avoidance of punishment. Salary, or the social prestige of the large house and luxury car it allows a person to buy, rather than the actual job, are examples of extrinsic rewards that motivate behavior. When a person does not seem to enjoy influencing and leading others, this can be a cue that their interest in a managerial position may come from extrinsic sources. Of course, people can be motivated for both intrinsic and extrinsic reasons. For example, a highly paid CEO may be very motivated by doing the job itself and also be motivated by the amount of pay and other extrinsic rewards she receives.

A helpful heuristic based on research findings is that Performance = Ability × Motivation. We all know brilliant individuals who struggle to get out of bed in the morning or who begin projects but cannot bring them to closure. By contrast, we have also seen people who work very diligently, but that does not fully compensate for their lack of innate talent. The most reliable predictor of job performance and career success is cognitive ability.[3] This means that intelligence should be a major criterion when we select job candidates. Nevertheless, determining candidates' motivation level is also crucial. Conscientiousness, a stable personality trait, is sometimes used to operationalize motivation. For example, a study of early career success in MBA graduates found that those who were both smarter and worked harder than their peers were more successful in their initial job search and earned higher salaries with more rapid pay raises and more promotions.[4] This may seem obvious, but not all hiring decisions hone in on these elements. Other factors may also contribute to career success—for example, researchers are currently looking more closely at the role of emotional intelligence, even in jobs that do not seem to require "people skills". To solve performance problems, we have to be able to discern whether we are dealing with a deficiency in ability or motivation or demotivators in the organizational context, because the resulting action scripts are very different. We will discuss ways to enhance ability in detail in Chapter 20, Performance Management and Appraisal.

Our understanding of human motivation is crucial because it explains why people behave as they do. It tells us why two people with the same job, the same pay, the same tenure in the same organization put in very different levels of effort. Knowledge about motivation has increased substantially over the past decades. Simplistic theories arguing that people work primarily for money or primarily for social gratification have been replaced with more complex theories of human nature. Even so, no single theory is adequate to explain human motivation, which is often the result of a complex set of needs and factors. Effective managers have an understanding of the various theories in this chapter and rely upon those that are most helpful in a given situation. The analogy that best describes how experts approach motivation is a mental rolodex of theories and mental models that they sort through until they find a match that explains the situation facing them. When people ask our help in decoding why an individual does not appear to be motivated to do their job, we generally take a close look at four areas: the person-job-reward fit, job design, the role of the leader, and the role of organizational policies and rewards.

THE PERSON-JOB-REWARD FIT

An art institute could not figure out why they had such high turnover among the clerks who processed course registrations. Interviews with current and former employees revealed minor, typical complaints, but we were struck by the recurring comment that what they really liked was art. When asked what drew them to the job, they answered that they wanted to be around art and to be connected with the institute, an organization they greatly admired. They had accepted the job hoping that it would transition into something more interesting, which was not possible given their skills and the organization's needs. When that did not happen and non-stop data entry and clerical work sucked the life out of their artistic souls, they quit. The most important cue in all the interview data was their love of art. Fixing minor problems or even redesigning their jobs to be more satisfying would not correct this basic lack of person-job fit. The recommended action script was simple—stop hiring people whose needs would never be met by this job and develop a hiring profile more suited to the actual task, in other words, people who enjoy clerical work.

A key step in understanding motivation problems is to identify the factors unique to an individual that energize, direct, sustain, and stop behavior. *Content theories focus on the specific internal needs that motivate people.* Failure to understand these needs may mean that individuals unwittingly seek jobs that leave them profoundly unmotivated. Or managers may promote employees into jobs where they fail or become very dissatisfied. Content theories include *Maslow's hierarchy of needs* and *McClelland's need theory.* The tenets of some theories (that of Maslow and Herzberg) have been disproved by subsequent research[5] or do not apply in all cultures.[6] Therefore, we will summarize the most useful, reliable contributions of content theories.

Maslow's Hierarchy of Needs

Maslow identified the following needs.[7] Physiological needs refer to the basic needs like food, water, and shelter that are necessary for survival. Organizations satisfy this need by providing salaries and wages so employees can live adequately. Security needs are defined as the need for security, stability, and protection from physical or emotional harm. Organizations satisfy this need by providing pension and health care plans, career paths within the organization, and a safe work environment. Social belonging needs reflect the human need for social interaction, friendship, affection, and love. Organizations can fulfill this need by permitting interaction with colleagues, work team structures, social and sports facilities, and parties. Self-esteem is the need to feel good about oneself and to be respected, appreciated, and recognized by others. Organizations can satisfy this need by providing feedback and recognition for high performance and accomplishments, seeking and respecting employee input, making employees visible to others (customers, board members, industry) and promoting them. Self-actualization refers to the need people have to realize their full potential. The military recruitment poster, "Be all that you can be" captures the idea of self-actualization. Organizations fulfill this need when they allow employees to use their skills and talents fully at work. Entrepreneurs who left large organizations to work for themselves so they could use more of their talents are good examples of people who are motivated by a strong need for self-actualization. Maslow's theory is typically called the "Hierarchy of Needs" because it stated that the needs are arranged in a hierarchy (starting with physiological and progressing through security, social, self-esteem, and self-actualization), and that lower order needs must be satisfied before higher level needs can be addressed. Although research on the theory has failed to suppport the existence of a need hierarchy, Maslow's theory can be useful in helping managers understand different types of human needs.

Not everyone has the same needs, nor are these needs given equal importance in different cultures.[8] For example, the security need is more important than self-actualization in Greece and Japan. Social needs are more important in collectivist African countries than the self-esteem and self-actualization needs that are more figural in an individualistic culture like the United States. Social needs are also more important in the Scandinavian countries where quality of life is generally more highly valued than career success. In a study of eight different countries, however, self-actualization was more important and security was less important to highly educated people than to their less educated colleagues.[9] In lesser-developed countries, where more people live at the subsistence level, physiological and security needs are very important. When working with people from another culture, managers should be acutely aware that needs and their relative importance may differ.

McClelland's Need Theory

Psychologists, most notably David McClelland, have made a great deal of progress over the past 40 years in scientifically measuring and defining human motives.[10] McClelland began by looking not at behavior but at the way people think and feel. He used the Thematic Apperception Test (TAT), which asks subjects to write stories in response to pictures; the thoughts in these stories are content-analyzed to reveal categories of dominant themes. McClelland and his colleagues found evidence of three human motives: need for affiliation, need for power, and need for achievement. Most people have a degree of each of these motives in their thoughts but seldom in the same strength. McClelland states that these motives are learned from our parents and culture. He discovered different motive patterns for different cultures. For example, the power motive is very pronounced in Latin America where power and control are dominant cultural themes. Because of its projective nature, the TAT test has been used successfully with people from different cultures. Nevertheless, Hofstede notes that the word achievement is not readily translated into all languages, and the need to achieve requires a certain tolerance of risk and concern with career success that is not found equally in all cultures.[11]

The *need for power (n-Power) is defined as the need to influence and lead others and be in control of one's environment*. A high need for power is very common among middle- and upper-level managers because, by definition, their job is to influence people and organizations. A strong need for power can be satisfied by working in professions and positions that allow people to influence and lead others, such as management, politics, police work, the military, and the law. There are two faces of the power need. The positive face is *socialized power*, which is *influence used for the good of others*. People driven by a need for socialized power seek a management position or political office to make their organizations better so that others will benefit. The negative face is *personalized power, an unsocialized concern for personal dominance*. People with the need for personalized power have less inhibition or self-control, and they exercise power impulsively. According to McClelland and Burnham's research, subjects with a high need for personalized power were often more rude, drank to excess, engaged in casual sexual exploitation (scoring), and collected prestige symbols like expensive cars.[12] Dictators and people who establish work fiefdoms are usually motivated by personalized power. An international health institute had a matrix structure in which employees had two bosses—one in their functional area and a project boss. The head of the community outreach department was driven by a need for personalized power. He established a fiefdom and engendered a strong sense of loyalty in his team members, but their loyalty was to him rather than the organization. As a result, the project bosses and team members complained frequently that the entire community outreach department was uncooperative. Thus, the matrix structure did not work until he retired and was replaced.

The *need for affiliation* is *the desire for friendly and close interpersonal relationships*. People high in n-Affiliation prefer cooperative situations to competitive situations, and they seek relationships involving a high degree of mutual understanding. As with the power motive, there are two faces of this need. The positive face, *affiliative interest*, is a *concern for interpersonal relationships but not at the expense of goal-oriented behavior*. People motivated by affiliative interest value good relationships and work at maintaining them, but their concern with relationships does not prevent them from giving negative feedback or making tough decisions.

The negative face of n-Affiliation is *affiliative assurance, a concern with obtaining assurance about the security and strength of one's relationships and avoiding rejection*. According to Boyatzis,[13] managers with a strong need for affiliative assurance look for proof that others are committed to them and avoid issues and conflicts that might threaten the stability of the relationship. They seek approval from others and devote more energy to maintaining relationships than to achieving work goals. They worry about being disliked.

Although a high need for affiliation does not correlate with job performance and is found more often in supervisors than high-level leaders, people with a need for affiliative interest make a valuable contribution by creating a friendly, cooperative atmosphere at work. High n-Affiliation managers spend more time communicating with others than do managers high in either n-Power or n-Achievement[14] and are good at creating the networks that are crucial for success in many organizations.[15]

The *need for achievement* is *a need to accomplish goals, excel, and strive continually to do things better.* Persons high in n-Achievement want to take personal responsibility for their success or failure, like to take calculated (moderate) risks, prefer situations in which they get immediate, concrete feedback on how well they are doing, and have a single-minded focus on accomplishing a task. Their sense of personal responsibility may keep them from delegating authority unless they value developing and empowering subordinates. Executives high in n-Achievement tend to have fewer meetings than other executives and prefer to work alone, despite the fact that many organizational problems would be better solved by collaborative effort.[16] Many entrepreneurs and small business owners are high in n-Achievement.

What pattern of needs is found in effective managers? Research results show that a manager needs a reasonably high n-Power to function as a leader.[17] Although many of today's managers seem uncomfortable talking about power, their job consists of influencing other people to get the work done. The most effective managers in McClelland and Burnham's research scored high on the need for power and self-control and low in the need for affiliation; they called this group institutional managers because of their concern for the organization.[18] Their direct reports exhibited more team spirit, responsibility, and clarity on organizational goals than employees with bosses who scored high in n-Affiliation or n-Achievement. The institutional managers also had greater maturity and used a democratic coaching style; rather than create dependence in their followers, they empowered them. Both these factors helped prevent them from using power for personal aggrandizement or manipulation. The institutional managers were also less defensive about their ideas and more willing to take advice from experts, more willing to self-sacrifice for the good of the organization, had a longer-range view, demonstrated a strong concern for justice and equity, and accumulated fewer material possessions.[19]

In AT&T's longitudinal, 20-year study of managers, people with a high need for power and a low need for affiliation were promoted to a higher level than managers with other profiles.[20] In small or decentralized companies, however, success depends more on a high need for achievement than a high need for power. The nature of such companies with their focus on constant improvement and cost-efficient growth is a better fit for people with a high need for achievement.[21] However, a high need for both power and achievement has been found in effective low- and middle-level managers.[22]

A manager's effectiveness depends not only on his or her need for power but also on the other values he or she brings to the job. John Andrew's classic study of two Mexican companies is striking in this regard.[23] Both companies had presidents who scored high in n-Power, but one firm was stagnating whereas the other was growing rapidly. The manager of the growing company, although high in n-Power, was also high in n-Achievement and was dedicated to letting others in the organization satisfy their own needs for achievement by introducing improvements and making decisions on their own. The stagnant company, although well capitalized and enjoying a favorable market, was constantly in turmoil and experienced a high rate of turnover, particularly among its executives. In this company, the president's high n-Power, coupled with highly authoritarian values, led him to make all the decisions himself, leaving no room for individual responsibility on the part of his personnel. A comparison of motivation scores of upper-level managers of the two companies showed that the dynamic company's managers were significantly higher in n-Achievement than were those of the stagnant company, who tended to be more concerned with power and compliance than with individual responsibility and decision making.

People can be motivated by a variety of these needs, and the salience of particular needs can vary. Alderfer argued that satisfied needs do not motivate behavior, although he stipulated that changing conditions may turn a previously satisfied need into a motivator.[24] For example, individuals' security needs may have been met earlier in their career, freeing them to focus on other needs until downsizing and proposed changes in pension and health care plans made security needs figural once again. Content theories show us that people have very different mental maps when it comes to motivation. Not everyone is motivated by the same needs, and certainly they are not motivated by the same needs we are. As a result, they behave differently and will respond differently to work outcomes and rewards. Rewards that fulfill innate human needs are more likely to motivate behavior. However, their efficacy also varies over time. Currently, some employees feel so overworked that they prefer time off to a raise. When employees at Bronson Healthcare Group in Kalamazoo, Michigan told management their lives were too busy (85 percent of its employees are female), management listened and adopted a concierge service. The service helps with errands like dry cleaning pick-ups, car servicing, travel plans, and shopping. Thus, this particular job reward is carefully designed to fit their needs. Southwest Airlines has a profit-sharing plan that invests a certain percentage of the firm's profits in company stock for employees. As a result, several employees with 18 or 20 years of service became millionaires.

JOB DESIGN

Although individuals come to organizations with previously learned motive patterns and unique needs, this is only part of the motivation puzzle. The intrinsic motivation of employees is very important, but job motivation is also affected by the environment in which workers find themselves, and, in particular, the way in which their jobs are designed.

Job Characteristics Model

Based on what we know about motivation, alienation, and worker/commitment, job situations that motivate people and lead to job satisfaction have the following characteristics:

1. **Skill variety**—The degree to which a job requires a range of personal competencies and abilities in carrying out the work.
2. **Task identity**—The degree to which a job requires completion of a "whole" and identifiable piece of work, that is, doing a good job from beginning to end with a visible outcome.
3. **Task significance**—The degree to which the job is perceived by the employee as having a substantial impact on the lives of other people, whether those people are within or outside of the organization.
4. **Autonomy**—The degree to which the job provides freedom, independence, and discretion to the employee in scheduling the tasks and in determining the procedure to be used in carrying out the task.
5. **Job feedback**—The degree to which carrying out the job-related tasks provides the individual with direct and clear information about the effectiveness of his or her performance.[25]

Skill variety, task identity, and task significance are geared toward increasing the sense of meaningfulness that is threatened whenever jobs are divided into small, repetitive segments. Granting employees autonomy over their jobs encourages them to feel responsible (powerful and in control) for the outcome of their work. It also reduces legalistic approaches to work, for example, "That's not my job" or "If they're gonna give me a robot's job to do, I'm gonna do it like a robot! Anyway, it just lowers my production record to get up and point out someone else's error."[26] Job feedback allows employees to receive immediate feedback from the work itself, not from a supervisor. This relates to one of the conditions McClelland found to be most favorable for people with high needs for achievement—immediate concrete feedback that allows them to adjust their performance to meet their personal and/or organizational goals. Jobs that involve dealing with others and have friendship opportunities are ways of encouraging social belonging and combating social isolation.

Jobs with these characteristics are termed "enriched." In their Job Characteristics Enrichment Model, which appears in Exhibit 5–1, Hackman and Oldham[27] show that the positive outcomes of job enrichment characteristics are high internal work motivation, high-quality work performance, high satisfaction with the work, and low absenteeism and turnover. However, these outcomes occur at maximum level only when all three of the critical psychological states are experienced: (1) experienced meaningfulness of the work, (2) experienced responsibility for the work outcomes, and (3) knowledge of the actual results of the work. Hackman and Oldham also note that there are three types of individual differences that must be taken into consideration

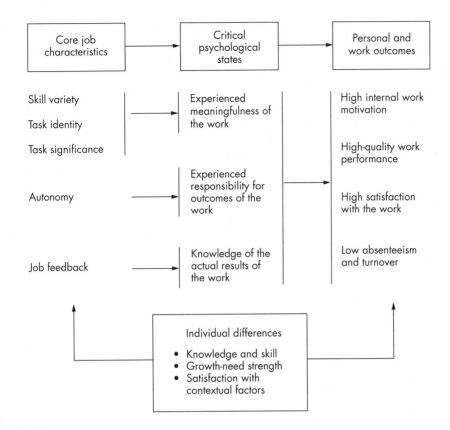

EXHIBIT 5-1 Job Characteristics Enrichment Model

Source: J. R. Hackman and G. R. Oldham, WORK REDESIGN ©1980, p. 90. Reprinted with permission of Pearson Education, Inc., Upper Saddle River, New Jersey.

when planning job redesign projects. The first is the knowledge and skill of the employee—is the employee capable of performing an enriched job? The second is growth-need strength, which refers to the individual's personal need for learning, self-development, and challenge. People with low growth needs may well prefer repetitive jobs to enriched ones. The final individual difference is satisfaction with contextual factors. Job redesign efforts are unlikely to be successful if employees are dissatisfied with other conditions at work.

Ensuring that the work situation is one that employees find motivating and involving is a major, ongoing task of managers. Because of the close relationship between well-designed jobs and productivity, it is an area that managers and organizations cannot afford to overlook. It is possible to design jobs that are more congruent with human needs and motivation. The major ways of doing so are briefly described later.

Job rotation programs move people from one job to another periodically to decrease their boredom and allow them to learn different skills.

Job enlargement policies increase the number of tasks performed by an individual. In an assembly-line example, a worker would perhaps install an entire door panel rather than securing only one tiny part of the door. Herzberg called the addition of interrelated tasks "horizontal job loading."[28] Job enlargement can meet employees' motivational needs because it allows more ownership over a product or process and decreases monotony. It also provides an opportunity for workers to feel more competent, as they may get to use more of their skills. Being responsible for a larger task may increase the meaningfulness of the job in the worker's eyes. However, remember the comment of one critic, "You combine seven boring jobs and what do you get?"

Job enrichment methods attempt to change the nature of the job by broadening responsibilities, giving more autonomy for decision making, creating client systems and direct feedback systems, and generally enlarging the scope of jobs. Herzberg called this type of job design "vertical job loading" because it also includes tasks formerly performed by someone at a higher level—planning and control functions.[29] For example, a sales support clerk who formerly handled only one piece of the paperwork for the entire sales staff is now given responsibility for all paperwork in one district. He is encouraged to deal directly with the sales staff and quickly becomes an important resource for them. He also has discretionary control over the scheduling of his work and the responsibility for making sure he has made no errors. A feedback system is established so he can gauge both the quality and quantity of his output. Both contact with the sales staff and the monitoring of his work were formerly performed by his supervisor.

What is motivating about job enrichment? It resolves the problems of meaninglessness, powerlessness, and isolation factors that cause worker alienation[30] rather than commitment. Job enrichment not only has the same motivational advantages as job enlargement, but the effects of job enrichment are stronger, and enrichment has the added benefit of granting workers autonomy. Autonomy allows people to utilize even more skills and to exercise their creativity and capacity to learn and develop. Research on work redesign programs indicates that they do reduce absenteeism and turnover; however, there are mixed results on productivity. Some job enrichment efforts result in much higher productivity, while others do not.[31]

Sociotechnical system interventions attempt to match the necessary technology of the job with the social needs of the employees. Their goal is to produce a fit or integration of these two components. It's noteworthy that the basic unit of work design here is usually the group rather than the individual. Job rotation, enlargement, and enrichment focus on individual rather than group needs.[32]

The most common example of sociotechnical systems are autonomous work teams. Such teams are totally responsible for assigning the work, determining the work schedule, work process, quality control procedures, reward structure, and so on. One of the most famous examples of autonomous work teams was found in the Volvo plant in Uddevalla, Sweden.[33] Instead of using an assembly line, the cars remained stationary while teams of 8 to 10 workers assembled three entire cars a day. This job design reduced tedium because the workers did a variety of jobs that required expanded skills. Furthermore, the workers experienced both greater task identity and control over their work. The team approach at Uddevalla resulted in increased quality and satisfaction, but productivity and absenteeism were still a problem.[34] The teams required 50 labor hours to build a car, twice the hours needed at Volvo's Belgium plant. The Japanese can build a car in less than 20 hours. To cut costs, Volvo shut down the Uddevalla plant and their Kalmar plant, which also used autonomous work teams. Many car manufacturers are utilizing some form of work teams, but they vary in terms of how many tasks they are responsible for and how much autonomy is granted to the teams.

Sociotechnical systems have the advantages of all the previous design systems plus the added benefit of group membership. Interdependent work teams anchor people firmly within a social system, thus avoiding isolation. Furthermore, groups often are more creative and productive than are individuals when it comes to complex decisions and tasks.

Self-managed work teams, highlighted in Chapter 10, share many similarities with sociotechnical systems. Both emphasize skill variety, task identity, task significance, autonomy, job feedback, and the social belonging that comes from group membership. In sociotechnical systems, however, more attention is specifically concentrated on balancing technical and human systems. Self-managed work teams decide how they will accomplish the goals for which they are responsible and allocate the necessary tasks. They are responsible for planning, scheduling, organizing, directing, controlling, and evaluating their own work process, which is usually an entire process or product. Some teams select and evaluate their own members.

None of the work redesign programs described in this section should be seen as a quick fix for organizations. The initial result may be a decrease in productivity until employees have mastered the new system and worked their way up the learning curve. Some programs never do succeed, but the reasons for failure may have more to do with the way they were implemented than with the merits of the program. Good redesign and implementation can pay off in higher employee motivation. For this reason, managers should carefully consider whether jobs are designed as well as they could be.

THE ROLE OF LEADERSHIP IN FOSTERING MOTIVATION

Managers and, to some degree, team leaders can affect how employees perceive their environment. They shape and direct motivation by establishing expectations and rewards that tap into employee motives and further the organization's goals. The manager's task is to make sure that there is a fit and a direct link—between employee needs and rewards, between performance and rewards, and between employees and jobs. The better the fit, the higher the employee motivation. For this reason, when there are motivation problems, we look closely at what managers and leaders are saying and doing. Leaders and managers must understand *how* employees are motivated and be sure that their words and actions support employee motivation.

Employees make conscious choices about their behavior at work. They calculate whether a certain level of effort will result in a particular goal; they determine whether the reward is worth the effort, and they also compare whether their efforts and rewards are comparable to those of other people. These decisions, which are based on employees' perception of the environment and previous experiences, affect their behavior and level of productivity. These assumptions underlie the second category of motivation theories, *process theories which attempt to describe how personal factors and environmental factors interact and influence each other to produce certain kinds of behavior.* In other words, these theories provide leaders and managers with understandings of how employees are motivated. Examples of these theories are goal-setting theory, equity theory, expectancy theory, and reinforcement theory.

Goal-Setting Theory

One of the easiest and most effective ways to spur motivation is through goal setting. *Goal Setting involves setting a clear objective and ensuring that every participant is aware of what is expected from him or her, if this objective is to be achieved.* Groups that set goals have higher average performance than those that do not. Why does simply setting target goals increase motivation and performance? Goals provide direction and a sense of how much effort is needed to be successful. They also promote the development of a strategy to achieve the goals, mobilize effort, focus attention, and encourage persistence.[35] There are several important lessons to be learned from the research on goal setting: (1) specific goals increase performance, (2) compared to easy goals, difficult goals that are accepted by employees result in higher performance, (3) feedback leads to higher performance than nonfeedback, and (4) people are more committed to goals that are made public and that they themselves set.[36] Goals should be challenging but feasible, and when projects are lengthy, they should have intermediate goals and celebrations. These actions encourage the need for achievement.

Equity Theory

The equity that people perceive in their situation also influences motivation. *According to equity theory, employees evaluate what they receive from a job (outputs such as pay, bonuses, job security, promotions, recognition, etc.) in relation to what they contribute (inputs such as time, skills, creativity, effort, etc.).* They compare their own input-output ratio with (1) relevant others, (2) system policies and precedents, and/or (3) criteria related to the "self," such as previous jobs or family commitments. When inequity exists and they are either overrewarded or underrewarded, people will attempt to correct this situation. Those who are overrewarded may increase production or the quality of their work, but they are also likely to simply find ways to justify the overreward to themselves and thus restore a sense of equity.[37] For example, they may adjust their perceptions of how much effort they really put in to the job, thinking, for example, "Wow, now that I think about it, I did work really hard and I really do deserve more pay than my coworker." Those who are underrewarded may also try a variety of methods to restore equity. They may ask for a pay raise or an increase in other rewards, decrease production or quality, increase absenteeism, and perhaps even resign. When compensation systems are perceived as equitable, employees report greater levels of job satisfaction, organizational commitment, and trust in their supervisors. Perceptions are not always accurate, either on the part of employees or management. For this reason, they should be periodically discussed and subjected to a "reality check."

Equality in workplace rewards, which means that everyone receives the same compensation, does not foster high motivation. If there are no negative consequences for low performance, some will not be motivated to work harder. Simultaneously, high performers who receive nothing more for their extra effort may eventually become demotivated, unless they are motivated by other factors, such as intrinsic needs, a strong sense of professionalism, or by the organizational mission.

Expectancy Theory

Expectancy theory, shown in Exhibit 5–2, assumes that motivation is a function of three linkages: (1) the effort-performance expectation that if a person makes an effort, it will result in good performance, (2) the performance-outcome expectation that good performance will result in a particular outcome or reward, and (3) the valence (value) of the reward to the person.[38] Ability also influences how much effort is necessary, since good performance is more difficult for people with less ability. For example, a student with good study habits may need to study only 10 hours for a test, while a student without the ability to extract and focus on key points may need to put in twice the hours. If a student believes that studying 10 hours for a test will make it possible for her to do extremely well on an exam, she will be more motivated to study than if she has no previous experience with hard work paying off in the classroom. Her professor's exams cannot be so difficult that she thinks her effort won't pay off. Our student must also believe that her good performance on an exam will be fairly graded and will yield an A outcome. If her professor has a reputation for being a biased, careless grader, our student will not put forth much effort because the payoff is uncertain. Finally, she has to think an A is a good thing, a reward that's worth her effort. If all these linkages are in place, she will be motivated.

Note how much the professor's actions in this example affected the student's decisions about how much effort to make and her subsequent behavior. Managerial actions have the same power to motivate or demotivate. To motivate effort, managers have to ensure that feasible performance goals and standards are clearly communicated and that employees have the ability to accomplish them. Managers have to pay attention to employee performance, recognizing whether they are doing well or poorly, and then reward good performance on time with something the employee values. For rewards to be motivating, managers must link them clearly, perhaps publicly, with good performance. Employees will differ in their preference for extrinsic or intrinsic rewards; some want bonuses, for example, while others prefer more autonomy and interesting work.

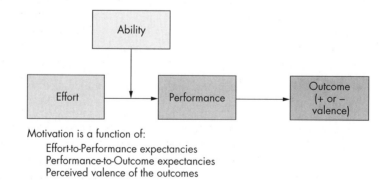

Motivation is a function of:
   Effort-to-Performance expectancies
   Performance-to-Outcome expectancies
   Perceived valence of the outcomes

EXHIBIT 5-2 Expectancy Theory

Source: Adapted from D. A. Nadler and E. E. Lawler III, "Motivation: A Diagnostic Approach," *Perspectives on Behavior in Organizations*, (New York: McGraw-Hill, 1977).

Reinforcement Theory

Our discussion of rewards in expectancy theory leads us to another theory that fosters motivation and influences performance. By mindfully linking performance with outcomes, or failing to do so, managers shape and reinforce employee behavior. Employees can also shape behavior as we say in the "How to Change Your Boss" vignette. Reinforcement theory ignores internal motives and focuses instead on learned behavior. B. F. Skinner developed *operant conditioning, the idea that people continue behavior that is rewarded and suppress behavior that does not lead to desired consequences.*[39] Thus, managers have to understand the effects of their behavior and policies on employees and how they are perceived, so they do not inadvertently reinforce the wrong behaviors. For example, highly productive employees are sometimes "rewarded" only by being assigned extra work that less responsible employees are not completing. Unless they are rewarded for the extra work, the productive employee may perceive this as working more for the same salary (i.e., a punishment), while irresponsible employees are "rewarded" by having less work to do and more free time to fool around at work. As a result, managers sometimes lose their high performers due to burnout or equity complaints. *The main tenets of reinforcement theory are that managers should reinforce desired behavior and discourage undesirable behavior by negative reinforcement, extinction or punishment.*[40]

The first step is to define what good performance looks like and clarify what behavior should be reinforced. Organizations don't always think this through logically. Steve Kerr's famous article about "The Folly of Rewarding A While Hoping for B" lists several examples of rewarding the wrong behavior, such as businesses that hope for long-term growth but reward quarterly earnings or businesses that hope for high quality but reward shipping on schedule, regardless of defects.[41] Another common folly is hoping for teamwork but rewarding individual effort in a manner that fosters competition rather than collaboration.

As the theory goes, if a behavior persists, it is somehow being rewarded. The trick for managers is to figure out where the reward is coming from and determine whether their own behavior is a contributing factor. An entrepreneur complained that he was overworked and wanted his employees to take on more responsibility and decisions. He insisted that he had effectively delegated work to them, but interviews with his staff revealed that he couldn't keep his fingers out of the pie. When they made decisions for their own departments, he overruled them abruptly and publicly, which was embarrassing. This was a *negative reinforcer—desired behavior results in punishment.* Continuing to refer decisions to him had a better pay-off. When asked what he got out of this setup, he realized that being the "all-knowing patriarch" was the reward that kept him from changing. He figured out a more constructive way to share his knowledge without disempowering his employees and started praising them for making decisions.

Positive reinforcement involves giving people positive outcomes when they perform the desired behavior, such as a bonus when their team finishes a product launch on time. Outcomes can consist of praise, pay, promotion, an attractive project assignment, and so on, whatever the individual views as desirable. Outcomes should occur in a timely, consistent manner to emphasize the link between the behavior and the positive result. It is better to create a positive environment and reward positive behavior than to focus primarily on punishing or disciplining negative behavior. Kouzes and Posner suggest that leaders "find people who are doing things right" and praise them.[42] Praise, however, can never be phony, and managers cannot simply ignore serious negative employee behavior without losing the respect of good employees or causing equity complaints.

When managers wonder why employees exhibit chronic negative or dysfunctional behavior, sometimes the answer is simply "because they can." There are no negative consequences to stop them. Office bullies can satisfy their need for power at no cost, as long as the boss does not confront them or discipline them. If employees are habitually late with their work but never suffer for this, they will continue. Unfortunately, it is often coworkers who pay the price, as they scramble to rearrange their own work schedule to accommodate a colleague's tardiness. To be effective, managers may have to punish negative behaviors that impede performance. *Punishment is defined as administering an undesired or negative consequence in response to undesired behavior.* Organizations substitute the word "discipline" for "punishment." Discipline can take the form of a reprimand, warning letter, suspension, pay cut, demotion, termination, loss of a hoped-for assignment and so forth. Punishment or discipline should take place shortly after the behavior occurs so the link is clear. It should be handled privately with tact and without emotion. Whenever possible, punishment or discipline should be couched as the natural consequences of the person's negative behavior. The chapter on performance management and appraisal discusses how to confront employees on performance problems.

Extinction occurs when the reinforcer for an undesired behavior is removed. A manager who was promoted from within realized that he could not continue to have all of the same types of social interaction with his buddies at work. Some of their conversation topics (gossip, ruminations about what senior management was thinking) were no longer appropriate for him, and yet he did not want to lose their friendship or act like he was too good for them. He maintained the friendships, but learned to walk away when certain topics came up; eventually his buddies realized which topics were off-limits because those topics were not rewarded by his attention and participation.

The Leader Role: The Importance of Words and Actions

So how do leaders' words and actions affect motivation? All of the following action scripts that foster motivation are drawn directly from the motivation theories discussed in the previous sections.

- **Creating the right vision** Leaders set a vision that is inspiring and motivating
- **Ensuring the employees are placed in the right jobs** They ensure that employees are placed in jobs that fit their unique needs and skills.
- **Setting challenging goals** Managers and leaders can establish high standards, which they themselves model. They can set clear goals and performance expectations, which are rewarded as promised.
- **Monitoring and rewarding performance** Effective leaders track, recognize, reward, and celebrate progress toward organizational goals, ensuring that the organization's reward system is effective and fair. And, they can reward good performance and punish inadequate performance.
- **Proactively managing low performers** When employees are not performing, expert leaders proactively deal with low performance—they don't ignore it and hope it gets better on its own. If low performance is caused by a lack of skill, they provide training for the employee. If the reward system is reinforcing the wrong behavior, they change the reward structure. But if these types of interventions are unsuccessful, they also work to reassign chronic low performers who cannot be salvaged to a better fitting job or ultimately fire them, sending a message to the rest of the organization that mediocrity is not tolerated.
- **Creating a culture that values employees and performance** Effective motivators show genuine concern about employees' personal development, investing in that development through training and coaching. They enact the self-fulfilling prophecy to think positively about their workers and peers and expect the best from them. They also create an organizational culture that values good performance and customer service. Along the way, they can develop supportive, respectful relationships with employees so there is less likelihood of disappointing the other party.

In addition to creating the right environment for motivation, leaders and managers also have to avoid doing the wrong things; there are many ways to demotivate employees. Common demotivators are: politics and favoritism, unclear expectations, unproductive meetings, hypocrisy (saying one thing and doing another), constant excessive change, withholding information, excessive criticism, and low-quality standards that prevent employees from taking pride in their work.[43] Employees have a long memory for the thoughtless words and actions of bad bosses, which may explain the popularity of the Dilbert comic strip, whose totty-headed manager both demotivates and infuriates employees. Obstacles are also demotivators, because they make good performance more difficult, if not impossible, and lead some employees to give up. Red tape, departmental wrangling that prevents employees from accomplishing their goals, and work overload that prevents employees from doing excellent work are typical obstacles. The job of managers, supervisors, and team leaders is to remove obstacles. Novice managers are more likely to forget that this is one of their key tasks. They demotivate workers unconsciously without understanding the negative consequences of their words or actions.

To summarize, leaders and managers play an important role in fostering an atmosphere that either encourages or discourages motivation. But, broader organizational factors also have to be taken into consideration.

THE ROLE OF THE ORGANIZATION IN FOSTERING MOTIVATION

There are many aspects of organizations that influence motivation, such as their vision, mission statement, culture, policies, and HR practices, so a systems approach to motivation is useful. Firms that are known for having highly motivated employees, such as Chick-Fil-A, Southwest Airlines, AptarGroup, Inc., and Lincoln Electric have a strong organizational culture with a team spirit, job stability, and growth opportunities, in addition to a carefully thought out compensation and reward systems. Employees have different needs and those needs can change over the course of their career. Therefore, many employers offer cafeteria benefits so workers can choose those that best suit their needs. Some employers are reducing long-term fixed pay and increasing variable performance based pay to give themselves more flexibility and to motivate workers. Because some employees have less trust in long-term payoffs for their efforts, they prefer short-term incentives, which are more successful for ensuring high productivity, morale, and retention.[44] Employee stock options and gain-sharing are options that allow employees to benefit when the organization as a whole performs well. In gain-sharing, the organization establishes a base period of performance. When performance gains occur, a formula is used to share the financial gains with all employees. Gain-sharing focuses attention on cost savings, continuous improvement, and higher performance from everyone, including managers.

Compensation is a complex issue. Some studies indicate that providing extrinsic rewards actually takes the intrinsic pleasure out of performing a task.[45] Money is very motivating to some people, but not to everyone. Not all rewards have to be extrinsic. In a survey of 1,800 American workers, the following items were ranked more highly than pay as major motivators for employees: recognition of the importance of personal and family time, organizational direction, opportunities for personal growth, ability to challenge the way things are done, satisfaction from everyday work, and employee participation in planning organizational change.[46] Some of these are similar to the motivators Herzberg identified in his earlier research: the work itself, achievement, challenge, responsibility, advancement, growth, and recognition.[47]

Companies cannot compete without motivated employees. CEO Howard Schultz attributes Starbucks' growth and success to sharing company profits in the form of stock options (Bean Stock) and health insurance benefits for both full- and part-time workers. To Schultz's knowledge, no other company provides benefits like these, but the payoff for Starbucks is low turnover and high productivity. "If people relate to the company they work for, if they will form an emotional tie to it, and buy into its dreams, they will pour their hearts into making it better."[48]

Costco also provides better-than-average wages and benefits in its industry and presents an interesting counterpoint to its closest rival Sam's Club, which is owned by Wal-Mart. The average hourly pay for Costco's 113,000 employees is US $17, 42 percent higher than Sam's Club.

Even though Wall Street analysts advise CEO Jim Sinegal to be less generous, he insists that Costco's policies are not altruistic but just good business; the results are very low rates of both turnover and employee theft. Furthermore, Costco shoppers, who tend to be more affluent than Sam's Club customers, appreciate that low prices are not the result of skimping on employees. Sinegal devotes the same intense energy to retaining both his customers and his employees. "Besides higher pay, Costco contributes generously to its workers' 401(k) plans, starting with 3 percent of salary the second year and rising to 9 percent after 25 years. Its insurance plans absorb most dental expenses, and part-time workers are eligible for health insurance after just six months on the job, compared with two years at Wal-Mart. Eighty-five percent of Costco's workers have health insurance, compared with less than half at Wal-Mart and Target. Costco also has not shut out unions, as some of its rivals have."[49]

In summary, managers and organizations cannot influence employee motivation unless they understand what motivates individual employees. Apparently this is easier said than done; studies repeatedly show that when workers and supervisors rank job factors in order of their importance to workers, their answers do not concur. In one study of ten job factors, the workers' first, second, and third ranked items—appreciation for their work, being in on things, and sympathetic help on personal problems—were ranked eighth, ninth, and tenth by their supervisors! The supervisors mistakenly assumed that good wages, job security, and promotional growth were most important to the workers.[50] We often hold mistaken assumptions about what motivates others, which is why it's important to hone our skills at decoding human behavior.

CLASS ACTIVITY: DIAGNOSING MOTIVATION IN THE DONOR SERVICES DEPARTMENT

The purpose of this activity is to provide you with an opportunity to recognize motivation problems related to theories we have studied and to counsel an employee on motivation issues. (Time allotted: 95 minutes)

STEP 1. Group Applications of Theory (20 minutes)

    a. Divide into groups of five to six (your learning groups). Each group will be assigned one of the following theories to discuss with respect to the Donor Services Department, on page 673.

        1. Maslow's Hierarchy of Needs
        2. McClelland's Need Theory
        3. Job Characteristics Model
        4. Goal-Setting Theory
        5. Equity Theory
        6. Expectancy Theory
        7. Reinforcement Theory

    b. As a group, answer the following two questions regarding your assigned theory and be prepared to present your answers to the rest of the class in a 2-minute presentation.

        1. What problems occur in the case that can be explained by this theory?
        2. What recommendations should be made based on this theory?

STEP 2. Group Presentations (20 minutes)

    Each group gives a two-minute presentation.

STEP 3. Motivation Counseling Session Role Play (20 minutes)

    a. Form trios and select one person to play the role of Sam, one to be Elena and the other to be the observer. Sam has told Elena he wants to meet with her to discuss her job performance because she seems less motivated now than she did in her old job. In the next 10 minutes, Sam and Elena should plan separately what they both want to accomplish during this session, based on the information in the case. During this period the observer can coach Sam and/or Elena on their goals and strategies for the meeting. Discuss what Sam will attempt to accomplish in the interview and how he will go about it. "Sam" should focus on the motivational factors affecting Elena and what would make her job more motivating. "Elena" should also prepare to speak with Sam, by thinking about (1) what motivates and demotivates her in her present job; and (2) how she would like to change her boss and shape his behavior (refer to the second vignette).

    b. Conduct the role-play during the next ten minutes. The observer should note (1) how well Sam does at drawing out and understanding Elena's views and (2) how successful Elena is at trying to change Sam's behavior.

STEP 4.   Plenary Role Play Debriefing (15 minutes)

    1. How well did "Sam" understand "Elena's" views and her situation in the office?
    2. What are the factors that play a role in her performance?
    3. How successful was Elena at attempting to change Sam's behavior?
    4. Did you find a solution?
    5. What have you learned about counseling employees on motivation issues?

STEP 5.   Plenary Case Discussion (20 minutes)

    1. What was Joanna Reed's diagnosis of the situation in the donor services department?
    2. What should she recommend to Sam Wilson?
    3. Describe the managerial styles of Sam, José, and Elena. What is the impact of their styles?
    4. How can motivation be improved in the department?
    5. What are the cultural factors that influence this case?

THE MOTIVATED CLASSROOM

The preceding chapter contained a class activity devoted to transforming your class into a learning organization. To make that a reality, we also need to think about the role motivation plays in a learning organization. The purpose of this exercise is to apply the lessons of motivation theory and practice to this course by devising a motivation program. (Time allotted: 55-75).

STEP 1.   Divide into groups of five to six (your learning groups). Each group will be assigned at least one (depending on the number of groups) of the following topics to discuss and apply. (20–30 minutes)

    a. Maslow's Hierarchy of Needs
    b. McClelland's Need Theory
    c. Job Characteristics Model
    d. Goal-Setting Theory
    e. Equity Theory
    f. Expectancy Theory
    g. Reinforcement Theory

Please answer these questions:

    1. How does this theory or concept relate to the classroom and the learning organization we want to create?
    2. Are there any practices that companies are successfully using to create a motivated workforce that you think we should borrow?
    3. Based on the discussion so far, brainstorm some ways to motivate yourself and your classmates. Decide on your top recommendation. Use these criteria to help you decide: Remember that the instructor should not be the sole source of motivation and make sure your recommendation is feasible and easy to implement.

STEP 2.   A representative from each group briefly explains how the group's theory applies to the classroom and presents the group's recommendation. (20 minutes)

STEP 3.   The class and the professor decide which recommendation(s) they want to adopt. (15 minutes)

LEARNING POINTS

1. Motivation refers to the psychological forces that determine the direction of people's behavior, their level of effort, and level of persistence.

2. Motivation is not something that is "done" to other people. It is an internal state that directs individuals toward certain goals.

3. The manager's job is to understand and channel the motivation employees already possess and direct it toward tasks that further the organization's objectives.

4. The sources of motivation are either intrinsic (e.g., the work itself) or extrinsic (e.g., external consequences like material or social rewards, avoidance of punishment).

5. Individuals are motivated by different needs, such as Maslow's physiological, security, affiliation, self-esteem, and self-actualization needs.

6. McClelland's theory of motivation focuses on three needs that are learned from one's culture and family: affiliation, achievement, and power. Almost everyone has these needs in varying degrees. Job performance is affected by people's motive patterns as well as by the values that individuals hold.

7. There are two faces, positive and negative, to n-Power (socialized and personalized) and n-Affiliation (interest and assurance).

8. According to McClelland, high achievers:
    a. Like to set their own goals.
    b. Tend to avoid either extremely difficult or extremely easy goals.
    c. Prefer tasks that provide immediate feedback on their performance.

9. Jobs that are motivating have the following characteristics:
    a. Skill variety
    b. Task identity
    c. Task significance
    d. Autonomy
    e. Job feedback

10. Job redesign efforts have been found to improve both satisfaction and productivity in some cases. However, job enrichment programs are also contingent on the individual worker's (1) knowledge and skill; (2) need for growth, self-development, and challenge; and (3) satisfaction with contextual factors.

11. Methods of job redesign and motivating employees are:
    a. Job rotation—switching different jobs.
    b. Job enlargement—horizontal job loading, which combines related tasks.
    c. Job enrichment—vertical job loading, which increases job scope by including planning and control functions formerly held by supervisors. It also includes client contact and direct output feedback.
    d. Sociotechnical systems—integration of the needs of both people and technology. The basic work unit is usually the group rather than the individual. Autonomous work teams are an example.
    e. Self-managed work teams decide how they will accomplish the goals for which they are responsible and allocate the necessary tasks. They are responsible for planning, scheduling, organizing, directing, controlling, and evaluating their own work process, which is usually an entire process or product.

12. According to research on goal setting, higher performance results when goals are specific, difficult (but accepted by employees), and when employees receive feedback on their progress. Publicly stated goals are more likely to be accomplished than private ones.

13. Equity theory maintains that employee motivation is affected by the perceived fairness of what people contribute and receive.

14. Expectancy theory assumes that motivation is a function of three linkages: (1) the effort-performance expectation that if a person makes an effort, it will result in good performance, (2) the performance-outcome expectation that good performance will result in a particular outcome or reward, and (3) the valence (value) of the reward to the person.

15. According to reinforcement theory, people learn to use behaviors that are rewarded and to suppress behavior that does not lead to desired consequences. Positive reinforcement, punishment or discipline, and extinction are used to shape employee behavior.

16. Managers can create an environment that fosters motivation by setting clear performance standards and ensuring there are fits between employee needs and jobs and between employee needs and rewards, and by ensuring that good performance is rewarded fairly.

17. While money is a highly valued reward for some people, other rewards are more important to other employees. For example, Herzberg identified these intrinsic factors as motivators: the work itself, achievement, challenge, responsibility, advancement, growth, and recognition.

 **ACTION SCRIPTS**

FOR EMPLOYEES

- Employees who are expert at self motivation view every work experience as an opportunity to learn more about their needs and figure out what type of work they find most motivating. In this respect, even "bad" jobs hold valuable lessons.

- They also take responsibility for becoming aware of what motivates them—take assessment tests, ask for feedback from people with good judgment who know them well, watch how they (and others) spend their time and what they enjoy doing. One of the characteristics of successful people is that they love what they do and do not perceive it as "work." Instruments like the Strong Campbell Personal Interest Inventory, available at many university counseling centers, are helpful for identifying the professions of people with similar interests.

- They seek out or create jobs and work settings that they find motivating. Rather than taking the first job that is offered, they make sure it is a good fit for them.

- They respond proactively to demotivation. If they have a demotivating boss or work environment, rather than working less and harming their work reputation, they either try to improve the situation, look for another job, or do a good job in spite of the demotivating boss. Being a professional means adhering to high standards of performance, regardless of the rewards or lack of rewards that come from the environment or one's superior. In some situations, this may be as good as it gets (other than the paycheck) (and others).

FOR MANAGERS

- Managers who are skilled motivators look for evidence of fit or lack of fit between employee needs and jobs and their rewards. They work hard to place people in jobs they find rewarding.

- Experts know that figuring out what motivates employees is not always a simple matter of asking them. Learning about employees' nonwork activities, observing what they do with discretionary time at work, and determining what type of work or projects they enjoy are indirect methods of gauging their motive patterns. Employee surveys can provide information about satisfaction with jobs and rewards. The yearly performance appraisal provides a good opportunity to check whether the manager's assumptions about what motivates an employee are accurate. There is a close relationship between understanding what motivates your workers and negotiating and renegotiating an effective psychological contract with them.

- Whenever they contemplate changes in the organization, skilled motivators consider employee needs and how they will be impacted. For example, a secretary with a very boring job that is redeemed only by a central location that allows her to satisfy a high need for affiliation will not be excited about a new workstation in an isolated location. The easiest ways to avoid making errors of this sort are to understand what makes the job challenging or at least palatable for each employee and to discuss possible changes with employees before they are made.

- Experts take pains to create an inspiring shared vision for their team, work unit, or department. Even if the job is miles away from the executive suite, all units can profit from being reminded about how their work will achieve the vision, and what progress has been made.

- They ask employees what is going on when the organization is at its best and encourage them to make this a daily reality.

- Expert motivators understand that they set the stage of motivation by creating an environment that helps employees achieve great performance by:
  - Communicating high expectations for employees or team members and thinking positively about workers and peers so that they live up to expectations, in keeping with the self-fulfilling prophecy.
  - Setting challenging but attainable goals.
  - Establishing clear work objectives and standards of good performance.
  - Providing appropriate feedback to encourage achievement among employees.
  - Providing feedback on an ongoing basis rather than waiting until projects are completed.
  - Removing demotivators that frustrate employees and sap their energy and morale.
  - Devoting time and effort to recognizing employee contributions as well as praising employees sincerely whenever doing something right.
  - Linking rewards to performance and behaviors that promote the organization's goals.
  - Ensuring that rewards are equitably distributed; people who produce more should receive greater rewards.
  - Using a variety of rewards that individual employees find valuable or motivating. Rewards can also be chosen with the participation of employees.
  - Analyzing whether the right behaviors are rewarded and whether there are negative consequences for negative behaviors, and when negative behaviors persist, figuring out what is rewarding them.

- Skilled motivators confront low performers to discover whether the problem is inability or unwillingness to do the job correctly. If the problem is inability, they provide coaching or training. If the problem is unwillingness, they explain the consequences of their performance on the work and the organization; describe what will happen if their performance does not improve; make sure the employees understand clearly what is expected of them; create an action plan with a timeline by which their performance must improve; and monitor their progress carefully.

FOR ORGANIZATIONAL ARCHITECTS

- Expert organizational architects recognize that organizational design and organizational policies can powerfully affect employee motivation. They take special care to align the organizational reward systems, job design processes, employee selection procedures, and performance appraisal policies with the organizational mission. They periodically check to make sure the alignment is correct and appropriate.

PERSONAL APPLICATION ASSIGNMENT

The topic of this assignment is to think back on a motivation experience that was significant for you. Choose an experience that intrigues you and that you want to learn more about.

A. Concrete Experience

   1. Objectively describe the experience (who, what, when, where, how) (2 points)

   2. Subjectively describe your feelings, perceptions, and thoughts that occurred during (not after) the experience. What did others seem to be feeling? (2 points)

B. Reflective Observation

   1. Looking back at the experience, what were the perspectives of the key actors (including you)? (2 points)

   2. Why did the people involved (including you) behave as they did? (2 points)

C. Abstract Conceptualization

    1. Relate concepts or theories from the assigned readings or the lecture to the experience. Explain thoroughly how they apply to your experience. Please apply at least two concepts or theories and cite them correctly. (4 points)

D. Active Experimentation

    1. What did you learn about motivation from this experience? (1 point)

    2. What did you learn about yourself? (1 point)

    3. What action steps will you take to be more effective in the future? (2 points)

E. Integration, Synthesis, and Writing

    1. Did you integrate and synthesize the four sections? (1 point)

    2. Was the Personal Application Assignment well written and easy to understand? (1 point)

    3. Was it free of spelling and grammar errors? (2 points)

ENDNOTES

[1] R. Kanfer, "Motivation Theory and Industrial and Organizational Psychology, " in M. D. Dunnette and L. M. Hough, eds., *Handbook of Industrial and Organizational Psychology*, 2nd Ed., *vol. 1* (Palo Alto, CA: Consulting Psychologists Press, (1990): 75–170.

[2] F. Herzberg, B. Mausner, and B. Snyderman, *The Motivation to Work* (New York: John Wiley, 1959).

[3] R. J. House, A. Howard and G. Walker "The Prediction of Managerial Success: A Competitive Test of the Person-situation Debate," *Academy of Management Best Papers Proceedings* (1991): 215–219; J. E. Hunter, "Cognitive Ability, Cognitive Aptitudes, Job Knowledge, and Job Performance," *Journal of Vocational Behavior 29* (1986): 340–362; L. S. Gottfreson, "Societal Consequences of the g Factor in Employment, *Journal of Vocational Behavior 29* (1986): 379-410; G. F. Dreher, and R. D. Bretz, "Cognitive Ability and Career and Career Attainment: Moderating Effects of Early Career Success, " *Journal of Applied Psychology 76*(3) (1991): 392–397; F. L. Schmidt, D. S. Ones, and J. E. Hunter, "Personnel Selection," *Annual Review of Psychology, 43* (1992): 627–670.

[4] C. O'Reilly and J. Chatman. "Working Smarter and Harder: A Longitudinal Study of Managerial Success," *Administrative Science Quarterly 39*(4) (1994): 603–627.

[5] Kanfer, "Motivation Theory and Industrial and Organizational Psychology.

[6] N. A. Adler, *International Dimensions of Organizational Behavior* (Cincinnati, OH: South-Western, 2001); G. Hofstede, "Motivation, Leadership and Organization: Do American Theories Apply Abroad?" *Organizational Dynamics 9*(1) (1980): 42–63.

[7] A. Maslow, *Motivation and Personality* (New York: Harper & Row, 1970).

[8] Adler, *International Dimensions of Organizational Behavior*; H. J. Reitz, "The Relative Importance of Five Categories of Needs among Industrial Workers in Eight Countries," *Academy of Management Proceedings* (1975): 270–273.

[9] Reitz, ibid.

[10] D. C. McClelland, *The Achieving Society* (Princeton, NJ: D. Van Nostrand, 1961) and *Human Motivation* (Glenview, IL: Scott, Foresman, 1985).

[11] Hofstede, "Motivation, Leadership and Organization: Do American Theories Apply Abroad?"

[12] D. C. McClelland and D. H. Burnham, "Power Is the Great Motivator," *Harvard Business Review 81*(1) (January 2003): 117–126.

[13] R. E. Boyatzis, "The Need for Close Relationships and the Manager's Job," *The Organizational Behavior Reader* (Englewood Cliffs, NJ: Prentice Hall, 1991):118–124.

[14] K. Noujaim, "Some Motivational Determinants of Effort Allocation," Ph.D. Thesis, Sloan School of Management, MIT (1968).

[15] G. A. Yukl, *Leadership in Organizations* (Upper Saddle River, NJ: Prentice Hall, 2002); Noujaim, "Some Motivational Determinants of Effort Allocation."

[16] Noujaim, "Some Motivational Determinants of Effort Allocation."

[17] H. A. Wainer and I. M. Rubin, "Motivation of Research and Development Entrepreneurs: Determinants of Company Success," *Journal of Applied Psychology 53*(3) (1969): 178–184.

[18] McClelland and Burnham, "Power Is the Great Motivator."

[19] McClelland and Burnham, "Power Is the Great Motivator."

[20] A. Howard and D. Bray, *Managerial Lives in Transition: Advancing Age and Changing Times* (New York: Guilford, 1988).

[21] D. C. McClelland, Retrospective Commentary to "Power Is the Great Motivator." In S. Kerr (ed.), *Ultimate Rewards* (Cambridge, MA: Harvard Business Review Books, 1997): 81.

[22] A. M. Harrell and M. J. Stahl, "A Behavioral Decision Theory Approach for Measuring McClelland's Trichotomy of Needs," *Journal of Applied Psychology 66* (April 1981): 242–47; M. J. Stahl and A. M. Harrell, "Evolution and Validation of a Behavioral Theory Measurement Approach to Achievement, Power, and Affiliation," *Journal of Applied Psychology 67* (6) (December 1982): 744–51; and M. J. Stahl, "Achievement, Power, and Managerial Motivation: Selecting Managerial Talent with the Job Choice Exercise," *Personnel Psychology 36*(4) (Winter 1983): 775–89.

[23] J. D. Andrews, "The Achievement Motive in Two Types of Organizations," *Journal of Personality and Social Psychology 6* (1967): 163–68.

[24] C. P. Alderfer, "A Critique of Salancik and Pfeffer's Examination of Need-Satisfaction Theories," *Administrative Science Quarterly 22* (1977): 658–672.

[25] This list is composed of factors identified by J. R. Hackman and G. Oldham, *Work Redesign* (Reading, MA: Addison-Wesley, 1980): 77–80.

[26] B. Garson, "Luddites in Lordstown," *Harpers*, (June 1972): 235.

[27] J. R. Hackman and G. R. Oldham, "Development of the Job Diagnostic Survey," *Journal of Applied Psychology 60* (1975): 159–70.

[28] F. Herzberg, "One More Time: How Do You Motivate Employees?" *Harvard Business Review 81*(1) (January-February 2003).

[29] Ibid.

[30] M. Seeman, "On the Meaning of Alienation," *American Sociological Review 24* (1959), 783–91; and "Alienation Studies," *Annual Review of Sociology 1* (1975): 91–123; and R. Blauner, *Alienation and Freedom: The Factory Worker and His Industry* (Chicago: University of Chicago Press, 1964).

[31] R. W. Griffin, "Effects of Work Redesign on Employee Perceptions, Attitudes, and Behaviors: A Long-term Investigation," *Academy of Management Journal 34* (June 1991): 425–35.

[32] An entire issue of *the Journal of Applied Behavioral Science 22* (3) (1986), edited by W. Pasmore and W. Barko, is devoted to sociotechnical systems and includes information about autonomous work teams.

[33] J. Kapstein, "Volvo's Radical New Plant: The Death of the Assembly Line?" *Business Week*, (August 28, 1989): 92–93.

[34] S. Prokesch, "Edges Fray on Volvo's Brave New Humanistic World," *New York Times*, (July 7, 1991): C5.

[35] E. A. Locke, and G. P. Latham, *A Theory of Goal Setting and Task Performance* (Upper Saddle River, NJ: Prentice Hall, 1990); and P. C. Early, G. B. Northcraft, C. Lee, and T. R. Lituchy, "Impact of Process and Outcome Feedback on the Relation of Goal Setting to Task Performance," *Academy of Management Journal 33*(1) (1990): 87–105.

[36] M. E. Tubbs, "Commitment as a Moderator of the Goal-Performance Relation: A Case for Clearer Construct Definition," *Journal of Applied Psychology 78*(1) (1993): 86–97.

[37] J. S. Adams, "Inequity in Social Exchanges," in L. Berkowitz (ed.), *Advances in Experimental Social Psychology* (New York: Academic Press, 1965): 16–23.

[38] V. H. Vroom, *Work and Motivation* (New York: Wiley, 1964). Please see the Nadler and Lawler article in the *Organizational Behavior Reader* on expectancy theory.

[39] B. F. Skinner. *Contingencies of Reinforcement*. New York: Appleton-Century-Crofts, (1969).

[40] F. Luthans and R. Kreitner, *Organizational Behavior Modification and Beyond: An Operant and Social Learning Approach* (Glenview, IL: Scott, Foresman, 1985). For excellent compilations of the research on this theory, see F. Andrasik, "Organizational Behavior Modification on Business Settings: A Methodological and Content Review," *Journal of Organizational Behavior Management, 10*(1) (1989): 59–77; and G. A. Merwi, Jr., J. A. Thomason, and E. E. Sanford, "A Methodology and Content Review of Organizational Behavior Management in the Private Sector: 1978–1986," *Journal of Organizational Behavior Management, 10*(1) (1989): 39–57.

[41] S. Kerr, "The Folly of Rewarding A While Hoping for B," *Academy of Management Executive 9* (1) (1995): 7–14; and the *Organizational Behavior Reader*.

[42] J. Kouzes & B. Posner. *The Challenge of Leadership* (San Francisco: Jossey-Bass, 2002).

[43] D. Spitzer, "The Seven Deadly Demotivators," *Management Review 84* (11) (November 1995): 56–61 and *SuperMotivation* (New York: Amacom, 1995).

[44] B. Tulgan, "Trends Point to a Dramatic Generational Shift in the Future Workforce," *Wiley Periodicals* (2004): 23–31.

[45] A. Kohn, "Why Incentive Plans Cannot Work," *Harvard Business Review 71*(5) (September-October 1993): 54–63.

[46] D. S. Campbell, "Firms Try to Adjust for Worker's New Career Expectations," *Knight-Ridder/Tribune Business News*, (October 6, 1998).

[47] F. Herzberg, B. Mausner, and B. Snyderman, *The Motivation to Work* (New York: John Wiley, 1959).

[48] L. Harman, "Starbucks' Schultz Reveals How Firm Keeps Perking," *San Diego Business Journal 18*(39): (September 29, 1997): 4.

[49] S. Greenhouse, "How Costco Became the Anti-Wal-Mart" *The New York Times*, (July 17, 2005): BU: 1, column 2.

[50] A. L. LeDuc Jr., "Motivation of Programmers," *DATA BASE 11*(4) (1980): 4–12.

Chapter 6

▲▲

VALUES
AND WORKPLACE ETHICS

OBJECTIVES By the end of this chapter, you should be able to:

A. Describe how organizations foster unethical behavior.

B. Explain how organizations can promote ethical behavior.

C. Define ethics and values.

D. Better articulate your own values.

E. Distinguish between ethical and nonethical values.

F. Explain and recognize the stages of moral reasoning.

G. Describe five different ethical models.

H. Explain corporate social responsibility and its benefits.

RAY ANDERSON AND THE NATURAL STEP

In 1994 Ray Anderson, 61-year-old founder of a commercial carpet company called Interface Inc., had an epiphany. It came during a period of soul searching that was triggered when his company slipped from the number 1 slot. An employee gave Anderson the "Ecology of Commerce," a book by Paul Hawken who believes that the Earth's living systems are in decline, the industrial system is the largest culprit in this decline, and therefore, businesses should take the lead in promoting sustainability.[1] Companies need to control the creation of harmful waste rather than focus solely on waste disposal. After reading about rapidly depleting natural resources and toxins that accumulate in the human body and pass on to the next generation, Anderson thought of his own grandchildren and wept. He realized that his company was guilty of consuming a disproportionate amount of hydrocarbons as well as producing harmful toxins.[2]

Anderson developed a new mission for Interface—create zero pollution with zero oil consumption while simultaneously advancing the interests of everyone involved in the company's endeavors (investors, employees, and customers). Interface calls this goal "climbing Mt. Sustainability," achieving zero footprint—leaving no impact on the environment—by 2020. With the help of environmental consultants and The Natural Step format, his employees examined their work processes and designed less wasteful ways of producing carpet. For example, Interface originated the idea of installing carpet tiles under a "perpetual lease" program: for a monthly rental fee Interface removes deteriorated individual tiles and recycles them into new carpet. This is less wasteful than the general industry practices of replacing an entire carpet that is only worn in heavy traffic areas and failing to recycle old carpet. Interface also considers its employees a part of nature. In an industry noted for poor working conditions, Interface's mill is relatively quiet, odor-free, and sunny.[3]

As a result of Interface's new environmental mission, the company has saved $262 million in costs for eliminating waste.[4] Furthermore, many other businesses want to buy carpet from a "green" (environmentally concerned) vendor, so Interface's market share increased.[5] However, Interface has not been profitable since 2000, which Anderson attributes to external factors like the dot.com bust, 9/11, and a 40 percent decline in office furnishing purchases.[6] While critics are beginning to wonder if the firm's heavy focus on sustainability has harmed the firm financially, Anderson, now chairman of the board, insists that this focus was the reason Interface survived the economic downturn. In addition to increased cost savings, Interface's sustainability program led to improved, creative products, highly motivated employees, and customer goodwill that no amount of advertising could produce.[7] In the last 10 years, Interface has reduced its global greenhouse gas emissions by 52 percent, reclaimed 66 million pounds of carpet that would otherwise have ended up in a landfill, and has some plants that rely completely on renewable energy sources like wind and solar power. As a result, both Anderson and Interface have won numerous awards.

Anderson has become one of the leading U.S. proponents of The Natural Step, a not-for-profit environmental education organization founded by Dr. Karl-Henrik Robèrt. Robèrt, a Swedish pediatric oncologist, was motivated by an anomaly he observed in his work with children suffering from cancer. The parents of these children frequently vowed to do anything they could to save their children, including sacrificing their own lives. Yet Sweden as a whole was fairly complacent about taking steps to eradicate the environmental causes of cancer. As Robèrt noted "After a time of pulling drowning bodies out of a river, the intelligent person wants to go upstream to see if he can't prevent them falling in in the first place." Robèrt began a process of dialogue and consensus building about sustainability with scientists; fifty scientists, after numerous iterations, agreed on four basic, non-negotiable system conditions for sustainability. Due to his extraordinary networking skills, Robèrt succeeded in sending a booklet and an audiotape on these Natural Step principles to every household and school in Sweden.[8]

Sustainability is defined as meeting the needs of present generations without compromising the ability of future generations to meet their own needs. The moral basis for sustainability is the ethical position that destroying the future capacity of the Earth to support life is wrong. The Natural Step program promotes sustainability because it encourages people in organizations to consider the following four system conditions whenever they make decisions.

1. Substances from the Earth's crust must not systematically increase in the ecosphere. This means that fossil fuels, metals and other minerals must not be extracted at a faster pace than their slow redeposit and reintegration into the Earth's crust. This requires a radically reduced dependence on mined minerals and fossil fuels. Businesses must ask themselves this question: "Which materials that are mined from the Earth's surface do we use (e.g., metals, fuels) and can we use less?"

2. Substances produced by society must not systematically increase in the ecosphere. Nature cannot withstand a systematic buildup of substances produced by humans, which means that substances must not be produced at a faster pace than they can be broken down and integrated into the cycles of nature or deposited into the Earth's crust. The question for business is: "Which unnatural substances does our organization depend on (e.g., plastics, chemical compounds) and can we use less?"

3. The physical basis for productivity and diversity of nature must not be systematically diminished. Nature cannot withstand a systematic deterioration of its capacity for renewal. In other words, societies cannot harvest or manipulate ecosystems in such a way that

productive capacity and biodiversity systematically diminish. This requires that all people critically examine how they harvest renewable resources and adjust consumption and land use practices to be well within the regenerative capacities of the planet's ecosystems. The question for businesses is: "Does our organization depend on activities that encroach on productive parts of nature (e.g., over-fishing) and can we decrease these activities?"

4. For the three previous conditions to be met, there must be fair and efficient use of resources with respect to meeting human needs. Satisfying basic human needs must take precedence over the provision of luxuries, and there should be a just resource distribution. This will result in the social stability and cooperation required to make the changes that will eventually ensure sustainability. The question for businesses is: "Is our organization economically dependent on using an unnecessarily large amount of resources in relation to added human value (e.g., cutting down forests inhabited by indigenous people whose way of life is thereby threatened) and can we lessen this dependence?"

The Natural Step has gained widespread popularity in Swedish municipalities and multinationals such as IKEA, Electrolux, OK Petroleum, and Scandi Hotels. The program has also spread to other countries. In the United States, The Natural Step has worked with Bank of America, Home Depot, McDonalds, Nike, and Starbucks among other organizations.[9] According to early adopters of The Natural Step, the program has helped companies to achieve the following benefits:[10]

- Reduce operating costs.
- Stay ahead of regulatory frameworks and protect long-term investments.
- Enhance the organization's standing among stakeholder groups including customers, suppliers, and employees.
- Incorporate environmental concern into the culture of the workplace.
- Spark creativity among employees, especially those in product and process design.
- Differentiate their products and services and build brand image.

Ray Anderson and Interface became more successful as a result of incorporating The Natural Step system conditions, but it's not simply a question of profit for Anderson. His introduction to the importance of sustainability came "as a spear in the chest for me, and I determined almost in an instant to change my company. Sometimes it seems very rapid; other times it's slow—but it began, frankly, in the heart, not in the mind. And I suspect that that's where the next industrial revolution has to begin—in the hearts of people—to do the right thing."[11]

Source: Adapted from J. S. Osland, B. H. Drake and H. Feldman, "The Stewardship of Natural and Human Resources." In C. J. Dempsey and R. A. Butkus (eds.) *All Nature Is Groaning* (Collegeville, MN: Liturgical Press, 1999): 168–192; P. Asmus, "100 Best Corporate Citizens for 2005" *Business Ethics Online* (Spring 2005) Accessed 10/15/2005. http://www.business-ethics.com/whats_new/100best.html.

 CLASS PREPARATION

A. Read "Ray Anderson and The Natural Step."

B. Fill out the Rokeach Values Survey on the following page and score it.[12]

C. Read "WEYCO's Ban On Employee Smoking" and answer the case questions that follow.

D. Fill out the Corporate Integrity Checkup.

E. While reading the chapter, make a list of cues that you will look for when dealing with values and ethics in the workplace.

Rokeach Values Survey

Please rate each of the values on these two pages in terms of their importance to you by circling the appropriate number (1 = of lesser importance, 7 = of greater importance). Think about each value *in terms of its importance to you, as a guiding principle in your life.* Is it of greater importance to you, or of lesser importance, or somewhere in between? As you work, *consider each value in relation to all the other values listed on each page.* Work slowly and think carefully about the importance you assign to all the values listed below. When you're done, follow the scoring and plotting instructions that appear below and at the end of the survey.

Terminal Values	Of Lesser Importance	Of Greater Importance		Weight	
A comfortable life	1 2 3 4	5 6 7		$\times 5 =$ _____	
An exciting life	1 2 3 4	5 6 7		$\times 4 =$ _____	
A sense of accomplishment	1 2 3 4	5 6 7		$\times 4 =$ _____	
A world at peace	1 2 3 4	5 6 7		$\times 5 =$	_____
A world of beauty	1 2 3 4	5 6 7		$\times 3 =$	_____
Equality	1 2 3 4	5 6 7		$\times 5 =$	_____
Family security	1 2 3 4	5 6 7		$\times 1 =$ _____	
Freedom	1 2 3 4	5 6 7		$\times 1 =$ _____	
Happiness	1 2 3 4	5 6 7		$\times 4 =$ _____	
Inner harmony	1 2 3 4	5 6 7		$\times 5 =$ _____	
Mature love	1 2 3 4	5 6 7		$\times 4 =$ _____	
National security	1 2 3 4	5 6 7		$\times 5 =$ _____	
Pleasure	1 2 3 4	5 6 7		$\times 5 =$ _____	
Salvation	1 2 3 4	5 6 7		$\times 3 =$ _____	
Self-respect	1 2 3 4	5 6 7		$\times 5 =$ _____	
Social recognition	1 2 3 4	5 6 7		$\times 3 =$ _____	
True friendship	1 2 3 4	5 6 7		$\times 4 =$ _____	
Wisdom	1 2 3 4	5 6 7		$\times 5 =$ _____	
				_____	_____
				P Total	*S* Total

P Total ÷ 53 = _____ P score   S Total ÷ 18 = _____ S score

P $-$ S $=$ T (Terminal Values)

_____ $-$ _____ $=$ _____

Scoring Instructions for Terminal Values

1. For all items, multiply the number you circled by the weighted value that appears under the heading "Weight." Write the total in the blank to the right.
2. Sum the numbers in the first column and write the total at the bottom where it says "*P* Total." Next, divide this total by 53. Your new score should be a value between 1 and 7. This is your *P* score. *P* stands for Personal Values.
3. Sum the numbers in the second column and write the total at the bottom where it says "*S* Total." Next, divide this total by 18. Your new score should be a value between 1 and 7. This is your *S* score. *S* stands for Social Values.
4. Subtract *S* from *P* to find your **Terminal Values Score.** A positive sum indicates a "personal" orientation, while a negative sum indicates a "social" orientation.

Instrumental Values	Of Lesser Importance				Of Greater Importance			Weight	
Ambitious	1	2	3	4	5	6	7	× 5 = _____	
Broadminded	1	2	3	4	5	6	7	× 2 = _____	
Capable	1	2	3	4	5	6	7	× 5 = _____	
Cheerful	1	2	3	4	5	6	7	× 4 =	_____
Clean	1	2	3	4	5	6	7	× 3 =	_____
Courageous	1	2	3	4	5	6	7	× 2 =	_____
Forgiving	1	2	3	4	5	6	7	× 5 =	_____
Helpful	1	2	3	4	5	6	7	× 5 =	_____
Honest	1	2	3	4	5	6	7	× 2 =	_____
Imaginative	1	2	3	4	5	6	7	× 5 = _____	
Independent	1	2	3	4	5	6	7	× 5 = _____	
Intellectual	1	2	3	4	5	6	7	× 5 = _____	
Logical	1	2	3	4	5	6	7	× 5 = _____	
Loving	1	2	3	4	5	6	7	× 5 =	_____
Obedient	1	2	3	4	5	6	7	× 1 =	_____
Polite	1	2	3	4	5	6	7	× 3 =	_____
Responsible	1	2	3	4	5	6	7	× 4 = _____	
								C Total	M Total

P Total ÷ 36 = _____ P score   S Total ÷ 30 = _____ S score

C − M = I (Instrumental Values)

_____ − _____ = _____

Scoring Instructions for Instrumental Values

1. For all items, multiply the number you circled by the weighted value that appears under the heading "Weight." Write the total in the blank to the right.
2. Sum the numbers in the first column and write the total at the bottom where it says "C Total." Next, divide this total by 36. Your new score should be a value between 1 and 7. This is your C score. C stands for Competence Values.
3. Sum the numbers in the second column and write the total at the bottom where it says "M Total." Next, divide this total by 30. Your new score should be a value between 1 and 7. This is your M score. M stands for Moral Values.
4. Subtract M from C to find your **Instrumental Values Score**. A positive sum indicates a "competence" orientation, while a negative sum indicates a "moral" orientation.

Plot your Terminal Values Score on the horizontal axis and your Instrumental Values Score on the vertical axis of 6-1 on page 137. Mark the point of intersection between the two scores.

WEYCO'S BAN ON EMPLOYEE SMOKING[13]

Located in Okemos, Michigan, WEYCO is a small company, founded in 1979, that specializes in managing employee benefit plans. It administers self-funded vision, dental, medical, and short-term disability plans. It also serves as an agent for other benefit plans. The company strives to be "the premiere benefit and healthcare information management organization." Here is WEYCO's company creed and vision:[14]

- We recognize we must work together to thrive.
- We understand another's point of view.

- We treat others as we would want to be treated, with courtesy, respect and dignity.
- We acknowledge and respond to fellow workers' requests with regard to each other's time and priorities.
- We are responsible for our own positive attitude.
- We treat problems as learning opportunities while working together toward resolution.
- We provide an atmosphere for open, honest and objective communication without fear.
- We strive for individual excellence that enables others to perform their jobs.
- We encourage initiative, new ideas and decisive problem solving.
- We acknowledge the equal importance of all fellow workers.

WEYCO has made a serious commitment to improving the health of its own employees. Their voluntary wellness program includes weight management, nutrition counseling, diabetic counseling, visits with a personal trainer that can result in a $110 bonus/month if fitness goals are met, and even a scale in front of vending machines that contain healthy foods.[15] WEYCO also has medical advisors on staff who provide health counseling to employees. But, as CEO Howard Weyers notes, "Our involuntary programs are more controversial."

WEYCO stopped hiring smokers in 2003 when they discovered there was no law in Michigan that prevented them from screening out tobacco users in the same way that firms regularly screen out drug users through testing. According to the ACLU, there are over 6000 employers who do not hire smokers.[16] Other firms, like U-Haul International, charge smokers $130 more annually for their health insurance.[17] WEYCO banned tobacco from company property and set up voluntary testing and classes and programs aimed at smoking cessation. In early 2004, Weyers assessed a $50 smoking fee for each employee who smoked. However, the company waived the fee for employees who passed a nicotine test or signed up for a smoking cessation class. WEYCO also provided a smoking counselor.[18] For those who continued smoking, WEYCO's policy was that employees would be suspended for 30 days without pay if they tested positive in a random test for tobacco use or were discovered to be using tobacco. The suspended employees would then be tested on return and would be subject to multiple random tests after that. If they failed a second test they would be dismissed.

CEO Howard Weyers adopted a no smoking policy on January 1, 2005, that stated that employees could not smoke anywhere, not even at home. To ensure their compliance with the policy, employees were forced to take a test to prove they had quit. One employee quit before the policy was implemented and four more were fired for refusing to take the test. An estimated 18–20 of the company's 200 employees had been smokers and as many as a dozen quit.[19]

Weyers is 70 years old, a former college football coach who exercises five times a week. He states there are no religious reasons behind his decision. Weyers defended the no smoking ban in the following press release. [*Why Business Should Get Serious about Smoking*, Howard Weyers, February 7, 2005 (http://www.weyco.com).]

> *"Rather than face the dangerous realities of smoking, critics of WEYCO's tobacco-free policy rush to the so-called "slippery slope" argument, imagining all kinds of dire consequences for workers. But the fact is, federal and state laws prohibit employers from discriminating on the basis of age, sex, race, weight, national origin, and other attributes — and smoking is not a civil right. It's just a poor personal choice. Moreover, for other lifestyle issues, WEYCO provides positive assistance — such as wellness counseling and subsidies for health club membership — in which participation is voluntary.*
>
> *So, let's get real. Employment is not a right, either. Businesses can hire whomever they wish based on desirable skills and characteristics, so long as the selection factors are lawful. Some call this a violation of privacy, pointing to the principle that "what you do in your own home is your own business." But they forget the part about "so long as it doesn't harm anyone else."*
>
> *Nor is health insurance a right, but it's darned expensive. Businesses generally need not provide it, and many don't, thanks to years of double-digit cost increases—and a big reason for those is self-destructive behavior by a small percentage of employees. The CDC reports that smoking costs $75 billion a year in excess medical bills and $82 billion in lost*

productivity. In Michigan alone, tobacco kills 16,000 people annually—more than alcohol, AIDS, car crashes, illegal drugs, murders, and suicides combined.

Businesses have the right to protect themselves from the horrendous damage smokers inflict upon themselves and others—except in states with "smokers' rights laws," mostly passed in the early 1990s with tobacco industry backing. Furthermore, standard company incentives to quit tobacco haven't worked.

WEYCO's mission is to help businesses improve employee health and cut costs with innovative benefit plans. WEYCO decided to take the lead by phasing in a tobacco-free employee policy over 15 months, with company-paid smoking-cessation assistance. It's not about what people do at home. It's about the acceptance of personal responsibility by people we choose to employ. WEYCO is proud of its position on tobacco and wellness. For every smoker who quits because of it, many others—family members, friends, co-workers—will be thankful the person has chosen a healthier lifestyle. It's not just about saving money. It's about saving lives."

According to Weyers, although some employees were initially negative about the policy: "We believe we have overcome any negativity. Our employees completely understood that employees had 15 months to decide what was most important, their job at WEYCO or the use of tobacco. Our employees understand that unhealthy lifestyle decisions made by other employees will affect their paychecks via higher deductibles, co-pays and contributions to the plan."[20] Weyers specified the payoff for the no-smoking policy.

Such steps may sound draconian, but they get results. By making employees responsible for their own health, and by establishing support programs for them, we have both lowered and stabilized our health care costs. Our insurance costs per employee—including medical and dental care, and prescription and vision coverage—average $300 per month compared with the state average of $500. Our health care costs have remained level for 27 months in a row.[21]

Cara Stiffler, one of the four WEYCO employees who was fired for failing to take the test for tobacco use, stated, "I don't believe any employer should be able to come in and tell you what you can do in your own home."[22] Another employee who quit, Anita Epolito, stated, "You feel like you have no rights. You're all alone. It's the most helpless feeling you can imagine. . . . I never, ever from day one conceded to go with his policy because I knew that it had nothing to do with smoking. It had to do with my privacy in my own home."[23]

In contrast, Christine Boyd felt, "I had to choose between whether I wanted to keep my job and whether I wanted to keep smoking. To me it was a no-brainer." She quit smoking.[24]

HEALTH AND CIGARETTE SMOKING

"Cigarette smoking has been identified as the most important source of preventable morbidity and premature mortality worldwide. Smoking is responsible for approximately one in five deaths in the United States. From 1995 to 1999, smoking killed over 440,000 people in the United States each year. This includes an estimated 264,087 male and 178,311 female deaths annually. Among adults, most smoking attributable deaths were from lung cancer (124,813), coronary heart disease (81,976) and chronic airway obstruction (64,735)."[25] Smoking can also significantly contribute to other cancers such as cancer of the esophagus, larynx, kidney, pancreas and cervix.[26] Estimates vary but the peer reviewed literature on the medical costs of smoking put it at 6–8 percent of annual personal health care expenditures in the United States, although this fails to take into consideration the physical and emotional toll imposed on the victims of smoking and their loved ones.[27]

SMOKING CESSATION

Of smokers who had reported smoking at least 100 cigarettes during their lifetime, only 42 percent reported abstaining from cigarettes during the previous year, and of this group, males reportedly abstained more often than females.[28] It is very difficult to quit smoking since smoking is habit forming (becoming associated with certain events and feelings) and nicotine (a product of tobacco) is a highly addictive substance that affects the brain.[29] When one tries to abstain from smoking, physical and emotional withdrawals arise such as irritability, weight gain, anxiety, sleeping problems, and fatigue. These physical and emotional withdrawals often prompt relapses within the first few weeks or months. It may take smokers up to three cessation attempts before they finally succeed and stop smoking.

Research shows mixed results on the relapse rates for ex-smokers. According to a study in Nicotine & Tobacco Research, the relapse rate for smokers within the first year of trying to quit smoking ranged between 60 percent and 90 percent.[30] For smokers who had abstained for at least two years, the relapse rate dropped significantly to 2–4 percent, and smokers who had abstained from smoking for 10 years or more had less than a 1 percent relapse rate. In contrast, the National Cancer Institute found that smokers who were able to cease from smoking for three months or longer did not usually relapse.[31]

Recent research by the National Institute on Drug Abuse (NIDA) discovered a genetically determined enzyme that might contribute to nicotine addiction. In the NIDA study, of the "426 smokers who participated in a 10-week smoking cessation program, those with a gene form that decreases activity of an enzyme that metabolizes nicotine, reported greater craving and were less likely to achieve abstinence during treatment than those with the gene form that increases the enzyme's activity."[32] This research suggests that genetics may make it more difficult for some smokers to quit than others, thereby contributing to higher relapse rates.

There are examples of patients in the advanced stages of lung disease in smoking cessation programs who, despite the severity of their illness and the threat of imminent death, fail to quit smoking.[33] Clearly for some individuals, smoking cessation is extremely difficult.

POLITICAL OPPOSITION

Some lawyers and the ACLU contend that WEYCO's termination of smokers goes too far and will not hold up in court. The Michigan legislature is considering joining 21 other states that passed legislation that prohibits employers from firing smokers. Michigan State Senator Virg Bernero introduced the bill because, "This is America. Your personal time should be your own."[34] WEYCO takes the position that this law would be a step backward for the businesses of Michigan.[35]

Please answer the following questions about this case and express your personal opinion. There are no "correct" answers. Provide careful and thorough explanations to support your opinions.

1. What are the views of the key stakeholders in this case?

2. What are the ethical issues to consider when deciding to fire tobacco users?

3. Is it appropriate for employers to impose restrictions on individual freedoms?

4. Is WEYCO doing the right thing? What reasons support your opinion?

5. Would you want to work at WEYCO? Why?

Corporate Integrity Checkup

Rate your current company (or former employer) against the following 25 best practices in ethics management. If you have never held a job, evaluate any type of organization to which you belong or have had the opportunity to observe closely.

Code of Ethics	Yes	Not Sure	No
1. Our company has an up-to-date code of ethics (or "code of conduct") that describes typical dilemmas in our industry, and defines ethical work practices.	❑	❑	❑
2. Our company's ethics policies have been developed in consultation with employees and other stakeholders.	❑	❑	❑
3. All employees undergo training in how to implement our code of ethics.	❑	❑	❑
4. Our company has published a set of values that reflect the expectation of ethical work practices.	❑	❑	❑
5. Our stated values recognize the importance of external stakeholders.	❑	❑	❑

Dialogue	Yes	Not Sure	No
6. Questions of ethics are openly discussed in our company.	❑	❑	❑
7. Our people have a safe source of guidance (i.e. other than their boss!) if they have a question about ethics or law.	❑	❑	❑
8. Our people have recourse to a confidential third party (such as an Ombuds office) if they perceive any wrongdoing by their peers or superiors.	❑	❑	❑
9. Our strategic planning process includes a discussion of personal and corporate values.	❑	❑	❑
10. The company's impact on a wide range of external stakeholders is considered as part of our strategic planning process.	❑	❑	❑

Leadership & Empowerment	Yes	Not Sure	No
11. Our company's commitment to ethics is reflected in specific actions, and not just rhetoric.	❑	❑	❑
12. Our managers demonstrate their understanding that ethical integrity trumps other business demands.	❑	❑	❑
13. There are clear consequences for those who do not adhere to our stated ethics policies.	❑	❑	❑
14. Our people are encouraged to accurately portray the limitations as well as the benefits and features of our products/services.	❑	❑	❑
15. Our managers (or other staff) are authorized to withdraw a product/service if it is found to be hazardous to public health or safety, or conflicts with our code of ethics.	❑	❑	❑

Human Resources	Yes	Not Sure	No
16. People in our company are well equipped to recognize and resolve ethical issues in our business.	❑	❑	❑
17. Ethical integrity is a critical factor when hiring and promoting people.	❑	❑	❑
18. Formal opportunities are provided for our people to review ethical issues with their peers, such as in orientation and training programs or facilitated meetings.	❑	❑	❑
19. Managers and executives receive extensive training in ethics as part of our leadership development program.	❑	❑	❑
20. Our managers are evaluated on their commitment to ethics, as well as other aspects of performance.	❑	❑	❑

Systems	Yes	Not Sure	No
21. Our incentive system (pay and career advancement) does not provide rewards for unethical behavior. [Take a moment to think about this one!]	❑	❑	❑
22. Our incentive system does not penalize ethical behavior, even if it costs us time, money or potential business. [Another tricky question!]	❑	❑	❑
23. Our company systematically verifies the accuracy of claims made to customers about our products/services.	❑	❑	❑
24. Our key suppliers are systematically monitored for product quality, product safety, and humane work practices.	❑	❑	❑
25. Our Board of Directors has approved mechanisms to ensure compliance with our code, and a schedule to revise the code on an ongoing basis.	❑	❑	❑

Add up your points in the "Yes" column ____. If you scored:

15 to 25 Well done! You're healthier than many other corporations. But of course there's always room for improvement managing ethics.

0 to 15 Pretty good score! But as you can see, you could be a lot healthier when it comes to managing business ethics.

Less than 0 It looks like you enjoy living dangerously! Get help soon.

Source: This survey is reprinted with permission of Larry Colero, a consultant who helps organizations develop corporate ethics programs. Available at http://www.crossroadsprograms.com/corporate.html. Accessed 9/30/06.

THE KNOWLEDGE BASE

As a purely pragmatic matter, a society cannot survive, let alone thrive, if it exempts its most influential and pervasive institutions from all notions of morality.

Lynn Sharp Payne, Harvard Business School

Interface is an example of a company that "does well by doing good," guided by strong core values and an inspiring vision. Some people have a mistaken perception that firms that act ethically have lower profits.[36] This may be the case in the short term, but companies that engage in unethical practices make themselves vulnerable to lawsuits, boycotts, governmental restrictions and regulations, and loss of reputation—all of which endanger profits. There is growing evidence that good corporate citizenship correlates with higher financial performance. Companies that look beyond maximizing wealth and profits and are driven by values and a sense of purpose outperform companies that focus only on short-term gain.[37] Ethical practices pay off in the long run, as trusting relationships with employees, stockholders, and well-satisfied customers are the basis of business success. Hartley contends that:

> *The interests of a firm are best served by scrupulous attention to the public interest and by seeking a trusting relationship with the various publics with which a firm is involved. In the process, society also is best served. Such a trusting relationship suggests concern for customer satisfaction and fair dealings. The objective is loyalty and repeat business, a durable and mutually beneficial relationship, which is contrary to the philosophy of short-term profit maximization, corporate self-interest, and coercive practices with employees and dependent suppliers.*[38]

There are many ethical businesspeople who prosper in large part because of their integrity. In recent years, we have seen an increase in companies that define themselves as socially responsible companies in their mission statement. For example, Levi Strauss voluntarily set up Global Sourcing Guidelines to carefully select contractors in overseas factories and ensure that their products are not made in sweatshops by children.[39] Organizations like Anita Roddick's Body Shop and Ben and Jerry's Ice Cream donate part of their profits to "good works," such as human rights groups, community development projects, environmental groups, and peace programs. Richard Branson, CEO of Virgin Group, donated all profits from his airline and train businesses to research and development on renewable energy initiatives.

These companies are well known for their value systems and for having a larger purpose than making money. They seek profits but maximizing shareholder wealth is not their only concern. Like the visionary premier companies that prosper over long periods of time and are widely admired (but are not necessarily socially responsible) that Collins and Porras reported on in *Built to Last*, they have a strong sense of mission based on a shared set of core values.

> *Contrary to business school doctrine, "maximizing shareholder wealth" or "profit maximization" has not been the dominant driving force or primary objective through the history of visionary companies. Visionary companies pursue a cluster of objectives, of which making money is only one—and not necessarily the primary one. Yes, they seek profits, but they're guided by a core ideology, values and a sense of purpose beyond just making money. Yet, paradoxically, the visionary companies make more money than the more purely profit-driving comparison companies.*[40]

When the profit motive is untempered by ethical values, white collar crime and corporate scandal result. Tyco executives' misuse of company funds, Boeing's irregular procurement of government contracts, Halliburton's overcharges, and Health South's Medicare fraud are prime examples of unethical behavior in the workplace. The extent of the accounting fraud at WorldCom, Enron, Qwest, and Adelphia in the United States prompted a good deal of discussion about an ethical decline, soul-searching, and tighter regulation. In Singapore, a greedy British financial trader in his late 20s was jailed for fraud and forgery, bringing about the collapse of Barings

Bank, Britain's oldest merchant bank. The Italian dairy and grocery company, Parmalat, and the Dutch retailer, Ahold, two of Europe's largest and most global firms, were both guilty of fraudulent accounting practices. The Swiss-based F. Hoffman-LaRoche and the German-based BASF A.G. were heavily fined for fixing prices in the vitamin market they dominate. Accounting scandals occurred at Kanebo Pharmaceuticals and Seibu Railway in Japan and at business conglomerate SK Group in South Korea. China is grappling with corruption in state-owned banks as well as *intellectual property theft (failure to respect patents and copyright laws or pay for using what other firms or individuals have created)* and *piracy (making imitations of brand name goods)*. [41] Given the growing number of business scandals, it is no surprise that one study found that only 58 percent of U.S. employees view their senior leaders as people of high integrity. [42]

There are significant costs of unethical behavior to firms:

- Losses in revenue due to customer defections and lost sales
- Revenue loss due to product recall and withdrawal
- Operational expenses to correct past errors
- Higher funding costs imposed by lenders and investors
- Decreased ability to borrow money
- Lower share price as shareholders opt to invest in more trustworthy firms
- Legal expenses
- Consulting expenses related to investigating allegations
- Fines, penalties, damages, and settlement costs
- Increased marketing and PR expenses to counteract the negative publicity of scandal
- Higher turnover due to employee defections
- Higher recruiting costs due to the firm's damaged reputation

Furthermore, when the business sector does not police itself, governments and international regulating bodies are more likely to intervene with laws and regulations that impact all companies, guilty and innocent alike. For example, the 2002 Sarbanes Oxley act, which requires more extensive accounting reports and transparency from all firms, was a direct result of corporate indiscretions at Enron and WorldCom and Arthur Andersen's failure to report them. Arthur Andersen, a top accounting firm, imploded after blurring the boundary between its consulting and auditing arms and losing the public's trust when it failed to report the transgressions of clients like Enron and WorldCom. The fear of losing consulting dollars made Andersen and other firms less rigorous in their auditing responsibilities. Andersen was found guilty of shredding two tons of Enron-related documents. Although the Supreme Court later overturned this decision and criticized the judicial instructions given to the jury, the ruling came too late to help approximately 28,000 Arthur Andersen employees who lost their jobs and felt their own reputations were unfairly tainted by the actions of unethical colleagues. Ironically, Arthur Andersen's ethics consultants helped other firms set up ethics programs, but the company itself refused to establish one. [43] Not only firms but also shareholders, employees, and taxpayers pay a price for corporate malfeasance. Employees have lost their jobs and pensions, shareholders have lost their income and savings, and taxpayers pay more when government has to police the business sector more carefully and occasionally pick up the tab for wrong-doing, as U.S. taxpayers did with the Savings and Loan scandal bailout which cost billions of dollars. [44] Business scandals in developed countries result in less stock market participation due to lack of trust. [45]

The increased corporate misconduct of recent years has focused more attention on corporate governance, and some boards of directors have begun to take their governance role more seriously. In theory, boards of directors are responsible for ensuring that the organizations comply with laws and ethical codes. In reality, many boards are only now beginning to live up to this responsibility, by providing more oversight and insisting that firms have ethics programs. The U.S. government provides incentives to firms that develop comprehensive ethics programs; for example, fines for breaking certain laws can be reduced by up to 95 percent and board members are not held personally liable for the firm's unethical actions when comprehensive ethics programs are in place. [46] A growing number of firms have ethics officers, who are responsible for developing ethics programs and ensuring that the company in is compliance with legal require-ments. Whether attention to ethics is just for show (called window dressing or, in the case of environmental initiatives, "green-washing") or a serious effort to respect the spirit of the law varies widely from organization to organization. The higher up ethics officers are found in the organizational chart, the greater likelihood that ethics is a serious concern. At UPS, Baxter Inter-national, and Raytheon, for instance, ethics officers report directly to corporate officers or direc-tors,[47] which increases their visibility and influence.

Both business and governments are lobbied by a growing number of non-governmental organizations (NGOs) and activists whose mission is to promote more socially responsible cor-porate behavior. *The "CNN effect," rapid international media coverage of corporate transgres-sions*, can result in global boycotts organized by NGOs via the Internet. When governments fail to take action against unethical corporate practices, NGOs take on that role. Although not all NGOs or activists are motivated by purely altruistic motives, they enjoy a higher level of trust that they are operating "in society's best interests" among a survey of people in 47 countries; 59 percent reported a lot or some trust in NGOs compared to 39 percent who trusted global corpo-rations and 42 percent who trusted large national companies.[48] Other surveys indicate that a minority of U.S. Americans currently believe that business strikes a fair balance between profit and the public interest.[49]

The recent proliferation of business scandals led business educators to question their own role in influencing the thinking of business practitioners.[50] According to Mitroff and Swanson, "Two of the most prominent theories in business education—transaction cost analysis and agency theory—assume that humans are ruthless, motivated solely by greed, opportunism, and selfishness. These theories complement a strain of Neoclassical Economics, which infects cur-riculum with the message that business decisions are 'value free.'"[51] If we teach that all humans are solely motivated by opportunism and selfishness, this can become a self-fulfilling prophecy. Instead, professors are encouraged to focus more attention on the consequences of business deci-sions on all stakeholders—employees, suppliers, customers, family, and the society as a whole—and to acknowledge that there is more to business than profit maximization.

Ethics refers to "standards of conduct that indicate how one should behave based on moral duties and virtues arising from principles about right and wrong."[52] The very nature of business means that managers may be confronted with numerous ethical questions without the benefit of a professional code of ethics, like many other professions have. Companies confront internal issues such as employee safety, discrimination and sexual harassment, theft of company prop-erty, and irregular accounting practices in an environment where the financial stakes are very high. In addition, companies have struggled with a host of external ethical dilemmas such as bal-ancing profit with environmental protection and consumer safety and doing business in cultures where bribes are commonplace.

While there are many highly ethical business people, there are unethical people in all types of organizations for whom money and power take precedence over all else. The key question is whether they are perceived as heroes or villains.[53] This is determined by societal values and by the ethical climate and norms created by each organization. In one U.S. study, 92 percent of the managers agreed that the ethical tone of their firm is determined by the behavior of those in charge, and one-third felt their bosses engage in unethical behaviors and are less concerned with ethics than they are.[54] Some companies place employees in positions that force them to choose between their careers and their personal sense of ethics.

Factors that lead to questionable business practices are:

1. Overemphasis on both individual and firm performance;
2. Mission statements, evaluation systems, and organizational cultures that focus on profit as the organization's sole objective;
3. Intense competition among firms, departments, and individuals;
4. Management concern for the letter of the law rather than the spirit;
5. Ambiguous policies that employees interpret as "window dressing" for outsiders rather than clear expectations for ethical behavior;

6. Inadequate controls so that managers get away with violating standards, allowing them to pursue greater sales and profits for personal benefit;

7. Expediency and indifference to the customers' best interest;

8. Management's failure to comprehend the public's ethical concerns;

9. Custom and local practice says "let the buyer beware;"

10. A "groupthink" mentality that fosters group decisions that individual members would not support.[55]

Companies that want to encourage ethical behavior need to (1) communicate their expectations that employees will behave ethically and define what that means; (2) hire top executives who set an example of moral behavior; (3) reward ethical behavior and punish unethical behavior; (4) teach employees the basic tools of ethical decision making; and (5) encourage the discussion of ethical issues.[56]

Ethical mistakes are responsible for ending careers more quickly and more definitively than any other errors in judgment or accounting.[57] Nevertheless, one of the factors that inhibits the discussion of ethics in the workforce is a reluctance on the part of managers to discuss the moral aspects of their decision making, even when they are acting for moral reasons.[58] Managers give several reasons for avoiding moral talk. First, people do not like to appear judgmental or intrusive, or lay themselves open to countercharges of wrongdoing. As a result, they often avoid confronting others who are not behaving ethically. Second, moral talk threatens efficiency when it simply muddies the waters and distracts attention from problem solving. Managers worry that it may be self-serving, simplistic, inflexible, or inexact. Finally, some managers fear that the esoteric and idealistic nature of moral talk is not in keeping with the image they want to convey, and they are leery about exposing their lack of training in ethics. Therefore, we find a norm in many businesses to justify decisions on the basis of organizational interests, practicality, and sound economic sense, even when moral considerations play an important role. Although managers struggle individually with ethical problems, in many firms, they seldom discuss them in groups of managers, which gives rise to the term "the moral muteness" of managers.[59] One purpose of this chapter is to provide you with a rudimentary understanding of ethical terms and principles so you can take part in ethical discussions.

VALUES

Both individuals and organizations have codes of ethics that are rooted in their values. One of the first steps in teaching ethics is to help people identify and articulate their own values. *Values are core beliefs or desires that guide or motivate attitudes and actions.* Whereas the study of ethics is concerned with how a moral person *should* behave, values concern the various beliefs and attitudes that determine how a person *actually* behaves. People, however, do not always act in accordance with their espoused values. For example, you may devote very little time to enacting some of the values you checked off in the Rokeach survey in the class preparation, even though you believe they are important.

Our values are shaped early in life; we learn them from our parents, friends, teachers, church, and the culture that surrounds us. As adults, we often seek environments that are compatible with our values. For example, values help determine what companies we are attracted to and how long we stay with them. They also affect how motivated we are at work; people who share the same values as the organization are more committed to the organization than those who do not.[60] *Shared systems of values between two entities is called value congruence.* Many business people, however, work in organizations whose values differ from their own, an example of value incongruence.

Employees may also choose to work in environments that match their ethical preferences. The better the ethical fit, the more likely employees are to continue with the organization and be committed to it.[61] Whenever people make decisions or talk about what constitutes appropriate behavior at work, we can observe the impact of values, or even conflicts between different values. For example, when companies consider whether to employ temporary or permanent employees, which values are more important—saving money for the company or providing benefits and job security to employees?

Within our personal value system, some values are more important than others. The exercise in the Class Preparation allows you to see which of the most common values, based on U.S. research, have the greatest significance for you. (In the following chapter on career development, you can see the link between values and career planning in the Class Preparation exercise.)

Rokeach,[62] who developed the list of values that you rated, believes that people possess a relatively small number of values that they hold to varying degrees. He classified these key values into two types. *Terminal values are desirable end states of existence or the goals that a person would like to achieve during his or her lifetime.* Terminal values can be subdivided further into two categories: personal values (a comfortable life, freedom, happiness, salvation) and social values (world peace, equality, national security).

Instrumental values are preferable modes of behavior or the means to achieving one's terminal values. There are two types of instrumental values: moral values and competence values. Moral values (cheerful, courageous, helpful, honest) tend to have an interpersonal focus; when they are violated, we feel pangs of conscience or guilt. Competence values (ambitious, capable, intellectual, responsible) have a personal focus. When they are violated, we feel ashamed of our personal inadequacy rather than guilty about wrongdoing.

Rokeach looked for a relationship between terminal and instrumental values and found that all combinations are possible, as shown in Exhibit 6–1 where you plotted your scores from the Rokeach Value survey. The personal-competence value orientation is most commonly preferred by managers. The personal-moral and social-moral value orientations are the least common for managers and a majority of U. S. Americans.[63] When we compare individual values of managers with those of the population at large, we find that "sense of accomplishment," "self-respect," "a comfortable life," and "independence" are more highly valued by managers.[64]

Building on Rokeach's work, Schwartz and Bilsky created a universal psychological structure of human values that applies to people from all cultures. Their theory presents seven types of values that motivate behavior:[65]

- *Prosocial*—Active protection or enhancement of the welfare of others.
- *Restrictive conformity*—Restraint of actions and impulses likely to harm others and to violate sanctioned norms.

Terminal Values (P – S)

		Personal Values			Social Values	
	Competence Values	Preference for Personal-Competence Values	+7 +6 +5 +4 +3 +2 +1		Preference for Social-Competence Values	
Instrumental Values (C minus M)		+7 +6 +5 +4 +3 +2 +1 0	0 −1 −2 −3 −4 −5 −6 −7			
	Moral Values	Preference for Personal-Moral Values	−1 −2 −3 −4 −5 −6 −7		Preference for Social-Moral Values	

EXHIBIT 6-1 Personal Values Orientation Typology

Refer to the Rokeach Values Survey that you completed earlier.

- *Enjoyment*—Pleasure, sensuous and emotional gratification.
- *Achievement*—Personal success through demonstrated competence.
- *Maturity*—Appreciation, understanding, and acceptance of oneself, others, and the surrounding world.
- *Self-direction*—Independent thought and action—choosing, creating, exploring.
- *Security*—Safety, harmony and stability of society, of groups with whom one identifies, of relationships, and of self.

These values have hold varying degrees of importance in different cultures.

ETHICAL VERSUS NONETHICAL VALUES

When ethical issues arise, we have to distinguish between ethical and nonethical values. *Ethical values directly relate to beliefs concerning what is right and proper* (as opposed to what is simply correct or effective) *or that motivate a sense of moral duty.* Core ethical values that transcend cultural, ethnic, and socioeconomic differences in the United States are (1) trustworthiness; (2) respect; (3) responsibility; (4) justice and fairness; (5) caring; and (6) civic virtue and citizenship.[66] The effort to identify these values is part of a trend toward character building as a remedy for the breakdown in societal values that is taking place in many countries. It is difficult for adults to act ethically if they have not been inculcated with ethical values when they were growing up.

Nonethical values deal with things we like, desire, or find personally important. Examples of nonethical values are money, fame, status, happiness, fulfillment, pleasure, personal freedom, and being liked. They are ethically neutral. One of the guides to ethical decision making is that ethical values should always take precedence over nonethical values.

MORAL REASONING

Values alone do not determine our actions. Our behavior is also influenced by our moral reasoning, organizational culture, culture, the influence of significant others, the type of harm that could result from a decision involving ethics, and who might be harmed.[67] The first factor, moral reasoning, is the process by which we transform our values and beliefs into action. This reasoning affects the way managers make decisions.[68]

Kohlberg conducted a longitudinal study of the moral reasoning reported by male subjects at various ages.[69] He identified three different levels of moral development which we will call self-centered, conformity, and principled. Kohlberg uses different labels here (preconventional, conventional, and postconventional),[70] but we think it is easier for you to remember titles that describe the major characteristic of each level. The progression through these levels can be summarized as moving from (1) a self-centered conception of right and wrong to (2) an understanding of the importance of conformity and social accord and finally to (3) universal principles of justice and rights. As shown in Exhibit 6–2, each level has two stages, the second of which is more advanced.[71]

Self-Centered Level (Preconventional)

This level of moral reasoning has a personal focus and an emphasis on consequences. It is usually found among children who see moral issues in the black and white terms of "good and bad" and "right and wrong." Actions are judged either by their consequences (punishment, reward, exchange of favors) or in terms of the physical power of those who lay down the rules.

Stage	What is Considered to be Right
Level One–Self-Centered (Preconventional)	
Stage One–Obedience and Punishment Orientation	Sticking to rules to avoid physical punishment. Obedience for its own sake.
Stage Two–Instrumental Purpose and Exchange	Following rules only when it is in one's immediate interest. Right is an equal exchange, a fair deal.
Level Two–Conformity (Conventional)	
Stage Three–Interpersonal Accord, Conformity, Mutual Expectations	Stereotypical "good" behavior. Living up to what is expected by peers and people close to you.
Stage Four–Social Accord and System Maintenance	Fulfilling duties and obligations of social system. Upholding laws except in extreme cases where they conflict with fixed social duties. Contributing to the society, group.
Level Three–Principled (Postconventional)	
Stage Five–Social Contract, Individual Rights	Being aware that people hold a variety of values; that rules are relative to the group. Upholding rules because they are the social contract. Upholding nonrelative values and rights regardless of majority opinion.
Stage Six–Universal Ethical Principles	Following self-chosen ethical principles of justice and rights. When laws violate principles, act in accord with principles.

EXHIBIT 6-2   **Three Levels of Moral Development According to Kohlberg**

Source: Linda K. Trevino, "A Cultural Perspective on Changing and Developing Organizational Ethics," in *Research in Organizational Change and Development*, W. A. Pasmore and R. W. Woodman (eds.) (Greenwich, CT: JAI Press, 1990): 198.

This level is divided into two stages:

Stage 1: *The Obedience and Punishment Orientation.* The physical consequences of an action determine its goodness or badness. An avoidance of punishment and unquestioning deference to power are valued but not because the individual believes in the importance of a moral order supported by punishment and authority.

Stage 2: *Instrumental Purpose and Exchange (Instrumental Relativist Orientation).* Interest in satisfying one's own needs is the most important consideration. Elements of fairness, reciprocity, and equal sharing are present, but they are always interpreted in a physical or pragmatic way. For example, reciprocity is a matter of "you scratch my back, and I'll scratch yours" rather than loyalty, gratitude, or justice.

Conformity Level (Conventional)

At this level, there is a group focus and an emphasis on social harmony. People are concerned with meeting the expectations of their family, group, or nation. They have moved beyond a preoccupation with consequences to focus on conformity and loyalty to the social order. They support, justify, and identify with the existing social order or with the people or group(s) involved in it. Like the self-centered individuals, this group also sees rules and laws as outside themselves, but they obey them because they have accepted them. At this level, we find the following two stages.

Stage 3: *Interpersonal Accord, Conformity, and Mutual Expectations (The "Good Boy–Nice Girl" Orientation).* Good behavior is defined as behavior that pleases or helps others and is approved by them. Conformity to stereotypical images of what is "natural" behavior (i.e., behavior that is characteristic of the majority of people) is a common guide. People are concerned with maintaining mutually trusting relationships with people. The Golden Rule, "Do unto others as you would have others do unto you," is common at this stage of moral reasoning. Judging behavior by its intention, for example, "she meant well," is also found for the first time at this stage.

Stage 4: *Social Accord and System Maintenance (The Law and Order Orientation).* At stage 4, the individual takes the perspective of a member of society. The individual perceives the social system as a consistent set of codes and procedures (legal, religious, societal) that applies impartially to all members in a society. There is an emphasis upon "doing one's duty" and showing respect for authority and maintaining the social order for its own sake.

Principled Level (Postconventional)

At this level, individuals have a more universal focus that emphasizes internalized ethical standards, rights, or duties. Individuals at this level examine society's rules and laws and then develop their own set of internal principles. These internalized principles take precedence over rules and laws.

Stage 5: *Social Contract and Individual Rights (The Social Contract Legalistic Orientation).* At this stage, the individual realizes that there is an arbitrary element to rules and the law. Right is relative and perceived as a matter of personal values and opinion. For the sake of agreement, the individual agrees to procedural rules such as respect for contracts and the rights of others, majority will, and the general good.

Stage 6: *The Universal Ethical Principles Orientation.* Right is defined by decisions of conscience, in accord with self-chosen ethical principles that are logically comprehensive, universal, and consistent. These principles are abstract and ethical, such as justice, the reciprocity and equality of human rights, and respect for the dignity of human beings.

The research of Kohlberg and others concluded that:[72]

1. People's reasoning tends to reflect one dominant stage, although they may occasionally be either one stage lower or higher than the dominant stage.
2. Most adults in Western urban societies reason at stages 3, 4, and 5. Stage 4 reasoning is the most common. Development can stop at any stage. Many prison inmates never get beyond stage 2 reasoning.
3. People develop moral maturity gradually, moving from step to step; they do not skip stages.
4. Development is not governed by age. Some young people reason at a higher stage than their elders. While cognitive development (which normally occurs during adolescence) is a necessary condition for abstract reasoning, it does not guarantee moral maturity.
5. Empathy, the capacity to feel what others are feeling, is also a necessary but not sufficient condition for moral development.
6. Managers whose values are categorized as social-moral in Exhibit 6–1 demonstrated a higher level of moral reasoning.[73]
7. Ethical decision making and intended ethical behavior generally increase as individuals utilize higher stages of moral reasoning.[74]

The major criticisms of Kohlberg's theory follow:

1. The highest stages of reasoning are based on abstract principles of justice rather than social considerations. Since women are more socialized than men to make care-based judgments (how will the people involved be affected?), Gilligan argued that Kohlberg's test was biased against women.[75] Originally, Kohlberg only studied men, a common practice before researchers came to appreciate gender differences, but he later incorporated women in his

samples. The controversy is not settled, although there is evidence that women and men do not reason differently when confronted with real-life dilemmas.[76]

2. Since Kohlberg's test consists of hypothetical dilemmas, the results might be different when people confront real-life ethical dilemmas. In Argyris's terms, their test answers might reflect their espoused theories rather than their theories-in-use.[77] In fact, research on real-life dilemmas showed that people reason at various stages, depending on the specific dilemma involved.[78] This contradicts Kohlberg's belief that people reason consistently at the highest possible level unless they are transitioning to a higher stage.

3. The theory is culturally biased. The roots of the model are Western European and North American, and the higher stages of the scale reflect individualism rather than an understanding of the demands and obligations owed to others in collectivist cultures. The Chinese, for example, do not seek universal norms for all situations; they balance respect for the individual with the individual's subordination to society and the state.[79]

Although Kohlberg's theory of moral development has been the target of various criticisms, it has been refined and clarified in response and is still the most widely accepted model of moral development. Both personal values and moral reasoning affect the way people make decisions.

ETHICAL FRAMEWORKS

In addition to moral reasoning, another set of tools that helps with ethical decision are various models of ethics, most of which come to us from the study of philosophy. These are the most helpful frameworks for guiding business decisions that involve ethics.[80]

1. **Utilitarianism** In utilitarian ethics, a moral act produces the greatest good for the greatest number of people. Therefore, the good of the group takes precedence over consideration for individuals. Actions, plans, and policies are judged by their consequences, not necessarily how they were achieved. This approach is quite common in business decisions. For example, when managers maximize profit, or opt for efficiency and productivity, they can argue that they are obtaining the greatest good for the greatest number. A disadvantage of this approach is that the rights of minority groups can be easily overlooked and the means used to produce the greatest good may not be viewed as ethical by everyone. The utilitarian orientation is often used with environmental issues.

2. **Individual Rights Principle** Unlike utilitarian ethics, this principle emphasizes *personal entitlements in the form of the legal and human rights of individuals*. Examples are a person's right to privacy, free speech, and due process. For example, if a person has the right to be paid for an eight-hour day, he or she is also obligated to contribute a "fair day's work" for a "fair day's pay." Business contracts reflect this approach, which is commonly used with occupational health and safety problems. A negative consequence of rights-based ethics is that it engenders a self-centered, legalistic focus on what is due the individual. Another difficulty with this approach is that the rights of different groups may be in conflict.

3. **Justice Principle** In this approach, people are guided by fairness, equity, and impartiality when treating both individuals and groups. Fairness is the criterion for distributing the benefits and burdens of society, the administration of rules and regulations, and sanctions. This approach is appropriate for issues such as employment discrimination.

4. **Caring Principle** The focus in this approach is the well-being of another person. An ethical person is aware of the needs and feelings of others and takes the initiative to respond to that need. The criteria used to judge behavior is, "Who will be harmed and what will happen to existing relationships?"[81]

5. **Environmentalism** While the preceding approaches concern person-person or person-society relationships, the environmental ethic extends the boundary to include the person-land relationship. A greater understanding of the interdependent relationship between humankind and the continuing sustainability of the earth has resulted in a growing acceptance of an environmental ethic.[82] The basis for sustainability is the belief that people have

an obligation and a duty to act as stewards who protect the earth and its resources and keep them intact for future generations. Many businesses have "gone green" due to global warming, their leaders' personal values, government regulations, or their agreement with some strategy gurus that environmentalism is a strategic competitive advantage.

ETHICAL DECISION MAKING

How can managers ensure that they are taking an ethical approach to decision making? Nash devised 12 questions for examining the ethics of a business decision.[83]

1. Have you defined the problem accurately? What are the factual implications of the situation rather than a biased perspective that reflects your loyalties?
2. How would you define the problem if you stood on the other side of the fence?
3. How did this situation occur in the first place? What is the historical background of events leading up to this situation?
4. To whom and to what do you give your loyalty as a person and as a member of the corporation?
5. What do you want to accomplish in making this decision?
6. How does this intention compare with the probable results?
7. Whom could your decision or action injure?
8. Can you discuss the problem with the affected parties before you make your decision?
9. Are you confident that your position will be as valid over a long period of time as it seems now?
10. Could you disclose without qualms your decision or action to your boss, your CEO, the board of directors, your family, and society as a whole?
11. What would this decision symbolize for others if they interpret it correctly? What could it symbolize if the decision is misinterpreted by others?
12. Under what conditions would you allow exceptions to your stand?

INTERNATIONAL ETHICS

The difficulty of making ethical decisions is exacerbated in international business due to different value systems and practices. Bribery, which is frowned upon (if still practiced) in many cultures, is a daily way of life in others. While bribes and kick-backs to win contracts at home and abroad are illegal for U.S. businesses, such practices were actually a valid tax deduction in some countries, such as Germany and Australia until a few years ago.[84] Nevertheless, ethical behavior is viewed as a competitive advantage in global business because it builds trust.[85]

Although bribing is an ancient custom, there is a growing movement to curb this practice. At the urging of the United States, the industrialized nations signed a treaty in 1997 that banned bribes and made bribes by businesses to foreign officials a crime. The World Bank, the OECD (Organization for Economic Cooperation and Development), and the International Monetary Fund are attacking various forms of corrupt practices that prevent countries from digging themselves out of poverty and joining the global economy. A common definition of *corruption is the abuse of public power for private gain.* Transparency International[86] publishes an annual list of the perceived corruption among public officials and politicians in various countries. This ranking is determined by expert surveys of businesspeople and analysts. Of the 159 countries evaluated for the 2005 Corruption Perceptions Index, seventy countries reportedly have high levels of corruption because they scored less than 5 on a 1–10 point scale where 10 indicates a corruption-free clean score. Exhibit 6–3 indicates the least corrupt countries, such as Iceland, which has the highest score at 9.7 out of 10, and the most corrupt countries, such as Bangladesh and Chad, each with a score of 1.7. The chairman of Transparency International, Peter Eigen, states that "Corruption is a major cause of poverty as well as a barrier to overcoming it."[87] Most European countries, Singapore, Hong Kong, Australia, Canada, the United States, Japan and Chile, rank in the top 23 positions with scores of 7 or higher. The United States, for example, is number 17 with a score of 7.6 while Japan ranks number 21 with a score of 7.3. China is ranked at number 78 with a score of 3.2, and India is ranked at number 88 with a score of 2.9.

Country Ranking	Highest Ranked Countries (least corrupt)	2005 CPI Score (1–10)	Country Ranking	Lowest Ranked Countries (most corrupt)	2005 CPI Score (1–10)
1	Iceland	9.7	152	Angola	2
2	Finland	9.6	152	Cote d'Ivoire	1.9
3	New Zealand	9.6	152	Equatorial Guinea	1.9
4	Denmark	9.5	152	Nigeria	1.9
5	Singapore	9.4	155	Haiti	1.8
6	Sweden	9.2	155	Myanmar	1.8
7	Switzerland	9.1	155	Turkmenistan	1.8
8	Norway	8.9	158	Bangladesh	1.7
9	Australia	8.8	158	Chad	1.7

EXHIBIT 6-3 **Corruption Perceptions Index 2005—Highest and Lowest Ranking Countries**

The degree of corruption in a country is determined primarily by cultural values.[88] In high power distance cultures, corruption is more likely since subordinates are less likely to question authority; society is less sympathetic to whistle-blowing, which is perceived as disloyalty or as challenging authority, and superiors are more likely to retaliate and use their power to punish whistle-blowing.[89] Achievement cultures (or masculinity, as Hofstede terms it) correlate with higher corruption because individuals are encouraged to be successful, ambitious and competitive, which often seems to justify cutting ethical corners.[90] Corruption is less likely when economic activity is moderately regulated; having no regulations is ineffective, but an overabundance of regulations leads to bribery since following all the rules is perceived as too difficult and time-consuming. Corruption is also less likely in countries with socio-political stability and a tradition of abiding by well-established law and order.[91] But, because corruption is a complex social phenomenon, it is difficult to eradicate with laws alone.

One of the common dilemmas in international business is whether or not to subscribe to cultural relativism. Does one accept the values of the local culture (when in Rome, do as the Romans) or continue to observe or even impose one's own values? Do you promote women and minorities in international subsidiaries where there is little or no concern for diversity issues? Do you sell the pesticide that has been banned in the United States as a hazardous product to a lesser-developed country that has no environmental or consumer safety laws? Many of these issues and their legal ramifications are extremely complex. It's important to identify the cultural values, historical precedents, and legal requirements that are involved. It's also helpful to consult with various people from the other culture to make sure you understand the foreign viewpoint.

The ethics and values the owners of Kingston Technology Corporation brought with them from Taiwan and Shanghai have resulted in spectacular growth. Based in Los Angeles, John Tu and David Sun sell add-on memory modules for personal computers. In a cutthroat business, they treat their employees, suppliers, and customers like family. They pay their employees, two-thirds of whom are ethnic minorities, higher than average salaries and have promised them one to two years of salary if the business fails. They do multimillion-dollar deals with a handshake. They don't pressure suppliers on price, but they do pay them ahead of schedule if possible and never cancel orders. Their philosophy of making customers, workers, and suppliers happy has translated into one of the highest revenue per employee figures anywhere.[92]

Several codes of conduct for global business have been developed by international organizations, such as the European corporate code of conduct, global Sullivan Principles, OECD Guidelines for Multinational Enterprises—2000, and the Caux RoundTable Principles for Business. The principles identified by this last group are (1) be responsible for stakeholders as well as shareholders; (2) contribute to the economic and social development of the world community; (3) behave ethically in accordance with the spirit of the law; (4) respect international and domestic rules; (5) support multilateral trade systems; (6) respect the environment; and (7) avoid illicit operations (bribery, money laundering, corruption).[93]

CORPORATE SOCIAL RESPONSIBILITY

In recent years, companies have come to realize the importance of intangible assets, such as company values, human and intellectual capital, reputation and brand equity.[94] Companies that demonstrate good corporate citizenship (an intangible asset) are likely to have a competitive advantage in business and in their ability to attract and retain employees,[95] particularly Gen Y employees who are reportedly more idealistic than some previous generations. A meta-analysis that looked at the aggregated results of 10 studies found that corporate social responsibility does pay off financially for firms due to the positive impact on the firms' reputations.[96] *Corporate social responsibility (CSR) is broadly defined as a company's commitment and contribution to the quality of life of employees, their families and the local community and society overall to support sustainable economic development.*[97] Business has long been involved in philanthropic causes, but current CSR efforts also encompass cause-related marketing, minority support programs, socially responsible employment and manufacturing practices, and environmental practices. Furthermore, many firms have begun to pressure their business partners, particularly overseas suppliers, to adhere to more universal workplace standards. The Web sites of more than 80 percent of *Fortune 500* companies contain a section on their CSR activities, which seems to indicate that business leaders perceive CSR as both an ethical/ideological and an economic imperative.[98] Although CSR programs seem to be proliferating, not everyone believes that business should use shareholder wealth for any purpose other than business. For example, economist Milton Friedman and others believe that corporations' only obligation is to shareholders and that the public good is the responsibility of government which is better equipped for this role.[99] These critics also argue that the money spent on CSR is better devoted to other priorities like research and development.

There is growing demand for more accountability and transparency in business, along with greater corporate social responsibility. The 1999 Millennial Poll of 25,000 people from 23 countries found that (1) people all around the world base their opinion of firms on their corporate citizenship; (2) 20 percent rewarded or punished firms (e.g., buying, investing or boycotting) for their social performance and would consider doing so again in the future; and (3) 66 percent want companies to go beyond a focus on profit to contribute to broader societal goals.[100] Sixty percent of global managers of various nationalities reported that CSR activities results in enhanced reputations and goodwill that facilitates relations and opportunities in local communities.[101] According to a 2004 survey, 82 percent of U.S. firms reported that corporate citizenship is beneficial to the bottom line, and 74 percent indicated that the public has a right to expect corporate citizenship.[102] Changing expectations about corporate responsibility has led to a shift from the shareholder to a stakeholder model in some firms with the result that communities and other groups affected by corporate decisions were brought into a dialogue.[103] Starbuck's efforts to pay higher prices to coffee growers, Hewlett Packard's attempts to alleviate poverty by bridging the digital divide between the haves and the have-nots in the United States and lesser-developed countries, and Chiquita Banana's environmental improvements for plantation workers and neighbors reflect a stakeholder approach.[104]

In the ranking of the 100 Best Corporate Citizens for 2005, published in Business Ethics Magazine, the number one firm is Cummins, the Indiana-based engine maker. To make this list, companies perform at a high standard and service a variety of stakeholders with excellence and integrity. Cummins won because it tripled earnings at the same time it greatly reduced air-emissions. Cummins employees have employee ownership and profit sharing. The firm publishes a sustainability report and funds schools in China and India, biodiversity in Mexico, and architecture in its local community.[105]

CLASS ACTIVITY: WEYCO'S BAN ON EMPLOYEE SMOKING

The purpose of this exercise is to provide an opportunity to discuss an ethical dilemma and identify different types of moral reasoning and value considerations (Time allotted: 60 minutes).

STEP 1.   In your learning group, discuss your answers to the case questions that you completed in the Class Preparation.

STEP 2.   If possible, come to a group consensus on whether WEYCO is doing the right or wrong thing with their smoking ban. What values can you identify in this discussion?

STEP 3.   Using Exhibit 6–2, what stage of moral development is reflected in the reasoning behind your group decision? What stage of reasoning is reflected in your individual decision in the class preparation? What stages of reasoning do Howard Weyer's statements reflect? (Steps 1–3—30 minutes)

STEP 4.   General Debriefing Questions. (30 minutes)
1. What are the views of the key stakeholders in this case?
2. What are the ethical issues to consider when deciding to fire tobacco users?
3. Is it appropriate for employers to impose restrictions on individual freedoms?
4. What values were evident in your group discussion? Was anyone thinking of different values when you made your individual decision prior to class? Which values took precedence—ethical or nonethical?
5. Did your group come to a consensus on whether WEYCO is doing the right or wrong thing? If so, what is your group decision? Describe the level of moral reasoning on which it was based.
6. What ethical framework is WEYCO using to support their anti-smoking ban—utilitarianism, individual rights principle, justice principle, caring principle, or environmentalism?
7. Would you want to work at WEYCO? Why?

ETHICS IN EVERYDAY WORKLIFE

The purpose of this exercise is to compare our views on workplace ethics. (Time allotted: 30 minutes)

STEP 1.   Please fill out the following survey.[106] (5 minutes)
How ethical are these behaviors?

1 = very unethical   2 = unethical   3 = neither ethical or unethical   4 = ethical   5 = very ethical

_____ Accepting gifts/favors in exchange for preferential treatment
_____ Giving gifts/favors in exchange for preferential treatment
_____ Divulging confidential information
_____ Calling in sick to take a day off
_____ Taking the organization's products without permission
_____ Using the organization's materials and supplies for personal use without permission (e.g., using company stationary, envelopes, sneaking food)
_____ Using the organization's services for personal use without permission (e.g., sending personal mail, asking the computer staff to fix your home computer at the office)
_____ Doing personal business on work time without permission (e.g., surfing the web, playing computer games, making personal phone calls)
_____ Taking extra personal time (additional breaks, long lunches)
_____ Blaming innocent co-workers for errors they did not make
_____ Claiming credit for someone else's work
_____ Not reporting other's violations of organizational policies
_____ Concealing your errors
_____ **Total** (sum your response)
_____ **Average** (divide your total score by 13)

STEP 2.   Discuss your answers with your learning group. (15 minutes)

    a.   Compare your scores in your learning group. Which items had the greatest consensus?

    b.   Which items showed the most disagreement? Discuss why you disagree on these items. What factors could explain why you perceive these behaviors differently? Approach this discussion like a scientist who is trying to understand, rather than simply judge, human behavior.

    c.   Were there any items that were difficult to rate due to the possibility of extenuating circumstances that you would want to consider?

STEP 3.   In the plenary group, discuss the following question. (10 minutes)

    a.   If you were the owner of the company, would you answer differently?

    b.   What did you learn about personal ethics from this discussion?

LEARNING POINTS

1. Ethics refers to standards of conduct that indicate how one should behave based on moral duties and virtues arising from principles about right and wrong.

2. Ethical practices pay off in the long run, as trusting relationships and well-satisfied customers are the basis of repeat business.

3. Companies create an environment in which unethical practices are more likely when they focus solely on profit and intense competition; when top management gives lip service only to ethical behavior and fails to establish clear policies and adequate controls; and when they are insensitive to the customer's best interests and public concerns about ethics.

4. Companies that want to encourage moral behavior (1) communicate their expectations that employees will behave ethically and define what that means; (2) hire top executives who set a good example; (3) reward ethical behavior and punish unethical behavior; (4) teach employees the basic tools of ethical decision making; and (5) encourage the discussion of ethical issues.

5. Values are core beliefs or desires that guide or motivate attitudes and actions.

6. Rokeach developed a list of the most common American values, which people hold to varying degrees.

7. Terminal values are desirable end states of existence or the goals people want to accomplish in their lifetime. Terminal values are either personal or social.

8. Instrumental values are preferable modes of behavior or the means to achieving one's terminal values. There are two types: moral and competence.

9. Schwartz and Bilsky created a universal psychological structure of human values that applies to people from all cultures, which consists of seven motivational types of values: prosocial, restrictive conformity, enjoyment, achievement, maturity, self-direction, and security.

10. Ethical values directly relate to beliefs concerning what is right and proper and motivate a sense of moral duty (trustworthiness, respect, responsibility, justice and fairness, caring, and civic virtue). Nonethical values are things we like, desire, or find important. Ethical values should always take precedence over nonethical values.

11. Kohlberg's theory of moral development consists of three levels: self-centered, conformity, and principled. Individuals move through these stages from a self-centered conception of right and wrong to an understanding of social contracts and internalized principles of justice and rights.

12. The five ethical models are utilitarian, rights and duties, justice, caring, and environmental ethics.

13. The difficulty of making ethical decisions is intensified in international business due to different value systems and business practices.

ACTION SCRIPTS

FOR EMPLOYEES

- "Experts" at ethics know their personal values and can readily articulate them. They have spent time figuring out what is most important in life to them.
- They can also decode what values seem to be guiding the behavior of others, which helps them discuss ethical dilemmas.
- When they have a choice, "experts" choose to work for an organization whose values are compatible with their own. They work at identifying the real values, not just the espoused values, that are manifested by prospective employers and colleagues in their actions, interviews, and written materials.
- When faced with ethical dilemmas, they know who would be the best people to go to for consultation and advice. Knowing who to go to is largely determined by political considerations as well as the integrity, discretion, and wisdom of the advisors. Novices are often less likely to seek help or less likely to consult the right advisors.
- They try to settle ethical issues internally first before going outside the company.
- When there is wrong-doing, "expert" employees analyze the source of the problem and know what actions are most likely to halt the behavior in a particular situation. If their first attempt doesn't succeed, they exert more pressure, take more formal action, go higher up the organizational hierarchy, or even resort to public whistle-blowing as the situation demands. They understand that there is an escalating progression of actions that they can employ, which is not formulaic but reflects their understanding of what will work with different people at different times. Novices are more likely to see themselves as having fewer options, for example, being stuck between a rock and a hard place—"either I go along with this or I'll be fired" or "If I speak up, I'll be fired."
- "Expert" employees see themselves as embedded in a network—they understand that their actions not only reflect on themselves personally but on their work unit and the company as a whole. They are able to identify everyone who might be impacted by unethical behavior on their part and how they would be affected. They can play out the consequences of their behavior.
- Whistle-blowing is legitimate when (1) it would benefit the public interest; (2) the revelation is of major importance and very specific; (3) the facts have been checked and rechecked for accuracy; (4) all other avenues within the organization have been exhausted; and (5) the whistle blower is above reproach and has no personal advantage to gain by revealing the information.[107]

FOR MANAGERS

- The top management of an organization sets the moral tone of the company. If they consistently behave in an ethical manner and set clear expectations that their subordinates should behave ethically, it is less likely that violations will occur. Some of the standards of moral behavior that are commonly expected of employees are (1) keeping one's promises, (2) not harming others, (3) helping others in need, (4) respecting others and not treating them merely as means to your own ends, and (5) not using company resources for one's own purposes.
- Expert managers encourage and promote the discussion of ethical dilemmas. Employees should not be punished for questioning a decision on moral grounds. However, ethics discussions become more difficult and polarized when people take the "moral high road" and criticize those who do not share their values. Experts work at identifying and understanding the different perspectives on an issue and then discuss the consequences of alternative actions that might be taken.
- Managers who are skilled at ethics help employees and co-workers see the broader picture, generate and evaluate various alternatives, and keep working the problem until they arrive at a creative option when there is no simple solution to ethical dilemmas.
- They learn how to coach others through ethical mindfields in a way that provides clear moral standards in a nonjudgmental fashion.

- Expert managers understand the symbolic nature of their actions and the message they send to the rest of the organization about the importance of ethical behavior. They see themselves as accountable to shareholders, owners, and society.
- They use systems thinking to analyze how ethical problems evolved and to foresee the long-term consequences of unethical behavior.
- When making decisions, they can identify all the different stakeholders that need to be considered and how they might be affected by the decision.
- Expert managers are skilled at generating various alternative strategies for resolving ethical dilemmas and can foresee and evaluate the consequences of each. unethical behavior.
- Expert managers have a finely tuned radar for recognizing questionable behavior and use the Ethics Warning System when they make a decision:[108]
  - Golden Rule—Are you treating others as you would want to be treated?
  - Publicity —Would you be comfortable if your reasoning and decision were to be publicized (i.e., how would it look on the front page of tomorrow's papers)?
  - Kid on your shoulder —Would you be comfortable if your children were observing you? Is your behavior an example of ethical behavior?
- When involved in global business, expert managers can read the cues in the local culture context and learn how to avoid bribery requests. They also develop relationships with decision-makers and people at the top of the organization in both relationship and hierarchical cultures to avoid having to bribe people lower in the organizational hierarchy to take their requests or messages up through the internal communication channels.[109]

FOR ORGANIZATIONAL ARCHITECTS[110]

- Expert organizational architects know that organizations begin with a mission statement that defines the values and beliefs of the organization and a vision that spells out their responsibilities to stakeholders. The next step is an up-to-date code of conduct with specific and measurable standards for which employees are held accountable in performance reviews. The code of conduct focuses on ethical dilemmas that are typical in the industry and clearly defines ethical work practices. All employees are trained in implementing the code of ethics.
- To help their organization promotes ethical behavior, expert designers work to ensure that the following practices are put in place:
  - Citizenship and ethical conduct are criteria in the performance evaluation process. Employees are not given incentives for unethical behavior, nor are they penalized for ethical behavior.
  - The company communicates and enforces clear consequences for those who do not behave ethically.
  - Employees have someone other than their boss, a confidential third party, whom they can go to with ethical questions and concerns about unethical actions.
  - The organization has a published set of values that includes the expectation of ethical work behavior and recognizes the importance of stakeholders. These values are not just rhetoric and public relations but are reflected in the organizational culture and norms of each work unit.
  - Because one's values are fairly well set by adulthood and difficult to change, ethical workplaces focus on developing selection and hiring practices that weed out candidates with questionable ethics. Ethical behavior and integrity are also important factors in determining who gets promoted.
  - Corporate strategic planning includes a discussion of personal and corporate values as well as the impact of decisions on a broad range of external stakeholders.
  - Ethics are considered in supplier contracts, and supplies are monitored for product safety, quality, and labor practices.
- Experts understand that firms send a strong message to their employees and benefit from striving toward and attaining the standards for inclusion in lists of well-respected companies, such as "100 Best Corporate Citizens."
- They develop a CSR program, they also begin with their mission, responsibilities to key stakeholders, standards of conduct, and metrics to measure their progress.[111]

- They know that a viable CSR strategy usually requires open dialogue and constructive partnerships with government at various levels, non-governmental organizations (NGOs) including activist groups, and local communities.
- When designing social and environmental programs, experts establishing successful CSR programs listen to the wishes of local communities and respect the beliefs (e.g., cultural, ethnic, or community beliefs) they may encounter. Since programs that work in one setting may not succeed elsewhere, local input and guidance are essential. Despite allowances for local variation, good CSR programs still maintain consistent global standards and policies.
- They obtain feedback from relevant stakeholders on how well they are meeting their social responsibility goals, as Royal Dutch/Shell does with its "Tell Shell" Web site.[112]
- They can develop social metrics to measure the organizational impact on society and the environment,[113] benchmark with others to learn best practices, and invite outsiders in to evaluate their ethics programs.
- Experts consider joining global organizations that promote CSR, such as Social Accountability International's Corporate Involvement Program, the Ethical Trading Initiative, and the United Nations' Global Compact.

PERSONAL APPLICATION ASSIGNMENT

Think back over the last few years and try to recall a specific event or situation at school, work, or home when you were confronted with an ethical dilemma or a difficult situation that called for a socially responsible action. Some examples might be taking something that did not belong to you, observing someone else's dishonest behavior, or having to decide between looking out for yourself and possibly harming another person.

1. In writing, describe the situation in some detail. How did this situation occur? Who else was there besides yourself? What were they doing? What were you doing? If you were on the receiving end of an unethical act, how were you treated? What were the issues involved?

2. How would you describe the main issues if you were on the other side of the fence?

3. What were the conflicts or dilemmas for you in this situation?

4. Why were they conflicts?

5. What did you do?

6. Why did you do it? What were your intentions? Were there extenuating circumstances that affected your decision?

7. What were the results of your actions?

8. At the time of the situation, did you think you did the right thing?

9. Now, looking back, what if anything would you do differently?

10. What conclusions or lessons can you draw from this reflection?

ENDNOTES

[1] P. Hawken, *The Ecology of Commerce: A Declaration of Sustainability* (New York: HarperBusiness, 1993).

[2] T. Petzinger, "Business Achieves Greatest Efficiencies When at Its Greenest," *Wall Street Journal*, (July 11, 1997): B1.

[3] Ibid.

[4] H. Bradbury and J. A. Clair, "Promoting Sustainable Organizations with Sweden's Natural Step," *Academy of Management Executive 13*(4) (1999): 63–74.

[5] R. C. Anderson, R. C., Speech, Shared Air Summit, Toronto, Canada (June 20, 2005).

[6] P. Asmus. "100 Best Corporate Citizens for 2005," *Business Ethics Online* (Spring, 2005) http://www.business-ethics.com/whats_new/100best.html. Accessed 10/15/2005.

[7] Anderson, Speech, Shared Air Summit.

[8] Bradbury and Clair, "Promoting Sustainable Organizations with Sweden's Natural Step."

[9] http://www.naturalstep.org/about/clients.php. Accessed 10/8/05.

[10] *The Natural Step: From Consensus to Sustainable Development* (Sausalito, CA: The Natural Step, 1997).

[11] Bradbury and Clair, "Promoting Sustainable Organizations with Sweden's Natural Step": 72.

[12] The authors would like to thank Bruce Drake, James Weber, and Asbjorn Osland for their contributions to this chapter. The instructions for scoring this version of the Rokeach Value Survey were developed by James Weber, "Managerial Value Orientations: A Typology and Assessment," *International Journal of Value Based Management 3*(2) (1990): 37–54, and adapted by Bruce Drake.

[13] This case was written by Asbjorn Osland and Pamela Wells, San Jose State University, 2005, and is excerpted here with permission of the authors.

[14] Information about the company, including the creed, was retrieved from http://www.wE.com/web. Accessed 6/3/05.

[15] Commentary by John Stossel, retrieved from http://abcnews.go.com/ 2020/GiveMeABreak/ story?id=650390&page=1. Accessed 6/6/05.

[16] http://www.workindex.com/ editorial/hre/hre0201-03.asp. Accessed 6/3/05.

[17] http://www.workrights.org/issue_1 ifestyle/ld_legislative_brief.html. Accessed 6/3/05.

[18] J. W. Peters, "Company's Smoking Ban Means Off-Hours, Too." *New York Times* (February 8, 2005): C.5.

[19] "WEYCO fires 4 employees for refusing smoking test." *Associated Press State & Local Wire* (January 24, 2005).

[20] Personal e-mail communication from Anne Lichliter, *Executive Assistant to Howard Weyers*, dated 6/5/05.

[21] H. Weyers, "HBR Case Commentary – Should Sid's weight be a factor in Bill's decision?" *Harvard Business Review 83*(5) (May 2005): 38.

[22] K. B. Hoffman (Associated Press). "Kick the habit—or get kicked off the job; Firm's policy fuels privacy concerns." *Chicago Tribune*, (February 9, 2005): 22.

[23] Peters, "Company's Smoking Ban Means Off-Hours, Too."

[24] Ibid.: C.5.

[25] American Lung Association, http://slati.lungusa.org/default.asp. Accessed 6/3/05.

[26] Retrieved from the National Cancer Institute: http://cis.nci.nih.gov/fact/10_19/htm on June 5, 2005.

[27] K. E. Warner, T. A. Hodgson, and C. E. Carroll, "Medical costs of smoking in the United States: estimates, their validity, and their implications," *Tobacco Control 8* (1999): 290–300.

[28] National Household Survey on Drug Abuse, http://www.oas.samhsa.gov/2k2/tobquit.htm. Accessed 6/5/05.

[29] National Institute on Drug Abuse Research Report Series, http://www.nida.nih.gov/researchreports/nicotine/nicotine.html. Accessed 6/5/05

[30] http://www.cfah.org/nbns/newsrelease/relapse2-27-02.cfm. Accessed 6/7/05.

[31] Household Survey on Drug Abuse, http://www.oas.samhsa.gov/2k2/tobquit.htm. Accessed 6/5/05.

[32] http://www.nida.nih.gov/NIDA_notes/NNVol18N3/Genetic/html. Accessed 6/5/05.

[33] W. A. Mojica, et al. Smoking-cessation interventions by type of provider: A Meta-analysis, *American Journal of Preventive Medicine 26*(5) (2004): 391–400.

[34] T. Martin. Michigan Senate Bill Would Protect Workers Who Smoke On Own Time. *Detroit Free Press*. (April 13, 2005).

[35] Personal e-mail communication from Anne Lichliter, Executive Assistant to Howard Weyers, June 5, 2005.

[36] R. F. Hartley, *Business Ethics: Violations of the Public Trust* (New York: John Wiley & Sons, 1993). This book describes ethics scandals and how companies handled them.

[37] J. C. Collins and J. I. Porras, *Built to Last* (New York: Harper-Collins, 1994).

[38] R. F. Hartley, *Business Ethics: Violations of the Public Trust*: 1 and 323.

[39] R. D. Haas, "Ethics—A Global Business Challenge," *Vital Speeches of the Day* (1994): 506–509.

[40] Collins and Porras, *Built to Last*: 8.

[41] C. Johnson, "Ahold Settles SEC Fraud Charges" *The Washington* Post (Thursday, October 14, 2005): E03; G. Edmondson and L. Cohn, "How Parmalat Went Sour" *BusinessWeek Online* (January 12, 2004). http://www.businessweek.com/magazine/content/04_02/b3865053_mz054.htm. Accessed 10/11/05. B. Bremner and D. Roberts, "Wanted: A Big Broom for China's Banks" *BusinessWeek Online* (May 9, 2005). http://www.businessweek.com/magazine/content/05_19/b3932074.htm. Accessed 10/11/05. "SK Group Owner Jailed on Fraud, Illegal Accounting Charges," *Business Times* (Singapore) (June 13, 2003). For a Web site on classic financial and corporate scandals, see: http://www.ex.ac.uk/~RDavies/arian/scandals/classic.html.

[42] Walker Information (personal communication October 27, 2005). This organization tracks ethics data.

[43] B. Toffler, *Final Accounting* (New York: Broadway Books, 2003).

[44] R. Elaydi, "A Meso Approach to Understanding Ethical Behavior," Paper presented at the Academy of International Business conference, Quebec, Canada, 2005.

[45] "America's Ague," *The Economist 377* (October 15, 2005): 75–76.

[46] A. Wheat, "Keeping an Eye on Corporate America," *Fortune 146*(11)(November 25, 2002): 44–46.

[47] Wheat, "Keeping an Eye on Corporate America."

[48] Environics and the Gallup Organization, "Voice of the People Survey" (2002).

[49] P. A. Argenti, *Corporate Communication*. 3rd Ed. (New York: McGraw-Hill, 2003).

[50] S. Ghoshal, "Business Schools Share the Blame for Enron," *Financial Times* (July 17, 2003): 19.

[51] I. I. Mitroff and D. L. Swanson, "An Open Letter to the Deans and the Faculties of American Business Schools: A Call to Action." *Academy of Management News 35* (2004): 7.

[52] M. Josephson, *Making Ethical Decisions* (Marina Del Rey, CA: The Josephson Institute of Ethics, 1993): 4.

[53] M. Josephson, *Ethical Obligations and Opportunities in Business: Ethical Decision Making in the Trenches* (Marina Del Rey, CA: Josephson Institute of Ethics, 1990).

[54] B. Z. Posner and W. Schmidt, "Values and the American Manager: An Update Updated," *California Management Review 34*(3) (Spring 1992): 80–94.

[55] Hartley, *Business Ethics: Violations of the Public Trust*: 5; and G. F. Cavanagh, *American Business Values* (Englewood Cliffs, NJ: Prentice Hall, 1984): 159.

[56] M. J. Baasten and B. H. Drake, "Ethical Leadership," *Social Sciences Perspectives Journal* (March 1990).

[57] R. C. Solomon, *Ethics and Free Enterprise in the Global 1990s* (Lanham, MD: Littlefield Adams, 1993).

[58] F. B. Bird and J. A. Waters, "The Moral Muteness of Managers," *California Management Review 32*(1) (Fall 1989): 73–88.

[59] Bird and Waters, "The Moral Muteness of Managers."

[60] R. E. Boyatzis and F. R. Skelly, "The Impact of Changing Values on Organizational Life," *The Organizational Behavior Reader* (Upper Saddle River, NJ: Prentice Hall, 1995).

[61] R. L. Sims, and E. G. Kroeck, "The Influence of Ethical Fit on Employee Satisfaction, Commitment and Turnover," *Journal of Business Ethics 13* (1994): 939–947.

[62] M. Rokeach, *The Nature of Values* (New York: The Free Press, 1973).

[63] J. Weber, "Exploring the Relationship Between Personal Values and Moral Reasoning," *Human Relations 46*(4) (1993): 435–463 and "Managerial Value Orientations: A Typology and Assessment," *International Journal of Value Based*

Management 3(2) (1990): 37–54; and G. F. Cavanagh, *American Business Values.*

[64] D. A. Clare and D. G. Sanford, "Mapping Personal Value Space: A Study of Managers in Four Organizations," *Human Relations 32* (1979): 659–666.

[65] S. H. Schwartz and W. Bilsky, "Toward a Theory of the Universal Content and Structure of Values: Extensions and Cross-Cultural Replications" *Journal of Personality and Social Psychology 58*(5) (1990): 878–891.

[66] These core ethical values were developed by a diverse group of 30 national leaders. M. Josephson, *Making Ethical Decisions*: 9.

[67] J. Weber, "Exploring the Relationship Between Personal Values and Moral Development," *Human Relations 46*(4) (1993): 459.

[68] L. K. Trevino and S. A. Youngblood, "Bad Apples in Bad Barrels: A Causal Analysis of Ethical Decision-Making Behavior," *Journal of Applied Psychology 75* (1990): 378–385.

[69] L. Kohlberg, "Stages of Moral Development as a Basis for Moral Education," in C. M. Beck, B. S. Crittenden, and E. V. Sullivan (eds.), *Moral Education: Interdisciplinary Approaches* (New York: Newman Press, 1971); and A. Colby and L. Kohlberg, *The Measurement of Moral Judgment, Vol. 1: Theoretical Foundations and Research Validations* (Cambridge, MA: University Press, 1987).

[70] These titles are taken from D. A. Whetton and K. S. Cameron, *Developing Managerial Skills* (New York: HarperCollins, 1991): 60.

[71] The more descriptive stage names are taken from L. K. Trevino, "A Cultural Perspective on Changing and Developing Organizational Ethics," in *Research in Organizational Change and Development*, W. A. Pasmore and R. W. Woodman (eds.) (Greenwich, CT: JAI Press, 1990): 195–230.

[72] L. Kohlberg, *Essays in Moral Development, Vol. I: The Philosophy of Moral Development* (New York: Harper & Row, 1981); and R. Duska and M. Whalen, *Moral Development* (New York: Paulist Press, 1975).

[73] J. Weber, "Exploring the Relationship Between Personal Values and Moral Development," *Human Relations 46* (4) (1993): 454.

[74] Ibid.: 441.

[75] C. Gilligan, *In a Different Voice* (Cambridge, MA: Harvard University Press, 1982); C. Gilligan, and J. Attanucci, "Two Moral Orientations: Gender Differences and Similarities," *Merrill-Palmer Quarterly 34*(1988): 223–237.

[76] G. R. Wark, and D. L. Krebs, "Gender and Dilemma Differences in Real-Life Moral Judgment," *Developmental Psychology 32*(2) (1996): 220–231.

[77] C. Argyris, *Overcoming Organizational Defenses: Facilitating Organizational Learning* (Boston: Allyn and Bacon, 1990).

[78] R. S. Snell, "Complementing Kohlberg: Mapping the Ethical Reasoning Used by Managers for Their Own Dilemma Cases," *Human Relations 49*(1) (1996): 23–50.

[79] S. K. Lau and H. C. Kuan, *The Ethos of the Hong Kong Chinese* (Hong Kong: Chinese University Press, 1988) and C. C. Ji,

"Collectivism in Moral Development," *Psychological Review 80*(3) (1997): 967–976.

[80] See Cavanagh, *American Business Values*: 139–145 and G. F. Cavanagh, D. J. Moberg, and M. Velasquez, "The Ethics of Organizational Politics," *Academy of Management Review 6*(3) (1981): 363–74 and "Making Business Ethics Practical," *Business Ethics Quarterly 5*(3) (1995): 399–318.

[81] C. Gilligan, *In a Different Voice.*

[82] G. Dutton, "The Green Bottom Line," *Management Review 87*(9) (1998): 59–64; C. Merchant, "Environmental Ethics and Political Conflict," *Environmental Ethics 12*(1) (1990): 45–68; A. Miller, *Gaia Connections* (Savage, MD: Rowman and Littlefield, 1991); R. A. Buchholz, *Principles of Environmental Management: The Greening of Business* (Upper Saddle River, NJ: Prentice Hall, 1998).

[83] Adapted from L. L. Nash, "Ethics Without the Sermon," *Harvard Business Review 59* (November–December 1981): 79–90.

[84] M. Milliet-Einbinder, "Writing Off Tax Deductibility," *OECD Observer*, (April 2000): 38–40.

[85] P. Buller and G. McEvoy, "Creating and Sustaining Ethical Capability in the Multi-national Corporation." *Journal of World Business 34*(4) (1999): 326–343.

[86] Transparency International, (http://www.transparency.org/). Accessed 7/1/06.

[87] *Transparency International Corruption Perceptions Index 2005.* http://ww1.transparency.org/cpi/2005/cpi2005_infocus.html. Accessed 10/19/05.

[88] B. Husted, "Wealth, Culture, and Corruption," *Journal of International Business Studies 30*(2) (1999): 339–360; H. Park, "Determinants of Corruption," *The Multinational Business Review 11*(2) (Fall 2003): 29–48.

[89] D. V. Cohen and K. Nelson, "Multinational Ethics Programs: Cases in Corporate Practice." In Hoffman, Kamm, Frederick, & Petry Jr. (eds.), *Emerging Global Business Ethics* (Westport, CT: Quorum, 1994).

[90] H. Park, "Determinants of Corruption," *The Multinational Business Review 11*(2) (Fall 2003): 29–48.

[91] Park, "Determinants of Corruption."

[92] "Doing the Right Thing," *The Economist 335*(7915) (1995): 64.

[93] "Caux Round Table Principles for Business." http://www.cauxroundtable.org/documents/Principlespercent20forpercent20Business.PDF. Accessed 10/15/05.

[94] L. Low and P. C. Kalafut, *Invisible Advantage: How Intangibles Are Driving Business Performance* (Cambridge, MA: Perseus Publishing, 2002).

[95] N. Lockwood, "Corporate Social Responsibility: HR's Leadership Role." *SHRM 2004 Research Quarterly* (2004): 4.

[96] M. Orlitsky, F. L. Schmidt, and S. L. Rynes, "Corporate Social and Financial Performance: A Meta-Analysis," *Organization Studies 24*(3) (2003): 403–411.

[97] World Business Council for Sustainable Development, *Corporate Social Responsibility: Making Good Business Sense*

(Conches-Geneva, Switzerland: World Business Council for Sustainable Development, 2000).

98 N. C. Smith, "Corporate Social Responsibility: Whether or How?" *California Management Review 45*(4) (Summer 2003): 52–76; K. B. Murray and C. M. Vogel, "Using a Hierarchy of Effects Approach to Gauge the Effectiveness of CSR to Generate Goodwill Towards the Firm: Financial versus Nonfinancial Impacts" *Journal of Business Research 38* (1997): 141–159. For guidance on maximizing the benefits of social and strategic initiatives in collaborative social initiatives, see J. A. Pearce, II and J. Doh, "The High Impact of Collaborative Social Initiatives." *MIT Sloan Management Review 46*(3) (2005): 30–39.

99 "The Good Company." *The Economist 374* (8410) (January 22, 2005): p3–s4; B. Frow, "The Debate Over Doing Good." *BusinessWeek*, 3947 (August 15, 2005): 76–78.

100 Environics International Ltd., The Prince of Wales Business Leaders and the Conference Board. *Millennium Poll on Corporate Social Responsibility*. Executive Briefing. Toronto, Canada: (1999).

101 S. A. Muirhead, C. J. Bennett, R. E. Berenbeim, A. Kao, and D. J. Vidal, *Corporate Citizenship in the New Century: Accountability, Transparency, and Global Stakeholder Engagement* (New York: The Conference Board, Inc., 2002).

102 The Center for Corporate Citizenship at Boston College and the U. S. Chamber of Commerce Center for Corporate Citizenship. *The State of Corporate Citizenship in the U. S.: A View from Inside 2003–2004"* (Chestnut Hill, MA: The Center for Corporate Citizenship at Boston College and the U. S. Chamber of Commerce Center for Corporate Citizenship, 2004).

103 For interesting case studies describing how well-known firms have struggled to develop their own brand of corporate social responsibility and for an extensive list of resources, see J. Hollender and S. Fenichell's *What Matters Most: How a Small Group of Pioneers Is Teaching Social Responsibility to Big Business, and Why Big Business Is Listening* (New York: Basic Books, 2004).

104 Hollender and Fenichell, *What Matters Most.*

105 P. Asmus. "100 Best Corporate Citizens for 2005," *Business Ethics Online.* (Spring, 2005), http://www.business-ethics.com/whats_new/100best.html. Accessed 10/15/2005.

106 These questions were adapted from T. Jackson, "Cultural Values and Management Ethics: A 10-Nation Study." *Human Relations 54*(10) (October, 2001): 1287–1288.

107 S. Bok, "Whistleblowing and Professional Responsibilities," in D. Callahan and S. Bok (eds.), *Ethics Teaching in Higher Education* (New York: Plenum Press, 1980): 277–295.

108 Josephson, *Making Ethical Decisions*: 40.

109 J. McNett and M. Søndergaard, "Making Ethical Decisions," in H. Lane, M. Maznevski, M. Mendenhall, and J. McNett (eds.), *The Handbook of Global Management* (Malden, MA: Blackwell, 2003): 152–169.

110 Many of these expert practices come from the "Corporate Integrity Checkup," which reflects best practices in ethics management. http://www.crossroadsprograms.com/ coporate.html. Accessed 10/15/05.

111 Some of this information about CSR programs was adapted from *Corporate Social Responsibility: Making Good Business Sense* by the World Business Council for Sustainable Development, January 2000, www.wbcsd.org.

112 P. H. Mirvis, "Transformation at Shell: Commerce *and* Citizenship." *Business and Society Review 105*(1) (2000): 63–84.

113 M. Kaptein and J Wempe, *The Balanced Company: A Theory of Corporate Integrity* (Oxford: Oxford University Press, 2002).

Chapter 7

▲▲▲

PERSONAL GROWTH AND WORK STRESS

OBJECTIVES By the end of this chapter, you should be able to:

A. Describe the characteristics of adult development.

B. Explain Levinson's concept of life structures.

C. Recognize career anchors and their significance.

D. Describe the functions that mentors perform.

E. Identify trends in career management and planning.

F. Explain the transactional model of career stress.

G. Assess your current life-career situation and develop a plan for the future.

OVERLOAD: WHAT'S CAUSING IT AND HOW TO SOLVE IT

Workloads never set out to hurt anybody. But doesn't it seem like over the past couple of years, someone named "Mr. Overload" muscled his way into all of our workplaces, sat down in our chairs, and took over our lives? Both the increased speed and complexity of work these days is leaving everyone from the executive suite to the factory floor throbbing from a massive migraine just trying to get all their work done.

Why this has happened, and why no one seems to be talking about it intelligently, let alone doing something constructive about it—is even more puzzling.

WHAT'S CAUSING OVERWORK AND WHY IS IT A PROBLEM?

You guessed it. Most employees don't just sign up to get overworked because they enjoy it. Economic, technological, and business factors such as downsizing, the skills shortage, and low unemployment have forced those American workers who were left sitting in the hot seat to give 150 percent (or more) just to stay on top of their workloads. Now, U.S. business leaders have come to expect and rely on this accelerated pace. What were once considered crises-mode workloads have now become business as usual. After all, the more people get done, the more our companies profit, right? True, the United States certainly is enjoying economic nirvana, but at what price? Collective burnout? Of course, burnout isn't new, but what is new is the way in which job overload—causing burnout—has elbowed its way into most of our work lives, sometimes without our even realizing it's a problem.

Take Jennifer Johnson, for instance. Johnson, who's now the principal strategist for Johnson & Co. in Santa Cruz, California, is a classic example of a fast tracker who was headed for burnout but jumped off the train before she crashed. "I was a corporate warrior for about 15 years," says Johnson. "When I first left college, I immediately began working 80-hour weeks in my first job at Novell in Provo, Utah." As a 22-year-old editor, she turned the company's in-house newsletter into an international consumer magazine that Novell sold three years later to The McGraw-Hill Companies for $10 million. She recalls nights when she'd stay at the office until 2 A.M., and was back in the office by 8 o'clock the next morning. "I realized it was the dues-paying time of my life, and I actually thrived on the fast pace," Johnson admits.

After she took a job in advertising at another firm, got married, and had kids, the pace became dizzying. She vividly remembers her breaking point 19 months ago when life and work clashed in the extreme. "My husband Scott, who headed the marketing function for one of 3Com's international-business units, was returning from a trip to Japan. The plan was for me to hand off the kids to him at the airport, and then I was going to catch a plane for the East Coast." It turns out her husband's plane was 20 minutes late. The moment he arrived, she threw the kids to him and sprinted to her own plane, luggage in tow.

In flight and exhausted, Johnson found herself writing a resignation letter. "I was laughing out loud as I wrote it because it was so obviously what I needed to do," she says. Johnson then started her own company—a virtual marketing organization that teams 17 contractors, mostly women, from across the country. Many of them were as desperate to balance their lives as she was. "I saw a lot of women who were forced to make the choice of either working or taking care of their families because their companies wouldn't be flexible," says Johnson. "I'm now seeing a world in which employees, after being downsized and rightsized, are turning the tables and they're my-sizing their jobs."

Workers who feel trapped in jobs in which they're powerless to do something about it tend to burn out faster. Ironically, those employees who are in fast-track careers are often the first ones to crash and burn, according to Beverly Potter, a workplace consultant and author of *Overcoming Job Burnout: How to Renew Enthusiasm for Work* (Ronin Publishing, 1998).

Although Johnson admits that when she was a 22-year-old she actually liked being what she calls a "fast burner," it wore her out after a while. Right before she left Novell the second time (she returned there after the ad agency job), she asked to be able to telecommute two days a week. "It really surprised me that they were unwilling to let me do that, even though they're a technology company," says Johnson. She found during her second maternity leave that she often got a lot more done working at home than when she was in the office—and having to contend with meetings, interruptions and mountains of extraneous information. "If HR and business line managers could start thinking outside the box about what really needs to get done, I think it would help relieve a lot of people's workloads."

If we can call it the bright side, all this overtime is helping push the recent surge in American workers' productivity. After growing at a brisk 2.9 percent annual rate in the 1960s and early 1970s, productivity slowed to a miniscule 1 percent from 1974 through 1995. Since then, it has been growing at around a 2 percent rate. That growth has led some economists to speculate that the economy has embarked on a new era of productivity growth, driven by computers and other high-tech innovations.

With the influx of technology, such as cellular phones and the Internet, workers are wired to the office 24 hours a day and are expected to achieve mind-boggling workloads. The Associated Press reported last May that the average business manager receives 190 messages per day.

Hundreds are quitting Corporate America daily because they're tired of the empty promises about companies helping them "balance their lives." The HR questions are: Have jobs grown too big for most workers? And what are companies really doing about it?

REENGINEERING JOBS TO FIT EMPLOYEES

One of the running jokes at Redmond, Washington–based Microsoft Corp. is you can work any 18 hours a day you want. Although it's well known that Microsoft employees reap hefty rewards for their intense productivity in terms of compensation, benefits, stock options, and the like, making overwork the corporate requirement can have its drawbacks. Many companies recognize the problem, and many think they've already solved it. But they should take another look at their solutions.

According to Terry Alan Beehr, professor of psychology at Central Michigan University in Mount Pleasant, Michigan, and an authority on organizational psychology, job stress is too often treated with medication or counseling rather than by making changes in the workplace and in workloads.

Companies need to take stock of where they're really at with their workloads and how those workloads piled up to where they are today. "This is a time when work needs to be trimmed just as firmly as the workforce has been trimmed," says William Bridges, consultant and author. He explains that companies have cut people out of the workforce (downsized) with razor-sharp accuracy, but haven't trimmed the workloads of the people who've remained with the same vigor. As a consultant, he has noticed there's a great deal of unnecessary work being done in U.S. companies. "Justifying work is very important," Bridges adds. It's a matter of figuring out what work is necessary and what isn't. It's essentially reengineering workloads. "I know that reengineering has a bad name," says Bridges, "but we need to take a close look at what we're making workers do." However, unlike reengineering, he says this is something workers themselves have to be very involved in.

For example, the HR leaders at Merck & Co., the giant pharmaceutical company based in Whitehouse Station, New Jersey, realized after hearing workers' complaints about overwork, inadequate training, schedule changes, poor new-hire screening, and lack of communication, among other things, that they needed to respond—quickly. In a major work redesign effort, Merck's management team assigned employees to teams that were devoted to solving these problems. Work was analyzed, dissected, and reorganized so that workers felt like they had more control over their workloads and schedules. "We focused on the things that are really important to our customers," says Michelle Peterson, senior director of work/life flexibility, who oversaw the effort.

In one area of the company, payroll employees weren't happy with the large amount of overtime they had to put in. During a series of meetings, team leaders realized that most of their work was more critical earlier in the week than toward the end of the week. Solutions included reducing peoples' commute time by allowing them to work at home more often and giving them compressed work weeks. They provided technology so payroll workers could input data at home. Solutions to the most difficult problems were implemented within three months, and turnover slowed from 45 percent to 32 percent, and is still dropping. In addition, overtime costs and absenteeism plummeted. And for the employees, overtime and commute time were slashed.

HR managers should also be willing to suggest that managers outsource tasks that are unnecessary, or could be done more effectively by a third party. "Who should do the work?" is the question every manager should ask about every bit of work. "And you may find some of the work could go outside, and you readjust what's left so it isn't so overwhelming," says Bridges.

Dell Computer Corp.'s direct-to-customer business model, for example, takes outsourcing to a new level. The firm doesn't just outsource a few tasks; it actually turns over three-quarters of its work to non-employees, particularly field service and manufacturing.

FOCUS ON WHAT'S MOST IMPORTANT

According to an article in the *Salt Lake Observer* in October 1998 called "The Zen of Managing Transition," one expert reminds us that you get what you focus on.

These days, in a 24-hour-a-day, global marketplace that moves faster than the speed of e-mail, it's important for HR managers to help their firms' management groups figure out what's most important to get done.

For example, this strategy has been a big focus at San Francisco–based AirTouch Communications Inc. this year. Tracey Borst, who heads the firm's HR team, says although she hears rumblings about overwork from time to time, the "noise level" about it hasn't gotten in the way lately. To nip the problem in the bud, the senior management team has been trying to get better at prioritizing work throughout the company by letting employees know which company goals are most important. "Even if we had all the money in the world, we still wouldn't have enough people and would have to let some things fall by the wayside," says Borst. "There's a limited number of resources to maintain customers and to create new products, so you have to focus on what's most important and create a balance."

Still, even with all the tweaking of processes and technological advances, why is it that companies are scrupulous about maintaining their inert equipment, but don't pay as much attention to giving their human assets workload tune-ups? Machines regularly get oiled, cleaned, and tuned. But when it comes to workers, we just expect they'll handle ever-increasing amounts of work without regard to regular check-ups.

When you come right down to it, perhaps we can't prevent "Mr. Overload" from coming to our offices altogether. But we can learn to work with him more consciously and intelligently. There are some new tools and ideas HR professionals can use to alleviate the work overload problem. Recognizing the problem exists and that it can be destructive is a good first step.

Source: Excerpted from Jennifer Koch, "Overload: What's Causing It and How to Solve It," *Work Force* 78 (January 1999): 30–37.

CLASS PREPARATION

A. Read "Overload: What's Causing It and How to Solve It."

B. How would you rate your current workload and stress level?

C. What strategies have you developed for coping with stress? Are they working?

D. Complete the Life Goal Inventory.

E. After reading the chapter, what cues and patterns will you look for with respect to personal growth, career development, and work stress?

LIFE GOAL INVENTORY

1. The purpose of the Life Goal Inventory is to give you an outline for looking at your life goals in a more systematic way. Your concern here should be to describe as fully as possible your aims and goals in all areas of your life. Consider goals that are important to you, whether they are relatively easy or difficult to attain. Be honest with yourself. Having fun and taking life easy are just as legitimate life goals as being president. You will have a chance to rate the relative importance of your goals later. Now you should try to just discover all the things that are important to you. To help make your inventory complete, we have listed general goal areas on the following pages. They are:
   * Career satisfaction
   * Status and respect
   * Personal relationships
   * Leisure satisfactions
   * Learning and education
   * Spiritual growth and religion
   * Material rewards and possessions

   These categories are only a general guide; feel free to change or redefine them in the way that best suits your own life. The unlabeled "Open" Section is for those goals that do not seem to fit into the other categories.

First fill in your own goals in the various sections of this inventory, making any redefinitions of the goal areas you feel necessary. Ignore for the time being the three columns on the right-hand side of each page. Directions for filling out these columns are on page 162.

Career Satisfaction

General Description: Your goals for your future job or career, including specific positions you want to hold. *Individual Redefinition:*	Importance (Hi, Med, Lo)	Ease of Attainment (Hi, Med, Lo)	Conflict with Other Goals (Yes or No)
Specific Goals			
1.			
2.			
3.			

Status and Respect

General Description: To what groups do you want to belong? What are your goals in these groups? To what extent do you want to be respected by others? From whom do you want respect? *Individual Redefinition:*	Importance (Hi, Med, Lo)	Ease of Attainment (Hi, Med, Lo)	Conflict with Other Goals (Yes or No)
Specific Goals			
1.			
2.			
3.			

Personal Relationships

General Description: Goals in your relationships with your significant other, colleagues, parents, friends, and people in general. *Individual Redefinition:*	Importance (Hi, Med, Lo)	Ease of Attainment (Hi, Med, Lo)	Conflict with Other Goals (Yes or No)
Specific Goals			
1.			
2.			
3.			

Leisure Satisfactions

General Description: Goals for your leisure time and pleasure activities—hobbies, sports, vacations, and interests you want to develop. *Individual Redefinition:*	Importance (Hi, Med, Lo)	Ease of Attainment (Hi, Med, Lo)	Conflict with Other Goals (Yes or No)
Specific Goals			
1.			
2.			
3.			

Learning and Education

General Description: What would you like to learn more about? What skills do you want to develop? What formal education goals do you have? *Individual Redefinition:*	Importance (Hi, Med, Lo)	Ease of Attainment (Hi, Med, Lo)	Conflict with Other Goals (Yes or No)
Specific Goals			
1.			
2.			
3.			

Spiritual Growth and Religion

General Description: Goals for peace of mind, your search for meaning, your relation to the larger universe, religious service, and devotional life. *Individual Redefinition:*	Importance (Hi, Med, Lo)	Ease of Attainment (Hi, Med, Lo)	Conflict with Other Goals (Yes or No)
Specific Goals			
1.			
2.			
3.			

Material Rewards and Possessions

	Importance (Hi, Med, Lo)	Ease of Attainment (Hi, Med, Lo)	Conflict with Other Goals (Yes or No)
General Description: What income level are you aiming for—upper class, middle class, voluntary simplicity?* What possessions do you want? *Individual Redefinition:*			
Specific Goals			
1.			
2.			
3.			

* Voluntary simplicity, both an inner and outer condition, is gaining popularity in the United States. It means deliberately organizing one's life around a purpose and avoiding exterior distraction and clutter, such as possessions, that are irrelevant to one's chief purpose in life. Some people who practice voluntary simplicity set a goal of earning only enough income to support a pared-down lifestyle, which allows them to work less than 40 hours a week. They then take the freed-up time and devote it to whatever purpose they have chosen for themselves.

Open–Other Goals

	Importance (Hi, Med, Lo)	Ease of Attainment (Hi, Med, Lo)	Conflict with Other Goals (Yes or No)
Description:			
Specific Goals			
1.			
2.			
3.			

Directions for Rating Goals

2. *Goal importance:* Now that you have completed the inventory, go back and rate the importance of each goal according to the following scheme:

Hi (High)   Compared with my other goals, this goal is very important.

Med (Medium)   This goal is moderately important.

Lo (Low)   A lot of other goals are more important than this one.

3. *Ease of goal attainment:* According to the following scheme, rate each goal on the probability that you will reach and/or maintain the satisfaction derived from it.

Hi (High)   Compared with my other goals, I could easily reach and maintain this goal.

Med (Medium)   I could reach and maintain this goal with moderate difficulty.

Lo (Low)   It would be very difficult to reach this goal.

Goal priorities: Select the goals from the inventory that seem most important to you at this time. Do not choose more than eight. Rank order them in terms of their importance. (1 = High, 8 = Low)

1.

2.

3.

4.

5.

6.

7.

8.

4. *Anticipating conflicts*: One of the major deterrents to goal accomplishment is the existence of conflict among goals.

People who ignore the potential conflicts between job and family, for instance, may end up abandoning goals because of the "either/or" nature of many decisions. Or years later they may come to regret sacrificing family needs for the sake of career demands or vice versa.

In the order you prioritized in the preceding step, list your goals on both axes of the Cross-Impact Matrix on the following page. Write your first goal where it says "Goal 1" on both axes, your second goal where it says "Goal 2," and so forth. Next, estimate the potential impact of the vertical goal statements you've written along the side of the chart on the horizontal goal statements you've written along the top. Please use the following symbols:

(+) for a helpful impact ("working on goal 1 will help me with goal 3")

(–) for a hindering impact ("working on goal 2 will make it more difficult to accomplish goal 5")

(0) for no impact of any kind

THE CROSS-IMPACT MATRIX

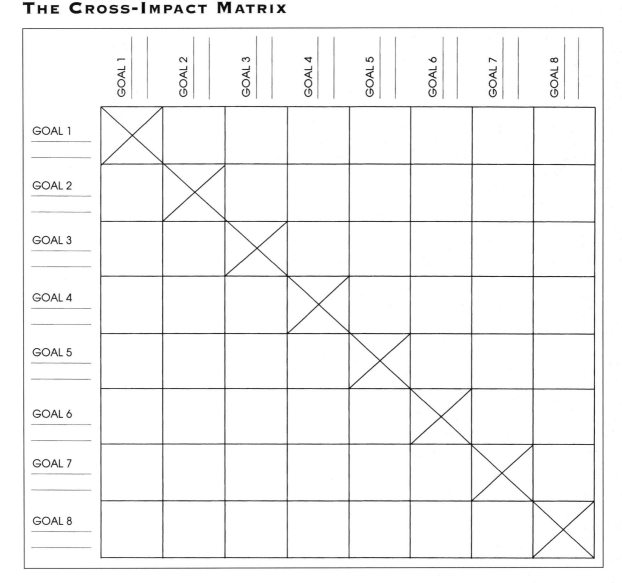

List conflicts in order of importance:

   1.
   2.
   3.
   4.
   5.

Note: The Personal Application Assignment for this chapter is a continuation of this exercise.

 ## THE KNOWLEDGE BASE

Taking responsibility for personal growth and career development is an important shared responsibility among employees, managers, and organizations. Theories of adult development provide insight into our personal experience and help us to understand the developmental phases and challenges facing our colleagues at work.

Theorists generally agree on the following characteristics of adult development.[1]

1. Personality development occurs throughout the life cycle as a succession of fairly predictable phases.
2. Each stage is characterized by a cycle of intensity and quiescence. In the latter, people achieve a state of quasi-stationary equilibrium that is eventually disrupted, initiating intense coping efforts and activity that often result in life changes. This is followed by another period of equilibrium and quiescence.
3. The disequilibrium of each stage is caused by a focal conflict or dilemma, which is created by internal forces, environmental demands, or both.
4. People cope with these focal conflict or dilemmas either positively through growth or negatively through defensiveness and regression.
5. Personal growth results from mastering the developmental tasks required to resolve the focal dilemma, satisfying both personal needs and social responsibilities.

Exhibit 7–1 portrays the stages three different researchers have identified. Gould[2] concentrates on the inner subjective experiences of individuals forming each period; his view asserts that we grow up with a mythical idea of adulthood and that, as we age, we need to let go of the myth and accept ourselves and the reality of our lives.

Age	Roger Gould	Gail Sheehy	Daniel Levinson
16	Escape from parental dominance	Provisional adulthood	Leaving the family
18			
20	Substitute friends for family		
22			
24	Aspiring builders of future		Getting into the adult world
26			
28	What am I doing and why?	First adulthood	
30			
32	A sense of urgency to make it		
34			
36			Transition period
38			Settling down and becoming one's own person
40			
42			
44	On terms with self as a stable personality		
46		Second adulthood	
48		Age of mastery	
50	Mellowing of friendships—valuing of emotions		
52			Midlife transition
54			
56			Restabilization and entering into middle age
58			
60			
62			Another transition
64			
66		Age of Integrity	
68			
70			
72			
74			
76			
78			
80			
82			
84			
86			

EXHIBIT 7-1 **Models of Adult Development**

Source: Dr. Eric Neilsen, Case Western Reserve University, Cleveland, Ohio.

Sheehy's stages reflect the current trends of taking longer to grow up and become full-fledged adults and longer to grow old. In the provisional adulthood of the "tryout twenties," the central task is to choose a life course. In first adulthood the focus on proving oneself and surviving gives way to mastery and a search for meaning in the first part of second adulthood. The final years of life are devoted to integrating the different parts of one's life.[3]

Levinson developed his theory of adult development from biographical interviews with 40 men; he later expanded his research to include women.[4] One of the gender differences Levinson found was that young men more easily formed a dream about what they would become than did young women. Another difference was that men were more likely to have a family and a career simultaneously if they so desired. In contrast, the women in the study made an either/or choice about family and career and had fewer cultural role models to guide them. Levinson's data was gathered two decades ago. Changing gender expectations about women's role and the increased number of women in the workplace may mean that young women today no longer feel the choice between family and career is quite so stark. Other factors may influence whether or not women decide to have children. There are more cultural models of business women juggling career and family up through middle management, although that is less true for women of color and women in senior level positions.[5]

Other differences have been found between male and female development.[6] Male development focuses on independence, self-sufficiency, and an emphasis on work and career. In contrast, female development emphasizes interdependence and a struggle to combine relationships and accomplishments. Generally speaking, development for men signifies increased autonomy and separation from others so that they can concentrate fully on their work. Whereas men gain their primary identity from their work, women are more likely to define themselves in relation to others, so they focus more on attachments than separation.

Levinson and his colleagues[7] concluded that both men and women face a recurring developmental task at different stages of their lives. They must establish a "life structure," which refers to the pattern or design of a person's life, which is appropriate for each era of life. Life structures last approximately six to eight years and constitute periods of stability. However, life structures become obsolete because no single structure could contain all aspects of the self or respond to the demands of different eras. For example, a man or woman who has been staying at home taking care of small children may no longer find this life fulfilling when the children become older and more independent. At this point, he or she may decide to return to work or develop an artistic side that was not possible given the previous child care demands. When a life structure no longer fits, people undergo a transition period that lasts four to five years. During this period, they reexamine their lives and eventually decide upon a new direction or life structure. The most widely recognized transition period is the *midlife crisis when people age 38 to 45 reevaluate what they have accomplished in comparison with their ambitions and decide where they would like to place greater priority in the coming years.* Transition periods are characterized by self-centeredness, introspection, and ambivalence about intimate relationships; during the periods of stability, people are more other-centered and dedicated to investing time and energy to key social relationships.[8]

The developmental challenge and dilemma facing people in their twenties (22 to 28) is to remain open enough to explore the world and stay committed enough to make something of themselves. Some people keep all their options open and make few commitments, whereas others marry young or invest in a serious career effort. Whatever options people build into their early adult life structure, they are likely to question these early decisions when they reach the age of 30 and have enough years of adult experience to reassess their dreams. Similar transitions occur around ages 40 and 50. During these transitions people make changes in their lives and try to build a life structure that is more attuned to the person they have become; they seek to create a life that allows them to place more priority on areas that are central to them, which they may have had to shortchange in their earlier life structure. There is some evidence that people who do not resolve these issues during one transition will eventually be forced to confront them in a later transition.

Whether or not these life transitions turn into full-blown crises depends on the individuals and their circumstances. For some people it's more a matter of reform than revolution. A crisis occurs when individuals find their current life structure intolerable but are not yet able to create a new one. How can managers help people through this process?

1. By expecting the phenomenon and seeing it as a normal stage of healthy adult development rather than a sign of instability.
2. By practicing active listening[9] or perhaps referring the individual to a professional counselor.
3. By being as flexible as possible regarding the changes the employee feels he or she needs to make.

CAREER ISSUES

In addition to a basic understanding of adult development, managers should also understand the key findings of career development research, which are presented in the following sections.

Career Stages

Douglas Hall identifies six different stages, beginning with exploration (a period in which the individual is open to a wide range of experiences); moving through establishment, mastery, and maintenance (periods directed at developing skills and achieving proficiency); and ending with disengagement (moving out of the field and reducing psychological involvement or transitioning into a different field) phases.[10] The tasks that must be accomplished in each stage vary tremendously. Yet, underlying all of them is the idea of what Hall terms the *protean career*. The term "protean" is taken from the Greek God Proteus, who changed shape and form at will. Hall uses this term to underscore *the new reality of the protean career that individuals must assume full responsibility for their continued career development, often must reinvent themselves in the course of their career, and must be capable of learning how to learn throughout their lives.*

Career Anchors

In the beginning of one's career, the major psychological issue is figuring out a career direction that meets one's needs and interests. Schein developed one of the most helpful models for diagnosing career interests, which he termed *career anchors*. As Schein defines them, "*Certain motivational, attitudinal, and value syndromes formed early in the lives of individuals apparently function to guide and constrain their entire careers.*"[11] When people stray too far from these key interests, they serve as an anchor that pulls people back to their original interest. Different types of career anchors are: (1) technical/functional competence, (2) managerial competence, (3) security and stability, (4) creativity/entrepreneurship, (5) autonomy and independence, (6) service, (7) pure challenge, and (8) lifestyle. These anchors, along with the characteristics of people with these anchors and their typical career paths, appear in Exhibit 7–2.

Career Patterns

Career patterns can vary tremendously. Recent research has identified four different categories of career paths.[12] They differ in the direction and frequency of movement within and across jobs and fields over time.

- **Linear careers** In linear careers, people progress through a series of jobs that increase in authority and responsibility. Individuals may stay with one company or may move through a series of companies as they advance up the organizational hierarchy.
- **Steady-state or expert careers** This type of career reflects a commitment to a field or specialty. Individuals focus on developing and refining their knowledge, technical proficiency, and skills within that field. They often view themselves as experts.

Career Anchor	Characteristics	Typical Careers Paths
1. Technical/functional competence	• Excited by work itself • Willing to forgo promotions • Dislikes management and corporate politics	• Research-oriented position • Functional department management job • Specialized consulting and project management
2. Managerial competence	• Likes to analyze and solve knotty business problems • Likes to influence and harness people to work together • Enjoys the exercise of power	• Vice-presidencies • Plant management and sales management • Large, prestigious firms
3. Security and stability	• Motivated by job security and long-term career with one firm • Dislikes travel and relocation • Tends to be conformist and compliant to the organization	• Government jobs • Small family-owned business • Large government-regulated industries
4. Creativity/entrepreneurship	• Enjoys launching own business • Restless; moves from project to project • Prefers small and up-and-coming firms to well-established ones	• Entrepreneurial ventures • General management consulting
5. Autonomy and independence	• Desires freedom from organizational constraints • Wants to be on own and set own pace • Avoids large businesses and governmental agencies	• Academia • Writing and publishing • Small business proprietorships
6. Service	• Enjoys work that manifests own values • Having an impact, not money, is central • Expect management to share own values	• Consultants • Financial analysts • Non-profit organizations • Socially responsible firms
7. Pure Challenge	• Wants to prove self • Seeks ever greater challenges • Enjoys competition and winning	• Strategy/management consultants • Naval aviators
8. Lifestyle	• Integrates needs of individual, family and career • Desires flexibility (part-time work, sabbaticals, maternity/paternity leaves, etc.) • Common with dual career families	• Consultants • Socially progressive companies

EXHIBIT 7-2 Career Anchors

Source: Adapted from the work of Edgar H. Schein, *Career Dynamics* (Reading, MA: Addison-Wesley, 1978); "Individuals and Careers," in Jay W. Lorsch (ed.), *Handbook of Organizational Behavior* (Upper Saddle River, NJ: Prentice Hall, 1987): 155–171; and adapted by the authors and R. Dunham and J. Pierce, *Management* (Glenview, IL: Scott, Foresman, 1989): 857.

- **Spiral careers** In spiral careers, individuals move across disciplines, moving from one field to a related one. The new field builds on skills developed in earlier fields but also fosters the development of new knowledge and skills.
- **Transitory careers** Transitory careers involve frequent job changes. Disciplines or fields may be unrelated, with each job different from the one before it.

Exhibit 7–3 presents key features of the four career patterns. Managers should pay attention to the type of careers their employees are pursuing and adapt learning and development opportunities to fit those patterns. For example, employees who prefer spiral careers want to expand their knowledge of various fields. Thus, rotating these employees across jobs would be a useful strategy. In

Career Patterns	Linear	Steady-state	Spiral	Transitory
Direction of movement	Upward	Little movement	Lateral	Lateral
Duration of stay	Variable	Life	7–10 years	3–5 years
Central motives	Power and achievement	Expertise and security	Personal growth and creativity	Variety and independence

EXHIBIT 7-3 **Central Features of Four Career Patterns**

Source: Adapted from J. Brousseau, M. Driver, K. Eneroth, and R. Larson. "Career Pandemonium: Realigning Organizations and Individuals," *Academy of Management Executive 10* (1996): 52–66.

contrast, individuals who want steady-state careers respond to opportunities that allow them to develop deeper knowledge and expertise in their chosen field.

Balancing Dual Careers

One of the most challenging aspects of modern life is balancing the demands of dual careers and raising a family. Just over half of U.S. families are dual-career couples, and in 2003 a quarter of the women in these families earned more than their husbands.[13] Although two salaries result in higher income, stress can be a common feature of many dual-career marriages when couples run up against relocation issues, child-rearing responsibilities, and demanding jobs that leave little time to take care of the home front. Working wives who still carry the major burden of household tasks experience a great deal of stress. Couples generally adopt one of the following strategies to manage dual careers.[14]

1. **Limiting the impact of family on work** Parents can delay having children or subcontract the child-rearing to day care centers or domestic help.
2. **Taking turns** Spouses trade off career opportunities and child care at different times.
3. **Participating in joint ventures** Both spouses have the same career or different careers in the same organization.
4. **Choosing independent careers** Both partners pursue their careers as fully as possible and learn to cope with long separations or commuter marriages.
5. **Subordinating one career to the other** One partner may leave the workforce or accept a job that is less demanding so that the other partner can optimize his or her career opportunities.

All of these strategies have advantages and disadvantages. The disadvantages have to do with who pays the cost—the children, the marriage, or the partner who is sacrificing so that the other can maximize career opportunities, and so forth. If couples can agree on a strategy and align the rest of their lives accordingly, some of the stresses found in dual-career marriages are more manageable.

Mentoring

A mentor is a senior person within the organization who assumes responsibility for a junior person. Mentors help socialize newcomers or junior members. Mentoring relationships occur either naturally or as part of a company program to develop junior employees. AT&T Bell Laboratories assigns mentors to women and minority hires and "technical mentors" to help new employees master their jobs. Research has shown that having a mentor was one of the characteristics that differentiated female executives who made it to the top from those who did not.[15] A study of both men and women found that those who were extensively mentored received more promotions, were more highly paid, and reported higher job satisfaction than those who received little mentoring.[16]

What is it that mentors do for their protégés? Kram identified two functions: career and psychosocial functions.[17]

Career functions consist of:

1. **Sponsorship** Actively nominating a junior manager for promotions and desirable positions.
2. **Exposure and Visibility** Matching the junior manager with senior executives who can provide opportunities and giving the junior person chances to demonstrate his or her ability (e.g., letting the junior person make important presentations that are attended by key executives).
3. **Coaching** Giving practical advice on how to accomplish objectives and achieve recognition.
4. **Protection** Shielding a junior manager from potentially harmful situations or senior managers.
5. **Challenging Assignments** Helping a junior manager develop necessary competencies through challenging job assignments and feedback.

The psychosocial functions are:

1. **Role Modeling** Giving a junior manager a pattern of values and behavior to imitate. (This is the most common of the psychosocial functions.)
2. **Acceptance and Confirmation** Providing mutual support and encouragement.
3. **Counseling** Helping a junior manager work out personal problems, thus enhancing his or her self-image.
4. **Friendship** Engaging in mutually satisfying social interaction.

Some firms have also implemented reverse mentoring in which young women and minorities mentor senior managers to provide them with a better understanding of diversity issues.

Career Management and Planning

There have been numerous changes in the area of career planning. In career management the necessity of tying strategic planning to human resource management has gained greater acceptance, along with the expectation that managers should be trained to provide career counseling to employees.[18] Leaner management hierarchies and the populous baby boom cohort have made assessment of management potential and succession management more appealing. Flatter organizations have also focused attention on the need for nontraditional career paths that provide alternatives to promotion, such as lateral or rotational moves, dual-career ladders, downward moves, and early retirement.

There is more emphasis on self-directed careers as a response to downsizing. The burden lies on employees to learn skills that are in demand to maintain their employability and reputational capital. Midcareer choice points seem to be occurring earlier due to the bulge of baby boomers in managerial jobs and the need for balance in dual-career families. Today's employees are more likely to question and reject transfers and even promotions. Opting for self-initiated *career plateauing (a cap to upward mobility)* due to family considerations or lack of desire to assume the burdens of greater management responsibility is becoming more common, although it is still seen as disloyal or un-American in some companies. Partly because of the glass ceiling that limits both women and minorities from reaching senior positions, more and more women are forsaking the corporate career path to become entrepreneurs. Freedom and flexibility are other reasons women give for starting a business. Women-owned U.S. businesses increased 42 percent from 6.4 million in 1992 to 9.1 million in 1999.[19] Between 1997 and 2004, the estimated growth rate in the number of women-owned firms was nearly twice that of all firms.[20]

There is currently a growing emphasis in the United States on spirituality and finding meaning at work.[21] According to John Renesch, editor and publisher of the New Leaders Business Press, "There is a core need within individuals to bring their entire selves to the workplace, not to turn off their heart and soul when they go to work."[22] "New Age" leaders like Tom Chappell of Tom's of Maine have designed companies "with soul" that respond to this need.

Because people can expect to have numerous jobs during their work life, numerous employers, and more than one career, they will face far more career decisions than their parents or grandparents. To make good decisions, self-awareness and an understanding of adult development in general are both helpful. The turbulent nature of today's careers also affects how we see ourselves. In earlier times, personal identity was maintained in a relatively stable environment of known expectations. Once on a life path, personal choice was primarily a process of affirming expectations. People obtained a college degree or M.B.A., gained experience, and worked their way up the organization. They were "managers" who also derived part of their identity from their employer ("I'm an IBMer"). In today's "future shock" world, environmental complexity and change have denied us the easy route to personal identity. Now, more than ever, identity is forged through personal choices. The challenge is to make the "right" choices and manage our careers wisely.

Goal setting is a critical aspect of personal growth and career development. The ability to conceptualize life goals and to imagine future alternatives for living can free us from the inertia of the past by providing future targets that serve as guides for planning and decision making. Research results from several areas—management, psychotherapy, and attitude change—all confirm the importance of goal setting for personal growth and achievement of one's goals.[23] The increased likelihood of change resulting from the setting and articulating of goals is illustrated, for example, by Kay, French, and Myer, who found that improvement needs among managers were accomplished only about one-fourth of the time when they were not translated into goals in performance appraisal interviews. When these needs were transformed into clearly stated goals, the likelihood of accomplishment increased to about two-thirds.[24] It is not enough just to think about how you would like to change. It is necessary to translate those visions into concrete goals.

Work Stress

In recent years, reengineering, downsizing, and increased competition have been responsible for increased career-related stress. Obsolescence, midcareer transitions, job loss or threat of job loss, diminished upward mobility, forced early retirement, dual-career pressures,[25] increased workloads for the survivors in downsized companies, and lack of balance between work and nonwork are all sources of stress. The World Health Organization estimates the global price tag for job stress at more than $200 billion in absenteeism, tardiness, worker's compensation, and health care.[26] A survey of the European Union member states found that the cost of stress at work was estimated to be 3–4 percent of gross domestic product (GDP).[27] By contrast, recent research suggests that positive "affect" or feelings can be very beneficial. Positive affect has been associated with cognitive flexibility, innovation, problem solving, creativity, and open-mindedness.[28]

Stress is defined as the nonspecific response of an organism to demands that tax or exceed its resources. There are three stages in the stress response: alarm, resistance, and finally, exhaustion.[29] Stress is positive when it motivates us to work harder and negative when the stress level exceeds our coping abilities. In the latter instance, stress interferes with our ability to perform at work and can result in illness.

The transactional model of career stress is portrayed in Exhibit 7–4.[30] We begin with a *stressor situation*, which can be either external, such as a new job or job loss, or internal, like a midcareer transition resulting from a shift in personal values. *Stressors take the form of demands, constraints, or opportunities.* A stressor does not result in a stress reaction unless it is first perceived as a stressor. What is stressful to one person may be merely challenging to another because people have different cognitions about stressor situations. *Cognitions are "the individual's perceptions that the situation poses uncertainty about obtaining outcomes, and the perceived importance of those outcomes."*[31] Thus, stress will be greater if people perceive that they

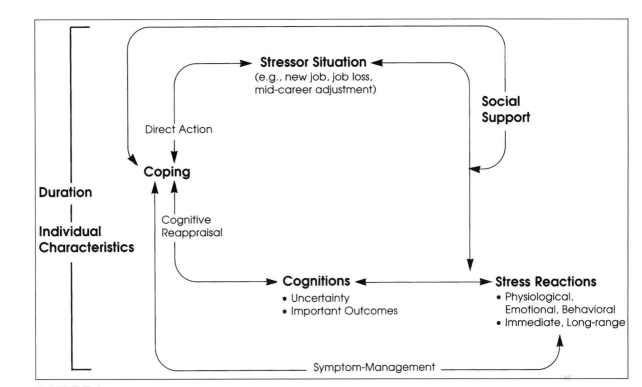

EXHIBIT 7-4 **Transactional Model of Career Stress**

Source: Janina C. Latack, "Work, Stress and Careers: A Preventative Approach to Maintaining Organizational Health,"
in M. B. Arthur, D. T. Hall, and B. S. Lawrence (eds.) *Handbook of Career Theory* (New York: Cambridge University
Press, 1989): 255.

have a lot at stake. For example, it is one thing to lose a job that you really enjoy with no other
prospects in sight and no money in the bank. It is quite another to lose a job you dislike intensely
when you have a sizable trust fund to fall back on.

The next category in the model is *stress reactions*, which *can be physiological (e.g., pulse
rate, blood pressure), emotional (e.g., anxiety, irritability), or behavioral (e.g., loss of sleep,
weight gain).* There are both immediate (e.g., job dissatisfaction) and long-term stress reactions
(e.g., illness or job change).

*Coping is the means by which individuals and organizations manage external or internal
demands that tax or exceed the individual's resources.* Coping strategies focus on (1) changing
the situation (direct action), (2) changing the way we think about the situation (cognitive reappraisal), or (3) focusing on the stress reaction (symptom management). Not all coping mechanisms that focus on symptom management are positive. For example, drinking alcohol and
overeating are harmful whereas meditation and exercise are positive. It is more effective to
reduce or eliminate the source of stress (the stressor situation) than to treat its symptoms through
stress management.[32] Coping mechanisms are an attempt to establish some degree of control
over the situation and prevent a stress reaction.

Social support is another factor that can prevent stress. *It is defined as receiving information
that tells people they are loved, respected, valued, and part of a network of mutual obligations.*[33]
People who receive social support from their supervisors, coworkers, families, or friends are
somewhat buffered from the effects of stress.

The *duration* of the stressor situation also plays a role in this model. The longer the stressful
situation lasts, the more likely that health problems will result. It is interesting that "daily hassles" may actually cause more stress than critical life events, such as divorce or the death of a
loved one.[34] Stress is additive, which means that a seemingly innocuous stressor may be "the

straw that breaks the camel's back" if the person has already been exposed to too many other stressors. Thus, the same stressful work event may impact individuals in different ways.

Finally *individual characteristics* also affect the stress process. For example, people who exhibit Type A behavior who are also quick to anger, mistrustful, and suspicious of other people are more likely candidates for stress-related heart disease than both Type A personalities who are not hostile and people with Type B behavior.[35] The characteristics of Type A behavior are an obsession with achieving more and more in less and less time, inability to cope with leisure time, doing two or more things at once, impatience with the time it takes to make things happen, constant movement, and rapid walking and eating. Many workaholics exhibit this behavior, but only when accompanied by a hostile attitude is it harmful to the individual's health. Type B behavior is characterized by the absence of time urgency and impatience, no felt need to display or discuss achievements, and playing for fun and relaxation without an accompanying sense of guilt.

People with *external locus of control*, who believe that their lives are controlled by outside forces, also perceive situations to be more stressful than people who believe they control their own destiny. The latter condition is referred to as *internal locus of control.*[36] When people have control over their tasks at work, they also feel less stress. [37]

There is very little research on cultural and ethnic differences with regard to work stress. We do know, however, that minorities in nontraditional careers experience their own particular brand of work stress. Having to prove their competence by working harder than others, dealing with racism and discrimination, and being observed more closely are sources of stress for African Americans.[38]

Companies should be aware of the cost of excessive work stress, not only for minorities, but for all employees—decreased job satisfaction and performance, and increased absenteeism, alcohol and drug abuse, and illness.

Overwork is a potential source of stress as well as a detriment to personal satisfaction and family and community life, according to social critics.[39] The overall statistics on average work hours are somewhat misleading since more individuals are working either long or short weeks. Many of those working long weeks (who tend to more skilled and highly educated) would like to reduce their hours, whereas some employees working short weeks would prefer a regular 40-hour week with full benefits. The percentage of employees working at least 50 hours a week has increased to 25 percent of men and 10 percent of women. In one study, 45 to 50 percent of all workers (and 80 percent of those working over 50 hours a week) reported that they would like to have more free time; 25 percent of them would be willing to take a pay cut to work fewer hours. Other research reports that 44 percent of employees report that they are overworked often or very often.[40]

Why haven't U.S. businesses responded and reduced work overloads? Many companies would rather overwork some employees and underwork others than pay costly benefits for more full-time employees. This practice may be beneficial to owners and stockholders in the short run; if we consider, however, the costs to a broader set of stakeholders—individual workers, their families, and their communities—the picture is less positive. Overworked people need time to nurture and maintain their families and relationships, to volunteer in their communities, and to replenish their energies and avoid burnout.[41] Finding a balance between work and nonwork is a personal challenge for many employees and an important HR issue for many organizations. Some suggestions for managing this balance follow.

- **Design the organization and jobs to support employee growth and achievement** One study found that employees who had jobs that provided them more opportunities to continue to learn, supportive supervisors, flexible work policies for managing job and personal lives, and input into the decision making process feel less overworked– even when they had demanding jobs and put in long hours at work.[42]

- **Develop policies that support both work and personal life interes** Families and Work Institute suggests that "employees who are dual- or work-centric are healthiest and most successful at work and at home. H work doesn't detract from work success—rather it appears to enhance nonwork activities appear to complement and support one another. Payi ance contributes to both individual and organizational effectiveness.

- **Recognize that the nature of work and careers have changed** Te possible for employees to work while at home and on vacation and accessible to their employers even when they are in remote location tributed to the sense of overwork that many employees report. Organ about the timing and pacing of work. For example, some companies ha baticals where employees take several months of paid time off to rejuvenate themselves. Intel employees can take a two-month sabbatical every seven years.[44] The accounting firm Deloitte and Touche has developed a Personal Pursuits initiative. The program allows Deloitte employees to take up to five years off unpaid, then return to the same or a new job. Deloitte will pay for any training, licenses, or professional association memberships the employees need to maintain. Employees also meet monthly with mentors who keep them apprised of office developments.[45]

In cultures that believe in fate and destiny (e.g., Arab countries and Latin America), people tend to be less proactive about planning their careers because "what will be will be." Cultures that believe people are the master of their own fate (such as Canada) place more emphasis on career planning. The disadvantage of the belief that humans control their destiny is that people blame themselves when they fail to achieve their career goals and ignore the role of luck. When economies undergo major restructuring, the careers of many people are disrupted through no fault of their own.

MY LIFE LINE

CLASS ACTIVITY: THE LIFE LINE, WHO AM I?, AND THE PAST EXPERIENCE INVENTORY

SELF-ASSESSMENT AND LIFE PLANNING

(Time allotted: 90 minutes)

STEP 1. **Form trios for life planning.** (5 minutes) These groups will act as sounding boards and coaches in the life planning activities that follow.

STEP 2. **Life line exercise.** (20 minutes) (a) Individually, trio members should draw a line in the box on the preceding page to describe their view of their whole life from beginning to end. Draw a line that corresponds to your own concept of your life line. Your life line can be any shape and can go in any direction. It could be a road, a river, a thread, a path, a graph line, or anything else you can imagine. Another way to think of it is as a route across a map with labels for the significant points of interest. Place a mark on this line to show where you are right now. (b) Next, interpret your life line for your trio and discuss the feelings and thoughts you had in drawing the line and in placing your mark.

Notice that each life line has three distinct portions: your past, the place you are now (the X), and the portion of the line that represents your view of your future life and career path. These three portions represent the three basic perspectives for self-assessment and career planning.

The Past

The past consists of your unique experiences, acquired skills, and personal history. With regard to career planning, these aspects of the past are important.

- The past has happened; we cannot change it.
- Our past has a place in our current lives; we need to accept it and use it creatively but not be inhibited by it.
- The past, creatively used, yields insight about our unfulfilled potential.
- The past creates expectations for ourselves and can influence or limit the goals we set for the future.

The Present

The present refers to the here-and-now of your life with all its joys and frustrations and your current priorities as they are embodied in your daily life situation and the way you spend your time. These aspects of the present play a role in career planning.

- Individuals can consciously plan their lives by assessing themselves, their environments, and their resources in the present.

- You can choose where you would like to go on the basis of what satisfies you now.
- We need symmetry and wholeness in our lives. Often we make choices in the present that lead to a lopsided future (e.g., being too career oriented at the expense of a private life of fun, friends, and family).
- Each person has a reservoir of undeveloped potential in the present that suggests directions for future development.

The Future

The future refers to your fantasies, dreams, goals, hopes, and fears, as well as specific commitments and responsibilities you have undertaken.

- In large part, we can create our own future.
- Our future becomes self-determined to a great degree through the choices we make in the present.
- We can try to create the future by the process of:

By using the combination of these three perspectives on your life, it is possible to develop a more fulfilling life plan. By taking all three perspectives into account, a kind of triangulation occurs that identifies common themes from your past, your present, and your future.

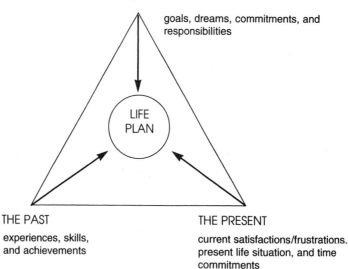

The next three exercises for your trio ask you to work together to assess yourselves from the present, past and future perspectives.

STEP 3.   **Who am I now?** (20 minutes)
- Write 10 separate short statements that answer the question, "Who am I?"
- Then rank these statements according to their importance to you.
- Discuss your answers and rankings with others in your trio.

Rank Order		Who Am I?
_____	1.	I am _____
_____	2.	I am _____
_____	3.	I am _____
_____	4.	I am _____
_____	5.	I am _____
_____	6.	I am _____
_____	7.	I am _____
_____	8.	I am _____
_____	9.	I am _____
_____	10.	I am _____

STEP 4.   **Past experience inventory.** (30 minutes) Complete the following questions and discuss them in your trio.

Approximate Dates

1. Who have been the most influential people in your life, and in what way have they been influential?

    _____   _____
    _____   _____
    _____   _____

2. What were the critical incidents (events) that made you who you are?

    _____   _____
    _____   _____
    _____   _____

3. What have been the major interests in your past?

    _____   _____
    _____   _____
    _____   _____

4. What were your significant work experiences?

_____   _____

_____   _____

_____   _____

5. What were the most significant decisions in your life?

_____   _____

_____   _____

_____   _____

6. What role have family, societal, and gender expectations played in your life?

_____   _____

_____   _____

_____   _____

7. Where do you feel fully alive, excited, turned on? Under what conditions does this occur?

_____   _____

_____   _____

_____   _____

8. Where do you feel dull, routine, turned off? What conditions produce that?

_____   _____

_____   _____

_____   _____

9. What are you really good at? What strengths do you have to build on?

_____   _____

_____   _____

_____   _____

10. What do you do poorly? What do you need to develop or correct?

_____   _____

_____   _____

_____   _____

11. What do you want to stop doing or do much less of?

_____   _____

_____   _____

_____   _____

12. What do you want to start doing or do much more of?

_____   _____

_____   _____

_____   _____

13. What do you want to learn or develop in yourself?

_____   _____

_____   _____

_____   _____

STEP 5.   **My future goals.** (20 minutes)

    a. Share your Life Goal Inventory, which you completed as part of the class preparation, with each other. Your work on the previous exercises may suggest changes to you. If so, make them.

 **LEARNING POINTS**

1. Adult development occurs in a succession of fairly predictable phases characterized by equilibrium and disequilibrium. The disequilibrium results from new psychological issues that arise from new internal forces and/or external demands or pressures. Once these issues are settled, people pass through a quiescent period of stability and equilibrium.

2. According to Levinson, the developmental task for adults is to establish a life structure—the pattern or design of a person's life—that is appropriate for each stage of their lives. These structures last approximately seven years.

3. People go through both stable and transitional periods. During the latter, individuals reevaluate and recreate their life structures. Transitions occur about the ages of 30, 40, and 50. If they are very turbulent, they are called crises, like the midlife crisis.

4. Career anchors are motivational, attitudinal, and value syndromes formed early in life that function to guide and constrain people's careers.

5. The different career anchors are (a) technical/functional competence, (b) managerial competence, (c) security and stability, (d) creativity/entrepreneurship, (e) autonomy and independence, (f) service, (g) pure challenge, and (h) lifestyle.

6. Four patterns of careers are: (a) linear, (b) steady-state, (c) spiral, and (d) transitory.

7. The five strategies for managing dual careers are (a) limiting the impact of family on work, (b) taking turns, (c) participating in joint ventures, (d) choosing independent careers, and (e) subordinating one career to the other.

8. A mentor is a senior person within the organization who assumes responsibility for a junior person.

9. People who were extensively mentored received more promotions, were more highly paid, and reported higher job satisfaction than those who received little mentoring. Mentoring is especially helpful for women and minorities.

10. The career functions of mentoring are (1) sponsorship, (b) exposure and visibility, (c) coaching, (d) protection, and (e) challenging assignments.

11. The psychosocial functions of mentoring are (a) role modeling, (b) acceptance and confirmation, (c) counseling, and (d) friendship.

12. People who set clearly stated career goals are more likely to achieve them.

13. Stress is defined as the nonspecific response of an organism to demands that tax or exceed its resources.

14. The transactional model of career stress consists of stressor situations, cognitions, and stress reactions. Social support and coping can prevent stress reactions. The stress process is also affected by the duration of the stressor and individual characteristics.

15. There are three types of coping mechanisms: direct action, cognitive reappraisal, and symptom management.

16. People who receive social support from their supervisors, coworkers, families, or friends are somewhat buffered from the effects of stress.

17. Individual characteristics that are related to greater susceptibility to stress are hostile Type A behavior and external locus of control.

18. The cost of excessive work stress is decreased job satisfaction and performance, increased absenteeism, alcohol and drug abuse, and illness.

ACTION SCRIPTS

FOR EMPLOYEES

- Career experts recognize that personal growth or change is not a steady progression but rather a series of fits and starts.
- They adopt a "protean" career strategy. This means that employees must be responsible for their own career development, create their own learning opportunities, and stay attuned to opportunities that allow them to refine existing skills and develop new ones.
- They seek out mentors, both inside and outside their organization.
- They make time to reflect on their career. One way to manage your career wisely is to identify your career pattern and analyze whether it is appropriate for your needs.
- Experts at managing stress use good time management skills.
- They proactively manage their stress by paying attention to how they balance work and non-work experiences.
- When change is looming on the horizon or hits their organization or industry, effective employees try to adapt quickly rather than getting stuck bemoaning the loss of "the way things were." They learn new skills and position themselves to weather inevitable changes.
- They are not a stress "carrier" who generates stress in others by being disorganized, putting employees in double binds, making impossible demands, and so forth.

FOR MANAGERS

- Managers who sincerely try to help employees reach their career goals are usually rewarded with loyalty and commitment.
- Managers with career management expertise recognize that employees have unique career goals and life situations. Too often managers who are single-mindedly pursuing a suite at the top find it difficult to value employees who are content to remain where they are or who have chosen a different career path. As long as employees perform their jobs well, lack of driving ambition should not be held against them.
- Experts take into consideration the different career stages of their employees. For example, a young "fast tracker" who may have many of the other skills needed for a managerial job may still be too involved in establishing his or her own career to mentor subordinates adequately. The best mentors are most likely to be found in the 40-to-60 age group because this coincides with a stage of adult development in which guiding the younger generation assumes greater importance.
- They help employees find a work/life balance, which they model. Managers who drive their employees so hard that it is impossible for them to have a personal life usually have a higher degree of turnover.
- They give workaholics a careful look. Sometimes working long hours is not a habit to admire but an indication of inefficient work habits and lack of social life outside of work. If this is the case, workaholics' need to socialize on the job may actually prevent other employees from getting their work done.
- Work schedules that change constantly do not allow employees to create a life outside of work. This is generally not healthy for an extended period. Most people need a balanced life to keep a perspective on problems and find a measure of contentment.
- Experts understand that some kinds of stress at work cause people to resign while other types help retain employees. Examples of "bad stress" include office politics, red tape, and stalled careers. "Good stress" includes the challenges that accompany increased job responsibility, high-quality assignments, and time pressure when employees have the skills to cope with these conditions. When employees perceive that stressful situations will result in money, new skills, or promotion, they are more likely to have a better attitude toward them and stay on the job.[46]

FOR ORGANIZATIONAL ARCHITECTS

- Organizations that evaluate their managers on their ability to develop employees will generally see more positive results in this area. It's not enough to state that career development is important; measuring and rewarding it provides a clearer message that career development is valued.
- Managers are more likely to provide effective counseling to employees if they themselves also receive it from their superiors. It should be modeled for them.
- Expert organizational architects take a pluralistic approach to career development for employees. Employees will differ in what they view as success and how they believe their careers should progress. Responding flexibly to those needs helps retain talented employees and leads to better performance from them.
- Organizational architects that take a proactive response to managing stress can reduce absenteeism, turnover, and health care costs. Training programs can give employees coping skills for dealing with stress and help educate people to realize that work and nonwork balance will often result in better, not worse, performance. HR managers can develop policies that allow employees to responsibly pursue their work and nonwork goals.
- They recognize that downsizing rarely results in less work that needs to be done. Instead, it usually results in *fewer* people having to do the same amount of work. When organizations are forced to reduce staff, managers should create a "Stop Doing" list with the help of employees to eliminate nonessential work and prevent overload.

PERSONAL APPLICATION ASSIGNMENT

Eisenhower once said, "A plan is nothing; planning is everything." In career planning, too, the plan itself is not as valuable as the act of planning. Plans must give way to outside contingencies. But the process of planning—taking stock, devising objectives and possible means of reaching a goal, and then checking to see how one is faring and coming up with a new plan if necessary—is extremely valuable.

This assignment is the Goal Achievement Plan and Achievement Progress Record. It is designed to help you create a plan for attaining a goal you select to work on in the immediate future. The steps in the plan are based on the factors that research has shown to be characteristic of successful goal achievers. Following these steps should help you improve your ability to achieve your goals.

A. From the Life Goal Inventory that you completed in the class preparation, pick the goal you most want to work on in the next six months. In choosing this goal you should consider the following issues. (See the ratings you made of goals.)

  1. Importance of the goal

  2. Ease of attainment

  3. Whether the goal is in conflict with other goals

B. The overall goal you choose to work on may include two or three of the goals you listed in the inventory. The main thing is to be clear about the future state you are striving for. To do this, complete the following Goal Definition form.

GOAL DEFINITION

1. State as specifically as possible what goal you want to achieve in the next six months.

    Now, think about your goal in terms of the following questions.

2. How important is it that you achieve your goal?

3. What conflicts are there with other goals? How will you manage the conflicts?

4. How will you feel when you attain this goal? (Try to imagine yourself with the goal achieved. What are your feelings?)

5. How will you feel if you do not attain this goal? (Try to imagine again. What are your feelings?)

6. What do you think about your chances of succeeding? What will happen if you do succeed?

7. What will happen if you fail?

C. Now that you have defined your goal, the next step is to plan how to achieve it. There are two issues to be examined: the personal shortcomings and external obstacles that may prevent you from reaching your goal.
    The questions on the accompanying Removing Obstacles and Planning Action form are designed to help you accomplish this.

REMOVING OBSTACLES AND PLANNING ACTION

What personal shortcomings might keep me from achieving my goal?

1.
2.
3.
4.

What external obstacles might keep me from achieving my goal?

1.
2.
3.
4.

What can I do to eliminate or lessen the effect of any of these obstacles or shortcomings? (Note that you need not eliminate the obstacle entirely. Anything you can do to lessen the force of the obstacle will start you moving toward your goal.)

Shortcoming/Obstacle	What I Can Do about It
_____	_____
_____	_____
_____	_____
_____	_____
_____	_____
_____	_____
_____	_____
_____	_____
_____	_____
_____	_____
_____	_____
_____	_____
_____	_____
_____	_____

What specific things can I do that will move me toward my goal?

1.
2.
3.
4.
5.

Circle the one that you are going to emphasize the most.

	Who Can Help Me Achieve My Goals?	What Will I Ask of Them?
1.	_____	_____
	_____	_____
	_____	_____
	_____	_____
	_____	_____
2.	_____	_____
	_____	_____
	_____	_____
	_____	_____
3.	_____	_____
	_____	_____
	_____	_____
	_____	_____
4.	_____	_____
	_____	_____
	_____	_____
	_____	_____
	_____	_____

PROGRESS REPORT

Now that you have made your plan, the next task is to put it into effect. Figure out what steps you must take to reach your goal and how you will measure your progress. Plan out what you need to do each week and how long it will take to meet your goal. You may want to choose a partner who will help you monitor your progress. You can agree on a contract that stipulates how often you will check in with each other and what kind of help you want from your partner.

ENDNOTES

[1] D. M. Wolfe and D. A. Kolb, "Career Development, Personal Growth, and Experiential Learning," *The Organizational Behavior Reader* (Englewood Cliffs, NJ: Prentice Hall, 1991): 147.

[2] R. L. Gould, *Transformations* (New York: Simon and Schuster, 1979).

[3] G. Sheehy, *New Passages* (New York: Ballantine 1995); and *Understanding Men's Passages* (New York: Ballantine, 1999).

[4] D. J. Levinson, "A Conception of Adult Development," *American Psychologist 41* (January 1986): 3–13.

[5] R. J. Burke and D. L. Nelson (Eds.) *Advancing Women's Careers* (Oxford: Blackwell, 2002).

[6] This section is taken from J. V. Gallos, "Exploring Women's Development: Implications for Career Theory, Practice and Research," in M. Arthur, D. T. Hall, and B. S. Lawrence (eds.), *Handbook of Career Theory* (Cambridge: Cambridge University Press, 1989): 110–32.

[7] D. J. Levinson, in collaboration with C. N. Darrow, E. B. Klein, M. H. Levinson, and M. Braxton, *Seasons of a Man's Life* (New York: Ballantine, 1978), and Levinson, "A Conception of Adult Development."

[8] D.C. Feldman, "Career Stages and Life Stages: A Career-Development Perspective," *The 1987 Annual: Developing Human Resources* (LaJolla, CA: University Associates, 1987): 231.

[9] For more details on active listening, see Chapter 8, Interpersonal Communication, and Rogers and Farson's article entitled "Active Listening" in the *Reader*.

[10] D. T. Hall. "Brand You: Building Your Protean Career," In A. R. Cohen (ed.), *The Portable MBA in Management* (New York: Wiley, 2002): 214–239.

[11] E. Schein, *Career Dynamics: Matching Individual and Organizational Needs* (Reading, MA: Addison-Wesley, 1978): 133, and "Individuals and Career," in J. W. Lorsch (ed.), *Handbook of Organizational Behavior* (Upper Saddle River, NJ: Prentice Hall, 1987): 155–71.

[12] J. Brousseau, M. Driver, K. Eneroth, and R. Larson, "Career Pandemonium: Realigning Organizations and Individuals," *Academy of Management Executive 10* (1996): 52–66.

[13] U.S. Bureau of Labor Statistics, "Employment Characteristics of Families Summary." http://www.bls.gov/news.release/famee.nr0.htm. Accessed July 3, 2006; U.S. Bureau of Labor Statistics, "Wives Who Earn More than Their Husbands," http://www.bls.gov/opub/ted/2005/jun/wk3/art04.htm. Accessed July 3, 2006.

[14] E. H. Schein, *Career Dynamics: Matching Individual and Organizational Needs*; and L. Bailyn, "Involvement and Accommodation in Technical Careers: An Inquiry into the Relation to Work at Mid-Career," in J. Van Maanen (ed.), *Organizational Careers: Some New Perspectives* (New York: John Wiley, 1977): 109–132.

[15] A. M. Morrison, R. P. White, E. Van Velsor, and the Center for Creative Leadership, *Breaking the Glass Ceiling: Can Women Reach the Top of America's Largest Corporations?* (Reading, MA: Addison-Wesley, 1987).

[16] G. Dreher and R. A. Ash, "A Comparative Study of Mentoring among Men and Women in Managerial, Professional, and Technical Positions," *Journal of Applied Psychology 75*(5) (October 1990): 539–46.

[17] K. E. Kram, *Mentoring at Work: Developmental Relationships in Organizational Life* (Glenview, IL: Scott, Foresman, 1985): 22–39. See also S. Donaldson, E. A. Ensher, and E. J. Grant-Vallone, "Longitudinal Examination of Mentoring Relationships on Organizational Commitment and Citizenship Behavior," *Journal Of Career Development 26*(4) (2000): 233–248; E. A. Ensher, E. J. Grant-Vallone, and W. D. Marelich, "Effects of Perceived Attitudinal and Demographic Similarity on Proteges' Support and Satisfaction Gained From Their Mentoring Relationships," *Journal of Applied Social Psychology 32* (2002): 1–26.

[18] M. B. Arthur, D. T. Hall, and B. S. Lawrence, *Handbook of Career Theory* (New York: Cambridge University Press, 1989); and D. T. Hall, *Career Development in Organizations* (San Francisco: Jossey-Bass, 1986).

[19] "Work Week," *Wall Street Journal*, (June 8, 1999), A-1.

[20] Center for Women's Business Research, "Top Facts About Women-owned Businesses," http://www.nfwbo.org/topfacts.html. Accessed 7/10/06.

[21] J. Conger, Spirit at Work: *Discovering the Spirituality in Leadership* (San Francisco: Jossey Bass, 1994).

[22] G. Rifkin, "Finding Meaning at Work," *Strategy & Business 1*(4) (Fourth Quarter 1996): 15–17.

[23] D. A. Kolb and R. E. Boyatzis, "Goal-Setting and Self-Directed Behavior Change," *Human Relations 23*(5) (1970): 439–457.

[24] E. Kay, J. R. P. French, Jr., and H. H. Meyer, *A Study of the Performance Appraisal Interview* (Management Development and Employee Relations Services, General Electric Co., New York, 1962).

[25] C. Latack, "Work, Stress and Careers: A Preventative Approach to Maintaining Organizational Health," in M. Arthur,

D. T. Hall, and B. S. Lawrence (eds.), *Handbook of Career Theory* (Cambridge: Cambridge University Press, 1989): 252.

[26] B. L. Seaward, "Job Stress Takes a Global Toll," *Safety & Health 151* (1) (1995): 64–66.

[27] World Health Organization. "Mental Health and Working Life," Briefing prepared for the WHO European Ministerial Conference on Mental Health (Helsinki, Finland, January 12–15, 2005).

[28] D. C. Ganster, "Executive Job Demands: Suggestions from a Stress and Decision-Making Perspective," *Academy of Management Review 30*(3) (2005): 492–502.

[29] H. Selye, *The Stress of Life* (New York: McGraw-Hill, 1956); and "The Stress Concept: Past, Present, and Future," in C. L. Cooper (ed.), *Stress Research: Issues for the 80's* (New York: Wiley, 1983).

[30] J. C. Latack, "Work, Stress and Careers: A Preventative Approach to Maintaining Organizational Health," in M.B. Arthur, D. T. Hall, and B. S. Lawrence (eds.) *Handbook of Career Theory* (Cambridge, UK: Cambridge University Press, 1989): 252-274.

[31] Latack, *Work, Stress and Careers*: 254.

[32] C. L. Cooper, and S. Cartwright, "Healthy Mind; Healthy Organization—A Proactive Approach to Occupational Stress," *Human Relations 47*(4) (1994): 455–472.

[33] S. Cobb, "Social Support as a Moderator of Life Stress," *Psychosomatic Medicine 38* (1976): 300–314.

[34] R. S. Lazarus and A. DeLongis, "Psychological Stress and Coping in Aging," *American Psychologist 38* (1983): 245–254.

[35] R.Williams, *The Trusting Heart: Great News about Type A Behavior* (New York: Times Books, 1989).

[36] K. R. Parks, "Locus of Control, Cognitive Appraisal and Coping in Stressful Episodes," *Journal of Personality and Social Psychology 46* (1984): 655–68.

[37] T. A. Beehr, *Psychological Stress in the Workplace* (London: Routledge, 1995).

[38] D. L. Ford, "Job-Related Stress of the Minority Professional: An Exploratory Analysis and Suggestions for Future Research," in T. A. Beehr and R. S. Bhagat (eds.), *Human Stress and Cognition in Organizations* (New York: Wiley, 1985): 287–323; C. McManus, B. Terry, D. Hicks, T. Rolle, and L. White, "Cumulative Experiences of Racism in African Americans: A Clear and Present Danger" Association for Psychological Science Convention (May 25–28, 2006).

[39] J. Jacobs and K. Gerson, "Individuals or Overworked Families: Explaining Trends in Work, Leisure, and Family Time,"*Work and Occupation*" 28(1) (2001): 40–63.

[40] E. Galinsky, J. Bond, S. Kim, L. Backon, E. Brownfield, and K. Sakai, *Overwork in America: When the Way We Work Becomes Too Much* (New York: Families and Work Institute, 2005).

[41] J. S. Osland, B. H. Drake and H. Feldman, "The Stewardship of Natural and Human Resources," in C. J. Dempsey and R. A. Butkus (eds.), *All Nature Is Groaning* (Collegeville, MN: Liturgical Press, 1999): 168–192.

[42] Galinsky, Bond, Kim, Backon, Brownfield, and Sakai, *Overwork in America*. See also S. Leka, A. Griffiths, and T. Cox, *Work Organization and Stress* (World Health Organization, Protecting Workers' Health Series, No. 3, 2003).

[43] Galinsky, Bond, Kim, Backon, Brownfield, and Sakai, *Overwork in America*: 10.

[44] C. Larson, "Time Out," *US News & World Report* (February 28, 2005) http://www.usnews.com/usnews/biztech/articles/050228/28eesabb.htm. Accessed 9/28/06.

[45] C. Larson, "Time Out."

[46] "Good Stress, Bad Stress," *HR Focus 76* (April 1999): 4.

Part 2

▲▲

CREATING EFFECTIVE WORK GROUPS

In Part 2, we will focus on developing the key skills needed by effective managers and employees.

Chapter 8

▲▲

INTERPERSONAL COMMUNICATION

OBJECTIVES By the end of this chapter, you should be able to:

A. Understand the transactional model of communication.

B. List common sources of distortion in communication.

C. Identify gender differences in communication.

D. Identify cultural differences in communication.

E. Describe and identify the five response styles.

F. Explain how to create a climate that encourages nondefensive communication.

G. Recognize assertive communication and utilize I-statements.

H. Improve your active listening skills.

COMMUNICATION MISTAKES ONLY REALLY SMART PEOPLE MAKE

When I first entered the workplace, I suffered the smugness shared by many young people who have had success in college. I could write well under the pressure of deadlines and felt comfortable speaking in public. I was quick to learn new skills and could solve technical problems that baffled more experienced colleagues. I had lots of energy, loved to work hard, and enjoyed succeeding at complex tasks. I was an up-and-coming star.

However, despite what I thought were my superior workplace skills, no one seemed to want to work with me. During meetings, my ideas were ignored. I was passed over for a promotion with the vague explanation that I needed to work on my interpersonal skills.

Although my technical skills were beyond reproach, I never seemed to progress in my career. My explanation: I wouldn't "suck-up" to the boss; I told the truth, particularly about the failings of my coworkers; and I intimidated other people with my intelligence and proficiency.

So I started the slow evolution into one of those bitter, sarcastic people I now see too often in the workplaces I visit. You probably know at least one.

I am one of the lucky ones. Because of the early intervention of several compassionate supervisors, I learned that the reason that I was not doing well had nothing to do with the jealousies or inadequacies of others.

To paraphrase one of my mentors, "The problem is not that you are so smart, Pat; the problem is that you are a jerk." ("Jerk" translates into "oblivious and/or unconcerned about how one's poor interpersonal skills impact others.")

Smart people are sometimes susceptible to "Jerkitude," because, if they are task oriented and have been rewarded only for measured success with computers, budgets, and other inanimate objects, they might ignore or even disparage the "soft" skills, such as negotiation, conflict management, and delegation. But, even if you are currently successful at building productive relationships, a change in your personal or professional situation can also change your behavior for the worse.

Here are some warning signs and prevention tips regarding three kinds of communication mistakes I have seen and heard in workplaces all over the United States, including universities, federal laboratories, high-tech companies, and research departments. Unfortunately, I am almost always there because the "jerk" factor is out of control, despite the fact that the majority of employees and administrators have postgraduate education and many years of experience. Being smart is not enough to protect you from these mistakes.

KEEPING IN THE BEST PERFORMANCE STATE

The first key to maintaining and improving excellent communication is to take your physical and emotional health seriously. How you feel, which is impacted by everything from the ugly situation with your daughter to the effects of the antibiotics you took for a gum infection, can impact your ability to assess accurately and respond effectively to situations in the workplace. You might not feel that your technical work has suffered, but did you slam that perfect budget report on the desk instead of handing it to the accountant with a smile?

At a radio station, one of the news anchors was coping with her mother, who was dying of cancer. Her way of dealing with the lack of control in her personal life was to become a raging perfectionist at work. When she realized what was happening, she asked a friend to give her a scorecard at the end of each day, particularly regarding her behavior during meetings with her producers and engineers. It took only two such scorecards for the news anchor to realize that she was not doing anyone a favor by staying on the job. She arranged a leave of absence, stayed with her family until her mother passed away, and then returned to work.

Of course, not everyone works for an institution where the policies allow for leeway during personal crises. And not everyone is fortunate to have honest and friendly coworkers. However, my experience is that you are deluding yourself if you think that willing away the effects of sadness, pain, and pharmaceuticals will ensure your workplace behavior is impeccable.

THE WRONG PROFESSIONAL ATTITUDE

Sometimes the cause of a smart person's behavior has nothing to do with a denial of the effects of stress. Sometimes an ineffective communication style is the result of years of conditioning, where the smart person is led to believe that being smart is the only measure of success, usually because he or she was rewarded for succeeding at taking tests or advancing through a hierarchical workplace, such as a university or large corporation. The smart person, in this case, thinks that all rank, authority, influence, and privilege in the workplace should be measured by "smart."

- "I have the most degrees, so I get to make the decisions for the group."
- "Only people who graduated from my prestigious college or its equivalent should be allowed into our program."
- "Hello, my name is Pat, and here is my IQ, as verified by a high-IQ organization. And what is your IQ? Oh, yes, and your name?"

My favorite story about ignoring rank comes from a pathologist, who ran a large laboratory. When a tissue sample defied diagnosis, he would recruit an ad hoc panel to comment on the problem. He always included young and relatively inexperienced lab technicians in the process. He had discovered that their fresh viewpoints were key to successfully analyzing the slides and specimens. This was true despite the fact that he, as a board-certified doctor with decades of experience and a wall full of degrees and awards, was supposed to have all of the answers.

"I am here to save lives, not to try to prove that I am the smartest person in the room," he said.

How do you prevent yourself from becoming sucked into a meaningless caste system where you begin to believe your own press releases? Two useful techniques fall under the heading of "career development."

First, get a life outside of work. (Some of your colleagues might suggest that you get a life, period, but we will ignore their sarcasm.) Volunteer activities, particularly ones not related to your field, are a great way to get a perspective on the relative importance of your title in the big scheme of things.

Second, seek out activities where you are going to meet people from different backgrounds. It can be disconcerting and refreshing to be around individuals who don't know what your credentials are, and don't care. You then have a way of judging your ability to influence other people outside of the familiar terrain of your business or profession, where they are reacting to your past successes, reputation, and so on, as much as to your actual skills as a communicator.

THE CLUELESS FACTOR

The most difficult flaw to self-diagnose and self-correct in the smart person is the conviction that one's failings are actually virtues. Here is a list of typical "smart" flaws that are easy to rationalize:

- "I don't talk too much. I simply have more to say."
- "I do not use sarcastic humor to hurt people. If my wit causes someone pain, perhaps it is deserved."
- "I do not indulge in chit-chat because it is a waste of time, not because I am not interested in other people."
- "The only reason I am asking that the rules be suspended for me is because I am more deserving."

Some of the smart people I have been asked to consult with about influencing their workplace behavior over the years are truly bulletproof. They use their intelligence to construct self-referential belief systems that are impenetrable.

- "Any criticism of my behavior is proof of the inferiority of the people doing the criticizing."
- "I believe I am perfect, and because I am perfect, my opinion of myself must be correct."

An attack on such a belief system is futile. Instead, I suggest a simple model of communication that can sometimes compel the person to change behavior in order to keep the belief system intact.

For example, the head of a government library was convinced that his behavior was beyond reproach. Trust me—it wasn't. The specific behavior that his colleagues complained about was his inability to delegate. I could not budge him off the idea that he was the only person who could do the job perfectly. However, I asked him if he was willing to take on the role of teacher, implying that he, of course, would do it perfectly. I suggested that one of the best ways to teach people was to let them create their own processes to get to the goal, which, as a learning exercise for them, he would create with them. Then, I said, he could demonstrate his expertise as a teacher by getting out of their way and stop micromanaging.

The library head did not become a changed man; he did do a decent job of stepping back and letting others do some of the work without interference. The trick is to appeal to the better nature of the smart person and suggest that because he or she can do anything well, this new behavior is another way to prove their competence to the world.

BUT ...

But what if you are the clueless person reading this article, scoffing at yet another "touchy-feely" approach to workplace productivity? The following exercise is sometimes enlightening. First, write a list of the behaviors that people in your workplace do that bother you. Then take the list to employees, colleagues, supervisors, and customers, and ask them if you do any of these behaviors. And when. And how often. Hopefully, you will have chosen to have enough truth-tellers in your life and will be able to elicit some valuable feedback about your own behavior. And, perhaps, if you are really smart, you will be able to do something with the information.

Source: Excerpted from P. Wagner, "Communication Mistakes Only Really Smart People Make," *Records Management Quarterly 31*(3) (July 1997): 13–17. Used with permission.

CLASS PREPARATION

A. Read "Communication Mistakes Only Really Smart People Make."

B. Fill out the Communication Climate Inventory that follows.

C. Please answer these questions:

    1. Is your own communication style defensive or supportive?

    2. What communication skills would you like to learn or improve?

    3. How do you plan on going about it? How can your learning group help you do this?

D. While reading the chapter, make a list of cues to consider with regard to communication.

Communication Climate Inventory

The following statements relate to how your supervisor and you communicate on the job. If you have never worked, evaluate the communication you have observed in another context (e.g., a coach, parent). There are no right or wrong answers. Respond honestly to the statement, using the following scale:

1=Strongly Agree 2=Agree 3=Uncertain 4=Disagree 5=Strongly Disagree

	Strongly Agree	Agree	Uncertain	Disagree	Strongly Disagree
1. My supervisor criticizes my work without allowing me to give any explanations.	1	2	3	4	5
2. My supervisor allows me as much creativity as possible in my job.	1	2	3	4	5
3. My supervisor always judges the actions of his or her subordinates.	1	2	3	4	5
4. My supervisor allows flexibility on the job.	1	2	3	4	5
5. My supervisor criticizes my work in the presence of others.	1	2	3	4	5
6. My supervisor is willing to try new ideas and to accept other points of view.	1	2	3	4	5
7. My supervisor believes that he or she must control how I do my work.	1	2	3	4	5
8. My supervisor understands the problems that I encounter in my job.	1	2	3	4	5
9. My supervisor is always trying to change other people's attitudes and behaviors to suit his or her own.	1	2	3	4	5
10. My supervisor respects my feelings and values.	1	2	3	4	5
11. My supervisor always needs to be in charge of the situation.	1	2	3	4	5
12. My supervisor listens to my problems with interest.	1	2	3	4	5
13. My supervisor tries to manipulate subordinates to get what he or she wants or to make himself or herself look good.	1	2	3	4	5
14. My supervisor does not try to make me feel inferior.	1	2	3	4	5
15. I have to be careful when talking to my supervisor so that I will not be misinterpreted.	1	2	3	4	5
16. My supervisor participates in meetings with employees without projecting his or her higher status or power.	1	2	3	4	5
17. I seldom say what really is on my mind because it might be twisted and distorted by my supervisor.	1	2	3	4	5
18. My supervisor treats me with respect.	1	2	3	4	5
19. My supervisor seldom becomes involved in employee conflicts.	1	2	3	4	5
20. My supervisor does not have hidden motives in dealing with me.	1	2	3	4	5
21. My supervisor is not interested in employee problems.	1	2	3	4	5
22. I feel that I can be honest and straightforward with my supervisor.	1	2	3	4	5
23. My supervisor rarely offers moral support during a personal crisis.	1	2	3	4	5
24. I feel that I can express my opinions and ideas honestly to my supervisor.	1	2	3	4	5
25. My supervisor tries to make me feel inadequate.	1	2	3	4	5
26. My supervisor defines problems so that they can be understood but does not insist that his or her subordinates agree.	1	2	3	4	5
27. My supervisor makes it clear that he or she is in charge.	1	2	3	4	5
28. I feel free to talk to my supervisor.	1	2	3	4	5
29. My supervisor believes that if a job is to be done right, he or she must oversee it or do it.	1	2	3	4	5
30. My supervisor defines problems and makes his or her subordinates aware of them.	1	2	3	4	5
31. My supervisor cannot admit that he or she makes mistakes.	1	2	3	4	5
32. My supervisor tries to describe situations fairly without labeling them as good or bad.	1	2	3	4	5
33. My supervisor is dogmatic; it is useless for me to voice an opposing point of view.	1	2	3	4	5
34. My supervisor presents his or her feelings and perceptions without implying that a similar response is expected from me.	1	2	3	4	5
35. My supervisor thinks that he or she is always right.	1	2	3	4	5
36. My supervisor attempts to explain situations clearly and without personal bias.	1	2	3	4	5

Source: J. I. Castigan, and M. A. Schmeidler, *The 1984 Annual: Developing Human Resources,* J. W. Pfeiffer and L. D. Goodstein (eds.): 115–116.
Copyright © 1984 by Pfeiffer & Company, San Diego, California. Used with permission.

COMMUNICATION CLIMATE INVENTORY
SCORING AND INTERPRETATION SHEET

Place the numbers that you assigned to each item statement in the proper blanks beneath each category in both Parts I and II. Now add them together to determine a subtotal for each climate category. Transfer these numbers to the correct blank in the "Subtotals for Defensive Scores" list on this page and in the "Subtotals for Supportive Scores" list on the next page and add your scores. Place an X on the graph at the bottom of the boxes to indicate your scores.

Part I: Defensive Scores

Evaluation

Question 1 _____

Question 3 _____

Question 5 _____

Subtotal _____

Neutrality

Question 19 _____

Question 21 _____

Question 23 _____

Subtotal _____

Control

Question 7 _____

Question 9 _____

Question 11 _____

Subtotal _____

Superiority

Question 25 _____

Question 27 _____

Question 29 _____

Subtotal _____

Strategy

Question 13 _____

Question 15 _____

Question 17 _____

Subtotal _____

Certainty

Question 31 _____

Question 33 _____

Question 35 _____

Subtotal _____

Subtotals for Defensive Scores

Evaluation _____

Control _____

Strategy _____

Neutrality _____

Superiority _____

Certainty _____

Total _____

18 25 30 35 40 45 50 55 60 65 70 75 80 85 90

Defensive   Defensive to Neutral   Neutral to Supportive   Supportive

Part II: Supportive Scores

Provisionalism

Question 2 _____

Question 4 _____

Question 6 _____

Subtotal _____

Empathy

Question 8 _____

Question 10 _____

Question 12 _____

Subtotal _____

Equality

Question 14 _____

Question 16 _____

Question 18 _____

Subtotal _____

Spontaneity

Question 20 _____

Question 22 _____

Question 24 _____

Subtotal _____

Problem Orientation

Question 26 _____

Question 28 _____

Question 30 _____

Subtotal _____

Description

Question 32 _____

Question 34 _____

Question 36 _____

Subtotal _____

Subtotals for Supportive Scores

Provisionalism _____

Empathy _____

Equality _____

Spontaneity _____

Problem Orientation _____

Description _____

Total _____

18   25   30   35   40   45   50   55   60   65   70   75   80   85   90

Supportive   Supportive to Neutral   Neutral to Defensive   Defensive

Note: See Jack Gibb's article on "Defensive Communication" in *Journal of Communication 11* (3) (1961): 141–148 or in *The Reader* for an explanation of the framework underlying this instrument.

THE KNOWLEDGE BASE

You can have brilliant ideas, but if you can't get them across, your brains won't get you anywhere. … I hadn't yet learned what I know now—that the ability to communicate is everything.

Lee Iacocca, former CEO of Chrysler

Communication is an essential skill at all levels of business. Poor written communication carries a high price tag for organizations.[1] Coleco lost $35 million in 1983 in just one quarter when frustrated customers returned its products because their instruction manuals were incomprehensible.

After discovering that military officers took as much as 23 percent less time to read clearly written documents, researchers concluded that the Navy could save over \$26.5 million in wasted person-hours by writing more simply and plainly. Clear writing is especially crucial in e-mails, which have become the dominant form of communication in many organizations. Our purpose in this chapter, however, is to focus on interpersonal rather than written communication.

Communication skills are the most important competency for entry-level job candidates, according to the managers who hire them.[2] At the M.B.A. level where technical proficiency is assumed, the top three characteristics recruiters look for in a job candidate are strong communication and interpersonal skills, proven ability to perform, and cultural fit with the company.[3] As an experienced executive recruiter noted, "There are lots of brilliant people who can't relate with others—we replace that kind of person every day."[4]

Mintzberg's ground-breaking study on the nature of managerial work identified communication as the most frequent and important of managerial activities.[5] He described the manager's work as essentially that of communication. Mintzberg claimed that many managers spend 80 percent of their time in verbal communication.[6] And even when managers are not trying to communicate, their actions (or lack thereof) are taken as messages. It's impossible to not communicate; rather the question for managers is, "Am I communicating effectively what I want to convey?" The definition of *communication is the process by which information is exchanged between communicators with the goal of achieving mutual understanding.*

To better understand this complex process of interpersonal communication, let's examine the basic model of communication that follows.

THE COMMUNICATION MODEL

The Greeks believed that the god Mercury plucked ideas from the brain of the speaker, impaled the ideas on the end of a spear, and plunged them into the listener's brain. Today, communication is viewed as a transactional process.

The model shown in Exhibit 8–1 has two communicators who participate equally and sometimes simultaneously in the communication process.[7] While Person A sends a message, Person B listens and responds, verbally or nonverbally, sending a message of his or her own. Thus, as

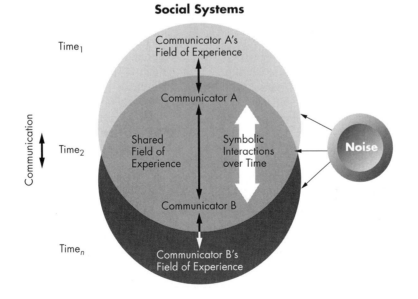

EXHIBIT 8-1 **Transactional Model of Communication**

Source: J. T. Wood, *Communication in Our Lives* (New York: Wadsworth, 1997): 21. Reprinted with permission.

Person A speaks, he or she is also "listening" and receiving a message from Person B. This is called a *transactional model because it acknowledges that our responses to speakers' messages lead them to modify what they say next.* Furthermore, the different time periods reflect the changing nature of communication over time, depending on what transpires between people. For example, we might communicate in a formal manner with a new boss ($Time_1$), more informally if we become good friends with the boss ($Time_2$), and even more formally and infrequently if we have a serious argument or falling out ($Time_{3n}$).

Communication occurs within social systems, and each communicator has a personal context, a field of experience (e.g., family, religious associations, friends). Our individual backgrounds and personality cause us to encode and decode messages in a unique fashion. This makes mutual understanding more challenging and explains why the two communicators must find a shared field of experience (e.g., shared town, culture, organization, views). The n in $Time_n$ in Exhibit 8-1 represents the infinite number of interactions that could occur between Communicators A and B. Both the personal and shared fields of experience can change over time.

The model also includes *noise, which is defined as anything that interferes with the intended communication.* There are three types of noise that prevent effective listening: (1) environmental (e.g., hot rooms, lawnmowers, etc.), (2) physiological (e.g., headaches or hunger pangs), and (3) emotional (e.g., worry, fear, anxiety). We can see how emotional states create noise in the following example: The employee who arrives late for an 8:30 A.M. meeting because of a domestic skirmish is unlikely to capture all the messages coming his or her way.

A rational mechanical view of the process of communication could be depicted in the following manner:

Person A ⟵————————————⟶ Person B

Person A says something to Person B who hears and understands what A said. If this were so simple, we would never experience what has been labeled the "arc of distortion,"[8] which is shown below. *The arc of distortion is the difference between what the sender intended to communicate and what the receiver actually understood.* Person A communicates something to Person B that was not intended; Person B reacts to this unintended communication, which confuses or even frustrates Person A. For example, a general manager spends little time at work with an experienced department head, who interprets this lack of attention as lack of interest and respect. When confronted about spending more time with some department heads than others, the general manager explained that he spent more time with employees whose work he did not trust. In this instance, the general manager's behavior communicated a lack of interest, rather than trust and recognition of a job well done. All behavior communicates a message even when it is not verbal. In the broadest sense, therefore, when we study the concept of interpersonal communication, we are dealing with interpersonal relationships. Communication is the process vehicle through which relationships form, are managed, and, occasionally, dissolve. Relationships are only one of several barriers to communication that are described in the following section.

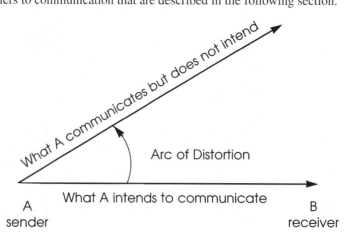

BARRIERS TO COMMUNICATION

The potential for distortion in the communication process is great, and there are numerous causes of distortion that function as barriers to mutual understanding.

Poor Relationships. Communications must be understood within the context of the interpersonal relationship. If two people have been involved in an ongoing, bitter argument over a business decision, it will be more difficult for them to hear the other's messages without distortion. We communicate in a different, more effective manner with people who are supportive than with people who are not. Poor relationships and poor communication go hand in hand when trust is lacking. Covey explains this in terms of an Emotional Bank Account that exists for each relationship.[9] We make deposits and build up a reserve when we are kind, courteous, honest, and dependable in our interactions with the other person. This results in a high level of trust that allows the other person to overlook our communication errors and give us the benefit of the doubt when interpreting what we mean. However, when we treat the other person in ways that indicate a lack of consideration (e.g., discourtesy, ignoring them, being arbitrary, etc.), our Emotional Bank Account with them becomes overdrawn. The level of trust is so low that each word must be chosen with great care so that the other person does not misinterpret the meaning and assume the worst. In reality, most people say many things that were better left unsaid or were better stated in a different manner. In the context of good relationships, such communications are tolerated and forgiven, and mutual understanding is much more likely to be achieved.

Lack of Clarity. The way Person A encodes the message may not accurately reflect the message he or she wants to transmit. "No, that's not what I meant," frequently accompanies communication attempts. Failure to consider how one's audience will perceive the message can result in unclear messages. Ambiguous language causes confusion, and jargon (technical language and acronyms as well as recognized words with specialized meanings) is incomprehensible to outsiders and newcomers. Poor communicators mistakenly assume that their meaning is obvious to others.

Individual Differences in Encoding and Decoding. The way Person A encodes messages and the way Person B decodes them is strongly related to their individual field of experience. Both encoding and decoding are heavily influenced by personal factors such as education, personality, socioeconomic level, family and child rearing, work history, culture, personal experience, and organizational role. This is one of the reasons that meaning lies in people, not in words. An "all-nighter" means staying up all night to finish a paper or study for an exam to a college student; but to people over fifty, it can mean sleeping through the whole night without waking. A feminist decodes a male boss's reference to "you girls" differently than a more traditional older woman. The recently hired low-level employee interprets a memo from the company president differently than a vice president with years of knowledge about the players and organizational history. The most effective communicators are "receiver oriented" because they gear their messages to the receiver. They ask themselves, "If I were the receiver, how would this message strike me? How would I interpret it?"

Gender influences how we encode communication. According to research,[10] women as a group are more concerned with connecting to others and maintaining the relationship with the person to whom they are speaking. Women focus on seeking and giving confirmation and support, and they are more likely to aim for consensus (cooperation). Men tend to be more concerned with status and trying to achieve or maintain the upper hand in a conversation (dominance). When groups argue, women are more likely to ask questions and agree with others and less likely to challenge the views of others and frame their arguments.[11] These are style differences that reflect gender role stereotypes and how men and women are socialized. Although gender alone does not influence how messages are decoded or interpreted, it can certainly influence how messages are sent and encoded.[12]

For example, gender affects the way we transmit messages and converse. Communication experts usually interpret gender differences in conversation as a reflection of power differences between men and women. For example, men and people with higher status speak more than women and people of lower status, invalidating a common stereotype that women are always more talkative than men. In formal meetings, men gain and keep "the floor" for more time, regardless of their status. Men are more likely to interrupt others who are talking, and women are interrupted more often than men. Women in powerful positions, however, sometimes interrupt others. Men are more likely to control the topic and redefine what women say ("What you mean is …"). Other characteristics of female communication are attributed to their lower power status. For example, women are more likely than men to soften their statements by the use of qualifiers such as "maybe, perhaps, sort of, I guess, kind of." When men use qualifiers, they are perceived as warm and polite; when women use qualifiers, they are perceived as weak and less assertive. Women are also more likely to use disclaimers that weaken their position ("I'm not really sure about this, but …" "This probably doesn't mean anything, but …"). Because women are socialized to be more polite than males, they tend to phrase orders more politely ("Please finish the report" as opposed to "Get that report done"). Women are also more likely to frame orders as questions ("Can you meet me at my office?" rather than "Come to my office"). Compared to men, women use more intensifiers, adverbs that exaggerate the strength of an expression ("I am so-o-o-o hungry," "It was a very, very productive meeting"). As a result, female speech is sometimes perceived as overemotional in the workplace.[13]

Perception. It is a fact of communication that people pay selective attention to the communication that comes their way and only hear some of the message. They may hear what they wish to hear or only hear messages that reinforce their own beliefs. Furthermore, people are likely to interpret messages they hear subjectively rather than objectively. Social perception is the name for this phenomenon, which will be explained in greater depth in the following chapter. Perception is another reason why meaning lies in people, not words. Perception is also culturally determined.

Culture. Differences in cultural backgrounds that can be another barrier to achieving a shared experience and mutual understanding. The ability to speak another language fluently does not guarantee that one understands all the nuances involved in a particular context. Words can have different meanings in different languages, and some concepts are nonexistent. There is no word for "late" in the Navaho language since their time is not measured by the clock.[14] A Spanish proverb observes that "*Mañana* is often the busiest day of the week." To a Spanish speaker, *mañana* is an imprecise term meaning "in the future" or "soon." This explains the confusion or frustration this causes for people from countries who define "tomorrow" as a precise term indicating the next 24 hours. Style differences also prevent people from accurately perceiving, analyzing, and decoding cross-cultural communication. People in collectivist cultures are more likely to encounter situations in which there is a preference for silence and high context, indirect, and self-effacing (modest) communication. The emphasis in collectivist cultures is to save face and not stand out (e.g., "The nail that sticks up is hammered down"). In contrast, individualists are more likely to encounter situations in which there is a preference for talkativeness, low-context, direct, and self-enhancing (bragging) communication.[15]

High-context versus low-context cultures vary in the extent to which they use language itself to communicate the message.[16] Low-context communication, found in individualistic cultures such as Germany, Switzerland, and the United States, relies on explicit verbal messages to convey intention or meaning. E-mail messages are the ultimate example of low-context communication because the message consists only of words, devoid of any context. By contrast, in high-context communication, found in collectivist cultures in Asia and Latin America, most of the information is either contained in the physical context or internalized in the person. Very little information lies in the coded or explicit part of the message. Therefore, in high-context communication, the onus lies on listeners to "read" meaning into the message based on their understanding of the historical context, social norms, roles, situational and relational context.

In low-context communication, the onus lies on the sender to craft and transmit a clear, explicit message that is easily decoded.

Silence is perceived and used differently according to cultural norms. A comparative study of 16 countries found that Finns had the highest preference for silence and succinct communication.[17] Silence plays an important role in high-context cultures in Southeast Asia, such as China, Japan, and Korea, where silence can indicate respect for someone with a higher status and careful consideration of the speaker's words. For traditional Chinese, silence is used as a social control, such as indicating their displeasure and disapproval of their children's behavior.[18] Silence in Japan implies harmony rather than lack of understanding, disagreement, or having nothing to say, which members of more talkative cultures may wrongly assume. In multicultural teams, members of highly verbal communication cultures who do not perceive that silence conveys meaning tend to fill in pauses and silence; by doing so, they do not allow enough room for people with a more succinct style to interact.

Direct versus indirect communication refers to the extent to which language and tone of voice reveals or hides the speaker's intent. Speakers using a direct style specify their intentions in a forthright manner, whereas speakers using the indirect style hide their meaning in nuances in their verbal statements. For example, if a Japanese neighbor compliments your piano playing, she may really be telling you to close your windows or not play when she is trying to sleep. To say that directly, however, would be impolite and involve a loss of face. The indirect style is generally found in Eastern and Middle Eastern cultures and most of Latin America, whereas the direct style is more common in Western cultures. A comparison of Hebrew, Canadian French, Argentinean Spanish, Australian English, and German speakers ranked them from most direct to least direct. The Argentinean Spanish speakers were the most direct, followed by the Hebrew speakers. The French Canadians and Germans were moderately direct, while the Australian English speakers were least direct of this group.[19] In multinational teams, it is not uncommon for different nationalities to need time to adjust to varying levels of direct and indirect speech. For example, Japanese members might be disconcerted if Israeli members of bluntly say, "You're wrong" or "Not true" in a business meeting.[20]

In all cultures, there are specific contexts in which both direct and indirect styles are utilized. For example, people in the United States tend to be very direct. However, they are less so when communicating to people of higher status. The following dialogue was transcribed and excerpted from the black box tape of the Air Florida plane that crashed in the Potomac River just after taking off from Washington, DC's National Airport in January 1982. The pilot failed to use the engine anti-icing system during takeoff or to de-ice the plane a second time while waiting in line to take off in a winter storm. The ice that had accumulated on the engine pressure probes caused incorrect readings on the Engine Pressure Ratio gauge, leading the pilot to assume there was more takeoff thrust than there actually was.[21] The copilot was more experienced than the pilot when it came to flying in icy weather and was diplomatically trying to warn the pilot.[22]

Copilot: Look how the ice is just hanging on his, ah, back, back there, see that? See all those icicles on the back there and everything?

Pilot: Yeah.

[The copilot also expressed concern about the long waiting time since de-icing.]

Copilot: Boy, this is a, this is a losing battle here on trying to de-ice those things; it [gives] you a false feeling of security, that's all that does.

[Just before they took off, the copilot expressed another concern—about abnormal instrument readings—but again, he didn't press the matter when it wasn't picked up by the pilot.]

Copilot: That don't seem right, does it? [3-second pause] Ah, that's not right. Well—

Pilot: Yes it is, there's 80.

Copilot: Now, I don't think that's right. [7-second pause] Ah, maybe it is.

A few minutes later, the plane crashed, killing all but five people on board. A linguist who analyzes black box tapes from airplane accidents like this found that the ambiguous indirect style employed by copilots and navigators with pilots caused accidents. Subsequently, copilots were trained to be more assertive in their communication to pilots.

The *self-enhancement versus self-effacement* style varies in terms of how one refers to one's effort or performance. The self-enhancement verbal style emphasizes the importance of boasting about or drawing attention to one's accomplishments and abilities. The self-effacement verbal style, on the other hand, emphasizes the importance of humbling oneself via verbal restraints, hesitations, modest talk, and the use of self-deprecation concerning one's effort or performance. Failures to establish shared meanings occur when people from self-enhancing cultures do not perceive the accomplishments and real worth of people from self-effacing cultures. Furthermore, employees from self-effacing cultures may find "selling themselves" to be hired or gain promotions in self-enhancing cultures very difficult. For example, a Chinese engineer working in a rural area in the United States was unhappy about being repeatedly overlooked for a promotion. An American coworker coached him, saying "Just tell the boss why you're the best person for the job and brag about all the good things you've done." The Chinese engineer couldn't bring himself to do this and opted instead to get a job at Intel, a firm that was relatively more cross-culturally sensitive and relatively accustomed to working with Asians. Negative perceptions can also occur when the boastful mode of self-enhancers is not well received in self-effacing cultures. Collectivist (Asian) cultures are generally self-effacing while Arab and African-American cultures are generally self-enhancing.[23]

Misinterpretation of Nonverbal Communication. Nonverbal communications convey important messages and are produced more automatically than words. They include body movements and gestures, facial expressions and facial gazing, tone of voice and the emphasis of certain words. Generally speaking, our nonverbal signals relate to the feeling level of the content we communicate. Even when words are used, more meaning is taken from nonverbal signals. Mehrabian and Weiner found that words account for only 7 percent of the meaning we make out of communications; 55 percent of the meaning comes from facial expressions and posture, while 38 percent comes from vocal intonations and inflection.[24] This means that managers who continue doing paperwork while their employees are trying to talk to them are severely handicapping the communication process.

According to some researchers, as much as 70 percent of communication between people in the same language group is nonverbal.[25] Furthermore, it is possible that people rely even more heavily on nonverbal messages in cross-cultural communications. However, the same nonverbal behavior can have very different meanings across cultures, and the same meaning is conveyed by different nonverbal cues in different cultures. For example, in Samoa people sit down to show respect, whereas in many cultures they stand up. Showing the sole of one's shoe in a Muslim society is a sign of great disrespect. Some common hand gestures in North America —repeatedly crooking the index finger with the palm up to beckon another person to come or the tip of the index finger to the tip of the thumb to signal "A-OK"— are obscene gestures in some cultures.

Defensiveness. Defensiveness is one of the most common barriers to good communication. Once people become defensive, they have difficulty hearing or interpreting messages accurately—they are too caught up in protecting or justifying themselves. Defensiveness in communication is usually caused by the sender's poor communication skills or by the receiver's low self-concept.

Carl Rogers, the famous psychologist, found that defensive communication in therapy sessions could be avoided by being descriptive rather than evaluative and by assuming an egalitarian rather than a superior stance.[26] Gibb contributed four more ways to avoid provoking defensive communication: (1) assuming a problem-solving orientation rather than trying to control the situation and telling others what to do, (2) being spontaneous (authentic) rather than strategic (calculating), (3) showing empathy (feeling what others feel) rather than neutrality (unfeeling), and (4) being provisional (open-minded) rather than certain (close-minded).[27]

An example of being certain rather than provisional is the manager who tears into employees when an error has been made before he or she has ascertained the facts of the situation. It's hard to repair the supervisor-employee relationship when this occurs because it signifies a lack of trust and respect for the employee and an unwillingness to give employees the benefit of the doubt. The Communication Climate Inventory you filled out as part of the class preparation measures the behaviors that create defensive and nondefensive climates.

Lack of Feedback and Clarification. Because the communication process is fraught with potential for distortion, the feedback aspect of communication is crucial. In this case, feedback refers to Person B's attempts to ensure that the message he or she decoded is what the sender really meant to convey. Asking for clarification and paraphrasing the sender's words ("Let me see if I have understood you correctly. Do you mean …?") are feedback methods. Senders also can check to see if their message got across. Managers often ask employees to paraphrase instructions to see if they are clear. The purpose of communication is mutual understanding. Unless we check with people, we may mistakenly assume that communication occurred when it did not.

Poor Listening Skills. The normal result of an attempt to communicate is a partial misunderstanding because of the uniqueness of senders and receivers and the absence of a shared field of understanding. Clarifying the message and active listening are ways to avoid communication failures. When communication does break down, people often waste time and energy trying to determine who is at fault, which provokes a defensive reaction that further inhibits mutual understanding. However, if we accept misunderstandings as a basic reality of communication, we can stop looking for blame and start seeking better ways to communicate. A more effective response to breakdowns is, "How can we arrive at a level of mutual understanding that will allow us to accomplish our objectives?" and "How can we prevent a breakdown like this from happening again?"

RESPONDING STYLES

Our responses to communications set the stage for subsequent communication and impact our relationship with the speaker. Most of our response styles (80 percent, according to some experts) fall into five categories:

1. **Evaluative** "What a great report!" "That idea will never work." An evaluative response indicates that the listener has made a judgment of the relative goodness, appropriateness, effectiveness, or rightness of the speaker's statement or problem. Such responses reflect either a positive or negative assessment. With this type of response, the listener implies what the sender should do.

2. **Interpretive** "You're just saying that because you lost the account." The interpretive response indicates that the listener's intent is to teach, to tell the sender what his or her statement or problem really means, and how the sender really feels about the situation. With this type of response, the listener implies what the sender should think.

3. **Supportive** "Don't worry, it'll work out." A supportive response indicates that the listener's intent is to reassure, to pacify, and to reduce the sender's intensity of feeling. The listener in some way implies that the sender need not feel as he or she does.

4. **Probing** "Why do you think you're going to be fired?" A probing response is a response that indicates that the listener's intent is to seek further information, provoke further discussion along a certain line, and question the sender. With this response, a listener implies that the sender needs to develop or discuss a point further.

5. **Understanding** "So, you think your job's on the line and you're pretty upset about it?" An understanding response indicates that the listener's intent is only to ask the sender whether the listener correctly understands what the sender is saying, how the sender feels about the problem, and how the sender sees the problem. With this response, the listener implies nothing but concern that the sender's message is accurately received.

Our natural tendency as listeners is to evaluate and judge what others say to us. The most common responses are evaluative, even though they are not always the most effective type of response to employ. Groups seeking creative solutions or resolution to a conflict are two examples of situations in which evaluative responses are clearly counterproductive.

These response styles communicate not only words but a message about the relationship between the two communicators. With the first four response styles, the responders put themselves in a one-up position in relation to the speaker. When we evaluate others, we assume the one-up position of a judge. The same is true when we interpret what others have said (as if we know best) or try to pacify them (as if they were children who shouldn't feel as they do), and even to some degree when we probe (as if they have not thought everything through). In contrast, the understanding response communicates that listeners have positioned themselves on the same level as the speaker, an egalitarian approach. This is the type of response that is used in active listening, which is explained later in the chapter. None of the responses described are appropriate for all situations. No response style can be said to be innately good or bad, but there are times when a certain type of response would be more appropriate or effective than another. A good communicator is aware of the type of response that is called for in each situation.

ASSERTIVENESS

Communication that is perceived as overly aggressive can provoke a defensive reaction. An assertive style, neither too aggressive nor too passive, is most likely to produce the desired results when we need to stand up for ourselves, express honest feelings, or exercise our rights. *Assertiveness is the ability to communicate clearly and directly what you need or want from another person in a way that does not deny or infringe upon the other's rights.* New supervisors often have difficulty finding the right balance in the nonassertive-assertive-aggressive continuum. Exhibit 8–2 provides a helpful description of the differences among these three styles. One characteristic of an assertive style is the use of I-statements, which are described in the following paragraph.

An I-statement is a feedback format designed to produce dialogue rather than defensiveness. I-statements have three components: (1) a specific and nonblaming description of the behavior exhibited by the other person, (2) the concrete effects of that behavior, and (3) the speaker's feelings about the behavior. Note that in the following examples of I-statements, they begin with "When you …"

Behavior	Effects	Feelings
When you come late to our project meetings,	we have to use valuable time bringing you up-to-date, and others end up doing your share of the work,	and I resent that.
When you interrupt me,	I lose my train of thought and don't get to make my point,	and that makes me angry.

I-statements differ from you-statements, such as "You are lazy and irresponsible," "You never pull your weight around here," or "You're rude and inconsiderate." More often than not, you-statements provoke a defensive response and an argument. I-statements are more likely to encourage an open dialogue because they are descriptive rather than evaluative, and they focus on communicating the speaker's feelings and needs to the other person. In some cases, simply becoming aware of the effects of one's behavior and the feelings it provokes is enough to make people change negative behaviors.

	Nonassertive (No Influence)	Assertive (Positive Influence)	Aggressive (Negative Influence)
Verbal	Apologetic words. Veiled meanings. Hedging; failure to come to the point. Rambling; disconnected. At a loss for words. Failure to say what you really mean. Qualifying statements with "I mean," "you know."	Statement of wants. Honest statement of feelings. Objective works. Direct statements, which say what you mean. "I-statements."	"Loaded" words. Accusations. Descriptive, subjective terms. Imperious, superior words. "You" statements that blame or label.
Nonverbal General demeanor	Actions instead of words, hoping someone will guess what you want. Looking as if you don't mean what you say.	Attentive listening behavior. Generally assured manner, communicating caring and strength.	Exaggerated show of strength. Flippant, sarcastic style. Air of superiority.
Voice	Weak, hesitant, soft, sometimes wavering.	Firm, warm, well modulated, relaxed.	Tensed, shrill, loud, shaky; cold, "deadly quiet," demanding; superior, authoritarian.
Eyes	Averted, downcast, teary, pleading.	Open, frank, direct. Eye contact, but not staring.	Expressionless, narrowed, cold, staring; not really "seeing" others.
Stance and posture	Leaning for support, stooped, excessive head nodding.	Well balanced, straight on, erect, relaxed.	Hands on hips, feet apart. Stiff, rigid. Rude, imperious.
Hands	Fidgety, fluttery, clammy.	Relaxed motions.	Clenched. Abrupt gestures, fingerpointing, fist pounding.

EXHIBIT 8-2 A Comparison of Nonassertive, Assertive, and Aggressive Communication

Source: Mastering Assertiveness Skills: Power and Influence at Work, © 1983 Elaina Zuker. Published by AMACOM, a division of the American Management Association. All rights reserved. Reprinted with permission of the publisher.

LATIN AMERICAN COMMUNICATION PATTERNS

Each culture has specific, learned communication patterns that must be deciphered for real understanding to occur. Unfortunately, we often make incorrect interpretations and negative attributions about cultural differences in communication. Although there are country differences in communication within Latin America, the following list summarizes the general characteristics of Latin American and Latino patterns of communication.[28]

- Emphasis on politeness and warm interpersonal relationships
- Use of indirect language in most countries to maintain harmonious social relations
- Use of affective style (process oriented and receiver focused), which avoids putting people in uncomfortable situations and relies more on nonverbal and intuitive meaning
- Use of the elaborate style, which involves a relatively high quantity of talk, great detail, repetition, and colorful language
- Value given to eloquence and expressive use of language
- Communication is high context, which means people convey more meaning through gestures, nonverbal communication, and reading between the lines and are less explicit than North Americans and Northern Europeans
- Frequent use of gestures
- Close proximity between people in face-to-face encounters
- Frequent touching, which is done in specific ways for specific occasions and relationships

- Preference given to personal, face-to-face communication over impersonal methods
- Respect may be shown to teachers by breaking eye contact and lowering the eyes

Based on this list, it is easy to see why people from this region may perceive the speech patterns of North Americans as too direct, too blunt, and too plain.

COMMUNICATION VIA ELECTRONIC MEDIA

More and more work communication takes place, not face-to-face, but via e-mail, teleconferencing, conference calls, and computer-mediated communication. The average U.S. employee devotes more than 1 3/4 hours to e-mail daily.[29] Over half of the 1,200 managers in another study spent at least two hours on e-mail at work; plus 30 percent of them spent yet another hour on work-related e-mail at home.[30] Some individuals and firms have learned the hard way that anything written on e-mail can come back to haunt to them; e-mail does not disappear when it is deleted and can be subpoenaed in lawsuits. In an ethics and e-mail scandal, Merrill Lynch was fined $100 million when its analysts belittled stocks in e-mails that they were publicly promoting to customers.[31]

Communication channels are described as either rich or lean. *Rich communication, such as face-to-face communication, involves multiple channels—verbal, visual, nonverbal, and emotional. Lean communication involves limited channels—language alone, with the possible addition of "emoticons" (e.g., ☺).* For this reason, e-mail messages are more likely to be misinterpreted because there are fewer cues to observe. Intended or unintended insults in e-mails, called flaming, are more likely when people feel less constrained about being rude online than they would face-to-face.[32]

Certain channels are more appropriate for some work processes than others. For example, studies of student project teams found that e-mail was effective in generating ideas, brainstorming, planning, and scheduling.[33] It was less effective when teams had to make decisions and choices, resolve conflicts and motivation problems, and execute at a high level of performance. Although experienced employees are more skilled at working virtually, some situations still require rich channels. Face-to-face meetings are better than e-mail for establishing relationships and trust. Once people have formed relationships, e-mail is an effective channel for maintaining them, but it is not appropriate for situations that require active listening.

ACTIVE LISTENING

When executives are asked to rank the communication skills they find most critical to their success on the job, they consistently place listening at the top of the list.[34] Executives spend 45 to 65 percent of their day listening, and this skill is related to higher performance, increased job satisfaction, and improved interpersonal relationships.[35] There are several filters that affect listening such as attitudes, biases, values, previous experiences, organizational roles (e.g., paying closer attention to what superiors say than to subordinates), poor listening skills, and lack of fluency in another language. These filters are minimized in active listening because people do not sit quietly like a bump on a log simply waiting for the other person to finish speaking. Instead, the listener takes personal responsibility to ensure that the messages sent are accurately received. If any distortions are uncovered, they are clarified before proceeding with the conversation.

Humans have a physiological excuse for being less than excellent listeners. The rate of speech is 100 to 150 words per minute, whereas our brains are capable of thinking at a rate of 400 to 500 words per minute. People often use this slack time to daydream, to judge what the sender is saying, or to prepare what they want to say next. In contrast, active listeners use this slack time to concentrate fully on the sender's message. Active listening involves a greater level of attending to the speaker.

The skills of active listening are demanding, but they can be learned using the guidelines in the paragraphs that follow.[36] Some of the behaviors suggested may seem awkward and forced at first, but with practice they will feel more natural. It is difficult to respond with patience, understanding, and empathy when the other person is expressing ideas that strike you as illogical, self-deceiving, or even morally wrong. However, the behaviors suggested will, if practiced faithfully, generate attitudes of tolerance and understanding that will make empathy and nonevaluative acceptance of the other person come more easily.

Being Nonevaluative

Active listening includes a variety of verbal and nonverbal behaviors that communicate to the speaker that he or she is heard and understood, that the feelings that underlie the words are appreciated and accepted, that regardless of what the individual says or thinks or feels, he or she is accepted as a person by the listener. The object is to communicate that whatever the qualities of the ideas, events, attitudes, and values of the person who is talking, the listener does not evaluate the person or his or her ideas or feelings. The listener accepts the person for what he or she is without making judgments of right or wrong, good or bad, logical or illogical.

Paraphrasing the Content

When we paraphrase the content, we put what the speaker has said in our own words and repeat it to the speaker to test whether we have understood correctly. The content includes both the thoughts and feelings manifested by the speaker. These phrases are used in paraphrasing.

> *As I understand it, what you're saying is ...*
> *Do you mean that ... ?*
> *So your feeling is that ...*
> *If I try to summarize what you've said ...*

The key to paraphrasing is listening intently to what the other party is saying. If we spend the time when the other is talking thinking of what we are going to say next, or making mental evaluations and critical comments, we are likely not to hear enough of it to paraphrase it accurately.

The emphasis at this level is comprehending the stated or manifest content, that which is explicitly communicated verbally and/or nonverbally. The more indirect the content, the more important are the next two active listening skills.

Reflecting the Implications

This requires going a bit beyond the manifest content of what the other is saying and indicating to the speaker your appreciation of where the content is leading. It may take the form of building on or extending the ideas of the speaker, using such phrases as

> *I guess if you did that, you'd then be in a position to ...*
> *So that might lead to a situation in which ...*
> *Would that mean that ... ?*
> *Are you suggesting that we might ... ?*
> *Would that help with the problem of ... ?*

It is important in reflecting the implications to leave the speaker in control of the discussion. When this technique is used to change the direction of the speaker's thinking or to show how much more clever the listener is by suggesting ideas the speaker has not thought of, it ceases to build trust and becomes a kind of skillful one-upmanship. When, however, this technique is genuinely used to help the speaker, it communicates very strongly that the listener has really heard and understood the drift of his or her thinking.

Reflecting Underlying Feelings

This technique goes still farther beyond the overt feelings content of what is said and brings into the open some of the underlying feelings, attitudes, beliefs, or values that may be influencing the speaker to talk in this way. One tries to empathize, to put oneself in the place of the speaker, to experience how it must feel to be in his or her situation. Then the listener tentatively expresses the feelings, using such phrases as

How does that make you feel?
If that happened to me, I'd be upset. Are you?
Times when I've been in that sort of situation, I've really felt I could use some help.
It sounds like you're proud of achieving that. Is that right?
It looks like you feel very strongly about this.

In reflecting the underlying feelings, delicacy is required so as not to overexpose the speaker or press him to admit to more than he would like to reveal. It is also important to avoid suggesting to the speaker that the feeling you reflect back is what she ought to feel in such a situation. This would tend to make the speaker feel evaluated, when what you are trying to do is to communicate acceptance of the underlying feelings. Often acceptance is communicated more by the manner and tone of the listener than by the words used.

Inviting Further Contributions

When listeners haven't heard or understood enough yet to follow up with indications of understanding, empathy, and acceptance, they can communicate interest in hearing more. Phrases such as the following are useful.

Tell me a bit more about that.
Help me understand ...
What happened then?

This differs from the probing response style described earlier because these questions are motivated solely by a desire to clearly understand what the speaker is trying to communicate. Specific requests for information may constitute a unilateral demand for openness on the part of the speaker. To maintain balance, questions should not be used exclusively but should be followed after a bit by rephrasing or reflecting. Generally, open-ended questions create a more supportive, trusting climate than do pointed questions fired in machine gun–like fashion.

Using Nonverbal Listening Responses

Active listening is often communicated as much by one's posture and nonverbal movements as it is by what one says. Nonverbal listening responses may vary from one culture to another. In the United States, these responses communicate interest and understanding: consistent eye contact, open body posture, leaning toward the speaker, head nodding, and receptive signals such as "um-hum." African Americans use less eye contact than whites.[37] In some cultures, lower status individuals make less eye contact.

When implemented in a climate of genuine concern and acceptance, the active listening skills described in this section help both parties understand as fully as possible the thoughts and the feelings in an interpersonal exchange. If, however, the listener is not being authentic—is not genuinely curious and caring—active listening will be perceived as just another technique to manipulate people.

CLASS ACTIVITY: ACTIVE LISTENING EXERCISE

The purpose of this exercise is to provide you with an opportunity to practice and receive feedback on your active listening skills. You will also have a chance to observe others and give them feedback on their active listening.
(Time allotted: 45 minutes)

STEP 1. Form groups of four and prepare for the role plays. In this exercise, everyone should have an opportunity to perform each role: expresser, active listener (or consultant), and observer. (5 minutes)

a. An expresser gets a chance to enhance his or her ability to express thoughts and feelings in a congruent, clear manner.

b. An active listener paraphrases what the expresser states and practices all the components of active listening. It is critical that active listeners resist the temptation to give advice or try to solve the problem for the expresser.

c. The two observers watch the interactions silently, use the observer sheet on page 210, and provide feedback afterward.

Participants can either choose a current topic that is controversial or one of the scenarios described on the following pages.

Controversial Topics. As a class, brainstorm a list of controversial topics to be written on the board. The first Expresser and Active Listener pair quickly choose a topic from the list. Expressers will give their opinion on the topic while the Active Listeners listen, without giving their own opinion or debating the issue. The interaction should last about 5 minutes until the Expresser feels the Active Listener really understands his or her position. Meanwhile, the observers watch. Then the Expresser and Active Listener switch roles, while the observers continue watching. After this second interchange, the observers give their feedback. Then the two observers quickly choose a topic and repeat the sequence described above.

Scenarios. Two people volunteer to be the first Expresser and Consultant pair, and the Expresser quickly chooses a scenario to use. For each scenario there will be (1) a stage-setting statement, (2) a scripted set of words to start the interaction, and (3) a suggested set of feeling states. The scenarios range from easy to hard as determined by the range and intensity of feelings associated with the scenario. Here's an example.

1. **Setting the stage** You are speaking with an outside consultant, brought in by your boss. The consultant has just delivered a copy of his or her final report.

2. **Script** I want to know why I wasn't consulted on that report! You were researching my territory and the decision will impact my people.

3. **Suggested feeling states** Bothered, insulted, left out, angry.

The roles needed in this scenario would be:

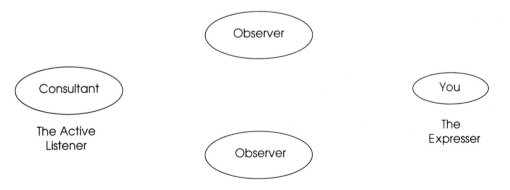

- The Expresser should pick a scenario that seems *real* to you (i.e., you have been or could imagine yourself actually being in that situation) and involves some suggested feeling states you would like to practice expressing that will stretch you but not immobilize you.

- "You" (the Expresser) would communicate the first line as scripted, for example, "I want to know why …" In so doing, you would try to express some or all of the suggested feeling states (insulted, left out, etc.). The "Consultant" would practice the active listening skills described in The Knowledge Base. "Observers" would watch the interaction carefully and critique it using the Observer Sheet.

- As the "Consultant" (in the scenario) actively listens, "you" would carry on and add to the conversation in a manner consistent with the thoughts and feelings reflected in the original scripted opening. Refrain from giving your opinion or gratuitous advice. Carry on the communication at least five minutes.

Although this is meant to be a play-acting situation, it is also intended to be a serious opportunity to develop your interpersonal communication skills as both expressers and active listeners.

STEP 2. **Role plays** (10 to 15 minutes each round) Each role play should consist of:
  a. 5 to 8 minutes conducting the role-play scenario.
  b. 8 to 10 minutes of feedback discussion initiated by the observers and then expanded by the expresser and the active listener.

During the feedback discussion, people should try to link insights gained from playing the different roles. For example, as an expresser, I may find out that I am more likely to give off mixed or confusing messages around high-intensity negative feelings than anything else. As the active listener, I may find that I am less likely to hear and pick up on high-intensity positive feelings.

Suggested Scenarios

1. **Setting the stage** You are speaking with an outside consultant, brought in by your boss. The consultant has just delivered a copy of his or her final report.
   Script I want to know why I wasn't consulted on that report! You were researching my territory and the decision will impact my people.
   Suggested feeling states Bothered, insulted, left out, angry.

2. **Setting the stage** You and a colleague are talking in your office. You are about to tell your colleague about an interaction you had with Ana, corporate vice president.
   Script After the meeting, I was walking down the hall, and Ana stopped me and said, "You did a really great job on that account!" (smiling) I thought so, too!
   Suggested feeling states Proud, happy, contented, a sense of accomplishment.

3. **Setting the stage** You are reporting to the boss on the status of your group. You know that in the boss's opinion the group just has not been pulling its weight.
   Script We finally had a breakthrough in that contract. After all the hours I spent researching the market, I finally got an idea that the client liked (longish sigh). For a while, I thought that the group would lose another one.
   Suggested feeling states Relieved, good, accomplished, productive, uncertain, scared.

4. **Setting the stage** You are a secretary whose boss feels that you have more promise and can utilize your talents better and move ahead. You are about to speak to your boss.
   Script Last week, you mentioned that I could read those articles and compose an annotated bibliography. I know that you want to make my job more interesting. Maybe you even think that I'm bored. But, really, I just don't want to be challenged any more. I guess that I like things as they are.
   Suggested feeling states Embarrassed, scared, resentful, frustrated.

5. **Setting the stage** You have just been offered a middle-management position of considerable prestige. You are talking to your boss about it.
   Script Frankly, I'm just not sure whether or not to accept the promotion. I should be overjoyed with the opportunity. It's a chance to influence some policy. Most people around here don't understand why I haven't left already. But parts of the job I have are very exciting. Marketing is always a challenge. So I just don't know.

Suggested feeling states Ambivalent, uncertain, frustrated, unfulfilled, afraid of success and/or failure.

6. **Setting the stage** You are the first and only female member of your audit team. You had hoped the marked increase in travel would not be a problem because you love the work and do it very well. You are talking to your boss.

   Script I know I said I would have no problem with the travel aspects of the job. I thought I would enjoy it. But I find that two to three weeks is too long. I'm not really happy when I'm traveling, and my husband and children are complaining.

   Suggested feeling states Dissatisfied, concerned, uncomfortable, worried, nervous.

7. **Setting the stage** You have just had an interaction with the division head, Ms. Sanchez, who is your boss's boss. You are now telling your boss about it.

   Script What was I going to say to her anyway? Ms. Sanchez—the division head!—pats me on the back and tells me how concerned she is for my image. I knew this place was pretty straight, but that's the most ridiculous thing that I ever heard—that I can't have my own painting in my office. Why does everything here have to be designer perfect?

   Suggested feeling states Adamant, determined, angry, resistant, feeling pressured to fit into a mold.

8. **Setting the stage** You and your boss have a lot of trouble agreeing on how things should be done and on priorities. Here we go again!

   Script No! This is not a smoke screen for something else! Look, I really don't understand why I have to analyze the reports that way. I want to do an excellent job and I will. However, I'd like a little latitude in bringing some of my ideas into action.

   Suggested feeling states Annoyed, confused, frustrated, unchallenged.

9. **Setting the stage** Given the problems you and your spouse have been having, it has been amazing to you that you've been able to function at all. Your boss has just called you in and read you the riot act.

   Script Don't you think that I know that my work has been poor? Holy smokes, nobody is cooperating around here. I just…look…so I haven't been too pleasant. But I'm doing the best I can under the circumstances.

   Suggested feeling states Exasperated, strung out, as if the "bottom has dropped out," tense, as if you have to keep up a front.

10. **Setting the stage** Your longtime friend and colleague, Abdel, has come to chat about his future career plans and long-term growth with the company. Your own career has been very much on your mind for months, so you almost interrupt Abdel in midstream.

    Script Abdel, you sound like I did about 15 years ago. I'm 50 years old. I'm one of, maybe, a hundred middle managers. I've been working my tail off to become a CEO. Nothing was more important to me than my career. Yeah, I'm good, but my wife and kids—they're strangers to me—and I'm not going to become a CEO. Look at the years I wasted working for a goal I'll never reach.

    Suggested feeling states Regret, frustration, bitterness.

STEP 3. Class Discussion (15 minutes) Answer the following questions:
   a. What was it like to practice active listening?
   b. What did you learn about yourself and others by doing this exercise?
   c. When should you use active listening?
   d. When would it be a mistake to use active listening?

OBSERVER SHEET

Your role is an important one. You should silently observe the interaction and note specific examples of effective and ineffective communication as you see them. These data will be important in the feedback discussion.

Active Listening Behaviors	Examples Where It Was Effectively Used by the Active Listener	Places Where It Could Have Been Used But Wasn't and/or Was Used Ineffectively*
1. Being nonevaluative		
2. Paraphrasing the content		
3. Reflecting possible implications		
4. Reflecting the underlying feelings		
5. Inviting further contributions		
6. Using nonverbal listening responses		

* The observations you note in this column will give you the chance to provide feedback to both the listener and to the expresser: (1) thoughts and feelings you heard expressed that the listener did not hear or pick up on and (2) mixed messages you observed being expressed (incongruence between words and nonverbal communication).

LEARNING POINTS

1. Communication is a major portion of a manager's job and an essential skill for anyone working in business.
2. Communication is the process by which information is exchanged between communicators with the goal of achieving mutual understanding.
3. The transactional model of communication consists of two communicators who participate equally from their own personal context or field of experience. To communicate, they must find a shared field of experience. Over time, the nature of their communication may change as well as their fields of experience. Noise can interfere with their intended communication.
4. The arc of distortion is the difference between what the sender intended to communicate and what the receiver understood the message to be.
5. There is much potential for distortion in the communication process. Therefore, it's best to assume that any communication can also involve a partial misunderstanding. Active listening, requesting clarification, and checking meaning with feedback are ways to ensure that the message received is the intended message.
6. Potential barriers to communication include: poor relationships, lack of clarity, individual differences in encoding and decoding, gender differences, perception, culture, misinterpretation of nonverbal communication, defensiveness, lack of feedback and clarification, and poor listening skills.
7. Meaning lies in people, not in words.
8. The most effective communicators are receiver-oriented because they take the perspective of the receivers and customize messages for them.
9. Men and women communicate in different ways, primarily because of societal socialization and status.
10. Common style differences in intercultural communication are: high-context versus low-context, direct versus indirect, and self-enhancement versus self-effacement. Cultures also use and interpret silence and nonverbal gestures in different ways.
11. More meaning is taken from (1) facial expressions and posture and (2) vocal intonation and inflection than from words themselves.
12. Defensiveness is a common barrier to communication because the energy devoted to defending oneself prevents attention to the message.
13. A nondefensive climate is created when people are descriptive, egalitarian, focused on problem solving, spontaneous, empathic, and provisional.
14. Five common response styles are: evaluative, interpretive, supportive, probing, and understanding. Evaluative responses are most common. These styles also contain a message about the relationship between the two parties. Only the understanding response reflects an egalitarian stance rather than a one-up position.
15. Assertiveness is the ability to communicate clearly and directly what you need or want from another person in a way that does not deny or infringe upon the other's rights.
16. I-statements (behavior, effects, feelings) are an effective way to provide feedback to others.
17. Communication channels can be rich (multiple channels) or lean (limited channels).
18. The components of active listening are:
    a. Being nonevaluative
    b. Paraphrasing the content
    c. Reflecting implications
    d. Reflecting underlying feelings
    e. Inviting further contributions
    f. Using nonverbal listening responses

 **ACTION SCRIPTS**

For Employees

- Expert communicators can distinguish between their thoughts and their feelings. They manage their emotion so that feelings do not unintentionally seep into the discussion and negatively influence communication. An example of a novice communicator would be the team member whose feelings have been hurt by a thoughtless remark who then vociferously attacks the group plan—not because he really thinks it's a bad plan, but because he is experiencing an emotional hijack.
- Effective communicators pay close attention to nonverbal clues when others communicate and make sure their own nonverbal communication conveys what they intend. To be congruent and consistent, both the verbal and nonverbal signals they send accurately reflect their thoughts and/or feelings.
- They understand that self-concept serves as a filter through which we see all communication. People with low self-concepts present the greatest communication challenge because they can become defensive with little or no provocation. The specific content of the message is less important than what you are communicating to them about your relationship with them; if it's anything less than fully supportive, they become defensive.
- Expert communicators seamlessly move in and out of active listening and can quickly identify when it should be used. Conflict situations, personal problems, customer complaints, performance appraisals, instruction-giving are all situations that benefit from active listening. It's difficult to maintain anger when the listener is making a concerted effort to understand both your point and your feelings.
- They learn to decipher and acknowledge the differences when communicating with people from a different culture, region, or gender without evaluating them.
- Experts can readily adapt their own communication style to match styles from different cultures or subcultures, which is called code-switching.
- Novices are more likely to misconstrue or overinterperet ambiguous e-mail messages.[38]
- Expert communicators use the appropriate channel for the message they need to convey. For example, they do not address sensitive issues on e-mail.
- In particular, they do not engage in arguments over e-mail. Such conflicts tend to escalate, and it is easy to misinterpret what has been written. Unlike face-to-face arguments, e-mail allows no opportunities to rephrase, soften one's statements, or change one's mind.
- Expert communicators understand that it is difficult to make amends for mistakes once words have been uttered and e-mail messages have been sent. Therefore, they think very carefully before talking and revise their e-mails repeatedly until they say exactly what they mean.
- They do not send unnecessary, unimportant e-mails that waste time, nor do they copy everyone on e-mails that only need to go to one person.

For Managers

- Managers who are effective communicators do the following:
  - Give other people confirmation or validation by acknowledging their presence and indicating acceptance of them and their ideas.
  - Do not exclude others or resort to in-group talk.
  - Avoid talking about themselves too much, do not "monologue," and try to listen as much as they talk.
  - Avoid both excessive criticism and undeserved praise in favor of honest appraisals given in a gentle manner.
  - Use language that neither offends nor demeans other people.[39]
- Expert managers take for granted that communication is a flawed process and try to eliminate as many pitfalls as possible. They paraphrase for employees the problems or requests that they receive (i.e., "Let me see if I've understood the problem correctly").

- To give instructions that get followed, effective leaders explain to followers their intent and do not overload them with too much detail. If leaders always use the same format, shown below, followers can more readily grasp what the leader wants and ask enough questions to figure out what they should do if the situation unexpectedly but probably inevitably changes. Karl Weick recommends using this format:[40]
  - Here's what I think we face
  - Here's what I think we should do
  - Here's why
  - Here's what we should keep our eye on
  - Now, talk to me
- Before they communicate at work, experts ask themselves the following questions: What do I want to accomplish as a result of this communication? Based on my knowledge of the receiver(s), how should I word this message and how should I transmit it? Am I the best person to communicate this message or does someone else have greater credibility or a better relationship with them? Will there be any likely resistance to the message that I need to take into consideration?
- Communication is a learned behavior, which means that people usually send messages that maximize rewards and minimize punishment. Managers who are expert at communication do not "kill the messenger" no matter how unpleasant the news. They know that bad news can be crucial to the organization's survival because it represents an opportunity to change course.
- Some managers deplore the power of the grapevine, the informal communication network, but all organizations have grapevines. Expert communicators use the grapevine for their own purposes, such as floating trial balloons to see how people react. The power of the grapevine can be decreased by more open sharing of information through formal channels. In a bureaucracy, information is often synonymous with power. Providing greater access to information means that employees will devote less energy to hoarding it or ferreting it out.
- Managers who are expert communicators make a concerted effort to seek information from employees at all levels. For senior managers, it is not always enough to talk only with the layer of people immediately beneath them because this group may have a vested interest in presenting only positive information or self-serving interpretations of situations. This is why the concept of "managing by walking around" is so important.
- Expert managers communicate enough so that others feel like they are in the loop and understand what their leaders are doing.

FOR ORGANIZATIONAL ARCHITECTS

- Because communication is such an important skill, skilled organizational designers and architects use it as a selection criterion in the hiring process. This not only saves money on training but helps to cut down on miscommunication errors.
- Even though new hires may bring good communication skills with them, different forms of communication training are needed for different levels of employees. Intercultural communication training, for example, is in greater demand as a result of the increasing numbers of multinational teams and global business ventures.
- Organizational architects concerned about good communication take steps to remove filters that keep communication from spreading up or down the hierarchy or across functional boundaries. They have mechanisms by which employees can communicate freely to top management (e.g., suggestion boxes, open door policies, e-mail access to the boss, informal meetings with the boss, etc.).
- Some organizational designers set communication norms (such as Intel's constructive confrontation, which is described in Chapter 13) that they believe will enhance their success and develop protocols for how they want employees to communicate. For example, GE encourages its employee to be blunt and brusque, especially in superior/subordinate communications to promote questioning assumptions, critical analysis of decisions, and accurate, candid communication.[41]

PERSONAL APPLICATION ASSIGNMENT

At the beginning of this chapter, you filled out an inventory in which you evaluated the type of communication climate your supervisor established. That question was based on Gibb's characteristics of defensive communication. This assignment is to gain insight into the type of communication climate you create. Choose one of the following ways to begin this assignment.

1. If you supervise employees, ask three of them to fill out a copy of the same questionnaire anonymously. If you're surprised at the results, discuss them and ask for clarification or examples from someone in your organization who you know will give you good, honest feedback. Take into consideration that your employees may be uncertain (or even terrified) about how you will accept feedback on your communication habits. Make sure they don't have to pay a price for their honesty.

2. Have a discussion on a controversial topic with someone (preferably someone with strong views that are different from your own so you can test out the skills you practiced in this chapter). Try to create a supportive climate according to Gibb's framework. Afterward, evaluate the conversation. If it's possible, get the other person's evaluation of the conversation. After you've completed (1) or (2), write up the experience in the usual format.

A. Concrete Experience

    1. Objectively describe the experience (who, what, when, where, how). (2 points)

    2. Subjectively describe your feelings, perceptions, and thoughts that occurred during (not after) the experience. What did others seem to be feeling? (2 points)

B. Reflective Observation

    1. Looking back at the experience, what were the perspectives of the key actors (including you)? (2 points)

    2. Why did the people involved (including you) behave as they did? (2 points)

C. Abstract Conceptualization

    1. Relate concepts or theories from the assigned readings or the lecture to the experience. Explain thoroughly how they apply to your experience. Please apply at least two concepts or theories and cite them correctly. (4 points)

D. Active Experimentation

    1. What did you learn about communication from this experience? (1 point)

    2. What did you learn about yourself? (1 point)

    3. What action steps will you take to be more effective in the future? (2 points)

E. Integration, Synthesis, and Writing

    1. Did you integrate and synthesize the four sections? (1 point)
    2. Was the Personal Application Assignment well written and easy to understand? (1 point)
    3. Was it free of spelling and grammar errors? (2 points)

ENDNOTES

[1] These examples come from S. Crainer and D. Dearlove, "Making Yourself Understood," *Across the Board 41*(3) (May/June 2004): 26.

[2] J. D. Maes, T. G. Weldy, and M. L. Icenogle, "A Managerial Perspective: Oral Communication Competency Is Most Important for Business Students in the Workplace," *The Journal of Business Communication 34*(1) (1997): 67–81.

[3] "What Corporate Recruiters Say," Graduate Management Admission Council Survey (2004). http://www.mba.com/mba/AssessCareersAndTheMBA/TheValueoftheMBA/TheMBAInTheMarketplace/WhatCorporateRecruitersSay.htm. Accessed 11/2/05; K. R. Kane, "MBA: A Recruiter's-Eye View," *Business Horizons 36* (1993): 65–68.

[4] K. Sandholz, "Do You Have What It Takes?," *Managing Your Career* (Fall 1987): 10.

[5] H. Mintzberg, *The Nature of Managerial Work* (New York: Harper & Row, 1973).

[6] Ibid: 171.

[7] J. T. Wood, *Communication in Our Lives* (New York: Wadsworth, 1997).

[8] H. Baumgartel, W. N. Bennis, and N. R. De (eds.), *Readings in Group Development for Managers and Trainers* (New York: Asia Publishing House, 1967): 151–156.

[9] S. R. Covey, *The 7 Habits of Highly Effective People* (New York: Simon and Schuster, 1989): 188–202.

[10] D. N. Maltz and R. A. Borker, "A Cultural Approach to Male-Female Miscommunication, " in J. J. Gumperz (ed.), *Language and Social Identity* (Cambridge: Cambridge University Press, 1982): 196–216; D. Tannen, *You Just Don't Understand: Women and Men in Conversation* (New York: Ballantine, 1990) and *Talking from 9 to 5* (New York: William Morrow, 1994); R. A. Meyers, D. E. Brashers, L. Winston, and L. Grob, "Sex Differences and Group Argument: A Theoretical Framework and Empirical Investigation," *Communication Studies 48* (1997): 19–41.

[11] Meyers, Brashers, Winston, and Grob, "Sex Differences and Group Argument."

[12] R. Edwards and M. A. Hamilton, "You Need to Understand My Gender Role: An Empirical Test of Tannen's Model of Gender and Communication," *Sex Roles 50* (7/8) (April 2004): 491–504.

[13] The findings in this paragraph are reported in L. P. Arliss, *Gender Communication* (Upper Saddle River, NJ: Prentice Hall, 1991); J. C. Pearson, "Language Usage of Women and Men, " in J. Stewart's *Bridges Not Walls* (New York: Random House, 1986): 283–300; and D. Borisoff and L. Merrill, *The Power to Communicate: Gender Differences as Barriers* (Prospect Heights, IL: Waveland Press, 1992).

[14] E. Hall, *The Silent Language* (New York: Doubleday and Co., 1959).

[15] S. Ting-Toomey, *Communicating Across Cultures* (New York: The Guilford Press, 1999): 103. This section on cultural communication styles is drawn from Ting-Toomey's work.

[16] The high- and low-context communication style was first identified by E. T. Hall, *Beyond Culture* (New York: Doubleday, 1976); See also S. Ting-Toomey, *Communicating Across Cultures:* 272.

[17] L. Zander, "Communication and Country Clusters," *International Studies of Management & Organization 35*(1) (Spring, 2005): 83–103.

[18] S. Ting-Toomey, "Talk as a Cultural Resource in the Chinese American Speech Community." *Communication 9* (1980): 193–203.

[19] S. Blum-Kulka and J. House, "Cross-Cultural and Situational Variation in Requesting Behavior," in S. Blum-Kulka, J. House, and G. Kasper (eds.), *Cross-Cultural Pragmatics: Requests and Apologies* (Norwood, NJ: Ablex, 1989): 123–154.

[20] S. Blum-Kulka, "Interpreting and Performing Speech Acts in a Second Language: A Cross-Cultural Study of Hebrew and English," in N. Wolfson and J. Elliot (eds.), *Tesol and Sociolinguistic Research* (Rowley, MA: Newbury House, 1983): 36–55.

[21] "January 13, 1982 Washington, DC, Air Florida, Flight 90, Boeing B-737-222, N62AF," http:www.planecrashinfo.com/cvr820113.htm. Accessed 10/31/05.

[22] This research on politeness among flight crews, attributed to linguist Charlotte Linde, was cited in D. Tannen, "The Power of Talk: Who Gets Heard and Why" *Harvard Business Review 73*(5) (September-October, 1995): 138–148.

[23] S. Ting-Toomey, *Communicating across Cultures* (New York: The Guilford Press, 1999).

[24] A. Mehrabian and M. Weiner, "Decoding of Inconsistent Communications," *Journal of Personality and Social Psychology 6* (1967): 109-114.

[25] Based on P. Noller, *Nonverbal Communication and Marital Interaction* (Oxford: Pergamon, 1984). See also "Why So Much Is Beyond Words," *Time* (July 13, 1981): 74.

[26] C. R. Rogers and R. E. Farson, *Active Listening* (Chicago: Industrial Relations Center, University of Chicago, 1975).

[27] J. Gibb, "Defensive Communication," *Journal of Communication 11* (3) (1961): 141–148 or *The Organizational Behavior Reader*.

[28] R. D. Albert, "A Framework and Model for Understanding Latin American and Latino/Hispanic Cultural Patterns," in D. Landis and R. Bagat (eds.), *Handbook of Intercultural Train-*

ing (Thousand Oaks, CA: Sage, 1996): 327–348; and W. Gudykunst, and S. Ting-Toomey, *Culture and Interpersonal Communication* (Newbury Park, CA: Sage, 1988); J. A. De Vito, *The Interpersonal Communication Book* (New York: Harper & Row, 1989): 197.

[29] Crainer and Dearlove, "Making Yourself Understood": 24.

[30] Crainer and Dearlove, "Making Yourself Understood."

[31] Crainer and Dearlove, "Making Yourself Understood," 23–27.

[32] S. Robbins, "Contexts of Uninhibited Online Behavior: Flaming in Social Newsgroups on Usenet," *Journal of the American Society for Information Science 49* (12) (1998): 1135–1141; L. Sproull and S. Kiesler, *Connections: New Ways of Working in Networked Organizations* (Cambridge, MA: MIT Press, 1992).

[33] E. V. Wilson, "Email Winners and Losers," *Communications of the ACM 45*(10) (October 2002): 121–126.

[34] J. Brownell, "Preparing Students for Multicultural Environments: Listening as a Key Management Competency," *Journal of Management Education 16* (1992): 81–93.

[35] Ibid.

[36] For an in-depth look at active listening, see D. Stone, B. Patton, and S. Heen, *Difficult Conversations: How to Discuss What Matters Most* (New York: Viking, 1999).

[37] G. Henderson, *Our Souls to Keep: Black/White Relations in America* (Yarmouth, ME: Intercultural Press, 1999).

[38] D. A. Morand, "Politeness and the Clash of Interaction Orders in Cross-Cultural Communication," *Thunderbird International Business Review 45*(5) (2003): 521–540.

[39] De Vito, *The Interpersonal Communication Book*: 179.

[40] G. Klein, "Why Won't They Follow Simple Directions?" *Across the Board 37*(2) (2000): 14–19.

[41] N. Tichy and S. Sherman, *Control Your Destiny or Someone Else Will* (New York: HarperCollins, 1994).

Chapter 9

▲▲

PERCEPTION AND ATTRIBUTION

OBJECTIVES By the end of this chapter, you should be able to:

A. Define perception and explain the perceptual process.

B. Identify the sources of misinterpretation in cross-cultural interactions.

C. Understand both the benefits and the drawbacks of the perceptual process.

D. Recognize common perceptual errors.

E. Describe the Johari window.

F. Explain attribution theory.

G. Understand the relevance of perception and attribution for managers.

THE BLIND MEN AND THE ELEPHANT

John Godfrey Saxe

It was six men of Indostan
To learning much inclined,
Who went to see the Elephant
(Though all of them were blind),
That each by observation
Might satisfy his mind.

The first approached the Elephant,
And happening to fall
Against his broad and sturdy side,
At once began to bawl:
"God bless me! but the Elephant
Is very like a WALL!"

The second, feeling of the tusk,
Cried, "Ho! what have we here
So very round and smooth and sharp?
To me 'tis mighty clear
This wonder of an Elephant
Is very like a SPEAR."

218

The third approached the animal,
And happening to take
The squirming trunk within his hands,
Thus boldly up and spake:
"I see," quoth he, "the Elephant
Is very like a SNAKE!"

The fourth reached out an eager hand,
And felt about the knee
"What most this wondrous beast is like
Is mighty plain," quoth he:
"'Tis clear enough the Elephant
Is very like a TREE!"

The fifth, who chanced to touch the ear,
Said: "E'en the blindest man
Can tell what this resembles most;
Deny the fact who can,
This marvel of an Elephant
Is very like a FAN!"

The sixth no sooner had begun
About the beast to grope,
Than seizing on the swinging tail
That fell within his scope,
"I see," quoth he, "the Elephant
Is very like a ROPE!"

And so these men of Indostan
Disputed loud and long,
Each in his own opinion
Exceeding stiff and strong,
Though each was partly in the right,
And all were in the wrong!

CLASS PREPARATION

A. Read "The Blind Men and the Elephant."

B. Think about an experience you've had or a situation you've observed when differing perceptions were the source of problems or misunderstanding. For example, have others ever falsely stereotyped you or have you ever had a mistaken impression about another person that was proved wrong?

1. Describe the situation.

2. What were the differing perceptions of the principal actors involved in this situation?

3. What was the impact of differing perceptions?

4. Were the differing perceptions ever discussed and resolved? If so, how did that come about? Who made that happen and how did they do it?

5. While did you learn about perceptions from this experience?

C. While reading the chapter, make a list of the cues you should keep in mind regarding perception and attribution.

THE KNOWLEDGE BASE

If somebody tells you that you have ears like a donkey, pay no attention. But if two people tell you, buy yourself a saddle.

Sholom Aleichem

In every chapter so far, we learned about various kinds of individual differences and mental maps. Yet another way in which people differ is the way we perceive the world. No individuals perceive stimuli in the exact same fashion. It is tempting to assume that human behavior is a response to an objective reality but, as the comedienne Lily Tomlin noted, "Reality is nothing more than a collective hunch." The same stimuli may be present in our environment, but how we process and interpret the stimuli is affected by individual differences. For example, if you talk with a rabid Republican and a fanatical Democrat the day after a U.S. presidential debate, it may be difficult to believe they both watched the same debate. Each claims his or her candidate "won" and the other candidate was a disaster. The same is often true of diehard fans of different sports teams talking about yesterday's game and why one team won. At work, we might see two managers with completely different impressions of an employee's performance; one manager wants to promote the employee, whereas the other recommends firing. How do we end up with such diverse and even contradictory impressions? Chalk it up primarily to individual differences in perception. *Perception is the process by which we select, organize, and evaluate the stimuli in our environment to make it meaningful for ourselves.* It serves as a filter or gatekeeper so that we are not overwhelmed by all the stimuli that bombard us. The three stages of the perceptual process are explained below.

Selection. A key aspect of the perceptual process is *selective attention, which is defined as the process of filtering the information our senses receive.* We simply do not see or hear everything that goes on around us. For example, when you live in another country and have reached a moderate level of fluency in a foreign language, you occasionally stumble on a new word that you have never heard before. Once you master the word, you realize to your chagrin that it is in fact a very common word—you just weren't "hearing" or attending to it before.

Both internal and external factors determine what sensory impressions we pay attention to. Internal factors that affect perception are motives, values, interests, attitudes, past experiences, and expectations. For example, hungry people are more attuned to references to food than people not currently motivated by the hunger need. Hungry people may even "hear" the word candy when the speaker says caddy because we often hear what we want to hear. People attend to only the stimuli that interest them or support what they are looking for, which explains the term selective attention. Studies of both low-level supervisors and middle-management executives revealed that these individuals perceived only those aspects of a situation that related to the goals and activities of their own departments.[1] Information that conflicts with what we believe is often ignored or distorted to conform to our preconceptions and expectations. Selective attention explains why two people can attend the same meeting or event and have contradictory stories about what occurred. The fervent political supporters mentioned in the opening paragraph heard and saw only what they wanted to hear (great points made by their candidate, indications of strong leadership potential, etc.) and blocked out the strengths of the opposing candidate. In this way, their preconceived attitudes about the debate affected their perception and interpretation of the actual event.

The external factors that influence perception are characteristics of the target we perceive. Our attention is drawn by motion, intensity, size, novelty, and salience. We notice things that are moving, the way a bull notices the cape waved by the bullfighter. Fire alarms grab our attention because the siren is loud, piercing (intensity), and rare (novel) in most neighborhoods. *Salience is the extent to which a given object or event stands out from the others around it*. The salient object or event is the "figure" that dominates what we see; the rest is "ground" or background in Gestalt psychology terms. What do you see in the picture in Exhibit 9–1? What is figural to some people is merely background to others. Furthermore, our perceptions tend to remain constant; once a perceived object is fixed in our minds, it is difficult to reinterpret the stimuli.

Organization. The second stage in the perceptual process is the organization of the stimuli that has been selected to make it simpler. Our thought processes automatically structure stimuli into patterns that make sense to us. Patterns of antithesis (opposites) and cause-and-effect relationships ("If … then") are two examples of common thought processes. It is easier to see cause-and-effect relationships in the physical world than it is with social interactions and human behavior. Nevertheless, we organize stimuli in the same patterns. For example, if an organization is successful, people in the United States tend to attribute this success to the leader whether or not the leader really had an impact.[2]

According to social cognition theory, we organize stimuli into schemas.[3] *Schemas are mental maps of different concepts, events, or types of stimuli that contain both the attributes of the concept and the relationship among the attributes.* Like geographical maps, schemas are representations of reality but not reality itself. Everyone's maps are different.

EXHIBIT 9-1

For example, each of us has a schema about "leadership" that includes the traits that we think describe a good leader. We tend to see these traits as a package deal; if someone has a few of these traits, we assume they also possess the other traits. Our leader schema might include attributes such as trustworthy, directive, courageous, enthusiastic, and value-driven. If we see a leader who is trustworthy and directive, we may mistakenly assume he or she is also courageous, enthusiastic, and value-driven. Once schemas have been established, they affect how we handle future information because they determine what we attend to and what we remember. We are less likely to notice and remember free-floating stimuli than stimuli that fit into existing schemas.

Evaluation. The final stage in the perceptual process is evaluation or inference. We interpret stimuli in a subjective rather than objective fashion. Our conclusions are biased by our individual attitudes, needs, experiences, expectations, goals, values, and physical condition at the time. Not only do interpretations differ from person to person, but the same person can have diverse perceptions of the same stimuli at different points in time. When large organizations are involved in major change efforts, it is easy to see examples of differential interpretations of the same stimuli in the diverse reactions to announcements about upcoming innovations. No matter how carefully such announcements are worded, employees reach vastly different conclusions, and harmful rumors are commonplace. People who are frightened about the changes are more likely to make negative inferences about the announcements than people who are looking forward to what they see as a much-needed improvement.

SOCIAL IDENTITY

Although no two people perceive the world exactly the same, social groups and cultures have shared perception. "Other things being equal, the higher the degree of similarity of perception among individuals, the easier communication among them is likely to be, and the more communication among them is likely to occur."[4] We communicate more with people we perceive to be like us. This group identification also determines how we perceive the world because we learn to see things as they do and to pay attention to the stimuli they view as important. Thus, social identity and perception are closely related. *Social identity theory is based on the belief that people tend (1) to perceive themselves and others in terms of social categories rather than as individuals (social categorization); (2) to assess the relative worth of groups as well as individuals by comparing them (social comparison); and (3) to perceive and respond to the world not as detached observers but in terms of their identity, which depends on the social groups to which they belong (social identification).*[5] Sharing a social identity means that people perceive themselves as similar along important dimensions (such as similar disposition, similar attitudes)[6] and define themselves in terms of the groups in which they are members. For example, people may define themselves by their ethnic group, religion, political party, fraternity or sorority, favorite sports team, and so on. They see their own group as more homogeneous and in a more favorable light than it really is. The more we perceive others as similar to us, the more likely we are to trust them as well as cooperate and exchange information with them.[7] However, the downside of this phenomenon is that when humans categorize others into groups, they tend to perceive other social groups as inferior.[8] This can lead to stereotyping.

STEREOTYPING

A common danger that may result from our perception of people who are somehow different from us is stereotyping. *Stereotyping occurs when we attribute behavior or attitudes to a person on the basis of the group to which the person belongs.* Much of the cynicism in organizations is expressed in terms of stereotypes about other groups, such as "Top management cannot be trusted," or "You'll never get those employees to participate and work harder." Furthermore, research in social cognition shows that people have an implicit bias against social categories, particularly racial minorities, despite their claims that they are not prejudiced. In other words, even when people sincerely believe that they are not racially biased, research studies find evidence that they are. For example, one researcher created a video game with pictures of individuals who were either holding a gun or other objects that were not dangerous. Subjects had to decide under time pressure whether to react to the presence of a gun and "shoot" the individual in the video game. When the individual was black, subjects were more likely to assume that he had a gun, even when he did not. Subjects also were more likely to mistakenly perceive that whites were unarmed, even when they were actually holding guns. This bias, which may be exacerbated by media coverage, was found in both blacks and whites.[9] Although implicit bias is difficult to eradicate completely, workplace efforts on managing diversity should cause people to challenge the incorrect stereotypes they hold about different groups in the workforce and be aware when biases from stereotypes might influence decisions.

A fairly common stereotype in many countries is that older workers contribute less than younger workers. This stereotype is reflected in European laws that encourage early retirement and in the lack of legal protection from discrimination in many countries. In reality, U.S. studies show that older workers are less likely to be absent, have half the accident rate of younger employees, and report higher job satisfaction.[10] Researchers have found no evidence that older U.S. workers are less productive than younger workers.[11] They use information technology more slowly but make fewer errors, according to research.[12] Although "conceptual innovators" are frame-breakers who do their best work when they are young (like physicists who dream of developing a major theory in their twenties), another group of "experimental innovators" are most creative when they are older and can rely on decades of experience and trial and error.[13] The decreased cognitive functioning that accompanies some geriatric diseases has been prevented by modern medicine. Older successful managers are actually experts at solving ill-defined problems using rules of thumb that "can't be put down on paper." What psychologist Colonia-Willner calls "practical intelligence" (like knowing how to deal with difficult bosses) seems to be expert intuition based on years of accumulated knowledge and judgment. She found no age-related difference in practical intelligence in the 200 bankers she tested, which led her to conclude that this is not something that people lose as they age.[14] Thus, when businesses opt to get rid of all managers over a certain age, they not only dismantle the institutional memory, but they are also dispensing with a great deal of wisdom and intellectual capital.

According to research, stereotypes are based on relatively little information, resistant to change even in light of new information, and rarely accurately applied to specific individuals.[15] For this reason, stereotyping is often viewed negatively as a source or excuse for social injustice. Nevertheless, the process of stereotyping is "a neutral, subconscious cognitive process that increases the efficiency of interpreting environmental information."[16] Stereotypes can be helpful if they are used effectively. According to Adler, helpful stereotypes are consciously held, descriptive rather than evaluative, accurate, and viewed as a "first best guess" about a group or person, which means they are subject to modification once we have firsthand experience with people.[17]

The drawbacks to perception are that it prevents us from taking in everything we should, makes our interpretations open to question, and promotes stereotypes. However, perception is an extremely useful process. It helps us to make sense of a world full of stimuli in three ways: first, by limiting the amount of information that enters our mind to prevent overload; second, by selecting what input we will attend to; and, third, by organizing and classifying the input we receive so we do not waste valuable time trying to make sense of behavior and situations that are in fact similar.

IMPACT OF PERCEPTION IN THE WORKPLACE

As W. I. Thomas stated, situations that are perceived to be real are real in their consequences. Managers and employees must deal with misperceptions, no matter how ridiculous they seem at times. We cannot ignore misperceptions with the comforting thought that they are untrue. For example, if employees perceive that their employer does not respect them or care about their welfare, there may well be tangible consequences in the form of high absenteeism, low productivity, and turnover. Recent research showed that hospital employees who perceived their employer as unfair took more sick days. Men who felt that decision making at work was arbitrary and did not take their views into consideration were 41 percent more likely to take sick days than men who did not have this perception.[18]

The determination of employee job performance is vulnerable to subjective perceptions that have surprisingly little to do with how people do their job. For example, two economists discovered that paychecks are correlated with beauty, particularly for men, which one scholar calls "the hunk differential."[19] People whose looks are above average are paid approximately 5 percent more than people whose appearance is average, and people with below-average looks receive 9 percent less than the average wage.[20] One of the economists, Daniel Hamermesh, decided to choose a profession where attractiveness should have no conceivable impact on productivity—college professors. With a student researcher, he looked at teaching evaluations for 463 courses taught by 94 faculty members at University of Texas-Austin. Six students rated the professors' photos on a beauty scale; their scores correlated strongly so they had a similar view of which profs were attractive and which were not. The highly attractive professors had average teaching evaluations of 4.5 on a five-point scale, whereas the least attractive had evaluations that averaged 3.5. Non-tenure-track faculty had higher evaluations than tenure track faculty, presumably because they are hired only for their teaching rather than both teaching and research. Minority instructors had lower evaluations than majority members, non-native English speakers had lower evaluations than native speakers, and females had lower evaluations than males. (No reasons were given for these differences, but we have to wonder whether stereotypes played a role in student perceptions.) However, good looks were more important in producing high teaching evaluations for men than women; men were more likely to get high evaluations if they were hunks and low evaluations if they were unattractive than women. Because this research deals only with perceptions about teaching performance rather than an objective comparison of teaching abilities by a panel of objective judges, it is hard to say whether good looks are the cause of a perceptual bias in students or whether attractive profs actually do a better job in the classroom. This is something for you to think about the next time you fill out evaluations!

PERCEPTUAL DISTORTIONS

Stereotyping is not the only perceptual distortion that influences how people are treated in the workplace. *Another distortion, the "halo effect," occurs when our evaluation of others is dominated by only one of their traits.* For example, a U.S. Army study showed that officers who were liked were evaluated as being more intelligent than those who were disliked.[21] The halo effect does not always work to an employee's advantage. A perceived negative trait such as sloppiness can prevent a boss from seeing the other positive characteristics an employee may have.

Two more perceptual distortions are also rooted in a limited consideration of the information. *The primacy effect means one's perception is dominated by the first impression of another person.* The initial impression of the person is never adjusted in light of more information about him or her. In contrast, *when one's perception is overly dominated by the most recent interactions with a person, this is called the recency effect.* If an employee makes a major error the week before his performance appraisal interview and his boss focuses primarily on this mistake and pays less attention to all the employee's other accomplishments during the year, the boss is biased by the recency effect.

Central tendency is a perceptual distortion that occurs when a person avoids extreme judgments and rates everything as average. We see this when managers rate all their employees as "3s" on a five-point scale, in spite of the fact that some employees really deserve a "5" or a "1." *Contrast effects are present when our evaluations are affected by comparisons with other people we have recently encountered who are either better or worse in terms of this characteristic.* For example, if a student has two of her university's best professors in the same semester, she may rate her other professors (who in reality are good professors) as only average or poor because she is comparing them with the excellent professors.

Another type of perceptual distortion is *projection, the tendency to attribute one's personal attitudes or feelings to another person, thereby relieving one's own sense of guilt or failure.* Projection is a defense mechanism that protects people from confronting their own feelings. It is most common in people who have little insight into their own personalities.[22] Some multinational corporations (MNCs) have been reluctant to transfer female executives abroad on the grounds that a woman could not be effective in a traditional, male-dominated culture. Sometimes, however, the MNC management is simply projecting upon the foreign culture its own feelings and prejudices about female managers. In reality, research has shown that female U.S. expatriates have been successful all over the world.[23]

The final source of perceptual distortion is known as the *perceptual defense. These defenses act as a screen or filter, blocking out that which we do not want to see and letting through that which we wish to see.*[24] The closer we get to schemas concerning our self-perceptions (self-image) and our relationships with important others, the more likely we are to call on these defensive screens.[25] These defenses help to create self-fulfilling or circular perceptual processes like the ones shown in the following examples.

Example 1   A Gender Stereotype

1. As a woman, I believe that men prefer women who are passive and unassertive.
2. Since I would like to develop meaningful relationships with men, I behave in a passive and unassertive manner.

3. I tend to develop relationships with men who expect women to be passive and unassertive.	or	3. I do not approach and/or am not approached by men who expect a woman to be active and assertive.
4. I am confirmed in my belief that men prefer women who are passive and unassertive.	or	4. I do not have the opportunity to develop my own assertiveness.

Example 2   A Managerial Dilemma

1. As a manager, I believe that subordinates are basically lazy and dislike work.
2. I assume, therefore, that to get the most out of subordinates I must watch over their every move.
3. I behave in a strict manner, delegating little responsibility, and demanding that everything be cleared through me first.
4. My subordinates react to this parent-like stance by acting like rebellious teenagers. I have to lean on them all the time, or they'll never do what I tell them.
5. Consequently, my original belief is confirmed; subordinates are basically lazy and dislike work.

The underlying pattern in these processes is one of (1) assumption or belief, (2) leading to behavior that is congruent with the assumption, followed by (3) observation of consequences, which, to the extent that selective perception is occurring, leads to (4) confirmation of the original assumption or belief. Testing the validity or desirability of this conceptual pattern is difficult for several reasons.

One important reason is that normal social interaction is basically conservative—social norms operate to preserve existing interaction patterns and perceptions. Sociologist Erving Goffman[26] has described the tendency of people to preserve the "face" that others present to them. When people act "out of character," social pressures are mobilized to force them back into their role. In social situations, we tend to act in such a way that we maintain our own self-image and the self-image we see others presenting. We resist telling someone that they have egg on their chin because we assume that this is not part of the image they want to present and we do not want them to "lose face" and be embarrassed. This conservative interaction norm tends to decrease the accuracy of interpersonal perception by relinquishing opportunities to test the accuracy of our perceptions of ourselves and others. The norm dictates that we cannot frankly tell others our impressions of them if these impressions differ from the face they are presenting. It also acts as an obstacle to our testing with others whether or not we are projecting the kind of self-image we think we are. "Do you see me the way I see myself?" When people present themselves as leaders, it is hard to tell them you do not feel like following. Thus, we are denied information about others' true thoughts and feelings by the face we present.

THE JOHARI WINDOW

A theoretical conceptualization of this process is depicted in the matrix, in Exhibit 9–2. *The Johari Window is an information processing model that consists of four regions determined by whether information about oneself is known or unknown to oneself and others.*[27]

When a person's arena is very small, communication is greatly hindered. The more we know ourselves and allow others to know us, the greater the potential for effective communication. There are two ways to increase our arena—self-disclosure and feedback from others. Self-disclosure means sharing information about oneself, which moves information from the façade to the arena. Feedback from others about information in our blindspot also moves information into the arena. Trust and psychological safety are prerequisites for both self-disclosure and feedback. We instinctively hold back personal information from people we do not trust, and it is too risky to give feedback to people who might react defensively or angrily. When we share a social identity with others and see them as one of "us," our arena is larger. Our arena is smaller and our façade is larger when communicating with people with whom we do not identify.[28]

One of the basic competencies of effective managers is self-awareness. This requires an ability to both seek feedback from others and to disclose one's own feelings and thoughts. Self-awareness is also important with regard to our perceptual biases. If we understand in what situations we are likely to be biased and listen to feedback from others that we appear biased, we can avoid perceptual distortions. For example, a high-level manager was informed that an employee was guilty of sexually harassing a subordinate. Because the manager herself had been falsely accused of harassment at one time, she was biased toward thinking that the employee, a good friend, also was innocent. Unfortunately, she did not listen when other subordinates suggested she might be letting her own experience and her friendship cloud her judgment, and the guilty employee was never held accountable.

	Known to Self	Not Known to Self
Known to others	Arena	Blindspot
Not known to others	Façade	Unknown

Arena	This cell includes information that I and others know about me—mutually shared perceptions. In other words, people see me the way I see myself (e.g., I feel confident, and people see me as confident).
Façade	This cell contains information that I know about myself but hide from others (e.g., I feel insecure, but I strive to project the image of a very secure person). In other words, people see a "false me," and I must always be on guard to prevent them from seeing the "real me."
Blindspot	This cell consists of information or characteristics that people perceive in me but that I do not see in myself (e.g., others see that my anxiety reduces my effectiveness, but I do not see—or will not admit to myself—that I am anxious). In other words, people know certain things about me that they may not tell me (like the old deodorant commercial, "Even your best friends won't tell you.").
Unknown	This cell is made up of information and characteristics that neither I nor others see in myself. Psychoanalysis might be necessary to unearth this type of information.

EXHIBIT 9-2 **The Johari Window**

CULTURAL INFLUENCE ON PERCEPTION

We know what we perceive; we don't know what we don't perceive. Since there is no way that we can know what we don't perceive, we assume that we perceive "correctly" —even if we don't.

Marshall Singer

Nowhere is it more obvious that different groups see and interpret the world in different ways than when we deal with people from different cultures or ethnic groups. For example, a West African tribe lives in round houses and, as a result, does not perceive perpendicular lines. The way that Africans do favors to gain allies conveys meaningful cues that are not even perceived, much less correctly interpreted by most non-Africans. Perceptual patterns are both learned and culturally determined.[29] They are also a barrier to effective cross-cultural communication when we fail to pay attention to cues that are important to another culture or when we misinterpret the behavior of a person from another culture. Asians and Westerners think and perceive in different patterns. Asians are more likely to "describe something in terms of what it is not," like the space that is not the figure.[30] Japanese subjects made 60 percent more references to objects they saw in the background of a fish tank (e.g., rocks, plants, small animals) than did U.S. subjects. There was no difference in their reports on the figure, the fish.[31]

Adler has identified three sources of misinterpretation in cross-cultural interaction:[32]

1. **Subconscious cultural blinders** We use our own cultural assumptions to interpret the events and behavior of a foreign culture.
2. **Lack of cultural awareness** We are unaware of our cultural values and norms and the way that other cultures perceive us. Without understanding our own culture, we cannot adapt our behavior so that it is perceived more accurately by others.
3. **Projected similarity** We assume that people from other cultures are more similar to us than they really are or that situations are similar when they are not. This is based on the ethnocentric view that there is only one way to be—like me.

D.I.E. MODEL

The D.I.E. model was developed to teach more accurate perceptions and attributions in cross-cultural interactions.[33] It stands for description, interpretation, and evaluation. Description refers to what you see—only observed fact. Interpretation refers to inferences, or what you think about what you see. Evaluation refers to judgments, what you feel about what you think. Evaluation can be positive or negative. For example, two team members, a Russian and an Israeli, are arguing in a team meeting. A Japanese woman observing this interaction could apply this model in the following fashion.

> *Description*: Ivan and Isaac are arguing vigorously and loudly about how the project report should be organized.
> *Interpretation*: I think that these two coworkers are very stubborn and might come to blows.
> *Evaluation*: Violent arguments like this among teammates make me uncomfortable. This is inappropriate behavior, which I don't want any part of.

In fact, Ivan and Isaac come from cultures characterized by the attached argument style. In the attached style, if an issue is important, it's worth getting excited about and worked up. In the detached argument style, found in Japan, if an issue is important, it should not be tainted by personal bias. In reality, this disagreement should help clarify what needs to be done on the report and result in a higher-quality product. The Japanese woman's interpretation is inaccurate because of her subconscious cultural blinders. Her evaluation, which is negative in this case, may prevent her from participating in an important discussion. Thus, reliance on description, rather than interpretation or evaluation, is more likely to promote effective intercultural interactions.

ATTRIBUTION

The most pertinent aspect of perception in terms of organizational behavior is social perception—how we perceive and judge other people. Our behavioral responses to others are based on our inferences about their behavior. *According to attribution theory, when people observe behavior, they attempt to determine whether it is internally or externally caused.*[34] For example, if a team member does not pull his weight on a project, other members may attribute his behavior to internal reasons that are under his control, such as "he's irresponsible and lazy." Or they may attribute it to external reasons, such as "he has too much other work to do a good job on this project." These attributions then determine the way peers and managers behave toward the person. If the employee is deemed irresponsible, his manager might take disciplinary measures or try coaching behavior. If the external cause is accepted, his manager might reorganize his work assignments, send him to time management courses, or negotiate with his other project leaders for more release time.

As shown in Exhibit 9–3, we use three types of information to help us make causal judgments about others:

1. *Consensus* refers to the extent to which others behave in the same manner.
2. *Consistency* is the extent to which the person acts in the same manner at other times.
3. *Distinctiveness* is the extent to which this person behaves in the same manner in other contexts.

Let's take the example of a human resources (HR) manager who is trying to figure out whether an employee complaint about his boss's managerial style is valid. The HR manager will consider whether other employees also have complained about this particular manager (consensus). She also will consider whether the employee has complained about this same boss on previous occasions (consistency) and whether the employee has a habit of complaining about all his bosses or just the current one (distinctiveness). If no one else has complained about the boss, and the employee's evaluation of the boss has been inconsistent (sometimes positive, sometimes negative), and if the employee is a habitual whiner, the HR manager will probably conclude that the problem lies within the employee (internal attribution) rather than the manager (external attribution). If other employees also have complained about the boss, the employee's complaints about this boss have been consistent over time, and the employee never complained about previous bosses, the HR manager is more likely to conclude that it is time to take steps to help the boss improve his style.

There are biases that distort our attributions about success and failure. The Chinese usually attribute personal success to luck and failures to personal failings.[35] In contrast, when Americans succeed, they attribute it to personal, internal factors (e.g., hard work, intelligence, initiative). However, when Americans fail they are more likely to blame it on external factors (such as tough competition, poor leadership, interdepartmental problems). This is called the *self-serving bias, the tendency*

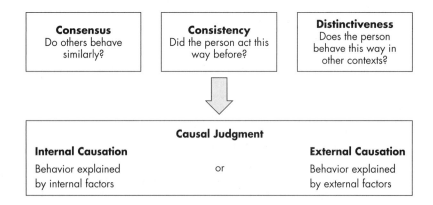

EXHIBIT 9-3 **Attribution Theory**

for people to attribute their successes to internal factors while blaming external factors for their failures. When some managers evaluate their employees, they are less generous and attribute low performance to the subordinates' personal failings rather than external factors. For example, rather than attributing low sales figures to being understaffed, a manager may attribute it to lack of motivation among the sales staff. This form of perceptual distortion is called *fundamental attribution error, the tendency to underestimate the influence of external factors and overestimate the influence of internal factors when making judgments about the behavior of others.*[36]

Given these natural tendencies, managers should make an extra effort to ensure that their attributions about employees are accurate. Katherine Whitehorn, a British writer, showed her understanding of human nature when she proposed the following conjugation of "irregular verbs."

I am firm.
You are obstinate.
He is a pig-headed fool.

Perception plays a major role in communication and decision making in the workplace, particularly in the areas of hiring and firing, performance appraisals, promotions, and work assignments. Effective managers acknowledge that their own perceptions may be uniquely biased and work hard at gathering and understanding the perceptions of other people so there is a greater chance of approximating "reality."

It is as difficult for humans to understand the impact of their own perceptual schema as it is for a fish to understand the concept of water. Yet our perceptual maps and the fish's water are equally important for survival. Without a conceptual system to simplify and order our experiences, we would become overwhelmed by stimuli. However, failure to recognize that our perceptions are to some extent our own creation can leave us closed, defensive, and unable to profit from new experiences. In the following Personal Application Assignment, an engineer analyzes his reactions to the perception chapter and struggles to understand his own way of perceiving others.

STUDENT PERSONAL APPLICATION ASSIGNMENT

Again it seems I am going to write a paper about myself rather than the suggested topic. Whenever I reflect on the subject matter we study, I can directly relate it to myself. I have always considered myself "free of hangups"; however, there are many things I do that I do not completely understand. Previously I have never taken the time to question myself, but now, being forced to think about a concept, I can see how I have been influenced by that concept and can attempt to explain, but not always justify, the way I feel toward many things. Well, here goes!

I am the perfect example of a person blinded by his own perception of the world. Not all of the time, mind you, but mainly in one case—the case being when I become "snowed" by a girl. I'll begin by relating my current project in this area—at least I think the project is current, although I'm not sure as of this moment because of a possible misperception on my part. Being alone in a new city, I engaged in the well-known game of mixer this autumn in the hope of meeting someone interesting. I accomplished my goal without any difficulties, and here is where my problem began—I committed my unpardonable sin of becoming snowed.

I do not have many difficulties with first perceptions. I think I am pretty objective and usually make good judgments. First impressions are almost solely objective! As long as I do not become emotionally involved, that is, as long as there is no filter between what I see and how I perceive what I have seen, I am quite able to understand what is communicated. However, once I am personally involved with the reason behind the attempted communication, my vision of what is actually happening is, I believe, distorted.

This weekend, for example, I did not take Mary (a fictitious name) out because of our last date and a phone call I made after the date. Even though I wanted to take her out, I didn't. Consequently, I have been asking myself all weekend what motivated me not to ask her out; and I do not have a specific answer—but I know it stems from how I perceived how she feels. However, maybe that's not how she really feels, and I do not let myself comprehend that there may be a difference between these two versions of the same feelings. I guess I feel that my logical reasoning of what a particular look or remark means is the correct idea. I completely leave out the possibility that everyone does not (thankfully) think about everything the same way I do.

Zalkind and Costello, in their article on perception, give five reasons why a person misperceives.[37] These are:

1. You are influenced by cues below your own threshold (i.e., the cues you don't know you perceived).
2. You respond to irrelevant cues to arrive at a judgment.
3. You are influenced by emotional factors (i.e., what is liked is perceived as correct).
4. You weigh perceptual evidence heavily if it comes from a respectable source.
5. You are not able to identify all factors (i.e., not realizing how much weight is given to a single item).

I feel I am guilty, if one can be "guilty," of most of the mentioned means of misperception. However, I feel that rather than imposing a perceptual defense on myself, I project a perceptual offense, and this greatly compounds my misperception. Rather than looking for favorable acts of communication and not allowing unfavorable perceptions, I am forever (when I become emotionally involved with a girl) on the lookout for any signs of displeasure. And at the slightest hint, my mind begins to work on such questions as "What if that means …?"

For example, to the question, "Did you have a good time?" I got the reply, "Yeah, I guess so." I did not perceive this as a positive statement. My perceptual offense was quickly in play and I have since been analyzing that statement. I don't know Mary well enough to say what anything she says really means, but because I was afraid the reply meant "I had a bad time," that is what I have convinced myself that she meant (although nothing else that was said even hinted at that idea; and to the friend who doubled with me, the opposite was obviously true). I didn't ask her out this weekend for reasons mainly based on this one perception of how she feels about dating me. Looking back on my action, I see I have committed three of the Zalkind-Costello misperception errors.

- I may have responded to an irrelevant cue—her remark probably just came out and didn't really have any deep meaning behind it.
- I was influenced by a (negative) emotional factor—I was so worried that she was not enjoying herself, and the impact this would have on my emotional happiness, that my perception might have been distorted.
- I did not realize how heavily I weighted this single cue.

Being apprehensive of how she felt, I ended up analyzing every little remark she made. I did not take time to think that my ways of comprehending a perception may be inaccurate—the thought never seemed to enter my mind. Our class handout on perception states, "These defenses act like a screen or filter … blocking out that which we don't want to see and letting through that which we wish to see." I, however, feel that I block out that which I want to see and let in that which I don't want to see. This is a definite problem, but one that I never thought of before. And to compound matters, the perceptions I let in are my own personal version of what is perceived and may be the opposite of what is being communicated.

I do not have this problem until I begin to like a girl. Trained as an engineer, I think I am able to cope with objective matters; but when I try to understand another person, I seem to fail—especially when my perceptions pass through an emotional filter.

To take a statement out of context, Zalkind and Costello say, "A little learning encourages the perceiver to respond with increased sensitivity to individual differences without making it possible for him to gauge the real meaning of what he has seen." Well, I have had only a little learning about perception, and their statement applies to me perfectly. I try to play psychologist without knowing the first thing about what I am looking for. This is a habit I have gotten myself addicted to, and one

I will have to break down in order to have a better understanding of the people around me. Right now the unknown (i.e., the human unknown—what people are thinking) confronts me and I am frustrated by it. In response to this frustration, I set up a perceptual defense (I guess my perceptual offense is nothing but a type of perceptual defense—there is an old football theory that the best offense is a good defense), which only adds to my frustration. Thus, to move from the unknown to perceptual understanding, I must first realize that I am reacting defensively to what is being communicated to me.

It seems I am now coming back to a familiar theme in all the topics we have covered so far. Zalkind and Costello say, "The person who accepts himself is more likely to be able to see favorable aspects of other people." I feel this is especially true of myself. If I stop and realize that my date is probably thinking of the same things that I am (at the initial stages of human relations, most of the time is spent in the unconscious, hidden, and blind areas of perception), then I may prevent my perceptual defense from operating at its current level. If I continually look at weak points and never strong points, and do not realize that I am doing this, I am not really aware of myself and, therefore, not aware of how others perceive me.

I feel I can improve myself in a number of ways. First, I must accept my own feelings and not worry or analyze them. As is stated in chapter 10 of the workbook, "Each of us has both his tender and tough emotions." Second, I should stop analyzing logically—it's hard for me to accept the fact that all of my world is not logical. Third, I should experiment more in the giving and receiving of perceptual feedback. I spend too much time analyzing a date's behavior and not enough time giving her feedback, thus blocking the understanding between us. Finally, the fourth area of improvement, and the factor that this paper has led me to explore, is increasing my own awareness and understanding of the causes of emotion. I hope I can put these steps into action and then build on them.

The following exercise is designed to help you develop perceptual skills that will be useful in the workplace.

CLASS ACTIVITY: THE SELECTION COMMITTEE

The purpose of this exercise is to understand the role of perception in personnel issues (Time allotted: 70 minutes).

STEP 1. Each class member will be assigned a role by your instructor, who will also assign you to groups composed of 4–6 other students who have been assigned the same role (10 minutes).

Selection Committee:

Gerilyn, Senior Loan Officer	Page 235
Mel, VP, Loans	Page 236
Maria, HR Manager	Page 237
Jason, Client Relations Supervisor	Page 238
Charlie, Senior Manager, Auditing	Page 239
Anne, Branch Manager	Page 240
Observer	Page 241

STEP 2. In your same-role group, read the role-play instructions for your character on the page indicated above. Do not read the instructions for any other role. Next read about The Situation, which follows, and discuss these questions: Do you think Lou should be a finalist for this job? Why? Each member should devise a list of reasons supporting their opinion. (20 minutes)

The Situation

Metro Bank has just acquired a smaller local bank, and the primary strategic goal is to merge the banks effectively without losing any customers or valuable employees. Most of the employees of the acquired bank are angry and afraid that they may lose their jobs. One of their bank managers quit so there is a new opening for a branch manager. Here is the job description followed by a list of general selection criteria for branch managers:

Branch managers have direct responsibility for managing and developing branch staff, supporting sales goals, and actively participating in the selling and delivery of all financial services. They must maintain and develop business relationships in the community. They report directly to the Regional Sales Manager and must ensure high quality customer service, which includes opening accounts, providing customers with information, and resolving banking problems. In staffing emergencies, they have to help the staff with day-to-day branch operations. They also ensure that the branch meets all regulatory compliance standards, develop the branch marketing plan, develop and execute the business development plan, manage sales efforts to meet sales goals, develop and execute customer service initiatives, including the resolution of customer complaints.

Selection Criteria for Branch Managers

1. Knowledge of sales, branch banking, and consumer lending
2. Strong business development skills
3. Excellent analytic skills
4. Strong written and verbal communication skills
5. Ability to oversee and administer human resource issues
6. Outstanding selling skills
7. Ability to build community relations
8. Strong interpersonal skills

Lou Welch has worked for 10 years at Metro Bank, beginning as a teller during college. Lou was later promoted to credit analyst and client relations supervisor. Lou has been working as a senior loan officer for the last year. There is an opening for a branch manager, and Lou wants the job. Below you will find a summary of Lou's previous performance appraisals. The bank uses a 1–5 scale, where 1 = unacceptable, 2 = poor, 3 = fair, 4 = good, and 5 = outstanding.

	2003	2004	2005	2006
Dependability	3	4	4	4
Initiative	4	4	5	5
Achieves work goals	4	4	5	5
Teamwork	2	3	3	3
Customer service	3	4	4	4
Leadership	3	4	4	4
Overall rating	3	4	4	4

STEP 3.   You will be assigned to a selection committee by your instructor, perhaps by counting off to form groups of six so that each committee has the same roster as the list shown in Step 1. Make a name tent (or tear out your role-play instruction sheet and fold it) so others can see your name.

If there are not enough participants to form equal groups of six, the person taking Anne's role can also speak for the missing person after reading his or her role instructions. (For example, "_____ is not here but sent me an e-mail with his or her opinion, which is _____.") If there are a few too many participants, they can be observers (5 minutes).

STEP 4.   Your task as a selection committee is to determine whether or not Lou should be one of the finalists to be considered for a management position. As branch manager, Anne will facilitate the meeting. Your committee has 20 minutes to make a decision about Lou. Mark your decision and list your reasons in the box below (20 minutes).

Decision: ____Select Lou as a finalist   ____Don't select Lou as a finalist

Reasons
_____

1. _____

2. _____

3. _____

4. _____

5. _____

STEP 5.   Plenary Debriefing (20 minutes)
   a. What was the impact of discussing Lou's application with other participants assigned to the same role before the selection committee meeting?
   b. What was your committee's decision? Why?
   c. Did you observe any perceptual distortions in other committee members? In yourself? If so, what were they?
   d. As a result of the selection committee's discussion, did you change your impression of Lou and whether Lou should be a finalist?
   e. How did your committee handle the members' individual perceptions of Lou? Did you share all the information you had about Lou with one another?
   f. What did you learn about social identity and perceptions from this exercise?

GERILYN
SENIOR LOAN OFFICER

Lou was hired the same year as you, so you have a long history. Lou is fairly conscientious when it comes to personal work goals. However, Lou really dropped the ball and let down the team on a big project you both worked on four years ago. You were the one who had to do Lou's part of this project, which meant you had to work several nights and weekends. Because of this experience, it's hard for you to see Lou as management material. You don't think Lou should be promoted because being a branch manager means leading the team and developing good relationships with everyone, although Lou does have pretty good financial analysis skills. You didn't apply for the branch manager job yourself because you and your family are moving out of state and you are resigning in three months.

MEL
VICE PRESIDENT, LOANS

You work at headquarters and are the boss of Lou's functional area. Lou's direct boss is Anne. You haven't supervised Lou's work directly, but you think Lou is a real up-and-coming star. Because you both play tennis, you have spent some time with Lou outside of work hours. You've become fairly good friends because you seem to have a lot in common. You go to the same church and belong to the same political party. Lou is always very polite and complimentary to you, frequently telling you what a good job you have done since taking over your position. Based on your experience with Lou, you think Lou should be promoted.

MARIA
MANAGER, HR

Over the years, you have received some complaints about Lou from coworkers who find Lou difficult at times. A secretary once came to your office in tears claiming that Lou was abrasive and harsh. You suspect that Lou might be one of those people who is good at ingratiating themselves with senior management but has little respect for lower-level employees like secretaries and the custodial staff. Lou comes from an upper-middle-class background and doesn't seem to understand what it's like for the less privileged employees or customers. Because your own family was working class, it makes you angry when the hourly workers are not given respect. You think Lou lacks the interpersonal skills to be a branch manager because Lou does not get along well with either coworkers or even customers who are different. You do remember that Lou does well at individual assignments.

JASON
CLIENT RELATIONS SUPERVISOR

You have a great deal of loyalty for Lou, who trained you when you were first hired. When you made a big mistake during your first year, Lou never told on you. Lou recommended you for your current job. After 10 years, you think Lou deserves to be a branch manager, and you know that Lou will be very disappointed if this promotion doesn't come through. You also think that Lou's financial analysis skills and knowledge of the lending process are terrific.

CHARLIE
SENIOR MANAGER, AUDITING

You realize that some of the data in Lou's performance file is not as favorable as it could be. But you imagine Lou has probably grown up during 10 years at the bank and rubbed off any rough edges that were observed in the past. Heck, you had a few rough edges yourself when you were young and look at how well you've done! Although you have heard rumblings that Lou is sometimes abrasive, you believe that Lou has great knowledge of how the branch works, especially in the financial area.

ANNE
BRANCH MANAGER

You have been the branch manager where Lou works for the last month. You don't really have a clear picture of this employee. Lou often stops by your office to chat and is very complimentary. You are hoping that other members of the committee will be able to tell you more about Lou's background and record than you've read in the personnel file. It's your job to wade through the different perceptions of Lou, get at the truth, and come up with a good decision based on valid reasons. Remember that you can't discuss Lou's personality but can only focus on Lou's work record. If a member from your selection committee is missing, please read that person's role instructions and bring his or her opinion into the meeting so that view is not overlooked.

Observer

Unobtrusively observe the group discussion, considering the following questions:

1. To what extent did the group focus on the selection criteria?

2. Which members of the group had the most influence on the group decision? Why?

3. Did you observe any perceptual distortions? If so, what were they?

4. To what extent did the members share information with each other?

5. What worked well? What could have been improved?

 **LEARNING POINTS**

1. Perception is the process by which we select, organize, and evaluate the stimuli in our environment to make it meaningful for ourselves.

2. Selective attention means that people perceive only some of the stimuli that is actually present.

3. Both internal factors (motives, values, interests, attitudes, past experiences, and expectations) and external factors (motion, intensity, size, novelty, and salience) affect what we perceive.

4. Perceived stimuli is organized into patterns, such as opposites, cause-and-effect relationships, and schemas.

5. Schemas are cognitive frameworks that represent organized knowledge about a given concept, event, or type of stimulus. Once established, they determine what stimuli we attend to and remember.

6. People evaluate and interpret the stimuli they perceive in a subjective fashion.

7. Social identity theory is based on the belief that people tend (1) to perceive themselves and others in terms of social categories rather than as individuals (social categorization); (2) to assess the relative worth of groups as well as individuals by comparing them (social comparison); and (3) to perceive and respond to the world not as detached observers but in terms of their identity, which depends on the social groups to which they belong (social identification).

8. Stereotyping occurs when we attribute behavior or attitudes to a person on the basis of the group or category to which the person belongs.

9. The drawbacks to perception are that it prevents us from taking in everything we should, makes our interpretations open to question, and promotes stereotypes.

10. On the positive side, the process of perception limits, selects, and organizes stimuli that would otherwise overwhelm us.

11. There are numerous perceptual distortions to avoid: stereotyping, the halo effect, primacy and recency effects, central tendency, contrast effects, projection, and self-fulfilling perceptual defenses.

12. The Johari window consists of four quadrants: the arena, blindspot, façade, and unknown. It is an information processing model that distinguishes among information about oneself that is either known or unknown to the self or the other in a social interaction. Good communication is most likely to occur when both parties are operating from their arena.

13. Three sources of misinterpretation in cross-cultural interactions are (1) subconscious cultural blinders; (2) lack of cultural self-awareness; and (3) projected similarity.

14. The D.I.E. model teaches people to distinguish among description, interpretation, and evaluation of cultural behavior. Description is the safest response because interpretation and evaluation are likely to result in misattributions or negative evaluations.

15. Attribution theory contends that when people observe others' behavior, they attempt to determine whether it is internally or externally caused. We look for information about consensus, consistency, and distinctiveness to decide on causation.

16. The self-serving bias occurs when people attribute their success to personal qualities while blaming their failure on external factors.

17. Fundamental attribution error is the tendency to overestimate the influence of personal factors and underestimate the influence of external factors when judging others' behavior.

✍ ACTION SCRIPTS

FOR EMPLOYEES

- Employees who are expert at perception are self aware and recognize their own biases. They are able to put their biases aside in an effort to be more objective.
- Experts are able to take the perspective of other people so they can imagine the types of perception that others hold.
- They are also able to empathize with others, which allows them to understand the internal and external factors that influence other people's behavior.
- When people give them feedback, they understand that the other's view of them may be distorted by personal perceptions. Therefore, they check out feedback with more than one person to discover whether it is accurate.
- Experts make an extra effort to clarify communication to and from others to ensure that perceptions are not acting as a barrier to understanding.
- People who have a greater degree of self-understanding are less likely to view the world in black-and-white terms and to make extreme judgments about others.[38]
- Experts understand that their own characteristics affect the characteristics they are likely to see in others. Traits that are important to us are the ones we look for in others. The truism that we see in others that which we most dislike in ourselves applies to perception. People who are self-critical are more likely to criticize others.

FOR MANAGERS

- Managers who are expert at understanding the role perception plays in the workplace understand that no one's perceptions are ever totally accurate or exactly the same. Therefore, they are humble and willing to accept the possibility that their perceptions are mistaken. They don't waste time arguing about what different people really saw or heard; they take a provisional approach that allows for different perceptions:

    Not: "I know I'm right; I heard him with my own ears!"

    But: "I thought he said that, but perhaps I'm mistaken."

    Not: "I'm positive the staff decided to approve my budget just as it is."

    But: "Well, if we have different perceptions about the outcome of the decision, we'd better check it out with the rest of the staff. We both may have heard only what we wanted to hear."

- Expert managers can distinguish between questionable perceptions that they need to verify with others and with solid, intuitive perceptions based on years of expertise.
- They make every effort to be fair when evaluating employees and put aside personal biases.
- They can readily recognize and warn against the different types of perceptual distortion they observe in others and themselves.
- They know that they must deal with misperceptions as seriously as if they were true. They take steps to prevent misperceptions by putting themselves in others' shoes and communicating clearly.
- Expert managers know how much self-disclosure is necessary to form relationships. Self-disclosure is like a bell-shaped curve. Too much disclosure scares people off and makes them nervous. Too little disclosure doesn't give others enough information about the person to form a relationship and they may fill in the gaps with their own projections.
- Expert managers don't make attributions about cultural behavior they don't fully understand. Instead they keep an open mind and seek explanations from cultural experts.

FOR ORGANIZATIONAL ARCHITECTS

- Expert organizational architects provide diversity and performance appraisal training so employees can recognize the dangers of stereotyping others.
- They provide training so that employees who make hiring, performance evaluation, and promotion decisions are trained to recognize the perceptual distortions that can influence these decisions.
- They make efforts to remove hiring and promotion barriers for minorities that reflect bias.
- Experts design training programs on cultural differences in the workplace to prevent mis-interpretations about behavior.
- To guard against against perceptual distortions, they develop performance appraisal systems that rely on facts and the judgments of multiple raters.

PERSONAL APPLICATION ASSIGNMENT

The topic of this assignment is to write about an experience that involved perception or attribution. Choose an experience that was significant to you and one about which you are motivated to learn more.

A. Concrete Experience

    1. Objectively describe the experience (who, what, when, where, how). (2 points)

    2. Subjectively describe your feelings, perceptions, and thoughts that occurred during (not after) the experience. What did others seem to be feeling? (2 points)

B. Reflective Observation

    1. Looking back at the experience, what were the perspectives of the key actors (including you)? (2 points)

2. Why did the people involved (including you) behave as they did? (2 points)

C. Abstract Conceptualization
    1. Relate concepts or theories from the assigned readings or the lecture to the experience. Explain thoroughly how they apply to your experience. Please apply at least two concepts or theories and cite them correctly. (4 points)

D. Active Experimentation
    1. What did you learn about perception or attribution from this experience? (1 point)

    2. What did you learn about yourself? (1 point)

    3. What action steps will you take to be more effective in the future? (2 points)

E. Integration, Synthesis, and Writing
    1. Did you integrate and synthesize the four sections? (1 point)
    2. Was the Personal Application Assignment well written and easy to understand? (1 point)
    3. Was it free of spelling and grammar errors? (2 points)

ENDNOTES

[1] D. Dearborn and H. Simon, "Selective Perception: A Note on the Departmental Identification of Executives," *Sociometry 21* (1958): 142; and A. Kofman, "Selective Perception Among First Line Supervisors," *Personnel Administrator 26* (September 1963).

[2] J. R. Meindl and S. B. Ehrlich, "The Romance of Leadership and the Evaluation of Organizational Performance," *Academy of Management Journal 30* (1987): 91–109.

[3] S. T. Fiske and S. E. Taylor, *Social Cognition* (Reading, MA: Addison-Wesley, 1984).

[4] M. R. Singer, *Perception and Identity in Intercultural Communication* (Yarmouth, ME: Intercultural Press: 1998): 99.

[5] S. A. Haslam, D. V. Knippenberg, M. J. Platow, and N. Ellemers (eds.), *Social Identity at Work: Developing Theory for Organizational Practice* (New York: Psychology Press, 2003): 6.

[6] N. R. Buchan, R. T. A. Croson, and R. M. Dawes. "Swift Neighbors and Persistent Strangers: A Cross-Cultural Investigation of Trust and Reciprocity in Social Exchange," *American Journal Of Sociology 108* (2002): 168–206.

[7] R. Cross, R. Rice, and A. Parker. "Information Seeking in Social Context: Structural Influences and Receipt Of Informational Benefits." *IEEE Transactions on Systems, Man and Cybernetics—Part C: Applications and Reviews 31* (2001): 438–448; D. J. McAllister. "Affect- and Cognition-Based Trust as Foundations for Interpersonal Cooperation in Organizations," *Academy of Management Journal 38* (1995): 24–59; G. R. Jones and J. M. George, "The Experience of and Evolution of Trust: Implications for Cooperation and Teamwork," *Academy of Management Review 23* (1998): 531–546.

[8] J. C. Turner, M. A. Hogg, P. J. Oakes, S. D. Reicher, and M. Wetherell, *Rediscovering the Social Group: A Self-Categorization Theory* (Oxford: Blackwell, 1987); S. Haslam, P. Oakes, K. Reynolds, and J. Turner, "Social Identity Salience and the Emergence of Stereotype Consensus." *Personality and Social Psychology Bulletin 25* (1999): 809–818.

[9] J. Correll, B. Park, C. M. Judd, and B. Wittenbrink, "The Police Officer's Dilemma: Using Ethnicity to Disambiguate Potentially Threatening Individuals," *Journal of Personality and Social Psychology 83*(6) (2002):1314–1329.

[10] W. Keichel III, "How to Manage Older Workers," *Fortune 122*(12) (November 15, 1990): 183–186.

[11] G. M. McEvoy and W. F. Cascio, "Cumulative Evidence of Relationship between Employee Age and Job Performance," *Journal of Applied Psychology 74*(1) (February 1989): 11–17.

[12] P. Coy, "Old. Smart. Productive." *BusinessWeek 3939* (June 27, 2005): 83.

[13] D. W. Galenson *Old Masters and Young Geniuses.* (Princeton, NJ: Princeton University Press, 2006).

[14] Coy, "Old. Smart. Productive": 82.

[15] D. Christensen and R. Rosenthal, "Gender and Nonverbal Decoding Skill as Determinants of Interpersonal Expectancy Effects," *Journal of Personality and Social Psychology 42* (1982): 75–87; and C. McCauley, C. L. Stitt, and M. Segal, "Stereotyping: From Prejudice to Prediction," *Psychological Bulletin 29* (1980): 195–208.

[16] L. Falkenberg, "Improving the Accuracy of Stereotypes Within the Workplace," *Journal of Management 16*(1) (1990): 108.

[17] N. J. Adler, *International Dimensions of Organizational Behavior.* (Cincinnati, OH: South-Western, 2002).

[18] K. B. Christensen, M. L. Nielsen, R. Rugulies, L. Smith-Hansen, T. S. Kristensen, "Workplace Levels of Psychosocial Factors as Prospective Predictors of Registered Sickness Absence," *Journal of Occupational and Environmental Medicine 47*(9) (September 2005): 933–940.

[19] H. Varian, "The Hunk Differential." *New York Times* (August 28, 2003). http://www.sims.berkeley.edu/ ~hal/people/hal/NYTimes/2003-08-28.html. Accessed 7/3/06.

[20] Ibid.

[21] S. S. Zalkind and T. Costello, "Perception: Implications for Administration," *Administrative Science Quarterly 7* (September 1962): 218–235.

[22] Ibid.: 226.

[23] N. Adler and D. N. Izraeli, *Women in Management Worldwide* (Armonk, NY: M. E. Sharpe, 1988); and M. Jelinek and N. Adler, "Women: World Class Managers for Global Competition," *Academy of Management Executive 2*(1) (1988): 11–19.

[24] M. Haire and W. F. Grunes, "Perceptual Defenses: Processes Protecting an Organized Perception of Another Personality," *Human Relations 3* (1950): 403–412; and M. Rokeach, *The Open and Closed Mind* (New York: Basic Books, 1960).

[25] For two excellent collections of material relevant to this point, see W. G. Bennis et al., *Interpersonal Dynamics,* rev. ed. (Homewood, IL: Dorsey Press, 1968), and R. Wylie, *The Self Concept* (Lincoln: University of Nebraska Press, 1965).

[26] E. Goffman, "On Face Work: An Analysis of Ritual Elements in Social Interaction," *Psychiatry 18* (1955): 213–231.

[27] J. Luft, "The Johari Window," *Human Relations and Training News* (January 1961): 6–7.

[28] M. R. Singer, *Perception and Identity in Intercultural Communication* (Yarmouth, ME: Intercultural Press, 1998).

[29] Adler, *International Dimensions of Organizational Behavior.*

[30] I. Varner and L. Beamer, *Intercultural Communication in the Global Workplace* (New York: McGraw-Hill, 2004): 34.

[31] R. Nisbett, *The Geography of Thought* (New York: Free Press, 2004).

[32] Ibid.: 78–84.

[33] M. Bennett, J. Bennett, and C. Stiller, "The D.I.E. Model." http://www.intercultural.org/pdf/die.pdf. Accessed 10/31/05.

[34] H. H. Kelley, "Attribution in Social Interaction," in E. E. Jones et al. (eds.), *Attribution: Perceiving the Causes of Behavior* (Morristown, NJ: General Learning Press, 1972).

[35] L. Pye, *Chinese Negotiating Style* (Cambridge, MA: Oelgeschlager, Gunn, & Hain, 1982).

[36] L. Ross, "The Intuitive Psychologist and His Shortcomings," in L. Berkowitz (ed.), *Advances in Experimental Social Psychology 10* (Orlando, FL: Academic Press, 1977): 174–220; and A. G. Miller and T. Lawson, "The Effect of an Informational Option on the Fundamental Attribution Error," *Personality and Social Psychology Bulletin 15* (June 1989): 194–204.

[37] Zalkind and Costello, "Perception."

[38] E. Weingarten, "A Study of Selective Perception in Clinical Judgment," *Journal of Personality 17* (1949): 369–400.

Chapter 10

GROUP DYNAMICS AND WORK TEAMS

chapter, you should be able to:

f teams.

be in place to set the stage for successful work teams.

development.

ent and group process.

process behaviors that either help or hinder group

maintenance behaviors.

MS

s. On hot teams work is engaging—and when the day
On hot teams everyone gets more done without some
llective neck. What's more, hot teams trust their leaders
w directions, improvising solutions on the spot and
llow through under changing conditions.
ompany project requires a hot team. Hot teams are vital
vel of "task interdependency." Task interdependency
ny single associate influence the success of another's
ple can do their jobs with their heads down—giving
le concern about the effect of their decisions or behavior
on others—and the group can still achieve its big objective, task interdependency is low and hot
teams are not crucial. On the other hand, when the individual's willingness to look beyond self-
interest and communicate, coordinate, and cooperate with others can make or break the team's
success, task interdependency is high and hot teams are critical. It's a hot team's need for each
member to recognize the effect of individual decisions and behavior on others and to adapt for
the good of the group's objectives that makes leading them a bigger challenge than managing an
ordinary work group. The challenge arises because becoming a hot team is a choice work groups
make based on how they feel. Those feelings are the result of how each associate relates from
day to day.

When relationships are poor, people are uninterested in the impact of their decisions and work style on others and unwilling to expend any extra effort to pull together as a team. Team members tend to be rigid, insensitive, and self-centered. However, when relationships are good, team members tend to be empathetic, flexible, and generous with each other—when there's a rift, a hot team will resolve it quickly. They take the initiative and look out for each other with an eye on the big picture.

Organizations fail to follow through on half of all management initiatives—and hot teams are an incredibly effective way to improve that terrible statistic. Tom Kelley, general manager of IDEO, an internationally respected and innovative design company, learned exactly what to do to turn ordinary work groups into hot teams.

A PROTOTYPE FOR CREATING HOT TEAMS

"Our learning [about hot teams] came from being in the trenches," Kelley, who is also the author of *The Art of Innovation*, told me. "That kind of 'Hey that worked. … Boy that was stupid. … Yikes, let's never do that again' knowledge you only get when you're busy doing. Most experts go from the general to the specific. Our understanding comes from the other direction. We didn't systematically toy with the variables. We just built a prototype. If something worked, we noticed it and stuck with it."

IDEO's simple prototype for creating hot teams started with the things that Kelley learned (through trial and error) you must remove from your environment to cultivate great relationships—what I've labeled the don'ts of hot teams. Here are two of the most important:

- Don't let your group become rule-bound.
- Don't be mean.

Don't Let Your Group Become Rule-Bound

Becoming rule-bound is a common and unintended outcome of a useful business practice called process. Process is all about standardizing tasks—highlighting inefficiencies and inconsistencies to reduce defects and increase reliability and repeatability. Process also helps create boundaries in the workplace so everyone can work together more easily. But most companies take the discipline of process too far and get rule-bound.

For example, a software firm needed a "process" for distributing office furniture. A committee met and decided, "Administrative assistants should not be given chairs with arms." Now Laura, an admin, was seven months' pregnant. She needed a chair with arms to sit comfortably. So her team swapped a chair (with arms) from an empty desk and gave it to her.

The operations manager heard about the swap. That night she took that chair back to the empty desk. The next day Laura's team brought the chair back. Again, when everyone was gone, the ops manager took the chair away. But this time she followed up with a company memo: "Policy states, Admins don't get chairs with arms."

This sort of thing happens all too frequently. Some rule-bound enforcer creates a process police state that represses any urge to become a hot team. Kelley says it isn't only over-the-top, uptight enforcement that kills hot teams. Every impulse to create a rule must be carefully scrutinized.

Don't Be Mean

Facing tough competition, demands for higher returns, and intense time pressures, many executives feel they have no choice but to take a hard line. "We need to become lean and mean," they'll announce. They are half right. Lean is a business necessity. But mean does more harm than good.

For example, the new CEO of a faltering enterprise insisted his 150 top executives get together every month on a conference call and report their results. During that call, he would single out anyone who'd missed budget to answer tough questions. "He'd ask you why in front of everyone," a former executive said.

When one executive said he believed anxiety and unrest in his business unit was affecting performance, the new CEO said, "This is a test of leadership. You show me an organization that's wringing its hands, listening to rumors, anxious about the future, and I will show you leadership that behaves the same way. People imitate their leaders. I can't believe this worry is fact-based. I believe their worry is ignorance-based. And if that's the case, it's your fault."

This kind of humiliation and manipulation usually produces bad outcomes. First, when executives are treated like "hand wringers" for saying something the boss doesn't want to hear, they learn to keep quiet and let problems turn into disasters. Second, most managers would do almost anything to avoid having to say in front of 150 of their peers, "I screwed up." Doing "almost anything" often gets companies in hot water.

And that's exactly what happened. Fifteen months after he was hailed for his tough minded-ness and sense of urgency, the company stumbled badly both ethically and financially and the stock price fell 71 percent. The CEO was asked to go away.

Mean managers believe they are enforcing accountability. But, there's a fine line between enough and too much accountability. Cross it and a leader becomes a bully who attacks people instead of problems, ignores the effect of feelings, and causes people down the line to look for payback.

Avoiding the don'ts won't produce a hot team all by itself, though. There are also things you must do.

Four Do's for Hot Teams

- Like your people.
- Listen to them.
- Make work engaging.
- Let them decide.

Like Your People

Mark Kuroczko created a hot team simply by liking his people. Kuroczko was in charge of a small department responsible for writing technical manuals and spec sheets for a big banking organization. But instead of hiring people with communications degrees and years in the financial business, Kuroczko hired painters, musicians, novelists, and even a sculptor—creative types that he liked to be around.

Because he liked them, Kuroczko was especially protective." I saw my job as manager to create a game preserve for creative beasts," he said. "I wanted to protect our little group of fun people, doing fun projects safe from the corporate types and bureaucratic interference." In return they showed Kuroczko something he never would have anticipated.

One day an executive VP who couldn't get the help he needed from the bank's main marketing communications department called Kuroczko and asked if he could take charge and do a critical four color brochure and some associated client proposals. Kuroczko said sure.

When his team got hold of the project they were unbelievably responsive and inventive. "We gave him a faster turnaround and an easier interface," he remembered. "Since we knew the products and services from the technical side and we were creative at heart, we were able to write a better proposal and brochure. And the people reporting to that executive felt like we actually enjoyed helping them, which we did."

Any manager who has dealt with creative types knows the difficulty of getting them to follow through fast. Kuroczko found the answer. Show creative people you like them and they'll move heaven and earth for you (another demonstration of hot teamwork).

Listen to Them

Dave La Pouple managed a team of twenty for Clear Channel Communications. He has discovered listening to associates is the key to making his team hot. "I've started giving everyone on my subteam, the six people of the twenty that are my direct reports, a weekly one-on-one. That one-on-one allows me to really listen to each person.

"I've got one person with me eighteen months. She came in so unsure of herself. She's had some bad bosses and bad situations. But just by listening every week and saying, 'You can do it,' I am reinforcing her belief in herself. It's made her a different person altogether. Listening works." Listening increases trust, makes expectations clearer, relaxes the barriers between people, and increases self esteem.

Make Work Engaging

A Stanford professor studied IDEO and found that IDEO employees are more engaged than employees at the average company. That's no accident, according to Kelley. "Creating a hot team is about mind set," he said. One of Kelley's favorite tactics is to create roles for everybody on the team to increase their sense of being "chosen." Look around your team to get a sense of the different roles people play, Kelley advised. He suggests that teams assign someone to be the Visionary, the Skeptic, the Technologist, and the Sympathizer, among other characters. Roles, Kelley believes, let people feel special. Roles also let you use people for their strengths while avoiding (and protecting them from) their weaknesses.

Let Them Decide

One of Kelley's other practices is to let people define their own work pace their own way, within budgets, never allocating space or creating rules controlling who does and doesn't get a chair with arms. He saw the great effects this "let them decide" mind set can have at one of the IDEO offices.

Kelley was in a weekly meeting with one of his teams when the head of that team said, "We've got a problem. We need to add some people, but we're out of room. Any ideas?" Kelley bit his tongue to let the team decide. One guy spoke up. "Everything is on wheels here. If each person gave up one foot of space, by the end of the row we'd have room for one person."

There were two rows of eight cubicles, and so both sides trimmed back one foot apiece so they could accommodate two additional people. Everybody agreed this was the way to solve the problem. What impressed Kelley was that everyone willingly gave up a little of their personal space to solve a business problem. "Did everyone get squeezed a little?" Kelley asked. "Yes. But did anyone complain or let that get them down? No!"

Giving employees the power to make decisions on their own is the opposite of being rule bound and hierarchical. And it has the wonderful side effect of making people behave more considerately and generously.

HOT TEAMS—IMPRACTICAL OR PRACTICAL?

"Morale is an expression of a work group's emotional health," organizational psychologist Harry Levinson wrote in his publication *The Levinson Letter*. "High morale groups (what we call hot teams) are built by managing in such a way that people's psychological needs [as well as their physical needs] are met."

A concerned executive wrote to Levinson with a familiar argument, "Yes, all that [about morale] is great, but our managers have to work under heavy pressure to get results." The executive explained to Levinson that perhaps in the future, his company's managers would have the time to cultivate such an ideal environment, where leaders met the psychological needs of their people in order to create hot teams. "But today," he told Dr. Levinson, "we can't afford the luxury of such idealism."

I believe that executive was both right and wrong. Good business demands practicality. Every team is under the gun, every manager under pressure. Any patience for wasted time, money, or efforts is gone. But that manager was wrong to assume that the activities that turn average workgroups into hot teams are impractical or idealistic. Let me illustrate why I disagree with his assumptions with the following puzzle:

Bob and Doug are lumberjacks in the Pacific Northwest. They both swing their ax at the exact same rate. Bob works nonstop from seven in the morning until three thirty in the afternoon, except for a 30 minute lunch break. Doug works the same schedule, but he takes an additional 10 minute break from swinging his ax every hour. That means Doug spends less time cutting trees (6 hours and 40 minutes a week less) than Bob. And yet, at the end of each week, Doug consistently cuts down more trees than Bob. Why?

Doug spends those 10 minutes every hour doing something very practical: he's sharpening his ax.

Hot teams are not a luxury. When your work group's willingness to look beyond their self interests and communicate, coordinate, and cooperate with others can make or break achieving the big objectives, hot teams are what Doug's sharper ax is to cutting down more trees— extremely practical.

Source: L. Haughton, "Creating Hot Teams," *Leader to Leader, 38* (2005): 7–12.

 **CLASS PREPARATION**

A. Read "Creating Hot Teams."

B. Answer and score the Team Assessment Survey.

C. Answer the following questions.

    1. Focus on an effective group to which you belong (or belonged).

        a. List the norms (unwritten rules of conduct) of this group.

        b. How do you think the group developed these norms?

    2. Now think about a poorly functioning group to which you belong(ed).

        a. List its norms.

        b. How do you think they developed?

    3. How would you go about changing the norms in a poorly functioning group?

    4. What are the norms in your learning group or class? How do they hinder or promote learning?

D. While reading The Knowledge Base, think about the cues that you will look for in teams to indicate whether they are managed well and functioning effectively.

Team Assessment Survey

Think about a team on which you are currently a member (or your latest team) and rate the extent to which these problems exist. Circle the number which best reflects conditions on this team (1= "Low Evidence", 5 = "High Evidence."

Team Problems	Low Evidence		Some Evidence		High Evidence
1. Unclear goals	1	2	3	4	5
2. Low commitment to goals	1	2	3	4	5
3. Unproductive meetings	1	2	3	4	5
4. Decisions not implemented	1	2	3	4	5
5. Lack of trust among members	1	2	3	4	5
6. Unequal work distribution	1	2	3	4	5
7. Communication problems	1	2	3	4	5
8. Lack of respect among members	1	2	3	4	5
9. Lack of innovation and creativity	1	2	3	4	5
10. Apathy or lack of involvement	1	2	3	4	5
11. No progress checks	1	2	3	4	5
12. Poor attendance	1	2	3	4	5
13. Conflict or hostility	1	2	3	4	5
14. Unclear task assignments	1	2	3	4	5
15. Lack of collaboration	1	2	3	4	5

Add up the points for each item to find your total score _____
What does your score mean?
15–30 = Your team is in good shape; congratulations!
31–53 = Some bumps but probably still a functional team
54–75 = Time to apply what you learn in this chapter or bring in a consultant and do some serious team building.

Source: Adapted from W. G. Dyer, *Team Building: Issues and Alternatives* (Reading, MA: Addison-Wesley, 1987): 42–43; and D. Jaques, "Teaching Small Groups," *BMJ* 326 (2003): 492–494.

THE KNOWLEDGE BASE

To build a great company, you must focus just as hard on your people as you do on customers, partners, communities and stakeholders. You must have talented individuals working together as a team, who share a commitment to common values and a collective determination to execute one vision.[1]

Michael Dell, Founder, Dell Computers

Teamwork has become so commonplace in global business that teamwork skills are one of the top ten qualities sought by recruiters. The move toward teamwork is one of the most significant trends in business. Most U.S. companies utilize work teams and this number is expected to grow.[2] One impetus for incorporating teams into organizational structures comes from the need for speed and flexibility. Other reasons include increases in the complexity, uncertainty, and scale of tasks that must be accomplished in organizations. As the opening vignette illustrates, teams that work well—that are "hot"—can be extremely effective. They often can make decisions faster and more accurately and can handle larger tasks than can individuals. The use of teams to make a decision can also result in greater understanding of the decision and commitment to that decision. But, even though there is currently a tendency to see work groups as a panacea, they are not appropriate for every organization nor are they appropriate for every project or decision. The use of teams can result in increased costs (as more people are devoted to a task), slower decision making, decreased accuracy, and hurt feelings and damaged relationships if not managed properly.[3] Indeed, groups can often make more extreme decisions than individuals—sometimes making more risky and sometimes more cautious decisions.[4] The key for managers, then, is to find ways to enhance the benefits and minimize the liabilities of teamwork. But first, we need to clarify what we mean by team effectiveness.

WHAT IS TEAM EFFECTIVENESS?

Although it is tempting to define group performance solely in terms of its production or efficiency, team effectiveness is a much richer concept that encompasses the following group, social, and individual components.[5]

1. **Output** The productive output of the team (i.e., its product, service, or decision) meets or exceeds the standards of quantity, quality, and timeliness of the team's clients—the people who receive, review, and/or use the output.
2. **Social Processes** The social processes the team uses in carrying out the work enhance members' capability of working together interdependently in the future.
3. **Learning** The group experience contributes positively to the learning and personal well-being of individual team members.

Creating Effective Work Teams

There are four questions that managers should ask themselves when working with teams.

- Is a team appropriate for this decision or task?
- How can I most effectively manage the team context?
- How can I most effectively manage the team members?
- How can I most effectively manage the team task and process?

These factors are discussed in the following sections.

Deciding When to Use a Team

Not all decisions or projects should be assigned to a work group. Groups are more likely to be effective when conditions are right. For example, groups are more likely to perform better when the task, the members, and the organization meet certain conditions.[6] When tasks are uncertain, complex, large in scale or scope, or require inputs from multiple sources, groups are likely to be an effective way to accomplish those tasks.

Other conditions also contribute to the use of teams as an effective method of solving problems. Members must have the requisite interaction and task skills and be willing and able to devote the necessary effort to accomplish the group task. In addition, managers should trust that team members will solve the problem in ways that meet organizational goals and not just team or personal goals. Finally, teams must be provided with the resources (e.g., technology, time, information) and must be given sufficient responsibility and authority to accomplish their tasks. In order to succeed, teams require a common purpose and specific goals.[7] It is also helpful to ensure that teams have a sense of *group efficacy—a feeling that the team has the capability to*

successfully accomplish its task and a shared *mental model, which refers to members' shared, organized understanding and mental represention of task-related and team-related knowledge.*[8] Shared mental models seem to contribute to team performance and effectiveness when the team task requires interdependence.

Managing the Team Context

It is particularly critical that teams recognize that they are embedded in an organizational context. That context needs to be actively designed and managed to ensure optimal team performance. A supportive organizational context that recognizes and welcomes teamwork; provides necessary resources such as information, technology, and raw materials; provides the administrative and human resource infrastructure (performance appraisals, rewards, performance management); and legitimizes team work through top management support is a significant factor in ensuring team success.

However, teams must also proactively manage their context. Often, team managers and members focus inward on the team process and fail to recognize that their external activities can be just as important as their internal ones. In fact, teams who proactively manage their external relationships tend to be more productive than those who do not. Exhibit 10–1 describes important external activities that teams should undertake.[9]

Managing Team Members

Team skills. Team members need to have the appropriate mix of necessary technical, social, and team management skills to accomplish their tasks. Recent research found that team members should be proficient in the following skills:[10]

- Collaborative problem solving—ability to structure the team interaction to achieve the appropriate amount of participation
- Conflict resolution—skill in handling cognitive conflict (conflict about ideas) and reducing emotional conflict (conflict about personalities, emotions, etc.)
- Communication—ability to enhance open communication and use active listening techniques
- Goal setting and performance management—skills in establishing goals and monitoring and coaching performance
- Planning and coordination—skill in coordinating tasks, establishing roles, balancing workloads across members

Motivation. In individualistic societies, such as the United States, working in groups does not always come as naturally as it does in more collectivist societies in which people feel a stronger sense of group loyalty. Phrases, such as "A camel is a horse put together by a committee," reflect reservations about group efforts. And in fact, U.S. Americans sometimes contribute less effort to

Role	Activity
Ambassador	Manage upward relationships; market the team; lobby for resources; manage the team reputation
Scout	Gather information in the organization, market, and industry; manage lateral and downward searches
Task Coordinator	Manage lateral connections among functions and interdependencies with other organizational units; coordinate deadlines and nudge other units to fulfill commitments; get feedback on how the team is meeting expectations

EXHIBIT 10-1 External Team Roles and Activities

Adapted from D. Ancona, H. Bresman, K. Kaeufer, "The Comparative Advantage of X-teams," *MIT Sloan Management Review, 43* (2002): 33–39.

group projects than when they work alone. This is known as *social loafing*. This phenomenon was not observed in a comparison study with Chinese groups, presumably because this behavior is less likely in a collectivist society.[11] Nor do we find this behavior in "hot" U.S. groups and teams described in the opening vignette.

Regardless of the cultural context, social loafing is not inevitable. It can be reduced by making sure that each team member's contribution is identifiable (e.g., communicating sales figures, profit margins, etc.). Designing tasks so that they are intrinsically involving, attractive, or engaging also tends to minimize social loafing as members become motivated to perform their tasks. Finally, assigning responsibility and making that responsibility public tends to reduce social loafing. In fact, when teams set their own goals, they are less likely to experience social loafing. In addition, teams with a social identity tend to have less social loafing. *Social identity refers to the perception of members as a "group," rather than as a set of unique individuals, and a shared (usually positive) image of the group.*[12]

Establishing the proper level and type of rewards for accomplishments is critical for team motivation. One central issue is how to balance individual and team rewards. Many of us have had personal experience with group members who try to grab the credit or who do not carry their fair share of the work. Sometimes, managers react by simply allocating rewards on an individual basis. On the other hand, it is important to reinforce *team* performance and reward the group as a whole. Research suggests that both types of rewards are appropriate at different stages in the group's work. For example, when the stage of the group's task involves individual contributions (e.g., generating ideas), individual rewards should be given. In contrast, when the task requires a group output, rewarding the group as a team makes sense. Failing to establish the right balance can have disastrous results.[13]

It is important to acknowledge cultural differences in rewarding teams and individuals.[14] Collectivist and individualistic cultures may differ in the value placed on each. Team-based rewards are generally more appropriate in collectivist cultures. The Japanese saying, "the nail that sticks up gets hammered down," indicates the cultural value placed on group rather than individual achievement. Many cultures have similar sayings. As a result, individuals in collectivist cultures are less likely to be motivated by incentives that cause them to stand out from their peers. For instance, rewarding the top sales team, rather than the top salesperson, is more effective in collectivist cultures.

At times, pressure from external groups that focus on individual achievement can harm collectivist team norms. For example, when New Zealander Sir Edmund Hillary's team climbed Mt. Everest for the first time in 1953, the whole team agreed not to speak about which individual reached the summit first. The important thing, they decided, was that the team reach the summit, and to do so, they had to travel in single file. No individual could possibly have made it without the team. Then the journalists and nationalists in the United Kingdom and Nepal got into the act. The Nepalese feted Tenzing Norkay, the Sherpa who guided the group, parading him in a seat of honor atop the royal carriage. The rest of the team rode inside that carriage, not visible to the crowd. A U.K. newspaper was incensed at such behavior, insisting that Tenzing was only a servant/guide and that Hillary, the real leader, was the first to set foot on Everest's summit.[15] The ensuing bickering damaged the friendship between the two men.

Composition and Diversity. Getting the right mix of team members is a critical component in assembling effective teams. In general, research shows that heterogeneous groups with a reasonable mix of task and interpersonal skills perform more effectively than more homogeneous groups. The trick is to establish the right level—too much heterogeneity and the group often becomes involved in unending conflict; too little and the group risks conformity and lack of innovation. Research on demographic diversity (e.g., race, age, gender differences) likewise shows the importance of developing heterogeneous groups. In general, the key seems to be incorporating the input of diverse, multiple perspectives and ensuring that group values and goals are shared. Groups who successfully do this perform more effectively and are more innovative than groups who do not.[16]

Managing the Team Process and Task

Groups are not static. As they change and evolve over time, the key issues and concerns of members also change. Managers need to understand how groups develop and how to manage the group interaction and task processes at each stage.

GROUP DEVELOPMENT

In spite of years of experience in various sorts of groups—families, clubs, sports teams, work teams—we don't always take the time to carefully observe what was going on in the group or reflect on why the members were behaving as they did.[17] One of the factors that affects behavior is the group's developmental age. We act differently in a brand-new group than we do in a group that has been functioning for several years. Therefore, it is helpful to have an understanding of how groups typically develop, even though not all groups are exactly alike.

Most groups evolve through stages. Effective team leaders help the group successfully weather each stage in which members confront specific issues that influence their behavior. The most well-known model of group development follows.[18]

- **Forming** In this stage, members focus on accepting each other and learning more about the group and its purpose. This is a period of uncertainty, self-consciousness, and superficiality. Effective group leaders help orient members, clarify the purpose of the group, and work on establishing trusting relationships. By the end of this stage, members feel like they belong to the group.
- **Storming** Members confront the issues of how much individuality they must relinquish to belong to the group and who will control the group. Tension, criticism, and confrontation are typical of this stage. The group becomes polarized, subdivides into cliques, and challenges the leader and others. Effective leadership involves helping the group focus on a common vision, modeling constructive conflict management, and legitimizing expressions of individuality that do not hinder productivity. Skilled leaders ensure that the group is a safe place for all members. They also reassure members that storming is a normal stage in a group's development, which paves the way for later productivity (unless the group becomes stuck in destructive conflict).
- **Norming** Members develop shared expectations about group roles and norms. This stage is characterized by collaboration, commitment, increased cohesion, and identification with the group. Effective leaders continue to help set norms, provide positive feedback on the group's progress, and prevent groupthink. *Groupthink is the tendency for members of a highly cohesive group facing a collective threat to seek consensus so strongly that they fail to explore alternative courses of action.*[19]
- **Performing** At this point, the group focuses its energy on achieving its goals and being productive. There is increased cohesion, acceptance of individual differences, and mutual support during this stage. Skilled leaders help the group run itself at this point, foster the development of group traditions, and encourage the group to evaluate its effectiveness.
- **Adjourning** Temporary groups disband and focus less on performance and more on closure. In this stage, members struggle with holding on (nostalgia) and letting go (looking ahead to the future). Effective leaders encourage the group to reflect on, learn from, and celebrate its achievements.

Another way to understand group development is the punctuated equilibrium model (see Exhibit 10–2). According to this model, the productivity of some groups can be described as periods of inertia or equilibrium that are punctuated by a transitional period of radical change that occurs at the midpoint of the group's calendar life.[20]

1. In the *first meeting,* the group sets its direction and does not reexamine it until the transition.
2. This is followed by *Phase I,* a period of inertia and equilibrium.
3. When the group has used up half its allotted time, a *transition* occurs that includes a burst of activity and a search for new ideas and perspectives. The group redefines its direction at this point.

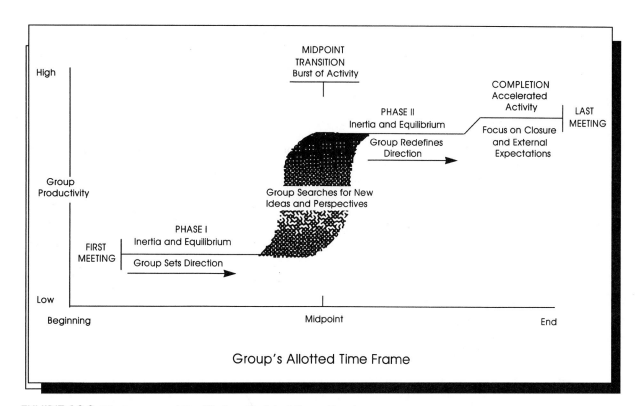

EXHIBIT 10-2 **The Punctuated Equilibrium Model of Group Development**

Source: Based on C. G. Gersick, "Time and transition in Work Teams: Toward a New Model of Group Development," *Academy of Management Journal 31*(1) (March 1988): 9-41 and "Marking Time: Predictable Transitions in Task Groups," *Academy of Management Journal 32*(2) (June 1989): 274-309.

4. A second phase of inertia and equilibrium, *Phase* 2, follows the transition.

5. Accelerated activity takes place during the group's last meeting in the *completion* phase.

Regardless of how long groups have to accomplish their task, some of them do not "get serious" until half of their time has been used up.

CONTENT AND PROCESS

In any group there are at least two classes of issues operating at any given point. One is the reason for the group's existence in the first place (e.g., to solve a particular problem). When we observe *what* a group is talking about, with regard to work that must be done, we are focusing on group *content*. When we try to observe *how* the group is functioning, we are talking about a second and equally important set of issues, group *process*. [21]

There are two types of group process: task process and maintenance process. *Task process focuses on how groups accomplish their work, including setting agendas, figuring out time frames, generating ideas, choosing techniques for making decisions and solving problems, and testing agreement. Maintenance process concerns how groups function with regard to meeting group members' psychological and relationship needs.* It includes issues such as leadership, membership, norms, communication, influence, conflict management, and dealing with difficult members and dysfunctional behaviors.

Effective group members pay attention to both group content and process, so they can intervene when necessary in an appropriate manner. In some ways, the appointment of a chairperson or facilitator recognizes that groups do not always "stay on track." While appointing a leader is often useful, there are two potential problems with this approach. First, seldom do the group members spend any time discussing *why* they are "off track." More often the chairperson will say something like "We're getting off the main track, let's get back to it!" and that's all that happens. It is extremely important to realize that if people are having difficulty staying on track, there are reasons for the behavior and simply saying "Let's get back to it" does nothing to eliminate the basic causes. Worse than that, this kind of behavior ("Let's quit wasting time and get to the task") may further accelerate the underlying reasons for lack of involvement and make the situation worse.

Second, there is no inherent reason that only one person in a group should have the responsibility for worrying about how the group is progressing. Everyone can and should share this responsibility. To delegate this function or role to just one individual is often a highly inefficient utilization of resources. People can learn to be skilled participant-observers in groups. In effective groups, *anyone* who feels that something is not right can and should raise the issue for the total group to examine. Anyone who observes a need for a particular kind of task or maintenance behavior can help the group. In a well-functioning group (working on something other than a routine programmable task), an observer looking in from the outside might not be able to pick out the formal leadership. The "leadership function" passes around according to the group's need at a particular point. It is important, in other words, to distinguish between leaders as persons and leadership as a function. For example, summarizing or gatekeeping (controlling the flow of information to the group) at the appropriate moment is performing an important act of leadership. To see the need and fail to respond can be viewed as a failure to fulfill one's membership responsibilities.

Although work groups spend most of their time on content, a failure to address process issues usually prevents a group from reaching its maximum potential and accomplishing its task in a timely manner. It is often argued that "We don't have the time to worry about people's feelings or to discuss how the group is working." Sometimes this is perfectly true, and under severe task pressure a different kind of process is necessary and legitimate. People can accept this, however, if they know from past experience that this situation is temporary. More often, however, lack of time is used as a defense mechanism to avoid the discussion completely. Furthermore, if a group is continually under severe time pressure, some time ought to be spent examining the effectiveness of the group's planning procedures.

A group that ignores individual members' needs and its own process may well find that it meets several times to make the same set of decisions. This happens because the effectiveness of many decisions is based on two factors—logical soundness and the level of psychological commitment among the members to the decision made. These two dimensions are not independent; in fact, some people who are uncommitted (often because of process issues) may withhold, on a logical basis, information necessary to make the soundest decision. In any event, the best decision (on a task or logical level) forged at the expense of individual commitment is not a very good decision at all. Effective facilitators are concerned with both productivity and commitment. The following sections focus on process issues that help us understand how groups function.[22]

COMMUNICATION AND DECISION MAKING

One of the most easily observed aspects of group process is the pattern of communication:

1. Who talks? For how long? How often?
2. At whom do people look when they talk?
   a. Individuals, possibly potential supporters
   b. The group
   c. Nobody
3. Who talks after whom, or who interrupts whom?
4. What style of communication is used (assertions, questions, tone of voice, gestures, etc.)?

These cues signal important group dynamics, such as who leads whom and who influences whom.

Group decisions are notoriously hard to undo. When someone says, "Well, we decided to do it, didn't we?" any budding opposition is quickly immobilized. We can undo the decision only if we reconstruct and understand how we made it and test whether this method was appropriate or not. Here are some typical decision making methods we see in groups.[23]

1. The *plop:* "I think we should appoint a chairperson." ... Silence.
2. The *self-authorized agenda:* "I think we should introduce ourselves. My name is Jane Allen ..."
3. The *handclasp:* Person A: "I wonder if it would be helpful to introduce ourselves?" Person B: "I think it would; my name is Pete Jones."
4. The *minority decision:* "Does anyone object?" or "We all agree, don't we?" Agreement or consensus may not be present, but it's difficult for others to object sometimes.
5. *Majority-minority voting:* "Let's vote and whoever has the most votes wins."
6. *Polling:* "Let's see where everyone stands. What do you think?"
7. *Consensus seeking:* Genuine exploration to test for opposition and to determine whether the opposition feels strongly enough to refuse to implement the decision. It's *not* necessarily unanimity but essential agreement by all. Consensus does *not* involve pseudo-"listening" ("Let's hear Joe out") and then doing what you were going to do in the first place ("Okay, now that everyone has had a chance to talk, let's go ahead with the original decision").

Group decisions can be facilitated by altering the decision making procedures used by the team. In general, the idea is to lengthen what is termed the "solution evaluation" phase (in which the group generates and evaluates ideas and alternatives). Some methods for accomplishing that goal are listed below.[24]

- **Structured discussion principles** Establish guidelines that emphasize analysis, solicitation of solutions, protection of individuals from destructive criticism, keeping the discussion problem-centered, and listing all solutions before evaluating them.
- **Second solution** Require the team to generate at least two solutions. This has the advantage of forcing the team to evaluate at least two alternatives, which in turn enhances performance quality. This technique is particularly useful when teams are reluctant to implement more elaborate decision making procedures.
- **Procedures for generating and protecting alternative viewpoints** Ask group members to assume the perspective of other stakeholders or constituencies (e.g., pretend you are a member of the marketing group; how will the marketing group react to this proposal?). Use the "two-column method" for all alternatives. For each alternative, members must identity genuine advantages and disadvantages (akin to drawing a line down a piece of paper and listing the pros and cons on each side of the line). The group can also appoint a *devil's advocate (a person assigned to specifically point out problems with the group decision and plans)*. It is important that this process generate authentic, rather than contrived, dissent. Sometimes groups generate "straw" arguments that appear to question the decision but actually are easy to refute. Rotating the devil's advocate role among members is typically a useful procedure as well.

GROUP COHESION

Group cohesion is the degree to which members are motivated to stay in the group.[25] Cohesiveness is a double-edged sword for managers because it can either enhance or impede group performance. Cohesive groups tend to be better at achieving their goals than are noncohesive groups.[26] Thus, cohesive groups that have the goal of increased productivity will be more productive. The converse is also true: cohesive groups that have goals that favor low performance indeed will perform more poorly.

Managers who want to increase group cohesiveness have a number of tools at their disposal. Group cohesion can be increased by:

- **Small size** Smaller groups tend to be more cohesive than larger ones.
- **Success** Groups who experience success have higher levels of cohesiveness than those who experience failure.
- **Common threat** Providing groups with a common, shared threat or a common enemy is also a way to increase cohesion. However, the group must be perceived by its members as capable of responding effectively to that threat or enemy. Cohesion actually will decrease if the group is viewed as ineffective.
- **Exclusivity** Groups that are more difficult to join or who have higher perceived prestige tend to be more cohesive.
- **Perceived similarity among members** Groups that emphasize member similarities have higher levels of cohesion than those that emphasize member differences. Similarities include values, attitudes, shared experiences, educational background, and so forth.
- **Competition** Competition with other groups or outsiders can increase cohesion—as long as the group has no interdependence with its competitors. For example, if two teams in one organization need to work together to accomplish a project, competition should not be encouraged because it may foster sabotage and other actions that decrease performance.[27]

TASK, MAINTENANCE, AND SELF-ORIENTED BEHAVIOR

Behavior in the group can be viewed in terms of what its purpose or function seems to be. When a member says something, is the intent primarily to get the group goal accomplished (task) or to improve or patch up some relationship among members (maintenance), or is the behavior primarily meeting a personal need or goal without regard to the group's problems (self-oriented)?

As the group grows and members' needs become integrated with group goals, there will be less self-oriented behavior and more task or maintenance behavior. Types of behavior relevant to the group's fulfillment of its task are the following:[28]

1. **Initiating** For any group to function, some person(s) must be willing to take initiative. These can be seemingly trivial statements such as "Let's build an agenda" or "It's time we moved on to the next item," but without them, little task-related activity would occur in a group. People would either sit in silence or side conversations would develop.
2. **Seeking information or opinions** The clear and efficient flow of information, facts, and opinions is essential to any task accomplishment. "What do you know about this situation?" and "What solution do you recommend" are examples of seeking information from others in the group. Because decisions should be based on full information, information-seeking statements not only help the seeker but the entire group.
3. **Giving information or opinions** In response to the seeking behavior described in #2 or at their own initiative, group members can offer both information and their opinions to aid the group. Examples of giving-type statements are — "I have some information that may be relevant" or "My own opinion in this matter is …"
4. **Clarifying and elaborating** Many useful inputs into group work get lost if this task-related behavior is missing. "Let me give an example that will clarify the point just made" and "Let me elaborate and build on that idea" are examples of positive behaviors in this regard. They communicate a listening and collaborative stance.
5. **Summarizing** At various points during a group's work, it is very helpful if someone takes a moment to summarize the group's discussion. This gives the entire group an opportunity to pause for a moment, step back, see how far they have come, where they are, and how much further they must go to complete their work.
6. **Consensus testing** Many times a group's work must result in a consensus decision. At various points in the meeting, the statement "Have we made a decision on that point?" can be very helpful. Even if the group is not yet ready to commit itself to a decision, it serves to

©1973 by Chicago Tribune NY News Synd, Inc. World Rights Reserved

Source: Reprinted by permission of the Chicago Tribune-New York News Syndicate.

remind everyone that a decision needs to be made and, as such, adds positive work tension into the group and clarifies how much consensus building remains to be done.

7. **Reality testing** Groups can take off on a tangent that is very useful when creativity is desired. However, there are times when it is important to analyze ideas critically and see whether they will hold up when compared to facts or reality. This helps the group get back on track.

8. **Orienting** Another way of getting a group back on track is through orienting behavior that helps the group to define its position with respect to goals and identify points of departure—from agreed-upon directions. When questions are raised about the direction the group is pursuing, everyone is reminded of the group goal and has an opportunity to reevaluate and/or recommit to meeting it.

The following behaviors are necessary to keep a group in good working order. These *group maintenance* roles help create a climate that permits maximum use of member resources:

1. **Gatekeeping** Gatekeeping, directing the flow of conversation like a traffic cop, is an essential maintenance function in a group. Without it, information gets lost, multiple conversations develop, and less assertive people get cut off and drop out of the meeting. "Let's give Joe a chance to finish his thought" and "If people would talk one at a time, I'd find it easier to listen and add to our discussion" are examples of gatekeeping behavior.

2. **Encouraging** Encouraging also ensures that all the potentially relevant information the group needs is shared, listened to, and considered. "I know you haven't had a chance to work it through in your mind, but keep thinking out loud and we'll try to help." "Before we close this off, Mary, do you have anything to add?"

3. **Harmonizing and compromising** These two functions are very important but tricky because their overuse or inappropriate use can serve to reduce a group's effectiveness. If smoothing over issues (harmonizing) and each party's giving in a bit (compromise) serve to mask important underlying issues, creative solutions to problems will be fewer in number and commitment to decisions taken will be reduced.

4. **Standard setting and testing** This category of behavior acts as a kind of overall maintenance function. Its focus is how well the group's needs for task-oriented behavior and maintenance-oriented behaviors are being met. All groups will reach a point where "something is going wrong" or "something doesn't feel right." At such points, effective groups stop the music, test their own process, and set new standards where they are required. "Is the way we're tackling the problem working for everyone?"

5. **Using humor** The use of humor to put people at ease and reduce tension is an important maintenance function. However, the inappropriate use of humor can prevent groups from reaching their goals quickly and stop them from tackling uncomfortable issues that need to be resolved.

For a group to be effective, both task-oriented behavior and maintenance-oriented behavior are needed.

EMOTIONAL ISSUES: CAUSES OF SELF-ORIENTED EMOTIONAL BEHAVIOR

The group process described so far deals with the work-facilitating functions of task and maintenance. But there are many active forces in groups that disturb work, which represent a kind of emotional underground or undercurrent in the stream of group life. These underlying emotional issues produce a variety of self-oriented behaviors that interfere with or are destructive to effective group functioning.[29] They cannot be ignored or wished away. Rather, they must be recognized, their causes must be understood, and as the group develops, conditions must be created that permit these same emotional energies to be channeled in the direction of group effort. What are these issues or basic causes?

1. **The problem of identity:** Who am I here? How am I to present myself to others? What role should I play in the group?
2. **The problem of control and power:** Who has the power in the situation? How much power, control, and influence do I have in the situation? How much do I need?
3. **The problem of goals:** Which of my needs and goals can this group fulfill? Can any of my needs be met here? To which of the group's goals can I attach myself?
4. **The problem of acceptance and intimacy:** Am I accepted by the others? Do I accept them? Do they like me? Do I like them? How close to others do I want to become?

Self-oriented behaviors tend to be more prevalent in a group at certain points in the group's life. In a new group, one can expect to see many examples of self-oriented behaviors. Members are unfamiliar with one another and a certain amount of "feeling out" is to be expected. Sometimes this takes place in after-hours social situations—"Why don't we get together after work for a drink?" Self-oriented behaviors can also be observed when a newcomer joins an already established group. It is not unlike the dynamics that develop when a new sibling arrives in a family. Everyone else may be sincerely happy with the newcomer ("We really need her resources"); nonetheless, this is now a "new" group. The old equilibrium has been changed and a new one must take its place.

The potential destructiveness of self-oriented behaviors is highest just when the group most needs to be effective—when it is under stress. Groups, like individuals, sometimes regress to previous stages of development in times of stress. Effective leaders try to predict difficult transitions or events and minimize their effect. Ford's global teams refer to stressful periods and cultural tension points as "bumps" (e.g., when team members transfer in or out and when the team moves from planning to implementation).

Types of emotional behavior that result from tension and from the attempt to resolve underlying problems follow.

1. **Tender emotions:** love, sympathy, desire to help, need for affiliation with others
   a. Supporting and helping others
   b. Depending on others
   c. Pairing up or affiliating with others
2. **Tough emotions:** anger, hostility, self-assertiveness
   a. Fighting with others
   b. Punishing others
   c. Controlling others
   d. Counterdependency
3. **Denial of all emotion**
   a. Withdrawing from others
   b. Falling back on logic or reason

Individuals have different styles of reducing tension and expressing emotion. Three "pure types" have been identified:

1. The "friendly helper" orientation: acceptance of tender emotions, denial of tough emotions—"Let's not fight, let's help each other", —can give and receive affection but cannot tolerate hostility and fighting.

2. The "tough battler" orientation: acceptance of tough emotions and denial of tender emotions—"Let's fight it out"—can deal with hostility but not with love, support, and affiliation.

3. The "logical thinker" orientation: denial of all emotion—"Let's reason this thing out"—cannot deal with tender or tough emotions; hence, shuts eyes and ears to much going on around him or her.

BUT ...

Friendly helpers will achieve their world of warmth and intimacy *only* by allowing conflicts and differences to be raised and resolved. They find that they can become close with people *only* if they can accept what is dissimilar as well as what is similar in their behavior.

Tough battlers will achieve their world of toughness and conflict *only* if they can create a climate of warmth and trust in which these will be allowed to develop. Logical thinkers will achieve their world of understanding and logic *only* if they can accept that their feelings and the feelings of others (both tough and tender) are also facts and contribute importantly toward our ability to understand interpersonal situations. Exhibit 10–3 portrays the different orientation and characteristics of each type. These three, as described, are clearly pure types; the average person has some elements of each. What differentiates people is their predisposition toward a particular type.

1. Friendly Helper	2. Tough Battler	3. Logical Thinker
Best of All Possible Worlds		
A world of mutual love, affection, tenderness, sympathy	A world of conflict, fighting, power, assertiveness	A world of understanding, logic, systems, knowledge
Task-Maintenance Behavior Demonstrated		
Harmonizing Compromising Gatekeeping by concern Encouraging Expressing warmth	Initiating Coordinating Pressing for results Pressing for consensus Exploring differences Gatekeeping by command	Gathering information Clarifying ideas and words Systematizing Procedures Evaluating the logic of proposals
Constructs Used in Evaluating Others		
Who is warm and who is hostile? Who helps and who hurts others? Who is nice and who is not?	Who is strong and who is weak? Who is winning and who is losing?	Who is bright and who is stupid? Who is accurate and who is inaccurate? Who thinks clearly and who is fuzzy?
Methods of Influence		
Appeasing Appealing to pity	Giving orders Offering challenges Threatening	Appealing to rules and regulations Appealing to logic Referring to "facts" and overwhelming knowledge
Personal Threats		
That he or she will not be loved That he or she will be overwhelmed by feelings of hostility	That he or she will lose his or her ability to fight (power) That he or she will become "soft" and "sentimental"	That his or her world is not ordered That he or she will be overwhelmed by love or hate

EXHIBIT 10-3 **Orientation of the "Pure Types"**

We can learn to use emotional resources more appropriately by:

1. Accepting our own feelings and acknowledging that each of us has both tender and tough emotions.
2. Understanding group behavior at the feeling level as well as at the logical level, as feelings are also part of the group's reality.
3. Increasing our awareness through observation and analysis of the causes of emotions. By learning to recognize which events in the here-and-now trigger emotions, we can gain better control of ourselves in a given situation and behave more appropriately.
4. Experimenting with expressing emotion differently and asking for feedback.

Within some companies, managers (and particularly males) are expected to be tough, hard, and aggressive. Any sign of "tender emotions" (warmth, affection) may be perceived as a sign of weakness. However, feelings do not go away simply because we ignore them, and there is no question that emotions can affect group decisions. Given the opportunity to experiment with and get feedback on our emotional behavior (and a climate that supports such behavior), we can become more aware of when it is appropriate to be tough, tender, or neither.[30]

GROUP NORMS

Another issue that must be addressed with respect to group process is group norms. *A norm is an unwritten, often implicit rule that defines what attitudes and behaviors characterize a "good" group member versus a "bad" group member or what constitutes acceptable behavior, attitudes, and feelings.* Norms are the group's shared beliefs about appropriate behavior, attitudes, and perceptions concerning matters that are important to the group.

All groups create norms as they develop and mature. In and of themselves, norms are neither good nor bad. The important point is whether or not the norms that exist support the group's work or act to reduce effectiveness. In this way, group norms control the behavior of members and make group life more predictable.

Let's take a real-world example. The president of a multimillion-dollar multinational corporation wanted to make a major change in the way he and his three vice presidents functioned. The general pattern of behavior was such that each vice president would argue for decisions that would benefit his or her particular department. Turf battles and tunnel vision were standard fare during group meetings.

It was the president's desire to create what he called the "Office of the Presidency." When he and the vice presidents met, he wanted everyone to look at the issues before them from an executive perspective. In other words, he wanted everyone to focus on the corporation as a whole, looking at decisions through the "eyes" of a president.

Clearly a host of group norms would have to change dramatically. Historically, no meeting ever began until the president arrived. After all, it was "his meeting." If the new philosophy was to be taken seriously, the "Office of the Presidency" had to function *irrespective* of who—as an individual—was present or absent.

One Monday morning the three vice presidents arrived for their normally scheduled meeting. But one "small" problem had arisen: a devastating weekend snowstorm caused the president to be stranded 1,000 miles away. Still, several critical topics were on the agenda. After considerable anxious grasping for solutions (conference calls, private jets, and even prayer) and much nervous laughter, they bit the bullet. The "Office of the Presidency" was called to order. An old norm had been changed.

The pinch point occurred Tuesday morning at 8:00 A.M., only now it was the president who felt the anxiety. To his credit, he asked to be *informed* as to the decisions taken by the Office of the Presidency in his absence. Any other behavior on his part, such as reopening decisions he personally did not like, would have violated and made a game of the new normative expectations. Fortunately, this president was aware of the importance of norms.

Too many groups operate under the norm: "In this group, no one ever dares to question or suggest that we examine our norms." As a result, there is an absence of standard setting and testing and an implied punishment for anyone who engages in such behavior. Such a "Catch-22" norm is unlikely to facilitate the development of an effectively functioning group.

CONCRETE EXPERIENCE AND REFLECTIVE OBSERVATION

Just as norms may vary from group to group, they also may vary from culture to culture. The following vignette relates the "concrete experience" of one expatriate professor who taught overseas in Latin America.

INTERNATIONAL EXAMPLE OF GROUP NORMS

I sat back in my chair, glancing around the handsome room with its graduation photographs of faculty members in full academic regalia, including some remarkably fetching scarlet robes and exotic headgear from a Spanish university. Finding it difficult to break an unconscious habit of punctuality, I have spent many moments alone in this room, waiting for colleagues to arrive. As a result, I learned to bring along small projects to occupy my time while waiting for those who live by a different internal clock. By now, other faculty members, all males except for myself, are dribbling in, responding to the external summons of a telephone call from on high, the Rector's (president's) secretary. They enter with a lot of good-natured greetings and jokes and, as always, it is a pleasure to see them.

In today's meeting, the dean is trying to get faculty support and compliance with policies and procedures that will improve academic standards and quality. As usual, I am intrigued by the norms in these meetings. Even though there are only 10 people present, the dean jots down the names of the professors who wish to speak in the order in which they signal him. This order is respected in the beginning but becomes more difficult to maintain when people want to respond immediately to the comments. At this point they are reminded by the dean or others that there are several people ahead of them in the queue. Occasionally, a senior faculty member is allowed to break in and make his comments without being reprimanded for being out of order. The result of the group's self-imposed structure is often a disjointed conversation with lots of looping back to previous points. There seems to be an unspoken expectation that everyone should speak at some point in the meeting, whether or not they are contributing a different opinion. The dean fields and reacts to each comment or question, immediately judging its worth. I am always surprised that one person, rather than the group, is granted the power to dispose of ideas that could possibly be developed and honed by more group discussion. If the communication pattern were graphed, it would show that a large majority of the comments are directed to and returned from a central hub, the dean. A much smaller percentage of the interactions occur laterally among the participants.

Since I agree with the policies and am already complying with the rules, my most fervent wish is to have the meeting end quickly so I can "return to work." I sense no similar urgency on the part of my colleagues; they are "at work." I decide to take advantage of the situation to clarify a practice I have never fully understood. I ask if students might not do better on future tests if their exams were returned to them. My suggestion is rapidly shot down with comments like, "This is the way it's always been done" and "Students would take advantage of the policy you are suggesting." Except for another expatriate, no one appears to find any merit in my suggestion and the discussion quickly moves on.

When the meeting ends, I head for yet another one with my departmental colleagues. I am immediately struck by the difference in atmosphere between the two meetings. Perhaps because we share many of the same values and because we have put in many hours and miles together, I feel more at ease, more listened to, and much more able to be myself in the second meeting. This group also has more experience working with women, so gender is not an issue. We are like a self-managed group in many ways. We begin a free-wheeling discussion in which everyone chimes in on a single topic until closure is reached, and then we move on to another point. We are tackling a topic that we chose ourselves—determining our regional strategy. Comments are directed to the entire group and everyone, including brand-new employees, apparently feels free to respond with his or her opinions, and even feelings. The group has a coordinator but not a formal leader. The coordinator helps keep the group on track at times but does not make the decisions. After vigorous discussion with clear differences of opinion, the group makes consensus decisions. It never occurs to me that I am a minority or an outsider in this meeting, even though I do not always agree with what my colleagues do or say. I don't find myself glancing at my watch in this meeting, and when we leave to return to our individual offices, I have a smile on my face.

When I reflect on this situation, I see numerous cultural differences between myself, an American, and the other faculty members who are primarily Latin American. Although not all individuals or organizations fit these stereotypes, the following cultural differences are generally acknowledged and appear to influence the norms in the first meeting. A major difference is a polychronic versus monochronic orientation. People in monochronic cultures tend to be punctual and do one thing at a time in a linear fashion. In polychronic cultures, people pay attention to several things at once; punctuality is less important than finishing other activities. In this example the monochronic American arrives on time and is disconcerted when one topic is not discussed until it is completed. The polychronic Latins arrive when it is convenient and easily track the various topics being discussed at once. For them, speaking out in the meeting may serve to maintain relationships and promote a sense of collegiality; in contrast, the norm that everyone should speak runs counter to a U.S. value of not wasting time.

Other differences are that Latins tend to respect tradition and resist policy changes while many Americans value change, sometimes for its own sake. Decision making is more centralized and leadership is generally more authoritarian in Latin America, which explains why people grant the dean the right to pass judgment on suggestions. In comparison, Americans tend to be more participative and egalitarian. The take-a-number-to-speak norm is not found in all Latin groups; it may be somewhat unique to the dominant organizational culture. Hierarchical power is much less important in the departmental meeting. In general, however, there is a greater emphasis on control and rules in Latin cultures, accompanied by attempts to get around these rules. People with high status or connections are more successful at evading rules, which explains why senior faculty are not always obliged to respect the queue. In U.S. universities, senior faculty are also privileged. What varies from school to school and country to country is the particular form that privilege takes.

In both meetings, there are norms that promote friendly relations and an institutional concern for excellence. Beyond these similarities, the two meetings are characterized by very different norms even though the cultural composition is fairly similar in both groups. Cultural differences are less significant in the departmental group than in the more formal faculty meeting. The smaller group is part of a cultural subgroup with values that are closer to my own and norms that I have helped create. As a result, only in the second group do I feel like a full-fledged member.

Source: Adapted from J. Osland, "International Diversity: An Essay on Expatriates and Advanced Acculturation," in *Diversity and Differences in Organization: An Agenda for Answers and Questions.* R. Sims & R. Dennehy (eds.)(Westport, Connecticut: Quorum,1993): 107-121.

TEAMBUILDING

It is foolhardy to assume that simply because a group of people assembles to perform a task, it will somehow automatically know how to work together effectively.[31] And yet many organizations make this assumption. Let's compare a football team with the typical management team. The football team spends untold hours practicing teamwork in preparation for the 60 minutes each week that its members' performance as a team really counts. In contrast, most management teams do not spend even 60 minutes per week practicing teamwork in spite of the fact that for 40 or more hours every week their behavior as a team really counts. For this reason, in recent years both management groups and work teams have undergone team-building training.[32]

Most team-building efforts encourage members to:

1. Establish their goals and priorities (What should we be working on?);
2. Define the roles that need to be performed (Who is going to do what?);
3. Examine and determine the procedures the team uses or should use (How are we going to do the work and make decisions?); and
4. Examine the team's interpersonal relationships and norms (How are we going to treat one another?).[33]

Common complaints about personality problems in teams often have their root in the failure to clarify goals, roles, and procedures, so the order in which teams tackle these issues is important.

TYPES OF TEAMS IN ORGANIZATIONS

Self-managed teams. Downsizing strategies have eliminated supervisors and middle managers and delegated many of their functions to self-managed or self-directed teams. When they function well, such teams allow their members to make a greater contribution at work and constitute a significant competitive advantage for the organization.

Self-managed work teams have the following characteristics. The teams determine how they will accomplish the goals they must achieve and how they will allocate the necessary tasks. Usually they are responsible for an entire product or process. The work teams take responsibility for planning, scheduling, organizing, directing, controlling, and evaluating their own work process. Some teams also select their own members and evaluate members' performance. Leadership varies in these teams—some have no formal leader, others elect a leader, while still others have a formal leader assigned by management.

Research shows that self-managed teams were rated as more effective in terms of productivity, costs, customer service, quality, and safety than traditionally managed teams.[34] Other company benefits are reduced absenteeism, lower turnover, and increased employee motivation. In terms of employee benefits, members of self-managed teams reported greater growth satisfaction, social satisfaction, and trust than did the members of traditionally managed groups.[35]

Virtual teams. As society and the global economy become more complex and as technology continues to advance, more and more of organizational life will revolve around a team or group structure. The "information explosion" will guarantee that no one person can expect to have all the facts necessary to make many decisions. *"Temporary systems" in which a group of people join for a short-term task and then disperse to form new and different task groups to tackle other problems* have become more prevalent. Virtual teams, in which members are geographically dispersed and seldom work face-to-face, have become more common. *Virtual teams are defined as teams that work across space, time, and organizational boundaries with links strengthened by webs of communication technologies.*"[36] Their popularity has necessitated a new term to distinguish virtual teams from conventional *teams,* which are now often referred to as—*collocated teams.* Some suggestions for effectively managing virtual teams follow:

- Begin with a face-to-face meeting to foster the development of trust among team members
- Clarify team goals and team roles that are not in conflict with commitments to other work units
- Designate a strong senior sponsor who protects the team and secures resources
- Carefully implement efficient communication and collaboration processes that prevent misunderstandings and conflict escalation
- Create experiences of interdependence within the team in order to compensate for feelings of disconnectedness, for instance via goal setting, task design, or team-based incentives
- Share measurement systems and metrics across sites—the more comprehensive, the more useful
- Align incentive systems across subunits and recognize team level efforts
- Create knowledge management systems such as a team intranet, archives, index, and templates
- Develop appropriate "kick-off" workshops and a team training concepts to prepare and support the teams for the specific challenges of virtual teamwork.[37]

Multicultural and multinational teams. Another consequence of our global economy is the development of teams that consist of members from multiple cultures. *Multicultural teams have representatives from various ethnic groups but share a common nationality. Multinational teams (also transnational teams or global teams) are a collection of individuals, small in number, with representatives from more than one national background among them, who are interdependent and mutually accountable for accomplishing a set of objectives, and who recognize themselves as a team.*[38] These teams present special challenges as they tend to involve greater difficulty in creating a team identity, dealing with communication barriers that include language, different communication styles, and computer-mediated communication, managing coordination and control issues, managing cultural diversity and conflict, adjusting to different interpersonal styles, and handling geographic distances and dispersion. Although much more research is needed, some suggestions for managing these types of teams include:[39]

- Clearly define the team charter outlining the scope of the project, the expected deliverables, and the timeline

- Overcome communication barriers by investing in language and cross-cultural training
- Agree on norms of behavior
- Adopt data-driven decisions
- Develop alternatives to enrich the debate (e.g., dialectical thinking and devil's advocates)
- Rotate meeting locations
- Cultivate a culture of trust
- Schedule face-to-face meetings to build a solid foundation and perform periodic team maintenance
- Rotate team leadership
- Link rewards to team performance
- Build social capital in the organization by helping managers build social networks outside their units
- Rotate personnel to different countries.

Teams play an important role in organizational life today, and every indication points toward their increased importance in the future.[40] Teams work best when they share common methods of problem solving, decision making, and conflict management—topics that are addressed in subsequent chapters.

CLASS ACTIVITY: THE INNER-OUTER EXERCISE

The purpose of this exercise is to provide an opportunity to experience and study group dynamics and discuss effective teams.[41] (Time alloted: 90 minutes)

STEP 1.   Divide the class into an even number of groups of 8 to 10 people by counting off. The instructor will ask for a volunteer coder from each group and ask them to go outside the classroom to read their instructions on page 267. Students should then sit with their group in the location their instructor indicates (all the Ones together, the Twos together, etc.). The groups will then be paired (the Ones paired with the Twos, the Threes paired with the Fours, etc., depending on how many groups there are in the class). The paired groups will sit in two concentric rings of chairs, forming a tight inner circle (the odd-numbered groups) surrounded by an outer circle (the even-numbered groups) sitting directly behind people in the inner circle. Both groups face inward. When the coders return, they will sit outside the outer circle at opposite points so each coder has a clear view of a different part of the inner circle.

STEP 2.   Each group will have one turn in the inner circle and one turn in the outer circle in each of four rounds; they will spend four minutes in the inner circle and four minutes in the outer circle (or whatever time periods your instructor chooses) in each round, as shown in the Activity Schedule on the next page. The team tasks you will perform when seated in the inner circle and the individual tasks you are to carry out when seated in the outer circle are described below.

Inner Circle Tasks:

In each round, when your team is sitting in the inner circle, your assignment is to
a. Be the most effective group you can; and
b. Create a list of the 10 characteristics of effective groups and rank-order them. You are allowed to work on this assignment (a & b) only when your group is seated in the inner circle. At this time, you should act as if the other group is not present.

Outer Circle Tasks:

In each round when your team is sitting in the outer circle, your individual role assignment is to act as observers and potential consultants to the other group.

c. Carefully observe how the other group functions and write down your observations on the bottom of the Role Observation Sheet on page 272. Try to identify what they are doing that either impedes or facilitates their accomplishment of their two tasks.

d. Use the Role Observation Sheet to keep track of the group roles carried out by the person who is sitting in the inner circle directly in front of you. (That same person should be observing you when you are working in the inner circle.) *Do not talk with the other members of your group while you are in the outer circle* because it will distract the other group.

To start, the Ones, for example, seated in the inner circle will have four minutes to work on a & b; the Twos will act as observers. When the four minutes are up and time is called; the Ones will immediately switch seats with the Twos and observe them at work for four minutes. Please switch seats quickly because the clock starts running for the following group as soon as time is called. The paired groups may borrow ideas from each other, but the goal is for each group to develop its own product.

To summarize, your team has two roles: "doers" when you are seated in the inner circle and "observers" when you are seated in the outer circle.

Time	Group	Location	Assignment
Round 1 0–4 min.	Group #1	Inner Circle	a. Be the most effective group you can be
			b. Create and rank a list of the 10 characteristics of effective groups
	Group #2	Outer Circle	c. Observe and take notes on group process of other group
			d. Keep track of group roles performed by the person seated in front of you
4–8 min.	Group #2	Inner Circle	a. Be the most effective group you can be
			b. Create and rank a list of the 10 characteristics of effective groups
	Group #1	Outer Circle	c. Observe and take notes on group process of other team
			d. Keep track of group roles performed by the person sitting in front of you
Round 2 8–12 min. 12–16 min.			Repeat same process as Round 1
Round 3 16–20 min. 20–24 min.			Repeat same process as Round 1
Consultation Period 24–29 min.	Group #1 Group #2	Outer Circle Inner Circle	Individuals consult with the person sitting directly in front/behind on the group process and roles they observed when seated in the outer circle

continues on next page

Round 4 29–33 min. 33–37 min.	Group #1 Group #2	Inner Circle Outer Circle	Repeat same process as Round 1
38–60 min.	New hete-rogeneous teams & Coder group	Assigned locations	Discuss assigned group process topic and prepare presentation
60–80 min.	Plenary		Team presentations and General Debriefing Questions
80–90 min.	Original groups	Assigned locations	Coders give feedback to their assigned group

STEP 3. After the third round, members of the group in the inner circle will turn around to face the members of the other group who are seated directly behind them. Both people should act as consultants to one another and the other group. Tell the other person what you saw occurring in his or her group and give some advice about how the other group could function more effectively. Then show the person what group roles s/he has been carrying out according to your Role Observation Sheet. The idea is for everyone to listen carefully to someone who has observed his or her group and take back suggestions for group and self improvement. Thus, members of both groups have the opportunity to both give and receive advice during a five-minute period. Then complete the final round of the exercise.

STEP 4. Each group submits its list of the characteristics of effective groups to the instructor and remains seated.

STEP 5. At this point, the coders will join together to prepare their feedback and discuss their observations. Everyone else counts off by four to form new heterogeneous teams. Each team will discuss a different aspect of group process that has a major impact on the life of any group or team. Our goal is to figure out what behaviors either hindered or helped group effectiveness during this exercise and become experts on one aspect of group process.

   a. **Team One's task** (all the number Ones) is to explore the concept of "goals" as they have influenced the life of the developing groups. You should look at goals from the perspective of those that were imposed on the group by the instructor, and those that evolved as the real group goals, which may or may not have anything to do with those established by the instructor. Did you see any individual goals that differed from the general goals of the group? Please develop specific examples of how individual and group goals influenced the life of the groups and helped determine their success. How can groups handle the problem of disparate goals?

   b. **Team Two's task** (all the Twos) is to look carefully at the "membership" criteria that prevailed in the groups. Membership in this case is equivalent to what behaviors were acceptable or not acceptable in terms of gaining entry to the group. During this exercise, some individuals gained greater membership than others because of their behavior. What kinds of behavior or circumstances made some people less than "full" members? Why? The group must understand not only what these criteria were but also how they influenced the feelings, motivation, and morale of the group itself. Please give examples of each of the criteria that you develop and examples of how they influenced the life of the groups. What can a group do to make everyone feel like a full member?

c. **Team Three's task** (all the Threes) is to take an in-depth look at the behavioral norms, the implicit or explicit "rules of the game," that influenced the life of each group. How did the groups handle conflict and stress, make decisions, listen, generate ideas, allow certain language to prevail, and so on? Be sure that with every norm that you identify you note specific examples and make comparisons among the groups when it is obvious that some of the norms differed radically. What can groups do to ensure that they develop norms that help rather than hinder group effectiveness?

d. **Team Four's task** (all the Fours) is to explore the kinds of leadership that developed in the groups—who had it, who took it, to whom it was given, and who if anyone was able to establish and maintain a real presence of leadership? What different kinds of behaviors did leaders demonstrate? What behaviors resulted in either resistance or a loss of leadership? Decision making is of specific importance here—how were decisions made, who made them, and how did this influence the group? The names of individuals are not important but specific behaviors are because we can then begin to understand how the life of each group was influenced. If you observed different types of leadership, what were the pros and cons of each leadership style? What can a group do to promote the type of leadership that is most effective for that group?

You will all have 20 minutes to develop an understanding of your particular concept and prepare a 2-3-minute presentation.

STEP 6. Each of the four teams presents its findings and examples.

STEP 7. General Debriefing Questions
a. Did your group act out all the characteristics on your list? Why or why not?
b. How would you describe the relationships between the paired groups?
Did you see any evidence of competition? If so, what triggered the competition?
Did the groups learn from watching each other? Why or why not?
c. What was the result of the consultation period? Why did this result(s) occur?
d. What did you learn about the way you behave in groups?

STEP 8. Students should reform into their original group so the coders can present their communication feedback to the group they observed. What are the implications of the communication pattern that emerged? What are the consequences of talking a lot in a new group and talking very little? (10 minutes)

ROLE OBSERVATION SHEET

Purpose: Learn to recognize specific group roles by watching a team member in action during the Inner-Outer Exercise. When you are sitting in the outer circle, put a hatch mark in the "Frequency Observed" column each time your assigned person (the one sitting directly in front of you) in the inner circle performs the following roles.

Group Task Roles	Frequency Observed
1. INITIATING—Proposes, suggests, recommends	
2. SEEKING INFORMATION—Asks for info, viewpoints, suggestions	
3. GIVING INFORMATION—Offers information, viewpoints, suggestions	
4. CLARIFYING—Clarifies and elaborates ideas	
5. SUMMARIZING—Sums up group's progress	
6. CONSENSUS TESTING—Checks for agreement	
7. REALITY TESTING—Asks whether ideas will work or fit the facts	
8. ORIENTING—Gets group on track, signals departure from goals	
9. ENERGIZER—Stimulates group to higher levels of productivity	
Group Maintenance Roles	**Frequency Observed**
1. GATEKEEPING—Directs flow of conversation, promotes participation	
2. ENCOURAGING—Expresses warmth, friendliness, encourages, acknowledges	
3. HARMONIZER—Mediates disagreements, reconciles differences	
4. STANDARD SETTING AND TESTING—Suggests standards for way group operates; checks for satisfaction	
5. USING HUMOR—reduces tension	

Also observe the group process of the other team as a whole. Is everyone participating? How are decisions made? Do they seem to enjoy working together? How are they accomplishing the task? Be prepared to coach your assigned person on how to improve his or her team's performance.

Your observations of their group process:

Your advice for that team:

CODER INSTRUCTIONS

Your task is to unobtrusively chart the communication that takes place in your group, using the Coder Chart on the following page. Please don't talk or distract the group in any way and don't tell them what you are doing.

1. In the Coder Chart, write down the names of the people in your group in the same order they are seated, both horizontally and vertically, before Round 1 begins.

2. Whenever your group is seated in the inner circle in Rounds 1-4, please code their communication as best you can. You won't catch everything, but it should be a good sample of what occurred. When your group is in the outer circle and during the consultation period, you can reflect on what you observed.

3. When a person speaks to another group member, please code who is speaking to whom and how often by putting a mark in the box that intersects the speaker's name on the side with the target of the communication, whose name is listed along the top. If it is a statement, write down a hatch mark. If it is a question, write down a question mark.

   The way to tell to whom a remark or question is addressed is to watch the eyes of the speaker. If the speaker is clearly making an effort to make eye contact with the whole group while talking (scanning) or is not looking at anyone when speaking, count the target as the "group" as a whole (the first column). Otherwise, count it as a communication directed at the person whom the speaker is looking at *when he or she finished talking.* That person is usually the one we are trying to influence or looking to for support. So even if the person has looked at other people while talking, code the communication in the box of the last person the speaker looked at.

4. Write down any observations you have about the way the group is communicating or functioning on the bottom of the Coder Chart. Does anyone seem left out of the discussion and, if so, why? Is there a dominant person or subgroup that is controlling the communication? Is anyone exhibiting task behavior? Is anyone exhibiting group task or maintenance behaviors?

5. After Round 4, add up the marks vertically and horizontally and prepare your feedback for the group. Stick to observable facts rather than interpreting the data you gathered and remember to deliver the feedback in a nonevaluative fashion so that no one becomes defensive. You can practice this feedback with the other coders while the heterogeneous groups are preparing their presentations.

Coder Chart—Who Speaks to Whom?

Target

Speaker	Group	1	2	3	4	5	6	7	8	9	10	Total
1												
2												
3												
4												
5												
6												
7												
8												
9												
10												
Total												

Code: Statements ⊞⊞   Questions ????
Observations:

LEARNING POINTS

1. To set the stage for successful work teams, organizations require supportive top management, an organizational climate and policies that promote teamwork, teams with a common purpose and specific goals, and supervisors and team members who have the necessary skills to make teams function. Teams need resources, authority and responsability and benefit from group efficacy and shard mental models.

2. To use teams effectively, managers should first determine if a team is the best way to make a decision. Managers also should be concerned with managing the team context, members, task, and process.

3. Managing the team context involves securing resources, managing the team's reputation, and coordinating with other organizational units.

4. Managing team members requires ensuring that members have the appropriate mix of skills, abilities, and other attributes.

5. The five-stage model of group development consists of forming, storming, norming, performing, and adjourning.

6. The punctuated equilibrium model describes group productivity as periods of inertia or equilibrium that are punctuated by a transitional period of radical change that occurs at the midpoint of the group's calendar life. Productivity accelerates again right before the group's time is completed.

7. In any group, there are two types of issues operating at any given time: content and process. Content issues refer to the task, "what" the group is working on. Process issues refer to "how" the group is functioning.

8. Task process focuses on how groups accomplish their work, including setting agendas, figuring out time frames, generating ideas, choosing techniques for making decisions and solving problems, and testing agreement.

9. Maintenance process concerns how groups function with regard to meeting group members' psychological and relationship needs. It includes issues such as leadership, membership, norms, communication, influence, conflict management, and dealing with difficult members and dysfunctional behaviors.

10. By observing communication patterns and decision-making procedures, we can understand better how a group functions.

11. Maintenance behaviors are geared toward creating a good climate for work and good relationships that permit maximum use of member resources. They are gatekeeping, encouraging, harmonizing and compromising, standard setting and testing, and using humor.

12. Task behaviors contribute to accomplishing the group task or goal. They consist of initiating, seeking or giving information or opinions, clarifying and elaborating, summarizing, consensus testing, and orienting.

13. Groups need both maintenance and task behaviors to be effective. Groups that emphasize content and ignore their process are just as likely to fail as groups that emphasize process at the cost of task.

14. Groups can adopt procedures such as structured discussion principles, second solutions, and procedures for generating multiple perspectives to help them be more effective.

15. Self-oriented emotional behavior interferes with effective group functioning. Issues of identity, inclusion, power, acceptance, intimacy, and goal agreement occur and reoccur at various points in a group's development.

16. The "pure types" that represent the three different styles of reducing tension and expressing emotion are:
    a. The "friendly helper" (tender emotions)
    b. The "tough battler" (tough emotions)
    c. The "logical thinker" (denial of all emotions)

17. However, each of these types can only create the type of climate in which they feel most comfortable by incorporating some of the perspectives of the other two types and accepting their dissimilarities.

18. We can learn to use our emotional resources better by:
    a. Accepting our personal feelings.
    b. Trying to understand the feelings that occur in a group.
    c. Trying to identify what causes our emotions to be triggered in a group.
    d. Experimenting with expressing emotion differently and asking for feedback.

19. Group norms are unwritten, often implicit, rules that define the attitudes and behaviors that characterize good and bad group members. All groups have norms. By making them explicit, a group can determine whether its norms help or hinder its effectiveness.

20. Ideally, all members of a group should be participant—observers so everyone can contribute to keeping the group on track and bringing up the need to discuss process issues that may be hindering the group. Group leadership should be performed by more than just the designated leader.

21. Groups that ignore their process often take longer to resolve content issues because process problems prevent commitment and full sharing of information.

22. It takes practice and effort to transform a group into an effective team.

23. Self-managed work teams are not appropriate in all situations, but they can be more effective and satisfying than traditionally managed teams.

24. Virtual teams consist of members who are not colocated. Multicultural teams consist of member who have different ethnic backgrounds but share the same national culture. Multinational teams consist of member who have different nationalities. Each type of team presents its own unique challenges that must be carefully managed.

ACTION SCRIPTS

FOR EMPLOYEES

- Employees who are expert team members understand that team effectiveness is everyone's responsibility. Whether or not they are the designated leader, they ensure that the team stays on track, manages its processes effectively, and performs well.
- They have developed the necessary team process skills as well as their technical skills. Both are crucial for being a successful group member.
- They exercise self discipline and do not disrupt the grap or pursue distracting personal agendas.
- They pay attention to group norms and work to set positive norms. When group norms are not useful, they speak up and initiate a discussion about whether they should be changed.
- They try to influence the team to adopt an effective decision making process and ensure that the team adequately listens to multiple perspectives. Teams are more effective when this is done.

FOR MANAGERS

- Expert managers pay careful attention to the factors that contribute to team effectiveness. In particular, they focus on the following characteristics:
  - Common agreement on high expectations for the team
  - A commitment to common goals
  - Assumed responsibility for work that must be done
  - Honest and open communication
  - Common access to information
  - A climate of trust
  - A general feeling that one can influence what happens

- Support for decisions that are made
- A win-win approach to conflict management
- A focus on process as well as results
- Expert team managers know that groups of employees can have either a positive or negative impact on productivity and the work environment, depending on the norms and stances they have taken. They build cohesion and set positive norms.
- Expert managers recognize that informal leaders of employee work groups are important communication links for getting input, sending out trial balloons, and disseminating information about upcoming plans or events.
- Asking a work group to help establish norms can be very effective. It can be done by asking group members:
  - What would be effective behaviors at work?
  - How should we treat each other at work?
  - How should we make decisions?
  - How should we communicate?
  - Do we have any norms that are keeping us from being effective?
- To avoid the problem of social loafing on a team, experts reward the team on the basis of its results and on the basis of individual contribution to those results. They also make contributions identifiable and design tasks that are intrinsically engaging.
- Managing the group context is a key activity of expert managers. They focus outward as well as inward.
- Expert managers are truly pros at running meetings. They recognize that meetings can be useful when group input into plans or decisions is important. But, they are also careful to avoid unnecessary meetings. When conducting group meetings, they:
  - Prepare an agenda that is distributed beforehand so participants have time to prepare for the meeting
  - Put difficult topics in the middle of the agenda
  - Go over the agenda at the beginning of the meeting and clarify what the group wants to accomplish in the meeting
  - Assign roles: scribe (note taker), timekeeper, secondary facilitator if needed. They rotate the responsibility for chairing the meeting, giving everyone an opportunity to develop leadership skills and see, at the same time, how difficult it is to run a good meeting.
  - Set ground rules with a new group about how the group will work and make decisions, involving the group in the process as much as possible
  - Start and end on time—some groups set time parameters for each issue on the agenda
  - Guide but do not dominate the discussion
  - Encourage participation and listen carefully to all members
  - Encourage the open discussion of ideas and differences while discouraging personal attacks and insults
  - Summarize, at the end of the meeting, what was accomplished and prepare a responsibility chart that describes what needs to be done before the next meeting by whom and by when
  - Circulate the meeting summary within 48 hours of the meeting

FOR ORGANIZATIONAL ARCHITECTS

- Organizational architects who know how to use teams well set the stage by designing a supportive organizational context. Their selection criteria, rewards, performance appraisal, technology, information access, and other procedures are congruent with how teams are used.
- They provide the training necessary for the various types of teams they employ.
- Their top management is committed to teamwork and works to remove obstacles that keep teams from succeeding.
- Organizational architects understand that virtual teams perform better if they have an initital face-to-face meeting that allows them to build trust.

PERSONAL APPLICATION ASSIGNMENT

The face-to-face group working on a problem is the meeting ground of individual personality and society. It is in the group that personality is modified and socialized; and it is through the workings of groups that society is changed and adapted to its times.

Herbert Thelen

The topic of this assignment is to think back on a group experience that was significant for you. Choose an experience that intrigues you and about which you want to learn more. (You may wish to write about one of the exercises your learning group did in this course.)

A. Concrete Experience

　　1. *Objectively* describe the experience (who, what, when, where, how). (2 points)

　　2. *Subjectively* describe your feelings, perceptions, and thoughts that occurred during (not after) the experience. What did others seem to be feeling? (2 points)

B. Reflective Observation

　　1. Looking back at the experience, what were the perspectives of the key actors (including you)? (2 points)

　　2. Why did the people involved (including you) behave as they did? (2 points)

C. Abstract Conceptualization

　　1. Relate concepts or theories from the assigned readings or the lecture to the experience. Explain thoroughly how they apply to your experience. Please apply at least two concepts or theories and cite them correctly. (4 points)

D. Active Experimentation
    1. What did you learn about groups or teams from this experience? (1 point)

    2. What did you learn about yourself? (1 point)

    3. What action steps will you take to be more effective in the future? (2 points)

E. Integration, Synthesis, and Writing
    1. Did you integrate and synthesize the four sections? (1 point)
    2. Was the Personal Application Assignment well written and easy to understand? (1 point)
    3. Was it free of spelling and grammar errors? (2 points)

ENDNOTES

[1] M. Dell, "Building Dell," *Global Agenda* (January 2005): 155.

[2] "Teams," *Training* (October 1996): 64. See also J. R. Hollenbeck, D. S. DeRue, and R. Guzzo, "Bridging the Gap Between I/O Research and HR Practice: Improving Team Composition, Team Training, and Team Task Design," *Human Resource Management*, 43 (2004, Winter): 353–366.

[3] N. R. F. Maier, "Assets and Liabilities in Group Problem Solving: The Need for An Integrative Function," *Psychological Review* 74(4) (1967): 239–249.

[4] M. E. Turner (Ed.). *Groups at Work: Theory and Research* (Mahwah, NJ: Erlbaum, 2001); J. A. F. Stoner, "Risky and Cautious Shifts in Group Decisions: The Influence of Widely Held Values," *Journal of Experimental Social Psychology 4* (1968): 442–459.

[5] J. R. Hackman and R. Wageman, "A Theory of Team Coaching," *Academy of Management Review, 30* (2005): 269–287; and J. R. Hackman, "The Design of Work Team," in J. W. Lorsch (Ed.), *Handbook of Organizational Behavior* (Englewood Cliffs, NJ: Prentice Hall, 1987): 315–342. For a recent review of the team literature, see S. W. J. Kozlowski and D. R. Ilgen, "Enhancing the Effectiveness of Work Groups and Teams," *Psychological Science in the Public Interest* (in press).

[6] See L. Thompson, *Making the Team: A Guide for Managers* (Upper Saddle River, NJ: Prentice Hall, 2004), and S. W. Kozlowski and D. R. Ilgen, "Enhancing the Effectiveness of Work Groups and Teams."

[7] J. R. Katzenback and D. K. Smith, *The Wisdom of Teams* (Cambridge, MA: Harvard Business School Press, 1992).

[8] S. M. Gully, K. A. Incalcaterra, A. Joshi, and J. M. Beaubien, "A Meta-Analysis of Team Efficacy, Potency, and Performance: Interdependence and Level of Analysis as Moderators of Observed Relationships," *Journal of Applied Psychology 87* (2002): 819–832; A. Bandura, "Social Cognitive Theory: An Agentic Perspective," *Annual Review of Psychology 52* (2001):1–27; R. Klimoski and S. Mohammed, "Team Mental Model: Construct or Metaphor," *Journal of Management 20* (1994): 407–437; S. W. J. Kozlowski and D. R. Ilgen, "Enhancing the Effectiveness of Work Groups and Teams;" J. E. Mathieu, T. S. Heffner, G. F. Goodwin, J. A. Cannon-Bowers, and E. Salas, "Scaling the Quality of Teammates' Mental Models: Equifinality and Normative Comparisons," *Journal of Organizational Behavior 26* (2005): 37–56.

[9] D. Gladstein, "Groups in Context: A Model of Task Group Performance," *Administrative Science Quarterly 29* (1984): 499–518; D. Ancona and D. Caldwell, "Bridging the Boundary: External Activity and Performance in Organizational Teams," *Administrative Science Quarterly, 37* (1992): 634–635; D. Ancona, H. Bresman, and K. Kaeufer, "The Comparative Advantage of X-Teams," *MIT Sloan Management Review 43* (2002): 33–39.

[10] M. A. West, *Effective Teamwork: Practical Lessons from Organizational Research* (Oxford, England: Blackwell, 2004); Thompson, *Making the Team: A Guide for Managers*; M. Stevens and M. Campion, "The Knowledge, Skill, and Ability Requirements for Teamwork," *Journal of Management 20* (1994): 503–530.

[11] P. C. Earley, "Social Loafing and Collectivism: A Comparison of the United States and the People's Republic of China," *Administrative Science Quarterly 34* (December 1989): 565–581.

[12] See S. J. Karau and K. D. Williams, "Understanding Individual Motivation in Groups: The Collective Effort Model," in M. E. Turner (Ed.), *Groups at Work: Theory and Research* (Mahwah, NJ: Erlbaum, 2001); B. Latane, "The Psychology of Social Impact," *American Psychologist 36* (1981): 343–356; S. Harkins and K. Szymanski, *Social Loafing and Social Facilitation: Old Wine in New Bottles* (Beverly Hills, CA: Sage, 1987); N. Ellemers, D. de Gilder, and S. A. Haslam, "Motivating Individuals and Groups at Work: A Social Identity Perspective on Leadership and Group Performance," *Academy of Management Review 29*(3) (2004): 459–478.

[13] J. R. Hollenbeck, D. S. DeRue, and R. Guzzo, "Bridging the Gap Between I/O Research and HR Practice: Improving Team Composition, Team Training, and Team Task Design," *Human Resource Management 43* (2004, Winter): 353–366.

[14] For more information on cultural differences in teams, see B. L. Kirkman and D. N. Den Hartog, "Performance Management in Global Teams," in H. W. Lane, M. L. Maznevski, J. E. Mendenhall, and J. McNett (eds.), *Handbook of Global Management: A Guide to Managing Complexity* (Malden, MA: Blackwell, 2004): 250–272 and *The Organizational Behavior Reader*, 2007.

[15] J. Lipman-Blumen and H. J. Leavitt, *Hot Groups* (New York: Oxford, 1999): 25.

[16] West, *Effective Teamwork: Practical Lessons from Organizational Research*, D. R. Ilgen, J. R. Hollenbeck, J. Johnson, and D. Jundt, "Teams in Organizations: From Input-Process-Output to IMOI Models," *Annual Review of Psychology 56* (2005): 517–543; D. A. Harrison, K. Price, J. Gavin, and A. Florey, "Time, Teams, and Task Performance: Changing Effects of Surface and Deep-Level Diversity on Group Functioning," *Academy of Management Journal 45* (2002): 1029–1045.

[17] The literature on group dynamics has grown to enormous proportions. See J. R. Hackman (Ed.), *Groups that Work (and Those that Don't)* (San Francisco: Jossey-Bass, 1990); K. Fisher, *Leading Self-Directed Work Teams* (New York: McGraw-Hill, 1993); A. Zander, *Groups at Work* (San Francisco: Jossey-Bass, 1977) and *Making Groups Effective* (San Francisco: Jossey-Bass, 1982); and Turner, *Groups at Work: Theory and Research*, 2001.

[18] B. W. Tuckman and M. C. Jensen, "Stages of Small Group Development Revisited," *Group and Organizational Studies 2* (4) (December 1977): 419–427; J. D. Rothwell, *In Mixed Company: Small Group Communication* (Fort Worth, TX: Harcourt Brace Jovanovich, 1992); and M. F. Maples, "Group Development: Extending Tuckman's Theory," *Journal for Specialists in Group Work 13*(1) (1988): 7–23.

[19] Groupthink is not as pervasive as the popular literature might lead us to believe. One form of groupthink tends to occur when highly cohesive groups face a collective threat that questions the group identity. See M. E. Turner and A. R. Pratkanis, "A Social Identity Maintenance Theory of Groupthink," *Organizational Behavior and Human Decision Processes 73* (1998): 210–235. For a review, see M. E. Turner and A. R. Pratkanis, "Twenty-Five Years of Groupthink Research: Lessons from the Evolution of a Theory," *Organizational Behavior and Human Decision Processes 73* (1998): 105–115.

[20] C. G. Gersick, "Time and Transition in Work Teams: Toward a New Model of Group Development," *Academy of Management Journal 31* (1) (March 1988): 9–41; and C. G. Gersick, "Marking Time: Predictable Transitions in Task Groups," *Academy of Management Journal 32* (2) (June 1989): 274–309.

[21] For a discussion of the differences between content and process issues, see E. H. Schein, *Process Consultation: Its Role in Organizational Development* (Reading, MA: Addison-Wesley, 1988) and *Process Consultation Revisited: Building the Helping Relationship* (Reading, MA: Addison-Wesley, 1998).

[22] Much of the following material has appeared in a variety of places and is a standard input into many training programs such as those conducted by the National Training Laboratory. This particular material was abridged with permission of the author from "What to Observe in Groups," from *Reading Book for Relation Training,* C. R. Mill and L. C. Porter (Eds.), (Arlington, VA: NTL Institute, 1982), 28–30; and B. E. Collins and H. Guestzkow, *A Social Psychology of Group Processes for Decision Making* (New York: John Wiley, 1964).

[23] This typology was developed by R. R. Blake.

[24] M. E. Turner and A. R. Pratkanis, "A Social Identity Maintenance Theory of Groupthink," *Organizational Behavior and Human Decision Processes, 73* (1998): 210–235; M. E. Turner and A. R. Pratkanis, "Mitigating Groupthink by Stimulating Constructive Conflict," in C. De Dreu and E. Van de Vliert (Eds.), *Using Conflict In Organizations* (London and Thousand Oaks, CA: Sage, 1997): 38–52.

[25] D. Cartwright and A. Zander, *Group Dynamics: Research and Theory* (Evanston, IL: Row, Peterson, 1953).

[26] S. E. Seashore, *Group Cohesiveness in the Industrial Work Group* (Ann Arbor: University of Michigan, 1954); M. E. Shaw, *Group Dynamics* (3rd ed.). (New York: McGraw-Hill, 1981); M. E. Shaw and L. M. Shaw, "Some Effects of Sociometric Grouping upon Learning in a Second Grade Classroom," *Journal of Social Psychology 57* (1962): 453–458.

[27] Shaw, *Group Dynamics*; West, *Effective Teamwork: Practical Lessons from Organizational Research* (Oxford, England: Blackwell, 2004); Thompson, *Making the Team: A Guide for Managers.*

[28] K. D. Benne and P. Sheats, "Functional Roles of Group Members," *Journal of Social Issues 2* (1948): 42–47; and E. H. Schein, *Process Consultation* and *Process Consultation Revisited.*

[29] This section is based on Schein's *Process Consultation.* For another view of emotional behavior in groups, see W. C. Schutz, "Interpersonal Underworld," *Harvard Business Review, 36*(4) (July–August 1958): 123–125, and W. W. Liddell and J. W. Slocum, Jr., "The Effects of Individual Role Compatibility upon Group Performance: An Extension of Schutz's FIRO Theory," *Academy of Management Journal 19* (1976): 413–426.

[30] One such process for learning how to work more effectively in groups is called broadly "laboratory training." For a full discussion of this and related educational techniques, see E. H. Schein and W. G. Bennis, *Personal and Organizational Change Through Group Methods: The Laboratory Approach* (New York: John Wiley, 1965).

[31] Ibid.

[32] For good descriptions of team building, see W. G. Dyer, *Team Building: Proven Strategies for Improving Team Performance (4th ed.)* (San Francisco: Jossey-Bass 2007); and R. Fry, I. Rubin, and M. Plovnik, "Dynamics of Groups that Execute or Manage Policy," in R. Payne and C. Cooper (Eds.), *Groups at Work* (New York: John Wiley, 1981), 41–57.

[33] R. Beckhard, "Optimizing Team-Building Efforts," *Journal of Contemporary Business 1*(3) (Summer 1972): 23–32.

[34] C. C. Manz, and C. P. Neck, "Teamthink: Beyond the Groupthink Syndrome in Self-Managing Work Teams," *Journal of Managerial Psychology, 10*(1) (1995): 7–16.

[35] S. G. Cohen and G. E. Ledford, Jr., "The Effectiveness of Self Managing Teams in Service and Support Functions: A Field Experiment," paper presented at the Academy of Management annual meeting, San Francisco, August 1990. See R. A. Guzzo, and M. W. Dickson, "Teams in Organizations: Recent Research on Performance and Effectiveness," *Annual Review of Psychology 47* (1996): 307–339. For a discussion of team empowerment and group effectiveness, see J. Mathieu, L. Gibson, and T. Ruddy, "Empowerment and Team Effectiveness: An Empirical Test of an Integrated Model," *Journal of Applied Psychology 91* (2006): 97-208.

[36] J. Lipnack and J. Stamps, *Virtual Teams* (New York: John Wiley & Sons, 1997): 7.

[37] G. Hertel, S. Geister and U. Koradt, "Managing Virtual Teams: A Review of Current Empirical Research," *Human Resource Management Review 15*(1) (March 2005): 69–95; S. Furst, M. Reeves, B. Rosen, and R. Blackburn, "Managing the Life Cycle of Virtual Teams," *Academy of Management Executive, 18*(2) (2004): 6–20; C. Gibson, "Virtuality and Collaboration in Teams," in J. Osland, D. Kolb, I. Rubin, and M. Turner (Eds.), *The Organizational Behavior Reader* (Upper Saddle River, NJ: Prentice Hall, 2007).

[38] C. P. Earley and C. B. Gibson, *Multinational Work Teams: A New Perspective* (Mahwah, NJ: Lawrence Erlbaum Associates, 2002).

[39] V. Govindarajan and A. K. Gupta, "Building an Effective Global Business Team," *MIT Sloan Management Review, 42*(4) (2001): 63–72.

[40] See Lipman-Blumen and Leavitt, *Hot Groups,* for an explanation and description of exciting, successful teams.

[41] Adapted from R. W. Napier and M. K. Gershenfeld, *Making Groups Work: A Guide for Group Leaders* (Boston: Houghton Mifflin, 1983), 114–120. Reprinted with permission.

Chapter 11

▲▲

PROBLEM SOLVING

OBJECTIVES By the end of this chapter, you should be able to:

A. Explain the four stages of problem solving.

B. Describe the red/green modes of problem solving.

C. Identify the different roles a facilitator or manager plays during the problem solving process.

D. Learn how to facilitate a problem-solving meeting.

E. Explain Six Sigma and Appreciative Inquiry.

Why Not?

IDEAS WAITING TO HAPPEN

While some people claim that the route to innovation is indescribable, we believe there's often a simple, recurrent structure to creative thinking. Most original ideas aren't completely original, but instead are the result of two basic things: problems in search of solutions and solutions in search of problems.

Both approaches have their advantages. If this seems odd, think of television game shows. *Who Wants to Be a Millionaire* looks for the right answer, while *Jeopardy!* starts with the answer and looks for the right question.

Once a problem has been identified, how do you go about finding a solution? Watching your customers is a fine place to start. Rather than invent a new solution from scratch, you can take the imperfect, often Rube Goldberg* solutions that people have already found and improve on them.

But consumer watching has its limits. While the unexpected reaction of consumers often signals that something is wrong with a product, there are many problems customers cannot solve on their own. This is because real-world consumers have limited resources.

So an alternative tool is to ask how an unconstrained consumer would solve the problem. We call this approach "What would Croesus** do?" as a shorthand for imagining solutions where price is no object. These may lead you to a solution that is affordable.

In his day, Howard Hughes had a Croesus-like flair for spending money to find solutions to problems. Imagine that it's 1966 and that you're Hughes. You sometimes have a hankering to watch old Bogart films. Unfortunately, the VCR has yet to be invented. What do you do?

Hughes bought a Las Vegas television station and used it as his private VCR. Whenever he wanted, he'd call up the station's general manager and tell him what movie to put on that night. We understand that the station played a lot of *Casablanca* and *The Maltese Falcon*.

---

*Rube Goldberg was a famous cartoonist known for drawing tremendously complex devices that perform simple tasks in convoluted ways.

**King Croesus ruled over Lydia in Western Asia Minor (now Turkey) from 560 to 546 BC. The expression "as rich as Croesus" was based on his legendary wealth. The Lydians were the first people to mint coins.

In this spirit, our "What would Croesus do?" approach begins by imagining a customized and very expensive solution. We don't begin with a view that the solution has to be practical. Instead, we ask: Are there any solutions at all?

Problem: Having to wait on hold at a customer service number Donald Trump or Bill Gates wouldn't spend much time on hold. They would have an assistant stay on the line and buzz them when the call goes through.

Mere mortals can't afford personal assistants. Is there any way ordinary folks could emulate this "personal assistant" strategy? Well, yes. Instead of waiting on hold to speak with an airline customer representative, why not have the airline call you back? With caller ID, you wouldn't even have to enter your number. Waiting on hold is not only a pain for the caller but also expensive for the company if it's paying for a toll-free line.

Huge sums are being spent right now on technology to move telephone support centers to low-wage countries. We invite airlines and other corporations to think about applying a little technology to the problem of making your customers less irate.

Problem: Cash management for the household Your checking account earns next to no interest, yet you may be paying 6 percent on your mortgage. Why don't you just take all your cash and prepay your mortgage? That way you would effectively earn an extra 6 percent on your money. Unfortunately, this proposal is impractical. You need to have some cash to pay bills and cover emergencies. If you put all of your money into your mortgage, you couldn't get it back when you needed it.

A modern Croesus—or any sizable corporation—could solve the liquidity problem by employing an assistant to do sophisticated cash management, using money market funds and a standby credit line. Ordinary folk can get the same result only by spending an inordinate amount of time shuffling balances back and forth. But what if the bank were willing to help out? What if the bank set up a combined mortgage/checking account that charges the homeowner only for the net indebtedness? A person with a $200,000 mortgage and a $10,000 checking balance would be charged mortgage interest only on $190,000.

If you are a retail banker, your first instinct is to reject the idea. Your profitability hangs on having a certain number of customers with idle cash balances. Why give the homeowner an easy means to shrink checking balances or to prepay high-rate mortgages? But think about all the time customers squander right now trying to manage their cash. Wouldn't it be possible to price the combo account in such a way that the bank is as profitable as before but the customer is still happy because he has been spared a lot of paperwork?

In 1997, Richard Branson's Virgin teamed up with AMP and the Royal Bank of Scotland to offer the Virgin One account, which nets cash balances against mortgage debt. Your salary is electronically deposited into this account. Any checks you write or credit card charges you incur are taken out of the account, thereby increasing your outstanding mortgage.

By late 2001, Virgin One had 70,000 customers. Today it's a very successful mortgage product in England. This creative idea was worth money. The Royal Bank of Scotland bought out Virgin and AMP's combined 50 percent share for $150 million in July 2001.

The combo account has come at long last to these shores. Wells Fargo launched a similar product in October 2002 and claims that it is its most successful product launch.

Sometimes it isn't helpful to start the problem-solving process by identifying a problem. The solution has to come first. Only after we've discovered a better way do we realize in retrospect that there was a problem to be solved. Take an existing solution and find a new application.

Solution: Round-the-clock rental start times Avis rents cars 24 hours a day, starting any time of the day (or night). What's the new application—that is, what other rentals should be flexible with the starting time? Anyone who's landed in Europe on an overnight flight can answer this question: hotel rooms. You arrive at 7:00 a.m. and want to shower and change, but it's six hours until check-in time.

Hotels would have to make an effort to provide this convenience. Coordinating room cleanings should be more challenging. And reservations would have to include a check-in time to ensure that a room would be available. But if Avis can program its computers to handle the problem, surely Sheraton can, too. Some airport hotels have begun offering this service. We think that some city center hotels should follow suit, perhaps dedicating one floor for this service.

Solution: Inflation-indexed bonds The U.S. Treasury protects you from unanticipated inflation by offering TIPS, or Treasury Inflation-Protected Securities. What else could be indexed? Municipal bonds. This has been done only a handful of times. They would be immensely attractive to investors who worry about both inflation and taxes. Right now investors in TIPS still face the risk of uncertain taxes on their returns because federal tax is due on both the real return (now about 2 percent) and the inflation kicker. If inflation hits 8 percent and the bonds start paying 10 percent, your aftertax, net-of-inflation return will be in the neighborhood of negative 1.5 percent. A state offering an indexed return could probably offer a real return not much more than 1 percent to 2 percent and still get a lot of takers.

Solution: Battery-operated spinners The Spin Pop, introduced in 1993, was one of the most successful new interactive candy launches ever. More than 85 million of these motorized lollipop holders have been sold worldwide. Hold your tongue steady and spin the candy against it. Now, what other question does the Spin Pop answer? After roaming the aisles of Wal-Mart, the Spin Pop creators found the right question: how to drive down the price of the electric toothbrush. Spin Pop gave birth to SpinBrush. In a little under four years John Osher and others turned a $1.5 million investment into a $475 million payout when Procter & Gamble bought them out.

Sometimes flipping things around provides a useful solution to a different problem. What we call symmetry takes an existing solution in a given context and turns it around to get a new perspective. Inflation-indexed bonds are a great idea. Turn this around. Would it also work to borrow at an inflation-indexed rate? This flip leads us to the inflation-indexed mortgage. Each year your payments go up with the rate of inflation. In countries with high inflation, such loans are standard. Even with low inflation, such as the 2 percent in the United States, these loans would allow people to borrow up to 50 percent more or to start off with payments that are a third less. Young families could suddenly afford to buy a lot bigger house.

For the most part, people find an answer that works and don't get in the habit of looking for an even better solution. Or we think there is some natural way of doing things and stop looking for alternatives.

Take the ketchup bottle. Did you ever store one upside down in order to make it flow faster? How long did it take for Hunt's and H.J. Heinz to figure out they could turn the label upside down? According to Heinz's Casey Keller, the change was no small matter: "We believe this is probably the biggest idea in ketchup since the invention of the plastic squeeze bottle." In the old days Heinz used Carly Simon's "Anticipation" in its marketing. The updated campaign is "No wait. No mess. No anticipation." Ketchup is not the only product to take advantage of this insight: Toothpaste, shampoo and even sour cream are now available upside down.

Coming up with a great idea is only the beginning of the battle. If you really want to change your company or the world, you need to sell the idea and you need others to buy in. In pitching an idea, try to make it familiar. It's hard enough for listeners to absorb a radically new idea. Don't make them also absorb a new context. Colgate has applied this rule brilliantly with its new Simply White tooth-whitening gel. The home-use tooth whitener is an unfamiliar product. Yet the Colgate product evokes a strong déjà vu—its packaging bears a powerful resemblance to that for Wite-Out, the familiar typo corrector.

Got a good idea? Don't get carried away with secrecy. If you can't make money on it yourself, share it The open-source movement in software development shows that a dispersed community of code writers can succeed in developing interlocking products that are free to the world.

We propose an open-source movement for everyday ingenuity. If you generate valuable ideas, even ones that seem to speak for themselves, you are likely to be in demand to help put them into practice. Being known as an idea person tends to pay big rewards in our society. Instead of hoarding ideas in hopes of a killer payoff, put the ideas out there and see what happens.

Join us in cyberspace at http://www.whynot.net. Add your ideas, come for inspiration and come to react to other people's ideas. We'll write about the best submissions in our FORBES column. We'll also challenge industry leaders to respond to your ideas: Why haven't they already put these ideas into practice, or why won't they?

Source: The preceding is adapted from *Why Not? How to Use Everyday Ingenuity to Solve Problems Big and Small*, by Barry Nalebuff and Ian Ayres. Reprinted by permission of Harvard Business School Press. Copyright 2003 by Barry Nalebuff and Ian Ayres. All Rights Reserved. *CreativityAtWork Newsletter*, January 2004.

CLASS PREPARATION

A. Read "Why Not?" and the following "Cardiotronics, Inc." case.

B. While reading the chapter, make a list of cues that you should look for with regard to problem solving.

C. Role-Play Preparation. Make a plan to conduct tomorrow's meeting of Assembly team D as if you were Marion Andrews. Write in the space below your planned introduction to begin the meeting. What can you say to get it off to a good start and ensure a productive problem-solving session? Then develop a list of questions that Marion can use to facilitate and lead the Cardiotronics team through each stage of Kolb's problem-solving model described in the chapter. What kinds of questions would facilitate good problem solving during the visioning stage, the priority-setting stage, and so on? For example, in the visioning stage, Marion could ask: "What would be the ideal situation here?"

What will you say to the team to get this meeting off to a good start? Your Introduction for the Cardiotronics Assembly Team D Meeting:

Write your facilitation questions for each stage below:

1. Visioning/Exploration

2. Priority Setting

3. Information Gathering

4. Problem Definition

5. Idea Getting

6. Decision Making

7. Participation

8. Planning

CARDIOTRONICS, INC.

Cardiotronics, Inc., was started 17 years ago in a small New Hampshire town by two bio-medical engineers whose goal was to produce a quality cardiac monitor (a device that continuously displays the wave pattern of the heart's function). The company originally produced customized monitors on a small scale. After five years, the owners had perfected a quality monitor that was significantly less expensive than custom monitors, and they decided to mass produce it.

The company currently has just over 200 employees. It remains nonunionized, but the labor union in this old New England milltown has from time to time made efforts to win a union election. For the past 11 years, the company has enjoyed a strong competitive edge and has gained a reputation for a quality product and prompt service. Recently, however, the company's top-management team has been informed that a similar monitor, reputed to be of equal or better quality than Cardiotronics', will soon be introduced into the U.S. market by a large Japanese electronics firm.

Monitor Assembly Process   The cardiac monitors (excluding cables) are produced in four stages. In the first stage, circuit boards are produced largely by a machine process. During the second stage, the circuit boards are placed by hand on a motherboard and are connected to one another. The final step in stage 2 is the attachment of the motherboard to the base panel. In the third stage, the casing is mounted by hand onto the base panel and external hardware and cables are placed. In the final stage, the monitors are tested for a week before shipping.

The Second-Stage Assembly Task   Four assembly teams are responsible for the second stage of monitor assembly, the manual assembly and the wiring of the motherboard. Each team consists of five workers operating in a U-shaped area. The motherboard is started at station 1. Each worker adds his or her circuit, connects it to the others, and passes it to the next worker. The assembly process requires some manual dexterity but is relatively easy to do. Each job on the line is of equal difficulty as determined by a recent industrial engineering study. The assembly arrangement for one of these teams, Team D, is as follows.

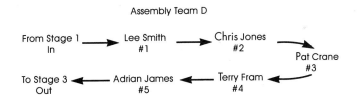

Assembly Team D

The following are the recently announced assembly team average daily production figures for the last month:

- Team A = 40 boards
- Team B = 32 boards
- Team C = 43 boards
- Team D = 35 boards

Your Problem as Marion Andrews, Supervisor of Team D   You are the new supervisor of Team D. You have been in the position for a month, having recently been promoted from the quality control section where you worked for five years. During your second week, you received a memo stating that all second-stage teams have to meet their minimum daily production rates. You passed on this information to the team in a brief meeting but had to leave for a week of supervisory training shortly thereafter. After returning from the training program, you note that the daily production has increased to 36, but your team is still 4 units below the daily minimum rate of 40 units. In looking into the problem you note the following:

- Work accumulates at Pat Crane's station #3 where there are typically several motherboards waiting. Pat is 58 years old and has been with the company for 13 years. The supervisors of the other production teams do not consider Pat acceptable for transfer.
- Only one monitor from your team has been rejected in the past month by quality control, a better quality record than the other teams have.
- Your team's assembly and test equipment is relatively new and in good working order.

Team D's assembly line will be closed for 30 minutes tomorrow, and you have decided to call a meeting for Team D. How will you conduct this meeting? Use the guidelines in the Class Preparation to think through what you will say.

THE KNOWLEDGE BASE

No problem can be solved from the same level of consciousness that created it.

Albert Einstein

For many scholars who study organizations and management, the central characteristic of organizations is that they are problem-solving systems whose success is measured by how efficiently they solve the routine problems associated with accomplishing their primary mission—be it manufacturing automobiles or selling insurance—and how effectively they respond to the emergent problems and opportunities associated with survival and growth in a changing world. Kilmann's view is representative of this perspective:

> *One might even define the essence of management as problem defining and problem solving, whether the problems are well structured, ill structured, technical, human, or even environmental. Managers of organizations would then be viewed as problem managers, regardless of the types of products and services they help their organizations provide. It should be noted that managers have often been considered as generic decision makers rather than as problem solvers or problem managers. Perhaps decision making is more akin to solving well-structured problems where the nature of the problem is so obvious that one can already begin the process of deciding among clear-cut alternatives. However, decisions cannot be made effectively if the problem is not yet defined and if it is not at all clear what the alternatives are, can, or should be.*[1]

In this view, the core task of management is problem solving. Views on problem solving, however, have expanded due to two major changes. First, more organizations are looking not at problems but at opportunities and what they do best. The discussion on Appreciative Inquiry is an example of this trend. Second, problem solving has been delegated in many organizations to employees, starting with employee involvement groups and total quality management to Six Sigma and project teams. Problem-solving techniques are now taught at all levels in companies that have a continuous improvement orientation. In addition to profiting from their ideas, involving employees in problem solving empowers them, gains their commitment to solutions, and develops their management skills.

General Electric's Work-Out program is a prime example of an organization-wide effort at involving employees in problem solving. Large companies have many competitive advantages due to their size. Unless they take special measures, however, they can also become inefficient, resistant-to-change bureaucracies characterized by rigid functional silos. GE addressed this danger with Work-Out, a program designed to cut through bureaucracy and across boundaries to solve problems fast with the help of people at all levels of the company. First, a large group of employees address a concern, a "target opportunity," identified by employees or senior management. Next, cross-functional and cross-level teams come up with recommendations. Finally, the teams present the recommendations to senior management who discusses the recommendations with them and, on the spot, accepts or rejects them. (This is similar to the action learning that takes place in the "Women and Global Leadership at Bestfoods" case, at the end of this book.) Work-Out has saved GE over $100 million.[2] Although it was designed to counter the disadvantages of a large bureaucracy, Work-Out has also been used successfully in small firms.

Groups are used in solving complex problems when no one person has all the necessary information, skills, and diverse perspectives. Other people contribute new dreams, new ideas, information, and help in getting things done. As such, problem solving is not just a mental puzzle but also a social process that requires communication, perception, creativity, conflict management, and group and facilitation skills. Employees at all levels are more likely to be committed to implementing the solutions to problems if they have participated in the problem solving process. Therefore, the decision about who is invited to problem solving groups is critical. As a general rule, those who are likely to be critical in the implementation stage of a solution should be members of the problem solving team, along with those who have the most knowledge about the situation and the most power to change it.

A MODEL OF PROBLEM SOLVING

Some of the frequent mistakes people make in problem solving are failing to see the potential opportunities in problems, leaping too quickly to discussing potential solutions before completely analyzing the problem, and not focusing enough on implementation issues. The Kolb model of problem solving as a dialectical process[3] shown in Exhibit 11–1 is designed to prevent these mistakes. This structured approach to problem solving is designed to facilitate a thorough consideration of complex problems. This is a normative model, which means that it shows how a process is done ideally. Not surprisingly, the model is based on Kolb's theory of experiential learning found in Chapter 3. It consists of four analytical stages that correspond to the four stages of the experiential learning cycle: Stage 1, situation analysis, corresponds to concrete experience; Stage 2, problem analysis, to reflective observation; Stage 3, solution analysis, to abstract conceptualization; and Stage 4, implementation analysis, to active experimentation. These four stages form a nested sequence of activities in that each stage requires the solution of a particular analytical task to frame the succeeding stage properly. The major focus of each stage is captured in these questions:

Situation Analysis: What's the Most Important Problem?
Problem Analysis: What Are the Causes of the Problem?
Solution Analysis: What's the Best Solution?
Implementation Analysis: How Do We Implement the Solution?

The stages will be described in depth after we introduce another key element of the model, the dialectics of problem solving.

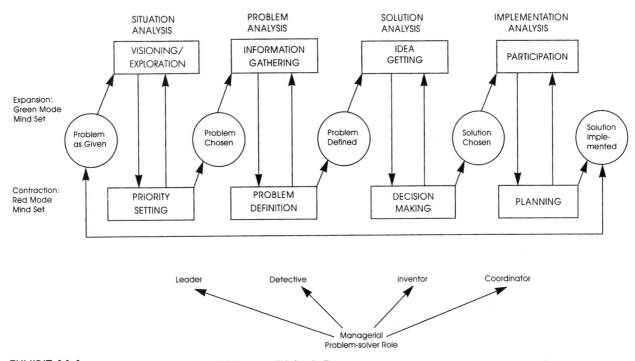

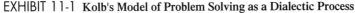

EXHIBIT 11-1 **Kolb's Model of Problem Solving as a Dialectic Process**

THE DIALECTICS OF PROBLEM SOLVING

The process of problem solving does not proceed in a logical, linear fashion from beginning to end. Instead, it is characterized by wavelike expansions and contractions alternatively moving outwardly to gather and consider alternatives, information, and ideas and inwardly to focus, evaluate, and decide. These expansions and contractions have been variously labeled as doubting/believing, green light/red light, and divergence/convergence.

Elbow's[4] description of "doubting" and "believing" games is one way to conceptualize the two different mind-sets required for problem solving. The first rule of the believing game is that people refrain from doubting or evaluating and instead focus on possibilities and how an idea could work. In contrast, the doubting game focuses on a reductive, structured, "objective" rationality. People with this orientation are constantly asking, "What's wrong with this?" As a result, they poke holes in ideas and arguments, torpedo assumptions, and probe in an analytical manner. Thus, problem solving is not the result of a single mental function such as logical thinking. Effective problem solving involves the integration of dialectically opposed mental orientations—these are often referred to as red- and green-mode mind-sets.

The green-mode mind-set facilitates creative imagination, sensitivity to the immediate situation, and empathy with other people. The green-mode mind-set encompasses the expansion phases of problem solving—visioning/exploration, information gathering, idea getting, and participation. The red-mode mind-set, by contrast, facilitates analysis, criticism, logical thinking, and active coping with the external environment. The red-mode mind-set is, therefore, most appropriate for the contraction phases of problem solving—priority setting in situation analysis, problem definition in problem analysis, decision making in solution analysis, and planning in implementation analysis. Effectiveness in problem solving is enhanced by approaching the expansion/contraction phases of each problem-solving stage in the appropriate mind-set. For problem solvers to accomplish this matching of mind-set and problem-solving task, they must first become aware of when they are in the red or green mode of consciousness and then learn to shift from one mode to the other. With some practice, this can be accomplished quite easily; practice in identifying and separating the two mind-sets usually has the effect of increasing the intensity of both modes. Managing the problem-solving process with groups of people requires the creation of a climate that stimulates and reinforces the appropriate mind-set in participants as they move through each of the stages described in the following section.

The problem-solving process is further guided by four roles that focus the dialectic interplay of red and green mind-sets on the relevant stage of the problem-solving process. In situation analysis, the problem solver adopts the role of a leader, focused on identifying goals and values in the situation in the green mode and setting priorities in the red mode. In problem analysis, the role is that of a detective, focused on gathering information in the green mode and building and evaluating models in the red mode. In solution analysis, the role is that of an inventor, generating ideas in the green mode and testing their feasibility in the red mode. In implementation analysis, the problem solver adopts the coordinator role, developing participation in the green mode and planning in the red mode. Conscious attention to these roles serves to focus attention on the priorities of each stage and signals the transition from one stage to another. We describe the stages of the problem solving model in more detail in the next sections. As you read through the discussion, think about how each of the roles comes into play during the various stages.

Situation Analysis—Visioning/Exploration and Priority Setting

In the situation analysis stage, our task is to examine the immediate situational context to determine the right problem to tackle. While problem-solving activity is often initiated by urgent symptomatic pressures, urgency alone is not a sufficient criterion for choosing which problems to address. As every manager knows, the press of urgent problems can easily divert attention from more important but less pressing long-term problems and opportunities. In reality, urgent problems are often the result of long-term unstructured problems that have never been addressed. For example, the continued urgent need to replace data entry clerks in a bank may result from the failure to address problems of low worker morale and lack of career opportunities within the organization. In this example, hiring to fill clerk vacancies is a structured problem, while low morale and the lack of a career ladder are unstructured problems. *Structured problems are repetitive and routine, and definite procedures are developed for dealing with them. Unstructured problems are novel and not covered by ready-made procedures because they occur infrequently or are very complex.* Situation analysis requires exploration to identify the problem that takes precedence by criteria of both urgency and importance. This is what is meant by the popular saying, "Managers do things right; leaders do the right thing." Problem finding is equally as important as problem solving. As Kaplan described it, "The manager gives form to a problem in the way a potter sees and then shapes the possibilities in a lump of clay. The difference is that managers practice their craft using an intangible medium: information."[5] For organizations in rapidly changing environments, aggressive opportunity seeking is essential to maintain stability and growth. Careful situation analysis is, therefore, most critical in those cases in which long-term adaptation to a changing environment takes precedence over expedient action.

Visioning/exploration The visioning/exploration stage of the situation analysis is concerned with envisioning what is possible. When people discuss problems, they devote time to talking about how they would like the situation to be. For example, the technique of visioning involves asking people to close their eyes and imagine their ideal organization or program. This reflects the green mode (whereas the exploration of current realities represents the red mode). The process of articulating desired goal states is called visioning. A common error at this substage is to simply accept a problem as given, without considering the opportunities it may hold. For example, a hospital was scheduled to undergo its accreditation review process, which demands a good deal of time and effort. Rather than view this solely as a burdensome bureaucratic requirement, the administration chose to see it as an opportunity to improve both service and efficiency. Framing the situation as an opportunity rather than a burden changed the problems they chose to tackle.

To be successful, the visioning process must overcome barriers that exist in some organizational settings. Foremost among these barriers is the organizational press to be realistic. Wishing, wanting, and visioning must be explored independently of reality for them to develop fully. Charles Lindblom[6] noted some time ago that it is easier to find agreement on a course of action than it is to get agreement on the goals for the action. Goals are a reflection of our values, and the discussion of values accentuates human individuality and emotional commitment with a resulting increase in conflicting viewpoints. In the dialectic view, such conflict is essential for the discovery of truth. Many managers, however, shy away from conflict because it is unpleasant and they do not know how to use disagreement constructively. A related barrier to visioning is the threat of isolation that comes from holding values or opinions that are different from those of the majority. This barrier gives rise to conformity and groupthink in problem finding.[7] A worker, for example, may suppress his or her genuine values for achievement and excellence so as not to violate group norms of mediocrity. For this reason an effective visioning process requires an environment that gives security and support for individuality. The result of visioning is a menu of problems and opportunities. The group may choose one that satisfies the decision criteria of both urgency and importance.

Priority Setting The contrasting pole to visioning in the situation analysis dialectic is priority setting. As with any dialectic, visioning and priority setting mutually enhance one another—visioning gives direction and energy to priority setting and priority setting gives substance and reality to visioning. Every managerial decision reflects values; choosing one problem as a priority reveals the values of the decision makers. Priority setting has three specific tasks: (1) to explore the current situation for those features that facilitate or hinder goal achievement, (2) to test the feasibility of changing those features, and (3) to articulate reality-based goal statements that give substance to values and allow them to be realized. Priority setting is not a rational, analytic process of reflective planning. It is an active, intuitive process of trial-and-error exploration of what is going on in the situation. It involves "knocking on doors," listening to people, trying things out, and taking risks.

Taken as a whole, the central issue in situation analysis is leadership, and the basic social role of the problem solver is that of a leader whose responsibility is to guide the attention of the organization to those problems and opportunities whose solution will be of maximum benefit to the long-run effectiveness of the organization. Someone once said that the key to successful leadership is to find out which way people are going and then run out in front of them. There is an element of truth in this, for the successful leader in situation analysis identifies the values and goals involved and then holds up those that are most important as priorities for action. The priority that is chosen should be phrased in very specific terms as a goal that can measured, for example, "Reduce cycle time for grant-proposal process by 20 percent within six weeks." In many instances, this stage identifies the gap between the ideal state and the current reality, the creative tension[8] that motivates people to take action. Once a problem or a target opportunity has been chosen, the group can move on to the next stage in the process.

PROBLEM ANALYSIS—INFORMATION GATHERING AND PROBLEM DEFINITION

The task of problem analysis is to understand and define the problem thoroughly. Common errors at this stage are defining the problem in terms of its solution or confusing symptoms with the problem's root cause. For example, the statement that "Our problem is not having enough meetings" probably indicates that one or both of these errors have been made (or maybe just insanity). A careful analysis of the problem may indicate that more of meetings is just one of several alternate solutions and lack of meetings is a symptom of a larger problem (e.g., overwork, a staff that does not get along). Without an accurate problem definition, the right solution cannot be identified.

Information Gathering In the expansion mode of problem analysis, the group makes an effort to gather all the necessary information surrounding the chosen problem. This is a receptive, open-minded phase in which information associated with the problem is sought and accepted.

Depending on the type of problem that has been chosen, this phase can involve a wide range of activities: talking with people familiar with the problem, running statistics, looking at policies and procedures, or brainstorming with groups about things that get in the way of progress. Information-gathering has both a cognitive and interpersonal component. Cognitively, it is important to avoid biases and preconceptions about the nature of the problem and its causes in favor of letting the data "speak for itself." Interpersonally, information gathering requires skills in developing trusting relationships so that others do not hold back or modify information to say "what the boss wants to hear" or to avoid reprisals. In many organizations, these two components negatively interact with one another to produce a climate that makes it difficult to gather accurate information. Mistrust and threat cause workers to withhold information, and this sometimes forces management to rely on its own preconceived notions about the nature of problems. In this sub-stage, facts have to be separated from opinion, so that the eventual solution will be data-driven and based on solid ground rather than assumptions.

Problem Definition In the contraction mode of problem analysis, the task is to define the problem based on the information gathered. Problem definition is basically a process of building a model portraying how the problem works—factors that cause the problem, factors that increase or decrease the strength of the problem, connections and relationships among elements, and symptoms of the problem. Complex problems usually need to be drawn visually so that everyone can follow the relationships. The resulting model of the problem separates out relevant and irrelevant information about the problem. Because it contains the factors and perhaps criteria that need to be managed to solve the problem, this problem definition guides the next stage, solution analysis. A task force at a community housing agency was trying to figure out why some of its grant proposals were not being funded. Some employees blamed the new grant writer. However, after interviewing everyone involved, including the funding agencies, the task force determined that the poor quality of certain grant proposals was due primarily to last-minute information from some programs. As a result, the grant writer did not have enough time to double check facts and intentions or to proofread all grants carefully before they were sent off. The task force then set off to gather more information to learn why some program heads did not respect the proposal deadlines. Apparently, the agency director had not communicated the financial importance of the grants to all program heads, so the grant writer's requests were viewed as less important than serving clients. These middle managers were never reprimanded for failing to collaborate with the grant writer. Finally, the grant writer was a new employee in a new position, whom these particular program heads perceived as having little power and influence. This model of the factors in the grant funding problem tells us what has to be included in the solutions chosen in the next stage.

The problem solver in the problem analysis stage takes on the role of detective—gathering clues and information about how the "crime" was committed, organizing these clues into a scenario of "who done it," and using that scenario to gather more information to prove or disprove the original hunch. The output of the problem analysis phase is a model of the problem validated through the interplay of information gathering and problem definition. Only when the problem has been thoroughly analyzed and defined is the group ready to begin thinking about solutions in the next stage.

SOLUTION ANALYSIS—IDEA GETTING AND DECISION MAKING

Solution analysis is achieved through the interplay between getting ideas about how the problem can be solved and decision making about the feasibility of the ideas generated. A common error in this stage is failing to separate the two stages of generating and evaluating ideas.

Idea Getting The expansive first phase of solution analysis focuses on creative imagination. Brainstorming is the most common technique used to produce an unstructured free-association of ideas. *Brainstorming is the generation of as wide a range of potential solutions as possible in an atmosphere that is free from criticism and evaluation.* The ban on evaluation is important to stimulate participation and creativity. Comments like these impede brainstorming: "That won't work." "That's too radical." "We've never done it that way before." "That's not practical." Common errors in this substage are assuming that there is only one right answer, getting "stuck" or attached to the first solution that arises and failing to consider other solutions (somewhat like the primacy effect in perceptual distortions), and being so anxious to finish that you settle for a solution that doesn't really work. A desire to take action and to reduce the uncertainty in a situation drives some people to leapfrog the other problem solving stages and discuss solutions well before they really understand the problem. This same factor may drive some people to hurry through the idea getting stage to converge on a best solution before they should. History and business alike are littered with examples of poorly thought out solutions to problems. For example, Gruenenthal Chemie's decision to market the drug thalidomide that caused numerous birth defects, Enron's decision to allow risky accounting practices that resulted in the company's bankruptcy, and NASA's decision to launch the space shuttle *Challenger* that ultimately exploded are all instances of extremely poor solutions that had disastrous consequences.[9]

Decision Making The second substage, the contracting phase, focuses-on sorting through the ideas generated in brainstorming and evaluating them systematically against the criteria that an effective solution must meet. The primary criterion of an effective solution is whether it solves the problem and produces the desired result. An efficient solution produces no harmful side effects.[10] Inexperienced problem solvers come up with recommendations that have little impact, are too expensive, or are too difficult to ever implement. Therefore, another way to evaluate solutions is to use the Payoff Matrix shown in Exhibit 11–2. GE uses this tool to help employees think about and categorize solutions in terms of their potential impact and achievability.[11]

If group members become competitive and fight over the best solution, they can list the criteria a good solution has to meet and evaluate each solution against those criteria. In the solution phase, the problem solver takes the role of inventor, creatively searching for ideas and then carefully evaluating them against feasibility criteria. When the best solution has been chosen, the group can move on to implementation in the next stage.

IMPLEMENTATION ANALYSIS—PARTICIPATION AND PLANNING

The final stage concerns the actions that must be taken to ensure that the solution is successfully implemented. This involves getting the appropriate people involved and coming up with a good plan. Three common errors in this stage are failing to gain the commitment of the people needed to implement the plan, failing to assign clear responsibility for each task, and failing to follow up and monitor the implementation process. Implementation analysis is accomplished through the interplay of planning and the process of carrying out plans.

Participation Since implementation of solutions in organizational settings is most often done by or with other people, the critical expansion task is participation, enlisting the appropriate

	Easy To Implement	Tough To Implement
Low Payoff		
Big Payoff		

EXHIBIT 11-2 **Payoff Matrix**

involvement of those actors in the situation who are essential to carrying out the problem solution. Three subtasks are involved here:

1. The anticipation of the consequences that will result from implementing the solution and the involvement of those who will experience these consequences in developing ways to deal with them.
2. The identification of those key individuals who by virtue of their expertise and/or motivation are best qualified to carry out the various tasks in the implementation process.
3. If the key individuals have not been involved in the problem-solving process to this point, it may be necessary to see if they agree with the group's outputs or have different ideas about the problem choice, definition, and proposed solution.

Receptivity and openness is also required in this substage, but here it is directed toward the concerns and ideas of people who will be involved in planning the implementation process.

Planning The planning phase of implementation analysis is an analytical process involving the definition of tasks to be accomplished in implementing the solution, the assignment of responsibility to qualified individuals, the setting of deadlines and planning for follow-up monitoring, and the evaluation of the implementation process. If the problem and its solution are very complex, planning may be quite complicated using network planning methods such as PERT (Program Evaluation Review Technique) or CPM (Critical Path Method). Often, however, a simple chart listing key tasks, responsible individuals, and time deadlines is sufficient for planning and monitoring implementation.

When groups develop plans for implementation and identify the potential consequences of implementing these plans, they may find that it is useful to use an iterative process. For example, they can scout potential issues that may arise in implementation, develop a rough plan, share it with those involved in the situation to get reactions, and then modify the plan. Another dialectic process relates to the "who's" and the "what's." Managers appear to have distinct stylistic preferences about how they deal with this issue. Some prefer to define the "what's" first—the plan and tasks to be accomplished—and then assign these tasks to individuals to carry them out. Others begin with the "who's," seeking to identify qualified and interested individuals and then developing plans with them. While the best approach probably varies with the situation and task, beginning with the "who's" has the advantages of giving priority to often scarce human resources and maximizing participation and delegation. In synthesizing these dialectics, the problem solver in implementation analysis adopts the role of coordinator, working to accomplish tasks with other people. The outcome of this stage is a coherent plan for the implementation and a follow-up evaluation.

Most experienced managers tend naturally to follow a problem-solving sequence that is close to that described in the four-phase model of situation analysis, problem analysis, solution analysis, and implementation analysis. There are, however, significant differences in the amounts of energy devoted to each of these phases, which sometimes inhibit effective problem solving. Perhaps the most significant of these is the tendency to spend too little time defining the problem at hand before generating possible solutions. This tendency to be solution oriented often results in the treatment of symptoms rather than causes of the problem, and time is wasted working on solutions before relevant information is known. If this process is typical of an organization's problem solving, a crisis fire-fighting atmosphere develops where symptom-oriented solutions fail to resolve basic problems that recur over and over. This further reduces the time available for thoughtful situation and problem analysis.

Effective problem solving requires balanced attention to each phase of the problem-solving process and equal emphasis on the expansion/green-mode and contraction/red-mode mind-sets. We learned in Chapter 3, "Individual and Organizational Learning," that individual learning styles emphasize different aspects of the experiential learning cycle. There is a strong correlation between people's learning styles and the way they approach problem solving. In the next section, we describe additional approaches to problem solving that have been used in organizations.

DIFFERENT APPROACHES TO PROBLEMS AND OPPORTUNITIES

Since not all problems or situations are exactly the same, different approaches to problem solving have been developed. Some problems are simply a matter of repairing something that has ceased to function correctly, particularly technical problems. This involves determining the cause and taking corrective measures. Other problems revolve around the need to improve the way something is working, so problem solving efforts focus on the constraints and modifications that are required. Finally, some situations require the creation of something new. In this instance, looking at causes and past functioning may be completely unnecessary since the focus is to develop something that is completely different. Two of the most highly developed and distinct approaches to problem solving, Six Sigma and Appreciative Inquiry, are explained below.

Six Sigma

Six Sigma, the next generation of the total quality movement (TQM), was initially developed at Motorola in the 1980s. Motorola was inspired by Japanese success in producing high-quality products. Decades earlier, the Japanese were known not for quality but for shoddy merchandise. In one of the most famous problem solving successes in business, Japanese products became synonymous with quality after they adopted Deming's principles of total quality management and *kaizen*, a commitment to continuous improvement and encouraged employees to contribute their ideas for improving products. Since the Japanese focused primarily on improving the quality of products, American firms such as Motorola, Allied Signal, and Texas Instruments thought they could compete with Japan if they focused on both products and work processes, and thus turned to Six Sigma.[12] Many companies have claimed that Six Sigma is responsible for millions or billions in cost savings or gains. GE reportedly saved $8 billion in one three-year period alone. Six Sigma squads from GE have expanded their internal focus to help their customers find inefficiencies and waste that will result in savings.[13]

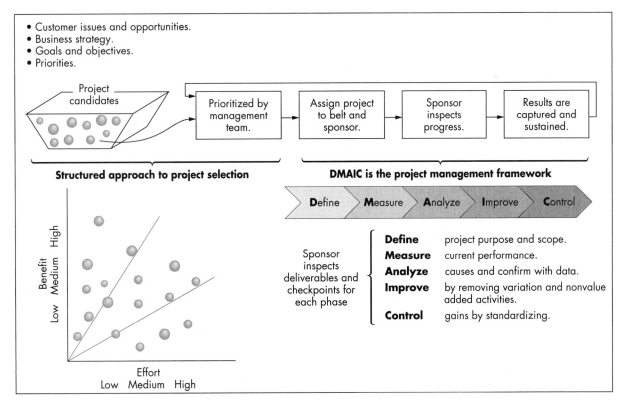

EXHIBIT 11-3 Lean Six Sigma Processes at Xerox

Source: Reprinted with permission from A. Fornari and G. Maszle, "Lean Six Sigma Leads Xerox," *Six Sigma Forum Magazine* (August, 2004): 12.

Sigma is a statistics term for a measure of variation from an expected outcome, in this case, a high quality product. A sigma of six refers to a near-perfect rate of only 3.4 defects per million parts. The basic formula for getting to SIX SIGMA is DMAIC:

- Define the requirements of a process or product to meet customer wishes
- Measure performance
- Analyze what's causing defects
- Improve the process to reduce them
- Control the process to maintain improvements.

Xerox has slightly modified the basic DMAIC formula for their own needs, as shown in Exhibit 11–3.

Like TQM, Six Sigma also relies heavily on statistical tools; it's been called "TQM on Steroids."[14] While TQM involved many, if not all employees in teams that chose their own improvement projects, Six Sigma relies primarily on employee experts with extensive Six Sigma training (green belts and black belts) who work with teams on projects chosen by management. Improved quality and savings are the benefits of a Six Sigma program that is effectively implemented. However, these strengths can be a double-edged sword if the focus on numbers leaves out other considerations. Circuit City's Six Sigma program produced a recommendation for variable staffing, which meant hiring part-time workers who receive no benefits. A department manager noted, "With Six Sigma, we're not supposed to look at the people any more, just meet the numbers. The pressure for the numbers is incredible."[15]

Appreciative Inquiry

Appreciative inquiry (AI) is an intervention used in organization development (efforts taken to make organizations and the people within them more effective), which differs radically from the traditional problem solving approach to organizational issues. Rather than focusing on problems, appreciative inquiry focuses on what the organization is like at its best. *Appreciative inquiry is defined as the study and exploration of what gives life to human systems when they function at their best.* This approach, developed by David Cooperrider, is based on the theory that questions and dialogue about what is positive in the organization results in the energy needed for transformation. In contrast, a problem-oriented focus generates negative emotions and perhaps feelings of helplessness, such as "This will never get any better." AI reflects the changing mindset that is found in the trend toward positive psychology, whose mission is to study human strengths and virtues rather than illness, deficiencies, or problems.[16]

Appreciative inquiry consists of the 4D cycle, which is applied to a topic that is strategically important to the organization:[17]

1. **Discover:** Appreciate "what is"
2. **Dream:** Imagine what could be
3. **Design:** Determine what should be
4. **Destiny:** Create what will be

AI takes various forms; one example is an AI summit lasting two to four days, which takes hundreds of employees and organizational stakeholders through the 4D cycle. One of the basic principles of AI is that positive questions lead to positive change.

"Appreciative inquiry asks questions such as: If your organization wants to enhance morale, what will you study—the causes of low morale, or the causes of high morale and enthusiasm?" As Whitney and Trosten-Bloom state, clearly, no amount of knowledge about low morale will sufficiently equip an organization to understand and create high morale. Imagine, on the other hand, an organization filled with inquiry and dialogue on the topic of "Whistle While You Work" or "Purposeful Work."[18]

This practice amplifies the organization's "positive core," which refers to its "wisdom, knowledge, successful strategies, positive attitudes and affect, best practices, skills, resources, and capabilities."[19] There are many case studies of successful AI programs in businesses, non-profits, and the military.

For any company-wide approach such as Work-Out, Six Sigma, and Appreciative Inquiry to be successful, the implementation of the program has to be skillfully done with the strong support of top management, the necessary resources, and often a change in the organizational culture. Firms usually hire consultants to ensure that such programs are successful.

CULTURAL DIFFERENCES IN PROBLEM SOLVING

Cultural differences can be seen in the way problems are defined and solved in different countries.[20] Fatalistic cultures with external locus of control (e.g., Thailand, Indonesia, and Malaysia) are more likely to accept situations as they are; therefore, they may be slower to identify and resolve problems. In Western cultures characterized by internal locus of control, where people are responsible for their own destiny, children are taught to solve problems in school.[21] Employees are rewarded for being troubleshooters or penalized for causing or failing to solve problems. U.S. managers take a problem-solving approach to most situations and often perceive problems as an opportunity to make improvements. Fixing problems is part of the U.S. orientation toward action. That same predisposition, however, sometimes results in pragmatic solutions that have not been thoroughly analyzed. In collectivist cultures, the responsibility for solving the problem is more likely to fall on the group.

In low-context cultures, problems are viewed as a time-consuming nuisance and are externalized, like the "bugs" that have to be knocked out before a software product launch. In process-oriented cultures such as Japan, however, problems are viewed as a normal part of the situation, not something that is external or even a nuisance. Thus, problems are defined differently. In collectivist cultures, problems are not the responsibility of the individual, and working together on the problem has the same value as solving the problem. This explains in part why quality circles were such a welcome import in Japan.[22]

As we have seen, part of the problem solving process includes gathering information; however, not all cultures collect, interpret, or even value business information in the same way. In high-context cultures, information is viewed in relation to a specific context whereas low-context cultures view information as objective and independent of the person who collected it.[23]

The alternative solutions developed in problem solving are also affected by cultural orientations toward time. Cultures that are oriented toward the past (England, Italy) tend to look for historical patterns and lessons. Future-oriented cultures, such as Australia, are more likely to generate new alternatives because they are less bound to the past.

CLASS ACTIVITY: CARDIOTRONICS ROLE-PLAY

PART I. ASSEMBLY TEAM D MEETING

The purpose of this role play activity is to allow you to practice problem-solving skills.
(Time allotted: 60-70 minutes)

STEP 1.   Divide the class into groups of six. In this role-play, each learning group will be Assembly Team D, with individuals in your group assuming the role of Marion Andrews, Lee Smith, and so on. (In groups of five, combine the Lee Smith role with that of Chris Jones; that is, "Chris can speak for his or her friend Lee who is sick today.") Groups larger than six should have observers. Observers should take notes on the group's problem-solving process during the role-play using the Cardiotronics Case Review form on page 299.)

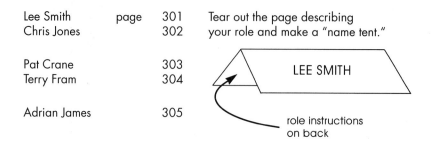

Lee Smith   page   301
Chris Jones   302

Pat Crane   303
Terry Fram   304

Adrian James   305

Tear out the page describing
your role and make a "name tent."

LEE SMITH

role instructions
on back

STEP 2. Group members should choose roles. One person should play Marion Andrews and prepare to conduct the meeting. Role descriptions for the other team members are on the pages cited. (5 minutes)

STEP 3. Marion begins the role play by calling the meeting to order and tackling the problem. (20-30 minutes).

Instructions for Team D Workers	Instructions for Marion Andrews
Place your name tent in front of you after you have read the role description and prepare to be the person described.	The assembly line just closed and the five workers from Assembly Team D have gathered in your office. As supervisor of Team D, you have 30 minutes to conduct the problem-solving meeting and find a solution to the problem described in the Cardiotronics Case before everyone goes back to work.

Four Tips on Role-Playing (Also see the tips presented in Chapter 4):
- Be yourself as much as you can.
- Imagine yourself in that person's life.
- Don't "ham it up."
- Talk loudly enough for the observers to hear.

STEP 4. Each team should write their solution and the reasons for this decision in the box below. (5 minutes).

In our group we decided on this solutiuon:

Based on these reasons:

STEP 5.   The group should prepare a group review of its problem-solving process by completing the Cardiotronics Case Review below (10 minutes). If you finish before the other groups, give Marion feedback on what s/he did that was effective or ineffective in the meeting

STEP 6.   Plenary discussion. (20 minutes)

Each group should share the solution it decided on and describe the highlights of the problem-solving process. Consider the following questions:

a. What differences were there in the problem-solving process followed in each group?

b. Were these differences related to the adequacy of the solutions arrived at (e.g., firing or removing Pat is not a particularly good solution because work would only pile up at Terry's position; realizing this requires green-mode information getting so that Terry feels free to share his or her role information)?

c. What common obstacles to effective group problem solving came up? How were these dealt with by Marion Andrews? By other Team D members?

d. How creative was your group's solution? Why?

e. Compare the Sample Facilitation Statements and Questions for Problem Solving at the end of the chapter to what you came up with in the Class Preparation and what Marion said in the role play. Any similarities?

CARDIOTRONICS CASE REVIEW

Cardiotronics Case Review

Describe what took place in each stage of the problem-solving process. What did you discuss or conclude in each stage?	Approximate percentage of total problem-solving time spent in this activity	Comparison averages with business executives*
Visioning/Exploration What opportunities did you discuss? What values were surfaced?		5.2%
Priority Setting What was the most important problem?		6.2%
Information Gathering What information did you gather?		7.7%
Problem Definition What were the causes, symptoms, connections in the problem?		5.2%
Idea Getting What ideas did you brainstorm?		43.0%
Decision Making Which solution was the best idea?		12.9%
Participation What other people need to be involved in planning the implementation? How should they be involved?		6.2%
Planning What is your implementation plan?		14.0%

*Averages for 60 managers in 10 groups
(1/2 female; 1/2 male)

STATION 1
LEE SMITH

You find you can easily do more work, but you have to slow down because Pat gets behind. So as not to make Pat feel badly, you hold back. You don't want to get Pat into trouble. Right now, the job lacks challenge and is boring.

STATION 2
CHRIS JONES

You and Lee work closely together, and you are usually waiting for the board from Lee. Waiting for the board is more prevalent in the latter part of the day than in the beginning. To keep busy, you often help out Pat who can't keep up. However, you are careful not to let the supervisor catch you helping Pat because Pat might be let go. Pat is a bit old for the pace set and feels the strain. For you, the job is easy, and you feel the whole job is slowed down too much because of Pat. "Why couldn't Pat be given less to do?" you ask yourself.

STATION 3
PAT CRANE

You work hard, but you just aren't as fast as the others. You know you are holding things up, but no matter how you try, you get behind. The faster you try to go, the more difficult it is to make correct connections. You feel quality is important, and you don't want to make mistakes. You are very proud of your reputation for making very few errors. The rest of the workers are fine people and have more energy than you do at your age.

STATION 4
TERRY FRAM

You are able to keep up with the pace, but on your last assembly job, you were pressed. Fortunately, Pat is slightly slower than you are, and this keeps that pressure off you. You are determined that Pat will not be moved off the job. Somebody has to protect people from speed-up tactics.

STATION 5
ADRIAN JAMES

You get bored doing the same circuit operations over and over. On some jobs you get variety by working fast for a while and then slowly. On this job you can't work fast because the boards aren't fed to you fast enough. Why can't the supervisor see that Pat is a problem and needs to be moved out of the group? It gets you down to keep doing exactly the same thing over and over in slow motion. You are considering getting a job someplace where they can keep a worker busy.

LEARNING POINTS

1. Organizations can be viewed as problem-solving systems whose success depends on how well they perform the problem solving process.
2. Historically, managers alone were responsible for problem solving, but today employees at all levels have been trained to take part in team efforts to solve problems.
3. Kolb's problem-solving model consists of four stages:
   a. Situation analysis
   b. Problem analysis
   c. Solution analysis
   d. Implementation analysis
4. Problem solving is not a logical, linear process. Instead, it is characterized by wavelike expansions and contractions alternately moving outwardly to gather and consider alternatives, information, and ideas and inwardly to focus, evaluate, and decide.
5. Each stage in the problem-solving model possesses two substages that reflect the two dialectics of problem solving: the expansion/green mode and the contraction/red mode. Effective problem solving requires balanced attention to each phase of the problem-solving process and equal emphasis on the expansion/green and contraction/red mode mind-sets.
6. The role of the facilitator or manager in problem solving is different for each stage and can be characterized as:
   a. Leader
   b. Detective
   c. Inventor
   d. Coordinator
7. Different types of problems or situations require different problem-solving approaches.
8. Six Sigma is a problem-solving approach that utilizes statistical methods to remove obstacles and create processes that lead to high-quality products and processes. DMAIC, the basic Six Sigma formula, stands for define the requirements of a process or product to meet customer wishes, measure performance, analyze what's causing defects, improve the process to reduce them, and control the process to maintain improvements.
9. Instead of focusing on problems, appreciative inquiry (AI) is the study and exploration of what gives life to human systems when they function at their best. The 4D cycle consists of: discover, dream, design, and destiny.
10. Cultures vary in the way they define problems, gather information, and solve problems. Cultural differences that influence problem solving are: locus of control, individualism versus collectivism, high- or low-context, and orientations toward time.

ACTION SCRIPTS

FOR EMPLOYEES

- Expert problem solvers can lead a group through a structured problem-solving approach, while paying attention to both content and process issues.
- They do not define the problem in terms of a solution. Instead they seek the source of the symptoms and then choose the most appropriate solution.
- During the early stages of problem solving, they keep the group from discussing solutions prematurely.
- They understand that problem solving is characterized by uncertainty and are willing to tolerate that uncertainty until the best solution is determined.
- They understand that feelings and perceptual biases influence the problem-solving process as do the mental ruts that prevent us from generating creative solutions. When necessary, they discuss the situation with neutral outsiders or objective insiders to get different perspectives.

- Experts take a systems view of problems and consider all the system links, both to define the problem and to ensure that implementation obstacles don't arise.

FOR MANAGERS

- Managers who are expert problem solvers are open to using new solutions, rather than relying too much on an action that was successful in the past. They employ a wide repertoire of creative solutions in response to the unique aspects of each problem they face.
- They are careful to invite people to meetings who are diverse (functions, learning styles, ethnic background) in ways that lead to creative ideas and then ensure that their disparate skills are both valued and utilized.
- Expert managers, as well as team leaders, prepare carefully for problem solving meetings by following these steps:
  - Clear, planned agenda
  - Only the necessary people are invited to the meeting
  - Clear ground rules
  - Clear, stated goals for the meeting and high expectations for meeting them (e.g., is their function advisory, information sharing, decision making?)
  - Assigned roles (chairperson, recorder, etc.)
  - Procedures in place for making decisions (voting or by consensus)
  - Group follows an orderly problem-solving sequence
  - Effective time management
  - Balanced discussion by members so the conversation is not dominated by high-status or aggressive members
  - Conflict is managed effectively
- Expert managers are highly skilled at gaining commitment to problem solutions or to opportunities by showing employees how this will benefit the organization or link to their personal goals and talents.
- They understand that executing a solution requires a great deal of energy and follow-up and keep evaluating whether solutions need to be tweaked.
- They know that solutions often have unanticipated consequences and try to predict and avoid consequences that simply result in another problem.
- They recognize that employee teams are fully capable of solving problems and facilitate their efforts by providing whatever training, information, or support they require.

FOR ORGANIZATIONAL ARCHITECTS

- Expert organizational architects and designers understand that organizational cultures may reinforce an approach to problems that can be either beneficial (proactively seeking opportunities and solutions) or harmful (ignoring problems or only relying on a small group of ineffective problem solvers). They realize that developing norms about the importance of surfacing and solving problems quickly and effectively should be designed into the organizational culture.
- Organizational designers train all employees in one method of problem solving to help save time and keep people on the same page. However, they are sure to periodically check to see that the method is effective and is not stifling creativity.
- They also develop procedures for communicating successful solutions to problems (a form of organizational learning) so that other employees benefit from the knowledge that's been acquired.
- Experts use action learning projects to bring together a carefully chosen team to work on a key organizational problem. In addition to solving problems, action learning projects also expose employees to competent people outside their normal networks and develop their management and leadership skills.

PERSONAL APPLICATION ASSIGNMENT

In this assignment, you will write about an experience involving problem management. Choose an experience about which you want to learn more.

A. Concrete Experience

    1. Objectively describe the experience (who, what, when, where, how). (2 points)

    2. Subjectively describe your feelings, perceptions, and thoughts that occurred during (not after) the experience. What did others seem to be feeling? (2 points)

B. Reflective Observation

    1. Looking back at the experience, what were the perspectives of the key actors (including you)? (2 points)

    2. Why did the people involved (including you) behave as they did? (2 points)

C. Abstract Conceptualization

    1. Relate concepts or theories from the assigned readings or the lecture to the experience. Explain thoroughly how they apply to your experience. Please apply at least two concepts or theories and cite them correctly. (4 points)

D. Active Experimentation

    1. What did you learn about problem solving or creativity from this experience? (1 point)

    2. What did you learn about yourself? (1 point)

    3. What action steps will you take to be more effective in the future? (2 points)

  E. Integration, Synthesis, and Writing
    1. Did you integrate and synthesize the four sections? (1 point)
    2. Was the Personal Application Assignment well written and easy to understand? (1 point)
    3. Was it free of spelling and grammar errors? (2 points)

ENDNOTES

[1] R. Kilmann, "Problem Management: A Behavioral Science Approach," in G. Zaltman (ed.) *Management Principles for Non-Profit Agencies and Organizations* (New York: American Management Association, 1979): 214–15.

[2] D. Ulrich, S. Kerr, and R. Ashkenas, *GE Work-Out* (New York: McGraw-Hill, 2002).

[3] The problem-solving model described here was developed by David Kolb in collaboration with Richard Baker and Juliann Spoth.

[4] P. Elbow, *Writing Without Teachers* (New York: Oxford University Press, 1973).

[5] R. Kaplan, "Creativity in the Everyday Business of Managing," *Issues and Observations* (Greensboro, NC: Center for Creative Leadership, 1983), and D. Kolb, I. Rubin, and J. S. Osland, *The Organizational Behavior Reader* ((Englewood Cliffs, NJ: Prentice-Hall, 1991).

[6] C. Lindblom, "The Science of Muddling Through," *Public Administration Review 2* (1959): 78–88.

[7] I. L. Janis, "Group Think," *Psychology Today* (November 1971); Kolb, Rubin and Osland, *The Organizational Behavior Reader* (1990).

[8] R. Fritz, *The Path of Least Resistance* (New York: Ballantine, 1989).

[9] B. Raven and J. Z. Rubin, *Social Psychology: People in Groups* (New York: Wiley, 1976); M. Swarz and S. Watkins, "Power Failure: "The Inside Story of the Collapse of Enron," (New York: Currency Doubleday, 2003); G. Moorhead, R. Ference, and C. Neck, "Group Decision Fiascoes Continue: Space Shuttle Challenger and a Revised Groupthink Framework," *Human Relations 44* (1991): 539–550. For a list of other fiascos and methods for preventing them, see M. E. Turner, A. R. Pratkanis, and T.

Samuels, "Circumventing groupthink by identity metamorphosis: Examining Intel's departure from the DRAM industry," in A. Haslam, D. van Knippenberg, M. Platow, and N. Ellemers (eds.). *Social Identity at Work: Developing Theory for Organizational Practice.* (Philadelphia, PA: Psychology Press, 2002): 117–136.

[10] C. Barnard. *The Functions of the Executive* (Cambridge, MA: Harvard University Press, 1938).

[11] Ulrich, Kerr, and Ashkenas, *GE Work-Out*: 34–35.

[12] R. Slater, *The GE Way Fieldbook* (New York: McGraw-Hill, 2000); M. Arndt, "Quality Isn't Just for Widgets," *BusinessWeek 3792,* (July 22, 2002): 72.

[13] Arndt, "Quality Isn't Just for Widgets."

[14] A. Gluckman, "Quality In, Workers Out? Companies Adopt Six Sigma," *Real World Micro* (Boston, MA: Dollars and Sense, 2002): 45–46.

[15] Ibid: 46.

[16] M. Seligman, and Csikszentmihalyi, "Positive psychology: An introduction," *American Psychologist 56*(1), (2001): 5–14.

[17] D. Whitney and A. Trosten-Bloom, *The Power of Appreciative Inquiry* (San Francisco: Berrett-Koehler, 2003)

[18] Ibid: 137.

[19] D. Whitney and A. Trosten-Bloom, *The Power of Appreciative Inquiry:* 67.

[20] N. J. Adler, *International Dimensions of Organizational Behavior* (Cincinnati, OH: South-Western College, 2002).

[21] I. Varner and L. Beamer, *Intercultural Communication in the Global Workplace* (New York: McGraw-Hill, 2005): 258.

[22] Ibid.

[23] Varner and Beamer, *Intercultural Communication in the Global Workplace.*

Sample Facilitation Statements and Questions for Problem Solving

Situation Analysis	Problem Analysis	Solution Analysis	Implementation Analysis
Visioning/Exploration Let's not discuss solutions until we thoroughly understand the problem. What do you think about the situation? How do you feel about it? What opportunities do you see in this situation? What do you hope is the outcome? Is there something else we should be looking at first? What's working well? What do we want to change? What values are involved in this situation?	Information Gathering Let's try to put our biases aside and take an objective look at the situation. What do we know so far? What do we need to know before we can really define the problem? Who else should we talk to? What's preventing us from reaching the desired state?	Idea Getting How could we make this change? Let's brainstorm possible solutions to the problem, but let's not evaluate them until all the ideas have been heard.	Participation Who would be affected by the implementation of this solution? Whose commitment is needed to successfully implement this solution? Who has the most at stake or the most energy to get this accomplished? How can we involve them in planning the implementation?
Priority Setting What's the most important problem that, if resolved, would cause other things to fall into place? Why? What do others in the organization and external stakeholders think about this? Do we all agree that this is the most important problem or opportunity?	Problem Definition Do we have enough information to put together a model of the problem? Can we draw a model of the problem? What factors caused the problem? What are the symptoms of the problem and the results? What other factors influence these relationships? Have we identified and verified the key cause?	Decision Making Are we ready to evaluate these suggestions? What criteria should our solution meet? Do these solutions get at all the causes in our problem definition? Which solution would have the biggest payoff and be the easiest to implement? Which of these solutions meets all the criteria? Are there any unintended consequences that might result from this solution?	Planning What tasks need to be done to implement this solution and when? By whom? What deadlines are we facing? What constraints? What potential implementation problems might arise? What should be our contingency plan? How will we monitor the progress of the implementation?

Chapter 12

▲▲

MANAGING CREATIVITY

OBJECTIVES By the end of this chapter, you should be able to:

A. List the five categories of characteristics that distinguish creative people from noncreative people.

B. Explain the personality traits of creative people.

C. Explain how the four cognitive creativity skills are promoted by creativity techniques.

D. Explain the organizational conditions that enhance or kill creativity.

E. Describe the steps in the creative process and "flow."

BEARS AND HONEY POTS

A small electric utility company located in a mountainous region of the Pacific Northwest was plagued by a problem it could not solve. Spring and fall ice storms coated the power lines with ice that was so heavy it often snapped the lines and cut off power to customers. Removing the ice, however, was a dangerous job for linemen who had to scale icy towers and poles to shake the wires with a long pole. A consultant brought together a diverse group of employees from different backgrounds to brainstorm a solution. There were linemen, accountants, secretaries, mailroom clerks, and supervisors in the group.

Several hours of brainstorming did not produce anything useful. During a break, the consultant overheard one lineman telling another that he really hated de-icing the lines. The last time out, a bear had chased him! When the group reconvened, the consultant related this tale in an effort to prod the group's thinking. A participant wondered if they could train bears to climb the poles; the bears' weight would shake the poles enough to knock off the ice. Once the group stopped laughing, someone suggested the group get back on task. But another lineman commented that the trick would be getting the bears to climb the poles sequentially so no poles would be overlooked. Someone else suggested they could get the bears to climb each pole by putting a honey pot at the top as a reward.

The group came up with several drawbacks to this idea. What would keep the bears from eating the honey in good weather rather than waiting for ice storms? What would keep raccoons or other animals from eating the honey? What if the bears eventually got tired of honey?

The tension level rose as conflict developed between two subgroups—the people who wanted to continue pursuing the bear-and-honey-pot idea and others who thought it was a deadend and wanted to move on to more practical ideas. A cynical lineman recommended using the executive helicopter that transported company VIPs around to put honey pots on top of each pole after an ice storm. The mention of helicopters brought a secretary into the discussion for the first time. As a former nurse's aide in Vietnam, she remembered that the helicopters bringing in wounded soldiers had a tremendous down wash. Would helicopter down wash be strong enough, she asked, to knock off the ice?

Bingo! That turned out to be the magic solution. The company, however, never would have hit on this idea if it had not put together a diverse group capable of tolerating ambiguity, conflict, and seemingly off-the-wall, impractical ideas—all essential elements for group creativity.

Source: Adapted from R. T. Pascale, "Intentional Breakdowns and Conflict by Design" *Planning Review* 22(3) (May/June 1994): 15.

Managing Creativity at SAS

The SAS Institute is the world's largest privately held software company. Located in North Carolina, the firm has a 3–5 percent turnover rate in an industry where the average is 20 percent. It has a regular spot on *Fortune's 100 Best Companies to Work For*. The company has an innovative way of selling its services to customers—in the form of subscriptions. Since 98 percent of those subscriptions are renewed, SAS has a steadier, more predictable income than if it sold products in the traditional way. Revenues have grown annually for the last 29 years. What explains the SAS success? According to Richard Florida, a public policy professor and creativity expert, and Jim Goodnight, SAS Institute CEO, the answer lies in the title of their recent *Harvard Business Review* article— "Managing for Creativity." Few companies have devoted as much time to designing a firm that promotes creativity as much as SAS has. Here's how they do it.

The SAS approach to creativity has three guiding principles, explained below:

1. Help employees do their best work by keeping them intellectually engaged and by removing distractions.
2. Make managers responsible for sparking creativity and eliminate arbitrary distinctions between "suits" (managers) and "creatives" (employees doing creative work).
3. Engage customers as creative partners to enable the company to deliver superior products.

Helping Employees Do Their Best Work

IT (information technology) workers are motivated more by challenging jobs than by salary and financial incentives according to an *Information Week* survey. SAS stimulates employees in various ways: training, employee white papers*, a constant stream of new products, and internal R&D expos where the technical staff explain new products to the nontechnical staff.

SAS doesn't want its workers to be distracted. Every year, HR surveys workers to discover what nonwork tasks are getting in the way. If the price is not exorbitant and the payoff is big enough, SAS meets their needs. If SAS can't do it, they explain why. After listening to employees, SAS established in-house medical facilities for workers and their families, a day care center and a cafeteria where kids can eat lunch with their parents, workout facilities, and a Work-Life Department that helps workers' children make the right college choice and finds home health care for workers' elderly parents. SAS also has dry cleaning, massage, haircut, and auto-detailing services on site at a discount. They figure the cost pays off in employee retention and productivity. SAS believes that long-term relationships among developers, support staff, salespeople, and customers is the home of creative capital.

SAS doesn't want workers distracted or frazzled by bureaucratic demands. No one likes bureaucratic hassles, but creative people in particular hate them as "the enemy of good work."

---

* White papers are reports that typically explain the results and conclusions of an investigation or a design and development effort written by a committee or research collaboration. Technology firms often publish white papers to explain the development, testing, and use of new technologies.

That means meetings are short, and work hours are flexible to make room for both creativity and family needs. Unlike many Silicon Valley companies where 70-hour work weeks are common, SAS encourages employees to take a break and recharge their creative batteries. An SAS proverb is: "After eight hours, you're probably just adding bugs (errors)."

SAS devotes a good deal of energy to hiring creative, collaborative people and hanging onto them. SAS figures their low turnover rate saves $85 million a year that would otherwise go to recruitment and replacement costs. Because the fit with SAS culture is so important, hiring decisions can take months to make. Employees are highly valued. No jobs are out-sourced, and all employees get the same benefits package. "SAS recognizes that 95 percent of its assets drive out the front gate every evening. Leaders consider it their job to bring them back the next morning."[†] Knowing their jobs are not dependent on quarterly earnings and shifting company fortunes allows employees to be more creative. This doesn't mean SAS doesn't fire workers who don't produce—Goodnight claims that they "hire hard, manage open, and fire hard." Employees are not fired for making mistakes, but if they don't meet performance expectations, they are given a corrective action plan that details what they need to improve. They can choose to have three months to improve their performance or quit immediately with a compensation package.

CREATING AN EGALITARIAN CULTURE

All SAS managers, even the CEO, do hands-on work in addition to managing. The CEO still writes code. This sends an important symbolic message that everyone in the firm is a creative (person doing a job requiring creativity), even when they wear a suit. Everyone is on the same team working toward the same goal. SAS believes bosses should be competent at doing the work their employees do. This creates more mutual understanding and respect and makes it easier for employees to seek out bosses to ask questions and make suggestions. The result is a culture that cares more about doing excellent work than titles and that values collegiality and trust. The manager's role is to stimulate creativity by asking lots of good questions, convening groups to exchange ideas, and removing obstacles and getting employees what they need. As the head of the software team, Larnell Lennon, says his job consists of "Go get it, go get it, go get it," which sounds a lot like servant leadership.

KEEPING THE CUSTOMER SATISFIED

Because SAS is privately held, they don't track stock price. What they do track is customer satisfaction and opinions, which then guides how they spend the 26 percent of their budget that goes to R&D. SAS stores customer complaints and suggestions in a database and also surveys customers annually about new features they would like to have. All this information is pulled out when it's time to design new products or updates.

SAS's user conference is not so much a sales job as an opportunity for both employees and customers to have creative interchanges. Customers can be a tremendous source of creativity because they have firsthand knowledge of product limitations and can imagine a better way. SAS tries to partner with customers to produce creative capital. "SAS may be the only company that prints the names of its software developers in product manuals. Customers can—and do—call them up. And because employee loyalty is so high, the developers actually answer the phone: they haven't moved down the road to start-up number seven."[‡] SAS seeks to build the same loyalty in customers by not releasing products until they are bug-free.

SAS has taken an integrative approach to managing creativity. All the pieces of organizational design fit together to attract the best global talent and build a competitive advantage in innovation, productivity, and business performance. This is the virtuous cycle that companies have to set in place if they want to excel at managing creativity.

† R. Florida and J. Goodnight, "Managing for Creativity," 127.
‡ R. Florida and J. Goodnight, "Managing for Creativity," 131.

CLASS PREPARATION

A. Read "Bears and Honey Pots" and "Managing Creativity at SAS."

B. Take a moment to reflect on this course. What are the underlying, integrative themes (e.g., appreciation of differences) that we have read about and discussed so far? Write at least three themes on a sheet of paper and bring them to class.

C. Fill out and score the Creative Personality Inventory on the following page before reading the chapter.

D. Then answer these questions:
  1. What was your most creative experience (at work or in a nonwork setting)?

  2. What factors were responsible for your high level of creativity?

E. While reading the chapter, make a list of the cues that you should look for with regard to creativity.

The Creative Personality Inventory

Answer the following questions as honestly as you can so you get a valid self-assessment. For each statement, write in the appropriate letter.

A. Agree   B. Undecided or don't know   C. Disagree

____ 1. I always work with a great deal of certainty that I am following the correct procedure for solving a particular problem.

____ 2. It would be a waste of time for me to ask questions if I had no hope of obtaining answers.

____ 3. I concentrate harder on whatever interests me than do most people.

____ 4. I feel that a logical, step-by-step method is best for solving problems.

____ 5. In groups, I occasionally voice opinions that seem to turn some people off.

____ 6. I spend a great deal of time thinking about what others think of me.

____ 7. It is more important for me to do what I believe to be right than to try to win the approval of others.

____ 8. People who seem uncertain about things lose my respect.

____ 9. More than other people, I need to have things interesting and exciting.

____ 10. I know how to keep my inner impulses in check.

____ 11. I am able to stick with difficult problems over extended periods of time.

____ 12. On occasion, I get overly enthusiastic.

____ 13. I often get my best ideas when doing nothing in particular.

____ 14. I rely on intuitive hunches and the feeling of "rightness" or "wrongness" when moving toward the solution of a problem.

____ 15. When problem solving, I work faster when analyzing the problem and slower when synthesizing the information I have gathered.

____ 16. I sometimes get a kick out of breaking the rules and doing things I am not supposed to do.

____ 17. I like hobbies that involve collecting things.

____ 18. Daydreaming has provided the impetus for many of my more important projects.

____ 19. I like people who are objective and rational.

____ 20. If I had to choose from two occupations other than the one I now have, I would rather be a physician than an explorer.

____ 21. I can get along more easily with people if they belong to about the same social and business class as myself.

____ 22. I have a high degree of aesthetic sensitivity.

____ 23. I am driven to achieve high status and power in life.

____ 24. I like people who are sure of their conclusions.

____ 25. Inspiration has nothing to do with the successful solution of problems.

____ 26. When I am in an argument, my greatest pleasure would be for the person who disagrees with me to become a friend, even at the price of sacrificing my point of view.

____ 27. I am much more interested in coming up with new ideas than in trying to sell them to others.

____ 28. I would enjoy spending an entire day alone, just "chewing the mental cud."

____ 29. I tend to avoid situations in which I might feel inferior.

____ 30. In evaluating information, the source is more important to me than the content.

___ 31. I resent things being uncertain and unpredictable.

___ 32. I like people who follow the rule "business before pleasure."

___ 33. Self-respect is much more important than the respect of others.

___ 34. I feel that people who strive for perfection are unwise.

___ 35. I prefer to work with others in a team effort rather than solo.

___ 36. I like work in which I must influence others.

___ 37. Many problems that I encounter in life cannot be resolved in terms of right or wrong solutions.

___ 38. It is important for me to have a place for everything and everything in its place.

___ 39. Writers who use strange and unusual words merely want to show off.

___ 40. Circle 10 words from the list below that best describe you.

energetic	persuasive	observant
fashionable	self-confident	persevering
original	cautious	habit-bound
resourceful	egotistical	independent
stern	predictable	formal
informal	dedicated	forward-looking
factual	open-minded	tactful
inhibited	enthusiastic	innovative
poised	acquisitive	practical
alert	curious	organized
unemotional	clear-thinking	understanding
dynamic	self-demanding	polished
courageous	efficient	helpful
perceptive	quick	good-natured
thorough	impulsive	determined
realistic	modest	involved
absent-minded	flexible	sociable
well-liked	restless	retiring

Source: E. Raudsepp, *How Creative Are You?* (New York: Perigee Books/G. P. Putnam's Sons, Inc.) copyright © by Eugene Raudsepp, Used by permission.

Scoring Key

Circle and add up the values assigned to each item. The values are as follows:

	A	B Undecided or Don't	C		A	B Undecided or Don't	C
	Agree	Know	Disagree		Agree	Know	Disagree
1.	0	1	2	21.	0	1	2
2.	0	1	2	22.	3	0	−1
3.	4	1	0	23.	0	1	2
4.	−2	0	3	24.	−1	0	2
5.	2	1	0	25.	0	1	3
6.	−1	0	3	26.	−1	0	2
7.	3	0	−1	27.	2	1	0
8.	0	1	2	28.	2	0	−1
9.	3	0	−1	29.	0	1	2
10.	1	0	3	30.	−2	0	3
11.	4	1	0	31.	0	1	2
12.	3	0	−1	32.	0	1	2
13.	2	1	0	33.	3	0	−1
14.	4	0	−2	34.	−1	0	2
15.	−1	0	2	35.	0	1	2
16.	2	1	0	36.	1	2	3
17.	0	1	2	37.	2	1	0
18.	3	0	−1	38.	0	1	2
19.	0	1	2	39.	−1	0	2
20.	0	1	2				

Subtotal ____ ____ ____   ____ ____ ____

40. *The following have values of 2:*

energetic	dynamic	perceptive	dedicated	
resourceful	flexible	innovative	courageous	
original	observant	self-demanding	curious	
enthusiastic	independent	persevering	involved	=_____

The following have values of 1:

self-confident	determined	informal	forward-looking	
thorough	restless	alert	open-minded	=_____

The rest have values of 0.   Total Score _____

Comparison Data

95–116	Exceptionally creative
65–94	Very creative
40–64	Above average
20–39	Average
10–19	Below average
Below 10	Noncreative

THE KNOWLEDGE BASE

Inventions have long since reached their limit, and I see no hope for further development.

Julius Sextus Frontinus, Highly regarded engineer in Rome, 1st century A.D.

Fortunately, Julius Sextus was really wrong. Inventions continue to fuel economic growth and corporate success. Research shows that employee creativity contributes to organizational innovation, effectiveness, performance and survival.[1] Employees utilize their creativity not only to create new inventions and solve organizational problems but also to develop new products, services, processes, approaches, and strategies.[2] Creative employees and innovative firms go beyond problem solving to look for the next opportunity. Examples of creativity run the gamut from small modifications to major breakthroughs. While some jobs (e.g., R&D, design, advertising) have more creative elements than others, there is room for creativity in almost every job.[3]

Before someone asks the perennial question, "Does this OB stuff apply to all types of employees, even janitors?," let us tell you about Bob Stahl. Stahl, a public high school facilities supervisor (the head custodian), is also an artist whose palette is the dazzling year-round display of flowers on the school grounds. People drive out of their way to admire his gardens, which is almost unheard of for a public school campus. Undeterred by lack of funds, he established fundraisers and asked for donations to pay for the cost of the flowers. In 2005, the school designated November 10th as Bob Stahl Day in his honor, and grateful students and community members came to help him plant 6,000 tulip bulbs.[4] Stahl's creative idea and problem solving was facilitated by his leadership skills in getting others to buy in to his vision, years of hard work to create the gardens, and by a principal who allows employees to realize their full potential.

Many examples of workplace creativity were never part of the job description. Bette Nesmith was a secretary who, in 1951, "wondered why artists could paint over their mistakes, but typists couldn't." In her blender, she mixed up a batch of water-based paint to match the company stationery. By putting the mixture into a nail polish bottle, she could use the brush to paint over and fix typos, thereby earning the gratitude of clerks, typists, and administrative assistants around the world. This magical mixture was what we now know as Liquid Paper. Nesmith sold her company to Gillette 28 years later for $48 million.[5]

Creativity is the development of ideas about products, practices, services, or procedures that are novel and potentially useful to the organization.[6] Creativity can be viewed as a precursor to *innovation, which is defined as the implementation of new ideas at the individual, group or organizational level.*[7] Many ideas never make it to the market. Ideas have to be recognized and funded, as well as overcome a variety of technical and organizational challenges before becoming an innovation. Because innovation in today's business environment is closely linked to organizational survival, creative thinking is an important skill and a competitive edge. For example, when Southwest Airlines needed 800 personal computers (PCs) for a new reservations center, the information systems group saved the company $1 million by purchasing parts from wholesalers and organizing an assembly line of employees to build the PCs themselves.[8]

3M, famous for its creative products and employees, has long been a benchmark for other firms that want to learn how to manage creativity.[9] The company sets an annual goal to have close to a third of its sales come from products developed within the last few years. This is what is known as a creativity goal. To make this happen, technical staff members at 3M are allowed to spend 15 percent of their time on any project they wish, on what are called "bootstrapping" activities. Post-It Notes came about in part because a 3M employee, Spence Silver, took advantage of this autonomy and became interested in a light adhesive glue. However, it wasn't until he hooked up with another employee, Art Fry, who'd encountered a problem with bookmarks for his church hymnal, that a practical application was found for the glue. Fry took equipment home to his basement and made a machine to manufacture prototypes. Incidentally, the machine grew to such a size that he had to break a hole in the wall of his basement to return the equipment to 3M! Other scientists and marketing people were pulled in to help with the project. Post-It Notes failed 3M's market tests, but the marketing people broke the rules by personally visiting test sites and giving away free samples to customers, who quickly became addicted to Post-Its. Although it took years to get this invention to market, 3M fortunately had an organizational culture that allowed employees to persist in championing a new idea. As a result, the company has earned a half-billion dollars in annual revenue from Post-It Notes.[10]

Silver and Fry are creative people working in a company known for innovation. Understanding how these two factors—personal and contextual—influence creativity is the focus of this chapter.[11]

THE CREATIVE PERSON

I make more mistakes than anyone else I know, and sooner or later, I patent most of them.

Thomas Edison

Although everyone can work on increasing their creativity skill level, some people are naturally more creative than others. The characteristics that distinguish more creative people from others, as shown in Exhibit 12-1, are: specific personality traits, tolerance of risk, cognitive creativity skills, domain-specific knowledge, and intrinsic motivation.[12]

In terms of *personality traits*, creative people tend to be self-confident, independent, attracted to complexity, tolerant of ambiguity, persistent, and intuitive. They are independent enough to follow their own path without being too concerned about conformity or how other people might view them.[13] They like to learn and are open and flexible. They are likely to have broad interests, high energy, and a concern with achievement. Not surprisingly, they see themselves as creative.

Other indications of creative potential are curiosity, focused interest on a topic, and self-discipline.[14] The Creative Personality Inventory scale that you filled out before class is one measure of overall creative potential. The "openness to new experience" dimension in the Five Factor Model (refer to your score on this inventory located in the beginning of Chapter 4) also correlates with various aspects of creativity and managerial ratings of creativity in employees.[15]

Thomas Edison, the famous inventor, had his own creativity test that he used to screen potential research assistants. He served them soup—if they salted it before tasting it, he did not hire them. Edison wanted employees with open minds who tested assumptions before they proceeded.[16]

Highly creative people tend to be *risk takers* who love their work.[17] The creative process involves trial and error, which by definition involves failure and learning from failure. People who are afraid to fail are more likely to stick with the status quo than gamble on a dream or a new idea. As Henry Ford said, "Whether you believe you can, or whether you believe you can't, you're absolutely right." As we'll see later, tolerance of risk also can be influenced by organizational reactions to failure.

In addition to personality traits, a particular skill set enables individuals to be more creative. These *cognitive creativity skills*, sometimes called "creativity relevant skills" include: the ability to think creatively, generate alternatives, engage in divergent thinking and suspend judgment.[18] Teresa Amabile found that the cognitive-perceptual style needed for creativity includes gathering and applying diverse information, accurate memory, use of effective heuristics, and the ability to concentrate deeply for long periods of time.[19] *Heuristics* are incomplete guidelines or rules of thumb. Heuristics such as "destroy judgment, create curiosity" and "ask dumb questions" can lead to learning or discovery.[20] Several of the skills needed for problem solving—problem finding, problem construction, combination and idea evaluation—are also essential in creativity.[21] The ability to make connections among various alternatives, example solutions or related ideas leads to creativity.[22] The green and red modes in the problem solving model we studied in the previous chapter are an example of divergent thinking, a creativity skill. As Carl Sagan, the famous astronomer, said: "It is the tension between creativity and skepticism that has produced the stunning and unexpected findings of science." Consider the following example.

In 1948, George de Mestral, a Swiss inventor and amateur mountaineer, returned home from a hike covered with burrs. He was curious about what made them stick and took a closer look at the burrs on his pants under a microscope. He decided to design a two-sided fastener with stiff hooks like those on the burrs on one side and soft loops like those on the pants fabric on the other. De Mestral named it "velcro" (combining "velour" and "crochet"). Critics laughed at his idea but he stuck to it (like you know what) and, after much trial and error, discovered that nylon sewn under an infrared light simulated the tough hooks of the burr. The design was patented in 1955, and de Mestral founded Velcro Industries, which became very successful.[23] Finding other applications of a phenomenon found in nature is an example of the cognitive connections made by creative people.

Another individual difference related to cognitive styles is captured in Kirton's Adaption-Innovation Theory, which assumes that people are predisposed to a particular style of creative problem solving.[24] All of us are creative to some degree, but we differ in how we prefer to solve problems. People who are more adaptive (adaptors) prefer more structure and are more likely to stay within the given and agreed-upon paradigm and rules without questioning. In contrast, people who are more innovative (innovators) are comfortable with less structure and more likely to go outside the given paradigm and devise qualitatively different solutions despite the given rules. Research has shown that innovators tend to be more creative.[25]

Domain-specific knowledge is another prerequisite for creativity. Occasionally a newcomer can look at a new area with fresh eyes and be struck with a creative idea, but most creativity comes from familiarity and expertise. Domain-specific knowledge is acquired via education, training, experience, and knowledge about a particular context. Johann Sebastian Bach, the famous music composer, not only devoted long hours to mastering the organ, he also learned how to build them and was an expert on the sound of organs.[26]

Finally, creative individuals possess the *intrinsic motivation* that allows them to persist with new ideas long enough to overcome adversity and bring them to fruition. Intrinsic motivation is the extent to which people are excited about an activity and do it for the sake of the activity itself rather than for external rewards. With regard to creativity, when people are intrinsically motivated, they are more likely to be curious, cognitively flexible, persistent despite obstacles, and to take risks.[27]

As Douglas Dayton, a high-level manager at the top-ranked IDEO industrial design firm, stated, "People work here for their personal enjoyment and for public recognition of the products they create, rather than for the money." IDEO was involved with the design of Apple's Lisa mouse, Palm V, and the Treo.

THE CREATIVE ENVIRONMENT

There ain't no rules around here! We're trying to accomplish something!

Thomas Edison, inventor

It is not coincidental that some organizations possess more creative employees than others. The social environment can influence both the level and frequency of creative behavior.[28] Therefore, managing creativity has become a hot topic in firms that understand its connection to high performance. Individual creativity can be enhanced by various contextual factors that are described below and illustrated in Exhibit 12–2.

Screening for creativity when hiring new employees is not enough to guarantee success, although it's a good place to begin. Lotus Development was an extremely successful start-up founded in 1982 to market Lotus 1-2-3. The firm grew to 1000 employees and senior management started hiring primarily MBAs who formerly worked at *Fortune 500* companies. They instituted management techniques that were appropriate for routine work in big firms, but not for creative work in a small company. This was one reason why Lotus had difficulty developing new products and marketing them. But the former CEO, Mitchell Kapor, who was then chairman of the board, and Freada Klein (head of organizational development and training) had a hypothesis about another cause of the lack of creativity. They decided to test it by carrying out an experiment. Taking the resumes of the first 40 people hired at Lotus, they changed the names on the resumes and put them into the current applicant pool. None of these "applicants" were even asked to come in for an interview! Their backgrounds had too many "wacko and risky things." Instead of a linear career in the business sector, some of them had worked in areas such as

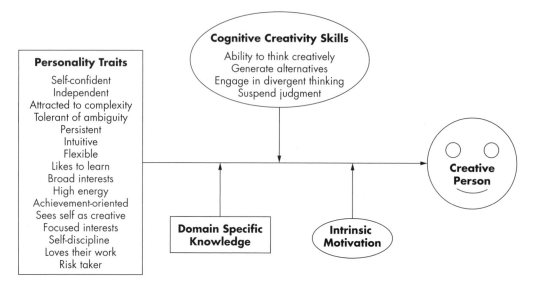

EXHIBIT 12-1 **Characteristics of Creative People**

community organization, transcendental meditation teaching, and clinical psychology. Kapor and Klein concluded that Lotus was systematically weeding out applicants like the creative people who were responsible for the firm's only hit product. [29] Getting creative people through the door and hiring them is the first step. The next step is designing jobs to unleash their creativity.

Job complexity, which fosters intrinsic motivation, enhances creativity.[30] Complexity is often operationalized in creativity research as the motivating job characteristics we studied in the motivation chapter, Chapter 5— jobs designed to include high levels of significance, identity, variety, autonomy, and feedback.[31] Jobs with these characteristics are not only more motivating but also result in higher creativity. More complex jobs correlate with higher supervisor ratings of creativity[32] and a greater number of creative ideas submitted to employee suggestion programs.[33] Jobs should be designed to be challenging enough to spark creativity, but not overwhelming.

Creativity requires time, a good deal of hard work, and strenuous mental energy.[34] Organizations can give employees the *time* to be creative and put in the necessary work and thought. Some studies show that this time to think creatively and play with ideas should be uninterrupted and free of pressure.[35] This is why firms such as Associated Enterprises gave its inventors one day a week to work on their own projects and why other firms allow employees doing creative jobs to work virtually on their own schedule. For some people, staring a deadline in the face lowers their ability to think creatively.[36] As we saw in the vignette, SAS takes the goal of freeing up employee time to an art form by removing as many distractions as possible. This is the impetus for their on-site medical services, haircuts, massages, dry cleaning, day care, athletic facilities, and referral service for family-related concerns. Leaders can also provide creative teams with the other resources they need to facilitate their work, such as funding, equipment, materials, and services. Thus, time is only one of the *resources* employees need to be creative.

Leaders can increase the level of creativity simply by setting *clear organizational goals* and *instructing employees to be creative* in doing their jobs.[37] When goals are unclear, employees are less creative. For example, a study of 400 project teams found that teams given a clear mission were able to focus their energies on new ideas, which resulted in successful innovations.[38] *Creativity goals are either "a stated standard that an individual's output should be creative (i.e., novel and appropriate) or that individuals should attempt to engage in activities that could lead to creative outcomes* (e.g., flexible thought, playing with ideas, environmental scanning, and data gathering)."[39] 3M's innovation goals are a good example. Thomas Edison set a quota for himself—one minor invention every 10 days and one major invention every 6 months.

As noted previously, creative people are more motivated intrinsically than extrinsically.[40] This means that organizations should hire people who enjoy being creative and like the process of the work as much as the result. Some research warns against indiscriminately using extrinsic rewards with creative employees.[41] This doesn't mean, however, that organizations shouldn't bother rewarding them financially for good performance.

Organizations that foster creativity do *recognize and reward creativity*. Managers and leaders reward creativity by listening to and supporting new employee ideas and by publicly recognizing successful ideas and implementations. For most creative people, the best reward is getting to work on yet another challenging project. Monetary rewards for both individuals and teams as well as praise sends a message that the organization values the creative efforts made by employees and encourages others to emulate them. MDA, a Canadian firm that provides advanced information solutions, has an ITUS award that stands for "I Told U So," which is given to employees who have heroically managed to get a successful idea past skeptical, sometimes indifferent colleagues and management.[42] Ericsson rewards employees who have made good suggestions by appointing them to a group that imports and adopts new ideas for improving the firm.

Another aspect of developing an innovative work setting is *encouraging risk-taking*. Creative organizations do not punish failure; they know that false starts are a normal part of the creative process. For this reason, a research and development company had Friday celebrations that included a hideous trophy that was jokingly awarded for the "Screw-Up of the Week."

We also know that organizations that successfully foster creativity grant their employees *autonomy*. Ed Catmull, president of Pixar Animation Studios, described what he learned from Steve Jobs, CEO of Pixar and Apple Computer: "His talent is identifying good people and giving them free rein. His style can best be summed up as "don't micromanage." …We have all these incredible people here and Steve doesn't tell them what to do or what stories to pick. Part of his genius is recognizing their genius and leaving them to it."[43] Idea exploration and creativity is linked to the degree of autonomy employees have in determining how they will spend their time on tasks and how their work goals will be accomplished.[44] Autonomy also makes work more intrinsically motivating.[45] Many creative firms give employees the freedom to design their own workspace. However, creative companies temper this autonomy with the clear goals mentioned earlier and the discipline of hard work.

Experts agree that *productivity*, in the form of action and hard work, pays off in more creativity. Simonton wrote that famous geniuses like Picasso and da Vinci simply produced more work, both successes and failures, than their colleagues. After studying various occupations, he concluded that creativity is a function of the quantity of work produced.[46] However, creative people also need down time to recharge their batteries.

Supportive supervision encourages creativity. This involves concern for employee feelings and openness to hearing their concerns. In contrast, critical supervision and negative feedback can impede creativity.[47] Therefore, supervisors and managers have to be careful how they deliver performance feedback and ensure that they are viewed as encouraging. When employees have the expectation that their work will be evaluated, are encouraged to learn from mistakes, and are provided with informational and helpful feedback, creativity improves after evaluation.[48] Creativity also improves when supervisors encourage creative self-efficacy in employees by building their confidence in their ability to innovate and modeling creative abilities for them.[49] In addition to being supportive, supervisors and leaders do not overcontrol or micromanage employees.[50] Employees are not pressured to conform or think in certain ways.[51] Supervisors should treat employees fairly with regard to the resources and rewards they receive. Creating a supportive climate is one of the most important contributions a leader can make to encourage creativity.

Supervisors and managers use a *participative leadership style*. Listening to employee concerns and getting input on decisions results in higher creativity.[52] Good relationships with supervisors and open interactions also increase innovativeness.[53] Employees can easily suggest new ideas that are considered. At Cisco, John Chambers, CEO, has birthday breakfasts with employees during the month of their birthday. At these breakfasts, he has an opportunity to get feedback and hear ideas. In contrast, when employees have to exert too much time and effort to get new ideas heard due to bureaucratic requirements, they may be less likely to try innovations.[54] SAS's efforts to remove distractions reflect their understanding that creative people intensely dislike unnecessary rules and regulations.

Creative organizations promote *internal diversity* and *interaction*, which means that they hire a heterogeneous work force and build in opportunities for them to interact and swap ideas. The Friday Beer Busts or ping pong games in some firms encourage cross-functional and cross-project conversations that promote new ideas and applications. Some organizations take this idea a step further and make sure their employees are also exposed to people with different ideas who are outside the organization. Weiden+Kennedy, an award-winning advertising firm in Portland, Oregon, carefully chose the organizations with which they wanted to share their headquarters building to maximize their exposure to other creative people. They have artists-in-residence, such as the Bebe Miller Dance Company, as well as the Portland Institute for Contemporary Art and the Portland Arts & Lectures as tenants. Weiden+Kennedy also provide rent-free space to some organizations in support of the arts in Portland.[55]

Diverse teams generally consider more alternatives, generate more solutions, communicate more both inside and outside the team and are more creative. However, they may require more help to develop a shared mental model.[56] Team leaders and members need process skills. For example, having more creative individuals in student teams was not an advantage unless the team also had the process skills to be inclusive, address conflict and communicate effectively.[57] New product development teams were more creative when their communication was inclusive and shared with all members rather than being filtered through a few dominant members.[58] SAS apparently recognizes the importance of process skills, which explains why it selects engineers and technical experts who are skilled at leadership, communication, and team building.

A supportive climate among peers is also important. People are more creative when they are not afraid of being laughed at or negatively judged for new ideas; this condition is called psychological safety.[59] Working alongside creative coworkers who challenge one another constructively also raises the level of creativity.

The *organizational culture* can either foster or impede creativity.[60] Shared organizational values have to include risk-taking, a high tolerance for uncertainty, challenge, and creativity itself. Some research has found that the key factor in determining R&D innovation is organizational climate.[61] IDEO, along with many creative organizations, encourages "an atmosphere of 'serious fun' that encourages nontraditional thinking and diverse points of view. The atmosphere is relaxed, open and collaborative."[62] In highly creative organizational cultures, stories are handed down about innovative people who are legends and creative role models. In such firms, however, everyone is expected to be creative. SAS prides itself on managers who also do "real work" and a CEO who still writes code; they have tried to create an egalitarian culture with little distinction between "suits" and "creatives."[63]

Creative organizations also have *flexible, flat structures* that encourage open, sustained contact with outsiders and information seeking from multiple sources.[64] IDEO's fairly flat, non-hierarchical organization structure promotes autonomy and decision making at the individual and team level rather than the managerial level.[65] IDEO recently experimented with its organizational structure to change from a geographic office-based structure to group employees by area of expertise. If this structure does not work, they will try something else.[66] As you can imagine, it is difficult to be creative in bureaucratic, authoritarian organizations.

Finally, extensive *contact with customers* results in greater creativity. Long-term relationships with customers results in a greater likelihood of "productive accidents."[67] Firms also turn to industrial design firms for help with understanding what customers want and how they experience products. IDEO, for example, puts together a team of people from diverse backgrounds (e.g., anthropologists) and takes them through three steps:[68]

Step 1. **Observation.** They watch people use the product or service and observe what challenges exist.

Step 2. **Brainstorming.** Guided by desired features, their goal is to generate 100 ideas an hour. They pair anthropologists with engineers to maximize creativity.

Step 3. **Prototyping.** They quickly make an unfinished prototype for customers to test while they discuss possible revisions.

A group from IDEO watched people mopping in the traditional manner. They saw the mop being put back into the increasingly dirty water. They saw how heavy a wet mop gets and how hard it is to clean afterwards. They also observed how long it took for a floor to dry. They figured there had to be a better way. This was the genesis for Procter and Gamble's Swiffer, a handle and flat surface to which a disposable cloth-like paper moistened with cleaning liquid is attached—no water and bucket needed.

Research has also discovered a list of organizational conditions that repress individual creativity, also shown in Exhibit 12–2. In addition to emphasizing extrinsic motivation and punishing failures, other "creativity killers" include focusing on how one's work will be evaluated, being under surveillance while working, competing with peers in a win-lose situation, and having one's limits dictated by superiors.[69]   Healthy competition does not impede creativity. For example, some organizations have multiple teams working on the same problem to generate more ideas, but "losing" teams do not lose their jobs. Time pressure, political problems at work, and an emphasis on the status quo rather than innovation also kill creativity.

Creativity Enhancers	Creativity Killers
Focus on intrinsic motivation	Excessive focus on extrinsic motivation
Creativity goals	Limits set by superiors
Developmental feedback	Critical evaluation
Supportive supervision	Close, controlling supervision
Healthy competition	Competition in a win-lose situation
Participative decision making	Control of decision making
Hire creative individuals	Control of information
Enriched, complex jobs	Time pressure
Provision of necessary resources, particularly time	Political problems
Clear organizational goals	Emphasis on the status quo
Instructions to be creative	
Recognition and rewards for creativity	
Encourage risk taking	
No punishment for failure	
Autonomy	
Productivity	
Workforce diversity	
Internal and external interaction	
Diverse teams skilled at working together	
Supportive climate	
Organizational culture that promotes innovation	
Flexible, flat structures	
Close interaction and relationships with customers	

EXHIBIT 12-2 **Contextual Effects on Creativity**

THE CREATIVE PROCESS

Studies of how creative people work have identified the following pattern of events. The catalyst is a problem or perceived need, which triggers these four stages in the creative process.[70]

1. **Preparation** This stage is akin to doing one's homework, and it requires a good deal of effort. People gather information and immerse themselves in everything that is known about the problem, often to the point of saturation.
2. **Incubation** This stage involves a process of reflective thought. The subconscious mind continues to mull over the problem, combining unrelated thoughts, even when people are no longer actively focusing on the problem.
3. **Illumination** Individuals have a flash of inspiration about the solution to the problem, often while engaged in an unrelated activity.
4. **Verification** The solution is tested by logic or experimentation and evaluated more rigorously to see whether it meets some standard of acceptability.

Csikszentmihalyi identified another aspect of the creative process, called *"flow." The phenomenon of "flow" (or autotelic experience), which when people experience a state of effortless concentration and enjoyment.*[71] Athletes and artists talk about flow as a special plane where they perform well almost without conscious thought. Flow is part of the creative process in business when people hit their stride and enjoy the challenge they are working on. Flow has the following key elements:[72]

- Clear goals every step of the way (you know exactly what to do)
- Immediate feedback to one's actions

- Balance between challenge and skills (neither bored that it's too easy nor anxious that you can't accomplish it)
- Action and awareness are merged (total concentration focused on what you're doing)
- Distractions are excluded from consciousness (intense concentration on the present without interruptions)
- No worry of failure
- Self-consciousness disappears (no monitoring of how we appear to others)
- Sense of time becomes distorted (feels longer or shorter than it actually is)
- The activity becomes an end in itself (enjoy the activity for its own sake)

Although some people are naturally more creative than others, anyone can be trained in creative thinking. Many companies provide workshops on creativity. Among other things, employees learn to break mental sets and take new perspectives on problems. They learn divergent thinking, which generates multiple solutions to problems, as well as learning to use heuristics such as analogies and metaphors and making associations. They also learn to avoid making premature judgments that kill off ideas before they have time to be fully developed.[73]

CREATIVITY TECHNIQUES

If at first the idea is not absurd, then there is no hope for it.

Albert Einstein Brainstorming Rules

There are numerous techniques for unleashing creativity. Two of the most well known are brainstorming and brainwriting. The rules for brainstorming are:[74]

1. **Expressiveness** Say whatever ideas come to mind without focusing on constraints.
2. **Nonevaluation** No criticism allowed; all ideas are valuable.
3. **Quantity** Produce as many ideas as possible.
4. **Building** Expand on other people's ideas.

Since individuals can sometimes produce better ideas than a brainstorming group,[75] brainwriting was developed as a hybrid of both individual and group brainstorming. Brainwriting produces more ideas than brainstorming.[76] To capture individual ideas first, the brainwriting technique gives people a set period to generate their own written ideas. Next, these are shared with a group, either face-to-face or via computer. The ideas are collected, categorized, and evaluated. In another variation, the ideas are written on separate note cards that are passed to a neighbor who is instructed to a) use the idea as a stimulus for another idea, b) build upon or modify the idea, or c) pass it on to the next person.

CULTURE AND CREATIVITY

Some research indicates that the personal and contextual characteristics shown in Exhibits 12–1 and 12–2 may not apply to all cultures, which is not surprising as most of the creativity research has been done in Western countries, primarily in the United States.[77] Researchers found greater expectations that employees share expertise and act in accordance with coworkers' expectations that they be creative in collectivist countries like Taiwan and China.[78] Another interesting finding is that creativity can flourish despite more authoritarian leadership styles in Egypt where employees are accustomed to more directive supervision; however, supportive communication and a caring atmosphere were still linked to greater creativity in the Egyptian study.[79]

Conservation is one of Schwartz's universal values discussed in Chapter 6. People who hold the value of conservation prize tradition, conformity, and security. In U.S. research, people who rate high on conservation tend to be less creative than those who rate low. This fits with the hypothesis that cultures (both national and organizational) characterized by high uncertainty avoidance tend to be less creative. However, a study of Korean employees found that conservation moderated the relationship between transformational leadership and creativity. The Korean employees high in conservation were more likely to follow their leaders and show creativity in their response to the leaders' call for change.[80] Despite some cultural differences, however, scholars have found more similarities than differences in comparative studies of creativity.[81]

There is a link between creativity and the mindfulness that is part of cultural competence. This is not surprising because dealing with people from other cultures frequently requires creativity. In fact, some research shows that students were more creative after studying abroad. Because they have observed different ways of doing things, people with international experience can serve as cross-pollinators and bring new ideas to the organization. The following list, originally developed as guidelines for cross-cultural interaction,[82] is an example of cross-pollination. It has been adopted and modified to serve as a guideline for stimulating creativity.[83]

1. Cultivate curiosity and interest in your immediate surroundings
2. Look at problems from as many viewpoints as possible (i.e., openness to novelty)
3. Be alert to complexity and distinctions within groups or cultures
4. Be sensitive to different types of situational uniqueness that may occur
5. Orient yourself to the present by attending to all five senses
6. Cultivate "flow" or enjoyment in your everyday interaction with others
7. Practice divergent thinking or sideways learning (multiple ways of carving up the same domain)

These guidelines may prove useful as you work through the activities in the next section.

CLASS ACTIVITY: CREATIVITY SKITS

Purpose: The goal of the activity is to work on a creative task as a team and analyze what conditions promote or hinder creativity. (Time allotted: 75 minutes)

STEP 1.   The class will be divided into teams of six to seven participants. The oldest member of the team will serve as the team leader. While the participants locate the underlying course themes they identified for the Class Preparation question, the instructor will give each team leader their instructions.

STEP 2.   With their leader's guidance, each team's task is to develop a creative five-minute skit that portrays the underlying course themes. All team members must participate in the skit except the leader. (25 minutes)

STEP 3.   Each team performs their skits. (Approximately 25 minutes depending on class size)

STEP 4.   Plenary Debriefing (25 minutes)
   a.   What did you observe from watching the skits?
   b.   How creative was your group? What was it like to work together on a creative task?
   c.   What factors helped you be creative?
   d.   Did any factors hinder your creativity?
   e.   What have you learned about managing creativity that you can apply in a real-life situation?

LEARNING POINTS

1. Creativity is the development of ideas about products, practices, services, or procedures that are novel and potentially useful to the organization.
2. Innovation is defined as the implementation of new ideas at the individual, group, or organizational level.

3. Creativity requires time, a great deal of hard work, and strenuous mental energy.

4. Personality traits of creative people include persistence, self-confidence, independence, attraction to complexity, tolerance of ambiguity, and intuitiveness. Creative types have broad interests, high energy, a concern with achievement, and a love of their work.

5. Risk taking is a characteristic of creative people that is also influenced by organizational reactions to failure.

6. Cognitive creativity skills include the ability to think creatively, generate alternatives, engage in divergent thinking and suspend judgment.

7. Individual creativity is based on domain-specific knowledge that has been developed via education, training, experience, and contextual knowledge.

8. Creative people are motivated by intrinsic motivation.

9. Organizations can foster creativity by hiring a creative, diverse workforce; designing complex, challenging jobs; setting clear goals, including creativity goals; and instructing employees to be creative. They should also recognize and reward creativity but not focus overmuch on extrinsic rewards.

10. The management style of creative organizations should encourage risk taking, autonomy, productivity, and a supportive climate and work group. The organizational culture should reinforce these values. The supervisory style should be supportive, and the decision making style should be participative (except in some cultures more accustomed to authoritarian leadership).

11. Managers can foster more creativity in employees by forming nurturing relationships and by encouraging and supporting them.

12. Creative employees should expect feedback on their work, and that feedback should be developmental and constructive.

13. The organization design that fosters creativity is a flexible, flat structure that promotes internal and external interaction, and close contact with customers.

14. The creative process, triggered by a problem, consists of four stages: preparation, incubation, illumination, and verification.

15. The flow state in creativity occurs when people experience a state of effortless concentration and enjoyment.

16. Two techniques that encourage creative thinking are brainstorming and brainwriting. The rules for brainstorming are: expressiveness, nonevaluation, quantity, and building.

 **ACTION SCRIPTS**

FOR EMPLOYEES

People who are creative look beyond the status quo to question why things are not done differently. As Anthony Jay noted, "The uncreative mind can spot wrong answers, but it takes a very creative mind to spot wrong questions."

- They make time to be creative and reduce distractions. This may mean going into a creative "bubble" in which they strip their lives down to nothing but the project at hand. They avoid multitasking.

- Creative people, almost by definition, tend to narrow their focus to the work at hand, overlooking the broader organization. Experts, however, understand that the success of their creation depends on obtaining organizational resources and support. Therefore, they devote energy to marshalling support.

- Experts know how to pitch a new idea so that it is more likely to be accepted by others—"catchers." Successful pitchers are neither lecturers nor zealots; instead they draw in catchers so they also feel that they are contributing to the idea and being creative themselves.[84] Experts know when it is most effective for catchers to think it was their own idea.

FOR MANAGERS

Managers who are skilled at managing creative people look for subordinates' natural talent and provide coaching to improve it.

- Leaders model creative behaviors and curiosity because they understand that creativity can be learned from role models.
- They include people with different thinking styles and disciplines on teams and committees. Expert managers champion and protect worthy ideas.
- They understand that top management support is a crucial factor in successfully developing new products. Therefore, they get senior management involved early in the development cycle and manage the political aspects of gaining organizational support.
- They understand which meetings are absolutely necessary and provide for interactions that spark creativity. Meetings that are simply distractions are eliminated. As Peter Drucker, the late management guru, said, "One either meets or one works."
- Experience teaches them where they can't compromise their judgment, and experts hold out for high standards. For example, when an engineering VP had a quality problem that required a creative solution, he insisted on recruiting the best possible team to help him. He had learned the hard way that it was better to hurt people's feelings who were excluded rather than satisfice and try to make do with employees who were not talented enough to do the work he envisioned.
- Although some people believe they are more creative under pressure, this is not generally the case. Experts ensure their employees have enough time to think, ponder, and let ideas incubate.

FOR ORGANIZATIONAL ARCHITECTS

Expert organizational architects adopt the following practices to increase innovation and creativity:

- Evaluation processes that evaluate innovations on their fit with strategic goals, rather than judging them only by financial controls and developmental costs.
- Selection practices that identify people who are more likely to be creative and who demonstrate breadth and depth of expertise.
- Placement mechanisms that ensure that more creative people are placed in jobs that require more creativity.
- An organizational culture that values diversity, autonomy, trust, collaboration, and productivity.
- A workspace designed to promote creativity. This often takes the form of both individual and common space, since creative employees may need both isolation and interaction. Research has found that people are less creative when they work in crowded, noisy areas.
- Mechanisms for soliciting and capturing employee ideas, like an open door policy, freedom to email the CEO, suggestion boxes, etc.
- Minimal bureaucratic rules and requirements.
- Training programs on creativity.
- Training for managers and leaders on how to manage creative people in innovative organizations.
- Procedures for setting and tracking creativity goals.
- A performance appraisal system that measures creativity but takes a developmental orientation with informational feedback.
- Rewards and incentives programs that further support and recognize creative contributions.

PERSONAL APPLICATION ASSIGNMENT

YOUR CREATIVE AUTOBIOGRAPHY

Twyla Tharp, the famous choreographer, created a test, the basis of the questions below, to help people know themselves better, by forcing them to go back to their roots and look for patterns.

Answer these questions quickly and honestly. Analyze your answers to see if you can identify your creative strengths and where you could focus your creativity. Where could you make your greatest creative contribution?

1. What is the first creative moment you remember?

2. Was anyone there to witness or appreciate it?

3. What is the best idea you've ever had?

4. What made it great in your mind?

5. Can you connect the dots that led you to this idea?

6. What is the dumbest idea you've ever had? (This question does not refer to previous failed relationships.)

7. What made it stupid?

8. What is your creative ambition?

9. What are the obstacles to this ambition?

10.   What are the vital steps to achieving this vision?

11.   Do you have any rituals that you use before setting to creative work?

12.   What is your first creative act each day?

13.   Which artists do you admire the most?

14.   Why are they your role models?

15.   What do you and your role models have in common?

16.   When confronted with superior intelligence or talent how do you respond?

17.   When faced with impending success or the threat of failure, how do you respond?

18.   When you work, do you love the process or the result?

19.   What is your ideal creative activity?

20. What is your greatest fear with regard to creativity?

21. What is the likelihood of either of the answers to the previous two questions happening?

22. What is your greatest dream?

If you want to see how Twyla Tharp answered many of these questions, go to pages 54–59 of her book on creativity.

Source: Adapted from T. Tharp, *The Creative Habit: Learn It and Use It for Life* (New York: Simon & Schuster 2003): 45–46.

INSTRUCTIONS FOR TEAM LEADERS

Count off by twos. The "ones" will be green leaders, and the "twos" will be red leaders. Your instructions are shown below. Please follow them as closely as possible.

Green Leaders — Supportive Leaders
1. Do not read them your instructions. Have the team members share their themes and ask them to quickly come to a consensus on the key themes they wish to present.
2. Tell them to be as creative as possible.
3. Tell them you are not allowed to act in the skit but that you are there to help them in any way you can. Offer to get them any resources they might need.
4. Be very positive—do not be critical in any way.
5. Make sure the team has a very supportive climate and try to make it fun for them.

Red Leaders — Directive Leaders
1. Do not read them your instructions. Ask them for the themes they identified and, <u>by yourself</u>, choose the 3-4 common themes you want them to include. Announce to them that these are the themes they will be acting out.
2. Tell them you are not allowed to act in the skit, but you are there to keep them on the right track and coordinate.
3. Ask them for their ideas and personally choose the idea you think is best. (Do not ask for their input into this decision.)
4. Make sure you watch the clock and remind them how much time they have left until the skit must be ready.

ENDNOTES

[1] T. M. Amabile, *Creativity in Context*, (Boulder, CO: Westview, 1996); I. Nonaka, "The Knowledge-Creating Company," *Harvard Business Review 69* (1991): 96–104.

[2] C. E. Shalley and L. L. Gilson, "What Leaders Need to Know: A Review of Social and Contextual Factors that Can Foster or Hinder Creativity," *Leadership Quarterly 15* (2004): 33–53; C. E. Shalley, J. Zhou, and G. R. Oldham, "The Effects of Personal and Contextual Characteristics on Creativity: Where Should We Go from Here," *Journal of Management 30*(6) (2004): 933–958.

[3] C. E. Shalley, L. L. Gilson, and T. C. Blum, "Matching Creativity Requirements and the Work Environment: Effects on Satisfaction and Intention to Leave," *Academy of Management Journal 43* (2000): 215–223; K. Unsworth, "Unpacking Creativity," *Academy of Management Review 26* (2001): 289–297.

[4] L. Zaragoza, "A Big Bloomin' Tulip Tribute," *Mercury News* (November 11, 2005): 1B–2B.

[5] B. Nalebuff and I. Ayres. *Why Not? How to Use Everyday Ingenuity to Solve Problems Big and Small* (Cambridge, MA: Harvard Business School Press, 2003): 5.

[6] Amabile, *Creativity in Context*; J. Zhou and C. E. Shalley, "Research on Employee Creativity: A Critical Review and Directions for Future Research," in J. Martocchio (ed.), *Research in Personnel and Human Resource Management* (Oxford, England: Elsevier, 2003): 165–217.

[7] Amabile, *Creativity in Context*; N. Anderson and N. King, "Innovation in Organizations," in C. L. Cooper, and I. T. Robertson (eds.), *International Review of Organizational Psychology* (Chichester: Wiley, 1993): 1–34; M. D. Mumford and S. B. Gustafson, "Creativity Syndrome: Integration, Application, and Innovation," *Psychological Bulletin 103* (1988): 27–43.

[8] K. Melymuka, "Sky King," *Computerworld 32*(39) (September 28, 1998): 68.

[9] R. M. Kanter, J. Kao, and F. Wiersema, *Innovation,* (New York: Harper, 1997); and "Ten Commandments for Managing Creative People," *Fortune 131* (January 16, 1995) 135.

[10] P. R. Nayak, and J. M. Ketteringham, *Breakthroughs!* (New York: Rawson Associates, 1986).

[11] For recent reviews of creativity, see C. E. Shalley and L. L. Gilson, "What Leaders Need to Know: A Review of Social and Contextual Factors that Can Foster or Hinder Creativity," *Leadership Quarterly 15* (2004): 33–53; M. A. Runco, "Creativity" *Annual Review of Psychology 55* (2004): 657–87.

[12] R. Woodman, J. Sawyer, and R. Griffin, "Toward a Theory of Organizational Creativity," *Academy of Management Review 18* (1993): 293–321. These authors also identified social and contextual factors that will be discussed later in the chapter.

[13] S. Z. Dudeck and W. Hall, " Personality Consistency: Eminent Architects 25 Years Later," *Creativity Research Journal 4* (1991): 213–32; H. E. Gruber, " The Life Space of a Scientist: The Visionary Function and Other Aspects of Jean Piaget's Thinking," *Creativity Research Journal 9* (1996): 251–65.

[14] M. D. Mumford, "Managing Creative People: Strategies and Tactics for Innovation," *Human Resource Management Review 10*(3) (2000): 313–51.

[15] For correlations between openness to experience and creativity, see G. J. Feist, "A Meta–Analysis of Personality in Scientific and Artistic Creativity," *Personality and Social Psychology Review, 4* (1998): 290–309; and R. R. McCrae and P. T. Costa, "Conceptions and Correlates of Openness to Experience," in Hogan, J. Johnson, and S. Briggs (eds.), *Handbook of Personality Psychology* (San Diego, CA; Academic Press, 1997): 825–847. For the relationship with managerial ratings of creativity, see L. S. Scratchley and A. R. Hakstian, "The Measurement and Prediction of Managerial Creativity," *Creativity Research Journal 13* (2000): 367–84.

[16] T. Tharp. *The Creative Habit: Learn It and Use It for Life,* (New York: Simon & Schuster, 2003).

[17] C. Martindale, "Personality, Situation, and Creativity," in J. A. Glover, R. R. Ronning, and C. R. Reynolds, (eds.), *Handbook of Creativity* (New York: Plenum, 1989): 211–32; F. B. Barron and D. M. Harrington, "Creativity, Intelligence, and Personality," *Annual Review of Psychology 32* (1982): 439–76; and M. Csikszentmihalyi, *Creativity: Flow and the Psychology of Discovery and Invention* (New York: HarperCollins, 1996); D. W. MacKinnon, "Assessing Creative Persons," *Journal of Creative Behavior 1* (1967): 303–04; E. Raudsepp, "Are You a Creative Manager?" *Management Review 58* (1978): 15–16; and R. J. Sternberg, "A Three–Faced Model of Creativity," in R. J. Sternberg, (ed.), *The Nature of Creativity* (London: Cambridge University Press, 1988): 125–47; D. R. Brophy, "Understanding, Measuring, and Enhancing Individual Creative Problem Solving Efforts," *Creativity Research Journal 11* (1998): 123–50; H. J. Walberg and W. E. Stariha, "Productive Human Capital: Learning, Creativity, and Eminence," *Creativity Research Journal 5* (1992): 323–40.

[18] T. M. Amabile, "A Model of Creativity and Innovations in Organizations," in B. M. Straw and L. L. Cummings (eds.), *Research in Organizational Behavior, vol. 10* (Greenwich, CT: JAI Press, 1988): 123–67.

[19] Ibid.

[20] M. Ray and R. Myers, *Creativity in Business* (New York: Doubleday, 1986): 4.

[21] A. S. Vincent , B. P. Decker, and M. D. Mumford, "Divergent Thinking, Intelligence, and Expertise: A Test of Alternative Models," *Creatvity Research Journal 14* (2002): 163–78.

[22] T. M. Amabile, R. Conti, H. Coon, J. Lazenby, and M. Herron, "Assessing the Work Environment for Creativity," *Academy of Management Journal 39* (1996): 1154–84.

[23] M. Bellis, "Microscopic View of Velcro." http://inventors.about.com/library/weekly/aa091297.htm. Accessed 11/13/05.

[24] M. J. Kirton, "Adaptors and Innovators: A Description and Measure," *Journal of Applied Psychology 61* (1976): 622–29; M. J. Kirton, *Adaptors and Innovators: Styles of Creativity and Problem Solving, 2nd ed.,* (New York: Routledge, 1994).

[25] R. T. Keller, "Predictors of the Performance of Project Groups in R&D Organizations," *Academy of Management Journal 29* (1986): 715–26; P. Tierney, S. M. Farmer, and G. B. Graen, "An Examination of Leadership and Employee Creativity: The Relevance of Traits and Relationships," *Personnel Psychology 52* (1999): 591–620.

[26] Tharp, *The Creative Habit.*

[27] C. H. Utman, "Performance Effects of Motivational State: A Meta-Analysis," *Personality and Social Psychology Review 1* (1997): 170–82; J. Zhou & C. E. Shalley, "Research on Employee Creativity: A Critical Review and Directions for Future Research," in J. Martocchio (ed.), *Research in Personnel and Human Resource Management* (Oxford, England: Elsevier, 2003): 165–217.

[28] Amabile, Conti, Coon, Lazenby, and Herron, "Assessing the Work Environment for Creativity."

[29] R. I. Sutton, "The Weird Rules of Creativity," *Harvard Business Review 79* (8) (2001): 8.

[30] T. M. Amabile and N. D. Gryskiewicz, "The Creative Environment Scales: Work Environment Inventory," *Creativity Research Journal 3* (1989): 231–52; S. M. Farmer, P. Tierney, and K. Kung-McIntyre, "Employee Creativity in Taiwan: An Application of Role Identity Theory," *Academy of Management Journal 46* (2003): 618–30.

[31] J. R. Hackman and G. R. Oldham, *Work Redesign* (Reading, MA: Addison–Wesley, 1980).

[32] P. A. Roos and D. J. Treiman, "Worker Functions and Work Traits for the 1970 U.S. Census Classification," in A. Miller (ed.), *Work, Jobs, and Occupations* (Washington, DC: National Academy Press, 1980): 336–89.

[33] L. Hatcher, T. L. Ross, and D. Collins, " Prosocial Behavior, Job Complexity, and Suggestion Contribution Under Gainsharing Plans," *Journal of Applied Behavioral Science 25* (1989):231–48.

[34] H. E. Gruber and S. N. Davis, "Inching Our Way Up Mount Olympus: The Evolving–Systems Approach to Creative Thinking," in R. J. Sternberg, et al. (ed.), *The Nature of Creativity: Contemporary Psychological Perspectives* (New York: Cambridge University Press, 1988): 243–70.

[35] T. M. Amabile and S. Gryskiewicz, *Creativity in the R&D Laboratory. Technical Report 30* (Greensboro, NC: Center for Creative Leadership, 1987); R. Katz and T. J. Allen, "Project Performance and Locus of Influence in the R&D Matrix," in R. Katz (ed.), *Managing Professionals in Innovative Organizations: A Collection of Readings* (Cambridge, MA: Ballinger, 1988): 469–84.

[36] T. M. Amabile, J. S. Mueller, W. B. Simpson, C. N. Hadley, S. J. Kramer, and L. Fleming, "Time Pressures and Creativity in Organizations: A Longitudinal Field Study," *HBS Working Paper 02–073* (2003).

[37] C. E. Shalley, "Effects of Productivity Goals, Creativity Goals, and Personal Discretion on Individual Creativity," *Journal of Applied Psychology 76* (1991): 179–85; C. E. Shalley, "Effects of Coaction, Expected Evaluation, and Goal Setting on Creativity and Productivity," *Academy of Management Journal 38* (1995): 483–505; Amabile and Gryskiewicz, *Creativity in the R&D Laboratory.*

[38] J. K. Pinto and J. E. Prescott, "Variations in Critical Success Factors Over the Stages in the Project Life Cycle," *Journal of Management 14* (1988): 5–18.

[39] C. E. Shalley and L. L. Gilson, "What Leaders Need to Know: A Review of Social and Contextual Factors that Can Foster or Hinder Creativity," *Leadership Quarterly 15* (2004): 38.

[40] T. M. Amabile, "Motivating Creativity in Organizations: On Doing What You Love and Loving What You Do," *Creativity Management Review 4*(1) (1997): 39–58.

[41] Amabile, *Creativity in Context.*

[42] L. Naiman, "Fostering Innovation in an IT World." http://www.creativityatwork.com/ articlesContent/ innovation–IT.htm. Accessed 11/28/05.

[43] J. Martin, "Inside the Pixar Dream Factory" *Fortune Small Business 13* (February 2003): 48.

[44] B. Ford and B. H. Kleiner, "Managing Engineers Effectively" *Business 37* (1987): 49–52.

[45] M. A. West, "Sparkling Fountains or Stagnant Ponds: An Integrative Model of Creativity and Innovation Implementation in Work Groups," *Applied Psychology: An International Review 51*(3)(2002): 355–424.

[46] D. K. Simonton, *Greatness: Who Makes History and Why* (New York: Guilford, 1994).

[47] Amabile and Gryskiewicz, *Creativity in the R&D Laboratory.*

[48] C. E. Shally and J. E. Perry–Smith, "Effects of Social–Psychological Factors on Creative Performance: The Role of Informational and Controlling Expected Evaluation and Modeling Experience," *Organizational Behavior and Human Decision Processes 84* (2001): 1–22; J. Zhou, "Feedback Valence, Feedback Style, Task Autonomy, and Achievement Orientation: Interactive Effects of Creative Performance," *Journal of Applied Psychology 83* (1998): 261–76; J. Zhou, "When the Presence of Creative Coworkers is Related to Creativity: Role of Supervisor Close Monitoring, Developmental Feedback, and Creative Personality," *Journal of Applied Psychology 88* (2003): 413–22.

[49] P. Tierney and S. M. Farmer, "Creative Self-Efficacy: Potential Antecedents and Relationship to Creative Performance," *Academy of Management Journal 45* (2002):1137–48.

[50] A. Cummings, and G. R. Oldham, "Enhancing Creativity: Managing Contexts for the High Potential Employee," *Creativity Management Review 40*(1) (1997): 22–38; Amabile, "Motivating Creativity in Organizations: On Doing What you Love and Loving What You Do;" E. L. Deci, J. P. Connell, and R. M. Ryan, "Self Determination in a Work Organization," *Journal of Applied Psychology 74* (1989): 580–90; R. F. Lovelace, "*Stimulating Creativity through Managerial Intervention*," *R&D Management 16* (1986): 161–74.

[51] R. W. Woodman, J. E. Sawyer, and R. W. Griffin, "Toward A Theory of Organizational Creativity," *Academy of Management Review 18* (1993): 293–321; Deci, Connell, and Ryan, "Self Determination in a Work Organization."

[52] F. M. Andrews and F. Farris, "Supervisory Practices and Innovation in Scientific Terms," *Personnel Psychology 20* (1967): 497–575.

[53] S. G. Scott and R. A. Bruce, "Determinants of Innovative Behavior: A Path Model of Individual Innovation in the Workplace," *Academy of Management Journal 37* (1994): 580–607; P. Tierney, S. M. Farmer, and G. B. Graen, "An Examination of Leadership and Employee Creativity: The Relevance of Traits and Relationships," *Personnel Psychology 52* (1999): 591–620.

[54] Shalley and Gilson, "What Leaders Need to Know: A Review of Social and Contextual Factors that Can Foster or Hinder Creativity."

[55] T. H. Davenport, S. Cantrell, and R. Thomas, "The Art of Work: Facilitating the Effectiveness of high-end Knowledge Workers" *Outlook Journal*, Accenture (1 January 2002): 44; T. Davenport, *Thinking for a Living: How to Get Better Performance Results from Knowledge Workers* (Harvard Business School Press, 2005).

[56] Shalley and Gilson, "What Leaders Need to Know."

[57] S. Taggar, "Individual Creativity and Group Ability to Utilize Individual Creative Resources: A Multilevel Model," *Academy of Management Journal 45* (2002): 315–330.

[58] R. T. Leenders, A. J. van Engelen, and J. Kratzer, "Virtuality, Communication, and New Product Team Creativity: A Social Network Perspective," *Journal of Engineering and Technology Management 20* (2003): 69–92.

[59] C. K. De Dreu and M. A. West, "Minority Dissent and Team Innovation: The Importance of Participation in Decision Making," *Journal of Applied Psychology 8* (2001): 1191–1201.

[60] P. E. Tesluck, J. L. Farr, and S. R. Klein, "Influences of Organizational Culture and Climate on Individual Creativity," *Journal of Creative Behavior 31* (1997): 27–41; L. D. McLean "Organizational Culture's Influence on Creativity and Innovation: A Review of the Literature and Implications for Human Resource, Development," *Advances in Developing Human Resources 7*(2) (2005): 226–46.

[61] A. Abbey and J. Dickinson, "R&D Work Climate and Innovation in Semiconductors," *Academy of Management Journal 26* (1983): 362–68.

[62] Davenport, Cantrell, and Thomas, "The Art of Work."

[63] R. Florida and J. Goodnight, "Managing for Creativity" *Harvard Business Review 83*(7)(July–August 2005): 125–131.

[64] D. G. Ancona and D. F. Caldwell, "Demography and Design: Predictors of New Product Team Performance," *Organization Science 3* (1992): 321–41.

[65] Davenport, Cantrell, and Thomas, "The Art of Work."

[66] N. C. Wong, "The Brains Behind IDEO," *Mercury News* (November 6, 2005): E1–E2.

[67] R. S. Burt "Structural Holes and Good Ideas, " *American Journal of Sociology 110*(2) 2004: 349–399.

[68] N. C. Wong, "The Brains Behind IDEO," *Mercury News* (November 6, 2005): E1–E2.

[69] T. Stevens, "Creativity Killers," *Industry Week 244*(2) (63, January 23, 1995): 63; and Amabile, "Motivating Creativity in Organizations: On Doing What You Love and Loving What You Do."

[70] D. G. Marquis, "The Anatomy of Successful Innovations," *Managing Advancing Technology 1* (1972): 34–48; and J. F. Mee, "The Creative Thinking Process," *Indiana Business Review 3* (1956): 4–9.

[71] M. M. Csikszentmihalyi, *Finding Flow: The Psychology of Engagement with Everyday Life* (New York: Basic Books, 1997).

[72] M. Csikszentmihalyi, "Happiness and Creativity: Going with the Flow" *The Futurist 31*(5) (September–October, 1997): 8–12.

[73] J. M. Higgins, "Creating Creativity," *Training and Development 48*(11) (November 1994): 11–16. Two of the most well–read authors on creativity are R. von Oech, *A Whack on the Side of the Head* (New York: Warner, 1983); and E. de Bono, *New Think* (New York: Basic Books, 1968).

[74] L. Thompson, *The Mind and Heart of the Negotiator* (Upper Saddle River, NJ: Prentice Hall, 2001).

[75] M. Diehl and W. Strobe, "Productivity Loss in Brainstorming Groups: Toward the Solution of a Riddle" *Journal of Personality and Social Psychology 61* (1987): 392–403; P. B. Paulus & V. Brown "Enhancing Ideational Creativity in Groups: Lessons From Research on Brainstorming," in P. B. Paulus and B. Nijstad

(eds.) *Group Creativity: Innovation Through Collaboration*, (Oxford: Oxford University Press, 2003): 110–136.

[76] A. B. VanGundy, "Brainwriting." http: //creativityatwork.com/articlesContent/brainwriting.htm. Accessed 11/12/2005.

[77] N. Anderson, C. K. W. De Dreu, and B. A. Nijstad, " The Routinization of Innovation Research: A Constructively Critical Review of the State-of-the-Science," *Journal of Organizational Behavior 25* (2004): 147–73; G. W. England and I. Harpaz, "How Working is Defined: National Contexts and Demographic and Organizational Role Influences," *Journal of Organizational Behavior 11*(1990): 253–266.

[78] S. M. Farmer, P. Tierney, and K. Kung–McIntyre, "Employee Creativity in Taiwan: An Application of Role Identity Theory," *Academy of Management Journal 46* (2003): 618–630; M. G. Martinsons and A. B. Martinsons, "Conquering Cultural Constraints to Cultivate Chinese Management Creativity and Innovation," *Journal of Management Development 15* (1996): 18–36.

[79] G. Rice, "Individual Values, Organizational Context, and Employee Creativity: Evidence from Egyptian Organizations," *Journal of Business Research 59 (2006): 233–241.*

[80] S. Shin and J. Zhou, "Transformational Leadership, Conservation, and Creativity: Evidence from Korea," *Academy of Management Journal 46* (2003): 703–714.

[81] Rice, "Individual Values, Organizational Context, and Employee Creativity: Evidence from Egyptian Organizations.

[82] S. Ting-Toomey, *Communicating Across Cultures* (New York: Guilford, 1999): 268.

[83] M. Csikszentmihalyi, *Creativity: Flow and the Psychology of Discovery and Invention.* (New York: HarperCollins, 1996); H. Gardner, *Leading Minds: Anatomy of Leadership* (New York: Basic Books,1995); E. Langer, *The Power of Mindful Learning* (Reading, MA: Addison–Wesley, 1997).

[84] K. D. Elsbach, "How to Pitch a Brilliant Idea," *Harvard Business Review 81*(9) (September, 2003): 117–123.

Chapter 13

▲▲

CONFLICT
AND NEGOTIATION

OBJECTIVES By the end of this chapter, you should be able to:

A. Describe behaviors that characterize conflict.

B. Identify common sources of conflict.

C. Explain the five conflict-handling modes.

D. Understand the functional and dysfunctional nature of conflict.

E. Differentiate between distributive and integrative bargaining.

F. Explain principled negotiation.

G. Describe how culture influences conflict.

COSTA RICA'S ALTERNATIVE TO LABOR CONFLICT—SOLIDARISMO

Once upon a time in Costa Rica, there was a great deal of conflict in the work environment. Many of the country's labor unions were viewed as radical or leftist, particularly by industry, government, and the ruling elite. Labor-management relations were often confrontational, and both sides took an adversarial approach. One large multinational company shut down a major agricultural operation in the 1960s because they were tired of dealing with a communist labor union (many labor unions in Latin America are based on communist ideology). Company officials believed they could work more harmoniously in neighboring countries. One indication of the degree of mistrust that had evolved was the union's insistence that the company's threats to shut down were simply bluffs. As the story goes, the company had already stripped everything out of their buildings, including the toilets, but the union leaders were still maintaining this was all a ruse. The company's departure dealt a serious blow to the economy. Some Costa Ricans worried that other companies interested in foreign direct investment would be put off by the strongly adversarial nature of labor-management relations. As Roberto Rojas, former minister of the economy, industry, and commerce, stated, "During the 1950s and 1960s, unions were politically part of the communist movement and disruptive to our work environment. Society decided we did not want unions in Costa Rica."*

*N. Sheppard, Jr., "AFL-CIO Asks U.S. Officials to Revoke Costa Rica's Special Trade Privileges," *The Journal of Commerce and Commercial Bulletin* 397(28035) (August 10, 1993) 4A.

What many see as a win-win solution to this problem is credited to two Costa Ricans. In the late 1940s, Alberto Martén Chavarría began advocating a concept called solidarismo (solidarity).† The idea caught hold in several companies but became even more widespread after a Catholic priest, Claudio Solano, founded an institute in 1963 that taught the principles of solidarismo. Its basic premises are that management and labor are interdependent and should share the common goal of making the organization succeed leading to benefits for both management and labor.

In practice, both employers and employees contribute a percentage of employee salaries to their organization's solidarismo association fund. From their peers, employees elect a board of directors to manage the fund. Unlike a traditional union setup or management-driven benefits, each organization's association decides for itself how the money will be used. Some funds may be invested in company stock, but they also may opt for loans, company cafeterias, recreation centers, transportation, education needs, housing assistance, or low-cost medical and dental care. These services are also supposed to benefit the families of employees.

Some companies include solidarismo membership as a job benefit in their newspaper advertisements. As of 1994, 200,000 of Costa Rica's 900,000 workers were members of solidarismo. According to a 1999 source, the membership totals about 43 percent of the working population.‡ Most employers like solidarismo because it allows them to resolve labor disputes and negotiate work contracts without strikes or violent confrontations. Solidarismo is credited with the transformation from adversarial to collaborative relations in Costa Rica's labor environment. The payoffs, a high level of foreign business investment and labor peace, have been important factors in making Costa Rica's economy the most stable in Central America.

Not everyone, however, is a fan. The most vociferous critics have been international labor organizations. For example, the ILO (International Labor Organization) based in Geneva claimed solidarismo interferes with trade union activity. In 1994, the AFL-CIO made an unsuccessful request that the United States drop Costa Rica's favorable trading privileges. In their argument, the U.S. labor union claimed that solidarismo functions like a union and that membership is a requirement of employment. Both the ILO and the AFL-CIO have urged Costa Rica to provide more protection to workers who are trying to form trade unions. Nevertheless, for a country that highly values democracy and peace (Costa Rica has no armed forces), solidarismo was an appropriate and innovative win-win solution.

 **CLASS PREPARATION**

A. Read "Costa Rica's Alternative to Labor Conflict—Solidarismo."
B. Fill out the Emotional Style Questionnaire.
C. Answer these questions.
   1. What was the worst experience you ever had with conflict? What was so bad about it?

---

†Information for this vignette is taken from N. Sheppard, Jr., "AFL-CIO Asks U.S. Officials to Revoke Costa Rica's Special Trade Privileges," *The Journal of Commerce and Commercial Bulletin 397,* (28035) (August 10, 1993): 4A; O. Bejarano, "La Fuerza del Solidarismo," *La Nacion,* (July 18, 1997); "Bananas," http://www.iuf.org/iuf/Ag/02.htm, Accessed on October 20, 1999. "The Real Record on Workers' Rights in Central America," AFL-CIO (April, 2005). http://www.globalpolicy.org/socecon/trade/2005/04realrecord.pdf#search=%22Solidarismo%20-%20Costa%20Rica%22. Accessed 10/2/06.

‡ R. Jiménez Vega, "Solidarismo in Costa Rica," http://www.edyd.com/solidarismo/englishgeneral.htm, Accessed on 10/20/99.

2. What are some of the things that caused the conflict?

3. Was the conflict ever resolved? How?

4. What would you like to learn about conflict?

D. While reading the chapter, make a list of the cues you will look for in conflict situations.

Emotional Style Questionnaire

Read each statement and indicate whether you think it is true or false for you in a negotiation situation. Force yourself to answer each one as generally true or false (i.e., do not respond with "I don't know").

Statement	Answer (T or F)
1. In a negotiation situation, it is best to keep a cool head.	_____
2. I believe in negotiations you can "catch more flies with honey."	_____
3. It is important to me that I maintain control in a negotiation situation.	_____
4. Establishing a positive sense of rapport with the other party is key to effective negotiation.	_____
5. I am good at displaying emotions in negotiations to get what I want.	_____
6. Emotions are the downfall of effective negotiation.	_____

7. I definitely believe that the "squeaky wheel gets the grease" in many negotiation situations. _____

8. If you are nice in negotiations, you can get more than if you are cold or neutral. _____

9. In negotiation, you have to "fight fire with fire." _____

10. I honestly think better when I am in a good mood. _____

11. I would never want to let the other party know how I really felt in a negotiation. _____

12. I believe that in negotiations, you can "catch more flies with a fly-swatter." _____

13. I have used emotion to manipulate others in negotiations. _____

14. I believe that good moods are definitely contagious. _____

15. It is very important to make a very positive first impression when negotiating. _____

16. The downfall of many negotiators is that they lose personal control in a negotiation. _____

17. It is best to keep a "poker face" in negotiation situations. _____

18. It is very important to get the other person to respect you when negotiating. _____

19. I definitely want to leave the negotiation with the other party feeling good. _____

20. If the other party gets emotional, you can use it to your advantage in a negotiation. _____

21. I believe that it is important to "get on the same wavelength" as the other party. _____

22. It is important to demonstrate "resolve" in a negotiation. _____

23. If I sensed that I was not under control, I would call a temporary halt to the negotiation. _____

24. I would not hesitate to make a threat in a situation if I felt the other party would believe it. _____

Scoring the Questionnaire

Computing Your "Rational" score: For items, 1, 3, 6, 11, 16, 17, 20, and 23, give yourself 1 point for every true answer and subtract 1 point for every false answer. The total is your "Rational" score. Rational score: _____

Computing Your "Positive" score: For items 2, 4, 8, 10, 14, 15, 19, and 21, give yourself 1 point for every true answer and subtract 1 point for every false answer. The total is your "Positive" score. Positive score: _____

Computing Your "Negative" score: For items 5, 7, 9, 12, 13, 18, 22, and 24, give yourself 1 point for every true answer and subtract 1 point for every false answer. The total is your "Negative" score. Negative score: _____

Source: S. Kopelman, A. Rosette, and L. Thompson, "The Three Faces of Eve: An Examination of Strategic Positive, Negative, and Neutral Emotional Styles in Negotiations," cited in L. Thompson, *The Mind and Heart of the Negotiator* (Upper Saddle River, NJ: Prentice Hall, 2005).

THE KNOWLEDGE BASE

The ability to avoid or resolve the ubiquitous conflicts that arise in organizations is a key skill for both managers and employees. *Conflict is a form of interaction among parties that differ in interests, perceptions, and preferences. Conflict is also defined as "the process that begins when one party perceives that the other has negatively affected, or is about to negatively affect, something that he or she cares about."*[1] Although it is true that some individuals are more likely to become enmeshed in conflicts than others, organizational factors also cause conflict.

A classic field experiment conducted by Muzafer and Carolyn Sherif shows how easily behavior may be changed by putting individuals in a competitive, limited contact situation with another group.[2] Their research is called the Robbers Cave experiment, named after a summer camp at Robbers Cave, Oklahoma. A homogenous group of 22 boys was divided into two groups of 11. During the first stage of the experiment, the boys were unaware of the existence of the other group. Each group did a variety of cooperative tasks and developed their own group norms and leadership. During the second stage, the groups were informed they would be competing against each other in a week-long grand tournament. The counselors manipulated the scores so that the two groups were neck and neck until the last event. The groups became very antagonistic; there were several "commando raids," and the losing team robbed the winning team of their medals. When members of one group passed the other, they held their noses. In addition to this robust qualitative evidence of intergroup conflict, the researchers employed quantitative measures, which proved that (1) the members of each group had an ethnocentric view of the other group, and strongly preferred "their own kind," (2) each group overvalued the performance of its own members and devalued the performance of the other group, and (3) each group stereotyped the other. One's in-group was "brave, tough, and friendly," whereas the out-group was comprised of "sneaks, stinkers, and smart-alecks." These adjectives and this story may seem humorous, but we frequently see the same dynamics with union-management conflicts, less than friendly mergers, and interdepartmental feuds.

What caused the intergroup conflict at Robbers Cave? We-they feelings are very common, but they don't always blaze into open conflict. The key variable in this instance was the competition with its scarce resources. The winning team would receive wonderful prizes, whereas the losing team would win nothing. Because both groups already thought more highly of themselves than of the other group, whichever team lost would think the tournament was unfair.

During the third stage of the experiment, the researchers tested two of the most effective methods for reducing intergroup tension: (1) noncompetitive contact in which the two antagonistic groups have equal status and (2) a superordinate goal that was important for all and attainable only by joint cooperation.[3] As the Sherifs suspected, the first solution, equal status contact, did not work with groups that had reached this level of antagonism. However, the superordinate goal technique was effective: the boys had to cooperate in finding a leak in their water supply; they had to pool their money to rent a movie; and they had to pull a broken-down bus to get back to camp on an outing. By the last week of camp, the boys had ceased hostilities, eaten meals together, and opted to share a single bus on the trip home. Furthermore, they had begun to treat each other as individuals and chose friends for reasons other than common group membership. (Incidentally, the boys had a wonderful time at camp!)

A test of stereotyping at the end of the research revealed that the boys thought the members of the other group had changed and become more like themselves. In fact, the only difference was because of an environmental change from competition to cooperation.

SOURCES OF CONFLICT

Conflict within organizations is inevitable and comes from several sources. In addition to we-they situations resulting from group membership, conflict is likely to occur anywhere in the organization where there are "joints" or interdependent interfaces between different functions. The current move toward boundaryless "horizontal corporations" that organize themselves around core processes rather than functions is, in part, an attempt to avoid conflict between the "silos" of functional departments.[4] Other common causes of conflict are differences in values, interests, personalities, education, culture, perceptions, goals, and expectations. Conflict also may result from deficient information that causes misunderstandings or when there are power or status differences. Ambiguity can cause conflict when people battle over power or turf that has not been clearly assigned. Competition over scarce resources in whatever form—recognition, money, or even offices with windows—is also a source of conflict. Whenever the work is structured in such a way that groups are interdependent and their output depends on that of another department, there is a potential for conflict.

To some degree, the human factor determines whether conflict will actually occur at some of these interfaces. Individuals and different ethnic groups are comfortable with varying degrees of conflict. In U.S. culture, for example, people receive two somewhat contradictory messages: (1) fight and stand up for yourself, but (2) only when it is acceptable. Part of being politically savvy is understanding when conflict is appropriate. Some people thrive on conflict and create it wherever they go; others go to great lengths to avoid it. Managers at either end of this continuum are likely to be less than effective in their jobs and in their ability to create a positive work environment for their employees.

FUNCTIONAL AND DYSFUNCTIONAL CONFLICT

Conflict can play both a positive or negative role in organizational life. Functional conflict can force us to articulate our views and positions, which usually results in greater clarification and understanding. It makes the values and belief system of the organization more visible and makes it easier to see organizational priorities. Conflict helps preserve groups when it serves as a safety valve that allows people to blow off steam and still maintain their relationships. When people band together in a conflict, group cohesiveness is increased. One of the most valuable contributions of conflict is the creativity that results when we are forced to find new ways to look at situations and seek innovative solutions and decisions. Thus, two types of conflict, if properly managed, can be beneficial. *Task conflict refers to conflict about the work itself such as its substance and goals; process conflict focuses on how the work gets done.* Both task and process conflict can lead to better performance if employees have the appropriate resolution skills.[5]

Conflict, unfortunately, can also be extremely dysfunctional for organizations. From the Robber's Cave study as well as other studies, we know that there are certain negative behaviors that are typical of conflict situations: stereotyping, overvaluation of one's own group, devaluation of the other group, polarization on the issues, decreased communication between groups, distortion of perceptions, and escalation. Kenneth Thomas, a well-known conflict researcher, notes "Escalation is reflected in such changes as increasing the number and size of the issues disputed, increasing hostility, increasing competitiveness, pursuing increasingly extreme demands or objectives, using increasing coercive tactics, decreasing trust, and enlisting other parties to take sides in the conflict."[6] Under conflict situations, *people often feel compelled to take sides and adopt extreme positions at the opposite poles of an argument, called polarization,* which leaves little room for compromise or agreement. Conflict often is characterized by an unwillingness to give the other party the benefit of the doubt with respect to motives or actions; instead, people often assume the worst about adversaries. In addition to blocking the achievement of organizational goals, dysfunctional conflict reduces productivity, morale, and job satisfaction and can cause heightened anxiety, absenteeism, and turnover.

Most of us have seen instances in which too much conflict has paralyzed groups and individuals. However, too little expressed conflict can be just as dysfunctional and can stifle innovation.[7] Brown maintains that conflict is a natural occurrence between groups and that the task of the manager is not necessarily to eliminate conflict but to maintain it at a level appropriate to the task. Too much conflict or the wrong kind of conflict can lead to defensiveness and an inability to work collaboratively toward organizational goals. Research has shown that most *relationship conflict* is dysfunctional. *Relationship conflict involves disagreements about interpersonal relations.*[8] This type of conflict frequently leads to friction, interpersonal animosity, and hurt feelings that can make future interaction extremely difficult. More and more companies and work teams are insisting that employees learn conflict management skills. Intel, for example, attempts to set the stage for healthy conflict by training employees in constructive confrontation. Questioning and arguing over ideas is encouraged—personal attacks and persisting after a decision or resolution has been made is not. After raising their objections, employees are expected to be committed to whatever decision has been made and move forward.

Sometimes managers will instruct groups or individuals in conflict to go off and solve a conflict themselves. Unless the employees already possess good conflict resolution skills, this can result in more harm than good. If we want the diversity of ideas that results when organizations encourage healthy conflict, we have to give employees the skills they need to manage conflict in a positive way. Work teams, in particular, need to be trained in conflict management. When groups share norms about how conflict should be handled and possess the requisite skills, people are less likely to suppress conflict out of fear that the situation will blow up or become worse if they try to address the conflict.

The manager who wishes to manage conflict productively needs to develop skills in diagnosing what type of conflict is involved and whether the system has an appropriate amount of conflict. Furthermore, effective managers have to be aware of larger societal or global conflicts (for example, race, ethnic background, religion, gender); they can then assess as clearly as possible the extent to which their organization reinforces them and work to change those attitudes, behaviors, and structures that institutionalize them.

LEVELS OF CONFLICT

Conflict can occur at many levels. Conflict may be *intrapersonal or within the individual*. Intrapersonal conflict can occur when an individual's roles, values, or goals conflict (for example, your need to study for an exam may conflict with your need to take a family member to a doctor's visit). Conflict also may occur among individuals, groups, organizations, or any combination of these.

Many organizations suffer from *intergroup conflict*. For example, in organizations there are different functional groups, professional specialties, geographical groupings, hierarchical levels, ethnic groups, genders, and social class distinctions. Any or all of these can serve as focal points for the creation of strong reference groups that provide their members with a sense of acceptance and identity in exchange for group loyalty and commitment. To the individual, these reference groups are often the most immediate and tangible sources of a sense of belonging to the organization. As a result, these groups are a vehicle for gaining commitment to organizational goals and motivation to work.

Yet group loyalty and commitment also lead group members to value their own priorities, goals, and points of view more highly than those of out-groups.[9] This often leads to a competitive we-they atmosphere between groups, which further strengthens internal group loyalty and out-group hostility in a cycle of increasing intensity. Each group sees itself as the best and the other group as the enemy. When groups are in conflict, other by-products can be more stress, conformity, and the acceptance of more structure and autocratic leadership. There is little tolerance for individual deviation.

Organizations may find intergroup conflict to be a major stumbling block in optimizing productivity and reaching the organization's goals. For example, the people in production see the marketing department as making inordinate demands on them for changes in products with insufficient lead time. Marketing, by contrast, may see production as intractable, a group that does not understand the necessity of meeting the competition from other companies. In the resulting conflict, the energy of both groups is expended in defense of their own position and attacking the position of the other group, all at the cost of organizational goals. Furthermore, in many cases, conflict is a major source of stress for the individuals involved.

Those who negotiate intergroup conflicts are not immune from repercussions. The negotiator who acts on behalf of a group often experiences significant role conflict between being a good judge and a good group member. People seldom realize how much responsibility a person feels when asked to represent a group and the tension that results from being put in such a position.

In addition, it is often unclear just how free representatives really are to be themselves as opposed to being what the group expects them to be. How much flexibility does the person have to deviate from the group's mandate in response to changes in the situation? Finally, if the group loses, the representative often feels guilty and responsible.

Is competition between groups always dysfunctional? Not necessarily. There are numerous examples in society of the advantages of intergroup competition. In the sports world, one team is always competing against another. This phenomenon produces much excitement for fans because they have an emotional identification with one of the teams and feel actively involved in the battle. The competitive nature of the encounter produces excitement for the players and motivates or induces them to exert maximum effort to reap the rewards of winning. In the business world, companies compete with one another for a larger share of the consumer market. Competition between organizations often increases the excellence of the product and customer service.

Situations in which competition between groups is productive have several distinguishing characteristics. First, they usually involve entities (groups) that are not part of the same formal organizational structure. The Packers and the Vikings are a part of the NFL, but they represent independent and autonomous operating organizations. Deliberate intergroup competition has been used by many government contracting agencies within the framework of parallel projects. The same task (usually a feasibility study) is given to two or more different companies with the understanding that the best proposal will win the follow-up contract. The assumption underlying this strategy is that the higher quality of the final product resulting from such a competitive structure will justify the duplication of effort and expenditure of funds. A second distinguishing characteristic is the competing organizations (groups) seldom have to work together to solve a common problem or to reach a common goal. Disparate units of the same organization can compete without harming the overall organization only when there is no interdependence or need for collaboration between them. The classic example of a failure to understand this distinction is found in manufacturing plants that initiate competitions among work shifts. Before long, equipment maintenance is put off so that downtime occurs during someone else's shift. Employees have even been known to hide supplies from other shifts.

CONFLICT-HANDLING MODES

Thomas developed a taxonomy of conflict handling modes, shown in Exhibit 13–1, that reflects a person's strategic intention in a conflict.[10] The two axes are (1) assertiveness—the degree to

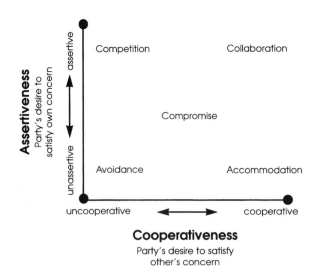

EXHIBIT 13-1 **Thomas's Five Conflict-Handling Modes**

Source: K. W. Thomas, "Conflict and Conflict Management," in M. D. Dunnette (ed.), *Handbook of Industrial and Organizational Psychology* (Chicago: Rand McNally, 1976): 889–935.

	Competition	Avoidance	Accommodation	Compromise	Collaboration
Gains	Chance to win everything	No energy or time expenditure	Little muss or fuss, no feathers ruffled	No one returns home empty-handed	Both sides win
	Exciting, games-manship	Conserve for fights that are "more important"	Others may view you as supportive	"Keeps the peace"	Better chance for long-term solutions
	Exercise own sense of power		Energy free for other pursuits	May or may not encourage creativity	Creativity in problem solving
					Maintains relation-ship
					New level of under-standing of situation
					Improves quality of solution and commitment
Losses	Chance to lose everything	Less stimulation	Lowered self-assertion and possibly self-esteem	Since neither side is totally satisfied, conflicts are likely to recur later	Requires more time, in the short run
	Alienates others	Less creative problem solving	Loss of power	Neither side realizes self-determination fully	Loss of sense of autonomy
	Discourages others from working with you	Little understand-ing of the needs of others	Absence of your unique contribution to the situation		
	Potentially larger-scale conflicts in the future (or more avoidance of conflict)	Incomplete comprehension of work environment	Others dependent on you may not feel you "go to bat" for them		

Source: Adapted from the work of R. Fry, J. Florian, and J. McLemore, Department of Organizational Behavior, Weatherhead School of Management, Case Western Reserve University, Cleveland, Ohio, 1984.

EXHIBIT 13-2   Gains and Losses Associated with Conflict Styles

which the individual wants to satisfy his or her own concerns and (2) cooperativeness—the degree to which he or she wants to satisfy the concerns of the other party. The *competitive* orientation implies winning at the other's expense. This is an example of a win-lose power struggle. In contrast, the *accommodation* style represents appeasement or satisfying the other's concern without taking one's own needs or desires into consideration. This is a lose-win situation (I lose—you win). *Compromising* reflects the midway point between these two styles and involves give-and-take by each party. Both parties gain and give up something they want. The *collaborative* orientation differs from compromising in that it represents a desire to satisfy fully the concerns of both parties. People search for solutions that are mutually beneficial, a win-win solution. The *avoidance* orientation implies lack of concern about the desire of either party, a lose-lose situation. As with any taxonomy, each conflict-handling mode has its advantages and disadvantages, shown in Exhibit 13–2. Exhibit 13–3 indicates when each mode is appropriate, according to 28 CEOs. Effective managers are capable of employing more than one mode and know which one to use in a given situation.

Competing
- When quick, decisive action is vital (i.e., emergencies)
- On important issues in which unpopular actions need implementing (e.g., cost cutting, enforcing unpopular rules, discipline)
- On issues vital to company welfare when you know you're right
- Against people who take advantage of noncompetitive behavior

Avoiding
- When an issue is trivial, or more important issues are pressing
- When you perceive no chance of satisfying your concerns
- When potential disruption outweighs the benefits of resolution
- To let people cool down and regain perspective
- When gathering information supercedes immediate decision
- When others can resolve the conflict more effectively
- When issues seem tangential or symptomatic of other issues

Accommodating
- When you find you are wrong—to allow a better position to be heard, to learn, and to show your reasonableness
- When issues are more important to others than yourself—to satisfy others and maintain cooperation
- To build social credits for later issues
- To minimize loss when you are outmatched and losing
- When harmony and stability are especially important
- To allow subordinates to develop by learning from mistakes

Compromising
- When goals are important, but not worth the effort or potential disruption of more assertive modes
- When opponents with equal power are committed to mutually exclusive goals
- To achieve temporary settlements to complex issues
- To arrive at expedient solutions under time pressure
- As a backup when collaboration or competition is unsuccessful

Collaborating
- To find an integrative solution when both sets of concerns are too important to be compromised
- When your objective is to learn
- To merge insights from people with different perspectives
- To gain commitment by incorporating concerns into a consensus
- To work through feelings that have interfered with a relationship

Source: K. W. Thomas, "Toward Multi-Dimensional Values in Teaching: The Example of Conflict Behaviors," *Academy of Management Review 2* (1977): 487. Copyright 1977 by *Academy of Management Review.* Reprinted by permission.

EXHIBIT 13-3 **Appropriate Situations for the Five Strategic Intentions**

A BIAS TOWARD COLLABORATION

According to Thomas, there are many advantages to a collaborative approach to conflict.[11] It results in greater satisfaction and self-esteem, and relationships characterized by trust, respect, and affection. From an organizational point of view, it also results in more open exchanges of information and better decisions. However, it is not appropriate in all situations. Collaboration does not work if there are competitive incentives and procedures already in place. It is also inappropriate when the two parties have insufficient problem-solving skills, do not trust each other, and when time is too short. Compromise or competition is more appropriate under these conditions.

However, collaboration is the direction in which modern businesses are moving. Even though we may be forced to use a competitive style in a given situation, Thomas recommends that we should try to change the context so that collaboration is possible in the future. The Standard Fruit Company wanted to improve its negotiations with union members in Costa Rica. They hired consultants to teach them the collaborative principled negotiation method presented in the following section. The consultants insisted and management agreed that the same training be given to the union representatives. In doing so, the company changed the situational context from one that promoted competitive negotiation to one that encouraged collaboration. The payoff was more positive outcomes and less time-consuming negotiations.

In the opening vignette, union and management in Costa Rica initially exhibited typical *intergroup* conflict behaviors, but the conflict was effectively resolved using a collaborative process. An overarching, superordinate goal was determined—establishing a stable economy that provided both jobs and profits. To achieve this goal, they had to give up an ingrained adversarial relationship and perceive themselves as members of the same team.

Once intergroup conflict is set in motion, it is extremely hard to reduce.[12] The strategy of locating a common enemy or a superordinate goal is a good starting point, but much work must be done to overcome the negative consequences that have already developed before such strategies become feasible. Educational techniques exist and are being used with considerable success to help organizations deal with conflict that has dysfunctional consequences.[13]

Schein's strategies for eliminating intergroup competition in the first place are very important. He suggests four steps that have proved to be effective in helping organizations avoid the dysfunctional consequences of intergroup conflict.[14] We add that these steps can be useful in preventing conflict at many levels, be it interpersonal, intragroup, or intergroup.

1. *Relatively greater emphasis is given to total organizational effectiveness* and the role of departments in contributing to it; departments are measured and rewarded on the basis of their *contribution to the total effort* rather than on their individual effectiveness.
2. *High interaction and frequent communication* are stimulated between groups to work on problems of intergroup coordination and collaboration; organizational *rewards are given partly on the basis of help* that groups give each other.
3. There is *frequent rotation of members* among groups or departments to stimulate high degrees of mutual understanding and empathy for one another's problems.
4. *Win-lose situations are avoided.* Groups should never be put into the position of competing for the same organizational reward. Emphasis is always placed on pooling resources to maximize organizational effectiveness; rewards are shared equally with all the groups or departments.

BARGAINING APPROACHES

At times, conflicts are resolved through bargaining and negotiation. Most negotiation strategies are based on two types of bargaining. *Distributive bargaining is the classical win-lose approach in which a fixed amount of resources is divided.* For example, if a union fails to negotiate a favorable salary contract, management wins at the union's expense. If the union gains a large increase, management loses because its costs have increased accordingly. Distributive bargaining has a short-term focus on relationships because, like the competitive conflict management style in Thomas's model, it often results in winning the battle and losing the war. The resentful losers try to figure out a way to get back at the winners, which creates an adversarial relationship.

Integrative bargaining is a win-win approach that is more suitable to maintaining long-term relationships; it does not assume that there is a fixed amount of resources to be divided because the parties search for various settlements that would be agreeable to both parties.[15] The settlements in integrative bargaining often consist of creative solutions. Costa Rica's "better idea" in the opening vignette is an example of integrative bargaining because union and management recognized their interdependence and sought solutions that were mutually advantageous. This form of bargaining is akin to the collaborative conflict-handling mode in Thomas's model.

PRINCIPLED NEGOTIATION

The negotiating scheme presented in the next section is based on integrative bargaining and a win-win approach. Fisher and Ury observed that some people are too soft and accommodating when they negotiate while others are too hard and competitive.[16] As a result, they developed an alternative called "principled negotiation" that consists of four principles.

1. **People: Separate the People from the Problem**
   This relates to the need to maintain a relationship with the other party. Fisher and Ury recommend being "soft on people and hard on the problem" and taking the stance of a partner working with the other side to solve the problem under negotiation. To do this, the negotiator should be empathetic with the other party and accept that human problems concerning perception, communications, and emotions will emerge in the negotiation process.

2. **Interests: Focus on Interests, Not Positions**
   When negotiators focus only on a predetermined position, it may be more difficult for them to achieve what they really want. The story that is often used to illustrate this point concerns two library patrons who were noisily arguing over the following positions. One wanted the window closed while the other wanted the window open. The librarian who came to investigate the ruckus asked the first man why he wanted the window open. He explained that he thought the library was too stuffy. In response to the same question, the other man explained that he had a cold and did not want to sit in a draught. The librarian thought for a moment and opened a window in an adjacent room. This solution pleased both men because it allowed the first man to have more air circulating and prevented the second man from getting any sicker than he already was. Had they continued arguing about their positions, it is doubtful such a creative solution would have surfaced.

   When parties enter a negotiation (or conflict) with a set position, they may become locked into it and develop a vested interest in saving face by not backing away from that position. The parties should assertively present their own interests and mutually identify those that are shared, opposed, and simply different.

3. **Options: Invent Options for Mutual Gain**
   Putting into practice the first two options makes it easier to come up with optimal solutions in the pressure of a negotiation setting. In this stage the parties brainstorm options that are favorable to both parties. This requires creativity and a commitment to joint problem solving.

4. **Criteria: Insist on Objective Criteria**
   Sometimes negotiators (and bosses, spouses, parents, etc.) take a hard line and insist on getting their way. To avoid a standoff, look for objective criteria, such as market value, expert opinion, custom, or law, that are agreeable to both parties. For example, a stalled salary negotiation moved forward after both parties agreed to use a salary survey of similar companies as an objective standard of reference. The Blue Book of car values is another example of objective criteria that can facilitate a negotiation over the price of a used car. When objective criteria exist, negotiators can resort to principles rather than pressure to reach agreements.

Another aspect to principled negotiation is the concept of BATNA. This acronym stands for Best Alternative To a Negotiated Agreement. Fisher and Ury recommend that negotiators arm themselves with an alternative in case the negotiation does not go as expected. For example, what alternative does a job candidate have if his or her salary negotiation does not turn out as planned? A BATNA in this case might be going to work in the family firm. Or what fall-back scheme can homeowners have if negotiations fail with a potential buyer? Their BATNA might be taking the house off the market and either remodeling it or renting it out. A BATNA liberates negotiators from thinking they have to reach an agreement at all costs because it provides the security of an alternative. During the important preparation period for a negotiation, people should determine their own BATNA as well as consider what the other party's BATNA might be.

	North Americans	Arabs	Russians
Primary negotiating style and process	Factual: Appeals made to logic	Affective: Appeals made to emotions	Axiomatic: Appeals made to ideals
Conflict: opponent's arguments countered with. . .	Objective facts	Subjective feelings	Asserted ideals
Making concessions	Small concessions made early to establish a relationship	Concessions made throughout as a part of the bargaining process	Few, if any, small concessions made
Response to opponent's concessions	Usually reciprocate opponent's concessions	Almost always reciprocate opponent's concessions	Opponent's concessions viewed as weakness and almost never reciprocated
Relationship	Short term	Long term	No continuing relationship
Authority	Broad	Broad	Limited
Initial position	Moderate	Extreme	Extreme
Deadline	Very important	Casual	Ignored

Source: Reprinted with permission from E. S. Glenn, D. Witmeyer, and K. A. Stevenson, "Cultural Styles of Persuasion," *International Journal of Intercultural Relations 1* (3) (1977) 52–56. Reprinted with permission of Elsevier.

EXHIBIT 13-4   **Cultural Styles of Persuasion**

In principled negotiation, three criteria determine whether or not a negotiation has been successful:

1. It should produce a wise agreement if agreement is possible.
2. It should be efficient and not waste time.
3. It should improve or at least not harm the relationship between the parties.[17]

The criteria for successful negotiations, as well as negotiating practices, vary from culture to culture. Exhibit 13–4 shows cultural styles of persuasion that influence negotiation. It's crucial to do your homework on cultural differences before attempting an international negotiation.[18]

EMOTION AND NEGOTIATION

Negotiations do not take place in a vacuum. They involve real people who have emotions and feelings that affect their thoughts and behaviors. Think about some of the conflicts you have experienced. It is likely that at least one of them has involved some heated reactions that affected the outcome. Traditionally, emotions have been viewed as obstacles that hinder effective conflict resolution. Negotiators have been counseled to control their emotions and to avoid expressing any feelings whatsoever when involved in the bargaining process. However, researchers now suggest that emotions can play both positive and negative roles in conflict and negotiations. Managers need to understand how emotions can affect the negotiating process and how to effectively handle those emotions. Exhibit 13–5 presents some effects that positive and negative emotions may have on various stages of the negotiating process.

But how can emotions be effectively managed? Well-known negotiation researcher Leigh Thompson suggests that an important step is to identify one's own negotiation style.[19] The survey you filled out before class in the Class Preparation helps you assess your own style. Thompson and her colleagues have identified three different emotional approaches to negotiation. It is

Negotiating Feature	Effects of Negative Emotions	Effects of Positive Emotions
Relationship between the parties	Tension and distrust	Cooperation and collaboration
Communication	Restricted	Open, two-way
Interests	Focus on own interests, increasing commitment to extreme demand	Openness to other's interests and concerns
Options	Focus on two options: ours and theirs	Attempt to invent multiple options that promote mutual gain
BATNA	May reject an agreement even if it surpasses BATNA	Commitment to getting the best option we can get, as long as it exceeds BATNA

Source: Adapted from R. Fisher and D. Shapiro, *Beyond Reason: Using Emotions as You Negotiate* (New York: Penguin, 2005).

EXHIBIT 13-5 **Emotions and the Negotiating Process**

important to remember that these styles refer to *expressed* rather than *felt* emotions. People have been known to feign anger or happiness in bargaining in an attempt to obtain a more favorable outcome while feeling very different emotions.

- **Rational** This approach suggests that controlling and suppressing emotional expression is important. In this approach, the negotiator remains calm at all times and does not express any emotion whatsoever.
- **Positive** This perspective attempts to "sweeten the pot." Three steps are critical in this approach: (a) feeling positive emotion, (b) expressing it, and (c) engendering it the opposing parties. This approach can result in more creative outcomes and greater joint gains.
- **Negative** In this approach, negative emotions such as anger, rage, and irritation are deliberately expressed by the negotiator in hopes of obtaining a more favorable outcome. This approach can be effective. Opponents may assume that the angry negotiator is close to breaking off negotiations and make concessions due to fear. Of course, these concessions may have negative effects on the relationships among the parties.

Roger Fisher and Daniel Shapiro suggest that the key to managing emotions during negotiations is to proactively address core concerns (what people really want) as opposed to only addressing expressed emotion.[20] They identify five concerns: appreciation (do I feel valued?), affiliation (do I feel treated as a colleague?), autonomy (is my independence validated?), status (am I being treated appropriately according to the differences in our standings?), and fulfilling roles and responsibilities (am I able to feel fulfilled and feel like I am contributing?). These core concerns can be used to help prepare and conduct the negotiation. Fisher and Shapiro suggest using these concerns as a checklist of sensitive areas to be aware of in yourself and others and to help you frame your negotiations. They can also be used to understand what might be motivating you and your opponent and prompting your reactions. When you feel attacked, for instance, try to identify the core concern that is being threatened and respond to that.

CULTURE AND CONFLICT

Cultural assumptions affect our approaches to conflict as well as our expectations and behaviors in conflict situations. For example, Hall's concept of high- and low-context communication influences conflict styles.[21] Low-context communication refers to a communication system that utilizes explicit verbal messages. Examples of low-context cultures include Germany, England, Switzerland, and the United States. In contrast, high-context communication involves transmitting intention or meaning via the context (e.g., social roles, positions) and nonverbal communication (such as pauses, silence, tone of voice). The listener is expected to "read between the lines" of high-context communication. High-context cultures include Japan, China, Egypt, France, and Saudi Arabia.

According to Ting-Toomey, in low-context cultures, conflict is instrumental, which means the world is viewed in analytic, linear, logical terms.[22] Issues are viewed as separate from people, which makes it less threatening to address conflict. Conflict is more direct, disclosing, and likely to contain verbal messages that threaten the "face" of the other party. *Face is defined as "upholding a claimed sense of positive public image in any social interaction."*[23] In high-context cultures, conflict is indirect to preserve face and the relationship.

Another cultural aspect that influences conflict is the individualism-collectivism dimension.[24] In individualistic cultures (e.g., many Western European cultures such as France, Germany, and Scandinavia, as well as Britain, Australia, and the United States), people are primarily concerned about themselves and their families. The individual, rather than the group, is important, and personal rights are valued. In collectivist cultures (e.g., many Asian, Mediterranean, Latino, Middle Eastern, and African cultures), people subordinate their personal interests for the good of the group and think in terms of "we" rather than "I."

Because harmonious relationships with the group are extremely important in a collectivist culture, conflict is approached more indirectly and face-saving behaviors are more common. In some collectivist cultures, the use of third-party mediators helps preserve the relationship between the two parties in conflict. In individualistic cultures, people are more likely to strongly assert their personal opinion, express personal emotions, and focus on individual rather than group accountability for problems. Conflict in individualistic cultures tends to center around violations of individual expectations ("I thought you would get me your report before Friday"). Collectivistic conflict focuses more on violations of group norms or expectations ("You've let the extended family down with your behavior").[25] Barnlund described the cultural differences between Japanese and Americans with regard to conflict:[26]

> *Conflict is far less common in Japanese society for a number of reasons. First, the emphasis on the group instead of the individual reduces interpersonal friction. Second, an elaborate set of standards emphasizes "obligations" over "rights," what one owes to others rather than deserves for oneself. Third, the value attached to harmony cultivates skill in the use of ambiguity, circumlocution, euphemism, and silence in blunting incipient disputes. The ability to assimilate differences, to engineer consensus, is valued above a talent for argument.*

Individualists tend toward an outcome-oriented model of conflict—they want to resolve the conflict and quickly achieve tangible outcomes. For them, settling the conflict is more important than facework. In contrast, collectivists are process-oriented—they take care of mutual face saving before they discuss outcomes. Issues related to face are pride, honor, insults, dignity, shame, disgrace, humility, trust, mistrust, respect, and prestige.[27]

Individualists also tend to be more self-oriented, controlling, and competitive than collectivists, who tend to use integrative and compromising styles. For example, Asians are more likely to use the avoiding and accommodation styles of conflict handling in the Thomas model and less likely to use the competitive style. Individualists may perceive collectivists, with their indirect style, as sidestepping the actual issues. By contrast, collectivists may perceive individualists as pushy, rude, and overbearing.[28] In the Gulf War and the Iraq War, it is very likely that the cultures involved did not always understand each other's approach to conflict or their typical ways of dealing with conflict. Exhibit 13–6 illustrates some of these differences. When engaged in conflict with people from other cultures, it is necessary to learn their unique style of handling conflict. And, of course, it is always helpful to understand one's own conflict style. Some key elements to consider are listed below.

- *Choose your representative carefully.* In hierarchical cultures, it is insulting to send a lower-rank employee to negotiate with a higher ranking one. Be sure that the power statuses are appropriate.

- *Understand the network of relationships.* Some cultures require multiple levels of approval before the negotiation can be completed. Be aware of all of the steps that must be completed and do not expect that an agreement between the negotiators is the final stage. Approval from those higher in the hierarchy may be necessary before the deal can be finalized.
- *Provide mechanisms for saving face.* Saving and giving face and maintaining dignity and status are important concerns in many cultures.
- *Understand how and when to show respect in the culture.*
- *Understand the communication style.* Cultures differ in the degree to which they rely on direct and indirect communications in negotiations and conflict. For example, in Japan, negotiators are often reluctant to say no and use silence as an indicator of disagreement.
- *Anticipate that cultural differences may influence integrative bargaining* and "expanding the pie." These differences may be used to help identify opportunities for mutual gain. But they can also blind negotiators to those opportunities.[29]

Virtues of Battle/Peace

Western: Battle is costly; peaceful resolution preferred.

Arab: War is not shameful; peace can be costly; struggle can be a progressive, invigorating, and purifying process.

Utilitarianism versus Pain

Western: Conflict brings discomfort that can be avoided or eliminated.

Arab: Discomfort and physical suffering are preferable to a loss of honor, loss of face, or perpetuation of an injustice.

Change: Optimistic or Pessimistic Outlook

Western: Change can be managed in ways that make people better off. Success comes through adaptation to or capturing of new technologies, market developments, and so forth. Joint gains are possible.

Arab: The forces of change lie outside one's control. Most changes have made Arabs worse off over time. Conflicts may be inherently unresolvable.

Scientific versus Moralistic World Views

Western: Conflicts can be reduced to objective problems that have objective solutions.

Arab: Conflict may reflect struggles between good and evil. Compromise may imply compromising on deeply held moral principles.

Interpersonal Styles

Western: Informality, personal self-revelation, openness to one's feelings, and development of positive interpersonal relationships among parties are to be encouraged. Mediators must be trusted and need to develop informal relationships with the parties.

Arab: Formality and clarity of social roles are important for self-identity and maintaining relationships with negotiating partners and opponents. Authority figures make better mediators than peers or others lacking a formal role.

Agreements

Western: Agreements are to be enforced by law, convention, or specified procedures.

Arabs: Agreements tend to be broken; agreeing to an enforcement procedure implies giving up control over the future.

Source: Paul E. Salam, "A Critique of Western Conflict Resolution from a Non-Western Perspective," *Negotiations Journal* 9 (1993): 361–369.

EXHIBIT 13-6 **Arab and Western Assumptions about Conflict Resolution**

The purpose of the following exercise is to simulate a set of organizational relationships among groups. As you go through the exercise, try to be aware of your feelings about your group and other groups; there will be time after the exercise to reflect on your feelings individually and to discuss them with your group and the entire class.

CLASS ACTIVITY: THE RED-GREEN GAME

The purpose of this exercise is to simulate the feelings and behaviors that may appear in a conflict situation (Time allotted: 60 minutes)

STEP 1.   Form a single-line human continuum based on your feelings about conflict. Stand at the right endpoint if you are "Very comfortable with conflict." Stand at the left endpoint if you are "Very uncomfortable with conflict" and toward the middle if you are neither comfortable nor uncomfortable with conflict. You will have to talk to other students to figure out where you stand in relation to them in order to form yourselves into a single line. (10 minutes)

STEP 2.   While still in line, the Ones will turn to the Twos beside them, and the Threes will face the Fours next to them and discuss this question: "Does your comfort level with conflict ever influence your behavior at work or school?" (5 minutes)

STEP 3.   Count off by fours, starting at one end of the continuum. The Ones, Twos, Threes, and Fours in groups composed of 3–12 people should sit in separate corners of the room. (For a large class, split into two groups and run the exercise concurrently.) Each group should take one piece of paper and tear it into eight pieces. Write your group number on each piece of paper.

Scoring Rules

GGGG	All teams win +50 points.
GGGR	The teams voting green lose 100 points. The team voting red wins 300 points.
GGRR	The teams voting green lose 200 points. The teams voting red win 200 points.
GRRR	The team voting green loses 300 points. The teams voting red win 100 points.
RRRR	All teams lose 50 points.

Scoring Chart

	Votes				Cumulative Scores			
Rounds	Team 1	Team 2	Team 3	Team 4	Team 1	Team 2	Team 3	Team 4
1								
2								
3R								
4R(2Xs)								
5								
6R								
7R								
8(10Xs)								

STEP 4.   Read your instructions, which follow, and begin the simulation (25-30 minutes).

Your Task: Your objective is to win as many positive points as possible. Your team will have two minutes to decide whether to vote green or red in each round of the game. To indicate your votes, write an R (red) or G (green) on one of your pieces of paper below your team number. The game director (usually your instructor) will collect your votes after each round and record your score but is not allowed to answer any questions. Before rounds 3, 4, 6, and 7, you may send a representative to discuss with the other team representatives in the center of the room for two minutes. During this time, representatives should speak very loudly so others can hear their discussion, and the rest of the class should remain silent so as not to distract them. Your representative does not always have to be the same person. Whatever you earn in round 4 will be doubled; your score in round 8 will be multiplied by 10. Remember, the purpose of the game is to win as many points as possible. The accompanying chart indicates how the game will be scored. You have two minutes to decide on your vote for round 1.

STEP 5.   Plenary debriefing. (30 minutes) Answer these questions:
   a. Did conflict occur in this simulation? Why? What was the cause?

   b. What role does trust play in this simulation? What made you trust or distrust certain teams or individuals?

   c. What did the conflict look like? What were its characteristics?

   d. What was it like to be a representative in this simulation?

   e. Did you see any examples of effective leadership among the representatives?

   f. What's the relationship between ambiguity and conflict?

   g. What can we learn about conflict from this simulation?

   h. What can you learn about your own conflict-handling style? Which of the styles in the Thomas model did you use in this simulation?

NEGOTIATION EXERCISE— THE FILM-MAKING EQUIPMENT

The purpose of this exercise is to allow you to practice principled negotiation. (Time allotted: 80 minutes)

STEP 1.   Divide the class so they can negotiate in groups of five people: two representatives from Ivy League U. and two representatives from Intelligentsia U. and one observer. (You can use two observers if the number of students is not divisible by five.)

STEP 2.   Determine who will play each role. Read only the role description for your university; please do not read the other role description. The two pairs of representatives in each group should go off together and prepare their negotiating strategy. Identify the interests of both parties. Think about potential options for mutual gain and objective criteria. What might be the BATNA for both parties? (20 minutes)

Observers should read both roles and go over the Observer Worksheet on page 356. Fill out the worksheet as you are observing and write down any interesting, funny, and/or outrageous comments you hear during the negotiation session. Be prepared to describe the strategy of each team and its results.

STEP 3. The negotiating session takes place between the two representatives from each university, under the careful eye of the observer. By the end of the assigned time period, be prepared to announce to the class the details of the agreement you made with the other representatives. (20 minutes)

STEP 4. Under the leadership of the observer, evaluate the negotiation that just occurred in your group of five students using the Observer Worksheet as a guide. (20 minutes)

STEP 5. Plenary debriefing. (20 minutes) Discuss these questions as a class.
   a. What outcome did your group reach? What strategy did you use?
   b. Was your group able to separate people from the problem? Did observers hear any interesting comments?
   c. What were the interests of Ivy League U.? Or Intelligentsia U.?
   d. How did you invent options? What were some creative options?
   e. What objective criteria did you use?
   f. What was the BATNA of Ivy League U.? Of Intelligentsia U.?
   g. What role did emotions play in your negotiation?
   h. How could you improve upon the negotiation?

Ivy League U. Role

A well-established university, Ivy League U., has a film-making department that it no longer wants. Its new president has decided to eliminate departments with small numbers of students and focus on more successful programs. Therefore, the department chair, Dr. Hitchcock (who fortunately had tenure and was switched to another department rather than fired) and Ivy League's business manager, Lou (the) Hatchet, have been ordered to sell the equipment quickly. They have only four weeks to remove the equipment so another department can take over the premises before the next semester begins. There is no space on campus to store the equipment, which is rather bulky. Hitchcock and Hatchet have succeeded in selling off some of the smaller equipment, such as lights, but the film-making department inventory still contains the following:

- 10 video cameras, two of which have never been used
- 2 television cameras
- 1 editing machine
- 3 computers that are two years old
- 1 nearly new computer that does state-of-the-art, digitized editing

The university paid a total of $75,000 for this equipment when it was new, and it was all top-of-the-line quality. A secondhand store is willing to pay $35,000 for the lot. However, Hitchcock heard via the grapevine that a small, private, liberal arts school, Intelligentsia U., wants to set up a film department and is looking for equipment. Hitchcock and Hatchet have made an appointment with its representatives to see if they can get a better deal by selling to Intelligentsia. But, first, they will sit down and plan out their negotiating strategy.

Intelligentsia U. Role

Intelligentsia U. is a small, relatively young, private liberal arts school that just became a university by adding on some different programs. It is hoping to increase its student body by offering more glamorous majors. Intelligentsia has decided to add a film-making department and is looking for equipment at a reasonable price. Since the school is still scrambling to establish itself, its resources are limited. Nevertheless, the chair of the new film-making department, Dr. Reel, wants to provide students with all the equipment they'll need to get a good background in film. An alumni donated some of the smaller equipment they require, but following is a list of things Reel needs to buy.

Observer Worksheet

1. Which conflict handling styles in the Thomas model were individual negotiators using?

2. What was the effect of these styles?

3. What type of bargaining occurred during the role-play?
    Distributive   1   2   3   4   5   Integrative
    Why?

4. Did the negotiators separate the people from the problem?   Yes_____   No_____
    Examples?

5. Did they focus on interests rather than positions?   Yes_____   No_____
    Examples?

6. Did they invent options for mutual gain?   Yes_____   No_____
    Examples?

7. Did they insist on objective criteria?   Yes_____   No_____
    Examples?

8. How could the negotiation have been improved?

- 10 video cameras
- 2 television cameras
- 1 editing machine
- 1 computer that does state-of-the art, digitized editing

If the university bought this equipment new, it would cost $90,000. Another alternative is to buy used pieces of equipment, which would cost $40,000.

The facilities are not yet ready for the equipment. The film studio will not be completed for two months. But Intelligentsia U. has a large warehouse where equipment could be stored until the studio is ready.

Dr. Reel heard via the grapevine that Ivy League U. is trying to sell off its film-making equipment because it is closing down its department. Reel wants to meet with Ivy League's representatives, not only to buy their equipment but also to establish a good relationship. Intelligentsia wants to set up an exchange program so that its students can go to Ivy League for classes they can't get at their own school, and vice versa. Reel has asked Intelligentsia's business manager, Pat Spreadsheet, to go along to meet and negotiate with the representatives from Ivy League U. Spreadsheet agreed, so now they will sit down and plan out their negotiating strategy.

 **LEARNING POINTS**

1. Conflict is a form of interaction among parties that differ in interests, perceptions, and preferences.
2. Groups in conflict tend to stereotype each other, see their own group as ideal, and overvalue the contributions of their own members, while devaluing those of the other group. Polarization on issues occurs along with decreased intergroup communication. Perceptions of the other group become distorted and hostilities tend to escalate.
3. The Sherifs' Robbers Cave experiment revealed that conflict behavior was induced by having two groups of boys compete for scarce resources—limited prizes. The hostility that resulted decreased greatly when the researchers introduced superordinate goals that were important to all the boys and required collaboration.
4. Two ways to resolve intergroup conflict are (a) noncompetitive contact in which the groups have equal status; and (b) establishing a superordinate goal that can only be attained through joint cooperation.
5. Organizations are full of reference groups that provide individuals with a sense of belonging and identity in exchange for loyalty and commitment. However, a we-they attitude often develops when these groups come into contact with each other.
6. We-they attitudes between internal groups can foster competition and a lack of collaboration that hinder productivity and achievement of the overall goals of the organization. In contrast, competition with external groups can be very productive.
7. Common sources of group conflict in organizations are we-they attitudes of reference groups, competition for scarce resources, ambiguous authority, interdependence, deficient information, and differences in values, interests, personalities, education, culture, perceptions, goals, and expectations.
8. Although dysfunctional conflict siphons energy away from organizational goals, functional conflict plays an important role in organizations. One way to ensure that conflict is functional is to train employees in conflict management skills.
9. The five conflict-handling modes are based on a person's strategic intentions along two axes:
   a. Assertiveness—desire to satisfy one's own concerns
   b. Cooperativeness—desire to satisfy the concerns of the other party

10. The five conflict-handling modes are:
    a. Competition
    b. Avoidance
    c. Accommodation
    d. Compromise
    e. Collaboration
11. Effective managers use the mode that is appropriate to the situation.
12. There are two types of bargaining: distributive (win-lose) and integrative (win-win).
13. Fisher and Ury's scheme of principled negotiation consists of four steps:
    a. Separate the people from the problem.
    b. Focus on interests, not positions.
    c. Invent options for mutual gain.
    d. Insist on objective criteria.
14. Too much or too little conflict are both dysfunctional states. Dysfunctional intergroup conflict can be avoided when organizations emphasize the contribution of departments to total organizational effectiveness, stimulate frequent interaction among groups, rotate members among departments, and avoid win-lose situations.
15. It is easier to create conflict than resolve it.
16. The three emotional approaches to negotiation are rational, positive, and negative.
17. The key to managing emotions in bargaining is to proactively address people's core concerns: appreciation, affiliation, autonomy, status, and fulfilling roles and responsibilities.
18. Cultural dimensions, such as high- and low-context communication and individualism-collectivism, influence conflict approaches, expectations, and styles.

 **ACTION SCRIPTS**

FOR EMPLOYEES

- Employees who are adept at managing conflicts take pains to understand the type of conflict they are facing. If they are faced with interpersonal or relationship conflict, they attempt to effectively manage the emotions associated with that type of conflict. They know that they need to address the underlying concerns (be they affiliation, appreciation, etc.) and focus on the other party's behavior rather than personality or other personal attributes.
- They are not invested in "being right" but in resolving the conflict.
- They devote energy to understanding the source of the conflict and the perspective of the other party.
- They acknowledge that their own perspective could be inaccurate and understand the role perception plays in conflict.
- Expert conflict handlers also understand that no one conflict resolution strategy fits all situations.
- Superb conflict resolvers recognize that creating outcomes in which all the opponents gain something results in better long-term relationships and easier conflict resolution in the future. They realize that attempting to get the most for themselves (and the least for their opponents) can actually have negative long-term consequences.

FOR MANAGERS

- To prevent conflict, expert managers ask the heads of other departments or units how their department can help the other departments be successful. They educate their own employees on the need to be collaborative and model that collaboration. In the process, they also identify what they need from other departments to create a win-win situation.
- Expert conflict managers often try to reframe conflict situations from a "we-they" position to a "we versus the problem" approach. For example, the manager of an auditing department realized

her efforts to incorporate the auditing department of a recently merged smaller bank were not succeeding. In fact, hostility between the two groups was increasing. Rather than fighting over whose procedures were better, the manager wisely reframed the situation and asked the entire group to start from scratch and use the merger as an opportunity to devise the best possible procedures. Their final product was "ours," and in the process, the two departments became a cohesive unit.

- When faced with intergroup conflict, managers who are skilled at conflict resolution look for mutual goals and values, or even a common enemy. They make sure common enemies are outside the company and not a person or group with whom it is important to have a collaborative relationship. Managers can set the stage for collaboration between departments or divisions by having a clear understanding of the contribution each group makes and continually communicating the importance of all groups.

- Managers can sometimes decrease conflict by the use of a liaison or a buffer. Liaisons or boundary spanners absorb heat from both sides and try to interpret the actions of both groups to each other. Buffers can also be inanimate objects that prevent two groups from having to interact, for example, the order wheel in restaurants and automatic reordering systems in warehouses.

- Managers who wish to establish collaboration can also show an interest in all groups and insist that they work together. The manager's attention is often one of the scarce resources in an organization. Therefore, managers who share their attention as equally as possible (or at least explain to the others why they are focusing on a certain area) are more likely to have a collaborative climate.

- When conflicts are brought to managers to be settled, expert managers take the following steps:
  - Listen with understanding rather than evaluation and recognize and accept the feelings of the people involved without judging them.
  - Analyze the source of the conflict and make sure all parties understand the nature of the conflict from everyone's perspective.
  - Suggest procedures and ground rules for discussing and resolving the differences:
    - Everyone will be treated with respect.
    - Although groups may be committed to their own position, they should still be open to other perspectives.
    - Avoid unproductive conflict strategies such as blaming, forcing, threatening, and manipulating.
    - Give all parties equal opportunity to present their views and arguments and ensure fair treatment.
    - Keep the focus on the current situation rather than past history that has no relevance.
    - Seek a win-win solution.
  - Suggest problem-solving procedures, such as brainstorming and agreement on objective criteria, to judge solutions.
  - Teach problem-solving skills so employees can resolve conflicts themselves in the future.

For Organizational Architects

- Organizational architects who are expert at managing conflict understand that conflict can be both functional and dysfunctional. They look for ways to minimize the dysfunctional conflict (conflict about personalities) but optimize functional conflict (conflict about tasks and processes). They also make sure that employees are given the necessary conflict resolutions skills (e.g., through constructive controversy training, etc.) so they can effectively handle conflict situations.

- They provide clear organizational goals that eliminate ambiguity and ensure that there are shared superordinate goals.

- Competition over scarce resources is eliminated or mitigated. For example, the budgeting process is designed to reinforce superordinate goals and avoid creating losers.

- Organizational architects design integrating mechanisms to bring together groups that have different goals and ways of working to avoid conflict (see Exhibit 21-8).

- They also understand that competition can have both benefits and disadvantages. They are careful to use it only when the individuals or groups do not depend on one another and when the competition will not interfere with organizational goals.

PERSONAL APPLICATION ASSIGNMENT

This assignment involves writing about a situation involving conflict or negotiation. Choose an experience about which you want to learn more. When you address the Reflective Observation section, make a special effort to take the perspective of all parties.

A. Concrete Experience

1. Objectively describe the experience (who, what, when, where, how). (2 points)

2. Subjectively describe your feelings, perceptions, and thoughts that occurred during (not after) the experience. What did others seem to be feeling? (2 points)

B. Reflective Observation

1. Looking back at the experience, what were the perspectives of the key actors (including you)? (2 points)

2. Why did the people involved (including you) behave as they did? (2 points)

C. Abstract Conceptualization

    1. Relate concepts or theories from the assigned readings or the lecture to the experience. Explain thoroughly how they apply to your experience. Please apply at least two concepts or theories and cite them correctly. (4 points)

D. Active Experimentation

    1. What did you learn about conflict on negotiation from this experience? (1 point)

    2. What did you learn about yourself? (1 point)

    3. What action steps will you take to be more effective in the future? (2 points)

E. Integration, Synthesis, and Writing

    1. Did you integrate and synthesize the four sections? (1 point)
    2. Was the Personal Application Assignment well written and easy to understand? (1 point)
    3. Was it free of spelling and grammar errors? (2 points)

ENDNOTES

[1] K. W. Thomas, "Conflict and Negotiation Processes in Organizations," in M. D. Dunnette and L. M. Hough (eds.), *Handbook of Industrial and Organizational Psychology,* 2nd ed. (Palo Alto, CA: Consulting Psychologists Press, 1991): 653.

[2] M. Sherif, and C. W. Sherif, "Ingroup and Intergroup Relations: Experimental Analysis," in *Social Psychology* (New York: Harper & Row, 1969); and M. Sherif, *Intergroup Relations and Leadership* (New York: John Wiley, 1962).

[3] M. Deutsch, "An Experimental Study of the Effects of Cooperation and Competition upon Group Process," *Human Relations 2* (1949): 199–231, and G. W. Allport, *The Nature of Prejudice* (Reading, MA: Addison-Wesley, 1954).

[4] J. A. Byrne, "The Horizontal Corporation," *BusinessWeek 3351* (December 20, 1993) 76–81.

[5] K. Jehn, "A Multimethod Examination of the Benefits and Detriments of Intragroup Conflict," *Administrative Science Quarterly 40* (1995): 256–282; K. Jehn, "Affective and Cognitive Conflict in Work Groups: Increasing Performance through Value-Based Intragroup Conflict," in C. K. W. DeDreu and E. Van de Vliert (eds.), *Using Conflict in Organizations* (London: Sage, 1997): 87–100; M. Turner and A. Pratkanis, "Mitigating Groupthink by Stimulating Constructive Conflict," in C. K. W. De Dreu and E. Van de Vliert (eds.), *Using Conflict in Organizations* (London: Sage, 1997): 39–52. But see also L. Weingart and C. K. W. De Dreu, "Task Versus Relationship Conflict, Team Performance, and Team Member Satisfaction: A Meta-Analysis,"

Journal of Applied Psychology 88 (2003): 741–749 for qualifications of this relationship.

[6] Thomas, "Conflict and Negotiation Processes in Organizations": 697.

[7] L. D. Brown, "Managing Conflict Among Groups," in D. Kolb, J. Osland, and I. Rubin (eds.), *The Organizational Behavior Reader* (Upper Saddle River, NJ: Prentice Hall, 1995): 317–328.

[8] Jehn, "A Multimethod Examination of the Benefits and Detriments of Intragroup Conflict"; Jehn, "Affective and Cognitive Conflict in Work Groups"; Turner and Pratkanis, "Mitigating Groupthink by Stimulating Constructive Conflict"; and Weingart and De Dreu, "Task Versus Relationship Conflict, Team Performance, and Team Member Satisfaction."

[9] E. H. Schein, *Organizational Psychology* (Upper Saddle River, NJ: Prentice Hall, 1965): 80–86.

[10] K. W. Thomas, "Conflict and Conflict Management," in M. D. Dunnette (ed.), *Handbook of Industrial and Organizational Psychology* (Chicago: Rand McNally, 1976): 889–935.

[11] K. W. Thomas, "Conflict and Conflict Management," *Journal of Organizational Behavior 13* (1992): 265–274.

[12] The reality of this is nowhere clearer than in our efforts to combat years of racial prejudice and discrimination.

[13] J. W. Anderson, M. Foster-Kuehn, and B. C. McKinney, *Communication Skills for Surviving Conflict at Work* (Cresswell, NJ: Hampton Press, 1996); J. P. Folger, M. S. Poole, and R. K. Stutman, *Working Through Conflict* (New York: Longman, 1997); and C. De Dreu, and E. Van De Vliert (eds.), *Using Conflict in Organizations* (Thousand Oaks, CA: Sage, 1997).

[14] Schein, *Organizational Psychology.*

[15] R. J. Lewicki and J. A. Litterer, *Negotiation* (Homewood, IL: Irwin, 1985): 280.

[16] R. Fisher and W. Ury, *Getting to Yes: Negotiating Agreement Without Giving In* (Boston: Houghton Mifflin, 1981); R. Ury, *Getting Past No: Negotiating Your Way from Confrontation to Cooperation* (New York: Bantam, 1993); and R. Fisher, W. Ury, and B. Patton, "Negotiation Power: Ingredients in an Ability to Influence the Other Side," in L. Hall (ed.), *Negotiation: Strategies for Mutual Gain: The Basic Text of the Harvard Law School Program on Negotiation* (Newbury Park, CA: Sage, 1993): 3–14. See B. McRae, *Negotiating and Influencing Skills* (Thousand Oaks, CA: Sage, 1998) for more detailed information on negotiation.

[17] Fisher and Ury, *Getting to Yes:* 4.

[18] For information on international negotiations, see N. J. Adler, *International Dimensions of Organizational Behavior* (Cincinnati, OH: South-Western College, 1997); S. E. Weiss, "Negotiating with 'Romans'—Part 1," *Sloan Management Review 35*(2) (Winter 1994): 51–61; S. E. Weiss, "Negotiating with 'Romans'—Part 2," *Sloan Management Review 35*(3) (Spring 1994): 85–99; and R. D. Lewis, *When Cultures Collide: Managing Successfully Across Cultures* (London: Nicholas Brealey, 1996).

[19] S. Kopelman, A. Rosette, and L. Thompson, "The Three Faces of Eve: An Examination of Strategic Positive, Negative, and Neutral Emotional Styles in Negotiations," cited in L. Thompson, *The Mind and Heart of the Negotiator,* (Upper Saddle River, NJ: Prentice Hall, 2005).

[20] R. Fisher and D. Shapiro, *Beyond Reason: Using Emotions as You Negotiate* (New York: Penguin, 2005).

[21] E. T. Hall, *Beyond Culture* (Garden City, NY: Anchor Press/Doubleday, 1976).

[22] S. Ting-Toomey, "Intercultural Conflict Competence" in W. R. Cupach, and D. J. Canary (eds.), *Competence in Interpersonal Conflict* (New York: McGraw-Hill, 1997): 121–147.

[23] Ibid: 132.

[24] H. C. Triandis, *Individualism and Collectivism* (Boulder, CO: Westview Press, 1995); G. Hofstede, *Culture's Consequences* (Thousand Oaks, CA: Sage, 1980).

[25] Ting-Toomey, "Intercultural Conflict Competence."

[26] S. Barnlund, *Communication Style of Japanese and Americans: Images and Reality* (Belmont, CA: Wadsworth, 1989): 3.

[27] Ting-Toomey, "Intercultural Conflict Competence."

[28] Ibid.

[29] The suggestions are adapted from L. Thompson, *The Mind and Heart of the Negotiator* (Upper Saddle River, NJ: Prentice Hall, 2005).

Chapter 14

▲▲

MANAGING DIVERSITY

OBJECTIVES By the end of this chapter, you should be able to:

A. Explain the broad definition of diversity.

B. List the reasons why diversity is a business issue.

C. Discuss ethnicity, gender, age, and culture in terms of workplace diversity.

D. Define ethnocentrism.

E. Provide examples of stereotyping and bias.

F. Explain what happens to minority tokens in organizations.

G. Understand how to design an inclusive workplace.

WHAT'S YOUR ECCENTRICITY QUOTIENT?

How weird can you be in a major corporation and still keep your job? Kathleen McDonald, a former organization development team leader who was responsible for a project on managing diversity at Exxon, devised an eccentricity model to help employees answer that very question.

According to McDonald, the employees' goal is to balance their perceived competence with their perceived eccentricity (PC = PE). She defines perceived competence as how you and your job performance are seen by others in your organization. But note that this perception can be different from reality; perceived competence is how good others in the organization "think" you are.

Perceived eccentricity refers to those parts of you or your actions that do not fit neatly into the profile of the "ideal organization person" as defined by your organization. As McDonald describes it, perceived eccentricity refers to the corners of the square peg if you work in an environment that rewards round pegs. Obviously, some of those corners can be worn down, while others are difficult, if not impossible, to remove. In the higher realms of most Fortune 500 companies, anyone who is female, foreign-born, or a person of color is likely to have a higher perceived eccentricity score than a WASP male. Likewise, people with different lifestyles, vocal religious beliefs, or a unique style of dress, mannerisms, or speech also may be perceived as eccentric in some organizations. In technical environments, perceived eccentricity can also relate to the degree of risk and innovation you display.

How you manage the perceived eccentricity side of your equation has to do with how much acceptance you seek and what that acceptance represents. How much of an insider can you be? How much of an insider do you want to be? How much of yourself are you willing to leave at home or to censor at work? These can be tough issues, especially for minorities who feel the strain of struggling to fit an "ideal type" that bears little resemblance to them.

McDonald described the experience of a white man who moved from a plant to a technical service position. At the plant he and just about everyone else wore jeans. For his new job he upgraded his wardrobe to wear a sport coat with his jeans. Eventually word drifted back to him that the salespeople did not want to take him with them on customer calls because of his "eccentric" dress. He had a choice to make: he could work at raising his perceived competence so that his new colleagues would see him as an invaluable resource even in a burlap sack, or he could invest in a new wardrobe and decrease his perceived eccentricity. He went out and bought suits—a quicker if more expensive route to correcting an imbalance in the eccentricity model.

However, it's easier to change clothes than skin color. The African-American female, who entered a predominantly white company and was assigned to a supervisor who was also brand new, had more difficulty in overcoming the perceived eccentricity of her race. Because the new supervisor couldn't inform her about the company's norms early on or interpret her competence to others in the organization, it took longer for the African American to establish her perceived competence.

McDonald says that you can be as eccentric as you are competent. And it's usually a good idea to establish your competence before you test the company's tolerance of eccentricity. How do you scope out your perceived competence and eccentricity? From performance appraisals, the rewards that come your way, and from feedback. And you may have to take an active role in seeking out feedback so you can decide how to manage yourself in the workplace. McDonald's eccentricity model is a good barometer for figuring out the consequences of your choices.

Examples of employees whose perceived eccentricity far outweighed their perceived competence come readily to mind. These are folks who are no longer around to tell their tale or who are continuously passed over for promotion. The danger of that kind of imbalance is clear. However, McDonald sees no advantage in the opposite kind of imbalance, even though there are typically many people in organizations who are perceived to be more competent than they are eccentric. The danger here is that employees will lose valuable opportunities to grow, both personally and professionally, by playing it safe. And organizations won't learn how to live with and profit from the diversity of their employees. So if your organization perceives you as more competent than eccentric, even up the equation and break out a little. Let those at work know how wonderfully weird or innovative you can be. You'll be doing everyone a favor.

Source: Adapted from an unpublished document by Kathleen McDonald.

 **CLASS PREPARATION**

A. Read "What's Your Eccentricity Quotient?"

B. Then complete the following exercises:

   1. Analysis of a Personal Experience of Being Different.

   2. Intensity of Differentness Rating.

C. While reading the chapter, make a list of cues that you should attend to with respect to diversity.

ANALYSIS OF A PERSONAL EXPERIENCE OF BEING DIFFERENT*

The experience of being different from others can be frustrating, isolating, and even painful. In our desire to avoid these feelings of difference, we are often tempted to deny our individual uniqueness and to "fit in"—to adopt the superficial characteristics of the majority. But doing so is not good for us as individuals for we are denying part of ourselves, which can result in feelings of alienation. It is ineffective as well because our skills lie with who we are, not who we pretend to be. Nor is this denial of differences good for the organization, for without a variety of perspectives and alternatives for action, organizations become rigid and less effective.

Think of a recent experience you have had in which you felt you were being treated as though you were "different," when others were not recognizing you as a unique person. It could be an experience in this course, at work, or anywhere. (Use a separate piece of paper if you need more space.)

1. Describe what happened in the situation.

2. How did you feel, think, and act?

3. How did others feel, think, and act?

4. What was the outcome of the situation?

5. What did you learn from the experience?

INTENSITY OF DIFFERENTNESS RATING

We are all unique individuals with unique cultural and subcultural backgrounds and identities. As a result, we all have experiences of being different, and of being stereotyped and discriminated against. These feelings are most pronounced and intense:

- When the situation is very important (e.g., when a job is at stake, in personal relationships, or when physical safety is at risk).

* These exercises were developed by David Akinnusi, Lyda Detterman, Rafael Estevez, Elizabeth Fisher, Mary Ann Hazen, David Kolb, Dennis O' Connor, and Michelle Spain, a diverse group if there ever was one!

- When our own cultural experiences are markedly different from the dominant culture around us.
- When these differences are visible to others (e.g., skin color, sex, age, language, manner of dress).
- When there are power differences between ourselves and the dominant culture (i.e., when we are "one-down" in influence or rank).
- When we are alone or isolated from others who share our culture or subculture.
- When others are stereotyping us in an obvious fashion.
- When we have strong emotional reactions of frustration, anger, or humiliation.

Look back over your description of the situation in which you felt "different." Score it on the following issues:

Intensity of Differentness Scale

	Circle the Number that Applies:		
1. How important was the situation to you?	0 Relatively unimportant	1 Important	2 Very critical
2. How different were you?	0 Very little difference	1 Some difference	2 Great difference
3. Were these differences visible to others?	0 No	1 A little	2 Yes
4. Were there power differences?	0 I was one-up, in charge	1 Equal	2 I was one-down
5. Were you isolated from others similar to you?	0 I had several others like me for support	1 One other person like me	2 I was alone
6. Were you stereotyped?	0 I was treated as a unique individual	1 I felt stereo- typed	2 There was direct evidence of stereotyping
7. Did the situation cause you to react emotionally?	0 No emotional reaction	1 I felt slightly upset	2 I had a strong emotional reaction

Add the numbers circled to get your total INTENSITY OF DIFFERENTNESS SCORE: _____ .

 **THE KNOWLEDGE BASE**

As companies become more global and as many national workforces become more diverse, we find ourselves working with more and more coworkers who differ from us. Diversity goes well beyond cultural and ethnic values and practices to include a broad definition of categories. *Diversity is broadly defined as differences and similarities with respect to ethnicity, race, culture, gender, age, functional and educational backgrounds, lifestyle preferences, tenure with the organization, personality traits, and ways of thinking.*[1] Each individual is a unique collection of the multiple cultural identities found in this definition, forming their own cultural mosaic.[2]

Diversity is not an issue until an employee is excluded or discriminated against based on one of these categories. Listen to the story of Joe Anderson, an African-American executive working at General Motors.

When I returned from the Harvard Program, General Motors was going through a restruc-turing. So I went on a temporary assignment to the reorganization team breaking down the barriers between brand name cars like Pontiac and Chevrolet. ... I went to work for a vice president in that organization. For the first time, I experienced somebody I knew who didn't want me there. This was not a race issue. I was a Pontiac guy, and he was from a different division of GM. I was not his guy. There were other guys from other places who were also not his guys.[3]

Many companies are already trying to take advantage of a diverse workforce by learning to (1) appreciate, understand, and benefit from differences; (2) communicate and work with diverse groups; (3) develop an organizational culture that welcomes all groups and their unique contri-butions; and (4) allow all kinds of people to reach their full potential. The purpose of this chapter is to focus on both cross-cultural and domestic diversity and inclusion issues.

THE BUSINESS CASE FOR DIVERSITY

In the past, some firms saw only moral and legal reasons for managing diversity well. Today, however, progressive corporations also see diversity as a business issue. The reasons are explained below and illustrated in Exhibit 14–1.

Diverse Viewpoints Businesses benefit from the multiple viewpoints of diverse employees. Ernest Drew, CEO of Hoechst Celanese, became an advocate of diversity when he attended a company conference in 1990. Hoechst's 125 top officers, mostly white males, were joined by about 50 lower-level women and minorities. To tackle the questions of how the corporate culture affected the business and what changes were needed to improve results, problem-solving groups were formed. Some groups were composed only of whites and males; other groups were heterogeneous in terms of race and gender. When the groups presented their findings, Drew became a believer in diversity. "It was so obvious that the diverse teams had the broader solutions," he recalls. "They had ideas I hadn't even thought of. For the first time, we realized that diversity is a strength as it relates to problem solving. Before, we just thought of diversity as the total number of minorities and women in the company, like affir-mative action. Now we knew we needed diversity at every level of the company where deci-sions are made."[4]

Diverse Customers A second business reason is that a diverse workforce has a better under-standing of the needs of diverse customers. Women make more than 85 percent of total house-hold purchasing decisions.[5] Avon, for example, has been very successful at understanding minority customers because of its diverse employees. PepsiCo estimates that approximately one percentage point of the company's 2004 8 percent revenue growth could be attributed to new products that came into existence as a result of the company's diversity efforts.[6] Consider the following example from Sempra Energy, ranked second on *Fortune Magazine's* Best Companies for Minorities.

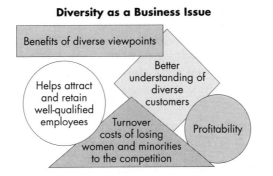

Diversity as a Business Issue

EXHIBIT 14-1 **Reasons Why Diversity Is a Business Issue**

Sempra's Southern California Gas Co. (SoCalGas) field employees alerted management to a trend among Vietnamese customers—they were altering floor furnaces to use as grills. The practice needed to stop, because such changes could cause carbon monoxide poisoning or an explosion. SoCalGas sprung to action at once, launching an education campaign and sending workers out to repair the furnaces. But, what seemed like a dilemma of culture versus safety didn't end there.

Many families would not let the workers into their homes. To comply with state and federal regulations, the SoCalGas employees wore steel-toed boots, which the homeowners demanded they remove before stepping inside.

Company officials were stumped, but they had a resource at hand—a large number of Vietnamese employees that reflected the growing number of Asian immigrants in Orange County. These employees came up with a novel [and effective] solution: to cover the required boots with paper booties.[7]

Attract and Retain Talent Many firms want to hire from the deepest possible talent pool, so inclusive firms have greater ability to attract and retain the best talent. Books and business magazines rate companies as to how well they treat women and minorities; these companies naturally become "preferred employers" for talented members of these groups.

A former CEO of Avon, James Preston, had his own epiphany regarding diversity in the late 1970s when the company's first female vice president, Patricia Neighbors, asked him if she could open a meeting of regional sales managers.[8]

She walked in, went to the podium and began greeting the assembled men. "Hello, Tom, you've changed your hairstyle, haven't you?" "Charlie, that suit looks great on you." "Jack, you're losing weight, aren't you?" She paused, Preston says, to let the astounded silence reign for a moment, and then said, "How do you feel?" Another pause. "That's how two thousand female sales reps feel when you talk to them in such an unprofessional way."

Avon has made great strides since that time. Today, Andrea Jung is the Chairman and CEO of Avon, and eight members of its senior management team are women.[9]

Costs of Losing Women and Minorities The turnover costs associated with losing women and minorities to the competition after investing in their early career development is a fourth reason why businesses are concerned about diversity. For nonunion employees, the turnover costs related to rehiring and training replacements are estimated to be between 90 to 150 percent of annual salary.[10] A recent survey of minority executives found that 50 percent were likely to leave their companies for more challenging positions. "A chronic issue for senior minority executives is that they feel underutilized," according to a managing director at the Korn/Ferry job search firm.[11] The swelling ranks of minority and female entrepreneurs who left the corporate world is partly to blame on poorly managed inclusion. Of the women who founded businesses during the past 10 years, 22 percent cited a corporate glass ceiling as one reason they became entrepreneurs.[12] Minorities sometimes find themselves limited to "racialized" jobs—Equal Employment Opportunity oversight, community relations, government affairs, and ethnic markets—that do not lead to senior executive positions. Although many corporations hire minorities with the ability to advance, very few corporations have the internal systems to ensure that people of color can rise through the ranks. Instead, most high-ranking minorities are hired from other firms. Thomas and Gabarro say the problem is not so much that minorities run into a glass ceiling but that the problems occur much farther down in the hierarchy. They blame "squishy floors" and "revolving doors" for preventing people of color from making it to the upper-middle-management jobs.[13]

Profitability. Finally, diversity is valued is because it can contribute to profitability. Some studies have demonstrated a link between workforce diversity and financial measures of firm profitability. A study of Fortune 500 firms showed that firms with the largest number of women on their senior management teams had 35 percent higher return on equity (ROE) and 34 percent higher total returns to shareholders (TRS).[14]

Cultural sensitivity is a prerequisite for international organizations that want to avoid costly mistakes with employees as well as foreign governments and customers. An example of clashing cultural viewpoints that had serious business consequences was the reaction of some Muslims to cartoons depicting the Prophet Mohammad in a Danish newspaper. Even though other Danish corporations were not responsible for the cartoons, their products were boycotted across the Middle East, resulting in millions of dollars in losses.

In the following sections, we will discuss in more detail four aspects of diversity: ethnicity, gender, age, and culture.

ETHNICITY

The U.S. workforce will likely become more culturally and racially diverse in the future. Women and minorities will represent 70 percent of new entrants into the U.S. workforce by the year 2008. By 2010, 34 percent of the U.S. workforce will be composed of non-Caucasians. Moreover, over the next decade, 75 percent of new entrants will likely be from Asia, with only 3 percent from North America and Europe.[15] In the United States, white males still earn more than people of color and women. For example, the median earnings of different racial groups indicate that black men earn 78 percent and Hispanic men earn 63 percent of the earnings of white males.[16] Some of this disparity is due to the types of occupations different groups tend to hold, but managers have to be careful that minorities and women are not paid less because of discrimination.

Minority advancement in business has seen slow but steady progress. For example, 84 percent of the top 200 S&P companies now have at least one African-American director.[17] Metrics on minority representation on Fortune 100 boards of directors indicate that minorities still form a small percentage of these boards; African Americans held 10 percent, Hispanics 3.9 percent, and Asian Americans 1 percent of the total board seats.[18] Up until 1998, when Franklin Raines became the CEO of Fannie Mae, no African American, Asian American, or Hispanic had ever been CEO of a Fortune 500 company. In 2005, only three African Americans lead Fortune 100 companies.[19] Persons of color have led other types of organizations—military, government agencies, universities, and large nonprofits—but scaling the heights of business organizations has proved more difficult. The odds of a person of color holding an executive position in a Fortune 500 corporation is 33 to 1, compared to those for whites.[20] This means that corporate leaders and board members are drawn from a limited pool that may not contain the best candidates. We know that managers tend to hire people who are similar to themselves, over people who are different, but greater comfort with people "like us" is not a valid reason for promotion and hiring. Thus, it is critical that managers and employees develop skills that allow them to effectively work in multicultural and multiethnic settings.

GENDER

Although the gap is narrowing, women in the United States still earn less than men; white women earn 77 percent, African-American women earn 68 percent, Hispanic women earn 57 percent, and Asian-American women earn 88 percent of men's earnings.[21] The gap is less for younger women, age 16–24, who earn 93 percent of men's earnings.[22] The pay equity gap also persists in Europe, where women generally earn about 15 percent less than men.[23] Much of the gap is a result of occupational choices and family responsibilities, but some women in the same occupations and positions as men still earn less.

Greater numbers of women are entering and progressing up the corporate ladder. Over half of U.S. accounting graduates hired by public accounting firms in 2004 were women. According to the U.S. Labor Bureau, women make up 46 percent of the labor force and hold 50 percent of managerial, professional, and related positions.[24] However, only 8 percent of the top corporate jobs are held by women, and there are only a handful of female CEOs. Low percentages of women at the top of corporations gave rise to concerns about the "glass ceiling." In 2005, 14.7 percent of Fortune 500 corporate board seats were held by women, 3.4 percent by women of color. This percentage increases by about half a percentage point every year—slow but steady progress. However, Catalyst president Ilene Lang concluded, "Our research reveals that if we continue at this pace, it could take 70 years for women to reach parity with men on corporate boards!"[25] On the global stage, 73.5 percent of the 200 largest companies in the world as ranked by *Fortune* magazine had at least one woman board member in 2004, but only 10.4 of total board seats were held by women. In Japan, the world's second largest economy, women hold less than 1 percent (0.7) of board seats.[26]

Women executives report that lack of general management or line experience, exclusion from formal networks, and stereotyping and preconceptions of women's roles and abilities are factors that serve as obstacles to their advancement. In contrast, they report that the following factors contributed to their success: consistently exceeding performance expectations, successfully managing others, developing a style with which male managers feel comfortable, having recognized expertise in a specific area, and seeking out difficult or highly visible assignments. Both female executives and their CEOs agreed that future progress for women is best served by holding senior leaders accountable for women's advancement.[27]

AGE

Understanding how to effectively attract, retain, and manage a multigenerational workforce is likely to become more important in future years as people live longer and expect to work longer. The age makeup of the workforce will likely change. The research group Catalyst predicts that by 2012, workers 55 and older will comprise 19.1 percent of the U.S. workforce (up from 14.3 percent in 2002), and their annual growth rate will be higher than that of all other age groups.[28] It is no wonder that Harriet Hankin, an author and business consultant who specializes in diversity issues, says that as many as five generations may be working together by the year 2050.[29] Each generation is shaped by unique historical and cultural forces that affect their wants, needs, and expectations about work and life. Exhibit 14–2 presents descriptions of the generations, key influences on their development, and their expectations about work and careers. Managing a multigenerational workforce will require that managers be sensitive not only to their workers' expectations about what the organization and work should provide but also about what their workers need at varying times in their lives. For example, a young worker with no children has no need for child-care benefits. A middle-aged worker with both children and elderly parents may be very interested in flexible scheduling options, whereas an older worker may be more interested in health care and retirement issues. Despite those differences, though, workers across generations do share some similar values including respect, fair treatment, equality, balance, flexibility, appropriate feedback, and job enhancement and advancement opportunities.[30]

CULTURE

Culture is a major determinant of human behavior. It provides us with ready-made solutions to basic human issues and a sense of self-identity. "But while humans gain so much from culture, they are also brainwashed, to some extent by the culture to which they are exposed from birth. Equipped with a collection of stereotypes with which to face the world, humans are apt to lose sight of possible alternative modes of behavior and understanding."[31] Part of this "brainwashing" or programming by culture determines how we expect others to behave. Consider the following example:

Wilfredo was a watchman and respected community elder who earned a modest salary at a non-profit development organization located in an isolated island community off the coast of Colombia. The American director offered him an opportunity to earn extra income by cutting down the diseased coconut palm trees that ringed the organization's large property. Wilfredo signed the contract, and the director told him he had a month to complete the task. Instead, Wilfredo hired a crew of community members that he knew, and they cut down all the trees in two days. Knowing that Wilfredo had a large family to feed, the director asked why he hadn't done the work himself and pocketed the money. Wilfredo replied, "Comen y comemos" (They eat and we all eat).

Generation	Born	Influences	Expectations About Work
The Silent Generation Veterans, the Greatest Generation	1922–1945	Great Depression, New Deal, World War II, Holocaust, Hiroshima, radio, movies	Disciplined, hard-working, loyal Respect for authority
Baby Boomers (other names: Boomers, Me Generation)	1946–1964	Vietnam War, assassinations of J. F. Kennedy, M. L. King, and R. F. Kennedy, landing on the moon, Watergate, television, women's liberation, environmental concerns	Optimistic, competitive, active in social causes, focused on personal accomplishment and gain Lack of respect for authority Belief in meritocracy
Generation X (other names: Baby Bust, X-ers)	1965–1976	Demolition of the Berlin Wall, Challenger space shuttle disaster, high technology start-ups, the dot.com boom and bust, 24-hour live remote news coverage, divorce	Independent, resilient, adaptive Expect work to be fun, work well in multicultural settings Loyal to their team and coworkers, not to organizations
Generation Y (other names: Baby Boom Echo, Nexters, Internet Generation)	1977–2000	Internet, Oklahoma City bombing, Columbine High School shooting, September 11, 2001, attacks, Y2K, corporate downsizings and layoffs, corporate scandals	Extremely comfortable with high tech Desire feedback, structure and direction, respectful of positions, titles, bosses Willing to work hard for their goals Expect balanced work and family life, clearly delegated assignments with balanced freedom and flexibility, ongoing training and learning opportunities, mentors, meaningful work
Millennium Generation	2000 and later	To be determined	To be determined

Source: Adapted from H. Hankin, *The New Workforce* (Amacom: New York, 2005); R. Zemke, C. Raines, B. Filipczak, *Generations at Work* (New York: Amacom, 2000); and S. Armour, "Generation Y: They've Arrived at Work with a New Attitude" *USA Today* (November 7, 2005): B1.

EXHIBIT 14-2 **Generations and Their Work Expectations**

Rather than focusing solely on the task or his individual benefit, Wilfredo was more concerned about his relationships with his neighbors and the common good of the community.[32]

The difference between their cultural perspectives can be explained by diverse cultural orientations, a focus on individualism versus collectivism and on task versus relationship. One orientation is not better than the other; they are simply different and, therefore, have to be taken into consideration when working across cultures.

In the "Setting the Global Stage" introduction to this book, we discussed major perspectives on culture and identified several values that can be used to compare and contrast cultural behavior. Although they help us predict and decode behavior, they fail to capture the complexity within a single culture. There are other values that are unique to each culture. And no culture is always, for example, individualistic or collectivist; how people behave depends in large part on the context. Therefore, we run the risk of stereotyping entire cultures with these bipolar dimensions unless we understand they are simply a helpful first step in decoding cultural behavior.[33] Exhibit 14–3 presents cultural influences at work in three cultures: China, India, and the United States. You can see examples of the unique cultural values in this exhibit, such as *guanxi* (network of personal connections) in China and *dharma* (duty) in India.

All cultures have advantages and disadvantages when considered objectively. Human nature sometimes prevents us from appreciating the advantages or the good points of other cultures. This quality is referred to as ethnocentrism.

EXHIBIT 14-3 Culture's Influence on Work

Core Cultural Axioms	Organization & Leadership/ Management Style	Decision-Making/ Problem-Solving	Motivation/ Recognition	Communication/ Procedures
China *Respect,* *Obedience, and* *Humility* *Face (Mianzi)* *Group Loyalty* *(Family, School,* *Work, Nation)* *Network of* *Personal* *Connections* *(Guanxi)* *Ordered* *Hierarchy*	• Respect and trust must be earned to do business • Hierarchical with varying levels of authority • High degree of dependence on leaders • Authority is not delegated downward with tasks • Seniority is important (often based on age) • Entrepreneurial • Heavily influenced by governmental authority and institutional policies and activities	• Complicated hierarchical decision-making process • Difficult to determine who makes decisions • Top-down, leader-mediated compromise based on input from group members • Takes a long time due to consensus building and approval seeking • Decision of the leader is the final word; others are expected to follow • Accountability for decisions is evaded • The order is generally not challenged	• Honor • Intragroup harmony • Conformity to group norms • Fulfilling the needs of one's groups • Status and rank • Wealth • Reciprocity • Education	• Senior members of business delegations lead discussion • Punctuality is important • Meticulous research, note-taking and documentation in negotiation process • Gifts and favors are expected to be reciprocated, and kept balanced • Indirect style • Overt criticism is discouraged • Laughter may indicate embarrassment or nervousness • Long-term focus
India *Collectivism/Group* *Cyclicality* *Fatalism (karma)* *Hierarchy* *Duty (dharma)*	• Older and larger organizations are more hierarchical and lines of authority are clearly defined • New companies are more collegial and entrepreneurial with a flat and flexible structure • High value on formal status and power, paternalism • Managers need to show greater intelligence and expertise than subordinates to secure and maintain their loyalty • Outsiders judged with caution • Superiors will not engage in work below their level	• Handle uncertainty well, are risk-takers and innovators • Decisions are made at the top and are centralized • Incentives for middle managers helps move proposals upward • Managers judge performance morally and by efficiency • Good deal of discussion, followed by long wait for a final decision, then whatever is meant to happen will happen • Based on mix of extensive research and intuition • High business acumen • Reluctance to deliver negative news; sometimes issues ignored in hopes they will "fade away"	• Earn a living • Care for family • Personal Accomplishments • Obtain power and status • Work is more of a place to earn a livelihood than to belong • Strong work ethic • Goal oriented, setbacks are taken in stride • Loyalty valued in general • Value for ability, professionalism and competence, less than for loyalty, in private sector firms, especially in south	• Punctuality is defined somewhat loosely • Information flow is vertical, up and down the organization • Negotiation proceeds slowly • Emotions can be shown • Communication is direct, but it is considered more polite to be indirect when expressing a refusal • Verbal agreements carry weight, but supported by detailed contracts • Pressure for individuals to share group values • English is common • Although collectivist and loyal to family/group, individually brilliant negotiators

Core Cultural Axioms	Organization & Leadership/ Management Style	Decision-Making/ Problem-Solving	Motivation/ Recognition	Communication/ Procedures
U.S. *Individualism* *Freedom/Equality* *Pragmatism* *Achievement and Material Gain*	• Explicit and transparent • Flat, flexible • Informal • Task-related • Tends to over simplify • Subordinates expected to know more than managers about how to do their jobs	• Quick • Action focused, can do attitude • Individual decision authority at most levels • Gather facts • Focus on new alternatives • Try it; if it works then implement • Likes risk • Optimistic, sometimes overly • Initiative at all levels	• Competitive • Individual achievement and advancement • External, often monetary • Based on merit	• Structured agenda, sequenced subjects • Managers listen to subordinates • Deadlines are strict and very serious • Interruptions are considered rude • Managers ask for info • Teamwork is common • Information is shared, distributed knowledge is efficient • Communication is direct and explicit

Source: J. C. Gluesing, Cultural Connections. Used with permission.

ETHNOCENTRISM

Ethnocentrism is defined as the "exaggerated tendency to think the characteristics of one's own group or race are superior to those of other groups or races."[34] Humans are preoccupied with the differences between their "own" kind and outsiders. Anthropologists have encountered many tribes whose name is literally translated as "the human beings"; this implies that those outside their tribe are not human and, therefore, not worthy of the same consideration.

Everyone possesses some degree of ethnocentrism. For anyone who deals with people who are different, the first step is to acknowledge one's ethnocentrism and try to curb the natural thought that one's own group or culture, by definition, is better than others. The next steps in cross-cultural relations include gaining an understanding of your own culture, followed by a serious attempt to understand the other culture or subculture. Until we understand the internal logic of another culture, we may be tempted to interpret their behavior using our own cultural norms and assumptions. This usually leads to misperceptions and false attributions about their behavior.

INTERCULTURAL SENSITIVITY

The Developmental Model of Intercultural Sensitivity (DMIS) is a taxonomy that describes how people react to cultural differences and develop intercultural competence.[35] The model assumes that as our attitudes and behaviors with regard to cultural difference become more sophisticated, we become more interculturally competent.[36] The DMIS model, shown in Exhibit 14–4, describes the worldviews that characterize each of the six stages. They are grouped into two major categories: ethnocentric and ethnorelative. In the first three stages, one's own culture is the central reference point, which is why they are called "ethnocentric." All other cultures are viewed and evaluated from the reference point of one's own culture. Differences are avoided by denying their existence (denial), by seeing one's own culture as superior and other cultures as inferior (defense), or by assuming that all

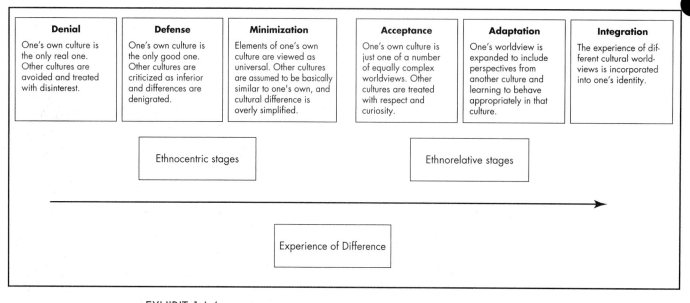

EXHIBIT 14-4 Development Of Intercultural Sensitivity Model

Source: Adapted from M. Bennett, "Towards Ethnorelativism: A Developmental Model of Intercultural Sensitivity," in R. M. Paige (ed.), *Education for the Intercultural Experience* (Yarmouth, ME: Intercultural Press, 1993): 21–71.

cultures are basically the same—"like mine" (minimization). In contrast, in the ethnorelative stages one's own culture is *not* the central reference point. Instead, it's simply one of many reference points that can be used to view and evaluate the social world. Cultures are interpreted in their own right and not judged by how they compare with one's own culture. They come to see their own culture as one of many equally complex worldviews (acceptance), they learn to take on the perspectives and behaviors of other cultures with whom they interact (adaptation), or they incorporate aspects of another culture into their own personal identity (integration). Bicultural people are an example of integration. The adaptation and integration stages involve the greatest degree of intercultural competence.

STEREOTYPING AND DISCRIMINATION

People entering organizations bring with them their own assumptions and preconceptions, and they use these ideas to form new impressions about other groups in the organization. When we act toward individual members of a group based on our assumptions about the group to which they belong, we are engaging in stereotyping behavior. Aronson describes this as follows: "*To stereotype is to assign identical characteristics to any people in a group regardless of the actual variation among members of the group.*"[37]

One common example are negative comments made about other departments or functions in organizations. Stereotypes abound in organizations. The common ones are based on gender, race, age, and professional groups. For instance, ageism may be responsible for the difficulty some people over the age of 55 have in finding jobs.[38] Exhibit 14–5 presents common stereotypical misinterpretations and the values that more accurately explain Asian American behavior. Stereotyping often results in misattributions about behavior.

Stereotypic perceptions of individual differences lead to prejudice and discrimination. Racial stereotypes can impact hiring and termination decisions and prevent organizations from realizing the potential of minority employees. For instance, more African Americans lost their jobs during the 1990–1991 recession than any other ethnic group.[39] Racial stereotypes can be a significant problem, even for highly successful minorities. Arthur Ashe was a world-famous African-American tennis star who contracted AIDS via a blood transfusion while undergoing heart surgery. Billie Jean King, a fellow tennis pro, once asked Ashe, "What's the most difficult thing for you?" He replied, "Most people would think it's HIV, AIDS, or my heart, but it's really

Observed Behavior of Asian Americans	Common Stereotypical Misinterpretations	Possible Cultural Explanation
Nonconfrontational	Passive; does not care one way or another	Values harmony; sees disagreements as being in disharmony
Quiet; reserved	Has no opinions	Values opinions of others and fitting in with group
Agreeable; dependable follower	Unassertive; no leadership qualities	Values what is good for group; can be assertive and a leader if needed for the group
Industrious	Make good "worker bees"	Values carrying their share of work; believes hard work will be recognized and rewarded
Technically and scientifically competent	No management competence or leader-type charisma	Values science as universal language crossing cultural barriers; believes leadership comes in many forms
Deferential to others	Not committed to own opinions, judgments, or preferences	Values being respectful of others; believes in "saving face" for self and others; values age and wisdom
Very American behavior	Looks Asian; must be of different culture	Born in United States; values both American and Asian heritage

EXHIBIT 14-5 Asian Americans: Common Stereotypes and Corresponding Cultural Explanations

Source: Reprinted with permission from NTL Institute from *Managing in the Age of Change,* edited by Roger A. Ritvo, Anne H. Litwin, and Lee Butler, 1995.

being a black man. Every time I walk out the door, I know my day could be difficult because of prejudice."[40]

As mentioned earlier, stereotyping is partly responsible for the glass ceiling facing female executives, but female executives and male CEOs have different perceptions about the impact of stereotyping. Fifty-two percent of female executives versus 25 percent of male CEOs responded that "male stereotyping and preconceptions about women" kept women from being promoted to executive positions.[41] Workplace stereotypes prevent people who are different from feeling accepted and living up to their full potential. They also deny individual uniqueness, which can lead to communication and cooperation problems as well as discrimination.

Although significant progress has been made in reducing workplace discrimination, a Gallup Poll found that 15 percent of U.S. workers experienced some kind of discrimination in the preceding year. Women (22 percent) reported over twice as much as men (9 percent). Asians (31 percent), Blacks (26 percent) and Hispanics (18 percent) also experienced discrimination. In sharp contrast, only 3 percent of white men did so. The specific types of discrimination were related to gender (26 percent), race/ethnicity (23 percent), age (17 percent), disability (9 percent), sexual orientation (4 percent) and religion (4 percent).[42]

THE MINORITY EXPERIENCE

Organizations exist in a multicultural environment and cannot avoid this reality. People in organizations bring with them aspects of their cultural experience and, thus, organizations come to mirror issues facing society and the world. Brown, for example, reminds us that the minorities in a society that allows discrimination tend to be particularly sensitive to discriminatory behaviors within the organizations that employ them.[43] They perceive discriminatory intent in behaviors that may seem appropriate and nondiscriminatory to members of the dominant culture. As a result, members of the majority may feel insulted if accused of discrimination. They do not recognize that they are beneficiaries of institutional discrimination and do not understand why minorities are "so sensitive."

Minorities in both cultures and organizations often pay a high price for their "differentness." Feeling the need to represent one's entire race, gender, or culture can be a burden. As one African-American man, who was tired of fielding questions in an all-white group, stated, "I'm not putting on a charm school course on blacks for white folk." Kanter's study of "tokens" in a large corporation found that three perceptual tendencies occur when there is a small number of minorities. This phenomenon can be observed with any tokens, including white males, when they constitute a small minority.[44]

1. Because tokens are more highly visible, they receive more attention and performance pressure. In Gestalt psychology terms, the tokens become the "figure" rather than the "ground." As a result, the tokens are constantly in the public eye, and their behavior is scrutinized for symbolic content because they represent their entire group, not just themselves. Performance pressures are thereby magnified.

2. Contrast between the token and the majority group results in exaggeration and polarization of the differences between the two groups. Exposure to a minority makes the majority self-conscious and, therefore, uncomfortable and uncertain. As a result, the boundaries of the dominant group become even stronger and isolation of the tokens occurs.

3. Assimilation via stereotyping occurs with tokens. A larger number of "token-type" people would allow the majority to perceive that there are, in fact, many individual differences among this group. However, because of their small numbers, tokens are forced into limited and caricatured roles, which Kanter refers to as "role encapsulation." Common stereotypes for tokens are mascot, cheerleader, sex object, and militant.

Sensitivity to the stress that accompanies tokenism can be partially alleviated by managers who understand the phenomenon. But the systemic answer to the problem is to hire and promote enough people from the minority group to make tokenism a moot point.

People who belong to similar diversity categories often develop a subculture or social network characterized by shared meanings, values, frameworks, and languages. Kinship, ethnic, and minority ties are among the strongest links that hold together a social network.[45] Such groups are likely to have common interests and to share needs that the formal organization seldom meets. As a consequence, these groups form their own networks in which they exchange the things they need and desire, such as support, advice, and collaboration. Many corporations encourage the development of formal minority networks.

DESIGNING THE INCLUSIVE ORGANIZATION

A recent Gallup poll found that employees who rate their company's diversity efforts highly report more company satisfaction and loyalty and are more likely to remain with the firm and recommend it to others.[46] Organizations that want to "maximize the benefits and minimize the drawbacks of diversity, in terms of workgroup cohesiveness, interpersonal conflict, turnover, and coherent action on major organizational goals, must create multicultural organizations."[47] The characteristics of an inclusive organization are:[48]

1. It actively seeks to capitalize on the advantages of its diversity, rather than attempting to stifle or ignore the diversity, and to minimize the barriers that can develop as a result of people having different backgrounds, attitudes, values, behavior styles, and concerns.

2. Organizational resources (key jobs, income, perquisites, access to information, etc.) are distributed equitably and are not determined or affected by cultural characteristics such as race and gender.

3. The ability to influence decisions and the way they are carried out is shared widely, not differentially by cultural characteristics.

4. Minority group members are fully integrated in the informal networks of the organization.

5. The organizational culture (assumptions about people and groups, take-it-for-granted norms, the way work gets done) is pluralistic in that it recognizes and appreciates diversity and all cultural groups respect and learn from each other. The culture acknowledges both the need for "being the same" in some ways to work together effectively and the need for "being different" in some ways to recognize individual and group interests, concerns, and backgrounds.

6. Institutional policies, practices, and procedures are flexible and responsive to the needs of all employees.

7. There is an absence of prejudice and discrimination.

8. Majority and minority members are equally identified with the organizational goals.

9. There is a minimum of intergroup conflict among diverse groups.

There are several steps businesses can take to help make their organizations more effectively make use of diversity.

1. Tangibly demonstrate top management commitment to diversity. Without the support of top management, diversity efforts will fail. Top executives must be committed to diversity and, importantly, visibly communicate and demonstrate that commitment. For example, Peggy Moore, senior vice president of human resources at PepsiCo, says CEO Steve Reinemund uses every opportunity to demonstrate the importance of diversity: "No matter what you want an agenda for a meeting to be, he will make sure it is included. For six years, he has been bringing it up, and after a while, people get that it isn't going to go away."[49]

2. Establish unambiguous, explicit, and focused qualifications criteria used in selection decisions and clearly communicate those criteria. Sometimes, women and minorities are believed to have obtained their jobs on the basis of a preferential selection process, which can lead to a perception that they are less competent. In turn, this may set in motion a self-fulfilling prophecy (see Chapter 1) by creating what is called "a threat in the air" or stereotype threat to members of a targeted group. This fear of being viewed in stereotypical terms can negatively affect their performance.[50] Negative consequences like these can be reduced by identifying and communicating the criteria used to make hiring decisions.[51]

3. Develop strategies to recruit a diverse workforce. A study by the National Urban League found that the following practices were effective:
   • Establish more aggressive diversity recruiting goals based on company need and workforce availability
   • Align reward systems with effective recruiting and hiring of a diverse workforce
   • Establish partnerships with recruiting sources that have a strong likelihood of successfully delivering desired results
   • Use partners as company recruiters
   • Create multiple exposures to potential candidates—internships, co-ops, classroom presentations, and company receptions to begin the relationship process early
   • Connect potential candidates with a variety of company resources across levels
   • Create a diverse pool of qualified candidates for final consideration
   • Highlight previous success stories in recruiting process
   • Get in touch and stay in contact with the candidates that have the greatest potential until they are on-board as new employees
   • Continue to recruit in places that yield the greatest results
   • Maintain presence and relationship (active and financial) regardless of fluctuations in annual recruiting needs[52]

4. Remove barriers to achievement and advancement. Efforts to ensure that all employees can achieve and contribute to the organization take many forms. For Starbucks, this means working hard to hire people with disabilities and to make their store hospitable to disabled customers. There are both ethical and business reasons driving Starbucks' programs—people

with disabilities have discretionary spending power of $220 billion annually in the United States alone. Starbucks has hired a senior diversity specialist in charge of disability issues who has launched a number of initiatives ranging from ensuring that the disabled have equal access to jobs to redesigning store layout to developing company-wide etiquette programs (e.g., helping employees understand how to effectively work with disabled customers; for example, employees are reminded to avoid petting or distracting guide dogs).[53]   Other companies set up mentoring and networking programs so that employees can cultivate relationships that will help them succeed. PepsiCo has created affinity groups consisting of people of a particular race, gender, sexual orientation, or disability. These groups meet to discuss their needs and perspectives. What is especially effective is that PepsiCo makes sure to assign an executive sponsor (thereby demonstrating top management support) who is from a different affinity group. For example, the sponsor of the women of color group is a white female division president while the sponsor of the white male affinity group is a black male executive. This helps to ensure that executives understand the needs of the group but also facilitates communication and understanding across members of different affinity groups.[54]

5. Encourage the development of a superordinate goal and a group identity. As we saw in the chapter on conflict, superordinate goals can help people work together—especially when they need each other in order to succeed. Establishing a group identity (for example, "we are all employees of X Company") also helps promote cooperation.

6. Establish appropriate training programs. Training programs should focus not only on diversity issues per se but also on the skills employees need to work effectively in a diverse environment. Recent efforts focus on developing the business case for diversity and on teaching employees the skills they need to reach a diverse customer base as well as to work in diverse teams. The jury is still out on whether these programs will be effective. However, a study by the National Urban League underscores the need for effective diversity initiatives. According to the study, just 32 percent of more than 5,500 U.S. employees believed that their companies did a good job of hiring and promoting people other than white males. Moreover, less than half of the executives believed their own efforts were working, and most believed it was partly a result of their own lack of involvement.[55]

7. Align organizational reward systems with recruiting, hiring, retaining, and advancing a diverse workforce. It is critical that performance evaluations, rewards, and compensation systems reinforce these goals.

8. Monitor the effectiveness of your diversity initiatives. Keeping track of relevant metrics is an important part of managing diversity effectively. One method is to establish a diversity scorecard, a measurement tool that includes both financial and nonfinancial measures.[56]

9. Train employees and managers to be interculturally competent.

People who are interculturally competent possess the competencies found in Exhibit 14–6.

Tolerance of differences
Tolerance of ambiguity
Open-mindedness
Positive attitudes toward people and experiences
Patience
Personal self-awareness
Behavioral flexibility
Empathy
Interpersonal sensitivity
Good communication skills, including active listening
Ability to connect with others

EXHIBIT 14-6 **Diversity/Intercultural Competencies**

CLASS ACTIVITY: CROSS-CULTURAL/DIVERSITY COMPETENCY SKITS

The purpose of this exercise is to give you an opportunity to practice and recognize effective and ineffective cross-cultural or intercultural interactions. (Time allotted: approximately 1 hour)

STEP 1.   If yours is a diverse, multicultural classroom, divide into small groups of no more than six members based on ethnic or cultural identity. If your class is not very diverse along these dimensions, your instructor may choose to divide you into small groups that represent other forms of diversity, such as gender, age, or ethnicity.

STEP 2.   As a group, make up a two-part skit that lasts no more than five to eight minutes. The first part should portray an ineffective way to handle a cross-cultural or intercultural interaction that you might face at work or elsewhere, due to your brand of diversity. For example, Thai students would present the wrong way and then the right way to communicate with Thais in a particular context. The second part should present effective handling of the same interaction, demonstrating the Diversity/Intercultural Competencies shown in Exhibit 14–6 on the previous page. Be as creative as possible and have fun with your skit. Prepare to ask the rest of the class to analyze "what's wrong with this picture?" after the first part and "What's right with this picture?" after the second part. (20–30 minutes)

STEP 3.   Each group presents its skit and asks the rest of the class to identify what was ineffective in the first part and effective in the second part. (30–40 minutes)

STEP 4   Plenary Debriefing. (10 minutes) Discuss this question: What did you learn from this exercise?

CROSS-CULTURAL TRAINING*

The purpose of this exercise is to design a cross-cultural training experience for people with varying levels of intercultural sensitivity. (Time allotted: 60 minutes)

STEP 1.   Divide the class into teams of no more than six people; each team should be numbered between one and six.

STEP 2.   Each team has been hired as outside contractors to do a training session on intercultural competence by a company that is seeking to develop its global operations. You have never met the group of employees you will be training. You can assume, however, that the entire group shares the same mind-set, even though the group itself is culturally diverse, both domestically and internationally. This will be their first experience with learning about cultural differences, and they are curious about what to expect. At work, these individuals have daily contact with dozens of different cultures. Your goal in the upcoming meeting is to discuss how you will develop their intercultural competence in the organization. Intercultural training can focus on knowledge, attitudes, and/or behavioral skills. The most effective training is multimethod, such as a combination of lectures, videos, role plays, simulations, and learning from real experiences.

Read the mind-set of the group assigned to your team, as shown in the following list.
- Team 1—Group A Mind-Set Page 380
- Team 2—Group B Mind-Set Page 380
- Team 3—Group C Mind-Set Page 381

* This exercise was adapted from an exercise developed by Janet Bennett, Executive Director of the Intercultural Communication Institute, and Ann Marie Lei, consultant, and is used with their permission.

- Team 4—Group D Mind-Set Page 381
- Team 5—Group E Mind-Set Page 381
- Team 6—Group F Mind-Set Page 381

Perhaps you have met others who have this mind-set in the classroom or workplace. Feel free to imitate their thoughts on these matters!

STEP 3. Answer these questions in your team and post #4 on the board/wall. (30 minutes) Choose a spokesperson to summarize your answers.

1. What forms of resistance would this training group have? What specific things might they say to you, or to others in the class?
2. What are the advantages individuals may experience having this mind-set? Name three.
3. What are the limitations or disadvantages of this mind-set? Name three.
4. What tactics should you use to help your training group become more interculturally competent? (Refer to Exhibit 14-4 and 14-6)

STEP 4. Plenary Debriefing. (30 minutes) Each group summarizes their answers and explains their tactics.

1. Which stage in Exhibit 14-4 describes the mindset of your training group?
2. What did you learn from this exercise?

GROUP A MIND-SET

This group both acknowledges and respects cultural difference. They are aware of their own culture(s), and they see that their own culture is just one of many ways of experiencing the world. When they think of people from other cultures, they imagine them as every bit as complex as themselves. The ideas, feelings, and behavior of other cultures may seem unusual to them, but they realize that others' experience is just as "rich" as their own.

They may not like everything about other cultures (or everything about their own, for that matter), but that fact does not make them think that the members of those cultures as a group are any less civilized than their own cultural group. They are curious about other cultures and seek opportunities to learn more about them, even if they do not have as many opportunities as they would like to interact with members of those cultures.

When they are around people who are culturally different, they may not act any differently than they do with members of their own culture, but they are aware that their behavior might be interpreted in unusual ways. They are careful to withhold quick judgments of members of other cultures and to consider how their behavior might mean something different than it would in their own culture. One of their clear strengths is in recognizing cultural differences between their own and other groups and seeing how these differences are valuable to society and to themselves.

GROUP B MIND-SET

They have gotten beyond feeling that people from other cultures pose a threat to their own. Their experience is that people from other cultures are pretty much like them, under the surface. They are quite aware that other cultures exist all around them, and they may be fairly knowledgeable about cultural differences in customs and everyday behavior.

They do not denigrate other cultures and they seek to avoid stereotypes by treating every person as an individual or by treating other people as they would like to be treated. They believe in the Golden Rule, because, deeply, we all share a common humanity. They enjoy sharing aspects of their culture with people from other places.

In many ways, they like it that people from other cultures speak and act in ways different from themselves, but they probably believe that there are some universal values that apply to all people, regardless of culture. One of their clear strengths is recognizing the essential humanity of every person and trying to behave in tolerant ways toward others.

GROUP C MIND-SET

They are comfortable with the familiar and are not anxious to complicate life with "cultural difference." They may simply not notice much cultural difference around them. Because they have many things on their mind, culture may not seem like a very important issue to them.

When they think about "culture," they may be most interested in familiar categories of food, clothing, and the arts instead of exploring the less familiar idea of cultural differences.

They also may maintain separation from others who are different. Perhaps they avoid contact because of the discomfort of dealing with strange people and situations. Or they might seek out meeting places, groups, or religious organizations with people who are as culturally similar to themselves as possible.

Essentially, they don't see how cultural differences affect their life or work, and sometimes they may wonder why people make such a big deal about it. They suspect that this is an issue that will eventually go away, or certainly won't impact them. One of their clear strengths is their adherence to traditional values and support for the community of like-minded people.

GROUP D MIND-SET

They enjoy the flexibility they have in living "dynamically in-between" at least two cultures. They have had the opportunity to internalize two or more cultures so deeply that they feel at home in both, using the styles, skills, and perspectives of each of the cultures easily in their life and work. They probably speak at least two languages fluently, and have deep and long-term relationships with members of multiple cultures. They may be in a bicultural marriage, with bicultural/biracial children.

They enthusiastically interpret one culture to another, and they are frequently able to think and interact using multiple worldviews. They are world citizens, even though they are somewhat removed from the cultural norms of their home culture. They know there are many ways to examine an issue and solve problems.

Their clear strengths are bicultural thinking, creative use of many cultural perspectives and deep cultural complexity.

GROUP E MIND-SET

They recognize the added value of having more than one cultural perspective available to them. They have deep knowledge of their own and at least one other culture, and they are able to shift their cultural perspective to look at the world through different eyes. When they shift perspective into another culture, they find that their behavior changes in a natural way to express that different view of the world.

They have a broad repertoire of behavior that allows them to act in culturally appropriate ways outside of their own culture. In fact, they are able to intentionally change their behavior to match that of other cultures, even if they are not around people from that culture.

They are often in situations in which they use this ability to facilitate intercultural discussions, conduct negotiations across cultures, manage teams, or direct projects. It is likely that they are bicultural in at least one other culture, although they can shift their behavior in more limited ways toward other cultures as well. They may routinely use this ability to act as a bridge across cultures.

Their clear strengths include the ability to communicate effectively across cultures, their flexible perspective, and their deep understanding of at least one other culture.

GROUP F MIND-SET

They have a strong commitment to their own worldview and some distrust of cultural behavior or ideas that differ from their own. They are aware of other cultures around them, but they may have a relatively incomplete understanding of them and they probably have some fairly strong negative stereotypes about some of them.

For instance, they might routinely attribute negative characteristics to many foreign cultures, many religions, many women, many gays, and so on. They may complain themselves about the failings of people from other culture groups. They probably do not seek out the company of people from other cultures because they object to one or more of their unpleasant traits.

If they do have a good relationship with a coworker, neighbor, or friend from another culture, they may consider that person an exception to the rule about the group to which he or she belongs. They believe their own culture has a lot to offer these people. One of their clear strengths is in dealing head-on with difficult international and multicultural issues and resisting the temptation to return to blissful ignorance about them.

 **LEARNING POINTS**

1. Diversity is becoming increasingly valued by business because of the following reasons:
   a. Increased diversity of viewpoints
   b. Ability to reach additional customers
   c. Attracting and retaining the best talent
   d. Decreased costs of turnover
   e. Linkages to profitability
2. Culture provides us with ready-made solutions for basic human problems and a sense of identity, but it also limits our ability to see and sometimes appreciate alternative behaviors.
3. All cultures have both positive and negative aspects and are best understood as a series of trade-offs.
4. Ethnocentrism is the tendency to think one's own group or race is superior to other groups or races.
5. Everyone possesses a degree of ethnocentrism, but it must be curbed to work effectively with people from other groups or races.
6. The Developmental Model of Intercultural Sensitivity (DMIS) is a taxonomy that describes how people react to cultural differences and develop intercultural competence. The ethnocentric stages of the model are: defense, denial, minimization; the ethnorelative stages are: acceptance, adaptation, and integration.
7. Stereotyping is assigning identical characteristics to any member of a group regardless of his or her individual differences. The prejudice that accompanies stereotypes prevents us from judging individuals fairly on their own merit.
8. Minorities in societies characterized by discrimination are especially sensitive to discriminatory behavior in the organizations that employ them.
9. Three perceptual tendencies and their results affect tokens:
   a. High visibility leads to performance pressures on tokens.
   b. Contrast that exaggerates differences between two groups leads the dominant group to heighten its cultural boundaries, which isolates tokens.
   c. Assimilation by stereotyping results in role encapsulation for the tokens.
10. These consequences, which cause stress for tokens, can be avoided by increasing the number of the minority group within the organization so minorities are perceived as individuals rather than tokens.
11. Minority groups often form networks within larger organizations to share common interests and meet needs that the formal organizations may not fill.
12. Managing diversity well (a) allows minorities and eccentric people to feel comfortable and contribute fully at work, (b) permits organizations to benefit from diverse viewpoints, (c) makes it easier to serve a diverse group of customers, and (d) helps organizations attract and retain high-quality minority employees.

13. The following steps can help create an inclusive organization:
    a. Tangibly demonstrate top management commitment to diversity.
    b. Establish unambiguous, explicit, and focused qualifications criteria used in selection decisions and clearly communicate those criteria.
    c. Develop strategies to recruit a diverse workforce.
    d. Remove barriers to achievement and advancement.
    e. Encourage the development of a superordinate goal and a group identity.
    f. Establish appropriate training programs.
    g. Align organizational reward systems with recruiting, hiring, retaining, and advancing a diverse workforce.
    h. Monitor the effectiveness of diversity initiatives.

ACTION SCRIPTS

FOR EMPLOYEES

* People who are experts at working with different cultural or ethnic groups follow the guidelines below:
  * Know and understand your own culture. (Why do we value certain things and behave in certain ways?)
  * Know the other culture.
  * Make an effort to understand why members of the other culture hold the values they do and behave as they do.
  * Look for strengths in the other culture rather than focus on weaknesses or differences.
  * Respect the other culture and bear in mind that it's the ability to create relationships and work through others that leads to effectiveness.
  * Recognize the degree to which you are ethnocentric and keep it in check.
  * Listen actively so that people from the other culture can guide you and so the organization will benefit from its diversity.
* Experts do not expect everyone to behave as they do or to always adapt to them. They find cultural and ethnic differences interesting, not annoying, and accept that people are programmed to act and think in different ways. They do not compare behavior from other cultures or ethnic groups to their own and judge it to be inferior.
* They practice mindfulness, which involves switching from our usual "cruise control" to paying closer attention in a reflective and creative way to cues in cross-cultural situations.[57]
* They develop a broad repertoire of behaviors that are appropriate in different cultures and with different groups of people.
* When communicating with people who have a different native language, they speak slowly, avoid jargon, and frequently check for understanding.
* People who are skilled at dealing with minorities accept that they may not fully understand the minority viewpoint and therefore are careful to ask for input and feedback rather than sticking to their own assumptions.

FOR MANAGERS

* Managers who are skilled at directing diverse workforces understand that multicultural groups can be a source of learning and creativity but only when groups can be open about their differences and use them to enhance understanding.
* They also recognize that some diversity training has pitted groups against each other, resulting in less rather than more understanding. A divisive approach (e.g., blaming the majority) only causes hard feelings and a backlash against minorities. Diversity training should emphasize

an appreciation of differences, a focus on similarities, and the ways in which diversity can be a competitive advantage. It should also incorporate training for skills needed to be effective in a diverse workplace (e.g., communication, listening, conflict resolution, teamwork). Training in skills for reaching a diverse customer base also should be included.

- Managers who effectively manage a diverse team will take the time to create a superordinate goal and to make sure that all team members make essential contributions toward achieving that goal. They will also work hard to develop a common team identity that includes all members.
- They use management techniques or intervention strategies that are appropriate for the given culture or subculture.
- Experts understand that virtually all aspects of management are influenced by cultural values. If they are unfamiliar with a specific culture with whom they might be negotiating, for example, they read up on cultural practices and/or ask for help from an expert in that culture.

FOR ORGANIZATIONAL ARCHITECTS

The last section in The Knowledge Base, entitled Designing the Inclusive Organization, includes many guidelines for organizational architects.

In addition, companies that understand the business value of a diverse workforce have learned the following lessons:[58]

- Get the CEO's commitment.
- Make diversity a business objective.
- Define diversity widely so all employees understand that they bring some diversity to the table.
- Adopt a plan for addressing the concerns of the dominant group so they do not feel excluded.
- Scrutinize compensation and career tracking for fairness.
- Identify high-potential employees so they are developed and considered for promotions.
- Avoid diversity training that is divisive.
- Celebrate differences.
- Improve the supply of diverse workers. College internships, for example, are a means of locating and attracting more minorities.

PERSONAL APPLICATION ASSIGNMENT

Quelle verité que ces montagnes burnent, qui est mensonge au monde qui si tient au dela? [What kind of a truth is this that is bounded by a chain of mountains and is falsehood to the people living on the other side?]

Montaigne, Essa is II, XII, p. 34

The topic of this assignment is to think back on a diversity experience that was significant for you. Choose an experience that intrigues you and that you want to learn more about.

A. Concrete Experience

   1. Objectively describe the experience (who, what, when, where, how). (2 points)

2. Subjectively describe your feelings, perceptions, and thoughts that occurred during (not after) the experience. What did others seem to be feeling? (2 points)

B. Reflective Observation
   1. Looking back at the experience, what were the perspectives of the key actors (including you)? (2 points)
   2. Why did the people involved (including you) behave as they did? (2 points)

C. Abstract Conceptualization
   1. Relate concepts or theories from the assigned readings or the lecture to the experience. Explain thoroughly how they help describe your experience. Please apply at least two concepts or theories and cite them correctly. (4 points)

D. Active Experimentation

1. What did you learn about diversity from this experience? (1 point)
2. What did you learn about yourself? (1 point)
3. What action steps will you take to be more effective in the future? (2 points)

E. Integration, Synthesis, and Writing

1. Did you integrate and synthesize the four sections? (1 point)
2. Was the Personal Application Assignment well written and easy to understand? (1 point)
3. Was it free of spelling and grammatical errors? (2 points)

ENDNOTES

[1] R. R. Thomas, Jr., *Beyond Race and Gender* (New York: AMACOM, 1991); R. R. Thomas, Jr., *Redefining Diversity* (New York: AMACOM, 1996).

[2] G. T. Chao and H. Moon, "The Cultural Mosaic: A Metatheory for Understanding the Complexity of Culture," *Journal of Applied Psychology 90*(6) (2005): 1128–1140.

[3] P. M. Cobb and J. L. Turlock, *Cracking the Corporate Code* (New York: AMACOM, 2003): 10.

[4] F. Rice, "How to Make Diversity Pay," *Fortune 130* (3) (August 8, 1994): 78.

[5] *Catalyst, Advancing Women in Business: The Catalyst Guide* (San Francisco: Jossey-Bass, 1998).

[6] C. Hymowitz, "The New Diversity," *The Wall Street Journal* (November 14, 2005): B1.

[7] Sempra, http://www.sempra.com/diversity.htm. Accessed 7/8/06.

[8] *Catalyst, Advancing Women in Business:* 14.

[9] Avon Senior Management, http://www.avoncompany.com/investor/seniormanagement/index.html. Accessed 7/13/06.

[10] Catalyst, *Advancing Women in Business*: xix.

[11] "Work Week," *Wall Street Journal* (April 13, 1999): A-1.

[12] P. Thomas, "Closing the Gender Gap," *Wall Street Journal* (May 24, 1999): R12.

[13] Ibid.

[14] N. R. Lockwood, "Workplace Diversity: Leveraging the Power of Difference for Competitive Advantage," *Research Quarterly* (Alexandria, VA: Society for Human Resource Management, June 2005); Catalyst, *The Bottom Line: Con-* necting Corporate Performance and Gender Diversity (New York: Catalyst, 2004); and National Urban League, *The American Worker Speaks* (New York: National Urban League, 2005).

[15] These statistics are reported in N. R. Lockwood, *Workplace Diversity.*

[16] "The Wage Gap, by Gender and Equity," National Committee on Pay Equity, http://www.infoplease.com/ipa/A0882775.html. Accessed 7/13/06.

[17] R. O. Crockett, "The Rising Stock of Black Directors," *BusinessWeek 3973* (February 27, 2006): 34.

[18] J. Preciphs, "Moving Ahead...But, Slowly," *The Wall Street Journal* (November 14, 2005): R3.

[19] Ibid.

[20] D. A. Thomas, and J. Gabarro, *Breaking Through: The Making of Minority Executives in Corporate America* (Boston: Harvard Business School Press, 1999). This book describes how companies can successfully promote diversity and how people of color can break through to senior management levels.

[21] "Wage Gap Remains," National Committee on Pay Equity. http://www.pay-equity.org/. Accessed 7/13/06.

[22] Bureau of Labor Statistics, *Highlights of Women's Earnings in 2002* (Washington, DC: U.S. Department of Labor, September, 2003).

[23] "Gender Pay Equity in Europe," European Foundation for the Improvement of Living and Working Conditions. http://www.eiro.eurofound.ie/2002/01/study/TN0201101S. html. Accessed 3/28/06; "Women's Pay: The Hand That

Rocks the Cradle," *The Economist 378*(8467) (March 4, 2006): 27.

24 U.S. Labor Bureau, *Women in the Labor Force 2005.* http://www.dol.gov/wb/factsheets/Qf-laborforce-05.htm. Accessed 3/30/06.

25 Catalyst, "2005 Catalyst Census of Women Board Directors of the Fortune 500 Shows 10-Year Trend of Slow Progress and Persistent Challenges" (March 29, 2006).

26 Corporate Women Directors International. Women Board Directors of *Fortune Global 200* Companies. http://www.globewomen.com/cwdi/global200_keyfindings. htm. Accessed 3/28/06.

27 Catalyst, *Women in Corporate Leadership* (New York: Catalyst, 2003).

28 Catalyst, "Quick Takes: Older Workers," http://www.catalyst.org/files/quicktakes/Quick%20Takes%20-%20Older%20Workers.pdf. Accessed 7/13/06.

29 H. Hankin, *The New Workforce* (New York: Amacom, 2005).

30 Ibid.

31 V. Barnouw in R. Webber, *Culture and Management* (Homewood, IL: Irwin, 1969): 69.

32 This example was contributed by Asbjorn Osland, San Jose State University.

33 J. Osland, and A. Bird, "Beyond Sophisticated Stereotyping: Cultural Sensemaking in Context," *Academy of Management Executive 14* (1) (2000): 65–77.

34 G. Hofstede, *Culture's Consequences: International Differences in Work-Related Values* (Beverly Hills, CA: Sage, 1984): 25.

35 M. Bennett, "Towards Ethnorelativism: A Developmental Model of Intercultural Sensitivity," in R. M. Paige (ed.), *Education for the Intercultural Experience* (Yarmouth, ME: Intercultural Press, 1993): 21–71.

36 J. Bennett and M. Bennett, "Developing Intercultural Sensitivity: An Integrative Approach to Global and Domestic Diversity," in D. Landis, J. M. Bennett, and M. Bennett (eds.), *Handbook of Intercultural Training,* 3rd ed. (Thousand Oaks, CA: Sage, 2004): 147–165.

37 E. Aronson, *The Social Animal* (San Francisco: W. H. Freeman, 1976): 175.

38 S. R. Rhodes, "Age-Related Differences in Work Attitudes and Behavior: A Review and Conceptual Analysis," *Psychological Bulletin 93* (March 1983): 328–367.

39 R. Sharpe, "Losing Ground," *Wall Street Journal* (September 14, 1993): A-1, col. 6.

40 Quoted in *The Oregonian* (Monday, February 22, 1999): C-2 from Billie Jean King's acceptance speech for the Arthur Ashe Award for Courage.

41 Catalyst, *Women in Corporate Leadership.*

42 K. M. Butler, "Workplace Diversity Can Increase Employee Loyalty," *Employee Benefit News 20*(3) (March 2006): 16–17.

43 L. D. Brown, *Managing Conflict at Organizational Interfaces* (Reading, MA: Addison-Wesley, 1983).

44 R. M. Kanter, *Men and Women of the Corporation* (New York: Basic Books, 1977): 206–242.

45 J. P. Lafargue, "A Survival Strategy-Kinship Networks," *American Journal of Nursing 80* (9) (1980): 480–495; M. F. Neitlin, L. Ann, and R. E. Ratcliff, "New Princes for Old? The Large Corporation and Capitalist Class in Chile," *American Journal of Sociology 80* (1974): 87–123; and R. D. Alba, "Ethnic Networks and Tolerant Attitudes," *Public Opinion Quarterly 42* (1) (1980): 1–16.

46 K. M. Butler, "Workplace Diversity Can Increase Employee Loyalty."

47 T. H. Cox and S. Blake, "Managing Cultural Diversity: Implications for Organizational Competitiveness," *Academy of Management Executive 5*(3) (1991): 52.

48 J. Merevitch and D. Reigle, *Toward a Multicultural Organization* (Cincinnati, OH: Proctor & Gamble, January 1979); T. H. Cox, "The Multicultural Organization," *Academy of Management Executive 5* (2) (May 1991): 34–47.

49 S. Sherwood, "PepsiCo's Reinemund Takes His Faith In Diversity To A New Level," *Diversity Inc.* (October 2005): 35–37.

50 C. M. Steele, "A Threat in the Air: How Stereotypes Shape Intellectual Identity and Performance," *American Psychologist 52* (1997): 613–629; C. M. Steele and J. Aronson, "Stereotype Threat and the Intellectual Performance of African Americans," *Journal of Personality and Social Psychology 69* (1995): 797–811.

51 A. R. Pratkanis and M. E. Turner, "Mr. Rickey Has His Way," *Across the Board 31* (July/August 1994): 42–47; A. R. Pratkanis and M. E. Turner, "Nine Principles of Successful Affirmative Action: Mr. Branch Rickey, Mr. Jackie Robinson, and the Integration of Baseball," *Nine: A Journal of Baseball History and Social Policy Perspectives 3* (1994): 36–65; A. R. Pratkanis and M. E. Turner, "The Proactive Removal of Discriminatory Barriers: Affirmative Action as Effective Help," *Journal of Social Issues 52*(4) (1996): 111–132.

52 National Urban League, *The American Worker Speaks.*

53 M. Corkery, "A Special Effort," *The Wall Street Journal* (November 14, 2005): R8.

54 Hymowitz, "The New Diversity."

55 A. Fisher, "How You Can Do Better on Diversity," *Fortune 150*(10) (November 15, 2004): 60; National Urban League, *The American Worker Speaks.*

56 Lockwood, *Workplace Diversity.*

57 D. C. Thomas and K. Inkson, *Cultural Intelligence* (San Francisco: Berrett-Koehler, 2003). This book has many good suggestions for improving the intercultural skills needed in global business.

58 F. Rice, "How to Make Diversity Pay": 78–84 and *Advancing Women in Business: The Catalyst Guide.*

Part 3

LEADERSHIP AND MANAGEMENT

Part 3 focuses on the knowledge and skills required of effective leaders and managers to accomplish their vision and goals with the help of other people.

Chapter 15

▲▲▲

LEADERSHIP

OBJECTIVES By the end of this chapter, you should be able to:

A. Describe what followers expect of leaders.

B. Differentiate between leadership and management.

C. Identify the traits that distinguish leaders from nonleaders.

D. Summarize the conclusions of behavioral theories of leadership.

E. Explain why path-goal theory and the leader-member exchange model are contingency theories.

F. Compare and contrast transformational, transactional, laissez-faire, and charismatic leadership.

G. Describe servant leadership and emotional intelligence.

H. Explain the role of trust in leadership.

I. Summarize the relationships between leadership and both culture and gender.

WHAT MAKES AN EFFECTIVE EXECUTIVE

An effective executive does not need to be a leader in the sense that the term is now most commonly used. Harry Truman did not have one ounce of charisma, for example, yet he was among the most effective chief executives in U.S. history. Similarly, some of the best business and non-profit CEOs I've worked with over a 65-year consulting career were not stereotypical leaders. They were all over the map in terms of their personalities, attitudes, values, strengths, and weaknesses. They ranged from extroverted to nearly reclusive, from easygoing to controlling, from generous to parsimonious.

What made them all effective is that they followed the same eight practices:

1. They asked, "What needs to be done?"
2. They asked, "What is right for the enterprise?"
3. They developed action plans.
4. They took responsibility for decisions.
5. They took responsibility for communicating.
6. They were focused on opportunities rather than problems.
7. They ran productive meetings.
8. They thought and said "we" rather than "I."

The first two practices gave them the knowledge they needed. The next four helped them convert this knowledge into effective action. The last two ensured that the whole organization felt responsible and accountable.

GET THE KNOWLEDGE YOU NEED

The first practice is to ask what needs to be done. Note that the question is not "What do I want to do?" Asking what has to be done, and taking the question seriously, is crucial for managerial success. Failure to ask this question will render even the ablest executive ineffectual.

When Truman became president in 1945, he knew exactly what he wanted to do: complete the economic and social reforms of Roosevelt's New Deal, which had been deferred by World War II. As soon as he asked what needed to be done, though, Truman realized that foreign affairs had absolute priority. He organized his working day so that it began with tutorials on foreign policy by the secretaries of state and defense. As a result, he became the most effective president in foreign affairs the United States has ever known. He contained Communism in both Europe and Asia and, with the Marshall Plan, triggered 50 years of worldwide economic growth.

Similarly, Jack Welch realized that what needed to be done at General Electric when he took over as chief executive was not the overseas expansion he wanted to launch. It was getting rid of GE businesses that, no matter how profitable, could not be number one or number two in their industries.

The answer to the question "What needs to be done?" almost always contains more than one urgent task. But effective executives do not splinter themselves. They concentrate on one task if at all possible. If they are among those people—a sizable minority—who work best with a change of pace in their working day, they pick two tasks. I have never encountered an executive who remains effective while tackling more than two tasks at a time. Hence, after asking what needs to be done, the effective executive sets priorities and sticks to them. For a CEO, the priority task might be redefining the company's mission. For a unit head, it might be redefining the unit's relationship with headquarters. Other tasks, no matter how important or appealing, are postponed. However, after completing the original top-priority task, the executive resets priorities rather than moving on to number two from the original list. He asks, "What must be done now?" This generally results in new and different priorities.

To refer again to America's best-known CEO: Every five years, according to his autobiography, Jack Welch asked himself, "What needs to be done now?" And every time, he came up with a new and different priority.

But Welch also thought through another issue before deciding where to concentrate his efforts for the next five years. He asked himself which of the two or three tasks at the top of the list he himself was best suited to undertake. Then he concentrated on that task; the others he delegated. Effective executives try to focus on jobs they'll do especially well. They know that enterprises perform if top management performs–and don't if it doesn't.

Effective executives' second practice–fully as important as the first–is to ask, "Is this the right thing for the enterprise?" They do not ask if it's right for the owners, the stock price, the employees, or the executives. Of course they know that shareholders, employees, and executives are important constituencies who have to support a decision, or at least acquiesce in it, if the choice is to be effective. They know that the share price is important not only for the shareholders but also for the enterprise, since the price/earnings ratio sets the cost of capital. But they also know that a decision that isn't right for the enterprise will ultimately not be right for any of the stakeholders.

This second practice is especially important for executives at family-owned or family-run businesses–the majority of businesses in every country–particularly when they're making decisions about people. In the successful family company, a relative is promoted only if he or she is measurably superior to all nonrelatives on the same level.

Asking "What is right for the enterprise?" does not guarantee that the right decision will be made. Even the most brilliant executive is human and thus prone to mistakes and prejudices. But failure to ask the question virtually guarantees the *wrong* decision.

WRITE AN ACTION PLAN

Executives are doers; they execute. Knowledge is useless to executives until it has been translated into deeds. But before springing into action, the executive needs to plan his course. He needs to think about desired results, probable restraints, future revisions, check in points, and implications for how he'll spend his time.

First, the executive defines desired results by asking: "What contributions should the enterprise expect from me over the next 18 months to two years? What results will I commit to? With what deadlines?" Then he considers the restraints on action: "Is this course of action ethical? Is it acceptable within the organization? Is it legal? Is it compatible with the mission, values, and policies of the organization?" Affirmative answers don't guarantee that the action will be effective. But violating these restraints is certain to make it both wrong and ineffectual.

The action plan is a statement of intentions rather than a commitment. It must not become a straitjacket. It should be revised often, because every success creates new opportunities. So does every failure. The same is true for changes in the business environment, in the market, and especially in people within the enterprise—all these changes demand that the plan be revised. A written plan should anticipate the need for flexibility.

In addition, the action plan needs to create a system for checking the results against the expectations. Effective executives usually build two such checks into their action plans. The first check comes halfway through the plan's time period; for example, at nine months. The second occurs at the end, before the next action plan is drawn up.

Finally, the action plan has to become the basis for the executive's time management. Time is an executive's scarcest and most precious resource. And organizations—whether government agencies, businesses, or nonprofits—are inherently time wasters. The action plan will prove useless unless it's allowed to determine how the executive spends his or her time.

Napoleon allegedly said that no successful battle ever followed its plan. Yet Napoleon also planned every one of his battles, far more meticulously than any earlier general had done. Without an action plan, the executive becomes a prisoner of events. And without check-ins to re-examine the plan as events unfold, the executive has no way of knowing which events really matter and which are only noise.

ACT

When they translate plans into action, executives need to pay particular attention to decision making, communication, opportunities (as opposed to problems), and meetings. I'll consider these one at a time.

Take responsibility for decisions. A decision has not been made until people know:

- the name of the person accountable for carrying it out;
- the deadline;
- the names of the people who will be affected by the decision and therefore have to know about, understand, and approve it—or at least not be strongly opposed to it—and
- the names of the people who have to be informed of the decision, even if they are not directly affected by it.

An extraordinary number of organizational decisions run into trouble because these bases aren't covered. One of my clients, 30 years ago, lost its leadership position in the fast—growing Japanese market because the company, after deciding to enter into a joint venture with a new Japanese partner, never made clear who was to inform the purchasing agents that the partner defined its specifications in meters and kilograms rather than feet and pounds—and nobody ever did relay that information.

It's just as important to review decisions periodically—at a time that's been agreed on in advance–as it is to make them carefully in the first place. That way, a poor decision can be corrected before it does real damage. These reviews can cover anything from the results to the assumptions underlying the decision.

Such a review is especially important for the most crucial and most difficult of all decisions, the ones about hiring or promoting people. Studies of decisions about people show that only one-third of such choices turn out to be truly successful. One-third are likely to be draws— neither successes nor outright failures. And one-third are failures, pure and simple. Effective executives know this and check up (six to nine months later) on the results of their people decisions. If they find that a decision has not had the desired results, they don't conclude that the person has not performed. They conclude, instead, that they themselves made a mistake. In a well managed enterprise, it is understood that people who fail in a new job, especially after a promotion, may not be the ones to blame.

Executives also owe it to the organization and to their fellow workers not to tolerate nonperforming individuals in important jobs. It may not be the employees' fault that they are underperforming, but even so, they have to be removed. People who have failed in a new job should be given the choice to go back to a job at their former level and salary.

A systematic decision review can be a powerful tool for self development, too. Checking the results of a decision against its expectations shows executives what their strengths are, where they need to improve, and where they lack knowledge or information. In areas where they are simply incompetent, smart executives don't make decisions or take actions. They delegate. Everyone has such areas; there's no such thing as a universal executive genius.

Take responsibility for communicating. Effective executives make sure that both their action plans and their information needs are understood. Specifically, this means that they share their plans with and ask for comments from all their colleagues—superiors, subordinates, and peers. At the same time, they let each person know what information they'll need to get the job done. The information flow from subordinate to boss is usually what gets the most attention. But executives need to pay equal attention to peers' and superiors' information needs.

We all know, thanks to Chester Barnard's 1938 classic *The Functions of the Executive*, that organizations are held together by information rather than by ownership or command. Still, far too many executives behave as if information and its flow were the job of the information specialist—for example, the accountant. As a result, they get an enormous amount of data they do not need and cannot use, but little of the information they do need. The best way around this problem is for each executive to identify the information he needs, ask for it, and keep pushing until he gets it.

Focus on opportunities. Good executives focus on opportunities rather than problems. Problems have to be taken care of, of course; they must not be swept under the rug. But problem solving, however necessary, does not produce results. It prevents damage. Exploiting opportunities produces results.

Above all, effective executives treat change as an opportunity rather than a threat. They systematically look at changes, inside and outside the corporation, and ask, "How can we exploit this change as an opportunity for our enterprise?" Specifically, executives scan these seven situations for opportunities:

1. an unexpected success or failure in their own enterprise, in a competing enterprise, or in the industry;
2. a gap between what is and what could be in a market, process, product, or service (for example, in the nineteenth century, the paper industry concentrated on the 10 percent of each tree that became wood pulp and totally neglected the possibilities in the remaining 90 percent, which became waste);
3. innovation in a process, product, or service, whether inside or outside the enterprise or its industry;
4. changes in industry structure and market structure;

5. demographics;

6. changes in mind-set, values, perception, mood, or meaning; and

7. new knowledge or a new technology.

Effective executives also make sure that problems do not overwhelm opportunities. In most companies, the first page of the monthly management report lists key problems. It's far wiser to list opportunities on the first page and leave problems for the second page. Unless there is a true catastrophe, problems are not discussed in management meetings until opportunities have been analyzed and properly dealt with.

Staffing is another important aspect of being opportunity focused. Effective executives put their best people on opportunities rather than on problems. One way to staff for opportunities is to ask each member of the management group to prepare two lists every six months—a list of opportunities for the entire enterprise and a list of the best-performing people throughout the enterprise. These are discussed, then melded into two master lists, and the best people are matched with the best opportunities. In Japan, by the way, this matchup is considered a major HR task in a big corporation or government department; that practice is one of the key strengths of Japanese business Run Productive Meetings.

Every study of the executive workday has found that even junior executives and professionals are with other people—that is, in a meeting of some sort—more than half of every business day. The only exceptions are a few senior researchers. Even a conversation with only one other person is a meeting. Hence, if they are to be effective, executives must make meetings productive. They must make sure that meetings are work sessions rather than bull sessions.

The key to running an effective meeting is to decide in advance what kind of meeting it will be. Different kinds of meetings require different forms of preparation and different results:

A meeting to prepare a statement, an announcement or a press release. For this to be productive, one member has to prepare a draft beforehand. At the meeting's end, a preappointed member has to take responsibility for disseminating the final text.

A meeting to make an announcement; for example, an organizational change. This meeting should be confined to the announcement and a discussion about it.

A meeting in which one member reports. Nothing but the report should be discussed.

A meeting in which several or all members report. Either there should be no discussion at all or the discussion should be limited to questions for clarification. Alternatively, for each report there could be a short discussion in which all participants may ask questions. If this is the format, the reports should be distributed to all participants well before the meeting. At this kind of meeting, each report should be limited to a preset time—for example, 15 minutes.

A meeting to inform the convening executive. The executive should listen and ask questions. He or she should sum up but not make a presentation.

A meeting whose only function is to allow the participants to be in the executive's presence. There is no way to make these meetings productive. They are the penalties of rank. Senior executives are effective to the extent to which they can prevent such meetings from encroaching on their workdays.

Making a meeting productive takes a good deal of self-discipline. It requires that executives determine what kind of meeting is appropriate and then stick to that format. It's also necessary to terminate the meeting as soon as its specific purpose has been accomplished. Good executives don't raise another matter for discussion. They sum up and adjourn.

Good follow-up is just as important as the meeting itself. The great master of follow–up was Alfred Sloan, the most effective business executive I have ever known. Sloan, who headed General Motors from the 1920s until the 1950s, spent most of his six working days a week in meetings—three days a week in formal committee meetings with a set membership, the other three days in ad hoc meetings with individual GM executives or with a small group of executives. At the beginning of a formal meeting, Sloan announced the meeting's purpose. He then listened. He never took notes and he rarely spoke except to clarify a confusing point. At the end he summed up, thanked the participants, and left. Then he immediately wrote a short memo addressed to one attendee of the meeting. In that note, he summarized the discussion and its conclusions and spelled out any work assignment decided upon in the meeting (including a decision to hold another meeting on the subject or to study an issue). He specified the deadline and the executive who was to be accountable for the assignment. He sent a copy of the memo to everyone who'd been present at the meeting. It was through these memos—each a small masterpiece–that Sloan made himself into an outstandingly effective executive.

Effective executives know that any given meeting is either productive or a total waste of time.

THINK AND SAY "WE"

The final practice is this: Don't think or say "I." Think and say "we." Effective executives know that they have ultimate responsibility, which can be neither shared nor delegated. But they have authority only because they have the trust of the organization. This means that they think of the needs and the opportunities of the organization before they think of their own needs and opportunities. This one may sound simple; it isn't, but it needs to be strictly observed.

We've just reviewed eight practices of effective executives. I'm going to throw in one final, bonus practice. This one's so important that I'll elevate it to the level of a rule: *Listen first, speak last.*

Effective executives differ widely in their personalities, strengths, weaknesses, values, and beliefs. All they have in common is that they get the right things done. Some are born effective. But the demand is much too great to be satisfied by extraordinary talent. Effectiveness is a discipline. And, like every discipline, effectiveness *can* be learned and *must* be earned.

Source: Excerpted from P. F. Drucker, "What Makes an Effective Executive," *Harvard Business Review* 82(6) (June 2004): 58–63. Reprinted with permission of Harvard Business School Press; all rights reserved.

CLASS PREPARATION

A. Read "What Makes an Executive Effective."

B. Think of four leaders who you have had occasion to observe or read about. If you have not observed a leader in a work setting, choose leaders from clubs, teams, neighborhoods, and so on. Write their initials in the box below.

_____ Leader 1	_____ Leader 2
_____	_____
_____	_____
_____	_____
_____	_____
_____	_____
_____ Leader 3	_____ Leader 4
_____	_____
_____	_____
_____	_____
_____	_____
_____	_____

1. Now write down the ways these leaders behave differently from each other. Be specific. For example, if one leader strikes you as being a better communicator than another, don't stop with "M.G. communicates well; B.D. communicates poorly." Write down the specific behavior that is different. For example, "M.G. makes expectations clear; B.D. doesn't explain what she wants us to do."

2. Using the list of behaviors or characteristics you generated for 1, rank these characteristics according to how important they are in terms of a leader's effectiveness. The most important characteristic should be number one, the second most important should be number two, and so on.

3. What are your own strengths as a leader?

4. How would you rate yourself on the characteristics you previously identified for the four leaders you described?

C. Answer the questions in The Leadership Job Interview.

1. Which of these interview questions, if you answered them with a "yes," are designed to be a red flag and identify candidates who do not have good senior-level leadership potential?

2. Write an action step that describes your plan to improve your own leadership skills. The action step should describe very specifically the behavior you wish to improve, the steps you will take to accomplish this, the date when you will finish, and how you will know that you have succeeded.

D. While reading the chapter, make a list of the cues you will look for with regard to leadership.

The Leadership Job Interview

Some consultants who help firms select senior leaders claim that the best way to evaluate candidates for leadership positions is to do a group evaluation by the individual's boss, the boss's boss, and other senior managers who have worked with the person. This group answers questions similar to those below and comes up with behavioral examples to support their opinions. As you answer these questions honestly about yourself, think of examples from your life that relate to each question.

1. Do you shade the truth or withhold important information to make yourself look good?

2. Do you take credit for work that others have done?

3. Do you always follow through with what you say you will do?

4. Do people know what your values are and where you stand on issues? Are you wishy-washy or likely to say what you think others want to hear?

5. Do people look up to you as an ethical person?

6. Are you capable of integrating a lot of diverse information and coming up with good ideas or solutions?

7. Do you come up with ideas or wait for others to give you orders?

8. How good are you at persuading others to accept your ideas?

9.   Do people at all levels at work respect you and pay attention to your views?

10. Can you make good intellectual arguments without offending others?

11. Do you procrastinate when the situation is ambiguous or complex?

12. Do you make decisions too quickly and fail to show sound judgment?

13. Do you have a vision for your company or your unit?

14. Do you pay attention to and adapt to trends that influence your organization?

15. Are you more of a tactical or a strategic thinker?

16. How good are you at executing a plan and getting things done?

17. Are your teams at work, school, and so on successful because of your leadership?

18. Are you threatened by people who are more experienced, smarter, or more skilled than you?

19. Do you work well with people who are different from you and who have different styles?

20. Are you aware of what motivates other people and are you capable of helping them to perform well?

21. How well do you delegate authority and responsibility to others? Do you have to do everything yourself?

22. Do you understand and take into consideration other people's feelings at work? Can you come up with an example?

Source: Adapted from M. Sorcher and J. Brant, "Are You Picking the Right Leaders?" *Harvard Business Review 80* (February 2002): 83.

THE KNOWLEDGE BASE

Possunt quia posse videntur. (They can because it seems to them they can.)

Virgil

Thumb through U.S. business magazines and you'll find a great deal of print devoted to descriptions of corporate leaders. Following the tradition in mythology and literature, there is a tendency to romanticize leadership and see leaders as "heroes." The high level of CEO compensation (413 times that of the average employee) indicates that some boards of directors actually believe they are paying for heroes. This results in either giving leaders more credit than they deserve or expecting them to work miracles when their hands are fairly well tied.[1] In reality, very few leaders succeed alone. When Steve Nash won the NBA's Most Valuable Player award in 2005, he called the whole Phoenix Suns team up to the podium to accept the award with him, acknowledging that he couldn't have done it without them. Business leaders are no different. Organizations do best when they have bench-strength in leadership—many leaders throughout the firm who are willing to take action for the good of the organization inside a system designed to help them be successful. GE is so well known for its leadership strength that some observers suggest their slogan could be, "Leaders (rather than progress) are our most important product."[2]

Whereas the business press likes to make celebrities of business leaders, Jim Collins found that it was the humble leaders with an intense will who made good firms great.[3] He describes these Level 5 leaders as modest and understated, quietly determined based on inspired standards rather than charisma, ambitious for the firm, rather than themselves, driven to achieve sustained success for the firm, and giving credit to others for success and taking blame for themselves. Some of these elements are the exact opposite of the profile of superstars who derailed at Pepsi. When the company did an internal study to determine why they derailed, they found three reasons: (1) arrogance (going beyond confidence to a belief that you are always right and others are always wrong, the opposite of being a team player); (2) lack of commitment in the sense of continuing to work away at a problem until it is solved; and (3) lack of loyalty (unwilling to put the good of the organization ahead of their own interests). Leaders don't have to be "heroic," bigger-than-life personalities.

There is strong evidence, however, that leaders do make a notable difference in organizations, particularly those undergoing crisis, growth, and change.[4] Not only do companies with effective leaders report higher net profits, but in times of increased competitive pressures and widespread demands for change, good leadership is not just a competitive advantage but an essential survival factor. Effective leadership helps provide employees with a sense of pride and with superordinate goals and values that take priority over individual interests; good leadership also makes it easier for employees to adapt to change.[5] Many people quit their jobs because their managers are bad leaders.[6] The increased demand for leadership skills, however, is not limited to people in executive suites. Given the flattened hierarchies in companies that have terminated middle managers and the move toward empowerment, teams, and networks, more and more companies are looking for leadership from people at all levels.

Leaders are "individuals who (1) establish direction for a group, (2) gain the group members' commitment, and (3) motivate and influence them to achieve goals to move in that direction."[7] An important aspect of this definition is that leaders make others "want" to follow them voluntarily. Leadership is generally held to be in the eye of the beholder because there are no leaders without followers. Zaleznik once wrote, "Leadership is based on a compact that binds those who lead with those who follow into the same moral, intellectual, and emotional commitment."[8] A title or office does not automatically confer leader status. We can all name people in high-level positions whom we would not call leaders. Instead, leadership is a point of view and the ability to change the status quo. Leaders see what needs to be done, no matter where they are found in society or organizations; they seek to understand all the underlying forces at play in a situation; and finally, they have the courage to take action to make things better.[9]

Leadership can be viewed as a social process rather than a specialized role. Yukl defines it as "the process of influencing others to understand and agree about what needs to be done and how to do it, and the process of facilitating individual and collective efforts to accomplish shared objectives."[10] Any member of a social system can exhibit leadership by behaving in ways that move the group toward its goals. *At different points in time, the leadership rotates and people with the most relevant skill take the initiative to influence the group*, which is called *shared* or *distributed leadership*. Depending on the situation, it can be just as effective as vertical leadership. Self-managed teams, in particular, encourage shared leadership among members. *Lateral leadership occurs when colleagues at the same level in the hierarchy collaborate and facilitate joint problem solving.* We could see lateral leadership, for example, in an action learning project composed of employees from different units who cannot rely on their position power to influence other members. Regardless of hierarchical position, today's employees have to develop their leadership and influence skills to get work done.

As individuals, we develop schemas about leaders and leadership that determine whether or not we perceive someone as a leader or whether a particular behavior equates with leadership in our eyes.[11] The characteristics you listed in the Class Preparation should give you a better idea about your own leadership schema because these are the factors you notice about leaders. These schemas also influence our expectations of leaders.

FOLLOWER EXPECTATIONS OF LEADERS

According to U.S. research, followers expect the following four characteristics of their leaders, in descending order of importance.[12]

1. **Honest** (truthful, trustworthy, consistent in word and deed, has character, has convictions)

2. Forward-looking (sense of direction and concern for the future)
3. Inspiring (enthusiastic, energetic, positive about the future)
4. Competent (capable, productive, effective)

In combination, these characteristics determine a leader's credibility. When employees perceive management to have high credibility and a strong philosophy, employees are more likely to:[13]

- Be proud to tell others they are part of the organization
- Have a strong sense of team spirit
- See their own values as consistent with those of the organization
- Feel a sense of ownership about the organization
- Feel attached and committed to the organization

In contrast, those who do not perceive management to be credible work primarily for money, produce only when watched, bad-mouth the organization in private, and would consider leaving the organization in rough times. In other words, there is a positive payoff for leaders and management teams that work hard at building and preserving their credibility with subordinates.

Leadership is closely related to organizational ethics. In a study of managerial values, 92 percent reported that "the behavior of those in charge is the principal determinant of the 'ethical tone' of my firm." To make matters worse, one-third of these managers felt their bosses engaged in unethical behaviors and were less concerned about ethics than they were.[14]

Our schemas of what constitutes good leadership vary by culture and can change over time. In this book's introduction, Setting the Global Stage, we described the rapidly changing global context. Traditional bureaucracies with centralized, authoritarian leadership styles are shifting toward information-centered organizations peopled by highly educated knowledge workers in teams. Given this context, more participative and transformational leadership styles have evolved, which focus on empowering employees, motivating people to contribute their knowledge and ideas, and making changes in response to customers and the environment. Latin Americans historically have preferred authoritarian leaders and centralized decision making,[15] but recent studies have found more evidence of participative leadership.[16] U.S. citizens now expect their leaders to provide or help create a vision that encompasses both environmental threats and opportunities and an appropriate response to situations. For example, some political pundits maintain that George Bush Sr. lost the 1992 presidential election primarily because he did not grasp the importance to U.S. citizens of what he called "the vision thing." Because leadership evolves over time in response to changing local contexts, we can expect to see cultural and generational differences in leadership schemas.

MANAGERS VERSUS LEADERS

Being a good manager and a good leader are not necessarily synonymous.[17] The basic functions of management are planning, organizing, leading, and controlling. Leading in this respect is usually viewed as motivating employees to perform well. Not all managers, however, function as leaders, as shown in Exhibit 15–1. As Warren Bennis stated, "While managers do things right, leaders do the right thing." Whereas leaders establish a vision, managers do planning and budgeting. Whereas leaders focus on imaginative ideas, managers focus on processes and systems. Leaders spend time and

Do things right	Do the right thing
Planning and budgeting	Vision
Processes and systems	Imaginative ideas
Organizing and staffing	Aligning people with vision
Control and problem solving	Motivate and inspire
Produce order, predictability, results expected by stakeholders	Produce change

Adapted from J. P. Kotter, *A Force for Change: How Leadership Differs from Management* (New York: Free Press, 1990).

EXHIBIT 15-1 **Managers Versus Leaders**

effort aligning people so that they understand and accept their vision and strategies, while managers focus on organizing and staffing. Whereas leaders motivate and inspire others, managers focus on control and problem solving. As a result, leaders tend to produce change, whereas managers tend to produce order, predictability, and the key results expected by stakeholders.[18]

Obviously, both leadership and management are important. In the opening vignette to this chapter, Drucker's description of what effective executives do is a mixture of both leadership and management with a heavy emphasis on the execution that is crucial for success. Leaders should not ignore the organization's core competencies (a Japanese concept that refers to well-developed operating capabilities) to focus solely on an abstract vision.[19] And, managers should not get so caught up in pushing the organization along that they lose sight of the broader picture or overlook opportunities and the importance of providing a vision that motivates people. In today's business world, it makes more sense to aim for both—to develop ourselves as leaders who also strive to be good managers with a thorough understanding of organizational functions.

THE EVOLUTION OF LEADERSHIP THEORY

Our conceptions of leadership and the theories we use to explain it have evolved over time. Although there are more than 7,000 books and articles on leadership, no one theory is universally accepted. The rest of the chapter presents the practical highlights of leadership research:[20] (1) leader traits; (2) behavior styles; (3) contingency theory; (4) transformational and charismatic leadership; and (5) recent leadership developments.

Leader Traits

The first leadership studies focused on the question of why some people become leaders and others do not. Years ago, common wisdom held that leaders were born, not made, so researchers began by looking at *leader traits*. This attempt to figure out what characteristics distinguished natural leaders from nonleaders yielded limited results, and leader skills came to be seen as more important than personality. We know, however, that these traits relate positively to leadership: self-confidence, emotional maturity, stress tolerance, need for achievement and power, internal locus of control, intelligence[21] and self-monitoring.[22] Good leaders read different situations and individuals and then adapt their leadership style accordingly, a talent that is aided by self-monitoring. Some leader traits can be a double-edged sword if balance is missing. Self-confidence is a desirable trait in a leader, particularly a charismatic leader, but excessive self-confidence can result in rash decisions based on overly optimistic assessments and an unwillingness to look at a plan's flaws.[23]

A study of successful business leaders found that they shared the following traits: drive, honesty and integrity, leadership motivation, self-confidence, cognitive ability, knowledge of the business, creativity, and flexibility.[24] There are only two leader traits, intelligence and high energy, on this list that are inherited, which means there is some truth to the statement that leaders are born. However, one's childhood experiences, such as socialization, opportunities, diversity, and so on, play a more important role than genes in determining leadership potential.[25] Furthermore, leaders can be developed, primarily through work experiences, challenging job assignments, role models, mentors, and training.[26] Opportunity and luck also determine who will become leaders. Many experts conclude that leaders are born and made. Remember Peter Drucker's comment: "There may be born leaders, but there surely are far too few to depend on them." For this reason, organizations actively develop leaders and, when it comes to selecting and promoting leaders, they consider other factors in addition to traits—their skills, attitudes, experience, and track record as a leader.

Behavior Styles

Once researchers gave up on the idea that all leaders were born, they started observing differences in behavior between leaders and nonleaders. Much of the early research identified two principal dimensions of *effective leader behavior*—a concern for task objectives and a concern for people, which were referred to as initiating structure and consideration by some researchers.

1. Initiating structure (task)—leader behavior that organizes and defines what group members should be doing to maximize output.

2. Consideration (people)—leader behavior associated with creating mutual respect or trust and that focuses on a concern for group members' needs and desires.

Research programs (Ohio State studies, University of Michigan studies, the Managerial Grid) reported that leaders who were rated as high on both these dimensions were generally more likely to have high subordinate performance and satisfaction. The results, however, were not conclusive because these studies did not take situational factors into consideration.[27] Not every situation requires leaders who employ a high degree of both initiating structure and consideration. For example, highly skilled employees who are self-motivating require neither of these behaviors on the part of leaders.[28] The enduring lesson, however, is that leaders should exhibit both behaviors appropriately, according to the needs of the particular situation. Furthermore, using these behaviors effectively is more important than using them frequently.[29] Leaders who provide excessive initiating structure or consideration are likely to be viewed as annoying rather than helpful. Other scholars have argued that a third category of effective behavior should be added—change–oriented behavior.[30]

After hundreds of studies on effective leadership behaviors, researchers and practitioners came to the conclusion that there is no "one best way" to lead; it depends on the situation. Effective leaders analyze the factors pertaining to the situation, task, followers, and the organization, and then choose the appropriate behavior or style. This is why the next wave of leadership theories are examples of contingency theories. As we saw in Chapter 2, there is no "one best way" in contingency theory—the most effective approach depends on the unique contingencies in each situation.

Contingency Theories

Contingency Theories of management include various leadership styles. One continuum, which appears in Exhibit 15–2, ranges from one extreme at which the manager has total freedom to make decisions to the other extreme at which managers and employees make joint decisions. In Chapter

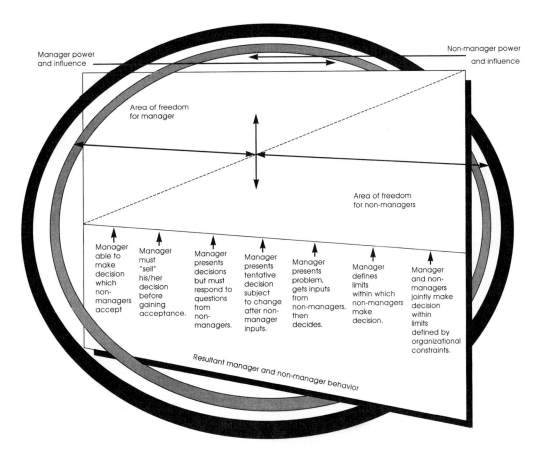

EXHIBIT 15-2
Continuum of Manager-Nonmanager Behavior

Source: R. Tannenbaum and W. H. Schmidt, "How to Choose a Leadership Pattern," *Harvard Business Review 36* (May–June 1973): 95–101. Copyright © 1973 by the President and Fellows of Harvard College; all rights reserved.

17, Vroom's leader-participation model of decision making is an example of a well-researched contingency theory that includes an autocratic-consultative-participative continuum of leader styles.

Path-Goal Theory. Other theories go beyond decision-making behavior styles to include concepts such as initiating structure and consideration behavior. For example, House's path-goal theory of leadership[31] takes into consideration both employee characteristics and environmental factors to indicate which leadership styles lead to leadership effectiveness. House believes that effective leaders compensate for what is missing in the environment or in subordinates themselves; for example, individual employees might need more clarification from their supervisor before they can perform effectively. He maintains that leaders motivate higher performance by helping subordinates attain individual goals that are aligned with organizational goals.[32] In House's latest version of this theory, leadership isn't limited to supervisors or managers; shared leadership can also be exercised by employees. Leaders enhance employee performance when they (1) clarify the path that will result in employee achievement, (2) provide the necessary guidance and support to get the job done, (3) remove the obstacles that block the path to goal achievement, and (4) link rewards to goal accomplishment, and so forth. Leader behavior is acceptable if subordinates perceive it as a source of either immediate or future satisfaction. Depending on both subordinate contingency factors (e.g., locus of control, self-perceived task ability, need for achievement, need for clarity, need for independence, and experience) and environmental contingency factors (e.g., task structure, stressful work, and work group dynamics), the leader employs one of the following leadership styles, which should result in employee motivation, satisfaction, and performance, leader acceptance, and work unit performance.[33] Exhibit 15–3 provides a general representation of this theory.

- **Path-Goal Clarifying Behaviors** The leader informs subordinates what is expected of them, sets performance standards, schedules activities, and provides specific guidance as to what should be done and how to do it. The leader also rewards employees positively or negatively contingent on their performance.
- **Achievement-Oriented Behaviors** The leader sets challenging goals, seeks improvement, emphasizes excellence, shows confidence that subordinates will attain high standards of performance, and encourages pride in their work and self evaluation in employees.
- **Work-Facilitation Behaviors** The leader plans, schedules, organizes, and coordinates work and provides mentoring and coaching to help them develop their skills. The leader empowers employees, removes obstacles, and provides necessary resources to get the job done.

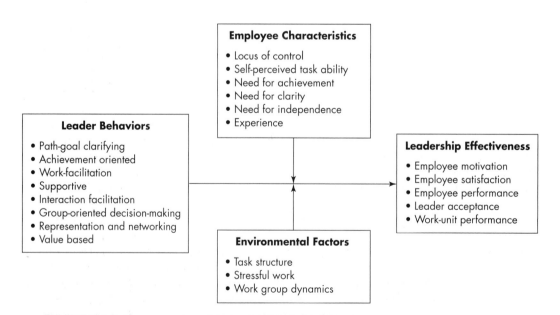

EXHIBIT 15-3 **Representation of the Revised Path-Goal Theory**

Source: Based on R. House, "Path-Goal Theory of Leadership: Lessons, Legacy, and a Reformulated Theory," Leadership Quarterly 7(3) (1996): 323–352.

- **Supportive Behaviors** The leader is friendly and approachable and shows concern for the needs, status, and well-being of subordinates. He or she treats subordinates as equals.
- **Interaction-Facilitation Behaviors** The leader facilitates communication and collaboration and teamwork. He or she resolves conflicts and fosters close relationships among employees.
- **Group-Oriented Decision-Making Behaviors** The leader encourages work group members to get involved in decision making and provides them with the information they need to make decisions.
- **Representation and Networking Behaviors** The leader represents the group to others, attends ceremonial functions, and maintains positive relationships with influential people.
- **Value-Based Behaviors** The leader creates and supports a vision, shows confidence in himself and others to accomplish the vision, and gives positive feedback.

House's theory has not been supported conclusively, because it is difficult to test in its entirety. However, we do know that leaders are more effective if they use a variety of behaviors, such as those described above. We included them to help you expand your repertoire of leader behaviors. Furthermore, we know that it's important to consider various contingencies before choosing to use a leader behavior. Although there is widespread acceptance of a contingency approach to leadership, no one theory contains all the possible contingencies. Some of the accepted connections between specific situational factors and leadership styles follow.

- Subordinates benefit from a directive style when they are working with an unstructured or stressful task. When they know how to do a routine job, further instruction not only wastes time and may be perceived as insulting.
- When subordinates perform boring, repetitive, unsatisfying tasks, leaders should consider restructuring the job (see Chapter 5, on Motivation) so that it would meet more of the employees' needs. If that proves impossible, leaders should use a supportive style that allows employees to meet their social needs on the job.
- In highly formalized organizations where everything is standardized, there is little need for a task-oriented leader. Cohesive work groups with norms that heavily influence employees make both consideration and initiating structure leader behavior redundant.
- Subordinates who do not want to take responsibility at work prefer autocratic rather than participative leaders.

Contingency theories usually focus on the fit between the situation and the appropriate leadership style. The next theory, however, describes what happens when the leader's relationships and behaviors themselves act as a contingency.

Leader-Member Exchange Model. Another theory that focuses on the relationship between leader and follower is the *leader-member exchange* (LMX) model. It goes beyond traits and behaviors to focus on the relationship between leader and follower and on one of the contingencies that affects this vertical dyad relationship. *Leaders behave differently with different followers, a basic tenet of the leader-member exchange model.*[34] Highly motivated, skilled, and trustworthy subordinates, as well as subordinates who are similar to the leader in terms of personality, age, or gender, are sometimes given preferential treatment and constitute an in-group. The leader's favoritism consists of giving them more attention, resources, and recognition[35] and inflating their performance ratings when they underperform.[36] As one would expect, research has generally shown that in-group members perform better and are more satisfied at work.[37] They are more committed to work goals and more satisfied with the leader;[38] they also report a better work climate and more manager-employee trust.[39] These employees also are less likely to resign.[40] The increased mentoring in-group members receive also helps them be more successful in their career.[41] Although it is natural for leaders to treat their in-group members differently, this practice usually results in jealousy and resentment among out-group members and reduced cooperation and communication between the two groups. Therefore, leaders should guard against favoring some followers over others.

Transformational Leadership

The effective leader is like a balloon man who is holding onto the strings of helium-filled balloons.

E. F. Schumacher

The helium-filled balloons in Schumacher's quotation are the efforts of empowered, involved employees who are motivated and encouraged to forge ahead, whereas the strings that link the balloon man to the balloons illustrate the all-important relationship between leaders and followers. The balloon man exemplifies transformational leadership, which grew out of the realization that both emotions and symbolic actions were involved in effective leadership. *Transformational leaders are value-driven change agents who make followers more conscious of the importance and value of task outcomes; they provide followers with a vision and motivate them to go beyond self-interest for the good of the organization.* The behaviors associated with transformational leadership are: articulating a vision of the future, fostering group-oriented work, setting high expectations, challenging followers' thinking, supporting followers' individual needs, and acting as a role model.[42]

Given the difficult challenges facing humankind, the need for leaders who can transform organizations is understandable. In several studies, researchers have listened to effective transformational leaders describe how they actually lead others. Bennis and Nanus found that highly effective and charismatic leaders manage four areas: attention, meaning, trust, and self.[43] They manage attention by being highly committed to a compelling vision or outcome. They manage meaning by making ideas seem real and tangible for others, by means of both words and symbols. They manage trust by being reliable and congruent so that people know what they stand for. And, finally, they manage self by knowing and using their skills effectively, learning from mistakes, and focusing on success rather than failure.

Kouzes and Posner asked leaders to describe their "personal best" leadership experience, a time when they accomplished something extraordinary in their organization.[44] From these critical incidents, they identified five leadership practices:

1. Challenging the process (questioning the status quo, seeking new opportunities to improve and grow, taking risks)
2. Inspiring a shared vision (envisioning an uplifting and ennobling future)
3. Enabling others to act (fostering collaboration and empowerment)
4. Modeling the way (setting a good example and planning small wins)
5. Encouraging the heart (recognizing individual contributions and celebrating team accomplishments)

Bass and Avolio developed a continuum, called the full range of leadership styles, that ranges from *laissez-faire* (*noninterference in the affairs of others*) to transactional and then transformational.[45] The laissez-faire approach is least effective. *Transactional leadership is an exchange process in which leaders clarify employee roles and task requirements and then reward or punish followers based on their performance.* Transactional leaders get subordinates to perform using promises and contingent rewards for good performance and using threats and discipline for poor performance. Transactional leaders are less effective than transformational leaders in making major organizational changes.[46] A recent meta-analysis of leadership studies compared all three styles of leadership and found that both transformational and transactional leadership resulted in higher levels of follower motivation, job satisfaction, and satisfaction with the leader.[47] The results for laissez-faire leadership, however, were not positive. Managers who use both transformational behaviors and contingent rewards have higher employee performance and satisfaction than managers who use only contingent reward behavior.[48] The lesson is to use both transformational and transactional leadership and avoid passivity.

Charismatic Leadership. Although charismatic leaders share some behaviors with transformational leaders, in *charismatic leadership, followers make attributions of extraordinary or heroic leadership abilities.* Charismatic leaders have special relationships with their followers and elicit high levels of performance, loyalty, sacrifice, and enthusiasm. They develop a vision to which they are strongly committed that touches the emotions of their followers. Charismatic leaders take risks and act in unconventional ways. They are sensitive to follower needs as well as environmental constraints. Such leaders are very self-confident and good at communicating.[49] Richard Branson, founder of the Virgin Group, and Mary Kay Ash, CEO of Mary Kay Cosmetics, are both examples of charismatic leaders.

There are two types of charismatic leaders. Ethical charismatic leaders use power to serve others, align their vision with their followers' needs and aspirations, accept and learn from criticism, encourage followers to think independently, work to develop followers into leaders, and rely on internal moral standards. In contrast, unethical charismatic leaders are motivated by personalized power, pursue their own vision and goals, censure critical or opposing views, encourage blind obedience, dependency, and submission in their followers, and lack an internal moral compass.[50]

Contemporary Developments

Servant Leadership. Robert Greenleaf, a longtime HR executive for IBM, argued that leaders should be stewards who choose service over self-interest.[51] In doing so, they are willing to be accountable for the well-being of the larger organization by operating to serve rather than control those around them. Servant leadership is rooted in spirituality, which is a growing trend in the U.S. workplace. Shell encourages servant leadership among its employees and defines a servant leader as one who:[52]

- recognizes that, as an individual, one does not have all the answers;
- is able to demonstrate a sense of humility and vulnerability;
- advances his or her own transformation, the personal transformation of others, and the transformation of the company; and
- builds the capability of the company and the people in it.

Looking for strong leaders to "save us" localizes the responsibility, power, ownership, and privilege at the top of the organization. Current thinking conceives of organizations more as a partnership. The organizational vision is not simply created and passed down from the top; each employee is responsible for articulating a vision for his or her own area of responsibility.

Emotional Intelligence. A recent addition to our thinking about leadership takes us back to traits and skills by focusing on the leader's emotional intelligence (known as EI or EQ). This theory is grounded in new research on how the brain processes emotions and on Gardner's multiple intelligence theory, which claims that human intelligence is more than IQ.[53] According to Mayer, Caruso, and Salovey, *"Emotional intelligence refers to an ability to recognize the meanings of emotions and their relationships and to reason and problem-solve on the basis of them."*[54] Goleman and his colleagues popularized the concept of emotional intelligence and argue that it is related to leadership effectiveness. Whereas high IQ and technical skills are threshold requirements for executive positions, their research found that emotional intelligence was the key distinguishing factor in outstanding leaders.[55] More research is needed to improve the measurement of EQ and to clarify the link between EQ, leadership, and performance; the organizational context also determines performance.[56]

Emotional intelligence consists of four dimensions:

- Self awareness—reading one's own emotions, realistic self-assessment, and self-confidence
- Self-management—emotional self-control, transparency in the form of integrity and trustworthiness, adaptability, achievement, initiative, and optimism
- Social awareness—empathy, organizational awareness, and service to clients
- Relationship management—inspirational leadership, influence, developing others, change catalyst, conflict management, building bonds, and teamwork and collaboration[57]

Goleman coined the term *emotional hijack, which occurs when the fight or flight reaction is triggered in the amygdala of the brain and an emotional reaction overcomes reason.* Impulse control is especially important for leaders, which begins with recognizing one's own emotions. Research has found a link between EI and transformational leadership wherein leaders who were better at recognizing emotion were rated more highly on transformational leadership behaviors.[58]

Although there appears to be a genetic component to emotional intelligence, it can be developed if people are highly and sincerely motivated to make a concerted effort.[59] The subordinates of a Wall Street executive were terrified of disagreeing with him or telling him bad news. When his family confirmed that they felt the same way, he was shocked and vowed to learn to become more empathetic and open to perspectives that differed from his own. He engaged a coach who sent him to vacation in a foreign country where he did not speak the language. Forced to listen and observe, he wrote down his reactions to an unfamiliar setting and people who were different. On his return, he asked his coach to observe how he treated people at work with different or new ideas. He practiced listening hard to new ideas at work and even videotaped his interactions and asked employees to critique his ability to interpret and react to other's feelings. After several months of hard work, he became more empathetic and improved his work performance.[60]

Theories about leadership have evolved from the original emphasis on traits to behavior styles theory and situational, contingency theories, to more recent research on transformational and charismatic leadership, leaders as stewards, and emotionally intelligent leaders. This evolution reflects both the progress that has been made in understanding a complex concept and our changing expectations and conceptions about leaders.

TRUST AND LEADERSHIP

Building and maintaining trust is one of the most crucial social processes of effective leadership. *Trust in this context refers to the confident expectations of followers about the leader's behavior and intentions.* Trust is an aspect of several leadership theories: charismatic and transformational leadership,[61] the consideration dimension (consideration vs. initiating structure),[62] and leader-member exchange theory.[63] Leader effectiveness studies found that trust relates to "positive job attitudes, organizational justice, psychological contracts, and effectiveness in terms of communication, organizational relationships, and conflict management."[64] A meta-analysis of four decades of leader trust research in various types of organizations (e.g., military, public, and business) found that trust relates to job performance, organizational citizenship behavior, turnover intentions, job satisfaction, organizational commitment, and commitment to the leader's decisions.[65]

Thus, employee trust in leaders is not something that is simply "nice to have"—it's a significant factor in organizational success. For example, the trust and behavioral integrity of hotel general managers predicted both customer satisfaction and profits.[66] A study of NCAA basketball teams found that trust in the head coach was responsible for 7 percent of the variance in the percentage of games they won, and the team with the highest level of trust won the national championship![67] It's worth noting that the level of trust in the head coach predicted team performance more than trust in their fellow players and was almost as important as team-member ability. As one player stated, "Once we developed trust in Coach, the progress we made increased tremendously because we were no longer asking questions or apprehensive. Instead, we were buying in and believing that if we worked our hardest, we were going to get there."[68]

There are two theoretical approaches to trust—relationship- and character-based. *The relationship-based perspective views trust as a social exchange process; rather than being bound by an economic contract, leaders and their followers operate on trust, goodwill, and perceived mutual obligations.*[69] If the leader treats followers well, they will reciprocate by performing as the leader wishes and perhaps by doing more than expected, which is called organizational citizenship behavior (OCB) (see Chapter 1). In contrast, in the *character-based approach, followers are concerned about the leader's integrity, sense of fairness, dependability, competence because the leader is in a position to make decisions that impact the follower* (e.g., job assignments, salary, promotions).[70] When followers trust their leader, they will put themselves at greater risk, for example, by sharing sensitive information.[71] In contrast, when they do not trust the leader, they will use energy to cover their backs that would otherwise be devoted to performance goals.[72] Research shows that the leader's personal integrity and ability to develop trusting relationships with followers are both important.[73]

One of the worst losses of trust in a leader occurred when Donald Carty, former CEO and chairman of AMR, successfully asked American Airlines' three major unions for pay concessions to avoid bankruptcy. However, he delayed an announcement that he had already arranged for executive perks in the form of pensions that were protected in case of bankruptcy and retention bonuses ($1.6 million for Carty himself) that were not tied to performance. When these perks became public knowledge, the unions were outraged that they had gone along with Carty's plea for a "shared sacrifice" while executives were reaping greater benefits. They demanded to vote again. Union leaders and board members struggled to hold together the concessions, but Carty was forced to resign. Carty lost the trust of his employees and the board by not being transparent and because he was not perceived to be fair; he also jeopardized the credibility of the union leaders who were blindsided by the perks.[74]

GENDER AND LEADERSHIP

Many scholars and practitioners alike have wondered whether women and men lead differently. Although the research results are sometimes contradictory, the similarities between the way women and men lead outweigh the differences, and neither gender is more suited to leadership.[75] Once given a leadership role and legitimized by the organization, women and men do not act very differently. Women do, however, prefer a more democratic leadership style than men, perhaps due to more developed social skills or to placate those who might otherwise resist female leadership.[76] Laissez-faire leadership and some aspects of transactional leadership are more common among males than females, while transformational leadership complemented by the use of contingent rewards (a component of transactional leadership) is more common among females.[77] These differences, however, were small. Gender differences in leadership are sometimes attributed to early socialization practices in which girls are expected to demonstrate care and consideration, whereas boys are expected to compete and perform. However, when women find themselves in situations that require a more autocratic style (e.g., working in a male-dominated or hypermasculine organization such as the military or the police), they tend to adapt their style accordingly.[78] The organizational context in which leadership takes place influences leadership style.

Gender stereotypes can influence the perceptions of leader effectiveness. If people have a leadership schema that includes masculine, rather than feminine traits ("the ideal leader acts like 'a man'"), they may be predisposed to see men as more likely and more effective leaders than women. In this way, gender stereotypes sometimes determine who is chosen for leadership positions and how they are evaluated. For example, one study that used 360-degree ratings to compare high-level male and female CEOs and senior VPs found that the only difference was that the women's bosses (not their direct reports or peers) rated them more negatively than they did the male subjects.[79] There is a slight tendency to evaluate female leaders more negatively than males, but a meta-analysis of research studies found that male and female leaders are equally effective.[80]

The crucial question with regard to gender and leadership is whether organizations provide equal opportunity for skilled women to exercise leadership. Many women with leadership ability have become entrepreneurs to bypass organizational constraints. In China, 46 percent of the urban workforce is composed of women; the majority still works in low-end jobs, despite their improved status over the last 50 years. However, 20 percent of China's entrepreneurs are women, drawn by the opportunity to call the shots, to put their stamp on their chosen field, and to be measured by their results rather than their gender.[81] In the United States, a woman starts a new company every 60 seconds, twice the rate of men.

Should corporations be concerned about retaining and promoting women leaders? When Deloitte Consulting established a professional development system to retain and advance women, the firm saved $250 million dollars in turnover costs and was chosen as the "#1 employer of choice for women."[82] A Catalyst study of 353 *Fortune* 500 firms found that companies in the top quartile, as determined by greater representation of women leaders in the top management team, reported 35 percent higher Return on Equity (ROE) and 34 percent higher Total Return to Shareholders (TRS) than firms in the bottom quartile with the fewest women leaders. In four of five industries studied, firms with the highest representation of women leaders in the top management team earned a higher ROE than companies with the least women leaders.[83] A 19-year study of 215 *Fortune* 500 firms discovered that companies that promoted women into executive positions were 18–69 percent more profitable than the median firms in their industries.[84] Studies showing correlations between senior women leaders and higher profits do not always prove causality—instead of senior women causing higher profits, perhaps companies that are already doing well are progressive and more open to promoting women. Nevertheless, firms should carefully consider the potential financial costs of organizational failure to hire, promote, and retain women leaders.

CULTURE AND LEADERSHIP

The field of comparative leadership studies the differences and similarities in national leadership styles. Leadership schemas and behaviors, as well as perceptions of what constitutes effective leadership often vary from one culture to another. These are lessons from Korean parables of leadership.[85]

- Listen to the unheard—the hearts of followers, their uncommunicated feelings, unexpressed pains, and unspoken complaints—rather than listening only to superficial words of followers.

- Humble rulers with deep-reaching inner strength who bring well-being to their followers are more effective than vain rulers.

- A leader's commitment and willingness to work alongside his or her followers are strong determinants of success.

- The wise leader earns the devotion of followers by placing them in positions that fully realize their potential and secures harmony by giving them all credit for their distinctive achievements.

In the United States people value charisma in their leaders; in West Germany, charisma is distrusted because it reminds people of Hitler. We find more participative leadership and shared governance in cultures with small power distance (e.g., Scandinavia). In contrast, cultures characterized by large power distance tend to have autocratic leaders (e.g., Russia).[86] A Russian study found that participative management techniques decreased rather than increased productivity.[87] Therefore, expatriate managers who work abroad with a participative style may find that subordinates in a high power distance culture are, at least initially, uncomfortable when the leader does not call all the shots. Asking for advice may be interpreted as incompetence or weakness in cultures in which leaders are supposed to be omnipotent experts, at least until leaders have earned the trust and confidence of followers. Villages in French West Africa have a different tradition of leadership. Villages have a "palaver" tree where the entire village meets to discuss important issues. Representatives from the elders, the young men, and the women express their opinions and talk until a consensus opinion is reached.

Despite documented national differences in leadership, recent research findings also point out commonalities. Project GLOBE, the largest such study, obtained data on indigenous leadership from 18,000 middle managers in 825 firms in 62 countries. The researchers developed their own cultural framework to distinguish among cultural practices.[88] They also asked middle managers about effective leadership styles and discovered that the transformational leadership style seems to be the most universally acceptable style around the globe.[89] They identified a list of leader traits that are universally acceptable, universally unacceptable, and culturally contingent (they work in some cultures but not in others), shown in Exhibit 15–4. Similar business conditions and practices, technology, more well-educated employees, and the presence of multinational enterprises may be responsible for at least partial convergence on leadership views. Effective leaders from different countries may have more practices in common with each other than they do with average, less effective leaders in their own cultures.

A new field of research focuses on *global leadership, which can be defined as a process of influencing the thinking, attitudes, and behaviors of a global community to work together synergistically toward a common vision and common goals.*[90] Unlike expatriate managers who usually work in just one foreign country or region at a time, global leaders have followers from numerous countries, which results in greater complexity, ambiguity, interdependence, and flux in the context in which they lead.[91] A review of the literature concluded that global leadership is a multidimensional construct with at least six core dimensions of competencies: cross-cultural relationship skills, traits and values, cognitive orientation, global business expertise, global organizing expertise, and visioning.[92]

Carlos Ghosn, President of Nissan Motors, Ltd and Automotive News' 2000 Industry Leader of the Year, has a reputation as an effective global leader. Born in Brazil and educated in France, Ghosn served seven years as head of Michelin in the United States and three years with Renault before becoming President and COO of Nissan. He is responsible for Nissan's turnaround effort and cross-border alliance with Renault. A background like this helps develop the necessary global mind-set and skills that global leaders require. Jack Welch, former CEO of GE once commented:

Universally Acceptable Traits	Universally Unacceptable Traits	Culturally Contingent Traits
Decisive	Ruthless	Enthusiastic
Informed	Egocentric	Self-sacrificial
Honest	Asocial	Risk-taking
Dynamic	Nonexplicit	Sincere
Administratively skilled	Irritable	Ambitious
Coordinator	Non-cooperative	Sensitive
Just	Loner	Self-effacing
Team builder	Dictatorial	Compassionate
Effective bargainer		Unique
Dependable		Willful
Win-win problem solver		
Plans ahead		
Intelligent		
Excellence-oriented		

Source: R. J. House, P. J. Hanges, M. Javidan, P. W. Dorfman, V. Gupta (eds.), *Culture, Leadership, and Organizations: The GLOBE Study of 62 Societies* (Thousand Oaks, CA: Sage, 2004).

EXHIBIT 15-4   **Project GLOBE Leadership Traits**

The Jack Welch of the future cannot be like me. I spent my entire career in the United States. The next head of General Electric will be somebody who spent time in Bombay, in Hong Kong, in Buenos Aires. We have to send our best and brightest overseas and make sure they have the training that will allow them to be the global leaders who will make GE flourish in the future.[93]

Bicultural backgrounds and exposure to other cultures during childhood, long-term international assignments, multicultural team projects, cultural mentors, and training play an important role in developing global leadership.[94]

When working with people from other cultures or ethnic groups, it is important to understand their accustomed leadership style and to be aware of how it differs from one's own style. The next step is finding a way to bridge these differences and determine the most effective style for a particular situation. Sometimes this means being flexible enough to adapt to the other culture's expectations about what constitutes good leadership; at other times it means educating people so they understand why a different style would work better, or coming up with synergistic style that is not indigenous to any of the cultures involved.

The following exercise allows us to look at the relationship between emergent leader behavior and the particular contingencies in a given situation.

 ## CLASS ACTIVITY: THE PERFECT SQUARE

The purpose of this exercise is to provide an opportunity to observe different types of leader and follower behavior. (Time allotted: 60–80 minutes)

STEP 1.   Break up into groups of between 8 and 18 people. Each group should form a circle in a large area of empty space, inside or outside, where they can spread out without running into chairs or walls.

STEP 2.   Ask for a volunteer(s) in each group to be observers. If your group is small, one observer will do. If your group has 18 people, you can have up to three observers. The observers should withdraw from the circle and carefully read the observer instructions found on page 411.

STEP 3. The members of the circle(s) should blindfold themselves. (Blindfolds will be provided by the instructor unless otherwise indicated.) If you wear glasses, place them in your pocket or give them to an observer to hold.

STEP 4. The instructor (or student facilitator) will read you the instructions for the exercise found on page 416. The blindfolded group has 20 minutes to complete the assigned task. (25 minutes)

STEP 5. Individual Reflection. After you have completed the exercise, please answer the following questions without talking in the next 10 minutes. (10 minutes)

   a. What different types of leadership emerged in this exercise? In your opinion, who were the leaders and why? What leader behaviors did they exhibit?

   b. What occurred in the group to help you solve the problem?

   c. What occurred in the group that hindered you from solving the problem or from solving it quickly?

   d. What did you learn about leadership from this exercise?

   e. What did you learn about yourself as a leader or follower in this exercise?

STEP 6. Group Discussion. Discuss the questions in Step 5 with your group. Ask the observers what they observed. Choose a representative to report to the entire class a summary of your discussion about the questions in Step 5. (20–30 minutes) (Instructors of small classes may skip this step and debrief Step 5 and 7 together.)

STEP 7. Plenary Debriefing Session. (25 minutes)

   a. Have an observer from each group briefly and objectively describe what happened when his or her group did the blindfolded exercise. Next, the group representative presents his or her report.

   b. Can you see any relationships between this exercise and the real world you experience at work or in other organizational settings?

   c. What are the important contingencies in this particular situation? What type of leadership works best in a situation such as this? What leader behaviors are needed? What's the difference between a leader and a facilitator?

   d. What examples of leadership behavior did you observe? Who took on a leadership role and what did they do to gain or lose leadership? Did anyone do anything to promote trust?

   e. There are no leaders without followers. In this exercise, what were the characteristics of a good follower?

   f. If you were to repeat this exercise, what would you do differently to be a better leader?

Observer Instructions

Please do not talk, laugh, or make any noises at all during the exercise so you do not disturb the group. Do keep an eye out for their safety; move any items that could trip them, and warn them if they are approaching obstacles, the edge of a cliff, etc. Otherwise, do not talk to them or to the other observers and no giggling, hard as that may be.

Please answer the following questions based on your observations.

1. Look for leadership behavior in the group. Who emerged as leaders and what exactly did they do to become leaders?

2. Please observe and describe the group's communication patterns and nonverbal language.

3. How did the group make decisions?

Be prepared to share these observations in your group discussion period.

Be prepared to give a brief description of your group's strategy and execution of the task during the plenary debriefing session.

LEARNING POINTS

1. Although Americans tend to romanticize leadership, there is evidence that leaders do make a notable difference in organizations, particularly organizations that are undergoing crisis, growth, and change.

2. Level 5 leaders are modest; quietly determined based on inspired standards rather than charisma; ambitious for the firm, rather than themselves; driven to achieve sustained results; and give credit to others for success and taking blame for themselves.

3. Leaders are individuals who (a) establish direction for a group, (b) gain group members' commitment, and (c) motivate and influence them to achieve goals to move in that direction.

4. The leadership point of view consists of seeing what needs to be done, understanding all the underlying forces in a situation, and having the courage to initiate action to improve things.

5. Shared or distributed leadership is rotated and the person with the most relevant skill assumes the leadership role at a particular time.

6. Lateral leadership occurs when colleagues at the same level in the hierarchy collaborate and facilitate joint problem solving. They learn to influence people without the aid of hierarchical status.

7. Followers expect their leaders to be honest, competent, forward-looking, and inspiring.

8. Not all managers are leaders. Leaders focus more on changing the status quo.

9. Successful business leaders possess the following traits: drive, honesty and integrity, leadership motivation, self-confidence, cognitive ability, knowledge of the business, creativity, and flexibility.

10. Whereas intelligence and high energy are inherited traits, leadership skills can be developed. Thus, leaders are born, then made.

11. Behavior styles in leadership focus on task (initiating structure) or people (consideration behavior). Generally speaking, effective leaders are high on both these dimensions; otherwise, it depends on the situation.

12. In House's path-goal theory, the effectiveness of the leadership styles depends on both employee and environmental contingency factors.

13. According to the leader-member exchange model, leaders give preferential treatment to an in-group that is therefore more satisfied and more successful. However, the leader's favoritism results in less communication and cooperation between the in-group and out-group.

14. Transformational leaders are value-driven change agents who make followers more conscious of the importance and value of task outcomes. They provide followers with a vision and motivate them to go beyond self-interest for the good of the organization.

15. According to Kouzes and Posner, effective leaders (a) challenge the process; (b) inspire a shared vision; (c) enable others to act; (d) model the way; and (e) encourage the heart.

16. Bass and Aviolo's full range of leadership styles is laissez-faire—transactional—transformational. The laissez-faire approach is least effective.

17. Transactional leadership is an exchange process in which leaders clarify employee roles and task requirements and then reward or punish followers based on their performance.

18. Charismatic leaders develop a special relationship with their followers that includes high levels of performance, loyalty, sacrifice, and enthusiasm. They are adept at communicating an inspiring vision and can be either ethical or unethical.

19. Servant leaders are stewards who are responsible for serving, developing, and transforming the organization and its people.

20. Emotional intelligence consists of self-awareness, self-management, social awareness, and relationship management.

21. Follower trust in leaders results in higher organizational performance.

22. There are few gender differences in leadership except that women are more participative and use a transformational style with contingent rewards more frequently than men. Men and women are equally effective as leaders.

23. Although leadership varies to some extent by culture, the transformational leadership style is viewed as universally effective.

ACTION SCRIPTS

FOR EMPLOYEES

- Being a good follower involves asking questions that clarify everyone's understanding about the vision and how it will be accomplished. According to research, good followers are also trustworthy, participative, loyal, capable of independent critical thinking so they can question the leader's orders, courageous communicators who give honest feedback, change agents, and they have collaborative team skills and integrity. [95]
- Employees who are skilled at managing the direct report-boss relationship give their bosses cooperation, reliability, and honesty and take the time to understand their needs.
- Experts are good at perceiving a need and coming up with an inspiring and feasible vision that will make a difference.
- They see leadership as a journey that involves figuring out their life's purpose.

  Because we believe that all employees should strive to take a leadership role in their organization, most of the manager scripts in the next section also apply to employees.

FOR MANAGERS

- Expert leaders scan the environment for opportunities and threats, stay current in their fields, and take time to think about the future and reflect on their performance.
- Expert leaders think of followers as volunteers who contribute their efforts, not because they are paid, but because their needs are met in the process. This prevents leaders from taking their followers for granted.
- Effective leaders analyze the factors pertaining to the situation, task, followers, and the organization, and then choose the appropriate leadership style.
- Leaders need to have an in-depth and up-to-date understanding of what makes both their followers (including ones from diverse backgrounds) and their organization tick.

- Many initially successful leaders let power go to their heads. A measure of humility and the ability to accept negative feedback and admit mistakes can prevent this common occurrence.
- Leaders model self-awareness and leader development by openly discussing the areas they themselves need to improve.
- Consistency, honesty, and fairness all contribute to a leader's respect and credibility. When followers perceive that they are being manipulated by leaders or that leaders are motivated by self-interest rather than the good of the organization, it may be impossible for leaders to regain their credibility.
- Managers usually have to take the first step to building trust with employees, and their actions and behaviors lay the groundwork for trust. These behaviors help develop trust: behavioral integrity, behavioral consistency, participative decision making, communication, and demonstration of concern.[96]
- Good leaders deliver bad news personally without procrastinating.
- They devote time and attention to maintaining the trust of their followers, which is easier to build than rebuild.
- Leaders should articulate a clear vision that appeals to followers, express confidence in their followers' capacity to achieve the vision, consistently serve as a good example, treat employees fairly and avoid favoritism, and celebrate successes and accomplishments.[97]
- Leaders cannot control what happens in their environment, but they can influence how it is seen. One of the symbolic roles of leadership is to frame meaning for followers, helping them to see the world the way their leaders do.[98]
- The leadership function is shared in many effective groups. Leaders rise to the occasion but return to follower status once their contribution is made. Such groups do not require a leader so much as a facilitator (rotating or fixed) who helps the group stay on track and allows people to be heard.
- Leaders act as teachers who educate their followers at times and as coaches who help them develop and achieve their goals.
- They are extremely skilled communicators who tailor their message to the specific audience that they are addressing and inspire them.
- Rather than ignoring emotions, leaders pay attention to their followers' emotions and figure out how to best handle the emotional toxicity that is a by-product of organizational life. They accomplish this by listening empathetically, focusing on healing, buffering pain by intercepting attacks, extricating people from painful situations when necessary, and trying to transform the pain by framing it more positively. They control their own emotions and avoid hijacks.[99]
- Expert leaders include cultural, ethnic, and gender differences in the list of contingencies that they consider when deciding how to behave in a given situation, and they find a way to bridge potential differences.

FOR ORGANIZATIONAL ARCHITECTS

- Expert organizational architects recognize that firms known for their best practices in leadership development are distinguished from other firms by:
  - The quantity and intensity of their interventions. Although the range of activities is similar, the best practices firms do more of these same activities with greater consistency and rigor.
  - The extent to which they measure their efforts at leadership development. They track potential leaders and catalogue projects, jobs, and bosses that provide greater developmental impact, and keep track of which potential leaders receive these experiences, and the result.
  - Senior management strongly supports leadership development.[100]
- Expert organizational architects pay close attention to leadership development in their organizations and work hard to adopt the following practices:
  - Leadership development is linked to business strategy and acknowledged as a source of competitive advantage.
  - Leadership development is often tied to succession planning.
  - Because leadership requirements vary by job and situation, leadership development is viewed as an ongoing process.

- Companies generally adopt a particular model of leadership, such as one of the theories in this chapter or a competency model based on their own organization, to guide and integrate leadership development.
- Coaching is available for employees who have transitioned to new situations and have special challenges (e.g., new managers, executives assigned to different areas or countries)
- Jobs, bosses, hardship, and special projects are the most useful experiences for leadership development.[101]
- Training is most helpful when it is customized around current organizational challenges and the lessons and skills learned can be directly applied on the job and reinforced.
- They also design their leadership selection, evaluation, and compensation systems with care. In particular, they:
    - Hire people with leadership potential for jobs at all levels, not just senior management, and they encourage and reward people for exerting leadership.
    - Have an accurate evaluation process that identifies potential leaders in an inclusive and objective manner. The ideal leader profile does not exclude minorities, women, or people from different cultures.
    - Provide high potential and high-performing leaders with more compensation, and track their turnover.
    - Evaluate managers on how well they develop talented employees and allow them to move ahead.
    - Use 360-degree feedback on leadership performance wisely and ensure that leaders then discuss the results with their direct reports. They also follow up to see that leaders have effectively responded to concerns, thus reinforcing accountability.
- Experts also know that trust in the organization's leadership is a valuable commodity, and they develop and sustain mechanisms to maintain trust (e.g., open door policy, dissemination of information, Q&A sessions with senior management, transparent personnel decisions).

PERSONAL APPLICATION ASSIGNMENT

The topic of this assignment is to think back on a leadership experience that was significant for you. Choose an experience that intrigues you and that you want to learn more about.

A. Concrete Experience

    1. Objectively describe the experience (who, what, when, where, how). (2 points)

    2. Subjectively describe your feelings, perceptions, and thoughts that occurred during (not after) the experience. What did others seem to be feeling? (2 points)

B. Reflective Observation

    1. Looking back at the experience, what were the perspectives of the key actors (including you)? (2 points)

    2. Why did the people involved (including you) behave as they did? (2 points)

C. Abstract Conceptualization

    1. Relate concepts or theories from the assigned readings or the lecture to the experience. Explain thoroughly how they help describe your experience. Please apply at least two concepts or theories and cite them correctly. (4 points)

D. Active Experimentation

    1. What did you learn about leadership from this experience? (1 point)

    2. What did you learn about yourself? (1 point)

    3. What action steps will you take to be more effective in the future? (2 points)

E. Integration, Synthesis, and Writing

    1. Did you integrate and synthesize the four sections? (1 point)
    2. Was the personal application assignment well written and easy to understand? (1 point)
    3. Was it free of spelling and grammatical errors? (2 points)

Facilitator Instructions for the Perfect Square

(For the Facilitator Only)

General Procedure: The groups should form a circle in a large empty area away from a wall or sidewalk they could use as a guide. Ask for the number of observers your instructor has designated and have them stand off to the side. Pass out the blindfolds, and instruct the students remaining in the circle to blindfold themselves. When they are blindfolded and cannot see, read them the instructions below and pass out the rope. Don't tell them anything that is not listed in your instructions. Do not let them see the rope beforehand—they shouldn't know how long it is. The last person to receive the rope should be the quietest person. Make your best guess about who that person is (don't ask) and give the first end of the rope to the person to his or her left and continue handing out the rope in that direction around the circle so that you finish distributing the rope to the quietest person. Take the slack (leftover rope) and lay it on the ground behind that person so he or she has to search for the end. This is a test to see whether the group listens to quiet people. Don't tell the group there is leftover rope. Watch their group process as they work, but don't intervene unless someone is in danger of falling or hurting themselves. Don't talk at all during the exercise except to read them the instructions and give them ten- and five-minute warnings. Once the group starts, check that the observers know what to do and remind them to be absolutely quiet. Note what time they start; when 10 minutes have passed, tell them they have ten minutes left. When you give them their 5-minute warning five minutes later, you can also tell them this: "If you want to have one of your members check the square, that person can go inside the circle and walk it, but both their hands have to stay on the rope at all times." When the 20 minutes are up, have them take off their blindfolds and answer individually the questions in Step 5. If they finish earlier, ask if they are satisfied with their square. If so, let them take off their blindfolds. Collect the blindfolds and the rope while they work on Step 5.

Read these instructions to the participants once they form a group:

1. Please form a circle. Who would like to observe this exercise? Please stand to the side and read your instructions. Everyone else should put on a blindfold so you cannot see. I'll give you the rest of the instructions once everyone is blindfolded.

2. Your task is to form a perfect square utilizing all the rope that I am passing out. Here are the rules:

   a. Use all the rope so that your square is taut, with no slack.

   b. You must keep both your hands on the rope at all times.

   c. You have 20 minutes to form a perfect square.

   I can repeat these rules if you like, but after that I cannot answer any questions. Shall I repeat the rules?

ENDNOTES

[1] S. Anderson, J. Cavanaugh, S. Klinger, and L. Stanton, *Executive Excess 2005* (Washington, D. C.: Institute for Policy Studies, 2005); J. R. Meindl and S. B. Ehrlich, "The Romance of Leadership and the Evaluation of Organizational Performance," *Academy of Management Journal 30* (1987): 91–109; J. Pfeffer, "The Ambiguity of Leadership," *Academy of Management Review 2*(1) (January 1977): 104–112; and A. B. Thomas, "Does Leadership Make a Difference to Organizational Performance?" *Administrative Science Quarterly 33*(3) (September 1988): 388–400.

[2] R. M. Fulmer, P. A. Gibbs, and M. Goldsmith, "Developing Leaders: How Winning Companies Keep on Winning," *Sloan Management Review 42*(1) (Fall 2000): 49.

[3] J. Collins, "Level 5 Leadership: The Triumph of Humility and Fierce Resolve," *Harvard Business Review 79*(1) (2001): 67–76.

[4] S. Motowidlo, "Leadership and Leadership Processes," in *Handbook of Industrial and Organizational Psychology*, 2nd ed., M. D. Dunnette (ed.) (Palo Alto, CA: Consulting Psychologists Press, 1992).

[5] A. Zaleznik, "The Leadership Gap," *Academy of Management Executive 4*(1) (1990): 7–22.

[6] J. M. Kouzes and B. Z. Posner, *The Leadership Challenge* (San Francisco: Jossey-Bass, 2002).

[7] Adapted from J. Conger, *Learning to Lead* (San Francisco: Jossey-Bass, 1992): 18–19.

[8] Zaleznik, "The Leadership Gap": 12.

[9] J. G. Clawson, *Level Three Leadership: Getting Below the Surface* (Upper Saddle River, NJ: Prentice Hall, 2006): 6.

[10] G. Yukl, *Leadership in Organizations* (Upper Saddle River, NJ: Prentice Hall, 2006): 8.

[11] J. G. Hunt, *Leadership: A New Synthesis* (London: Sage, 1991).

[12] B. Z. Posner and W. H. Schmidt, "Values and the American Manager: An Update Updated," *California Management Review 34*(3) (Spring 1992): 80–94; and Kouzes and Posner, *The Leadership Challenge: How to Get Extraordinary Things Done in Organizations* (San Francisco: Jossey-Bass, 2002).

[13] Kouzes and Posner, *The Leadership Challenge*: 26–27.

[14] Posner and Schmidt, "Values and the American Manager."

[15] F. Quezada and J. E. Boyce, "Latin America," in *Comparative Management*, R. Nath (ed.) (Cambridge, MA: Ballinger, 1988): 247–69.

[16] J. S. Osland, L. Hunter, and M. M. Snyder, "A Comparative Study of Managerial Styles in Nicaraguan and Costa Rican Female Executives," *International Studies of Management and Organization 28*(2) (1998): 54–73; E. Kras, *Modernizing Mexican Management Style: With Insights for U.S. Companies Working in Mexico* (Las Cruces, NM: Editts, 1994).

[17] A. Zaleznik, "Managers and Leaders: Are they Different?" *Harvard Business Review 55*(3) (May–June, 1977): 67–78.

[18] J. P. Kotter, *A Force for Change: How Leadership Differs from Management* (New York: Free Press, 1990); J. P. Kotter, "What Leaders Really Do," *Harvard Business Review 79*(11) (December 2001): 85–96.

[19] L. R. Sayles, "Doing Things Right: A New Imperative for Middle Managers," *Organizational Dynamics 21*(4) (Spring 1993): 5–14.

[20] See G. Yukl's book, *Leadership in Organizations* (Upper Saddle River, NJ: Prentice Hall, 2006), for a comprehensive treatise on leadership theories. C. Stiver's *Gender Images in Public Administration* (London: Sage, 1993) looks at leadership theory from a feminist perspective.

[21] Yukl, *Leadership in Organizations*.

[22] S. J. Zaccaro, R. J. Foti, and D. A. Kenny, "Self-Monitoring and Trait-Based Variance in Leadership: An Investigation of Leader Flexibility across Multiple Group Situations," *Journal of Applied Psychology 76*(2) (April 1991): 308–315.

[23] Yukl, *Leadership in Organizations*: 190.

[24] S. A. Kirkpatrick and E. A. Locke, "Leadership: Do Traits Matter?" *Academy of Management Executive 5*(2) (1991): 48–60.

[25] Conger, *Learning to Lead*: 22–24.

[26] J. Kotter, *The Leadership Factor* (New York: Free Press, 1988) details best practices of companies that create talented management teams.

[27] Yukl, *Leadership in Organizations*.

[28] J. P. Howell, D. E. Bowen, P. W. Dorfman, S. Kerr, and P. M. Podsakoff, "Substitutes for Leadership: Effective Alternatives to Ineffective Leadership," *Organizational Dynamics 19*(1) (Summer 1990): 20–38.

[29] F. Shipper and C. S. White, "Mastery, Frequency, and Interaction of Managerial Behaviors Relative to Subunit Effectiveness," *Human Relations 52*(1) (January 1999): 49–66.

[30] G. Yukl, *Leadership in Organizations*; G. Ekvall and J. Arvonen, "Change-Centered Leadership: An Extension of the Two-Dimensional Model," *Scandinavian Journal of Management 7*(1) (1991): 17–26; M. Lindell, and C. Rosenqvist, "Management Behavior Dimensions and Development Orientation," *Leadership Quarterly 3*(4) (1992): 355–377.

[31] R. J. House, "A Path-Goal Theory of Leader Effectiveness," *Administrative Science Quarterly 16*(3) (September 1971): 321–338; House revised his theory in this article "Path-Goal Theory of Leadership: Lessons, Legacy, and a Reformulated Theory," *Leadership Quarterly 7*(3) (1996): 323–352.

[32] See "Motivation: A Diagnostic Approach" by D. A. Nadler and E. E. Lawler III, in *Perspectives on Behavior in Organizations* (New York: McGraw-Hill, 1977): 26–34 or the *Organizational Behavior Reader*, 2007 for an explanation of this theory.

[33] Adapted from R. J. House, "Path-Goal Theory of Leadership": 323–352.

[34] R. C. Liden and G. Graen, "Generalizability of the Vertical Dyad Linkage Model of Leadership" *Academy of Management Journal 23* (1980): 451–465.

[35] G. B. Graen and M. Wakabayashi, "Cross-Cultural Leadership-Making: Bridging American and Japanese Diversity for Team Advantage," in H. C. Triandis, M. D. Dunnette, and L. M. Hough, (eds.), *Handbook of Industrial and Organizational Psychology,* 2nd ed., vol. 4 (Palo Alto, CA: Consulting Psychologists Press, 1994): 415–466.

[36] N. T. Duarte, J. R. Goodson, and N. R. Klich, "How Do I Like Thee? Let Me Appraise the Ways," *Journal of Organizational Behavior 14* (1993): 239–249.

37 R. J. Deluga and J. T. Perry, "The Relationship of Subordinate Upward Influencing Behavior, Satisfaction and Perceived Superior Effectiveness with Leader-Member Exchanges," *Journal of Occupational Psychology 64* (1991): 239–252.

38 O. Janssen and N. W. V. Yperen, "Employee's Goal Orientations, the Quality of Leader-Member Exchange, and the Outcomes of Job Performance and Job Satisfaction," *Academy of Management Journal 47*(3) (2004): 368–384.

39 B. Erdogan, M. L. Kraimer, and R. C. Liden, "Work Value Congruence and Intrinsic Career Success: The Compensatory Roles of Leader-Member Exchange and Perceived Organizational Support," *Personnel Psychology 57*(2) (Summer 2004): 305–332.

40 G. R. Ferris, "Role of Leadership in the Employee Withdrawal Process: A Constructive Replication," *Journal of Applied Psychology 70* (1985): 777–781.

41 T. A. Scandura, and C. A. Schriesheim, "Leader-Member Exchange and Supervisor Career Mentoring as Complementary Constructs in Leadership Research," *Academy of Management Journal 37* (1994): 1588–1602.

42 P. M. Podsakoff, S. B. MacKenzie, R. H. Moorman, and R. Fetter, "Transformational Leader Behaviors and their Effects on Followers' Trust in Leader, Satisfaction and Organizational Citizenship Behaviors," *Leadership Quarterly 1* (1990): 107–142.

43 W. Bennis and B. Nanus, *Leaders* (New York: Harper & Row, 1985).

44 Kouzes and Posner, *The Leadership Challenge*: 14.

45 B. J. Avolio and B. M. Bass, *The Full Range of Leadership Development: Basic & Advanced Manuals* (Binghamton, NY: Bass/Aviolo and Associates, 1990).

46 N. Tichy and D. O. Ulrich, "The Leadership Challenge—A Call for the Transformational Leader," *Sloan Management Review 26*(1) (Fall 1984): 59–68; B. M. Bass, "Does the Transactional-Transformational Leadership Paradigm Transcend Organizational and National Boundaries?" *The American Psychologist 52*(2) (1997): 130–140.

47 T. A. Judge and R. F. Piccolo, "Transformational and Transactional Leadership: A Meta-Analytic Test of Their Relative Validity," *Journal of Applied Psychology 89*(5) (2004): 755–768.

48 C. A. Schriesheim, S. L. Castro, X. Zhou, and L. A. deChurch, "An Investigation of Path-Goal and Transformational Leadership Theory Predictions at the Individual Level of Analysis," *The Leadership Quarterly 17*(1) (2006): 21–38.

49 J. Conger and R. N. Kanungo, (eds.), *Charismatic Leadership* (San Francisco: Jossey-Bass, 1988) and a chapter in the same book, by B. Bass, "Evolving Perspectives on Charismatic Leadership": 40–77.

50 J. Howell, "Two Faces of Charisma: Socialized and Personalized Leadership in Organizations," in J. Conger and R. Kanungo, (eds.), *Charismatic Leadership* (San Francisco: Jossey-Bass, 1988): 213–36 and J. Conger, "The Dark Side of Leadership," *Organizational Dynamics 19*(2) (Autumn 1990): 44–55.

51 P. Block, *Stewardship: Choosing Service over Self-Interest* (San Francisco: Berrett-Koehler, 1993). The founder of servant leadership is a Quaker, Robert Greenleaf, who wrote the original essay in the 1970s that sparked this movement. See R. K. Greenleaf, *Servant Leadership: A Journey into the Nature of Legitimate Power and Greatness* (New York: Paulist Press, 1991).

52 W. B. Brenneman, J. B. Keys, and R. M. Fulmer, "Learning Across a Living Company: The Shell Companies' Experience," *Organizational Dynamics 27*(2) (1998): 61–71.

53 H. Gardner, *Frames of Mind: Theories of Multiple Intelligences* (London: Fontana, 1993).

54 J. D. Mayer, D. R. Caruso, and P. Salovey, "Emotional Intelligence Meets Traditional Standards for an Intelligence," *Intelligence 27* (1999): 267.

55 D. Goleman, R. Boyatzis, and A. McKee, *Primal Leadership: Realizing the Power of Emotional Intelligence* (Boston, MA: Harvard Business School Press, 2002); R. Boyatzis, and A. McKee, *Resonant Leadership: Renewing Yourself and Connecting with Others Through Mindfulness, Hope, and Compassion* (Boston, MA: Harvard Business School Press, 2005).

56 C. Dulewicz and M. Young, "The Relevance of Emotional Intelligence for Leadership Performance," *Journal of General Management 30*(3) (2005): 71–87.

57 Goleman, Boyatzis, and McKee, *Primal Leadership*: 39.

58 R. S. Rubin, D. C. Munz, and W. H. Bommer, "Leading from Within: The Effects of Emotion Recognition and Personality on Transformational Leadership Behavior," *Academy of Management Journal 48*(5) (2005): 845–858.

59 D. Goleman, "What Makes a Leader?" *Harvard Business Review 76*(6) (November-December, 1998): 93–102.

60 Ibid.

61 Kirkpatrick and Locke, "Leadership: Do Traits Matter?"; P. M. Podsakoff, S. B. MacKenzie, R. H. Moorman, and R. Fetter, "Transformational Leader Behaviors and their Effects on Followers' Trust in Leader, Satisfaction and Organizational Citizenship Behaviors," *Leadership Quarterly 1*(1990): 107–142.

62 E. Fleishman and E. F. Harris, "Patterns of Leadership Behavior Related to Employee Grievance and Turnover," *Personnel Psychology 15* (1962): 43–56.

63 C. A. Schriesheim, S. L. Castro, and C. C. Cogliser, "Leader-Member Exchange (LMX) Research: A Comprehensive Review of Theory, Measurement, and Data-Analytic Practices," *Leadership Quarterly 10*(1), (1999): 63–113.

[64] K. T. Dirks and D. P. Skarlicki, "Trust in Leaders: Existing Research and Emerging Issues," in R. M. Kramer and K. Cook (eds.), *Trust and Distrust in Organizations* (New York: Russell Sage, 2004): 22.

[65] K. T. Dirks, and D. L. Ferrin, "Trust in Leadership: Meta-analytic Findings and Implications for Organizational Research," *Journal of Applied Psychology* 87(4) (2002): 611–628.

[66] T. Simons and J. McLean Parks, "Empty Words: The Impact of Perceived Managerial Integrity on Employees, Customers, and Profits." Working Paper (2001).

[67] K. T. Dirks, "Trust in Leadership and Team Performance: Evidence from NCAA Basketball," *Journal of Applied Psychology* 85(6), (2000): 1004–1012.

[68] Dirks and Skarlicki, "Trust in Leaders": 27.

[69] P. Blau, *Exchange and Power in Social Life* (New York: Wiley, 1964).

[70] Dirks and Skarlicki, "Trust in Leaders."

[71] R.C. Mayer, J. H. Davis, F. D. Schoorman, "An Integrative Model of Organizational Trust," *Academy of Management Review* 20(3) (1995): 709–734.

[72] R. C. Mayer and M. Gavin, "Trust for Management and Performance: Who Minds the Shop While the Employees Watch the Boss?" Paper Presented at the Annual Academy of Management, Chicago, IL (1999).

[73] Dirks and Skarlicki, "Trust in Leaders."

[74] H. Meyerson, "CEOs You Don't Want in the Cockpit," *The Washington Post*, (April 22, 2003): A-19; W. Zellner: "What Was Don Thinking?" *BusinessWeek* (May 5, 2003): 32; "AMR Names New CEO," CNNMoney.com (April 24, 2003). http://money.cnn.com/2003/04/24/news/amr_jake/index.htm. Accessed 8/11/06.

[75] G. N. Powell, *Women and Men in Management* (Thousand Oaks, CA: Sage, 1993); R. P. Vecchio, "Leadership and Gender Advantage," *Leadership Quarterly* 13(6) (December 2002): 643–671.

[76] A. H. Eagley, and S. J. Karau, "Gender and the Emergence of Leaders: A Meta-Analysis," *Journal of Personality and Social Psychology 61* (1991): 685–710; A. H. Eagley, M. G. Makhijani, and B. G. Klonsky, "Gender and the Evaluation of Leaders: A Meta-Analysis," *Psychological Bulletin 108* (1992): 3–22.

[77] A. H. Eagley, M. C. Johannesen-Schmidt, and M. L. van Engen, "Transformational, Transactional, and Laissez-Faire Leadership Styles: A Meta-Analysis Comparing Women and Men," *Psychological Bulletin 95* (2003): 569–591.

[78] T. Melamed and N. Bosionelos, "Gender Differences in the Personality Features of British Managers," *Psychological Reports 72* (1992): 979–986.

[79] R. Kabacoff, "Gender and Leadership in the Corporate Boardroom" (Portland, ME: Management Research Group, 2000): 1–10.

[80] Eagley, Johannesen-Schmidt, and van Engen, "Transformational, Transactional, and Laissez-Faire Leadership Styles: A Meta-Analysis."

[81] A. Newcomb, "Four Women Who Shape Beijing," *Christian Science Monitor*. www.csmonitor.com_2005_0816_p10s01-woap.html. Accessed 8/17/05.

[82] K. Porter, "Women Leaders: Strategic Yet Invisible Assets," *Link & Learn* (May 2003). http://www.linkageinc.com/company/news_events/link_learn_enewsletter/archive/2003/05_03_women_leaders_porter.aspx. Accessed 8/21/06.

[83] "The Bottom Line: Connecting Corporate Performance and Gender Diversity," *Catalyst*, (2004). http://www. catalystwomen.org/knowledge/titles/title.php?page=lead_finperf_04. Accessed 7/15/06.

[84] R. D. Adler, "Women in the Executive Suite Correlate to High Profits," Glass Ceiling Research Center, Pepperdine University, 2002 http://www.equalpay.nu/docs/en/adler_web.pdf. Accessed 8/11/06.

[85] W. C. Kim and R. A. Mauborgne: "Parables of Leadership," *Harvard Business Review* 7(16) (July–August 1992): 123–128.

[86] G. Hofstede, "Motivation, Leadership, and Organization: Do American Theories Apply Abroad?" *Organizational Dynamics 9* (1980): 42–62.

[87] D. H. B. Welsh, F. Luthans, and S. M. Sommer, "Managing Russian Factory Workers: The Impact of U.S.-Based Behavioral and Participative Techniques," *Academy of Management Journal 36*(1) (1993): 58–80.

[88] M. Javidan and R. J. House, "Cultural Acumen for the Global Manager: Lessons from Project Globe," *Organizational Dynamics 29*(4) (2001): 289–305.

[89] D. N. Den Hartog, R. J. House, P. J. Hanges, S. A. Ruiz-Quintanilla, P. W. Dorfman, and Associates, "Culture Specific and Cross-Culturally Generalizable Implicit Leadership Theories: Are the Attributes of Charismatic/Transformational Leadership Universally Endorsed?" *Leadership Quarterly 10*(2) (Summer 1999): 219–256.

[90] This definition was combined from work by N. J. Adler, "Global Leadership: Women Leaders," in *Developing Global Business Leaders: Policies, Processes, and Innovations*, M. Mendenhall, T. M. Kuhlmann, and G. Stahl (eds.) (Westport, CN: Quorum, 2001): 73–97, and M. Festing, "The Effects of International Human Resource Management Strategies on Global Leadership Development," in *Developing Global Business Leaders: Policies, Processes, and Innovations*, M. Mendenhall, T. M. Kuhlmann, and G. Stahl (eds.) (Westport, CN: Quorum, 2001): 37–56.

[91] H. Lane, M. Maznevski, M. Mendenhall, and J. McNett (eds.), *Handbook of Global Management* (Oxford: Blackwell, 2004).

[92] M. Mendenhall and J. S. Osland, *"An Overview of the Extant Global Leadership Research,"* Paper presented at the Academy of International Business Conference, Puerto Rico, June, 2002. See also J. Osland, A. Bird, M. Mendenhall, and A. Osland, "Developing Global Leadership Capabilities and Global Mindset: A Review," in *International Human Resources Handbook*, G. Stahl and I. Bjorkman (eds.) (London: Elgar, 2006): 197–222.

[93] Cited in H. Gregersen, A. Morrison and J. S. Black, "Developing Leaders for the Global Frontier," *Sloan Management Review 40*(1) (1998): 22.

[94] Osland, Bird, Mendenhall, and Osland, "Developing Global Leadership Capabilities and Global Mindset."

[95] R. Kelley, E. Whitener, S. E. Brodt, M. A. Korsgaard, and J. M. Werner, "Managers as Initiators of Trust: An Exchange Relationship for Understanding Managerial Trustworthy Behavior," *Academy of Management Review 23*(3) (1998): 513–530.

[96] S. M. Latour and V. J. Rast, "Dynamic Followership: The Prerequisites for Effective Leadership," *Air & Space Journal 18* (Winter, 2004): 102-111.

[97] Yukl, *Leadership in Organizations*.

[98] G. T. Fairhurst and R. T. Sarr, *The Art of Framing: Managing the Language of Leadership* (San Francisco: Jossey-Bass, 1996). This book provides explicit advice on framing and communicating with employees.

[99] P. J. Frost, "Handling Toxic Emotions: New Challenges for Leaders and their Organization," *Organizational Dynamics 33*(2) (2004): 111–127.

[100] J. Conger, "Developing Leadership Capability: What's Inside the Black Box?" *Academy of Management Executive 18*(3) (2004): 136–139.

[101] Ibid.

Chapter 16

▲▲

ORGANIZATIONAL CULTURE

OBJECTIVES By the end of this chapter, you should be able to:

A. Define organizational culture and explain its function.

B. Explain how organizational culture evolves and is transmitted.

C. Contrast the characteristics of strong and weak cultures.

D. Explain the relationship between strong cultures and high performance.

E. Describe the importance of organizational justice.

F. Explain the impact of organizational culture in mergers.

G. Describe how leaders can manage culture.

H. Identify the four stages in the organizational life cycle.

THE FABRIC OF CREATIVITY

When *Fast Company* set out to find the most innovative company in America, we wanted to rely on objective measurements, but that proved daunting. How can you quantify something as intangible as innovation? So we gave up crunching numbers and focused on other criteria. For starters, we looked for a company with a long history of innovation that is adept at product innovation as it is at process innovation. Pound for pound, the most innovative company in America is W. L. Gore & Associates.

You've no doubt heard of its most famous product: Gore-Tex fabrics, which have a transparent plastic coating that makes them waterproof and windproof but keeps them breathable. Gore is big—with $1.58 billion in annual revenues and 6,300 employees—but not gargantuan like 3M, GE, or IBM. Still, Gore makes so many products that the total is hard to pin down—with all the variations, the count rises above 1,000. It makes the number one products in industrial and electronics niches ranging from filters for reducing air pollution at large factories to the assemblies for fuel cells that convert hydrogen to electricity. Gore, a privately owned company, doesn't release its annual financial data, but a spokesperson says that the company has had "double-digit" revenue growth for the past couple of years. In many businesses, Gore has come out of nowhere and seized the market lead, as it did with its smooth Glide dental floss, the first floss that resisted shredding, and its Elixir guitar strings, which last three to five times longer than normal strings. When Gore's people think they can create a much better product, they are fearless about attacking new markets.

Epiphany in the Car Pool

What really distinguishes Gore is its culture, which goes back to 1958, when Wilbert ("Bill") L. Gore left DuPont, where he had worked as an engineer for 17 years, and launched his start-up. Bill liked to say that "communication really happens in the car pool." At a hierarchical company, the car pool is the only place where people talk to one another freely without regard for the chain of command. He also observed that when there's a crisis, a company creates a task force and throws out the rules. That's when organizations take risks and make big breakthroughs. Why, he wondered, should you have to wait for a crisis?

So Bill Gore threw out the rules. He created a place with hardly any hierarchy and few ranks and titles. He insisted on direct, one-on-one communication; anyone in the company could speak to anyone else. In essence, he organized the company as though it were a bunch of small task forces. To promote this idea, he limited the size of teams—keeping even the manufacturing facilities to 150 to 200 people at most. That's small enough so that people can get to know one another and what everyone is working on, and who has the skills and knowledge they might tap to get something accomplished—whether it's creating an innovative product or handling the everyday challenges of running a business.

Gore doesn't have an impressive campus that proclaims the company's success. It consists of several dozen bland, low-rise buildings scattered near the Delaware-Maryland border. They're separated enough from one another so that each can house a small, autonomous team. You can drive by and think you're passing farmland rather than corporate sites.

What goes on inside those nondescript buildings is hard to understand unless you've actually worked there for at least a year or two. Consider the case of Diane Davidson, whom the company hired to work on Citywear, an effort that has persuaded designers such as Prada, Hugo Boss, and Polo to use Gore-Tex fabrics in clothing that people can wear to the office or out to a party. Nothing in Davidson's 15 years of experience as a sales executive in the apparel industry prepared her for life in a place where there are no bosses and no clear-cut roles.

"I came from a very traditional male-dominated business—the men's shoe business," she recalls. "When I arrived at Gore, I didn't know who did what. I wondered how anything got done here. It was driving me crazy." Like all new hires, Davidson was given a "starting sponsor" at Gore—a mentor, not a boss. But she didn't know how to work without someone telling her what to do.

"Who's my boss?" she kept asking.

"Stop using the B-word," her sponsor replied.

As an experienced executive, Davidson assumed that Gore's talk was typical corporate euphemism rather than real practice.

"Secretly, there are bosses, right?" she asked.

There weren't. She eventually figured out that "your team is your boss, because you don't want to let them down. Everyone's your boss, and no one is your boss."

What's more, Davidson saw that people didn't fit into standard job descriptions. They had all made different sets of "commitments" to their team, often combining roles that remained segregated in different fiefdoms at conventional companies, such as sales, marketing, and product design. It took a long time to get to know people and what they did—and for them to get to know her and trust her with responsibilities. Eventually, Davidson went on to oversee the sales force and product development for Citywear. She describes herself as a "category champion" involved in marketing, sales, and sponsorship, a good example of how Gore associates create roles that aren't easily defined by traditional corporate departments.

Her experience is commonplace. "You join a team and you're an idiot," says John Mongan, who has switched into new teams five times over a 20-year tenure. "It takes 18 months to build credibility. Early on, it's really frustrating. In hindsight, it makes sense. As a sponsor, I tell new hires, 'Your job for the first six months is to get to know the team,' but they have trouble believing it—and not contributing when other people are."

LEADERS ARE TALENT MAGNETS

Gore's knack for innovation doesn't come from throwing money or bodies at a challenge, or from building a great ivory tower of an R&D lab. It springs from a culture where people feel free to pursue ideas on their own, communicate with one another, and collaborate out of self-motivation rather than a sense of duty. Gore enshrines the idea of "natural leadership." Leaders aren't designated from on high. People become leaders by actually leading, and if you want to be a leader there, you have to recruit followers. Since there's no chain of command, no one has to follow. In a sense, you become a talent magnet. You attract other talented people who want to work with you. You draw them with your passion for what you're working on and the credibility that you've built over time.

Natural leadership is how Gore, which has no experience whatsoever in the music business, wound up inventing Elixir, the top-selling acoustic guitar string and a big advance in a field that had gone three decades without a technological breakthrough. Elixir came out of an unlikely place: one of Gore's medical-product plants in Flagstaff, Arizona. Dave Myers was an engineer there who helped invent new kinds of plastic heart implants. Gore encourages its associates to spend some of their time—typically around 10 percent—on speculative new ideas. Myers had a Eureka moment in 1993. He was experimenting by coating guitar strings with plastic for another project, when he asked himself, "Gosh, would this make a good guitar string?" Myers wasn't a guitarist himself, so he sought out help from a colleague who was. The pair experimented for two years without success. Then another colleague who had just finished working on Glide heard about their project and joined up.

Gore puts its R&D technologists and its salespeople in the same building as its production workers, so the entire team can work together and roles can blend. The trio in Flagstaff persuaded a half-dozen colleagues to help with improving the strings. They all did it in their spare time. Finally, after three years of working entirely out of their own motivation—three years without asking for anyone's permission or being subjected to any kind of oversight—the team sought out the official support of the larger company, which they needed to actually take the product to market.

BREAKTHROUGH IDEAS NEED BREAKOUT MARKETING

Beginning in 1958, Bill Gore tried to create the ideal environment for a guy like himself—a geeky buttoned-down engineer. Longtime associates say Gore feels like a university as much as a corporation. And Gore's strategy still depends on its engineering prowess: The company still insists that its new ideas have to be "unique and valuable"—dramatic improvements, not me-too products. But since the 1980s, the company has learned that superior technology often isn't enough. You also need breakthrough marketing to push past entrenched but inferior market leaders.

Gore's first marketing coup came with Gore-Tex, where the challenge was to find a way past the middlemen to talk directly to potential consumers. The solution: Gore created tags for the final garments that said "Gore-Tex: Guaranteed to Keep You Dry." After trying to interest consumer-products manufacturers in its technology for creating a better dental floss for 20 years, Gore took Glide to market itself and built a following by giving out free samples to dentists and hygienists. It was an early example of viral marketing. Gore followed the same tactic with Elixir guitar strings, which retailed for $15 apiece—so expensive that merchants refused to carry them.

But the Gore people figured that consumers would demand the product when they realized how much better it sounded. They gave away 20,000 samples in the first year, sending the product to the subscriber lists of guitar magazines. With a 35 percent share, Elixir now leads the market for acoustic guitar strings.

INNOVATION FOR THE LONG RUN

Gore's humanistic culture is the legacy of Bill Gore, who died in 1986. Colleagues describe Bill as quiet, humble, and completely approachable. His wealth was considerable, but inconspicuous. He never moved from the house where he started the company along with his wife, Genevieve, and their son, Bob. Bill and "Vieve" raised seed capital from their bridge club. Their early employees slept in the basement and set up a production line in the backyard, often raiding Vieve's kitchen for cooking equipment they could adapt for manufacturing. They used an egg-beater to coil the cables. Early customers were surprised to find blades of grass mixed in with the cables they bought.

Forty-six years later, Vieve still lives in that house. When Bob took over as CEO in the 1980s, he still drove a 1955 station wagon. His associates say that they would be embarrassed to pull up to one of the company's parking lots in a fancier car. Joe Rowan, who works in medical products at Gore, says he once used frequent-flier miles to upgrade to business class on a flight, only to look back to the economy-class section and see Vieve Gore sitting there with a member of the company's board of directors. Colleagues say that success never went to the heads of any of the Gores, and the family's values are still strong in Bob's children, the third generation to work for the company.

Gore's patient, private ownership has allowed it to sustain innovation over the years. Without the pressure of reporting quarterly reports, the company can comfortably take many years to bring a new product from invention to profitability. Gore isn't a cult. But its culture is much like Gore-Tex. As Gore grows, it must continue to invent ways to protect its people from the harsh outside elements, even as it lets their big and creative ideas breathe—and prosper.

Source: Excerpted with permission from A. Deutschman, "The Fabric of Creativity," *Fast Company 89* (December 2004): 54. http://www.fastcompany.com/magazine/89/open_gore.html. Accessed March 9, 2006.

 **CLASS PREPARATION**

A. Read "The Fabric of Creativity."

B. Fill out the Organizational Culture Questionnaire and answer questions 8-13 based on an organization to which you belong(ed).

C. Read the Ecoquest Case, Part I, and prepare your individual analysis by answering the questions at the end of the case.

D. While reading the chapter, make a list of the cues you should look for with respect to organizational culture.

Organizational Culture Questionnaire

> For each of the seven organizational culture dimensions described, place an (a) above the number that indicates your assessment of the organization's **actual** position on that dimension and an (i) above the number that indicates your assessment of where the organization should **ideally** be on this dimension.

1. **Conformity**. The feeling that there are many externally imposed constraints in the organization; the degree to which members feel that there are many rules, procedures, policies, and practices to which they have to conform rather than being able to do their work as they see fit.

Conformity is very characteristic of this organization.

1 2 3 4 5 6 7 8 9 10

Conformity is not characteristic of this organization.

2. **Responsibility**. Members of the organization are given personal responsibility to achieve their part of the organization's goals; the degree to which members feel that they can make decisions and solve problems without checking with superiors each step of the way.

No responsibility is given in the organization.

1 2 3 4 5 6 7 8 9 10

There is a great emphasis on personal responsibility in the organization.

3. **Standards**. The emphasis the organization places on quality performance and outstanding production, including the degree to which the member feels the organization is setting challenging goals for itself and communicating these goal commitments to members.

Standards are very low or nonexistent in the organization.

1 2 3 4 5 6 7 8 9 10

High, challenging standards are set in the organization.

4. **Rewards**. The degree to which members feel that they are being recognized and rewarded for good work rather than being ignored, criticized, or punished when something goes wrong.

Members are ignored, punished, or criticized.

1 2 3 4 5 6 7 8 9 10

Members are recognized and rewarded positively.

5. **Organizational clarity**. The feeling among members that things are well organized and that goals are clearly defined rather than being disorderly, confused, or chaotic.

The organization is disorderly, confused, and chaotic.

1 2 3 4 5 6 7 8 9 10

The organization is well organized with clearly defined goals.

6. **Warmth and support**. The feeling that friendliness is a valued norm in the organization, that members trust one another and offer support to one another. The feeling that good relationships prevail in the work environment.

There is no warmth and support in the organization.

1 2 3 4 5 6 7 8 9 10

Warmth and support are very characteristic of the organization.

7. **Leadership**. The willingness of organizational members to accept leadership and direction from qualified others. As needs for leadership arise, members feel free to take leadership roles and are rewarded for successful leadership. Leadership is based on expertise. The organization is not dominated by, or dependent on, one or two individuals.

Leadership is not rewarded; members are dominated or dependent on hierarchical leaders; leadership attempts by others are resisted.

1 2 3 4 5 6 7 8 9 10

Shaded leadership based on expertise is accepted and rewarded.

8. What are the dominant values of this organization?

9. What are some of the behavioral norms of the organization that an outsider or a newcomer would quickly notice?

10. How do the leaders of the organization reinforce these values and norms?

11. How are newcomers socialized in this organization?

12. Does this culture help or hinder the organization in terms of performance?

13. What do you want to learn about organizational culture and socialization?

THE ECOQUEST CASE, PART I

Ecoquest is a Memphis consulting firm specializing in environmental analyses used by businesses and developers. Because the firm helps clients comply with environmental laws, its work has to be very reliable. If mistakes are made, both the firm and its clients could be sued. The company was founded two years ago by two women and a man with various backgrounds in environmental science and engineering. They had become friends while employed at a large firm in Atlanta with clients all over the Southeast. Fed up with the poor management and red tape at their former firm, they became convinced that they would do better on their own. A year after the founders launched Ecoquest, an environmental policy expert with a finance background bought into the company, making a total of four principals.

Due to the principals' reputation for giving clients what they want, Ecoquest quickly gained a respectable share of the market and no longer has to worry daily about bringing in enough business to survive. The firm has added employees over time and currently employs 21 staff members. The four principals work directly with clients and also supervise the work of 14 environmental experts and technicians, who form project teams. Three support staff are responsible for administrative work and the final preparation of client reports. Most of the staff are idealistic and very pleased to be working in the environmental field. What they like best about the company are its flexible work hours and the opportunity to work with knowledgeable, team-oriented colleagues. The principals are concerned about both attracting and retaining good staff.

Preparing the analyses for clients involves a good deal of teamwork. The office becomes very hectic around deadlines because the work of several people must be pulled together and compiled into flawless reports. Each project is supervised by one of the principals. Given the liability concerns in the field, a second principal always reviews each report before it goes out the door to make sure there are no errors.

Ecoquest is housed on the first floor of a small office building on the fringe of downtown Memphis. Its quarters are cramped and utilitarian. In some offices, reports are stacked in formidable piles on the floor. One of the principals shares her office with two other employees. The CEO's office is slightly more elegant than the others but still fairly small. The lobby has one modest chair in close proximity to the receptionist's desk. Although the principals have offices with windows, most of the employees work in cubicles located in the center of the office. Employees have all the equipment they need, and the computer system and laboratory are state of the art. The only works of art in the office are posters with environmental themes. Employee cubicle decor varies widely from family pictures to red chile pepper lights. The bulletin board by the coffeemaker is overflowing with announcements of training courses, outdoor recreational events, and cartoons poking fun at environmentalists. Casually dressed employees walk around quickly as if they are on deadline, but they take the time to tease each other as they go. The office is known for bantering and practical jokes.

When they planned the company, the original principals wanted to create a firm that provided quality service to customers in a fun, participative workplace. They wanted their employees, all well-educated professionals, to feel empowered—something that was lacking in the large firm they came from. They also wanted to make more money, which has become a reality for the principals. At present, however, the firm is experiencing growing pains. They were not planning to grow so quickly, if at all, but it seemed foolish to turn down business. In addition to the outgrown office space, employees are starting to complain about unclear policies, lack of input into decisions, and not knowing whom to go to with certain requests. (Actually, the more savvy employees have figured out which principal is likely to say yes to which request.) It takes the principals longer to make decisions than employees think it should. Employees receive year-end bonuses based on a joint decision by the principals, but there is no formal performance evaluation process. The major problem facing Ecoquest, however, is the unexpected illness of its CEO, Chel (pronounced like "shell") Morrison.

Chel, the majority owner of the firm, is a dynamic environmental engineer in her late forties. She is extremely good with clients and goes all out to provide them with the service they want. Some say she goes too far and asks for too many sacrifices on the part of both employees and the firm's bottom line to satisfy clients. For example, when legitimate extra expenses are involved in a project, Chel refuses to charge clients more than the estimated cost. Chel is popular with the staff. She wants them to enjoy their work, and she and the other principals are generous with benefits. Her major flaw is lack of delegation, which has turned into a vicious circle. Chel's excuse is that her employees do not have the experience or skills that she does, which is partly true. As a result, she works 80 to 100 hours a week and has no time to develop the employees. Last month, Chel was diagnosed with a serious autoimmune deficiency disease that is usually related to stress.

Chel's illness has thrown the company into turmoil. Someone else has to take over the CEO position because Chel's doctors do not think she will be able to return to work any time soon, if ever. The other three principals talked the succession issue over but could not agree which of them should be the CEO. All of them are interested in the position. Since the discussion looked as if it might turn into a divisive argument, the principals suggested that their two outside board members should make the decision with Chel's guidance. There may well be some hard feelings no matter who is chosen. However, the three contenders have agreed to accept whatever decision is made and support the new CEO. They refuse, however, to consider bringing in an outsider to be CEO. Chel and the two outside board members have opted to hire a small business consulting firm (you) to help them select Chel's successor. Their goal is to choose a CEO who will contribute to the firm's continued success. The profiles of the candidates, the three principals, follow.

Mike Lewis

Mike is an environmental engineer in his late 40s. He is very knowledgeable and has a good reputation in his field. Mike bought into the firm a year later than the other principals because he was working overseas at the time. He is an exacting boss who is very detail oriented. He expects a lot of himself as well as others. Unlike the other principals who want as little structure and bureaucracy as possible, Mike likes to set up policies and track figures. Mike has often argued with Chel about overemphasizing client service at the expense of making a profit. He caused a ruckus in the office by distributing a ranked list of employees from the most to the least profitable. This was perceived as unfair by employees who did more administrative work or who worked on long-term projects that appeared less profitable than short-term projects in his rating system. Those at the bottom of the list were embarrassed or somewhat demoralized. Nevertheless, employees respect Mike and his expertise.

Anita Sanchez

Anita, a woman in her mid-40s, has a Ph.D. in environmental biology. She is good at developing employees, working on teams, and building a sense of community. Anita was the one who insisted on company outings, such as the annual "in-tents" camping trip. She has also been encouraging the other principals to create a mentoring program for employees. She and Chel have been good friends for 15 years. Since the firm's inception, they have worked together so closely in getting new business that it is difficult to know whether Anita is capable of bringing in business on her own. Anita is, however, a very hard worker. She has more people skills than financial skills. In the past, she has taken less interest in the financial side of the business, and the board does not know whether that is due to a greater preoccupation with projects or an inability to master that area. Recently Anita has been scuffling with Mike over his ranking system. She is afraid employees will start to cut corners on quality just to look good on paper and get a higher bonus.

Kent Chang

Kent, in his late 50s, worked in corporate finance before going back to school to study environmental policy. He handles financial matters for Ecoquest and interprets government environmental regulations for clients. Kent is a bit less entrepreneurial than the others, but he enjoys good relationships with clients that Chel and others bring in. His relations with other employees are cordial but a little distant and more formal. Because his work is somewhat more specialized, he is used to working more independently than the others. Like Chel, he is not as used to delegating as are Mike and Anita. While he dislikes paperwork and bureaucracy, Kent has a slightly more traditional approach to management and believes that decisions should be made quickly by the CEO. As the firm becomes larger, he thinks it will need "a stronger hand" to hold things together and avoid confusion. Kent sees himself as the best replacement for Chel because he has the most years of work experience and a financial background that will become increasingly important as Ecoquest continues to grow. Although he promised to support the new CEO, he seems the most likely candidate to be offended if he is not chosen.

Your Task

The concerns of succession and continuity are complex problems, and many factors are involved in successfully dealing with such problems. Please analyze this case by answering the following questions. Be prepared to back up your opinions in class when you will work with a team of consultants to prepare your final report for Ecoquest.

1. How would you describe the organizational culture of Ecoquest? List the firm's values and the evidence that supports your claim.

2. What do you see as the major strengths and weaknesses of the three candidates?

3. Which candidate would you recommend as the new CEO of Ecoquest?

4. What is your rationale for this choice? What kind of leadership style does the company need now?

5. How would you rank the other candidates?

6. A change of leadership is a good opportunity to make sure that all aspects of the organization are in alignment. Without this "fit," new leaders might fail or current problems may not be addressed. What organizational changes should be made to ensure that your recommended CEO candidate is successful?

7. What should the new CEO do to maintain or change Ecoquest's organizational culture?

THE KNOWLEDGE BASE

Organizational culture is one of the key elements that determine organizational performance.[1] Organizational culture can either facilitate or impede the organization's mission as well as change efforts to improve performance. Today, consultants and businesspeople talk about culture as the DNA of the organization and the "personality of the firm."[2] Many companies identify and communicate their values and try to develop a culture that will help them achieve their strategy, such as high-performance cultures or customer-oriented cultures. More and more firms use selection practices that identify prospective employees who fit the culture. "In an organization whose employees are self-motivating and largely self-directed, the compass that steers them in the way the organization wants them to go is its culture. Toyota has 580 different companies around the world, 51 factories outside Japan, and sells cars in more than 170 countries. What holds these operations together and makes them part of a single entity, says Takis Athanasopoulos, the head of its European operations, is the company's strong corporate culture."[3] Cultural values and traditions can be a roadblock to achieving strategic goals and needed organizational changes. Therefore, understanding organizational culture and how it is created, maintained, and changed has become a necessity for all organization members and, in particular, for the managers and leaders who are its stewards.

   Schein defines organizational culture as follows:

Organizational culture is the pattern of basic assumptions that a given group has invented, discovered, or developed in learning to cope with its problems of external adaptation and internal integration, and that have worked well enough to be considered valid, and, therefore, to be taught to new members as the correct way to perceive, think, and feel in relation to those problems.[4]

In simple terms, organizational culture is the pattern of shared assumptions, values and beliefs that lead to certain norms of behavior,[5] in other words, "the way we do things around here." Schein refers to three levels of culture:

1. Artifacts that are visible or tangible (e.g., organizational stories, buildings, rituals and ceremonies, stories, language)
2. Espoused values, such as strategies, goals, and philosophies (e.g., the company mission)
3. Assumptions, which are unconscious, taken-for-granted beliefs, perceptions, thoughts, and feelings (e.g., it's more important to save face than correct a problem)

The "Toyota Way" describes the espoused values that comprise Toyota's culture and, ideally, guide its employees' daily decision making:

- **Kaizen**—Continuous improvement which is embedded in the belief that employees should come to work each day with the goal of becoming better than the day before.
- **Genchi genbutsu**—Translates roughly as "go to the source" for facts rather than relying on hearsay. Consensus is easier to build around arguments based on facts instead of opinions.
- **Challenge**—See problems as challenges that will help improve performance.
- **Teamwork**—Share knowledge and put the firm's interests ahead of individual interests.
- **Respect for other people**—Express different opinions in ways that are respectful to others, as people and for their skills and knowledge.[6]

Many organizations have a list of values posted on their walls. Some companies take it even further and pass out laminated cards for employees carry in their wallets or purses. The key point, however, is whether employees actually enact or live by espoused values. The opening vignette, "The Fabric of Creativity," seems to prove that the values Bill Gore identified years ago, shown here, do successfully guide the way employees work and treat others:[7]

- Fairness to each other and everyone with whom we come in contact
- Freedom to encourage, help, and allow other associates to grow in knowledge, skill, and scope of responsibility
- The ability to make one's own commitments and keep them
- Consultation with other associates before undertaking actions that could impact the reputation of the company

In a large organization, there is usually a dominant culture accompanied by various subcultures.[8] The *dominant culture manifests the values shared by a majority of the organization's members. Subcultures usually share the dominant culture's core values as well as other values that characterize their own department, geographical unit,* and so on. For example, the accounting department at Gore may be more structured than the dominant culture, because accountants have a professional subculture that influences their behavior no matter where they work. Some organizations also have *countercultures, whose values are in opposition to those of the dominant culture.* We should be on the lookout for subcultures and countercultures and try to figure out why they exist and what function they serve. When they have more contact with customers or the environment, these groups sometimes develop unique values that are exactly what the larger organization will need for future adaptation.

What is the function of organizational culture? Culture serves as the glue that holds the organization together. Culture also provides members with a sense of identity, generates commitment to something larger than self-interest, and helps people make sense of what occurs in the organization and the environment. Furthermore, strong organizational cultures serve the same control function as the cultural rules we learn in childhood. When groups of people share the same behavioral norms, there is less need for external controls and close supervision. Corporate cultures can be either ethical or unethical, depending on the values, traditions and norms they have developed. Cultures that promote ethical behavior were high in both risk and conflict tolerance and have members who identify with the professional standards of their job.[9]

When dealing with unfamiliar organizations, one of our first tasks is to determine whether they really believe in the values they espouse. The rest of this chapter describes the elements that will help you decode organizational cultures.

SOURCES OF ORGANIZATIONAL CULTURE

The sources of organizational culture are basically: "(1) the beliefs, values, and assumptions of the founders, (2) the learning experiences of group members as their organization evolves; (3) new beliefs, values, and assumptions brought in by new members and leaders."[10] Other factors that influence the culture of an organization are the specific industry, the environment, and national culture.

Many organizational cultures reflect the personalities and values of their founders. For example, people who knew Bill Gates pre-Microsoft, during the early collaborative days of the computer revolution, noted his fierce competitiveness. This strong sense of competition is now synonymous with Microsoft and its dealings with other companies. Founders are natural role models for their employees. Schein states, "Founders often start with a theory of how to succeed; they have a cultural paradigm in their heads, based on their experience in the culture in which they grew up."[11] Similarly, founding groups (for example, the partners in Ecoquest) begin with some degree of consensus on their basic assumptions. Founders then hire and retain people who think like they do and take steps to socialize employees into this way of thinking and behaving.[12] Thus, it comes as no surprise that a study of organizational effectiveness found that the culture managers create is one of the most important contributions a manager can make.[13]

Invgar Kamprad, the founder of IKEA, the Swedish home furnishing company currently operating in 31 countries, has been especially good at transmitting his theory for success. A budding entrepreneur from an early age, he began IKEA at the age of 17 with a gift from his father for doing well in school. His theory of success was hard work and frugality, which he learned growing up in a poor farming region of Sweden. His words give you an idea about how he approaches life: "You can do so much in 10 minutes' time. Ten minutes, once gone, are gone for good. Divide your life into 10-minute units and sacrifice as few of them as possible in meaningless activity." Although the title for richest man in the world gets traded back and forth between Kamprad and Bill Gates depending on the exchange rate, Kamprad is notoriously thrifty. He takes the subway to work, drives an old Volvo, and, according to rumor, replaces whatever he takes from hotel wet bars with purchases from a nearby convenience store to avoid paying the higher hotel prices.[14] IKEA's goal is to provide home furnishings and accessories that are functional and well-designed at low prices that many customers can afford. This goal reflects Kamprad's frugality and his belief that IKEA exists to improve people's lives as well as the people themselves. The value he places on self-sufficiency is reflected in the self-service design of the stores and the easily assembled furniture (although less-mechanically inclined souls might argue about just how easy the assembly process is).

The values of the founder are clearly evident in IKEA's organizational culture, but so is the impact of solutions they developed for problems. Early in its history, IKEA was the target of a supplier boycott as a result of pressure from its competitors. IKEA's solution to this problem was to design its own furniture, which led to their current reputation for innovation and lower costs. An employee came up with the idea of folding a table's legs underneath when he was unable to fit a table into a car. This was the genesis of their flat packaging designs, which saved even more money.

Kamprad may live frugally, but IKEA is known for its community outreach, global philanthropic causes, and generosity to employees. The company is on 2005 *Working Mothers* list of "100 Best Companies" and on the list of *Fortune*'s "100 Best Companies to Work For." IKEA provides all employees, who are referred to as "coworkers," their domestic partners, and their children with medical and dental benefits. IKEA also gives the same benefits to its part-time coworkers, which is not common practice in today's retail industry. They offer paid maternity/paternity leaves and flexible work arrangements (flextime, job share, telecommuting, and condensed work weeks) to facilitate child care. Coworkers can eat for $2.00 during their shift and have 2–5 weeks of yearly paid vacation. IKEA helps both undergraduate and graduate students with tuition assistance. They offer so many training programs that they also appear on *Training Magazine's* "Training Top 100" list.

According to the North American president of IKEA, Pernille Lopez, the firm values respect and caring for each other, the environment, the community, and for those in need. The values of IKEA's organizational culture include diversity, openness, equality, cost consciousness, and competitiveness. These values, like the sense of style found in IKEA's products, may reflect Swedish culture. Kamprad understands the importance of organizational culture: "Maintaining a strong IKEA culture is one of the most crucial factors behind the continued success of the IKEA concept."[15]

One of the keys to maintaining a strong successful culture is acknowledging the importance of both internal and external "fit." Organizational effectiveness is more likely to occur when the following aspects are in alignment:

- The people in the organization, and their abilities and motives
- The organization's tasks and the kinds of behavior needed to accomplish those tasks most effectively
- The organization's external environment and the demands it makes on the organization for creativity, flexibility, quality, and so on
- The strategy, which dictates how an organization attempts to position itself in relation to its competitors
- The organization's culture as determined by the leadership styles of management and the organization's structure and values

The goal of organization design is to match people with tasks that inspire them and best utilize their abilities and to design tasks and a strategy that can cope with environmental demands and opportunities. The organizational culture should reinforce these efforts. One of the reasons Toyota has been so successful for so many years is the alignment among these aspects. Their focus on lean production reflects the values of Toyota's leaders.

Two important aspects of culture are internal integration of new members and external adaptation to the environment.

Internal Integration and Strong Cultures. One of the key aspects of culture is to foster the internal integration of new members and ensure that its members fit the culture. This is especially pronounced in strong cultures, which have the following characteristics:[16]

- People in the organization can easily identify the dominant values.
- The selection processes target people who are likely to fit into the culture and find it satisfying.
- Socialization and training convey to newcomers the "ropes" they need to learn.
- Employees who do not fit the culture or produce in accordance with its values are sometimes fired.
- People within the company are rewarded for acting in accordance with the dominant values of the organization.
- By their behavior, leaders and managers send clear, consistent signals about desired values and norms.
- Managers measure and control what is important to the culture.

Examples of organizations with strong cultures are Southwest Airlines, Intel, Hyundai, and The Body Shop.

Strong cultures are "thicker" than weak cultures. *Strong cultures have core values and beliefs that are intensely held, more widely shared and more ordered.* By this we mean that cultural members know which values are more important relative to other values. For example, the value of customer service trumps (is given priority over) a value like informality.[17] Employees are less likely to resign from organizations with a strong culture[18] because they are generally more cohesive and committed. A stable workforce contributes to a strong culture since employees themselves are the carriers and the institutional memory; excessive downsizing or turnover can weaken or even break down an organizational culture.

Because of the intensity and consensus of shared values in a strong culture, the individual-culture fit is important. Employees are more likely to succeed in an organization that has values similar to their own. During the hiring process, both candidates and the company should attempt to determine whether this fit is present.

External Adaptation. Although organizational cultures result in control, alignment, and motivation, these contributions do not yield high performance unless there is a fit with the environment. This brings us to the second aspect of culture, external adaptation. Lack of external adaptation or fit was the impetus for some of the widespread restructuring that industries have undergone in recent years. In addition to outdated strategies, structures, technology, and employee skills, many companies had cultures that did not fit a rapidly changing global economy.

Because so many excellent companies had strong organizational cultures, there seemed to be a relationship between strong culture and high performance. Research has found that companies with strong cultures perform better than companies with weak cultures.[19] One study supports this assumption when leadership is also present. Kotter and Keskett found that corporate culture can in fact have a significant impact on a firm's long-term economic performance. Firms with strong cultures that focused on all the key constituencies (customers, stockholders, and employees) and that had leadership from managers at all levels outperformed other firms without these characteristics. "Over an 11-year period, the former increased revenues by an average of 682 percent versus 166 percent for the latter, expanded their work forces by 282 percent versus 36 percent, grew their stock prices by 901 percent versus 74 percent, and improved their net incomes by 756 percent versus 1 percent."[20] They predict that corporate culture will probably be an even more important factor in determining company success or failure in the next decade. Cultures, even strong ones, that are not adaptive or change oriented may not survive. Thus, the culture-environment fit warrants a good deal of attention.

In addition to high performance under certain conditions, the advantages of a strong culture include the following: clear sense of purpose, commitment and loyalty, pride in working for the organization, and values that serve as standards of reference for decision making. Strong corporate cultures are also difficult to copy, so they can constitute a competitive advantage, which is increasingly important to success.[21] However, strong cultures also have the disadvantages of resistance to change and conformity.[22] Strong cultures exert more pressure for conformity than weak cultures, which may decrease the tolerance for individual differences unless valuing diversity is one of the culture's values. Strong cultures run the risk of becoming obsolete if the company does not value learning and staying attuned to its environment and customers.

Many companies with strong cultures that were successful in the past failed to adapt as the environment changed. Their cultures became arrogant, inwardly focused, politicized, and bureaucratic. Managerial self-interest took precedence over concern for customers, stockholders, and employees when effective leadership was lacking. Previous success often led the companies to resist innovation and continue with strategies and policies that were no longer viable.[23] Employees who wanted to change such companies often became discouraged and quit because they no longer fit the culture. If a culture is self-sealing and refuses to consider new assumptions, its very strength can become a weakness.

Many outstanding organizations have followed ... paths of deadly momentum—time-bomb trajectories of attitudes, policies, and events that lead to falling sales, plummeting profits, even bankruptcy. ... Productive attention to detail, for instance, turns into an obsession with minutia; rewarding innovation escalates into gratuitous invention; and measured growth becomes unbridled expansion.[24]

The banking industry was once known for its strong organizational cultures; when the external environments changed due to deregulation, these stable and inbred cultures became a threat to their survival. The survivors learned to play a different game and developed more competitive and innovative organizational cultures. IBM was also known for its strong culture, complete with an extensive language all its own. At one point, they even had what amounted to a "uniform"—

dark blue suits and white shirts. Historically, IBM culture was seen as an advantage. In the early 1990s, however, its slowness and arrogance was blamed for preventing IBM from adapting rapidly to environmental changes. The company broke with tradition and hired an outsider as CEO, Lou Gerstner. He had the following reaction to IBM culture, "I have never seen a company that is so introspective, caught up in its own underwear, so preoccupied with internal processes. People in this company tell me it's easier to do business with people outside the company than inside. I would call that an indictment."[25]

Gerstner was successful in turning around IBM and making the culture more cooperative and customer oriented. He was succeeded by Sam Palmisano, a veteran IBM-er, who has emphasized the strengths of the firm's original culture. Palmisano dismantled the 92-year-old executive management committee, claiming it just slowed down decisions, and replaced it with three diverse teams of people from various parts of the firm. Palmisano dislikes the idea of a celebrity CEO and expects creativity to come from all over a large organization, not just the CEO. He had the board cut his 2003 bonus and put it into a pool to be shared as a performance bonus with about 20 top executives. Palmisano's guiding strategy is called e-business on demand, in which computing power functions like electricity or water and customers pay only for what they use. His blue prints for making this happen? An egalitarian culture that fits with the reliance on teamwork; bureaucracy-busting big decisions; a unifying goal—e-business on demand—that cuts across fiefdoms; becoming an agenda setter once again; being a talent magnet by training managers to lead rather than control their staff; squeaky clean finances; and good works.[26] IBM employees have held the record for the highest number of community volunteer hours.

Palmisano wanted IBM to model the concepts it was selling, so the company transformed its own technological infrastructure to foster collaboration. The company had a 72-hour online chat session with employees that resulted in the selection of three values for the 21st century: (1) "Dedication to every client's success"; (2) "Innovation that matters, for our company and for the world"; and (3) "Trust and personal responsibility in all relationships."[27] IBM created an online suggestion box, named "Think Place," where all employees can read and modify suggestions; 300 of the first 4,500 were adopted. Linda Sanford, senior vice-president, described how IBM resolved a technical problem caused by Hurricane Katrina: "Using our Blue Pages Plus expertise locator on the corporate intranet, we found the right people within the space of an hour or two, and had a wiki [a Web page that can be edited by anyone with access] up and running. Using the wiki as a virtual meeting room, a team of IBMers from the US, Germany, and the UK were able to offer a solution to the problem in the space of just a few days."[28]

In a company once known for lifelong employment of men in blue suits, 50 percent of its current employees have been with the firm for less than five years, 30 percent are women, and 40 percent are "mobile," which means that they do not go to work every day at the same IBM facility.[29] IBM's financial success rests in part on their ability to adapt to a changing environment and to modify the elements of their culture that impede adaptation without losing the essential values that make the company unique.

Organizations need people who question cultural values and suggest different assumptions. For this reason, it comes as no surprise that one study found that companies with well-organized workplaces and strong participative cultures performed better than other firms.[30] Presumably, the value placed on participation would allow for the expression of different opinions and assumptions about the external environment. Another alternative is to hire managers from the outside who bring in fresh perspectives and are more likely to question cultural assumptions. One of the dilemmas in organizations is finding the right degree of stability and flexibility. Managers need to understand and respect past history while simultaneously ensuring that organizational learning and adaptation are taking place.

Leaders can affect an established organizational culture, but they cannot unilaterally determine what that culture should be.[31] Culture emerges from a consensus held by people in a social system. Cultures take time to develop and are slow to change because cultural values are internalized and provide us with part of our identity. Thus, managers should not see cultural change as a quick fix. Nevertheless, it is possible to instill certain values and reward certain behaviors. Consistency is essential in managing culture. Too many companies have an official set of cultural values that does not represent the real values that are acted out in the organization. Employees quickly spot the hypocrisy when managers do not "walk the talk."

TRANSMITTING CULTURE

Culture is transmitted through various mechanisms: socialization, stories, symbols, jargon and language, rituals and ceremonies, and statements of principles.[32]

Socialization

Socialization is the systematic process by which organizations bring new members into their cultures. Socialization is the process of becoming a member of a group, learning the ropes, and being taught how to communicate and interact to get things done.

Strong cultures use a socialization process that consists of the following seven steps:[33]

1. **Careful selection of entry-level candidates** Candidates who do not fit the culture are encouraged to deselect themselves and apply elsewhere.
2. **Humility-inducing experiences that cause newcomers to question prior behavior, beliefs, and values** Boot camp performs this function in the military; businesses may put new employees through extensive and demanding training programs that leave them with no time to do anything else. Other companies use upending experiences to induce the humility that allows newcomers to learn with an open mind. In one company, newly graduated engineers are given a problem to solve that does not conform to the theories learned in school. When they inevitably fail, they realize they still have more to learn at the company. The humility and self-examination triggered by experiences such as these make it more likely that newcomers will buy into the company's values.
3. **In-the-trenches training that leads to mastery of one of the business's core disciplines** Employees work their way up the ranks, and promotion depends on a proven track record.
4. **Meticulous attention given to rewards and control systems** The company's critical success factors (the limited number of factors that are central to a firm's performance) and corporate values are monitored. They are included in the performance appraisal system, and employees are rewarded and promoted for contributing to the success factors and behaving in accordance with cultural values.
5. **Careful adherence to the firm's core values** Managers ensure that their own decisions and actions are consistent with stated values. As a result, employees are more likely to make personal sacrifices for the organization.
6. **Reinforcing folklore** The company stories and legends told to newcomers always reinforce the values of the corporate culture. For example, there is a Procter & Gamble story about one of its best brand managers who was fired for exaggerating a product's features. The moral of this story is that making ethical claims is more important than making money.[34]
7. **Consistent role models** Cultural heroes and "winners" consistently exhibit the traits valued by the organization's culture. For example, the Morgan and Stanley employees identified as having high potential exhibit the energy, aggressiveness, and team play demanded by their culture.

The consistency and careful thought that characterize this socialization process make it possible to effectively transmit and maintain a strong organizational culture.

Stories

The importance of stories as reinforcing folklore was mentioned in the socialization process. All organizations have stories that are repeated to newcomers. They often explain what's important in the culture and legitimize how the organization does things. Many of these stories contain a moral that prescribes how members should act. Others describe how the organization overcame hardship or the shining moments that make members proud. To transmit its culture to newcomers, Hewlett-Packard has several stories that are told in various settings—training classes, management meetings, retirement parties, and newsletters. Some of the most common HP stories describe:[35]

- How Bill and Dave (as Hewlett and Packard are commonly addressed) started the company with $538 in the garage behind Dave's rented house. Bill rented a spare room there.
- How they called their first instrument the 200A (rather than using a lower number) so that people would not know they were just starting out.
- How Bill Hewlett challenged HP labs to build a scientific calculator he could put in his shirt pocket, which led to the introduction of the world's first small scientific calculator and one of HP's most important business segments.

Symbols

Symbols also transmit culture and convey meaning. The famous pink Cadillacs awarded to successful saleswomen symbolize Mary Kay Cosmetics' cultural values of determination and achievement. Company slogans also communicate the company's values. Material objects such as the type of building and office decor often tell us something about a company's culture—whether it values, for example, informality, prestige, or frugality. In the opening vignette, Gore's facilities are described as functional, rather than ostentatious, barely visible to those driving by, and designed to be small enough to facilitate teamwork and cross-fertilization. This seems consistent with a privately held firm that values substance over style, and innovation and collaboration over hierarchy and structure. The frugality of the family founders may also be expressed in the choice of buildings.

In many organizations, the hiring office is a sterile, utilitarian setting, even though it represents the first contact and the first impression with a potential employee. Most of us can probably remember sitting uncomfortably on folding chairs in a hiring office hidden away in the bowels of a large building. If anything, such offices communicate that employees are not very important in the grand scheme of things. In contrast, Disney takes great care to convey a symbolic message about its cultural values and mission to potential employees who go to their employment office, which is called the Casting Center. The building itself looks like a Venetian palace, and the doors are replicas from Alice in Wonderland. "The physical design reminds everyone of the magic that Disney seeks to create for its guests and employees. ... The message communicated to the applicant through this physical design is: "You are entering a different world; this isn't your typical employment office. Be prepared for new and unusual things; also be prepared to have some fun."[36]

Jargon and Language

Organizations sometimes develop their own language or slang. Some organizations, such as the military and government bureaucracies, use so many acronyms that outsiders and newly hired employees do not understand what they are talking about. The employees' use of a shorthand form of communication identifies them as members of the culture. Microsoft employees use the term 'dogfood' to indicate that a new product is being used and tested by Microsoft employees before it is sold to the public.

> *Apparently the term comes from that old advertising industry joke about the agency that just couldn't seem to come up with a successful campaign for a dogfood company. Punchline: "The dogs just didn't like the dogfood," meaning, no amount of effort can sell a lousy product. At Microsoft they like to say, "We eat our own dogfood."*[37]

The choice of language that organizations use is another indication of its culture. Volunteers are responsible for 95 percent of the programmatic experiences that 26,000 girls receive from the Girl Scouts—Arizona Cactus Pine Council. Without them, the paid staff could not deliver their programs. Yet, Tamara Woodbury, council CEO, concluded that the language they used led volunteers to think that they were not trusted:[38]

> *In a four-page brochure to introduce new volunteers to Girl Scouting, the words must, mandatory, or required came up 84 times in a simple word search. In our zeal to promote the health and safety of the girls, we had unknowingly used command-and-control language that implicitly communicated that we did not trust our volunteers to make their own decisions in the best interest of the girls. When we further examined our organizational practices and training curricula, we realized we had assumed that the behavior of our volunteers and staff could be controlled through the use of rulemaking, mandatory training, rigid boundary-setting, and organizational authority. ... Over time, these practices had begun to generate unintended consequences in our organization's culture ... we had, in effect, exiled innovation, creativity— and anyone who wanted to do things differently.*

Woodbury concluded that leaders throughout her organization must not only "walk the talk" but also "talk the talk." As a result, they rewrote their materials to present information, guidelines, and tips and cut way down on rules and paperwork. The guiding principle behind these and other cultural changes were to promote, rather than command, the personal commitment of volunteers to do what is best for the girl scouts for whom they are responsible.

Rituals and Ceremonies

Rituals are programmed routines of daily life that reflect the values of a corporate culture. How employees communicate with one another and how meetings are run are both examples of rituals. The Friday beer busts in some high-tech companies symbolize the informality and cross-fertilization valued in these cultures. Ceremonies are planned events for the benefit of audiences, such as induction ceremonies for new members or graduation-like ceremonies when members pass to another level. The award ceremonies in many organizations emphasize the accomplishments of organizational "heroes." In organizations that value loyalty, these ceremonies may simply celebrate the number of years employees have worked for them.

Statements of Principles

Many organizations create and distribute a list of their values and basic assumptions. It is not uncommon to see such principles displayed on office walls. Sometimes they are included in a firm's code of ethics. Southwest Airlines lives by and emphasizes the following fundamentals in every training course it offers to 25,000 employees a year.

Fundamental 1: Hire for Attitude; Train for Skill. Employees must have a sense of humor, positive attitude, and a desire to have fun at Southwest Airlines.

Fundamental 2: Do It Better, Faster, Cheaper. Cost control is viewed as the personal responsibility of all employees.

Fundamental 3: Deliver Positively Outrageous Customer Service (POS) to Both Internal and External Customers. Put employees first and they will automatically take care of customers, who come second.

Fundamental 4: Walk a Mile in Someone Else's Shoes. Employees volunteer to spend a day learning other jobs so they understand the whole operation.

Fundamental 5: Take Accountability and Ownership. Employees are encouraged to take initiative and think for themselves.

Fundamental 6: Celebrate and Let Your Hair Down. Based on studies showing that productivity and performance improves when people have fun on the job, Southwest has zany parties and celebrations, like chili cook-offs and Christmas in July, to keep employees motivated.

Fundamental 7: Celebrate Your Mistakes as Well as Your Triumphs. Southwest wants employees to continue learning and trying new ideas.

Fundamental 8: Keep the Corporate Culture Alive and Well. Southwest has a culture committee headed by an Executive Vice-President that travels around the country inculcating the culture so it is not lost.[39]

ORGANIZATIONAL JUSTICE

One of the most important values of organizational cultures is fairness. Employees are concerned about three types of justice in the workplace that, in combination, are referred to as *organizational justice*.[40] *Distributive justice* refers to fairness regarding the distribution of resources—pay, rewards, promotions, and dispute resolutions. *Procedural justice* describes the fairness of decision-making procedures that are used to determine how resources are distributed. *Interactional justice* refers to the treatment employees receive from others, particularly authority figures.

Within organizational cultures, members develop expectations about fairness. When their expectations are met, positive outcomes result—performance and compliance. For example, smokers who were personally informed and given information about a smoking ban were more likely to comply with the ban, even though it went against their personal interests.[41] Employees are also more likely to trust managers, cooperate with coworkers, and engage in organizational citizenship behavior when organizational justice exists.[42]

When employee expectations about justice are disappointed, negative outcomes result. Some take the form of withdrawal behaviors: higher turnover, absenteeism, and employee silence (failure to speak up). For example, in one study employees who perceived that work decisions were arbitrary and failed to take their views into consideration were more likely to take sick days; sick days increased by 41 percent for men and 12 percent for women who perceived their workplace as unfair.[43] Lack of organizational justice is a stronger predictor of turnover intent than job satisfaction.[44] This means that even when employees are otherwise satisfied with their work, they will go elsewhere if they have been treated unfairly. This makes organizational justice a key factor in retention. Rather than quit, some employees react to unfair treatment with workplace violence and counterproductive behaviors like theft, sabotage, disciplinary problems, and so forth.

MERGERS

The failure rate for mergers and acquisitions (M&A) is roughly 50 percent.[45] Seventy percent of mergers fail to generate the expected revenue synergies and shareholder returns diminished in two-thirds of mergers.[46] The reasons behind failed mergers range from economic problems or a lack of fit, to poor implementation in getting the merger to work. When companies are considering a merger or acquisition, they typically perform due diligence by analyzing the strategic and financial aspects and identifying potential problems. However, an audit of their respective organizational cultures is equally important because mergers often fail due to cultural clashes. Such audits identify the artifacts, espoused values, and assumptions for each firm and determine whether they constitute potential problems or common ground. Integration teams then figure out ways to reduce or eliminate cultural clashes and enhance the synergy that can result from combining the best of two corporate cultures. Other options occur when the acquiring firm adopts the culture of the acquired firm, or the two firms try to work independently and retain their individual cultures. Until recently, many acquiring firms have assumed that the merged firm should adapt to their culture because they are the buyers. Simply imposing the culture of one firm on the other usually results in serious problems rather than the shared values that merger partners need to move forward.[47]

The challenges are even more complex in international mergers, such as Daimler-Chrysler, where cultural differences play a role.[48] Unlike the Daimler-Chrysler merger, the Nissan-Renault alliance has been touted as an example of a successful international merger in the automotive industry. CEO Carlos Ghosn attributed its success to making business goals the priority rather than getting bogged down in the process, to the attitudes and behavior of top management (e.g., their integrity and accountability) and to these behavioral dimensions: being open-minded, listening carefully to everyone, focusing on the prize (goal-oriented), and acting fast.[49] Some experts recommend that companies considering a merger first work together on joint ventures to see whether their cultures are compatible.[50]

One of the most interesting mergers to watch is K-Mart and Sears, Roebuck & Company. Both cultures have been described as inward looking rather than focused on customers. To address this problem, changes in the work flow were implemented to provide employees with more time on the floor interacting with customers. All Sears headquarters employees have to spend a day toiling in a store—something many of them have never done. CEO Aylwin Lewis identified 500 high potential leaders who are required to attend a one-day course in groups of forty; the course is entitled, "Sowing the Seeds of Our Culture," and is run by Lewis himself. This indicates the importance he places on building a joint culture that is more collaborative and competitive.[51]

MANAGING ORGANIZATIONAL CULTURE

Creating, maintaining, or changing a corporate culture that employees value is an important managerial task. Changing an organizational culture is not a quick process because of all the organizational elements that are aligned with the values that are targeted for change. Often the first step in changing a culture is introducing a more participative management style that allows people to openly discuss the culture and its impact.

How do leaders create and change organizational culture? Schein identified a set of primary and secondary mechanisms.[52]

Primary Mechanisms

1. **What leaders pay attention to, measure, and control on a regular basis** If managers talk about the importance of continuous improvement (TQM) but show no interest in the improvements suggested by employee groups, employees correctly discern that quality is not a value of this organizational culture. In contrast, if managers monitor and evaluate quality improvements, this sends out the opposite message and reinforces the value of producing quality products. Similarly, when the CEO visits the R&D lab the first thing every morning, this is a clear signal that innovation is a value of the organizational culture.

2. **How leaders react to critical incidents and organizational crises** What happens, for example, when the company faces a downturn in business or a cash flow problem? Does upper management immediately start firing lower-level employees or does everyone make sacrifices (e.g., four-day workweeks or across-the-board pay cuts for everyone) and start looking for creative solutions? The response shows employees what the company values.

3. **How leaders allocate scarce resources** What criteria are used to make decisions about resources? How does the organization create its budgets? What gets funded? What are acceptable levels of financial risk? Budget decisions and the budget process itself reflect cultural values and beliefs. For example, a company that utilizes bottom-up budgets may do so because it values entrepreneurial managers. A top-down process may reflect a paternalistic culture that does not value participation.

4. **Deliberate role modeling, teaching, and coaching** One international manager was a master at recreating the organizational culture in new overseas offices. Since he was the only person in the office with in-depth knowledge of how the organization functioned, he had new employees come to his office to review their work during the first month. He used this opportunity to correct their mistakes, teach them the finer points of their jobs, answer their questions, hear their suggestions, and explain how their work fit into the broader picture of the local office and the international organization. He told them stories about the organization's heroes and success stories from other countries. At the same time, he developed a personal relationship with them and gained their loyalty and commitment. As a result, they felt comfortable going to him in the future with their concerns and ideas, even after the office had grown much larger and he no longer supervised their work directly. By doing this, he transmitted to them the values of the international headquarters and created a strong culture.

5. **How leaders allocate rewards and status**   We can analyze what type of behavior is rewarded to determine what the organization values. Are whistle-blowers who point out unethical practices congratulated and promoted, or are they shunned or even fired? Those who enact the key values of the organizational culture should be rewarded and respected. Otherwise, we cannot tell who are the cultural heroes whom we should try to emulate.

6. **How leaders recruit, select, promote, and excommunicate**   The question of who fits and does not fit the organizational culture and who deserves to play a key role figures either consciously or unconsciously in these personnel decisions. Companies that are concerned with creating a strong culture devote time and energy to hiring and promoting only those people whose values are compatible with those of the company. It is very difficult, if not impossible and unethical, to change people's personalities. Service companies in particular find it easier to hire people who already have a service ethic. There is, however, a danger in trying to obtain a perfect person-culture fit with every employee. Cultural deviants often keep organizations "honest" by questioning the culture's dominant assumptions and behaviors. Too much conformity is not healthy, so organizations are wise to pay attention to deviant views. Excommunication takes the form of either firing or being given a less important job (perhaps kicked upstairs) and isolated. Leaders sometimes fire senior managers who do not support their efforts to change corporate culture.

Secondary Mechanisms

1. **Organizational design and structure** (decision making, coordination, reporting, structure)
2. **Systems and procedures** (performance appraisal, information, control, decision support systems, etc.)
3. **Rites and rituals**
4. **Design of physical space, facades, and buildings**
5. **Stories about important events and people** (anecdotes, legends, myths, and parables)
6. **Formal statements of organizational philosophy, creeds, and charters**

A. G. Lafley was chosen as one of *Business Week's* 2005 Best Leaders because he utilized many of these mechanisms. Lafley "transformed a stodgy, insular culture into one that is nimbler and more open—P&G now gets 35 percent of its product ideas from outside companies or inventors. It has also outflanked rivals in design and innovation: The company had 5 of the top 10 best-selling consumer-product launches in 2005."[53] It is not impossible to change a culture, but it is a difficult task and one that is not accomplished overnight. Some experts claim it is a 4- to 10-year process. Successful cultural changes usually involve effective leaders, with either an outsider's perspective or an insider's long-term view of the culture's strengths and weaknesses, who take advantage of a propitious moment or crisis to mobilize support for a cultural change. Leaders create a new vision that they communicate with optimism and enthusiasm.[54] However, it is also important to "honor the past" and maintain some aspects of a culture for the sake of continuity.[55] According to Trice and Beyer, all cultural change is partial, and we cannot expect to completely eradicate a previous culture.[56]

We usually associate cultural change with a strong, visionary leader, but some cultural changes have bubbled up from the bottom of organizations, when management planted the seed and allowed workers the autonomy to make the necessary changes. Ford's focus on quality and customer service was a bottom-up change effort that changed the organizational culture.[57] Corning Glass Works' switch to a total quality culture used widespread education and training programs as the catalyst.[58]

Research studies on best practices identify common practices that result in high performance. In well-managed firms, executives and employees are encouraged to look for best practices outside their company that they can adopt to help them keep up with industry leaders. This is called "bringing the outside in." After studying high-performing companies, Gratton and Ghoshal also advised executives to "bring the inside out" by articulating and developing the "signature processes" that can give them a unique advantage.[59] Because these processes embody a company's values, history, and top executive team, they only fit and work successfully for the organization that develops them. They are not easily imitated by other firms, as shown in the following example.[60]

Nokia, the Finnish telecommunications firm, is ranked among the top 10 most valuable brands in the world by Interbrand Corporation. According to best practices for strategic planning, firms engage in an annual planning exercise with a small group of people. Nokia's unique adaptation, however, involves as many as 400 people every six months in a modular structure. The people are carefully chosen from all across the company to form teams that are asked to explore between five and fifteen themes, which senior management deems crucial for the firm. The teams interview experts, both internal and external to Nokia, during a two-month period and then meet for two days to compile their findings and identify any missing gaps in the information. Subsequently, they prepare reports, called Strategy Road Maps, for key employees. Due to the complexity of their technology and the fast cycle time in their industry, Nokia's signature process in strategic planning is a better fit for the firm even though it employs more speed and involvement than is generally found in best practices for strategy creation.[61]

SERVICE CULTURES AND ALIGNMENT

Many service firms today are trying to develop or maintain organizational cultures that result in excellent customer service.[62] Nordstrom and Singapore Airlines, for example, are known for their service cultures. Nordstrom employees ("Nordies") are encouraged to follow the company motto: "Respond to Unreasonable Customer Requests!" and engage in daily acts of "heroics" to go out of their way to provide extra customer service.[63] For starters, such firms take pains to hire friendly employees who come with a predisposition toward serving others, and then they teach them to be good listeners. Managers treat employees well because you can't chew out or exploit employees and then expect them to turn right around and be sweet to customers. Managers give employees the autonomy to meet customer needs by not handcuffing them with unnecessary red tape and the need for supervisor approval. Some firms, and hotels in particular, set a limit of how much money or complementary services employees have at their disposal to compensate for poor service. Companies analyze the contact points with customers, "the moments of truth" where customers decide whether or not their expectations of quality service have been met and set standards for quality service in these moments. But there is much more to creating and maintaining a customer-oriented culture. Exhibit16–1 lists many of the processes that need to be in alignment and provides suggestions for how they can be audited to ensure excellence in customer service.[64]

EXHIBIT 16-1 **Service Mission Alignment Factors and Possible Audit Items**

Internal Processes	Sample Audit Items
Strategic and Tactical Practices	
1. Departmental goals are aligned with customer service mission	Management specifically rewards unit/ department managers on how well they score on customer service measures
	Management specifically rewards managers on how well their unit/department provides excellent service to other units/departments
2. Environmental setting/physical design communicates customer service mission	Physical layout is customer friendly
	Temperature, lighting, and environmental conditions are customer friendly
3. Stories and celebrations focus on customer service excellence	Formal celebrations for employees who provide excellent customer service
	Formal recognitions and rewards for excellent

Internal Processes	Sample Audit Items
	customer service in the reward system
4. Top management walks the service talk	Management shows its commitment by setting an example for customer service
5. Performance standards are aligned with the service mission	Customer service excellence is part of each manager/supervisor's annual plan/goals/ objectives
	Established standards of service quality for all aspects of the service experience that customers or guests say are important to them
6. Budget allocations are aligned with the service mission	Departmental/unit supervisors have the financial resources to train employees on how to provide service excellence
	Employees are reminded that customer service is equally important with financial goals
Staffing Policies and Processes Factors	
7. Job descriptions include service mission	Every job description includes a responsibility for excellent customer service
8. Job ads include service mission	Recruitment literature mentions commitment to excellent customer service
9. Interviews include questions about commitment to service mission	Applicants are routinely asked about their customer service commitment
	One criterion used to determine who gets hired is customer service commitment
10. Orientation programs stress service mission	Orientation programs explain customer service commitment to new employees
11. Performance appraisals include and reward service mission	Commitment to excellent customer service is part of everyone's annual performance evaluation
	Poor customer service can lead to disciplinary action or termination
System Procedures and Design Factors	
12. Service quality systematically measured	Information on customer satisfaction is consistently gathered
	A procedure exists to fix customer service problems
13. Feedback on service quality systematically provided to all	Customer feedback is consistently shared with employees
	Unit/department customer service performance scores are systematically tracked over time and publicly shared across units/departments
14. Service delivery system design reflects service mission	The length of time customers wait for service is consistently recorded

Source: Adapted from J. C. Crotts, D. R. Dickson, R. C. Ford, "Aligning Organizational Processes with Mission: The Case of Service Excellence," *Academy of Management Executive* 19(3) (2005): 57.

THE ORGANIZATIONAL LIFE CYCLE

The leader's role in managing culture varies according to the stages of organizational growth that are explained in the following paragraphs. Organizations (like people) go through stages of growth and development.[65] Although the time spent in each stage varies, most organizations evolve in a predictable sequence. The typical stages in the organizational life cycle are the entrepreneurial stage, the collectivity stage, the formalization stage, and the elaboration stage, as shown in Exhibit 16–2.

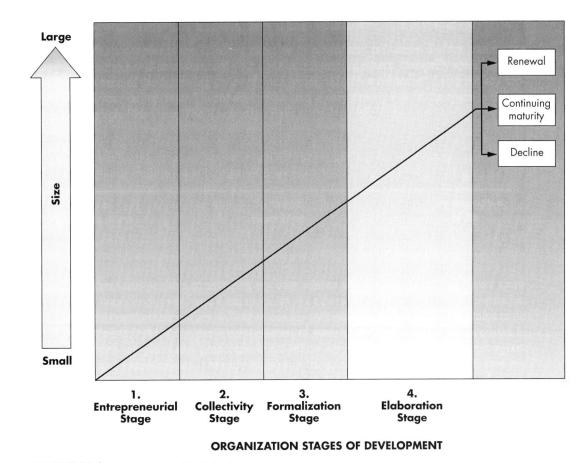

EXHIBIT 16-2 Organizational Life Cycle

1. **Entrepreneurial Stage** This is the start-up phase, driven by an entrepreneur with vision, energy, and a strong desire to succeed. At this point, the organization seldom has a formal structure; people pitch in to help wherever they are needed. The goals are to create a product and survive. Communication is informal and face-to-face. The entrepreneur makes most of the decisions and there is little formal planning. In this stage, creativity and morale are often high because people enjoy the challenge of being in on the ground floor of a new venture.

2. **Collectivity Stage** If the organization survives the entrepreneurial stage (and many do not), it moves to stage 2, collectivity. Some form of hierarchical authority has to be defined so employees know whom to go to for decisions and orders. Although some formal aspects of organization are beginning to appear, such as an initial division of labor, communication and control are still likely to be fairly informal. Employees identify with the organization and its mission. The name of this stage, collectivity, refers to this sense of a highy committed group that is working together to make the organization succeed. A more directive leadership style is needed in this stage.

    Organizations are often characterized by growing pains such as lack of coordination among newly created departments, missed deadlines, overrun budgets, poor or uneven quality control, and overworked CEOs and employees. If these normal stresses and strains are not managed effectively, the organization may find itself on a sharp downward spiral. While the forces are undoubtedly many and complex, a critical variable appears to be the organization's ability to reorganize and accept the fact that at different points in its life it needs different kinds of top-management motivation and leadership and a different organizational culture. These transitional issues are particularly disconcerting to the entrepreneur-owner. The organization is his or her "baby" and letting go in certain areas and recognizing the need for more teamwork and group problem solving and conflict resolution, for example, is by no means simple. Some entrepreneurs inherently dislike adding bureaucracy to their business, even though a certain degree of organization is necessary to support their growth. Many companies are "underorganized" during this stage, which sometimes results in conflict over issues that are "fought out" by employees rather than resolved by policies and hierarchical authority.

3. **Formalization Stage** A greater degree of formalized organization and bureaucratization, in the form of rules, policies, and control systems, is needed to sustain growth in this stage. The management style is less entrepreneurial and more professional, relying on analytical tools and focusing on efficiency. The morale and excitement, so high in the early years, may start to disappear. That old feeling of personal contact and easy access to the boss begins to wane as the organization grows in size. Top management concentrates on strategy rather than operations, which is taken over by middle management. The leader in forced to delegate more authority to others, and the organization becomes more decentralized.

4. **Elaboration Stage** This is the mature stage of the organizational life cycle, evidenced by large size and bureaucratic systems. By this point, companies usually have multiple products or service lines. Communication has become very formal, and there are numerous rules and regulations concerning the planning process. Long-term planning is common. Too much bureaucracy is perceived as a major threat, so organizations in this stage often rely on decentralization and teams to maintain responsiveness. There is a focus on streamlining bureaucracy and using social control and self-discipline rather than formal bureaucratic controls. Leadership is concerned with creating a complete organization and making sure the necessary coordination and controls are functioning.

The elaboration stage can result in continuing maturity, organizational decline, or renewal. When organizations are not successful in balancing the right degree of bureaucracy with their need to learn, adapt, and innovate, they may go into decline. Decline is characterized by rigid, top-heavy, and overly complex organizational structures. Communication breakdowns are common. There is often blind adherence to a "success formula," regardless of environmental changes that make this formula obsolete. Decision making emphasizes form rather than substance, and self-serving politics are the norm. There is an excess of conformity and compromise. There are nine early warning signals of organizational decline:[66]

1. Excess personnel
2. Tolerance of incompetence
3. Cumbersome administrative procedures
4. Disproportionate staff power
5. Replacement of substance with form (e.g., the planning process is more important than results)
6. Scarcity of clear goals and decision benchmarks
7. Fear of embarrassment and conflict prevents problem identification
8. Loss of effective communication
9. Outdated organizational structure

Experts say decline is almost inevitable unless management takes steps to avoid it. This is best done before the organization finds itself in difficulty. Some organizations manage to halt a decline and enter a renewal stage that allows the organization to shift itself back to a previous stage. To fight off organizational decline, reengineering efforts closely examine how the organization functions and then take action to streamline and improve processes and the structure.

Each stage requires a different type of leadership that is capable of tackling the major growth challenges. Leaders should also manage organizational culture differently in each stage.[67] In the entrepreneurial and collectivity stages, an organizational culture is often the glue that holds the organization together and makes growth possible. The leader should elaborate, develop, and articulate the cultural values. In the formalization stage, culture tends to be taken for granted. The culture often becomes more diverse as subcultures form in the different areas of the organization. Leaders can reward the subcultures whose values are in the organization's best interests. In the elaboration stage, the culture may become dysfunctional, and the leader's task is to change the culture and make it more adaptive.

Beatty and Ulrich suggest that the probability of renewal of mature organizations increases if four principles are understood and practiced.[68]

1. **Mature organizations renew by instilling a customer perspective and focusing on customer demands** This involves seeking a sustained competitive advantage that comes from understanding and meeting customer needs in unique ways. Companies question whether their mind-sets, or mental models, and practices really meet customer requirements and expectations.

2. **Mature organizations renew by increasing their capacity for change** Organizations have an internal clock about how long it should take to make decisions. In many cases, the challenge is to decrease the cycle time for decisions. Companies have to focus more on alignment so that all aspects of the organization are moving toward consistent and shared goals. Symbiosis is also emphasized so that companies can learn and benefit from removing boundaries both inside and outside the organization. Reflexiveness, the ability to learn from previous actions, is a necessity.

3. **Mature organizations renew by altering both the hardware and software within the organization** The hardware (strategy, structure, and systems) is where many renewal programs begin. However, hardware has to be supported by software (employee behavior and mental models).

4. **Mature organizations renew by creating empowered employees who act as leaders at all levels of the organization** Individuals have both responsibility and accountability in their areas.

 CLASS ACTIVITY:
THE ECOQUEST CASE

The purpose of this exercise is to give you an opportunity to think about organizational culture and succession issues. (Time allotted: 65 minutes)

STEP 1.   The class should divide up into their learning groups (approximately five to six persons per group).

STEP 2.   Each group should discuss the questions below, which you considered individually in the Class Preparation, and come to a consensus. Next, prepare a four-minute summary analysis of the Ecoquest case to share with the total class. Use the accompanying Ecoquest Case Summary form to write down your group's conclusions. (25 minutes):
   a. What do you see as the major strengths and weaknesses of the three candidates?
   b. Which candidate would you recommend as the new CEO of Ecoquest?
   c. What is your rationale for this choice?
   d. What other organizational changes would you recommend to help the new CEO be successful?
   e. How should the organizational culture be maintained or changed?

STEP 3.   Group Analyses. Each of the groups should share its analysis with the entire class. Others should ask clarification questions during the process to ensure understanding. (20 minutes)

STEP 4.   Plenary discussion. Before giving your opinions on the Class Discussion Questions at the end of this section, the class should take a few moments to read over the Ecoquest Case, Part II on page 453. (20 minutes)

Ecoquest Case Summary

	Mike Lewis	Anita Sanchez	Kent Chang
Major Strengths			
Major Weaknesses			

Group Choice for the New CEO:

Rationale for Group Choice:

Organizational Changes to Help CEO Succeed:	Recommendations for Maintaining or Changing Ecoquest's Culture:

Class Discussion Questions

1. What can you learn about leadership and succession from this case?
2. What type of leadership does Ecoquest need at this stage in their development? Where are they in the organizational life cycle in Exhibit 16-2?
3. What is your analysis of Ecoquest's organizational culture?
4. What threats to Ecoquest's organizational culture appeared in the case?

ASSESSING THE ORGANIZATIONAL CULTURE OF YOUR LEARNING GROUP

The purpose of this exercise is to give your learning group an opportunity to assess the organizational culture you have created and see where improvements are needed.

This exercise utilizes a technique known as the nominal group technique, developed by Andre Delbecq. It is designed to gather ideas or data quickly in a democratic fashion. The round-robin nature of this technique prevents influential people from controlling the air time or the vote. Once ideas are mentioned, they become the property of the group, not ideas advocated by specific individuals. (Time alloted: 60-70 minutes)

STEP 1. Write three to five statements that describe the following: (5 minutes)
   a. The ideal state of your learning group.
   b. The current state of your learning group.

   Note: (1) It's not necessary to write complete sentences as long as your words or phrases will be understood by others. (2) For the "ideal state" questions, give yourself free rein here to be creative and think beyond the constraints of the current situation. (3) For the "current state" questions, try to think of both positives and negatives to "cover the waterfront." Don't limit yourself by merely reversing positive characteristics you may have identified for the ideal state.

STEP 2. Students form into their learning groups and choose a facilitator to lead them through the following steps. The facilitator goes around the group in a round-robin manner asking each participant to read out loud one statement from his or her "ideal state" list and then writes it on a flipchart or blackboard. Number each idea and write down whatever the person says, without judging or rewriting their idea. This continues until all participants have exhausted their lists. Participants say "pass" when all the statements on their list have been recorded. Do the same on a different section of the blackboard or different flip chart paper for the "current state" list. (15 minutes)

STEP 3. The individual learning groups then examine the statements in both the ideal and current lists to see if all are comprehensible and that there are no duplicates. Some statements may need to be combined if the people who contributed them agree that they have the same meaning. Do not argue about the ideas since you will have an opportunity to vote on them. (10 minutes)

STEP 4. Participants approach the board or flip chart as a group and individually mark the three statements that are most significant to them as individuals by putting a hatchmark with a marker or chalk beside them. (Do not call out your votes to the facilitator because your votes are actually more private when all of you are marking them at the same time.) This is a way of quickly prioritizing group opinion. (5 minutes)

STEP 5. Count up the marks for each item and identify the five ideas that received the most votes. Include all ideas that were ties and received the same number of votes in your top-five ranking. These results identify the major issues regarding the organizational culture in your learning group. Discuss how you can close the gap between the current and the ideal situation. Brainstorm ways your group can become more ideal and then write an action plan that your group agrees to carry out. (For example, one group realized they wanted to replace a clique-like subgroup with a norm of inclusiveness. Their action plan included changing their seating pattern, working with the members they knew the least, and planning a social event for the whole group.) (20 minutes)

STEP 6.   Each group briefly shares their action plans with the whole class. (10–20 minutes)

Note: Another option with this exercise, with a small class, is to focus on the organizational culture of the learning organization as a whole—the course. Substitute for "learning group" in a. and b. of Step 1 the words "learning organization" and do the nominal group technique in a plenary session. Afterwards, discuss what the class and the professor can do to close the gap between the ideal and current state of the course.

 **LEARNING POINTS**

1. Organizational culture is defined as a pattern of shared values and beliefs that produces certain norms of behavior.
2. Organizational culture has three levels: artifacts, espoused values, and assumptions.
3. The dominant culture in a large organization manifests the values shared by the majority, while subcultures usually share those values as well as other values that characterize their own group. The values of countercultures are in opposition to those of the dominant culture.
4. Organizational culture provides members with a sense of identity, generates commitment, helps people make sense of what occurs in the organization and the environment, and serves as a control mechanism.
5. The sources of organizational culture are (1) the beliefs, values, and assumptions of the founders, (2) the learning experiences of group members as their organization evolves; (3) new beliefs, values, and assumptions brought in by new members and leaders.
6. There should be a fit among the people, the organization's task, environment, strategy, and culture.
7. Strong cultures have the following characteristics:
   a. People in the organization can easily identify the dominant values.
   b. The selection processes target people who are likely to fit into the culture and find it satisfying.
   c. Socialization and training convey to newcomers the "ropes" they need to learn.
   d. Employees who do not fit the culture or produce in accordance with its values are sometimes fired.
   e. People within the company are rewarded for acting in accordance with the dominant values of the organization.
   f. By their behavior, leaders and managers send clear, consistent signals about desired values and norms.
   g. Managers measure and control what is important to the culture.
8. Compared to weak cultures, strong cultures have core values and beliefs that are intensely held, more widely shared and more ordered.
9. A strong culture does not guarantee good performance unless it focuses on all its key constituencies (customers, stockholders, and employees) and has leadership from managers at all levels.
10. The advantages of strong organizational cultures are high performance under certain conditions, clear sense of purpose, more value-driven decision making, and employee commitment, loyalty, and pride. Two disadvantages of strong cultures are their pressure for conformity and potential resistance to change.

11. Culture is transmitted through socialization, stories, symbols, jargon and language, rituals and ceremonies, and statements of principles.

12. Organizational justice consists of distributive justice (fair distribution of resources), procedural justice (fair decision-making procedures), and interactional justice (fair treatment from others). Treating employees fairly results in higher performance, compliance, trust, cooperation with coworkers, organizational citizenship behavior and less turnover, absenteeism, employee silence, and counterproductive behaviors.

13. Since clashing organizational cultures sometimes cause mergers to fail, the firms should analyze their cultural compatibility beforehand as part of the due diligence process and seek to develop shared values.

14. Leaders can affect an organizational culture, but they cannot unilaterally determine what that culture should be. The primary mechanisms a leader can use to create, transmit, or change culture are:
    a. What leaders pay attention to, measure, and control on a regular basis
    b. The reactions of leaders to critical incidents and organizational crises
    c. Observed criteria by which leaders allocate scarce resources
    d. Deliberate role modeling, teaching, and coaching
    e. Criteria for allocating rewards and status
    f. Criteria for recruitment, selection, promotion, retirement, and excommunication

15. Most organizations go through predictable stages of growth—the entrepreneurial stage, collectivity, formalization, and elaboration. Each stage requires a different type of leadership.

 **ACTION SCRIPTS**

FOR EMPLOYEES

- Before experts on organizational culture join an organization, they try to read its culture and determine whether or not their values are compatible with those of the organization. They talk with as many contacts as possible and in their job interviews, they ask the same questions (e.g., see the questions in the following Personal Application Assignment) of different interviewers to see if their answers are consistent.
- New employees decode the cultural artifacts they observe and analyze the stories about the organization that are commonly told. Emotional outbursts often signal when a key value has been violated. They watch what leaders pay attention to and ignore.
- They ask different people for explanations about the culture so they get a balanced view, rather than the perception of one person who may belong to a subculture or a counterculture or who is incapable of explaining culture.
- They check with mentors before taking action that might be taboo or that could result in negative repercussions.
- They create traditions and events that emphasize cultural values (e.g., the Glorious Booboo Award in the R&D lab, roasts for people who get promoted or retire, and Friday afternoon TGIF parties).

FOR MANAGERS

- Every action a manager takes either creates, reinforces or breaks down organizational culture. Whenever decisions are made, managers should ask the question, "Is this decision in keeping with our cultural values?" Maintaining or changing corporate culture requires consistency. What managers do to reinforce cultural values is stronger than what they say.
- Managers see building culture as yet another component of their job description that requires goal-setting and execution.

- Experts figure out their organization's cultural characteristics and use that understanding when making analyses and decisions. Awareness of the history of the organization and its key values can keep new managers from making errors.
- They respect the past, but make sure the culture is adapting and learning in the present.
- Expert managers encourage a certain degree of nonconformity. Although it is sometimes more difficult to handle people who don't fit the culture well, they are often valuable in pointing out the assumptions that guide the dominant culture. Sometimes deviants see the need for change more clearly than others.
- Like national culture, one of the disadvantages of organizational culture is that it blinds us to other values and other ways of doing things. Managers can help work groups make their norms explicit and then identify which values need to be reinforced or changed.
- Managers who are expert at managing culture tell stories that transmit cultural values to employees. Stories and parables are easy to remember and help guide employee behavior.

FOR ORGANIZATIONAL ARCHITECTS

- Organizational architects who are expert at managing culture understand that it has to be aligned with their mission, strategy, and employees and adaptable to their environment.
- They explain repeatedly to employees why the organization was founded and what makes it unique. They use language that reflects desired cultural values.
- They maintain their culture by articulating and celebrating their values, selecting employees who share those values and socializing them, and rewarding employees for behaving in accordance with the desired values.
- They hold each manager accountable for the culture they build in their unit.
- They design celebrations and create traditions that foster cultural values.
- They measure the culture with survey instruments or focus groups and take actions to remedy aspects that are not aligned with the desired cultural values.
- Some organizational cultures are less hospitable to minorities and women, even though this can have an adverse impact for both individuals and the organization. This problem can be remedied by including diversity as a key cultural value and by making diversity a priority and evaluating the inclusiveness of the culture.
- They pay attention to the special cultural needs and values of nomadic workers and telecommuters, since the internal integration of such workers is a unique challenge.[69] Half of Sun Microsystem's 31,000 employees worldwide work at home or at "drop-in"centers owned by the company.
- The organization's culture must be taken into consideration whenever changes are planned, because culture can be a major impediment to change. Changes that build on or leverage cultural values, rather than go against them, are more likely to succeed. Even so, cultural change can be a slow, evolutionary process that requires patience.
- When rapid growth and the absorption of so many new members that they will outnumber the original workforce, special measures are needed to maintain the organizational culture and socialize the newcomers.
- They pay special attention to organizational justice and are careful to treat employees fairly. They design systems for grievance procedures so that employees can complain and seek redress if unfair actions do occur.
- Due diligence for possible mergers should include information and analysis on the organizational cultures of both entities, as well as potential problems stemming from differences in managerial style, employee behavior, culture, and ethical standards.
- Merger targets with similar cultures make for smoother integration.
- The acquiring firm in mergers should develop trust with the other firm and demonstrate their commitment to them by treating them fairly.[70]
- The acquiring firm attempts to create shared values rather than imposing their values on the other company.

PERSONAL APPLICATION ASSIGNMENT

Your assignment is to analyze the culture of an organization you know well (a work setting, church, club, or even the school where you are taking this course).

1. What is the background of the founders?

2. What explains the organization's growth and survival?

3. What does the organization stand for? What is its motto?

4. What values does the organization talk about?

5. What values does the organization act out?

6. How do people get ahead? What does it take to do well in this organization? To stay out of trouble?

7. What kind of mistakes are not forgiven?

8. Who is considered deviant in the culture and why? How does the organization treat them?

9. How are good employees rewarded?

10. What are the main rules that everyone has to follow in this organization?

11. How does the organization respond to crises?

12. What message is conveyed by the physical setting?

13. How do things get done in this organization?

14. How do people spend their time at work?

15. How does the organization take in new members?

16. What kinds of stories are told about the organization?

17. Who are the heroes and why?

18. Is there anything that cannot be talked about?

19. How do people exercise power?

20. What is the organization's code of ethics?

21. Based on the answers to these questions, what is your analysis of this organizational culture?

Ecoquest, Part II—The Aftermath

(Please do not read until directed to do so during the class session.) The consultant team recommended promoting Mike Lewis to the CEO position on the grounds that he had the organizing skills needed at this point in the company's development.

Both Kent and Anita were disappointed. In Kent's case, it was more a matter of hurt pride because he was the eldest. Kent eventually acknowledged that he did not really want the added responsibility of the CEO position and the pressure of bringing in new clients, even though he had been tempted by the title. Anita, however, chafed under Mike's increasingly autocratic controls. She and Mike argued quite a bit in the first few months over the service-versus-profit issue and the need for more organization. Kent resented decisions Mike made without consulting him, even though he had been in favor of centralized decision making in principle (or when he was the one making the decisions). Anita and Kent were still operating with the mind-set that policies and structure led straight to rigid bureaucracy. The conflict over these competing values began to spill over onto the rest of the organization when the principals started grousing about each other.

Mike established job descriptions and policies, but he did so without any input. Some policies had a nit-picky flavor, causing a mini-rebellion among staff. Morale dropped, some key employees quit, and a few clients started complaining about the service they received and Mike's "bean-counter" mentality. Finally, the board (and Chel from her sickbed) insisted that the principals resolve their differences.

After acknowledging that their arguments had taken much of the fun out of work, Anita, Mike, and Kent took a hard look at the business and what they needed to accomplish. In a long emotional meeting, Kent pointed out that both service and profit were important and had to be balanced. The principals agreed to monitor the firm's critical success factors and develop some guidelines about what they considered quality service. In a surprise move, Mike resigned as CEO, saying he wasn't cut out for the job.

The principals and the board chose Anita as his replacement and the person best suited to solve Ecoquest's current problems. She quickly put into place a mentoring program that made Ecoquest a preferred employer. Her people skills helped repair relations with staff and clients. Once the conflict and competition died down, both Anita and Mike realized that their differences could be complementary rather than divisive. Anita became more open to Mike's suggestions about clearer roles and policies. Anita and Kent agreed that they had grown to a point where more organization was needed. She asked an employee task force to revise the policies. Then Anita showed them to the entire staff and asked for their suggestions. The resulting, new-improved policies were accepted, and the firm ran much more smoothly. Over time, Mike took on more and more administrative functions while Kent focused on the financial aspects. This allowed Anita to concentrate on bringing in new clients and managing and developing staff. In this way, the strengths of all three principals were available to the company. Mike's organizing abilities were essential to keep operations running smoothly and Kent's experience and financial background kept the firm's growth on a steady path, but Anita's values and skills were a closer fit with Chel's and the organizational culture. One of the most important lessons the principals learned, however, was to make sure they maintained the organizational culture that was so crucial to their early success. They became more skilled at recognizing decisions and behaviors that threatened their cultural values. As a reminder, there's a new sign by the bulletin board—"How to Avoid Becoming an Endangered Species—Quality Service, Fun, and Empowerment."

ENDNOTES

[1] R. T. Pascale and A. G. Athos, *The Art of Japanese Management: Applications for American Executives* (New York: Simon and Schuster, 1981); T. Peters and R. H. Waterman, *In Search of Excellence* (New York: Harper and Row, 1982); T. Peters and N. A. Austin, *A Passion for Excellence* (New York: Random House, 1985); T. E. Deal and A. A. Kennedy, *Corporate Cultures: The Rites and Rituals of Corporate Life* (Reading, MA: Addison-Wesley, 1982); and J. P. Kotter and J. L. Heskett, *Corporate Culture and Performance* (Toronto: The Free Press, 1992).

[2] "The X and Y Factors: What Goes Around Comes Around," *The Economist 378*(8461) (January 21, 2006): 17–18.

[3] "Inculcating Culture," *The Economist 378*(8461) (January 21, 2006): 11.

[4] E. H. Schein, "Coming to a New Awareness of Organizational Culture," *Sloan Management Review 25*(2) (Winter 1984): 3.

[5] L. Smircich, "Concepts of Culture and Organizational Analysis," *Administrative Science Quarterly 28*(3) (September 1983): 339-358.

[6] "Inculcating Culture," *The Economist.*

[7] "Corporate Culture." http://www.gore.com/en_xx/aboutus/culture/index.html. Accessed 1/15/06.

[8] S. A. Sackmann, *Cultural Complexity in Organizations: Inherent Contrasts and Contradictions* (Thousand Oaks, CA: Sage, 1997).

[9] B. Victor. and J. B. Cullen, "The Organizational Bases of Ethical Work Climates," *Administrative Science Quarterly 33*(1) (March 1988): 101–125.

[10] E. H. Schein, *Organizational Culture and Leadership* (San Francisco: Jossey-Bass, 2004): 225.

[11] E. H. Schein, "The Role of the Founder in Creating Organizational Culture," in *Psychological Dimensions of Organizational Behavior*, B. M. Staw (ed.) (Upper Saddle River, NJ: Prentice Hall, 2004): 321.

[12] Schein, *Organizational Culture and Leadership.*

[13] D. Denison, *Corporate Culture and Organizational Effectiveness* (New York: John Wiley, 1990).

[14] About Entrepreneurs.Com. http://entrepreneurs.about.com/cs/famousentrepreneur/p/ingvarkamprad.htm. Accessed 2/18/06.

[15] "IKEA's Innovative Human Resource Management Practices and Work Culture," Case available from ICFAI Center for Management Research, (2005): 1-15; "IKEA Named a 2005 Working Mother 100 Best Company by Working Mother Magazine. http://www.ikea.com/ms/en_US/about_ikea/press_room/press_release/national/working_mother. Accessed 2/18/2006.

[16] Schein, *Organizational Culture and Leadership.*

[17] V. Sathe, "Implications of Corporate Culture: A Manager's Guide to Action," *Organizational Dynamics 12*(2) (Autumn 1983): 4–23.

[18] R. T. Mowday, L. W. Porter, and R. M. Steers, *Employee-Organizational Linkages: The Psychology of Commitment, Absenteeism, and Turnover* (New York: Academic Press, 1982).

[19] J. C. Collins and J. I. Porras, *Built to Last* (New York: HarperBusiness, 1994); D. R. Denison and A. K. Mishra, "Toward a Theory of Organizational Culture and Effectiveness," *Organization Science 6*(2) (March–April 1995): 204–223.

[20] Kotter and Heskett, *Corporate Culture and Performance*: 11.

[21] J. Pfeffer, *The Human Equation: Building Profits by Putting People First* (Boston, MA: Harvard Business School Press, 1998).

[22] R. T. Pascale, "The Paradox of 'Corporate Culture': Reconciling Ourselves to Socialization," *California Management Review 27*(2)(Winter 1985): 26–41.

[23] Kotter and Heskett, *Corporate Culture and Performance*: 142.

[24] D. Miller, *The Icarus Paradox* (New York: HarperBusiness, 1990): 3.

[25] J. H. Dobrzynski, "Rethinking IBM," *BusinessWeek 3339* (October 4, 1993): 88. See also G. Lewis, "One Fresh Face May Not Be Enough," *BusinessWeek 3314* (April 12, 1993): 33.

[26] S. E. Ante, "The New Blue," *BusinessWeek 3824* (March 17, 2003): 8–15.

[27] "Big and No Longer Blue: A Totally New, Improved IBM," *The Economist 378*(8461) (January 21, 2006): 15.

[28] Ibid.

[29] "The New Organisation," *The Economist 378*(8461) (January 21, 2006): 3.

[30] R. D. Denison, "Bringing Corporate Culture to the Bottom Line," *Organizational Dynamics 13*(2)(Autumn 1984): 5–22.

[31] H. Trice and J. Beyer, *Culture of Work Organizations,* (Englewood Cliffs, NJ: Prentice Hall, 1993): 356–57.

[32] J. S. Ott, *The Organizational Culture Perspective* (Chicago: Dorsey, 1989).

[33] Pascale, "The Paradox of 'Corporate Culture'."

[34] Ibid.

[35] R. O. von Wessowets, "Human Resources at Hewlett-Packard," *Harvard Business School Case #482-125* (1982): 6.

[36] J. C. Crotts, D. R. Dickson, and R. C. Ford, "Aligning Organizational Processes with Mission: The Case of Service Excellence," *Academy of Management Executive 19*(3) (2005): 60.

[37] M. Kinsley, "Company Man," *The New Republic 215*(10), (September 2, 1966): 42.

[38] T. J. Woodbury, "Building Organizational Culture—Word by Word," *Leader to Leader 39* (Winter 2006): 49–50.

[39] A. Bruce, "Southwest: Back to the FUNdamentals," *HRFOCUS* (March 1997): 11.

[40] J. A. Colquitt, J. Greenberg, and C. P. Zapata-Phelan, "What is Organizational Justice? An Historical Overview," in *The Handbook of Organizational Justice,* J. Greenberg, and J. A. Colquitt (eds.), (Mahwah, NJ: Erlbaum, 2005): 3–56.

[41] J. Greenberg, "Using Socially Fair Procedures to Promote Acceptance of a Work Site Smoking Ban," *Journal of Applied Psychology 79* (1994): 288–297.

[42] E. A. Lind, "Fairness Heuristic Theory: Justice Judgments as Pivotal Cognitions in Organizational Relations," in *Advances in Organizational Justice,* J. Greenberg and R. Cropanzano (eds.), (Stanford, CA: Stanford University Press, 2001): 56-88, D. E. Conlon, C. J. Meyer, and J. M. Nowakowski, "How Does Organizational Justice Affect Performance, Withdrawal, and Counterproductive Behavior?" in Greenberg and Colquitt (eds.) *Handbook of Organizational Justice*: 301-328; Colquitt, Greenberg, and Zapata-Phelan, "What is Organizational Justice?".

[43] "Perception of Fairness Linked to Sick Days," *San Jose Mercury News* (December 31, 2002): 3E.

[44] R. C. Dailey and D. J. Kirk, "Distributive and Procedural Justice as Antecedents of Job Dissatisfaction and Intent to Turnover," *Human Relations 45*(3) (1992): 305–316.

[45] D. D. Bergh, "Predicting Divestiture or Unrelated Acquisitions: An Integrative Model of Ex Ante Conditions," *Strategic Management Journal 18*(9) (1997): 715–731.

[46] K. Frieswick, "Fools Gold" *CFO* (February 2005): 27; D. Henry, "M&A Deals: Show Me" *BusinessWeek 3857* (November 10, 2003): 38-40.

[47] B. B. Allred, K. B. Boal, and W. K. Holstein, "Corporations as Stepfamilies: A New Metaphor for Explaining the Fate of Merged and Acquired Companies," *The Academy of Management Executive 19*(3) (2005): 23–37.

[48] For information on the role of culture in global mergers, see G. Stahl and M. Mendenhall's book, *Mergers and Acquisitions: Managing Culture and Human Resources* (Palo Alto: Stanford University Press, 2005).

[49] V. Emerson, "An Interview with Carlos Ghosn, President of Nissan Motors Ltd. and Industry Leader of the Year," *Journal of World Business 36*(1), (Spring 2001): 3–10.

[50] S. Cartwright and C. L. Cooper, "The Role of Culture Compatibility in Successful Organizational Marriage," *Academy of Management Executive 7*(2) (1993): 57–70.

[51] "At Sears, A Great Communicator," *BusinessWeek 3957* (October 31, 2005): 50–52.

[52] Schein, *Organizational Culture and Leadership*: 246.

[53] S. Woolley (ed.), "Best Leaders," *BusinessWeek 3964* (December 19, 2005): 62.

[54] Kotter and Heskett, *Corporate Culture*: 147; and Trice and Beyer, *Culture of Work Organizations:* 399–413.

[55] A. L. Wilkins, *Developing Corporate Character* (San Francisco: Jossey-Bass, 1989). See J. Thorbeck's "The Turnaround Value of Values," *Harvard Business Review 69*(1) (January–February, 1991): 52–62 for a firsthand account by a manager

who took company history into account and successfully revived company values.

[56] Trice and Beyer, *Culture of Work Organizations.*

[57] R. T. Pascale, *Managing on the Edge: How the Smartest Companies Use Conflict to Stay Ahead* (New York: Simon and Schuster, 1990).

[58] L. Schein, "A Manager's Guide to Corporate Culture," (New York, The Conference Board, 1989).

[59] Gratton, and Ghoshal, "Beyond Best Practice," *MIT Sloan Management Review 46*(3) (Spring 2005): 49–57.

[60] Gratton, and Ghoshal, "Beyond Best Practice,": 56.

[61] Ibid.: 52.

[62] See B. Schneider, D. E. Bowen, M. G. Erhart, and K. M. Holcombe, "The Climate for Service: Evolution of a Construct," in *Handbook of Organizational Culture and Climate,* N. M. Ashkanasy, C. P. M. Wilderom, and M. F. Peterson (eds.), (Thousand Oaks, CA: Sage, 2000): 21–36; R. Peccei and P. Rosenthal, "Delivering Customer-Oriented Behaviour Through Empowerment: An Empirical Test of HRM Assumptions," *Journal of Management Studies 38*(6) (September 2001): 831–856; S. D. Pugh, J. Dietz, J. W. Wiley, and S. M. Brooks, "Driving Service Effectiveness Through Employee-Customer Linkages," *Academy of Management Executive 16*(4) (November 2002): 73–84.

[63] R. T. Pascale, "Intentional Breakdowns and Conflict by Design," *Planning Review 22*(3) (May–June 1994): 17.

[64] J. C. Crotts, D. R. Dickson, and R. C. Ford, "Aligning Organizational Processes with Mission: The Case of Service Excellence," *Academy of Management Executive 19*(3) (2005): 57.

[65] K. G. Smith, T. R. Mitchel, and C. E. Summer, "Top Level Management Priorities in Different Stages of the Organizational Life Cycle," *Academy of Management Journal 28*(4) (December 1985): 799–820; R. E. Quinn and K. Cameron, "Organizational Life Cycles and Shifting Criteria of Effectiveness: Some Preliminary Evidence," *Management Science 29* (1983): 33–51; and L.E. Greiner, "Evolution and Revolution as Organizations Grow," *Harvard Business Review 76* (May-June 1998): 55–64; P. Lorange and R. T. Nelson, "How to Recognize and Avoid Organizational Decline," *Sloan Management Review 28*(3) (Spring 1987): 41–48.

[66] Lorange and Nelson, "How to Recognize and Avoid Organizational Decline": 43–45.

[67] Schein, *Organizational Culture and Leadership.*

[68] R. W. Beatty and D. O. Ulrich, "Re-Energizing the Mature Organization," *Organizational Dynamics 20*(1) (1991): 16–30.

[69] L. Chen and R. Nath, "Nomadic Culture: Cultural Support for Working Anytime, Anywhere," *Information Systems Management 22*(4) (Fall 2005): 56–64.

[70] Allred, Boal, and Holstein, "Corporations as Stepfamilies: A New Metaphor for Explaining the Fate of Merged and Acquired Companies."

Chapter 17

▲▲▲

DECISION MAKING

OBJECTIVES By the end of this chapter, you should be able to:

A. Explain why decision making is a social process.

B. Define and explain how bounded rationality influences decision making.

C. Describe five models of decision making.

D. Explain groupthink and how it can be avoided.

E. Explain how experts make decisions.

F. Identify your personal approach to organizational decision making.

G. Apply the leader-participation model of decision making.

Pajama Talk

The Sleepytime Pajama factory was going great guns. Sales were up. The workforce was expanding. There was only one hitch. To remain competitive, factory managers were constantly adapting both work techniques and products. Workers were often transferred to different jobs or had parts of their job modified, either in the name of progress or as a result of high turnover and absenteeism. The biggest problem facing Sleepytime was worker resistance to these changes. As soon as they became proficient at one job, they'd be switched to another. They worked on a piece-rate incentive system, and it wasn't easy to work their way up to producing 60 units per hour, the standard efficiency rate. Some suspicious souls thought management just switched workers to new jobs when they had finally mastered their tasks and could begin to earn bonuses for producing more than 60 units. Even though workers received a transfer bonus that made up for the money lost learning new jobs, it didn't make up for the loss in status of being a "green-horn" on a new task. Workers still hated to be transferred to a new job, and some quit rather than change. Others complained bitterly about management and fought with their supervisors and the time-study engineers. Statistics showed that experienced workers took longer to relearn new jobs and get up to speed than did new employees with no work experience! This convinced the company that the problem was really a question of motivation and resistance to change.

Mr. Sleepytime himself, Joe Berg, had the production people organize the output figures in relation to the changes that had been introduced during the last year. He was surprised to find that the work groups supervised by Kathy Johnson seemed to have fewer problems with changes. Her groups got back to speed more quickly after the changes and had a higher level of output than the others. She also had fewer terminations, even after the job transfers. So Berg sent his industrial relations expert out on the floor to figure out what was going on.

After observation, the expert discovered that the difference lay in how the supervisors handled the changes. Supervisors of the low-productivity groups simply announced to their employees that a job had to be changed, explained the new piece rate, and answered questions.

In contrast, Johnson used physical demonstrations with her workers in which she showed them samples of pajamas made using new and old techniques, explained the cost differential, and asked them if they could tell the difference between them. Or she'd bring in pajamas made by a competitor who was underselling them and show them why changes had to be made to respond to this challenge. Next, she'd ask the group how the new jobs should be designed. They'd come up with a blitz of ideas for improving the job, and then they worked with the time-study engineer to test out the innovations. Johnson let the workers do most of the talking and planning. She didn't have in her head a "one best way" to make the changes; she let them figure it out for themselves. As a result, they bought into the changes and became committed to making them work. Johnson made the factory workers participants in the change process rather than victims of it. And so it was that Berg learned that the sooner people are brought into a change effort and allowed to participate in the decision making, the better.

Source: Based on Lester Coch and John R. French, Jr., "Overcoming Resistance to Change," *Human Relations 1* (1947): 515–531.

JIM COLLINS ON TOUGH CALLS

When he's not out scaling mountains (he's a world-class rock climber), author Jim Collins eats, drinks, and sleeps business. So when *Fortune* senior writer Jerry Useem (a sometime Collins collaborator) asked him to discuss the art of decision-making, he got so into the idea that he pored over 14 years of research and interviews he had amassed in the course of writing his business blockbusters *Built to Last* and *Good to Great*. Then, in a series of conversations, he and Useem explored the intriguing insights he had gleaned from analyzing the processes behind key decisions in business history. For example, lasting excellence in corporations seems to stem less from decisions about strategy than decisions about people, and seeking consensus is not the way to make the tough calls. Here are edited highlights of their talks.

What were the surprises when you reexamined your research through the lens of decision-making?

We tend to think that decisions are very much about "what." But when I look at my research notes and I look at interview transcripts from the executives we've interviewed, one theme that comes through is that their greatest decisions were not "what" but "who." They were people decisions.

Why are people decisions so important?

Fundamentally, the world is uncertain. Decisions are about the future and your place in the future when that future is uncertain. So what is the key thing you can do to prepare for that uncertainty? You can have the right people with you.

Let's take a nonbusiness case and a business case to illustrate the importance of the people piece. In 1978, Jim Logan and his partner, Mugs Stump, became the first people to climb the Emperor Face of Mount Robson in the Canadian Rockies. And to this day, everybody else who's tried the face has either died or failed on the route. When I asked Logan, "Why were you able to do the Emperor Face?" he said, "Because I made the single most important decision, I picked the right partner."

He told me that there was this one place, the "death zone," and once they went above it, they really couldn't retreat. They were going to either summit or die—no going back. They didn't know what they were going to find beyond that point, and they didn't know what the weather was going to be. And so, therefore, what's your greatest hedge against uncertainty? Having people who can adapt to whatever the mountain throws at you.

Give us the business example

Let's take the story of a company heading into a very uncertain world: Wells Fargo in the late 1970s. Everybody knows the storm of deregulation is going to hit. But nobody knows precisely how it's going to shake out. When is it going to hit? What exact form is it going to take? What impact is it going to have on the banking industry? Dick Cooley, chief executive of Wells Fargo at that time, was very clear with us when we did our research. He said, in essence, "I did not know what we were going to have to do to prevail through deregulation, because it was an uncertain set of contingencies. Too many of them. But I did know that if I spent the 1970s building a team of the most capable executives possible, they would figure out what to do when deregulation hit." He couldn't lay down a plan for what was going to happen, because he didn't know what was going to happen. So his decision was actually a bunch of decisions about getting the people who could deal with whatever deregulation turned out to be.

Okay, but once you have great people in place, you still have to make decisions

Great decisions begin with really great people and a simple statement: I don't know. The research evidence on that is very clear—that the leaders who ended up setting things in place that produced extraordinary results over time, and a series of great decisions over time, really were very comfortable saying "I don't know" until they knew.

And really, they were just being honest. I mean, which is best? Lying—meaning saying you don't know when you've already made up your mind? Or presuming to know when you don't and therefore lying to yourself? Or speaking the truth? Which is, "I don't yet know, but I know we have to get it right."

How do you say that without looking irresolute? Don't people expect leaders to say clearly, "Here's where we're headed"?

That's the typical thing that happens in companies. The CEO has already made a decision, and his definition of leadership is to get people to participate so that they feel good about the decision he's already made.

What's wrong with that?

For one thing, you're ignoring people who might know a lot that would be useful in making the decision. You're accepting the idea that because you're in the CEO seat, you somehow know more or you're smarter than everyone else. But what you're really doing is cutting yourself off from hearing options or ideas that might be better.

How do you create the kind of atmosphere where information flows freely?

You have to recognize that your position can be a hindrance to getting the best information. And so can your personality. My own greatest enemy is my personality—I can convince the people on my team of a point of view. I'm older than they are. I've done more research than they have. I know more than they do. I can influence them perhaps too much and therefore not get the best answers. So when we were doing the research for *Good to Great*, I built a culture that began with disagreements, that set people up to disagree with each other and disagree with me.

I tried to increase what I call my questions-to-statements ratio. I learned this from the *Good to Great* leaders we were studying. They were just marvelous at igniting dialogue and debate with Socratic questions. And I tried to make heroes out of those on my team who identified flaws in my thinking. At the next meeting I might say, "I really want to give Leigh or Brian or Stefanie credit. She really pushed my thinking, and I wasn't looking at this right."

I looked for people with a streak of irreverence and independent thought. One of my favorite researchers is a young man who went to Princeton, majored in medieval literature, and then joined the Marine Corps. Now, that's independent thinking. I wanted him on my team because he's not going to care what I think.

The really critical part came in designing the research so that for every piece of the puzzle—for every case, every analysis—someone on the team knows that piece as well as I do or better. This was a key mechanism to reduce the odds that my authority and strong personality would override the evidence.

Does having that kind of team make it harder to reach consensus?

I really want to underscore something. This is not about consensus.

You mean it depends on conflict?

That's the key. What we found in companies that make good decisions is the debate is real. When Colman Mockler at Gillette is trying to decide whether to go with cheaper, disposable plastic razors or more expensive ones, he asks marvelous questions. He's Socratic. He pushes people to defend their points of view. He lets the debate rage. And this is, by the way, not an isolated case. We found this process in all the companies we studied, when they made a leap to greatness. The debate is real. It is real, violent debate in search of understanding.

And then in the end, the leader makes the call?

Yes. It's conflict and debate leading to an executive decision. No major decision we've studied was ever taken at a point of unanimous agreement. There was always some disagreement in the air.

Doesn't that make it hard to carry out the decision?

Our research showed that before a major decision, you would see significant debate. But after the decision, people would unify behind that decision to make it successful. Again, and I can't stress this too much, it all begins with having the right people—those who can debate in search of the best answers but who can then set aside their disagreements and work together for the success of the enterprise.

Okay, so creating a debate is crucial. What are some other ingredients of great decisions?

Most people start with the outside world and try to figure out, How do we adapt to it? Greatness doesn't happen that way. It starts with an internal drive. And there's a really key question with big decisions: What is the truth of this situation? There are three parts to this question. The first is internal: What are our real core values and our real aspirations? I mean, what do we really stand for? What do we really want to get done? What is internally driving us? I believe that it is the internal imprint that drives all the action. Everybody harps about "It's all about responding to the outside world." But the great companies are internally driven, externally aware.

So the first question is, What is really driving us internally? The second question is, What is the truth about the outside world? And in particular, What is the truth about how it operates and how it is changing?

And the third question is, When you intersect our internal drive with external reality, what's the truth about what we can distinctively contribute potentially better than anyone else in the world?

Now, let's look at Boeing's decision to build the 707. What are the factors? First, you have the values of Boeing, which had to do with "We're adventurers, for goodness' sake. We like doing big, adventurous things. We'd rather not be in business than not do that." And second, the aspiration to make Boeing even greater than it was. Those are internal drives. They had nothing to do with adapting to the outside world.

But the second question—What was the truth about the outside world and how it was changing?—well, the war was over. There wasn't going to be as much demand for bombers. And there was a major change in technology, from propellers to jets. And the demand for military aircraft was going to decline relative to demand for commercial aircraft. So that's how the outside world was changing.

On to question No. 3: What could Boeing do better than anyone else in the world? Well, they had jet technology. They'd been building those big strato bombers, the B-47 and the B-52. They had experience, so they knew they could build a large-scale jet. Boeing confronted the truth, internal and external, and grasped that it could make a distinctive impact by bringing the world into the Jet Age—and that's when Bill Allen pulled the trigger on the 707.

We've been talking about big decisions, but there's a lot more to running a business than making one life-or-death decision, right?

No decision, no matter how big, is any more than a small fraction of the total outcome. Yes, some decisions are much bigger than others, and some are forks in the road. But as far as what determines outcomes, the big decisions are not like 60 of 100 points. They're more like 6 of 100 points. And there's a whole bunch of others that are like 0.6, or 0.006. They add up to a cumulative result. Business schools have regrettably taught us that it's all about the singular case decision. And when you and I write, we like the dramatic moment of decision.

Right. So-and-so leaned back in his chair, looked out the window, and said, "Should I do X or Y?"

But that's not the way life really happens. Yes, there are pivotal decisions, but it's really the stream of decisions over time, brilliantly executed, that accounts for great outcomes.

What elements of a leader's psychology, or the company's psychology, affect decision-making?

One big factor is, Do you believe that your ultimate outcomes in life are externally determined— "I came from a certain family, I got the right job"? Or do you believe that how your life turns out is ultimately up to you, that despite all the things that happen, you are ultimately responsible for your outcomes?

Consider the airline industry, and think of all the events and factors outside managerial control that have hit it since 1972: fuel shocks, interest rate spikes, deregulation, wars, and 9/11. And yet the No. 1 performing company of all publicly traded companies in terms of return to investors for a 30-year period from 1972 to 2002 is an airline. According to Money magazine's retrospective look in 2002, Southwest Airlines beat Intel, Wal-Mart, GE—all of them! Now what would have happened if the folks at Southwest had said, "Hey, we can't do anything great because of our environment"? You could say, "Yeah, the airline industry is terrible. Everyone in it is statistically destined to lose money." But at Southwest they say, "We are responsible for our own outcomes."

Are you saying that you can control your own destiny with good decisions?

Not entirely. Luck is still a factor. But overall our research is showing that the primary factors reside more inside your control than outside. Yes, the world throws a lot at us, but the fundamental assumption needs to be like Southwest's—the ultimate responsibility for your destiny lies with you. The question is not what the world does to you but how you make an impact on the world. Decision-making is ultimately a creative act.

So it's hard to make good decisions if you don't really think they're going to make that much difference in the end. What else counts?

Our research shows one other variable to be vitally important for both the quality of decisions and their implementation. If you look at some of the great decisions in business history, the executives had the discipline to manage for the quarter-century, not the quarter. Look at Andy Grove deciding to abandon memory chips at Intel, Bill Allen and the Boeing 707, Reg Jones choosing Jack Welch to run GE, Darwin Smith selling the mills at Kimberly-Clark, Jim Burke standing firm in the Tylenol crisis, Tom Watson Jr. and the IBM 360. Those leaders were very clear that their ambition was for the long-term greatness of the company. And where decisions can go awry is when there's ambiguity or confusion about what you are really making decisions for—yourself or the company. Why should people throw their full creative energies into a decision that is ultimately about you?

Can you give us a preview of your current project?

My colleague Morten Hansen, formerly a professor at Harvard and now at Insead, and I conceived a simple question: Why do some prevail in brutally turbulent environments, while others do not? How do you retain control over your destiny when you are vulnerable to an environment that seeks to rip that control away from you or where you are statistically destined to fail? Think of it this way: If you wake up at Everest base camp and an unexpected storm hits, you'll probably be fine, but if you're high on the mountain when that storm hits, you just might die. Morten and I believe leaders increasingly feel they are high on the mountain, facing storms they never anticipated. We want to know, How do you build greatness anyway?

And the answer is?

We're early in our research, and we don't yet know. But one thing we're learning is a great relief to me, because I'm so hard on myself. You can make mistakes, even some big mistakes, and still prevail. That's a wonderful thing to know. You don't need a perfect hit rate. You might need to go four out of five on the really big ones, and there are some killer gotcha mistakes from which you can't recover, but you don't have to go five out of five. And I didn't know that before.

Source: J. Useem, "Jim Collins on Tough Calls," *Fortune 151*(13) (2005): 89–94.

⬭ CLASS PREPARATION

A. Read "Pajama Talk" and "Jim Collins on Tough Calls."

B. Analyze a significant organizational decision that you observed first-hand. Why was it effective or ineffective?

C. Read the descriptions of decision-making styles in Exhibit 17–1 shown below and describe how you would handle each of the three decision-making cases that follow. Indicate which decision-making approach you would use, and explain your rationale. This will allow a comparison between your decision-making style and the recommendations of the decision-making model described in this chapter.[1]

D. While reading the chapter, make a list of the cues that you will pay attention to when making decisions.

Decide	Consult Individually	Consult Group	Facilitate	Delegate
You make the decision alone and either announce or "sell" it to the group. You may use your expertise in collecting information that you deem relevant to the problem from the group or others.	You present the problem to the group members individually, get their suggestions, and then make the decision.	You present the problem to the group members, in a meeting, get their suggestions, and then make the decision.	You present the problem to the group in a meeting. You act as facilitator, defining the problem to be solved and the boundaries within which the decision must be made. Your objective is to get concurrence on a decision. Above all, you take care to ensure that your ideas are not given any greater weight than those of others simply because of your position.	You permit the group to make the decision within prescribed limits. The group undertakes the identification and diagnosis of the problem, developing alternative procedures for solving it, and deciding on one or more alternative solutions. While you play no direct role in the group's deliberations unless explicitly asked, your role is an important one behind the scenes, providing needed resources and encouragement.

Source: Reprinted with permission of Elsevier; V. H. Vroom, "Leadership and the Decision-Making Process," *Organizational Dynamics 28*(4) (2000): 84.

EXHIBIT 17-1 **Decision-Making Styles**

CASE 1: THE FINANCE CASE

You are the head of a staff unit reporting to the vice president of finance. The vice president has asked you to provide a report on the firm's current portfolio including recommendations for changes in the selection criteria currently employed. Doubts have been raised about the efficiency of the existing system in the current market conditions, and there is considerable dissatisfaction with prevailing rates of return.

You plan to write the report, but at the moment you are quite perplexed about the approach to take. Your own specialty is the bond market, and it is clear to you that detailed knowledge of the equity market, which you lack, would greatly enhance the value of the report. Fortunately, four members of your staff are specialists in different segments of the equity market. Together they possess a vast amount of knowledge about the intricacies of investment. Although they are all dedicated employees, they seldom agree on the best way to achieve anything when it comes to investment philosophy and strategy. While staff meetings are argumentative, they do eventually arrive at decisions on problems.

You have six weeks before the report is due. You have already begun to familiarize yourself with the firm's current portfolio and have been provided by management with a specific set of constraints that any portfolio must satisfy. Your immediate problem is to come up with some alternatives to the firm's present practices and select the most promising for detailed analysis in your report.

How would you deal with this situation?

Indicate the style that most closely describes the action you would take with a checkmark in the top row.

Decide	Consult Individually	Consult Group	Facilitate	Delegate
You make the decision alone and either announce or "sell" it to the group.	You present the problem to the group members individually, get their suggestions, and then make the decision.	You present the problem to the group members in a meeting, get their suggestions, and then make the decision.	You present the problem to the group in a meeting. You act as a facilitator but take care that your ideas are not given any greater weight than those of others.	You permit the group to make the decision by themselves within prescribed limits.

Why would you use this style?

CASE 2: THE ENGINEERING WORK ASSIGNMENT

You are supervising the work of 12 civil engineers. Their formal training and work experience are very similar, permitting you to use them interchangeably on projects. Yesterday, your manager informed you that a request had been received from an overseas affiliate for four engineers to go abroad on extended loan for a period of six to eight months. For a number of reasons, she argued and you agreed, this request should be met from your group.

All your engineers are experienced in and are capable of handling assignments such as this. From the standpoint of present and future work projects, there is no particular reason why any one should be chosen over any other. The problem is somewhat complicated by the fact that the overseas assignment is in what is generally regarded in the company as an undesirable location. However, some of the engineers may be attracted by hardship pay and the opportunity to gain international experience. The engineers sometimes decide on project assignments as a group.

How would you deal with this situation?

Indicate the style that most closely describes the action you would take with a checkmark in the top row.

Decide	Consult Individually	Consult Group	Facilitate	Delegate
You make the decision alone and either announce or "sell" it to the group.	You present the problem to the group members individually, get their suggestions, and then make the decision.	You present the problem to the group members in a meeting, get their suggestions, and then make the decision.	You present the problem to the group in a meeting. You act as a facilitator but take care that your ideas are not given any greater weight than those of others.	You permit the group to make the decision by themselves within prescribed limits.

Why would you use this style?

CASE 3: THE OIL PIPELINE

You are general supervisor in charge of a large gang laying an oil pipeline. It is now necessary to estimate your expected rate of progress to schedule material deliveries to the next field site.

You know the nature of the terrain you will be traveling and have in your records the historical data needed to compute the mean and variance in the rate of speed over that type of terrain. Given these two variables, it is a simple matter to calculate the earliest and latest times at which materials and support facilities will be needed at the next site. It is important that your estimate be reasonably accurate. Underestimates result in idle supervisors and workers, and overestimates result in tying up materials for a period of time before they are to be used.

Progress has been good, and your five supervisors and other members of the gang stand to receive substantial bonuses if the project is completed ahead of schedule.

How would you deal with this situation?

Indicate the style that most closely describes the action you would take with a checkmark in the top row.

Decide	Consult Individually	Consult Group	Facilitate	Delegate
You make the decision alone and either announce or "sell" it to the group.	You present the problem to the group members individually, get their suggestions, and then make the decision.	You present the problem to the group members in a meeting, get their suggestions, and then make the decision.	You present the problem to the group in a meeting. You act as a facilitator but take care that your ideas are not given any greater weight than those of others.	You permit the group to make the decision by themselves within prescribed limits.

Why would you use this style?

THE KNOWLEDGE BASE

To a manager, executive, or administrator, no other job function encapsulates the frustrations and joys of leadership more dramatically than decision making. Grappling with tough calls brings home the responsibilities, the power, and the vulnerability of their jobs. This central focus of decision making is illustrated in the autobiographies of political leaders, who characteristically organize their life stories around major decision points they faced, the dilemmas and pressures they experienced, and how in the end the "buck" stopped on their desks. Most of us in our life and work face decisions of less magnitude; nonetheless, from time to time we share the existential loneliness of making an important decision.

Yet there are two things wrong with using this admittedly powerful subjective experience of decision making as the focus for analyzing and improving the decision-making process in organizations. First, these experiences suggest that decisions can be thought of as independent, solitary events that are relatively unconnected to other decisions and the process that brought the decision point to a head. If there is anything to be learned from the Bay of Pigs fiasco or the Vietnam War experience, it is that the organizational process of problem identification, information sharing, and problem solving, if mishandled, can undo the work of the most logical, and experienced individual decision maker.

Second, these political memoirs suggest that decision making is an individual process and, therefore, the skills of logical analysis and problem solving (described in Chapter 11) should be sufficient to produce high-quality decisions. In reality, decision making in organizations is also a social process. Organizational functioning requires an unending stream of decisions great and small. These decisions are identified, made, and communicated by individuals and groups throughout the organization. As a manager, you depend on the decisions of others, their perceptions, and the information they bring you. You also delegate decisions and share information about them with others. Part of a manager's role is determining who in the organization has the information, experience, and wisdom needed to make a particular decision. Another part is understanding who are the stakeholders in each issue who need to be involved because their acceptance of the outcome is crucial. Seeing decision making as a social process means that the manager is responsible for determining how the problem is to be solved, but not necessarily the solution. The sense that any decision is made alone in an organization is an illusion.

The focus of this chapter is on managing the process of decision making as opposed to the problem-solving skills of making a specific decision. It underscores the social aspects of that process and the alternative ways of making decisions with other people: the costs and benefits and the appropriate application of these decision-making methods in different situations.

Studies of 356 decisions in Canadian and U.S. organizations revealed that half the decisions failed (were never put into practice, only partly used, or completely dissolved).[2] The primary cause of failure can be traced to poor managerial tactics rather than factors outside managers' control. Although two tactics are commonly used by managers, they are less likely to result in successful decisions: persuasion (selling expert opinions to convince employees about a decision) and *edicts (directives that announce decisions on which employees have not been consulted)*. In one of the opening vignettes to this chapter, Jim Collins recounts how he tries to avoid persuading his own employees by creating a culture of debate and independent thinking and increasing his questions-to-statements ratio to elicit their views. The repeated use of edicts depletes a manager's *social credit (the store of goodwill created by honest dealings and positive accomplishments)* and may result in sabotage, token compliance, delays, and outright refusals to comply.[3] Employees are more likely to overlook the merits of a decision made by edict and devote their energies to complaining about how the decision was made. Companies are forced to expend unnecessary time, money, and effort to counteract the employee resistance that is a natural outgrowth of many edicts. The managers studied were not aware of the high failure rates associated with edicts and persuasion. Nor were they aware that the following set of tactics has a higher success rate: (1) setting realistic objectives for the decision (e.g., lower costs, higher market share) before moving on to consider options; (2) intervention (pointing out performance gaps and the need for the decision, networking, calling attention to ideas that might work, and identifying and justifying new performance norms); (3) participation (task forces with key individuals); and (4) integrated benchmarking (studying several organizations to learn from their best practices). Decisions are also more likely to be successful if managers involve themselves in the implementation process.

MODELS OF DECISION MAKING

The Rational Decision-Making Process

The process of rational decision making is somewhat similar to the problem-solving model we studied in Chapter 11:

1. Recognize and define the problem.
2. Identify the objective of the decision and the decision criteria.
3. Allocate weights to the criteria.
4. List and develop the alternatives.
5. Evaluate the alternatives.
6. Select the best alternative.
7. Implement the decision.
8. Evaluate the decision.

By decision criteria, we mean the factors that a decision must satisfy. Cost, time needed for implementation, and fairness are examples of decision criteria. The model of rational decision making is an outgrowth of classical economic theory with its view of rational man (and woman). Although this model is useful in guiding our general approach to decision making, the circumstances surrounding most decisions are seldom so simple or so rational that this model works perfectly and predictably.

Bounded Rationality

With this in mind, Herbert Simon won a Nobel Prize for his theory of *bounded rationality, which maintains that people are restricted in the information they possess to make decisions, engage in limited search for solutions, and settle for less than optimal solutions.*[4] In other words, there are limits or bounds on rationality. Bounded rationality is based on these assumptions:

1. Managers *select the first alternative that is minimally acceptable, which is called satisficing.*
2. Both the available information and the definition of the situation are incomplete and inadequate to some degree.
3. Managers are comfortable making decisions without first determining all the alternatives.
4. Managers use judgment shortcuts to make decisions, which are called heuristics.

Managers satisfice (i.e., accept a decision that is "good enough") because the costs of maximizing are too great. Maximizing would be analogous to searching the Internet to find the very best Web site to help you write an assigned report; satisficing is searching the Web only until you find a site that provides enough information to allow you to produce an acceptable report. Another constraint on the decision-making process is *bounded discretion, which limits decision alternatives to those that fall within the bounds of current moral and ethical standards.* Optimal solutions are not always best because they may involve unethical behavior. For example, when Beech-Nut sold adulterated apple juice for babies, it optimized its profit in the short term However, this decision was viewed as unethical, and the company was penalized.[5]

Heuristics are rules of thumb based on past experience that managers use to simplify decision making. For example, when a stock drops a set number of points, some investors automatically sell rather than analyze a wide array of factors that influence the stock. People also tend to compare one decision against another in an incremental approach rather than carry out a comprehensive consideration of all possible decisions.[6] Exhibit 17–2 presents some other decision biases and ways to overcome them.

Garbage Can Model

The garbage can model of decision making diverges even more radically than bounded rationality from the conception of decision making as a rational process.[7] In the garbage can model, four factors—problems, participants, solutions, and choice opportunities—all float randomly inside an organization, described metaphorically as a garbage can. If they connect, a decision results. The garbage can model assumes that decision making is haphazard, chaotic, unpredictable, and sometimes depends on sheer luck.

The following section explains some of the human factors that influence and sometimes distort the decision-making process.

EXHIBIT 17-2 Common Decision Biases

Bias	How It Works	Example	How to Avoid It
Anchoring and adjusting	Initial information (the anchor—e.g., a first offer in a negotiation) is overweighted. The decision maker then fails to adequately take into account new information (fails to adjust).	Initial asking price for a house becomes the anchor when real estate agents are asked to estimate the value of the home.	As a buyer, pay little attention to initial offers; as a seller, make the first offer. Gather hard data to help ensure that your initial information is accurate.
Representativeness	The probability that an event will occur is estimated based on how closely that event resembles some other event.	Relying on small sample sizes to make estimates. For example, using a few reviews of a product to make a judgment about its quality.	Gather as large a sample size as possible to get a realistic picture of possible outcomes. Understand that chance events are not related; extreme performances are often followed by more average performances. Be sure to make comparisons between situations or events that are as similar as possible.

Continued on next page

Bias	How It Works	Example	How to Avoid It
Availability	Things that we remember easily heavily influence our judgments and perceptions.	Overestimating the probability of events that are heavily covered in the media or that are available in memory. Film producers release films closer to the Academy Award date because voters may be more likely to recall movies they saw in the previous month than those seen 11 months earlier.	Expand your experiences so that you have a variety of events and experiences readily available in memory. Get additional data about how frequently events occur and other decisions. Don't just rely on your memory.
Overconfidence	Holding unrealistically optimistic views of your own accuracy in decisions.	Employees generally estimate that they perform better than about 75 percent of their peers.	Gather realistic data about events, opinions, and performance. Ask for feedback about your performance and adjust your self-evaluations accordingly.
Bounded awareness	Awareness or perception narrows so that information that may be useful to the decision maker falls outside awareness and is not attended to.	In times of threat or crisis, perception and attention tends to be focused on narrow alternatives. In the *Columbia* space shuttle disaster, managers failed to consider that the broken foam shields could result in explosions.	Imagine alternative scenarios. Use multiple role playing procedures to imagine how other people and stakeholders would react to decisions. Conduct PreMortems for your decisions.
Emotional involvement	Unrealistic optimism can lead to the belief that the future will be more positive than it will really be; pessimism can lead to more negative evaluations.	Commodities and products tend to be more positively evaluated when people own them than when they do not; fear and anxiety result in risk-averse behavior.	Check your mood. If you are emotionally involved, take a "breather" from the decision process. Re-evaluate after your emotions subside.
Self-serving reasoning	Taking credit for success and avoiding blame for failure.	In responding to a survey, 85 percent of the respondents said their opponent should reimburse the respondents for legal costs when the opponent lost the suit. In the same survey, only 45 percent of the respondents said they should pay their opponent's legal costs if the respondents were the losing party in a legal proceeding.	Realistically assess your role in the outcome. Ask for feedback from trusted friends, colleagues, and other people who can give you realistic appraisals of your accountability and responsibility.

Adapted from S. R. Robbins, *Decide and Conquer* (Upper Saddle River, NJ: Financial Times Prentice Hall, 2004), and M. Bazerman, *Judgment in Managerial Decision Making* (6th ed.) (New York: Wiley, 2006).

FACTORS THAT INFLUENCE DECISIONS

Decisions are affected by individual differences and biases. For example, some people are more risk averse than others and have less tolerance of uncertainty. As a result, their decisions tend to be more cautious and conservative. Other people are more risk-tolerant and may be less cautious and conservative. Interestingly, however, people sometimes support riskier or more cautious decisions in a group setting than they would individually. This is known as the *choice shift*.[8] *The determining factor is the premeeting position of the members; group discussion seems to cause individuals to exaggerate their initial stance and move toward extremes*.[9] For example, a cautious shift is more likely when individual members are leaning toward a cautious decision before the group meeting, whereas a risky shift is more likely when members are favoring a riskier alternative.

Groupthink refers to the tendency for members of a highly cohesive group to seek consensus so strongly that they fail to do a realistic appraisal of other alternatives, which may be more correct.[10] Ford's decision to produce the Edsel, President Kennedy and his advisors' decision on the Bay of Pigs invasion into Cuba, Morton-Thiokol's decision to recommend launching in the Challenger disaster, and Salomon Brothers' illegal purchases at U.S. Treasury auctions are all examples of decisions characterized by groupthink. In each case, individuals "went along" with consensus-driven group decisions that should have been questioned. When groupthink occurs, members censor their misgivings about a decision, or they pressure dissenters to stifle their opinions. Thus, there is pressure toward uniformity and an illusion of unanimity that does not really exist. There is also an illusion of invulnerability that makes the group overly optimistic and more likely to make high-risk decisions. The illusion of morality occurs when groups feel they are morally correct and should, therefore, not be criticized. They collectively rationalize their actions and often stereotype out-group members who may be likely to criticize their actions.[11]

To avoid groupthink, groups can (1) encourage all members to express their doubts, (2) assign a devil's advocate in each meeting who challenges assumptions and arguments, (3) adopt the perspectives of other constituencies with a stake in the decision, (4) bring in qualified outsiders to discuss decisions, and (5) after a tentative decision has been reached, schedule a "let's sleep on it one last time" meeting for final concerns and doubts. Group leaders have to demonstrate their own willingness to be criticized and should avoid laying out their own opinions first.

Recent reviews of the groupthink literature suggest that the phenomenon is not quite as prevalent as previously believed, nor has Janis's original theory been validated completely. Researchers have begun to refine the concept of groupthink to adapt to different situational characteristics.[12] Some researchers have highlighted the importance of social identity maintenance in producing groupthink. When facing a shared, collective threat, a cohesive group may become focused on the maintenance, protection, and even enhancement of its threatened image—to the detriment of the group's performance. To prevent poor performance under these conditions, group leaders and managers can adopt two different types of approaches. One approach is to provide ways for the group to maintain its positive image while also focusing on performing well.[13] This could be done, for example, by providing groups with a face-saving mechanism that reduces the risk of poor performance. Providing an excuse for potential poor performance appears to reduce the group's need to focus solely on ways to maintain the group image or identity and allows them to increase their focus on problem-solving, which in turn enhances performance. A second approach to helping cohesive groups perform well under threat involves designing methods to allow groups to evaluate different decision alternatives fully and to engage in constructive conflict about ideas and solutions (what we call cognitive or task conflict).[14] One way to do that is via guidelines on how to conduct their discussions. For example, group performance can be improved by giving groups guidelines that emphasize generating ideas before evaluating them, listening to all group members' opinions, systematically evaluating the advantages and disadvantages of different solution alternatives and developing contingency plans. Another method for improving performance is called the multiple role-playing procedure, in which group members assume the perspectives of other constituencies with a stake in the decision or of another group member.[15]

Intel's decision to exit the computer memory market (the market that had formed the backbone of Intel's revenues for years) reflects this process. The company had been losing money on memory components for some time. When business slowed during the recession of the early eighties, other products could not compensate and losses mounted. Andrew Grove, former CEO and Chairman of the Board, reports how role-playing factored in the decision-making process:

> *"The need for a different memory strategy . . . was growing urgent. We had meetings and more meetings, bickering and arguments, resulting in nothing but conflicting proposals. . . . It was a grim and frustrating year. I remember a time in the middle of 1985, after all this aimless wandering had been going on for almost a year. I was in my office with Intel's chairman and CEO, Gordon Moore. Our mood was downbeat. I looked out the window at the Ferris wheel of the Great America amusement park revolving in the distance, then I turned back to Gordon and I asked, "If we got kicked out and the board brought in a new CEO, what do you think he would do?" Gordon answered without hesitation, "He would get us out of memories." I stared at him, numb, then said, "Why shouldn't you and I walk out the door, come back and do it ourselves?"* [16]

Intel is known for putting all employees through a training program in constructive conflict that encourages debate but also emphasizes the need to unite behind the final decision (disagree and commit). Such programs improve the quality of decision making and are part of what makes the Intel culture special, which links the role of critical evaluation to their social identity. When organizations do not have the time, resources or motivation to institute such programs, they can also enhance decision making by simply instructing group members to follow structured discussion principles and pay attention to minority opinions. [17]

Surprisingly, negative feedback is not always enough to deter groups and individuals from continuing to support bad decisions. *Escalation of commitment occurs when people continue to commit resources to a failing course of action.* [18] In spite of evidence that a previous decision was a mistake, people sometimes focus on what they have already invested and become even more committed. Two examples of escalating commitment are countries that continue with wars they cannot win, arguing that it makes the deaths of soldiers or money spent "in vain," and people who persist in buying shares of a failing stock, based on their rationale that they have already invested so much money. It is difficult to know when to reverse course in light of negative feedback on prior decisions and when to hold firm. Avoiding arguments based on escalation of commitment in favor of objective analysis can make the distinction easier to discern.

THE LEADER-PARTICIPATION MODEL

The decision-making alternatives you used in the Class Preparation reflect a contingency theory of leadership. The continuum ranges from autocratic decision-making behavior (in which the leader decides alone) to participative styles, ranging from consultation to joint decision making (facilitation) and delegation. The choice of style depends on the problem at hand. Once again, managerial effectiveness depends on having the skills required to analyze the problem in question and the ability to vary one's leadership behavior accordingly.

The leader-participation model is based on evidence that the choice of leadership style can affect these four outcomes of the decision-making process. [19]

1. **Decision Quality** The quality of the decision relates to how wise, well-reasoned, and sound it is. This depends on where the information and expertise needed for a particular decision reside, whether the decision makers care about the good of the organization, and whether the decision team is synergistic rather than dysfunctional.
2. **Decision Implementation** Many high-quality decisions are never implemented because employees are not committed to doing so. Allowing people to participate in decisions yields greater acceptance and commitment, which usually translates into more effective implementation of the decision.
3. **Costs of Decision Making** Decision quality and decision implementation refer to a decision's effectiveness. However, efficiency is also a factor because decision making consumes

resources, such as time and energy. For example, more participative decisions require more time and utilize more person-hours than autocratic decisions.

4. **Development** The greater costs of participative decision making are offset by the development opportunity they offer. Team members have a chance to practice problem solving, create a collaborative team, and, because they have a greater voice, employees are more likely to identify with the organization.

Depending on the decision in question, these four outcomes vary in importance. For example, the decision about how the office support staff will cover the phones at lunch time doesn't demand much in the way of decision quality. Any one of the support staff can do the job, but it must be acceptable to the people involved. Efficiency is usually an important consideration in everything we do in organizations, but developing subordinates or encouraging organizational learning sometimes take priority. Effective managers can skillfully diagnose decision situations to determine the outcome requirements and the appropriate method of decision making. No single decision-making method or management style is appropriate for all jobs or even all decisions in a single job.

Victor Vroom and his associates have developed a formal model that helps us to analyze specific decision situations and to determine the decision-making approach that is likely to be most effective.[20] The model is constructed in the form of a decision matrix based on six rules (shown in Exhibit 17–3) that were derived from research on problem solving and decision making. It poses seven questions for managers to ask about a decision, shown on the following page.

Rules to Protect the Quality of the Decision

1. **The leader information rule.** If the quality of the decision is important and the leader does not possess enough information or expertise to solve the problem by himself or herself, then the Decide style is not appropriate.

2. **The goal congruence rule.** If the quality of the decision is important and subordinates are not likely to pursue the organizational goals in their efforts to solve the problem, then the Facilitate and Delegate styles are not appropriate.

Rules to Protect the Acceptance of the Decision

3. **The acceptance rule.** If the acceptance of the decision by subordinates is critical to effective implementation and if it is not certain that an autocratic decision will be accepted, the Decide style is not appropriate.

4. **The conflict rule.** If the acceptance of the decision is critical, an autocratic decision is not certain to be accepted, and disagreement among subordinates in methods of attaining the organizational goal is likely, the methods used in solving the problem should enable those in disagreement to resolve their differences with full knowledge of the problem. Accordingly, under these conditions, the Decide and Consult Individually styles, which permit no interaction among subordinates, provide no opportunity for those in conflict to resolve their differences. Their use runs the risk of leaving some of the subordinates with less than the needed commitment to the final decision.

5. **The fairness rule.** If the quality of the decision is unimportant but acceptance of the decision is critical and not certain to result from an autocratic decision, it is important that the decision process used generate the needed acceptance. The decision process used should permit the subordinates to interact with one another and negotiate over the fair method of resolving any differences, with full responsibility on them for determining what is fair and equitable. Accordingly, under these circumstances, the Decide and Consult styles are not appropriate.

6. **The acceptance priority rule.** If acceptance is critical and not certain to result from an autocratic decision, and if subordinates are motivated to pursue the organizational goals represented in the problem, then methods that provide equal partnership in the decision-making process can provide greater acceptance without risking decision quality. Accordingly, the Decide and Consult styles are not appropriate.

Source: Adapted from V. H. Vroom, "A New Look at Managerial Decision Making," *Organizational Dynamics 2* (Spring 1973): 67.

EXHIBIT 17-3 **Rules Underlying the Leader-Participation Model**

A. Decision Significance—How significant is the decision to the success of the project or organization?

B. Importance of Commitment—How important is the team members' commitment to the decision?

C. Leader's Expertise—Does the leader (you) possess the knowledge or expertise related to this problem?

D. Likelihood of Commitment—If you were to make the decision yourself, what is the likelihood that the team would commit itself to the decision?

E. Group Support for Objectives—To what degree does the team support the organization's objectives at stake in this problem?

F. Group Expertise—Do team members' possess the knowledge or expertise related to this problem?

G. Team Competence—Do team members have the ability to work together in solving problems?

By answering these questions sequentially and tracing the answers through the model's decision matrix (see Exhibit 17–4 on the next page), managers are led to the most effective leadership alternative for the problem. The time-driven model shown here emphasizes efficiency rather than employee development. This matrix functions like a funnel. Beginning on the left with a particular decision situation in mind, you answer the questions as either "high" (H) or "low" (L) and continue answering each relevant question to the right until eventually you arrive at the right-hand column of recommended decision making processes, or leadership styles. The leadership styles are described in detail in Exhibit 17–1 on page 463 in the Class Preparation section. To understand how the model works, let's analyze an actual problem using the decision matrix.

You were hired last month as vice president in charge of purchasing for a large manufacturing company that has thirty plants located throughout the United States. For the last 20 years, the company operated in a decentralized fashion with corporate executives providing a minimal amount of control and direction to autonomous plant managers. Each local purchasing manager reports directly to the plant manager and makes his or her own purchasing decisions. There is little or no coordination among the purchasing managers in different plants, and relationships among them are best described as competitive rather than collaborative.

The president predicted that the company would have increasing difficulty in procuring certain essential raw materials and, as a result, created your position so purchasing decisions would be centralized. You were selected for this job due to your extensive background in corporate purchasing in a different industry. The president announced your appointment in last week's newsletter. Because the peak buying season is approaching, you want to quickly establish a procedure that will decrease the chance of serious shortages and maximize the advantages of centralized buying (greater leverage with suppliers, lower costs due to greater volume).

You are anxious to meet the purchasing agents and pick their brains about their purchasing practices. You have heard that they are a conscientious group that tends to resent interference from headquarters. They are likely to interpret a move toward centralized purchasing as a loss of power on their part. You will need both their input and cooperation for centralized purchasing to work effectively. Furthermore, any solution that does not receive the active support of the various plant managers is likely to fail.[21]

Exhibit 17-5 shows the answers to the appropriate diagnostic questions in the Time Driven Model of the decision matrix (Exhibit 17–4). Therefore, the model predicts that the Consult Group style, sharing the problem in a group meeting to obtain their ideas and suggestions and then making the decision alone, will be the most effective style for handling this situation.

Time-Driven Model

Instructions: The matrix operates like a funnel. You start at the left with a specific decision problem in mind. The column headings denote situational factors which may or may not be present in that problem. You progress by selecting High or Low (H or L) for each relevant situational factor. Proceed to the right judging only those situational factors for which a judgement is called for, until you reach the recommended process.

Problem Statement	Decision Significance	Importance of Commitment	Leader's Expertise	Likelihood of Commitment	Group Support for Objectives	Group Expertise	Team Competence	
	H	H	H	H	–	–	–	Decide
				L	H	H	H	Delegate
							L	Consult (Group)
						L	–	Consult (Group)
					L	–		Consult (Group)
			L	H	H	H	H	Facilitate
							L	Consult (Individually)
						L	–	Consult (Individually)
					L	–		Consult (Individually)
				L	H	H	H	Facilitate
							L	Consult (Group)
						L	–	Consult (Group)
					L	–		Consult (Group)
		L	H	–	–	–	–	Decide
			L	–	H	H	H	Facilitate
							L	Consult (Individually)
						L	–	Consult (Individually)
					L	–		Consult (Individually)
	L	H	–	H	–	–	–	Decide
				L	–	–	H	Delegate
							L	Facilitate
		L	–	–	–	–	–	Decide

EXHIBIT 17-4 The Revised Leadership-Participation Model

Source: Adapted and reprinted with permission of Elsevier: V. H. Vroom, "Leadership and the Decision-Making Process," *Organizational Dynamics* 28 (4) (2000): 87.

A. **Decision Significance?**	High. Running out of essential raw materials would threaten the company's performance.
B. **Importance of Commitment?**	High. A solution that does not receive active support of the plant managers and the purchasing managers will not succeed.
C. **Leader's Expertise?**	Low. You need to pick their brains and get the purchasing managers' input, and you came from a different industry.
D. **Likehood of Commitment?**	Low. You are an unproven newcomer trying to exert authority over employees who report directly to someone else.
E. **Group Support for Objectives?**	Low. The purchasing managers will probably resist giving up their power to make autonomous decisions, and their primary allegiance may lie with their plant rather than with Headquarters.

EXHIBIT 17-5 Vice President of Purchasing Case—Example

Another situational contingency, which appeared in an earlier version of Vroom's model, is whether or not the problem is structured or unstructured. A problem is well structured if we know the current state of the problem, the desired state, and the alternative courses of action that can remedy it. *Structured problems are repetitive and routine problems for which a definite procedure has been developed.* In contrast, *unstructured problems are novel, and no procedures have been developed to handle them because they occur infrequently and/or are very complex.* For example, repairing an airplane is a structured problem; designing a completely new spaceship is an unstructured problem. Because a situation involving an unstructured problem requires more ideas and brains, a more participative leadership style is required.

Vroom and Jago's latest version of the leadership-participation model includes four new contingencies: time constraints, geographical dispersion (which acknowledges the difficulty of getting people together for a discussion), motivation to minimize the time needed to make the decision (so that time can be devoted to more pressing items), and motivation to develop subordinates.[22] Designed for the computer, the new version utilizes a continuum ranging from 1 to 5 rather than a simple yes or no response to each question. It has four decision matrices, two for group decisions and two for individual decisions. At the individual and group level, there are separate matrices for use when decisions must be made quickly, as in Exhibit 17–4, and when time is not such an important consideration. Vroom also developed a further extension of the model that incorporated managers' needs to expand their employees' decision-making capabilities. The "employee development" matrix recognizes that managers may decide to delegate decisions in order to help employees expand their decision-making skills.[23]

A normative model, such as the leader-participation model, raises three questions: (1) When managers utilize this model, how likely are their decisions to be effective? (2) Do managers really make decisions in this manner? (3) If not, why not?

First, research on a previous, slightly different version of Vroom's model found that a greater percentage of managerial decisions were effective when they chose leadership styles that agreed with Vroom's model.[24] In six studies, when managers used the leadership style indicated by the model, 62 percent of their decisions were effective; when they did not, only 37 percent of their decisions were successful.[25] Another study of 45 retail cleaning franchises revealed that managers whose leadership behaviors conformed to the leadership-participation model had more satisfied employees and more profitable operations than other managers.[26]

Second, research comparing the leadership-participation model with the actual behavior of managers has shown that there is a general correspondence between the model recommendations for a specific situation and a manager's behavior in that situation. Vroom and Jago report, "In approximately two-thirds of the problems, nevertheless, the behavior which the manager reported was within the feasible set of methods prescribed for that problem, and in about 40 percent of the cases it corresponded exactly to the minimum person-hours solution."[27] Thus, managers seem to be using an intuitive notion similar to the leader-participation model to manage the decision-making process in their organizations.

In some ways, however, the differences between model recommendations and managerial behavior are more interesting, because they shed light on the assumptions on which the model is based and on particularly difficult issues in managing the decision-making process. For example, when we have asked managers how they would solve the engineering work assignment case described in the Class Preparation for this chapter, many of them chose a Decide style. Some resisted strongly the idea of bringing the group together for decision making in the other more participative styles, saying "No way!" or "It will never work!" Further discussion revealed the following assumptions that underlie their opinion that the Decide style was the only feasible choice:

- "The group wouldn't be able to deal with a difficult problem like this."
- "I wouldn't know how to control the conflict this situation creates if it became a group decision."
- "In most groups the members would expect the manager to make this decision, and they would have to live with it."

The leadership-participation model also makes three assumptions, shown below, that may prove to be problematic when the model is applied:

1. Managers are equally skilled in using the different decision-making alternatives.
2. Groups are equally skilled in their adaptation to these decision-making alternatives.
3. Organizational history and the resulting organizational culture have no impact on a single decision analyzed by the model.

What the model does is analyze a specific decision dispassionately in terms of its outcome requirements without regard to the preceding assumptions about managerial and group skill or organizational culture. Yet in any specific situation, these issues must be considered to ensure that decisions are effective.

In conclusion, we suggest the following considerations, based on research findings, in applying the leader-participation model to actual managerial situations:

- Intuitive managerial decision-making models are more simplified than the leader-participation model. They do not account for some of the interactions among decision rules portrayed in Exhibit 17–4.
- Managers tend to underemphasize the importance of the acceptance and commitment components of decision effectiveness.
- Managers tend to use decision-making styles they are skilled at and avoid styles they feel uncomfortable with. For many, this means avoiding the more difficult group decision-making procedures.
- Organizational history and culture will affect the decision-making method chosen, independent of the logical dictates of the situation. Organizational culture affects decision making in several ways:
  a. Group members will adjust to norms about "the way things are decided around here" and may have little experience or skill using other styles, such as group consensus.
  b. Managers may use a particular decision-making method because their boss uses it and be constrained in their flexibility of decision making by the style dictated from above. If your boss is autocratic with you, it may be more difficult to be participative with your own subordinates. The boss may neither understand nor appreciate a style different from his or her own.

These considerations suggest that the leader-participation model is useful in determining how the decision-making process should be conducted, but the application of this ideal requires managerial skill training in all of the decision-making methods, team development in the various forms of group decision making, and organizational development to create norms that value quality, acceptance, and efficiency as the primary criteria for effective decision making. See Exhibit 17–6 for realities in organizational decision making and suggestions for dealing with them.

Some Things Individual Managers Cannot Expect to Do Much About	Some Things Individual Managers Can Do	Some Things the Organization Can Do
The fact that decision making in organizations is not a totally rational, orderly process	Exercise choices in the problems to work on, which battles to fight and where, and when to cut losses	Set values and tone to support problem solving and risk
The nature of managerial work: the juggling of problems and conflicting demands	Develop intimate knowledge of the business and good working relationships with the people in it	Design organizational structure, reward, and control systems to support action rather than bureaucracy
People are flawed: They are limited information processors, have biases and emotions, and develop vested interests	Know yourself: Know your strengths, weaknesses, and hot-buttons, and when to ask for help	Provide assignments in which decision-making skills can be developed
Fundamental forces in the business environment	Develop the diverse set of skills necessary to act in different situations	Keep business strategy focused on areas about which management is knowledgeable
Basic organizational components determined largely by the business one is in		

Source: M. M. McCall and R. E. Kaplan, *Whatever It Takes: The Realities of Managerial Decision Making* (Upper Saddle River, NJ: Prentice Hall, 1990): 120. Reprinted by permission of the publisher.

EXHIBIT 17-6   **Some Apparent Realities of Decision Making in Complex Organizations**

The leader-participation model gives us a partial answer to the question, "What are the pros and cons of group decisions?" The advantages are more complete information and knowledge, diverse views, increased commitment to the decision, and the increased legitimacy of a democratic decision. However, group decisions can also be time-consuming and overly influenced by conformity pressures or a dominant person or subgroup.

THE ZONE OF INDIFFERENCE AND CULTURAL DIFFERENCES IN DECISION MAKING

Chester Barnard, one of the first management writers and a former CEO of New Jersey Bell Telephone, introduced the concept of the "*zone of indifference, the range within each individual in which he or she willingly accepts orders without consciously questioning authority.*"[28] When applied to decision making, employees willingly accept decisions made by their boss on topics that fall within their zone of indifference (e.g., the font of the lettering on the new office stationery). Asking for participation on such topics wastes employee time and can even frustrate employees ("How can we get our work done if management keeps bugging us with stupid little decisions? Don't they get paid to make decisions?"). However, employees do want to have a voice in decisions that lie outside their zone of indifference. For example, a U.S. consultant redesigning a department in a Guatemalan agency repeatedly asked employees for their input on the new systems and processes. They rubber-stamped whatever she proposed to them and seemed more than content to let her make all the decisions. However, the employees revolted when she and the director surprised them by replacing their traditional desks with new workstations that inadvertently prevented them from being able to see and talk to other employees. Unlike the consultant's previous decisions, the new workstations did not fall into the employees' zone of indifference. She took measures to make the workstations more palatable for the employees, regaining some of the social credit she'd lost with the employees. However, it is always better to avoid causing rebellions in the first place—understanding what falls inside and outside the zone of indifference for one's employees is an important managerial competency.

In terms of the leader-participation model, the zone of indifference relates to the Likelihood of Commitment diagnostic question, "If you were to make the decision yourself, what is the likelihood that the team would commit itself to the decision?" This question will have different answers in different settings as well as different cultures. For example, in high power distance cultures (e.g., Korea), employees are less likely to expect to influence decisions and more likely to expect bosses to make autocratic decisions. Their zone of indifference will be larger. Participative decision making is more likely in cultures with low power distance, as well as in individualistic cultures in which individual opinions are valued (e.g., the Netherlands). As the global labor force becomes more educated, however, employees may expect to be consulted more frequently about decisions at work.

Japan is noted for *ringisei*, decision making by consensus. Proposals in document form are circulated for approval among employees before a decision is implemented. Thus, employees can voice an opinion before a manager makes the final decision. *Ringisei* is time-consuming up front, but this participative process eliminates resistance to decisions, thereby improving implementation quality and speed.[29]

As we noted in the chapter on problem solving, cultures vary in terms of how accepting or proactive they are with regard to problems that may require decisions. Fatalistic cultures are more accepting of situations and, therefore, usually slower to make a decision to resolve a problem. The alternatives considered in the decision-making process are also affected by cultural values. Cultures oriented to the past (e.g., Italy) are more likely to make decisions in keeping with tradition and precedents. Present-oriented cultures (e.g., the United States) focus on short-term solutions, whereas future-oriented cultures (e.g., Japan) are more likely to focus on long-term solutions. Innovative solutions are generally welcomed and more accepted in cultures that are less tied to the past.

INTUITION AND DECISION MAKING: THE RECOGNITION PRIMED DECISION MODEL

Cultures also vary in the way they search for information pertaining to a decision, which relates to the value given to rationality. In the United States, where rationality is highly valued, even intuitive decisions may be couched in rational terms so they are more readily accepted. Other cultures

Source: Reprinted by permission of Tribune Company Syndicate, Inc.

(e.g., Sweden) are more comfortable with intuitive decision making. Cultures that value rationality rely more on their senses (facts) while others rely on intuition (ideas, images, and possibilities).

There is a growing recognition that rational analysis has been overemphasized in U.S. business. Intuition is becoming more acceptable in the workplace. In a recent study, two-thirds of the professionals interviewed stated that intuition led to better decisions.[30] Intuitive skills are usually developed through experience or working with people who have intuitive qualities. *Intuition is a "cognitive conclusion based on a decision maker's previous experiences and emotional inputs."* [31] Thus, intuition and rational analysis are complementary aspects of good decision making.

Take a few moments to review the Recognition-Primed Decision Model (RPD),[32] which we discussed in the introduction to this book. Gary Klein developed this model as a result of his work with expert decision makers.[33] In a particular situation, cues are generated, which allows a decision maker to recognize patterns. Pattern recognition tells what cues will be important and have to be monitored. It also tells what types of goals the decision maker can accomplish in this situation—what's possible—and gives a sense of what is expected to happen next. Finally, when patterns look typical, decision makers also recognize the typical ways to respond. These patterns tell you what to do and lead to specific action scripts that tell you how to do it. Rather than comparing and evaluating numerous action scripts to find the best one, the patterns experts observe activate certain action scripts, which they assess through mental simulation. Rather than comparing numerous possible actions to select the best one, experts quickly perceive the action script or scripts that fit the pattern and then "mentally game out an option to see if it will work."[34] In mental simulation, they try to foresee how events and consequences might unfold. If they like what they "see," they proceed with that action. These simulations are driven by "mental models" of how things work. These models direct expectations and explanations.

One particularly useful aspect of the RPD model is the "PreMortem Exercise." The PreMortem is designed to expose vulnerabilities in planning. The term is derived from autopsy or postmortem—a procedure conducted to learn how a person died. In a PreMortem, the investigation is conducted *before* the project or plan is implemented. Through mental simulation, all weaknesses of a plan are identified. Importantly, the next step involves designing ways to counter, avoid, or minimize those weaknesses. The advantage of this kind of procedure is twofold. Individuals become more adept at mentally simulating how a plan will work in reality, which also strengthens their intuition. This in turn helps them become better planners.

A PreMortem conducted with a team has the following steps:

1. **Preparation** Participants thoroughly review the plan.
2. **Imagine a fiasco** In this stage, decision makers imagine that the project or plan is a complete and utter failure. They ask themselves what the possible causes of this might be.
3. **Generate reasons for failure** Participants write down all the reasons why they believe failure occurred. Individuals will have different reasons based on their own experiences and intuitions.
4. **Consolidate the lists** Each member states one reason for failure. This process continues until all reasons have been shared.
5. **Revisit the plan** Participants address two or three issues of major concern. Another meeting is scheduled to address the remaining issues.
6. **Review the list** Periodically, the team reviews the list of concerns. This allows the team to check the list to ensure that all concerns have been addressed.

The RPD model is not effective in all circumstances. It should not be used when decisions are extremely complex and uncertain. Under these conditions, decision makers often fool themselves into believing they recognize a pattern. For example, predicting the stock market is a task that is far too complex to rely on intuition. The RPD model is also ineffective when decision makers have not had a chance to acquire sufficient expertise. This may be due to a simple lack of experience with the task or to lack of feedback about performance on the task. A third situation in which the RPD model should not be used is when the decision maker's experience base is distorted or limited. If the decision maker is only exposed to a few different circumstances and cue patterns, then he or she will develop intuition based on an incomplete set of cues. Consequently, intuition will be unreliable because the pattern-matching mechanism will be inaccurate. Finally, the individual's mindset or frame can be a source of error. In this case, the decision maker becomes wedded to a particular way of thinking or perceiving cue patterns. Thus, expertise can help ignore irrelevant cues, but it can also mean that the decision maker misses novel cues or information, ignores new opportunities, and disregards potential new strategies.[35]

CLASS ACTIVITY: TEAM ANALYSIS OF DECISION CASES

The purpose of the group exercise is to provide an opportunity to practice using the decision matrix and identify and discuss reasons for differences between what the model recommends and your own decision-making style. Use this exercise to develop your skills at cue recognition, pattern matching, and mental simulation. (Time allotted: 50 minutes)

STEP 1.   Form learning groups of 5-6 students. Select one person from the group to record the style each group member selected for the three cases in the Class Preparation. Record these styles on the form below or on the chalkboard or flipchart so that all members can view the results. The following Case Analysis Record Form provides a format for recording this data. (5 minutes)

Case Analysis Record Form

Participant Names	Case 1	Case 2	Case 3
Group recommendations after using the decision tree			

STEP 2.   The learning groups should work through the decision matrix in Exhibit 17–4 for each case and arrive at a group recommendation on which leadership style should be used. Trace your decision steps with a different color for each case or utilize a matrix in a different textbook for each one so that you can track the answers to each question. (20 minutes)

STEP 3.   Each group should post its recommended leadership style for each case on the Case Analysis Record Form and on the board. (5 minutes)

STEP 4.   Plenary Debriefing. (20 minutes) After comparing the group answers with those of Vroom and Yetton, answer the following questions:

   a. Did your group come up a different style than Vroom and Yetton, and if so, how and why did you differ?
   b. Sometimes students end up with different answers than Vroom and his colleagues because of assumptions they have made about the decision. Can you identify any assumptions you made in the cases?
   c. What factors, if any, are missing from this model?
   d. When you compare your individual answers from the Class Preparation with those of Vroom and his colleagues, what can you learn about your natural decision-making style from this exercise?

LEARNING POINTS

1. Individual decisions are not independent, solitary events. Instead, they are closely connected to previous decisions and are influenced by the process that brought the decision point to a head.
2. Although decision making at very high levels is frequently characterized as a lonely, individual struggle, decision making is also a social process. Decision making involves information sharing and interdependence among organization members. The manager's job is to manage the decision process by assessing which information and which players need to be involved.
3. The model of rational decision making is an outgrowth of classical economics, but the decision-making process is seldom completely rational.
4. The theory of bounded rationality maintains that people are restricted in the information they possess to make decisions, engage in limited search for solutions, and settle for less than optimal solutions. They satisfice, selecting the first minimally acceptable alternative that is satisfactory.
5. In the garbage can model, four factors—problems, participants, solutions, and choice opportunities—all float randomly inside the organization, described metaphorically as a garbage can. If they connect, a decision results.
6. Choice shift occurs when groups make more extreme decisions than individuals. When people support riskier decisions in a group setting than they would individually, this is called the risky shift. When the group decision is more conservative than individual positions, this is the cautious shift.
7. Groupthink refers to the tendency for members of a highly cohesive group faced with a collective threat to seek consensus so strongly that they fail to do a realistic appraisal of other alternatives, which may be more correct.
8. Escalation of commitment occurs when people continue to commit resources to a failing course of action.
9. The leader-participation model is a contingency theory of leadership. The continuum of leadership styles ranges from autocratic to participative styles: Decide, Consult Individuals and Groups, Facilitate, and Delegate.

10. The choice of leadership style affects these outcomes of the decision-making process:
    a. Decision Quality
    b. Decision Implementation
    c. Costs of Decision Making
    d. Development
11. Utilizing groups to make decisions involves more time but results in more perspectives, greater acceptance of the decision, and more likelihood of successful implementation.
12. The leader-participation model helps managers analyze specific decision situations and determine which leadership styles are most appropriate by diagnosing these factors: decision significance, importance of commitment, leader's expertise, likelihood of commitment, group support for objectives, group expertise, and team competence.
13. Structured problems are repetitive and routine problems for which a definite procedure has been developed. Unstructured problems are novel, with no procedures to handle them because they are infrequent and/or complex.
14. Managers whose leadership behavior approximates the leader-participation model are more likely to make effective decisions than managers whose behavior does not conform to the model.
15. The zone of indifference refers to the range within each individual in which he or she willingly accepts orders without consciously questioning authority. Employees willingly accept decisions made by their boss on topics that fall within their zone of indifference. They want to participate, however, in decisions that fall outside that zone.
16. Intuition is a cognitive conclusion based on a decision maker's previous experiences and emotional inputs.
17. Intuition and rational analysis are complementary aspects of good decision making.
18. The Recognition Primed Decision (RPD) model has the following steps: cue recognition and pattern matching, action script activation, and mental simulation driven by mental models.

ACTION SCRIPTS

FOR EMPLOYEES

- Expert decision makers proactively seek diverse experiences that allow them to develop rich bases of expertise. In that way, they become adept at recognizing cues and matching patterns.
- Some decisions eventually become obvious with time. The trick lies in knowing which decisions (or which parts of them) can be postponed and which need to be made immediately. This is learned by experience.
- Experts sometimes test the water about possible solutions with carefully chosen people such as informal opinion leaders, greybeards (wise, older employees), and powerful people who are interested in the issue. In contrast, yes-men and -women and people with a narrow perspective or a self-serving approach are not good sounding-boards.

FOR MANAGERS

- One of the most important factors expert managers bear in mind when decisions are being made is the concept of setting precedents. They take the time to consider whether they want a given decision to be a guide for future ones. The criteria used for making any decision should reflect both fairness issues and the cultural values they are trying to promote within the organization.
- Because decision making is learned by experience, expert managers start employees out making decisions at the lowest possible level and help them develop this skill. They teach employees

good decision-making techniques by explaining why they made their own decisions as they did, asking employees what decision they would make in the manager's shoes, and by delegating as many decisions as possible. Effective managers encourage the development of decision expertise by using techniques like PreMortems. Providing employees with decision-making practice prevents them from being overwhelmed or making poor decisions in their first supervisory or management job.

- Decisions are only as good as the information on which they are based. Therefore, experts ensure that they have reliable and accurate information sources. In some organizations the higher one goes, the more difficult it is to have accurate information because people are busy telling you either what they think you want to hear or information that reflects well upon them. Kotter found that the aggressiveness with which managers sought out information distinguished effective managers from less effective ones.[36]

- It is not uncommon to have second thoughts about decisions. Indeed, it's a natural cognitive phenomenon called cognitive dissonance. Knowing this helps experts be more patient when employees (or even they themselves) have second thoughts, even when a decision seemed to be final and everyone was in agreement.

- People can only process so much information because our brains have limited capacity. Furthermore, it is sometimes impossible to have all the information that is needed to make a good decision. Thus, there is often an element of ambiguity involved with decision making. People have different tolerance levels for ambiguity, which affects their decision-making process. Expert managers pay attention to the tolerance levels of their employees and adapt accordingly.

- Part of the psychological contract regarding employee input on decisions concerns the manager's response. When managers request input from employees, they "owe" them the courtesy of explaining what the final decisions were and why employee suggestions were or were not used. When managers do not do this, employees are likely to say, "I don't know why I bothered; they just went ahead and did what they wanted to anyway." In the future, such employees may be less forthcoming with their input. However, when managers do explain how decisions were made and why an employee suggestion could not be used, they are both recognizing the employees' contributions and training them to make decisions in the future. Employees are not always aware of the broader contingencies their managers face. Sharing the rationale behind decisions is a way to develop employees.

- Managers who are expert decision makers don't let disruptive debates over a decision drag on too long. When a group cannot come to an agreement after a reasonable amount of time, the manager should step in and make the decision.

FOR ORGANIZATIONAL ARCHITECTS

- Organizational designers who are experts at creating situations in which effective decisions can be made invest significant resources to ensure that all employees have the necessary skills. They incorporate programs such as job rotation that allow employees to develop wide bases of experience and incorporate decision making in training curriculum. They also make sure to align performance appraisal and reward systems with the development of diverse experiences and with the development of effective decision-making skills.

- They develop a climate that encourages constructive, healthy debate followed by commitment to final decisions.

- Expert organizational architects also ensure that information is appropriately distributed throughout the organization and that the bearers of bad news are not punished.

- They periodically review the decision processes used by the organization to ensure that they are effective. People have a way of slipping back into old, less beneficial ways of doing things and often need reminders and skill refresher programs. They work hard to ensure that the organizational structure, reward, and control systems promote action rather than bureaucracy.

PERSONAL APPLICATION ASSIGNMENT

The topic of this assignment is to think back on a decision-making experience that was significant for you. Choose an experience that intrigues you and that you want to learn more about. One possibility is to analyze a previous decision using the leadership-participation model.

A. Concrete Experience

1. Objectively describe the experience (who, what, when, where, how information). (2 points)

2. Subjectively describe your feelings, perceptions, and thoughts that occurred during (not after) the experience. What did others seem to be feeling? (2 points)

B. Reflective Observation

1. Looking back at the experience, what were the perspectives of the key actors (including you)? (2 points)

2. Why did the people involved (including you) behave as they did? (2 points)

C. Abstract Conceptualization

1. Relate concepts or theories from the assigned readings or the lecture to the experience. Explain thoroughly how they apply to your experience. Please apply at least two concepts or theories and cite them correctly. (4 points)

D. Active Experimentation

    1. What did you learn about decision making from this experience? (1 point)

    2. What did you learn about yourself? (1 point)

    3. What action steps will you take to be more effective in the future? (2 points)

E. Integration, Synthesis, and Writing

    1. Did you integrate and synthesize the four sections? (1 point)

    2. Was the Personal Application Assignment well written and easy to understand? (1 point)

    3. Was it free of spelling and grammatical errors? (2 points)

Decision-Making Case Answers

	Decision Significance	Importance of Commitment	Leader's Expertise	Likelihood of Commitment	Group Support	Group Experience	Team Competence	STYLE
Case #1	H	L	L		H	H	H	Facilitate
Case #2	L	H		L			H	Delegate
Case #3	H	L	H					Decide

ENDNOTES

[1] The decision making styles material in this unit is based on the research of Victor Vroom and his colleagues Phillip Yetton and Arthur G. Jago. Cases used with permission of the University of Pittsburgh Press and the American Institute for Decision Sciences. Further information about training programs based on the model can be obtained from Kepner-Trego Associates, Inc.

[2] P. C. Nutt, "Surprising But True: Half the Decisions in Organizations Fail," *Academy of Management Executive 24*(4) (1999): 75–89.

[3] E. Bardack, *The Implementation Game* (Cambridge, MA: MIT Press, 1977).

[4] H. A. Simon, *Administrative Behavior* (New York: Free Press, 1976).

[5] V. Haller, "Baby Juice Scam Nets Executives Fine, Prison Time," *Mesa Tribune* (June 17, 1988): A10, 3.

[6] C. E. Lindholm, "The Science of Muddling Through," *Public Administration Review 19*(2) (Spring 1959): 79–88.

[7] M. D. Cohen, J. G. March, and J. P. Olsen, "A Garbage Can Model of Organizational Choice," *Administrative Science Quarterly 17*(1) (1972): 1–25.

[8] J. A. F. Stoner, "Risky and Cautious Shifts in Group Decisions: The Influence of Widely Held Values," *Journal of Experimental Social Psychology 4*(4) (1968): 442–459; N. Kogan and M. A. Wallach, "Group Risk Taking as a Function of Members' Anxiety and Defensiveness," *Journal of Personality 35*(1) (1967): 50–63.

[9] D. G. Myers and H. Lamm, "The Group Polarization Phenomenon," *Psychological Bulletin 83*(4) (1976): 602–627; M. E. Kaplan, "The Influencing Process in Group Decision Making," in *Group Processes*, C. Hendrick (ed.) (Newbury Park, CA: Sage, 1987): 189–212.

[10] I. L. Janis, *Victims of Groupthink* (Boston: Houghton-Mifflin, 1972) and *Groupthink* (Boston: Houghton-Mifflin, 1982). See also G. Whyte, "Groupthink Reconsidered," *Academy of Management Review 14*(1) (1989): 40–56.

[11] Janis, *Victims of Groupthink* and *Groupthink.*

[12] J. K. Esser, "Alive and Well after 25 Years: A Review of Groupthink Research," *Organizational Behavior and Human Decision Processes 73*(2/3) (1998): 116–141; S. R. Fuller and R. J. Aldag, "Organizational Tonypandy: Lessons from a Quarter Century of the Groupthink Phenomenon," *Organizational Behavior and Human Decision Processes 73*(2/3) (1998): 163–184; M. E. Turner and A. R. Pratkanis, "Twenty-Five Years of Groupthink Theory and Research: Lessons from the Evaluation of a Theory," *Organizational Behavior and Human Decision Processes 73*(2/3) (1998): 105–115; and R. M. Kramer, "Revisiting the Bay of Pigs and Vietnam Decisions 25 Years Later: How Well Has the Groupthink Hypothesis Stood the Test of Time?," *Organizational Behavior and Human Decision Processes 73*(2/3) (1998): 236–271.

[13] M. E. Turner and A. R. Pratkanis, "Social Identity Maintenance Prescriptions for Preventing Groupthink: Reducing Identity Protection And Enhancing Intellectual Conflict" in E. van de Vliert and C. K. de Dreu (eds.), *Optimizing Performance Through Conflict Stimulation* [special issue], *International Journal of Conflict Management 5* (1994): 254–270; M. E. Turner and A. R. Pratkanis, "Mitigating Groupthink by Stimulating Constructive Conflict," in *Using Conflict in Organizations,* C. de Dreu and E. Van de Vliert (eds.) (London: Sage, 1997): 53–71; M. E. Turner and A. R. Pratkanis, "A Social Identity Maintenance Theory of Groupthink," *Organizational Behavior and Human Decision Processes 73*(2/3), (1998): 210–235.

[14] N. R. F. Maier, *Principles of Human Relations* (New York: John Wiley & Sons., Inc., 1952).

[15] R. Fisher, E. Kopelman, and A. K. Schneider, *Beyond Machiavelli: Tools for Coping With Conflict* (New York: Penguin, 1996); M. E. Turner, A. R. Pratkanis, and T. Samuels, "Circumventing Groupthink by Identity Metamorphosis: Examining Intel's Departure from the DRAM industry," in *Social Identity at Work: Developing Theory for Organizational Practice,* A. Haslam, D. van Knippenberg, M. Platow, and N. Ellemers (eds.) (Philadelphia, PA: Psychology Press, 2003): 117–136.

[16] A. S. Grove, *Only the Paranoid Survive: How to Exploit the Crisis Points that Challenge Every Company* (New York: Currency Doubleday, 1996): 88–89.

[17] C. Neck and G. Moorhead, "Jury deliberations in the Trial of U. S. v. John DeLorean: A case analysis of groupthink avoidance and an enhanced framework," *Human Relations 45*(10) (1992): 1077–1091.

[18] B. M. Staw and J. Ross, "Commitment in an Experimenting Society: An Experiment on the Attribution of Leadership from Administrative Scenarios," *Journal of Applied Psychology 65*(3) (1980): 249–260.

[19] V. H. Vroom, "Leadership and the Decision Making Process," *Organizational Dynamics 28*(4) (2000): 82–94.

[20] V. H. Vroom and P. Yetton, *Leadership and Decision Making* (Pittsburgh, PA: University of Pittsburgh Press, 1973); V. H. Vroom and A. G. Jago, *The New Leadership: Managing Participation in Organizations (Upper Saddle River, NJ: Prentice Hall, 1988)*; V. H. Vroom and A. G. Jago, "Situation Effects and Levels of Analysis in the Study of Leader Participation," *Leadership Quarterly 6*(2) (1995): 169–81; and V. H. Vroom, A. G. Jago, D. Eden, P. W. Yetton, and J. F. Craig, "Participative Leadership," in *Leadership: The Multiple-Level Approaches: Classical and New Wave 24,* F. Dansereau and F. J. Yammarino, (eds.) (Stamford, CT: JAI Press, 1998): 145–89; V. H. Vroom, "Leadership and the Decision Making Process," *Organizational Dynamics 28*(4) (Spring 2000): 82–94.

[21] A version of this case appears in Vroom and Jago, *The New Leadership:* 166–168.

[22] Vroom and Jago, *The New Leadership.*

[23] Vroom, "Leadership and the Decision Making Process."

[24] R. H. Field and R. J. House, "A Test of the Vroom-Yetton Model Using Manager and Subordinate Reports," *Journal of Applied Psychology* 75(3) (1990): 362–366.

[25] Vroom and Jago, *The New Leadership*: 79.

[26] C. Margerison and R. Glube, "Leadership Decision Making: An Empirical Test of the Vroom and Yetton Model," *Journal of Management Studies* 16(1) (1979): 45–55.

[27] V. H. Vroom and A. G. Jago, "Decision Making as a Social Process: Normative and Descriptive Models of Leader Behavior," *Decision Sciences* 5 (1974): 743–769.

[28] C. Barnard, *The Functions of the Executive* (Cambridge, MA: Harvard University Press, 1938).

[29] W. Ouchi, *Theory Z. How American Businesses Can Meet the Japanese Challenge* (New York: Avon, 1989).

[30] L. A. Burke and M. K. Miller, "Taking the Mystery Out of Intuitive Decision Making," *Academy of Management Executive* 13(4) (1999): 91–98.

[31] Ibid: 93. For another interesting discussion of intuitive decision making, see G. Klein, *Sources of Power: How People Make Decisions* (Cambridge, MA: MIT Press, 1999).

[32] G. Klein, *The Power of Intuition* (New York: Doubleday, 2004): 26–28.

[33] G. Klein, *Intuition at Work* (New York: Currency, 2003).

[34] G. Klein and K. Weick, "Decisions: Making the Right Ones. Learning from the Wrong Ones," *Across the Board* 37(6) (2000): 18.

[35] Klein, *The Power of Intuition.*

[36] J. Kotter, *The General Managers* (New York: Free Press, 1982).

Chapter *18*

▲▲▲

POWER AND INFLUENCE

OBJECTIVES By the end of this chapter, you should be able to:

A. Identify the three possible outcomes of an influence attempt.

B. Describe the various sources of power.

C. Identify the influence tactics people use at work.

D. Describe and utilize the four influence styles.

GETTING YOUR IDEAS HEARD

Samantha knew she had good ideas, but she felt invisible in staff meetings. In the beginning, she'd piped up with suggestions or proposals, but the response was either a dismissive "That won't work" or worse, dead silence. Not even her boss acknowledged her ideas. Eventually, she gave up trying to have an impact. This wasn't her best long-term solution because she was passed over for promotions since she didn't "look" like a leader. Eventually she quit in disgust. When asked why, Samantha attributed her problems at the company to sexist coworkers. However, since other women were able to advance, the more likely culprits were Samantha's own inability to exercise influence with her peers and her boss–and her boss's inability to help her develop this crucial skill.

People with power have a ready audience for their ideas and an easier time in influencing others. But most of us have to put more effort into exerting influence. Sometimes that means figuring out in advance whom you need to talk with before meetings and laying the groundwork. Consultant Kim Barnes recommends identifying people who are opinion leaders and asking them what their decision criteria will be for new proposals. Based on that information, you can adapt your proposal and frame your presentation to address their goals and concerns. You can also meet with the opinion leaders beforehand to seek their support before presenting your idea, but this should not take the form of backroom deals that others could resent. Your ideas and proposals should be well researched and presented clearly and concisely. Succeeding at this type of influence means putting yourself in the shoes of other people and considering their perspective; in other words, to influence others, you must also allow yourself to be influenced by their views.

It never occurs to many employees like Samantha that they also have to manage the boss. Peter Drucker, management guru, insisted that bosses are also human and deserve the same considerations we try to give subordinates. He encouraged employees to focus on their relationship with their boss. Every boss is an individual with different needs, preferences, and strengths. Once subordinates figure out what these are, they can help their bosses be more effective and, within reason, adapt to their idiosyncrasies. If the boss is not a morning person, wait till afternoon before dropping into his office. If the boss prefers to read information rather than receive oral briefings, communicate in writing rather than always attempting to meet face to face. If the boss tends to get bogged down unnecessarily in details, get her to sign off on the project concept and agreed-upon milestones. That way she won't be tempted by your detailed implementation plan, and you can help her stay focused on what her own boss expects of her.

Some employees are good at coaching their boss to be more effective, but this requires mutual trust. Employees who earn the boss's trust do not underrate or bad-mouth them. Neither do they zap their bosses with unexpected surprises that make them look incompetent or poorly informed. They try not to cause the boss unnecessary grief. They do, however, sincerely have the boss's best interest at heart and try to help him or her succeed. They empathize with the difficulty of the boss's job. By managing this relationship well, subordinates are more likely to have a boss who listens to their ideas and tries out their suggestions. If they follow this up with learning to influence others skillfully, they won't have to worry about feeling invisible when trying to get their ideas heard.

Based on P. Drucker, "How to Manage the Boss," *The Wall Street Journal* (August 1, 1986) and B. K. Barnes, *Exercising Influence* (Berkley, CA: Barnes & Conti, 2000).

CLASS PREPARATION

A. Read "Getting Your Ideas Heard."

B. Answer the following questions:

    1. Think about someone who handles power very well. How does he or she do it?

    2. What differences in behavior have you observed between someone who has power and influence and someone who does not?

    3. What do you want to learn about power?

C. Complete the Personal Influence Style Self-Diagnosis.

D. While reading the chapter, make a list of the cues you should pay attention to with regard to power and influence.

PERSONAL INFLUENCE STYLE SELF-DIAGNOSIS

The focus of this chapter is the effective exercise of power and influence. Before reading the chapter, do a simple self-assessment of your style of influencing others. Generally speaking, how descriptive is each of the following styles of your typical influence behavior? Using the key provided, record your rating (from 1 = not descriptive to 5 = very descriptive) in the space to the left of each paragraph. Then read The Knowledge Base.

1	2	3	4	5
Not at all descriptive of me		Somewhat descriptive		Very descriptive of me

_____ I am direct and positive in asserting my own wishes and requirements. I let others know what I want from them, and I am quick to tell others when I am pleased or dissatisfied with their performance. I am willing to use my influence and authority to get others to do what I want. I skillfully use a combination of pressures and incentives to get others to agree with my plans and proposals, and I follow up to make sure they carry out agreements and commitments. I readily engage in bargaining and negotiation to achieve my objectives, using both tough and conciliatory styles according to the realities of power and position in each situation.

_____ I am open and nondefensive, being quick to admit when I do not have the answer, or when I have made a mistake. I listen attentively to the ideas and feelings of others, actively communicating my interest in their contributions, and my understanding of their points of view. I am willing to be influenced by others. I give credit to others for their ideas and accomplishments. I make sure that everyone has a chance to be heard before decisions are made, even when I do not agree with their position. I show trust in others, and I help them to bring out and develop their strengths and abilities.

_____ I appeal to the emotions and ideals of others through the use of forceful and colorful words and images. My enthusiasm is contagious and carries others along with me. I bring others to believe in their ability to accomplish and succeed by working together. I see and can communicate my vision of the exciting possibilities in an idea or situation. I get others to see the values, hopes, and aspirations that they have in common, and I build these common values into a shared sense of group loyalty and commitment.

_____ I produce detailed and comprehensive proposals for dealing with problems. I am persistent and energetic in finding and presenting the logic behind my ideas and in marshalling facts, arguments, and opinion in support of my position. I am quick to grasp the strengths and weaknesses in an argument and to see and articulate the logical connections among various aspects of a complex situation. I am a vigorous and determined seller of ideas.

THE KNOWLEDGE BASE

Power and influence have negative connotations for many people. They conjure up unpleasant images such as the misuse of power by politicians, the high-pressure tactics of some salespeople, and the destructive behavior occasionally exhibited by military dictators. We often see examples of poor organizational decisions that reflect the self-serving motives of powerful individuals or groups rather than a concern for the good of the organization. By contrast, the ability to get things done is a crucial requirement for both personal and organizational success. Managers need a certain degree of power and influence to obtain the necessary resources for their units, to ensure that good ideas are heard and decisions are implemented, and to place competent people in key positions. Another advantage of power is having access to top decision makers and receiving early information on decisions and policy shifts. Therefore, understanding and knowing how to manage power is a key skill for employees and managers alike.

In a comparative study of successful and unsuccessful executives, almost all the following characteristics of the unsuccessful executives can be traced to an abuse or misuse of power. Their personal inadequacies were (1) insensitive, abrasive, and intimidating; (2) cold, aloof, and arrogant; (3) betrayed others' trust; (4) overly ambitious and political; (5) unable to delegate or build a team; and (6) overly dependent on others (a mentor, for example).[1]

In contrast, the personal characteristics of people who successfully obtain and exercise a great deal of power are (1) energy, endurance, and physical stamina; (2) the ability to focus their energy and avoid wasted effort; (3) sensitivity so they can read and understand others; (4) flexibility—the ability to consider different means to achieve goals; (5) personal toughness—a willingness to engage, when necessary, in conflict and confrontation; and (6) the ability to submerge one's ego and be a good subordinate or team player to enlist the help and support of others.[2]

The power and status differences that exist in hierarchies, between supervisors and subordinates, for example, are real and natural. They cannot be ignored or wished away. Indeed, in its simplest, most basic form, your role as a manager is to make a difference in the behavior of your subordinates. Your responsibility as a manager is to behave in ways that add to your subordinates' ability to do their jobs effectively and efficiently. The issue is not, therefore, whether or not managers have power, but how they choose to exercise the power demanded by the role and with what consequences. One does not "make a difference" without exercising power and influence.

Power is defined as the capacity to influence the behavior of others. Influence is the process by which people successfully persuade others to follow their advice, suggestions, or orders. In general, there are three possible outcomes to an influence attempt—commitment, compliance, or resistance. Whereas *commitment* implies internal agreement, *compliance* is merely going along with a request or demand without believing in it. *Resistance* occurs when a person's influence attempt is rejected. This can take the form of a flat refusal, passive-aggressive tactics (making excuses or pretending to agree while resorting to delaying actions or sabotage), or seeking out a third party or superior who has the power to overrule the request.

SOURCES OF POWER

Traditionally, managers have relied almost exclusively on the power inherent in their position. An extreme form of this sounds like, "I'm the boss. I have the right and responsibility to tell you what to do, and if you don't perform, I retain the ultimate power of reward and punishment." Increasingly, managers are being forced to develop other influence skills. The greater need for different forms of influence is a result of (1) a shifting value structure among younger generations who have less respect for traditional authority; (2) rapid organizational change; (3) the diversity of people, goals, and values; and (4) increased interdependence.[3] Many managers spend the majority of their time on interdependent lateral relationships with people who are neither subordinates nor superiors.[4] In the lateral relationships that we find in staff positions, self-directed work teams, and network organizations (discussed in Chapter 21), power comes from expertise, effort, and relationships, rather than one's position or the ability to reward or punish others (coercive power). Charisma (magnetic personality, rare ability to attract others) is another source of power; it is an extension of referent power, which is based on desirable personal traits or resources.[5] We admire and identify with people who have referent power, such as celebrites who endorse products.

Power also comes from "being in the right place." A good location is one that provides (1) control over resources, and (2) control and access to information, in addition to (3) formal authority (position).[6] *Units that cope with the critical uncertainties facing an organization also acquire a measure of power that they would not otherwise have; this is termed the strategic contingency model of power.*[7] For example, John Zeglis, a corporate lawyer, became a powerful figure at AT&T, and eventually its former president, because he helped lead the company through regulatory changes. "Chief counsels rarely rise so far in corporate America, but Mr. Zeglis . . . is a special case. AT&T's single most important operational concern remains regulation and how telecommunication laws might impede the company's ability to boost earnings and expand beyond its long-distance franchise. Nobody knows these rules better than Mr. Zeglis, who helped write them."[8]

The more dependent people are on someone else, the more power that person has over them.[9] For example, if a person has a scarce skill or resource that is not easily substituted, he or she has power.[10] A highly valued and hard-to-replace employee has the power to negotiate a higher salary and perks than an employee who is less essential to the success of the organization. The former can always threaten to leave the organization; such a threat by a less essential employee is not a source of concern. Thus, it's important to understand the relationship between dependency and power.

INFLUENCE TACTICS

In addition to understanding the sources of power, effective managers need to know what influence behavior looks like. When people were asked to describe incidents in which they had influenced others at work, researchers identified nine generic influence tactics that appear in Exhibit 18–1.[11] U.S. managers prefer rational persuasion, consultation, and inspirational appeals over more coercive tactics. They often begin with the softer influence tactics and, if they are not successful, move to harder tactics, such as threats. Managers who use a variety of tactics tend to be more successful than those who rely on a single tactic. Robert Cialdini, a social psychologist and internationally recognized expert on persuasion, has identified several influence tactics that are commonly used in many settings; Exhibit 18–2 lists six influence strategies, along with descriptions of how they can be implemented.

Complex and vital influence attempts, such as those required for major strategies or new projects, always require multiple influence tactics. A successful attempt is likely to begin with gathering facts, citing parallel examples (who is doing this?), marshaling the support of others (perhaps insured by an effective web of influence), precise timing and packaging of a presentation, and, in the case of initial resistance, persistence and repetition over weeks or even months. Less frequently, but sometimes successfully, managers may resort to manipulation, threats, or pulling rank.[12] When people are trying to obtain benefits or favors from others, they are more likely to use ingratiation or friendly behavior.

The organizational culture affects the type of influence tactics used. Norms and values determine which tactics are acceptable. For example, threats and sanctions are frowned on in informal, egalitarian cultures. Newly hired managers should carefully observe successful influence attempts rather than assuming that acceptable tactics in their previous job will work in a different organizational culture.

Rational Persuasion	The agent uses logical arguments and factual evidence to persuade the target that a proposal or request is viable and likely to result in the attainment of task objectives.
Inspirational Appeals	The agent makes a request or proposal that arouses the target's enthusiasm by appealing to target values, ideals, and aspirations, thereby increasing the target's self-confidence.
Consultation	The agent seeks the target's participation in planning a strategy, activity, or change for which target support and assistance are desired, or is willing to modify a proposal to deal with target concerns and suggestions.
Ingratiation	The agent uses praise, flattery, friendly behavior, or helpful behavior to get the target in a good mood or to think favorably of him or her before asking for something.
Personal Appeals	The agent appeals to the target's feelings of loyalty and friendship toward him or her when asking for something.
Exchange	The agent offers an exchange of favors, indicates willingness to reciprocate at a later time, or promises a share of the benefits if the target helps accomplish a task.
Coalition Tactics	The agent seeks the aid of others to persuade the target to do something, or uses the support of others as a reason for the target to agree also.
Legitimating Tactics	The agent seeks to establish the legitimacy of a request by claiming the authority or right to make it, or by verifying that it is consistent with organizational policies, rules, practices, or traditions.
Pressure	The agent uses demands, threats, frequent checking, or persistent reminders to influence the target to do what he or she wants.

EXHIBIT 18-1   **Definition of Influence Tactics**

Source: Adapted from Gary Yukl, *Leadership in Organizations* (Upper Saddle River, NJ: Prentice Hall, 1994): 225.

A common mistake is using influence strategies that fail because they are "too much too soon or too little too late."[13] Effective managers understand that there is a continuum of influence attempts, and they use the appropriate degree of "muscle" when influencing others. Generally, it works best if you begin with Level 1 in the following continuum and move up the scale if your influence target does not respond as you wish.

- Muscle Level 1 is a polite request: "I'd like you to let us know when you can't come to a steering committee meeting."
- Muscle Level 2 is a request that is stronger in word choice, voice characteristics, and body language: "When you don't let us know that you're going to miss a meeting, we sometimes end up meeting without a quorum, which is useless. I need to know when you can't make a meeting."
- Muscle Level 3 is a statement of consequences if the behavior doesn't change: "If you can't let us know when you'll miss a meeting, we will have to ask you to resign from the committee."
- Muscle Level 4 is the application of the consequences stated in Level 3: "Because you have not been keeping us informed about your attendance, I will have to ask you to leave the committee."[14]

If you escalate too quickly to the higher muscle levels, you can cause a backlash or ruin relationships. If you fail to escalate at all, the other person will simply continue with the unacceptable behavior and you may be perceived as weak and ineffectual.

INFLUENCE STYLES

In the class activity, we will focus on the influence styles identified by Berlew and Harrison that readily lend themselves to skill-based training and practice.[15] Effective managers need to

Influence Strategy	How It Works	Application
Reciprocity	People repay in kind	• Give what you want to receive • Do favors • Make concessions
Social proof	People follow the lead of similar others	• Use peer power when available • Get buy-in from peers and bosses who are well-regarded by others • Demonstrate how many people agree with you
Consistency	People align with clear, public commitments	• Make commitments active, public, and voluntary • Ask people to circulate email messages, memos, or other public communications that state their commitment to a particular decision or course of action
Scarcity	People want more of scarce items	• Highlight unique benefits and exclusive information
Expertise and Authority	Task/application relevant expertise and experience persuades	• Demonstrate specialized knowledge and expertise • Exhibit indicators of legitimate authority (e.g., doctors wear lab coats and stethoscopes)
Liking	People respond to those who are pleasant, likable, and charismatic	• Identify similarities (likes, dislikes, anything that is shared) • Offer sincere praise and compliments

EXHIBIT 18-2 Interpersonal Influence Strategies

Source: Adapted from R.B. Cialdini, *Influence: Science and Practice* (Boston: Allyn & Bacon, 2000) and R.B. Cialdini, "Harnessing the Science of Persuasion," *Harvard Business Review 79* (2001): 72–79.

develop the capacity to analyze a situation and determine which influence tactic will be most effective. Although people often use a combination of influence tactics, we tend to be predisposed to certain styles that feel more natural. In the class preparation, you were asked to determine how much each style describes your influence behavior. These styles are described more fully in the following paragraphs. Two of the styles rely on "pushing" energy, whereas the others utilize "pulling" energy.

Assertive Persuasion

In the assertive persuasion style, we "push" others with our intellect. Assertive persuasion is considered the bread and butter of the business world. The essential quality of assertive persuasion as an influence style is the use of facts, logic, rational argument, and persuasive reasoning. Although the influencer may argue forcefully with great élan and spirit, the power of assertive persuasion does not come from an emotional source. Facts and logic are, by definition, emotionally neutral. A person may react to a fact emotionally and thereby be persuaded to behave in a certain way. However, the feelings of the person using assertive persuasion should not enter into their argument. The facts are supposed to speak for themselves.

People using assertive persuasion to persuade others are usually highly verbal and articulate. They confidently present their ideas, proposals, and suggestions and can support their proposals with rational reasons. They structure their arguments and enumerate the points they want to make so listeners can follow their logic. Sometimes they are guilty of selectively listening to others' attempts at assertive persuasion, hoping to find a weak spot so that they can effectively reason against others' proposals.

This style is most appropriate when the issue in question is suited to a logical approach, which is not the case with emotional or value-laden issues. Assertive persuasion also works best when the person exerting influence is already respected and enjoys a certain prestige.

Reward and Punishment

The second "pushing" style is reward and punishment, in which we are "pushing our will" onto other people. Reward and punishment involves the use of bargaining, incentives, and pressures, and demanding certain behavior from other people. People who use this style state their expectations for how others will behave and also evaluate that behavior.

Rewards may be offered for compliance, and punishment or deprivation may be threatened for noncompliance. Naked power may be used, or more indirect and veiled pressures may be exerted through the use of status, prestige, and formal authority.

This influence style is characterized by contingent, if-then consequences: "If you do X, then I'll do Y" or "If you don't do this, then Y will happen to you." At times, the consequence (Y) is left implicit or vaguely defined, but people using this style clearly state the behaviors or results (X) they want to see. They use negotiation, threats, and promises to influence others.

Both reward and punishment and assertive persuasion involve agreeing and disagreeing with others. The difference is that in assertive persuasion, one agrees or disagrees with another's proposal or idea because it is more or less effective, correct, accurate, or true. In reality, other factors can bias logical judgments, such as emotions, relationships, and personal agendas. When using reward and punishment, the judgment of right or wrong is an evaluation based on a moral or social standard, a regulation, or an arbitrary performance standard. The person making the evaluation usually sets himself or herself up as the judge instead of appealing to a common and shared standard of rationality.

People using reward and punishment are very comfortable, generally, in conflict situations. They are comfortable giving clear feedback—both positive and negative—and are very direct about prescribing their goals and expectations. They are comfortable evaluating the work of others and saying what they like and don't like about it. People who use this style should state their expectations clearly in a direct manner. They must be assertive rather than wishy-washy or tentative, so that it is clear what will happen if the other party does not do what the influencer is demanding. This style is not appropriate with individuals or groups who have a strong need to be in control or not be controlled by a strong desire to others.

As you reflect on the description just given, it will be clear that any individual, regardless of formal position, can effectively utilize many reward and punishment behaviors. Anyone, theoretically, can make evaluative statements involving praise and criticism. Similarly, if a meeting were dragging, anyone could prescribe a goal and expectation ("We've got to finish our work by six o'clock"). However, not everyone can utilize the same incentives and pressures. The ability to follow through on an evaluation or a prescribed goal or expectation depends on one's access to and control of meaningful rewards and punishments (incentives and pressures). Nevertheless, by withholding support, dragging their heels, and other forms of subtle "sabotage," subordinates demonstrate that bosses are not the only ones who have reward and punishment power.

Participation and Trust

Unlike the first two styles that involve pushing energy, the use of the participation and trust style pulls others toward what is desired or required by involving them. By actively listening to and involving others, an influencer using participation and trust increases the commitment of others to the target objective or task. This is in sharp contrast to the reward and punishment style in which compliance (not commitment) must be monitored frequently.

People who use participation and trust are generally rather patient and have developed the capacity to be very effective listeners. They are very good at reflecting back to people (paraphrasing) both the content and feelings of what the person has said. They build on others' ideas and are quick to credit others for their contributions.

People who use participation and trust as an influence style also effectively use personal disclosure. By sharing personal information about themselves, others are encouraged to reciprocate, which is one of the first steps in developing a trusting relationship. People who use this style readily admit their own areas of uncertainty and mistakes. By openly acknowledging their own limitations and taking a nondefensive attitude toward feedback, they help others to feel more accepted for what they are.

On the surface, participation and trust may appear to some to be a weak and wishy-washy style of influence when contrasted, for example, with the toughness of assertive persuasion or reward and punishment. It is not. Its power derives from building the trust and commitment needed to implement actions and with it a willingness to be influenced. As with the other influence styles, participation and trust can be misused to manipulate others. For example, managers who involve subordinates in a consensus decision-making process even though they have already chosen a solution are treading on thin ice.

Common Vision

Another influence style that pulls rather than pushes is the common vision style. It aims to identify a common vision for the future and to strengthen the group members' belief that through their collective efforts, the vision can become a reality. This style appeals to people's emotions and values, activating their personal commitment to private hopes and ideals and channeling that energy into working toward a common purpose. People using this style clearly articulate goals and the means to achieve them. The well-known speeches of Martin Luther King Jr. and John F. Kennedy are classic examples of the effective use of common vision, although it is by no means a style that is useful only in large-group or political settings. This style is especially important in organizations undergoing major change efforts.

Within the everyday world of organizations, there are numerous opportunities for the effective use of common vision. Many organizational meetings become exercises in competing assertions. In such situations, the ability to help the group to pull together around a common goal can provide a much needed spirit of collaboration and inspiration: "What we can accomplish if we work together."

People who use common vision are generally emotionally expressive. They are enthusiastic and skilled at projecting and communicating their feelings in an articulate manner. They talk in emotionally vivid imagery and metaphors. People using this style look for common ground and the synergy that can result from working together. People who use this style well are described as charismatic leaders.

Please return to the Personal Influence Style Self-Diagnosis and determine which style is described in each paragraph.

THE VALUE ISSUES—POSITIVE VERSUS NEGATIVE POWER

None of these four styles is inherently right or wrong. The key to effectiveness is using them in the appropriate situation and paying attention to how others experience your use of power. For example, when people are uplifted by an inspiring vision or when their competence is recognized and rewarded, they are empowered and feel stronger. There are other times, however, when the use of power and influence makes others feel weak and powerless—put down by intimidating bosses, run over by autocratic people, or exploited by ambitious people.

The important distinction, therefore, has to do with how the exercise of power and influence is experienced: What is its impact? Assertive persuasion, reward and punishment, participation and trust, and common vision can be used in a way that results in other people feeling stronger. They can also be used to make people feel weaker—to feel like pawns in the hands of someone else. Common vision, for example, will result in people feeling weaker if it is used only to raise people's hopes and expectations without anything ever being realized or gained.

Conger has expanded the definition of persuasion to incorporate aspects of participation and trust and common vision. The effective persuasion he observed in successful managers includes four steps:[16]

1. Establish credibility.
2. Frame goals in a way that identifies common ground with those you intend to persuade.
3. Reinforce your position using vivid language and compelling evidence.
4. Connect emotionally with your audience.

We learned in the chapter on motivation that McClelland identified a need for power as a basic motivator, even though it is somewhat difficult in U.S. society to acknowledge this need because we are often suspicious of power. McClelland resolved this dilemma by referring to the two faces of power.[17] Although a need for power always refers to a desire to have a strong impact on others, one face of power, personal power, is an unsocialized concern for personal dominance. It is characterized by an I win–you lose perspective and a need to dominate others. The second face of power is socialized power. People motivated by a high need for socialized power show a concern for group goals, empowering others, and a win-win approach. This second face of power, the socialized version, is required for long-term success in organizations. In some cultures people maintain that "power corrupts" and even people who started out with a need for socialized power degenerate into a selfish concern for personal dominance. Although this may not always be the case, it is essential for people to know themselves and their need for power.

Influence attempts have both content and relationship outcomes. You may be successful at winning what you want (content) from the other party, but if they resent being coerced or manipulated, you have harmed your relationship with them. In order to balance the content and relationship outcomes, it is helpful to plan out beforehand what it is that you want from the other party (content objective) and what impression you want the other party to have of you as a result of this influence attempt (relationship objective).

In their day-to-day work, managers are continually faced with a host of questions about the process of leadership. How can I get the job done most effectively? What is the "best" leadership style? How can I build commitment and loyalty among the members of my work team to the company and its objectives? When should I listen and when should I give orders? If I become too friendly with my subordinates, will I lose their respect? How can I get others to do their work well? These are all contingency questions—there is no one right or wrong answer for every occasion.

Some managers mistakenly believe that the more power they give to their employees, the less power they have for themselves. This is true only if you impose a win-lose framework on the situation and see power as a limited commodity. In fact, power is often paradoxical—the more one gives away, the more one has for oneself. Managers who work hard to develop and empower their employees are examples of people who accrue power by giving it to others.

Researchers have identified the steps that practicing managers use to establish sustained managerial influence:[18]

1. **Develop a reputation as a knowledgeable person or an expert** This is the most commonly reported form of gaining influence. This requires keeping up to date in one's field or area. However, it is not sufficient to be knowledgeable; others must also be aware of this fact, so it is sometimes necessary to market oneself or use impression management.

2. **Balance the time spent in each critical relationship according to the needs of the work rather than on the basis of habit or social preference** Managers should spend their time where it will do the most good in advancing organizational goals. This may necessitate switching from a narrow focus on subordinates or technical areas to developing both lateral and upward relationships and external relationships in order to have greater influence.

There are two interesting findings related to building relationships and personal advancement. First, women are more likely to assume that hard work will result in promotion whereas men tend to believe that political contacts within the organization are essential to their advancement.[19] Second, there is some research evidence, which is not gender-related, that managers who spend time networking and trying to "look like a star" are more likely to win promotions in U.S. companies than effective, competent managers who devote their energies to their jobs and subordinates.[20] In organizations that allow this to happen, impression management and political skills rather than merit and performance are rewarded, and the people who make it to the top will be more dedicated to their personal career than to the company and, in some cases, be less competent than others. Once again, the concept of the two faces of power helps us determine what type of networking and relationship building we want to encourage—networking for the good of the organization or unit (social power) as opposed to networking that only benefits the individual (personal power).

3. **Develop a network of resource persons who can be called on for assistance** In many cultures in Latin America, Asia, and Africa, things get done in organizations primarily because of personal relationships. People who take the time to cultivate good relationships within the organization usually receive better service and cooperation than those who do not. Although this phenomenon is less striking in the United States, relationships are still extremely important. As mentioned in Chapter 2, Luthans and his colleagues observed managers at work and identified networking as one of four key behavioral categories that emerged. He defined networking as "socializing/ politicking and interacting with outsiders."[21] (The other three categories were communication, traditional management, and human resource management).

4. **Implement influence tactics with sensitivity, flexibility, and adequate levels of communication** As with any strategy, it is necessary to understand one's audience and do no harm to the long-term relationship with the other party—in this case, the target one wishes to influence. Therefore, good influencers analyze the target and use the communication style that will be most effective with him or her. Managers who are good at influencing others are usually good listeners who can adapt their tactics to the responses they hear from the target.

Exhibit 18–3 lists some of the key questions managers should ask themselves as they design their influence strategies.

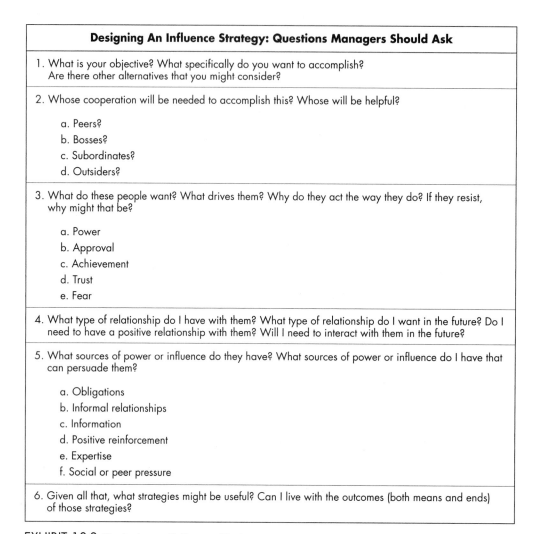

Designing An Influence Strategy: Questions Managers Should Ask
1. What is your objective? What specifically do you want to accomplish? Are there other alternatives that you might consider?
2. Whose cooperation will be needed to accomplish this? Whose will be helpful? a. Peers? b. Bosses? c. Subordinates? d. Outsiders?
3. What do these people want? What drives them? Why do they act the way they do? If they resist, why might that be? a. Power b. Approval c. Achievement d. Trust e. Fear
4. What type of relationship do I have with them? What type of relationship do I want in the future? Do I need to have a positive relationship with them? Will I need to interact with them in the future?
5. What sources of power or influence do they have? What sources of power or influence do I have that can persuade them? a. Obligations b. Informal relationships c. Information d. Positive reinforcement e. Expertise f. Social or peer pressure
6. Given all that, what strategies might be useful? Can I live with the outcomes (both means and ends) of those strategies?

EXHIBIT 18-3 Designing an Influence Strategy

Adapted from J. Kotter, *Power and Influence* (New York: Free Press, 1985); J. Pfeffer, *Managing with Power* (Cambridge: Harvard Business School Press, 1992); A. Pratkanis and E. Aronson, *Age of Propaganda: The Everyday Use and Abuse of Persuasion* (New York: Freeman, 2000).

DO MEN AND WOMEN DIFFER IN THEIR INFLUENCE STYLES AND USE OF POWER?

There are contradictory findings concerning gender differences in the use of influence tactics; some studies find no differences between men and women,[22] whereas others find that the only difference is that women are less assertive with their superiors[23] and more likely to appeal to altruism and rationale-based strategies than threats of punishment with their subordinates.[24]

The longitudinal study of AT&T employees revealed the following gender differences with regard to power. Women are more consensus-oriented than men, which has been confirmed in many other studies. Women and men view and utilize power in different ways.

Women see it as a "resource that can be used to influence outcomes on the job and to focus the competencies of the people who work for them. Men in the study, by contrast, tended to think of power more as an end in itself, as something they can use to react against or take power away from others in authority. Men saw power as a way to supersede others in power, women rarely did."[25] Recent interviews in an on-going study found that both male and female high-tech managers in the Silicon Valley viewed power as something to be used sparingly and only as a last resort.

SEXUAL HARASSMENT AND POWER

Sexual harassment refers to unwelcome advances, requests for sexual favors, and other verbal or physical conduct of a sexual nature. Subjects of harassment, female or male, find themselves in especially difficult situations when their superiors, with their power to reward and punish them, are the ones doing the harassing. People sometimes fear that refusing to go along with sexual advances will result in termination, poor performance appraisals, and decreased promotion opportunities and salary. Therefore, power can be a factor in sexual harassment when those in higher positions abuse their power to harass people in lower-ranking positions. Sometimes, however, the initiators are people in lower-ranking positions who offer sexual favors to obtain advantages at work from a powerful person. Sexual harassment is both illegal and unethical.

CULTURAL DIFFERENCES

Because of cultural values and history, power is perceived and exercised differently around the world. For example, power is one of the dominant values in Latin American cultures. It is the principal theme in the organizational literature indigenous to this region.[26] Therefore, the flagrant use of power is more acceptable in Latin America than in cultures with a more ambivalent view of power.[27] In high–power distance cultures (e.g., Venezuela, Yugoslavia, and France), leaders are expected to behave differently from people of lower rank, and differences in rank are more apparent. In low–power distance cultures, people are less comfortable with differences in power, and there is less emphasis on social class distinction and hierarchical rank. Power is more likely to be shared in these cultures (e.g., Denmark, the Netherlands, and Israel).[28]

In any setting, it's important to decipher who has the power. Different cultures and organizations use various artifacts and symbols to designate power. Office size, private space (the executive restroom), large staffs, and immediate access to important people are symbols of power in many U.S. businesses. However, these objects may have no symbolic meaning whatsoever in other cultures, or even in specific organizational cultures in the United States. Thus, decoding the symbols and behaviors that indicate the location of power is an important skill. It is also wise to determine the norms and expectations about the exercise of power and influence in various cultures so you can adapt your behavior accordingly.

CLASS ACTIVITY: INFLUENCE ROLE PLAY

The purpose of this exercise is to allow you to practice the influence styles and increase your own behavioral flexibility. (Time allotted: 100 minutes)

STEP 1. Divide into three- or four-person groups (preferably with students from your learning groups whom you have worked with repeatedly) and discuss the following questions. (15 minutes)

   a. Self-assessments. Which style(s) do you use most frequently? Do the descriptions in the Personal Influence Style Self-Diagnosis in the Class Preparation accurately describe how you try to influence others?

   b. Which styles have you seen the other members in your four-person group use most often throughout this course?

   c. By which style(s) are you most likely to be influenced? Which style(s) are you least likely to be influenced by and most likely to resist?

STEP 2. Preparing for role plays: individual work. (15 minutes)

   On the pages that follow you will find six potentially stressful influence situations. Individuals should read these situations carefully and select one (to start) that best meets the following criteria:

   a. It seems real to you (i.e., you have been in that situation and/or could easily imagine yourself being in that situation).

   b. You would expect yourself to experience at least a moderate level of stress in dealing with that situation.

   c. It calls for an influence style that you would like to develop.

   If none of these situations appeal to you, choose a real-life situation that you can quickly explain to your group.

   Jot down your response to questions (1) through (4) in each situation in the space provided following the situation you have chosen to work on.

STEP 3. Conducting and critiquing the role plays. (1 hour)

Each person in the group should have an opportunity to play all of the following roles.

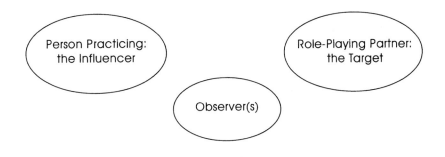

Please follow this sequence:

a. One person volunteers to go first. That person (the influencer) selects a partner (the target). The other(s) are to be silent observers who can use the observation forms that precede each situation.

If the influencer chose a real-life situation, very briefly (2 to 4 minutes), he or she tells his or her partner what the other person (boss, co-worker, etc.)—the target—is like and how he or she is likely to act. Partners should behave in a way so as to produce the moderate stress level desired—neither outrageously stubborn nor a pushover.

b. Enact the situation. (5–6 minutes)

c. Feedback discussion. (8–10 minutes)

   1. The influencer begins by stating:

      a. Which response style he or she was planning to use and which one(s) was actually used.

      b. His or her content and relationship objectives. Were they achieved?

   2. The observers and the target person relate:

      a. Which styles they thought the influencer was using based on the specific behavior they observed (e.g., "It looked like you were using trust and participation when you began talking about your previous personal experiences"—personal disclosure).

      b. What influencer behaviors made the target feel stronger? Weaker?

      c. What two or three specific suggestions would you offer the influencer to enhance his or her impact in a situation such as this?

The influencer should focus on listening to and understanding this feedback (i.e., use of participation and trust style) and not try to convince the others why their observations are wrong or misinformed (i.e., use of reward and punishment and/or assertive persuasion).

Then repeat the procedure so that each person has at least one practice opportunity. (If time permits, select a second stressful influence situation and repeat Step 3.)

STEP 4. General debriefing (10 minutes)

   a. What did you learn about influencing other people from doing these role-plays?

Observations Category	INFLUENCE STYLES			
	Assertive Persuasion	Reward and Punishment	Participation and Trust	Common Vision
	Logic, Facts, Rationality, Ideas, Proposals, Reasons For and Against	Evaluations, Use of Incentives and Pressures, Bargains, Stating Own Personal Goals and Expectations	Active Listening, Recognizing Others' Contributions, Involving Others and Getting Their Contributions, Disclosing Own Areas of Uncertainty	Building a Sense of Group Spirit, a We-Feeling, Creating a Superordinate Group Goal, Shared Identity
Which styles did the influencer use most frequently? 1 = most frequently 4 = least frequently				
Examples of influence behavior that strengthened the other person (positive power)				
Examples of influence behaviors that weakened the other person (negative power)				
Missed opportunities (i.e., example of where the style might have had a positive impact but was not used)				
Which style did the influencer use most effectively? 1 = most effective 4 = least effective				

Situation 1—Pushing a Change Effort

You are concerned that the other managers in your somewhat conservative company have not completely grasped the need to be more competitive. Even though the firm's profit and loss statement and other statistics have been slipping steadily, most of them do not yet perceive a need for change. You want to encourage them to reexamine the firm's strategy and implement a Customer Service program.

Planning Questions:
1. Which style(s) do you think would be most effective in this situation? Do you require compliance or commitment in a situation such as this?

2. What is it that you want the person you are trying to influence (the target) to do; that is, what is your content objective?

3. What kind of an outcome are you looking for in terms of your relationship with the other party; that is, what is your relationship objective?

4. Plan out how you will handle this influence attempt.

After the Role-Play:
5. What were the content and relationship outcomes?

6. Is there any way this influence attempt might have been improved?

Observations Category	INFLUENCE STYLES			
	Assertive Persuasion	Reward and Punishment	Participation and Trust	Common Vision
	Logic, Facts, Rationality, Ideas, Proposals, Reasons For and Against	Evaluations, Use of Incentives and Pressures, Bargains, Stating Own Personal Goals and Expectations	Active Listening, Recognizing Others' Contributions, Involving Others and Getting Their Contributions, Disclosing Own Areas of Uncertainty	Building a Sense of Group Spirit, a We-Feeling, Creating a Superordinate Group Goal, Shared Identity
Which styles did the influencer use most frequently? 1 = most frequently 4 = least frequently				
Examples of influence behavior that strengthened the other person (positive power)				
Examples of influence behaviors that weakened the other person (negative power)				
Missed opportunities (i.e., example of where the style might have had a positive impact but was not used)				
Which style did the influencer use most effectively? 1 = most effective 4 = least effective				

SITUATION 2—THE LESS-THAN-EXPECTED SALARY INCREASE

You and your boss had what you thought was a really great performance appraisal session last month. You were clearly led to expect a 6 percent salary increase and have begun to plan on it. Wham! Your increase notice comes through with only a 3 percent cost-of-living increase. You are about to enter your boss's office to "have a talk."

Planning Questions:

1. Which style(s) do you think would be most effective in this situation? Do you require compliance or commitment in a situation such as this?

2. What is it that you want the person you are trying to influence (the target) to do; that is, what is your content objective?

3. What kind of an outcome are you looking for in terms of your relationship with the other party; that is, what is your relationship objective?

4. Plan out how you will handle this influence attempt.

After the Role-Play:

5. What were the content and relationship outcomes?

6. Is there any way this influence attempt might have been improved?

Observations Category	INFLUENCE STYLES			
	Assertive Persuasion	Reward and Punishment	Participation and Trust	Common Vision
	Logic, Facts, Rationality, Ideas, Proposals, Reasons For and Against	Evaluations, Use of Incentives and Pressures, Bargains, Stating Own Personal Goals and Expectations	Active Listening, Recognizing Others' Contributions, Involving Others and Getting Their Contributions, Disclosing Own Areas of Uncertainty	Building a Sense of Group Spirit, a We-Feeling, Creating a Superordinate Group Goal, Shared Identity
Which styles did the influencer use most frequently? 1 = most frequently 4 = least frequently				
Examples of influence behavior that strength-ened the other person (positive power)				
Examples of influence behaviors that weak-ened the other person (negative power)				
Missed opportunities (i.e., example of where the style might have had a positive impact but was not used)				
Which style did the influencer use most effectively? 1 = most effective 4 = least effective				

SITUATION 3—SIGNING THE JOB CANDIDATE

It's taken you a few months, but you have finally located the perfect job candidate to fill the position of your assistant. This candidate, who will graduate with a Bachelor's/Master's degree in business this June, has all the qualities you have been looking for. The candidate is highly skilled and has the service orientation and values that you need in your company, which prides itself on being a socially responsible company that focuses on the double bottom line. However, at least two other companies are also trying to hire this person. Convince the candidate to come to work for you.

Planning Questions:

1. Which style(s) do you think would be most effective in this situation? Do you require compliance or commitment in a situation such as this?

2. What is it that you want the person you are trying to influence (the target) to do; that is, what is your content objective?

3. What kind of an outcome are you looking for in terms of your relationship with the other party; that is, what is your relationship objective?

4. Plan out how you will handle this influence attempt.

After the Role-Play:

5. What were the content and relationship outcomes?

6. Is there any way this influence attempt might have been improved?

Observations Category	INFLUENCE STYLES			
	Assertive Persuasion	Reward and Punishment	Participation and Trust	Common Vision
	Logic, Facts, Rationality, Ideas, Proposals, Reasons For and Against	Evaluations, Use of Incentives and Pressures, Bargains, Stating Own Personal Goals and Expectations	Active Listening, Recognizing Others' Contributions, Involving Others and Getting Their Contributions, Disclosing Own Areas of Uncertainty	Building a Sense of Group Spirit, a We-Feeling, Creating a Superordinate Group Goal, Shared Identity
Which styles did the influencer use most frequently? 1 = most frequently 4 = least frequently				
Examples of influence behavior that strengthened the other person (positive power)				
Examples of influence behaviors that weakened the other person (negative power)				
Missed opportunities (i.e., example of where the style might have had a positive impact but was not used)				
Which style did the influencer use most effectively? 1 = most effective 4 = least effective				

SITUATION 4—SEEKING DEPARTMENTAL COLLABORATION

You are one of five department heads in a software company. As the person in charge of production, you have no authority over the other department heads. However, you are worried that lack of collaboration among departments is costing the company business. Therefore, you have scheduled lunch with the head of Marketing and Sales because you think this department promises customers things that your department cannot produce.

Planning Questions:

1. Which style(s) do you think would be most effective in this situation? Do you require compliance or commitment in a situation such as this?

2. What is it that you want the person you are trying to influence (the target) to do; that is, what is your content objective?

3. What kind of an outcome are you looking for in terms of your relationship with the other party; that is, what is your relationship objective?

4. Plan out how you will handle this influence attempt.

After the Role-Play:

5. What were the content and relationship outcomes?

6. Is there any way this influence attempt might have been improved?

Observations Category	INFLUENCE STYLES			
	Assertive Persuasion	Reward and Punishment	Participation and Trust	Common Vision
	Logic, Facts, Rationality, Ideas, Proposals, Reasons For and Against	Evaluations, Use of Incentives and Pressures, Bargains, Stating Own Personal Goals and Expectations	Active Listening, Recognizing Others' Contributions, Involving Others and Getting Their Contributions, Disclosing Own Areas of Uncertainty	Building a Sense of Group Spirit, a We-Feeling, Creating a Superordinate Group Goal, Shared Identity
Which styles did the influencer use most frequently? 1 = most frequently 4 = least frequently				
Examples of influence behavior that strength-ened the other person (positive power)				
Examples of influence behaviors that weak-ened the other person (negative power)				
Missed opportunities (i.e., example of where the style might have had a positive impact but was not used)				
Which style did the influencer use most effectively? 1 = most effective 4 = least effective				

SITUATION 5—SHAKING LOOSE THE LATE REPORT

One of your subordinates has been promising to finish a report for three weeks. Every time you inquire as to how it's going, what you get back is, "Oh, it's coming along. It's more complicated than either one of us imagined." The grapevine has informed you that your subordinate's marriage is going through some rocky spots. Although you want to be fair, your boss is putting the screws on you to get the report in. The pressure on you is really mounting and something has to give. The "last recourse" meeting you called is about to begin.

Planning Questions:
1. Which style(s) do you think would be most effective in this situation? Do you require compliance or commitment in a situation such as this?

2. What is it that you want the person you are trying to influence (the target) to do; that is, what is your content objective?

3. What kind of an outcome are you looking for in terms of your relationship with the other party; that is, what is your relationship objective?

4. Plan out how you will handle this influence attempt.

After the Role-Play:
5. What were the content and relationship outcomes?

6. Is there any way this influence attempt might have been improved?

Observations Category	INFLUENCE STYLES			
	Assertive Persuasion Logic, Facts, Rationality, Ideas, Proposals, Reasons For and Against	Reward and Punishment Evaluations, Use of Incentives and Pressures, Bargains, Stating Own Personal Goals and Expectations	Participation and Trust Active Listening, Recognizing Others' Contributions, Involving Others and Getting Their Contributions, Disclosing Own Areas of Uncertainty	Common Vision Building a Sense of Group Spirit, a We-Feeling, Creating a Superordinate Group Goal, Shared Identity
Which styles did the influencer use most frequently? 1 = most frequently 4 = least frequently				
Examples of influence behavior that strengthened the other person (positive power)				
Examples of influence behaviors that weakened the other person (negative power)				
Missed opportunities (i.e., example of where the style might have had a positive impact but was not used)				
Which style did the influencer use most effectively? 1 = most effective 4 = least effective				

SITUATION 6—STOPPING SEXUAL HARASSMENT

You have heard several accounts from reliable sources that one of your top performers, a man in his fifties, has been sexually harassing the young women in his department. You would hate to lose this employee, but you strongly disapprove of people who abuse their power in this fashion. You want him to stop this behavior before the company loses the young women as employees or is slapped with a lawsuit. You summoned him to your office to discuss the situation and are awaiting his arrival.

Planning Questions:

1. Which style(s) do you think would be most effective in this situation? Do you require compliance or commitment in a situation such as this?

2. What is it that you want the person you are trying to influence (the target) to do; that is, what is your content objective?

3. What kind of an outcome are you looking for in terms of your relationship with the other party; that is, what is your relationship objective?

4. Plan out how you will handle this influence attempt.

After the Role-Play:

5. What were the content and relationship outcomes?

6. Is there any way this influence attempt might have been improved?

LEARNING POINTS

1. Power often has negative connotations for people, but it is a crucial part of leading and managing. A manager cannot "make a difference" without exerting power and influence over employees.
2. Power is defined as the capacity to influence the behavior of others.
3. Influence is the process by which people successfully persuade others to follow their advice, suggestions, or orders.
4. In general, there are three possible outcomes to an influence attempt: commitment, compliance, or resistance.
5. Managers traditionally relied on the power inherent in their position. Changes in both society and the workplace demand that managers rely on others sources of power and be proficient in several influence styles.
6. Sources of power are expertise, effort, relationships, the ability to reward or punish others (coercive power), position, charisma, and referent power. People also gain power when they have control over resources, have control and access to information, and work in units that cope with the critical uncertainties facing the organization.
7. Nine commonly used influence tactics are rational persuasion, inspirational appeals, consultation, ingratiation, personal appeals, exchange, coalition tactics, legitimating tactics, and pressure.
8 Cialdini's social influence tactics include reciprocity, social proof, consistency, expertise, and authority scarcity, and liking.
9. U.S. managers prefer consultation, rational persuasion, and inspirational appeals over more coercive tactics.
10. Managers who use a variety of influence tactics tend to be more successful than those who rely on a single tactic. In designing influence strategies, managers should ask themselves questions such as: Whose cooperation do I need? How can they be persuaded? What are my sources of influence? Can I live with the outcomes of my tactics?
11. Berlew and Harrison identified four influence styles:
    a. Assertive persuasion
    b. Reward and punishment
    c. Participation and trust
    d. Common vision
12. Power has two faces: a negative, unsocialized need to dominate others and a socialized concern for group goals and empowering others.
13. Power is paradoxical in that the more a leader empowers others, the more power he or she receives.
14. When working across cultures, it's important to decode the symbols and behavior that denote who holds power, determine the norms and expectations about how power and influence are exercised, and adapt one's style accordingly.

ACTION SCRIPTS

FOR EMPLOYEES

• Employees who are expert at wielding influence are ambitious in appropriate ways. They realize that naked ambition generates distrust when others sense that ambitious people will not let human considerations stand in the way of their quest for success.
• Employees can be powerful, even when they don't hold supervisory or managerial positions. Possessing a scarce expertise, developing a reputation as a hard worker, serving as a liaison between two groups that have difficulty getting along, being likable, having access to information or people with hierarchical power, having a personal network that facilitates both tasks and information gathering, as well as being seen as an objective source of sound judgment are all ways to accrue power.
• Experts at influence do not make others feel that they are being manipulated; instead, they are perceived by others as sincere.

- Expert persuaders use a variety of influence tactics and adapt their strategies to the specific audience they face and the goals they want to accomplish.
- They make an effort to understand what motivates the target of their influence attempt and which tactics and styles will be most effective.

FOR MANAGERS

- Managers who are expert influencers likewise are adept at varying their influence style. They also understand that sometimes more subtle tactics can be more effective. For example, controlling and limiting the number of options is a way to ensure that a desired outcome is selected (e.g., making sure that only job candidates acceptable to the manager are interviewed). Similarly, controlling who makes a decision is often an effective way to influence a decision. Selecting committee members who are favorable to the manager's decision alternative is a common way of delicately slanting a decision.[29]
- Managers can deal with existing political fiefdoms by removing or splitting the most dysfunctional subgroups and warning individuals who are motivated by personal power.
- When appropriate, managers skilled at influencing others take pains to reduce the status gap that may exist between them and their target audience. They communicate in ways that do not put the other person in a one-down position. By contrast, they also recognize that authority and expertise can be highly influential and make use of that in situations in which it is warranted. For example, occupational therapists found that patients were not following their instructions because the patients believed that the therapists had no expertise or special knowledge. Simply displaying the therapist's advanced degree in the consultation room increased patient compliance with instructions significantly.[30]
- Expatriate managers know when to emphasize their power to gain compliance and when, paradoxically, to downplay their power to gain participation and commitment. High–power distance cultures may expect managers to be more authoritarian, but because they are less knowledgable in a foreign culture than the locals, expatriate managers are more dependent on local guidance.[31]

FOR ORGANIZATIONAL ARCHITECTS

- Skilled organizational architects recognize that certain conditions can contribute to increased political behavior. This behavior occurs when there is too much uncertainty in the organization. Managers can reduce political jockeying by establishing clear evaluation criteria that distinguish between high and low performers and reward them accordingly. Managers will be less likely to resort to political influence when organizational goals are clearly specified and when they do not have to compete for scarce resources.[32] Interdependence among people, groups, or organizational units also can contribute to political behavior.[33]
- Although this may not completely eliminate such behavior, leaders can establish a norm that political jockeying is not acceptable and consistently reprimand such behavior.
- Reward systems play an important role in how people use power and politics. Top management should identify "an apolitical attitude that puts organizational ends ahead of personal power ends" as an important promotion criteria.[34]
- Companies can train employees to develop their persuasioin and influence skills and teach them to use power appropriately.

PERSONAL APPLICATION ASSIGNMENT

The topic of this assignment is to think back on a significant experience involving power or influence. Choose an experience that intrigues you and that you want to learn more about.

A. Concrete Experience

    1. Objectively describe the experience (who, what, when, where, how information). (2 points)

    2. Subjectively describe your feelings, perceptions, and thoughts that occurred during (not after) the experience. What did others seem to be feeling? (2 points)

B. Reflective Observation

    1. Looking back at the experience, what were the perspectives of the key actors (including you)? (2 points)

    2. Why did the people involved (including you) behave as they did? (2 points)

C. Abstract Conceptualization
   1. Relate concepts or theories from the assigned readings or the lecture to the experience. Explain thoroughly how they apply to your experience. Please apply at least two concepts or theories and cite them correctly. (4 points)

D. Active Experimentation
   1. What did you learn about power and influence from this experience? (1 point)

   2. What did you learn about yourself? (1 point)

   3. What action steps will you take to be more effective in the future? (2 points)

E. Integration, Synthesis, and Writing
   1. Did you integrate and synthesize the four sections? (1 point)
   2. Was the personal application assignment well written and easy to understand? (1 point)
   3. Was it free of spelling and grammatical errors? (2 points)

ENDNOTES

[1] M. W. McCall, Jr. and M. M. Lombardo, "What Makes a Top Executive?" *Psychology Today 17*(2) (February 1983): 26–31.

[2] J. Pfeffer, *Managing with Power: Politics and Influence in Organizations* (Boston, MA: Harvard Business School Press, 1992): 166.

[3] B. Keys and T. Case, "How to Become an Influential Manager," *Academy of Management Executive 4*(4) (1990): 38–51.

[4] L. Sayles, *Leadership: Managing in Real Organizations* (New York: McGraw-Hill, 1989). See the Bradford and Cohen, "Influence Without Authority: The Use of Alliances, Reciprocity, and Exchange to Accomplish Work," article in *The Organizational Behavior Reader* for advice on influencing people over whom one has no authority.

[5] J. R. P French, Jr. and B. Raven, "The Bases of Social Power," in D. Cartwright (ed.), *Studies in Social Power* (Ann Arbor: University of Michigan, Institute for Social Research, 1959).

[6] Pfeffer, *Managing with Power*: 69. See also D. Mechanic's "Source of Power of Lower Participants in Complex Organizations," *Administrative Science Quarterly 7* (1962): 349–364.

[7] G. R. Salancik and J. Pfeffer, "Who Gets Power—And How They Hold Onto It: A Strategic Contingency Model of Power," *Organizational Dynamics 5* (Winter 1977): 3–21.

[8] J. K. Keller, "Who Is John Zeglis and Why Is a Lawyer on AT&T's Short List?" *The Wall Street Journal* (September 5, 1997): A-1.

[9] R. E. Emerson, "Power-Dependence Relations," *American Sociological Review 27* (1962): 31–41.

[10] H. Mintzberg, *Power In and Around Organizations* (Upper Saddle River, NJ: Prentice Hall, 1983).

[11] G. Yukl, *Leadership in Organizations* (Upper Saddle River, NJ: Prentice Hall, 1994): 225. These tactics are a modification of the exploratory work described in D. Kipnis, S. M. Schmidt, and I. Wilkinson, "Intraorganizational Influence Tactics: Explorations in Getting One's Way," *Journal of Applied Psychology 65* (1980): 440–452. See also D. Kipnis, S. M. Schmidt, C. Swaffin-Smith, and I. Wilkinson, "Patterns of Managerial Influence: Shotgun Managers, Tacticians, and Bystanders," *Organizational Dynamics* (Winter 1984): 58–67; and G. Yukl, H. Kim, and C. M. Falbe, "Antecedents of Influence Outcomes," *Journal of Applied Psychology 81*(3) (1996): 309–317.

[12] Keys and Case, "How to Become an Influential Manager": 47.

[13] B. McRae, *Negotiating and Influencing Skills* (Thousand Oaks, CA: Sage, 1998): 58.

[14] S. S. Drury, *Assertive Supervision: Building Involved Teamwork* (Champaign, IL: Research Press, 1984): 49–50.

[15] The ideas and materials here (with permission of Situation Management Systems, Inc.) are part of a series of training programs originally developed by David Berlew and Roger Harrison on positive power and influence. For more detail on the actual program, contact Situation Management Systems, Inc., Box 476, Center Station, Plymouth, MA 02361. Http://www.smsinc.com.

[16] J. A. Conger, "The Necessary Art of Persuasion," *Harvard Business Review 76*(3) (May/June 1998): 85.

[17] D. C. McClelland, "The Two Faces of Power," in D. A. Kolb, I. M. Rubin, and J. McIntyre, (eds.) *Organizational Psychology: Readings on Human Behavior in Organizations*, 4th ed. (Upper Saddle River, NJ: Prentice Hall, 1984): 59–72.

[18] Keys and Case, "How to Become an Influential Manager": 43.

[19] M. Henning and A. Jardim, *The Managerial Woman* (New York: Anchor Press/Doubleday, 1977).

[20] F. Luthans, "Successful vs. Effective Real Managers," *Academy of Management Executive 2*(2) (May 1988): 127–132; and F. Luthans, R. M. Hodgetts, and S. Rosenkrantz, *Real Managers* (Cambridge, MA: Ballinger, 1988).

[21] Luthans, "Successful vs. Effective Real Managers": 129.

[22] G. F. Dreher, T. W. Doughtery, and W. Whitely, "Influence Tactics and Salary Attainment: A Gender-Specific Analysis," *Sex Roles 20* (May 1989): 535–550.

[23] A. Rizzo and C. Mendez, "Making Things Happen in Organizations: Does Gender Make a Difference?," *Public Personnel Management 17*(1) (Spring 1988): 9–20.

[24] N. L. Harper and R. Y. Hirokawa, "A Comparison of Persuasive Strategies Used by Female and Male Managers: An Examination of Downward Influence," *Communication Quarterly 36*(2) (Spring 1988): 157–168.

[25] D. C. McClelland and D. H. Burnham, "Power Is the Great Motivator," *Harvard Business Review 73* (January/February 1995): 138.

[26] G. Hofstede, *Culture's Consequences: International Differences in Work-Related Values* (Beverly Hills, CA: Sage, 1980).

[27] J. S. Osland, S. De Franco, and A. Osland, "Organizational Implications of Latin American Culture: Lessons for the Expatriate Manager," *Journal of Management Inquiry 8*(2) (June 1999): 219–234.

[28] Hofstede, *Culture's Consequences*.

[29] J. Pfeffer, *Managing With Power*.

[30] R. B. Cialdini, "Harnessing the Science of Persuasion," *Harvard Business Review 79* (2001): 72–79.

[31] J. S. Osland, *The Adventure of Working Abroad* (San Francisco: Jossey-Bass, 1995).

[32] D. R. Beeman and T. W. Sharkey, "The Use and Abuse of Corporate Politics," *Business Horizons 30*(2) (March–April 1987): 30.

[33] J. Pfeffer and G. Salancik, *The External Control of Organizations* (New York: HarperCollins, 1978).

[34] Beeman and Sharkey, "The Use and Abuse of Corporate Politics": 30.

Chapter 19

▲▲▲

EMPOWERMENT AND COACHING

OBJECTIVES By the end of this chapter, you should be able to:

A. Describe the characteristics of high-performance organizations.

B. Distinguish between the command-and-control and involvement-oriented approaches of management.

C. Define empowerment.

D. Explain the four aspects of empowerment.

E. Describe how managers can empower employees.

F. Identify five different types of coaching.

G. Explain how culture can impact empowerment and coaching.

A PIECE OF WORK

In 1973, a book appeared that would define the conversation about the American workplace for the next generation. *Work in America* was an unlikely hit, the report of a task force commissioned by Elliot L. Richardson, President Nixon's secretary of health, education, and welfare. It was a rather academic assessment, rooted in research papers and scientific surveys. But the findings were explosive: They described "the alienation and disenchantment of blue-collar workers," "the search by women for a new identity," and "the quest of the aged for a respected and useful social role."

The chairman of that task force was James O'Toole, then a young special assistant to Richardson; Edward E. Lawler III was part of a University of Michigan research team that produced the report's key data. Now, 33 years later, O'Toole and Lawler—both at the Center for Effective Organizations at the University of Southern California—have prepared a sequel using the same methods: *The New American Workplace* (Palgrave-Macmillan, July 2006).

The New American Workplace is, in a way, an optimistic updating—not least because work actually has, for many people, become more fulfilling and democratic in the manner *Work in America* prescribed. But it also reckons with technological forces and a global economy that are radically and rapidly disrupting business organizations. "Our general conclusion," the authors write, "is that, in far too many instances, the United States is attempting to implement tomorrow's competitive strategies with yesterday's managerial ideas and public policy infrastructure."

We asked O'Toole and Lawler to revisit *Work in America* in the context of their more recent work. Their assessments follow excerpts from the original book, shown in italics.

ON JOB SATISFACTION

"Significant numbers of American workers are dissatisfied with the quality of their working lives. Dull, repetitive, seemingly meaningless tasks offering little challenge or autonomy are causing discontent among workers at all occupational levels."

Good news here: Surveys show that American workers are more satisfied with their jobs today than they were in the 1970s. Much to our surprise, Americans also report higher satisfaction with their work than they do with other aspects of their lives. Have jobs become better or have personal relationships gotten worse?

ON SELF-EMPLOYMENT

"Our economic, political, and cultural system has fostered the notion of independence and autonomy, a part of which is the belief that a hardworking person . . . can always make a go of it in business for himself. This element of the American dream is rapidly becoming a myth. . . . The trend of the past 70 years or more . . . has been a decrease in small, independent enterprises and self-employment, and an increase in the domination of large corporations and government in the workforce."

Thank goodness that trend reversed itself: In 2002, the Census Bureau reported that 17.6 million Americans worked for, and by, themselves. When enterprising Americans are laid off by corporations, they increasingly become independent consultants, contractors, landscape gardeners, and computer coaches. If it hadn't been for the growth in self-employment during the prolonged 2001–2003 recession and accompanying downsizing, the nation's unemployment rate would have been really alarming.

Indeed, it appears that working alone in homes, cars, hotel rooms, libraries, Wi-Fi cafés, Starbucks, and FedEx Kinko's is gradually replacing working with others in traditional offices, factories, and stores. We find that one of the major sources of societal discontent is the loss of the "community" that was once found in traditional workplaces. While freedom is a good thing, it is hard to put a happy face on the increasing social isolation of the American worker.

ON WOMEN AT WORK

"What is the quality of working life for women in the labor force? The job of secretary is perhaps symbolic of the status of female employment in this country, both qualitatively and quantitatively. There are 9 million secretaries, and they compose nearly one-third of the nation's female workforce. Judy Klemesrud has written that the secretary is often stereotyped as a 'gum-chewing sex kitten; husband hunter; miniskirted ding-a-ling; slow-witted pencil pusher; office gofer; reliable old shoe.' Certainly, many secretaries have very poor jobs by the accepted standards of job satisfaction."

Here is an area of clear progress: The government does not even keep statistics on "secretaries" anymore, and the great majority of women are no longer trapped in low-paying "women's jobs" as they were in the past. The gender wage gap has closed remarkably—particularly as women are now more likely than men to attend college and thus, get better jobs.

On Retirement

"The thrust toward 'early' retirement calls into doubt the very meaning of 'retirement.' . . . [R]ecent analysis of census data indicates that older men increasingly do not and will not want to retire at age 65."

Wow, did we get that right! Americans' deferral of retirement is good news for corporations as we head toward a labor crunch with the aging of the boomer generation. Alas, the willingness of Americans to soldier on is not simply a voluntary response among work-loving men and women who are living longer, healthier lives and want to feel productive. Many workers want to retire, but they are not able to do so "in comfort": Boomers are discovering that the once-prevalent company pension plans that funded their parents' retirements will not be able to pay for theirs.

On Trade Unions

"As Irving Bluestone of the UAW writes, 'Just as management is beginning to ponder the new problems of discontent and frustration in the workforce, so must unions join in finding new ways to meet these problems.' If new ways are to be charted and accepted, the trade-union movement must be among the initiators of new demands for the humanization of work."

The unions had their chance and blew it. Inexplicably, union leaders did not play a significant role in the efforts in the 1970–1980s era to improve the quality of work life in America. Their failure undercut their power and credibility. It might also be argued that when unions walked away from promising experiments to improve American industrial competitiveness through worker participation in decision making and profit sharing, they contributed to the decline in the number of manufacturing jobs in U.S. Rust Belt industries. And there is no doubt that their failure to respond to their members' desire for improved working conditions contributed to the decline of industrial trade unionism.

On Worker Involvement

"Most of the work redesign effort has confined itself to small work groups. Little of it has embraced the wider implications of the system's viewpoint and involved a plant or a corporation as a whole. The major exception to this trend is a General Foods manufacturing plant that was designed to incorporate features that would provide a high quality of working life, enlist unusual human involvement, and achieve high productivity. . . . [I]ndustrial engineers had indicated that 110 workers would be needed to man the plant. But when the team concept was applied . . . the result was a manning level of less than 70 workers. . . . [And] the major economic benefit has come from such factors as improved yields, minimized waste, and avoidance of shutdowns."

The Gaines dog-food plant in Topeka, Kansas, became the most talked about factory in America since Henry Ford's first assembly line in Dearborn, Michigan. The bad news: Within a few years, General Foods executives decided against applying its high-involvement management approach at the company's other facilities. They then added layers of managers and supervisors in the plant until the productivity of the once-self-managing workers was whittled down to the company average!

The good news: Over the next few years, other companies (most notably Procter & Gamble) copied practices introduced in the plant, including the empowerment of work teams to choose their methods of production, to allocate their own tasks, to set their own schedules, and to recruit new members. Today, many U.S. manufacturing plants and customer-service organizations operate with self-managing work teams, flat hierarchies, and financial-gain-sharing plans.

ON OBSTACLES TO CHANGE

"So far, we have seen that the redesign of work is feasible, that a careful alteration of jobs can lead to participation in responsibility and profits, and that the precise nature and extent of participation is a matter for experimentation within each workplace. [So] why not simply get out of the way to avoid being crushed in the stampede? The answer is, of course, 'it isn't as easy as it looks.' Single remedies (e.g., 'job enrichment,' 'job rotation,' 'management by objectives') abound for the ills of work. Such efforts have failed because there is no single source of job dissatisfaction. In brief, the bad experiences of employers in the past have led them to ask: 'Whom can I trust?' "

We were naive. We failed to recognize that the greatest obstacles to high-involvement workplaces are the attitudes and assumptions of top executives. Many are still threatened by the prospect of worker participation. And too many leaders of American corporations still believe they have "no choice" but to match the working conditions and employment practices of their lowest-wage competitors at home and, increasingly, abroad.

They are wrong. In 2006, the most promising fact we are able to document is the existence of high-involvement, high-wage, high-profit companies in almost every industry—for example, Southwest Airlines, Nucor Corp., W.L. Gore & Associates, Xilinx Inc., Harley-Davidson Inc., UPS, Costco Wholesale Corp., and Alcoa Inc., to cite just a few. These are productive and growing companies that have lower labor costs overall than their low-wage competitors. Because these companies involve their workers in decision making, reward them fairly for their efforts, and provide them with good training and career opportunities, their employees reciprocate the favor in terms of much higher productivity than workers in comparable low-wage companies. As executives at Starbucks explain, they are able to offer unusually high benefits to their employees not because they charge a premium for their product, but because their productive, customer-sensitive employees allow the company to realize a premium for the products and services they offer.

The bottom line: All the evidence shows that workers who participate in decision making, training, profit sharing, and stock ownership are so much more productive than workers who don't enjoy these working conditions that they pay for their own higher salaries and benefits. They also work to keep jobs in America.

Source: Reprinted with permission from James O'Toole and Edward E. Lawler III, *Fast Company 106* (June 2006): 87.

 **CLASS PREPARATION**

A. Read "A Piece of Work."

B. Fill out the Empowerment Questionnaire on the following page.

C. Practice building the spaceship Enterprise following the blueprints on pages 541–544.

D. While reading the chapter, make a list of the cues you should look for with regard to empowerment and coaching.

THE EMPOWERMENT QUESTIONNAIRE

The following questionnaire consists of managerial behaviors that promote empowerment. How frequently does your manager (or coach) do each of the following? If you have never worked, interview someone else about their manager. Please circle the response that best describes your manager's behavior. (1 = Very Infrequently, 5 = Very Frequently)

My Manager:	Very Infrequently	Infrequently	Sometimes	Frequently	Very Frequently
1. Lets me do my job without interfering	1	2	3	4	5
2. Makes an effort to locate and remove barriers that reduce efficiency	1	2	3	4	5
3. Encourages all of us to work as a team	1	2	3	4	5
4. Clearly defines what is expected of me	1	2	3	4	5
5. Provides me with honest feedback on my performance	1	2	3	4	5
6. Openly recognizes work well done	1	2	3	4	5
7. Keeps me focused on customer needs	1	2	3	4	5
8. Encourages me to monitor my own efforts	1	2	3	4	5
9. Makes sure I have the training I need to do my job	1	2	3	4	5
10. Allows me to make decisions about my own work	1	2	3	4	5
11. Listens to me before making decisions affecting my area	1	2	3	4	5
12. Provides me with an environment conducive to teamwork	1	2	3	4	5
13. Rewards me for meeting company goals	1	2	3	4	5
14. Informs me regularly about the state of the business	1	2	3	4	5
15. Encourages me to make suggestions	1	2	3	4	5
16. Makes sure I have all the information I need to do my work	1	2	3	4	5
17. Behaves in ways that demonstrate respect for others	1	2	3	4	5
18. Explains how my job fits into the company objectives	1	2	3	4	5

Add up your total points _____ to determine in which category your manager belongs.

Low empowerment = 18–36   Moderate empowerment = 37–63   High empowerment = 64–90

THE KNOWLEDGE BASE

Any company trying to compete . . . must figure out a way to engage the mind of every employee.

Jack Welch, former CEO, General Electric

Did you notice that the opening vignette stated that high-involvement, high-wage, high-profit companies have lower labor costs than their low-wage competitors? The psychological contract in these firms is employee involvement in decision making, fair rewards for their efforts, good training, and career opportunities on the part of the company; in return, the employees contribute their brains, enthusiasm, higher productivity, and responsiveness to customers. This is not only a good deal for both sides but also a source of competitive advantage. The consumer electronics retailer Best Buy has a metric that measures employee engagement; if CEO Brad Anderson had to use only one metric to gauge their success, this is the one he'd pick.[1] Convincing cynical employees that they shouldn't check their brains at the door when they come to work can be challenging, but the payoffs are high. There is a direct correlation between good people management and profits. High-commitment companies have a 30 to 40 percent higher productivity rate than other companies, according to years of research.[2] The Ritz Carlton, Whole Foods Market, and ServiceMaster have climbed to the top of their industries by distinguishing themselves from the competition with their people-centered management practices. More and more companies are realizing, as research shows, that the only way to ensure profits, and even survival, is to develop a work environment that attracts, focuses, and retains highly talented employees.[3]

Companies that survive and flourish in today's business environment are those that focus on high performance, which translates into the cost competitiveness, high-quality products and services, innovation, and speed that is necessary to gain a competitive advantage. Harris reported the following characteristics of high-performing companies.[4]

- Joint goal setting by managers and workers with objectives and targets that are always a bit beyond current levels to promote greater achievement.
- Employees reach a consensus on norms of competence and high performance and standards of excellence that are incorporated into the corporate culture by means of logos and slogans.
- Continual reinforcement of positive behavior and accomplishment.
- Constructive feedback to redirect worker energies from ineffective to effective work habits and activities so that people learn from failure.
- Capitalizing on human assets and potential by giving individuals and work groups more flexibility, responsibility, and autonomy—while maintaining accountability.
- Encouraging and modeling a spirit of innovation and entrepreneurialism.
- Recruiting, selecting, promoting, and rewarding top performers, and identifying them as role models.
- Fostering synergy and collaboration so that individual competition is replaced by teamwork and group achievement.
- Using training, education sessions, and self-learning methods to develop people's potential for success and high performance.
- Eliminating underachievers who do not respond positively to demands for high performance.
- Altering organizational structure so that it is more decentralized, mission oriented, and responsive.
- Making work meaningful and fun by cultivating informality and fellowship in a context of achievement and accomplishment.
- Staying close to personnel, suppliers, and customers so that managers respond quickly to market and employee needs.
- Providing a mix of benefits, rewards, and incentives to encourage talented performance.

COMMAND-AND-CONTROL VERSUS INVOLVEMENT-ORIENTED MANAGEMENT APPROACHES

Creating high-performance organizations, in which people see themselves as businesspeople rather than employees, requires a different style of management.[5] There has been a gradual shift from a command-and-control model to an involvement-oriented approach centered on employee commitment and empowerment (see Exhibit 19–1). *The command-and-control model is based on the assumption that hierarchy and vertical relationships are the best way to organize. Managers working with a command-and-control mentality perceive their job as making decisions, giving orders, and ensuring that subordinates obey.* The limited role of subordinates in this model ("Do what you're told") can result in passive workers with little commitment to organizational goals. When this occurs, management often finds itself shouldering the lion's share of the responsibility and prodding employees to get the work done. People talk in terms of "we and they" (workers versus management) rather than "us."

The involvement-oriented approach is based on the belief that the best way to organize is to give employees the freedom and responsibility to manage their own work as much as possible.[6] In addition to the work itself, employees also do the thinking and controlling aspects that only supervisors and managers do in the command-and-control model. *In the involvement-oriented approach, employees are given both the information and the power to influence decisions about their work.* Not surprisingly, high-involvement organizations require a special breed of employee—people who are capable and skilled at basic problem solving, communication, and quantitative techniques. They must also be responsible and willing to make a commitment to learning, to developing themselves, and to being a productive member of an organization. For their part, supervisors and managers in high-involvement organizations must be willing to share both power and information and listen to employees.

The command-and-control model was more fitting in an earlier time. It is certainly not appropriate for highly competitive, rapidly changing global businesses that employ highly educated workers. Even firms that employ poorly educated workers have improved their performance by involving and empowering their workers. Companies that still operate in the command-and-control fashion find it more difficult to compete against firms that utilize their human resources more fully.[7] With a command-and-control approach, one can obtain satisfactory performance, but high performance only results when employees are truly committed to the success of the organization. Although the research has some limitations, the involvement-oriented approach is more

	Command-and-Control	Involvement-Oriented
Best Way to Organize	Hierarchy and vertical relationships	Employee self-management
Role of Managers	Make decisions, give orders, ensure that subordinates obey	Share power and information, listen to employees
Role of Employees	Obey orders	Carry out thinking and controlling functions of their jobs, make decisions
Required Employee Skills	Job skills	Basic problem solving, communication, quantitative techniques, commitment to learning and self-development

EXHIBIT 19-1 **Command-and-Control versus Involvement-Oriented Approach**

productive than a control-oriented approach, except for companies that produce simple products or services in a stable environment.[8] High-involvement organizations also have less turnover because employees find them a more attractive place to work.[9] Listen to the differences in how these two employees talk about their managers.[10]

> *Down on the floor (in a GM plant), you can see the operation, and you know how it's sup-posed to be done. Up there, upper management's saying, "Nah, nah, we can do it cheaper and more efficient if we do it our way." So these people up there that are calling all the shots are not experiencing what really needs to take place on the floor. And they don't really care, because they're thinking, "Short-term dollars and cents, it looks real good" and we're here down on the floor thinking, "Long-term, it's our job." Plus we want to give a person exactly what they bought: a perfect vehicle for the price. Any auto worker would tell you that. . . . They should not concentrate so much on quantity—and let us work on the quality. (GM worker)*

> *Honda's thing is, the guy on the line is the gut professional on his job, and he knows what is best for that process at that time. He knows best how to make it better. You give us an oppor-tunity to have a say-so, and we can do a good job. (Honda worker)*

Management can be either a competitive advantage for a company or an obstacle to high performance. Most experts agree that to succeed in the current business environment, companies need managers who see themselves less as bosses and more as facilitators and coaches.

Rather than calling all the shots, the new breed of manager or supervisor focuses on devel-oping subordinates and encouraging them to become involved and take responsibility for their own output. "The key assumption in the involvement-oriented approach is that if individuals are given challenging work that gives them a customer to serve and a business to operate they can and will control their own behavior."[11] The new managers talk about "working themselves out of a job" as subordinates are trained to take over duties formerly done by supervisors or middle managers. This frees up management time to concentrate on areas that are more likely to ensure the organization's survival. For example, managers can utilize the time they formerly spent checking up on employees to focus on obtaining the resources subordinates need to do their jobs, adding value to the product, looking for and learning from problems, and creating the best possi-ble environment for employees.[12]

EMPOWERMENT

Managers consistently delude themselves about how much good they're doing. The oath for man-agers should be the same as physicians: First do no harm.

Robert Sutton, professor, Stanford University

Empowerment is the term that describes a large part of what the new breed of managers actu-ally do. *Empowerment is defined as granting employees the autonomy to assume more respon-sibility within an organization and strengthening their sense of effectiveness.* We have known for many years that certain types of charismatic leaders, such as John F. Kennedy, empower their followers by making them feel stronger and more capable of taking action.[13] His famous quotation is a call for empowerment: "And so, my fellow Americans: ask not what your coun-try can do for you—ask what you can do for your country. My fellow citizens of the world: ask not what America will do for you, but what together we can do for the freedom of man."[14] The term empowerment, however, has become popular only within the last 15 years. It refers to an enabling process that increases the intrinsic task motivation for employees[15] as well as their *self-efficacy, which is the individual's belief that he or she is capable of performing a task.*[16] Higher self-efficacy is correlated with higher work performance.[17] Empowerment, which has been called an effort to "white-collarize" factory workers, has been adopted by many manu-facturers, in addition to service and knowledge industries.

Empowerment is a mind-set with these characteristics:[18]

1. **Meaning** People feel that their work is important to them. They care about what they do. There is often a connection between their personal values and the work they do.

2. **Competence** People are confident about their ability to do their work well; they know they can perform and, as a result, have a sense of self-efficacy.

3. **Self-determination** People are free to choose how to do their work; they are not micro-managed.

4. **Impact** People believe they can have influence on their work unit; others listen to their ideas.

Employees have to choose to be empowered, but organizations can encourage this mind-set by the following actions:[19]

- Reduce hierarchical and bureaucratic structures (e.g., design organic systems that emphasize flexibility, adaptability, and innovation).
- Increase access to sources of system power (e.g., access to strategic information, resources, and managerial support).
- Foster an organizational culture that values the human assets of the organization.
- Establish direction and boundaries relating to empowerment.

Some experts say empowerment is primarily about limiting the amount of power that is taken away from employees.[20] Teams are a good example of organic systems that make organizations less bureaucratic and increase the power held by individual workers. Employees at Frito-Lay have access to strategic information; they can log on to see the company's entire product development system and track the volume of each product line. The Levi Strauss mission statement provides an example of an empowerment culture: "We want our people to feel respected, treated fairly, listened to and involved. We want a company that our people are proud of and committed to, where all employees have an opportunity to contribute, learn, grow, and advance."

However, senior management has to agree on what they mean by empowerment and provide direction and boundaries. Unrestrained empowerment can do serious damage. The Barings Bank, for example, collapsed under a mountain of debt created by a young trader who worked without checks and balances. Many companies set limits on employee discretion so that mistakes cannot threaten the firm's survival. Dick Brown, chairman and CEO of EDS, stated: "Freedom is greatest when the ground rules are clear. Chalk out the playing field and say, within those lines, make any decisions you need."

The outcomes of empowerment are employees who are more effective, innovative, and capable of exerting upward influence than disempowered employees and who have higher levels of job satisfaction and lower levels of stress.[21]

Empowerment is predicated on the beliefs reflected in both Theory Y (Chapter 2) and the Job Characteristics Enrichment model (Chapter 5) that people want to make a contribution and desire greater autonomy and meaning at work. Herbert Simon, Nobel Laureate, states that many people are motivated by a sense of altruism that translates into organizational commitment. However, not everyone shares these values or can break the old habits of the command-and-control model. Thus, it comes as no surprise that some employees and managers have found the transition to an "empowered" workplace exceedingly difficult.[22] Of the managers who have made the shift, some did so because empowerment fits their own value system; others use empowerment simply because it is a more effective management technique.[23]

Not all workers enjoy being empowered. Being held accountable, worrying about tasks that were formerly the concern of management, disciplining fellow workers or being disciplined by them is not for everyone. In addition to personal values and habits, another barrier to empowerment can be organizational cultures with norms that work against employee involvement. For example, at one university new faculty members are cautioned by senior faculty not to jeopardize their chances for tenure by making suggestions to the administration or getting involved in controversial topics. They are also told stories about professors who have been fired in the past for disagreeing with the administration on topics that fell within the professors' area of expertise.

This perception of a closed-minded administration may no longer be true, but faculty members are still fearful of rocking the boat. Even when they believe the administration is making a serious mistake, they muzzle themselves and narrow their focus to their individual job or department. "I'll just teach my classes and let them stew in their own juices." Thus, the norms of silence and centralized decision making are perpetuated by the organizational culture. Faculty perceive themselves as a relatively powerless group. They complain about the administration, but they are not proactive about making improvements.

In contrast, high performance–high commitment work cultures have these characteristics: delegation, teamwork across boundaries, empowerment, integration of people and technology, and a shared sense of purpose.[24] Employees who have the most relevant information or the most appropriate work skills are delegated the responsibility for completing the work. Integrating people with technology signifies that employees control the technology rather than being controlled by it. A shared sense of purpose implies a common vision of the organization's purpose and the methods for accomplishing this purpose.

THE MANAGER'S ROLE IN EMPOWERMENT

An outstanding manager at high-tech start-up, Janet was well known for her problem-solving skills and institutional memory. Because she had an open door policy, numerous employees from all parts of the organization came to her for quick solutions and answers. Although it was flattering to be seen as the repository of valuable knowledge and information, she eventually saw herself as a bottleneck and as a manager who was failing to develop her employees adequately. So she set up a buddy system; if one partner asked a work question that his or her buddy could not answer, the questioner was then responsible for digging up the answer and using it to cross-train the buddy and the rest of the project team. Janet jokingly announced that she herself would be charging a $5.00 fee for each question that came her way. She only collected $10.00 in the first year after the buddy system was up and running, because it successfully broke the employees' habit of overreliance on her knowledge. The employees were motivated to rise to her challenge to develop their own knowledge base.[25]

When organizations introduce the idea of an empowered workforce, they are usually changing the psychological contract that exists between management and employees. New behavior and expectations are required of both groups, but not everyone can adapt to these changes. Middle managers, who feel the pinch most personally in change efforts, sometimes find it difficult to relinquish their traditional ways of dealing with subordinates and carve out a new role for themselves. One tactic that has been used to prevent managers from micromanaging subordinates is to give them more direct reports than one person could ever supervise. Eventually, they realize that the only way to survive is to allow subordinates and teams greater autonomy. Managers can then focus on spotting and transferring best practices in the units they manage rather than peering over employees' shoulders.[26]

Managers can use these strategies to encourage an empowerment mind-set:[27]

- Solicit input from employees on a regular basis.
- Ask for their help in solving problems.
- Teach employees to make sound decisions by allowing them to gain experience with carefully selected decisions. As their judgement improves, let them make progressively more complex decisions.
- Remove any bureaucratic obstacles that stop employees from taking initiative and responsibility. In many organizations, people feel powerless to fix things because both procedures and management practices promote the status quo and get in the way of positive changes.
- Rather than automatically supplying answers to employees, ask questions that encourage them to come up with answers. "What would you do if you had to make this decision?" "What factors do we need to consider here?"
- Provide workers with all the information they need to make decisions about the business.
- Let employees know it's up to them to do whatever is necessary within reason to serve the customer, without having to request permission.

- Provide a positive emotional atmosphere that promotes self esteem and self-development.
- Reward achievements in visible and personal ways.
- Serve as a role model for employees.
- Coach people so they can successfully master tasks.

Based on surveys of 80,000 managers in 400 companies, the following questions identify the levers management should use to engage good employees and make them more productive and less likely to quit and work elsewhere. Ideally, all employees should be able to answer yes to these questions:[28]

- Do I know what is expected of me at work?
- Do I have the materials and equipment I need to do my work?
- Do I have the opportunity to do what I do best, every day?
- In the past seven days, have I received recognition or praise for good work?
- Does my supervisor, or someone at work, seem to care about me as a person?
- Is there someone at work who encourages my development?

One of the common concerns supervisors and managers have about employee empowerment is whether it means relinquishing all their own authority. When managers share power with subordinates, their own power does not diminish as it would if power were really a zero-sum commodity. When power is shared, it expands. Managers who practice empowerment are still responsible for setting the direction for their subordinates, or for seeing that a direction is set in a participative fashion. Furthermore, wise managers do not simply turn over power to subordinates without first ensuring that they have the necessary information and skills to make good decisions. Managers who empower their employees still have to:[29]

- Know what is going on.
- Set or communicate the direction for the department or unit.
- Make decisions subordinates cannot make.
- Ensure that people are on course.
- Offer a guiding hand and open doors to clear the way.
- Make sure that employees have the necessary skills to assume greater autonomy and responsibility.
- Ensure that employees have the necessary information to make good decisions.
- Assess performance.

Mary Parker Follett, one of the earliest management writers, noted, "Authority, genuine authority, is the outcome of our common life. It does not come from separating people, from dividing them into two classes: those who command and those who obey. It comes from the intermingling of all, of my work fitting into yours and yours into mine."[30]

Follett first proposed the idea of depersonalizing authority and adopting the law of the situation in which "the situation is the boss."[31] She observed that workers react to receiving orders by becoming more passive and taking less and less responsibility. However, by examining the situation, it becomes evident to almost everyone, regardless of their hierarchical position, what needs to be done. In this way, the situation becomes the boss. It is much easier to examine situations when employees have access to both information and data-analysis skills. When employees and managers engage in a "databased dialogue," the inherent tensions of a superior-subordinate relationship are reduced.[32]

ORGANIZATIONAL BACKUP FOR EMPOWERMENT

There are many actions organizations can take to foster empowerment. Some organizations, such as Cadillac, have turned their organizational chart upside down to form an inverted pyramid. This communicates that management's primary purpose is to serve the employees who are serving the customers. Federal Express not only has an inverted structure, but management reinforces it by having employees fill out yearly Survey/Feedback/Action (SFA) forms on their managers. The form includes items such as those found in the Empowerment Questionnaire you filled out in the Class Preparation section. Upper management at Federal Express is evaluated on its openness to ideas and suggestions, its fairness, and whether or not it keeps employees informed. The survey results affect the managers' bonuses and future with the company. Thus, Federal Express has modified its structure, evaluation system, and rewards to encourage managers to empower their employees.

Dick (Sethi) Depak, assistant director of executive education at AT&T, uses this "seven R" model to develop a culture of high performance and high self-esteem among today's knowledge workers.[33]

1. **Respect** Not platitudes but a sincere belief that people at all levels of the organization have unique contributions to make. Too often, only people at the top of organizations can get a hearing for their ideas.
2. **Responsibility and Resources** Employees perform best when they have a discrete and well-defined area of responsibility and the resources needed to make it successful. In contrast, micromanaging implies a lack of trust in employees.
3. **Risk Taking** In order to promote innovation, employees have to learn to take risks—some of which will inevitably result in mistakes. Mistakes have to be viewed as opportunities for lessons rather than career-ending triggers.
4. **Rewards and Recognitions** Talented, hardworking employees should receive both monetary rewards and recognition for a job well done. The major reasons good people leave corporations are lack of recognition, lack of involvement, and poor management.[34]
5. **Relationship** "When people on all levels get to know one another in a respectful and benevolent way and get to understand one another's strengths, shortcomings, hopes, dreams, and fears, a context is established in which trust can flourish, as mutual and meaningful feedback is given and received."[35]
6. **Role Modeling** Managers "walk the talk" by acting, rather than "speechifying," in accordance with these values. Senior executives serve as inspiring role models.
7. **Renewal** A culture that promotes organizational learning at all levels results in the expanded consciousness needed for renewal.

COACHING

Raul Burgos Miranda, vice president and general manager of AT&T Wireless in Puerto Rico, is a leader in the telecommunications industry. When asked about his success, he gave the following explanation.

If I have done something successful, it is to allow people room to feel and know that they matter, that what they say is heard and know that what they do will have an impact; to know at the end of the day, when they close the door, that this is part of their home—this is theirs." He believes that age-old bureaucratic channels have to be replaced by a "no-door policy" in communication. "We have taken empowerment to the level that it truly needs to be," he affirmed. "Many companies say they give you empowerment . . . , but they do so without real responsibility or even the trust to do so. We give you empowerment with responsibility and trust, and in that process, coaching—because empowerment cannot be sustained long-term without real coaching behind it. I think that is very important. . . . I think that has made all the difference in the world.[36]

Empowerment implies a strong commitment to employee development. Managers see themselves as resource people who are responsible for developing their subordinates. One of the primary skills managers need for this task is coaching. *Coaching is defined as a conversation that follows a predictable process and leads to superior performance, commitment to sustained improvement, and positive relationships.*[37] Coaching generally takes place in a one-on-one conversation. Although it is usually performed by managers with subordinates, coaching can also be initiated by skilled coworkers or subordinates (e.g., the case of the young manager who is taught the ropes by an older subordinate or the manager with low emotional intelligence who relies on a subordinate with people skills for advice) or by executive coaches who coach others for a living. Coaching is one of IBM's core leadership competencies; more and more firms expect managers to master coaching as a way to develop their subordinates.

There are five general types of coaching.[38]

1. **Tutoring** Tutoring is used to teach employees necessary job skills they have not yet learned. For example, when employees do not know how to run a team meeting, they must be taught the specific steps in the process and given both practice and feedback.

2. **Counseling** In counseling sessions, the purpose is to help employees gain personal insight into their feelings and behavior. Counseling is appropriate for employees with attitude problems they themselves do not recognize. The focus in counseling is problem recognition and solution.

3. **Mentoring** In mentoring sessions, the objective is to help employees gain a better understanding of the organization, its goals, and advancement criteria. This approach is used, for example, when employees ask why other employees have been promoted and they have not. In such sessions, managers try to make employees more politically savvy and warn them of possible traps. They also help employees live up to their full potential and encourage them to be more proactive in managing their careers.

4. **Confronting** The purpose of confronting is to improve substandard employee performance. Confronting is used, for example, with an employee who is consistently late to work. Performance standards are clarified, the discrepancy between the standard and the employee's performance is pointed out, the cause of the discrepancy is identified, and both parties problem-solve to find a solution.

5. **High performance coaching** The purpose of high-performance coaching is to discover and unleash employee potential to reach meaningful, important objectives.[39] This approach to coaching is described below in the section on Professional Coaching. It focuses on the coachee's desires and talents rather than the organization's need for them to learn job skills (tutoring), learn the ropes (mentoring) or conform (confronting).

Knowing which type of coaching to use in specific situations with specific people requires expertise and experience. The correct approach to take with employees who are not performing well depends on the cause. Unsatisfactory performance often has multiple causes, some of which lie within the control of the employee and some that do not. Fournies suggested that managers use the following guidelines to determine what action they should take.[40] When employees are unaware that their performance is unsatisfactory, the manager (or team) provides feedback. When poor performance occurs because employees are not really sure what is expected of them at work, the manager (or team) provides clear expectations. When employee performance is hampered by obstacles that are beyond their control, the manager removes the obstacles. When the employee simply does not know how to do a task, the manager provides training. The manager should also make sure that good performance is followed by positive rather than negative consequences, and that poor performance is not rewarded by positive consequences. If all these steps have been taken to ensure good performance, and the employee is still not able or willing to perform well, it is time for confrontation coaching.

There are certainly differences in how one performs each type of coaching, but the following steps can be used as a general guideline for coaching sessions.[42]

Before the coaching session:

- Does the supervisor/manager have all the facts about the situation?
- What type of coaching does the situation require?
- How might the employee react and feel about the discussion?
- Think about the best way to present what you want to say to the employee.

During the session:

- Discuss the purpose of the session.
- Try to make the employee comfortable.
- Establish a nondefensive climate characterized by open communication and trust.
- Praise the employee for the positive aspects of his or her performance.
- Mutually define the problem (performance or attitude).
- Mutually determine the causes. Do not interpret or psychoanalyze the employee's behavior; instead, ask questions such as, "What's causing the lack of motivation you describe?"
- Help the employee establish an action plan that includes specific goals and dates.
- Make sure the employee clearly understands what is expected of him or her.
- Summarize what has been agreed upon in the session.
- Affirm your confidence in the employee's ability to make needed changes based on his or her strengths or past history.

After the session:

- Follow up to see how the employee is progressing.
- Modify the action plan i f necessary.

STEPS IN THE COACHING PROCESS

The tutoring process for teaching new skills consists of the following steps.[41]

1. Explain the purpose and importance of what you are trying to teach.
2. Explain the process to be used.
3. Demonstrate how it is done.
4. Observe while the person practices the process.
5. Provide immediate and specific feedback (coach again or reinforce success).
6. Express confidence in the person's ability to be successful.
7. Agree on follow-up actions.

PROFESSIONAL COACHING

Coaching as a profession (as opposed to what skilled managers do with subordinates) began in the 1990s in the United States. It is a rapidly growing profession. According to the International Coach Federation:

> *Professional coaches provide an ongoing partnership designed to help clients produce fulfilling results in their personal and professional lives. Coaches help people improve their performances and enhance the quality of their lives. Coaches are trained to listen, to observe and to customize their approach to individual client needs. They seek to elicit solutions and strategies from the client."* [43]

The steps in personal coaching include: discovering the client's real needs, assessing their situation, setting target goals, and identifying the steps that will achieve the coachee's goals. A trusting relationship with the coach forms the foundation for this process, as shown in the following example.

Roger Seldon is a co-founder and CEO with a hard-nosed, hard-driving, and brusque style. Worried about losing several key executives, he wanted to learn to become a more compassionate leader. His coach asked him what he wanted out of life and for his own future and that of the company. Because he was close to retirement, Roger wanted his legacy to be seen as a great leader who was not known, as he was currently, for his intimidating style and Machiavellian tactics. He also wanted to spend more time with his family and hoped that they would see that as a positive rather than a negative change. His coach obtained feedback from his direct reports who described Roger as "stubborn, bullies people with his strong opinions, dominates discussions, constantly makes decisions lower level employees are charged to make, and rarely appears to listen to other's opinions."[44] This feedback was not a surprise to Roger. His rationale for not changing before was his fear that company results would suffer if he became "soft." His coach suggested that he first try behaving in a different way outside the work setting. Roger devised a plan with the coach's help to act like the leader he wanted to be during an overseas church mission trip that involved constructing a schoolhouse. The plan was a success, and Roger learned that other people also have good ideas and are capable of making good decisions without him calling all the shots. Next, he practiced being more patient and a better listener at home, which was noticed and appreciated by his family. Finally, after experiencing these small wins, Roger tried using these behaviors at work. Although he slipped up occasionally, which is to be expected, he was successful enough that employees realized he was making a concerted effort to develop a new leadership style that was far more effective.[45]

Coaching worked with Roger because he finally saw the negative costs of his management style and received good coaching that moved him step by small, successful step to adopting new behaviors. However, coaching is not indicated with all employees, nor is it always successful. When people have psychological problems (e.g., depression, chronic substance abuse), are narcissistic and see no need to change their behavior, or have highly developed defenses (lack of self-awareness and denial), they are poor candidates for coaching. In contrast, good candidates for coaching are people who are willing to accept feedback, have a sincere desire to improve and an intrinsic need to grow, and who are lifelong learners.[46]

POSITIVE REGARD

Coaching and developing employees is a type of helping relationship. Carl Rogers, the famous psychologist, discovered the importance of unconditional positive regard in his own helping relationships.[47] "I feel that the more acceptance and liking I feel toward this individual, the more I will be creating a relationship which he can use. By acceptance I mean a warm regard for him as a person of unconditional self-worth—of value no matter what his condition, or his feelings. . . . This acceptance of each fluctuating aspect of this other person makes it for him a relationship of warmth and safety, and the safety of being liked and prized as a person seems a highly important element in a helping relationship." Positive regard for employees is also one of the competencies of high-performing managers.[48] When bosses assume that employees want to do a good job, this encourages employees to live up to their boss's good opinion, creating a self-fulfilling prophecy.

THE ROLE OF CULTURE

The cultural dimension, power distance, influences the relationship between empowerment and job satisfaction. Empowerment techniques were less likely to increase job satisfaction in Chinese employees and students, who reported higher power distance scores, when compared to Canadian employees and students with lower power distance scores. Similar results were found in a study of 33 nations.[49] However, employees in high-power distance cultures can become accustomed to greater autonomy and self-determination if their boss coaches them, ensures that they are competent to make decisions, and creates an organizational culture that promotes and rewards empowerment.

Cultural differences play a major role in coaching——they can be potential obstacles or leverage points. Organizations hire coaches to help new executives decipher three types of culture: professional, organizational, and national culture. Coaches also serve as a safe sounding board for bosses from high–power distance cultures who are uncomfortable discussing weaknesses or areas where they lack knowledge with peers or subordinates.

In cross-cultural coaching, mindful communication is important.[50] Essential skills include frequent paraphrasing, suspension of judgment, and careful attention to the words as well as the person and their context. Cultural differences and multiple interpretations are acknowledged and discussed ("How is that kind of behavior viewed in your culture?"). Cross-cultural coaches also help people understand different ways of behaving and doing business. For example, an American consultant who is an expert on Japanese culture coaches executives in newly formed U.S.-Japan mergers. She helps both sides understand the behavior of the other culture and teaches them how to modify their own behavior to be more effective with the other group. The ultimate goal of many culture coaches is to help people leverage cultural differences to create synergy and higher performance. For instance, in Chubb Insurance's Asia/Pacific leadership development program, executives were coached to learn from the example of other cultures. The Australians learned the value of silence and listening more carefully from the Asian executives who, in turn, learned from the Australians to speak up and challenge the group's harmony on decisions when it made good business sense. As a result, the firm's leaders are learning to blend the best aspects of the different cultures.[51]

A direct communication style may not be acceptable with clients accustomed to indirect communication. Therefore coaches with a direct style can utilize these indirect communication strategies:[52]

- Mediation: a third person is used as a go-between
- Refraction: statements intended for person A are made to person B while person A is present
- Metaphors: analogies are used to deliver the message
- Hints: subtle suggestions are made.

CLASS ACTIVITY: THE ENTERPRISE MERGER GAME

The Enterprise Merger game is designed to simulate the dynamics that occur when companies are merged or acquired. The class will divide into Enterprise Teams, which manufacture spacecraft, and Merger Teams, which have recently acquired Enterprise. The exercise focuses on the Merger Team's visit to the Enterprise production facility; the Merger Team's purpose is to improve Enterprise's productivity. (Time allotted: 105-110 minutes)

STEP 1. Choose one or two game coordinators (instructors often play this role or assign it to students ahead of time). The role of the game coordinator is to (1) act as a leader and timekeeper for the simulation; (2) function as the government inspector and buyer of Enterprise's products, and (3) guide the class debriefing.

STEP 2. The class should be divided in half to form two corporations—Enterprise and Merger. Teams of approximately five people from each corporation should be assigned to work together.

STEP 3. Go over the timetable and game procedure shown in Exhibit 19–2.

STEP 4. The game coordinator and the Enterprise and Merger Teams should read their own instructions, which follow.

INSTRUCTIONS FOR THE GAME COORDINATOR

Read the instructions for the entire exercise. Your most important tasks are to:

- Keep to the time schedule described in Exhibit 19–2 (or set by your instructor).
- Ask Enterprise Teams how many spacecraft they want to buy and sell them these materials before production periods 1 and 2 so they are ready to begin construction at the exact moment the production periods begin.

Step	Activity		Time
A	Select Game Coordinator; Form Teams Read Simulation Instructions		10 min.
B	**Merger Team** – Develop plan for helping Enterprise improve productivity – Observe Enterprise's management and production process without intervening	**Enterprise Team** – Organize management and production process – Build spacecraft mockups – Buy materials from coordinator – Prepare to produce	20 min.
C	Continue observation	First production period	5 min.
D	Coordinator evaluates and buys; teams compute and post profit		3–5 min.
E	Merger team consults with Enterprise Team; buys materials from coordinator		20 min.
F	Merger Team observes	Second production period	5 min.
G	Coordinator evaluates and buys; teams compute and post profit		5 min.
H	Teams average their evaluation scores in the consultation process (Step 5) and discuss Step 6 questions		20 min.
I	Class Debriefing; discuss Step 7 questions		20 min.
		Total Time	105–110 min.

EXHIBIT 19-2 **Timetable for the Enterprise Merger Game**

- Inspect and buy acceptable spacecrafts from Enterprise Teams after production periods 1 and 2. *Don't buy the spacecraft unless they fully meet the quality criteria at the end of the blueprints.*
- Ask the Enterprise Teams to compute and post the number of material sets bought and sold and their profit and loss after each production period on the blackboard. Use the Enterprise Team Accounting Form on page 539 as a guide.
- Once the profit and loss figures have been determined after the second production period, ask each individual to evaluate the Merger Team's intervention, as shown in Step 5. Ask each team to average its scores, compare its average with that of the team assigned to work with it, and fill out the form in Step 6.
- Record the two team averages for each pair of Enterprise-Merger Teams on the blackboard and lead the discussion of the questions in Step 7.

INSTRUCTIONS FOR THE ENTERPRISE TEAM

Your previous successful experience in the aerospace industry has just won you a government contract to produce as many Enterprise spacecraft as your production facilities will allow during the next two months (represented in this exercise by the two five-minute production periods). The government has just given you a set of blueprints for the spacecraft accompanied by a number of quality criteria. You must buy raw materials from the game coordinator as determined by the price schedule in Exhibit 19–3.

Your profit is determined by the number of spacecraft you sell to the government at a price of $5 million each minus the cost of materials (other factors, such as overhead, materials, and

Sets of Raw Materials Purchased	Cost Per Set
0–4	$ 4,500,000
5–9	4,400,000
10–14	4,300,000
15–19	4,200,000
20–24	4,100,000
25–29	4,000,000
30–34	3,900,000
35–39	3,800,000
40–44	3,750,000
45–49	3,700,000
50–100	3,650,000
Over 100	3,600,000

Caution: The materials you buy may be slightly faulty. Apparently it is difficult to print the spacecraft perfectly. If you receive raw materials with nose cone lines that don't start at the exact corner of the paper, ignore the lines and make your fold from the true corner of the paper. We're sorry for the inconvenience, but we hear that real-life government contractors sometimes have the same problem.

EXHIBIT 19-3 **Cost of Enterprise Spacecraft Materials**

waste, have been eliminated for simplicity's sake). Only completed vehicles of acceptable quality can be sold. See the Quality Criteria at the end of the blueprints. No materials can be returned; nor can leftovers from period 1 be used in period 2.

In the 20-minute preparation time, you can organize your members in any way you wish to make purchasing and production decisions. During this time, your team is allowed two free sets of materials for each member to use in any way the team wants to establish production techniques and time estimates. You can tear them from your book at the back of the chapter. Any additional materials used during this time must be purchased at full cost. These materials cannot be used during the production periods.

Your agreement with the Merger Team is that it may observe your activities during this time, but it is not to interfere in any way.

When you have decided how many units you want to produce, tell the game coordinator how many sets of materials you want to buy and record that information on the Enterprise Team Accounting Form (page 539) and the blackboard.

INSTRUCTIONS FOR THE MERGER TEAM

Your task during the 20 minutes of preparation period (B) is to decide how best to work with the Enterprise Team after the first production period to help it increase its profit during production period 2. You can organize yourself in any way you want (e.g., you can choose one or two members to act as consultants and feed information and ideas to them, work one-on-one with members of the Enterprise Team, or use any other model you may choose). During the 20-minute preparation period and the first production period, you can observe the Enterprise Team at work, but please do not intervene or speak to its members until Step E. If you want to try building a spacecraft, tear one sheet from the back of the chapter. It cannot be used in the production rounds.

During the 20 minutes before production period 2 begins (E), help the Enterprise Team in any way you see fit. Once the second production period begins, however, you are only allowed to observe. During round 2 (E), the Enterprise Team can have no more members than it had during round 1. Personnel transfers are, however, legitimate. In other words, the total number of people on the Enterprise Team during round 2 must be the same, but specific people can be shifted from the Merger Team to replace someone on the Enterprise Team.

Enterprise Team Accounting Form

	Material Sets Purchased	Cost Per Set	Total Cost	Number Of Units Sold at $5 million Per Unit	Total Receipts	Profit or Loss
PRODUCTION PERIOD 1						
PRODUCTION PERIOD 2						
					Total	Total

ANALYSIS OF THE CONSULTATION PROCESS

STEP 5. The Merger Team has just attempted to effect an improvement in a way in which the Enterprise Team produces spaceships. On the whole, how successful do you think the Merger Team was? (Enterprise Team members evaluate their Merger Team; Merger Team members do a self-evaluation.) Draw a circle around the number that most closely represents your personal opinion:

1   2   3   4   5   6   7

Completely   Completely
unsuccessful   successful

STEP 6. Group Discussion. Average the scores of your team (Enterprise or Merger) and compare it with that of the other team you worked with in the simulation (e.g., the Enterprise Team's evaluation average for Merger Team compared to the self-evaluation average of the Merger Team). The two teams should discuss together the following questions and choose a representative to report your findings back to the class as a whole.

  a. Did the two teams perceive the Merger Team's intervention in the same way?

  b. What did both teams do that either helped or hindered a successful collaborative effort? Use the following chart to record your answers.

Enterprise Team Actions That		Merger Team Actions That	
Helped	Hindered	Helped	Hindered

STEP 7.   Class Debriefing. After presenting the group findings, the class discusses the following questions.

   a. What attributions did the Merger Team make about the performance of the Enterprise Team during the first production period? What was Merger's opinion of the Enterprise team?

   b. Was the Merger Teams' definition of the problem the same as that of the Enterprise Teams?

   c. What was the Merger Team's strategy for helping the Enterprise Team? Did it work?

   d. Was the psychological contract clarified between the two teams in the consultation period?

   e. Did the Merger Team do anything to empower or disempower the Enterprise Team with regard to:

   1. Meaning?

   2. Competence?

   3. Self-determination?

   4. Impact?

   f. Can you draw any analogies between this simulation and real-life merger situations?

DIRECTIONS FOR MAKING THE SPACESHIP ENTERPRISE

The following are directions for making the spaceship. After each step, there is a picture showing what to do and another picture showing what it should look like. Make sure you check this picture before going on to the next step. There are 11 steps.

1. You should have a piece of paper that has one blank side, and one side that looks like this:

2. Turn the paper over so that the blank side is facing up and the word ENTER-PRISE is on the left-hand underneath side. It should now look like this:

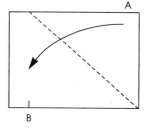

3. Fold corner A to B at the bottom of the paper.

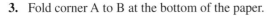

It should now look like this:

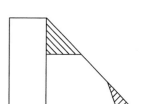

4. Fold corner C to D.

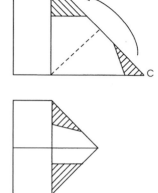

It should now look like this:

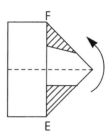

5. Fold E to F.

It should now look like this:

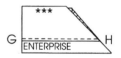

6. Fold on GH by starting with the part with the stars (***) on it and folding down so that the fold comes along the printed solid line. *There are three thicknesses of paper—make sure you only fold the first layer.*

It should now look like this.

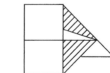

7. Make a fold (up direction) about one inch from the bottom along JK.

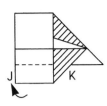

It should now look like this:

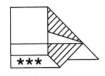

8. Turn the spaceship over and round so that L is on the left side.

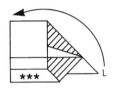

It should now look like this:

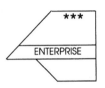

9. Fold on MN by starting with the part with the stars (***) on it and folding down so that the fold comes along the printed solid line. *There are two thicknesses of paper—make sure you only fold the top one.*

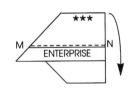

It should now look like this. Make sure this cockpit sticks up in the center.

10. Make a fold (up direction) about one inch from the bottom along OP to make wingtips that show the stars.

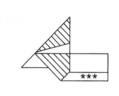

It should now look like this:

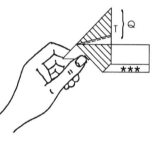

Read all of step 11 and then go back and do it part by part.

11. **a.** Hold spaceship in hand.
    b. Open up Q with finger and flatten the lined area (/////) by bringing central point R toward the main body of the plane. Leave room for the pilot in the cockpit.
    c. Fold along ST to keep it flat.
    d. Make wings level so that plane can fly.
    e. Make the JK fold from #7 and the OP fold from #10 a 90° angle so the wingtips point straight up.

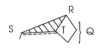

Finished plane should look like this:

top view   side view   front view

QUALITY CRITERIA

1. Printed lines should be in the position shown on the diagram.
2. The wingtips must be one inch tall and point straight up.
3. The "pilot's cabin" (step 11) must be puffed out noticeably. Skinny cabins crowd the astronauts. Cabin folds must be creased on printed lines wherever possible.
4. The two wings must be even with each other (i.e., the entire wing deck should be perfectly level).
5. The nose of the spaceship should be pointed.

The game coordinator will buy only those spacecraft that meet these quality control standards.

LEARNING POINTS

1. Companies that survive and flourish in today's business environment are high-performance companies characterized by cost competiveness, high-quality products and services, innovation, and speed.
2. The command-and-control model is giving way to an involvement-oriented management approach in high-performance organizations because committed workers are more productive.
3. In the command-and-control model, managers make decisions, give orders, and make sure they are obeyed.
4. In the involvement-oriented approach, managers develop employee commitment by sharing both power and information, and developing the employee skills needed to plan and control their own work.
5. Empowerment is defined as granting employees the autonomy to assume more responsibility within an organization and strengthening their sense of effectiveness.
6. The four aspects of empowerment are meaning, competence, self-determination, and impact.
7. The characteristics of high performance-high commitment work cultures are delegation, teamwork across boundaries, empowerment, integration of people and technology, and a shared sense of purpose.
8. Empowerment does not imply that managers and supervisors relinquish all their own authority. They are still responsible for setting the direction, knowing what is going on, removing obstacles, ensuring that employees are on course, ensuring that employees have the necessary skills and information, and assessing performance.
9. Coaching is a conversation that follows a predictable process and leads to superior performance, commitment to sustained improvement, and positive relationships.
10. There are five types of coaching: tutoring, counseling, mentoring, confronting, and high-performance coaching.
11. Positive regard for others is a characteristic of both effective helper/coaches and high-performing managers.

ACTION SCRIPTS

FOR EMPLOYEES

- Employees who are experts at empowering fellow co-workers allow them to determine for themselves where and how to devote their efforts at work as much as possible.
- They look for opportunities to contribute and take initiative.
- When they identify problems, they also suggest solutions. They don't expect the boss or the organization to solve problems when they are capable of doing so themselves.
- They understand when others are good candidates for coaching and when coaching would not work.
- They understand that self-determination is a key role in behavioral change and do not impose their own views on employees they are trying to coach.

FOR MANAGERS

- Managers who are expert at empowering employees make sure they know what is expected of them and understand the limits of their discretion in making decisions.
- They provide employees with the materials and equipment they need to accomplish their work and remove any obstacles in their path.

- They are committed to developing employees and place them in jobs that allow them to utilize current skills as well as learn new skills.
- They understand that employees have varying experience and comfort levels with empowerment and adapt their expectations accordingly. Not everyone wants to be empowered or should be empowered to do all tasks. When employees are not accustomed to empowerment, managers coach them to accept an increasing degree of autonomy, without expecting them to change overnight.
- Unlike some new managers, they understand that a great deal of their time must be spent developing employees and dealing with employee problems.
- They are good at judging which employee problems are beyond their expertise and should be referred to professional counselors.
- Because they know their employees well, they can pick up on behavioral cues that indicate whether or not employees are engaged and involved in their work.
  - They encourage employees to call meetings when they think an issue requires attention, rather than reserving that power for themselves alone.
  - They try to avoid being seen as the source of all wisdom. Instead, they use the Socratic method to ask questions that model for employees the thought processes needed to make good decisions.
  - They are open to feedback and coaching from employees and model the willingness to learn from both superiors and subordinates.
  - To develop employees, they make sacrifices, like turning over enjoyable tasks at which they excel to subordinates. They are patient and understand that employees may initially perform a new task at a lower level until they have mastered it. They understand that letting go of tasks and delegating is an investment that will pay off in the future because competent employees will free up their time to look at the broader picture.
- They give employees the autonomy to do tasks in a different manner than they themselves might use, as long as the final product is acceptable. This is why some people say that engineers can't really be good bosses until all their subordinates possess more state-of-the-art technical knowledge than they do; they have to trust their subordinates to do the right thing because they no longer completely understand how to do it themselves.
- Active listening is a key part of coaching because people often determine what is bothering them or what decision they want to make by talking things out with another person. In presenting their story to a listener, many people imagine how the listener is reacting and this provides the speaker with another perspective.
- The leader's behavior determines the level of trust within a group. When leaders micromanage or fail to delegate, employees assume they are not trusted—and, in return, their trust in the leader diminishes. Employees who trust their immediate supervisor are more likely to be high performers.[53]

FOR ORGANIZATIONAL ARCHITECTS

- Organizational architects who are expert at empowerment train managers to coach and empower their subordinates and evaluate them on how effectively they put these skills into practice.
- They provide executive coaching when needed.
- They design organic systems that emphasize flexibility, adaptability, and innovation.
- They develop stream-lined procedures with as few bureaucratic obstacles as possible.
- They provide employees with the necessary resources and materials.
- They set up systems to provide employees with the information needed to make decisions.
- They develop and post performance metrics that provide employees with motivating data.
- They measure how many employees are actually engaged at work.
- They establish clear direction for employees and map out the boundaries within which they are empowered to make decisions and take initiative.
- The reward system provides recognition and rewards for empowerment and coaching behavior.

- They pay employees to learn new skills and to teach others new skills.
- They have suggestion boxes that require workers to take action and come up with solutions, not just ideas.
- They develop an organizational culture that values employee participation and development and supportive management.

 PERSONAL APPLICATION ASSIGNMENT

The topic of this assignment is to write about a significant experience that involved coaching or empowerment, or the lack thereof. Choose an experience that intrigues you and that you want to learn more about. Alternatively, you may want to experiment with the skills taught in this unit and write about the outcome.

A. Concrete Experience

    1. Objectively describe the experience (who, what, when, where, how information) (2 points)

    2. Subjectively describe your feelings, perceptions, and thoughts that occurred during (not after) the experience. What did others seem to be feeling? (2 points)

B. Reflective Observation

    1. Looking back at the experience, what were the perspectives of the key actors (including you)? (2 points)

    2. Why did the people involved (including you) behave as they did? (2 points)

C. Abstract Conceptualization

   1. Relate concepts or theories from the assigned readings or the lecture to the experience. Explain thoroughly how they apply to your experience. Please apply at least two concepts or theories and cite them correctly. (4 points)

D. Active Experimentation

   1. What did you learn about empowerment and coaching from this experience? (1 point)

   2. What did you learn about yourself? (1 point)

   3. What action steps will you take to be more effective in the future? (2 points)

E. Integration, Synthesis, and Writing

   1. Did you integrate and synthesize the four sections? (1 point)
   2. Was the Personal Application Assignment well written and easy to understand? (1 point)
   3. Was it free of spelling and grammatical errors? (2 points)

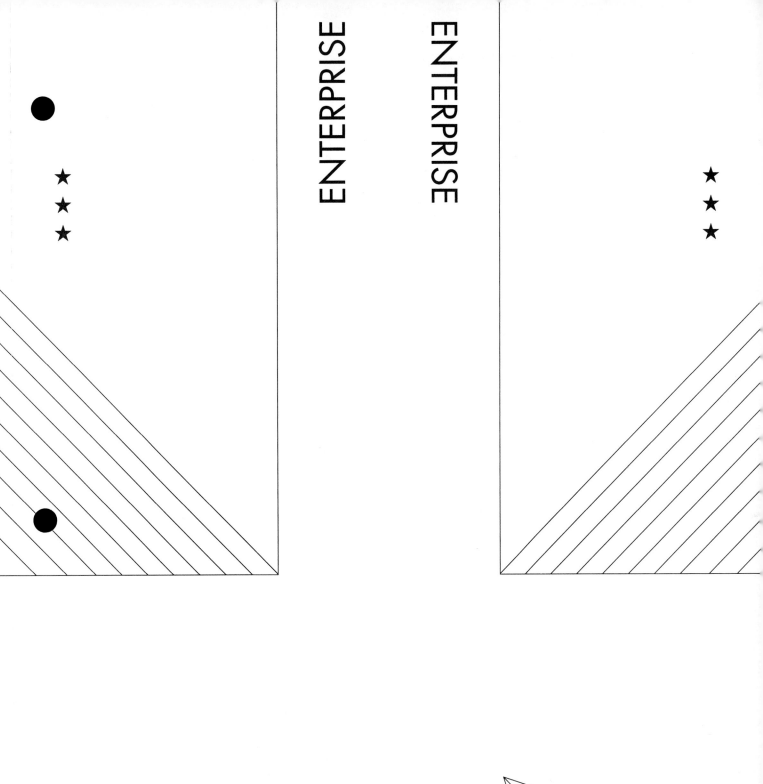

ENTERPRISE

ENTERPRISE

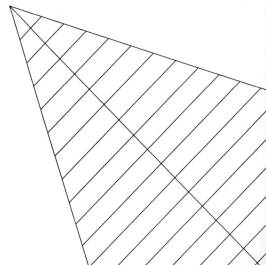

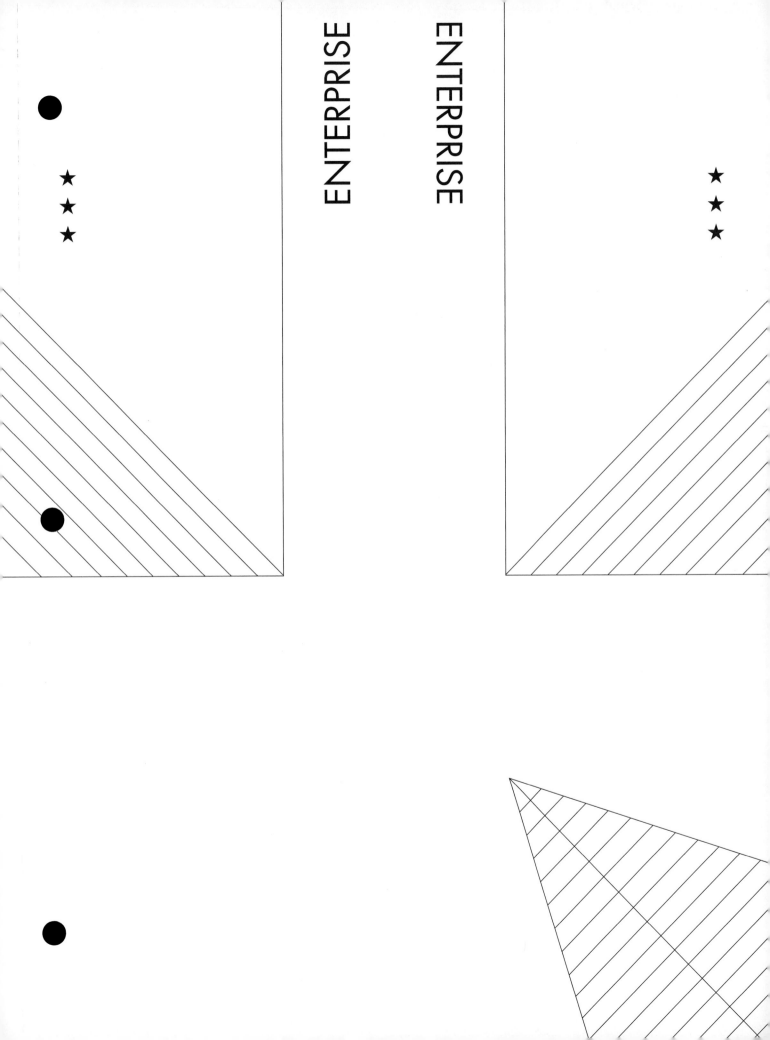

ENTERPRISE

ENTERPRISE

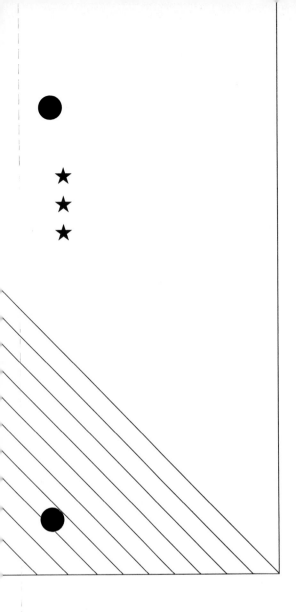

ENTERPRISE

ENTERPRISE

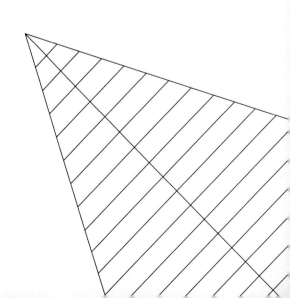

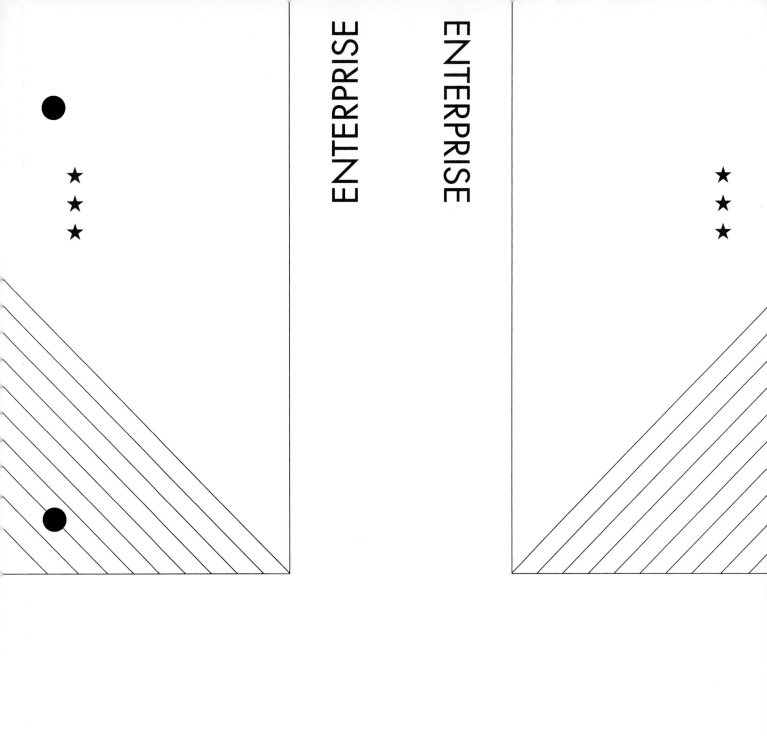

ENTERPRISE

ENTERPRISE

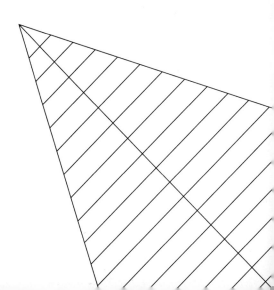

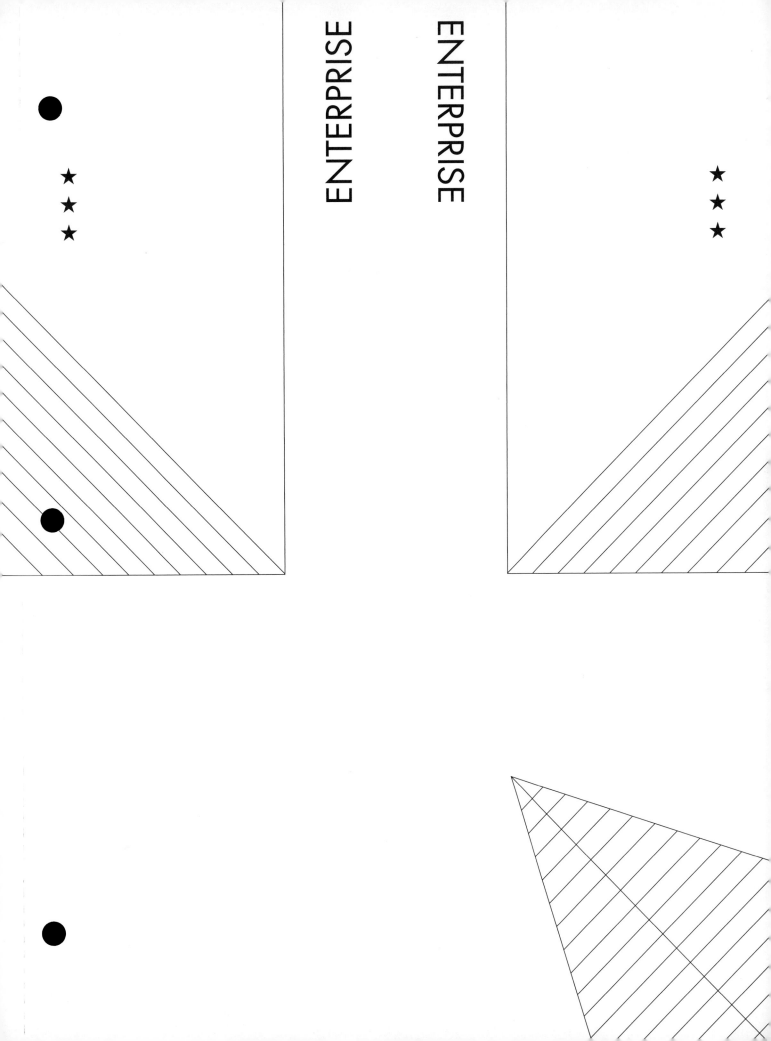

ENTERPRISE

ENTERPRISE

ENTERPRISE

ENTERPRISE

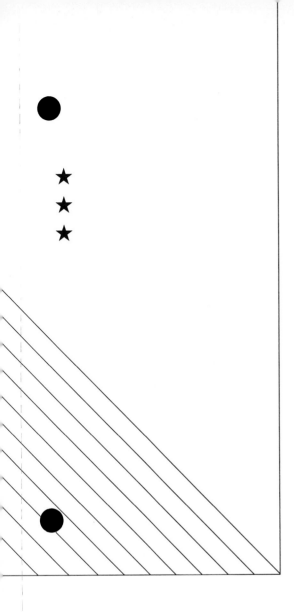

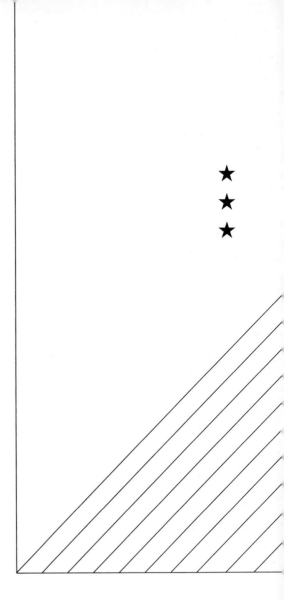

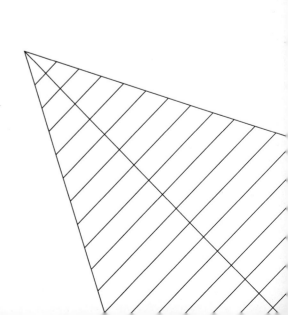

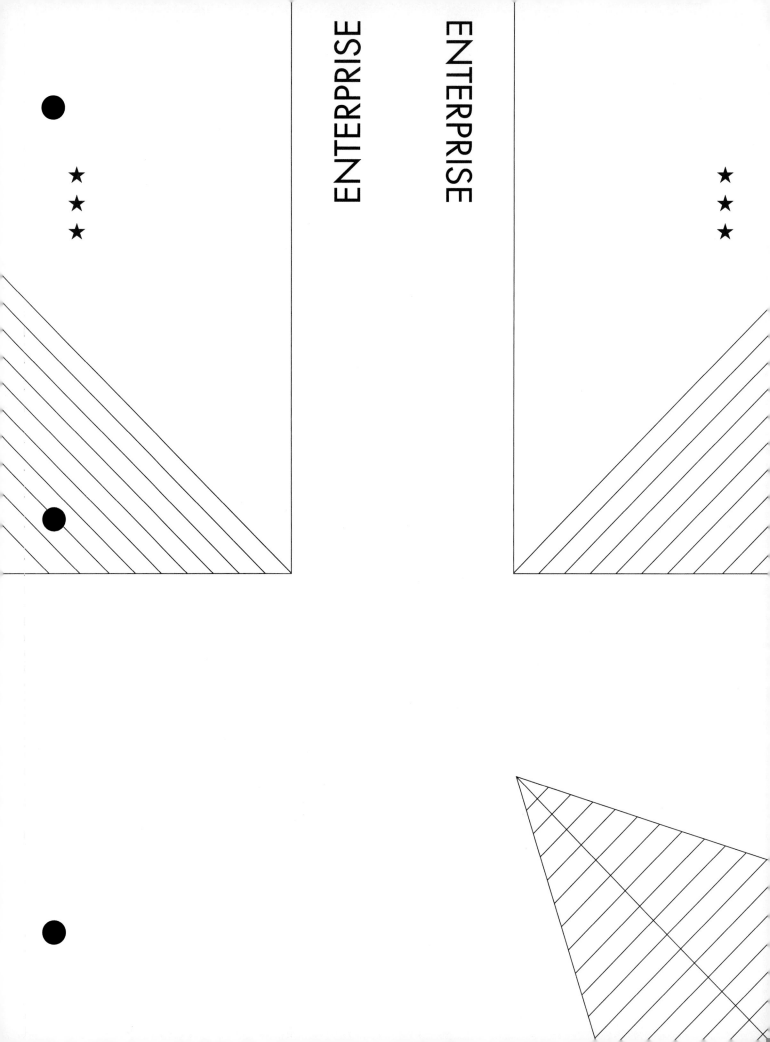

ENTERPRISE

ENTERPRISE

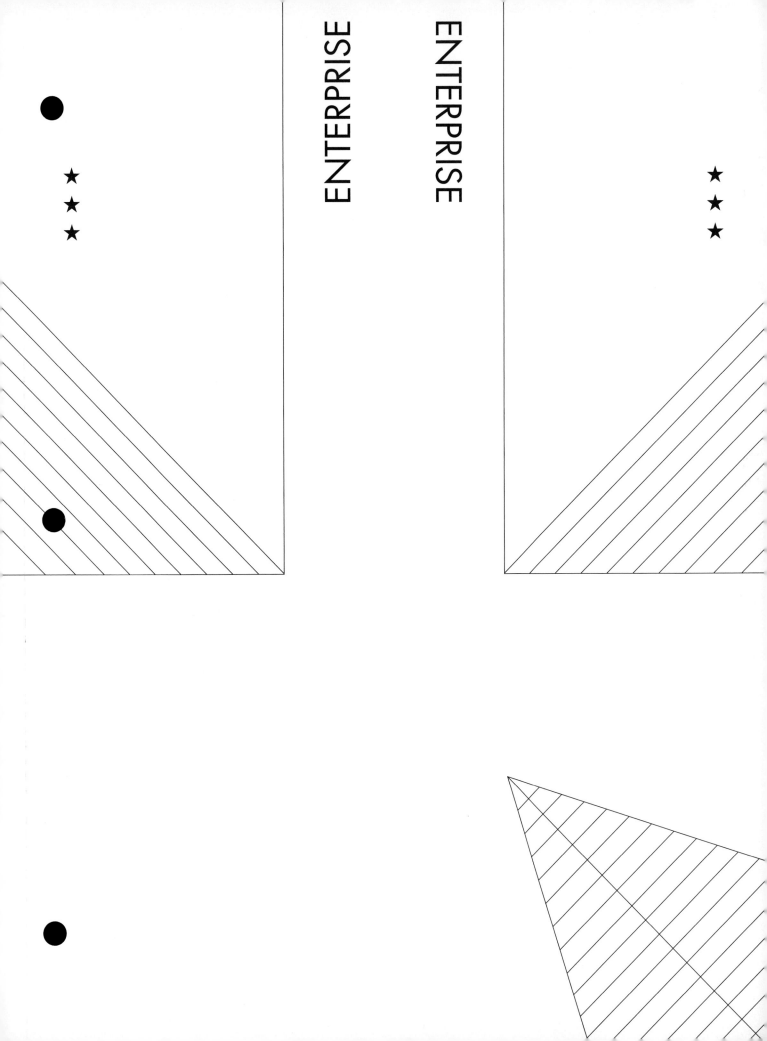

ENTERPRISE

ENTERPRISE

ENTERPRISE

ENTERPRISE

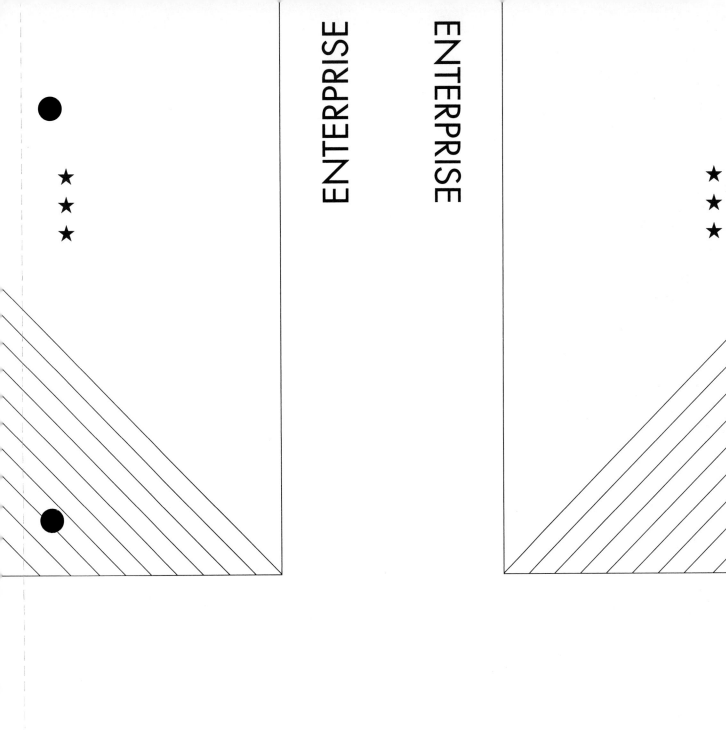

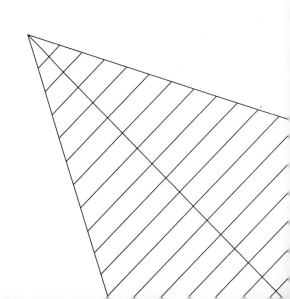

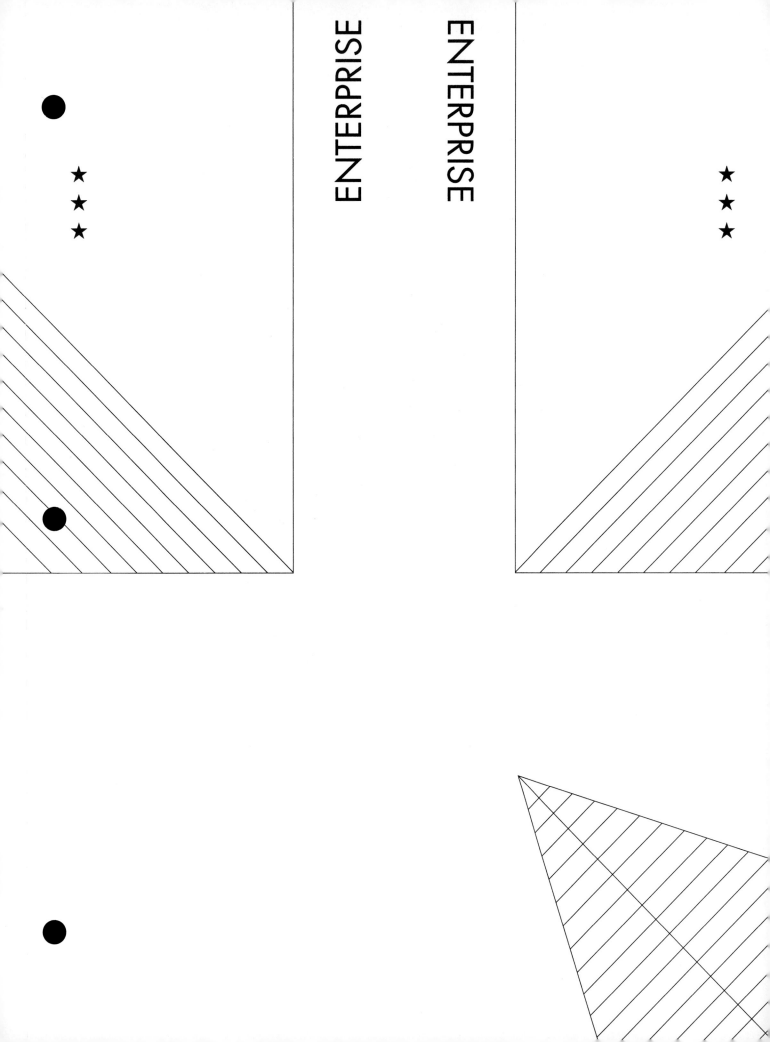

ENTERPRISE

ENTERPRISE

ENDNOTES

[1] B. Breen, "The Clear Leader," *Fast Company 92* (March 2005): 65.

[2] J. Pfeffer, *The Human Equation: Building Profits by Putting People First* (Cambridge, MA: Harvard Business School Press, 1999).

[3] J. Heskett, W. E. Sasser, and L. Schelsinger, *The Human Profit Chain* (New York: Free Press, 1997); B. N. Pfau and I. T. Kay, *The Human Capital Edge* (New York: McGraw-Hill, 2002).

[4] This list is paraphrased from P. R. Harris, *High Performance Leadership* (Glenview, IL: Scott, Foresman and Company, 1989): 14–15.

[5] T. Peters, *Liberation Management* (New York: Alfred A. Knopf, 1992).

[6] E. E. Lawler III, *The Ultimate Advantage* (San Francisco: Jossey-Bass, 1992): 28–29.

[7] R. E. Walton, "From Control to Commitment in the Workplace," *Harvard Business Review 63*(2) (March-April 1985): 76–84.

[8] Lawler, *The Ultimate Advantage*: 44.

[9] Ibid.: 41.

[10] M. Magnet, "The Truth About the American Worker," *Fortune 125*(9) (May 4, 1992): 58 and 64.

[11] Lawler, *The Ultimate Advantage*: 29.

[12] W. H. Schmidt and J. P. Finnigan, *The Race Without a Finish Line* (San Francisco: Jossey-Bass, 1992): 46. Although these authors are writing about managers in TQM programs, which are not synonymous with high-involvement companies, this statement holds true for any manager who has empowered workers.

[13] D. C. McClelland, *Power: The Inner Experience* (New York: Irvington, 1975) and J. A. Conger and R. N. Kanugo, "The Empowerment Process: Integrating Theory and Practice," *Academy of Management Review 13*(3) (1988): 471–482.

[14] J. F. Kennedy, "Inaugural Address," Washington, D.C. (January 20, 1961). Available at http://www.jfklibrary.org/j012061.htm. Accessed 3/21/06.

[15] K. W. Thomas and B. A. Velthouse, "Cognitive Elements of Empowerment: An Interpretative Model of Intrinsic Task Motivation," *Academy of Management Review 15*(4) (October 1990): 666–681.

[16] A. Bandura, "Self-efficacy: Toward a Unifying Theory of Behavioral Change," *Psychological Review 84*(2) (1977): 191–215; and A. Bandura, *Self-Efficacy: The Exercise of Control* (New York: W. H. Freeman and Company, 1997).

[17] A. Stajkovic and F. Luthans, "A Meta-Analysis of the Effects of Organizational Behavior Modification on Task Performance," *Academy of Management Journal 40*(5) (1997): 1122–1149.

[18] R. E. Quinn and G. M. Spreitzer, "The Road to Empowerment: Seven Questions Every Leader Should Consider," *Organizational Dynamics 26*(2) (Autumn 1997): 41; G. M. Spreitzer, "Toward a Common Ground in Defining Empowerment," in W. A. Pasmore and R. W. Woodman (eds.), *Research in Organizational Change and Development 10* (Greenwich, CT: JAI Press, 1997): 31–62.

[19] G. M. Spreitzer, "Social Structural Levers for Workforce Empowerment," *Academy of Management Journal 39*(2) (1996): 483–504.

[20] D. Geisler, "The Next Level in Employee Empowerment," *Quality Progress 38*(6) (2005): 48–52.

[21] G. M. Spreitzer, "An Empirical Test of a Comprehensive Model of Interpersonal Empowerment in the Workplace" *American Journal of Community Psychology 23*(5) (1995): 601–629; K. W. Thomas and W. G. Tymon, "Does Empowerment Always Work: Understanding the Role of Intrinsic Motivation and Personal Interpretation," *Journal of Management Systems 6*(2) (1994): 1–13; and H. K. Spence Laschinger, J. E. Finegan, J. Shamian, and P. Wilk, "A Longitudinal Analysis of the Impact of Workplace Empowerment on Work Satisfaction," *Journal of Organizational Behavior 25*(4) (2004): 527–545.

[22] B. Argyris, "Empowerment: The Emperor's New Clothes," *Harvard Business Review 76*(3) (May-June 1998): 98–105; J. Gandz and F. G. Bird, "The Ethics of Empowerment," *Journal of Business Ethics 15*(4) (1996): 383–392; and T. Appel, "Not All Workers Find Idea of Empowerment as Neat as It Sounds," *Wall Street Journal* (September 8, 1997): A-1.

[23] See R. Frey's "Empowerment or Else," *Harvard Business Review 71*(5) (September-October 1993): 80–94, for a vivid description of one manager's experience in empowering his workers; and K. Blanchard, J. P. Carlos, and A. Rudolph, *The Three Keys to Empowerment* (San Francisco: Berrett-Koehler, 1999).

[24] J. J. Sherwood, "Creating Work Cultures with Competitive Advantage," *Organizational Dynamics 16*(3) (Winter 1988): 5–27.

[25] This example came from a leadership interview written by Marcia Trask, MBA student at San Jose State University, (2003).

[26] J. and S. Welch, "Ideas The Welch Way," *BusinessWeek 3973* (February 27, 2006): 102.

[27] These suggestions come from a variety of sources including Bandura, *Self-Efficacy*; and W. C. Byham with J. Cox, *Zapp!*

The Lightning of Empowerment (Pittsburgh, PA: DDI Press, 1989).

[28] M. Buckingham and C. Coffman, *First, Break All the Rules* (New York: Simon & Schuster, 1999).

[29] Adapted from Byham, *Zapp!*: 108.

[30] M. P. Follett, *Freedom and Coordination: Lectures in Business Organization* (London: Management Publications Trust, 1949): 46.

[31] E. M. Fox and L. Urwick (eds.), *Dynamic Administration: The Collected Papers of Mary Parker Follett* (New York: Hippocrene Books, 1982).

[32] A. Osland, "The Role of Leadership and Cultural Contingencies in Total Quality Management in Central America," *Journal of Business and Management 3* (1996): 64–80.

[33] S. Deepak, "The Seven R's of Self-Esteem," in F. Hesselbein, M. Goldsmith, and R. Beckhard (eds.), *The Organization of the Future* (San Francisco: Jossey-Bass, 1997): 231–238.

[34] M. Goldsmith, "Retaining Your Top Performers," in Hesselbein, Goldsmith, and Beckhard (eds.), *The Organization of the Future*: 262.

[35] Deepak, "The Seven R's of Self-Esteem": 235.

[36] R. Velazquez, "Raul Burgos Takes Organizational Empowerment to the Next Level," *Carribean Business* (Thursday, December 2, 2004): 39.

[37] C. C. Kinlaw, *Coaching for Commitment* (San Diego, CA: Pfeiffer & Company, 1993): 31.

[38] The first four types of coaching are described in Kinlaw's *Coaching for Commitment*, ibid., while high-performance coaching is discussed in P. Rosinski, *Coaching Across Cultures* (London: Nicholas Brealey, 2003).

[39] Ibid.

[40] F. Fournies, *Coaching for Improved Work Performance* (New York: Van Nostrand Reinhold, 1978).

[41] Byham, *Zapp!*: 129.

[42] Kinlaw provides more detailed instructions for each type of coaching in *Coaching for Commitment*.

[43] International Coach Federation. Available at: http://www.coachfederation.org/ICF/For+Coaching+Clients/What+is+a+Coach/. Accessed 3/20/06.

[44] R. E. Boyatzis, A. Howard, B. Rapisarda, and S. Taylor, "Coaching Can Work, But Doesn't Always," *People Management 10* (5) (March 11, 2004): 28.

[45] Boyatzis, Howard, Rapisarda, and Taylor, "Coaching Can Work, But Doesn't Always": 26–32.

[46] T. R. Bacon and M. I. Spear, *Adaptive Coaching: The Art and Practice of a Client-Centered Approach to Performance Improvement* (Palo Alto, CA: Davies-Black, 2003).

[47] D. Rogers, *On Becoming a Person* (Boston: Houghton Mifflin, 1961): 34.

[48] R. E. Boyatzis, *The Competent Manager: A Model for Effective Performance* (New York: John Wiley, 1982).

[49] The data in this paragraph is reported in M. K. Hui, K. Au, and H. Fock, "Empowerment Effects Across Cultures," *Journal of International Business Studies 35*(1) (2004): 46–60.

[50] Ibid.

[51] Rosinski, *Coaching Across Cultures*.

[52] Rosinski, *Coaching Across Cultures*:161.

[53] L. R. Offermann, "Leading and Empowering Diverse Followers," in G. R. Hickman (ed.), *Leading Organizations*: *Perspectives for a New Era* (Thousand Oaks, CA: Sage, 1998): 397–403.

Chapter 20

▲▲

PERFORMANCE MANAGEMENT

OBJECTIVES By the end of this chapter, you should be able to:

A. Explain the importance of performance feedback.

B. Describe the process of performance appraisal.

C. Identify the components of effective appraisals.

D. Demonstrate the skills required for a good appraisal.

E. Describe 360-degree feedback.

F. Explain the opposition to appraisal systems.

G. Distinguish between effective and ineffective feedback.

LEADER AS DEVELOPER

During the conference when we were discussing difficult subordinates, I realized that I had completely written Mike off and had stopped any effective communication with him. Mike was a 53-year-old sales representative who had been with the company for over 12 years. He was well liked by the central office staff but had not met his sales plan for five of the last six years. Furthermore, I was starting to hear complaints about him from some of our clients.

I first tried to put myself in Mike's shoes. What must it be like to be near the end of one's career and starting to go downhill? If I were Mike, how receptive would I be to criticism? I might then be able to understand one of his habitual behaviors that had been particularly annoying to me: his tendency to look only to external factors for his failures, to blame "bad luck," the market, competitors who used unfair tactics, and the like.

Still, before meeting with Mike, I did two things. I considered what would be a reasonable goal for him in six months—what exactly did I expect of him in terms of sales level, generating new business, and the like. Then I thought, "What is it in Mike's behavior that would cause him trouble in making sales? Is it something in his style or is some knowledge lacking?"

I then sat down with Mike and began by acknowledging that our relationship had deteriorated, that I had been dissatisfied with him but hadn't confronted him before, and also that I probably hadn't helped him as much as I could have. Mike immediately blamed me for everything that had gone wrong. It was fortunate that I had thought this out before, because my first response was defensive, to attack back. What helped was that I had already thought about why Mike must be hurting—clearly his pain was greater than anything I was now feeling about his comments.

After Mike had vented his feelings, I repeated that I wanted to change our relationship so that I could be more helpful. In return, we needed to get agreement on some specific goals for Mike. Although I would help him, it would be his responsibility to meet certain objectives. He was to be accountable for them, and if he failed to meet or substantially reach them in six months, he would be placed on probation. We mutually negotiated these goals. When I felt he was setting them too low, I pointed out what other sales personnel would do. We ended up with my original list modified, but in a way both of us could live with.

I then asked Mike what he thought might cause him difficulty in going about reaching his goals. In what areas did he need more training, and were there ways he behaved that caused problems? (I also asked him to discuss what he thought was easy for him—what his especially strong areas were.) As he shared his self-perception, I also shared my perception. I tried to point to specific behaviors at specific times that illustrated the problem areas I saw. At one point, he got very defensive and offered external reasons why the problems I identified were not his fault. I used his response as an illustration of what I was pointing out in his behavior.

In this discussion, we agreed to specific areas in which he could benefit from training. I sent him to a training program to work on his time-management problem. Also, we set up regular meetings (every two weeks) when we would review progress. I said that I was always available if he had a question, but that the initiative was up to him.

Mike did not meet the goals at the end of six months. I placed him on probation, with notice of termination in three months. I again met with him on a regular basis to offer assistance and coaching. Seven days before the end of his probation, Mike came in and said that the fit between him and the job was not right and quit.

As a result of this process, there was minimal reaction by the office staff (who had very much liked Mike). There was neither a decrease in morale nor a rise in paranoia among the others. Mike found another job in an area both of us had discussed as being more in line with his skills. Perhaps most gratifying to me, he expressly thanked me for my concern. He is doing well in his new position and is much happier.

Source: David Bradford and Allen R. Cohen, *Managing for Excellence* (New York: John Wiley, 1984): 157–158.

 **CLASS PREPARATION**

A. Read "Leader as Developer."

B. Think back on the best performance appraisal you ever received or gave regardless of where it occurred (work, school, or extracurricular activity). Write down what was good about it.

C. Think about the worst performance appraisal you ever received or gave. What made it so ineffective?

D. Write a list of the conditions you think are necessary for an effective performance appraisal.

E. Consider your performance in this course and write your answers to these questions. Bring them to class:

1. What have you done so far that has contributed to your own learning and that of your learning group?

2. What have you contributed to the general atmosphere of the class?

3. Are there extenuating circumstances that have affected your performance in the course?

4. What have your weaknesses and strengths been so far?

5. What would you like to improve in your performance?

6. How do you plan to do it between now and the end of the semester?

F. While reading the chapter, make a list of cues that you should look for with respect to performance management.

 **THE KNOWLEDGE BASE**

A *performance management system is a process of establishing performance standards and evaluating performance to ensure that goals are being effectively accomplished.* It encompasses the performance methods, measures, processes, and systems that can be applied to an organization, subunit, process, subsystem or employee.[1] Best practices companies utilize their performance management systems to:[2]

- Replace a "best-effort" culture with a results-driven culture
- Establish and reinforce the importance of core competencies
- Target poor performers for termination

The performance management process is a method of translating goals and strategies into action by establishing measurable goals, communicating those goals, monitoring goal accomplishment, and providing feedback on performance.[3] At the organizational level, one very popular approach is the *balanced scorecard*, created by Robert Kaplan and David Norton.[4] This approach was developed to assist managers in considering all important aspects of organizational performance. Many performance systems have a limited focus. For example, they may consider only financial measures or target only operational efficiency measures. By using a balanced scorecard, managers look at organizational performance from four perspectives:[5]

1. **Customer Perspective:** How do customers see the organization?
2. **Internal Business Perspective:** What must the organization excel at in order to succeed?
3. **Innovation and Learning Perspective:** How can the organization continue to improve and create value?
4. **Financial Perspective:** How does the organization look to shareholders?

For each perspective, managers translate their general strategy and mission into goals and measures. For example, Electronic Circuits Incorporated established general goals for customer performance such as getting products to market sooner and then developed measures for those goals (e.g., percentage of sales from new products). They monitored performance on those measures and communicated results to employees.[6]

Managers attempting to implement performance management systems often face a number of challenges. Aligning goals with strategy throughout the organization can be a key issue. Managers need to be sure that organizational units, teams, and individual employees are working together to achieve compatible rather than conflicting goals. Music and video distributor Handelman Company addressed this challenge by establishing a Center for Performance Management. The center is responsible for strategy alignment (ensuring that all levels of the organization are aligned with its strategy); communication and education about the organization's strategy; managing initiatives to execute the strategy; defining measures; change management; and working with senior administration to shape strategic review and learning.[7]

As we saw in the chapter on motivation, one of the key issues in fostering performance is defining the right measure of performance and rewarding performance on those measures appropriately. Using an ill-defined or poorly chosen measure can lead to results that are the opposite of what managers intended. For example, let's suppose that you wanted to be sure that your employees don't abuse your organization's sick leave policies. You might, for example, implement what is called "well-pay" or paying employees only when they come into work. You can probably guess what often occurs under these types of systems. Employees come to work, even when they are ill—with frequently negative repercussions for their performance and their co-workers!

Performance measures may not always provide managers with the whole story, or even the right story. For example, William Starbuck, a management scholar and professor, notes that stock prices can reflect a number of factors other than company performance. They may be affected by the optimism and pessimism of investors and societal or economic forces (such as oil supply fluctuations and political upheavals).[8] Thus, managers must be careful in the selection, implementation, and interpretation of performance measures. Most appraisal systems focus on either outcomes or behavioral criteria.

Another challenge that managers face in implementing performance management systems is the monitoring of performance and results. Efficiently obtaining and reporting performance data in ways that are useful for the organization can be difficult issues for managers. Some managers compile too little data; while others overload employees with too much data. Both information overload and underload can have negative effects on future decisions. Managers must be careful to achieve the proper balance of information that facilitates accountability and effective decision making.

Finally, managers must also pay attention to who must achieve the results and the consequences for meeting—or not meeting—performance goals and targets. Experts note that managers should:

- **Develop rigorous systems that differentiate between three groups of employees:** The outstanding contributors, the satisfactory or successful employees, and those who aren't performing acceptably. Along with this objective, companies should strive to get the best people in the most important jobs, or the jobs with the most critical links to performance and organizational goals.
- **Create conditions that foster goal accomplishment** by establishing clear performance expectations, removing obstacles to performance, and rewarding performance.

- **Establish a culture of accountability** so that managers and employees are held responsible for meeting their goals.[9]

One of the most important methods for ensuring that performance management systems operate effectively is the performance appraisal process. We'll examine that process in depth in the next sections of the chapter.

PERFORMANCE APPRAISAL PROCESS

Performance appraisals are often one of the least favorite activities of managers. Yet they can be a valuable managerial tool for maintaining and improving performance and reinforcing what's important in an organization. Without such systems, managerial decisions about promotions, raises, and terminations might have little objective basis. Research on performance management shows that "the higher the quality of the appraisal process, the more the appraisal event results in performance improvement, improved working conditions for the subordinate, and better working relations between the subordinate and the supervisor."[10]

Performance appraisal systems attempt to evaluate employees fairly using a standardized model, but because humans operate these systems we cannot guarantee total objectivity. Given what we know about the correlation between feedback and high performance,[11] it is surprising that some organizations still do not evaluate employees in a systematic fashion. Even when organizations have systems in place, many managers fail to comply. In such instances, employees often interpret skipped or late reviews, accurately or inaccurately, as an indication that their manager is not concerned about them and does not appreciate their work. It is not uncommon to find organizations in which reviews hold great significance for employees but are perceived as little more than a waste of time by their managers.

Why the difference in opinion about performance reviews? At the organizational level, some appraisal systems are outdated and cumbersome and seem to measure only that which is easily quantified. It's difficult for managers to take such systems seriously and see how they have any positive results. On the personal level, some managers resent the time consumed by appraisals and feel uncomfortable sitting in judgment on another person. McGregor argued that the conventional approach to performance appraisal:

> *Unless handled with consummate skill and delicacy, [performance appraisal] constitutes something dangerously close to a violation of the integrity of the personality. Managers are uncomfortable when they are put in the position of "playing God." The respect we hold for the inherent value of the individual leaves us distressed when we must take responsibility for judging the personal worth of a fellow human being. Yet the conventional approach to performance appraisals forces us, not only to make such judgements and to see them acted upon, but also to communicate them to those we have judged. Small wonder we resist!*[12]

Some supervisors and managers are uncomfortable giving negative feedback and fear that doing so may make a bad situation even worse, maybe even prompt disgruntled employees to engage in workplace violence. Others disagree philosophically with having to rank all their employees or place them into a forced distribution and fire the bottom ten percent, a practice currently used by many U.S. firms.[13]

In contrast to these reasons why managers tend to avoid appraisals, we know that managers who see appraisals as a useful tool can utilize their human resources more effectively. Research has shown that monitoring and providing feedback on performance is one of the most effective ways to improve performance.[14] Appraisals allow managers the opportunity to give feedback on performance and set goals for future performance, which are highly effective ways to motivate employees.

In addition, performance feedback serves a variety of functions for employees:[15]

- Contributes to the development of employees' self-concept.

- Reduces uncertainty about whether their behavior is on track and how it is perceived by others.
- Signals which organizational goals are most important in relation to others.
- Helps individuals to master their environment and feel competent.

An awareness of these functions may help managers to realize that a performance appraisal session means more to employees than just finding out what their salary will be for the next year.

Let's return to McGregor's statement that managers feel uncomfortable when they are put in the position of "playing God." To an extent, this is determined by the attitude the manager has toward appraisal. If the manager's underlying approach is to help the employee develop, his or her feedback is more likely to be effective and well received. The theory-in-use that underlies this approach is one that acknowledges the role of enlightened self-interest. In other words, if employees understand what is required of them and what they need to do or stop doing to be promoted or receive good performance ratings, they will do it. Managers utilizing this approach see their function as presenting employees with objective feedback about their performance and career plans. A less successful managerial approach to appraisal is the judgmental "gotcha," which is more likely to result in defensiveness than in the behavioral changes the manager desires. Thus, the performance appraisal activity requires leaders and managers to switch into a coaching mind-set.

Although the specific mechanics of implementation will vary across organizations, the "ideal" performance appraisal system is designed to achieve five basic objectives:

1. Provide feedback to subordinates to facilitate their ability to achieve organizational and personal goals.
2. Provide management with data to make personnel decisions (salary, promotional, termination).
3. Recognize skill acquisition and identify skill deficits for further professional training and development.
4. Motivate employees to be more effective workers.
5. Comply with equal opportunity regulations and ensure fairness.

Depending on how this process gets implemented, managers often find themselves in a role conflict. On the one hand, they are asked to be helper-coaches in the feedback process; on the other hand, they serve as judges, linking performance assessment to salary and promotion decisions. Some research on the performance appraisal process points strongly to the need to separate these roles.[16] In addition to mastering the coaching skills described in the last chapter, it's important for managers to understand the unique aspects of the performance appraisal process, which are presented in the next section.

LAYING THE GROUNDWORK FOR EFFECTIVE PERFORMANCE APPRAISAL

Too often managers see appraisals as a once-a-year event. In reality, appraisal is a process that begins long before the appraisal interview and consists of the following steps:

1. Review legal requirements.
2. Translate organizational goals into individual job objectives or requirements.
3. Set clear expectations for job performance and communicate both expectations and instructions clearly.
4. Provide employees with the job training or coaching they require to meet the expectations.
5. Supply adequate supervision, feedback, and coaching throughout the year.
6. Choose a measurement system that accurately measures performance.
7. Acknowledge employee accomplishments, diagnose employees' relative strengths and weaknesses, and present all of these objectively during the appraisal interview.

8. Use the appraisal interview to establish performance goals and a development plan with the employee, which includes an action plan for improved performance or further education and the efficient future use of the employee's abilities.

Framing performance appraisal as a ongoing process rather than an annual interview means that appraisal is better integrated with the rest of the organization's functions. Once their annual goals are set, managers usually begin worrying about whether employee performance is on track or requires feedback or more serious intervention.

A basic truism about human behavior is that people generally focus their energies on that which is measured or evaluated. If managers measure only tangible factors (such as financial and output figures), the intangibles (such as service orientation, ability to get along with co-workers, organization building, etc.) are given less importance. This means, we have to be very careful about what we include in the performance appraisal form. The same caveat applies to supervisors and managers: if they are evaluated and rewarded based on how well they develop and evaluate their own subordinates, they will be more likely to give performance management the attention it deserves.

There are four common responses to appraisals that wise managers seek to avoid:

1. "I never knew that's what the boss expected me to do!"
2. "Why didn't they tell me before that they weren't happy with my work?"
3. "I wish I had known all along that they liked my work. I wouldn't have wasted so much time worrying about it or looking for other jobs!"
4. "I got a poor review because my boss doesn't like me."

By clarifying expectations carefully, giving immediate feedback throughout the year, and demonstrating a concern for fairness, managers can avoid some of these reactions. Providing immediate feedback has several advantages. First, it offers an opportunity to improve performance. Second, it gives employees an idea about how their supervisor sees them so that the appraisal does not come as a shock. Third, it can keep the channel of communication open between managers and employees. Often new supervisors see an employee doing something incorrectly but are unsure how to give feedback. Instead, they become more and more angry with the employee and either "dump" the feedback when they can no longer contain themselves (think emotional hijack) or save it for the appraisal interview. This is called "gunny-sacking." In the meantime, their relationship with the employee usually suffers, and they may have rounded out the employee's character with negative attributions that are inaccurate. The feedback given during the appraisal interview, be it positive or negative, should never come as a total surprise to employees.

The fairness issue with appraisals relates to the necessity for managers to know themselves and their personal tendencies. The research on similarity and attraction indicates that people prefer those who are similar to themselves. They also tend to give higher ratings to subordinates who are similar to them.[17] The result can be what Moore termed a "bureaucratic kinship system" based on "homosexual reproduction," in which men with the power to hire and promote "reproduce" themselves.[18] It is not uncommon to look around a table of senior managers and discover that they resemble one another, either physically or socially. Thus, it is easy for managers to perceive an employee they like more positively than that person really deserves. The opposite can occur with employees whom managers either dislike or perceive as different than themselves.

When certain appraisal conditions are met, the potential sources of bias such as age, race, sex, and being different are less likely to have a negative effect on performance appraisals. These conditions are:

- When employees make their work visible to the appraiser;
- When appraisers and appraisees together clarify objectives and task responsibilities; and
- When the appraiser uses the behaviorally-based appraisal scales.[19]

Attribution theory (see Chapter 9) maintains that we make attributions about the causes of behavior of both others and ourselves to understand what we see occurring.[20] We guess or infer the causes of people's behavior and base our reactions to their behaviors on these inferences rather than on the way they really behave. A practical example of attribution theory might be the "golden boys or girls" who surface, to the puzzlement of their peers, in some organizations. Although such people usually possess a certain degree of talent, they are seldom as outstanding as their superiors apparently need to believe.

Perhaps this is explained by the finding that managers are more likely to attribute excellent performance to internal causes (effort, ability) in the case of people who are members of their in-group than if they are members of their out-group.[21] Attributions, like perceptions, sometimes have more to do with the observer than with the person being observed. Appraisals are yet another instance when managers have to step back and ensure that their decisions and evaluations are not overly biased, either positively or negatively, by their personal values and preferences. If you recall, the chapter on perception and attribution contains examples of perceptual biases that can affect performance evaluation (stereotyping, halo effect, central tendency, contrast effects, projection, and perceptual defenses).

Does performance appraisal work? A meta-analysis of feedback interventions found that feedback generally improves performance, but it can also diminish performance.[22] Appraisals that are used for developmental rather than administrative reasons are more likely to produce positive reactions.[23] The impact of multisource feedback, discussed in team appraisals and 360-degree feedback below, is limited when:[24]

- Ratees are not held accountable for using the feedback
- Raters are not accountable for the accuracy or usefulness of their feedback
- Management does not accept accountability for providing resources to support behavioral change of those evaluated.

TEAM APPRAISALS

The move toward team structures and geographically dispersed team members caused a major reexamination and shift in performance appraisal. Companies could no longer evaluate individual performance alone, because this did not foster the collaboration successful teams need. In the worst examples, when people had to choose between efforts that would make the team look good or make themselves look good, they opted for self-interest. Effective appraisal systems have to both reward good team players and discourage behaviors that hinder team effectiveness. The first step was then to figure out what knowledge, skills, and abilities (KSAs) each team requires. In addition to task-specific KSAs related to the team's job, the general process-oriented KSAs critical to team success are conflict resolution, collaborative problem-solving, communication, decision-making, and team member support.[25] The next step was determining who should be involved in evaluating teams (peers, supervisors, customers), and finally, coming up with ways to measure and evaluate team members fairly. The fairness question raises the issue of social loafing (see Chapter 10), which can occur when individuals are not held accountable for their individual team contribution. If free riders are not dealt with, "social loafing spreads among team members like flu, poisoning the work climate."[26] Therefore, a combination of both individual and team performance measures is often recommended, particularly in more individualistic cultures. The use of peer feedback meant that performance appraisal training had to extend beyond supervisors and managers to team members.

360-DEGREE FEEDBACK APPRAISAL SYSTEMS

One of the most popular forms of performance appraisal is *360-degree feedback, defined as multirater assessment or multisource feedback (MSF)*. Superiors, peers, subordinates, suppliers, and customers can all be asked to evaluate the person being rated, the ratee, as shown in Exhibit 20–1. The ratee then compares these ratings with his or her own self-ratings, sometimes with the help of a consultant or performance coach. This full-circle feedback is assumed to be more valid and reliable than assessment by a sole source or supervisor. It is also based on the assumption that greater self-awareness will lead to behavioral change.

The Basic Industry Division of Nalco implemented a 360-degree feedback program to solve its turnover problem. Managers estimated that it cost $50,000 to replace a sales representative

EXHIBIT 20-1 **360-Degree or Multi-rater Feedback**

who has been with the company for six months and $250,000 to replace a seven-year veteran. After they cleaned up some pay and career path issues, they discovered that the primary reason people still quit was problems with the boss. Thus, the goal of their multisource performance appraisal system was to improve the leadership skills of their district sales managers. As a result, the company decreased its turnover rate from 15 to 18 percent to 8 to 10.5 percent.[27]

The various sources who evaluate an employee in 360-degree feedback perceive the employee in different ways and, therefore, their evaluations are not always similar. To some degree, effective managerial behavior is in the eye of the beholder.[28] Varying appraisal perspectives are positive when they provide a more well-rounded view of the ratee, but negative if they are overwhelming and confusing. Whose opinion do you take? This is why it's so important to help ratees make sense of the feedback. Another aspect of 360-degree appraisal that can be both positive and negative is its anonymity. On the positive side, employees can rate their boss (or others), which provides a fuller view of the person; on the negative side, anonymity allows for overly harsh criticism without fear of repercussions. 360-degree feedback has two additional advantages. Employees feel that their input makes a difference, especially if their bosses actually try to change their behavior in response to the feedback, and managers can gain more insight into factors that impact employee morale and organizational goals.

The success of 360-degree feedback depends on how well raters have been trained and whether employees receive follow-up help in interpreting their scores and appropriate coaching and support for changing their behavior.[29] Assessment alone does not change behavior. Like any program, 360-degree feedback has to be tailored to the particular organization, supported by and integrated with other organizational processes, and effectively implemented. The ratees have to be willing to change, and this does not happen without confidence, trust, and an understanding of 360-degree feedback and a strong belief in its importance. Such programs require both time and money to function well.[30]

INNOVATIVE APPRAISAL SYSTEMS

Appraisal systems should fit the organizational mission, culture, structure, and type of employees, which has led to some interesting innovations. When managers at the Air Force Research Lab in Dayton, Ohio were pressed to cut staff, they discovered that virtually all their 3,200 scientists and engineers received uniformly positive performance ratings. Only one employee was judged marginal, and none were rated as unsatisfactory! Because this system failed to distinguish among employees, a group of lab scientists was assigned the job of designing a new system. Their solution was to assume that all employees are performing well and evaluate them on the contribution their particular job makes to the lab's mission. "They naturally gravitate toward the toughest jobs they can competently perform, and their pay is based on the value of those jobs to the lab."[31]

The move toward team-based work has resulted in different appraisal systems such as the one described below.

If knowledge work depends on teams, it makes sense to reward them, not individuals. People who move from project to project cannot be paid according to the number of direct reports they have. Top industrial-design firm Ideo Product Development ... is a good example. It has several "vice presidents" who awarded themselves the title to get the free subscriptions some magazines give VPs. Ideo's performance reviews used to be done by a person's boss and two peers of the employee's own choosing, but that system, offbeat though it was, had to be scrapped a couple of years ago when the company realized that for many employees (more than one in ten) it was impossible to identify a boss. Now people pick two peers plus one from a slate of six "management types." According to Tom Kelley, people tend to pick demanding evaluators: "The culture says don't pick softies, because this is about improving performance, not about getting ahead."[32]

Eastman Chemical Company, winner of the 1993 Malcolm Baldrige National Quality Award, decided that its old appraisal system no longer fit an organizational culture that emphasized teamwork and more open and trustworthy communications. Therefore, a team designed a system that responded to these employee suggestions: eliminate forced distributions, eliminate performance categories, obtain performance input from sources other than the supervisor, enhance coaching and development, minimize individual performance and teamwork conflicts, identify only extremes in performance (the superstars and the below-average employees), and separate the systems for handling selection (promotion, transfer, and layoffs), compensation, and coaching. The design team concluded that self-esteem is critical to motivation and that employees like to believe, not only that they are above average performers but that they are growing and improving from year to year.[33]

RECOMMENDATIONS RESULTING FROM CRITICISM OF CURRENT PERFORMANCE MANAGEMENT PRACTICES

Not everyone is enchanted with the concept of performance management as it is currently practiced. Below you will find four major criticisms.

1. **Eliminate traditional performance appraisals** Deming, the total quality guru, was very opposed to performance appraisals and referred to them as one of the seven deadly diseases plaguing U.S. management. He and his disciples criticize appraisal systems for the following reasons.[34] Appraisals usually lack objectivity and attribute variations in performance to employees rather than crucial factors that are outside their control. Appraisals encourage an individual focus rather than a team orientation. When appraisals are based on measurable goals, they promote both short-sightedness and a short-term focus. Furthermore, employees come to see the boss as their "customer" rather than the real customer (the next person in the process, be they external or internal). When the main goal of employees is to gain the approval of their superior, fear, rivalry, and politics can result. Deming criticized merit rewards for rewarding people for doing well "in the system" rather than rewarding attempts to improve the system.

    So how do we measure performance in a total quality program? TQM writers suggest that outstanding performers should receive recognition and poor performers should be coached. Groups should gather continuous data on their own performance and should receive coaching whenever necessary. Companies should base compensation on market rate, seniority, or the company's prosperity. However, U.S. companies that implemented total quality programs have been slow to relinquish their performance appraisal systems.

2. **Eliminate forced distribution systems** In forced distribution systems, managers have to fit their employees into a predetermined distribution. This often involves ranking every employee, which is why this is also referred to as forced ranking. Only a certain percentage of employees are allowed into each category. Before it was sued by executives who claimed the system was discriminatory, Ford graded its managers as A, B, or C. Ten percent had to be graded "C", which meant they were obliged to receive coaching and counseling. Ford executives complained that the system was a source of low morale. Eventually, Ford dropped the 10 percent requirement.[35] Some firms automatically fire the bottom 10 percent. This approach is a quick fix when a company is loaded with dead wood because they have failed to distinguish between their best and worst performers and fire incompetent employees. But if you keep carving away annually, eventually a manager could end up firing good employees simply to comply with a bureaucratic requirement. Your unsatisfactory employees may make up 2 percent of your total workforce, but managers are being forced to give bad evaluations to another 8 percent that does not deserve them. If we applied this system to the classroom, a professor would decide before the course started that he would only give A's to the top 10 percent and F's to the bottom 10 percent of the class. If all the students were in fact B and C students, the highest B students would end up with an undeserved A, while the lowest C students would fail the course. A system like this does not reflect people's actual performance but where they stand in relation to others.

   Jack Welch popularized the forced distribution system, and one-third of U.S. firms followed GE's example. HR managers and organizational behavior experts question its effectiveness and criticize businesses for copycatting an unproven system that may not fit their organizational culture or goals. A recent survey of HR managers reported that forced ranking leads to skepticism and lower levels of productvity, collaboration, and morale.[36] Breaking up well-functioning teams to replace the lowest ranked members and taking the time to hire and socialize new team members carries a high cost. Forced ranking encourages competition, requires difficult judgment calls by managers that may or may not be accurate, and can demotivate the employees who don't come out in the top percentile.

3. **Develop strengths, not weaknesses** Management guru Marcus Buckingham cautions that focusing on employee weaknesses is less productive than further developing their strengths for the following reasons. Our ability to learn how to fix weaknesses is determined in part by our genetic makeup, particularly when flaws relate to our personality. Focusing on our flaws evokes negative memories and emotions, which means we are less motivated and energized than when we focus on developing our strengths, which are linked to positive memories and emotions. Focusing on weaknesses may rob employees of the self-assurance they need to be successful and cause them to doubt themselves. As people age, it becomes more difficult for them to develop new synaptic connections in their brain. They can learn more by "piggybacking" on existing connections, which neuroscientist Joseph LeDoux likens to growing new buds on a branch rather than growing a new branch from scratch.[37] These branches are the strengths we have already developed. Buckingham advises managers to discover each employee's unique strengths, capitalize on them, and work around their weaknesses. Based on numerous interviews with outstanding managers and executives, he argues that sustained success will result from orienting your life around your strengths and keeping your primary focus on using those strengths as much as possible. Too many people are victims of career creep—they end up doing tasks or jobs that are not fulfilling because they stray from their strengths. Only 17 percent of people polled by Buckingham spend 75–100 percent of the day doing things they really like to do; only 25 percent reported that their managers discuss how to build their strengths in performance discussions, whereas 40 percent had managers who focused on weaknesses and 35 percent had managers who discussed neither strengths nor weaknesses with them.[38]

   Does this mean we should simply forget about weaknesses? Not necessarily. Remember that successful executives at the top of the food chain have the power to hire people whose skills make up for their own weaknesses or flat sides. In fact, their bosses may only want these executives to do nothing more than their strengths. This is not the case with younger, less experienced employees who are generally asked to make up skill deficits and work on weaknesses. Furthermore the consequences of some employee weaknesses are too serious for managers to ignore, such as fatal flaws that might get them fired.

4. **Rely Less on financial incentives and use them more wisely** Most businesses rely primarily on financial incentives to motivate performance, but research does not prove that incentives always work. In fact, they can do more damage than good if they are poorly designed and implemented. According to Pfeffer and Sutton, for good or ill, incentive systems have three potential effects: motivational, informational, and selection.[39] They can have a *motivational effect* when they spur employee effort. They increased productivity by 44 percent with installers who worked alone replacing car windshields, because it was easy to measure the output (number of windshields completed), detect quality problems (presence of cracks), and assign blame for poorly done work (by keeping track of the installers).[40] However, not all performance outcomes are under the control of individual employees, and not all employees can actually make a difference in organizational performance.

Financial incentives can have an *informational effect* when they indicate to employees what senior management really cares about. Granting bonuses for specific behaviors sends a clear signal about what's important, and the good news is that employees will usually respond and refocus their efforts if rewarded. The bad news is that many incentive systems are too blunt and narrow, leading employees to overlook other important behaviors. For example, management wants higher numbers but does that mean they don't care how those numbers are achieved, even if it means reducing quality, customer service or ethics?

Finally, incentive systems can have a *selection effect* if they serve to attract the right kind of employees and deter the wrong kind. For example, some people might choose to work for a firm that offers the highest performance-based pay and wages. But are these the employees you want to attract? As James Treybig, former CEO of Tandem Computers, said, "if people come for money, they will leave for money." For some CEOs, the "right kind" of employees who will remain with the firm longer are people who receive intrinsic enjoyment from the work and who like the culture, management, and their co-workers.

The heavy reliance on financial incentives may reflect what Heath called an *"extrinsic incentives bias," the tendency to overestimate how much employees care about extrinsic job features such as pay and to underestimate how much employees are motivated by intrinsic job features like autonomy and meaningful work.*[41] Heath found that people assume others are motivated primarily by money, even though they themselves rank other factors as more important. In a recent survey of 1,700 high-performing employees in various organizations, 'expecting a significant financial reward' was ranked 9th out of 10 factors. 'Maintaining a positive reputation' was first, 'being appreciated' was second, and 'important work' and 'interesting assignments' were third and fourth, respectively.[42] The bottom line is that we should be careful not to overuse financial incentives or fail to carefully consider their unanticipated consequences.

EFFECTIVE FEEDBACK

Effective performance coaching utilizes the communication skills we have studied in previous chapters—active listening, empathy, creating a nondefensive climate, response styles, assertive communication, the use of I-statements, and understanding the role of perception in communication. Communication has to be supportive so employees can absorb the message. Another crucial coaching communication skill is providing effective feedback. Feedback helps individuals to keep behavior "on target" and, thus, better achieve their goals. Achievement-oriented people, in particular, want and need frequent and specific feedback to continue performing at optimal levels. The purpose of feedback in general is to provide people with information that they may or may not choose to utilize. In a work setting there may well be consequences for not utilizing the information, but feedback offered in the spirit of helpful data is less likely to arouse defensiveness. Before offering feedback, check with others to make sure your perceptions are valid and unbiased. Effective feedback has the following characteristics, which are summarized in Exhibit 20–2:

1. **Effective feedback is descriptive as opposed to evaluative** For example, telling a person "When you interrupt and don't let me finish my statements (description), it makes me feel as if you don't value my ideas (personal reactions)," has a very different impact from the evaluative statement, "Boy, you sure are a power-hungry s.o.b." The latter is bound to cause a defensive reaction. Although the former may not be totally pleasant, it is nonetheless easier to hear because it is more descriptive than evaluative.

2. **Effective feedback is specific and data-based rather than general** To be told that one is "not performing well" will not be as useful as being told "your last three shipments were sent without the proper paperwork." Vague feedback based on fuzzy impressions is generally very hard to translate into the specific developmental goals that are so important to improvement.

3. **Effective feedback is directed toward behavior that the receiver can control** To be told that "short people don't get ahead very fast in this company" is frustrating. We cannot ask people to change their personality or immutable characteristics.

4. **To the extent possible, it is better for feedback to be solicited rather than imposed** If people can formulate the questions they feel a need to explore, their motivation to listen carefully is significantly enhanced. This is the ideal circumstance, particularly in nonwork situations. Nevertheless giving an employee unsolicited feedback is an important aspect of any supervisory or managerial job. Even in this instance, however, you can share the control and provide the employee with an opportunity to participate by saying, for example, "I've noticed a few things I think it would be good for us to talk about. Is now a good time to talk? If not, when would be a good time for you?"

5. **Effective feedback is well timed** As seen in the preceding example, feedback must be offered when the receiver can best accept it. For example, the end of a hectic day or when an employee is worried about a family-related problem are not the most propitious times to give feedback.

6. **Feedback should be immediate and continual rather than delayed and sporadic** It does the receiver little good to find out that six months ago he or she did something "wrong." Feedback is generally most effective at the earliest opportunity after the behavior in question has occurred.

7. **Good feedback suggests rather than prescribes avenues for improvement** Demanding that other people change their behavior in a certain way is similar to the control-oriented communication that provokes a defensive reaction and disempowers people.[43] Furthermore, we lose sight of the crucial role of self-determination in behavioral change. This means that people must decide for themselves what they want to do and take responsibility for their own actions and their consequences.

8. **Effective feedback is intended to help** Feedback is ineffective when the person giving feedback seems driven to do so for his or her own needs (e.g., venting one's personal frus-

Effective	Ineffective
• Descriptive	• Evaluative
• Specific and data-based	• General
• Directed toward controllable behaviors	• Directed at personality traits/characteristics
• Solicited	• Imposed
• Close to the event under discussion	• Delayed
• Occurs when the receiver is ready to accept it	• Occurs when giver is ready
• Suggests ways to improve	• Prescribes ways to improve
• Intended to help	• Intended to punish

EXHIBIT 20-2 **Characteristics of Effective versus Ineffective Feedback**

tration on an employee). Feedback is not punishment, although ineffective feedback may feel that way. It simply provides information that the receiver's behavior is off target.

Positive and negative feedback has to be balanced if you don't want people to see you as overly critical. Because people tend to remember negative feedback more than positive feedback, your ratio of positive feedback has to be even higher. One rule of thumb suggests that if you want employees to see you as giving 50 percent positive and 50 percent negative feedback, you actually have to provide 80 percent positive feedback to 20 percent negative feedback.[44] Furthermore, pointing out people's weaknesses in a feedback session may be less effective than asking them about their desired future and what kind of person they want to be. When people reflect on those who have had a lasting impact on their lives, the great majority (80 percent) recalled moments when people helped them extend their dreams and reflect on what it means to be a good person or to be successful. Rather than focusing on their weaknesses, they endorsed their strengths, which led to behavioral change.[45] So consider carefully whether negative feedback is the best strategy for helping someone to change their behavior.

There are also guidelines for receiving feedback. The most important is to take feedback as helpful information that warrants serious consideration. In many cases the person giving the feedback is taking a risk and should be thanked for what is often a "gift," even though you may not be feeling particularly grateful at the moment. If the feedback is not clear, request more information or examples. If the feedback does not seem accurate, which is a possibility given what we know about perception, seek a second opinion by asking others how they perceive your behavior. Try to avoid becoming defensive or arguing about how your behavior impacts others (you have no first-hand experience here and they do). Feedback is worthless if (1) we automatically deny its validity; (2) rationalize our behavior; or (3) assume others are only telling us this because they do not like us or are trying to manipulate us.

THE PERFORMANCE APPRAISAL INTERVIEW

Doing appraisal interviews may be uncomfortable in the beginning, but it is a skill that can be mastered with practice. The opening vignette, "Leader as Developer," is an example of a successful performance appraisal process with a problem employee. Managers who use performance appraisals well can utilize their human resources more fully. It is a mechanism for increasing the communication and dialogue that is so crucial to high performance. One of the truisms that is repeatedly mentioned when we discuss this topic is that the appraisal instrument itself is only as good as the people who use it. Therefore, it is important that managers, supervisors, and team members who evaluate peers be trained in appraisal and interview techniques.

The common interview guidelines that describe what to do before, during, and after the interview are shown in Exhibit 20–3. Because you will be practicing an interview during the Class Activity, let's focus on the steps that take place during the interview. Some employees are anxious or nervous about the interview, which is why we begin by explaining its purpose and the format we will cover. The next step is the employee self-appraisal, which gives them an opportunity to present their view before supervisors give their own evaluation. There are several reasons for letting the employee go first. They may mention important factors that supervisors either don't know or have forgotten, giving the supervisor a chance to correct their feedback. If supervisors go first, employees may react negatively and become either defensive or intimidated. By listening to the employee's self appraisal, supervisors can determine the employee's level of self-awareness and perceptual accuracy; they can then respond more appropriately. For example, when employees are overly self-critical, supervisors can emphasize their strengths and downplay any weakness. They don't need you to be critical when they do such a good job of that all by themselves. When employees seem to be out of touch with reality and have an inflated sense of their contributions, supervisors know in advance they need to tread carefully and emphasize facts and figures that other employees might not need.

Before the interview

1. Set a time and date for the interview that allows the employee enough time to prepare the self-appraisal.

2. Ask the employee to prepare the self-appraisal and provide an outline for doing so.

3. Don't postpone the interview or come late to it. Employees interpret these actions as a lack of interest in them and the appraisal process. To do any good, appraisals have to be taken seriously by managers.

4. Choose a private location where you will not be interrupted.

5. Set aside enough time (one to two hours) so that you will have time to complete your discussion.

6. Gather all the materials and relevant information about the employee's performance. Some managers also give copies of this information to the employee in advance.

7. Determine which aspects of the employee's performance (e.g., strengths, areas for improvement) should be addressed in the interview. Decide how to phrase these points.

During the interview

8. Explain the format and purpose of the performance appraisal interview:
   a. To discover the employee's opinions regarding his or her performance and career goals.
   b. To provide the supervisor's appraisal of the employee's performance.
   c. To problem solve together about performance if necessary.
   d. To plan for the next period.

9. Ask the employee to present his or her self-appraisal.

10. Respond to the employee's self-appraisal and convey feedback. First, tell the employee the parts of the self-appraisal with which you agree and then identify parts with which you disagree, if there are any. Next, provide other feedback that would impact performance. In doing this,
    a. Be appreciative of the employee's accomplishments.
    b. Support the employee even when you are criticizing his or her behavior.
    c. Avoid defensiveness (on both your parts).
    d. Encourage participation.

11. Ask if there are any conditions or problems that have been hindering the employee's work.

12. Problem solve with the employee regarding what both of you could do to improve the employee's performance.

13. Set objectives and design a plan for the next period together.

14. Discuss the employee's long-term career goals and the training and experience needed to reach them.

After the interview

15. Fill out the performance appraisal form after the interview so the employee sees that his or her input was included.

16. Follow up on training and coaching needs identified in the interview.

Source: Adapted from P. King, *Performance Planning and Appraisal* (New York: McGraw-Hill, 1984): 73–74, 88.

EXHIBIT 20-3 **Performance Appraisal Interview Guidelines**

Being evaluated evokes authority issues for many individuals and results in defensive communication. Taking care to posture yourself more as a counselor than a judge and creating a nondefensive climate by the way you communicate are two ways to decrease defensiveness. Gibb's recommendations for creating a supportive climate (see Chapter 8) are important to bear in mind—descriptive, egalitarian, focused on problem solving, spontaneous, empathic, and provisional.

When you as a supervisor ask whether there are any conditions or problems that hinder employees' performance, they may well say that your management style is a negative factor. This is when you yourself need to avoid becoming defensive. Sessions involving mutual feedback between the supervisor and subordinate can be very effective if the supervisor is skilled enough to model how one should receive feedback effectively and respond positively by coming up with a future solution. The interview ends with a good action plan for the next evaluation period and the future so employees know exactly what they need to do in the short-term to perform well and in the long-term to prepare themselves for the career they desire.

CULTURE AND PERFORMANCE APPRAISAL

Performance appraisals have different characteristics and purposes in different cultures. In Arab cultures, appraisals are generally informal and held on an ad hoc basis. Their purpose is to set employees on track or reprimand them for bad performance.[46] In Japan, reviews tend to be informal, ad hoc, and based on continuous feedback; their objective is to find out why the employee's performance is not in harmony with that of the group.

Several cultural values also impact how appraisals are handled: harmony and face-saving, power distance, uncertainty avoidance, and individualism-collectivism. In Eastern cultures such as Japan, China, and the Philippines, negative feedback is likely to be interpreted as a loss of face and a public humiliation.[47] Asian team members are often reluctant to evaluate other members negatively if this means disrupting the harmony of the group.[48]

Employees in low–power distance cultures, such as Norway, are more willing to question superiors than employees in high–power distance cultures, such as Mexico and Thailand. Employees in high–power distance cultures are more fearful of disagreeing with their boss.[49] A Thai senior management team did not want to implement a 360-degree feedback process for reasons related to high power distance. "They felt that subordinates would be uncomfortable because Thai workers do not see it as their business to evaluate their bosses, and the bosses would be insulted because Thai managers do not think subordinates are in any way qualified to assess them."[50] In cultures characterized by high uncertainty avoidance, appraisal systems are more formalized with more detailed regulations and procedures.[51]

The individualism-collectivism dimension affects performance appraisal practices in several ways.[52] Individualists are geared more toward personal goals whereas collectivists focus more on group goals. Individualistic cultures emphasize individual achievement, individual incentive schemes, formal appraisal processes with feedback on performance, and merit-based hiring and promotion. In contrast, collectivist cultures emphasize group achievement, group incentive schemes, informal appraisals, and they hire and fire based on loyalty and seniority.[53] Collectivists tend to be more generous than individualists when they evaluate coworkers, especially when they are in-group members.[54] Formal appraisal systems are more prevalent in the United States than in collectivist countries such as Japan and Korea as a result of the emphasis placed on individual rather than group performance.[55]

A cultural preference for direct versus indirect communication also influences the way feedback is conveyed informally or during the performance appraisal interview. Given all these cultural differences and the varied forms performance appraisal takes around the world, we cannot assume that an appraisal system that functions well in one culture (or one company) can be easily transferred to another.

CLASS ACTIVITY: PERFORMANCE APPRAISAL ROLE PLAYS

This exercise provides you with an opportunity to practice and observe the "consummate skill and delicacy" required in a performance appraisal. You will also receive feedback on your course performance. (Time allotted: 70 minutes)

STEP 1.   The class should divide into three-person teams, consisting of learning group members. The exercise simulates a performance appraisal interview between two group members who will take on the roles of supervisor and employee, while the other member acts as an observer. Rotate the roles so each person has a chance to perform every role. Decide whom each person will evaluate and be evaluated by. Student A evaluates the performance of student B while student C observes; B evaluates C while A observes; and C evaluates A while B observes. The "employee" performance to be evaluated is your course performance; you already prepared your self-evaluation for the interview when you answered the questions in #E of the Class Preparation. (5 minutes)

STEP 2.   Individual Supervisor Preparation (10 minutes)

Take 10 minutes alone to plan the appraisal interview for the person you will evaluate. Use the following questions to help you prepare for the supervisor role; the "employee" is the student you will be evaluating, so answer these questions with that person in mind.

a. What has the employee done so far that has contributed to his or her own learning and that of your learning group?

b. What has the employee contributed to the general atmosphere of the class?

c. Are there any extenuating circumstances that have affected the employee's performance in the course?

d. Is there anything you personally are doing that has hindered the employee's performance in the class? What could you do to help the employee improve his or her performance?

Observer Worksheet

1. Did the supervisor explain the purpose of the appraisal interview?

2. Did the supervisor give the employee sufficient time to present his or her self-appraisal?

3. Did the supervisor do a good job of presenting his or her feedback?

4. Did the supervisor use active listening, or did he or she do most of the talking?

5. Did the supervisor create a nondefensive climate and refrain from becoming defensive himself or herself?

6. Did the supervisor take a problem-solving approach, or did he or she spend too much time giving advice or orders to the employee?

7. Did the supervisor jointly set goals and an action plan for the future with the employee?

8. Other comments:

    e. What are the employee's weaknesses and strengths so far?

    f. Choose at least one strength and one weakness that you have observed in the employee's performance in class to discuss during the five-minute interview. Base your choice on which behaviors could make a significant difference if they were to be either enhanced (a strength) or changed (area for improvement). Write down how you could phrase the employee's weak point to him or her using the characteristics of effective feedback.

    g. What kind of action plan for the rest of the course might help improve the employee's performance? Is there anything you could suggest that might utilize the employee's talents or strengths better in the classroom or learning group?

STEP 3. Review the "During the Interview" portion of Performance Appraisal Interview Guidelines on page 585 and the Observer Worksheet on page 588. (5 minutes)

STEP 4. Each supervisor should conduct a five-minute performance appraisal interview with his/her employee while the observer watches and fills out the Observers' Worksheet (page 588). After each interview all three participants should talk about how it went and what, if anything, could have been done differently. (30 minutes)

STEP 5. Plenary debriefing session (20 minutes):
    a. What did you learn about performance appraisal interviews from this exercise?
    b. What did you learn about yourself in this process?
    c. Did you observe any supervisor behavior that was especially effective?
    d. Will the appraisal affect your future performance in this course? Why?

 **LEARNING POINTS**

1. Performance appraisals are intended to improve performance and motivate employees.
2. Feedback serves the following functions for employees:
    a. Helps to form their self-concept.
    b. Reduces uncertainty about whether their behavior is on track.
    c. Signals which organizational goals are most important.
    d. Helps them master their environment and feel competent.
3. The attitude managers bring to performance appraisal contributes to the effectiveness of that appraisal. Managers who are sincerely trying to develop their employees and provide them with objective feedback are more successful than those who take a judgmental approach.
4. Performance appraisal requires that managers take on the role of coaches.

5. The "ideal" performance appraisal system is designed to achieve five basic objectives:
   a. Provide feedback to subordinates to facilitate their ability to achieve organizational and personal goals.
   b. Provide management with data to make personnel decisions (salary, promotional, termination).
   c. Recognize skill acquisition and identify skill deficits for further professional training and development.
   d. Motivate employees to be more effective workers.
   e. Comply with equal opportunity regulations and ensure fairness.
6. Performance appraisal is a process that begins with translating organizational goals into clear expectations for each individual, training people to do their jobs, providing effective supervision and coaching, determining strengths and weaknesses, and developing plans for each employee. It is not a once-a-year event but an ongoing activity.
7. Providing immediate feedback gives the employee an opportunity to improve, ensures that the appraisal is not a surprise, and keeps the employee-manager channel of communication open. Saving up negative feedback and "dumping" can cause a defensive reaction.
8. Fairness is always a matter of concern with appraisals because people tend to rate those who are similar to themselves more highly than those who are different.
9. Attributions or inferences about why people behave the way they do can also bias the appraisal process.
10. Multirater or multisource feedback, such as 360-degree feedback, incorporates feedback from various sources, such as: superiors, peers, subordinates, suppliers, and customers.
11. Total quality experts suggest that companies stop doing performance appraisals and focus more on collecting data that provides continuous feedback and coaching individuals and teams that are not performing well.
12. Forced ranking systems lead to skepticism and lower levels of productvity, collaboration, and morale.
13. Some evidence indicates that it is more effective to develop employee strengths rather than focusing on their weaknesses.
14. Financial incentives can have motivational, informational and selection effects that produce either positive or negative consequences.
15. The extrinsic incentives bias is the tendency to overestimate how much employees care about extrinsic job features such as pay and to underestimate how much employees are motivated by intrinsic job features.
16. Effective feedback is descriptive rather than evaluative, specific and data-based rather than general, directed toward controllable behavior, solicited rather than imposed, and well timed. It is immediate rather than delayed, suggests rather than prescribes avenues for improvements, and is intended to help, not punish.
17. Different cultures have different perceptions about the purpose of performance appraisal and how it should be carried out. These cultural values should be taken into consideration when appraising people from other cultures: harmony, face saving, power distance, uncertainty avoidance, individualism-collectivism, and direct versus indirect communication.

 **ACTION SCRIPTS**

FOR EMPLOYEES

- Employees who are expert at managing their own performance proactively set goals, seek feedback, acquire training, and practice new skills until they achieve a high level of performance. They are also skilled at helping others go through this process.
- They have enough self-awareness to understand when they are being overly critical or projecting their own flaws on others.

- When giving someone feedback, they prepare mentally by focusing on the desired positive outcome. If there is no constructive purpose for the feedback, they do not give it. They briefly state what they want to cover ("I have a concern about . . . ") and tie the feedback to a common goal ("I'm not sure this system is meeting our customer service goals. Let's look at what we can improve."). They explain the impact of the person's behavior (one or two key consequences). Next they invite the other person to respond ("What is your view of the situation?") and listen objectively and actively. They do not explain too much or become defensive if the other party denies the accuracy of the feedback. They state their expectations for a change in behavior and focus on what has to be done next ("A win-win solution here could involve your taking steps to ... "). To increase the likelihood of change, they allow the other person to determine the details and take responsibility for action. They do not come across as either bossy or a know-it-all.

FOR MANAGERS

- Managers who are expert at performance appraisal meet with employees to discuss plans for the coming year with respect to the appraisal form. They write these plans down so both parties have a copy. These plans then form the basis of the subsequent appraisal.
- They provide the interviewees with data that will allow them the opportunity to change negative behavior. Although they cannot force employees to change their behavior, they outline the likely consequences of their behavior in an objective fashion.
- The appraisal interview can be an occasion of great anxiety for some individuals. This means that their ability to take in information may be impaired, so verbal or written summaries of what has been said are useful. People with low self-concepts may hear only the negative feedback, whereas others will hear only positives and completely miss the improvements you would like to see made.
- Experts understand the role that attribution may play in performance appraisal. When people succeed, they are likely to attribute their success to the internal qualities they possess (e.g., tenacity, intelligence). When they fail, some are likely to blame external conditions (e.g., their boss, the company's policies). Assigning blame is not as important as trying to figure out ways to improve performance in the future.
- No matter how objective managers try to be, there is always a possibility of bias or misperception. Incorrect evaluations are very demotivating. Experts at performance appraisal collect robust data and check out their perceptions with other colleagues. They take a provisional approach to the interview and assume that the employee may mention a contrasting view in their self-appraisal that needs to be taken into consideration.
- They focus more on what employees do right than wrong, and they motivate people by focusing on their strengths and managing around their weaknesses.
- When employees publicly set specific rather than general goals for the future, their performance is more likely to improve.
- Above all, expert managers make sure the process is fair.

FOR ORGANIZATIONAL ARCHITECTS

- Organizational architects who that are expert at designing performance management systems make sure their system is aligned with the company mission and philosophy.
- They differentiate among outstanding, satisfactory, and unsatisfactory contributors.
- They set clear expectations, remove obstacles, and reward outstanding and satisfactory performance.
- They have consistent systems in place to deal effectively with unsatisfactory performers.
- All employees are held accountable for meeting performance goals.
- Managers are trained in performance management and held accountable and evaluated on their own effectiveness in developing employees to meet both organizational and career goals.
- Raters who participate in 360-degree feedback are trained to do this accurately and objectively.

- Performance appraisal and management is taken seriously rather than viewed as a necessary evil.
- The feedback and coaching process is ongoing.
- The organizational culture fosters open feedback, supportive professional development, goal setting, and accountability.
- They ensure that the performance appraisal process fosters ethical behavior rather than rewarding employees for unethical behavior.
- The performance management system is characterized by fairness and a concern for organizational justice.

PERSONAL APPLICATION ASSIGNMENT

The topic of this assignment is to write about a significant experience that involved performance appraisal. Choose an experience that intrigues you and that you want to learn more about.

A. Concrete Experience

    1. Objectively describe the experience (who, what, when, where, how information). (2 points)

    2. Subjectively describe your feelings, perceptions, and thoughts that occurred during (not after) the experience. What did others seem to be feeling? (2 points)

B. Reflective Observation

    1. Looking back at the experience, what were the perspectives of the key actors (including you)? (2 points)

2. Why did the people involved (including you) behave as they did? (2 points)

C. Abstract Conceptualization

    1. Relate concepts or theories from the assigned readings or the lecture to the experience. Explain thoroughly how they apply to your experience. Please apply at least two concepts or theories and cite them correctly. (4 points)

D. Active Experimentation

    1. What did you learn about performance appraisal from this experience? (1 point)

    2. What did you learn about yourself? (1 point)

    3. What action steps will you take to be more effective in the future? (2 points)

E. Integration, Synthesis, and Writing

    1. Did you integrate and synthesize the four sections? (1 point)
    2. Was the personal application assignment well written and easy to understand? (1 point)
    3. Was it free of spelling and grammatical errors? (2 points)

ENDNOTES

[1] G. Cokins, *Performance Management,* (Hoboken, NJ: Wiley, 2004); S. P. Robbins and D. DeCenzo, *Fundamentals of Management* (Upper Saddle River, NJ: Pearson Prentice Hall, 2005).

[2] R. G. Epstein and N. Hatch Woodward, "Best Practice Tips for Performance Appraisals," Available at: http:www.careerbank.com/resource/articleview.cfm/133.htm. Accessed 10/31/05.

[3] C. McNamara, "Performance Management: Performance Management Plans," Available at: http://www.managementhelp.org/perf_mng. Accessed 10/31/05.

[4] R. S. Kaplan and D. P. Norton, "The Balanced Scorecard: Measures That Drive Performance," *Harvard Business Review 70*(1) (July-August 2005): 71–80; R. S. Kaplan and D. P. Norton, *Strategy Maps: Converting Intangible Assets into Tangible Outcomes,* (Boston, MA: Harvard Business School Press, 2004).

[5] Kaplan and Norton, "The Balanced Scorecard: Measures That Drive Performance"; Kaplan and Norton, *Strategy Maps.*

[6] Kaplan and Norton, "The Balanced Scorecard: Measures That Drive Performance."

[7] R. H. Russell and J. Kock, "A Profile of Handleman Company's Center for Performance Management," *Balanced Scorecard Report 6*(8), (September–October 2004).

[8] W. H. Starbuck, "Performance Measures: Prevalent and Important But Methodologically Challenging, *Journal of Management Inquiry 14*(3) (2005): 280–286.

[9] L. Gary, "Performance Management That Drives Results," *Harvard Management Update*, (September 2004). Available at: http://harvardbusinessonline.hbsp.harvard.edu/b02/en/common/item_detail.jhtml;jsessionid=5DR5HMJOFDJD0CTE-QENB5VQKMSARWIPS?id=U0409A&referral=8871&_requestid=36032. Accessed 9/23/06; D. Whetton and K. Camerson, *Developing Management Skills* (6th ed.) (Upper Saddle River, NJ: Pearson Prentice Hall, 2005).

[10] P. Cunneen, "Improve Performance Management, *People Management 12*(1) (January 12, 2006): 42–43.

[11] G. P. Latham and K. N. Wexley, *Increasing Productivity through Performance Appraisal* (Reading, MA: Addison Wesley, 1993). This book is a good compendium of knowledge on performance appraisal.

[12] D. McGregor, "An Uneasy Look at Performance Appraisal," *Harvard Business Review 35*(3) (May–June 1957): 90.

[13] J. Pfeffer and R. I. Sutton, *Hard Facts, Dangerous Half-Truths & Total Nonsense: Profiting From Evidence-Based Management* (Boston, MA: Harvard Business School Press, 2006).

[14] D. A. Nadler, C. Cammon, and P. Mirvis, "Developing a Feedback System for Work Units: A Field Experiment in Structural Change," *Journal of Applied Behavioral Science 16*(1) (1980): 41–62; and D. R. Ilgen, C. D. Fischer, and M. S. Taylor, "Consequences of Individual Feedback on Behavior in Organizations," *Journal of Applied Psychology 64*(4) (1979): 349–371.

[15] S. J. Ashford and L. L. Cummings, "Feedback as an Individual Resource: Personal Strategies of Creating Information," *Organizational Behavior and Human Performance 32* (1983): 370–398.

[16] H. H. Meyer, E. Kay, and T. R. P. French, Jr., "Split Roles in Performance Appraisal," *Harvard Business Review 43*(1) (1965): 123–129.

[17] E. D. Pulakos and K. N. Wexley, "The Relationship among Perceptual Similarity, Sex, and Performance Ratings in Manager-Subordinate Dyads," *Academy of Management Journal 26*(1) (1983): 129–139.

[18] W. Moore, *The Conduct of the Corporation* (New York: Random House, 1962): 109.

[19] Latham and Wexley, *Performance Appraisal*: 152.

[20] J. Jaspars, F. D. Finchman, and M. Hewstone, *Attribution Theory and Research: Conceptual Developmental and Social Dimensions* (London: Academic Press, 1983).

[21] R. L. Heneman, D. B. Greenberger, and C. Anonyo, "Attributions and Exchanges: The Effects of Interpersonal Factors on the Diagnosis of Employee Performance," *Academy of Management Journal 32*(2) (1989): 466–476.

[22] A. N. Kluger and A. DeNisi, "The Effects of Feedback Interventions on Performance: A Historical Review, a Meta-analysis, and a Preliminary Feedback Intervention Theory," *Psychological Bulletin 119*(2) (1996): 254–284.

[23] K. L. Bettenhausen and D. B. Fedor, "Peer and Upward Appraisals: A Comparison of Their Benefits and Problems," *Group and Organization Management 22*(2) (June 1997): 236–263.

[24] M. London, J. W. Smither, and D. J. Adsit, "Accountability: The Achilles' Heel of Multisource Feedback," *Group and Organization Management 22*(2) (June 1997): 162.

[25] M. A. Campion, E. M. Papper, and G. J. Medsker, "Relations Between Work Group Characteristics and Effectiveness: A Replication and Extension, *Personnel Psychology 49*(2) (1996): 429–452; D. E. Hyatt and T. M. Ruddy, "An Examination of the Relationship Between Work Group Characteristics and Performance: Once More Into the Breech," *Personnel Psychology 50*(3) (1997): 533–585.

[26] S. G. Scott and W. O. Einstein, "Strategic Performance Appraisal in Team-Based Organizations: One Size Does not Fit All," *Academy of Management Executive 15*(2) (2001): 109.

[27] B. Flannigan, "Turnaround from Feedback," *HR Focus* *74*(10) (October 1997): 3–4.

[28] S. Salam, J. F. Cox, and H. P. Sims, Jr., "In the Eye of the Beholder," *Group and Organization Management 22*(2) (June 1997): 185–209; and A. Fumham and P. Stringfield, "Congruence in Job-Performance Ratings: A Study of 360-Degree Feedback Examining Self, Manager, Peers, and Consultant Ratings," *Human Relations 51*(4) (April 1998): 517–531.

[29] B. R. Fisher, "Listen to What's Really Going On," *Supervision 65*(8) (August 2004): 9–11.

[30] W. Tornow and M. London (eds.), *Maximizing the Value of 360-Degree Feedback: A Process for Successful Individual and Organizational Development* (San Francisco: Jossey-Bass and Greensboro: Center for Creative Leadership, 1998).

[31] D. Grote, " Performance Appraisal Reappraised," *Harvard Business Review 78*(1) (January–February 2000): 21.

[32] T. Stewart, "The Great Conundrum—You Vs. the Team," *Fortune 134*(10) (November 25, 1996): 165.

[33] R. C. Jines, S. Quisenberry and G. W. Sawyer, "Business Strategy Drives Three-Pronged Assessment System," *HRM Magazine* (December 1993): 68–72.

[34] W. E. Deming, *Out of the Crisis* (Cambridge: MIT Press, 1986). Other sources on this topic are M. Walton, *Deming Management at Work* (New York: Putnam, 1990); P. R. Scholtes, *An Elaboration on Deming's Teachings on Performance Appraisal* (Madison, WI: Joiner Association, 1987); and W. M. Fox, "Improving Performance Appraisal Systems," *National Productivity Review 7*(1) (Winter 1987–1988): 20–27.

[35] N. Shirouzu and J. B. White, "Ford May Change White-Collar Job Rating System," *The Wall Street Journal* (July 9, 2001): A3-4; N. Shirouzu, "Ford Stops Using Letter Rankings to Rate Workers," *The Wall Street Journal* (July 16, 2001): B1, B4.

[36] Pfeffer and Sutton, *Hard Facts, Dangerous Half-Truths & Total Nonsense: Profiting From Evidence-Based Management.*

[37] M. Buckingham, *The One Thing You Need to Know ... About Great Managing, Great Leading, and Sustained Individual Success* (New York: Free Press, 2005): 242.

[38] M. Buckingham, "When Your Manager Discusses Your Performance With You, Do You Spend More Time Talking About How to Build your Strengths or How to Improve Your Weaknesses?" The Marcus Buckingham Company. Available at: http://www.marcusbuckingham.com/ resources/ attitudesStudy/Question3.jpg. Accessed 3/20/06.

[39] J. Pfeffer and R. Sutton, *Hard Facts, Dangerous Half-Truths & Total Nonsense*. This section is based on their chapter, "Do Financial Incentives Drive Company Performance?". 109–133.

[40] E. P. Lazear, "Performance Pay and Productivity," *American Economic Review 90* (2000): 1346–1361.

[41] C. Health, "On the Social Psychology of Agency Relationships: Lay Theories of Motivation Overemphasize Extrinsic Incentives," *Organizational Behavior and Human Decision Processes 78* (1999): 25–62.

[42] Watson Wyatt Worldwide company report, "Strategic Rewards: Maximizing the Return on Your Reward Investment" (2004): 11.

[43] J. Gibb, "Defensive Communication," in Osland, Turner, Kolb and Rubin (eds.), *The Organizational Behavior Reader* (Upper Saddle River, NJ: Prentice Hall, 2007): 290–294.

[44] Rosinski, *Coaching Across Culture.* (London: Nicholas Brealey, 2003)

[45] R. E. Boyatzis, A. Howard, B. Rapisarda, and S. Taylor, "Coaching Can Work, But Doesn't Always," *People Management 10*(5) (March 11, 2004): 26–32

[46] F. Elashmawi and P. R. Harris, *Multicultural Management* (Houston: Gulf Press, 1993): 152.

[47] P. C. Earley, *Face, Harmony, and Social Structure: An Analysis of Organizational Behavior across Cultures* (New York: Oxford University Press, 1997).

[48] B. L. Kirkman and D. N. Den Hartog, "Performance Management in Global Teams," in Osland, Turner, Kolb and Rubin (eds.), *The Organizational Behavior Reader* (Upper Saddle River, NJ: Prentice Hall, 2007): 614–636.

[49] D. J. Adsit, M. London, S. Crom, and D. Jones, "Cross-Cultural Differences in Upward Ratings in a Multinational Company," *International Journal of Human Resource Management 8*(4) (1997): 385–401.

[50] D. A. Light, "Cross-Cultural Lessons in Leadership," *MIT Sloan Management Review 45*(1) (Fall 2003): 5.

[51] N. Lindholm, "National Culture and Performance Management in MNC Subsidiaries." *International Studies of Organization & Management 29*(4) (Winter 1999/2000): 45-67.

[52] H. C. Triandis, *Individualism and Collectivism* (Boulder, CD: Westview, 1995); and G. Hofstede, *Culture's Consequences* (Thousand Oaks, Sage, 2005).

[53] S. J. Carroll and N. Ramamoorthy, "Individualism and Collectivism Orientations and Reactions toward Alternative Human Resource Management Practices," *Human Relations 51*(5) (May 1998): 571–589.

[54] C. B. Gomez, B. L. Kirkman, and D. L. Shapiro, "The Impact of Collectivism and Ingroup/Outgroup Membership on the Evaluation Generosity of Team Members," *Academy of Management Journal 43*(6) (2000): 1097–1106.

[55] K. Kim, H. Park, and N. Suzuki, "Reward Allocations in the United States, Japan, and Korea: A Comparison of Individualist and Collectivist Cultures," *Academy of Management Journal 33*(1) (1990): 188–198. See also L. R. Gomez-Mejia and T. Welbourne, "Compensation Strategies in a Global Context," *Human Resource Planning 14*(1) (1991): 29–41.

Part 4

▲▲▲

MANAGING EFFECTIVE ORGANIZATIONS

In this section of the book, we're going to make a more obvious transition from micro-level topics in organizational behavior dealing with individuals and groups to macro-level issues that affect the entire organization. In addition to a thorough grounding in the topics we have already covered, organization design and change are heavily dependent on systems thinking and analytical skills. These final chapters examine how managers can design and change organizations to make them more effective and successful.

CHAPTER 21 Organization Design
CHAPTER 22 Managing Change

Chapter 21

▲▲

ORGANIZATION DESIGN

OBJECTIVES By the end of this chapter, you should be able to:

A. Distinguish between mechanistic and organic structures.

B. Describe the three traditional types of organizational structures and their advantages and disadvantages.

C. Describe horizontal and network structures and their advantages and disadvantages.

D. Distinguish between formal and informal organizational structure.

E. Describe the boundaryless organization.

F. Explain the differentiation-integration issue in organization design.

PERMEABILITY IN ACTION: CASE STUDY OF A BOUNDARYLESS ORGANIZATION

Retailer Financial Services (RFS) is one of GE Capital's approximately two dozen businesses. Headquartered in Stamford, Connecticut, it provides private label credit card services to various retail chains in the United States and overseas, and through its "bank," it offers its own credit card programs. RFS customers include retail chains such as Macy's, Burton, Filenes' Basement, Harrods, IKEA, and hundreds more. Seeing this level of success, few people remember that less than a decade ago, GE was trying desperately to sell Retailer Financial Services, then named Private Label. It had been in business for 50 years, yet its market share was a mere 3 percent. To make matters worse, its own strategic planners did not believe it had much of a future. "Why," they reasoned, "would consumers want to carry multiple credit cards when they could carry just one or two? And if that's the case, we don't have a business here!"

Holding fast to his pledge to sell off businesses that could not become the number one or two performers in their industries, GE Chairman and CEO Jack Welch put the company on the block. Fortunately for GE, potential buyers agreed with GE's assessment that Private Label was a dying business. They stayed away. With little choice other than to make the best of it, GE Capital promoted David A. Ekedahl, who had spent his whole career at Private Label, to run the business. His mission: Keep it going as long as you can without losing money. Ekedahl did better than that. He created a successful boundaryless corporation.

Reformulating External Boundaries

As Ekedahl describes it, the initial objective was to keep the wolves at bay by aggressively adding new customers. However, Ekedahl and his managers first had to decide who the customers were and how to win their business. That analysis led them to an important insight—the company needed to concentrate not just on the consumer (the end-user of private label cards) but on the retailer as well.

By changing the long-standing external boundary that defined the customer, Ekedahl began a transformation that was to take Private Label light-years forward. He realized that fast and flexible processing would be the critical success factor for retailers. If Private Label could get the retailers online quickly, manage the volume of business efficiently, provide error-free processing, maintain balances and credit information accurately, and manage customer databases, it would have tremendous leverage with retailers. But at this time, both putting systems in place for a new retailer and keeping them going for an existing one was an incredibly cumbersome process.

Loosening Horizontal Boundaries

To achieve fast and flexible processing, Dave Ekedahl had to open up another boundary.

We had just signed up a new company to do their private label credit cards, and I wanted to go through the process of getting that client on board. I found that in order to do that, I had a lot of people in the room, but none of us had any idea what to do by ourselves. We needed dozens of other people. So I figured if this was what it took to get something done, I might as well organize around these kinds of processes. So we began to recreate our own organization around the major processes that needed to get done rather than just do it ad hoc all the time.

Making organizational structure mirror the way work actually got done, Ekedahl gradually transformed Private Label, leveling horizontal boundaries between systems and other business functions. The change was especially difficult because the systems resources were all part of GE Capital's corporate organization, a centralized organization well defended by solid functional walls.

Early in 1989, Ekedahl tried to bridge the functions by sponsoring a joint working conference between his business people and the central systems organization. At a rancorous concluding meeting, the systems people complained that they were not consulted in the early stages of new customer conversions and were given unrealistic requirements and deadlines. On the other side, the marketing people accused the systems professionals of not delivering on their promises. Ekedahl found himself caught in the middle, wanting to create a cross-functional team yet forced to arbitrate between disagreeing sides.

Ekedahl did not give up. First, he influenced the head of GE Capital's systems to dedicate a particular group of systems professionals to his business. Then he insisted that the systems and marketing people find new ways of working together, and he encouraged them to rethink their basic work processes.

In 1990, Rich Nastasi, head of the group of systems people, began a process of working with the other business functions to radically reduce the time required to bring a new retailer online as a customer, an average of eight weeks. Nastasi then brought together a group of systems, marketing, finance, and customer service people and challenged them to complete new customer conversions in a matter of days, not weeks.

Over the next few months, as the solutions were implemented, customer conversion times began to drop dramatically, to less than a week for all but the largest new customers. Equally significant, the different functions put the solutions in place together.

Less than a year later, Nastasi and his people were reporting directly to Dave Ekedahl, as full-fledged members of business team for what was now called Retailer Financial Services.

Flattening Vertical Boundaries

As RFS organized around key processes, a different organization gradually took shape. Essentially, the company shifted from a centralized model, in which such functions as systems, credit, marketing, and customer service were all run out of Stamford, to a hybrid model with both centralized and decentralized processes. The guiding idea was that processes to support specific customers should be managed in the field, close to those customers. Processes requiring consistency and control across all customers—financial reporting, credit scoring, systems processing, and telecommunications—should be handled by the head office. Additional head office roles were to facilitate the sharing of best practices, the movement of key personnel, and the allocation of investment resources.

To shift processes to the field, RFS created "regional business centers." The business processes they managed for the retailer customers in their regions included training of retailer staff in systems and procedures, developing mailing and promotional programs with the retailers, providing management information for the retailers, and handling the whole range of customer service for cardholders, both through the mail and on the phone. The key and single focus of these centers was to help retailer customers become more successful.

Setting up regional centers, however, was expensive. Ekedahl was under pressure to reduce costs by increasing productivity. So the cost-cutting pressure led to a radically different way of organizing the regional business centers. As Ekedahl explains: "We originally came at it from a productivity point of view. We figured maybe we could save costs by not having so many management levels. So we asked a group of our associates how to do this. The exempt and the nonexempt people got together for a week and went way beyond what we had been expecting. They recommended that we organize around teams, with no managers whatsoever. I said, 'what the heck, let's try it.' So we did, starting with one business center in Danbury."

The dissolution of hierarchical boundaries within the business centers represented a fundamental revolution. And as in any revolution, there were casualties—managers who could not adjust, supervisors who were no longer needed, and in particular, frontline associates who were not willing or able to handle increased accountability. For the first few years, an abiding issue in several centers was a high level of associate turnover.

Eventually, by involving everyone in the center in a dialogue helped along by a few outside experts in team processes, a pattern for success emerged. Teams were set up to service all the needs of one large or several small retailers and the retailers' customers. All team members were cross-trained in all the skills needed to provide effective service, including handling billing problems and collections, changing credit lines, and changing customer data. The more senior or experienced people (in most cases, former supervisors) became roving trainers, documenters of procedures, and problem solvers.

Gradually, the teams learned to police their own performance against an agreed-upon set of goals, setting up performance improvement programs for team members not performing up to standard. In essence, the teams were given all the same levels of authority as managers had held in the past.

The payoff from the first boundaryless business center was so great that Ekedahl and his team never seriously considered going back to the traditional vertical organization. Even with high levels of turnover, productivity was still many times greater and overall costs far lower. More important, the customers loved the service they were now getting from a dedicated team that knew the customers' business, their consumers, their systems, and their issues. They began to see the business teams as extensions of their own companies and not just as service providers.

RFS became a true boundaryless corporation, consciously evolving ways to function across different boundaries with speed, flexibility, integration, and innovation. RFS journeyed successfully from the traditional structural paradigm to the boundaryless paradigm of the 21st century. But that journey took a full decade. At times, it was marked by internal pain, struggle, and doubt. And any organization that intends to become boundaryless must prepare itself for resistance, both from within and without.

Source: Excerpted from R. Ashkenas, D. Ulrich, T. Jick, and S. Kerr, *The Boundaryless Organization* (San Francisco, CA: Jossey-Bass, 1995): 13–21.

CLASS PREPARATION

A. Read "Permeability in Action: Case Study of a Boundaryless Organization."

B. Analyze your organization (e.g., work setting, team, church, academic department, university, etc.) using the 7-S Model.[1] All seven components are important; they are interconnected and should complement one another. This "fit" among the components is a major source of organizational effectiveness. Describe the following components of your organization and, as you do this, start thinking about how well they complement one another.

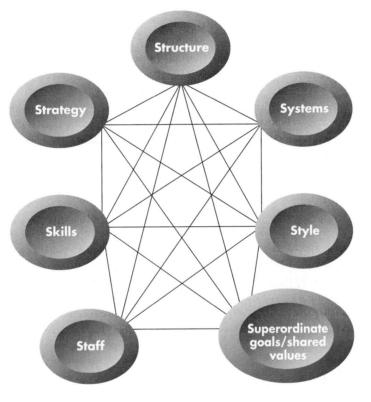

The 7-S Model

Source: Based on R. T. Pascale and A. G. Athos, *Art of Japanese Management* (New York: Simon & Schuster, 1981).

1. **Strategy** The goals and objectives to be achieved as well as the values and missions to be pursued, the basic direction of the company. The strategy lays out the projects or services to be provided, the markets to be served, and the value to be offered to the customer. Strategy also specifies sources of competitive advantage.

2. **Structure** The anatomy of the organization that shows the formal reporting relationships and how job tasks are formally divided, grouped, and coordinated. The organizational chart is a representation of structure.

3. **Systems** The formal and informal procedures that make the organization work: capital budgeting systems, recruitment systems, training systems, compensation systems, cost accounting procedures, planning, reports, and so on.

4. **Style** The way managers behave to achieve the organization's goals; how they generally interact with employees.

5. **Staff** A demographic description of important personnel categories. What types of people work in the organization (e.g., software designers, new immigrants whose limited language skills prevent them from working in their own fields, Ph.D. research scientists, part-time college students, etc.)?

6. **Skills** The distinctive capabilities of key personnel or the competencies for which the firm is noted.

7. **Superordinate Goals/Shared Values** The guiding concepts of the organization, the values and aspirations that are taught to members. These are the fundamental principles around which the organization is built (e.g., innovation, customer service, integrity).

C. Analyze the fit among the 7-Ss you just described.
   1. Which components work well together and which do not?

   2. What changes would you recommend so there is greater complementarity among these components?

3. Finally, what are the pros and cons of your organization's structure?

D. While reading this chapter, make a list of the cues you will look for with regard to organizational design.

THE KNOWLEDGE BASE

Leaders in highly layered organizations are like people who wear several sweaters outside on a freezing winter day. They remain warm and comfortable but are blissfully ignorant of the realities of their environment.

Jack Welch, former CEO, GE

Peter Senge, the organizational learning guru, regularly asks groups of managers to imagine their organization as an ocean liner and themselves as the "leader." "What is your role?" he asks them. Most answer, "The captain." Some reply, "The navigator determining the direction" or "the helmsman." Others see themselves as "the engineer stoking the fire, producing energy" or "the social director communicating with and involving everyone." Rarely do they mention the role of ship designer. Senge, however, maintains that "no one has a more sweeping influence than the designer. What good does it do for the captain to say, 'Turn starboard 30 degrees,' when the designer has built a rudder that will only turn to port, or which takes six hours to turn to starboard? It's fruitless to be the leader in an organization that is poorly designed."[2]

This chapter addresses the essential skill of organizational design. There are various models, such as the 7-S model, that portray the basic organizational building blocks. Galbraith, an expert on organizational structure, proposed the star model, which consists of the following five components. He suggests managers begin by determining the strategy and then move to processes, people, rewards, and motivation.[3] Although the components in design models may be slightly different, all of them emphasize the importance of fit and complementarity among interconnected aspects. And none of them view structure as the only aspect of an organization that needs to be designed. However, because some design aspects have been covered in previous chapters or in other business courses (organizational theory, strategy, human resources), this chapter will focus primarily on structure.

Organizational design is a challenge that must be revisited again and again as companies grow and other conditions change. At present many corporations are restructuring to respond more quickly and with greater flexibility to changing environments and customer demands.[4] Large companies worry about becoming rulebound bureaucracies and losing the entrepreneurial spark that fueled their early growth. For example, Dow Jones recently reorganized around their three markets—consumer media, enterprise media, and community media to better align their structure with strategic and financial goals. Previously they were organized by distribution channels.[5]

In general, we can categorize organizational structures as either *mechanistic or organic. Mechanistic organizations are rigid bureaucracies with strict rules, narrowly defined tasks, top-down communication, and centralized decision making.* They are best suited to routine functions within stable environments. A banana plantation is mechanistic because everyone has assigned jobs, and the work is very predictable. McDonald's is another example of a mechanistic organization. There are rules to ensure that customers receive a more or less standardized product all over the world, and the work is broken down into specific, standardized tasks. Walk into any McDonald's, and you will find employees performing the same tasks in the same way.

Mechanistic	Organic
1. Tasks broken down into specialized, separate parts	1. Employees contribute to the common task of the unit
2. Rigidly defined tasks	2. Broadly defined tasks
3. Centralized authority and control	3. Decentralized authority and control
4. Vertical communication	4. Horizontal communication
5. Rigid departmentalization	5. Cross-functional teams
6. Clear chain of command	6. Cross-hierarchical teams
7. Narrow span of control	7. Wide span of control
8. High formalization	8. Low formalization

EXHIBIT 21-1   **A Comparison of Mechanistic and Organic Structures**

In contrast, *organic organizations are flexible, decentralized networks with broadly defined tasks.* One example of an organic structure is a new start-up firm in which employees do whatever needs to be done at a given moment rather than follow a fixed job description. They also communicate directly with anyone in the company rather than limiting their communication to their direct superior or subordinates and unit co-workers. Organic structures are most appropriate for complex, changing environments that require flexibility. A "skunkworks" where a relatively small, multidisciplinary group of employees sequesters itself until it comes up with a new computer design is another example of an organic organization. One seldom finds organizations that are totally mechanistic or totally organic. For example, although a skunkworks is organic, other parts of the same company may be mechanistic. Exhibit 21–1 depicts the differences between mechanistic and organic structures.[6]

THE LANGUAGE OF STRUCTURE

Organization structure refers to the pattern of roles, authority, and communication that determines the coordination of the technology and people within an organization.

To discuss structure, we need to equip you with definitions of the key terms, found in Exhibit 21–2.

Hierarchy	Distribution of authority among organizational positions. The power to influence and direct others resides in the higher levels of a hierarchy.
Centralization	Authority to make decisions is concentrated at the top of the organization.
Decentralization	Authority to make decisions is granted to those closest to the situation.
Complexity	Number of levels in the hierarchy (vertical differentiation) and the number of departments or jobs (horizontal differentiation). Large organizations, therefore, tend to be more complex than small organizations.
Specialization	Degree to which organizational tasks are subdivided into separate jobs. If specialization is high, employees perform a narrow range of tasks. If it is low, they perform a wide range of tasks.
Standardization	The extent to which similar work activities are performed in a uniform manner.
Routine technology	Technology characterized by little task variety and formalized, standardized tasks (assembly lines). Nonroutine technology has high task variety and involves problem analysis based on experience and technical knowledge (strategic planning, basic research).
Formalization	Extent to which explicit rules, regulations, policies, and procedures govern organizational activities.
Span of control	Number of employees who report to a single supervisor or manager.

EXHIBIT 21-2   **Organizational Design Terms**

TRADITIONAL ORGANIZATIONAL STRUCTURES

There are various forms of organizational structure, each with a particular focus and unique advantages and disadvantages. We'll describe some of the more common forms in this section. Organizational charts represent structure; in particular, they illustrate how employees have been grouped, who has authority over whom, and how certain forms of communication are directed. We'll use organizational charts from hospitals as an example for the first three traditional types of structure: functional, divisional, and matrix.

Functional Structure

In this model, the organization is differentiated primarily by the functional specialties (e.g., nurses, physicians) required to accomplish the organization's mission. Each organization member, throughout the chain of command, reports to his or her functional superior (e.g., a nurse reports to a head nurse who reports to a nursing director). A health care delivery system may be functionally organized as shown in Exhibit 21–3.

Functional structures have various advantages. They enable the system to develop and maintain higher levels of expertise in the various functional areas or specialties. Organization members' loyalties are to the function, or specialty, and its standards of performance. In addition, each functional department can maintain subspecialists in various areas and allocate their time across the various services (e.g., inpatients, outpatients) being performed by the organization. One cardiologist, for example, could serve inpatients, outpatients, and the operating room. Thus, duplication of resources is reduced with functional designs. They promote standardization; with everyone doing similar work, it is easier to work in a uniform fashion. Functional designs also allow companies to centralize certain activities; for example, a central purchasing department may handle all transactions and facilitate buying leverage.

On the other hand, under a functional structure, it is often very difficult to perform the integration and coordination of services and inputs required by the organization. Problems in different services areas become difficult to manage because the various functional representatives in that department often do not have a strong direct reporting relationship to the service director. For example, pediatricians in the outpatient department under a functional structure may hold themselves more responsible to the chief of pediatrics than to the outpatient director. If coordination of doctors, nurses, and social workers is important in the outpatient department, and each health professional is responding to a different functional director, then coordination becomes

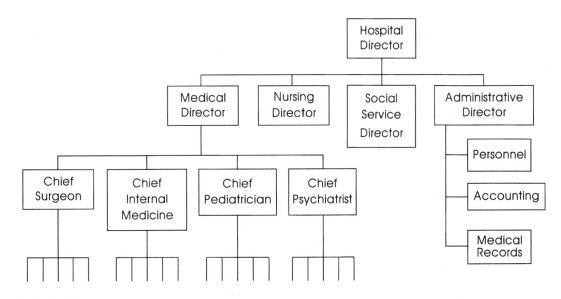

EXHIBIT 21-3   **Functional Structure**

difficult and problems may develop. These problems may take the form of inability to agree on schedules to ensure proper coverage, difficulty in developing work responsibilities for each function in a given service, problems in developing procedures for coordinating activities in the service, or even trouble agreeing on the goals and objectives of the service.

Other disadvantages of the functional structure relate to slow decision making. Because decisions are sent up the hierarchy to the top of functional areas, sometimes called *functional silos*, decision making may be slow. The priorities of the functional silos may assume greater importance than those of the organization as a whole. The barriers between different functions inhibit cross-functional collaboration, coordination, and information sharing.[7]

A functional structure is appropriate when the organization is small, when there is a single product line or service, when the number of markets served is limited, and when product life and development cycles are long. When survival depends on responsiveness to variety and speed, functional structures often are replaced by product, market, or process structures and by lateral cross-functional processes.[8]

Divisional Structure

As shown in Exhibit 21–4, the divisional structure is differentiated by its outputs—usually its products or services. This structure is also referred to as a product structure or strategic business units. As an organization grows in size and adopts a strategy of product diversification, many companies switch from a functional to a divisional structure. Each department or division contains representatives from the various functional areas. Each organization member in this system reports directly or indirectly to a manager in charge of a particular product or service (e.g., a pediatric nurse reports to the director of the pediatric clinics). In larger companies, divisions can consist of business divisions, businesses, or profit centers.

Divisional structures have several advantages. The concentrated focus on one area often results in improvements as well as increased customer satisfaction. Because customers deal directly with the unit, there is a stronger possibility that their customized needs will be met and

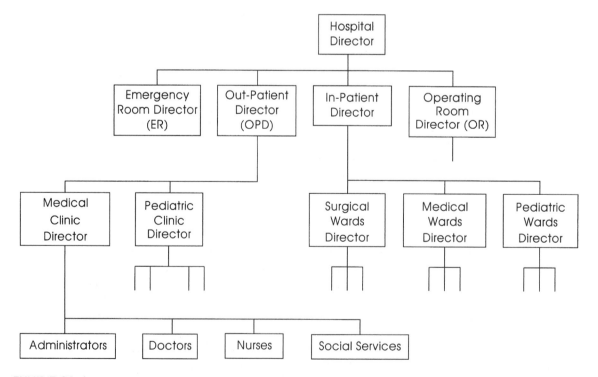

EXHIBIT 21-4   **Divisional Structure**

their suggestions incorporated into product design and service procedures. Changes in the environment or in customer taste can be speedily addressed. Ideas for improvements and adaptations do not have to compete internally for attention with all the company's other products or services and wait for a decision to come from on high. The product development cycle is most easily speeded up in divisional structures divided into product units.[9] This structure allows for coordination across functions and decentralized decision making. Decisions that are best for the product or service can be made closer to the customer.

Divisional structures also have their disadvantages. Because each department or division has representatives from each functional area, there is duplication of effort and resources. There may not be enough work for each department to have full-time specialists. Each unit may need equipment for functional specialists that could be shared in a functional structure. Divisions may buy their materials from different vendors rather than consolidating their orders. Therefore, various economies of scale are lost with divisional structures. Different divisions sometimes reinvent the wheel. Furthermore, because specialists no longer work only with people in their own field, there is decreased opportunity for in-depth competence and technical specialization. Standardization across product lines is also more difficult. It is not uncommon, for example, to find departments using different procedures with customers or using different computer systems and software that eventually create compatibility problems. Coordination across the boundaries of different departments or divisions is difficult, so opportunities for shared learning and collaboration are often lost. And, finally, customers who want to buy more than one product from the company cannot do "one-stop shopping" and deal with only one department or division. This is less efficient for the customer. Finally, employee loyalty may be to the division rather than to the company as a whole.

Divisional structures are appropriate when the company has several products or services that differ from one another, when the environment is rapidly changing and unpredictable, when the technology is nonroutine and depends on several functional areas, when the organization's goals are external effectiveness, adaptation, and customer satisfaction, and when organizations are large.[10]

A variation of the divisional structure is a *geographic structure, divided into regions.* For example, before it was bought by Unilever, Bestfoods International, one of the largest global food companies, had four geographic divisions: Europe, Asia, Latin America, and North America. Divisions could stay close to their customers and reduce travel and distribution costs. The company understood that different regions (and countries) have different tastes in food and, therefore, allowed a great deal of local autonomy. In yet another variation, *market structures, the most rapidly increasing type of structure, divide the company into units that serve particular customers, markets, or industries.*[11]

Many companies have adopted *hybrid structures, which are combinations of different structures*, because they are better suited to their needs and avoid the disadvantages of the pure structures. For example, eBay, the Internet auction company, has elements of both functional and divisional structures. The company has centralized human resources, finance, operations, and legal departments but also has divisional structures that are organized along geographic (e.g., North America) and product (e.g., marketplace, PayPal) lines. Matrix structures, discussed next, are another example of hybrid structures.

Matrix Structure

Matrix structures, allow companies to have a dual focus, usually product and function. They evolved out of the need to provide both the advantages of functional specialization and the coordination of products or service activity. The structure is differentiated by both product and function as shown in Exhibit 21–5. For example, a nurse working in the pediatric ward would report to the pediatric clinic director and to the hospital's nursing director.

Matrix structures have the advantages of facilitating the communication and coordination required to meet dual demands from the environment. The organic nature of the matrix (e.g., project groups) makes it flexible and adaptable to environmental changes. They allow for flexible and efficient sharing of human resources across products, which avoids duplication of resources. They provide the opportunity for both functional and product skill development.

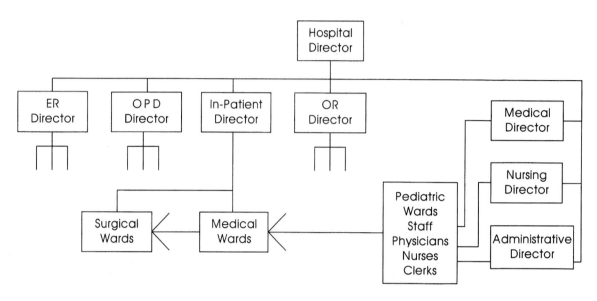

EXHIBIT 21-5   **Matrix Structure**

By maintaining the functional organization, the subspecialists can be retained and allocated where needed in the organization. The functional director can provide for in-service education and screening to maintain professional standards. At the same time, the product or service managers' authority over the functional representatives when they are in their service areas allows for better coordination.

The disadvantages of matrix structures are rooted in the dual structure. Matrices are time-consuming because employees attend meetings in both areas and sometimes have to resolve conflicts between them. The dual authority is confusing for some employees, and if organizational members do not develop the special skills required by a matrix structure (e.g., handling ambiguity, competing demands, and shared authority), this structure does not work. As a manager once noted, "The challenge is not so much to create a matrix structure as it is to create a matrix in the minds of our managers."[12]

Matrix structures are only appropriate under very specific conditions:

1. Pressure exists to share scarce resources (people and equipment) across product lines.
2. Environmental pressure exists for two or more critical outputs (e.g., new products and high technical specialization and quality).
3. The organization's environment is both complex and uncertain. There are frequent changes that require both vertical and horizontal coordination and information sharing.[13]

Matrix structures are appropriate when the technology is nonroutine and interdependent or when the strategy has a dual focus, such as product innovation and technical specialization.[14] Matrix structures work best in medium-sized organizations with multiple, but not too many, products. In addition, employees should have superior conflict resolutions skills and be able to cope with uncertainty and ambiguity.

NEW ORGANIZATIONAL FORMS—HORIZONTAL AND NETWORK ORGANIZATIONS

Galbraith contends that organizations need to develop *lateral capability, which refers to the coordination of different functions without the need to communicate through the hierarchy* in today's environment.[15] He identifies three types of lateral capability:

1. Coordination across functions
2. Coordination across business units in a diversified corporation
3. International coordination of activities across countries and regions

Both horizontal structures, sometimes called *process structures*, and network structures are organic structures that increase lateral capability. Both are gaining in popularity.

Horizontal Structures

Horizontal structures, as shown in Exhibit 21–6, focus on a complete flow of work, which means managing across rather than up or down a hierarchy. *Horizontal corporations are flat structures with minimal layers of management and self-managing, multidisciplinary teams organized around core process.* Their primary goal and benefit is customer satisfaction, which is attained by reducing the boundaries with suppliers and customers alike and empowering employees.

Any work that does not add value is eliminated. Teams are the central organizational building block, and to reduce the need for supervisors, they manage themselves. Employees are trained to make their own analyses and decisions and then share the raw data. Employees are rewarded for skill acquisition and team performance. The use of multidisciplinary teams

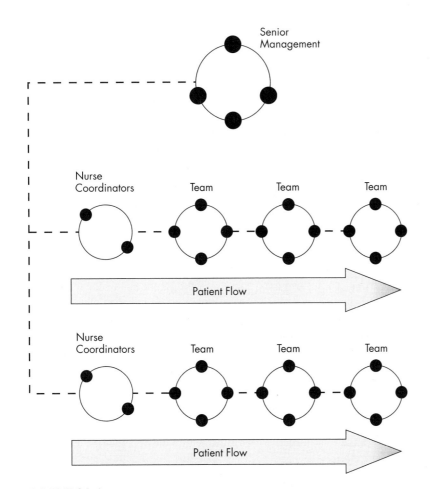

EXHIBIT 21-6 **Horizontal Hospital Structure**

Source: Karolinska Hospital in Stockholm, Sweden, as described in R. Rao, "The Struggle to Create an Organization for the 21st Century," *Fortune 131* (April 3, 1995): 90–99; and J. A. Byrne, "The Horizontal Corporation," *Business-Week 3351* (December 20, 1993): 76–81.

means that companies can decrease the number of "disconnects" and "handoffs" that occur whenever work is passed from one functional area or department to another.[16] Chrysler used a horizontal structure with the Neon car, thereby reducing both development time and costs. Examples of units within a horizontal structure might be new-product development process, order fulfillment process, and customer acquisition and maintenance.

Because horizontal structures are a fairly recent innovation, there is less research on their advantages and disadvantages. In general, the benefits of leaner, flatter structures are lower management costs, more widely shared communications and decision making, and greater employee involvement. The advantages of horizontal structures are customer satisfaction and the potential redesign and improvement of processes, resulting in increased efficiency, speed, and reduced costs. Because one manager is responsible for the entire process, the resistance to improving the process sometimes found in functional departments is reduced. It is easier to measure entire processes and hold process units accountable than to determine what bits and pieces of functional units have contributed to a process. Horizontal structures eliminate duplication of effort across functions. Because many tasks are delegated to self-managed teams, administrative overhead is reduced. Decentralized decision making in the teams makes for rapid decisions. Empowered, involved employees report improved morale. Administrative overhead is reduced because of the teams. By coordinating functions across the process, cycle times can be reduced, making some companies more competitive.[17]

One disadvantage of horizontal structures is figuring out how to define the numerous processes in most large organizations. Employees have to be trained to work in self-managed teams, and managers have to work as coaches rather than bosses. This structure may be viewed as a threat by middle managers. More time may be spent in meetings to make sure efforts are coordinated.

Horizontal structures are appropriate in companies with short product life and development cycles, when customer satisfaction is the goal, and when the environment is uncertain.

Few companies are making a total transition to a horizontal structure, perhaps because there will always be a need for some managers with functional expertise.[18] In the future, we can expect to see more hybrid structures that organize multifunctional teams around core processes whenever possible.

Network Structure

Network structures are found in network organizations, sometimes called modular or virtual corporations. Shown in Exhibit 21–7, they made their appearance in the 1980s. *Network organizations consist of brokers who subcontract needed services to designers, suppliers, producers, and distributors linked by full-disclosure information systems and coordinated by market mechanisms.* These organizations are also referred to as hollow corporations because some activities are farmed out to other companies that form the network. For example, Nike, Apple Computer, Reebok, and Emerson Radio do virtually no manufacturing. Some employees never touch their company's product. Instead, these brokers form relationships with other companies that are responsible for manufacturing, selling, and transporting their products. Their contribution, as the center of the network, is the design, marketing, advertising, and integration of the network.[19]

The characteristics of networks are:

1. **Vertical disaggregation** Functions normally performed within the organization are carried out by independent organizations.
2. **Use of Brokers** Networks of designers, suppliers, producers, and distributors are assembled by brokers.
3. **Market mechanisms** The key functions are tied together by market mechanisms rather than plans and controls.

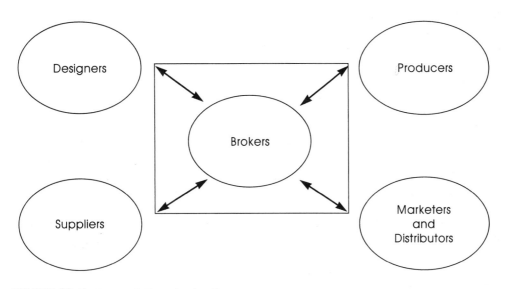

EXHIBIT 21-7   Network Organization Structure

4. **Full-disclosure information systems** Broad-access, computerized information systems substitute for extensive trust-building processes based on experience.[20]

In 1999 Benetton had 5,000 franchises, with 22 factories in Europe, and 900 subcontractors in Italy manufacturing the company's clothing that interact via an extensive, worldwide telecommunications network. Benetton's core is modern information technology that tracks each purchase from the cash registers in every franchise, so they can reportedly respond to market changes in 10 days' time. Benetton is relieved of the headaches of the manufacturing work that is subcontracted out to companies that work exclusively for Benetton and are guaranteed both work orders and a set profit margin.[21]

Network organizations have given rise to new ways of collaborating with other companies. Network partners must agree to ground rules that result in trustworthy relationships and transactions. Companies often develop close and helpful relationships with several suppliers and customers so they do not become overdependent on one particular relationship.

The primary benefit of network structures is that they allow organizations and managers to concentrate on what they do well and subcontract activities that lie outside their specialty. Network structures help companies deal with complex relationships both within and outside the organization in rapidly changing environments. For example, when labor costs become too high in one country, firms simply look for subcontractors in countries with lower labor costs (a practice that disturbs critics of globalization).

Network structures are also lean with few administrative overhead costs. They make it possible to break into a market without incurring prohibitive start-up costs.[22] Network structures can be large (centralizing purchasing at the lead company) and small (subcontracting to small flexible shops) when it is to their advantage.[23] Companies in rapidly changing industries can avoid investing in factories and technologies that will quickly become obsolete, because their sourcing is flexible.

One of the disadvantages of network organizations is limited control over subcontractors. For example, how do you ensure quality and acceptable worker conditions in a company owned by a subcontractor? Brokers are vulnerable to allegations of human rights abuses committed by subcontractors. Subcontractors have been known to raise their prices once a broker has become dependent on them. (Similarly, brokers can pressure subcontractors without other options.) Brokers risk losing proprietary knowledge to companies that become competitors. "Apple taught independent software vendors about the Macintosh's operating system so that they could write application programs that would run on the Mac. One of those vendors was Microsoft. Microsoft did, indeed, write programs for the Mac, but it also incorporated what it learned into its own operating system, Windows. Once Windows 3.0 appeared, Apple had lost its competitive advantage."[24] Networks have limited loyalty because contractors can be replaced at any time in favor of a better deal. Network organizations also have the disadvantage of making it difficult to capture and share learning across different segments of the organization.[25] GE is currently experimenting with bringing in outside experts so that the company creates and takes advantage of industry experts.[26] Network organizations are especially appropriate for fast-paced, changing industries in uncertain environments.

Networked Idealists. What do Kazaa, Skype, and Craigslist have in common other than they are free of cost to the user? They are all examples of a new, innovative organizational form, called networked idealists (NIs), which has been revolutionizing the marketplace and providing services via the Internet that traditional businesses do not offer. *Networked idealists are "initially non-profit entrepreneurs who develop organic, cellular distributed network structures to accomplish their work."*[27] To circumvent the usual barriers to entry that plague new organizations, they use financial, transportation, and communications networks in unique and creative ways. They tend to rely on viral marketing and word-of-mouth buzz. Unlike most firms, they tap into their customers/users' idealism or shared values, who then partner with them to innovate. Open source software is one example. Linux came about because Finnish student Linus Torvalds couldn't afford IBM's Unix operating system; he sent off an email to a list-serve and asked if anyone would like to help him create an operating system he could run on a PC. You can see the results below:

Open source software is free in the sense that anyone may have access to the source code and modify it, but not copyright their innovations. Linux, the foremost example of open source, now runs a third of the world's web servers and is invading other areas of computing, phones, and other devises. It's an ideally structured NI business. It's global, distributed, and cellular, and its leaders almost all work for other companies, rendering them invulnerable to direct business attack. [28]

According to Lowy and Hood, NIs are distinguished from other businesses by five strategies or characteristics:[29]

- **Guerilla infrastructures and radical architectures** They bypass traditional barriers to entry by using guerilla approaches (e.g., Skype bypasses the phone network by using the Internet.)
- **Winning by not trying** They do not want to succeed by the measures of incumbent firms. They are visualizing "a different game."
- **Value-based motivations** They are idealistic and believe that doing good and making money are not antithetical but complementary.
- **Attack strengths** Rather than seeking unfilled niches, they attack incumbent strengths directly. Linux went after Microsoft's OS (operating system) monopoly and Moveon.Org, a grassroots political organization, directly attacked the fundraising advantage of political incumbents who usually have greater access to big donors.
- **Knowledge from the people** NIs typically involve partners, customers, and supported deeply in value creation, if not decision-making. For example, Kazaa users uploaded their song libraries to the web for others to download.

The structure of NIs is a series of concentric circles:[30]

- The *founder* is in the center circle
- The *inner circle* of advisors, mentors and perhaps funders are located in the second circle
- The *active users* who co-create the content of the organization are in the third circle
- The *passive users* in the fourth circle are the public supporters or customers who provide funding and word-of-mouth support

These circles are linked by public networks. Power tends to be hierarchical and rest with the founder, but decision authority is determined by expertise.

BOUNDARYLESS ORGANIZATIONS

Boundaryless organizations work at eliminating or diminishing the boundaries between both internal and external entities in order to be more effective. Good ideas are welcomed whatever their source, whether inside or outside the company. People should collaborate and make things happen without waiting for permission from a central authority.[31] For example, Daimler Chrysler and Ford use cross-disciplinary teams that include designers, engineers, plant managers, and people from finance, marketing, and human resources. In the past, the plans for a new car would have been passed sequentially and bumpily from department to department, taking a great deal of time. Some companies also include customers in the product phase. Others, such as Johnson & Johnson, have computers located within their customers' facilities that keep them abreast of inventory. Honda believes that helping its suppliers become better companies makes Honda a better company. To this end, Honda assigned a team of engineers to work with and train employees at ParkerHannifin. The benefits to Parker-Hannifin were cost savings and faster production time.

The Informal Organizational Structure

So far, we have been discussing formal organizational structures. An organizational chart, as we have noted, specifies the nature of the formal organizational authority and communication patterns. However, these charts do not always reflect the reality of life within an organization. For example, a young boss may not have the necessary technical expertise so employees turn to an older employee as the real source of authority in their department. Employees and managers typically leave people out of the communication loop who are not respected, trusted, or powerful. The in-groups in companies in collective cultures (e.g., Latin America) often call the shots and share information, regardless of where these members appear on the organizational chart. All these examples of variations from the formal structure reflect the organization's social system. Thus, organizations have both a formal structure and an informal structure that determine how both authority and communication really function. *The informal structure refers to natural formations, informal leadership, and communication patterns that evolve in an organization and run parallel to the formal structure.*

The importance of understanding the distinctions between formal versus informal organizations and the problems that can arise if the two are not understood is at no time clearer than when one attempts to introduce a technological change into an organization. In Trist's classic study of an attempt to change the process by which coal was mined, the anticipated production increases from the new method were not being realized.[32] On investigation, it was observed that the new technology substantially altered the social system that had developed within this mine. The men were used to working in close-knit teams characterized by loyalty and mutual help. The new technology involved factory-like, individualized workstations that disrupted the informal group patterns that had made their jobs satisfying. Whereas a formal organizational chart can be redrawn to account for the effects of a technological change, the informal social system, which does not appear on an organizational chart, is also influenced by the technological change. Both must be taken into account.

KEY ISSUES IN ORGANIZATION DESIGN
Differentiation and Integration

A key design issue, called differentiation and integration, was identified by Lawrence and Lorsch.[33] Organizations divide up their tasks among employees. As employees focus more and more on their particular tasks, differentiation occurs. *Differentiation is "the differences in cognitive and emotional orientations among managers in different functional departments, and the difference in formal structure among these departments."*[34] For example, accountants develop a particular mind-set toward their work that is quite different from

Characteristic	R&D Department	Manufacturing	Sales Department
Goals	New developments, quality	Efficient production	Customer satisfaction
Time horizon	Long	Short	Short
Interpersonal orientation	Mostly task	Task	Social
Formality of structure	Low	High	High

EXHIBIT 21-8   Differences in Goals and Orientations Among Organizational Departments

Source: Based on P. R. Lawrence and J. W. Lorsch, *Organization and Environment* (Homewood, IL: Irwin, 1969): 23–29.

that of salespeople. Departments differ from one another, as shown in Exhibit 21–8, because of the nature of their work. They develop particular goals, time horizons, interpersonal orientations, and levels of formality. Sometimes these differences are the source of intergroup conflict. When organizations have complex tasks and operate in dynamic environments, they become more differentiated than when their tasks are simple and their environments stable. The natural result of high differentiation is the difficulty in coordinating the work of the various units. Therefore, organizations have a variety of integration mechanisms that promote collaboration. Some examples are coordinators, committees, liaison positions, and task forces.[35] *Integration is defined as the behaviors and structures used by differentiated organizational subunit to coordinate their work activities.*

Deciding Which Structure Is Best

Choosing the most appropriate structure is a matter of making trade-offs, because all structures have advantages and disadvantages. A starting point for determining the right structure for a particular organization is the design principle: "Form follows function." The task (function) should determine the structure (form). This explains why departments or divisions with very diverse tasks are usually structured in different ways. Champy suggests this principle be modified to "form follows customers." In his opinion, structures should mirror the customers and cater to their specific needs.[36]

There are other contingencies that affect the choice of structure: the company's strategy, the environment, technology, size, national culture, and the people and their shared values. The Quaker religion, for example, is predicated on a direct relationship to God and personal conscience. These beliefs translate into a highly developed form of participative decision making in most Quaker organizations that is seldom found elsewhere and a predisposition toward decentralized structures.[37]

Strategy and Structure. Galbraith recommends setting strategy first and then choosing the structure most likely to make that strategy a reality.[38] This involves identifying key success indicators, understanding the unique organization qualities the strategy attempts to exploit, and determining the organizational capabilities the design should support. For example, if the company's competitive advantage is fast cycle times, a horizontal, process-oriented structure is more appropriate than a functional structure.

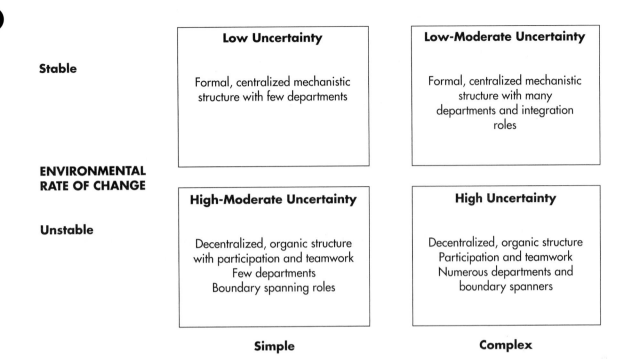

EXHIBIT 21-9   **Environmental Characteristics and Recommended Organizational Designs**

Source: Based on R. B. Duncan, "What Is the Right Organization Structure? Decision Tree Analysis Provides the Answer," *Organizational Dynamics* 7(3)(Winter 1979): 59–80.

The Environment and Structure. The environment has a major effect on the choice of structure. Two dimensions are used to analyze an organization's environment: the simple-complex dimension and the stable-unstable dimension. Both concern the elements in an organization's domain, such as customers, competitors, suppliers, government regulators, unions, financial resources, and so on.

The *simple-complex dimension* refers to environmental complexity, the heterogeneity or the number and dissimilarity of external elements relevant to an organization's operations. Small, family-owned businesses usually have a simple environment—few, fairly similar, external elements that influence the organization. In contrast, global corporations have complex environments.

The *stable-unstable dimension* gauges whether the elements in the environment are dynamic. Stable environments remain the same for a relatively long period. Unstable environments change quickly.

Environmental uncertainty is high when information on environmental factors is insufficient and it is difficult to predict what will happen. The more uncertain the environment, the more information the organization needs about the environment. People in boundary-spanning roles often gather information on the environment as well as represent the interests of the organization to the environment. Two examples of boundary spanners are people engaged in market research and corporate lawyers who specialize in government regulations.

A matrix of the simple-complex and stable-unstable dimensions, shown in Exhibit 21–9, provides more guidance about organizational structure.[39]

Low uncertainty environments exist when the environment is both stable and simple (e.g., beer and soft-drink industry). The most appropriate structure for this type of environment is a formal, centralized mechanistic structure with few departments.

Low-moderate uncertainty environments exist when the environment is stable and complex (e.g., chemical companies and universities). The most appropriate structure for this category is a formal, centralized mechanistic structure. The complexity of the environment makes it necessary to have more departments along with integration roles to coordinate them. High-moderate uncertainty environments exist when the environment is unstable and simple (e.g., cosmetics and toy industries). The most appropriate structure is a decentralized, organic structure characterized by participation and teamwork. Because there are few elements in the environment, few departments are necessary; however, boundary-spanning roles are prevalent to keep on top of information and changes in the environment.

High uncertainty environments exist when the environment is both unstable and complex (e.g., computer firms, airlines, telecommunications). The most appropriate structure is a decentralized, organic structure characterized by participation and teamwork. Because of the complexity of the environment, however, numerous departments and boundary spanners are necessary.

Technology and Structure. Changes in technology have had a far-reaching impact on organizational design. Successful Internet companies may have organizational charts with only three full-time employees. Geographical location ceases to matter when people make their purchases online. Telecommuting and groupware mean that many colleagues are no longer physically grouped, even though they work "together." Flexible manufacturing processes ensure that factories produce a greater variety of products and provide more customization for customers. E-mail makes it easier for subordinates to gain access to decision makers; hitting "send" on your keyboard is simpler than trying to get past the executive secretary guarding the president's office in many companies. Automation and information technology make possible wider spans of control, resulting in flatter hierarchies.[40] Advanced information technology has been credited with broader participation in decision making, faster decision making, and better organizational intelligence.[41]

In some cases, information technology has revolutionized industries. Before Wal-Mart, most small-town retail stores in the United States were "mom and pop" operations in which the owners made business decisions without knowing what was happening in stores outside the area. Sam Walton of Wal-Mart changed this scene forever by centralizing pricing, buying, and promotional decisions on a national level, thanks to the company's state-of-the-art electronic ordering and inventory control systems. As a result, Wal-Mart was able to deliver better-quality products at lower prices, and many of its competitors were forced out of business. Wal-Mart has, however, designed in some decentralized decision making. Local managers have some latitude on decisions about ordering stock and allocating space. There are also price-sensitive items for which local store managers can determine their own prices, depending on the local competition.[42] As Wal-Mart's CIO (Chief Information Officer) said: "I think the challenge... is to enable a chain as big as Wal-Mart to act like a hometown store, even while it maintains its economies of scale."[43]

Size and Structure. Start-ups usually have functional or organic structures, depending on the founder(s). As organizations grow and begin to experience coordination costs, they often adopt more complex and decentralized structures. Extremely large organizations are prone to routinization and stagnation, as we saw in Chapter 16, Culture. To stimulate innovation and responsiveness, large organizations may restructure to disrupt the existing decision making, coordination, and communication patterns and change their focus.

International Structures

Expanding the business into a foreign country for the first time often means entering a highly uncertain environment. Companies may choose to minimize the risk and uncertainty via a range of strategic alliances. Some *license their products or technology to be sold for a fee by foreign companies that have access to global markets and distribution channels.* Other companies enter into joint ventures with companies that are well established in the target country or region. *Joint ventures are separate business entities designed to enter new markets, formed by two or more firms that share development and production costs.* Other companies join *consortia—groups of independent companies (e.g., suppliers, customers, and competitors) that join together to share skills, resources, costs, and access to one another's markets.*

Corporations that have established a presence abroad may use some variation of the structures described in the chapter. Their choice of structure may depend partly on the stage of their international development, how many products they sell internationally, and the importance of their international sales.[44] Bartlett and Ghoshal recommend an integrated network model for transnational corporations that are truly global.

> *In such companies, key activities and resources are neither centralized in the parent company, nor decentralized so that each subsidiary can carry out its own tasks... . Instead, the resources and activities are dispersed but specialized, so as to achieve efficiency and flexibility at the same time. Furthermore, these dispersed resources are integrated in an interdependent network of worldwide operations.[45]*

Integrated network models consist of (1) distributed, specialized resources and capabilities; (2) large flows of components, products, resources, people, and information among interdependent units; and (3) complex processes of coordination and cooperation in an environment of shared decision making.[46] They can be illustrated as a network (no top or bottom to denote authority) with interconnecting lines to all units.

CULTURE AND STRUCTURE

Family businesses are the most common form of business organization throughout the world. As a general rule, they are characterized by paternalistic, centralized decision making—the male leader or owner makes the decisions—and decisions are often based on kinship considerations rather than rational business judgment. For example, providing jobs for relatives may be more important than maximizing performance and profit. Family businesses may or may not follow bureaucratic rules.

In Chinese family businesses, the dominant values are patrimonialism, which includes paternalism, hierarchy, mutual obligations, responsibility, familialism, personalism, and connections. With the exception of Chinese businesses that employ nonfamily members and operate as a clan or extended family, many businesses remain small and, therefore, have simple structures. They do not have systematic sets of rules, systems, or roles. Workers do not specialize and are switched from task to task at the owner's whim. Given the absence of formal structure, cliques occasionally form as a substitute; intergroup conflict sometimes results, an indication of the factionalism found in Chinese family businesses.[47]

The Japanese *keiretsu* and Korean *chaebols* are structures that originated in family businesses and have played a major role in the economic development of these countries. *Keiretsu are complex interfirm networks that combine market exchange and noneconomic social relations.* Each member firm buys a small percentage of stock in the other firms in the group. They generally participate in a large number of industries and have a bank at their core. *Keiretsu* networks, such as Mitsubishi, reduce costs and risks and safeguard member firms by ensuring trusting, reliable business dealings and a certain degree of protection from competition with nonmember firms.[48] Korean *chaebols are "a business group consisting of large companies owned and managed by family members or relatives in many diversified business areas."*[49] *Hyundai, Samsung*, and *Daewoo* are *chaebols*.

National culture affects the choice of structure. High-power-distance cultures tend toward organizational structures with centralized decision making. Low-power-distance cultures prefer decentralized decision making. The uncertainty avoidance dimension relates to the degree of formalization—the need for formal rules and specialization. High uncertainty avoidance cultures generally prefer formalized structures. Matrix structures were not widely accepted in France because they go against the French respect for the hierarchy and unity of command.[50]

CLASS ACTIVITY: STRUCTURE, INC.

The purpose of this exercise is to develop a good understanding of different organizational structures and experience what it is like to work within them. (Time allotted: 110 minutes)

STEP 1. Divide into groups of approximately 8-10 students (unless your instructor decides otherwise). These groups will form different companies whose product is the transfer of knowledge to their customers, in this case, your classmates. Each group will be assigned one of the following structures: functional structure, divisional structure, matrix structure, horizontal structure, or network structure.

STEP 2. Preparation Stage. (40 minutes)
The groups have two tasks during the preparation stage, which could be done either in class or as homework. Don't start on a. until you've read b.
  a. Prepare a 10-minute class presentation with the following minimum components. If you want to exceed these requirements (except for the time constraint), please do so.
    1. Explain how your assigned structure works, based on the information in the chapter. (If you were assigned this project ahead of time, please try to obtain an organizational chart from a company using this structure.)
    2. Describe the strengths and weaknesses of the structure.
    3. Under what conditions is a structure such as this most appropriate?
    4. Prepare a one-page handout for your classmates (to be copied and distributed as instructed).
    5. Design a presentation that is as interesting and creative as possible—the goal of your group (a service business) is to transfer knowledge about your structure to your audience. Your presentation should also model symbolically your structure.
  b. Carry out the preparation and delivery of the presentation by organizing your group using the type of structure you were assigned. For example, if your group has the network structure, two of you might constitute the core organization and the rest of the members will be subcontractors who produce different services. Please adhere strictly to this requirement so we can compare afterward what it was like to work in the different structures.
  Depending on your structure and the type of presentation you choose, some of the specialized tasks in your company might be research, writing, design, graphics (e.g. Power Point, overheads, posters), talent (presenters or actors), and management.

STEP 3. Each group makes its presentation. (40 minutes)

STEP 4. Plenary debriefing. (20-30 minutes) As a class, discuss the following questions.
  a. How did you organize your group?
  b. What effect did your structure have on your preparation phase?
  c. Were there any differences in the presentations that might be traced back to different structures?
  d. Did any other design-related issues surface in this project?
  e. Did you like working with the type of structure you were assigned?
  f. What did you do to ensure communication? Coordination? Quality control?

LEARNING POINTS

1. Mechanistic organizations are rigid bureaucracies with strict rules, narrowly defined tasks, top-down communication, and centralized decision making. They are best suited to routine functions within stable environments.
2. Organic organizations are flexible, decentralized networks, with broadly defined tasks, horizontal communication, and cross-functional teams. They are most appropriate for complex, changing environments that require flexibility.
3. Organizational structure refers to the pattern of roles, authority, and communication that determines the coordination of the technology and people within an organization.
4. The functional form of organizational structure centers around the functional specialties required to accomplish the organization's mission. It allows for greater development of functional expertise but may make organizational coordination more difficult.
5. The divisional structure is organized around outputs such as products or services, business divisions, businesses, or profit centers. The concentrated focus and decentralized decision making improve the chances of customer satisfaction and rapid adaptation and change.
6. Matrix structures have a dual focus, usually products and functions. It is an attempt to profit from the advantages of both functional and product structures. However, having both a product boss and a functional boss can cause confusion and conflict.
7. Horizontal corporations are flat structures with minimal layers of management and self-managing multidisciplinary teams organized around core processes.
8. Network organizations consist of brokers who subcontract needed services to designers, suppliers, producers, and distributors linked by full-disclosure information systems and coordinated by market mechanisms.
9. Networked idealists are initially non-profit entrepreneurs who develop organic, cellular distributed network structures to accomplish their work.
10. Boundaryless organizations work at eliminating or diminishing the boundaries between both internal and external entities in order to be more effective.
11. The informal structure refers to natural formations, informal leadership, and communication patterns that evolve in an organization and run parallel to the formal structure.
12. Because they do different tasks, employees become differentiated and develop dissimilar goals and orientations; therefore, organizations need mechanisms for integrating various units. Integration refers to the behaviors and structures used by differentiated organizational subunit to coordinate their work activities.
13. A guiding rule in design is "form follows function." Thus, different parts of the organization may have different structures.
14. Organizational design is influenced by these contingencies: strategy, environment, technology, size, national culture, and the people and their shared values.
15. The simple-complex dimension (environmental complexity) and the stable-unstable dimension (rate of environmental change) can be used to determine the level of environmental uncertainty organizations face.
16. Corporations may gain access to foreign markets via strategic alliances such as licensing agreements, joint ventures, and consortia.
17. Family businesses are the most common form of business structure throughout the world.

ACTION SCRIPTS

FOR EMPLOYEES

Employees who are experts in organization design understand the pros and cons of different structures.

- They take the time to analyze how their own organizational structure impacts the workplace.
- They can distinguish between problems that are rooted in the structure versus individual personalities.
- They make recommendations for ways to improve structures that are not optimal.
- They do not let themselves be handicapped by the structure. For example, if they work in a functional structure, they take the initiative to communicate and coordinate with essential people outside their department.
- They learn the skills their structure requires.
- They try to adapt quickly when restructuring occurs.

FOR MANAGERS

- When experts look at an organizational problem, they ask, "What is the problem, not who?" Unless managers are sophisticated about design issues, they are likely to see individuals, rather than structure, as the problem.
- When a succession of people fail in a position, it is often a signal that the design of position or structure is at fault. Some jobs and even departments are simply doomed to failure by poor designs, and it's a manager's job to determine that and rectify it.
- Managers who are expert at organization design make sure the informal structure is well understood before any changes are made. Some organizations succeed in spite of their structure because the informal structure is stronger than the formal structure.
- They try to forecast the unanticipated consequences that will result from new structures, which is not always easy. Without doubt, there will be some. Therefore, it makes sense to brainstorm possible consequences and leave some room for later modifications.
- They know that a change in organizational design often results in resistance. It is upsetting to most people to participate in reorganization. Getting employee participation in the process of developing a new design is one way to reduce resistance.

FOR ORGANIZATIONAL ARCHITECTS

- As always in management, balance is important. Some companies go overboard with bureaucracy busting. Organizations need enough bureaucracy to facilitate the work, provide structure, and avoid reinventing the wheel and enough chaos to promote initiative and creativity.[51]
- Organizational architects who are expert at design strive to match the internal organizational structure to the external environment, strategy, environment, technology, size, national culture, and the people and their shared values.
- There is a saying, "When in doubt, reorganize." Experts don't reorganize, however, unless they have undertaken a thorough analysis and are fairly certain that the design issues are really the culprit. Above all, they don't choose a structure simply because it's in fashion.
- When determining a structure, they consider the following design questions:
  - What structure is most likely to support development of required organizational capability?
  - What new roles are required and what are the points of interface among them?
  - How can the design be tested before doing a full-scale implementation?
  - How should others be involved in mapping the design?

- How should others be involved in implementing the design?
- They know that organization structure is but one aspect of effective organizational design. A well-designed organization focuses on complementarity among its strategy (vision, direction, competitive advantage), people practices (staffing, selection, performance feedback), reward systems (goals, metrics, compensation, rewards), and lateral processes (integrative processes, teams, networks).[52]

PERSONAL APPLICATION ASSIGNMENT

In this assignment you are to write about the design of an organization you know well (e.g., workplace, church, volunteer group) by answering the following questions:

1. How would you diagram the formal structure of your organization?

2. How would you describe the communication and coordination among different departments?

3. How would you diagram the informal structure of your organization?

4. How does your organization deal with the differentiation-integration issue?

5. What are the strengths and weaknesses of your organization's design?

6. What improvements could you suggest?

ENDNOTES

1 R. T. Pascale and A. G. Athos, *Art of Japanese Management* (New York: Simon & Schuster, 1981).

2 P. Senge, "The Leader's New Work: Building Learning Organizations," *Sloan Management Review 32*(1) (Fall 1990): 10.

3 J. R. Galbraith, *Designing Organizations* (San Francisco: Jossey-Bass, 1995): 11–17. See also J. R. Galbraith, D. Downey, and A. Kates, *Designing Dynamic Organizations* (New York: AMACOM, 2002).

4 C. Handy, *The Age of Unreason* (London: Hutchinson, 1988).

5 "Dow Jones Sets New Structure and Leadership Team." Available at: http://www.dowjones.com/Pressroom/Press Releases/Other/US/2006/0222_US_DowJones_6022.htm. Accessed 9/25/06.

6 T. Burns and G. M. Stalker, *The Management of Innovation* (London: Tavistock, 1961) was the original source describing organic and mechanistic structures; a few additional descriptors included in the chart are taken from G. Zaltman, R. Duncan, and H. J. Holbeck, *Innovations and Organizations* (New York: Wiley, 1973): 131.

7 The advantages and disadvantages of the functional, divisional, and matrix structures are described in R. B. Duncan, "What Is the Right Organization Structure? Decision Tree Analysis Provides the Answer," *Organizational Dynamics 7*(3) (Winter 1979): 59–80; and R. L. Daft, *Organizational Theory and Design* (Cincinnati, OH: SouthWestern, 1998).

8 Galbraith, *Designing Organizations*: 27.

9 Ibid.

10 Daft, *Organizational Theory and Design*: 218.

11 Galbraith, *Designing Organizations*: 30.

12 C. A. Bartlett and S. Ghoshal, "Matrix Management: Not a Structure, a Frame of Mind," *Harvard Business Review 68*(4) (1990): 45.

13 S. M. Davis and P. R. Lawrence, *Matrix* (Reading, MA: Addison-Wesley, 1977).

14 Daft, *Organizational Theory and Design*: 228. For a discussion of problems associated with matrix structures, see L. Bryan C. Joyce, "The 21st Century Organization," *McKinsey Quarterly 3* (2005): 24–33 and T. Sy and L D'Annunzio. "Challenges and Strategies of Matrix Organizations: Top-Level and Mid-Level Managers," *Human Resource Planning 28*(1) (2005): 39–48.

15 J. R. Galbraith, *Competing with Flexible Lateral Organizations* (Reading, MA: Addison-Wesley, 1994). See also J. R. Galbraith, D. Downey, and A. Kates, *Designing Dynamic Organizations* (New York: AMACOM, 2002).

16 J. A. Byrne, "The Horizontal Corporation," *BusinessWeek 3351* (December 20, 1993): 76–81.

17 Galbraith, *Designing Organizations;* and Daft, *Organizational Theory and Design*: 253.

18 Byrne, "The Horizontal Corporation."

19 E. E. Lawler, III, *The Ultimate Advantage* (San Francisco: Jossey-Bass, 1992): 69–70.

[20] R. E. Miles and C. Snow, "Organizations: New Concepts for New Forms," *California Management Review 28*(3) (1986): 62–73; R. Johnston and P. R. Lawrence, "Beyond Vertical Integration—The Rise of the Value-Adding Partnership," *Harvard Business Review 66*(4) (1988): 94–101; C. C. Snow, R. E. Miles, and H. J. Coleman, Jr., "Managing 21st Century Network Organizations," *Organizational Dynamics 20*(3) (1992): 5–19; see also R. E. Miles, C. C. Snow, J. A. Mathews, G. Miles, and H. J. Coleman, Jr., "Organizing in the Knowledge Age: Anticipating the Cellular Form," *Academy of Management Executive 11*(4) (November 1997): 7–35.

[21] S. R. Clegg, *Modern Organizations* (London: Sage, 1990); J. Mantle, *Benetton—the Family, the Business, and the Brand,* (London: Warner, 2000); T. Waterstone, "The Colour of Money," *Management Today* (April 1999): 48. See also United Colors of Benetton at: www.benetton.com.

[22] R. E. Miles and C. C. Snow, "The New Network Firm: A Spherical Structure Built on a Human Investment Philosophy," *Organizational Dynamics 23*(4) (Spring 1995): 5–18.

[23] Galbraith, *Designing Organizations.*

[24] Ibid.: 130.

[25] Galbraith, Downey, and Kates, *Designing Dynamic Organizations.*

[26] Brady, D. "The Immelt Revolution," *BusinessWeek 3926* (March 28, 2005): 64–73.

[27] A. Lowy and P. Hood, "The Networked Idealist's Advantage," *Strategy and Leadership 33*(3) (May–June, 2005): 4.

[28] Lowy and Hood, "The Networked Idealist's Advantage": 5. For more on open source software, see J. Dedrick and J. West, "Movement Ideology vs. User Pragmatism in the Organizational Adoption of Open Source Software," in K. L. Kraemer and M. Elliott (eds.), *Computerization Movements and Technology Diffusion: From Mainframes to Ubiquitous Computing* (Medford, NJ: Information Today, 2007): in press.

[29] Based on Lowy and Hood, "The Networked Idealist's Advantage": 5-6.

[30] Ibid.: 7.

[31] R. Ashkenas, D. Ulrich, T. Jick, and S. Kerr, *The Boundaryless Organization* (San Francisco: Jossey-Bass, 1995).

[32] Eric Trist as reported in W. G. Bennis et al., *The Planning of Change,* 2nd ed. (New York: Holt, Rinehart and Winston, 1969): 269–81.

[33] P. R. Lawrence and J. W. Lorsch, *Organization and Environment* (Homewood, IL: Irwin, 1969).

[34] J. W. Lorsch, "Introduction to the Structural Design of Organizations" in G. Dalton, P. R. Lawrence, and J. W. Lorsch (eds.), *Organizational Structure and Design* (Homewood, IL: Irwin and Dorsey, 1970): 5.

[35] J. W. Lorsch and P. R. Lawrence, "Environmental Factors and Organizational Integration," in J. W. Lorsch and P. R. Lawrence (eds.), *Organization Planning: Cases and Concepts* (Homewood, IL: Irwin and Dorsey, 1972): 38–48.

[36] J. Champy, "Management Strategies: Form Follows Customers," *Forbes* (March 8, 1999): 130–131.

[37] M. J. Sheeran, *Beyond Majority Rule: Voteless Decisions in the Religious Society of Friends* (Philadelphia Yearly Meeting, 1983).

[38] Galbraith, *Designing Organizations*: 12.

[39] Duncan, "What Is the Right Organization Structure?"

[40] Galbraith, *Designing Organizations.* See also Galbraith, Downey, and Kates, *Designing Dynamic Organizations.*

[41] Daft, *Organizational Theory and Design*: 144.

[42] M. Stevenson, "The Store to End All Stores," *Canadian Business Review 67* (May 1994): 20–29.

[43] T. W. Malone, "Is Empowerment Just a Fad? Control, Decision Making and IT," *Sloan Management Review 38*(2) (Winter 1997): 26.

[44] J. M. Stopford and L. T. Wells, *Strategy and Structure of the Multinational Enterprise* (New York: Basic Books, 1972).

[45] C. A. Bartlett and S. Ghoshal, *Transnational Management* (Boston: Irwin McGraw-Hill, 2000): 13.

[46] Bartlett and Ghoshal, *Transnational Management.* See also C. A. Bartlett and S. Ghoshal, *Managing Across Borders: The Transnational Solution* (Boston: Harvard Business School Press, 2000) and G. Hedlund and D. Rolander, "Action in Hetarchies: New Approaches to Managing the MNC," in C. A. Bartlett, Y. Doz, and G. Hedlund (eds.), *Managing the Global Firm* (New York: Routledge, 1990): 15–46.

[47] M. Chen, *Asian Management Systems: Chinese, Japanese, and Korean Styles of Business* (New York: Routledge, 1995).

[48] R. Lincoln, M. L. Gerlach, and C. L. Ahmadjian, "Keiretsu Networks and Corporate Performance in Japan," *American Sociological Review 61*(1) (1996): 67–88.

[49] S. Yoo and S. Lee, "Management Style and Practice of Korean Chaebols," *California Management Review 24*(4) (1987): 97.

[50] A. Laurent, "The Cultural Diversity of Western Conceptions of Management," *International Studies of Management and Organizations 13*(1–2) (1983): 75–76.

[51] P. S. Adler, "Building Better Bureaucracies," *Academy of Management Executive 13*(4) (November 1999): 36; H. Leavitt, "Why Hierarchies Thrive," *Harvard Business Review 81*(3) (March 2003): 96–102.

[52] J. R. Galbraith, D. Downey, and A. Kates, *Designing Dynamic Organizations* (New York: AMACOM, 2002).

Chapter 22

▲▲▲

MANAGING CHANGE

OBJECTIVES By the end of the chapter, you should be able to:

A. Describe the nature of change.

B. Explain the essential components in the change process.

C. Understand the leader's role in the change process.

D. Define resistance to change and its function.

E. List tactics for dealing with resistance to change.

MAKING CHANGE

Change or die.

What if you were given that choice? For real. What if it weren't just the hyperbolic rhetoric that conflates corporate performance with life and death? Not the overblown exhortations of a rabid boss, or a slick motivational speaker, or a self-dramatizing CEO. We're talking actual life or death now. Your own life or death. What if a well-informed, trusted authority figure said you had to make difficult and enduring changes in the way you think and act? If you didn't, your time would end soon—a lot sooner than it had to. Could you change when change really mattered? When it mattered most?

Yes, you say?

Try again.

Yes?

You're probably deluding yourself.

You wouldn't change.

Don't believe it? You want odds? Here are the odds, the scientifically studied odds: nine to one. That's nine to one against you. How do you like those odds?

This revelation unnerved many people in the audience last November at IBM's "Global Innovation Outlook" conference. The company's top executives had invited the most farsighted thinkers they knew from around the world to come together in New York and propose solutions to some really big problems. They started with the crisis in health care, an industry that consumes an astonishing $1.8 trillion a year in the United States alone, or 15 percent of gross domestic product. A dream team of experts took the stage, and you might have expected them to proclaim that breathtaking advances in science and technology—mapping the human genome and all that—held the long-awaited answers. That's not what they said. They said that the root cause of the health crisis hasn't changed for decades, and the medical establishment still could not figure out what to do about it.

Dr. Raphael "Ray" Levey, founder of the Global Medical Forum, an annual summit meeting of leaders from every constituency in the health system, told the audience, "A relatively small percentage of the population consumes the vast majority of the health-care budget for diseases that are very well known and by and large behavioral." That is, they're sick because of how they choose to live their lives, not because of environmental or genetic factors beyond their control. Continued Levey: "Even as far back as when I was in medical school"—he enrolled at Harvard in 1955—"many articles demonstrated that 80 percent of the health-care budget was consumed by five behavioral issues." Levey didn't bother to name them, but you don't need an MD to guess what he was talking about: too much smoking, drinking, eating, and stress, and not enough exercise.

Then the knockout blow was delivered by Dr. Edward Miller, the dean of the medical school and CEO of the hospital at Johns Hopkins University. He turned the discussion to patients whose heart disease is so severe that they undergo bypass surgery, a traumatic and expensive procedure that can cost more than $100,000 if complications arise. About 600,000 people have bypasses every year in the United States, and 1.3 million heart patients have angioplasties—all at a total cost of around $30 billion. The procedures temporarily relieve chest pains but rarely prevent heart attacks or prolong lives. Around half of the time, the bypass grafts clog up in a few years; the angioplasties, in a few months. The causes of this so-called restenosis are complex. It's sometimes a reaction to the trauma of the surgery itself. But many patients could avoid the return of pain and the need to repeat the surgery—not to mention arrest the course of their disease before it kills them—by switching to healthier lifestyles. Yet very few do. "If you look at people after coronary-artery bypass grafting two years later, 90 percent of them have not changed their lifestyle," Miller said. "And that's been studied over and over and over again. And so we're missing some link in there. Even though they know they have a very bad disease and they know they should change their lifestyle, for whatever reason, they can't."

Changing the behavior of people isn't just the biggest challenge in health care. It's the most important challenge for businesses trying to compete in a turbulent world, says John Kotter, a Harvard Business School professor who has studied dozens of organizations in the midst of upheaval: "The central issue is never strategy, structure, culture, or systems. The core of the matter is always about changing the behavior of people." Those people maybe called on to respond to profound upheavals in marketplace dynamics—the rise of a new global competitor, say, or a shift from a regulated to a deregulated environment—or to a corporate reorganization, merger, or entry into a new business. And as individuals, we may want to change our own styles of work—how we mentor subordinates, for example, or how we react to criticism. Yet, more often than not, we can't.

CEOs are supposedly the prime change agents for their companies, but they're often as resistant to change as anyone—and as prone to backsliding. The most notorious recent example is Michael Eisner. After he nearly died from heart problems, Eisner finally heeded his wife's plea and brought in a high-profile number-two exec, Michael Ovitz, to alleviate the stress of running Disney. But Eisner proved incapable of seeing through the idea, essentially refusing to share any real power with Ovitz from the start.

The conventional wisdom says that crisis is a powerful motivator for change. But severe heart disease is among the most serious of personal crises, and it doesn't motivate—at least not nearly enough. Nor does giving people accurate analyses and factual information about their situations. What works? Why, in general, is change so incredibly difficult for people? What is it about how our brains are wired that resists change so tenaciously? Why do we fight even what we know to be in our own vital interests?

Kotter has hit on a crucial insight. "Behavior change happens mostly by speaking to people's feelings," he says. "This is true even in organizations that are very focused on analysis and quantitative measurement, even among people who think of themselves as smart in an MBA sense. In highly successful change efforts, people find ways to help others see the problems or solutions in ways that influence emotions, not just thought."

Unfortunately, that kind of emotional persuasion isn't taught in business schools, and it doesn't come naturally to the technocrats who run things—the engineers, scientists, lawyers, doctors, accountants, and managers who pride themselves on disciplined, analytical thinking. There's compelling science behind the psychology of change—it draws on discoveries from emerging fields such as cognitive science, linguistics, and neuroscience—but its insights and techniques often seem paradoxical or irrational.

Look again at the case of heart patients. The best minds at Johns Hopkins and the Global Medical Forum might not know how to get them to change, but someone does: Dr. Dean Ornish, a professor of medicine at the University of California at San Francisco and founder of the Preventative Medicine Research Institute, in Sausalito, California. Ornish, like Kotter, realizes the importance of going beyond the facts. "Providing health information is important but not always sufficient," he says. "We also need to bring in the psychological, emotional, and spiritual dimensions that are so often ignored." Ornish published studies in leading peer-reviewed scientific journals, showing that his holistic program, focused around a vegetarian diet with less than 10 percent of the calories from fat, can actually reverse heart disease without surgery or drugs. Still, the medical establishment remained skeptical that people could sustain the lifestyle changes. In 1993, Ornish persuaded Mutual of Omaha to pay for a trial. Researchers took 333 patients with severely clogged arteries. They helped them quit smoking and go on Ornish's diet. The patients attended twice-weekly group support sessions led by a psychologist and took instruction in meditation, relaxation, yoga, and aerobic exercise. The program lasted for only a year. But after three years, the study found, 77 percent of the patients had stuck with their lifestyle changes—and safely avoided the bypass or angioplasty surgeries that they were eligible for under their insurance coverage. And Mutual of Omaha saved around $30,000 per patient.

FRAMING CHANGE

Why does the Ornish program succeed while the conventional approach has failed? For starters, Ornish recasts the reasons for change. Doctors had been trying to motivate patients mainly with the fear of death, he says, and that simply wasn't working. For a few weeks after a heart attack, patients were scared enough to do whatever their doctors said. But death was just too frightening to think about, so their denial would return, and they'd go back to their old ways.

The patients lived the way they did as a day-to-day strategy for coping with their emotional troubles. "Telling people who are lonely and depressed that they're going to live longer if they quit smoking or change their diet and lifestyle is not that motivating," Ornish says. "Who wants to live longer when you're in chronic emotional pain?"

So instead of trying to motivate them with the "fear of dying," Ornish reframes the issue. He inspires a new vision of the "joy of living"—convincing them they can feel better, not just live longer. That means enjoying the things that make daily life pleasurable, like making love or even taking long walks without the pain caused by their disease. "Joy is a more powerful motivator than fear," he says.

Pioneering research in cognitive science and linguistics has pointed to the paramount importance of framing. George Lakoff, a professor of those two disciplines at the University of California at Berkeley, defines frames as the "mental structures that shape the way we see the world." Lakoff says that frames are part of the "cognitive unconscious," but the way we know what our frames are, or evoke new ones, springs from language. For example, we typically think of a company as being like an army—everyone has a rank and a codified role in a hierarchical chain of command with orders coming down from high to low. Of course, that's only one way of organizing a group effort. If we had the frame of the company as a family or a commune, people would know very different ways of working together.

The big challenge in trying to change how people think is that their minds rely on frames, not facts. "Neuroscience tells us that each of the concepts we have—the long-term concepts that structure how we think—is instantiated in the synapses of the brain," Lakoff says. "Concepts are not things that can be changed just by someone telling us a fact. We may be presented with facts, but for us to make sense of them, they have to fit what is already in the synapses of the brain. Otherwise, facts go in and then they go right back out. They are not heard, or they are not accepted as facts, or they mystify us: Why would anyone have said that? Then we label the fact as irrational, crazy, or stupid." Lakoff says that's one reason why political conservatives and liberals each think that the other side is nuts. They don't understand each other because their brains are working within different frames.

The frame that dominates our thinking about how work should be organized—the military chain-of-command model—is extremely hard to break. When new employees start at W.L. Gore & Associates, the maker of Gore-Tex fabrics, they often refuse to believe that the company doesn't have a hierarchy with job titles and bosses. It just doesn't fit their frame. They can't accept it. It usually takes at least several months for new hires to begin to understand Gore's reframed notion of the workplace, which relies on self-directed employees making their own choices about joining one another in egalitarian small teams.

Getting people to exchange one frame for another is tough even when you're working one-on-one, but it's especially hard to do for large groups of people. Howard Gardner, a cognitive scientist, MacArthur Fellow "genius" award winner, and professor at Harvard's Graduate School of Education, has looked at what works most effectively for heads of state and corporate CEOs. "When one is addressing a diverse or heterogeneous audience," he says, "the story must be simple, easy to identify with, emotionally resonant, and evocative of positive experiences."

In Louis V. Gerstner Jr.'s successful turnaround of IBM in the 1990s, he learned the surprising importance of this kind of emotional persuasion. When he took over as CEO, Gerstner was fixated on what had worked for him throughout his career as a McKinsey & Co. consultant: cool-headed analysis and strategy. He thought he could revive the company through maneuvers such as selling assets and cutting costs. He quickly found that those tools weren't nearly enough. He needed to transform the entrenched corporate culture, which had become hidebound and overly bureaucratic. That meant changing the attitudes and behaviors of hundreds of thousands of employees. In his memoir, Gerstner writes that he realized he needed to make a powerful emotional appeal to them, to "shake them out of their depressed stupor, remind them of who they were—you're IBM, damn it!" Rather than sitting in a corner office negotiating deals and analyzing spreadsheets, he needed to convey passion through thousands of hours of personal appearances. Gerstner, who's often brittle and imperious in private, nonetheless responded admirably to the challenge. He proved to be an engaging and emotional public speaker when he took his campaign to his huge workforce.

Steve Jobs's turnaround at Apple shows the impact of reframing and telling a new narrative that's simple, positive, and emotional. When he returned to the company after a long exile, he recast its image among employees and customers alike from a marginalized player vanquished in the battle for market share to the home of a small but enviable elite: the creative innovators who dared to "Think different."

When leaders are addressing a small group of people who have a similar mind-set and shared values, the reframed message can be more nuanced and complex, Harvard's Gardner says. But it still needs to be positive, inspiring, and emotionally resonant. A good example is how chairman and publisher Arthur Sulzberger Jr. rescued *The New York Times* from crisis. Former editor Howell Raines had alienated much of the newsroom's staff, undermining its communal spirit with a new culture of favoritism. Raines fell when a star reporter he had shielded from criticism was exposed for fabricating news stories. The scandal threatened the famed paper's credibility. Gardner says that Sulzberger successfully reframed the narrative this way: We are a great newspaper. We temporarily went astray and risked sacrificing the community spirit that made this an outstanding place to work. We can retain our excellence and regain our sense of community by admitting our errors, making sure that they don't happen again, and being a more transparent and self-reflecting organization. To achieve these goals, Sulzberger replaced Raines with a new top editor, Bill Keller—a respected veteran who reflected the lost communal culture—and he appointed a "public editor" to critique the paper in an unedited column. Now, Gardner says, "the *Times* is a much happier place and the news coverage and journalistic empire are in reasonable shape."

RADICAL CHANGE

Reframing alone isn't enough, of course. That's where Dr. Ornish's other astonishing insight comes in. Paradoxically, he found that radical, sweeping, comprehensive changes are often easier for people than small, incremental ones. For example, he says that people who make moderate changes in their diets get the worst of both worlds: They feel deprived and hungry because they aren't eating everything they want, but they aren't making big enough changes to quickly see an improvement in how they feel, or in measurements such as weight, blood pressure, and cholesterol. But the heart patients who went on Ornish's tough, radical program saw quick, dramatic results, reporting a 91 percent decrease in frequency of chest pain in the first month. "These rapid improvements are a powerful motivator," he says. "When people who have had so much chest pain that they can't work, or make love, or even walk across the street without intense suffering find that they are able to do all of those things without pain in only a few weeks, then they often say, 'These are choices worth making.'"

Although it's astonishing that most patients in Ornish's demanding program stick with it, studies show that two-thirds of patients who are prescribed statin drugs (which are highly effective at cutting cholesterol) stop taking them within one year. What could possibly be a smaller or easier lifestyle change than popping a pill every day? But Ornish says patients stop taking the drug because it doesn't actually make them feel any better. It doesn't deal with causes of high cholesterol, such as obesity, that make people feel unhealthy. The paradox holds that big changes are easier than small ones.

Research shows that this idea applies to the business realm as well. Bain & Co., the management consulting firm, studied 21 recent corporate transformations and found that most were "substantially completed" in only two years or less while none took more than three years. The means were drastic: In almost every case, the CEOs fired most of the top management. Almost always, the companies enjoyed quick, tangible results, and their stock prices rose 250 percent a year on average as they revived.

IBM's turnaround hinged on a radical shift in focus from selling computer hardware to providing "services," which meant helping customers build and run their information-technology operations. This required a momentous cultural switch—IBMers would have to recommend that a client buy from competitors such as Hewlett-Packard and Microsoft when it was in the client's interest. But the radical shift worked: Services have grown into IBM's core business and the key to its success.

Of course, radical change often isn't possible in business situations. Still, it's always important to identify, achieve, and celebrate some quick, positive results for the vital emotional lifts that they provide. Harvard's Kotter believes in the importance of "short-term wins" for companies, meaning "victories that nourish faith in the change effort, emotionally reward the hard workers, keep the critics at bay, and build momentum. Without sufficient wins that are visible, timely, unambiguous, and meaningful to others, change efforts invariably run into serious problems."

SUPPORTING CHANGE

Even when leaders have refrained the issues brilliantly, it's still vital to give people the multifaceted support they need. That's a big reason why 90 percent of heart patients can't change their lifestyles but 77 percent of Ornish's patients could—because he buttressed them with weekly support groups with other patients, as well as attention from dieticians, psychologists, nurses, and yoga and meditation instructors.

Xerox's executives learned this lesson well. Four years ago, when the company was in crisis, they came up with a new vision that required salespeople to change the way they had always worked. "Their whole careers, salespeople had done one thing," says James Firestone, president of Xerox North America, who leads a sales force of 5,400. "They would knock on doors, look for copiers, see how old they were, and sell a refresh. They knew how to do that." The salespeople had such predictable routines that they could plan their days, weeks, even years. It was comforting. But it just wasn't succeeding any longer.

Under the new strategy, the salespeople were supposed to really engage with customers so they could understand the complexities of how their offices operated and find opportunities to sell other products, such as scanners and printers. Maybe they would find that the customer actually needed fewer machines that could do more than the old ones had. Learning about the client's needs meant that the sales reps had to take a lot more time and talk to more people about broader issues. It undermined the cozy predictability of their routines. The reps became anxious, Firestone recalls. "They'd say, 'I know how to sell and make a living the old way, but not the new way.'"

Their anxiety was compounded by the fact that Xerox lagged in giving them the support they needed. It often took a couple of months before the salespeople received their scheduled training in the new approach. And it took two years before the company changed its incentive pay system to fit better with the new model, in which the reps had to invest a lot more time and effort before they signed deals. Eventually, though, the change effort, by expanding the sales focus to a larger range of products, helped Xerox avoid bankruptcy and return to profitability. "People need a sense of confidence that the processes will be aligned internally," Firestone says. "For large companies, this is where change usually fails." Even if change starts at the top, it can easily die somewhere in the middle. That's why Xerox now holds "alignment workshops" that ask middle managers—the people who make processes work—to outline the ways its systems could inhibit its agendas for change.

THIS IS YOUR BRAIN ON CHANGE

Are most of us like the fearful copier salespeople who dread disruption to their routines? Neuroscience, a field that has exploded with insight, has a lot more to say about changing people's behavior—and its findings are guardedly optimistic. Scientists used to believe that the brain became "hardwired" early in life and couldn't change later on. Now researchers such as Dr. Michael Merzenich, a professor at the University of California at San Francisco, say that the brain's ability to change—its "plasticity"—is lifelong. If we can change, then why don't we? Merzenich has perspective on the issue because he's not only a leading neuroscientist but also an entrepreneur, the founder of two Bay Area start-ups. Both use PC software to train people to overcome mental disabilities or diseases: Scientific Learning Corp. focuses on children who have trouble learning to read, and Posit Science Corp. is working on ways to prevent, stop, or reverse cognitive decline in older adults.

Merzenich starts by talking about rats. You can train a rat to have a new skill. The rat solves a puzzle, and you give it a food reward. After 100 times, the rat can solve the puzzle flawlessly. After 200 times, it can remember how to solve it for nearly its lifetime. The rat has developed a habit. It can perform the task automatically because its brain has changed. Similarly, a person has thousands of habits—such as how to use a pen—that drive lasting changes in the brain. For highly trained specialists, such as professional musicians, the changes actually show up on MRI scans. Flute players, for instance, have especially large representations in their brains in the areas that control the fingers, tongue, and lips, Merzenich says. "They've distorted their brains."

Businesspeople, like flutists, are highly trained specialists, and they've distorted their brains, too. An older executive "has powers that a young person walking in the door doesn't have," says Merzenich. He has lots of specialized skills and abilities. A specialist is a hard thing to create, and is valuable for a corporation, obviously, but specialization also instills an inherent "rigidity." The cumulative weight of experience makes it harder to change.

How, then, to overcome these factors? Merzenich says the key is keeping up the brain's machinery for learning. "When you're young, almost everything you do is behavior-based learning—it's an incredibly powerful, plastic period," he says. "What happens that becomes stultifying is you stop learning and you stop the machinery, so it starts dying." Unless you work on it, brain fitness often begins declining at around age 30 for men, a bit later for women. "People mistake being active for continuous learning," Merzenich says. "The machinery is only activated by learning. People think they're leading an interesting life when they haven't learned anything in 20 or 30 years. My suggestion is learn Spanish or the oboe."

Meanwhile, the leaders of a company need "a business strategy for continuous mental rejuvenation and new learning," he says. Posit Science has a "fifth-day strategy," meaning that everyone spends one day a week working in a different discipline. Software engineers try their hand at marketing. Designers get involved in business functions. "Everyone needs a new project instead of always being in a bin," Merzenich says. "A fifth-day strategy doesn't sacrifice your core ability but keeps you rejuvenated. In a company, you have to worry about rejuvenation at every level. So ideally you deliberately construct new challenges. For every individual, you need complex new learning. Innovation comes about when people are enabled to use their full brains and intelligence instead of being put in boxes and controlled."

What happens if you don't work at mental rejuvenation? Merzenich says that people who live to 85 have a 50-50 chance of being senile. Although the issue for heart patients is "change or die," the issue for everyone is "change or lose your mind." Mastering the ability to change isn't just a crucial strategy for business. It's a necessity for health. And it's possibly the one thing that's most worth learning.

Five Myths About Changing Behavior

1. MYTH Crisis is a powerful impetus for change

   REALITY Ninety percent of patients who've had coronary bypasses don't sustain changes in the unhealthy lifestyles that worsen their severe heart disease and greatly threaten their lives.

2. MYTH Change is motivated by fear

   REALITY It's too easy for people to go into denial of the bad things that might happen to them. Compelling, positive visions of the future are a much stronger inspiration for change.

3. MYTH The facts will set us free

   REALITY Our thinking is guided by narratives, not facts. When a fact doesn't fit our conceptual "frames"—the metaphors we use to make sense of the world—we reject it. Also, change is inspired best by emotional appeals rather than factual statements.

4. MYTH Small, gradual changes are always easier to make and sustain

   REALITY Radical, sweeping changes are often easier because they quickly yield benefits.

5. MYTH we can't change because our brains become "hardwired" early in life

   REALITY Our brains have extraordinary "plasticity," meaning that we can continue learning complex new things throughout our lives—assuming we remain truly active and engaged.

Source: A. Deutschman, "Making Change," *Fast Company,* (May 2005): 52–59.

Rate Your Readiness to Change

Executives say that as many as two-thirds of total quality management efforts flop. Michael Hammer and James Champy, authors of the best-selling *Reengineering the Corporation*, estimate that well over half the radical change programs they advocate fade into similar oblivion. Take a bittersweet tour of your own company's failed attempts to shape up: Walk down to the galley and check out the slogans on the mugs on the shelf above the coffeemaker—"No. 1 in '01," "A team's for you in '02," "Qual-i-tee in '03," and this year's "Try once more in '04." They're almost enough to make you feel young again, like songs from the fifties.

If it's any comfort, the problem isn't new. According to the very first management consultant, Niccolo Machiavelli, "There is nothing more difficult to take in hand, more perilous to conduct, or more uncertain in its success than to take the lead in the introduction of a new order of things." Yet some companies do take to change readily, if not always painlessly. Think of Motorola, which grabbed TQM in a bear hug early in the 1980s and hasn't let go, continuously raising its standards and its profits. Or General Electric, which uses a set of management tools—maps of its processes, the study of other companies' best practices, and its bureaucracy-subverting Work Out program—to build a machine that churns out change the way a turbine makes electricity.

Why does one organization thrive on change while another sulks like a teenager? For Andrea Sodano, who holds a Ph.D. in psychology, the question is of more than academic interest. A consultant at Symmetrix, a firm in Lexington, Massachusetts, that specializes in reengineering, Sodano fretted as she saw some jobs go smoothly while others bogged down. Says her boss, Symmetrix CEO George Bennett: "Some places, we've gone in with our best people and broken our picks. That's a waste of our resources and those of our clients."

People and culture—the human systems of a company—are what make or break any change initiative. Last year the Wyatt Co., an actuarial and human resources consulting firm in Washington, DC, surveyed executives of 531 companies that had restructured their operations. It found that the most-often-cited barriers to change were employee resistance and "dysfunctional corporate culture." A dysfunctional culture, says Wyatt's John Parkington, is one whose shared values and behavior are at odds with its long-term health: For example, a high-tech company might celebrate individual star performers even though teamwork produces the innovation on which its future depends.

Sodano and several colleagues at Symmetrix have studied signs of change readiness and resistance. They looked for specific characteristics that tend to keep things in place and fuel resistance to changing behavior, as well as the common traits of companies that adopt new business practices successfully.

The quiz that follows is an adaptation of their work. Its first aim is to assess your company's or your business unit's versatility. The higher you score, the better able you are to change when change is needed. Conversely, says Bennett, "trying to reengineer a company that scores low is like sending troops into battle against superior forces." The old culture will rise up and overwhelm you.

The quiz serves a second, equally important purpose: Because it reveals likely causes of failure, it creates an agenda, a list of ways to make a big restructuring or reengineering more likely to take. Says Sodano: "The problem with the 'soft side' of management is getting good data, numbers that business people are willing to accept. This quiz gives you specifics." Last autumn, Sodano used the quiz with a British chemical company, a potential client. Afterward, the company's reengineering head realized that she needed more public support from top management if the project was to succeed, and she used the findings to get it.

Now to see how you measure up, pull out your pen or pencil. Ready? Begin.

A QUIZ

The left-hand column lists 17 key elements of change readiness. Rate your organization on each item. Give three points for a high ranking ("We're good at this; I'm confident of our skills here"); two for medium score ("We're spotty here; we could use improvement or more experience"); and one point for a low score ("We've had problems with this; this is new to our organization"). Be honest. Don't trust only your own perspective; ask others in the organization, at all levels, to rate the company too. The consultants at Symmetrix believe—no surprise—it helps to have an outsider do the assessment with you.

CATEGORY	SCORE

Sponsorship

The sponsor of change is not necessarily its day-to-day leader; he or she is the visionary, chief cheerleader, and bill payer—the person with the power to help the team change when it meets resistance. Give three points—change will be easier—if sponsorship comes at a senior level; for example, CEO, COO, or the head of an autonomous business unit. Weakest sponsors: midlevel executives or staff officers.

Leadership

This means the day-to-day leadership—the people who call the meetings, set the goals, work till midnight. Successful change is more likely if leadership is high level, has "ownership" (that is, direct responsibility for what's to be changed) and has clear business results in mind. Low-level leadership, or leadership that is not well connected throughout the organization (across departments) or that comes from the staff, is less likely to succeed and should be scored low.

Motivation

High points for a strong sense of urgency from senior management, which is shared by the rest of the company, and for a corporate culture that already emphasizes continuous improvement. Negative: tradition-bound managers and workers, many of whom have been in their jobs for more than 15 years; a conservative culture that discourages risk taking.

Direction

Does senior management strongly believe that the future should look different from the present? How clear is management's picture of the future? Can management mobilize all relevant parties—employees, the board, customers, etc.—for action? High points for positive answers to those questions. If senior management thinks only minor change is needed, the likely outcome is no change at all; score yourself low.

Measurements

Or in consultant-speak, "metrics." Three points if you already use performance measures of the sort encouraged by total quality management (defect rates, time to market, etc.) and if these express the economics of the business. Two points if some measures exist but compensation and reward systems do not explicitly reinforce them. If you don't have measures in place or don't know what we're talking about, one point.

Organizational Context

How does the change effort connect to other major goings-on in the organization? (For example: Does it dovetail with a continuing total quality management process? Does it fit with strategic actions such as acquisitions or new product lines?) Trouble lies ahead for a change effort that is isolated or if there are multiple change efforts whose relationships are not linked strategically.

Processes/Functions

Major changes almost invariably require redesigning business processes that cut across functions such as purchasing, accounts payable, or marketing. If functional executives are rigidly turf conscious, change will be difficult. Give yourself more points the more willing they—and the organization as a whole—are to change critical processes and sacrifice perks or power for the good of the group.

Competitor Benchmarking

Whether you are a leader in your industry or a laggard, give yourself points for a continuing program that objectively compares your company's performance with that of competitors and systematically examines changes in your market. Give yourself one point if knowledge of competitors' abilities is primarily anecdotal—what salesmen say at the bar.

Customer Focus

The more everyone in the company is imbued with knowledge of customers, the more likely that the organization can agree to change to serve them better. Three points if everyone in the work force knows who his or her customers are, knows their needs, and has had direct contact with them. Take away points if that knowledge is confined to pockets of the organization (sales and marketing, senior executives).

Rewards

Change is easier if managers and employees are rewarded for taking risks, being innovative, and looking for new solutions. Team-based rewards are better than rewards based solely on individual achievement. Reduce points if your company, like most, rewards continuity over change. If managers become heroes for making budget, they won't take risks even if you say you want them to. Also: If employees believe failure will be punished, reduce points.

Organization Structure

The best situation is a flexible organization with little churn—that is, reorganizations are rare and well received. Score yourself lower if you have a rigid structure that has been unchanged for more than five years or has undergone frequent reorganization with little success; that may signal a cynical company culture that fights change by waiting it out.

Communication

A company will adapt to change most readily if it has many means of two-way communication that reach all levels of the organization and that all employees use and understand. If communications media are few, often trashed unread, and almost exclusively one-way and top-down, change will be more difficult.

Organizational Hierarchy

The fewer levels of hierarchy and the fewer employee grade levels, the more likely an effort to change will succeed. A thick impasto of middle management and staff not only slows decision making but also creates large numbers of people with the power to block change.

Prior Experience with Change

Score three if the organization has successfully implemented major changes in the recent past. Score one if there is no prior experience with major change or if change efforts failed or left a legacy of anger or resentment. Most companies will score two, acknowledging equivocal success in previous attempts to change.

Morale

Change is easier if employees enjoy working in the organization and the level of individual responsibility is high. Signs of unreadiness to change: low team spirit, little voluntary extra effort, and mistrust. Look for two types of mistrust: between management and employees, and between or among departments.

Innovation

Best situation: The company is always experimenting; new ideas are implemented with seemingly little effort; employees work across internal boundaries without much trouble. Bad signs: lots of red tape, multiple signoffs required before new ideas are tried; employees must go through channels and are discouraged from working with colleagues from other departments or divisions.

Decision Making

Rate yourself high if decisions are made quickly, taking into account a wide variety of suggestions; it is clear where decisions are made. Give yourself a low grade if decisions come slowly and are made by a mysterious "them"; there is a lot of conflict during the process, and confusion and finger pointing after decisions are announced.

TOTAL SCORE

If Your Score Is

41–51: Implementing change is most likely to succeed. Focus resources on lagging factors (your ones and twos) to accelerate the process.

28–40: Change is possible but may be difficult, especially if you have low scores in the first seven readiness dimensions. Bring those up to speed before attempting to implement large-scale change.

17–27: Implementing change will be virtually impossible without a precipitating catastrophe. Focus instead on (1) building change readiness in the dimensions above and (2) effecting change through skunkworks or pilot programs separate from the organization at large.

Source: T. A. Stewart, "Rate Your Readiness to Change," *Fortune 129*(3) (February 7, 1994): 106–108.

CLASS PREPARATION

A. Read "Making Change" and evaluate your organization in "Rate Your Readiness to Change."

B. Please answer the following questions:

   1. Think back on a time when a major change effort took place within your organization or group. What was the change? What preceded it? What happened when the change occurred? How did people react to it? Was it successful? Why or why not? What could have been done to make it more successful?

   2. What theories do you have about organizational change? What factors might determine success or failure?

   3. What skills are necessary for instituting change?

C. What do you want to learn about organizational change and development?

D. While reading this chapter, make a list of the cues that you will look for with regard to organizational change.

THE KNOWLEDGE BASE

How are you supposed to change the tires on a car when it's going 60 miles per hour?
Epitaph of a change agent

Change is a way of life in today's business environment, and the ability to manage change is a key factor in organizational survival. Foreign competition, deregulation, and rapid technological advances are some of the common triggers for change in business. As a result, organizations are merging, restructuring, reengineering, revitalizing, and rethinking how they do business in an effort to keep pace with the changes they confront. Therefore, managers and employees alike need to understand the nature of organizational change.

In spite of environmental pressures for change and the amount of resources devoted to change efforts, they are not always successful. Large organizations are notoriously hard to change. There are several common roadblocks to organizational change.[1]

- Changes often upset the political system in organizations and come into conflict with the vested interests of people who prefer the status quo.
- Managers are limited in their power to make changes in part because complex systems resist change.
- Changes are hard to sustain; some innovations succeed initially, but conditions eventually revert to their previous state.
- What works in one part of an organization cannot always be transferred successfully to another area, so standardized change efforts may not be possible.
- Sometimes when organizations most need to change, they may lack the resources (will, energy, money, trust, slack time) to do so.
- In some U.S. companies, top management looks for quick fixes and suffers from a short attention span. Change programs are not given time to work before the next change fad comes along. This results in employee cynicism about management's commitment to change.

THE NATURE OF CHANGE

Organizational change is usually categorized in terms of magnitude as either incremental or transformative. *Incremental change, also known as first-order change, is linear, continuous, and targeted at fixing or modifying problems or procedures. Transformative change, also called second-order change or gamma change, modifies the fundamental structure, systems, orientation, and strategies of the organization.*[2] Transformative change is radical and tends to be multi-dimensional and multilevel. It involves discontinuous shifts in mental or organizational frameworks.[3] Whereas incremental change is analogous to rearranging the furniture in a room and making it more comfortable, transformative change means asking whether this is even the room or floor where we should be.[4] Organizational transformation implies not only new behaviors but also new ways of perceiving and thinking by members. The current trend toward organizational learning is based on a model of continuous change and adaptation.

Change is usually neither easy nor fast, except when there exists a strong consensus about what the organization needs to change and a pent-up demand for change among employees. Although a successful change effort generally requires top-management support, that alone is not sufficient to change a large system. There must be a critical mass of people who support the change. *Critical mass is defined as the smallest number of people and/or groups who must be committed to a change for it to occur.* Successful changes often begin at the periphery of the organization with dedicated general managers who focus energy on work improvements rather than abstract principles such as participation or organizational culture.[5] Their success then moves to the core of the organization as other units imitate their example.

Another requirement for successful change efforts is a sufficient level of trust within the organization so that people are willing to give up the known for the unknown and question some of their basic assumptions. Change almost always requires reexamining and rethinking the assumptions people hold about the environment, the way the organization functions, and their working relationship with other people. People often undergo a mourning period before they can let go of previous ways of behaving, psychological contracts, conceptions of their organization, and relationships. Change requires both new behaviors and organizational learning, which must eventually be institutionalized so that the change can endure. Previously, it was assumed that changes in attitudes led to changes in individual behavior. In reality, the opposite is more likely to occur. Behavior is shaped by the roles people are expected to play within organizations. Therefore, new roles, responsibilities, and relationships force people to develop new attitudes and behaviors.[6]

The study of human behavior reveals that people do not easily change long-term behaviors. Anyone who has tried to give up a cherished "bad habit" understands that behavioral change can be tricky, if not downright difficult or impossible. Lewin described the process of change as unfreezing, moving, and refreezing.[7] Unfreezing is accompanied by stress, tension, and a strong felt need for change. The moving stage refers to relinquishing old ways of behavior and testing out new behaviors, values, and attitudes that have usually been proposed by a respected source. Refreezing occurs when the new behavior is either reinforced, internalized, and institutionalized, or rejected and abandoned. One study of multinational organizations expands this framework to describe the sequence as follows: *incubation* (questioning the status quo), *variety generation* (middle-up experimentation) leading to *power shifts* (change in the leadership structure), and then the process of *refocusing*.[8] Ghoshal and Bartlett observed the following sequential but overlapping process— *simplification, integration,* and *regeneration*—in successful large-scale transformations at GE, ABB, Lufthansa, Motorola, and AT&T. Simplification targets a change such as GE's "being number one or two in the industry," which clarifies the strategy. The integration phase involves the "software," bringing people together with shared values such as Welch's focus at GE on interunit collaboration and sharing best practices. The last phase, regeneration, attempts to build an organization capable of renewing itself. This was the purpose of Welch's "boundarylessness" push at GE.[9]

There are some aspects of companies that should rarely be changed, such as their core values. Figuring out what should not change is just as important as figuring out what to change.[10] Furthermore, too much simultaneous change is disturbing. There has to be some stability for people to hang on to so that they can cope with the seeming chaos of large complex changes.[11]

Based on the preceding lessons, it should be obvious that change is a process rather than an event or a managerial edict or order. Furthermore, it is a process that is somewhat unpredictable since it is difficult to foresee how all the actors and interconnected parts of a system will react. Once we start tweaking a system, there are usually unanticipated consequences that require some modification in the change plans. Although there may always be a few surprises in a change effort, managers can avoid many problems if they are careful not to move immediately from a superficial diagnosis of a problem to the action steps. There will be more effective results and fewer tensions if a more thorough diagnosis is made of the situation to be changed and if the change process is managed systematically.

THE CHANGE PROCESS

There is no exact blueprint for change that works in every situation, but the essential components in this sequential process are described next and illustrated in Exhibit 22–1. As with most models of behavior, the steps may blur into one another, but the articulation and recognition of each step can help steer a clearer course through a change effort.

Determining the Need for Change

The first step is to determine the organization's readiness for change. Is a change really necessary and who perceives this need? Changes have a greater likelihood of success when people with power believe the status quo is no longer good enough and when there is a critical mass that supports the change.

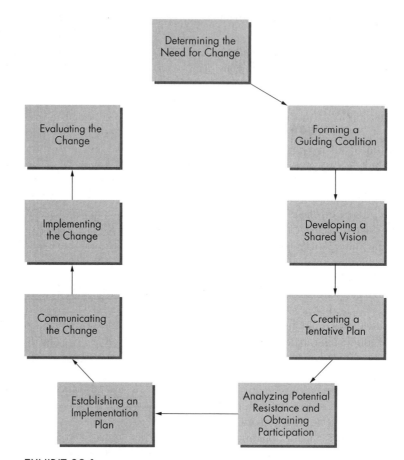

EXHIBIT 22-1 **Steps in the Change Process**

In this stage, potential change agents consider the costs and whether conditions are favorable for change. This formula helps change agents determine whether it's worthwhile to "rock the boat."[12]

$$C = (D \times S \times P) > X$$

where:

C = change

D = dissatisfaction with the current state of affairs or status quo

S = an identifiable and desired end state

P = a practical plan for achieving the desired end state

X = the cost of change to the organization

As Beckhard states: "For change to be possible and for commitment to occur, there has to be enough dissatisfaction with the current state of affairs to mobilize energy toward change. There also has to be some fairly clear conception of what the state of affairs would be if and when the change were successful. Of course, a desired state needs to be consistent with the values and priorities of the client system. There also needs to be some client awareness of practical first steps or starting points toward the desired state."[13]

It is possible to increase the level of dissatisfaction with the status quo by sharing productivity information about competitors with employees or by survey-feedback techniques that present employees with the aggregated results of their individual opinions. In this manner, more people perceive the need for change and form the necessary critical mass. However, Kotter and Cohen argue that touching people's emotions, rather than appealing to their logic, creates a greater sense of urgency and commitment to the change.[14] Showing a video of dissatisfied customers or assigning employees to work at a supplier's company gives employees a closer look at the results and costs of the status quo. These experiences involve emotions in a way that a PowerPoint graph cannot.

Diagnosing the situation carefully is another way to ascertain whether there is a real need for change. As any consultant can tell you, it is not uncommon for managers to attribute organizational problems to the wrong source. For example, a hospital administrator received complaints about customer service in the emergency room. He identified the problem as poor communication skills among the nurses and hired a consultant to train them. In the beginning of the seminar, she asked the nurses what they hoped to get out of the training. They erupted and quickly let her know that, in their opinion, nothing was wrong with their communication skills—the real problem was understaffing and poor management. Managers (and consultants) have to poke around and talk to several people at different levels to find the root causes of problems. Otherwise, changes may not address the real issues. Furthermore, diagnosis should be a collaborative effort involving as many people as possible. When people participate in data gathering and diagnosis, they have greater ownership of the results and more commitment to making change happen.

Lewin saw change as a dynamic balance of forces working in opposite directions.[15] He devised the *"force field analysis," which assigns pressures for change and resistance to change to opposite sides of an equilibrium state*. For example, several years back, Ford found itself pressured by foreign competition, declining market share, and stakeholder complaints to change the company. These were some of the forces that promoted change at that time. However, within Ford there were also forces that inhibited change such as an entrenched adversarial union-management relationship, and both managers and workers who were accustomed to a way of working that was less efficient and innovative than much of their competition. Eventually a critical mass of employees became convinced of the need to change in order to keep their jobs. The pressures for change were stronger than the resistance, allowing the company to make major innovations in a fairly short period of time. Today Ford faces pressures for change that include high gas prices, global warming, strong competition, and legacy costs. Identifying the major forces for and against change is a useful aid in diagnosing the situation. Managers have three choices: to increase the strength of a pressure(s) to change, to decrease or neutralize the strength of a resistance(s) to change, or to try to convert a resistance into a pressure for change. The key point here is the conception of change as a dynamic process in which a state of equilibrium is reached.

Many change efforts utilize the principle of creative tension.[16] *Creative tension results from perceiving the gap between the ideal situation (the organization's vision) and an honest appraisal of its current reality*. The natural tension that results from the gap between the vision and current reality can be resolved by either changing the vision to reflect reality or by improving current conditions so they match the vision. Most change efforts focus on the latter; understanding the gap often motivates people to change the current reality. The nominal group technique found in Chapter 16 is often used in change efforts to diagnose the vision and the reality and then determine how to close the gap.

The capacity to envision a feasible and powerful future is one of the ways a single person can influence a large organization. Larry Bossidy, Honeywell International's Chairman and CEO, is a believer in the "burning platform" theory of change. When the foreman on an oil rig orders the workers to jump in the water, they won't obey (fear of sharks, etc.) until they see the actual flames burning the platform. He provides a clear explanation of how a global manager can be a catalyst for change.

> *The leader's job is to help everyone see that the platform is burning, whether the flames are apparent or not. The process of change begins when people decide to take the flames seriously and manage by fact, and that means a brutal understanding of reality. You need to find out what the reality is so that you know what needs changing. I traveled all over the company with the same message and the same charts, over and over. Here's what I think is*

good about us. Here's what I'm worried about. Here's what we have to do about it. And if we don't fix the base problem, none of us is going to be around. You can keep it simple: we're spending more than we're taking in. If you do that at home, there will be a day of reckoning." [17]

In contrast, some organizations suffer from the Boiled Frog Phenomenon.[18] A frog placed in a pan of cold water fails to notice that the water temperature is gradually rising. The frog continues to sit in the pan and ultimately boils to death. Don't go home and experiment with your own frog, but do remember that organizations that don't pay close attention to environmental changes end up in hot water.

Some leaders raise the heat in their organizations by creating a sense of urgency. Peter Lewis, CEO of Progressive Insurance, paid attention to the finding that customers who bought his high-risk insurance were unhappy with high premiums. Convincing his employees that "our customers actually hate us," they significantly reduced the time it took to process claims and improved customer service.[19] Progressive was not doing poorly before this "crisis," but Lewis wanted to counteract complacency and spur his company on to greater improvements.

Like boiled frogs, successful companies can easily become complacent. John Kotter suggests these methods for turning up the heat.[20]

- Create a crisis by allowing a financial loss to occur or an error to blow up.
- Eliminate obvious examples of excess such as corporate jet fleets and gourmet dining rooms (that lull people into seeing only success).
- Set targets such as income, productivity, and cycle time so high that they can't be reached by doing business as usual.
- Share more information about customer satisfaction and financial performance with employees.
- Insist that people talk regularly to unsatisfied customers, unhappy suppliers, and disgruntled shareholders.
- Put more honest discussions of the firm's problems in company newspapers and management speeches. Stop senior management happy talk!

Not all change efforts are problem driven. As we discussed in the chapter on problem solving, appreciative inquiry, a change approach developed by David Cooperrider, focuses on "the best of what is."[21] Members identify when their organization is working at its best, create a vision to reflect that state, and work toward making the vision an even greater reality.

Forming a Guiding Coalition

Change efforts are more likely to be successful with a powerful leadership coalition at the helm.[22] Coalition members should be carefully chosen for characteristics such as expertise, good relationships, powerful position, access to information, respected reputation, and dynamic nature and ability to get things done.

General Motors was considering closing a factory when its newly promoted manager asked for another chance. He was convinced that the factory could improve its performance if workers were involved in making decisions and recommendations. The consulting team he hired to design an employee involvement training program insisted on working with a steering committee composed of factory workers. The committee members met many of the criteria mentioned earlier—they were dynamic, informal leaders and respected workers. One of them was vociferously opposed to this change effort; his inclusion on the team was an attempt to co-opt him. By involving him in the project, the consultants believed he could voice his concerns and have an impact on the design; at the same time, greater exposure to the project and the consultants might lead him to develop more trust and confidence in both. This gamble paid off, and he became a valuable member of the committee and an active champion of the program. The consultants had the steering committee envision an ideal program and its immediate and long-term effects on the factory. Based on the needs and hopes they identified, the consultants designed a tentative training design and presented it to them for their approval, asking how it could be improved. The consultants then incorporated the committee's suggestions into the final design. The committee

funneled information about the program to the rest of the factory employees and gener
enthusiasm for the initial training workshop. The employee involvement program was hi
successful, primarily because of the manager's vision and support and the guidance of the s
ing committee. The factory's performance increased so significantly that it became a benchi
for other factories and was taken off the closure list.

Developing a Shared Vision

Creating a shared vision makes people more committed to the change. Any major change means
asking people to leave the known for the unknown. That won't happen unless there is a clear
and compelling vision pulling them away from the status quo. Their participation in shaping
what the desired end state should look like gives them a greater sense of control and makes the
change less threatening. Successful visions often contain a persuasive idea or an inspiring
metaphor. Visions have to be communicated over and over again so people don't lose sight of
where they are headed. It has to become part of people's shared mental model.

Creating a Tentative Plan

Once a vision is established, it must be operationalized into a plan. People need as much certainty
as possible about what will happen in the change. However, plans should not be completely *prec-
ocinado* or "precooked," as they say in Latin America. It's important to let organizational members have an opportunity to tweak the plan and put their imprint on it. They may be able to see
with greater clarity what will or will not work and point out other aspects the planners may not
have considered. In the GM example, the consultants presented a tentative training design to the
steering committee so the design could be improved by their input. The final plan is created after
employees have a chance to provide their input.

Analyzing Potential Resistance and Obtaining Participation

Whenever there is change, some form of resistance to change is likely to appear. Analyzing possible sources of resistance ahead of time means that preventive measures can be taken. Including
a resistant informal leader on the GM steering committee was an example of proactively managing resistance.

   Because participation is the quick answer to the question of how to deal with resistance to
change, change agents try to involve those who will be affected by the change. Their input almost
always improves the plan. Formal meetings, focus groups, and asking for written comments or e-
mail responses are all vehicles for employee participation. When resistance is systemic (embedded in the overall system), changes must be made to align other areas of the organization.

Establishing an Implementation Plan

Having a time line with a set schedule for each component of a change process eliminates some
of the uncertainty caused by change. Nevertheless, few large-scale change programs play out
exactly as planned because complex human systems are somewhat unpredictable. Unforeseen
crises, delays, and factors outside the change agents' control will require flexibility. Implementation generally takes more time than anticipated.[23]

Communicating the Change

The general rule of thumb for disseminating changes is to communicate at least three different
times in three different ways. Because of the anxiety change evokes, perception sometimes prevents accurate listening. Managers should assume that misunderstandings will occur, no matter
how carefully they explain what is to happen. Therefore, communication should be frequent and
honest. In-depth communication helps counter the ubiquitous rumors that accompany change
projects. There should be some vehicle for two-way communication, whereby employees can get
their questions answered and their suggestions heard.

Change announcements should:[24]

- Be brief and concise.
- Describe where the organization is now, where it needs to go, and how it will get to the desired state.
- Identify who will implement the change and who will be affected by it.
- Appeal to the heart and emotions as well as the mind.
- Address timing and pacing issues regarding implementation.
- Explain the change's success criteria, the intended evaluation procedures, and the related rewards.
- Identify key things that will not be changing.
- Predict some of the negative aspects that people should anticipate.
- Convey the leader's commitment to the change.
- Explain how people will be kept informed throughout the change process.
- Capitalize on the diversity of the communication styles of the audience.

Implementing the Change

There are numerous pitfalls that may occur during the implementation stage. Some are inevitable and outside the change agents' control, such as industry- or government-related conditions that impede implementation. However, some problems can be avoided by building strong support for the change, clearly defining the expectations and goals, providing sufficient training for employees who are expected to take on new behaviors and skills, involving everyone affected by the change, listening respectfully to complaints, and carefully coordinating implementation activities.[25]

Begin by targeting "low hanging fruit"—highly visible projects that are easily achieved—and then work up to more difficult targets. Once the change looks as if it will succeed, more people will jump on board. To sustain the momentum of the change effort, organizations have to provide resources, build a support network for change agents, help employees develop new competencies and skills, and reinforce new behaviors.[26] When employees act in ways that support the change, they should be rewarded with bonuses, recognition, praise, and so forth.

Evaluating the Change

An evaluation of the change provides another opportunity to ensure the change is accomplishing its purpose and has been institutionalized. Evaluations can be done via surveys, focus groups, large-scale meetings, and so on. Sometimes external evaluators are used in this stage to ensure objectivity. It is not uncommon to find areas that need further improvement or alignment.

If the change process has been successfully implemented passing through all the steps we've outlined, there is a natural tendency to experience a letdown after all the hard work and excitement about reaching the change goals. However, it's not time to completely switch focus to new projects. This is still a crucial time. Institutionalization should not mean a rehardening of the organization's arteries but a new way of working that combines stability and flexibility. If the change is seen as "complete," those arteries will harden. If it is seen as "continuous," there will be mechanisms in place for continuing to flex and change as situations demand. Some of these conditions necessary for the maintenance of the change are as follows:[27]

1. Management must pay conscious attention to the "continuous transition."
2. Explicit process or procedures for setting priorities for improvement should be instituted.
3. There should be systematic and continual processes of feedback.
4. The reward system should reward people for time and energy spent on these processes.

LEADING A CHANGE

Change agents are people who act as catalysts and assume the responsibility for managing change activities. Managing change can be exhilarating, exasperating, and exhausting, which is why it's important to create a supportive network for change agents.

How people feel about a change often depends on their position in the hierarchy and what they stand to lose or gain. For top-level managers, change is viewed as an opportunity "to strengthen the business by aligning operations with strategy, to take on new professional challenges and risks, and to advance their careers. For many employees, however, including middle managers, change is neither sought after nor welcomed. It is disruptive and intrusive. It upsets the balance."[28] Therefore, change agents seek first to understand and respect the different views people have toward a change.

According to Beer and his colleagues, top-down mandated change seldom works. Therefore, the manager's ideal role in the change process is a series of six steps that they call the critical path.[29] The steps are sequential and their exact timing is of critical importance:

1. Mobilize commitment to change through joint diagnosis of business problems.
2. Develop a shared vision of how to organize and manage for competitiveness.
3. Foster consensus for the new vision, competence to enact it, and cohesion to move it along.
4. Spread revitalization to all departments without pushing it from the top.
5. Institutionalize revitalization through formal policies, systems, and structures.
6. Monitor and adjust strategies in response to problems in the revitalization process.

Tichy and Devanna identified three similar roles for transformational leaders who are attempting to make fundamental organizational change:[30]

1. **Envisioning** Executives must articulate a clear and credible vision of the new strategic orientation. They also must set new and difficult standards for performance and generate pride in past accomplishments and enthusiasm for the new strategy.
2. **Energizing** Executives must personally demonstrate excitement for the changes and model the behaviors that are expected of others. They must communicate examples of early successes to mobilize energy for change.
3. **Enabling** Executives must provide the resources necessary for undertaking significant change and use rewards to reinforce new behaviors. Leaders must also build an effective top-management team to manage the new organization and develop management practices to support the change process.

Kotter and Cohen have identified eight steps that are characteristic of successful changes. They suggest that change leaders must begin with finding ways to create a sense of urgency—to make employees really *feel* that change must happen or the organization will truly perish—and finish with finding ways to make sure that the change becomes a way of life. Exhibit 22–2 presents each stage of the change process they recommend and lists actions that leaders can take to help make each step more effective and cautions us against actions that do not work.

Organizational culture, with its well-entrenched norms and beliefs, can be a serious obstacle to change. Therefore, leaders and change agents need to thoroughly understand the culture and use it to leverage change efforts. They can emphasize the aspects of the organizational culture that fit with a proposed change. For example, a traditional value of excellent service might be refocused on the current definition of service rather than an outmoded definition. An in-depth understanding of the culture allows leaders to know what resources to use and how hard to push for a change. It also guides them in gaining participation and knowing how best to implement the change. When cultural norms and assumptions lie in direct opposition to the goals of a change program, determining a way to change the norms has to be part of the implementation plan.

RESISTANCE TO CHANGE

Resistance to change is a natural reaction to change and part of the process of adaptation. This resistance, when it occurs, is often treated as an irrational negative force to be overcome by whatever means necessary; yet, in some cases, resistance to change can be functional for the survival of a system if it helps us perceive the basic flaw or potential problems of a planned change. If an

EXHIBIT 22-2   **The Eight Steps for Successful Large-Scale Change**

Step	Action	New Behavior	What Works	What Does Not Work
1	Increase urgency	People begin saying, "Let's go, we need to change things!"	• Showing the need for change with something they can actually, see, touch, and feel and that touches their emotions • Showing people incontrovertible, dramatic evidence for change from outside the organization • Reducing complacency • Acknowledging the complacency and negative emotions in the organization	• Focusing exclusively on building a "rational" business case, getting top management approval while ignoring the feelings that are blocking change • Leaping immediately to create a vision and strategy without creating urgency • Giving up because there's no crisis or you're not the top person
2	Build the guiding team	A group powerful enough to guide a big change is formed and they start to work together well as an effective team.	• Showing enthusiasm and commitment to attract the right people into the group • Modeling trust and teamwork • Designing meetings to minimize frustration and increase trust	• Leading a change with weak task forces, single individuals, complex governance structures, or fragmented top teams • Trying to leave out or work around unit heads because they are "hopeless"
3	Get the vision right	The guiding team develops the right vision and strategy for the change effort.	• Trying to see possible futures • Clear visions that can be articulated in one minute or written up on one page • Inspirational moving visions • Bold strategies for bold visions • Determining how quickly to introduce change	• Assuming that linear or logical plans and budgets are enough to guide behavior • Overly analytic, financially based vision exercises that leave no room for dreams • Negative visions—(e.g., slashing costs)—that elicit negative emotions
4	Communicate for buy-in	People begin to understand and buy into the change, and this shows in their behavior.	• Keeping communication simple and heartfelt • Doing your homework before communicating and trying to understand what people are feeling • Addressing anxieties, confusion, anger, and distrust • Uncluttering communication channels so that important messages are heard • Using new technologies (intranet, satellites, etc.)	• Undercommunicating • Speaking as though you are only transferring information rather than faith and hope • Fostering cynicism by not 'walking the talk'

Step	Action	New Behavior	What Works	What Does Not Work
5	Empower action	More people feel able to act on the vision and obstacles are removed from their path.	• Finding individuals with change experience who can inspire others • Well thought out recognition and reward systems • "Retooling" managers who block change by transferring them jobs where the need for change is hard to ignore	• Ignoring bosses who block their subordinates from supporting the vision • Disempowering problem bosses, which makes them mad and scared and further entrenched against the change • Giving in to pessimism and fears
6	Create short-term wins	Momentum builds as people realize successes and are rewarded for doing so, while fewer and fewer resist change.	• Early easy and visible wins that come fast—"low-hanging fruit" • Wins that have symbolic meaning and penetrate emotional defenses • Early wins that convince powerful players to support the change	• Launching too many projects at once • Providing the first win too slowly • Exaggerating accomplishments
7	Don't let up	People make wave after wave of changes, tackling more difficult challenges, until the vision is fulfilled.	• Cutting out or delegating tasks that wear you down or distract from attaining the vision • Looking constantly for ways to maintain urgency • Using new situations opportunistically to launch the next wave of change • Eliminating unnecessary, exhausting, demoralizing work to focus on tasks crucial to the vision	• Developing a rigid four-year plan with no room for opportunism • Declaring victory too early before the job is done and moving on • Convincing yourself that you don't really need to tackle embedded bureaucratic and political behaviors that are obstacles to change • Working so hard you physically or emotionally collapse (or sacrifice home life)
8	Make change stick	New behavior continues despite the pull of tradition, turnover of change leaders, etc.	• Not stopping at step 7—it isn't over until the change is rooted in the culture • Using new employee orientation to inculcate recruits with new values and inspire them • Promoting people who act according to the new norms into influential and visible positions • Repeated storytelling about the new organization, what it does, and why it succeeds • Ensuring the continuity of behavior and results that help a new culture grow	• Relying on a boss or compensation scheme, or anything but culture, to maintain the change

Source: Adapted from J. Kotter and D. Cohen, *The Heart of Change: Real-Life Stories about How People Change Their Organizations* (Cambridge, MA: Harvard Business School Press, 2002).

organization tried every new scheme, product, or process that came along, it would soon wander aimlessly, flounder, and die. The positive function of resistance to change is to ensure that plans for change and their ultimate consequences are thought through carefully.

Resistance may occur immediately in the form of criticism about the change or the process, or it may surface months later. Some resistance is passive—people go through the motions to avoid trouble but don't really support the change, or they quietly sabotage it. Change agents should expect resistance and carefully analyze its sources, which can be categorized as inadequate change goal, inadequate process, personal resistance, political resistance, and systemic resistance.

Inadequate Change Goal. A successful change requires a high-quality idea or goal (e.g., a technical solution to an organizational problem, or a strategic mission that fits the environmental demands and provides competitive advantage) and acceptance by organizational members. People become resistant when they believe the proposed change is a poor idea—they know it won't do what planners say it will accomplish, or they know it will cause other problems.

Inadequate Process. People also resist changes, actively or passively, when the process is not carefully managed. For example, when change is decreed from on high without employee input or when the members of a system do not fully understand why a change is necessary or how it will play out, resistance will be strong. Unfortunately, an inadequate change process can overshadow and engender resistance to the most brilliant idea for change. More changes fail as a result of a poorly managed process than to technical flaws in the suggested change.

Kanter identified the following sources of resistance that occur when the change process is inadequately managed: (1) feeling out of control, (2) excess uncertainty from not knowing where the change will lead, (3) lack of time to mentally adjust to changes, (4) stress caused by too many changes and forced attention to issues that were formerly routine, (5) feeling compelled to defend the status quo because doing otherwise would involve a loss of face, (6) concerns about future competence when the ground rules seem to be changing, (7) ripple effects to personal plans that will be affected by the change, (8) greater work and energy demands necessitated by the change, (9) past resentments prevent people from supporting the change, and (10) the real threat posed by a change in which some people will be winners and others will be losers.[31]

Personal Resistance. Individual resistance can result not from a considered opinion that the proposed change or the process is inappropriate, but from personal discomfort with change. Some people fear the unknown and dislike change of any kind. Others worry about whether or not they can learn the new skills a change may require of them. Employees who can readily find work elsewhere if the change does not turn out as they hope may be less resistant than people who feel trapped and insecure about their jobs.

Political Resistance. Political resistance can occur when change threatens people who hold power. Resources (including employees) are often allocated differently as a result of changes; therefore, some people win power while others lose power in the aftermath of change. Furthermore, the status quo is generally the result of past decisions made by people in power. When change agents insist that the status quo is no longer acceptable, those responsible for former decisions may feel insulted and become defensive. One solution to this problem is emphasizing that former innovations or decisions were appropriate when they were made; because times have changed, however, new decisions and directions are necessary for organizational success.[32]

Systemic Resistance. At the organizational level, resistance often occurs due to habit ("This is the way we've always done things"), sunk costs invested in the status quo,[33] and problems caused by lack of internal congruence or alignment. Changes hit a roadblock when only one aspect of the system is changed without modifying the other components.

To implement most changes, we also need to modify the performance review system, recruiting, compensation policies and systems, career planning, and human resources planning systems.[34] For example, when a chemical company decided to adopt a global strategy, it was not enough to change its production standards and capacity. It also started recruiting employees with international backgrounds and foreign language skills. The company established a policy that overseas experience was a prerequisite for senior management positions. These complementary changes in the system removed any obstacles that may have prevented employees from adopting an international focus.

In the preceding chapter, we wrote that fit among the components of an organization promotes effectiveness. Internal congruence among strategy, structure, culture, and people is responsible for short-term performance.[35] When major changes occur in the environment and organizations are forced to adapt or fail, however, that same congruence may turn into systemic resistance. Changing an organization that is meticulously aligned to an obsolete strategy or product takes on mammoth proportions. The solution, according to Tushman and O'Reilly, is to seek congruence during stable, evolutionary periods when change is primarily incremental but be willing to destroy that alignment and start over again when confronted with discontinuous, revolutionary change.[36] This is easier said than done because organizations, particularly successful organizations, cling to traditional ways.

Successful global change always requires a certain degree of alignment of organizational design components. For example, a new strategic thrust often requires concomitant changes in policies, employee skills, staffing, systems, cultural norms, and structure. Organizations are interdependent systems, so changing one component is usually insufficient. Ensuring the 'fit' among components is a way to institutionalize change. For example, a study of 500 of the largest European firms found significant performance benefits only in firms that changed structures, processes, and boundaries. Firms that changed only structures and boundaries but not processes actually did worse."[37]

The evolutionary nature of organizations, however, means that global managers cannot expect their alignments to last. They face the paradoxical demands of "increasing the alignment or fit among strategy, structure, culture, and processes, while simultaneously preparing for the inevitable revolutions required by discontinuous environmental change."[38] Organizational evolution usually consists of periods of incremental change punctuated by discontinuous or revolutionary change. This means that global managers have to keep an eye on the future and be willing to tear apart what they've just painstakingly cobbled together. With regard to organizational capability, Lew Platt, former HP CEO, stated, "We have to be willing to cannibalize what we're doing today in order to ensure our leadership in the future. It's counter to human nature, but you have to kill your business while it is still working."[39] Alignment can be a double-edged sword—both a necessity for institutionalizing change and a barrier to perceiving the need for subsequent changes.

TACTICS FOR DEALING WITH RESISTANCE

Resistance to change is not irrational, and managers who understand the reasons for resistance are better able to deal with it constructively. Managers often resent and become angry with employees who resist change. However, this reaction does nothing to reduce the resistance and often exacerbates an already difficult situation. Empathy is the starting point for dealing with resistance—trying to understand how others view the change without judging their reactions. Other effective tactics for dealing with resistance to change are:[40]

1. **Education and Communication** Help people understand the reasons for the change, the form it will take, and the likely consequences. This clears up misunderstandings that often cause resistance.

2. **Participation and Involvement** Encourage others to help with the design and implementation of the changes. This creates commitment to the change and usually improves the quality of the change decisions. The disadvantages of this tactic are the time it consumes and, if the participants lack the necessary expertise, their solutions may be inadequate.

3. **Facilitation and Support** Provide encouragement, support, training, counseling, and resources to help the people who are affected by the change.

4. **Co-optation** Co-optation occurs when the leaders of the resistance are "bought off" by allowing them a role in the change process. This is positive when previously unrepresented factions are given a voice, as in the GM example. Co-optation is sometimes used manipulatively to simply silence critics.

5. **Negotiation and Agreement** Offer incentives in return for decreased resistance to the change.

6. **Manipulation** Manipulation usually takes the form of distorting or withholding information or starting false rumors so that employees agree to a change. For example, one multinational wanted their employees to switch to a less expensive retirement plan. HR staff were told to present only the attractive features of the new plan and suppress the information that employees would fare worse under the new plan. Employees were understandably angry at both the company and the HR staff who went along with the deception. When people realize they have been manipulated, they lose the trust that is so essential to the change process and can become even more resistant.

7. **Coercion** When people are threatened with negative incentives (e.g., unwanted transfers, denial of promotion and pay raises, negative performance evaluations, etc.) if they do not accept a change, this is called coercion. Most people resent coercion, and its use may irreparably harm relationships. However, at times there is no other alternative to reduce resistance.

The first three tactics, although more time-consuming, are more likely to result in commitment to the change. The last three tactics may yield compliance with the change but not commitment. The result of co-optation depends on the intentions behind it.

Johnson & Johnson devised a method for decreasing resistance to change. Although size is a competitive advantage in maintaining financial strength and market leadership, the company was concerned that its size (170 distinct operating companies) could prevent rapid adaptation to emerging opportunities and environmental changes. Its nine-member executive committee devised a management process called FrameworkS because they wanted "frameworks" to better understand issues that cut across the company's decentralized structure, such as markets, customer expectations, and new opportunities. The capital S helps remind them that there are multiple frames through which they must view the diverse businesses in their global organization. The company forms FrameworkS teams—task forces comprised of members from various companies, countries, and functional areas who extensively research topics important to the company's future. Their findings are presented to and discussed by all the other FrameworkS teams and the executive committee. After including this input, the teams develop action plans, which are then implemented. The FrameworkS program has paid off in tangible results, such as setting up new businesses and entering new markets. However, the intangible results are equally impressive. The executive committee is more in touch with how employees and customers think, operating has learned it can push ahead to take advantage of opportunities without waiting for edicts from the top of the hierarchy, and "there is a greater receptivity to deal with change that did not exist five years ago."[41]

TYPES OF ORGANIZATIONAL CHANGE PROGRAMS

Organization development (OD) is a specialized area of organizational behavior focused on planned change. It is a *"system-wide process of data collection, diagnosis, action, planning, intervention, and evaluation aimed at: (1) enhancing congruence between organizational structure, process, strategy, people, and culture, (2) developing new and creative organizational solutions, and (3) developing the organization's self-renewing capacity. It occurs through collaboration of organizational members working with a change agent using behavioral science theory, research, and technology."*[42] Many change agents are external consultants, but large corporations employ internal OD consultants. OD emphasizes organizational effectiveness and health and tries to improve organizational capacity to solve problems and cope with changes in the external environment.[43] Unlike traditional consulting, which involves diagnosis and recommendations by outside experts, OD consultants facilitate a process in which organizational members participate in diagnosing the system and agreeing on the changes that should be made. The rationale is that greater participation and involvement increase the likelihood that change will actually happen.

There are numerous OD interventions, such as survey feedback, process consultation, and team building to name just a few.[44] In *survey feedback*, organization members are surveyed or interviewed, the results are often shown first to top management (to avoid surprising them and give them time to prepare a constructive response) and then fed back to the surveyed group. The group discusses its diagnosis and decides on action steps to pursue. Survey feedback raises employee expectations that improvements will be made once the data are presented. Therefore, managers have to commit beforehand to implementing suggested changes and perhaps changing their own managerial style if that is identified as a problem.

In *process consultation*, a process facilitator observes a work group or a manager in action and provides insight about what is occurring around, within, and between people. For example, a process facilitator may point out to a management team how it handles disagreement and coach team members so they have more skills to deal with conflict in the future.

In *team-building* interventions, consultants usually take work team members to a retreat location where they can get to know one another better and establish a more effective way of working together. Consultants often provide performance data that show why change is necessary and guide them through discussions and clarifications of the team's goals, roles, procedures for working together, and interpersonal norms. Many outdoor challenge activities and ropes courses are used in team building, but the design of the intervention depends on the team's unique needs or vision.

OD programs do not always work, but when implemented correctly, they can have positive effects on performance. Their success depends, among other factors, on management commitment, organizational readiness for change, the skill of the change agents involved, the appropriateness of the intervention for the specific organization, and enough slack to devote time and resources to the change. Using multiple methods in change interventions that are clearly related to the ongoing work of the organization (e.g., team building, survey feedback, and skill training in the same change program) is more successful than using a single method.[45]

Culture and Change

The values that underlie OD are:[46]

- Respect for people
- Trust and support
- Equality and power sharing
- Candor and confrontation
- Participation
- Collaboration

These values naturally reflect those of the U.S. culture, where OD was developed. One could argue that, more accurately, they reflect the values of a humanistic, democratic U.S. subculture—otherwise, we would not require special programs to encourage companies to adopt behaviors more in keeping with OD values. OD values fit low-context cultures characterized by low power distance, individualism, masculinity, and moderate levels of uncertainty avoidance.[47] OD is used successfully all over the world, primarily in developed nations, but it has to be adapted to the local culture.

Cultures vary in terms of their comfort with change. Few countries value change more than the United States. Bridges noted, "In the Old World, respect came from a valuable heritage, and any change from that norm had to be justified. In America, however, the status quo was no more than the temporary product of past changes, and it was the resistance to change that demanded an explanation. A failure to change with the times was more than just a private misfortune; it was a socially and organizationally subversive condition. This attitude still persists in America, particularly in the corporate world."[48] Cultures that are high in uncertainty avoidance or order, rather than flexibility, are more likely to view change and the risks it involves with greater caution. They will expect the change process to be very clearly delineated. Cultures with a stronger value for the past and tradition are generally more resistant to change. In such cultures, managers will tend to be less proactive about making changes, and change processes are likely to take more time. The same is true of cultures that believe more in fate than in human control of one's destiny.

Cultural values also affect the change implementation process. In cultures where human nature is viewed as unchangeable or untrustworthy, people are more likely to be skeptical about the success of a change effort, and it may take longer to build trust and commitment. Participation is the best way to allow employees to feel some sense of ownership of the change process in low power distance cultures. Employees from cultures characterized by high power distance, however, are more likely to expect leaders to make decisions without their input.

Influence is exerted in different ways in different cultures. Both formal and informal leaders play a major role in encouraging others to support a change effort. Determining who is the best person to communicate a change and who should be included in a coalition depends on the culture. Whereas participation is the best way to allow U.S. employees to feel some sense of ownership of the change process, other cultures expect their leaders to make decisions without their input.

Cultures also vary in their beliefs about how change occurs. When most European and Japanese companies want to make a change, they begin by trying to change the attitudes and mentalities of their key people. Next, they modify the flow of communication and decision-making processes. Finally, they consolidate the changes by realigning the structure to mirror the changes that have already occurred. U.S. companies, however, have opposite assumptions about change. They tend to assume that modifying the organizational structures results in organizational change. This line of thought presupposes that a new structure causes changes in interpersonal relationships and processes, which leads eventually to changes in individual attitudes and mentalities. Bartlett and Ghoshal note that these different national biases seem to be disappearing as global companies learn different approaches from one another.[49]

These are the stereotypical cultural differences one should be aware of in multicultural change projects; however, global managers also need to take into consideration unique, indigenous cultural values (emic values), the country's history, and the organizational culture and the occupational culture of the particular group involved in the change effort. One of the paradoxes inherent in global change is the simultaneous need for a universal (global) and particularistic (local) solution. Even the best corporate-wide changes have to be *contextualized*—modified to fit the local context. This is one of the major lessons about global change. Those who know the local people and culture best should be granted the necessary autonomy and discretion to tailor the change effort so it is appropriate.

Managers in cross-cultural or multicultural settings need to understand the various cultural values about change and recognize that change interventions that work in one country may not succeed elsewhere.[50]

TOTAL QUALITY MANAGEMENT (TQM)

The quality movement was started by Edward Deming, an American management consultant who taught his famous 14 principles to the Japanese in the 1950s; where at the time, the "Made in Japan" label was synonymous with poor quality.[51] Japan's current reputation for producing goods of extremely high quality is credited in large part to Deming. Is there a cultural reason why TQM was so readily adopted in Japan? Several theories have been advanced to answer this question. Japan had a long history of fine craftsmanship among artisans that was transferred to the factory floor and technicians via TQM. Furthermore, Japan's scarce natural resources and cultural orientations of collectivism and harmony with nature created a belief that technology was a resource to be used frugally and carefully to obtain the maximum value. This resulted in systems thinking as well as an internal focus on productivity and manufacturing operations. The resulting organizational structures and mind-set made Japanese companies fertile soil for TQM.[52]

In addition to improving quality, other basic goals of quality programs are to lower costs; speed up the flow of information, materials, and products; increase flexibility; reduce inventory; and improve customer satisfaction. Quality programs focus on managing the process of the work rather than people and give workers the challenge of constantly trying to improve the quality of the work processes, placing primary emphasis on the customer. This provides workers with a sense of meaning. Such programs teach statistics as a common language that is used to measure variances from the perfect quality standard. Each employee is taught to inspect his or her own work so that defects and reworks are reduced or even eliminated. This emphasis on immediate feedback on quality stimulates the need for achievement. Quality programs generally involve group problem-solving efforts, which meet people's need for affiliation. Quality programs focus on the requirements of the task, but their manner of doing so also meets the motivational needs of employees.[53] The Six Sigma method discussed in the problem-solving chapter in this book is another example of a quality management program that continues to be popular.

Continuous improvement, *kaizen* in Japanese, is a key factor in total quality programs. This term is sometimes used interchangeably by companies to describe their total quality effort. Continuous improvement programs are designed to take advantage of employee experience and commitment to improving the products, services, and work practices of the organization.[54] In recognition of the importance of quality in global competition, the U.S. government initiated the Malcolm Baldridge Quality Award to honor organizations that attain "world-class" quality in their products, services, and operations. The competition criteria are:

- A plan to keep improving all operations continuously
- A system for measuring these improvements accurately
- A strategic plan based on benchmarks that compare the company's performance with the world's best
- A close partnership with suppliers and customers that feeds improvements back into the operation
- A deep understanding of the customers so that their wants can be translated into products
- A long-lasting relationship with customers, going beyond the delivery of the products to include sales, service, and ease of maintenance
- A focus on preventing mistakes, rather than merely correcting them
- A commitment to improving quality that runs from the top of the organization to the bottom.[55]

TQM is a good example of a program that was treated like a fad in some companies and later dropped while it produced (and is still producing) impressive results at other organizations. Although some firms no longer use all the technical practices, TQM's core ideas, particularly its emphasis on quality and continuous improvement, are still visible in many companies.

Transforming companies into learning organizations, which are described in Chapter 3, and Appreciative Inquiry in Chapter 11 are recent examples of large scale organizational change interventions. Some interventions are viewed as short-lived management fads. Read what Stanley Bing, a corporate veteran and chronicler of corporate life, has to say about management fads in the box below.

How to Live in a Fad Environment

Every so often a guy like Kip Breen descends from corporate Mecca, all teeth and gray twill, to spread ultrasenior management's latest instant credo with beamish zeal and a steel fist. That year it was something called Negative Task Evaluation, and it made us dance like Saint Vitus before it disappeared into the mists of corporate time, as fads do.

"It's pretty simple," Kip said benignly, easing a glossy, user-friendly packet across my blotter. "We want each manager to break down his or her ongoing activities, then derive the amount of time each chore requires as a percentage of the total workweek. Then you just work out a couple of simple graphs to see who is spending an inappropriate amount of time on matters of minor importance."

And then fire them, I thought.

In the coming months, I filled out more graphs than an infertile couple. People were evaluating one another all over the place, and relationships grew formal. We needn't have worried, though, because while middle management was diddling with its new Tinkertoy, the big guys were seized by a more terrible trend then careening around the horn: decentralization. Out of the window went the assiduously kept charts. With them flew 400 nice folks, willy-nilly. Nothing has been heard of Kip since, except over booze, when we survivors haul out his memory just for a hoot. Then we get back to work.

You'll have to excuse us guys on the inside if we get a little giggly each time the next new dogma comes along. We've been converted before, after all. We've managed in a minute and Theory Z'd, spotted megatrends, spun matrices, woven grids; we've hammered ourselves into hard-networking intrapreneurs, and sat in stupefaction before lanky preachers nagging us to Be Excellent! Some of us, thank God, have even found Wellness. We're willing to give each new creed a chance, until its hasty priests begin torturing the innocent into false confessions. The damned thing is, when the right idea is given the chance to mellow, spread, and ooze deep into the culture, it can actually do some good. But don't hold your breath.

Even when the idea is right—which it rarely is—most corporations still get it wrong. "You can go back to Management-by-Objective, Son of Management-by-Objective, Management-by-Objective meets Appraisal-and-Counseling," says E. Kirby Warren, professor at Columbia University's Graduate School of Business. "Most of these fads would have some real value if senior management took the time to ask themselves: (1) How do I adapt the idea to our culture and business? (2) What has to be changed to reinforce that thing we're talking about? and (3) Are we committed to staying with it long enough to make it work?"

But in today's overheated environment, most firms are too desperate to wait for results. "When we're facing intense competition from Asia, and money is relatively expensive, and technology is available and moves rapidly, it's not surprising that people reach out for what you call fads," says Joseph Bower, professor at Harvard Business School. "If you take almost any of them and discuss it with the author, it's a perfectly qualified view of how a set of ideas can run a company. But if it's treated as a kind of cookbook, as a single tool carried to an extreme, you get nonsense."

Still, when the guys with liver spots get that nutsy gleam in their eyes, you may have to snap to. Here are some pointers on how to survive.

It must be an autocracy, because democracy doesn't squeeze like that. The guys put in charge of forging the new culture aren't usually the Mother Teresa type. They take things personally, and they're not long on patience. Don't be fooled by warm and fuzzy verbiage designed to win your heart. This is a full blown drill. Get out on deck and run around.

Keep your mouth shut. Yes, the anal graphs and rah-rah lingo may seem absurd, but develop some instant naiveté—I've seen more than one astute critic mailed overnight to the Elmira office for being a party pooper. "It's a religion," says a friend currently being strangled in the noose of a Quality circle. "To openly question or be cynical about it—you're more than grumpy, you're an apostate."

Charts are not enough. The need to play with neat fad gewgaws doesn't call off your actual job. "I had this subordinate who insisted on spending six months doing a PERT chart, while completely ignoring his other duties," recalls Wes, strategic-planning director at a multinational. "I love the memory of Frank pouring over a chart as big as a barn door that was supposed to govern our actions for the next year. He finally finished it, and we never looked at it again." Frank is out on the Coast now, by the way, teaching people how to do PERT charts.

General Pinochet! I had no idea you were dropping by. There's a healthy whiff of authoritarian zealotry in many fads, and some big boosters may think they've been named Ayatollah. Push them gently off your back. Unostentatious resistance to excess—even excess orthodoxy—is rarely questioned. "One of the darker moments last year was when the Productivity Czar asked everyone to sign a Petition of Commitment," recalls my friend Andy, a marketing manager at a retail firm. "It was invasive and ridiculous. I tried to kid him out of it. It turns out a lot of other people did, too. He was even advised against it by some of his peers, who felt it was sort of like reading the Bible in the office." The loathed petition now resides on the czar's wall, half full. Not one of the missing was punished.

Dare to be sold. A little credulity can be a beautiful thing. Several years ago I worked for a manufacturing company that decided to dedicate itself to Excellence. The propaganda campaign we inflicted on our workers was fierce. Management spent actual money to improve service. Worker initiative was rewarded. And, unbelievably, the elephantine organism began to lumber forth, to feel pride and a determination to succeed. It was corny and inspirational. We were a team, suddenly, and felt it. I wouldn't have missed it for the world.

A year into the program, the corporation was abruptly sold to a group of midwestern investors who broke it down and resold its body parts for cash. So long, Excellence. Hello, Leverage. What the hell: One good fad deserves another.

Source: Stanley Bing. Reprinted from *Esquire 106* (August 1986): 36. With permission of the author.

 # CLASS ACTIVITY: THE HOLLOW SQUARE EXERCISE[56]

Materials: Each group should bring one pair of scissors and four envelopes unless the instructor will provide the necessary materials.

This exercise is designed to simulate the stage in the change process when the planners of a change must communicate it to the people who will implement the change. (Time allotted: 95 minutes)

STEP 1. The class divides into groups of eight people. These groups will then further subdivide into four planners and four implementers. If there is an odd number of students, place three to five people on the planning team. The implementation teams, however, should always consist of exactly four people (5 minutes).

STEP 2. Once the groups have decided who will be planners and implementers, the implementers will wait in a separate area until the instructor has given the planners their instructions. Please do not read the instructions for the other team.

STEP 3. The instructor reads the planning teams their instructions (page 660) and either provides them with the materials they need to perform the exercise or explains how to obtain them.

STEP 4. The planning teams have 30 minutes to plan how they will communicate the instructions to their implementation team (30 minutes).

STEP 5. The instructor reads the implementation teams their instructions (page 655).

STEP 6. All implementation teams begin the 15-minute assembly period at the signal of the instructor. The first team to complete the assembly wins. During this time, the planning team can only observe and must refrain from making any noises that might distract or influence the implementing team (15 minutes).

STEP 7. When the assembly period is completed, each participant should complete both sections of the Team Evaluation Form that follows. Then each subgroup should average its scores for each question (i.e., the implementation team comes up with its own team average and the planning team does likewise) (5 minutes).

Comparison of Scores	Implementation Team Subtotal	Planning Team Subtotal
Planners		
Implementers		

STEP 8. Group Discussion. The two subgroups that worked together compare their evaluation scores. Discuss the following questions and choose a representative to present your answers to the class during the plenary session. (10 minutes)
   a. Are there any differences in the way the planning and implementation teams perceived and evaluated each other? Why or why not?

b. What did the planning team do that helped the implementation team? Did they do anything that hindered the implementers? Use the chart on the next page, Analysis of the Hollow Square Exercise, to record these factors.

c. What did the implementation team do that helped it succeed in this exercise? Did the team do anything that hindered its success?

TEAM EVALUATIONS FORM
EVALUATION OF THE IMPLEMENTATION TEAM

a. How well was the puzzle completed?   **Team average**

    Not at all well   1   2   3   4   5   6   7   Very well   _____

b. How faithfully did the implementers follow the planning team's instructions?

    Not at all well   1   2   3   4   5   6   7   Very well   _____

c. How well organized was the implementation team?

    Not at all well   1   2   3   4   5   6   7   Very well   _____

d. How well did the implementation team understand the planning team's instructions?

    Not at all well   1   2   3   4   5   6   7   Very well   _____

e. To what extent did the implementation team try to clarify the planning team's instructions (e.g., asking questions, paraphrasing instructions, etc.)?

    Not at all well   1   2   3   4   5   6   7   Very well   _____

                        Implementation Team Subtotal (a–e)   _____

EVALUATION OF THE PLANNING TEAM

f. How clear (explicit, unequivocal) were the instructions given by the planning team?

    Not at all well   1   2   3   4   5   6   7   Very well   _____

g. How well organized was the planning team?

    Not at all well   1   2   3   4   5   6   7   Very well   _____

h. To what extent did the planning team involve the implementation team in their strategies?

    Not at all well   1   2   3   4   5   6   7   To a large degree   _____

                                Planning Team Subtotal (f–h)   _____

Analysis of the Hollow Square Exercise

Planning Team Actions That		Implementation Team Actions That	
Helped	Hindered	Helped	Hindered

STEP 9.   Plenary debriefing (30 minutes). Each group presents its findings, and the class as a whole discusses the following questions:

   a.   What feelings and thoughts did the implementation teams experience while awaiting the instructions for an unknown task?
   b.   How did the implementation teams organize to accomplish this task?
   c.   How did the planners transfer the instructions? What was your strategy?
   d.   How much time did the planning teams devote to figuring out how to transmit their message to the implementation teams?
   e.   At what time did the implementation teams enter and how did that occur? Why did the planning teams bring or allow the implementation teams in when they did?
   f.   Did the time at which the planners brought the implementers into the process (early on or just before the assembly period) have an effect upon the proceedings? If so, what was the effect and why did it occur?
   g.   What can we learn about communicating an organizational change from this exercise?
   h.   What parallels can you draw between this simulation and organizational change efforts you have observed or experienced?

Look at Exhibit 22–4 on page 669 for lessons about communicating changes.

INSTRUCTIONS FOR THE IMPLEMENTATION TEAMS

1.   You have the responsibility for carrying out a task for four people in accordance with the instructions given to you by your planning team. Your planning team can call you back to the classroom to receive these instructions at any time during their 30-minute preparation period. However, if they have not called you by_____ (five minutes before you are scheduled to carry out your task), you should report to them. Your task is programmed to start exactly at _____. Once you begin, your planning team cannot provide you with any more instructions.

ur mission is to complete the assigned task as quickly as possible.

ile you are waiting for the planning team to call you in to receive your instructions,
e discuss and take notes on the following questions. Your notes will be useful during
enary debriefing session.

.at feelings and thoughts are you experiencing as you await the instructions for an
unknown task?

b. How can the four of you organize yourselves as a team to accomplish this task?

LEARNING POINTS

1. Managing change has become a crucial skill for both managers and employees.
2. Incremental change is linear, continuous, and targeted at fixing or modifying problems or procedures. Transformative change is radical, discontinuous, multidimensional, and multi-level, and modifies the fundamental structure, systems, orientation, and strategies of the organization.
3. Critical mass is defined as the smallest number of people and/or groups who must be committed to a change for it to occur.
4. Successful changes often begin at the periphery of the organization with dedicated general managers who focus energy on work improvements rather than abstract principles.
5. Lewin described the process of change as unfreezing, moving, and refreezing.
6. Change is a process rather than an event or a managerial edict.
7. The essential components of the change process are determining the need for change, forming a guiding coalition, developing a shared vision, creating a tentative plan, analyzing potential resistance and obtaining participation, establishing an implementation plan, communicating the change, implementing the change, and evaluating the change.
8. To diagnose the situation, a force field analysis assigns pressures for change and resistance to change to opposite sides of an equilibrium state.
9. Creative tension, which sometimes motivates people to change, results from perceiving the gap between the ideal situation (vision) and an honest appraisal of its current reality.
10. Change agents are people who act as catalysts and assume the responsibility for managing change activities.
11. The role of a transformational leader consists of envisioning, energizing, and enabling.
12. Resistance to change is a natural reaction and part of the process of adaptation.
13. Managers should seek to understand the source of resistance and listen carefully to concerns employees have regarding proposed changes rather than seeing those who resist as adversaries.
14. Resistance to change can be caused by inadequate change goals, inadequate change processes, personal resistance, political resistance, and systemic resistance.
15. Tactics for dealing with resistance include empathy, education and communication, participation and involvement, facilitation and support, co-optation, negotiation and agreement, manipulation, and coercion.

16. Organization development (OD) is a systemwide process of data collection, dia. action, planning, intervention, and evaluation aimed at enhancing organizational fit, p. lem solving, effectiveness, health, and self-renewal.

17. International OD interventions and change programs have to be contextualized so they fit the local cultural context.

 ## ACTION SCRIPTS

FOR EMPLOYEES

- Employees who are proficient at handling change recognize their own orientations and biases toward change. They take the time to understand the basis for their reactions to change and then respond appropriately.
- They also realize that they can be sources of change. When acting as change agents, these employees carefully survey the political landscape to determine allies and opponents and work to reinforce their allies and persuade their opponents.
- Expert change agents do not give up if their ideas are not immediately accepted. They focus on developing alliances at all levels of the organization. They recognize that peers and managers are important sources of support and can be critical for successfully implementing change.

FOR MANAGERS

Many managerial action scripts, as well as actions to avoid, are found in Exhibit 22-2 and 22-4.

- Managers who are adept at implementing change don't make changes simply to be taking action or to look good. Too much change in a system is just as frustrating to employees as the feeling that any change is impossible. They think through the pros and cons of potential changes very carefully before taking action. For some people, making changes has more to do with their own need to impact the system than with the needs of the system.
- They analyze the political landscape and seek to understand why employees are reacting negatively to a proposed change. They deal with the specific sources of resistance for each employee.
- Employees often undergo a period of "mourning" in large-scale change projects. Accepting this difficulty, acknowledging it with employees, allowing them to vent their feelings, and planning ritual celebrations like farewell parties help people to get through this period more easily.[57]
- Expert managers realize that trust is an important aspect of any change effort. Employees do not believe management's sense of urgency or new visions for the future unless their trust has been won. Experts know that making promises regarding a change that cannot be kept or promising too much diminishes trust.
- They understand that change is not always a rational, linear process. When major organizational transformation is required, change involves a leap of faith to move the organization to another plane that cannot always be seen from the point of departure. For this reason, such changes require shared values and symbolic gestures by managers.
- Expert managers recognize the importance of "small wins"—quick, tangible results that can be clearly linked to the change effort. These results provided needed reinforcement for supporters and help convince opponents. Smart change agents build those wins into their plan for change right from the start.
- They devote a great deal of time to communicating the change message and signal to others in the organization that the change is significant enough to warrant changing the previous rules of the game and making sacrifices.

FOR ORGANIZATIONAL ARCHITECTS

- Almost all organizations should focus energy on innovation and change on a regular basis. But not everyone in the organization needs to be involved in this. Expert organizational architects utilize parallel or collateral organization structures. Parallel organizations have the freedom and flexibility to do the innovating and problem solving, whereas the "maintenance organization" carries on with business as usual. People who dislike uncertainty and who cherish a fondness for the status quo are more satisfied in maintenance organizations, while the creative, entrepreneurial types prefer the parallel organization. Architects and managers who point out that both of these structures and types of employees are equally valuable to the organization can avoid potential conflict between these groups.[58]
- New programs require careful attention and nurturing. Successful change designers often have the heads of major new programs report directly to the CEO or senior managers until the programs are well established.
- Expert organizational architects recognize that making change "stick" is one of the greatest challenges they face. They build reinforcements and continued resources for implementation in their change plan. They also monitor the progress of the change effort and make any needed adjustments based on the feedback they receive.

PERSONAL APPLICATION ASSIGNMENT

The topic of this assignment is to think back on a significant experience involving organizational change. Choose an experience that intrigues you and that you want to learn more about.

A. Concrete Experience

1. Objectively describe the experience (who, what, when, where, how information). (2 points)

2. Subjectively describe your feelings, perceptions, and thoughts that occurred during (not after) the experience. What did others seem to be feeling? (2 points)

B. Reflective Observation

1. Looking back at the experience, what were the perspectives of the key actors (including you)? (2 points)

2. Why did the people involved (including you) behave as they did? (2 points)

C. Abstract Conceptualization
    1. Relate concepts or theories from the assigned readings or the lecture to the experience. Explain thoroughly how they apply to your experience. Please apply at least two concepts or theories and cite them correctly. (4 points)

D. Active Experimentation
    1. What did you learn about change from this experience? (1 point)

    2. What did you learn about yourself? (1 point)

    3. What action steps will you take to be more effective in the future? (2 points)

E. Integration, Synthesis, and Writing
    1. Did you integrate and synthesize the four sections? (1 point)
    2. Was the personal application assignment well written and easy to understand? (1 point)
    3. Was it free of spelling and grammatical errors? (2 points)

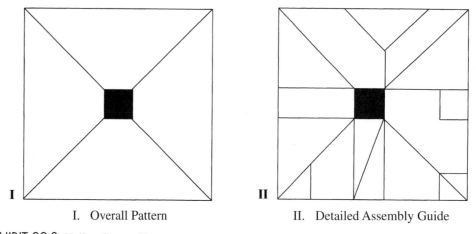

I. Overall Pattern II. Detailed Assembly Guide

EXHIBIT 22-3 **Hollow Square Key**

INSTRUCTIONS FOR THE PLANNING TEAMS

Unless your instructor provides you with different materials, each member should cut out the shapes on either the A, B, C, or D pages found at the end of the chapter. Please do not mix these pieces up (keep all A pieces separate, etc.). Thus, each of the four members of the planning team will have a separate group of four shapes in front of them as we read the following instructions. (If there are five members on the team, two members can share one set of shapes.) These sets, when properly assembled with pieces from other participants, will make a hollow square design.

During the next 30 minutes, your task is to:

1. Plan how these pieces, distributed among you, should be assembled to make the design shown in Exhibit 22–3.
2. Instruct your implementation team on how to implement your plan so as to complete your task ahead of the other teams. You may begin instructing your implementation team at any time during the 30-minute planning period—but no later than five minutes before they are to begin the assembly process at _____.

General Rules

1. You must keep all your four pieces in front of you at all times.
2. You may not touch the pieces of other planning team members or trade pieces with other members of your team during the planning or instructing phase.
3. You may not show Exhibit 22–2 to the implementation team at any time. Nor may you provide them with written instructions or drawings.
4. **You may not actually assemble the entire square at any time** (this is to be left to your implementation team at the moment the assembly period begins).
5. You may not number or otherwise mark the pieces at any time during the exercise.
6. **Members of your implementation team must also observe the preceding rules until the signal is given to begin the assembly.**
7. Just before the assembly time starts, place your four pieces into an envelope and give the envelope to an implementer. This will allow the implementers on each team to start from an equal position.
8. When your instructor announces the start of the contest and your implementation team begins assembling the pieces, you may give no further instructions. Just step back and observe the implementation team at work without making any noises that might distract or influence the implementers.

A

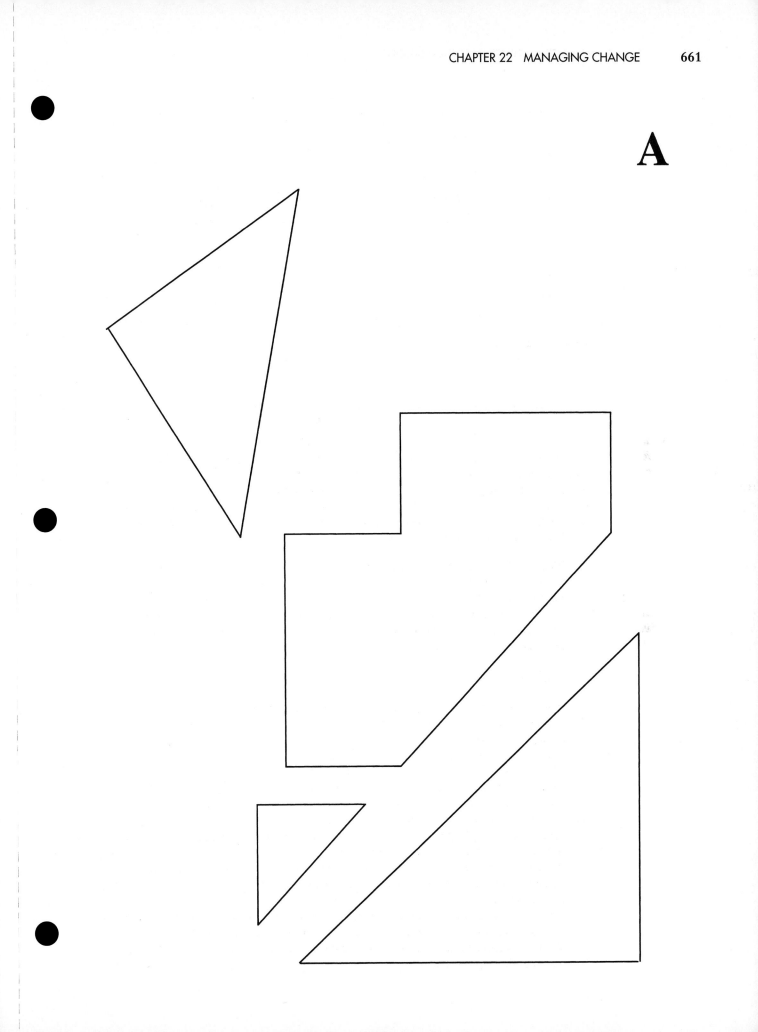

B

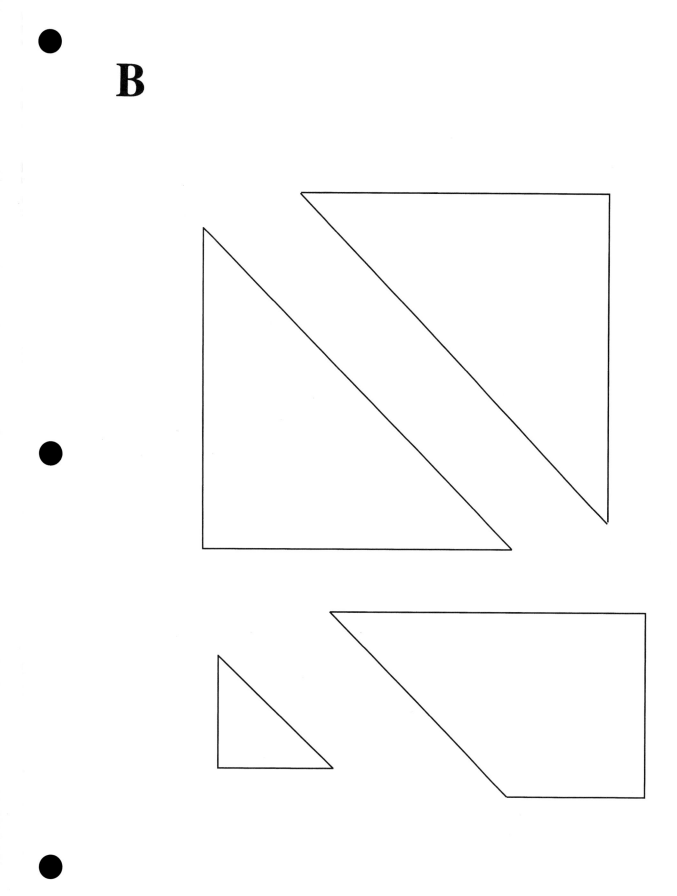

C

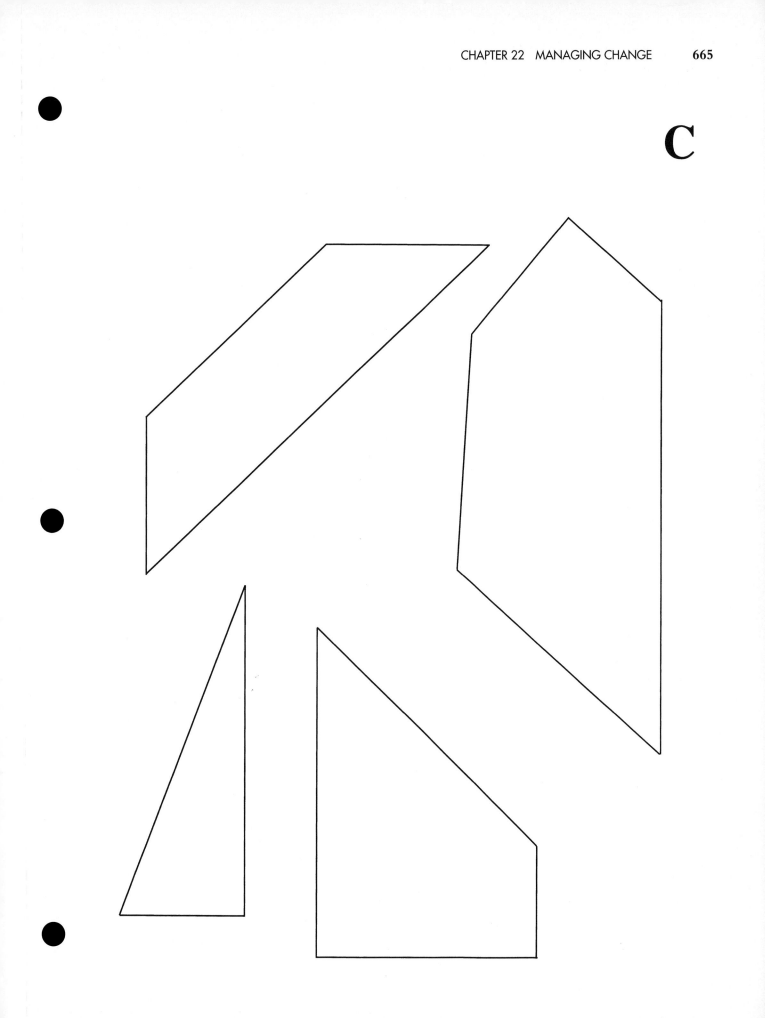

D

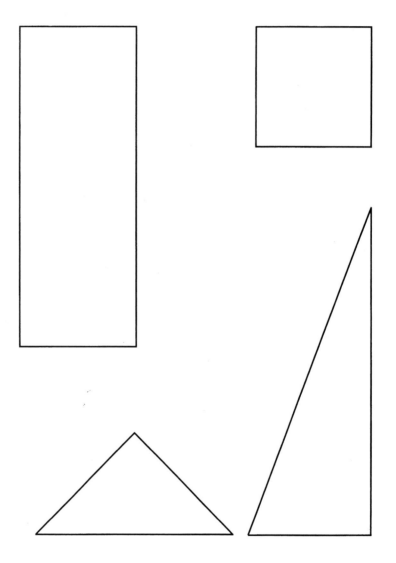

Problems that may occur when one group makes plans that another group is to carry out:

1. Planners sometimes impose restrictions on themselves that are unnecessary.
2. It is sometimes difficult for planners to see the task from the point of view of the implementers.
3. Sometimes in planning, more attention is given to details while the larger clues and possibilities go unnoticed.
4. Planners sometimes fail to apportion their time wisely because they plunge into the act of planning before they think through their entire task and the amount of time available to them.
5. Planners sometimes have different understandings of their task and the boundaries in which they must operate.
6. When members of a planning team fail to listen to one another, time is lost in subsequent efforts to clarify what each party meant.
7. Sometimes planners fail to prepare a proper physical setup for the implementation team.
8. Sometimes planners become so involved in the planning process that they do not plan their method of instructing the implementers.

Common problems when planners instruct implementers:

1. Sometimes the planners do not consider the implementers' anxieties when they orient them to the environment and task.
2. Planners may not allow enough time for instruction and fail to help the operators feel prepared and comfortable about doing their job.
3. Planners may not encourage questions from the implementers and, therefore, assume greater understanding on the part of the implementers than really exists.
4. The planners' own feelings of anxiety or insecurity are likely to be transmitted to the implementers.
5. Planners sometimes give detailed instructions before giving the implementers an overall feel for the task.
6. Planners sometimes stress minute problems instead of more important points.
7. The instructions may be given in a way that discourages members of an operating group from working as a team.

Common problems when implementers carry out the plans of others:

1. If instructions are confusing, implementers tend to display irritation toward each other and the planners.
2. If instructions are unclear, considerable time will be spent in clarification.
3. Members of an implementation team will often have different perceptions of their instructions.
4. The factor of pressure will influence different implementers in different ways—the efficiency of some will go up and the efficiency of others will decline.
5. If members of an implementation group do not feel themselves to be a team, they will usually perform less efficiently.

EXHIBIT 22-4   Lessons About Communicating Changes
Source: Based on B. Bass, "When Planning for Others," *Journal of Applied Behavioral Science* 6(2) (1970): 151–71.

ENDNOTES

[1] Some of these pitfalls appear in R. M. Kanter, B. A. Stein, and T. D. Jick, *The Challenge of Organizational Change: How Companies Experience It and Leaders Guide It* (New York: The Free Press, 1992): 5–8.

[2] W. W. Burke and G. H. Litwin, "A Causal Model of Organizational Performance and Change," *Journal of Management* 18(3)(1992): 523–545.

[3] Gamma change is described in R. Golombiewski, K. Billingsley, and S. Yeager, "Measuring Change and Persistence in Human Affairs: Types of Changes Generated by OD

Design," *Journal of Applied Behavioral Science* 12(2) (1975): 133–157. First- and second-order change is discussed in A. Levy, "Second-Order Planned Change: Definition and Conceptualization," *Organizational Dynamics* 15(1) Summer 1986: 4–20.

[4] This analogy was created by Ken Wilbur, *A Sociable God* (New York: McGraw-Hill, 1983).

[5] M. Beer, R. A. Eisenstat, and B. Spector, "Why Change Programs Don't Produce Change," *Harvard Business Review* 68 (6) (November–December 1990): 158–166.

[6] Ibid.

[7] K. Lewin, "Frontiers in Group Dynamics," *Human Relations* *1*(1) (1947): 5–41.

[8] Y. Doz and C. K. Prahalad, "A Process Model of Strategic Redirection in Large Complex Firms: The Case of Multinational Corporations," *in The Management of Strategic Change*, A. M. Pettigrew (ed.) (Oxford: Basil Blackwell, 1988): 68–83.

[9] S. Ghoshal and C.A. Bartlett, "Rebuilding Behavioral Context: A Blueprint for Corporate Renewal," *Sloan Management Review 37*(2) 1996: 23–37.

[10] J. C. Collins, "Change Is Good—But First Know What Should Never Change," *Fortune 131*(10) (May 29, 1995): 141.

[11] L. D. Goodstein and W. W. Burke, "Creating Successful Organization Change," *Organizational Dynamics 19*(4) (1991): 5–17.

[12] This formula was originally developed by D. Gleicher of Arthur D. Little and later modified by M. Beer, *Organization Change and Development: A System View* (Glenview, IL: Scott, Foresman, 1980). See also A. Armenakis, M. Harris, and K. Mossholder, "Creating Readiness for Large-Scale Change," *Human Relations 46*(6) (1993): 681–703.

[13] R. Beckhard, "Strategies for Large System Change," *Sloan Management Review 16* (1975): 43–55.

[14] J. P Kotter and D. S. Cohen, *The Heart of Change: Real Life Stories about How People Change Their Organizations* (Cambridge, MA: Harvard Business School Press, 2002).

[15] K. Lewin, *Field Theory in Social Science* (New York: Harper & Row, 1951).

[16] R. Fritz, *The Path of Least Resistance* (New York: Ballantine, 1989) and *Creating* (New York: Ballantine, 1990).

[17] L. Bossidy in N.M. Tichy and R. Charan, "The CEO as Coach: An Interview with AlliedSignal's Lawrence A. Bossidy," in J. Champy and N. Nohria (eds.), *Fast Forward: The Best Ideas on Managing Business Change* (Cambridge, MA: Harvard, 1996): 247–248.

[18] N. M. Tichy and S. Sherman, *Control Your Destiny or Someone Else Will* (New York: Harper, 1994). This book describes the principles and actions Jack Welch used to make major changes at General Electric. The appendix contains a "Handbook for Revolutionaries," a step-by-step guide to change.

[19] B. Dumaine, "Times Are Good? Create a Crisis," *Fortune 127* (13) (June 28, 1993): 123–130.

[20] J. P. Kotter, "Kill Complacency," *Fortune 134*(3) (August 5, 1996): 170.

[21] C. Cooperrider and S. Srivastva, "Appreciative Inquiry in Organizational Life," in R. Woodman and W. Pasmore (eds.), *Organizational Change and Development 1,* (Greenwich, CT: JAI Press, 1987): 129–170. The Woodman and Pasmore annual series is an excellent source of current research in this field. See also D. Whitney and A. Trosten-Bloom, *The Power of Appreciative Inquiry.* (San Francisco: Berrett-Koehler, 2003).

[22] J. P. Kotter, "Leading Change: Why Transformation Efforts Fail," *Harvard Business Review 73*(2) (March–April 1995): 59–67.

[23] L. Alexander, "Successfully Implementing Strategic Decisions," *Long Range Planning 18*(3) (1985): 91–97.

[24] T. D. Jick, "Implementing Change," in his book *Managing Change: Cases and Concepts* (Boston: Irwin, 1993): 200.

[25] Jick, "Implementing Change"; Alexander, "Successfully Implementing Strategic Decisions"; and Kotter and Cohen, *The Heart of Change.* See also T. D. Jick and M. Peiperl, *Managing Change: Cases and Concepts* (New York: McGraw-Hill, 2003).

[26] T. C. Cummings and C. G. Worley, *Organization Development and Change* (Cincinnati, OH: South-Western, 1997).

[27] R. Beckhard and R. Harris, *Organizational Transitions: Managing Complex Change* (Reading, MA: Addison-Wesley, 1987).

[28] P. Strebel, "Why Do Employees Resist Change?" *Harvard Business Review 74*(3) (May–June 1996): 86.

[29] Beer et al., "Why Change Programs Don't Produce Change": 161–165.

[30] N. M. Tichy and M. A. Devanna, *The Transformational Leader* (John Wiley & Sons, Inc., 1986).

[31] M. Kanter, *The Change Masters* (New York: Simon & Schuster, 1983).

[32] Ibid.

[33] Cummings and Worley, *Organization Development and Change.*

[34] R. Beckhard and W. Pritchard, *Changing the Essence* (San Francisco: Jossey-Bass, 1992).

[35] D. Nadler and M. Tushman, *Competing by Design* (New York: Oxford University Press, 1997).

[36] M. Tushman and C. A. O'Reilly, "Amibidextrous Organizations: Managing Evolutionary and Revolutionary Change," *California Management Review 38*(4) (1996): 8–30.

[37] R. Whittington, A. Pettigrew, S. Peck, E. Fenton, and M. Conyon, "Change and Complementarities in the New Competitive Landscape: A European Panel Study, 1992–1996," *Organization Science 10*(5) (1998): 583–600.

[38] Tushman and O'Reilly, "Ambidextrous Organizations: 11.

[39] P. Evans, V. Pucik, and J. L. Barsoux, *The Global Challenge: Frameworks for International Human Resource Management* (New York: McGraw-Hill, 2002): 423.

[40] J. P. Kotter and L. A. Schlesinger, "Choosing Strategies for Change," *Harvard Business Review 57*(2) (March–April 1979): 106–14.

[41] R. S. Larsen, "Frameworks: Turning the Challenges of Change into Opportunities for Growth," *Chief Executive 144* (May 1999): 12.

[42] M. Beer, *Organization Change and Development,* Monica, CA: Goodyear Publishing, 1980).

[43] W. L. French and C. H. Bell, Jr., *Organizational Development: Behavioral Sciences Interventions for Organizational Improvement* (Upper Saddle River, NJ: Prentice Hall, 1999).

[44] See French and Bell, *Organizational Development*, and Cummings and Worley, *Organization Development and Change*, for comprehensive descriptions of interventions. See S. Schein, *Process Consultation II: Its Role in Organizational Development* (Reading, MA: Addison-Wesley, 1987); and *Process Consultation Revisited: Building the Helping Relationship* (Addison-Wesley, 1999) for in-depth reviews on process consultation. For team building, see W. G. Dyer and J. H. Dyer, *Proven Strategies for Improving Team Performance (4th ed.)* (San Francisco: Jossey-Bass, 2007); and J. Katzenbach and D. Smith, *The Wisdom of Teams* (Cambridge, MA: Harvard Business School Press, 1993).

[45] J. B. Nicholas, "The Comparative Impact of Organization Development Interventions on Hard Criteria Measures," *Academy of Management Review 7* (October 1982): 531–542; and J. I. Porras and P. O. Berg, "The Impact of Organization Development," *Academy of Management Review 3* (1978): 249–266.

[46] Cummings and Worley, *Organization Development and Change.*

[47] K. Johnson, "Estimating National Culture and O. D. Values," in P. Sorenson, Jr., T. Head, K. Johnson, N. Mathys, J. Preston, and D. Cooperrider (eds.), *Global and International Organization Development*, (Champaign, IL: Stipes, 1995): 266–281; and A. Jaeger, "Organization Development and National Culture: Where's the Fit?" *Academy of Management Review 11* (1986): 178–90.

[48] W. Bridges, "Managing Organizational Change," in (ed.) W. W. Burke, *Managing Organizational Change* (New York: American Management Association, 1995): 20.

[49] C. A. Bartlett and S. Ghoshal, *Transnational Management* (Boston: Irwin McGraw-Hill, 2000).

[50] For a description of the various forms of organizational change efforts that emerge in different cultures, see C. Faucheux, G. Amado, and A. Laurent, "Organizational Devel-

opment and Change," *Annual Reviews of Psychology 33* (1982): 343–370. See also K. E. Weick and R. E. Quinn, "Organizational Change and Development," *Annual Review of Psychology 50* (1999): 361–386; and J. Osland, "Managing Global Change by Building Community," in the *Handbook of Global Management: A Guide to Managing Complexity*, H. Lane, M. Mendenhall, M. Maznevski, & J. McNett (eds.) (Oxford: Blackwell, 2004): 134-151.

[51] M. Tribus, "Deming's Redefinition of Management," in D. Kolb, J. Osland, and I. Rubin (eds.), *The Organizational Behavior Reader*, (Upper Saddle River, NJ: Prentice Hall, 1995): 654–664; M. Walton, *Deming's Management at Work* (New York: Putnam, 1990); J. M. Juran, "Made in U.S.A.: A Renaissance in Quality," *Harvard Business Review 71* (1993): 42–50; and A. V. Feigenbaum, "How Total Quality Counters Three Forces of Internal Competitiveness," *National Productivity Review 13* (1994): 327–330.

[52] A. Bird and S. Kotha, "U.S. and Japanese Perceptions of Advanced Manufacturing Technologies: Revitalizing the Convergence/Divergence Debate," in S. Beechler and A. Bird (eds.), *Research in International Business and International Relations 6* (1994): 73–102; J. Liker, *Engineered in Japan* (New York: Oxford, 1995); W. M. Fruin, *Knowledge Works: Managing Intellectual Capital at Toshiba* (New York: Oxford, 1997).

[53] D. A. Garvin, *Managing Quality: The Strategic and Competitive Edge* (New York: Free Press, 1988) and W. H. Schmidt and J. Finnigan, *The Race Without a Finish Line* (San Francisco: Jossey-Bass, 1992) provide a good starting place for reading about the quality movement.

[54] D. M. Schrodoeder and A. G. Robinson, "America's Most Successful Export to Japan: Continuous Improvement Programs," *Sloan Management Review 32* (3) (Spring 1991): 67–81; L. S. Vansina, "Total Quality Control: An Overall Organizational Improvement Strategy," *National Productivity Review 9* (1) (Winter 1989/1990): 59–73.

[55] See Schmidt and Finnigan, *The Race Without a Finish Line*, for lessons from the Baldrige Award winners.

[56] This exercise was developed by Dr. Bernard Bass, Director, the Center for Leadership Studies, SUNY Binghamton, and is used with his permission.

[57] Bridges, "Managing Organizational Change": 20–28.

[58] "For more information on parallel organizations, see B. A. Stein and R. M. Kanter, "Building the Parallel Organization: Creating Mechanisms for Permanent Quality of Work Life," *Journal of Applied Behavioral Science 16* (1980): 37 -388; and G. R. Bushe and A. B. Shani, *Parallel Learning Structures* (Reading, MA: Addison-Wesley, 1991).

Integrative Cases

▲▲▲

The Donor Services Department *

Joanna Reed was walking home through fallen tree blossoms in Guatemala City. Today, however, her mind was more on her work than the natural beauty surrounding her. She unlocked the gate to her colonial home and sat down on the porch, surrounded by riotous toddlers, pets, and plants, to ponder the recommendations she would make to Sam Wilson. The key decisions she needed to make about his donor services department concerned who should run the department and how the work should be structured.

Joanna had worked for a sponsorship agency engaged in international development work with poor people for six years. She and her husband moved from country to country setting up new agencies. In each country, they had to design how the work should be done, given the local labor market and work conditions.

After a year in Guatemala, Joanna, happily pregnant with her third child, had finished setting up the donor services department for the agency and was working only part-time on a research project. A friend who ran a "competing" development agency approached her to do a consulting project for him. Sam Wilson, an American, was the national representative of a U.S.-based agency that had offices all over the world. Wilson wanted Joanna to analyze his donor services department because he had received complaints from headquarters about its efficiency. Since he had been told that his office needed to double in size in the coming year, he wanted to get all the bugs worked out beforehand. Joanna agreed to spend a month gathering information and compiling a report on this department.

What Is a Donor Services Department in a Sponsorship Agency Anyway?

Sponsorship agencies, with multimillion dollar budgets, are funded by individuals and groups in developed countries who contribute to development programs in less developed countries (LDCs). Donors contribute approximately $20.00 per month plus optional special gifts. The agencies use this money to fund education, health, community development, and income-producing projects for poor people affiliated with their agency in various communities. In the eyes of most donors, the specific benefit provided by sponsorship agencies is the personal relationship between a donor and a child and his or her family in the LDC. The donors and children write back and forth, and the agency sends photos of the child and family to the donors. Some donors never write the family they sponsor; others write weekly and visit the family on their vacations. The efficiency of a donor services department and the quality of their translations are key ingredients to keeping donors and attracting new ones. Good departments also never lose sight of the fact that sponsorship agencies serve a dual constituency—the local people they are trying to help develop and the sponsors who make that help possible through their donations.

The work of a donor services department consists of more than translating letters, preparing annual progress reports on the families, and answering donor questions directed to the agency. It also handles the extensive, seemingly endless paperwork associated with enrolling new families and assigning them to donors, reassignments when either the donor or the family stops participating, and the special gifts of money sent (and thank you notes for them). Having accurate enrollment figures is crucial because the money the agency receives from headquarters is based on these figures and affects planning.

The Cast of Characters in the Department

The Department Head

Joanna tackled the challenge of analyzing the department by speaking first with the department head (see the organizational chart in Exhibit 1). José Barriga, a charismatic, dynamic man in his forties, was head of both donor services and community services. In reality, he spent virtually no time in the donor services department and was not bilingual. "My biggest pleasure is working with the community leaders and coming up with programs that will be successful. I much prefer being in the field, driving from village to village talking with people, to supervising paperwork. I'm not sure exactly what goes on in donor services, but Elena, the supervisor, is very responsible. I make it a point to walk through the department once a week and say hello to everyone, and I check their daily production figures."

Like José, Sam was also more interested in working with the communities on projects than in immersing himself in the details of the more administrative departments. In part, Sam had contracted Joanna because he rightfully worried that donor services did not receive the attention it deserved from José, who was very articulate and personable but seldom had time to look at anything beyond case histories. José never involved himself in the internal affairs of the department. Even though he was not considered much of a resource to them, he was well liked and respected by the staff of donor services, and they never complained about him.

The Supervisor

This was not the case with the supervisor José had promoted from within. Elena had the title of departmental supervisor, but she exercised very little authority. A slight, single woman in her thirties, Elena had worked for the organization since its establishment 10 years earlier. She was organized, meticulous, dependable, and hardworking. But she was a quiet, nonassertive, nervous woman who was anything but proactive. When asked what changes she would make if she were the head of the department, she sidestepped the question by responding, "It is difficult to have an opinion on this subject. I think that the boss can see the necessary changes with greater clarity."

Elena did not enjoy her role as supervisor, which was partly due to the opposition she encountered from a small clique of longtime translators. In the opinion of this subgroup, Elena had three strikes against her. One, unlike her subordinates, she was not bilingual. "How can she be the supervisor when she doesn't even know English well? One of us would make a better supervisor." Bilingual secretaries in status-conscious Guatemala see themselves as a cut above ordinary

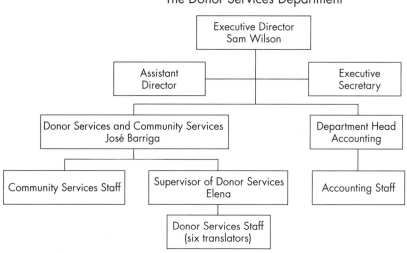

EXHIBIT 1   Organizational Chart—Donor Services Department

secretaries. This group looked down on Elena as being less skilled and less educated than they were, even though she was an excellent employee.

Second, Elena belonged to a different religion than the organization itself and almost all the other employees. This made no difference to Sam and José but seemed important to the clique who could be heard making occasional derogatory comments about Elena's religion.

The third strike against Elena was her lack of authority. No one had ever clarified how much authority she really possessed, and she herself made no effort to assume control of the department. "My instructions are to inform Don José Barriga of infractions in my daily production memo. I'm not supposed to confront people directly when infractions occur, although it might be easier to correct things if I did." ("Don" is a Latin American honorific used before the first name to denote respect.)

This subgroup showed their disdain and lack of respect for Elena by treating her with varying degrees of rudeness and ignoring her requests. They saw her as a watchdog, an attitude furthered by José who sometimes announced, "We (senior management) are not going to be here tomorrow, so be good because Elena will be watching you." When Sam and José left the office, the clique often stopped working to socialize. They'd watch Elena smolder out of the corner of their eyes, knowing she would not reprimand them. "I liked my job better before I became supervisor," said Elena. "Ever since, some of the girls have resented me, and I'm not comfortable trying to keep them in line. Why don't they just do their work without needing me to be the policeman? The only thing that keeps me from quitting is the loyalty I feel for the agency and Don José."

THE WORKERS

In addition to the clique already mentioned, there were three other female translators in the department. All the translators but one had the same profile: in their twenties, of working class backgrounds, and graduates of bilingual secretarial schools, possessing average English skills. (As stated earlier, in Latin America, being a bilingual secretary is a fairly prestigious occupation for a woman.) The exception in this group was the best translator, Magdalena, a college-educated recent hire in her late thirties who came from an upper-class family. She worked, not because she needed the money, but because she believed in the mission of the agency. "This job lets me live out my religious beliefs and help people who have less advantages than I do." Magdalena was more professional and mature than the other translators. Although all the employees were proud of the agency and its religious mission, the clique members spent too much time socializing and skirmishing with other employees inside and outside the department.

The three translators who were not working at full capacity were very close friends. The leader of this group, Juana, was a spunky, bright woman with good oral English skills and a hearty sense of humor. A long-time friend of José's, Juana translated for English-speaking visitors who came to visit the program sites throughout the country. The other translators, tied to their desks, saw this as a huge perk. Juana was the ringleader in the occasional mutinies against Elena and in feuds with people from other departments. Elena was reluctant to complain about Juana to José, given their friendship. Perhaps she feared Juana would make her life even more miserable.

Juana's two buddies (*compañeras*) in the department also had many years with the agency. They'd gotten into the habit of helping each other on the infrequent occasions when they had excessive amounts of work. When they were idle or simply wanted to relieve the boredom of their jobs, they socialized and gossiped. Juana in particular was noted for cutting sarcasm and pointed jokes about people she didn't like. This clique was not very welcoming to the newer members of the department. Magdalena simply smiled at them but kept her distance, and the two younger translators kept a low profile to avoid incurring their disfavor. As one of them remarked, "It doesn't pay to get on Juana's bad side."

THE ORGANIZATION OF THE DEPARTMENT

Like many small offices in Latin America, the agency was located in a spacious former private home. The donor services department was housed in the 40 by 30 foot living room area. The women's desks were set up in two rows, with Elena's desk in the back corner. Since Sam and

José's offices were in former back bedrooms, everyone who visited them walked through the department. Inevitably they stopped to greet and chat with the longtime employees (Elena, Juana, and her two friends). Elena's numerous visitors also spent a good deal of time working their way through the department to reach her desk, further contributing to the amount of socializing going on in the department.

Elena was the only department member who had "official" visitors since she was the liaison person who dealt with program representatives and kept track of enrollments. The translators each were assigned one work process. For example, Marisol prepared case histories on new children and their families for prospective donors while Juana processed gifts. One of the newer translators prepared files for newly enrolled children and did all the filing for the entire department (a daunting task). Most of the jobs were primarily clerical and required little or no English. The letter translations were outsourced to external translators on a piece-work basis and supervised by Magdalena. Hers was the only job that involved extensive translation; for the most part, however, she translated simple messages (such as greeting cards) that were far below her level of language proficiency. The trickier translations, such as queries from donors in other countries, were still handled by Sam's executive secretary.

Several translators complained that: "We don't have enough opportunity to use our English skills on the job. Not only are we not getting any better in English, we are probably losing fluency because most of our jobs are just clerical work. We do the same simple, boring tasks over and over, day in and day out. Why did they hire bilingual secretaries for these jobs anyway?"

Another obvious problem was the uneven distribution of work in the office. The desks of Magdalena and the new translators were literally overflowing with several months' backlog of work while Juana and her two friends had time to kill. Nobody, including Elena, made any efforts to even out the work assignments or help out those who were buried. The subject had never been broached.

The agency was growing at a rapid pace, and there were piles of paperwork sitting around waiting to be processed. Joanna spent three weeks having each department member explain her job (in mind-numbing detail), drawing up flow charts of how each type of paperwork was handled, and poking around in their files. She found many unnecessary steps that resulted in slow turnaround times for various processes. There were daily output reports submitted to José but no statistics kept on the length of time it took to respond to requests for information or to process paperwork. No data were shared with the translators, so they had no idea how the department was faring and had little sense of urgency about their work. The only goal was to meet the monthly quota of case histories, which only affected Marisol. Trying to keep up with what came across their desks summed up the entire focus of the employees.

Joanna found many instances of errors and poor quality, not so much from carelessness as from lack of training and supervision. Both José and Sam reviewed the case histories, but Joanna was amazed to discover that no one ever looked at any other work done by the department. The employees were very accommodating when asked to explain their jobs and very conscientious about their work (if not the hours devoted to it by the clique). However, they were seldom able to explain why things were done in a certain way because they had received little training for their jobs and only understood their small part of the department. Morale was obviously low, and all the employees seemed frustrated with the situation in the department. Nevertheless, with the exception of Magdalena who had experience in other offices, none of them could offer Joanna any ideas about how the department could be improved.

THE DONOR SERVICES DEPARTMENT CASE— DISCUSSION QUESTIONS

1. What was Joanna Reed's diagnosis of the situation in the donor services department?
2. What should she recommend to Sam Wilson?
3. Describe the managerial styles of Sam, José, and Elena. What is the impact of their styles?
4. How can motivation be improved in the department?
5. How should Juana be handled?
6. What are the cultural factors that influence this case?

Custom Chip, Inc.*

INTRODUCTION

It was 7:50 on Monday morning. Frank Questin, Product Engineering Manager at Custom Chip, Inc., was sitting in his office making a TO DO list for the day. From 8:00 to 9:30 A.M. he would have his weekly meeting with his staff of engineers. After the meeting, Frank thought he would begin developing a proposal for solving what he called "Custom Chip's manufacturing documentation problem"—inadequate technical information regarding the steps to manufacture many of the company's products. Before he could finish his TO DO list, he answered a phone call from Custom Chip's human resource manager, who asked him about the status of two overdue performance appraisals and reminded him that this day marked Bill Lazarus' fifth year anniversary with the company. Following this call, Frank hurried off to the Monday morning meeting with his staff.

Frank had been Product Engineering Manager at Custom Chip for 14 months. This was his first management position, and he sometimes questioned his effectiveness as a manager. Often he could not complete the tasks he set out for himself due to interruptions and problems brought to his attention by others. Even though he had not been told exactly what results he was supposed to accomplish, he had a nagging feeling that he should have achieved more after these 14 months. On the other hand, he thought maybe he was functioning pretty well in some of his areas of responsibility given the complexity of the problems his group handled and the unpredictable changes in the semiconductor industry—changes caused not only by rapid advances in technology, but also by increased foreign competition and a recent downturn in demand.

COMPANY BACKGROUND

Custom Chip, Inc. was a semiconductor manufacturer specializing in custom chips and components used in radars, satellite transmitters, and other radio frequency devices. The company had been founded in 1977 and had grown very rapidly. Most of the company's 300 employees were located in the main plant in Silicon Valley, but overseas manufacturing facilities in Europe and the Far East were growing in size and importance. These overseas facilities assembled the less complex, higher volume products. New products and the more complex ones were assembled in the main plant. Approximately one-third of the assembly employees were in overseas facilities.

While the specialized products and markets of Custom Chip provided a market niche that had thus far shielded the company from the major downturn in the semiconductor industry, growth had come to a standstill. Because of this, cost reduction had become a high priority.

THE MANUFACTURING PROCESS

Manufacturers of standard chips have long production runs of a few products. Their cost per unit is low and cost control is a primary determinant of success. In contrast, manufacturers of custom chips have extensive product lines and produce small production runs for special applications. Custom Chip, Inc., for example, manufactured over 2,000 different products in the last five years. In any one quarter the company might schedule 300 production runs for different products, as many as one-third of which might be new or modified products which the company had not made before. Because they must be efficient in designing and manufacturing many product lines, all custom chip manufacturers are highly dependent on their engineers. Customers are often first concerned with whether Custom Chip can design and manufacture the needed product *at all*, secondly with whether they can deliver it on time, and only thirdly with cost.

After designing a product, there are two phases to the manufacturing process. (See Exhibit 1.) The first is wafer fabrication. This is a complex process in which circuits are etched onto the various layers added to a silicon wafer. The number of steps that the wafer goes through plus inherent problems in controlling various chemical processes make it very difficult to meet the exacting specifications required for the final wafer. The wafers, which are typically 8 inches in diameter when the fabrication process is complete, contain hundreds, sometimes thousands of tiny identical die. Once the wafer has been tested and sliced up to produce these die, each die will be used as a circuit component.

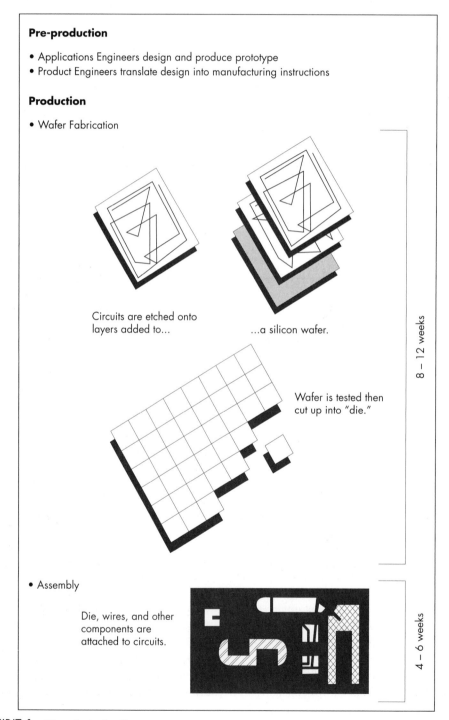

Pre-production

- Applications Engineers design and produce prototype
- Product Engineers translate design into manufacturing instructions

Production

- Wafer Fabrication

Circuits are etched onto layers added to...

...a silicon wafer.

Wafer is tested then cut up into "die."

8 – 12 weeks

- Assembly

Die, wires, and other components are attached to circuits.

4 – 6 weeks

EXHIBIT 1   **Manufacturing Process**

If the completed wafer passes the various quality tests, it moves on to the assembly phase. In assembly, the die from the wafers, very small wires, and other components are attached to a circuit in a series of precise operations. This finished circuit is the final product of Custom Chip, Inc.

Each product goes through many independent and delicate operations, and each step is subject to operator or machine error. Due to the number of steps and tests involved, the wafer fabrication takes 8 to 12 weeks and the assembly process takes 4 to 6 weeks. Because of the exacting specifications, products are rejected for the slightest flaw. The likelihood that every product starting the run will make it through all of the processes and still meet specifications is often quite low. For some products, average yield[1] is as low as 40 percent, and actual yields can vary considerably from one run to another. At Custom Chip, the average yield for all products is higher than 90 percent range.

Because it takes so long to make a custom chip, it is especially important to have some control of these yields. For example, if a customer orders one thousand units of a product and typical yields for that product average 50 percent, Custom Chip will schedule a starting batch of 2,200 units. With this approach, even if the yield falls as low as 45.4 percent (45.4 percent of 2200 is 1,000) the company can still meet the order. If the actual yield falls below 45.4 percent, the order will not be completed in that run, and a very small, costly run of the item will be needed to complete the order. The only way the company can effectively control these yields and stay on schedule is for the engineering groups and operations to cooperate and coordinate their efforts efficiently.

ROLE OF THE PRODUCT ENGINEER

The product engineer's job is defined by its relationship to application engineering and operations. The applications engineers are responsible for designing and developing prototypes when incoming orders are for new or modified products. The product engineer's role is to translate the application engineering group's design into a set of manufacturing instructions, then to work alongside manufacturing to make sure that engineering-related problems get solved. The product engineers' effectiveness is ultimately measured by their ability to control yields on their assigned products. The organization chart in Exhibit 2 shows the engineering and operations departments. Exhibit 3 summarizes the roles and objectives of manufacturing, application engineering, and product engineering.

The product engineers estimate that 70 to 80 percent of their time is spent in solving day-to-day manufacturing problems. The product engineers have cubicles in a room directly across the hall from the manufacturing facility. If a manufacturing supervisor has a question regarding how to build a product during a run, that supervisor will call the engineer assigned to that product. If the engineer is available, he or she will go to the manufacturing floor to help answer the question. If the engineer is not available, the production run may be stopped and the product put aside so that other orders can be manufactured. This results in delays and added costs. One reason that product engineers are consulted is that documentation—the instructions for manufacturing the product—is unclear or incomplete.

The product engineer will also be called if a product is tested and fails to meet specifications. If a product fails to meet test specifications, production stops, and the engineer must diagnose the problem and attempt to find a solution. Otherwise, the order for that product may be only partially met. Test failures are a very serious problem, which can result in considerable cost increases and schedule delays for customers. Products do not test properly for many reasons, including operator errors, poor materials, a design that is very difficult to manufacture, a design that provides too little margin for error, or a combination of these.

On a typical day, the product engineer may respond to half a dozen questions from the manufacturing floor, and two to four calls to the testing stations. When interviewed, the engineers expressed a frustration with this situation. They thought they spent too much time solving short-term

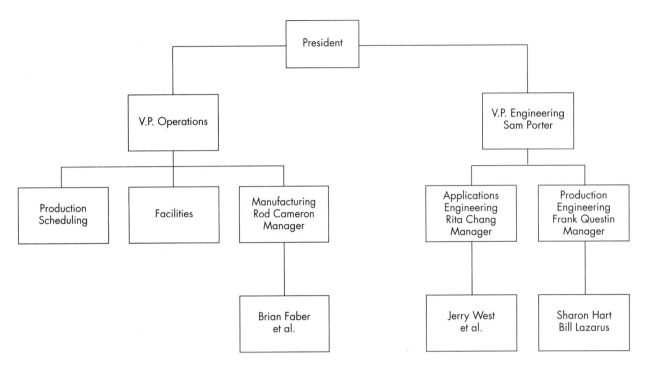

EXHIBIT 2 Custom Chip, Inc. Partial Organization Chart

Department	Role	Primary Objective
Applications Engineering	Design and develop prototypes for new or modified products	Satisfy customer needs through innovative designs
Product Engineering	Translates designs into manufacturing instructions and works alongside manufacturing to solve "engineering-related" problems	Maintain and control yields on assigned products
Manufacturing	Executes designs	Meet productivity standards and time schedules

EXHIBIT 3 Departmental Roles and Objectives

problems, and consequently they were neglecting other important parts of their jobs. In particular, they felt they had little time in which to:

- **Coordinate with applications engineers during the design phase** The product engineers stated that their knowledge of manufacturing could provide valuable input to the applications engineer. Together they could improve the manufacturability and thus, the yields, of the new or modified product.
- **Engage in yield improvement projects** This would involve an in-depth study of the existing process for a specific product in conjunction with an analysis of past product failures.
- **Accurately document the manufacturing steps for their assigned products, especially for those that tend to have large or repeat orders** They said that the current state of the documentation is very poor. Operators often have to build products using only a drawing showing the final circuit, along with a few notes scribbled in the margins. While experienced operators

and supervisors may be able to work with this information, they often make incorrect guesses and assumptions. Inexperienced operators may not be able to proceed with certain products because of this poor documentation.

WEEKLY MEETING

As manager of the product engineering group, Frank Questin had eight engineers reporting to him, each responsible for a different set of Custom Chip products. According to Frank:

> *When I took over as manager, the product engineers were not spending much time together as a group. They were required to handle operation problems on short notice. This made it difficult for the entire group to meet due to constant requests for assistance from the manufacturing area.*
>
> *I thought that my engineers could be of more assistance and support to each other if they all spent more time together as a group, so one of my first actions as a manager was to institute a regularly scheduled weekly meeting. I let the manufacturing people know that my staff would not respond to requests for assistance during the meeting.*

The meeting on this particular Monday morning followed the usual pattern. Frank talked about upcoming company plans, projects, and other news that might be of interest to the group. He then provided data about current yields for each product and commended those engineers who had maintained or improved yields on most of their products. This initial phase of the meeting lasted until about 8:30 A.M. The remainder of the meeting was a meandering discussion of a variety of topics. Since there was no agenda, engineers felt comfortable in raising issues of concern to them.

The discussion started with one of the engineers describing a technical problem in the assembly of one of his products. He was asked a number of questions and given some advice. Another engineer raised the topic of a need for new testing equipment and described a test unit he had seen at a recent demonstration. He claimed the savings in labor and improved yields from this machine would allow it to pay for itself in less than nine months. Frank immediately replied that budget limitations made such a purchase unfeasible, and the discussion moved into another area. They briefly discussed the increasing inaccessibility of the application engineers, then talked about a few other topics.

In general, the engineers valued these meetings. One commented that:

> *The Monday meetings give me a chance to hear what's on everyone's mind and to find out about and discuss company wide news. It's hard to reach any conclusions because the meeting is a freewheeling discussion. But I really appreciate the friendly atmosphere with my peers.*

COORDINATION WITH APPLICATIONS ENGINEERS

Following the meeting that morning, an event occurred that highlighted the issue of the inaccessibility of the applications engineers. An order of 300 units of custom chip 1210A for a major customer was already overdue. Because the projected yield of this product was 70 percent, they had started with a run of 500 units. A sample tested at one of the early assembly points indicated a major performance problem that could drop the yield to below 50 percent. Bill Lazarus, the product engineer assigned to the 1210A, examined the sample and determined that the problem could be solved by redesigning the wiring. Jerry West, the applications engineer assigned to that product category was responsible for revising the design. Bill tried to contact Jerry, but he was not immediately available and didn't get back to Bill until later in the day. Jerry explained that he was on a tight schedule trying to finish a design for a customer who was coming into town in two days and could not get to "Bill's problem" for a while.

Jerry's attitude that the problem belonged to product engineering was typical of the applications engineers. From their point of view there were a number of reasons for making the product engineers' needs for assistance a lower priority. In the first place, applications engineers were rewarded and acknowledged primarily for satisfying customer needs through designing new and modified products. They got little recognition for solving manufacturing problems. Secondly, applications engineering was perceived to be more glamorous than product engineering because of opportunities to be credited with innovative and groundbreaking designs. Finally, the size of the applications engineering group had declined over the past year, causing the workload on each engineer to increase considerably. Now they had even less time to respond to the product engineers' requests.

When Bill Lazarus told Frank about the situation, Frank acted quickly. He wanted this order to be in process again by tomorrow and he knew manufacturing was also trying to meet this goal. He walked over to see Rita Chang, head of applications engineering (see Organization Chart in Exhibit 2). Meetings like this with Rita to discuss and resolve interdepartmental issues were common.

Frank found Rita at a workbench talking with one of her engineers. He asked Rita if he could talk to her in private and they walked to Rita's office.

> Frank: We've got a problem in manufacturing in getting out an order of 1210A's. Bill Lazarus is getting little or no assistance from Jerry West. I'm hoping you can get Jerry to pitch in and help Bill. It should take no more than a few hours of his time.
>
> Rita: I do have Jerry on a short leash trying to keep him focused on getting out a design for Teletronics. We can't afford to show up empty handed at our meeting with them in two days.
>
> Frank: Well, are we going to end up losing one customer in trying to please another? Can't we satisfy everyone here?
>
> Rita: Do you have an idea?
>
> Frank: Can't you give Jerry some additional support on the Teletronics design?
>
> Rita: Let's get Jerry in here to see what we can do.

Rita brought Jerry back to the office, and together they discussed the issues and possible solutions. When Rita made it clear to Jerry that she considered the problem with the 1210A's a priority, Jerry offered to work on the 1210A problem with Bill. He said, "This will mean I'll have to stay a few hours past 5:00 this evening, but I'll do what's required to get the job done."

Frank was glad he had developed a collaborative relationship with Rita. He had always made it a point to keep Rita informed about activities in the Product Engineering group that might affect the applications engineers. In addition, he would often chat with Rita informally over coffee or lunch in the company cafeteria. This relationship with Rita made Frank's job easier. He wished he had the same rapport with Rod Cameron, the Manufacturing Manager.

COORDINATION WITH MANUFACTURING

The product engineers worked closely on a day-to-day basis with the manufacturing supervisors and workers. The problems between these two groups stemmed from an inherent conflict between their objectives (see Exhibit 3). The objective of the product engineers was to maintain and improve yields. They had the authority to stop production of any run that did not test properly. Manufacturing, on the other hand, was trying to meet productivity standards and time schedules. When a product engineer stopped a manufacturing run, he was possibly preventing the manufacturing group from reaching its objectives.

Rod Cameron, the current manufacturing manager, had been promoted from his position as a manufacturing supervisor a year ago. His views on the product engineers:

> The product engineers are perfectionists. The minute a test result looks a little suspicious they want to shut down the factory. I'm under a lot of pressure to get products out the door. If they pull a few $50,000 orders off the line when they are within a few days of reaching shipping, I'm liable to miss my numbers by $100,000 that month.

Besides that, they are doing a lousy job of documenting the manufacturing steps. I've got a lot of turnover and my new operators need to be told or shown exactly what to do for each product. The instructions for a lot of our products are a joke.

At first, Frank found Rod very difficult to deal with. Rod found fault with the product engineers for many problems and sometimes seemed rude to Frank when they talked. For example, Rod might tell Frank to "make it quick, I haven't got much time." Frank tried not to take Rod's actions personally and through persistence was able to develop a more amicable relationship with him. According to Frank:

Sometimes, my people will stop work on a product because it doesn't meet test results at that stage of manufacturing. If we study the situation, we might be able to maintain yields or even save an entire run by adjusting the manufacturing procedures. Rod tries to bully me into changing my engineers' decisions. He yells at me or criticizes the competence of my people, but I don't allow his temper or ravings to influence my best judgment in a situation. My strategy in dealing with Rod is to try not to respond defensively to him. Eventually he cools down, and we can have a reasonable discussion of the situation.

Despite this strategy, Frank could not always resolve his problems with Rod. On these occasions, Frank took the issue to his own boss, Sam Porter, the Vice President in charge of engineering. However, Frank was not satisfied with the support he got from Sam. Frank said:

Sam avoids confrontations with the Operations VP. He doesn't have the influence or clout with the other VPs or the president to do justice to engineering's needs in the organization.

Early that afternoon, Frank again found himself trying to resolve a conflict between engineering and manufacturing. Sharon Hart, one of his most effective product engineers was responsible for a series of products used in radars—the 3805A-3808A series. Today she had stopped a large run of 3806A's. The manufacturing supervisor, Brian Faber, went to Rod Cameron to complain about the impact of this stoppage on his group's productivity. Brian felt that yields were low on that particular product because the production instructions were confusing to his operators, and that even with clearer instructions, his operators would need additional training to build it satisfactorily. He stressed that the product engineer's responsibility was to adequately document the production instructions and provide training. For these reasons, Brian asserted that product engineering, and not manufacturing, should be accountable for the productivity loss in the case of these 3806A's.

Rod called Frank to his office, where he joined the discussion with Sharon, Brian, and Rod. After listening to the issues, Frank conceded that product engineering had responsibility for documenting and training. He also explained, even though everyone was aware of it, that the product engineering group had been operating with reduced staff for over a year now, so training and documentation were lower priorities. Because of this staffing situation, Frank suggested that manufacturing and product engineering work together and pool their limited resources to solve the documentation and training problem. He was especially interested in using a few of the long-term experienced workers to assist in training newer workers. Rod and Brian opposed his suggestion. They did not want to take experienced operators off of the line because it would decrease productivity. The meeting ended when Brian stormed out, saying that Sharon had better get the 3806A's up and running again that morning.

Frank was particularly frustrated by this episode with manufacturing. He knew perfectly well that his group had primary responsibility for documenting the manufacturing steps for each product. A year ago he told Sam Porter that the product engineers needed to update and standardize all of the documentation for manufacturing products. At that time, Sam told Frank that he would support his efforts to develop the documentation but would not increase his staff. In fact, Sam had withheld authorization to fill a recently vacated product engineering slot. Frank was reluctant to push the staffing issue because of Sam's adamant stance on reducing costs. "Perhaps," Frank thought, "if I develop a proposal clearly showing the benefits of a documentation program in manufacturing and detailing the steps and resources required to implement the program, I might be able to convince Sam to provide us with more resources." But Frank could never find the time to develop that proposal. And so he remained frustrated.

LATER IN THE DAY

Frank was reflecting on the complexity of his job when Sharon came to the doorway to see if he had a few moments. Before he could say "come in," the phone rang. He looked at the clock. It was 4:10 P.M. Rita was on the other end of the line with an idea she wanted to try out on Frank, so Frank said he could call her back shortly. Sharon was upset and told him that she was thinking of quitting because the job was not satisfying for her.

Sharon said that although she very much enjoyed working on yield improvement projects, she could find no time for them. She was tired of the applications engineers acting like "prima donnas," too busy to help her solve what they seemed to think were mundane day-to-day manufacturing problems. She also thought that many of the day-to-day problems she handled wouldn't exist if there was enough time to document manufacturing procedures to begin with.

Frank didn't want to lose Sharon, so he tried to get into a frame of mind where he could be empathetic to her. He listened to her and told her that he could understand her frustration in this situation. He told her the situation would change as industry conditions improved. He told her that he was pleased that she felt comfortable in venting her frustrations with him, and he hoped she would stay with Custom Chip.

After Sharon left, Frank realized that he had told Rita that he would call back. He glanced at the TO DO list he had never completed and realized that he hadn't spent time on his top priority—developing a proposal relating to solving the documentation problem in manufacturing. Then, he remembered that he had forgotten to acknowledge Bill Lazarus' fifth year anniversary with the company. He thought to himself that his job felt like a roller coaster ride, and once again he pondered his effectiveness as a manager.

ENDNOTE

1. Yield refers to the ratio of finished products that meet specifications relative to the number that initially entered the manufacturing process.

CUSTOM CHIP, INC.—DISCUSSION QUESTIONS

1. What are the key problems facing Frank?
2. What are the pros and cons of Frank's managerial style? His conflict handling style
3. What is the source of conflict among the different departments? How could it be resolved?
4. What are the advantages and disadvantages of Custom Chip, Inc.'s organizational structure?
5. What steps should Frank take to improve this situation?

Celestial's Global Customer Team*

COMPANY

Celestial Corporation (fictitious name) is a *Fortune* 500 firm that manufactures and sells products for consumer markets all over the world. Over its history, the company has usually enjoyed strong profits and has been widely admired for its excellence. Celestial is headquartered in the United States, and has large regional divisions in North America, Europe, Latin America, and Asia. About half of its employees are based in the United States, with another third in Europe and the remainder in other regions. The company's products are sold in retail establishments in over 100 countries. Celestial is thus dependent on retailers' cooperation for its success. One of Celestial's largest retail customers is a traditional French-based firm called Voila (also fictitious), headquartered in Paris, with retail outlets worldwide. For each of its major global retailers, Celestial established a cross-functional team dedicated to strengthening and maintaining its customer relationship. Such teams typically were located in proximity to the customers' headquarters.

GLOBAL RESTRUCTURING

During the 1990s, Celestial experienced increasing pressure from rising global competition in its markets around the world. Threatened with declines in market share and profits for some of its major brands, the company engaged in rethinking its strategy. A key outcome of this process was a plan for global restructuring, called "Global 2020." This plan would transform the firm's traditional geographical and functional structures to make them fully global with respect to product manufacturing, marketing, and services. One component of the plan involved the globalization of Celestial's major customer relationship teams, including the Voila-dedicated team. This team would be transformed from one that was essentially Franco-centric to one that was global both in terms of the composition and location of the core team, and its scope of responsibility. The creation of a globally distributed team to serve Voila was made possible by the rapid evolution of telecommunications technologies during the late 1990s, and the increasing availability and/or falling cost of communication tools such as videoconferencing, electronic meeting systems, knowledge repositories, workflow tools, and a suite of other options. To address escalating cost pressures, Global 2020 envisioned a downsizing of 15,000 employees over the next six years, and by 2003 the company had indeed eliminated about 8,000 positions.

ECONOMIC ENVIRONMENT

During the late 1990s and early part of 2000, the economic picture in the United States was dominated by a technology boom fueled in part by the Y2K frenzy. Consumer markets in the United States and Europe were strong, while Asia was experiencing the effects of a long-term recession. Older line companies such as Celestial were challenged by the rhetoric of a "new economy" that in some ways was threatening to their established way of doing business. This external environment inspired the appointment of a CEO at Celestial who espoused internal revolution and culture change. Making "breakthrough" was encouraged, while business as usual was frowned on.

* Excerpted from M. L. Baba, J. Gluesing, H. Ratner and K. H. Wagner, "The Contexts of Knowing: Natural History of a Globally Distributed Team," *Journal of Organizational Behavior 25* (2004): 547–587.

THE AMERICAN CORPORATE CONTEXT

One aspect of Celestial's globalization plan was the formation of a few select global teams to manage relationships with Celestial's largest global retail customers. Each team would be responsible for creating and executing strategy that would lead to improvements in business results worldwide with respect to a particular retailer. This responsibility included work related to daily interaction with retail customers and long-range efforts aimed at improving the overall business relationship.

Traditionally, the relationship between Celestial and its largest retail customers had been characterized by zero-sum dynamics; if you win, I lose. The two parties would negotiate the wholesale price of goods, the range of goods selected for sale, the terms of retail offering to consumers, and other matters of trade. Antagonism sometimes developed during these negotiations as a result of haggling over terms, and that occasionally led to a breakdown in the trade relationship. In the case of Celestial's largest France-based global customer, Group Voila, tension became acute. One individual commented: "Voila couldn't stand Celestial." This comment pertains to the relationship between the two corporate entities, not the individuals involved in the negotiations.

Towards the end of the 1990s, the relationship between Celestial and Voila became so strained that the French retailer threatened to cut off purchases of Celestial goods. Celestial deployed a special study team to investigate the matter, led by James Morris, a Celestial executive based at corporate headquarters. This executive's experience included several international assignments and a very successful term as leader of another Celestial customer team for the North American retail firm Americart. During the mid 1990s, when Americart faced bankruptcy, Morris's team helped turn around the situation by implementing with the customer a new merchandising methodology known as Product Family Management (PFM).

PFM is an innovative system of management practices that creates a strategic business plan around specific families of products (e.g., food). PFM is grounded in detailed research about shoppers' purchases, practices, and preferences. A multifunctional team of experts from the manufacturer and the retailer leads the research and planning effort. Based on research data, the team designs and implements a store-level plan to offer product groups in ways that increase the volume of shoppers' purchases and their profitability. PFM requires close collaboration between the manufacturer and retailer, as well as cooperation across different functions inside both companies. Marketing, logistics, information technology, finance, production, and other functions must coordinate and collaborate effectively to successfully plan and execute the strategy.

The PFM approach improved business results for both Celestial and Americart (i.e., higher sales and profits for both), and also improved the firms' relationship. Previous to Morris's tenure as head of Celestial's Americart customer team, the relationship between these two firms also had been highly strained and antagonistic. The introduction of PFM required Morris to reorganize not only the customer relationship, but also the internal relations on his own customer team. These changes caused a prolonged period of turmoil at Celestial, as traditional functional leaders and reporting lines were transformed into flatter, multifunctional teams that included customer representatives.

Study of the situation at Voila convinced Morris that PFM was the solution for improving relationships with that retailer as well. In 1998, his recommendations for reorganizing the work of Celestial's Voila customer team were approved by Celestial's corporate leadership, and Morris was named head of Celestial's new global customer team for Voila. The primary goals of the global team were to work with Voila's corporate headquarters to set the terms and conditions of trade on a global basis, to solve problems related to the global supply of products to Voila, and to improve the overall business relationship between Celestial and Voila such that, over the long run, both firms would experience improvements in sales and profits. The principal strategy to reach the latter goal would be implementation of PFM at Voila.

By late 1998/early 1999 Morris was recruiting new talent onto the Paris-based customer team. One person he approached was an internal consultant, Cathleen Drummond, who had previously worked with him at Americart and was highly skilled at implementing PFM. She was now in charge of paper products in Asia, with an office based in Tokyo. Morris planned to have Drummond lead the PFM work at Voila. Morris also recruited a talented member of the organizational development group at corporate headquarters, who had a wealth of experience leading organizational change at Celestial. This individual, Geraldine (Gerry) Hanover, would serve as facilitator of global team meetings and as the consultant on human and organizational aspects of the change to PFM. Gerry and as an academic colleague had conducted a detailed case study of PFM at Americart the year before, and it was thought that knowledge from this case could be transferred to the Voila situation. Gerry also had a thick binder of operating procedures documenting the working knowledge gained from Americart's experience.

THE FRENCH CUSTOMER CONTEXT

The new global team was not established in an historical or cultural vacuum. There had existed previously a Celestial Voila multifunctional customer team of about 10 members, based in Paris, near the Voila headquarters. This team was comprised primarily of French nationals (plus one English member) who focused on selling products to Voila, conducting business in the French language exclusively. The team leader (Henri Couture) concentrated his efforts on the Voila headquarters, with regional managers directing sales activity in local areas outside France where Voila had stores. This Paris-based team, which had established a very good working relationship with Voila executives and others in Paris, had responsibility for negotiating the terms and conditions of sale with Voila, but this group did not create or execute global strategy. Over the years, the Parisian team had become familiar with several key individuals at Voila and with customer operations in Paris and across Europe.

James Morris's new global customer team was built upon the foundation of the original team in Paris. Four of the original French nationals (including their team leader), plus the English member, continued to be members of the new global team. One of the original French members became the regional manager for Latin America. To this core, Morris gradually added eight new members (including himself). Five of these new members were Americans. One American was stationed in Paris, one became a regional manager in South Asia, while three others would remain at their home locations and commute to Paris only for meetings (Morris, Drummond, and Hanover). Also added to the new team were one Belgian in finance, one French national in logistics (both stationed in Paris), and one additional French national who became regional manager for North Asia. All of the regional managers were relocated to regional offices and only visited Paris occasionally.[1] Cathleen Drummond would continue to work out of her office in Tokyo and essentially hold two jobs. The reward for her double duty would be a promotion to director level. Both Morris and Hanover had personal reasons for not relocating to Paris but remaining at Celestial's U.S. headquarters (even though the new team's charter called for the team leader to collocate in Paris).

Exhibit 1 shows the composition of the newly constituted global team and their geographical locations. The new global team was larger than the original team, with 13 members. Like the original team, it continued to have a collocated group of French nationals (six) in Paris (plus one English and one American member), for a total of eight located near the customer's headquarters. In addition, the team's membership now included an extended global network of non-collocated regional managers (one each in Latin America (French), North Asia (French), and South Asia (American)). In addition, there were two Americans based at the U.S. headquarters, plus Drummond in Tokyo. In general, then, the French members primarily were clustered in Paris, while the Americans primarily were distributed over four locations on three continents. The new global team would conduct quarterly face-to-face meetings in Paris and hold weekly meetings facilitated by audio, video, and data conferencing. Team meetings would be conducted in English.

An important difference between the original team and the new globally distributed team was the fact that the former did business following the French model, while Morris expected the latter to follow the American business model. The French tend to rely on long-term, personal relationships and networks for the conduct of daily business and generally respect the organizational hierarchy for purposes of communication and coordination (Hall & Hall, 1990; Platt, 1996). On the other hand, some observers of American corporate practices have noted that U.S. businesspeople tend to be action-oriented and thus focused pragmatically on getting the job done; the

---

[1] An exception was the regional manager for Europe. This position was given to Henri Couture, the original French team leader, and it was based in Paris.

EXHIBIT 1 **Global Team Member Composition**

Team origin	Nationality	Location	Role
Original	French	Paris	Regional manager (Europe)[a]
Original	French	Caracas	Regional manager (Latin America)[b]
Original	French	Paris	Merchandising
Original	French	Paris	Information technology
Original	English	Paris	Customer relations
New global	American	U.S. HQ	Team leader
New global	American	Tokyo	Product family management
New global	American	U.S. HQ	Organizational development
New global	American	Paris	Marketing
New global	American	Thailand	Regional manger (South Asia)
New global	French	Hong Kong	Regional manager (North Asia)
New global	French	Paris	Logistics
New global	Belgian	Paris	Finance
Merger	French	Paris	Customer business development
Merger	Italian	Brussels	Human resources
Merger	Belgian	Brussels	Finance
Merger	French	Paris	Information technology
Merger	German	Brussels	Logistics
Merger	Belgian	Brussels	Marketing
Merger	Belgian	Brussels	Customer relations

[a]This role was assigned to the former French team leader, Henri Couture.

[b]On the original team, this individual was co-located in Paris; he was assigned to Caracas when the global team was reconstituted.

organizational hierarchy may be more or less salient, depending upon corporate culture and the conditions at hand (Stewart & Bennett, 1991; see also Carroll, 1988). Previously, members of the original team in Paris relied on their French team leader's personal contacts within Voila to carry out many business tasks. This individual, Henri Couture, had married into an "old money" French family. Because of the close intertwining of business and social relations in France, Couture had developed many personal relationships with other elite French business leaders, including executives at Voila. In fact, he had attended school with some of the Voila executives. The French nationals on the Celestial customer team gained a sense of security and strength from Couture's personal contacts with Voila, which assured they would continue to get business done, even if things were not so good at the corporate level.

When anyone on the Celestial Voila team needed to meet with a Voila manager, Couture would call the appropriate person at Voila and set up the appointment. This was virtually the only way to access Voila's management; other members of the Celestial customer team lacked contacts with Voila's top managers. Even James Morris (who was Couture's boss) had to go through Couture to get an appointment at Voila. James Morris, like most Celestial executives, had no connections to the French elite and did not speak French. It was well known that Voila managers preferred speaking French over English, making it very difficult to establish contacts on one's own if one did not speak French (or have preexisting personal ties). Thus, Morris was dependent on Couture.

When Morris was appointed global team leader, the Voila business in France was doing well, accounting for 70–80 percent of Celestial's Voila business worldwide. No one in Paris thought that the system was "broken" or needed a fix. The three key Americans, however, shared a very American belief that good results can always be bettered. Gerry Hanover described Morris's stance:

> *Jim Morris is a person who is very experienced. He's pulled together multi-resource customer teams to meet the needs of the customer as they're known today and as they should be approached in the future. His approach places a lot of focus on breakthrough. Why don't I call him a pioneer, somebody who is not quite satisfied with the status quo.*

Morris had big ideas for changing the way business got done with Voila, and he saw PFM as the vehicle for doing so. Morris wanted what, in the French view, were radical changes in the behavior of the Celestial global customer team members, and in the relationship with the customer. Voila was a traditional French firm, with a bureaucratic structure and functionally compartmentalized activities. But PFM required Voila to enter into a close partnership with Celestial that many in Voila's leadership believed was inappropriate (and potentially unethical). Voila believed that all suppliers should be treated equally, held at arm's length (especially Americans), and not given special privileges. Further, suppliers were not always held in high esteem in retail organizations, making close partnership difficult, as one French team member explained:

> *I could give you some stories about people (suppliers) visiting customers here in France, and not being physically hurt, but being really sent back, kicked back out of the offices of retailers, and I mean this is really true . . . in general, the French retailer is rude, and doesn't have any respect for suppliers . . . there is a kind of relationship that American people will have great difficulty understanding.*

Another change required by PFM involved day-to-day customer interface. Just as Henri Couture controlled access to Voila's top management, each functional manager on the Celestial customer team had a more or less exclusive relationship with his or her functional counterpart at Voila. The quality of these relationships, resting on carefully nurtured personal interactions, was the basis for Celestial employees' knowledge of the customer and created a deep sense of self-worth. PFM would alter this interface, making contact with the customer more diffuse and multifunctional. A Celestial team with multiple functions would work across all of the same functions at Voila, opening the possibility that people from one function at Celestial would be working with people from a different function at Voila. Such an arrangement was viewed as threatening by functional heads at Voila, since it would weaken their power and authority.

Leadership of the PMF effort posed another threat. As a PFM expert with eight years experience implementing the new technique, Cathleen Drummond would become prominent in directing the multifunctional team. In the past, only Henri Couture held the director title, and he was accustomed to being the undisputed authority. Having two directors on the team seemed to him like a loss of face, and potentially status and power as well. The Americans had not considered this to be an issue at the time Drummond was promoted. Yet, it is no wonder Couture was uncomfortable, given Drummond's explicitly stated goal. In her words:

> *We're trying to shift, I should say, it's my goal, and I think Jim is trying to do this too, and Gerry, to shift the team to a place where the main agenda we have with Voila is driven by the work that we do, not the relationships. Not because relationships aren't important, they're hugely important, it's just because more people can play if it's the work that [establishes] your value and your relationships. Because then, everybody can play, everybody can take the keys and go do work . . .*

Drummond wanted to shift the focus of interaction between the two firms from 80 percent relationship/20 percent work (which she believed the original distribution to be) to 40 percent relationship/60 percent work. She believed this shift would enable women and minorities to play a stronger role on the team, since they could bring knowledge, skills, and experiences to the table even if they did not always have the advantage of elite social relationships to rely upon. It was Drummond's strong belief that, ultimately, such changes would strengthen business results.

At first, Couture responded to the arrival of the Americans on what formerly had been his "turf" by simultaneously threatening to leave Celestial and attempting to negotiate an enhanced position for himself. Initial discussions with Morris succeeded in creating new responsibilities for the former French team leader as director of European operations for Celestial's work with Voila. It was even hinted that Couture might ultimately succeed his boss as overall global team leader. Ultimately, however, the speed with which changes were taking place, and their magnitude, overwhelmed his efforts to seize a key role for himself and ultimately led him to resign from Celestial later on.

Interactions between Celestial's French and American people also reflected the long-standing macro-level tensions between France and the United States around American "cultural imperialism." American corporations have a long history of introducing not only U.S.-born products and services to France, but also organizational innovations such as management-by-objectives and cross-functional teams (and with these more and more English language terms). Some French people are less than enthusiastic about the "invasion" of U.S. concepts, material artifacts, and language, expressing a national resistance to what they saw as a further incursion on French culture. The introduction of PFM and other American ways of doing business were viewed by some as an instance of American (and English language) domination, as this French team member suggests:

> . . . there is still . . . and this is probably coming from history, probably from the time where the goal here was empowering France . . . probably France is one of the countries where you still feel some kind of, I wouldn't call it anti-American but, still some kind of feeling that they are important, as important as the U.S., when you come from a cultural point of view, and they don't understand why the French is not a language that is recognized around the whole globe.

THE ASIAN CUSTOMER CONTEXT

During the late 1990s, the economic recession in Asia, together with increasing competition, pressured the Voila organization in Hong Kong. The Voila leader in Hong Kong, Jacques Clement, called in an American consulting firm to help re-engineer business processes to enable cost savings. The consultants told Clement about actions taken by Americart retailers several years earlier to turn around their financial difficulties, one of which was to work more closely with Celestial and to institute PFM with Celestial's help. (Recall that it was Jim Morris who led this work for Celestial.) Clement, intrigued by this information, met with Morris in the United States to learn more about Celestial's role in Americart's turn-around. As a result, Clement decided to run a small-scale test of PFM in the baby care product group. Although this test did not privilege Celestial, it did halt the decline in Voila profits in Hong Kong. This success renewed the debate within Voila regarding collaboration with suppliers and whether such action violated Voila's sense of propriety. Clement asked the American consulting firm to incorporate PFM principles into their reengineering work. He called this effort Nourriture Excellente.

Subsequently, Clement visited Americart's U.S. headquarters to meet with an executive there (David Hyde) who had been instrumental in implementing PFM. The two executives must have made a strong impression on one another, because soon after they met Hyde left Americart and went to work for Voila in France as their chief merchandising officer. Part of Hyde's agreement on joining Voila was that he and Clement would undertake a full test of PFM in Hong Kong, complete with Celestial partnership. This agreement was made with top executives at Voila, who wanted to see whether PFM really could deliver the kind of results Hyde promised, once implemented in a Voila retail store (but not in Paris, given the resistance of middle managers there).

David Hyde's arrival at Voila changed the situation for Celestial significantly. Morris no longer needed to access Voila through his French subordinate, Henri Couture. He could simply call Hyde, a fellow American with whom he had worked closely in the past. The two Americans became partners in an effort to change the way Voila related to Celestial, using PFM as the primary driver. Celestial would provide full support to the pilot, including help from an information technology expert (for shopper data analysis), and from Cathleen Drummond who would personally lead the PFM pilot, while maintaining her former position in Tokyo. Clement acted as local sponsor for the project.

The objective of the pilot, from Celestial's standpoint, was to demonstrate with hard business results the power of PFM. Only then would the Voila executives engage Celestial in a corporate-level partnership to implement PFM in Voila stores around the world, including those in France (or, at least, that is what Morris believed). Much was at stake for Morris and company, yet success was not ensured. There was no proven "Voila approach" to PFM as Celestial conceptualized it. The details of PFM at any given retailer were contingent on that specific customer's merchandising structures and practices; implementation would vary dependent upon these context-specific factors. Thus, an understanding gained from the implementation of PFM at Americart could not be transferred intact to Group Voila because the two firms were organized differently. Rather, PFM had to be "reinvented" in a French context, based on understanding the French customer's organization and consumers. Since Celestial had implemented PFM in the United States only, no one really knew exactly what to do or how to do it in a way that would ensure Voila buy-in. Drummond explains:

> . . . we had no Voila approach per se; they weren't doing this work (at Voila) ... This is fundamentally work you have in your head and you know how to do. I had stuff I'd done at Americart, and so you know, to the degree that I could, if it was stuff I created for Americart, then I could doctor it up and use it for Voila. It was essentially helping them take this approach . . . to try to get learning for David Hyde if he was going to be the champion for this work with the Voila Executive Committee . . . He wanted to have some kind of general idea of, you know, am I going to have to turn the organization upside down to get this done, or can I just tweak it a little . . . to get results, you have to learn enough about the organization, so . . . I had a chance to learn about Voila.

David Hyde decided to keep the pilot "off the radar screen" of resistant parties in Paris by providing his Parisian subordinates very little information about it. The effect was an American-based communication network, in which Hyde maintained close contact with Morris, who was in constant communication with Drummond and Hanover. This network did not share much, if any, information with Voila middle managers in Paris. The middle managers, in turn, became uneasy about the pilot, and some of them started to champion an alternative to PFM—Nourriture Excellente (created for Jacques Clement in Hong Kong, combining elements of PFM with reengineering methods). Some managers at Voila were convinced that Nourriture Excellente represented a less threatening "French way" to get the same benefits promised by PFM. Nourriture Excellente shared one key component with PFM—exposing Voila buyers to research on consumer shopping patterns, enabling better buying decisions. Shifting to multifunctional teams or manufacturer–retailer partnerships was not required. With an alternative method to champion, Voila managers stiffened their resistance to the PFM pilot in Hong Kong and promoted Nourriture Excellente as the way to go. Since French members of the Celestial global customer team relied heavily on good working relationships with their Voila counterparts, they could hardly ignore such suggestions. As a result, the Celestial team in Paris was not supportive of the pilot in Hong Kong, as Drummond explains:

> . . . [in Hong Kong] we had no organization, we had no infrastructure, we had no data, we had nobody who knew how to do the work except for me. We could not draw upon the global team here [in Paris] because what we thought we could draw upon turned out to be very dysfunctional. People here were not trying to support, and didn't necessarily want, did not understand why this test was good for them. So we were pretty isolated in Hong Kong.

Yet, anxiety among French global team members mounted as they realized that the Hong Kong pilot might represent the future for Celestial. One team member commented:

> *. . . there was huge angst (on the team in Paris) about non-French people doing anything that would be considered breakthrough or doing anything that would be considered important with this French company [i.e., Voila].*

This anxiety explains the seemingly contradictory reaction of Celestial's French team members upon receiving information about the PFM pilot. Unlike Hyde, Morris did not try to hide the pilot from his team members. On the contrary, face-to-face and virtual meetings of the global customer team always included an agenda item on the latest developments in Hong Kong, even showing video clips of changes being made in the store display to boost sales. These reports invariably were greeted with polite questions, mild congratulations, and, once, applause. In these meetings, there was never a hint that French team members were anxious.

As a result of Morris's efforts to enlighten his team, the French national members were learning about PFM. Everyone had access to the detailed case study of PFM as it had been implemented at Americart. This case was available on a Celestial Web site, and many of the French Celestial global team members had read it. The case study described PFM and its objectives, how it was implemented, its consequences for Americart, and the changes it required on the customer team and at the customer interface. Also, a second case study describing in detail the Hong Kong pilot was under preparation by Drummond, and was discussed at global team meetings. French team members gave input to this case during its creation. This case would support a first ever presentation by Celestial to new Voila store managers at NSEAD (a French business school). In addition, the French nationals attended seminars presenting some of the product family ideas, and they also received informal reports from their French teammate who was the regional manager for North Asia. Yet, as much as team members discussed PFM and compared it to Nourriture Excellente (and they did discuss it at every team meeting, and sometimes spent entire afternoons talking about it), there were lingering doubts about whether they all had the same idea in mind. One French team member commented:

> *I have a quite good understanding of what PFM means. I've been taught what PFM means. But the thing I don't know is, if what I'm thinking is PFM is the same that Cathleen, for example, is thinking of PFM?*

Gerry Hanover agreed that people were learning and understanding, but that their ideas had not been fully integrated:

> *. . . as we're now learning, and people have commented, we've all been doing [PFM] in the way we understand it. In a vacuum. And so, it's not as holistic as it will be when we link our thinking together . . . [The vacuum relates] to people's mind-sets, as well as our internal behaviors that might have us think that the enemy is the person we're competing with in thinking power in the company.*

Since team members in Paris did not participate actively in the Hong Kong pilot, their understanding of PFM probably did not advance as far as it might have if they were involved "hands on" through direct observation and practice. Thus, it is likely that Drummond's expert knowledge of PFM differed from that of her Parisian teammates. But it is also clear that the Parisians' knowledge was increasing.

THE MERGER CONTEXT

Anxiety regarding the PFM pilot test in Hong Kong might not have been so pronounced if not for another unanticipated turn of events: the merger of Voila and its major rival, Jardin. Jardin was a large French retail organization with globally distributed stores, similar to Voila. Celestial also sold goods through Jardin's stores, meaning that Celestial had Jardin customer teams operating in countries where Jardin stores were located. Celestial also had a Jardin Global Customer Team based in Brussels. The merger announcement meant that Celestial's Voila and Jardin globally distributed customer teams needed to merge too, and many of Celestial's teams did so immediately, including the two global teams serving the corporate customer (i.e., many local teams serving these two customers also merged). James Morris was designated leader of the merged Global Customer Team.

In all, seven new members were added to Morris's global team as a result of the merger, bringing the total number to 20. Two of these new members were French, based in Paris, bringing the total number of Parisian French on the team to eight. The other five were Belgian (three), Italian, and German, and all were based in Brussels. (See Exhibit 1 for roles, nationalities, and locations of the new team members.) The merged global team now had a core of about 10 people in Paris (eight French), a smaller cluster of five in Brussels (Europeans of various nationalities), and a global network of five other French and Americans, all located singly with the exception of Morris and Hanover, who were collocated at the American headquarters.

Unfortunately, after Celestial's Voila and Jardin global teams merged, the European Union (EU) determined that additional time would be required to review the proposed merger from a regulatory standpoint. In fact, the formal merger was not approved by the EU until January 2000. This meant that for at least 3 months the newly merged Celestial Voila–Jardin global team could not operate as it would normally. Celestial global teams are responsible for understanding the goals and strategies of their customers, and building work plans that maximize sales and minimize problems in the exchange relationship. During the period of merger limbo, however, it was not possible to do any of this, since the future direction of the merged company was not clear. In the meantime, there were proprietary restrictions on information that could be shared between the companies while they were still separate legal entities. This created an awkward situation in which it was not clear exactly who at Celestial should be speaking to whom at the customer companies about what. Productive activity on the team in Paris thus ground to a near-halt.

To make matters more difficult, the merger of Celestial's global teams created a single merged team with double the number of people necessary. Each function (e.g., finance, information technology, marketing, logistics) now had two people: one from Celestial's Voila global team, and one from Celestial's Jardin global team (see Exhibit 1). It was not at all clear whether two people were really needed for each function, especially since the customer's organization and direction were up in the air. The "double heads" situation made many global team members nervous, since it could turn out that any one of them (except for Morris, Drummond, and Hanover, who held unique roles) might be deemed redundant and eventually asked to leave the team. Members of the merged team were eager to know whether or not they would have a permanent place on the team. Their concerns were heightened by the enforced idleness caused by the premature merger of the two global teams; team members worried that their failure to generate work products during this period would reflect negatively on them as individuals. These questions were especially urgent and anxiety-producing within the Celestial "Global 2020" context, where 15,000 jobs were scheduled to be eliminated. People without a firm assignment under these circumstances might find out they had no job.

Jim Morris's response to European team members' worries about the merger was to advise them to work things out among themselves. He directed each team member to get together with his or her functional counterpart (i.e., from the "other" customer team) and decide what functional work needed to be done over the near and intermediate terms, and, by implication, who would remain on the team. This laissez-faire direction was not a problem for people in functions such as information technology (IT), where there was so much work to do that they easily justified two people. In other areas of the team, however, things were less simple. In some areas, there probably would not be enough work to go around, so one person had to leave. It was not always clear who this should be, or where the person departing would go.

Some team members were very uncomfortable and unhappy with this state of affairs and later described the situation as "horrible," "miserable," or "a disaster." One member commented that he and his counterparts felt as if they had been thrown into a bag, shaken, and left to see who would crawl out. For some individuals, this was a competitive situation that created anxiety and detracted from the possibility of collaboration across the team. Yet, these reactions were not communicated openly, either in virtual or in face-to-face settings, but were shared only behind closed doors. A French team member said:

> . . . *people were very concerned [about the merger], but they would never "put their mouths on the table." They were not doing that in meetings, they were doing it personally, in person-to-person conversations.*

Meanwhile, Jim Morris was not in Paris often enough to help. He visited Paris for face-to-face meetings once every two or three months, and the rest of the time he was at headquarters in America or visiting regional markets. Jim Morris's absence drew this comment from one team member who worked in Paris:

> . . . *Jim has been remote. You know, the fact that he's not here, in fact, he hasn't been with any-one, he's by himself, has been a huge problem for us. And, ultimately, when the team was going through turmoil trying to figure out how to deal with this new customer, trying to figure out how we're going to organize ourselves, you had double faces on every function . . . Not having a team leader present either as father figure, guide, counsel, authority, all the parts that our team leader needs to take . . . none of this was happening . . . The fact of him never being here meant that he never really got to know the people. And he doesn't know about that yet. He never met them personally, I don't know if he really understood exactly the work they were doing. And, if you don't know personally the work we're doing, I mean you really don't understand.*

Morris's knowledge of the situation also was limited by interaction dynamics during team meetings, which were formal and tightly controlled. Both Morris and Hanover expressed a sense of urgency regarding the limited time available for face-to-face and virtual meetings. Agendas often were rushed, with no time for protracted discussion. The team usually tried to cover a dozen or more agenda items in two to three hours, and Hanover carefully steered the discussion so that they could get through everything "in time." There was little diversion from the agenda, and lit-tle or nothing on the agenda that dealt squarely with the issues underlying French fears (e.g., the impending downsizing, the merger, and uncertainty regarding their own futures). People in French organizations may tend to expect 'open space' in meetings that encourages expression and ex-ploration of people's ideas and responses (Hall & Hall, 1990). Due to the Americans' tight con-trol over the agenda, however, the underlying issues were not acknowledged or addressed. In fact, the Americans believed (erroneously) that everyone was in agreement throughout much of the case, although Hanover later acknowledged that the time crunch prevented her from determining whether or not agreement had been reached.

This entire situation undermined the legitimacy of Jim Morris's authority in the minds of some team members. In a French organization, the top manager typically is expected to provide guidance to his subordinates and does not leave them to work things out on their own. Further, here was the American Morris inviting the Americans Gerry Hanover and Cathleen Drummond to join the team when it was not clear whether all of the French people would have jobs. Meanwhile, Henri Couture was on site through it all. Couture did little to discourage the French team mem-bers from continuing to look to him as the legitimate team leader.

THE GLOBAL TEAM CONTEXT

Much to the surprise of the Americans, Voila's top executives did not respond favorably to the un-veiling of the PFM pilot's results in Hong Kong, even though the pilot was a clear financial suc-cess. The reasons for their displeasure were unclear to the Americans, which is not surprising since the two groups rarely communicated directly. Some said that the test was not acceptable because, according to the French, it didn't teach Voila anything not already known. Others felt that the test was not acceptable because it was not conducted in France. Whatever the reason, the in-terest of the Voila executives in PFM waned, providing an opening for the Voila middle managers in Paris to push ahead with their plan to adopt Nourriture Excellente. They induced Henri Couture (just before he departed the scene) to sign an annual agreement with Voila that committed Celestial to collaborating with Voila on Nourriture Excellente.

The Americans (especially Morris, Drummond, and Hyde), on the other hand, continued to be dead set against Nourriture Excellente, since they felt it did not go far enough in rethinking what is offered at a retail store. Open arguments broke out between the Parisian French and more scattered American members of the Celestial global customer team regarding what is "real Product Family Management," and which of the two projects had the greatest potential for improving business results and being accepted by the customer. Each side tried to "kill" the other side's project, using their contacts within the customer organization. David Hyde indicated his interest in "killing" Nourriture Excellente at Voila, while Henri Couture reported that his contacts would "kill" PFM in Hong Kong. There were also rumors that David Hyde was about to be fired because he was "too American." Both sides believed that they had superior knowledge of how to lead innovative business development with the customer. Cathleen Drummond had her eight years of experience with PFM to draw upon, and Morris had led the Celestial–Americart team during implementation of PFM at that retailer. But the French team members in Paris claimed to have equally valuable knowledge of the Voila organization and the French consumer.

Everyone on the global team was feeling pressure to resolve the dispute over these competing projects before the next face-to-face meeting, to be held the following month. James Morris ordered the French nationals in Paris to work with Drummond to figure out how to link their two projects together, and he gave team members a short deadline for reaching an agreement. The key parties arranged a face-to-face meeting in Paris to negotiate a resolution to their differences. The meeting was explicitly organized as a means to share knowledge and use shared knowledge to make a decision. Some of the "nonaligned" parties (e.g., Belgians, other Europeans) were brought into the meeting to act as neutral observers and mediators. Drummond explains:

> . . . the idea in December was, let's increase people's knowledge of both projects. And then maybe we can figure out a solution. So I talked about the Hong Kong work and Jim, who had been there, talked about the Hong Kong work, and then Henri who was still here talked about the Nourriture Excellente work . . . So the theory was, OK, you get a number of people in the room who aren't aligned, who are not very close to either one of the projects, and if they hear about both projects, they'll help to facilitate a common understanding of what we're going to do about it. And it didn't work that way, because other dynamics in the team fell into it . . . [the other non-aligned] people didn't have ownership in either one of the projects, and they didn't have the knowledge to know which one was really better, so they couldn't use their intellectual capability, which they would have been happy to do . . .

This meeting demonstrated that there was no clearly superior approach, but there were two factions, each with power sufficient to result in a stalemate. Due to "baggage on the table" (as Drummond put it), this meeting did not result in a "solution," but participants did agree on an approach that might work in the long run. They agreed to continue both projects and attempt to merge them over time, and in the meanwhile to change the name of the Hong Kong project from PFM to Nourriture Excellente. Since Nourriture Excellente was a relatively new concept, it was believed that Celestial could influence or shape it to be more like PFM, but under the French name. It was agreed that Drumond would relate this plan to David Hyde and convince him not to kill Nourriture Excellente. At this point, no one knew for certain how the two projects would be merged in operational terms.

Early next month, two members of the Celestial team (both marketing managers, one the sole American in Paris and the other a Belgian from Brussels) flew to Hong Kong to learn more about the PFM pilot. They were to develop a firsthand understanding of PFM and transfer what they learned to the Nourriture Excellente project as it unfolded in Paris. In Hong Kong, these two joined Cathleen Drummond and the French regional manager for North Asia. This quartet worked on a plan that would allow PFM to be gradually incorporated into Nourriture Excellente, based on what all of them together knew about both projects. They also carried out their part of the agreement and tried to persuade David Hyde not to kill Nourriture Excellente.

To report on progress, the foursome in Hong Kong requested a videoconference with their colleagues in Paris. The Belgian team member would lead the Hong Kong side of the call to avoid the impression that Drummond was dominating the interaction. On the Parisian side, the call was led by the young French successor-elect to Henri Couture (previously a member of the original team, assigned to the role of regional manager for Latin American). All of the key French team members were present (including Couture, who had not yet left Celestial). Gerry Hanover in the United States had difficulty establishing her video connection, as did the French, so the videoconference started 20 minutes late.

The video facility in Hong Kong was crowded and hot. It was in a room about the size of a closet, with a stationary camera and space for only one person to be seen on the monitor. It was difficult for the people in Hong Kong to see who was at the other end of the connection in Paris—only one face could be seen on each monitor, one in Paris and one in Hong Kong. (Gerry Hanover was plugged into the videoconference from the United States, but no one could see her.) The people in Hong Kong could not see that Henri Coutour was in the video room in Paris, nor could those in Paris see Drummond, who became increasingly upset as the proceedings unfolded.

The call started with the people in Hong Kong asking their French colleagues to provide an update. Hong Kong learned that their French teammates had revealed the plan to merge the two projects to the Voila middle managers. Not surprisingly, the Voila middle managers were dead set against the plan. They wanted PFM to end and to proceed with Nourriture Excellente alone. In fact, they wanted to do a major market test of the hybrid method. This news set off a negative reaction in Hong Kong (the following conversation is reconstructed from interviews). "Why did you tell Voila about our plan? You knew they wouldn't be receptive!" demanded the Belgian marketer. Then, "We already considered the idea of doing a test of Nourriture Excellente and rejected it!" The French call leader tried to mediate: "Hold on, you don't understand. Henri had a wonderful opportunity here, it was an opportunistic approach to dealing with the customer, working on Nourriture Excellente. Would you suggest that we not do that? And do you really think that the French organization doesn't know what it's doing? They've been working with this for a long time. Of course, they have lots of knowledge and if we can pull this together, we'll be better off." Then Drummond came in, angry: "How could you have held these meetings with the customer and not involve me? I am the global director for this work!" This was met by a contemptuous denial on the part of the young Frenchman leading the call in Paris, who viewed the comment as "pulling rank": "You can't even speak French so how can you expect to work with the customer? The customer doesn't want to do PFM with you, so we don't have a choice." Then, the French regional manager for North Asia broke in and attacked: "How dare you? How can you criticize when you don't even know what it is? You guys need to come here and see for yourselves!" The so-called videoconference from hell drew to a close as Drummond left the videoconference room visibly distraught and on the verge of tears, determined to resign from the Celestial Corporation.

People remaining in the videoconference suddenly realized that something had gone terribly wrong, something that could damage their company and their own careers. Everyone understood how reputations are built and destroyed at Celestial and, realizing they were in danger, became very interested in repairing the damage. Gerry Hanover quickly made arrangements to talk on the phone with each individual privately, and then to get the group back together to resolve differences. Over the next week, Hanover spent most of her time in telephonic "shuttle diplomacy" that gained her access to the points of view of each participant, which she then shared with the others one-on-one. The anxieties and tensions that had been buried below the surface emerged as a result of this process, so that team members came to recognize the pressures and anxieties facing their colleagues.

A number of issues surfaced from this exchange. First, there was uncertainty and confusion over the nature of the work to be done and roles on the team. The globalization of the team, plus the merger, had brought several new people into the team setting, many of whom had potentially overlapping roles. It was difficult to resolve this issue while Voila was in merger limbo, since no one knew what the future customer organization would look like. As a result, the nature of the work that was to be done was unclear and unstable, as one of the Americans based in Paris explains:

At each of our team meetings, we would go through a redefinition of what the work was going to be . . . And we'd leave the meeting with a joint sense of future and promise and all the rest, because we thought we had a good idea what the work was going to be. And for whatever reason, you know, it would change again. And you know, people's morale, I think there was a drop rate down to say probably nothing. And then we would have another meeting again, and we would redefine what the work was going to be . . . So each time the work would change, this co-work in the team would change and because of that, a constant state of flux . . . people's understanding of what they, of what their role was going to be, how they were going to contribute, how to interact with each other, who is responsible for what, you know, the principles for how a team is going to run, projects, changed every seven or eight weeks.

It also became clear that much of the conflict during the videoconference stemmed from unresolved tensions around who was going to have power with the customer. Indeed, the two competing projects symbolized two very different ways of relating to the customer: one following the French tradition, the other, American. Drummond pointed out, for example, that Couture's successor had been introduced to the key Voila managers through a series of dinners arranged by Couture. Drummond, on the other hand, had not even been invited to meet the customer, much less go to a "power dinner." Thus, it seemed to her that some individuals had privileged access to the customer, and in the French tradition they certainly did. The PFM approach encouraged power sharing, while the traditional approach maintained exclusive hierarchical rights to this power.

Another problem was a question in the minds of some team members regarding Drummond's role on the team. Many in Paris viewed her not as a "real team member," but peripheral to the team, doing work on the other side of the world that involved virtually no one based in Paris. For her to suddenly claim that she needed to be involved in meetings with the customer in Paris seemed unreasonable. Drummond's legitimacy was questionable, especially because she had been added to the team during a period when some French team members either did not have a role, or still did not know what their role would be.

A major insight gained in the post-video discussions was that Voila was not ready for PFM. Of course, the French knew this all along and it was clear from the Voila middle managers' behavior, but the Americans would not accept it. The Americans believed that by proving the business superiority of PFM through hard results, they could virtually "force" the French to agree. However, after all they had experienced, the Americans finally came to realize that the Voila managers simply were not at a point where they could accept such a radical departure from the status quo, regardless of business results. The Americans learned that they needed to slow down. Gerry Hanover comments:

> *. . . the other thing we discovered, and this is a big one, is we are way too fast. We've gotta walk before we can run, and the customer's not ready. We all know this, but it's not gonna get done by the top telling the top to do it. We've gotta get plans, and details, and engage a lot of people. And so, you know, this takes some of the pressure off rushing through these high-intensity phone calls, and thinking we agree, but not having time to check the agreement.*

From her individual conversations with each party, Gerry Hanover was able to construct a holistic explanation for what happened. The explanation showed the role that each person had played in the incident, drawing attention to the responsibility that each had for repairing the damage and moving forward. In her own words, Gerry explains the process:

> *. . . it was piecing together the fabric, and the people know the answers, when you get it all together, you know what the overlap is, and playing that back to people about what the other one was saying, and to the credit of all of these people, they are principle-based, and they were talking to each other within a couple of days, and they were over it.*

Chastened by their crisis and having a better understanding of the forces shaping their difficulties, the French and American groups came back together, first in an audio conference format (video was discontinued), and later face-to-face in Paris where they worked in earnest on a plan to connect the competing projects. The French and Americans now were able to work out a substantive agreement, with concrete activities and goals, for merging their two approaches under a new name—Produits Exemplaires—a negotiated term that brought together elements from both the French and American perspectives (*produits* is the French word for products, as in Product Family Management, while *exemplaires* is close to *excellente*, as in Nourriture Excellente). The joint French–American team agreed to conduct three projects under this new title. One project was called "Changing Attitudes," and its objective was to improve the support and understanding of Voila people for Produits Exemplaires. Two people were named as co-leaders of this project: Couture's successor and Cathleen Drummond, a first in Franco-American teamwork. The other two projects under Produits Exemplaires were focused on the food product family, something that Voila was very keen to do. There would be two components, each on opposite ends of a continuum: one called "Ready to Eat" and the other called "Gourmet Cuisine" (symbolically reflecting the distance between American and French dining customs). There was laughing and joking all around when these projects were presented to the whole team at a face-to-face meeting. One French team member said: "A second passion of Cathleen is cooking!" To which she replied "Eating, forget cooking, it isn't necessary!" This brought on more laughter.

On reflection, a number of team members believed that the "videoconference from hell" was a positive development, as comments from a French and an American participant attest:

> . . . *we had our famous videoconference . . . from my point of view, it's a great thing that this happened. Because everybody was like rrrrr . . . Everybody exploded, and then, you know we started trying to build something instead of destroying. So I think it is the best thing that happened on the team . . . We are starting to get a team spirit, people joking, people talking to each other, and people get to know each other . . . everybody has the feeling of wanting to find a common—common work, to do a common something. And we're very happy that this is happening, and I mean it's incredible the progress we have been doing in a month. (French team member)*

> . . . *everything since then has been pretty much of a steady, you know, march upwards. It drove a very healthy round of meetings and discussions, thinking, good thinking from a lot of people . . . And everyone's pretty happy with how that streams in. So the videoconference was the epiphany, it really is what drove this final work around what the team's gonna do and how it's gonna do it . . . I think people really like each other. People have very positive feelings, which I think gets a lot of respect for each other on the team. (American team member)*

Ironically, business results for Voila and Celestial had been strong during the entire period described above. After the Voila–Jardin merger was finalized, however, business results began to decline, largely as a result of problems experienced during implementation of the corporate merger (which finally was approved by the EU). Voila lost interest in any new project with Celestial until sales volume and profits improved. The Celestial team turned its attention fully to the problem of boosting immediate business results. This was a traditional area of work for everyone on the team, an area in which all of the team members had excellent track records. Everyone on this team was steeped in deep knowledge of the core business function of selling and marketing (that is why they had been selected as team members), and their shared knowledge in this domain was associated with high emotional energy, since lower sales meant fewer rewards. Shared knowledge had been shaped by many years of interacting with the larger corporate context of Celestial, which was heavily results-oriented all over the world, not only in the United States. As a consequence, the team members began to collaborate intensely, engaging in detailed discussions of core business issues, and using teleconferences as means to identify problems and create solutions that required cooperation across the team.

From this point on, the content and style of the team's virtual meetings changed from largely passive information sharing on a wide range of topics to an intense and exclusive focus on business results. Interaction dynamics reflected collaborative give-and-take, a higher content of problem-solving dialogue, and creativity. For example, during one virtual meeting, the team members invented, as a solution to an internal funding problem they were facing, a new template that would display comparative global spending data to senior management. In a lengthy discussion on how to assemble quickly the data for this template, someone on the team suggested that they use the team Website as a means to share ideas and coordinate their activity. The Website had been in place from the beginning, but had never been utilized as a team resource previously, primarily because the team as a whole had not been collaborative up until now. But things were changing:

> *. . . why don't we use one of the tools in the team space to have that discussion on ideas we can use? Would that not be a good way to do that? The chat room part of it, let's go ahead, let's dedicate the chat room, and then we can see other ideas and we can do some virtual brainstorming, OK?*

"Excellent!" was the reply.

The team also displayed several forms of behavioral convergence. For example, Gerry Hanover read a book called *MindYourManners* (Mole, 1995), and as a result came to the realization that Celestial often tried to force-fit processes and methods from its American headquarters on to organizations and people in Europe, and that this may not be the best way to achieve performance gains. The team discussed this issue at a face-to-face meeting, the first time such a topic ever surfaced on a team agenda, and considered organizational approaches that would feel more natural to European members of the team. Another form of collaboration was the team decision to send subgroups that combined people from different locations to important meetings with the customer, specifically to encourage a shared understanding of situations and problems across sites. Probably the most significant form of convergence, however, was the decision to relocate Cathleen Drummond and her family to Paris, and to identify a new team facilitator who also would relocate to Paris. Finally, the global team charter was being fulfilled.

As our research team prepared to depart the field in November 2000, we said farewell to a team whose members were working together actively across time and space to develop plans for boosting business results with their French customer. Collaboration was a hard-earned achievement, based on team members' shared experiences:

> *. . . we have strength because we have been through a lot of pain, through a lot of frustration, up and down, and now we are . . . [in] a period that allows you to start building, to start to have trust, and that is very important, to operate efficiently as one team . . . (French team member)*

CELESTIAL'S GLOBAL CUSTOMER TEAM—DISCUSSION QUESTIONS

1. What role do cultural differences play in this case? Specify which values are responsible for some of the virtual team problems and for the tension between Celestial and Voila.
2. What typical problems of virtual teams can be seen in this case?
3. How effective was Morris in leading Celestial's global customer team? Describe his leadership style.
4. Analyze the role of power and influence in furthering or hindering the acceptance of PFM. Which individuals were powerful and why?
5. What factors contributed to the initial lack of collaboration on the team? What factors and interventions eventually resulted in successful team collaboration?
6. What should Morris, Drummond, Couture, and Hanover have done to avoid the PFM-Nourriture Excellente conflict that developed on the global customer team and between Celestial and Voila?

Women and Global Leadership at Bestfoods*

Laura Brody had just finished analyzing the progress she'd made in her first two years as director of diversity and development for Bestfoods International, formerly known as CPC. Brody is a stylish woman in her forties, possessed of a droll sense of humor. She had begun working for Bestfoods 10 years earlier in management development. The position provided Brody the opportunity to meet and develop good relationships with many of the managers who were identified as having senior management potential and who were now in senior executive positions. Brody spent eight years coordinating the company's well-respected annual Senior Management Development Program. The program, taught by world-famous professors, was for managers who had been tapped to become leaders. She also had helped organize Bestfoods' global action-learning programs (where knowledgeable people were brought together from all parts of the company to tackle strategic, systemwide issues). These programs were often held at Arrowwood, an off-site corporate conference center just outside New York City.

Brody came to Bestfoods in 1988 and was surprised to find that the company seemed to be far behind most leading companies in promoting diversity, particularly in the company's proportion of women and minorities. She found herself revisiting what it was like to work with senior men who had limited experience working alongside high-level professional women. Corporate efforts to date had been limited primarily to diversity awareness training. When Brody was asked to take over the diversity function in 1995, she wanted to be sure that real, substantive change was possible. Brody explained to her prospective boss, Dick Bergeman, senior vice president of human resources, that she needed to be assured of the company's sincerity and willingness to support progress and changes in this area. Bergeman is an engaging, well-respected, 22-year veteran with Bestfoods who spearheaded the transformation of human resources from an administrative function to an integral part of the global strategy team. He replied, "I can't tell you I will automatically agree to everything you propose, but I will agree that it is your job to make change happen. And if I say 'no' the first time, then it is your job to figure out a different way to approach it or structure it and come back at me again and again and again." Since Brody was not expecting "carte blanche" up front, she was sufficiently reassured by his response and took the job. Brody's diagnosis of her new job was that the company supported diversity, but there were few specific strategies in place for her to implement. She saw her position as "a double-edged sword."

> *It was a wonderful opportunity to stand out on my own, set an agenda and implement it. As this was a senior position, I was expected to establish the goals and strategies for the company-wide diversity function. If I was successful, I could be well positioned for future career progress. If not, like my two predecessors, I might have to look for future career growth elsewhere.*

Bestfoods has had a diversity function since 1989. It evolved from traditional EEO[1] compliance reporting and had two previous directors, a male Hispanic and a male African American. Unlike Brody, both were disadvantaged by not having an established network throughout the organization, since one was brought in from outside the company and the other had experience only in the U.S. division in labor relations. Brody suspected that the climate had not really been ripe for change in the area of diversity until the last few years. Another advantage Brody enjoyed was the fit between her personality and the challenges of this particular job. In the early years of her career, she had received feedback that she was too direct and not easily deterred from pursuing a

* Copyright © Joyce S. Osland and Nancy J. Adler. Reprinted by permission of the authors. The devolopment of this case was funded by the CIBER program at the University of Washington under a grant from the U.S. Department of Education.

certain path. Brody was counseled to "go along to get along." Characteristics that had formerly been seen as weaknesses, however, were now perceived as her strengths:

> *In my current job, I am expected to be the conscience of the organization. Like an Old Testament prophet, I am frequently expected to preach fire and brimstone, nudging the company in a certain direction even though they may not want to go that way. For once my style and the type of person I am fit exactly with what my job demands and what my boss expects me to do. I love my job! As I told Dick Bergeman, "I can't believe you pay me to make trouble— I would have done that for free!"*

COMPANY BACKGROUND

Bestfoods is among the largest global food companies, with annual sales in 1999 of $8.6 billion. Its most well-known brands include Hellmann's and Best Foods condiments and dressings; Mazola corn oil and margarine; Knorr soups, sauces, and bouillon; Skippy peanut butter; Thomas' English muffins; and Entenmanns's baked goods. Bestfoods also has a catering division that is known as Caterplan in most global markets. Bestfoods has operations in more than 60 countries and markets products in 110 countries. The 93-year-old company is well positioned internationally with over 90 years of operating experience in Europe, 70 years in Latin America, and more than 68 years in Asia. Although headquartered in the United States, the company earns 60 percent of its revenues from non-U.S. sources. The company projects future growth to continue to come primarily from outside the mature markets of North America and Western Europe. Africa, Asia, Eastern Europe, the Middle East, Latin America, and the countries of the former Soviet Union are projected to lead increases in twenty-first century revenue. At present the company has four geographic divisions: Europe, North America, Asia, and Latin America.

Bestfoods has a highly decentralized structure, which gives general managers and local management the autonomy to adapt and modify changes suggested by corporate headquarters. One of the company's strengths is its global strategic vision combined with a consistent local focus and decision making. CEO Dick Shoemate appreciates the difficult balance between giving the local divisions power to make their own decisions and integrating these units into a coherent whole. "It's our strength, but it's also a challenge when we try to make changes."

The company's vision (see Case Appendix A) is to be the best international food company in the world by building on the organization's core businesses, values, and strengths. Bestfoods has three global *core businesses*: savory products (e.g., soups, bouillon, sauces), dressings, and catering. The company's *core values* are:

- Growing (financial success, business growth, people development, and diversity)
- Caring (adherence to the law and highest moral and ethical standards, respect for individual worth and ability, satisfying customer and consumer needs, safe workplaces, and protecting the environment)
- Sharing (valuing teamwork, internal and external partnering, learning from experience and transferring learning with pride)
- Daring (courage, candor, conviction, pioneering and leadership, quick decision making, and aggressiveness in seizing new markets).

The company's identified *core strengths* are:

- A unique culture combining global strategic vision with local focus, decision making, and action.
- A proven ability to transfer and use products, skills, technology, and people from all parts of the world.

To best link employee actions with the company's vision, Bestfoods uses a strategic performance measurement system called the Balanced Scorecard. "The Balanced Scorecard provides a framework that helps shape our activities and measure our performance in four critically important areas (customer satisfaction, people development, business practices, and innovation and learning) which together result in a fifth critical area, financial performance, the ultimate measure of the best."[2] Instead of one uniform global measurement system, each division, affiliate, department, and functional group within the company creates its own Balanced Scorecard that identifies the key activities, or "strategic drivers," that will move its particular business closer to the company's goals. Nevertheless, the CEO may announce specific new goals to add to the Corporate Balanced Scorecard at WorldTeam Meetings, which the company holds about every three years. At the WorldTeam meetings, approximately 150 of the most senior executives from around the world spend several days together focusing on strategic issues, sharing innovative implementation plans, and learning together. The WorldTeam meetings are another way to coordinate the far-flung global company.

Dick Shoemate is chairman, president, and chief executive officer of Bestfoods. He joined the company in 1962 and held positions in manufacturing, finance, and business management in the consumer foods and corn refining businesses. Shoemate was president of the Corn Refining division before assuming the corporate presidency in 1988. Shoemate is not only bright but unassuming and down to earth. He is both approachable and an excellent listener. Shoemate is equally as impressive and comfortable dealing with board members as with the 60 children of employees he addressed on "Take Your Child to Work Day." Shoemate, in his late fifties, wants one of the marks he leaves on Bestfoods to be increased diversity worldwide and at the most senior levels.

Diversity at Bestfoods

Of the corporation's 44,000 employees, two-thirds currently work outside of the United States. In the U.S. division, Bestfoods has 10 to 15 percent more minorities than the industry norm, but 5 to 10 percent fewer women. Bestfoods has been known as a company where people spent most of their career. Similar to many companies, however, a disproportionate number of women and minorities leave Bestfoods within their first three to five years. Historically, women at Bestfoods tended to hit the "glass ceiling" at the middle-management level. Women have succeeded primarily in staff positions, such as the corporate legal department, which has the highest representation of women. There are numerous entry-to-midlevel women in human resources, but the division-level executives are all male. There are women in marketing who have attained midlevel jobs and some who have been promoted into senior-level positions, but only one woman has successfully made the leap from marketing to a general manager position. The usual career path that men followed in Bestfoods to become senior executives has gone from general manager positions to operating division presidents to corporate officers. Women have remained a small percentage of the candidate pool for senior executive jobs because they tended to be scarce in the usual career pipelines to the top—line positions and high-level positions outside the United States.

Not surprisingly, the 1997 employee survey in the United States showed that minorities and women perceived less opportunity for advancement and career development than did whites or men. Similarly, they perceived their performance to be less linked to compensation than did whites or men. It surprised many at the company, however, that men ranked "workload and pace interfere with work/life balance" as the number one issue among the five diversity-related issues they would like the company to address. Although women ranked this issue last at number five, the work/life integration issue cut across gender and hierarchy. For example, while female administrative staff might worry about making it to a day care center by 5 or 6 P.M., some senior men grumbled that their wives were "threatening to divorce them" if they missed one more family event.

Retention analyses revealed that at every management level, women and minorities had more turnover than males and whites. As a result of these findings, Brody's objective within the United States was to have better retention and development of both women and minorities.

When Brody and her staff did a global analysis of female employees, they discovered that 15 percent of the employees who had been designated as "high potential" were women. They also found that there were more U.S. women in management positions when compared to other regions, although Europe appointed the first woman as a country general manager. Among the approximately 264 participants who attended the Senior Management Development Programs from 1988 to 1998, the company sent only 15 female managers. It wasn't until 1998 that a senior female manager attended who was not an American. Brody knew that attitudes toward promoting women varied widely throughout the company, from extremely supportive to indifferent—or even chauvinistic in a few cases. For the most part, she believed that although managers were well intentioned, they were uncertain about what improvements could be made regarding career advancement for women. The company was committed to advancing diversity as a key competitive element in its overall business strategy.

Bestfoods has a diverse board of directors. Of their 14 directors, two are female CEOs, one is an African American CEO, seven are white U.S. American male CEOs, and four are male CEOs from other countries. Bestfoods has three female corporate officers, one each from manufacturing, marketing, and public relations. By 1997, 14 percent of the members of the board of directors, 15 percent of the corporate officers, and 13 percent of directors and vice presidents were women.

The Reasons Behind the Figures

When Brody and her staff ponder the barriers that women face at Bestfoods, they think some attitudes and behaviors may be due to generational rather than gender issues. For example, most of the corporate officers are in their late 50s and early 60s and have stay-at-home wives. They have never watched their wives struggle to climb the corporate ladder or juggle the competing demands of work and home life. Nor have their own careers been affected by the demands of a dual-career marriage. As a result, Brody wonders how well some of the senior male executives really understand the barriers or challenges today's women often face.

For example, a common complaint among women is that men have the luxury of coming to work early and staying late if they want to attempt to impress the boss in this fashion. Because many women are responsible for dropping off and picking up children at school or day care and then supervising them at home while preparing dinner, they have to work more regular hours. This does not mean the women work fewer hours or less hard. However, to the extent that the corporate culture values time spent in the office (rather than actual time spent working and achieving results) as an indicator of loyalty and promotability, working mothers (and some fathers) are at a disadvantage. One division manager has the night watchman keep track of the time employees leave at the end of the day; accurately or not, his employees interpret this as a clear signal that, "If you want to get ahead, you must work late."

Another factor that could be hindering development and ultimately retention is that the company has few women at high enough levels to be selected for senior management development opportunities. The corporation's senior-level management training programs are offered to senior managers whom the company has already promoted up the hierarchy. Few women attain that level and, therefore, receive little in the way of company-sponsored, formal management and career development opportunities, or the executive-level exposure and visibility that such opportunities provide.

Diversity as a Strategic Issue

While the number of senior women, corporate officers, and board members at Bestfoods is respectable when compared to many companies, neither Brody nor Shoemate think it is adequate to support the future they envision for Bestfoods. Consumer foods, not unlike many other industries, has become increasingly competitive; only the companies with top talent and top brands survive. Moreover, whereas many consumer foods companies used to be able to operate as loose confederations of fairly autonomous country operations, global competition is now forcing all members of the industry to more closely coordinate their worldwide operations.

To succeed in such an environment, Bestfoods needs to attract and retain the best talent available globally and have local employees from each country in which they operate reflect the consumer base. With women making more than 80 percent of purchasing decisions for Bestfoods' products, the company will suffer if it fails to understand women's perspectives, needs, and decision-making criteria. Shoemate sees promoting women into senior management positions not primarily as a matter of diversity but rather as an issue of strategic competitive advantage. On numerous occasions, he has explicitly expressed his commitment to developing the most highly talented women and men from around the world:

> We believe that one of Bestfoods' unique competitive strengths is a management team that delivers outstanding performance in the local marketplace and also works together to build the "Best International Food Company in the World." ... We actively seek to identify and to develop high performing Bestfoods' managers throughout the company, including men and women from all countries and ethnic backgrounds.

Shoemate knows, however, that words are not enough to change an organization. He personally appointed all three of Bestfoods' female corporate officers during his tenure as CEO. Nevertheless, he wants to see more rapid progress on the goal of including more women in senior management and leadership. He made a note to himself to discuss with Brody what form this change should take at Bestfoods.

MANAGING CHANGE AT BESTFOODS

No CEO can simply mandate change in a highly decentralized multinational that values local autonomy. Focusing on diversity further complicates change efforts because it is sometimes viewed as a "U.S. issue." Within some cultures, equity among women and men is not a well-publicized concern, and diversity is locally defined to refer to other groupings within the population. Therefore, for companies headquartered in the United States, the leadership has to tread carefully. Both within the food industry and within Bestfoods, employees tend to work their way up, and executives brought in from the outside often do not adjust to the informal norms and values of the company. This practice has the advantage of providing continuity and a strong organizational culture, but the downside is less new blood and fewer innovations. Bestfoods' U.S. employees tend to reflect "Middle America"—conservative, traditional people with "old-fashioned American values." Brody affectionately describes the company as a Norman Rockwell painting. While the pace and pressure has picked up in recent years, it is neither an industry nor a company with a prior reputation for being "fast-paced." Brody describes Bestfoods' culture as traditional, conservative, polite, "gentlemanly," and nonconfrontational. While the politeness contributes to the pleasant relations Bestfoods is noted for, it also makes face-to-face confrontations rare; criticism and dissent tend to go underground. The emphasis on tradition makes change slow and risky. Some executives are leery of being blamed if changes they initiate don't work. As a result, some managers use the "drip method" of change—small changes over time that eventually add up to progress.

While individuals may approach change somewhat cautiously, Bestfoods has developed a very effective group method for taking advantage of opportunities and resolving problems that affect all divisions. When the global action-learning task forces come together, they analyze situations and, toward the end of the meeting, present their recommendations to top management. The CEO and his direct reports immediately consider each recommendation and respond to the task force before the meeting ends.

As a result of all these factors, Brody's strategy has been to focus on getting the decision makers "on board" and then making incremental changes. Her style is to plant the seeds of ideas and provide information and options to the executive team so they can begin thinking about diversity more broadly and from different perspectives.

BRODY'S PHILOSOPHY
ON HUMAN RESOURCE DEVELOPMENT

Brody has a very clear idea of the role of human resources, as seen in the following description of her job.

> *As an HR executive, I do not see myself as merely an ombudsperson for employees. I have always seen HR as a critical management responsibility. There are several aspects of HR in which one is required to be the conscience of the organization. I spent many of my formative years as a consultant working with clients on diagnostic and implementation issues to help make organizations more effective. So my focus is more proactive and action-oriented, trying to create programs that lead to long-term change rather than compliance. My goal has always been to "make a difference" at work. I've learned that everything has to be linked to the business. Line management has to have an itch they want to scratch, and it's my responsibility to make them feel that itch—whether they know it or not. So I don't see HR as an administrative staff function, but as an organization development function that needs to work with line managers. Although people like me are sometimes seen as mavericks, I think you have to understand the needs of the business, create effective relationships with line management, and bend rules to solve problems. Traditionally, HR has a reputation for writing the policies and then telling people why they* can't *do things.*

Brody went on to explain that the traditional HR roles are switched at Bestfoods. In most companies, corporate HR establishes policy and procedures and then administers them, while the operating divisions creatively try to bend the rules to meet the needs of local line managers. At Bestfoods, HR policies are frequently developed and implemented at the divisional level, while the corporate group often has more freedom to experiment and be innovative.

LAYING THE GROUNDWORK FOR CHANGE

Bestfoods already had a Diversity Advisory Council (DAC) when Brody took over. It continues today and is composed of 14 members—senior executives in the U.S. business, corporate staff, and the vice presidents of human resources from each unit. The council is chaired by the CEO and facilitated by Brody. Her predecessor met with the council a few times a year, and their primary achievement was coming to consensus on a common diversity training program for senior managers throughout North America. By contrast, Brody adopted a team-building approach with the council. She knew they had to establish a common vision, so Brody spent almost her entire first year working with them to craft a vision and to agree upon a definition of diversity. Brody worked to ensure that Bestfoods defined diversity very broadly (see Case Appendix B) for two reasons: (1) to avoid excluding white males; and (2) so that other countries would not see diversity only in light of U.S. EEO requirements. The council also developed a Balanced Scorecard for diversity that mirrors the Corporate Balanced Scorecard (see Case Appendix B). As Brody states,

> *In corporate life, you only make progress on things you measure, and you only measure things that are important—such as operating income, profitability, ROI, ROA, and market share. These things are all measured and tracked very, very frequently. So in terms of making progress on diversity, the measurable goal was increased career opportunity—promotions, salary levels, and representation at senior management levels—and not the "nice-to-haves," like calendars with every ethnic holiday posted or "feeling included"; it was in fact about being included. I preached that you could not have an effective diversity function without, at a minimum, having effective equal employment policies and actions in place.*

Brody and the council also linked diversity to the corporate vision.

> *It's very simple. We could not be the best food company in the world if we weren't recruiting and retaining the talented women and minorities who make up large proportions of current M.B.A. programs and who bring different perspectives and experiences from those of whites and men. Since the number of minorities we have is fairly good, one of the first things I did was to focus on the representation of women, an area in which our numbers were not so good. I had industry measures to justify doing this. I also had my own personal experience in the organization and the frustration at seeing a lot of diversity awareness training going on but not seeing many tangible results coming out of it.*

Consistent with the CEO's perspective, Brody sees diversity as a business issue and insists on promoting it as such. She does not see her job as reengineering society or changing societal attitudes; her primary focus is on behaviors and practices that will benefit the company. Brody's team building with the Diversity Advisory Council paid off. After about two years, the council wanted to raise the bar on diversity and chose to go forward in a proactive way. To learn what leading companies were doing about leveraging workforce inclusion to increase their business competitiveness, Brody invited outside practitioners who were involved in best-practice efforts to make presentations to the council. She also gathered a variety of benchmarking and best-practice studies and reports for council members.

In addition to the groundwork Brody was laying with the Diversity Advisory Council, she established a program called Cultural Connections, an employee-driven education and awareness program, and a peer coaching and mentoring program for new hires called SOS, "Sponsoring Our Success." Brody's new initiatives complemented Bestfoods' long history of involvement with INROADS (Bergeman is on the board of directors for the northern New Jersey chapter). INROADS is an internship program for high school and college-age minority students that had proven successful for the company in recruiting top talent, as many interns later joined Bestfoods. Brody's department, which consisted of one other professional and a secretary, coordinated entry-level diversity awareness training, sexual harassment prevention training, and diversity training for the most senior 300 managers and executives in the company. At her suggestion, Shoemate sent out an open letter to all employees in 1997 regarding the company's diversity initiative (see Case Appendix B) and another "state of diversity" letter to U.S. employees in 1998 (see Case Appendix C). Brody's job is made easier by both Shoemate's and Bergeman's sincere belief in the strategic importance of diversity.

While these efforts have been successful, Brody knows that still more has to be done, and she too would like to pick up the pace of change. Among others, she has been considering three alternatives that might have an even larger impact.

1. Conduct a survey that would compare the differences in perception between women and men regarding development and retention in the company and more clearly identify the unique barriers women face.
2. Hold a meeting modeled after the global action-learning programs to tackle the problem of retaining and promoting women.
3. Offer a leadership development program for midlevel women managers.

One day Brody was in Shoemate's office getting his signature on some letters. He was in the midst of reviewing the 1997 employee survey data and said, "Laura, if you could do one thing to improve things for women in this company, what would it be?" Brody knew this was a big opportunity. The mental Rolodex in her head started spinning as she quickly considered a variety of options she'd been pondering. Brody took a deep breath and pitched her best idea.

> *I really cannot speak for all women. But if I were the CEO, what I would want to do is to engage a significant number of women in this dialogue. What about sponsoring a global forum for high-potential and senior women representing all the businesses from around the world*

and bringing them to Arrowwood? They could help us better understand the environment and culture in the company and how it impacts women. We could do what we always do with a business issue that needs to be driven from the center—have an action-learning program with outside experts to design and facilitate it. We could receive both information and recommendations from participants on how to proceed and make progress, and we could also do some leadership training at the same time.

Shoemate asked a few probing questions and suggested she flesh it out with Bergeman. Brody and Bergeman prepared a position paper that Bergeman discussed with the Corporate Strategy Council (CSC) at its next meeting in April. The CSC is composed of the six most senior corporate officers, who are responsible for the four geographic divisions, the baking business, and the corporate staff. The CSC immediately approved the forum idea. Shoemate requested that it take place no later than the end of July. That meant Brody had only 90 days to organize her company's first-ever Women's Global Leadership Forum.

Brody and her staff dove into preparations, and the plans began to fall into place. The question that continued to nag Brody was how to ensure that the forum resulted in real organizational change. She worried that participants might leave feeling good, with raised expectations about what the company would do for women, only to be disillusioned if the recommended changes didn't materialize afterward. As it turned out, senior management shared Brody's concern about unrealistically heightened expectations. Some of them also wondered how they could participate and interact with the attendees so that neither group would feel threatened.

Forum Invitations and Reactions

To create a comprehensive list of senior and high potential women, Brody solicited nominations from all division presidents, which she personally reviewed along with the corporate high-potential lists and succession plans. Next, the CEO sent a letter to all six members of the Corporate Strategy Council describing the forum and requesting that they rank order their nominees. As Bestfoods does with its Senior Management Development Program, the company allocated spaces at the Women's Global Leadership Forum according to the relative size of each division and geographical area to ensure balanced representation. Brody's goal was to invite 50 participants, of which at least half were to come from outside the United States. As an early indication of the high level of support, every division requested additional spaces. Brody responded by increasing the number of participants to 60 and choosing 10 of these as facilitators for small group sessions. Shoemate personally sent a letter of invitation to each participant. Fifty-five women from 25 countries were able to accept the invitation.

Brody knew that merely asking the division presidents to identity their high potential women, thereby adding them to the recognized and visible talent pool for the company's future leadership, was a significant intervention in and of itself. "Even if we'd never held the forum, it was a good exercise for the senior executives to stop and consider how many highly talented women managers they had and where they were in the company. One president promoted a woman a few months earlier than he had planned to as a result of thinking about whom he wanted to nominate for the forum!"

The reactions to the forum announcement were, for the most part, very positive. Several people commented that this was one of the most exciting and forward-looking initiatives the company had ever tackled. Many women were gratified to be identified as participants. Not all women, however, reacted positively. Some senior women, primarily Americans, worried that attending an all-women forum might encourage others to think their success was owed primarily to their status as women rather than to their competence; they had no desire to be at the forefront of women's issues. Some women who were not invited, from secretaries to directors, felt excluded from yet another "private club." Some invitees were also concerned about the potentially negative reactions from their male colleagues and bosses, including worrying about the likelihood of a male backlash.

There were sporadic dismissive and skeptical comments by both men and women who doubted that the forum would result in anything more than a "bitch session." One senior male manager told his female subordinate, "Have a good time at the koffee-klatch" as she left for the forum. Some men complained of discrimination because they were not invited. However, other men thought the forum was long overdue and emphasized their support. Brody kept Shoemate and Bergeman informed of the resistance she encountered so there would not be any surprises regarding this controversial program among the senior managers. At one point, Brody sent Shoemate a note saying, "You know how women get crabby and lose their sense of humor when they're left out? Well, guess what—it seems that men also get crabby and lose their sense of humor when they are excluded!" Given her strict deadline, Brody didn't feel she had enough time to deal with the backlash in depth, other than being aware of it and trying to deflect it with humor and an ongoing reiteration of the CEO's rationale and goals for championing the forum.

Planning the Forum

As far as Brody was aware, no other company had ever held a global meeting for its most senior and high-potential women with the intent of opening a dialogue on global leadership and organizational change. There were no models to follow, so she began searching for outside consultants to help design and implement the forum. One of the consultants she hired began by interviewing Shoemate, Bergeman, all corporate officers including the three female corporate officers, and one of the female board members to get a feel for the organization. She and Brody began designing a program to fit Bestfoods' needs and to meet the forum's goals:

- Increase the global competitiveness of Bestfoods.
- Develop the global leadership skills of Bestfoods' most highly talented and senior women.
- Create an internal network among Bestfoods' women leaders to facilitate their global effectiveness.
- Develop both global and local recommendations for enhancing Bestfoods' ability to support the career advancement and success of an increasing number of highly talented and senior women.

Early in the process, Brody warned Bergeman that the cost of the program would be higher than the original estimate. His response was, "Spend whatever you need to put on an outstanding program." Bergeman was aware that some people who were ambivalent about the program might try to find reasons for it to fail. He, therefore, insisted that everything about the program be first rate. While Bergeman remained available when Brody wanted his support or advice, he allowed her to take full responsibility for the program.

Pre-Forum Survey

Brody's team carried out a survey-feedback process aimed at producing data that would serve as a baseline and cause people to reexamine their thinking about the opportunities and barriers for women's career advancement. Brody was especially interested in surveying both senior women and men, so both groups' views would be visible at the forum. She developed a survey modeled after the Catalyst[3] report, "Women in Corporate Leadership: Progress & Prospects" (Wellington, 1996). A primary purpose of the survey was to determine whether there were significant differences of opinion between the views of women and men in Bestfoods regarding individual and corporate strategies that would most benefit women, common reasons preventing women from advancing, beliefs about women, and personal experiences in the company. Brody sent the survey to all corporate officers, the 125 most senior executives who were being invited to this year's WorldTeam meeting, and the 60 women who had been invited to the forum. The response rate for the survey was 70 percent. Brody understood quite clearly that for any significant organizational change to occur, the senior levels of management, almost exclusively male, had to be part of a coalition for change. For that to happen, they had to be included on the front end as part of the overall organizational change process. Brody sent the survey results to all the survey participants after the forum.

The survey data revealed the following key points:

1. Although women and men agreed on most of the barriers perceived to be inhibiting women's career advancement (women's lack of mobility for international assignments and lack of both general management and line experience), the women reported a number of barriers that appear to have been invisible to the men:
   - Senior men's discomfort with ambitious women
   - Senior men's negative stereotyping and preconceptions of women
   - Senior men's difficulty in reporting to a woman

2. While women and men agreed on the three most important strategies for women's career success at Bestfoods (consistently exceeding performance expectations; gaining line management experience; and seeking difficult and high-visibility assignments), they disagreed on other key strategies.
   - The majority of women believed that they had to "develop a style that men are comfortable with" in order to succeed, whereas men ranked this strategy next to last in terms of importance.
   - Women were more likely than men to believe they had to develop a relationship with an influential mentor in order to succeed.
   - More men than women stressed the importance of gaining international experience.
   - None of the men stated that they would consider changing companies to get ahead whereas 14 percent of the women stated that they would consider leaving Bestfoods for another company.

3. Men and women agreed on the five most important corporate strategies that would benefit women (more assignments managing people; include more women on divisional and global strategic task forces; include more women in the Senior Management Development Program; hold managers more accountable for identifying, developing, and advancing high potential women; and include a higher percentage of women in succession plans). However, women placed greater importance on each of these corporate strategies than did their male colleagues.

4. It was noteworthy that both women and men perceived the barriers facing women to be greater than the reality of what women actually experience. For example, although some men hold stereotypical assumptions about women in general, they reported that these assumptions usually disappear when they actually work with or for a woman manager. However, the specific women they know and work with are typically viewed as "exceptions" to the rule.

Brody and her team worked long hours to analyze the extensive survey data and present them in such a way that both women and men in the company would be able to understand each other's different views of reality. She hoped the survey results would trigger more in-depth discussion at the forum, so more people would be motivated to eliminate the gap in perceptions and find new ways for women and men to work together.

The Women's Global Leadership Forum

Brody and the consultants wanted to ensure that the forum was more than just an effective leadership training seminar for women that developed recommendations for organizational change. They had confidence that the participants would develop recommendations that were appropriate for Bestfoods, but what would happen afterward? Much depended on the continued support of senior executives and their reaction to the forum. To encourage their growing support, the majority of Bestfoods' most senior executives (CEO, Corporate Strategy Council, Diversity Advisory Council, corporate officers, and a board member) joined the women participants at the welcome dinner, as well as at other sessions (at which their presence would not be inhibiting), and at the all-important presentation of recommendations on the final morning of the 4 1/2-day Women's Global Leadership Forum. The senior executives' inclusion allowed them to see the women participants in action, hear their opinions firsthand, and learn for themselves what the company needed to do, and to avoid doing, in order to succeed.

The design of the forum tried to enhance the women's preparation for proactive roles in the company's future leadership. The forum design included three types of sessions: (1) individual professional development sessions focusing on global leadership skills; (2) organization development sessions aimed at gathering information and making recommendations to the company on women's retention, development, and advancement; and (3) sessions facilitating the formation of a women's network. At the participants' request, the design was modified to allow more time in small groups to formulate recommendations for presentation to the senior executives at the final session. Leadership development activities included "herstories" about significant women who influenced the values and leadership styles of the participants, skill assessment, skill building and coaching, experiential exercises, a panel of female CEOs and Bestfoods' highest-ranking women, and another panel of Bestfoods' senior male executives who gave career advice, and Brody's presentation of the survey results.

As predicted, the forum had some intense and challenging moments as the widely diverse group of 55 women with differing goals, opinions, experiences, and communication and behavior styles met and discussed key corporate and personal challenges. Nevertheless, the participants judged the forum to be a resounding success.

Forum Recommendations and Executive Response

A highlight of the forum was the participants' presentation to the CEO, Corporate Strategy Council, and the Diversity Advisory Council on the last day. The women stayed up late the night before, working in teams on the various recommendations. In an offer that reflected their skills as mentors and coaches, the senior American women graciously suggested that younger women from outside the United States do the actual presenting so that they could benefit more directly from the high visibility. Before the presentations began, Shoemate requested that the participants be candid and assured them that they could be totally honest in their feedback. All participants were visibly pulling for the presenters. At one point, a highly articulate and self-assured Chinese woman in her late twenties brought down the house when she assured Shoemate that "There's no need to feel threatened by us—we don't want your job. We want to be CEOs of bigger, better companies than Bestfoods!" Their specific recommendations (found in Case Appendix D) focused on three key areas: career development (enhancing career opportunities), diversity (increasing representation of women in senior and high-level positions), and work/life balance (enabling women to perform to their highest capabilities while recognizing their multiple roles). In addition to recommending what the company should do, the participants also identified what they themselves should do to enhance their own career opportunities.

While the women participated in a final small group session, Shoemate and the senior executives discussed the recommendations and planned their response. Shoemate suggested separating the recommendations into three categories:

- Current company initiatives—recommendations the company is already doing but which need to be accelerated and better communicated to employees.
- New corporatewide recommendations, which the Corporate Strategy Council could consider at its next meeting.
- New "local" recommendations best addressed within specific countries, regions, or divisions.

When the women rejoined the executives, Shoemate responded to each recommendation, some of which he immediately accepted. He was very open to feedback and did not argue with or become defensive about any points the women raised. He promised to look into existing programs and policies that were not consistently working to the benefit of women's development and retention. Shoemate eloquently referred to his belief that the company's strength lies in its local decision making and explained why he hesitates to mandate most policies from corporate headquarters. However, he also clarified what he could do as CEO to make change happen and assured the women that he would communicate to them the outcome of each recommendation as soon as possible. Shoemate's obvious sincerity and thoughtfulness made a positive impression, as did the response of other CSC members. Shoemate closed the session with an inspirational story about his first experience as a very young manager whose orders were obeyed because, like the women at the Forum, he had the backing and utter confidence of his boss. Shoemate and Bergeman then led a standing ovation for Brody and her staff.

Two hours later, after bidding goodbye to participants about to jet off to all corners of the globe, Brody gratefully collapsed on a lawn chair on Arrowwood's manicured grounds. She was delighted that the forum had ended on such a positive note. The immediate feedback at least seemed to indicate that it had indeed been the catalyst she was hoping for. Nevertheless, Brody still had that nagging question, "What next steps have to take place so that real change in the company and its leadership occurs and becomes institutionalized?"

NOTES

1. Equal Employment Opportunity (EEO) laws, under the provisions of Title VII of the Civil Rights Act of 1964, were created in the United States to ensure work environments free from illegal discrimination on the grounds of race, color, religion, disability, age, national origin, or sex.
2. 1998 Vision and Policies pamphlet.
3. Catalyst, located in New York City, is a well-respected research and education institute that focuses on corporate women in senior leadership and management positions.

Case Appendix A

The Bestfoods Vision

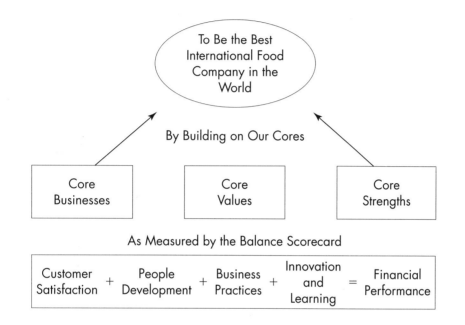

International

CPC INTERNATIONAL INC., INTERNATIONAL PLAZA, ENGLEWOOD CLIFFS, NEW JERSEY 07632

C.R. SHOEMATE
CHAIRMAN AND PRESIDENT   January 10, 1997

An open letter to all CPC Employees ...

Subject: CPC's Diversity Initiative

CPC's strong culture and proud traditions are deeply rooted in our core values of honesty, integrity, fairness, and respect. They are also the best foundation on which to build our future. Our values have not changed over time but the way we demonstrate them continues to change. Our customers and consumers, business partners and investors, our own workforce and managers reflect a more diverse society in the growing global economy. Our World Team vision, To Become The Best International Food Company in The World, our core values and company policies challenge every one of us to help in our drive toward becoming the best. That is only possible when every one of us truly believes we will have the opportunity to fulfill our potential at CPC.

Our diversity initiative is an ongoing process that affects everyone in the company. In order to ensure a more inclusive environment that values the contributions of all, we need to engage every person in this effort. The diversity vision that follows highlights the business rationale for increasing and leveraging our diversity, so that CPC employees can develop a shared understanding of why this is a strategic imperative.

The diagram that depicts elements of diversity in the workplace clearly demonstrates our commitment to a broad spectrum of differences that go far beyond equal opportunity programs, which are often limited to race and gender.

The Diversity Advisory Council has embraced four long-term objectives for CPC: Preferred Employer, Balanced Workforce, Equitable Workplace, and Enhanced Business Results. The Balanced Scorecard that follows identifies the drivers and measures to which Corporate Staff, Corn Refining North America, Best Foods and the Baking Business are committed. Division Presidents will be reviewing their progress with me every year.

But progress throughout CPC is everyone's responsibility. Increase your own awareness of people who are different from you and understand how your own assumptions affect the way you treat others. Support our Diversity initiative by following and reinforcing equal treatment and respect for all. Challenge others and speak up if you see inappropriate behavior or hear derogatory comments or jokes and talk to other people about your concerns and suggestions.

On the back cover of this brochure are additional questions and answers about our progress in this important area.

I hope you join me in continued learning and self improvement to reach our vision for the future.

CM Shoemate

OUR DIVERSITY VISION FOR THE FUTURE

WE WILL VALUE, LEVERAGE, AND INCREASE VARIETY AND DIFFERENCE IN OUR WORKFORCE SO THAT OUR DIVERSITY IS THE PERPETUAL STIMULANT OF INNOVATION, CREATIVITY, AND EFFECTIVE PROBLEM SOLVING, PROVIDING US WITH A SUSTAINABLE COMPETITIVE ADVANTAGE THAT HELPS US REACH THE HIGHEST LEVELS OF QUALITY, PRODUCTIVITY AND PROFITABILITY IN ACHIEVING CPC'S VISION TO BECOME THE BEST INTERNATIONAL FOOD COMPANY IN THE WORLD.

We envision a workplace where diversity is fully integrated into the organization to create an environment that encourages, values, and respects the uniqueness of the individual; fosters achievement; and optimizes business opportunities.

ELEMENTS OF DIVERSITY RECOGNIZED IN THE WORKPLACE

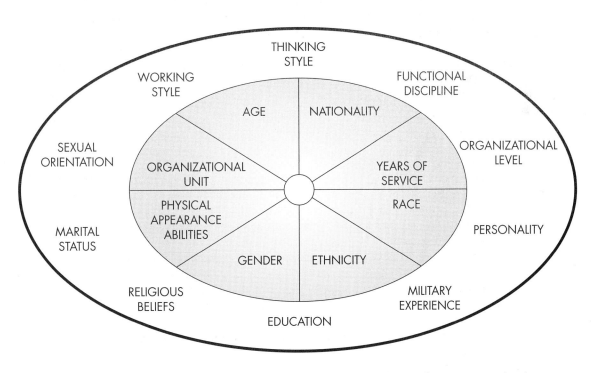

A myriad of characteristics make us who we are. The whole person contributes to the diversity of CPC International and to our success as a company.

LONG-TERM OBJECTIVES

■ PREFERRED EMPLOYER ESTABLISH BEST PRACTICE STANDARDS OF EXCELLENCE THAT EARN THE CORPORATION INTERNAL RECOGNITION BY EMPLOYEES AND EXTERNAL RECOGNITION BY THE MARKETPLACE FOR BEING THE PREFERRED EMPLOYER TO ALL SEGMENTS OF THE POPULATION.

■ BALANCED WORKFORCE ENSURE EVERY CPC ORGANIZATION'S WORKFORCE REFLECTS VARIETY AND DIFFERENCE AT ALL LEVELS.

■ EQUITABLE WORKPLACE ENSURE AN EQUITABLE WORKPLACE IN WHICH OPPORTUNITIES AND REWARDS ARE SUPPORTED BY POLICIES AND PRACTICES BASED ON ACHIEVEMENT, FAIRNESS, AND EQUITY. OUR CORE VALUES DEMAND THAT WE TREAT ONE ANOTHER WITH RESPECT AND DIGNITY AT ALL TIMES, TAKING INDIVIDUAL RESPONSIBILITY FOR DEVELOPMENT AND PERFORMANCE IN AN ENVIRONMENT FREE FROM BIAS AND DISCRIMINATION.

■ ENHANCED BUSINESS RESULTS ENSURE THAT VARIETY AND DIFFERENCE IN THE CPC WORLD TEAM IS LEVERAGED TO REACH THE HIGHEST LEVELS OF INNOVATION, CREATIVITY, EFFECTIVE PROBLEM SOLVING, AND PERFORMANCE FOR THE BENEFIT OF OUR CUSTOMERS, CONSUMERS, EMPLOYEES, AND SHAREHOLDERS.

DIVERSITY BALANCED SCORECARD

OBJECTIVES	DRIVERS	MEASURES
■ PREFERRED EMPLOYER	RECOGNITION BY EMPLOYEES	EMPLOYEE SURVEY RESULTS
	RECOGNITION BY EXTERNAL EMPLOYMENT CANDIDATES	TURNOVER/RETENTION RATES
		RECRUITING RESULTS
■ BALANCED WORKFORCE	REPRESENTATIVE OF CONSUMER BASE AND WORKPLACE AVAILABILITY	TRENDS IN CONSUMER AND WORKFORCE DEMOGRAPHICS
	REFLECTIVE OF CUSTOMER BASE	CUSTOMER DEMOGRAPHICS
	INCLUSIVE OF WORLDTEAM	VARIETY AND DIFFERENCE REFLECTED IN ALL ORGANIZATION LEVELS
	WORKFORCE DIVERSITY PLAN BY EACH OPERATING UNIT BASED ON PEOPLE DEVELOPMENT CHALLENGES FOR THE YEAR 2000	PEOPLE DEVELOPMENT COMPONENT OF THE BALANCED SCORECARD
■ EQUITABLE WORKPLACE	FREEDOM FROM BIAS AND DISCRIMINATION AS RECOGNIZED BY LOCAL EMPLOYMENT LAW AND OUR EMPLOYEES	EMPLOYEE SURVEY RESULTS (I.E., EMPLOYEE SATISFACTION WITH CAREER DEVELOPMENT COMPONENTS OF THE PERFORMANCE ENHANCEMENT PROCESS)
	EFFECTIVE POLICIES AND PRACTICES	LEGAL CLAIMS FILED AND (LITIGATED) RESULTS
■ ENHANCED BUSINESS RESULTS	BUSINESS GROWTH	SHAREHOLDER RETURN, NET SALES AND EARNINGS

SELECTED QUESTIONS AND ANSWERS

Q: Why is CPC interested in diversity?

A: A highly competent and motivated workforce that is characterized by variety and fully qualified to advance in the CPC WorldTeam is a critical element of realizing our vision, "TO BECOME THE BEST INTERNATIONAL FOOD COMPANY IN THE WORLD."

Q: A new member of our department recently transferred from another unit of CPC. He is standoffish and makes me uncomfortable. Another team leader told me to join in making him feel more welcome, that this is part of diversity. I thought diversity referred to race and gender.

A: People are unique individuals and "diversity" encompasses a wide range of things that make us different from others. Organization unit can be one of them. Share your department's "informal" rules with a newcomer. Make an extra effort to include a new employee in your lunch plans. Learning and growing is a two-way street. Ask about the unit he came from and what he sees as some differences. Take the opportunity to broaden your horizons by learning from him.

Q: Sometimes at staff meetings my peers repeat ethnic jokes they've heard recently. I am uncomfortable with this type of humor. What can I do?

A: Part of supporting diversity is challenging others when they make ethnic, cultural, gender-related, or sexually derogatory jokes. But sometimes we are hesitant to speak up in group because we think we are the only one with that concern. Often that is not the case. If you find something offensive, chances are others do too. You are not "off the hook" because you didn't tell the joke. Creating an inclusive environment at CPC means each of us has the responsibility to help educate others when certain behavior is objectionable.

Q: Who can I talk to to find out more about our diversity efforts?

A: Many people at CPC are actively involved and committed to these initiatives. A good place to start is with your immediate manager or your local Human Resources department. You can also contact the Workforce Diversity and Development Unit at Englewood Cliffs.

CPC'S U.S. EEO STATISTICS—1996

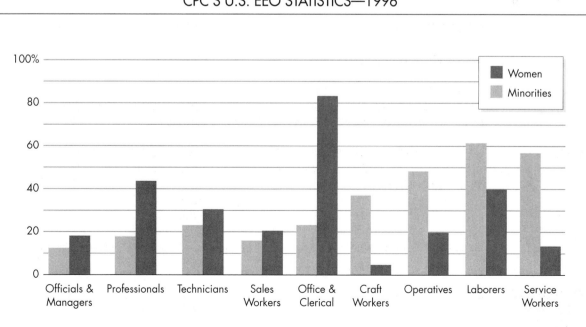

Case Appendix C

▲▲

BESTFOODS

January 12, 1998

An open letter to all Bestfoods North American Salaried Employees ...

Last year at this time, I introduced our Diversity Initiative and our diversity vision for the future. The Diversity Advisory Council, of which I am Chairman, defined a global diversity strategy. Our goal is to establish a workplace where diversity is fully integrated into the organization creating an environment and culture that encourages, values, and respects the uniqueness of the individual; fosters achievement; and optimizes business opportunities.

Our long-term objectives have four components: Preferred Employer, Balanced Workforce, Equitable Workplace, Enhanced Business Results. Each of our business units, as well as the corporate staff, has been engaged in specific actions this past year to ensure that Bestfoods benefits fully from the contributions, creativity, energy, and commitment of the broadest range of men and women representing different cultures, religions, ages, abilities, ethnic and racial backgrounds, and points of view. This is a competitive asset that every one of us must wholeheartedly embrace and actively foster if we are to achieve the outstanding growth that we seek. What are some of the specific accomplishments from this past year?

In order to measure our progress as **preferred employer**, we have committed to our second employee survey. Once again, there are a group of core questions that will be asked around the world. Several questions relate specifically to the amount of respect, inclusiveness, and fair treatment accorded to every Bestfoods employee.

We intensified our efforts to make faster progress in establishing a **balanced workforce** with more variety and difference reflected in all organization levels. We have begun breaking down glass ceilings and walls across the company. As a result of opening up our posting program globally for senior management positions, we have created more cross functional, cross divisional, and international moves than ever before.

We have made great strides in enhancing our career development practices resulting in a more **equitable workplace**. Our Performance Enhancement Process is being used worldwide. Every employee participating now has an individual development plan linked to our Bestfoods Leadership Competencies. And our WorldTeam Development Process, which drives our succession planning, has been revitalized.

All of these efforts are helping to reenergize the organization and are contributing to our **enhanced business results**. At a time when we must achieve more, often with fewer available resources, we are still meeting our financial targets. This was confirmed last year by Wall Street and our shareholders when our stock-price went above 100 for the first time ever!

Our Diversity Initiative is more than a training program, it is the way we do business and live our core values. It is hard work and sometimes frustrating. It requires full participation. Each one of us must be willing to act as a diversity change agent. This means acting as a role model and it often takes personal courage to do so.

In the past I have asked you to join me in continued learning and self-awareness. We are making progress and moving in the right direction. I now ask you to join me in becoming a change agent for the future.

[signature]

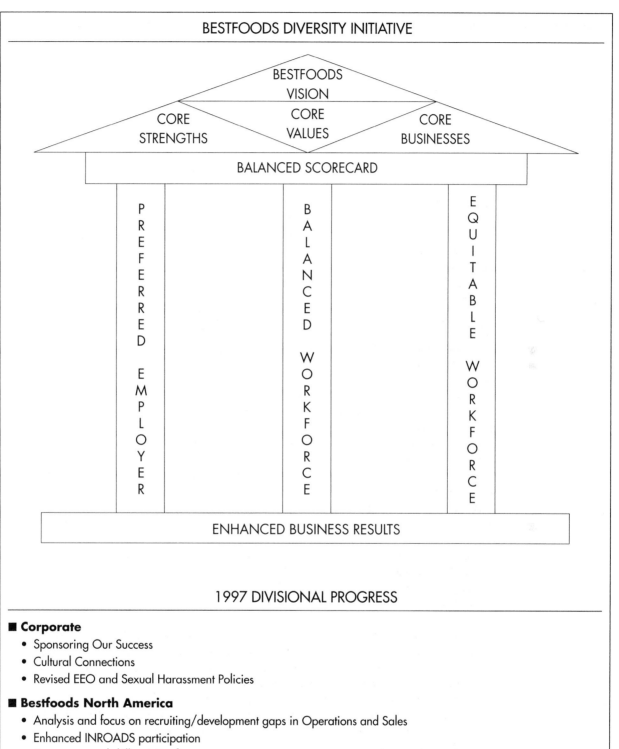

BESTFOODS DIVERSITY INITIATIVE

BESTFOODS
VISION

CORE
STRENGTHS

CORE
VALUES

CORE
BUSINESSES

BALANCED SCORECARD

PREFERRED EMPLOYER

BALANCED WORKFORCE

EQUITABLE WORKFORCE

ENHANCED BUSINESS RESULTS

1997 DIVISIONAL PROGRESS

■ **Corporate**
- Sponsoring Our Success
- Cultural Connections
- Revised EEO and Sexual Harassment Policies

■ **Bestfoods North America**
- Analysis and focus on recruiting/development gaps in Operations and Sales
- Enhanced INROADS participation
- Awareness and skill training for managers

■ **Baking Business**
- Mentoring Program
- Enhanced entry-level college recruiting and career development: Mfg; Sales; Fin; Mktg.
- 1st time INROADS participation: five interns

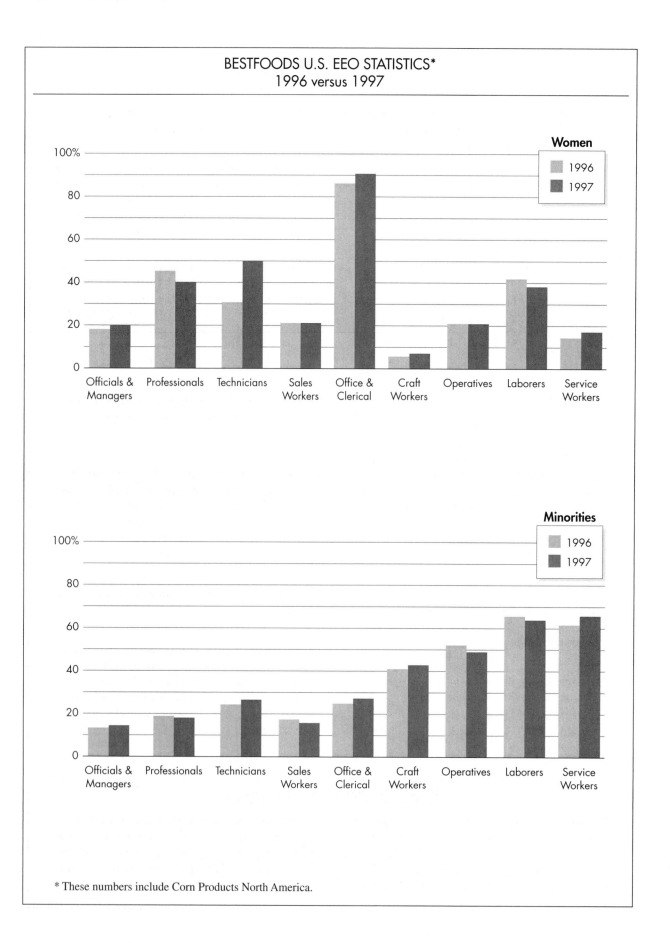

BESTFOODS U.S. EEO STATISTICS*
1996 versus 1997

* These numbers include Corn Products North America.

SELECTED QUESTIONS AND ANSWERS

Q. **What are the critical factors that we need to address in order to be successful with our Diversity Initiative?**

A. The Conference Board recently conducted a survey with leading edge organizations in diversity. The companies identifying the greatest progress with diversity efforts had two things in common: active support and involvement by their CEO and integrating diversity efforts into business and organizational objectives.

Q. **How do we compare to other companies that are implementing diversity programs?**

A. Although our Corporate initiative is fairly recent, Dick Shoemate's leadership on this issue has helped Bestfoods rapidly catch up with "best practice" companies. We have made great strides in integrating diversity into many of our business practices. Some of the key areas where this is occurring include: ongoing management and employee communications, employee awareness, education and involvement, management accountability measured by the balanced scorecard, the Performance Enhancement and Career Development Planning Process, community involvement and outreach, and divisional diversity action plans.

Q. **What impact has the recent restructuring had on minority representation in our workforce?**

A. There has been virtually no negative impact on minority representation despite a difficult year. In fact, we exceed the industry average for minority white collar workers by 5% and for blue collar by 10%.

Q. **Does Bestfoods think diversity is only an issue in the United States?**

A. We are deeply committed to extending our Diversity Initiative beyond the United States. Our definition of workforce diversity includes nationality, religion, age, and gender. These are just some of the elements of diversity that often resonate outside the United States. While legislation is increasing in many countries, our own U.S. heritage of equality and democracy tends to put emphasis on these issues here. However, the drivers of diversity are clearly universal. Ranked in order of importance they are customers and markets, global diversity, productivity, external workforce demographic trends, and internal workforce demographics.

Q. **How many international employees are there in Bestfoods? How many are women?**

A Bestfoods has approximately 130 employees on international assignments representing 34 nationalities. China, Hong Kong, Spain, and Colombia each have a female expatriate on assignment. We expect this number to continue to grow. Of our global posting applicants, 17% were women.

Q. **Has Bestfoods ever had a class-action suit filed?**

A. We have never had a class-action suit filed against us in our 90-year history. In fact, the number of discrimination charges filed by our 17,000 U.S. employees is very small. Year-to-date, we have only had 10 charges of discrimination filed with the EEOC, three of which have been dismissed for "no reasonable cause."

EQUAL EMPLOYMENT OPPORTUNITY

Bestfoods is committed to prohibiting discrimination in all employment practices including recruiting, hiring, pay, training, promotion, discipline, and termination on the basis of race, color, sex, age, religion, national origin, sexual orientation, disability, or veteran status. The Company prohibits harassment, including sexual harassment of its employees, in any form. The Company is also committed to an affirmative action policy, which will promote and ensure equal opportunity for minorities, women, individuals with disabilities, and covered veterans.

Case Appendix D

▲▲

Women's Global Leadership Forum Recommendations

CAREER DEVELOPMENT

To enhance career opportunities:

- Increase participation in high-visibility projects/assignments
  - Senior management development program
  - Task force assignments via posting and self-nomination
- Create flexible international assignments
  - Include assignment not involving relocation
  - Shorter-term assignment (six months to one year)
  - Job swapping/exchange
- Clarify career path and development opportunities
  - Provide honest, clear, consistent feedback
  - Full and consistent use of PEP (employee development program)
  - Management accountability for implementing action plans (PEP + employee interest)
- Take same level of risk with women as with men in promoting people
- Post all eligible job openings consistently

DIVERSITY

To increase representation of women in high-level positions:

- Have CEO communicate expectations to *all* global managers
- Create ombudspersons
- Appoint global representation on Corporate Diversity Advisory Council
- Share full results of Women's Global Leadership Forum survey with all divisions
- Benchmark with other companies and recognized experts
- Ensure appropriate measures in Balanced Scorecard

WORK/LIFE BALANCE

To enable women to perform to their highest capabilities, provide options for:

- Telecommuting
- Flexible work schedule, including maternity leave
- Job sharing
- Part-time opportunities

PERSONAL REPONSIBILITIES FOR CAREER DEVELOPMENT

- To take responsibility for your own personal career development
  - Identify goals
  - Communicate personal willingness for high-risk, challenging assignments
  - Self-nominate for those assignments as available
- Learn how to better develop personal networks to facilitate access to career opportunities

- To prepare for future opportunities
  - Develop leadership skills
  - Increase cultural sensitivities
  - Develop language skills
  - Maintain open-minded attitudes
  - Support, nurture, and develop career growth opportunities for those we manage

PERSONAL RESPONSIBILITIES FOR WORK/LIFE BALANCE

- Communicate personal needs and offer alternatives to meet those needs
- Set priorities and recognize the need for trade-offs
- Be sensitive to the needs of individuals we manage

WOMEN'S GLOBAL LEADERSHIP FORUM GROUP RESPONSIBILITIES

- Support diversity initiatives and share forum results
- Network on the basis of relationships developed at the forum
- Borrow with pride
- Share best-practice local learnings with other forum participants

WOMEN AND GLOBAL LEADERSHIP AT BESTFOODS—DISCUSSION QUESTIONS

1. Should the headquarters of U.S.-based multinationals promote diversity initiatives in their worldwide subsidiaries? If so, what's the best way to accomplish this?
2. Do you agree with Brody's idea to hold the forum? Why or why not? Can you suggest an alternative that would accomplish the same purpose or be even more effective?
3. What challenges and problems do Brody and Shoemate face in getting their diversity strategy implemented?
4. Prior to the opening session of the forum, what steps have Brody and her HR colleagues taken to promote diversity efforts throughout the company?
5. What actions or factors contributed to making this a successful change effort?
6. What else should Brody and Bestfoods do to institutionalize the changes begun at the Women's Global Leadership Forum?

Index